EARL H. BELL

DATE DU

Contemporary Social Issues

Preface

THIS VOLUME represents the results of four years of experimentation that began as an attempt to create greater student interest in the integrated social studies course at Stephens College. The initial criteria—to stimulate class discussion and debate, to provoke controversy, and to sharpen the classroom atmosphere—have been met through the use of (1) the problems approach and (2) readings that reflect the dynamics of the problem and relate theoretical material to the contemporary social scene. The selections have been sifted through classroom use at Stephens College, Colorado College, and State Teachers College (Indiana, Pennsylvania), and the contents presented here have proved effective in each of these different types of institutions.

The problems approach has proved its value as a teaching method in several ways. First, it presents to the student concrete issues in our society to which the theories of social science pertain and calls for analysis of those theories in terms of actual social settings.

Second, it stimulates critical thinking among students by providing the basis for controversy. Critical thought, so essential to civic competence, cannot be developed in a vacuum, and we have therefore chosen authors who are zealous defenders of a point of view rather than judicious compromisers. The student is presented the nature of the controversy and challenged to analyze it. We have also rejected the traditional introduction in favor of short passages that pose critical questions and encourage the student to raise further questions. And once critical thinking becomes a part of the student's approach, other rewards follow: we have noted among our students an increased social awareness and a growing tendency to bring to the classroom problems from their own experience and related reading.

Third, the problems approach provides a "guaranteed" medium for lively and penetrating class discussion, which is a necessary adjunct to instruction in social science. Since no pat answers are given—since there is no final voice of unimpeachable authority—the student is encouraged to participate in discussion.   The class becomes the testing ground for his own thinking.

Experience has demonstrated that the materials are presented in manageable and integrated units.   The several readings concerning each problem are closely related and provide a rather full treatment of the issue, thus they avoid the sketchiness that results from an attempt to cover everything. We do not offer readings on all social issues; rather, we have chosen to give more comprehensive treatment to vital problems.

Finally, this volume has proved suitable for use at almost any level of comprehension simply by increasing the analytical demands on the student. Freshmen may read mostly to gain facts and to apply a fairly elementary analysis.   Seniors may be asked to read the articles and to test them against various theories demanding more penetrating insight and analysis.

R. L. L.

J. A. B.

V. B. S.

Acknowledgments

THE EVOLUTION of *Contemporary Social Issues* has involved the cooperation, suggestions, and friendly criticisms of many persons, including whole departments and intercollegiate committees. In addition to the authors of the selection, without whose consent the book would have been impossible, we acknowledge here the assistance of those who have been most intimately connected with the project.

Special regard is due to John A. Decker, Chairman of the Social Science Division at Stephens College, who guided the course through many years and whose friendly counsel was always available.* Likewise, we have profited from the comments of Dr. Ralph W. Cordier, Dean of Instruction, State Teachers College, Indiana, Pennsylvania.

We have also drawn heavily upon the knowledge and teaching experience of those who were our colleagues while the book was in preparation: Howard Baker, John Crighton, Helen Elwell, Ray Kelch, Dorothy Martin, and John T. Mitchell, all of Stephens College; Orden Smucker, Michigan State College; Harry Jackson, Utica College; Daniel Tuttle, University of Hawaii; Ward Whipple, Teachers College, Columbia University; William Form, Michigan State College; Toimi Kyllonen, University of Missouri; and Halvor Melom, Long Beach College.

John L. Harr of Northwest State College, Meyer Weinberg of Wright Junior College, Wendell Bash of Colgate University, and Frances Outler of Atlanta, Georgia, deserve thanks for the informal but perceptive comments and encouragements they gave from time to time on the problems approach to the teaching of social science.

A grant from the research department of Stephens College made possible the use of the material in the classroom before its appearance in book form. In this connection, special thanks are due to B. Lamar Johnson of the University of California at Los Angeles, who, as Dean of Instruction at

---

* A summary description of the Decker-directed course may be found in Earl J. McGrath (ed.), *Social Science in General Education* (Dubuque, Iowa: W. C. Brown Co., 1948), pp. 210–16.

Stephens College, encouraged the writing of a problems textbook. His successor, James G. Rice, has followed the progress of the book with equal interest and enthusiasm.

The development of the book was also furthered by our association with intercollegiate committees, which alerted us to trends, movements, and values in the social sciences that have influenced the form and content of this volume. The Inter-College Committee on the Evaluation of Social Science Objectives, sponsored by the American Council on Education, sharpened our awareness of the place of critical thinking in the teaching of social science. Paul Dressel of Michigan State College, who directed the over-all study, and Paul Hanna of the University of Florida, who chaired the social science section, and fellow participants, who shared teaching materials and classroom experience, deserve our thanks. A pilot study of citizenship education at the college level, sponsored by Citizenship Education Project, Teachers College, Columbia University, proved a challenging experience. William S. Vincent, Executive Officer; Willis Griffin, Head, Program Development Division; Edward S. Evenden, Head of College Relations; and others who took part in the program furnished a climate of opinion that forced us to re-examine critically our objectives and tools for achieving them. Mention should also be made of the stimulating ideas generated by the Citizenship Clearing House of Western Pennsylvania under the leadership of Professor William C. Seyler, University of Pittsburgh.

To all who have contributed to the final publication in greater or less measure we express our sincere thanks. Whatever merits our volume may have must be attributed in part to their help; its shortcomings we accept as our own responsibility.

R. L. L.
J. A. B.
V. B. S.

Contents

CHAPTER THREE

The Politics and Administration of American Government

CHAPTER FOUR

Personal Maladjustment and Crime

CHAPTER FIVE

The Family in a Changing Society

CHAPTER SIX

Racial and Cultural Minorities

CHAPTER SEVEN

Rival Economic Ideologies

CHAPTER EIGHT

Evolution of American Capitalism

CHAPTER NINE

The United States in World Affairs

CONTENTS

CHAPTER ONE

Society and Social Change

THE MODERN scientific study of human society came into existence during the nineteenth century as the result of the accumulation of a vast amount of knowledge on diverse groups of people. This information was studied and classified. At the same time scholars began to look objectively at their own societies, and the pioneers of anthropology sought admission into primitive tribes in order to observe at first hand group living under simple conditions. From this large body of scientific fact there emerged the concept of *culture*. As defined by sociologists and anthropologists, culture is that complex whole which includes knowledge, techniques, religion, art, beliefs, and all else that people acquire as members of a society.

The implications of the cultural approach are comprehensive and far-reaching. Some of the more significant aspects of the thesis might be summarized as follows: (1) The social heritage is more important than blood, race, or national origin in influencing behavior and belief. (2) Groups of social institutions are important to the point of being indispensable. They help us to live together by providing common goals, habits, and ready-made solutions to the problems that continually recur in the life experience. Without these social lifelines society would soon come apart at the seams; culture, as Ruth Benedict points out, is the cement that binds men together. (3) Although culture is essential to the process of group living, it can also be a handicap. The customary way of doing things is not always the best way, and rigid acceptance of ideas and institutions may stand in the way of beneficial change. (4) A completely static society does not exist; change is present in all societies. However, there is no consistency in the rates of change for the total society or for its component parts. For example, both individuals and groups adapt themselves differently to material and to nonmaterial forces. Social change is characterized by both cultural "leads" and "lags." A new invention or idea reacts upon all phases of a culture, which always tries to fit it into the traditional complex of habits and beliefs. Sometimes there is a great disparity between the new and the traditional, and this is known as *cultural lag*.

This chapter deals with three specific problems. First, what is the role of culture in influencing thought and behavior and in molding national character? Does culture determine human thoughts and actions or merely influence them? Is culture the only factor, the most important single factor, or just one force in the highly complex area of the action and interaction of human beings? Second, to what extent can the terms "American character" and "American way of life" be justified? Are Americans a unique people, or are the differences between American and other cultures superficial, rather than basic, variations? Finally, where does American culture now stand and in what direction is it traveling? Within broad limits, is it possible to predict the road ahead?

Problem 1: What Role Does Culture Play in Regulating Human Behavior?

The cultural approach supports the thesis that men are not born human but acquire human characteristics through the learning of language, customs, moral beliefs, and the social behavior of the group. Thus, man learns how to behave, what to believe, what language to speak. These things are not biologically inherited, but they are socially inherited. Every person is caught in the web of culture and, subsequently, becomes a carrier of culture, transmitting the social experience to others.

Following this line of thought to its ultimate conclusion—that is, to cultural determinism—presents a strong temptation to regard human beings not as subjects but as objects. In other words, if individuals are regulated by the social milieu, they are not the regulators; if they are acted upon, they are not the actors. Such reasoning, of course, forces one to accept what is close to a philosophy of fatalism. If the culture is the all-determining force, the individual becomes a neutral, passive agent. On the other hand, it is possible that the cultural approach has neglected to assess correctly the role of the individual. Does not individuality have something to do with behavior responses? Does not the interplay of personalities have a great effect upon thought and action?

Although neither Stuart Chase nor Robert Lynd, the authors of the following articles, can properly be considered a cultural determinist, the idea itself has a bearing on each reading. Of greater importance, perhaps, is the different—and, to a degree, contrasting—emphasis each author gives to the role of culture. Stuart Chase acknowledges the importance of other factors but consistently stresses the prominence of the cultural background. Robert Lynd recognizes the overriding effects of culture, but maintains that no thesis on culture has any validity if it loses sight of the individual.

On Being Culture Bound [*]

As the result of his upbringing and the social climate in which he lives, the American will choose a convertible in preference to a rickshaw, ask for a coke instead of a glass of saki, and prefer soap to a powdered stone for hand bathing. Children all over the world quickly become conscious of the habits and the thinking of those around them and, hence, acquire varying religious, political, economic, and social beliefs. By the time adulthood is reached these cultural encasements bind men very tightly. After surveying the role of culture, Stuart Chase asks whether we will insist on clinging to ideas acquired in a preatomic age even though the consequences of these ideas may destroy us. Does the article overstress the influence of culture? What is the importance of knowledge and intelligence in regulating thought and modifying behavior?

When boys and girls of the Subanee tribe in the Philippines reach puberty, they grind and blacken their teeth. It is the logic of the Subanee that pearly white teeth belong to dogs, cats and other animals. Man must change his teeth if he is to maintain supremacy over the lower orders.

Moving half way around the world, a radio advertiser promises that his product will whiten your teeth in just one brushing. Otherwise you get your money back.

Fung Kwok Keung was born Joseph Rinehart on Long Island, New York. At the age of three he lost his parents and he was adopted by a Chinese gentleman. At 19 he left China, and came back to the United States. Here is a photograph of him before a blackboard in an "Americanization" class. He is writing down both Chinese and English words, painfully learning the latter. "He had become so thoroughly Chinese in manner, speech, habit and outlook that he was distinguishable from members of that race only by his features."

* Stuart Chase, *The Antioch Review*, Fall, 1949, pp. 293–306. Copyright, The Antioch Review, Inc., 1949.

Whatever Joseph Rinehart's inherited characteristics may have been, they were thickly coated over by his sixteen years as a Chinese boy, and we see him at the blackboard as a product of the culture of the East. The American boy is buried deep. Would he ever have appeared had Joseph-Fung remained in China?

Travel in the Canadian Arctic is difficult and the various tribes of Eskimos and Indians are comparatively isolated from each other. Anthropologists who studied them some years ago reported that they were co-operative and honest in their own communities, but relations between the tribes were marked by fear and ignorance. One particular tribe warned the explorers against another tribe that had long claws instead of hands ready to tear strangers to pieces! In their insularity each seemed to believe that they were the only genuine human beings, the other tribes being something less than men. "We are good people, we never steal. It is the Coppermine River people who steal." So constantly did they praise themselves that even seasoned anthropologists were surprised, terming it "a kind of personal vanity enlarged to embrace the group or tribe."

But the Copper Eskimos are only an extreme case of what the members of every society believe. Are we not all pretty sure that, in the last analysis, wisdom and virtue rest with our way of life, and are not to be found among those foreigners?

The crew with which Columbus sailed firmly believed in dog-faced men, and were prepared for all sorts of anatomical marvels on the other side of the world. The people of Western civilization no longer hold such expectations. They have moved around enough to expect a more normal anatomy. For those who cannot get around, there are photographs. Contrast between cultures has dissolved some tribal righteousness, but the recent progress of the U.S. Army through North Africa, the Mediterranean and Western Europe shows how much remains to be done. Just ask almost any GI what he thought of the A-rabs.

It is the thesis of this paper that every human being, whether in darkest Borneo or on enlightened Beacon Hill, is culture-bound beyond his remotest appreciation. The greater part of his system of values, of right and wrong, has been given him intact by his tribe. This is not a new idea. Boas and other anthropologists were expounding it a generation ago. You will find it in Sumner's *Folkways*. Much new evidence has come in, however, and since Hiroshima it has taken on a new urgency. It is now a matter of concern not only to specialists but to plain citizens in every country—ours most of all, as the chief power center of the planet.

By becoming aware of our cultural bondage, we can in a sense rise above it. We can look over the walls a little and meet the gaze of others trying to do the same thing in different cultures—Chinese, Russians, Argentinians. Unless we do this can we hope to establish One World?

To social scientists, a human being is the end product of three major influences: his genes; his unique personal experience; his learned culture.

The genes which he gets from his parents provide his bodily characteristics and the raw material for his personality.   If one is born feeble-minded, no training can help much.   But for normal individuals the limits of development set by the genes are wide.

Everyone meanwhile has unique experiences, especially in the formative years, which mould his personality.   A debilitating illness, a terrifying exposure to darkness, praise from an admired teacher, fire, a savage dog, a dead man on the lawn, a drunken father—such experiences are accidental and unpredictable except in the statistical sense that everybody has some of them.   Psychiatrists devote untold hours to dredging them up from a patient's unconscious memories.   Gillin calls them "unpatterned experiences."

Culture is the third and perhaps the major influence on personality.   "In all societies," says Gillin, "the greater part of life experiences to which the individual is exposed is of this type—patterned, arranged and structured by the culture.   The individual in the process of socialization is either purposely trained, or otherwise learns to react to these experiences in ways which are considered acceptable to his group."

If an infant can somehow survive without older people to pattern his behavior, he learns no culture.   In the few recorded cases where this has happened, the child becomes a gibbering idiot, without language, without standards of any kind, lower than the apes.   This pretty well disposes of that school of progressive education which held that the child arrived equipped like a beautiful flower to grow and expand, if only allowed freely to express himself.

Here is Alan at 15 months in his bath.   Although Alan does not talk yet he is far from unconscious, and the bath delights and gratifies him— the warm water, the rubber ducks, his mother laughing and playing with him.   Afterwards in clean pajamas beside the fire, he will have supper and enjoy that too.   In later life Alan will certainly not remember today's bath, the fire, or how his mother looked, yet all these impressions will influence his character.   Even if he reacts against cleanliness for a few years of boyhood, he will grow up an adult, bath-taking Anglo-Saxon, not a "filthy" Arab or Siberian.   Should he ever have to deal with any of these people, say on some international committee, negotiations might be gravely handicapped by their several concepts in regard to bathing.

So far Alan is only a baby, but since his birth he has been absorbing cultural patterns. Starting with a sensitive body, a sucking reflex, a minimum of primitive fears, he has been conditioned deliberately with many planned experiences.

First, the nurses in the hospital, then his mother, went to work on him. Then the other members of the family, the doctor, for a time a nurse of his own. A discipline is worked out—when he shall eat, when he shall sleep, when he shall play. If he does not like it, he can howl, but that is "naughty," and subject to special penalties.

These more or less systematic habits give Alan his first map of his world. It is apparently established in his nervous system before language or conscious memory, and his early map, buried in the unconscious, is important in forming Alan's standards of what is "right" and "wrong."

So with every child the world over.

Margaret Mead has described how the Indians of the Pueblos give responsibility to young children as soon as they are capable of it—close the door, take out the goat, sweep the floor. Such responsibility is not at all inconsistent with the feeling of emotional security which social scientists also tell us is so essential to the child and a well adjusted later life.

Says Karl Llewellyn:

Not human group-ways, but the group-ways of my particular group, are what each budding "I" is slowly shaped to fit into and so to demand of others. The American child does not grow up speaking French. He plays "Farmer in the Dell," not "Sur le pont d'Avignon." He knows of Washington, Lincoln, Roosevelt, not of Charlemagne, Jeanne d'Arc, Petain. His heart rises to the Stars and Stripes. . . .

The experts analyze culture as partly habits and partly material things. They break it down into three specific elements by which every child is molded:

1. The patterns of behavior which older and stronger people enforce upon him.

2. The belief systems they expect him to follow, with or without verbal explanations. These include religious, political, economic and other faiths and ideologies.

3. The artifacts or material equipment which he must learn to manipulate and adjust to in his immediate vicinity. These include such things as mugs, spoons, toilet seats, hair brushes, chairs, tables, electric lights, bows and arrows, ox carts, automobiles, igloos, elevators, and so on, depending on the society in which he lives.

It is somewhat frightening to reflect that W. F. Ogburn, the Chicago sociologist, finds that inventions, and the artifacts which flow from them, grow at a compound interest rate. In Western societies, Alan already has a perplexing number to deal with. At what point the human organism can deal no longer has not yet been calculated. Perhaps we are nearer to it than the manufacturers think. A compound interest curve, running in the open, is a formidable phenomenon for any organism to keep up with!

At the present time cultures all over the world are changing at an abnormally high rate. Mass production, atomic energy, supersonic aircraft, cotton picking machinery, artificial insemination, television, photo-electric cells—each brings a series of cultural changes. To change a pattern requires a change in the human nervous system, to the confusion, for a time at least, of the individual. A habit pattern is automatic by definition, one follows the path without thinking, as in driving a car. But changes in the culture demand new habits, which require conscious thought, sometimes painfully conscious, as when one is learning to drive a car. Often the new are in sharp conflict with the old. Too much of this and the nervous system rebels—which seems to be one of our main troubles today.

The artifacts of culture are tangible objects and will last a while, subject to the laws of depreciation. Behavior patterns and belief systems, on the contrary, are intangibles in the central nervous system. If all adults in a given society should suddenly die of a plague, the culture would vanish with them, save for the surviving artifacts and what the children had learned. But so long as enough members remain alive, the culture lives with them, a seamless web, forever passing into the hands of the next generation, forever changing as it passes. The individual merges into the fabric, but without the individual there is no fabric.

Every individual is both a creature of his culture and a carrier of it, in that he passes it along. He may also be a creator of culture, if and when he introduces changes in it. Confucius, Jesus, Mahomet, Gandhi, Galileo, Watt, Lincoln, come to mind, but many little people also are responsible for little changes. Consider that unnamed hero who first ate an oyster.

To hear about the culture concept is amusing and perhaps enlightening, but only when one applies it to his own behavior does he begin to test the strength of the walls by which he is encircled.

I have been jotting down a few rough notes on the cultural patterns which I personally follow, a writer living in a rural town in Connecticut, getting to New York occasionally, and around the country on lecture trips now and then. Aspirants to doctorates in social science could well do similar studies of individuals, with scholarly detachment and accuracy. My patterns can be tentatively divided into:

1. Those common to nearly all normal persons in the U.S.A.
2. Those shared by all American males.
3. Class patterns shared by most Americans in my income bracket.

4. Occupational patterns shared by those practicing my three professions of accounting, lecturing, writing.

5. Recreational patterns for various sports and leisure time activities. Some of these duplicate class behavior, but by no means all.

Let us consider each group briefly, not as a research project but simply to open up the subject.

The cultural patterns I share with all Americans begin with our language —the most important single culture trait. Although spoken words are common to all members of the human race, specific languages clearly exclude each other and tend to divide mankind. Foreigners not only look queer, they talk gibberish. I cannot learn to talk, to communicate, even to think, except by learning a unique and exceedingly complex set of conventional sounds and symbols known as language, no part of which is inherited.

Like all other Americans today I use dollars—which have been defined as moving numbers, now that the metallic base has all but disappeared. I also share the motor car complex with practically all Americans. If most of us do not learn the rules of the road, many of them unwritten, the automobile becomes too lethal for society to tolerate.

Other common customs and behavior patterns include monogamy, public schools, the use of knives and forks at table, coffee drinking, burying the dead with ceremony and respect, standing up for the national anthem, deportment in church, facing forward in elevators, listening to radio, reading newspapers, using electric lights, riding in trains, belief in the Constitution, and so on and so forth. The Ph.D.'s will find thousands of customs, belief systems and artifacts which all Americans share—the fundamental matrix which makes us one people.

Every other society has its matrix, too. The functions which the patterns serve in all societies can be analyzed down to a common human denominator—universals shared by all human beings everywhere.

On the next level, I join in a series of customs and beliefs with nearly all American males. I must give deference to women, at least in public, but I am permitted a so-called "double standard" of morality. I must wear shoes, trousers, shirt and coat in church or in company; but I may strip to the waist on a bathing beach—a custom only about a decade old. I am supposed to bear pain without flinching. I must be touchy of my "honor," and defend it with my fists if necessary. But for 100 years or so I have been discouraged from fighting duels with lethal weapons. I am directed to take the lead in affairs of the heart. I must not boast too loudly or throw my weight around.

My class patterns are more restricted in their application. I share them with what Lloyd Warner has defined in his Yankee City series as the "upper middles," and the "lower uppers" of the Eastern seaboard. In "upper upper" circles I seldom move, and I think it was Struthers Burt who once called this rarified group the "coastal tribes."

My class customs are specific about what clothes I may appear in, at what times and places, without humiliation. For a man to wear a pair of brown shoes with a dinner coat is as unthinkable as for a woman to wear cotton stockings at a cocktail party. There is a very extensive catalogue of taboos covering house furnishings, kitchen equipment, eating habits, what shops to patronize, what section of town to live in, what resorts to go to.

Warner found that the "upper uppers" without exception sent their children to private preparatory schools, but on my cultural level we do not penalize a member too severely who allows a child to go to high school.

The uniquely dynamic character of the American class structure is also pointed out by Warner. In most parts of the world, classes are fixed; one is born into them, and they are social rather than economic. In America classes are fluid, and tend to be economic. Like the escalators in a department store, people are forever riding up and riding down. The depression shook countless families out of the higher brackets; the war's black markets hoisted other families up.

Turning next to the occupational level, I find that each of my three professions—accountant, lecturer, writer—carries a great cluster of special customs. Every occupation listed in the census has its special culture patterns. Most of them, though known in detail only to members of the craft, are recognized and expected by the rest of society. Thus we freely allow a doctor to perform indignities on our person which we would not tolerate from anyone else.

Trying to analyze my occupations, I wonder how I ever learned this vast complex of procedures. For example: an accountant, like a lawyer, must preserve complete secrecy in respect to his client's affairs. The human tendency to gossip must be rigorously bottled up, no matter how succulent the details—and financial details can sometimes be very succulent. The accountant's demeanor while on duty must be grave if not positively funereal. The proper procedure and terminology in respect to books, records, working papers, is highly stylized. The report to the client is by convention dull and forbidding. To make a report genuinely interesting and readable would constitute, I am afraid, a grave offense.

A lecturer has a different series of specific taboos—for instance, he must assume that anyone in the audience who asks a question is a brother of Socrates, no matter how pointless the question. A writer has still another series—for instance, it is becoming for him to be officially photographed

in tweeds and a pipe. In my double role of accountant and writer, apparently I perplex some of my neighbors. . . . "The fellow looks tweedy
enough, but where does he get all those figures?"

Finally, we will glance at another future paradise for Ph.D. theses, the
patterns of sport and leisure activities in America. A monograph on baseball language would have more than academic interest. It is proper, for
example, for spectators at professional baseball games, particularly in
Brooklyn, to abuse the umpire. Such is the convention about umpires.
Reports of games are composed by the sports writers in a special terminology
practically unintelligible to a stranger.

Another monograph could be written on skiing centers. Here is a mass
sport hardly 20 years old in America in which already elaborate taboos have
been laid down, along with the skill itself. It is not good form, for instance, to stay long at a ski resort without actively participating. It is bad
form for students to copy the costume of instructors. No man, except an
expert, is expected to wear knickerbockers. No woman, unless a great expert, is expected to ski in a short, flaring skirt.

A Caribbean cruise ship is as full of culture patterns as of portholes.
Whatever examples of island cultures the tourists see are strictly classified
as entertainment. Old cruise hands break in the freshman by effective
methods, ridicule being the chief form of punishment. Indeed, ridicule
is the major guardian of culture in all societies, according to the anthropologists, stronger than the policeman's club, stronger than jails, stronger
than the gallows.

So the Ph.D.'s might continue, filling one monograph after another with
the patterns of Americans in their leisure hours. I have only tried to show
that leisure is not an escape from cultural bonds, not a leap into freedom.
Rather, it is like exchanging one suit of cultural clothes for another, as we
shift from work to play. The rules are precise in both departments.

Where do culture patterns come from? One can see new ones form, as
television is now being introduced, as we have seen the motor car form them
over the past few decades. But many are ancient. We live in rings of culture patterns, one within the next. Again take the man from Connecticut.

From civilization in general he gets such customs and artifacts as city
living, minute division of labor, a storable grain, writing, architecture,
mathematics, schools for the young, money and banking.

From Western civilization as such he gets, among other things, Christianity, Arabic numerals, the idea of the sovereign state, modern science,
mass production, music in the diatonic scale, property rights in land, military conscription.

From Anglo-Saxon culture, as part of the West, he gets his language—
the most important single culture trait of all, as noted earlier. He gets

parliamentary government, habeas corpus, free speech and press, the idea of progress, romantic love as the proper basis for marriage, a relatively puritanical moral code.

From North America, he gets corn, canoes, turkeys, tobacco, a number of Indian names and customs, the frontier pattern of marked individualism, an irresponsible attitude towards natural resources, a flexible class structure, a federal form of government with checks and balances, and many more.

From New England he gets clam chowder made with milk, baked beans, the town meeting, a nasal twang in his speech, a disposition to be close-mouthed about personal affairs, to count his pennies, to be suspicious of the neighbors, and to keep his house painted white and his woodpile full.

No wonder specialists sometimes refer to a culture complex. But it makes little difference to the child where the various patterns come from. An untrained baby could just as easily learn Chinese ways, or Eskimo ways, or the ways of Athens in the time of Pericles.

Even this random survey indicates clearly enough the great load of culture which all of us must bear. The amazing thing is that every last particle of it has to be learned *de novo* by Alan and his sister. There are no short cuts, no predigested courses. If you or I do not feel the weight too much, it is because we are not conscious of other ways to behave. For active and imaginative minds—which come probably from the genes—the burden is felt mostly in what the scientists call the cultural lag. This is that very common situation where people believe in doing things that they are no longer doing—such as observing the gold standard, or where they resist desirable changes because they contravene an established belief. Thus the need for child labor legislation anticipated the actual passage of the law in Congress by about one hundred years. We are right now caught in a lag covering medical care for all Americans. A large-scale approach to the problem is seriously needed, as the draft figures show, but there are formidable taboos against it.

How can these lags, this bondage, be reduced?

One way is for specialists to study the patterns of the tribe and then deliberately try to change or simplify them. This is a difficult and dangerous business, and techniques for doing it are not well understood. Reformers are forever trying to set up procedures in defiance of the culture, with the most lamentable results.

Meanwhile there is another road to constructive action, which does not involve such heroic measures. It lies in education, for adults as well as children. If enough people can become aware of their culture, and think about it, and respect its strength, they may occasionally rise above it. This does not mean ceasing to conform; it means realizing that one is bound, and that other peoples of the world are similarly bound. With such a realization—which may come like a thunder clap—one begins to suspend judgment on other people, to put oneself in their place by an act of the imagination, and for the first time to understand them.

Edmond Taylor in his book *Richer by Asia* makes a profound observation. "Not only between East and West, but wherever cultural or ideological factors play a major role in human conflict, it is less because men's values clash than because their delusions collide. . . ." Few societies today, for example, glorify war; most people want peace the world over. Yet their belief systems contain delusions about national honor, the rights of sovereign states, sacred soil, which act as catalysts for wars.

We return to the question asked at the beginning of this paper. How in the interests of achieving a world society can people learn to rise above their particular culture walls? I have been appealing to the reader to attempt this for himself, but fortunately he does not have to do it quite alone. There are precedents and expert help for this purpose. Many years ago the U.S. Indian Service revolutionized its approach by calling in anthropologists under John Collier to study Indian cultures in an objective way. It worked well. The British colonial services have used anthropologists to smooth their road with subject peoples. This has worked too, and saved much cruelty and suffering, but British administrators do not easily forget white supremacy.

The U.S. Navy now is the guardian of native peoples all over the Pacific Ocean, and the greatest project in the history of anthropology is under way to determine a scientific method for carrying out the mandate. "Scientific" in this connection means humane, and it will be a test of both humanity and science to see how far native cultures are respected and preserved. UNESCO is initiating a series of research studies on cross cultural relations which could be a brake on nationalist expansion.

The U.S. State Department operates a Foreign Service Institute which teaches the culture concept to career men and others going overseas. How can an American hope to understand a foreign society without such training? While waiting and planning for One World, how can America indeed carry on her new role of the number one Great Power without a working application of the culture concept? A State Department release puts it this way:

The great problem in international relations and in everyday dealing with foreign people is that most of us tend to identify our traditional ways of meeting problems, of organizing life, and of reacting to situations, as "human nature," whereas all of it is learned. Other peoples have developed different solutions to the same problems, and consequently have different "human natures." . . . Each people tends to regard its own particular culture as the best, furnishing the only proper solution to problems, and to think of all others as either quaint, queer or "cussed."

This statement is quite obvious as applied to the Copper Eskimos. The thing is to apply it to ourselves. A State Department man going abroad with such training is in a strong position to deal with the local people and perform his duties.

It is still harder to realize that foreigners regard many American customs and beliefs as queer if not downright perverted. The State Department tries to give its men a thorough briefing on this. For instance, to paraphrase its handbook:

The American culture assumes that every chain of action is directed toward a goal—"success" or whatever. But many societies interpret life as a series of activities, each satisfying in itself without a long-term goal to suffer and deny oneself for. To such people, American behavior is meaningless and quixotic.

Again, Americans assume that achievement is best furthered by competition. We are trained and encouraged to compete in many areas: school ranking, athletics, competition for mates, professional work, publicity seeking, business, even in labor unions. This pattern releases a great deal of energy, but also produces nervous breakdowns, bitter feelings towards the Joneses with whom we are directed to keep up, stomach ulcers, and a prodigious waste of natural resources. Other peoples cannot understand why Americans drive themselves so remorselessly.

Another belief mentioned by the State Department is the American's distrust of government. Europeans cannot understand this. They note that American business men, farmers and workers often receive government benefits on an extensive scale, but denounce nationalization programs in Europe. Europeans find this attitude hypocritical. A State Department man abroad should be aware of this, particularly while the Marshall Plan is in active operation.

White Western civilization has given its members an unprecedented opportunity to see other cultures in perspective. As the steam engine encircled the globe, its representatives might have become in a sense citizens of the world. They might have observed and recorded the ways of other cultures, and refrained from imposing Western standards on other people, sometimes by extremely rugged methods.

Records have been made from Marco Polo on, but mostly the adventurers have had their own consuming goals—trade, gold, the Cross, real estate—and on the whole they only learned enough of native cultures to corrupt them. Ruth Benedict says that the net effect of expansion has been to insulate Westerners from any consciousness of other cultures. Where many primitive people "have seen their religion, their economic system, their marriage prohibitions, go down before the white man's . . . the white man has had a different experience. . . . He has very likely been around the world without ever staying outside a cosmopolitan hotel."

Scientists are making what belated amends they can. The American Anthropological Association has submitted to the United Nations a code of understanding between peoples, consisting of three short principles:

1. That the individual realizes his personality through his culture, hence respect for individual differences entails a respect for cultural difference.

2. Respect for differences between cultures is validated by the scientific fact that no technique of qualitatively evaluating cultures has been discovered.

3. Standards and values are relative to the culture from which they derive. Any attempt to extend the beliefs or moral codes of one culture must weaken the applicability of any Declaration of Human Rights to mankind as a whole.

Since Hiroshima, for better or worse, mankind has entered a wholly new phase in its evolutionary path. It takes atomic physicists fully to understand this, but after what they have accomplished I am not disposed to dispute their conviction that it is so. The logic of Hiroshima is that large-scale war must cease. This points to the end of the sovereign state as we have known it since the Peace of Westphalia. It means the creation of some sort of planetary organization in control of world affairs.

People on the councils of such an organization cannot represent America, or Russia, or Ruritania, they must represent mankind. The difficulty with the United Nations, and the League before it, lies right here. Most delegates place the interest of Ruritania first, and so the sovereign state pursues its anarchic way in the very heart of Lake Success. This is not nearly good enough; delegates must learn to become citizens of the world, world men. They will need the support of world men everywhere. The most practical method for learning this unprecedented viewpoint would seem to lie in mastering the culture concept.

World men. The idea itself is not new, but consummation hitherto has been a romantic dream. Poets like Tennyson have written songs about it, but anthropologists have only just defined the exacting terms on which it might conceivably be achieved. Now, thanks to their efforts, we know the general direction.

The next great task of humanity is to develop world men. They may not be developed fast enough to save us, but the challenge reaches across the sky, and at last they have not only poets but scientists to help them.

CULTURE AND THE INDIVIDUAL *

A recognition of the importance of culture in social organization is an illuminating perception. By providing insights into diverse ways of living among different groups, the cultural concept refutes the innateness of behavior. The social-heritage approach contradicts the idea that biological heredity is responsible for national characteristics or that the unattractive behavior habits of a minority group are permanent and inflexible.

Like all significant ideas, however, the cultural concept can be carried too far. Does not the cultural approach ignore the action and interaction of human beings? Is there not a tendency in this view to regard the individual as neutral and passive rather than active and dynamic? In the following selection Robert S. Lynd replies to these questions by urging that in the study of social science the center of attention be focused on the individual.

. . . Beginning with the useful discrimination between the culture (or the institution) and the person, we then proceed by imperceptible shifts in emphasis to treat culture as something *apart from* the persons who live by it; next, we slide over into the acceptance of culture as *independent of* the persons who live by it; and then we are tempted to move on to acceptance, overt or tacit, of *culture determinism,* viewing culture as a self-contained force, operating by inner laws of its own to coerce and to shape people to its ends. Now every one of these steps is warranted to a certain extent: the culture and the persons who live by it are different conceptual foci, and it is important to study culture-as-such and persons-as-such; and culture patently does things to persons in a highly coercive way, the culture of a metropolitan city, for instance, having a momentum *qua* culture to which most persons find it necessary to bend and adapt in order to survive in such a city. But the trouble comes for the social scientist when, in grappling with the monopolizing immediacies of his problem, he forgets that these useful conceptual discriminations are only true to a certain extent, as methodological tools—when he begins to accept them neat, without qualification.

For the most part, social scientists have lost "the person" below their horizon, as they move along busily ploughing their respective research furrows. Most of them just have not quite known what to do with indi-

* Robert S. Lynd, *Knowledge for What?* (Princeton University Press, 1939), pp. 22–25, 27, 32, 38–40.

viduals, dwarfed as the latter are by the magnitude and power of current institutions. Many, when their attention is called to individuals, shrug their shoulders and pass them off with a sigh of relief to the psychologist, trusting that the unseen hand of this disciplinary division of labor will eventually fit the jig-saw puzzle of science together. Others lapse into an economic or other determinism that dismisses individuals outright in the face of the inner teleologies of capitalism, social classes, and the like.

Obviously, this is an unsatisfactory situation for the sciences that deal with social institutions and, in their more expansive moods, speak of themselves as "the sciences of human behavior." For cultural institutions can continue to "work" only so long as people abide by and support them; and the most patent aspect of many current institutions is that they are not working well, and people seem to differ in the degree to which they are willing to help to make them work. What appears to be needed is a recovery of persons-in-culture by social science.

It is here proposed, therefore, that the social sciences, in addition to viewing the institutions with which they work as parts of a total culture, take the further step of viewing culture as living in and operating as the learned habits and impulses of persons. This, like every useful conceptualization of a gross situation, can be overdone. It should not blind us to the facts that the culture and individuals interact; that culture does do things to people at the same time that people are doing things to culture; that a culture has at any given moment a coercive momentum that may usefully, for certain purposes of analysis, be regarded as "its own." Analysis must go forward on many levels. There is a rough, shorthand utility in lumping together the impacts of many specific individuals upon my decision to stop wearing an old suit to my office and to buy a new one, or upon my political views, or even upon such subtle things as my desiring to marry a pretty wife with money, and in saying that "the culture prompts me to do these things." Likewise, there is obvious utility in statistical prediction, on the basis of past experience, as to what masses of people will do, even though we do not know what individual persons will do; and the influence of inventions and other material aspects of our cultural environment may usefully be analyzed in many ways without forever stopping to stress the fact that these material tools are operative only because enough people have learned a meaning and use for them to keep them in operation. It is important to continue to study *the* price system, *the* securities market, *the* automotive industry, *the* family, *the* law, *the* tariff, *the* class structure, *the* city, *the* Federal administrative machinery, economic determinism, sequences in change in the cultural structure, and so on; for these things are necessary parts of our analysis. But, in so doing, the ultimate relation between persons and the culture must not be forgotten. The emphasis upon persons as the active carriers, perpetuators, and movers of culture performs for us the indispensable service of resolving the dualism of "culture *and* the person," and of placing the primary emphasis where it basically belongs, upon people.   Cultural institutions occupy a derivative, though important and active, role as a set of learned instrumental ways of behaving with which human beings seek to realize their needs. . . .

When "economic man," "political man," and "social man" are accepted as one and the same person, truly heroic abstraction is necessary if one is to view economic behavior apart from social behavior, political behavior apart from economic behavior, and so on.   Motivation may not then be viewed as single and consistent, as economics tends to view it, and such objects of study as citizenship, saving, conservatism, demand, occupation, marital satisfaction, social status, social classes, health, law observance, housing, and leisure break their dykes and flow together in the living persons whose behavior forms our institutions.   It is not extravagant to say that scarcely any area of institutional analysis can fail to take on new meanings when set thus in the close context of the totality of individuals' living.

When we view culture and institutions as the behavior of individuals, we are able to assign a normal place to deviations from "the" assumed normal way of doing a given thing in the culture.   A chronic embarrassment of social science theory is the explanation of "exceptions to the general rule." Some of these exceptions are so egregious as to defy explaining away by such qualifying phrases as "by and large," "in the main," and "other things being equal."   The deviations refuse to "cancel each other out."   In some cases these departures from the assumed norms are so striking that they have become standard "problems" with a semi-independent status as the object of research.   As a result, social science is full of dichotomies composed of the norm and a prominent deviation from it: "competition *and* monopoly," "voting *and* non-voting," "law observance *and* crime," "marriage *and* divorce," or "*and* prostitution," "employment *and* unemployment," "free *and* administered prices," and so on.   Even this overt recognition of departures from the norm belies the situation, for this Aristotelian emphasis upon classes and paired opposites hides the fact that one is dealing not with two contrasted poles but with a distribution of frequencies ranging from one extreme to the other.

The stubborn, unavoidable fact that confronts social science at every point is the presence, in every institutional trait that it seeks to analyze, of a subtly graded, unevenly distributed, and continually changing array of behavior. Individuals vary in their capacities and in their definitions of situations, and the pressures upon them to act in given ways or to depart from these ways of acting vary from moment to moment.   The Securities and Exchange Commission is not so much concerned with honest and dishonest brokers as it is with an infinite variety of specific practices employed in some degree at one time or another by most brokers, which practices blur imperceptibly from "performing a highly useful social function" at the one extreme into "gross exploitation of the public" at the other. New and more realistic possibilities of analysis will follow upon the frank recognition that each institution represents a distribution of individual conformities and dissents, and that the whole array of behavior must be studied if we are to understand what the institution is.

Edward Sapir of Yale University has stated acutely this necessity for driving cultural analysis down to the level of variant groups and individual differences:

It is no exaggeration to say that cultural analysis as ordinarily made is not a study of behavior at all. . . . Culture, as it is ordinarily constructed by the anthropologist, is a more or less mechanical sum of the more striking and picturesque generalized patterns of behavior. . . . [As such, these culture constructs] are not, and cannot be, the truly objective entities they claim to be. No matter how accurate their individual itemization, their integrations into suggested structures are uniformly fallacious and unreal. . . . If we make the test of imputing the contents of an ethnological monograph to a known individual in the community which it describes, we would inevitably be led to discover that, while every single statement in it may, in the favorable case, be recognized as holding true in some sense, the complex of patterns as described cannot, without considerable absurdity, be interpreted as a significant configuration of experience, both actual and potential, in the life of the person appealed to. Cultures, as ordinarily dealt with, are merely abstracted configurations of idea and action patterns, which have endlessly different meanings for the various individuals in the group. . . .

The complete, impersonalized "culture" of the anthropologist can really be little more than an assembly or mass of loosely overlapping idea and action systems which, through verbal habit, can be made to assume the appearance of a closed system of behavior. What tends to be forgotten is that the functioning of such a system, if it can be said to have any ascertainable function at all, is due to the specific functionings and interplays of the idea and action systems which have actually grown up in the minds of given individuals.

Professor Sapir concludes by suggesting the need for the close genetic study of the learning of a culture by individuals. "I venture to predict," he says "that the concept of culture which will then emerge, fragmentary and confused as it will undoubtedly be, will turn out to have a tougher, more vital, importance for social thinking than the tidy tables of contents attached to this or that group which we have been in the habit of calling 'cultures.' "

Analysis of institutional phenomena which seeks to proceed in disregard of the patent fact of wide individual differences is inevitably superficial and distorted. The assumption that differences "cancel each other out" is unwarranted because these differences are not identical quanta; they are qualitatively different; they carry therefore different weights, and they are thrown into the scales in different combinations and at different moments. Look at the range of these differences: In health we run the whole gamut, and what we do and the way we think is colored by how we feel when we get up in the morning and at each succeeding moment during the day. The energy of some of us is the despair of others. Some of us are confident, while others swing uneasily to the tides of anxiety and defensiveness. Some of us were born into a favored race or class, while others are forced to live uphill against set brakes because we belong to a minority group. Some of us have attractive, forceful personalities, physiques, and chins, while others must try "to win friends and influence people" with less auspicious endowments. For some of us "the future" runs reliably ahead, and for others it is no longer than tomorrow, or the end of the month. Then, too, as individuals we differ importantly in our capacity to learn; and we learn seemingly common things in a personal context that orients the thing learned, if and to the extent that it is learned, in different ways. We were all born little animals with unique endowments. We have been "house-broke" in varying ways—gently or roughly, consistently or erratically—by people bigger and stronger than ourselves and able to exercise authority over us. For convenience, we say we have "grown up," "become socialized," "been acculturated." What we mean is that we have learned, under the sharp sting of necessity, how to "get by" and get what we want and avoid trouble in terms of the habit systems of our coercive elders, who in turn had picked up their habits from the retrospective habits of their elders. What a social scientist deals with, therefore, is not a unit institution carried evenly by all persons, similarly learned in and responding to the institution in question. The problems that social science wrestles with derive to an important extent from the fact that different individuals and masses of individuals react differently to supposedly common institutions.

The viewing of culture as the behavior of individuals is important because it helps to counteract the over-easy acceptance of the officially promulgated norms (legal and "right" ways of doing things) or of assumed central tendencies (usual or most frequent ways of doing things) as the operating reality of an institution. It helps to keep prominently in focus all types of varying behavior around the problem in question; it also breaks down the false rigidities between "the" norm and all deviants by substituting a continuum, all parts of which are normal behavior to the particular persons involved. . . .

We watch culture change and say that "it changes." But culture does not "work," "move," "change," but is worked, is moved, is changed. It is *people* who do things, and when their habits and impulses cease to carry an institutional folkway, that bit of the culture disappears. "When one system of habits and mores is offered by one group to another, and the second refuses to adopt the new ones, there is a temptation to think in terms of a disembodied entity, a cultural pattern, which is incapable of 'assimilating' the new features. . . . The important thing is that it is *the Indians* that resist, and not their 'cultural pattern.' " The Patent Office has registered thousands of changes that never "went" because people did not "take them up" and make them "go"; and the suppression of patents by corporations like the Bell Telephone Company shows the relative helplessness of useful patents ready to go when strategically placed people elect to suppress them.

The culture does not enamel its fingernails, or vote, or believe in capitalism, but people do, and some do and some do not. When I give away a still warm and comfortable overcoat because it is beginning to look worn, I feel myself to be responding to people—my wife, my business associates, people at the club—and what they will think of me, and only incidentally and remotely, if at all, am I motivated by a non-personalized "cultural standard." When I stop my car at a red traffic light, it is an abstraction to say that I am "obeying the law"; what I *feel* in the situation is that *people* will do inconvenient things to me if I do not stop. Or to state this point from the viewpoint of comparative cultures: Objects and experiences that trip the trigger that releases a long line of associated actions in one habituated to a given culture may either be without meaning or have a different meaning to persons from another culture. A man in a blue uniform at a traffic intersection blowing a whistle when a light changes from green to red means to me as I drive toward him, "Stop my car—or else he will give me a ticket and I will have to lose time from my work and go to court and have to pay a fine and get on the court records as a traffic violator." But to an Eskimo he would mean none of these things. Likewise, a bank building with Corinthian columns would mean to an Eskimo only an extra-gorgeous shelter from wind and snow, while a calf-bound law book costing us fifteen dollars might mean to him a chunk of fuel, a nice chopping block on which to slice up fish, or perhaps an object to hurl at an enemy. Abstracted from the persons who live them, cultural institutions become dimmed, and often distorted, shadows on the wall.

Problem 2: How Unique Are the Culture and Character of America?

If a completely objective picture of American life could be drawn, it would have to be created by that legendary but often quoted visitor, the Man from Mars. And even his observations would probably be written off as one man's opinion. No formula has yet been devised to eliminate entirely the bias of subjectivity. We have attempted to avoid some pitfalls inherent in evaluating a phenomenon as complex as a national culture by selecting diverse sources. The commentaries include those of a ranking Russian journalist, a British cultural anthropologist, and an American anthropologist. Each interpretation, however, may contain personal judgments that not only warrant, but also demand, analysis and discussion.

For hundreds of years the distressed, the unwanted, the dispossessed looked to America as the land of the second chance. America's reputation as the land of opportunity was sung in song and saga, and the American, too, was heralded far and wide. Crèvecoeur, writing in 1782, referred to the American as "this new man." Throughout the nineteenth century a steady stream of journalists, novelists, historians, and philosophers visited the United States and found everything from a new country or a new people to an inferior segment of Western civilization. What is the situation today? Have the differences that were so apparent to earlier observers now disappeared? Is America still unique in its spirit and character? What are the strengths and shortcomings of American culture?

ILYA EHRENBURG'S AMERICA *

Americans have always been interested in the foreign visitor's impressions of their institutions and culture. During the nineteenth century the observations of European writers were often critical, sometimes penetrating, and occasionally banal. The twentieth-century commentaries on American life were generally still critical, but the criticisms took on a somewhat milder tone.

The following remarks are of interest not only as the commentary of

* Reprinted from *Harper's Magazine*, December, 1946, pp. 563–66, 568–74, 576.

a visitor but also because Ilya Ehrenburg is the foremost Soviet journalist, and his views on the United States, which appeared in *Izvestia*
during July and August, 1946, were written for Russian consumption.
Which comments appear to have validity?   Which do not?   Why do
you suppose Ehrenburg devotes so much attention to problems of
racial discrimination?   Is this preoccupation justifiable in terms of
what has been accomplished?   What techniques does he use to indict
democracy and American culture without openly stating that this is his
purpose?   How would you reply to this article?

. . . Modernity cannot be understood without understanding America.
Hundreds of odes and pamphlets have been dedicated to her; she can be
exalted or ridiculed with ease.   But this is not merely a peculiar country,
but also a diverse one, difficult to understand.   It is hard to set forth vivid,
often contradictory, impressions in brief notes.   Behind the complexity of
technology there is sometimes concealed spiritual simplicity, and behind
this simplicity—unexpected complexity.

I rate American literature very highly.   It is not easy now to find writers
in Western Europe equal to Hemingway, Faulkner, Steinbeck, or Caldwell.
I might venture to add two or three more names.   Right behind them is
a vacuum—stories in illustrated weeklies which are so cheap and stupid
that even the most unexacting readers in Europe would recoil from them.
There is no intermediate literature here, just as there are no four- or five-
story houses.   The skyscrapers of New York are justified by geography;
this is a huge city built on small islands.   But in a provincial city one may
see several skyscrapers surrounded by thousands of single-story houses.

At the railway station in Atlanta I was amazed by the automatic checking booths which have replaced the cloakroom.   You insert a coin, receive
a key, and can lock up your luggage yourself.   I was about to say to my
American companion, "You know how to make human existence easier,"
but before I could speak I noticed a dark, noisome room marked "For non-
Whites" in which Negroes and mulattoes were dozing.   In the state of
Mississippi I saw the home of a plantation owner.   It had a refrigerator,
a washing machine, a marvelous radio, and wonderful ventilators.   The
planter calmly explained that black-skinned people aren't people at all.
Neither the radio nor the ventilators had any reflection on the mental development of this slaveowner.

I stayed in several university towns.   In America a great deal is done to
elevate knowledge to its proper height.   I saw superb libraries and laboratories: I saw scientists surrounded with attention.   But in Tennessee professors told me they were not allowed the right to expound the theory of
evolution in the schools: the law forbids any departure from the biblical
myth of Adam and Eve.

In all American cities there are "lions'" clubs: I was fortunate enough to attend a luncheon at such a club in one town. Respectable business men assembled there, each one wearing a tag indicating the place and nature of his business; luncheons are closely associated with business. Before those present at the luncheon began to eat their compotes and mayonnaise and ham with raisins, the chairman banged the table with a wooden hammer and explained: "Greetings, lions!" The middle-aged business men at once rose and chorused: "Woo-woo-woo-woo." I quailed, but they explained that they were imitating the lion's roar.

Naturally, the sound-imitations of dealers in suspenders are an innocent affair. There are worse ideas. A parade of the Ku Klux Klan recently took place in Georgia. The members of this supposedly secret society donned fools' hoods and took an oath of loyalty to the local fascist *fuhrer,* whom they call the "Grand Dragon." They then swore to hang several Negroes and kill several freethinkers.

Everyone knows that in America money is surrounded with respect. Apart from many hundreds of registered churches and sects there is still another cult—the dollar. An art critic, after introducing a young artist to me, reeled off his surname and then, enunciating precisely, said "Three thousand dollars." A master of ceremonies at a cabaret announced that eminent visitors were present: an actress, a senator, and a business man "who has tripled his capital turnover since the war." I attended many dinner meetings with a program much like this one; first, everybody quickly chews the chicken, then orators give lengthy speeches; then a female singer renders a sentimental ballad; and finally a pastor takes a collection for charity. He recites the names of the liberal donors: "Mr. Smith gave five hundred dollars." Everyone applauds and Mr. Smith rises and bows.

It is not well known that, along with brisk business men, there are also many naive day-dreamers and noble idealists in America. I met a prominent inventor who renounced a fortune, fearing that the machine he invented would deprive hundreds of thousands of workers of their bread. I spoke to provincial Utopians who go without food and sleep, devoting their money and energy to the fantastic project of creating a "world government." In one town I found a circle of eccentrics who were convinced that they could render the atomic bomb harmless with the aid of Esperanto. Everywhere there are societies to protect the rights of Negroes. Every year innocent Negroes are condemned and put to death in the electric chair, and every year the best people in America protest against racial barbarism. Yes, the cult of the dollar does exist in America, but in America there are also people who deny themselves a pair of shoes and tickets to the cinema in order to send gifts to Yugoslav children.

There is much that is childish in Americans. They are not artificial;

they are frank, curious, and noisy. The oldest part of America is called New England. Everything in America is new; everything is young. In New Orleans, however, houses built in the seventeenth and eighteenth centuries have been preserved in the French Quarter. Such houses are legion in Europe and are ignored by even the most painstaking tourists. But the "Old Quarter" of New Orleans is like Pompeii—a real center of pilgrimage. There is either an antique shop or a stylized tavern in almost every house. I was in New Orleans on a very sultry day (the tropics are not far off), and a fire was burning in the grate of one house—to re-create the atmosphere of a bygone epoch. Perspiring Americans were sitting by the fire drinking iced water; they wanted to spend several minutes in an *old* house. One must remember the age of the country to understand Americans.

People here like to wander about. If they are sitting in a room, they jump up from time to time and change seats; they move readily from city to city and from state to state. They regard a person who lives in the place where he was born as a rarity.

There is nothing more the reverse of the British character and customs than the character and customs of the average American. The Englishman is polite and phlegmatic; he loves to live out his life in the house of his grandfather; he orders his suit of first-quality material, expecting to wear it, if not until he dies, at least until the next elections. The American likes only new clothes. Hardly has he furnished his apartment than he is looking for another. He never has a suit made to order; why should he? In any shop he can find a cheap, well-made suit; can wear it a little and then throw it out. He will buy a shirt that is not worth washing. He respects old stones, but loves flashy new ties—and noise.

The history of the United States is indeed a new history. I might say, incidentally, that history studied by school children appears to vary in different states; in the North the Southerners are called "defenders of slavery," and in the South the Northerners are called "oppressors." Vexed issues here frequently hide the feeling of history. For the average American nearly a whole epoch passes between the morning and evening papers; he doesn't always remember in the evening exactly what disturbed him in the morning. One lady told me: "Don't read this novel. It's not a new one; it came out two years ago."

I spoke to Professor Einstein about the campaign now being waged by various large newspapers against the Soviet Union. I pointed to an article which portrayed the restoration of Stalingrad almost as an act of "Soviet imperialism." Professor Einstein answered: "Such articles are designed for readers who have already forgotten what Stalingrad is." And he went on to tell me about a certain African tribe in which the members were

named after objects or phenomena: "mountain," "palm," "dawn," "hawk."
When a member of the tribe died, his name became taboo, and it became
necessary to think up new nouns for these things. Obviously such a tribe
would have neither legends nor traditions.

Anti-Soviet ideologists like to depict our country as a sort of barracks in
which everyone is deprived of individuality. The Soviet reader will be
amused by the surprise of some American editors who, on seeing us three
visitors, said "Why, they don't look much like one another."

As a matter of fact, I don't know of any country which has achieved such
perfection of standardization as the United States. I was in dozens of
American cities which were impossible to distinguish from each other.
Every city has its Main Street—the principal street—with fashion shops,
a cinema, and lighted signs advertising cigarettes or Coca-Cola. Not a
single American can distinguish Main Street in one town from Main Street
in one of a hundred others from a photograph. Naturally, New York
has its own distinctive character, yet Americans usually complain that
"New York is not America." For the inhabitant of Birmingham or St.
Louis, gigantic New York, with its many different races, is like a headquarters of a den of freethinkers. The visitor is shaken by the external
appearance of New York. The architect Le Corbusier called this city "a
catastrophic fairyland." It seems to me that it can also be called "a fairy-
like catastrophe." It has grown exclusively upward and has become a tall
forest of reinforced concrete. At night it resembles mountains with lighted
huts. It is multicolored, noisy, and fatiguing. It contains dozens of
separate towns—Negro, Jewish, Italian, Puerto Rican, German, and others.
In Chinatown barbers promise on their placards to remove bruises from
the face without trace. In Negro Harlem there are "shirt hospitals" and
private pawnshops where torn trousers may be pawned. On 57th Street
dealers sell masterpieces of European art. The wives of millionaires wander down Fifth Avenue in beaver coats. New York is the center of political thought and art. Officially it is not even the capital of a state but only
an insignificant town. It is, however, the real capital of America. Two
or three other towns—San Francisco, New Orleans, and Boston—have preserved their individual aspects. But the remaining towns are without personality; they are simply aggregations of a given number of Americans.

Trousers, percolators, and armchairs are standardized, too. I do not say
this reproachfully, for Americans have succeeded in raising the material
level of life, thanks to mass production. I think we can learn something
from the Americans: how to turn out shoes or saucepans quickly and well.
However, almost all luxury articles in America are imported and a salesman who wishes to explain why this or that is expensive says, "But this is
imported."

There is a certain depression in such uniformity: the same houses, the same furniture, the same crockery; men in identical suits; women in identical dresses. But still I do not agree with the European aesthetes who have ridiculed the standardization in America. Perhaps all the suits are alike; on the other hand, they are accessible to all.

Much more deplorable is a certain spiritual standardization. Americans are fond of speaking about their liberty; but their views, tastes, emotions, and consequent behavior are regulated from outside. The cinema, for instance, lays down the standard for beauty, and the papers supply all the details of the "ideally shaped" woman. This is the standard of desire. All American women are guided by these references in their efforts to resemble some film star, while men fall in love according to the same references without noticing it. There are no books with average circulation. Even the most remarkable book will not be circulated in more than several thousand copies unless it has been pronounced worth reading by some "book club," in which case it will be published in hundreds of thousands of copies. Since the average American does not like to choose, he entrusts the right to choose to his "club." The press and cinema de-personalize the ideas of people who stroll along thousands of Main Streets in the evening. This forms the key to the sense of depression which is linked with leisure in America. . . .

. . . It would seem that in this country of diverse races united by patriotism, national equality would prevail. However, America, which never knew feudalism, has established a *racial* hierarchy. The aristocracy are the English, Scotch, and Irish. After them come the Scandinavians and Germans, then the French and Slavs; much lower are the Italians, even lower still the Jews and Chinese; lower still the Puerto Ricans, and finally, at the bottom of the scale, the Negroes.

In the war against Hitlerism America played a prominent part; yet racialism here has a legal standing. When I entered America I had to fill out a questionnaire which contained the question: "Race—White or Colored?" If a person has a "colored" great-grandfather he is designated as "colored" and is subject to various restrictions. We were the guests of the government, and I was often amused by the thought of the reaction the representatives of the State Department might have had if Pushkin had come to America. I met a lawyer in Nashville who spent a long time trying to persuade me that there are "inferior and superior races." He reiterated the theories of Rosenberg and other ideologists of the Third Reich. Then he showed me the portrait of his brother, who was killed on the Rhine; he was proud of his brother, who had perished in the struggle against racialists.

Anti-Semitism is an ordinary phenomenon to most Americans; it seems quite natural to them that some institutions accept only Aryans and that certain hotels do not admit Jews. On the West Coast the Chinese are the pariahs. There are organizations in which Italians are not accepted as members. The fate of the Negroes is especially tragic. There are twelve million of them in the United States, and it may be said that one out of every ten Americans is deprived of all human rights.

Natives of New York like to emphasize the liberalism of the North— "*Our* grandfathers fought against slavery." In any Southern town, on the other hand, you may see a monument to the soldiers of the Southern army. This is a monument to the vanquished, because in the war which shook America the Southerners were defeated. However, it seemed to me more than once that these were monuments, not to the vanquished, but to the victors; since the South not only preserved the principles of slavery but was able, in some degree, to inject them into the North. Certainly equal rights among the races exist *theoretically* in New York. A Negro may not be ejected from a restaurant because he is a Negro, but not a single well-ordered American restaurant will admit a Negro. If it occurs to him to persist, he is told that the empty tables are reserved. A Negro cannot rent a room anywhere except in a Negro "ghetto." He may work in the most different sort of quarters, but he is obliged to live in Harlem, a Negro city within a city—dirty and impoverished, unhappy but still gay. New Yorkers amuse themselves in the cabarets in Harlem. The Negroes are the best dancers and musicians in America; they are gifted with a high sense of rhythm and are not as inherently mechanical as other Americans. In the center of New York there are theaters where Negro troupes perform excellently and are willingly applauded by the whites. But if a Negro wants to have a snack in a restaurant near the theater in which he is playing, he is calmly evicted.

Real estate speculators have a favorite trick; they buy a house in a good residential district and settle a Negro in it. The quarter than becomes taboo immediately, and all the whites depart. The speculator then buys the neighboring houses for a song, moves out the single Negro, and the section again becomes respectable—and the houses rise in price.

Still, in order to understand the place of the Negro in America, it is essential to see the South. When we were asked which part of America we wanted to see, my fellow-travelers chose California and Chicago. I wanted to see the Southern states. Remembering stories I had read—the novels of Steinbeck and Faulkner—I wanted to find out if reality resembled literature. Thus, after the skyscrapers of New York I saw Uncle Tom's Cabin, and I can say that this cabin has changed little.

In all the Southern states there is a "segregation of the races" law. Negroes are not forbidden to use railroads, but they must travel in special cars (always overcrowded). In streetcars, seats are set aside for Negroes in the rear. A car frequently leaves almost empty while Negroes stand and wait for the next one, as the seats for them are occupied. Negroes may not attend meetings of whites, they dare not enter a church where white people are praying, and of course they must not even dream of entering theaters or cinemas for whites.

The Constitution of the United States guarantees that all citizens, male and female, have the right to take part in elections. However, the Negroes in the Southern states do not possess the right to vote. In the state of Alabama there are three million inhabitants, of whom 1,100,000 are Negroes. Among the voters of the state are 496,000 whites and 4,000 Negroes. In Birmingham, Alabama, there are 130,000 Negroes who have reached the age of twenty-one, but the total number of Negro voters is only 1,400. How do the Southern states get around the federal Constitution? There are several ways: one, the poll tax; another, examinations. The qualified voter must know and "be able to interpret" the Constitution. Clearly the examiners can cut out many Negroes. Finally, if the Negroes pay their poll tax, pass the examination, and go to the voting places, the guardians of slavery frighten away the unwanted voters with sturdy clubs. Obviously they do indeed know how to "interpret" the Constitution in the Southern states! In the state of Mississippi, Negroes form half of the population; half the inhabitants of the state are deprived of the right to vote. All this is done cynically and is well known to all Americans both in the North and in the South.

When I was in Mississippi I remembered how certain American journalists had been indignant when the Yugoslav National Front government had deprived about 200,000 people who had aided the Germans of the right to vote. These same American journalists consider it quite natural, however, that millions of American Negroes (among them soldiers who took part in the war for the freedom of America) are not allowed to vote. I would ask a question of my American readers: which is more fair—to take away the right to vote from people with black consciences or with black skins?

The Northerners know that Negroes in the South are deprived of political rights, but they cannot imagine the fearful life of Southern Negroes. When Sam Grafton, one of New York's brilliant journalists, saw the hovel in which two or three Negro families made their home, he lost his self-control. "Is this really possible?" he gasped. Uncle Sam had met Uncle Tom.

The delta of the Mississippi is made up of many cotton plantations. The land is owned by the whites and rented to the blacks. The tenants must deliver half their cotton to the landowners; they are also bound to sell the other half to the same owners. The sum which the Negroes receive may be spent only in the shops of the same landlords. This may be legally close to tenantry, but in reality it is slavery. The landowner, who is also the purchaser of the cotton, dealer in shoes, kerosene, and salt, goes around his plantation shouting at the Negroes, issuing orders, and behaving like a king and a god.

I saw a family which earned $300 in a year and another which earned $200. The owner of the plantation on which they lived said to me that last year had been "unsuccessful," and that he had earned only $25,000. I saw one house in which twenty-three people lived, sleeping side by side on the floor. How far this is from the renowned American comfort, the refrigerators, elevators, and chewing gum! The Mississippi, a broad and bright yellow river, sees grief—the black grief of the blacks.

I was often told in New York that all American children under sixteen must go to school. An illusion. In the South I saw youths who cannot read, who have not seen schools, and since early youth have known only one thing—hard labor. In super-hygienic America, people are living in stalls. When births are difficult women cannot have medical assistance; a visit from the doctor costs $60, and the yearly income is only $200. But the slaveowners smile: "You don't know the Negroes. They are living in paradise. Of course they don't need anything more."

. . . I was in a Negro university where there are about seven hundred students of both sexes. They will become doctors, teachers, and lawyers; but they will only be able to help Negroes and teach Negro children. "Colored" professors and students have no access to the public library. Professor Brady, a chemist of high reputation, told me that he did not have the right to work in a state university laboratory.

In Fisk University there is a Russian girl student whose mother is from Odessa and whose father is a Negro. She speaks Russian and does not have negroid features. But her passport declares her "colored," and she comes under the law on the "segregation of the races." In New Orleans I knew an architect—a ginger-haired man with freckles—who was one of the best educated persons in the city. I wanted him to go with me to a cafe, but he declined. Afterward friends explained to me that this light-skinned man was a Negro and consequently did not have the right to go into a cafe.

There are also unwritten laws in the South. A white man may rape a Negro woman but is not punishable for this. On the other hand, if a Negro cohabits with a white woman, he is accused of rape and condemned to the electric chair. Justice in the South is close to "lynch law." Not long ago six whites in Albeville raped a Negro girl. The court found "no case of crime." In Pessemor a Negro traveling in a streetcar stepped over the permitted "border" several inches. The driver wounded him. What happened then? The police arrested not the white driver but the Negro and killed him as a precaution. In the city of Columbia thirty Negroes were brought up for trial. Why? The whites, in organizing a pogrom, which is called a "racial disorder" in the South, killed two Negroes and injured twelve. It is not the murderers who have to answer, but the fathers, brothers, and sons of those murdered. A lawyer in Jackson who was trying to save the life of an innocent Negro told me that no one really doubted the innocence of the Negro, but that white people had given evidence against him; the court could not believe black men's testimony contrary to the evidence of whites, even if the latter were false witnesses. There are no Negro jurors in the South, and the courts do not acquit Negroes. On the other hand, if by any chance the people who have lynched a Negro land on the prisoner's bench, their acquittal is guaranteed.

At the head of the slaveowners stands Senator Bilbo, a red-haired demagogue who attracts hearers with stormy appeals to "bridle the blacks." Bilbo has proposed removing all American Negroes to Liberia. The slaveowners would look well without slaves! However, everyone knows that this was only said by the Senator in jest. He is a Senator of the state of Mississippi, where Negroes are no fewer than the whites, and where the whites often shiver when they think of the mass of destitute, embittered people who may someday become fed up with singing hallelujah in expectation of the regular hanging.

Not a few Negroes have been in Europe; many fought for America against racialist Germany. They saw that in Paris or Rome no one looked at them as though they were plagued, and they returned home with even greater bitterness. The South is on the eve of a decisive event: either the owners will yield, or the Negroes—yesterday's men of the front line—will open the struggle for equality.

I am convinced that in the end racialism will be overthrown in America; but it must be understood that this disease has penetrated deeply into the mind of the average American. I did not meet a single white in the South who was not contaminated with racialism. One of the most fervent opponents of the slaveowners admitted to me in a frank and intimate conversation: "Yes, I defend the Negroes, but just the same, for me these are not people. I was playing yesterday with our Negro maid's child and found myself thinking that I was playing, not with a child, but with a nice puppy." Racialism has infected even the persecuted; I met Negro anti-Semites and Jews convinced of the superiority of whites over blacks.

Americans love to drink mixtures of different liquors. Among the multitude of cocktails there is one which resembles the rainbow—yellow, emerald, and red liquors which do not mix in the glass but lie in multi-colored layers. They are mixed only in the mouth of the drinker. I could compare this drink with the racial layers of America. How strange it is that the idea of racial "purity" finds fervent supporters in a country which is strong through the mixture of different races! Cocktails may be liked or disliked, but it is difficult to imagine a bartender preparing a mixture for a customer who will insist on purity, organic nature, and maturity in his drink. I have seen racialists in America defending the idea of the racial superiority of Americans over other peoples. For what did the American soldiers die in Normandy and on the Rhine?

. . . At night the roads in America and especially near the cities sparkle with hundreds of lighted advertisements—Coca Cola, cigarettes, furniture, candidates for the Senate, and even the Bible. The different churches and sects advertise their services—the beauty of the music, the eloquence of the preacher, and the comfort of the building—extensively in the press.

If you switch on the radio you will inevitably hear an advertisement for tinned goods, medicines, or ties in the middle of symphony music or radio comedies. In many American cities I saw the following advertisement: "500,000,000 people are starving. Be economical. Heinz—57 varieties." Although I have been able to acquaint myself with certain peculiarities of this country, I have still been amazed as to why human solidarity is preached not by the government, but by a firm making sausages and fifty-seven renowned varieties. I voiced my feeling to a chairman of a Chamber of Commerce. He was surprised to find I didn't understand such an elementary fact. "If such an appeal were signed by the government," he explained, "Americans would not believe it. But everyone believes Heinz, because it is a really reliable firm."

The press, radio, and cinema are in the hands of various reliable and unreliable firms. The editor of a large provincial newspaper said to me with a sigh: "Our independent paper depends entirely on advertisements. If we were to lose our advertising, we would not last a week." The wireless stations are owned by private firms and also depend upon advertising for their existence.

I was reminded again of the book I wrote many years ago about the cinema "dream factory." The American's desire to forget and divert himself by day-dreaming in the evening has given birth to a vast industry; in Hollywood mass dreams are turned out just as skillfully and quickly as tinned meat in Chicago. However, the dream factory is more dangerous than the hash factory; film producers organize the spiritual world of the average American, inculcating him with portable morals and guiding his thoughts and feelings. The producers may compete with each other over directors and actresses, but they are all subordinate to their own internal censorship, the Hays Office, which ruthlessly cuts out everything that may resemble free thinking.

Hollywood is a dangerous den for Quakers and slaveowners. Indeed, art claims its own and scores of talented people work in Hollywood; but they are surrounded by a wall. Chaplin himself found out what going against the wall of money means. The average American is convinced that he is inwardly independent, and he is terrified by "propaganda." In actual fact he repeats what he has read in the paper, heard on the radio, and seen on the screen. I often had occasion to meet representatives of the press; I inspected the offices of large papers, and I learned how public opinion is formed in them.

How do the huge trusts organize public opinion? Not by articles, because few people read them and the readers are incredulous. The majority of American newspapers wrote against Roosevelt, but the readers preferred Roosevelt to Dewey. The President's activity was apparent for all to see, and every American was a competent judge—all the more so as Roosevelt and his supporters spoke at thousands of meetings refuting the distortions of the newspapers. When I said to my American friends that the press poisoned readers they usually answered: "You over-emphasize the importance of newspapers. We do not submit to propaganda; we know how to think independently."

However in order to think independently, one must know of what one is thinking. The average American knew Roosevelt's tax policy, but can he know exactly what is going on in Iran, Germany, or Bulgaria? He thinks "independently" about the distortions which are brought to him by the first page of the newspaper. He asks himself whether the Russians are doing right or wrong in moving their tanks on Teheran and whether or not the Bulgarians are right in striving to retain the Greek Rhodopes; he does not know the data of the problem which he is attempting to solve. He does not suspect that Soviet tanks were never moved to Teheran; nor that there is not a single Greek in the Bulgarian Rhodopes.

The papers controlled by the trusts or by individual magnates of the printed word occupy themselves in misinforming people under an appearance of information. They are crafty and pretend to be objective: for every ten anti-Soviet articles showing that our country allegedly wishes to swallow the whole world right up to Guatemala and the Honduras, a small article is invariably published praising the works of a Soviet botanist or the skill of Soviet sportswomen. Many papers publishing monstrous fables about our country requested me to write something for them. The misled reader repeats: "Whatever you may say, our press is the most objective in the world."

. . . On the front page of a Birmingham newspaper I saw a huge picture of a girl; I decided that this good-looking individual had either murdered someone or had married a millionaire. It turned out that she had merely gone to Hollywood hoping to become a film star and had there become pregnant. There was nothing else worthy of note in her history, but just the same she had hit the front page.

Reporters in general are energetic people but not overeducated. I noted down several questions which one reporter put to me and herewith quote them in order: "Are you wearing an American or a Russian suit? Do the Russian people know that America helped them in the war? How do people in Moscow find out the latest trends on the stock market? Have you been married long? Why do you have only one political party in Russia and not two? Do you get up late? Why do you want to take possession of Albania?"

I will stipulate, however, that misconceptions occur not only among reporters. In New Orleans a lady professor of sociology who sat next to me at an official dinner asked me, "Are you a Red or a White Russian?"

I am convinced that the American reader is usually more intelligent than the newspaper which he reads, but involuntarily he yields to a lot of nonsense. The day before yesterday he was frightened to death by the atom bomb tests. Yesterday, disillusioned, he was saying that "Gilda" (the nickname for the bomb) had made a laughing-stock of herself. Today he is struck with emotion by the death of the goats and pigs which perished in the tests, since the paper told him in detail that a memorial would be erected in honor of the dead animals. He does not even think that perhaps his children are threatened with death from some sort of "Gilda."

. . I have told of a conspiracy of evil. I do not believe in the success of this plot. True, the average American possesses neither political maturity nor a knowledge of Europe. But he has a healthy mind and a heart. He has not always been well educated, he is poisoned with race prejudice, and he naively worships the paper dollar, although he hears the pastors in the churches condemning the cult of the golden calf. Perhaps he is too self-confident. But he is not wicked and certainly not a stupid person. America is growing; I speak not of skyscrapers but of people. Each year there are more and more people who are dimly referred to as "progressive." These people demand human rights for Negroes, ridicule prejudices and hypocrisy, condemn support for Franco, desire to uproot fascism, both in Germany and beyond its borders, and are passionately interested in our culture, our books, and our films. Granted that these people are a minority, they are a minority which thinks, fights, and seeks the truth. These people see the salvation of America not in the fact that the Russians will have few saucepans but in each American having, in addition to saucepans, profound thoughts and true feelings.

I left many sincere friends in America—not only personal friends, but friends of the Soviet people, friends of thought and conscience. Americans are fond of directness. I stated frankly what I liked and did not like in America. Only the sick and impotent should have their feelings spared. Americans have a super-abundance of youth and health. Besides, they now have many European flatterers, eager for loans, trousers, and canned goods. And the Americans themselves love to judge—to judge and condemn. I know that they will receive my words as the words of a friend. This great people has great strength and great will. Its history must be worthy of it.

———◆•••◆———

THE AMERICAN CHARACTER *

Geoffrey Gorer, the author of the following selection, describes himself as a British "cultural anthropologist." He has a wide background in this field as well as a thoroughgoing work experience in the United States. While doing research on projects for the Rockefeller Foundation and Yale University's Institute on Human Relations, he visited all but two of the forty-eight states. Since Gorer is a British social scientist, it is important to ask, Does the author's detachment from American culture contribute to his objectivity? Are his observations pertinent and impartial or are they merely interesting?

The following selection is condensed from a prepublication article containing a portion of the author's book, *The American People: A Study in National Character*. In the article, as in the book, Gorer attempts to present an integrated psychoanalytical study of the American scene. In doing so he examines such typical relationships as children and parents, husband and wife, boys and girls, and Americans and foreigners. The passage reprinted here discusses dating habits, the accent on youth, and the relationship among American men.

. . . Since dating is uncommon in the rest of the world and, indeed, unknown in most of it, a note of introduction is necessary to a fuller discussion of the subject. For the American child, "Am I successful?" comes to mean "Am I loved?" for from the very beginning the mother's unquali-

* Geoffrey Gorer, *Life*, August 18, 1947. Copyright 1947, Geoffrey Gorer.

fied love and approval has been given to her child in proportion to its success. By adolescence most Americans have inextricably confused the two ideas: to be successful is to be loved, to be loved is to be successful.

To gain one's mother's love, the prototype of all future love, it is not necessary that one should show love in return; one is loved for one's accomplishments vis-a-vis one's age-mates, not in the first place for one's attitude and behavior toward one's mother. Love in America therefore tends to have a nonreciprocal quality: to be loved it is not necessary to love in return but rather to be worthy of love. Because the child is pushed to the very limits of its capacity, because the conditions for its success are often so vague or so far outside its control, the child becomes insatiable for the signs of love, reassuring itself that it is worthy of love and therefore a success. Now, the least of these signs of love is the attention of other people (in the first place the parents) or, at the minimum, their presence, so that their attention, if not immediately fixed on one, may be momentarily so directed. If nobody is there, if one is alone, how can one still the gnawing doubts that maybe one is not a success, not lovable, not worthy of love?

It is these feelings which make loneliness intolerable to well-adjusted Americans and account for the numerous social features which are designed to obviate it: the absence of doors in all but the most private parts of most houses, the wedged-open doors of offices and studies, the innumerable clubs and fraternal and patriotic associations, professional organizations and conventions. They account also for the dating which occupies so much of nearly every American's leisure time from before adolescence until betrothal. Dating is a highly patterned activity or group of activities, comparable in some ways to a formal dance, in others to a very complicated competitive game. As in dances and games, the activity is felt to be enjoyable and rewarding for its own sake, and the more enjoyable the more nearly the partners or players are matched in skill and other necessary qualifications. There is one aspect, however, in which the comparison to a game breaks down. In a successful date there should not be a loser; both parties should feel their self-esteem, their assurance enhanced.

Because dating is so idiosyncratic of Americans (though most Americans do not suspect this, believing, like the rest of the world, that the behavior they are used to is "human nature") and because it employs the form—but not the content—of love-making, it has been the cause of innumerable and serious misunderstandings whenever young Americans have come in contact with foreigners of the opposite sex. An invitation to a date—a pleasant and mutually profitable evening to enhance each other's self-esteem and demonstrate one's skill in the game—is almost always interpreted by a non-American as an attempt at seduction. If it is indignantly repudiated both parties are left angry and dissatisfied; if it is immediately acceded to, the American at least feels defrauded, as if one had set out for a hunt and the fox had insisted on sitting down in one's backyard.

The date starts as an invitation from a boy or young man to a girl for an evening's public entertainment. The entertainment offered depends on the young man's means and aspirations and the locality. But it is in a public place always and nearly always includes eating food together, the food being anything from an ice-cream soda at the local drugstore to the most elaborate and expensive meal that the locality can provide. Besides the food the most usual entertainment is dancing—the place of the dance ranging anywhere from the cheap roadside cafe with a juke box to the most expensive cabaret or country club. The male (the "escort") should call for the girl in a car (unless he be particularly young or poor) and should take her back in the car. If the entertainment proposed is of a formal or expensive nature, the man should provide a corsage—flowers for the girl to wear on her dress or in her hair. "Showing the girl a good time" is the essential background for a date, but it is not its object, as far as the man is concerned; its object is to get the girl to prove that he is worthy of love and therefore a success.

Since on first dates the pair are normally comparative strangers to one another, a certain amount of autobiography is necessary in the hopes of establishing some common interest or experience, at the least to prove that one is worthy of the other's attention. These autobiographies, however, differ at most in emphasis, in tone of voice, from those which should accompany any American meeting between strangers. What distinguishes the date from other conversation is a mixture of persiflage, flattery, wit and love-making which was formerly called a "line" but which each generation dubs with a new name.

The line is an individual variation of a commonly accepted pattern which is considered to be representative of a facet of a man's personality. Most men are articulately self-conscious about their lines and can describe them with ease. They are constantly practiced and improved with ever-differing partners. The object of the line is to entertain, amuse and captivate the girl, but there is no deep emotional involvement. It is a game of skill.

The girl's skill consists in parrying the line without discouraging her partner or becoming emotionally involved herself. To the extent that she falls for the line she is a loser in this intricate game. But if she discourages her partner so much that he does not request a subsequent date in the near future she is equally a loser. To remain the winner she must make the nicest discrimination between yielding and rigidity.

The man scores to the extent that he is able to get more favors from the girl than his rivals, real or supposed, would be able to do. The proving time is the return journey from the place of public entertainment to the girl's home. A goodnight kiss is almost the minimum repayment for an evening's entertainment, but how much more depends on the enterprise of the man, the self-assurance of the woman and the number of dates the pair have had together.

Dating is normally ended by betrothal, which is the almost inevitable sequel of a boy's concentration on one girl. The majority of Americans marry young, in many cases directly after graduation from high school or college. Marriage is meant to be founded on romance, on love, without any other considerations being involved. Because the ecstatic phase of love is rarely long-lasting, even though it be the sole reason for marriage, and is usually succeeded by domestic irritations and difficulties and the responsibilities of rearing a family, a very great value is placed by Americans on the period between adolescence and, say, the birth of the first child. By almost everybody this is considered the peak of life, after which there is a gradual but continuous decline.

This period, roughly from 12 to 25, is Youth—the Best Years of Our Lives—and is almost without exaggeration the *raison d'être* of our living. One of the major duties of those who have passed this period is to make certain that their successors can enjoy it at least as much as they did. One of the reasons why so much guilt was obscurely felt by older people for the depression which started in 1929 was that it marred the Youth of a whole generation; and one of the chief reasons advanced against sending American "boys" overseas before America entered the war and for bringing them back as soon as possible after military victory was that otherwise the irreplaceable years of their Youth would be frittered away. This emphasis on Youth is overwhelming in American popular entertainment, in films, in magazine stories and novels, in advertisements and so on. In point of fact Americans have nearly the greatest expectation of life of any peoples in the world and, like other urban societies, an ever-increasing number of old people in the population. But no medium of mass communication would enable one to learn this. Americans wish to think of themselves, to be presented as they were when they were at the peak of their lives; they identify themselves with their children rather than with their parents. By the same reasoning Americans constantly refer to themselves as a "Young Nation." On many counts they could be considered the "oldest" nation, for no other major power is living under an 18th Century constitution, and few are more politically conservative. But Youth is so pre-eminently desirable that it is inevitably ascribed to the nation as a whole.

The relationship between American men is normally of very low intensity. All Americans want to be popular with their fellows, but this popularity is easily obtained and demonstrated. Little is needed beyond the use of first names, the jokes and the slap on the back, the easy sharing of drink and hospitality, fluency in conversation. Nearly all Americans have a fear of rejection and stigmatize people who do not easily give these overt signs of friendship as "high hat," "snooty," or "snobbish," attempting to reject before they are rejected. For to be rejected, even by an overformal and unsmiling servant, suggests that one may be a failure, may be unworthy of love. In contrast, people who are prodigal with such simple signs of friendship, particularly to their economic and social inferiors, are praised as "regular guys," as "truly democratic." As a description of character, "democratic" is generally used in such a way that his or her inferiors are not reminded of their inferiority. It has no political connotations.

Because of their diffuseness and lack of intensity most American friendships between men are strictly temporary. Nostalgia for lost Youth keeps some old relationships alive between people who have shared the same experiences. But most Americans after marriage replace the friendly competitive group of age-mates by their present nearest rivals—their business or professional associates and often their neighbors, the parents of their children's friends. Americans change both residence and job with the greatest of ease, and with each change of either, friends are changed too. This does not mean that people are not conscious of preferences. But these are seldom important enough to be worth the effort of keeping alive when propinquity or common pursuits have disappeared. For many American men sufficient friendships are found in the numerous service and patriotic clubs and associations—Rotary, Lions, Kiwanis, Elks, Free Masons, American Legion and so on—which they join so frequently and with such enthusiasm.

This should not be taken to imply that Americans are friendless compared with Europeans. The converse would be more nearly true. But generally American friendship has extension rather than depth and is founded more on common interest than on congeniality of character. As nearly every Western European must have experienced in recent years, the American is remarkably ready to give and receive affection. But like so much of the household equipment which the Europeans also envy, friendship is not a luxury to Americans. It is a necessity.

An Anthropologist Looks at the United States *

The stimulating remarks of Ilya Ehrenburg and Geoffrey Gorer illustrate the complexity, diversity, and the contradictory aspects of the many facets of American life. They also indicate, perhaps, something of the background of the observer. Ehrenburg, a journalist, and Gorer, a social scientist, see different things in the same phenomenon. Possibly the cultural conditioning of each has a bearing on his interpretations. In any event, it is fitting to turn to the observations of an American writer, particularly when the author is one of America's most brilliant scholars. Mr. Clyde Kluckhohn has written numerous articles and books on the science of man and at the present time is Professor of Anthropology at Harvard University.

A reading of Ehrenburg, Gorer, and Kluckhohn raises obvious questions: To what extent is life in the United States different from that of other countries? What factors help to explain these variations? Are differences between countries and between various nationalities greater or less than they were a century ago?

American culture has been called a culture of paradoxes. Nevertheless national advertising and a national moving picture industry would be impossible were there not certain terms in which one can appeal to the vast majority of this capturable people. Though sectional, economic, and religious differences are highly significant in some respects, there are certain themes that transcend these variations. Some life goals, some basic attitudes tend to be shared by Americans in every region and of all social classes.

To start with the commonplace: even the most bitter critics of the United States have conceded us material generosity. In spite of the romanticism of "public-spirited disinterestedness" most Americans are outgoing and genuinely benevolent. Sometimes, to be sure, American humanitarianism is linked with the missionary spirit—the determination to help others by making the world over on the American model.

Perhaps no huge society has ever had such generalized patterns for laughter. In older civilizations it is commonly the case that jokes are fully understood and appreciated only by class or regional groups. It is true that it is some distance from the sophisticated humor of *The New Yorker* to the slapstick of popular radio programs. But the most widespread

---

* Clyde Kluckhohn, *Mirror For Man* (McGraw-Hill, 1949), pp. 230–37, 246–48.

formulas reach all Americans. Some of the most characteristic of these are related to the cult of the average man. No one becomes so great that we cannot make fun of him. Humor is an important sanction in American culture. Probably the ridicule of Hitler did more than all the rational critiques of Nazi ideology to make the man in the street contemptuous of Nazism.

All European travelers are struck by American attitudes toward women. They often note that "Americans spoil their women," or that "America is dominated by petticoats." The truth is more complicated. On the one hand, it is clear that a very large number of American women of privileged economic position are freed by labor-saving devices from much household drudgery—particularly after their few children have entered school. Their abundant leisure goes into women's clubs, community activities, "cultural" organizations, unhealthy devotion to their children, other mildly or seriously neurotic activities. It is also true that many American men are so wrapped up in pursuit of the success goal that they largely abdicate control over their children's upbringing to their wives. The responsibility of American women for moral and cultural questions is tremendous. On the other hand, it is too often forgotten that in 1940, 26 out of every 100 women of working age worked outside the home, that almost every girl who graduates from high school or college has had some job training. We interest women in careers but make it difficult for them to attain a full life in one. In a culture where "prestige" is everything we have felt it necessary to set aside Mother's Day as a symbolic atonement for the lack of recognition ordinarily given to domestic duties.

In Japan a year ago Japanese of many classes complained to me that it was difficult to understand American democracy because Americans seemed to lack an explicit ideology that they could communicate. The Japanese contrasted the Russians who could immediately give a coherent account of their system of beliefs. Various Americans have remarked that what the United States needed more than a good five-cent cigar was a good five-cent ideology. Such explicit ideology as we have derives largely from the political radicalism of the late eighteenth century. We repeat the old words, and some of the ideas are as alive now as then. But much of this doctrine is dated, and a new latent ideology inherent in our actual sentiments and habits is waiting for popular expression.

Particularly since the drastic disillusionment that followed the fine Wilsonian phrases of World War I, Americans have been shy at expressing their deepest convictions and have been verbally cynical about Fourth of July oratory. Yet devotion to the American Way has been none the less passionate. It is significant that aviators in this past war who were under narcotics in the course of psychotherapy would not only talk freely about personal emotional problems but were equally articulate on the ideological reasons for American participation in the war.

The pattern of the implicit American creed seems to embrace the following recurrent elements: faith in the rational, a need for moralistic rationalization, an optimistic conviction that rational effort counts, romantic individualism and the cult of the common man, high valuation of change—which is ordinarily taken to mean "progress," the conscious quest for pleasure.

Mysticism and supernaturalism have been very minor themes in American life. Our glorification of science and our faith in what can be accomplished through education are two striking aspects of our generalized conviction that secular, humanistic effort will improve the world in a series of changes, all or mainly for the better. We further tend to believe that morality and reason must coincide. Fatalism is generally repudiated, and even acceptance seems to be uncongenial—though given lip service in accord with Christian doctrine.

The dominant American political philosophy has been that the common man would think and act rationally. The same premises are apparent in typical attitudes toward parental responsibility. The individual, if "let alone" and not "corrupted by bad company," will be reasonable. If a child does not turn out well, the mother or both parents tend to blame themselves or to explain the failure by "bad blood"—as if action-guided-by-reason could of itself always produce well-adjusted children when the biological inheritance was adequate.

While many Americans are in some senses profoundly irreligious, they still typically find it necessary to provide moral justifications for their personal and national acts. No people moralizes as much as we do. The actual pursuit of power, prestige, and pleasure for their own sakes must be disguised (if public approval is to be obtained) as action for a moral purpose or as later justified by "good works." Conversely, a contemplative life tends to be considered "idleness."

The American mother offers her love to her child on the condition of his fulfilling certain performance standards. No conversational bromides are more characteristically American than "Let's get going"; "Do something"; "Something can be done about it." Although during the thirties there was widespread devaluation of present and future and though pessimism and apathy about the atomic bomb and other international problems are certainly strong currents in contemporary national thinking, the dominant American reaction is still—against the perspective of other cultures—that this is a world in which effort triumphs. A recent public opinion study showed that only 32 per cent of Americans were concerned about social security—for themselves.

Countless European observers have been impressed by "enthusiasm" as a typically American quality. During the war military analysts noted repeatedly that the British were better at holding a position but the Americans at taking one. As Margaret Mead has observed, the British cope with a problem; Americans start from scratch and build completely anew.

Americans are not merely optimistic believers that "work counts." Their creed insists that anyone, anywhere in the social structure, can and should "make the effort." Moreover, they like to think of the world as man-controlled. This view about the nature of life is thus intimately linked with that conception of the individual's place in society which may be called "romantic individualism."

In the English-speaking world there are two principal ideologies of individualism. The English variety (which may be tagged with the name of Cobden) is capitalistic in its basic outlook. American individualism has agrarian roots and may be associated with Jefferson. To this day Americans hate "being told what to do." They have always distrusted strong government. The social roles most frequently jibed at in comic strips are those that interfere with the freedom of others; the dogcatcher, the truant officer, the female social climber (Mrs. Jiggs) who forces her husband and family to give up their habitual satisfactions. "My rights" is one of the commonest phrases in the American language. This historically conditioned attitude toward authority is constantly reinforced by child-training patterns. The son must "go farther" than his father, and revolt against the father in adolescence is expected.

However, as de Tocqueville pointed out, Americans are characteristically more interested in equality than in liberty. "I'm as good as the next man," seems at first a contradiction of the American emphasis upon success and individual achievement within a competitive system. It is true that there are relatively few places at the top in a social pyramid—*at any one time.* But the American faith that "there is always another chance" has its basis in the historical facts of social mobility and the fluidity (at least in the past) of our economic structure. "If at first you don't succeed, try, try again." The American also feels that if he himself does not "get a break," he has a prospect for vicarious achievement through his children.

American individualism centers upon the dramatization of the individual. This is reflected in the tendency to personalize achievement, good or bad. Americans prefer to attack men rather than issues. Corporations are personified. Public power projects were advertised as much as means of beating the Utility Devil as a way of getting better and cheaper service.

The less opportunity, the greater the merit of success. "You can't keep a good man down." Conversely, failure is a confession of weakness, and status distinctions and even class lines are rationalized on such grounds as, "he got there by hard work," "it's his own fault that he didn't get on." Such attitudes—and the idealization of the "tough guy" and the "red-blooded American" and the fear of "being a sucker"—derive both from the Puritan ethic and from the American pioneer era. Aggressive activity and rapid mobility were effectual in the rapid development of a new country, and it made sense then that the rewards in money and status should be high.

The worship of success has gone farther than in any known culture, save possibly prewar Japan. This is reflected in countless staple phrases such as "bettering yourself," "getting ahead," and "how are you getting on?" The opposition to Roosevelt's proposal for a taxation program that would limit net income to $25,000, attests to the depth of feeling for slogans like "the sky's the limit." But the striving for money is not simply the pursuit of purposeless materialism. Money is primarily a symbol. The deeper competition is for power and prestige. "Aggressive" is, in American culture, a descriptive adjective of high praise when applied to an individual's personality or character. "You have to be aggressive to be a success." The obvious crudities of aggression are, as Lynd says, explained away by identifying them with the common good.

But there is a defensive note in this aggressiveness which is also symptomatic. Competitive aggressiveness against one's fellows is not just playing a part in a drama. The only way to be safe in American life is to be a success. Failure to "measure up" is felt as deep personal inadequacy. In a phrase, the American creed is equality of opportunity, not equality of man.

The cult of the average man might seem to imply disapproval of outstanding individuals of every sort. Certainly it is true that a great deal of hostility is directed upward. However, under the influence of the dramatic and success aspects of the "romantic individualism" orientation, the typical attitude toward leaders may best be described as one of mixed feelings. On the one hand, there is a tendency to snipe at superior individuals with a view to reducing them to the level of their fellows. On the other hand, their very success is a dramatic vindication of the American way of life and an invitation to identification and emulation.

The cult of the average man means conformity to the standards of the current majority. To de Tocqueville this was "enfeeblement of the individual." A more recent observer, Fromm, who also looked at the American scene from a European viewpoint, likewise finds this conformity repressive to self-expression. But he fails to see that the American is not a passive automaton submitting to cultural compulsives like European provincials. The American voluntarily and consciously seeks to be like others of his age and sex—without in any way becoming an anonymous atom in the social molecule. On the contrary, all the devices of the society are mobilized to glamorize the individual woman and to dramatize every

achievement of men and women that is unusual—but still within the range
of approved aspirations of the conforming majority. "Miss America" and
"the typical American mother" are widely publicized each year, but an
announced atheist (no matter of what brilliance and accomplishment) cannot be elected President.

American devotion to the underdog must be linked to this attitude. As
Lynd points out, we worship bigness yet we idealize "the little man."
"Griping" is a characteristic American trait, but the griping of American
soldiers against the officer caste system is to be understood in terms of
American egalitarian notions and especially of the cult of the average man.
The fact that officers and enlisted men do not have equal access to various
facilities for recreation and transportation enraged what were felt to be the
most basic sentiments in the American code. To some extent this aspect
of the cult of the average man doubtless represents a refuge for those who
fail "to rise," a justification for envy of those who do.

Because of the cult of the average man, superficial intimacy is easy in
America. People of every social class can talk on common topics in a way
that is not so easy in Europe where life is based more on repetition of patterns of early family routines that are differentiated by class. However,
American friendships tend to be casual and transitory.

Thanks to our expanding economy and to national folklore created by
various historical accidents, the nineteenth-century faith in "progress" became intrenched in the United States as nowhere else. As Lovejoy and
Boas have pointed out, America's golden age has been located mainly in
the future rather than in the past. To some extent, to be sure, the future
has been brought into the present by installment plan buying, the philosophy of "spend, don't save," etc. But the basic underlying notions have
been well made explicit by Carl Becker.

By locating perfection in the future and identifying it with the successive
achievements of mankind, the doctrine of progress makes a virtue of novelty
and disposes men to welcome change as in itself a sufficient validation of their
activities.

Assembly-line factories and skyscrapers must, in part, be understood in
terms of the frontier. Our so rapid development in invention and technique, our gigantic financial and industrial systems—in general, the fact
that we adjusted so completely and quickly, albeit so inharmoniously, to
the Technical Age is to be traced to the absence of an ancient order of
society and the presence of the frontier where we had to adapt ourselves
to vastness with decision, speed, and skill. In an old culture there is a
belief in the established order, a rooted opposition to change, a constitutional imperviousness to new ideas which would involve radical altera-

tion in the mode of life. The frontier liberated the American spirit. It developed generosity and radiant vitality, together with a restlessness which was both good and ill, but did certainly bring with it a resiliency of mind, fluidity of idea and of society, a willingness for bold experiment.

Mass education, like mass suffrage and mass production, is a leading trait of our code. During the last generation education has supplanted the frontier as a favorite means of social mobility, for we have continued to define success in terms of mobility rather than in terms of stability. Our educational system has recently been built upon a kind of watery intellectualism. We have too often naively assumed that, if people were "well informed" and taught to reason in accord with accepted canons of logic, their characters would take care of themselves, and they would automatically acquire the point of view requisite in the citizen of a great society. Meanwhile, the toughening influences of frontier conditions were becoming steadily more dilute. Children of the economically dominant classes were being brought up in relative luxury. Parents failed to condition their offspring to rigorous standards of conduct because they were themselves confused. Actually many educative functions formerly carried out by the family have been surrendered to the school. The existing educational system is hopelessly irresolute on many fronts. It vacillates between training girls to be housewives or career women; it is torn between conditioning children for the theoretically desirable cooperative objectives or to the existing competitive realities. In spite of the terrific demands made upon them, elementary and high-school teachers are underpaid and lack social status. Psychiatrists are agreed that the elimination of social disorganization, as well as of personal disorganization, can be furthered only by more consistent educational practices both in the home and in the school because automatic actions based on the habits of early life are the most stable.

The anthropologist must also characterize our culture as profoundly irreligious. More than half of our people still occasionally go through the forms, and there are rural and ethnic islands of our population where religion is still a vital force. But very few of our leaders are still religious in the sense that they are convinced that prayer or the observance of church codes will affect the course of human events. Public figures participate in public worship and contribute financially to a church for reasons of expediency or because they know that churches represent one of the few elements of stability and continuity in our society. But belief in God's judgments and punishments as a motive for behavior is limited to a decreasing minority. Feelings of *guilt* are common but the sense of *sin* is rare.

Problem 3: What Is the Promise of American Life?

Every culture resists revision of its central beliefs, is hostile to ideas that disturb social customs, and constantly attempts to maintain equilibrium against social change. Much of the conflict in American life today reflects cultural derangement. During the past hundred years societies all over the world have felt the effects of industrialism, recoiled from its impact, and then sought to adjust the older institutions to the new cultural milieu.

In replacing a simple agrarian society, industrialism destroyed many of the controls around which life formerly revolved. At the same time new controls have not emerged rapidly enough to stabilize society during the transitional period. In the words of the poet Matthew Arnold, "we are placed between two worlds; one dead, the other struggling to be born." The breakdown of institutions has projected the individual into an anonymous, impersonal position, isolated and alone. Unable to attach meaning to the complexities around him, the individual often finds himself a stranger in a world he never made. Eugene O'Neill describes this sense of loneliness, the lack of a feeling of belonging, as "the sickness of today," while W. H. Auden identifies our times as "the age of anxiety."

The symptoms of social disorganization provide a background for more serious questions. What are the permanent and far-reaching consequences of industrialization? Has the concentration upon wealth and material production dimmed Whitman's dream of America, "the great Ideal nationality of the future, the Nation of the Body and the Soul," which would produce "the most splendid race the sun ever shone upon." Have industrialism, with its emphasis on production, and the acquisitive society led us to confuse progress with bigness, materialism with greatness? Today communities are judged by census returns, the increase in the size of telephone directories, and total building permits. Do we place the same emphasis upon accomplishment in the fields of art, literature, and music? Do we have the same passion for progress in human relations that we insist upon in automobile design and aeronautical engineering?

More threatening, perhaps, to democracy and individualism are the effects of uniformity and sameness. Must the inevitable end of an industrial society be the turning out of "generations of humanity like uniform iron castings"? Does the emphasis upon efficiency and standardization weaken the role of diversity in thought and behavior and thus pave the way for

Groupthink and *Brave New World?* On the other hand, may not science
and industry with their tremendous contributions of increased productivity, higher standard of living, and greater leisure prepare for "things farther onward." Now that the struggle against the raw American continent
is over and the system of urban industrialism firmly established, will the
United States not turn its energies and its best talents to the arts? The
editors of the *Partisan Review* and Frederick Lewis Allen seem to think so.
They are optimistic in their belief that the tide is already turning and that
the United States is approaching the position that Europe once held as the
sanctuary of the writer and the artist.

In this section we focus attention on the changing character of American
culture and the future of American life. How far have Americans come
on the road to the good society and in what direction are they now heading? What are America's accomplishments? Where will it stand in the
pages of history? Will America be known for achievement in commerce
and business or for its contributions to democratic government, the arts
and sciences, and knowledge and learning?

Brave New World *

Did the revolutionary ideas, symbolized by Henry Ford, of mass
production, efficiency systems, and time schedules mark the advent of
the good life, the rich society of abundance, the era of unsurpassed
human happiness? Or was the coming of urban industrialism a para-
sitical force that fixed upon us a robot-like society that in the end will
siphon away our liberty and individualism? Speculating along the
latter lines, Aldous Huxley writes of a society in which the individual
is guided and at the same time exploited by the efficiency expert, the
psychologist, and the technologist. In *Brave New World* there are
no maladjusted people, no radicals, no deviators, no erratic geniuses—
there is not room for them. Such individuals interfere with economic
and social efficiency.

Mr. Foster was left in the Decanting Room. The D.H.C. and his students stepped into the nearest lift and were carried up to the fifth floor.

Infant Nurseries. Neo-Pavlovian Conditioning Rooms, announced
the notice board.

The Director opened a door. They were in a large bare room, very

* Aldous Huxley, *Brave New World* (Harper, 1946), pp. 20–32. Copyright, 1932, by
Aldous Huxley.

bright and sunny; for the whole of the southern wall was a single window Half a dozen nurses, trousered and jacketed in the regulation white viscose-linen uniform, were engaged in setting out bowls of roses in a long row across the floor. Big bowls, packed tight with blossom. Thousands of petals, ripe-blown and silkily smooth, like the cheeks of innumerable little cherubs, but of cherubs, in that bright light, not exclusively pink and Aryar, but also luminously Chinese, also Mexican, also apoplectic with too much blowing of celestial trumpets, also pale as death, pale with the posthumous whiteness of marble.

The nurses stiffened to attention as the D.H.C. came in.

"Set out the books," he said curtly.

In silence the nurses obeyed his command. Between the rose bowls the books were duly set out—a row of nursery quartos opened invitingly each at some gaily colored image of beast or fish or bird.

"Now bring in the children."

They hurried out of the room and returned in a minute or two, each pushing a kind of tall dumbwaiter laden, on all its four wire-netted shelves, with eight-month-old babies, all exactly alike (a Bokanovsky Group, it was evident) and all (since their caste was Delta) dressed in khaki.

"Put them down on the floor."

The infants were unloaded.

"Now turn them so that they can see the flowers and the books."

Turned, the babies at once fell silent, then began to crawl towards those clusters of sleek colors, those shapes so gay and brilliant on the white pages. As they approached, the sun came out of a momentary eclipse behind a cloud. The roses flamed up as though with a sudden passion from within; a new and profound significance seemed to suffuse the shining pages of the books. From the ranks of the crawling babies came little squeals of excitement, gurgles and twitterings of pleasure.

The Director rubbed his hands. "Excellent!" he said. "It might almost have been done on purpose."

The swiftest crawlers were already at their goal. Small hands reached out uncertainly, touched, grasped, unpetaling the transfigured roses, crumpling the illuminated pages of the books. The Director waited until all were happily busy. Then, "Watch carefully," he said. And, lifting his hand, he gave the signal.

The Head Nurse, who was standing by a switchboard at the other end of the room, pressed down a little lever.

There was a violent explosion. Shriller and ever shriller, a siren shrieked. Alarm bells maddeningly sounded.

The children started, screamed; their faces were distorted with terror.

"And now," the Director shouted (for the noise was deafening), "now we proceed to rub in the lesson with a mild electric shock."

He waved his hand again, and the Head Nurse pressed a second lever. The screaming of the babies suddenly changed its tone. There was something desperate, almost insane, about the sharp spasmodic yelps to which they now gave utterance. Their little bodies twitched and stiffened; their limbs moved jerkily as if to the tug of unseen wires.

"We can electrify that whole strip of floor," bawled the Director in explanation. "But that's enough," he signalled to the nurse.

The explosions ceased, the bells stopped ringing, the shriek of the siren died down from tone to tone into silence. The stiffly twitching bodies relaxed, and what had become the sob and yelp of infant maniacs broadened out once more into a normal howl of ordinary terror.

"Offer them the flowers and the books again."

The nurses obeyed; but at the approach of the roses, at the mere sight of those gaily-colored images of pussy and cock-a-doodle-doo and baa-baa-black sheep, the infants shrank away in horror; the volume of their howling suddenly increased.

"Observe," said the Director triumphantly, "observe."

Books and loud noises, flowers and electric shocks—already in the infant minds these couples were compromisingly linked; and after two hundred repetitions of the same or a similar lesson would be wedded indissolubly. What man has joined, nature is powerless to put asunder.

"They'll grow up with what the psychologists used to call an 'instinctive' hatred of books and flowers. Reflexes unalterably conditioned. They'll be safe from books and botany all their lives." The Director turned to his nurses. "Take them away again."

Still yelling, the khaki babies were loaded on to their dumb-waiters and wheeled out, leaving behind them the smell of sour milk and a most welcome silence.

One of the students held up his hand; and though he could see quite well you couldn't have lower-caste people wasting the Community's time over books, and that there was always the risk of their reading something which might undesirably decondition one of their reflexes, yet . . . well, he couldn't understand about the flowers. Why go to the trouble of making it psychologically impossible for Deltas to like flowers?

Patiently the D.H.C. explained. If the children were made to scream at the sight of a rose, that was on grounds of high economic policy. Not so very long ago (a century or thereabouts), Gammas, Deltas, even Epsilons, had been conditioned to like flowers—flowers in particular and wild nature in general. The idea was to make them want to be going out into the country at every available opportunity, and so compel them to consume transport.

"And didn't they consume transport?" asked the student.

"Quite a lot," the D.H.C. replied. "But nothing else."

Primroses and landscapes, he pointed out, have one grave defect: they are gratuitous. A love of nature keeps no factories busy. It was decided to abolish the love of nature, at any rate among the lower classes; to abolish the love of nature, but *not* the tendency to consume transport. For of course it was essential that they should keep on going to the country, even though they hated it. The problem was to find an economically sounder reason for consuming transport than a mere affection for primroses and landscapes. It was duly found.

"We condition the masses to hate the country," concluded the Director. "But simultaneously we condition them to love all country sports. At the same time, we see to it that all country sports shall entail the use of elaborate apparatus. So that they consume manufactured articles as well as transport. Hence those electric shocks."

"I see," said the student, and was silent, lost in admiration.

There was a silence; then, clearing his throat, "Once upon a time," the Director began, "while our Ford was still on earth, there was a little boy called Reuben Rabinovitch. Reuben was the child of Polish-speaking parents." The Director interrupted himself. "You know what Polish is, I suppose?"

"A dead language."

"Like French and German," added another student, officiously showing off his learning.

"And 'parent'?" questioned the D.H.C.

There was an uneasy silence. Several of the boys blushed. They had not yet learned to draw the significant but often very fine distinction between smut and pure science. One, at last, had the courage to raise a hand.

"Human beings used to be . . ." he hesitated; the blood rushed to his cheeks. "Well, they used to be viviparous."

"Quite right." The Director nodded approvingly.

"And when the babies were decanted . . ."

" 'Born,' " came the correction.

"Well, then they were the parents—I mean, not the babies, of course; the other ones." The poor boy was overwhelmed with confusion.

"In brief," the Director summed up, "the parents were the father and the mother." The smut that was really science fell with a crash into the boys' eye-avoiding silence. "Mother," he repeated loudly rubbing in the science; and, leaning back in his chair, "These," he said gravely, "are unpleasant facts; I know it. But then most historical facts are unpleasant."

He returned to Little Reuben—to Little Reuben, in whose room, one evening by an oversight, his father and mother (crash, crash!) happened to leave the radio turned on.

("For you must remember that in those days of gross viviparous reproduction, children were always brought up by their parents and not in State Conditioning Centres.")

While the child was asleep, a broadcast program from London suddenly started to come through; and the next morning, to the astonishment of his crash and crash (the more daring of the boys ventured to grin at one another), Little Reuben woke up repeating word for word a long lecture by that curious old writer ("one of the very few whose works have been permitted to come down to us") George Bernard Shaw, who was speaking, according to a well-authenticated tradition, about his own genius. To Little Reuben's wink and snigger, this lecture was, of course, perfectly incomprehensible and, imagining that their child had gone mad, they sent for a doctor. He, fortunately, understood English, recognized the discourse as that which Shaw had broadcasted the previous evening, realized the significance of what had happened, and sent a letter to the medical press about it.

"The principle of sleep-teaching, or hypnopaedia, had been discovered." The D.H.C. made an impressive pause.

The principle had been discovered; but many many years were to elapse before that principle was usefully applied.

The case of Little Reuben occurred only twenty-three years after Our Ford's first T-Model was put on the market." (Here the Director made a sign of the T on his stomach and all the students reverently followed suit.) "And yet . ."

Furiously the students scribbled. "Hypnopaedia, first used officially in A.F. 214. Why not before? Two reasons (a) . . ."

"These early experimenters," the D.H.C. was saying, "were on the wrong track. They thought that hypnopaedia could be made an instrument of intellectual education . . ."

(A small boy asleep on his right side, the right arm stuck out, the right hand hanging limp over the edge of the bed. Through a round grating in the side of a box a voice speaks softly.

"The Nile is the longest river in Africa and the second in length of all the rivers of the globe. Although falling short of the length of the Mississippi-Missouri, the Nile is at the head of all rivers as regards the length of its basin, which extends through 35 degrees of latitude . . ."

At breakfast the next morning, "Tommy," someone says, "do you know which is the longest river in Africa?" A shaking of the head. "But don't you remember something that begins: The Nile is the . . ."

"The - Nile - is - the - longest - river - in - Africa - and - the - second - in-length-of-all-the-rivers-of-the-globe . . ." The words came rushing out. "Although-falling-short-of . . ."

"Well now, which is the longest river in Africa?"

The eyes are blank. "I don't know."

"But the Nile, Tommy."

"The-Nile-is-the-longest-river-in-Africa-and-second . . ."

"Then which river is the longest, Tommy?"

Tommy bursts into tears. "I don't know," he howls.

That howl, the Director made it plain, discouraged the earliest investigators. The experiments were abandoned. No further attempt was made to teach children the length of the Nile in their sleep. Quite rightly. You can't learn a science unless you know what it's all about.

"Whereas, if they'd only started on moral education," said the Director, leading the way towards the door. The students followed him, desperately scribbling as they walked and all the way up in the lift. "Moral education, which ought never, in any circumstances, to be rational."

"Silence, silence," whispered a loud speaker as they stepped out at the fourteenth floor, and "Silence, silence," the trumpet mouths indefatigably repeated at intervals down every corridor. The students and even the Director himself rose automatically to the tips of their toes. They were Alphas, of course; but even Alphas have been well conditioned. "Silence, silence." All the air of the fourteenth floor was sibilant with the categorical imperative.

Fifty yards of tiptoeing brought them to a door which the Director cautiously opened. They stepped over the threshold into the twilight of a shuttered dormitory. Eighty cots stood in a row against the wall. There was a sound of light regular breathing and a continuous murmur, as of very faint voices remotely whispering.

A nurse rose as they entered and came to attention before the Director.

"What's the lesson this afternoon?" he asked.

"We had Elementary Sex for the first forty minutes," she answered. "But now it's switched over to Elementary Class Consciousness."

The Director walked slowly down the long line of cots. Rosy and relaxed with sleep, eighty little boys and girls lay softly breathing. There was a whisper under every pillow. The D.H.C. halted and, bending over one of the little beds, listened attentively.

"Elementay Class Consciousness, did you say? Let's have it repeated a little louder by the trumpet."

At the end of the room a loud speaker projected from the wall. The Director walked up to it and pressed a switch.

". . . . all wear green," said a soft but very distinct voice, beginning in the middle of a sentence, "and Delta children wear khaki. Oh no, I don't want to play with Delta children. And Epsilons are still worse. They're too stupid to be able to read or write. Besides they wear black, which is such a beastly color. I'm so glad I'm so glad I'm a Beta."

There was a pause; then the voice began again.

"Alpha children wear grey. They work much harder than we do, because they're so frightfully clever. I'm really awfully glad I'm a Beta, because I don't work so hard. And then we are much better than the Gammas and Deltas. Gammas are stupid. They all wear green, and Delta children wear khaki. Oh no, I don't want to play with Delta children. And Epsilons are still worse. They're too stupid to be able . . ."

The Director pushed back the switch. The voice was silent. Only its thin ghost continued to mutter from beneath the eighty pillows.

"They'll have that repeated forty or fifty times more before they wake; then again on Thursday, and again on Saturday. A hundred and twenty times three times a week for thirty months. After which they go on to a more advanced lesson."

Roses and electric shocks, the khaki of Deltas and a whiff of asafoetida—wedded indissolubly before the child can speak. But wordless conditioning is crude and wholesale; cannot bring home the finer distinctions, cannot inculcate the more complex courses of behavior. For that there must be words, but words without reason. In brief, hypnopaedia.

"The greatest moralizing and socializing force of all time."

The students took it down in their little books. Straight from the horse's mouth.

Once more the Director touched the switch.

". . . so frightfully clever," the soft, insinuating, indefatigable voice was saying. "I'm really awfully glad I'm a Beta, because . . ."

Not so much like drops of water, though water, it is true, can wear holes in the hardest granite; rather, drops of liquid sealing-wax, drops that adhere, incrust, incorporate themselves with what they fall on, till finally the rock is all one scarlet blob.

"Till at last the child's mind is these suggestions, and the sum of the suggestions is the child's mind. And not the child's mind only. The adult's mind too—all his life long. The mind that judges and desires and decides —made of these suggestions. But all these suggestions are our suggestions!" The Director almost shouted in his triumph. "Suggestions from the State." He banged the nearest table. "It therefore follows . . ."

A noise made him turn round.

"Oh, Ford!" he said in another tone, "I've gone and woken the children."

GROUPTHINK *

Huxley's *Brave New World* is a challenging speculation regarding the new era when omnipotent experts will take us by the hand and lead us into the land of adjustment, integration, and contentment. Yet it is difficult to believe that these are real and present threats to our society, however ill they may augur for the future. As *Fortune* Magazine aptly points out, the danger that the layman will be guided by the social engineer is not nearly as disturbing as the possibility that the average man "will become one himself." "Rather than the pawn of the experts, he will be the willing apprentice. . . ." The climate of conformity that seems to be growing increasingly more intense, the stress on adjustment and integration, the emphasis on group-mindedness, threaten to do violence to America's traditions. Conceivably the effect of these forces on the American heritage could easily be more decisive than the alterations evolving out of political and economic change.

A very curious thing has been taking place in this country—and almost without our knowing it. In a country where "individualism"—independence and self-reliance—was the watchword for three centuries, the view is now coming to be accepted that the individual himself has no meaning—except, that is, as a member of a group. "Group integration," "group equilibrium," "interpersonal relations," "training for group living," "group dynamics," "social interaction," "social physics"; more and more the notes are sounded—each innocuous or legitimate in itself, but together a theme that has become unmistakable.

In a sense, this emphasis is a measure of success. We have *had* to learn how to get along in groups. With the evolution of today's giant organizations—in business, in government, in labor, in education, in big cities—we have created a whole new social structure for ourselves, and one so complex that we're still trying to figure out just what happened. But the American genius for cooperative action has served us well. "Human relations" may not be an American invention, but in no country have people turned so wholeheartedly to the job of mastering the group skills on which our industrial society places such a premium.

. . . Groupthink being a coinage—and, admittedly, a loaded one—a working definition is in order. We are not talking about mere instinctive

---

* William H. Whyte, Jr. Reprinted from the March, 1952, issue of *Fortune,* pp. 114–17, 142, 146, by special permission of the Editors. Copyright, 1952, Time, Inc.

conformity—it is, after all, a perennial failing of mankind. What we are talking about is a rationalized conformity—an open, articulate philosophy which holds that group values are not only expedient but right and good as well. Three mutually supporting ideas form the underpinning: (1) that moral values and ethics are relative; (2) that what is important is the kind of behavior and attitudes that makes for the harmonious functioning of the group; (3) that the best way to achieve this is through the application of "scientific" techniques.

Once grasped, as the work of the social engineers makes clear, these principles lead us to an entirely new view of man. And what a dismal fellow he is! For the man we are now presented with is Social Man—completely a creature of his environment, guided almost totally by the whims and prejudices of the group, and incapable of any real self-determination of his destiny. Only through social engineering—*i.e.,* applied groupthink—can he be saved. The path of salvation, social engineers explain, lies in a trained elite that will benevolently manipulate us into group harmony. And who's to be the elite? Social engineers modestly clear their throats.

. . . While youngsters are not inclined to philosophize, their attitude toward life adds up to a fairly discernible set of values. It could be described as a "practical" relativism. The old absolute moral values are disappearing. There is still black and white, to be sure, but it is no longer determined by fixed precepts; it is determined rather by what the group thinks is black and white—and if someone does things the way his group does, well, who is to censure him for his loyalty?

The colleges furnish documentation of the drift. If recent surveys are any indication (*Fortune,* June, 1949), a startling swing has taken place among students to the twin ideals of group harmony and expertism. "These men," one of their mentors says in praise, "don't question the system. Their main aim is to make it work better—to get in there and lubricate the machinery. They're not rebels; they'll be social technicians for a better society."

The registrar's records bear him out. Along with a concurrent drift from the humanities, there has been a tremendous increase in specialized courses —and of specialization within specialties. Significantly, the courses that enjoyed the most phenomenal popularity among postwar classes were those connected with personnel work. "I like people" became a universal cry, and in droves students aiming for business turned thumbs down on the idea of general, executive apprenticeship in favor of personnel work; here, with stop watch and slip stick in hand, they could measure away, safe from the doubts and intangibles of the world without. The picture was a mirage, of course, but it was only by the most strenuous efforts of placement officers and corporation personnel people that students gave it up. . . .

The System Lovers

Turn to the image of the good life in popular cultures and you find the same phenomenon at work. Slick-magazine fiction tells the story. It has never, of course, exactly called for a rebellion against the status quo, but back in the thirties it did present heroes and heroines who engaged in some kind of mild strife with their environment, told the boss off, or did something equally contentious. No longer. A *Fortune* analysis of 1935-36 plots and 1950-51 plots indicates that heroes and heroines have been growing remarkably submissive. Not only is the system they abide by—be it an Army camp, a business office, or a small-town environment—shown as more benevolent; in some cases the system itself becomes the *deus ex machina* that solves the problem.

So in serious fiction. More and more, writers are concerning themselves with the relationship of the individual to the group, and more and more resolving it in favor of the latter. The system—and they don't mean God or the universe—is eventually revealed to the hero as bigger than any of us, and thus it is not only foolish but wrong for him not to reconcile himself to it. From the extreme of the angry, to-hell-with-the-whole-lousy-setup tracts of the 1930's we seem to be going whole hog in the opposite direction.

Let us have a look at the current bestseller, Herman Wouk's *The Caine Mutiny*. Since it is about the Navy, the system shown has some aspects peculiar to service life. The basic question posed, however—the individual's place in the system—has great universality, and in an excitingly told tale Wouk sketches one point of view with such striking overtones that the book could almost go down as a landmark in the shift of American values.

The story tells of the terrible dilemma facing the officers of a mine sweeper; their captain, one Queeg, is a neurotic, cowardly incompetent. A typhoon brings the problem to the breaking point. Through hysteria and cowardice, Queeg is about to sink the ship. In vain, Maryk, the stolid, conventional executive officer, tries to get him to keep the ship headed into the wind. Queeg refuses. In the nick of time, Maryk makes his decision. Under Article 184 of Navy Regulations, he relieves Queeg of his command. The ship is saved.

What is the moral? Maryk, we find, shouldn't have done it. Says the author's protagonist, Lieutenant Willy Keith in a letter to his girl (p. 463); ". . . I see that we were in the wrong . . . The idea is, once you get an incompetent ass of a skipper—and it's a chance of war—there's nothing to do but serve him as though he were the wisest and the best, cover his mistakes, keep the ship going, and bear up. So I have gone all the way around Robin Hood's barn to arrive at the old platitudes, which I guess is the process of growing up."

In other times, perhaps, this definition of maturity might have been regarded as downright parody. Obedience and discipline few could have caviled at. But would they have applauded the counseling of an obedience, so abject, so *unquestioning,* that we are asked, in effect, not only to put up with the evils of a system but to regard them as right—to reach out, as Norbert Weiner's phrase goes, and kiss the whip that lashes us? Would they have joined in censuring an act to which the only logical alternative is the passive sacrifice of several hundred lives? Hardly. The executive officer's action might well have been seen as an act of great moral courage and one, furthermore, in true allegiance to the service; it did, after all, save the ship. The other byproduct, the withdrawal of Queeg from line command, might also have been interpreted as something less than a disaster to the system.

Not so A. D. 1952. The moral, to judge from what critics and readers have been saying about it, has struck exactly the right chord. The exec, as the dust jacket has it, was merely a well-meaning man "beyond his depth," and more to be pitied than censured. It is not for the individual to question the competence of the Queegs a system may contain. Queeg was a teacher. Queegs are necessary. We needed Queegs to win the war. So goes the assent. "It is about time that more books of this sort were written," says J. P. Marquand. "The lesson the newcomer must learn is in many ways the antithesis of democracy. It is essentially a final acceptance of the doctrine that full and unquestioning obedience must be accorded to a superior officer, no matter how personally odious or stupid this individual may be—and that without this individual surrender we can never win a war."

Love that system.

. . . A half-century has gone by and the relativistic, social view of man idea is still gaining. The appetite for cultural anthropology, for example, has been growing at such a rate that Ruth Benedict's *Patterns of Culture,* first published in 1931, has reached, after a phenomenal newsstand sale, the No. 1 best-seller spot in the Mentor paper-back series.

In several essentials, however, the nature of the movement against formalism has changed drastically. What started as a healthy revolt against dogmatism has produced an offshoot that has succeeded in becoming the new dogmatism itself. And since, like all dogmatisms, it promises respite from uncertainty, a society still shell-shocked by the upheavals of the twentieth century hasn't bothered yet to question its effects too closely. To be sure, those of the groupthink leaning customarily speak of themselves as rebels fighting an uphill battle against the enemy ("medievalists," "academicians," "absolutists") but the dog they are kicking is practically dead. They won that battle long ago.

Certainly so in one sector of education. Thanks to a strenuous academic controversy, the momentum of the militantly "progressive" brand was slowed down some time back. Groupthink, however, cannot be contained by a label, and to a formidable body of educators the basic ideal of adjustment to group values is so taken for granted that the only remaining job would appear to be working up better ways of bringing it about. "The American educator," writes one of them, Professor Stewart Cole, "(must) treat pupils as persons-in-groups-in-American-culture at every stage of their social learning." To do this the teacher should borrow from such disciplines as anthropology, the social sciences, psychology, and group dynamics. "The social interactions" of teachers and pupils should be "the primary channel of learning the good life for America." *

In this free, permissive atmosphere, the idea that the individual should be regarded as personally accountable for the way he behaves is, of course, old hat. And in the popular view as well. "If your young son sticks his tongue out at you and calls you a nasty old stinkpot," an article in *American Magazine* good-humoredly, but approvingly, counsels, "just ignore the insult and rejoice secretly that you have such a fine normal child. He is simply channeling his aggressive, aggrieved feelings harmlessly by verbal projection."

Where "social interaction" is the watchword, the attitude conditioning is left, in large part, to the child's peers. Even more than his elders, they are quick to reward deviance with hefty interaction; and thus in the natural distaste of the crowd for the individualist we now have a social tool. And this, the child learns from the books written for him, is as it should be. In these tales of fire engines and trains, as David Riesman has documented in his disturbing study, *The Lonely Crowd,* the neophyte groupthinker is taught that one wins by being directed by others—and that the most important thing in the world is to be a team player.

To further ensure that the child need never be a person-not-in-groups, the necessity for little groupthinkers to think as individuals *all by themselves* may soon be obviated altogether. Individual homework is now to be eliminated. Writes Amy Selwyn in the *Reader's Digest,* "Now authorities generally agree that children learn best if they do their learning in groups and talk out loud about lessons as they work. 'No homework' spokesmen also say if children were not required to spend their leisure studying they would not develop the resentment against study which often kills all incentive to learn anything. . . ."

---

* Educators of this bent cannot be accused of swimming against the current. As a recent Elmo Roper poll indicates, most Americans now feel the second most important reason for sending children to high school is "to teach them to get along better with other people." (No. 1: to get them ready for a job.)

Lest the layman presume to question the drift, groupthinkers explain that their work is rooted in the Scientific Method, and that now being a holy phrase, it is made plain that the debate is closed to outsiders—if indeed any grounds for debate exist at all.*

OUR COUNTRY AND OUR CULTURE †

It is usually more interesting and more dramatic to be a prophet of gloom than it is to be a harbinger of optimism. Speculations of disaster, decay, and disintegration often fall on willing ears even though their counterpoints might make sounder predictions. The first two readings, by Huxley and Whyte, describe trends that are dangerously current and could easily destroy a free society.

Yet there is another part of the story—the achievements and promise of American culture. America has come a long way from the intellectually and artistically barren days of the nineteenth and early twentieth centuries. She is beginning to fill out her hand in her shortest suit—the failure to appreciate and to encourage art, music, and literature. The United States is no longer regarded as a cultural Sahara. Instead, in a number of these fields America has become a leading center of activity.

The following excerpt is taken from an editorial statement in the *Partisan Review,* prefacing a discussion of American culture. Although the introduction is very favorable, it is not uncritical, and certainly deserves examination.

The purpose of this symposium is to examine the apparent fact that American intellectuals now regard America and its institutions in a new way. Until little more than a decade ago, America was commonly thought to be hostile to art and culture. Since then, however, the tide has begun to turn, and many writers and intellectuals now feel closer to their country and its culture. The following quotations illustrate the earlier pattern and the change that has recently occurred.

Here, for example, is the artist-hero of a James story speaking in 1879:

---

* "I should like to see teachers and professors as sure of themselves, as confident in their training and experience, as surgeons are, and as impatient of lay advice."—Margaret B. Pickel (Dean of Women, Columbia University), *New York Times Magazine,* June 3, 1951.

† Editorial Statement, *Partisan Review,* May–June, 1952, pp. 282–85. Copyright, 1952, by *Partisan Review.*

We are the disinherited of art! We are condemned to be superficial. We are excluded from the magic circle. The soil of American perception is a poor, little barren, artificial deposit. Yes! we are wedded to imperfection. An American, to excel, has just ten times as much to learn as a European. We lack the deeper sense: we have neither taste, nor tact, nor force. How should we have them? Our crude and garish climate, our silent past, our deafening present, the constant pressure about us of unlovely circumstances are as void of all that nourishes and prompts and inspires the artist as my sad heart is void of bitterness in saying so! We poor aspirants must live in perpetual exile.

—*The Madonna of the Future*

Ezra Pound in 1913:

O helpless few in my country,
O remnant enslaved!

Artists broken against her,
Astray, lost in the villages,
Mistrusted, spoken against . . .

Van Wyck Brooks in 1918:

How, then, can our literature be anything but impotent? It is inevitably so, since it springs from a national mind that has been sealed against that experience from which literature derives all its values.

—*Letters and Leadership*

John Dos Passos in 1937:

. . . The business of the day . . . was to buttress property and profits with anything usable in the debris of Christian ethics and eighteenth century economics that cluttered the minds of college professors, and to reinforce the sacred, already shaky edifice with the new strong girderwork of science Herbert Spencer was throwing up for the benefit of the bosses.

—*The Big Money*

And, finally, Edmund Wilson in 1947:

My optimistic opinion is that the United States at the present time is politically more advanced than any other part of the world. . . . We have seen in the last fifty years a revival of the democratic creativeness which presided at the birth of the Republic and flourished up through the Civil War. This began to assert itself strongly during the first two decades of this century, was stimulated by the depression that followed the blowing-up of the Stock Market, and culminated in the New Deal. It was accompanied by a remarkable renascence of American arts and letters.

—*Europe without Baedeker*

The American artist and intellectual no longer feels "disinherited" as Henry James did, or "astray," as Ezra Pound did in 1913. Van Wyck Brooks himself has by now entirely repudiated the view that "the national mind has been sealed against that experience from which literature derives its values." John Dos Passos in 1951 would deny precisely what he affirmed in 1937. And what Edmund Wilson wrote in the conclusion to his book describing a visit to post-war Europe represents a new judgment of American civilization. It is a judgment that would have been inconceivable twenty-five years ago, yet it is one which seems natural to most serious writers today. We have obviously come a long way from the earlier rejection of America as spiritually barren, from the attacks of Mencken on the "booboisie," and the Marxist picture of America in the thirties as a land of capitalist reaction.

Essential in the shift of attitudes is the relationship of America to Europe. For more than a hundred years, America was culturally dependent on Europe; now Europe is economically dependent upon America. And America is no longer the raw and unformed land of promise from which men of superior gifts like James, Santayana, and Eliot departed, seeking in Europe what they found lacking in America. Europe is no longer regarded as a sanctuary; it no longer assures that rich experience of culture which inspired and justified a criticism of American life. The wheel has come full circle, and now America has become the protector of Western civilization, at least in a military and economic sense.

Obviously, this overwhelming change involves a new image of America. Politically, there is a recognition that the kind of democracy which exists in America has an intrinsic and positive value: it is not merely a capitalist myth but a reality which must be defended against Russian totalitarianism. The cultural consequences are bound to be far-reaching and complex, but some of them have already become apparent. For better or worse, most writers no longer accept alienation as the artist's fate in America; on the contrary, they want very much to be a part of American life. More and more writers have ceased to think of themselves as rebels and exiles. They now believe that their values, if they are to be realized at all, must be realized in America and in relation to the actuality of American life. In one way or another, this change has involved us all, but it has not yet been the subject of critical reflection and evaluation. Hence we think there is much to be gained by the exchange of impressions which a symposium fosters.

The problem as we see it is this: the affirmation attitude toward America which has emerged since the Second World War may be a necessary corrective of the earlier extreme negation, but the affirmation cannot be unequivocal. For American economic and political institutions have not suddenly become ideally beneficent, and many intellectuals are not prepared to give up all criticism of them. In addition, the enormous and ever-increasing growth of mass culture confronts the artist and the intellectual with a new phenomenon and creates a new obstacle: the artist and intellectual who wants to be a part of American life is faced with a mass culture which makes him feel that he is still outside looking in. Ortega y Gasset has formulated the difficulty in an extreme way: "The mass crushes beneath it everything that is different, everything that is excellent, individual, qualified and select. Anybody who is not like everybody, who does not think like everybody, runs the risk of being eliminated." By "mass" Ortega y Gasset does not mean any social or economic class of society. "By Mass," says Ortega y Gasset, "is not to be specially understood the workers, it does not indicate a social class, but a kind of man to be found today in all social classes, who consequently represents our age, in which he is the predominant ruling power."

We cannot however accept the views of Ortega y Gasset without serious qualifications, for he ignores the fact that political democracy seems to coexist with the domination of the "masses." Whatever the cultural consequences may be, the democratic values which America either embodies or promises are desirable in purely human terms. We are certain that these values are necessary conditions for civilization and represent the only immediate alternative as long as Russian totalitarianism threatens world domination. Nevertheless, there are serious cultural consequences: mass culture not only weakens the position of the artist and the intellectual profoundly by separating him from his natural audience, but it also removes the mass of people from the kind of art which might express their human and aesthetic needs. Its tendency is to exclude everything which does not conform to popular norms; it creates and satisfies artificial appetites in the entire populace; it has grown into a major industry which converts culture into a commodity. Its overshadowing presence cannot be disregarded in any evaluation of the future of American art and thought. Its increasing power is one of the chief causes of the spiritual and economic insecurity of the intellectual minority.

Apparently, cultural democracy is an outgrowth of political democracy under conditions of modern industrial development. And the democratization of culture involves an inevitable dislocation though it may in the end produce a higher culture and demonstrate that a political democracy can nourish great art and thought. But whatever the future may promise, we cannot evade the fact that at present America is a nation where at the same time cultural freedom is promised and mass culture produced. This paradox, we think, creates many difficulties for American writers and intellectuals who are trying to realize themselves in relation to their country and its cultural life.

———◄•••►———

THE SPIRIT OF THE TIMES *

To say that few men are better qualified to comment on the spirit of our times than Frederick Lewis Allen may sound trite, but it is also a truism. His two books, *Only Yesterday* and *Since Yesterday,* are outstanding commentaries on the social history of the twenties and thirties. Besides being a leading writer on recent American history, Frederick Lewis Allen was Editor in Chief of *Harper's Magazine* and author of numerous articles on the current American scene.

In the following selection the author examines some of the charges that the United States is in the midst of widespread ethical and cultural decay. His optimistic conclusions raise provocative questions. Would anyone argue, for example, that we recognize achievement in the arts as we do in business and commerce? Just how much actual encouragement does our society give young people to enter into artistic careers? How many persons outside the upper ten per cent in painting, writing, and music are able to make an adequate living in the field without resorting to a side line?

. . . In his introduction to the book *Twentieth Century Unlimited* Bruce Bliven says that in his opinion "the most significant fact about the changes in the past half-century" has been "the alteration in the moral climate from one of overwhelming optimism to one which comes pretty close to despair."

"Half a century ago," continues Mr. Bliven "mankind, and especially the American section of mankind, was firmly entrenched in the theory that this is the best of all possible worlds and getting better by the minute. . . . There was a kindly God in the heavens, whose chief concern was the welfare, happiness, and continuous improvement of mankind, though his ways were often inscrutable."

Today, says Mr. Bliven, we have lost faith and are "frightened to death"— of war, atom bombs, and the looming prospect of a general brutalization and deterioration of the human species.

Have we, then, become since 1900 a comparatively irreligious and rudderless people? Church statistics do not help us far toward an answer to this question. They show steady gains in membership for most church groups, roughly comparable to the gain in population; but they are suspect because of a very human tendency to keep on the rolls people who never go to church any more except for weddings and funerals, and there is no

---

* Frederick Lewis Allen, *The Big Change* (Harper, 1952). Copyright, 1952, by Frederick Lewis Allen. Reprinted from *Harper's Magazine,* July, 1952, pp. 67–70, 72–74.

way of knowing whether the compilers of church statistics have become more or less scrupulous in the past few decades. My own definite impression is that during the first thirty or forty years of the half-century there was a pretty steady drift away from church attendance and from a feeling of identification with the church and its creed and institutions at least on the part of well-to-do Americans (except perhaps among the Roman Catholics, who were under an exceptionally rigid discipline). It became customary among larger and larger numbers of the solid citizenry of the land to sleep late on Sunday morning and then grapple with the increasing poundage of the Sunday paper, or have a 10:30 appointment at the first tee, or drive over to the Joneses' for midday cocktails, or pack the family into the car for a jaunt to the shore or the hills. I, myself, making many weekend visits every year over several decades, noted that as time went on it was less and less likely that my host would ask on Saturday evening what guests were planning to go to church the next morning; that by the nineteen-twenties or -thirties it was generally assumed that none would be. And although the households in which I visited may not have been representative, they at least were of more or less the same types throughout this whole period. Today I should imagine that in the heavy out-of-town traffic on a Friday afternoon there are not many people who will be inside a church on Sunday morning.

It has been my further observation that during at least the first thirty and perhaps the first forty years of the century there was an equally steady drift away from a sense of identification with the faiths for which the churches stood. Among some people there was a feeling that science, and in particular the doctrine of evolution, left no room for the old-time God, and that it was exceedingly hard to imagine any sort of God who was reconcilable with what science was demonstrating and would at the same time be at home in the local church. Among others there was a rising moral impatience with an institution which seemed to pay too much attention to the necessity of being unspotted by such alleged vices as drinking, smoking, card-playing, and Sunday golfing, and too little to human brotherhood; the churches, or many of them, made a resolute effort to meet this criticism by becoming complex institutions dedicated to social service and the social gospel, with schools, classes, women's auxiliaries, young people's groups, sports, and theatricals, but not many of them held their whole congregation—at least on Sunday morning. Still others felt that the clergy were too deferential to wealthy parishioners of dubious civic virtue, or too isolated from the main currents of life. Among many there was a vague sense that the churches represented an old-fashioned way of living and thinking and that modern-minded people were outgrowing their influence. And as the feeling of compulsion to be among the churchgoers and church workers weakened, there were naturally many to whom the automobile or the country club or the beach or an eleven o'clock breakfast was simply too agreeable to pass up.

Whether or not this drift away from formal religion is still the prevailing tide, there was manifest during the nineteen-forties a counter-movement. In many men and women it took no more definite form than an uneasy conviction that in times of stress and anxiety there was something missing from their lives: they wished they had something to tie to, some faith that would give them a measure of inner peace and security. The appearance on the best-seller lists in recent years of such books as *The Robe, The Cardinal, Peace of Mind,* and *The Seven Storey Mountain* has indicated a widespread hunger and curiosity. Some have returned to the churches—or entered them for the first time. In families here and there one has noted a curious reversal: parents who had abandoned the church in a mood of rebellion against outworn ecclesiastical customs have found their children in turn rebelling against what seemed to them the parents' outworn pagan customs. The Catholic Church in particular has made many converts, some of them counterrebels of this sort, and has spectacularly served as a haven for ex-Communists who have swung all the way from one set of disciplinary bonds to another. Whether the incoming tide is yet stronger than the outgoing one, or what the later drift may be, is still anybody's guess; but at least there is a confusion in the flow of religious feeling and habit.

Meanwhile, in quantities of families, the abandonment of church allegiance has deprived the children of an occasionally effective teacher of decent behavior. Some parents have been able to fill the vacuum themselves; others have not, and have become dismayed that their young not only do not recognize Bible quotations but have somehow missed out on acquiring a clear-cut moral code. There are other parents whose conscientious study of psychological principles, including the Freudian, and whose somewhat imperfect digestion of the ideas of progressive educators have so filled them with uncertainty as to what moral teachings to deliver and whether any sort of discipline might not damage young spirits that these young spirits have become—at least for the time being—brats of a singular offensiveness. And even if there have always been brats in the world, it has been easy for observers of such families to conclude that moral behavior is indeed deteriorating, and that basketball scandals and football scandals and teen-age holdup gangs and official corruption in Washington are all signs of a wide-spread ethical decay.

This conclusion is of doubtful validity, I am convinced. There has probably never been a generation some members of which did not wonder whether the next generation was not bound for hell in a handcar. It may be argued that at the mid-century the *manners* of many teen-agers have suffered from their mothers' and fathers' disbelief in stern measures; but that their *ethical standards* are inferior to those of their predecessors seems to me doubtful indeed. As for today's adults, there are undoubtedly many whose lack of connection with organized religion has left them without any secure principles; but as I think of the people I have actually known over a long period of time, I detect no general deterioration of the conscience: those I see today do a good many things that their grandparents would have considered improper, but few things that they would have regarded as paltry or mean. And there has been taking place among these people, and in the country at large, a change of attitude that I am convinced is of great importance. During the half-century the ancient question, "Who is my neighbor?" has been receiving a broader and broader answer.

There are still ladies and gentlemen who feel that they are of the elect, and that the masses of their fellow-countrymen are of negligible importance; but their snobbery is today less complacently assured, more defiant, than in the days when Society was a word to conjure with. The insect on the leaf is less often found "proclaiming on the too much life among his hungry brothers in the dust." There are still business executives with an inflated sense of their own value in the scheme of things, but the "studied insolence" which Mark Sullivan noted among the coal operators of 1902 when confronted by the union representatives and the President of the United States, and which magnates often displayed on the witness stand in those days, is no longer to be seen (except perhaps among such underworld gentry as Mr. Frank Costello). People who today look at what were originally the servants' quarters in an old mansion, or even in a swank apartment of the 1920 vintage, are shocked at their meagerness: is it possible, they ask themselves, that decent men and women could have had such disregard for the human needs of men and women living cheek by jowl with them?

The concept of the national income, the idea of measuring the distribution of this income, the idea of the national economy as an entity affected by the economic behavior of every one of us, the very widespread interest in surveying sociologically the status of this and that group of Americans the country over, in the conviction that their fortunes are interdependent with ours; all these have developed during this half-century. The ideal of equality of educational opportunity never before commanded such general acceptance. In recent years there has been a marked shift of attitudes toward our most disadvantaged group, the Negroes, and no less noticeably in the South than elsewhere. One notes a widespread gain in group tact, as when the Hospital for the Ruptured and Crippled is renamed the Hospital for Special Surgery, and the Association for Improving the Condition of the Poor becomes the Community Service Society. The concept of responsibility to the general public has become more and more widespread among the managers of pivotal businesses. The amount of time which individual men and women give to good works in the broadest sense— including church work, volunteer hospital work, parent-teacher associations, the Boy Scouts, the Red Cross, the League of Women Voters, local symphony orchestras, the World Federalists, the American Legion, the service activities of Rotary, and so on endlessly—is in its total incalculable. (There are communities, I am told, where the number of people who engage in money-raising for the churches is larger than the number of churchgoers.) In sum, our sense of public obligation has expanded.

The change has had its amusing aspects. There comes to one's mind Anne Cleveland's cartoon of a Vassar girl dining with her parents and exclaiming, "How can I explain the position of organized labor to Father, when you keep passing me chocolate sauce?" One thinks of a banker's daughter of one's acquaintance, who in her first job was much more deeply interested in the plight of the file clerk whom she regarded as underpaid, than in helping the company make money. And of the receipt by Dr. Ralph Bunche in June, 1951, of no less than thirteen honorary degrees in rapid succession, the singular unanimity of his choice by so many institutions undoubtedly reflecting in part a delight at finding an unexceptionable opportunity to pay tribute to a Negro.

That the change should meet, here and there, with heated resistance, is likewise natural. The democratic ideal imposes a great strain upon the tolerance and understanding of humankind. So we find a conscious and active anti-Semitism invading many a suburban community which once took satisfaction in its homogeneity and now finds it can no longer live to itself; or a savage anti-Negro feeling rising in an industrial town in which Negroes were formerly few and far between. And here one should add a footnote about the behavior of our armed forces abroad. For a variety of not easily defined reasons—including undoubtedly the traditionally proletarian position of the foreign-language-speaking immigrant in the United States—there is an obscure feeling among a great many Americans that the acceptance of the principle of human dignity stops at the water's edge: that a man who would be fiercely concerned over an apparent injustice to a fellow-private in the American Army may be rude to Arabs, manhandle Koreans, and cheat Germans, and not lose status thereby—and this, perhaps, at the very moment when his representatives in Congress are appropriating billions for the aid of the very sorts of people of whom he is so scornful.

Yet in spite of these adverse facts there has been, I am convinced, an increasing over-all acceptance in America of what Dr. Frank Tannenbaum has called "the commitment to equality . . . spiritual equality." Whether, as Walter H. Wheeler, Jr., has suggested, we may be "depleting and living off inherited spiritual capital" is far from certain. Yet at any rate this may be said: If we as a people do not obey the first and great commandment as numerously and fervently as we used to, at least we have been doing fairly well with the second. . . .

One who has worked for a great many years for a magazine which nowadays can pay its authors no more than it did a decade ago, because it has to pay its typographers and shipping men so much more, is not likely to be complacent about the lot of the man of letters today. Nor is one who has felt he was waging a steady uphill fight on behalf of what he perhaps fondly considered distinguished journalism—uphill because there were constantly appearing new magazines aimed at readers by the millions, and because advertisers tended to want to reach those millions—likely to be complacent about the conditions of literary institutions. It seems to me undeniable that the great success of the mass-circulation magazines and the rise of the staff-written magazines have between them made life harder for the free-lance author who lacks the popular touch and who will not do pot-boiling, or cannot do it successfully, and who has no other assured source of income. But then he almost never has had things very easy financially. And there is this to be said: one reason why magazines with severely high standards find the going difficult is that they have no monopoly on material of high quality, for during the past few decades an increasing amount of such material has been finding a place in the mass periodicals. (For a couple of random examples, let me cite Winston Churchill's memoirs, appearing in *Life,* and Faulkner's short stories, coming out in the *Saturday Evening Post.*) Furthermore, the number of writers of talent who make good incomes by writing for the mass magazines without the sacrifice of an iota of their integrity is much larger than one might assume from the talk of the *avant-gardists.* The picture is a mixed one.

So too with regard to books. The market for the output of the "original" publishers, meaning those who sell newly-written books at standard prices, chiefly through the bookstores, is somewhat larger than before the war, but it is manifest that price increases, reflecting high labor costs, have been deterring buyers. The share of a few very successful writers in the total revenue of authors increases; and it becomes more difficult than it used to be for those whose books are not likely to sell more than a few thousand copies (these include nearly all poets) to get their work accepted. Yet here again the situation is not as black as it has been painted. I agree with Bernard DeVoto that no book really worth publishing fails of publication by some unit of a very diversified industry; and I would add that while there is trash on the best-seller lists, most of the books which reach those lofty positions, with very pleasant results for their authors' pocketbooks, are among the best of their time.

And there is more to it than this. For there are also numerous book clubs, at least two of which—the Book-of-the-Month Club and the Literary Guild—sell books by the hundreds of thousands each month. There are the quarterly Condensed Books brought out by the *Reader's Digest*—four or five novels or non-fiction books condensed in one volume—which, launched in 1950, were selling by early 1952 at a rate of more than a million apiece. And there are the paper-bound reprint houses, whose volumes, priced at 25 to 35 cents for the newsstand and drugstore trade, are bought in phenomenal lots. In the year 1950 the total was no less than 214 million; in 1951 the figure had jumped to 231 million.

Two-thirds or more of these paper-bound books, to be sure, were novels or mysteries—thus falling into classifications too inclusive to be reassuring as to the public taste—and some were rubbish by any tolerable standard (the publishers of such wares having learned, as one cynic has put it, that you can sell almost anything adorned on the cover with a picture connoting sex or violence, or preferably both, as in a picture of a luscious girl getting her dress ripped off by a gunman). But consider these sales figures (as of January, 1952) for a few paper-bound books: Tennessee Williams' *A Streetcar Named Desire,* over half a million; George Orwell's *Nineteen Eighty-Four,* over three-quarters of a million; Ruth Benedict's *Patterns of Culture,* 400,000; and—to cite an incontrovertibly classical example— a translation of *The Odyssey* (with an abstract cover design), 350,000. And remember that these sales and regular bookstore sales, have been achieved in a nation of avid magazine readers. It is true that the financial returns to the author from such low-priced books are meager: he gets less revenue from a million of them than from 20,000 sold at standard prices. Nevertheless there is an interesting phenomenon here. There is a big American market for good writing if it and the price are within easy reach.

Let us look at the market for art. The painter of today faces two great difficulties. The first is that his work is offered to the public at high prices (if he can get any price at all) because he can sell only his original work, to one collector or institution, and cannot dispose of thousands at a time; and the collectors with money are scarce. The second is that the abler young painters of the day have mostly swung all the way to the abstract, which to most potential buyers is pretty incomprehensible. Yet the signs of interest among the public are striking. Forbes Watson is authority for the statement that there were more sales of paintings in the 1940's than in all the previous history of the United States; that in the year 1948 there were a hundred exhibitions of American art in American museums; and that the total attendance at art exhibitions that year was over 50 million.

One should also take note of the greatly enlarged number of local museums; of the lively promotion of an interest in art by many universities and colleges; the rising sale of reproductions, in book form and otherwise; and the recent sharp increase in the number of Sunday amateur dabblers with a paintbrush. Sales of artists' materials had a tenfold increase between 1939 and 1949. The suspicion comes over me that there is something stirring here, too, and that the plight of the contemporary artist, like the plight of the contemporary writer, may be partly due to the fact that the market for his output may not yet be geared to the potential demand.

We turn to music—and confront an astonishing spectacle.

In 1900 there were only a handful of symphony orchestras in the country; by May, 1951, there were 659 "symphonic groups"—including 52 professional, 343 community, 231 college, and a scattering of miscellaneous amateur groups. Fifteen hundred American cities and towns now support annual series of concerts. Summer music festivals attract audiences which would have been unimaginable even thirty years ago. To quote Cecil Smith in *Twentieth Century Unlimited,* "The dollar-hungry countries of Europe are setting up music festivals by the dozen, not to give American tourists the music they would not hear at home, but to make sure they do not stay at home because of the lack of music in Europe. The programs at Edinburgh, Strasbourg, Amsterdam, Florence, and Aix-en-Provence are designed as competition for Tanglewood, Bethlehem, Ravinia, the Cincinnati Zoo, and the Hollywood Bowl." Mr. Smith cites further facts of interest: that the Austin, Texas, symphony recently took over a drive-in movie for outdoor summer concerts; that Kentucky hill people come in their bare feet when the Louisville Orchestra plays in Berea; and that "an all-Stravinsky program, conducted by the composer, strikes Urbana, Illinois, as a perfectly normal attraction."

During the nineteen-twenties the phonograph record business was threatened with virtual extinction by the rise of radio. But presently radio began giving millions upon millions of Americans such a variety of music—popular, jazz, and classical—in such quantity, year after year, that a good many of these people began to want to hear music on their own terms, and the record business went into a prolonged and phenomenal boom. The expansion was accelerated by the wild vogue of jazz, whose more serious votaries soon learned that if you were to become a really serious student of what Benny Goodman and Duke Ellington were producing, you must collect old recordings and become a connoisseur of Handy, Beiderbecke, and Armstrong. By the middle and late nineteen-forties, young people who in earlier years would have gone off dancing of an evening were finding that it was very agreeable to sit on the floor and listen to a record-player, with a few bottles of beer to wash the music down. Many people whose taste in books and in art was very limited were not only becoming able to identify the most famous symphonies by their first few notes, but were developing a pride in their acquaintance with the works of Bach's obscure contemporaries, and in their connoisseurship of the comparative merits of recordings by various orchestras. A very rough estimate of the sales records during the year 1951, made by *Billboard* magazine, put the grand total at some 190 million—more than one for every man, woman, and child in the United States—and the total sale of records in the "classical" category at perhaps 10 to 15 per cent of that 190 million: let us say something like twenty to thirty million classical records. To give a single example: as many as 20,000 sets of Wanda Landowska's harpsichord recordings of the Goldberg Variations were sold in the first three months after they were issued. And a shrewd student of American culture tells me that as he goes about the United States he keeps being told, in place after place, "Our town is sort of unusual. I suppose the most exciting thing, to us, that's going on here isn't anything in business but the way we've put over our symphony orchestra (or our string quartet, or our community chorus)."

Verily, as one looks about the field of the arts, the picture is confused. Here is an incredible boom in public interest in music, along with expanding audiences for the ballet, old-style and new-style. Here is the Broadway theater almost ready for the pulmotor—and local civic theaters and college theaters in what looks like a promising adolescence. Here are the movies, beloved by millions (and berated by highbrow critics) for decades, losing audiences little by little to television, which has not yet outgrown a preposterous crudity. Here is architecture, which has outgrown its earlier imitation of old European styles and is producing superb industrial buildings along with highly experimental and sometimes absurd modern residences—while the peripheries of our great cities, whether New York or Chicago or St. Louis or Los Angeles, display to the bus traveler from airport to town almost no trace of the handiwork of any architects at all. Here are lovely (if monotonous) motor parkways—and along the other main highways a succession of roadtown eyesores—garages, tourist courts, filling stations, billboards, junk dealers, and more billboards—which makes the motor parkways seem, by contrast, like avenues for escapists.

Is not the truth of the situation perhaps something like this: Here is a great nation which is conducting an unprecedented experiment. It has made an incredible number of people, previously quite unsophisticated and alien to art or contemptuous of it, prosperous by any previous standard known to man. These multitudes offer a huge market for him who would sell them equipment or entertainment that they can understand and enjoy. Let us say it in italics: *This is something new; there has never been anything like it before.*

The job before those Americans who would like to see the United States a Greece rather than a Carthage is to try to develop, alongside the media of entertainment and equipment which satisfy these people's present needs, others which will satisfy more exacting tastes and will be on hand for them when they are ready for more rewarding fare. The problem is an economic one as well as an artistic one. Whether it can be solved is still anybody's guess. But in a day when, despite the discouragement of many literati, much of the best writing in the world is being done in the United States; when the impoverishment of foreign institutions of learning has made American universities no mere followers on the road of learning, but leaders despite themselves, attracting students from many continents; and when, willy nilly, a burden of responsibility for the cultural condition of the world rests heavily upon America, it should do us good to look at the army of music-lovers that we have produced. For if this is what auspicious economic conditions can bring in the area of one of the great arts, possibly the miracle may be effected elsewhere too, and the all-American culture may prove to have been, not the enemy of excellence, but its seed-bed.

CHAPTER TWO

Democracy and the Ideologies

THE WORD *democracy* is a study in semantics. A multitude of definitions have been advanced to explain its meaning; countless books have been written; and the flow of oratory on the subject matches the ocean tide in volume and regularity. To some spokesmen democracy is individualism; to others it is nineteenth-century liberalism. Certain groups link democracy with capitalism and free enterprise; some identify the ideal democratic society with government ownership or active regulation; still others think of democracy as social equality, economic opportunity, majority rule, or that vague thing, "a way of life."

Such a diversity of opinion need not undermine or threaten the democratic state. As long as there is a recognition of the importance of the individual, a trust in the wisdom of the people, an acceptance of majority rule, and a recognition of civil liberties that government cannot violate, diversity of democratic thought constitutes a source of strength and vitality. Only out of the interplay of conflicting ideas can a democratic society change, progress, and develop. Should the goals of democracy ever become accepted without dissent, it would lose its greatest asset—the character of experimentalism that challenges rigidity and defies dogma. Democracy demands a state of mind that is constantly seeking fresh perspectives, raising new banners, solving old conflicts. As such, democracy depends not so much upon the mechanics as upon the spirit of the people. It can exist under such diverse forms of government as a republic or a constitutional monarchy. Except in broad outline, therefore, democracy cannot be reduced to a credo, a catechism, or an ideology. Therein lies one of the major distinctions between democracy and rival philosophies of government.

It is tragic and ironic that World War I, fought to make the world safe for democracy, spawned the two great antidemocratic ideologies of our time—Fascism and Communism. Although the threat of Fascism reached a high-water line under Hitler and Mussolini, the future of free nations is still far from secure. Fascism has been superseded by an equally foreboding menace, Russian Communism. Today the Western democracies and world Communism are locked in a life-or-death struggle for the minds of men.

Democracy also faces vexing internal problems. Tension and hostility generated in the international conflict of ideologies have produced a domestic atmosphere of frustration and irrationalism. These forces, in turn, breed a demand for conformity that labels all unpopular ideas as subversive. In some quarters this desire to coerce and shackle expression into accepted molds borders on hysteria. Americans are thus faced with serious questions. Can democracy repel the attacks of foreign and domestic foes without resorting to totalitarian methods? Will freedom be lost in the defense of freedom?

Specifically, this chapter poses three problems. First, what is the meaning of democracy; what are its implications? Second, what are the true natures of the ideologies that now threaten the free nations of the world? Finally, how can a free society protect itself from nondemocratic groups without stifling independent thought and nonconformity? Should a free society allow native Communists to exercise those freedoms that Communists would deny to others?

Problem 4: The American Political System-- Doctrine or Direction?

Ignoring polished definitions of democracy, we bring together in this problem sharp and conflicting interpretations of the nature of the American political system. Hence, the following readings describe the American political experiment in diverse terms—individualism, group welfare, economic balance, political liberty, social class, social democracy, and a philosophy of life—the sum of all of these being, perhaps, that democracy does and should mean different things to different people. It is only in this role that democracy can continue to be a dynamic, ever-evolving system of government.

On the other hand, there are basic fundamentals that must exist before democracy can operate effectively—an acknowledged importance of the individual, a guarantee of civil liberties, a respect for the rules of the game. Herein lies the objection to Vyshinsky's allegations that Russia has a democracy, for one can question the honesty of his acceptance of the basic premises. Within the frame of reference, however, certain questions arise. Is democracy as much a parcel of doctrine as it is an attitude toward life, a direction, or an approach to the treatment of the problems of government? Individuals like Henry Wallace and Herbert Hoover are far apart in their ideas of what a democratic government should do. Is it necessary for individuals to be aligned on specific governmental programs in order to have a democratic society? Does not the presence of a blueprint defeat the democratic idea of experimentation?

The American System and Individualism *

> There is a strong and articulate feeling that individualism is the foundation stone of the American system. Many hold that liberty and even democracy turn on this factor. In the following article Ayn Rand, author of *The Fountainhead*, gives a concise expression to this philosophy.

The greatest threat to mankind and civilization is the spread of the totalitarian philosophy. Its best ally is not the devotion of its followers but the confusion of its enemies. To fight it, we must understand it.

Totalitarianism is collectivism. Collectivism means the subjugation of the individual to a group—whether to a race, class or state does not matter. Collectivism holds that man must be chained to collective action and collective thought for the sake of what is called "the common good."

Throughout history no tyrant ever rose to power except on the claim of representing "the common good." Horrors which no man would dare consider for his own selfish sake are perpetrated with a clear conscience by "altruists" who justify themselves by—the common good.

No tyrant has ever lasted long by force of arms alone. Men have been enslaved primarily by spiritual weapons. And the greatest of these is the collectivist doctrine of the supremacy of the common good over the individual. No dictator could rise if men held as a sacred faith the conviction that they have inalienable rights of which they cannot be deprived for any

* Ayn Rand, *The Only Path to Tomorrow* (Committee for Constitutional Government, 1945).

cause whatsoever, by any man whatsoever, neither by evildoer nor bene-
factor; that no cause is higher than these rights.

Individualism holds that man is an independent entity with an inalienable right to the pursuit of his own happiness in a society where men deal
with one another as equals in voluntary, unregulated exchange.

The American system is founded on individualism. If it is to survive,
we must understand the principles of individualism and hold them as our
standard in any public question, in every issue we face. We must have
a positive credo, a clear, consistent faith.

We must learn to reject as total evil the conception that "the common
good" is superior to individual rights. General happiness cannot be created
out of general suffering and self-immolation. The only happy society is
one of happy individuals. One cannot have a healthy forest made up of
rotten trees.

The power of society must always be limited by the basic, inalienable
rights of the individual. Such was the conception of the founders of our
country, who placed individual rights above any and all collective claims.

The right of liberty means man's right to individual action, individual
choice, individual initiative and individual property. Without the right
to private property no independent action is possible.

The right to the pursuit of happiness means man's right to live for himself, to choose what constitutes his own, private, personal happiness and
to work for its achievement. Each individual is the sole and final judge
in this choice. A man's happiness cannot be prescribed to him by another
man or by any number of other men.

These rights are the unconditional, personal, private, individual possession of every man, granted to him by the fact of his birth and requiring no
other sanction.

From the beginning of history, two antagonists have stood face to face,
two opposite types of men: the Active and the Passive. The Active Man
is the producer, the creator, the originator, the individualist. His basic
need is independence—in order to think and work. He neither needs nor
seeks power over other men—nor can he be made to work under any form
of compulsion. Every type of good work—from laying bricks to writing
a symphony—is done by the Active Man. Degrees of human ability vary,
but the basic principle remains the same; the degree of a man's independence and initiative determines his talent as a worker and his worth as man.

The Passive Man is found on every level of society, in mansions and in
slums, and his identification mark is his dread of independence. He is a
parasite who expects to be taken care of by others, who wishes to be given
directives, to obey, to submit, to be regulated, to be told. He welcomes

collectivism, which eliminates any chance that he might have to think or act on his own initiative.

When a society is based on the needs of the Passive Man it destroys the Active; but when the Active is destroyed, the Passive cannot survive. When a society is based on the needs of the Active Man, he carries the Passive ones along on his energy and raises them as he rises, as the whole society rises. This has been the pattern of all human progress.

Some humanitarians demand a collectivist state because of their pity for the incompetent or Passive Man. For his sake they wish to harness the Active. But the Active Man cannot function in harness. And once he is destroyed, the destruction of the Passive Man follows automatically. So if pity is the humanitarians' first consideration, then in the name of pity, if nothing else, they should leave the Active Man free to function, in order to help the Passive. There is no other way to help him. The Active, however, are exterminated in a collectivist society.

The history of mankind is the history of the struggle between the Active Man and the Passive, between the individual and the collective. The countries which have produced the happiest men, the highest standards of living and the greatest cultural advances have been the countries where the power of the collective—of the government, of the state—was limited and the individual was given freedom of independent action. As examples: The rise of Rome, with its conception of law based on a citizen's rights, over the collectivist barbarism of its time. The rise of England, with its system of government based on Magna Carta, over collectivist barbarism of its time. The rise of the United States to a degree of achievement unequaled in history—by grace of the individual freedom and independence which our Constitution gave each citizen against the collective.

While men are still pondering upon the causes of the rise and fall of civilizations, every page of history cries to us that there is but one source of progress: Individual Man in independent action. Collectivism is the ancient principle of savagery. A savage's whole existence is public, ruled by the laws of his tribe. Civilization is the process of setting man free from men.

We are now facing a choice: to go forward or to go back.

Collectivism is not the "New Order of Tomorrow." It is the order of a very dark yesterday. But there is a New Order of Tomorrow. It belongs to Individual Man—the only creator of any tomorrows humanity has ever been granted.

INDIVIDUALISM AND DEMOCRACY INCOMPATIBLE *

In the foregoing article Ayn Rand contends that individualism is superior to the common good, that collectivism is totalitarianism, and that the American way is predicated on the individual. Taking a position diametrically opposed to that point of view, Oliver Cromwell Cox sees the good society thwarted by competitive individualism. According to Cox, overemphasis on individual liberty places insurmountable roadblocks in the path of a progressive democracy. Only by regulating excessive individualism, he believes, can democracy fulfill its promise to modern man. What, then, is the true role of individualism in a democratic society?

Quite frequently, even among persons who call themselves socialists, it is not clearly seen that, the greater the advancement of democracy, the greater also will be the limitations upon individualism. Yet the process of democratic development may be defined as a continually increasing limitation of individual freedom (i.e., individualism) in favor of greater social equality and freedom for the masses. Although his purpose is to condemn democracy, Hayek is essentially right in saying:

There can be no doubt that most socialists . . . still believe profoundly in the liberal ideal of freedom and that they would recoil if they became convinced that the realization of their program would mean the destruction of freedom.

It must be admitted that the opportunities which bourgeois freedom presents, the remote chances of the worker's becoming economically powerful and of his ruling over the lives of others privately and individualistically, are precious values of capitalism. Yet nothing should be clearer than that we cannot have "freedom" as Professor Hayek conceives of it—i.e., the *laissez faire* individualism of capitalism—and have democracy also. In this regard J. A. Hobson states, ". . . excessive stress on individual liberty becomes an obstacle to the true growth of democracy." Thus, democracy and competitive individualism are incompatible; and the trend of modern civilization is inevitably against this sort of freedom. As Henry Pratt Fairchild observes: "What is of importance to the modern man is not freedom to do as he likes as an individual, but freedom to decide the kind of society he wishes to live in. Social liberty is the twentieth-century desideratum. . . . Only through social liberty can there be attained that form of personal freedom which is harmonious with the conditions of modern life."

* From: *Caste, Class, and Race* by Oliver Cromwell Cox, pp. 236–40. Copyright, 1949, by Oliver Cromwell Cox, reprinted by permission of Doubleday and Company, Inc.

If the resources of a people are to be controlled by that people in the interest of its own welfare, the economic interest of the individual cannot be allowed to stand in the way. And, conversely, if the profit-making interest of the entrepreneur is to be served, the welfare of the people cannot be allowed to stand in the way, here the people's welfare could never become a primary purpose of production.

Under capitalism a profit maker is free to exploit the human and natural resources of the people in his own interest; a slum dweller is free to live and die in filth. The new freedom of democracy is the freedom of the people so to govern themselves that they may be able to make judgments which can limit these minor freedoms. The people in a democracy may decide without hindrance both that slums should be cleared and that the individual who makes a profit from slums should give up that right. There is a loss of one kind of freedom and a gain of another; we cannot have them both. A labor union, the core of proletarian action, tends to destroy the freedom of the employer to develop and to patronize the cheapest labor market; it also destroys the freedom of the worker to sell his labor in such a market. If "freedom from want" is not just another euphonious cliche of "the democracies," it must necessarily mean some substitution of proletarian freedom for capitalist freedom. Sir William H. Beveridge is in point when, in consideration of employment specifically, he declares: "To ask for full employment while objecting to these extensions of State activity is to will the end and refuse the means." It is both a practical and an ideological contradiction to desire bourgeois freedom and social equality at the same time. In the words of Professor Fritz Fleiner, "Demokratie und individuelle Freiheit sind Gegensatze." [Democracy and individual freedom are opposites.]

Sometimes it is intimated that capitalism is basically interested in "the fundamental value and dignity" of the individual. This conclusion is seldom if ever demonstrated, but it is ordinarily associated with individualism. As a matter of fact, however, democracy is the supreme champion of individual worth and personal value because it reaches down irresistibly and facilitates the political upthrust of that major group of persons known as the masses; it concerns itself with the personalization of the least privileged individuals. Democracy tends to confer upon every individual a priceless sense of wantedness in the society—a sense of being a recognized part of a supremely vital organization. By this means alone the individual is able to form a positive conception of himself as a responsible social object. On the other hand, individualism champions the cause of the successful few and of the ablest; it despises the weak and jealously withholds its privileges and recognition from the common people.

As we have seen, the social system in which individualism functions typically is deaf and icy toward the welfare of individuals who cannot compel the attention of the oligarchy. In this system the individual is ordinarily presumed to be worthless until he is able to prove his worth. Therefore, paradoxically, the greater the measure of capitalist individual liberty, the greater the tendency to define the individual as having no intrinsic social worth. Capitalism seeks to atomize and segregate the individuals who constitute the masses of common people, not because of an inherent solicitude and respect for the rights and political influence of these individuals but because by means of their atomization their political influence and economic power may be nullified. Thus, the same ideal of individualism, which augments the dignity and power of the members of the ruling class, serves, when applied to the masses, as a powerful weapon of oppression and abasement. The value which individualism recognizes in the common people is a "use value."

There seems to be no theoretical reason for believing that in a society which abhors individualism the people will feel any need for it. Socialism, the system of democracy, is not simply capitalism without individualism; it is rather a distinct social system in which bourgeois individualism does not function. In a democracy one cannot "spend" his individualism because it is not one of the values of democracy. In a democracy one derives his life satisfactions through the welfare of his fellows and not by "objectively" seeking to wring as much as he can out of them for his private enjoyment. Democracy will probably give social reality to Christianity, a perennial desideratum of Western society. Those highly atomized conflicts and rivalries among individuals under capitalism will be quieted, so that the power of the group will be pooled and augmented for the task of mastering its environment expeditiously and economically. When individualism has lost its claim to indispensability in the social system, it may be viewed critically; and the likelihood is that it will then seem so absurd that only its disadvantages, which certainly are many, will be emphasized. For it cannot be gainsaid that individualism, in its negative aspects, is a separative, indifferent, unbrotherly, selfish, gloating, antagonistic, predatory, antisocial attitude. Those who desire individualism with the abolishment of capitalism are not socialists but anarchists, and consequently unpredictable utopians.

DEMOCRACY AND ECONOMIC BALANCE *

Throughout the nineteenth century democracy was largely identified with political concepts. However, the impact of urban industrialism in the twentieth century created economic tensions and conflicts that no government could safely ignore. For many years Henry A. Wallace has emphasized the importance of government action in 'ne area of economic problems. The following excerpt, taken from one of his earlier speeches, illustrates his views on an effective and progressive democracy.

. . . Democracy—and that term includes free science—must apply itself to meeting the material need of men for work, for income, for goods, for health, for security, and to meeting their spiritual need for dignity, for knowledge, for self-expression, for adventure and for reverence. And it must succeed. The danger that it will be overthrown in favor of some other system is in direct proportion to its failure to meet these needs. We may talk all we like about the beauties of democracy, the ideals of democracy, the rightness of democracy. In the long run, democracy or any other political system will be measured by its deeds, not its words.

The survival and the strength of American democracy are proof that it has succeeded by its deeds thus far. But we all know it contains the seeds of failure. I for one will not be confident of the continued survival of American democracy if millions of unskilled workers and their families are condemned to be reliefers all their lives, with no place in our industrial system. I will not be confident of the survival of democracy if economic crises every few years continue to put fear into the hearts of millions of skilled and professional workers. I will not be confident of the survival of democracy if half our people must continue to be below the line of decent nutrition, while only one-tenth succeed in reaching really good nutritional standards. I will not be confident of the survival of democracy if most of our children, which means most of our future citizens, continue to be reared in surroundings where poverty is highest and education is lowest.

These are the conditions that made possible what we are now witnessing in certain large areas of the world. They are the seeds of danger to democracy. Given a healthy, vigorous, educated people, dignified by work, sharing the resources of a rich country, and sure that their political and economic system is amply meeting their needs—given this, I think

---

* Henry A. Wallace, *Democracy Reborn* (Reynal and Hitchcock, 1944), pp. 157–58.

we can laugh at any threat to American democracy.   But democracy must continue to deliver the goods.

Let us dedicate ourselves anew to the belief that there are extraordinary possibilities in both man and nature which have not yet been realized, and which can be made manifest only if the individualistic yet co-operative genius of democratic institutions is preserved.   Let us dedicate ourselves anew to making it possible for those who are gifted in art, science and religion to approach the unknown with true reverence, and not under the compulsion of producing immediate results for the glorification of one man, one group, one race or one nation.

————◆•••◆————

POLITICAL FREEDOM *

During the 1928 presidential campaign Herbert Hoover replied to the argument that the government must assume a larger role in providing for the general welfare.   Hoover contended that government intervention in the economy would destroy liberty and freedom, since "Free speech does not live many hours after free industry and free commerce die."

There has been revived in this campaign a series of proposals which, if adopted, would be a long step toward the abandonment of our American system and a surrender to the destructive operation of governmental conduct of commercial business.   Because the country is faced with difficulty and doubt over certain national problems—that is, prohibition, farm relief and electrical power—our opponents propose that we must thrust government a long way into the businesses which give rise to these problems. In effect, they abandon the tenets of their own party and turn to State socialism as a solution for the difficulties presented by all three.   It is proposed that we shall change from prohibition to the State purchase and sale of liquor.   If their agricultural relief program means anything, it means that the Government shall directly or indirectly buy and sell and fix prices of agricultural products.   And we are to go into the hydro-electric power business.   In other words, we are confronted with a huge program of government in business.

There is, therefore, submitted to the American people a question of fundamental principle.   That is, shall we depart from the principles of

* Herbert Hoover, *The New York Times*, October 23, 1928.

our American political and economic system, upon which we have advanced beyond all the rest of the world, in order to adopt methods based on principles destructive of its very foundations? And I wish to emphasize the seriousness of these proposals. I wish to make my position clear; for this goes to the very roots of American life and progress.

The Government in commercial business does not tolerate amongst its customers the freedom of competitive reprisals to which private business is subject. Bureaucracy does not tolerate the spirit of independence; it spreads the spirit of submission into our daily life and penetrates the temper of our people not with the habit of powerful resistance to wrong but with the habit of timid acceptance of irresistible might.

Bureaucracy is ever desirous of spreading its influence and its power. You cannot extend the mastery of the Government over the daily working life of a people without at the same time making it the master of the people's souls and thoughts. Every expansion of Government in business means that Government in order to protect itself from the political consequences of its errors and wrongs is driven irresistibly without peace to greater and greater control of the nation's press and platform. Free speech does not live many hours after free industry and free commerce die.

It is a false liberalism that interprets itself into the Government operation of commercial business. Every step of bureaucratizing of the business of our country poisons the very roots of liberalism—that is, political equality, free speech, free assembly, free press, and equality of opportunity. It is the road not to more liberty but to less liberty. Liberalism should be found not striving to spread bureaucracy but striving to set bounds to it. True liberalism seeks all legitimate freedom, first in the confident belief that without such freedom the pursuit of all other blessings and benefits is vain. That belief is the foundation of all American progress, political as well as economic.

Liberalism is a force truly of the spirit, a force proceeding from the deep realization that economic freedom cannot be sacrificed if political freedom is to be preserved. Even if governmental conduct of business could give us more efficiency instead of less efficiency, the fundamental objection to it would remain unaltered and unabated. It would destroy political equality. It would increase rather than decrease abuse and corruption. It would stifle initiative and invention. It would undermine the development of leadership. It would cramp and cripple the mental and spiritual energies of our people. It would extinguish equality and opportunity. It would dry up the spirit of liberty and progress. For these reasons primarily it must be resisted. For a hundred and fifty years liberalism has found its true spirit in the American system, not in the European systems.

I do not wish to be misunderstood in this statement. I am defining a general policy. It does not mean that our Government is to part with one iota of its national resources without complete protection to the public interest. I have already stated that where the Government is engaged in public works for purposes of flood control, of navigation, of irrigation, of scientific research or national defense, or in pioneering a new art, it will at times necessarily produce power or commodities as a by-product. But they must be a by-product of the major purpose, not the major purpose itself.

Nor do I wish to be misinterpreted as believing that the United States is free-for-all and devil-take-the-hindmost. The very essence of equality of opportunity and of American individualism is that there shall be no domination by any group or combination in this Republic, whether it be business or political. On the contrary, it demands economic justice as well as political and social justice. It is no system of laissez-faire.

I feel deeply on this subject because during the war I had some practical experience with governmental operation and control. I have witnessed not only at home but abroad the many failures of Government in business. I have seen its tyrannies, its injustices, its destructions of self-government, its undermining of the very instincts which carry our people forward to progress. I have witnessed the lack of advance, the lowered standards of living, the depressed spirits of people working under such a system. My objection is based not upon theory or upon a failure to recognize wrong or abuse, but I know the adoption of such methods would strike at the very roots of American life and would destroy the very basis of American progress.

Our people have the right to know whether we can continue to solve our great problems without abandonment of our American system. I know we can. We have demonstrated that our system is responsive enough to meet any new and intricate development in our economic and business life. We have demonstrated that we can meet any economic problem and still maintain our democracy as master in its own house and that we can at the same time preserve equality of opportunity and individual freedom. . . .

And what have been the results of our American system? Our country has become the land of opportunity to those born without inheritance, not merely because of the wealth of its resources and industry, but because of this freedom of initiative and enterprise. Russia has natural resources equal to ours. Her people are equally industrious, but she has not had the blessings of one hundred and fifty years of our form of government and of our social system.

By adherence to the principles of decentralized self-government, ordered liberty, equal opportunity, and freedom to the individual our American experiment in human welfare has yielded a degree of well-being unparalleled in all the world. It has come nearer to the abolition of poverty, to the abolition of fear of want, than humanity has ever reached before. Progress of the past seven years is the proof of it. This alone furnishes the answer to our opponents who ask us to introduce destructive elements into the system by which this has been accomplished.

Let us see what this system has done for us in our recent years of difficult and trying reconstruction and let us then solemnly ask ourselves if we now wish to abandon it.

As a nation we came out of the war with great losses. We made no profits from it. The apparent increases in wages were at that time fictitious. We were poorer as a nation when we emerged from the war. Yet during these last eight years we have recovered from these losses and increased our national income by over one-third, even if we discount the inflation of the dollar. That there has been a wide diffusion of our gain in wealth and income is marked by a hundred proofs. I know of no better test of the improved conditions of the average family than the combined increase in assets of life and industrial insurance, building and loan associations, and savings deposits. These are the savings banks of the average man. These agencies alone have in seven years increased by nearly 100 per cent to the gigantic sum of over fifty billions of dollars, or nearly one-sixth of our whole national wealth. We have increased in home ownership, we have expanded the investments of the average man. . . . We have in this short period decreased the fear of poverty, the fear of unemployment, the fear of old age; and these are fears that are the greatest calamities of human kind. . . .

In bringing this address to a conclusion I should like to restate to you some of the fundamental things I have endeavored to bring out.

The foundations of progress and prosperity are dependent as never before upon the wise policies of government, for government now touches at a thousand points the intricate web of economic and social life.

I have dwelt at some length on the principles of relationship between the Government and business. I make no apologies for dealing with this subject. The first necessity of any nation is the smooth functioning of the vast business machinery for employment, feeding, clothing, housing, and providing luxuries and comforts to a people. Unless these basic elements are properly organized and function, there can be no progress in business, in education, literature, music, or art. There can be no advance in the fundamental ideals of a people. A people cannot make progress in poverty.

I have endeavored to present to you that the greatness of America has

grown out of a political and social system and a method of control of
economic forces distinctly its own—our American system—which has carried this great experiment in human welfare further than ever before in
all history. We are nearer today to the ideal of the abolition of poverty
and fear from the lives of men and women than ever before in any land.
And I again repeat that the departure from our American system by injecting principles destructive to it which our opponents propose will
jeopardize the very liberty and freedom of our people, will destroy equality
of opportunity, not alone to ourselves but to our children. . . .

◄►•◄►

DEMOCRACY AND THE CLASS SOCIETY *

How important is social mobility? Can democracy exist side by
side with class stratification? Is social equality as important as economic balance or political democracy?

These questions are often ignored or brushed aside with the conviction that there are no class barriers in America. The idea that ours
is a classless society is deeply entrenched. It is persuasively thrust
upon us by magazine fiction, Hollywood movies, and our national
advertising. Yet, what are the realities of the situation? In a speech
entitled, "You Can Do It Better Democratically," Robert Lynd, noted
sociologist, argues that the prevailing social barriers are one of democracy's greatest hurdles.

The first thing that I want to stress is that the most fundamental social
fact about the United States is that the people are divided into classes, and
the walls between the classes, instead of growing less, are getting higher.
Class barriers are increasing. Business is staging a big campaign to tell
us that classes don't exist in the United States, and that if you talk about
classes you are un-American. You people have seen these ads. Here, for
instance, is one by a steel company which says:

What does America want with a "class" system? That's easy. We don't
want one. But a class system is being pushed on us just the same by the wall
of differences—in some cases actual hatred—that is growing up between employers and employees in many industries. A relatively few men are building
that wall, some for un-American reasons, other for personal power; and it's

* Excerpt from a speech made by Robert S. Lynd before the U.A.W.-C.I.O. at Milwaukee,
Wisconsin, January, 1949, pp. 6–10.

being built of words, not facts. Certainly it doesn't belong in a country where more than 90 per cent of all employers and managers were once shop employees themselves; and where the ladder of promotion for all leads directly from the lowest jobs to the highest, depending only on individual merit.

Is that how the "ladder of promotion" looks from where you fellows stand?

There is a continuous barrage of such ads. Did you see the one showing a gray-haired old lady, who looks like the mother of any of us, asking the nice, clean brakeman on the rear-end of the caboose, "How's our railroad doing, young man?" The text goes on to say, "That's the beauty of America—the voice of the people is the voice that runs things." And then *Life* magazine in its splurge last summer on "The Pursuit of Happiness" (remember our right to "life, liberty, and the pursuit of happiness" in the Declaration of Independence?) came up with the conclusion that happiness comes "from within"—from your guts or somewhere—and that it can't be got by economic changes. So don't any of you radicals start to stir up anything! Over in England the London *Economist* said last summer that it would like to have Aneurin Bevan psychoanalyzed to see why he keeps injecting his dislike of Tories into the polite business of politics. I suspect from your reaction that I don't have to warn you hard-boiled people not to let this propaganda kid you. However, I do think that it is influencing a lot of Americans.

Class-Stratified Society

We are a class-stratified society and we are getting more so. And no amount of talk about "labor-management cooperation" can disguise this fact. We have had a lot of opportunity in our American past and, judged by the standards of the more closely-packed European nations, we have been pretty lucky. But the open frontier is gone; the continuous stream of cheap European labor that put a privileged floor under American-born labor is gone, too; monopoly is growing and our government can't stop it; and here, as elsewhere in all capitalist nations, the middle class which labor has aspired to join is being thwarted and squeezed. The picture is becoming clearer and clearer: on the one side, big industry, property and its managers; and on the other side, labor.

When they talk to you about "classless America" and "unlimited opportunity," tell them to go read page 55 of Monograph 11 of the Senate Temporary National Economic Committee, which says: ". . . it is a widely recognized fact that substantial opportunity for promotion does not exist for a large proportion of the workers (either in large corporations or in small companies) . . Most of them, therefore, must look forward to remaining more or less at their current levels, despite the havoc this may visit upon the American tradition of getting ahead."

It is this arbitrary power to force people to live out their lives on the level at which they happen to be born that is the bone and gristle of the capitalist class system. Jennie Lee, the British Labor bob-cat and wife of Aneurin Bevan, said after a visit to the United States a few years ago, "I hate the foul business of a nation pretending to be one nice big family when it is no such thing. No class society can be a reputable 'family'." (And, parenthetically, this is the same Jennie Lee who said to me in the summer of 1943 when I was in England that she thought the Reuther brothers represented the hope and future of American labor.)

Class and Power

So the point I am making here is that, when we talk about doing things "democratically," we have got to bear in mind that a class society is an arbitrary system of power that works directly against democracy, and that class barriers are becoming stronger. I should be interested to know the reaction of you labor-education people to my strong belief that your educational work should be pitched in terms of making members of the UAW aware, in season and out, of the nature of classes; why classes exist; and how classes mess up and thwart the things that democracy tried to do and, in the end, render real democracy impossible. I don't mean to wave the bloody shirt, but the discussion of this fundamental fact about our society seems, from what I have heard at this conference, rather startlingly lacking. Class seems to be just one of those "also-rans" of which a speaker here might say, if somebody jogged his memory about it, "Oh yes, of course, there are also classes in our society, and that causes trouble, too." But we don't seem to be talking straight out about the important fact that our arms are pinned to our sides before we ever start when we try to do things "democratically" in a class system.

CREDO OF AN AMERICAN *

The distinguished public servant David E. Lilienthal made the following unrehearsed statement on the meaning of democracy before the Congressional Committee on Atomic Energy. Not only are the

* David E. Lilienthal, *The New York Times*, February 5, 1947.

ideas significant, but the circumstances that impelled the utterance were unusually dramatic.   After being relentlessly badgered by an old political enemy, Senator Kenneth McKellar, and being criticized for not carrying certain TVA statistics in his head, Mr. Lilienthal began his comments with the sentence, "This I do carry in my head."

This I do carry in my head.   I will do my best to make it clear.   My convictions are not so much concerned with what I am against as what I am for: and that excludes a lot of things automatically.

Traditionally, democracy has been an affirmative doctrine rather than merely a negative one.   I believe—and I do so conceive the Constitution of the United States to rest upon, as does religion—the fundamental proposition of the integrity of the individual; and that all Government and all private institutions must be designed to promote and to protect and defend the integrity and the dignity of the individual; and that is the essential meaning of the Constitution and the Bill of Rights, as it is essentially the meaning of religion.

Importance of Men Supreme

Any form of government, therefore, and any other institutions which make means rather than ends, which exalt the State or any other institutions above the importance of men, which place arbitrary power over men as a fundamental tenet of government or any other institutions, are contrary to that conception, and therefore I am deeply opposed to them.

The communistic philosophy, as well as the communistic form of government, fall within this category, for their fundamental tenet is quite to the contrary.   The fundamental tenet of communism is that the State is an end in itself, and that therefore the powers which the State exercises over the individual are without any ethical standard to limit them.   That I deeply disbelieve.

It is very easy simply to say one is not a Communist.   And of course, if my record requires me to state that very affirmatively, then it is a great disappointment to me.   It is very easy to talk about being against communism.   It is equally important to believe those things which provide a satisfying and effective alternative.   Democracy is that satisfying affirmative alternative.

Its hope in the world is that it is an affirmative belief, rather than being simply a belief against something else and nothing more.

One of the tenets of democracy that grow out of this central core of a belief that the individual comes first, that all men are the children of God and their personalities are therefore sacred, carries with it a great belief in civil liberties and their protection, and a repugnance to anyone who would steal from a human being that which is most precious to him—his good name; either by impugning things to him by innuendo or by insinuations.

And it is especially an unhappy circumstance that occasionally that is done in the name of democracy. This, I think, can tear our country apart and destroy it if we carry it further.

Democracy a Daily Need

I deeply believe in the capacity of democracy to surmount any trials that may lie ahead, provided only we practice it in our daily lives. And among the things we must practice is that, while we seek fervently to ferret out the subversive and anti-democratic forces in the country, we do not at the same time, by hysteria, by resort to innuendo and smears, and other unfortunate tactics, besmirch the very cause that we believe in, and cause a separation among our people, cause one group and one individual to hate another based on mere attacks, mere unsubstantiated attacks upon their loyalty.

I want also to add that part of my conviction is based on my training as an Anglo-American common lawyer. It is the very basis and the great heritage of the English people to this country, which we have maintained, that the strictest rules of creditability of witnesses be maintained and hearsay and gossip shall be excluded in courts of justice. And that, too, is an essential of our democracy.

And, whether by administrative agencies acting arbitrarily against business organizations, or whether by investigating activities of the legislative branches, whenever those principles of the protection of an individual and his good name against besmirchment by gossip, hearsay and the statements of witnesses who are not subject to cross-examination are not maintained, then, too, we have failed in carrying forward our ideals in respect to democracy. That I deeply believe.

Problem 5: Rival Political Ideologies-- Dictatorship or "The Heavenly City"? *

Political unrest and social upheaval in the twentieth century have been marked in colored ink by wars, revolutions, changes in culture, and the rise of totalitarian governments. Democracy, which seemed to be the wave of the future up to World War I, suddenly found itself with many adversaries. Authoritarian regimes sprang up and challenged the basic values of our Christian democratic heritage. Their antidemocratic ideologies continue to disturb the countries of the world. Although Fascism in Germany, Italy, and Japan suffered a military defeat in World War II, the ideology survives as a potent force in Spain and Argentina. Russian Communism emerged from the war with more power and prestige than ever before. Its star is still on the ascendancy. Whether the Soviet Union will continue its present plans pointing toward global domination or will accept a policy of coexistence is a question that cannot be answered at this moment.

Although Communism and Fascism have different origins and vary considerably in their outward manifestations, the two systems have much in common. In each case totalitarianism submerges the individual, glorifies the state, regiments the economy, and suppresses civil liberty. Both types of government have monolithic, one-party political systems in which force and violence are standard procedures for rooting out opposition and quieting dissent. Finally, both ideologies grow best in the fertile seed bed of a sick society, among people who are without hope, and in areas of economic distress and spiritual despair.

By presenting contrasting portraits of Communism and Fascism the following readings attempt to provide insight into the clash of ideologies and to emphasize the tremendous cleavage between dictatorship and democracy. In each case the official statement of goals and accomplishments of an authoritarian government is balanced by the commentary of a more objective observer.

---

* See Carl L. Becker, *The Heavenly City of the Eighteenth Century Philosophers* (1932).

RUSSIAN COMMUNISM—FOR HOME CONSUMPTION *

The following article invites attention, if for no other reason, solely on the basis of the dominant role that Joseph Stalin played in the development of modern Communism. By the same criterion, the reading also prompts questions and criticisms. Is Stalin an objective, unbiased commentator? Do the facts established by other sources justify Stalin's interpretations? No prepared eulogy should be accepted uncritically. In a political document such as this one must constantly attempt to separate fact from fiction, truth from opinion, evidence from propaganda.

. . . The draft of the new Constitution of the U.S.S.R. proceeds from the fact that the capitalist system has been liquidated, from the fact that the socialist system is victorious in the U.S.S.R. The main foundation of the draft of the new Constitution of the U.S.S.R. consists of the principles of socialism, its main pillars, which have already been won and achieved: the socialist ownership of the land, forests, factories, works and other implements and means of production; the abolition of exploitation and of exploiting classes; the abolition of poverty for the majority and of luxury for the minority; the abolition of unemployment; work as an obligation and "He who does not work, neither shall he eat." The right to work, i.e., the right of every citizen to receive guaranteed employment; the right to rest and leisure; the right to education, etc., etc. The draft of the new Constitution rests on these and similar pillars of socialism. It reflects them, it gives them legislative consolidation.

Bourgeois constitutions tacitly proceed from the premise that society consists of antagonistic classes, of classes which own wealth and classes which do not own wealth, that no matter what party comes into power the guidance of society by the state (the dictatorship) must be in the hands of the bourgeoisie, that a Constitution is needed for the purpose of consolidating a social order desired by and beneficial to the propertied classes.

Unlike bourgeois constitutions, the draft of the new Constitution of the U.S.S.R. proceeds from the fact that there are no longer any antagonistic classes in society, that society consists of two friendly classes, of workers and peasants, that it is these classes, the toiling classes, that are in power, that the guidance of society by the state (the dictatorship) is in the hands of the working class, the most advanced class in society, that a Constitution

* Joseph Stalin in Morris R. Werner (ed.), *Stalin's Kampf* (Howell, Soskin and Company, 1940), pp. 220–23, by permission of Crown Publishers, Inc.

is needed for the purpose of consolidating a social order desired by and beneficial to the toilers.

Further, bourgeois constitutions tacitly proceed from the premise that nations and races cannot have equal rights, that there are nations with full rights and nations without full rights, and that, in addition, there is a third category of nations or races, for example in the colonies, which have even fewer rights than the nations without full rights. This means that, at bottom, all these constitutions are nationalistic, *i.e.,* constitutions of ruling nations.

Unlike these constitutions, the draft of the new Constitution of the U.S.S.R. is, on the contrary, profoundly internationalistic. It proceeds from the fact that all nations and races have equal rights. It proceeds from the fact that neither difference in color or language, cultural level or level of political development, nor any other difference between nations and races, can serve as grounds for justifying national inequality of rights. It proceeds from the fact that all nations and races, irrespective of their past and present position, irrespective of their strength or weakness, must enjoy equal rights in all spheres of the economic, social, political and cultural life of society.

The fifth specific feature of the draft of the new Constitution is its consistent and thoroughgoing democracy. From the standpoint of democracy bourgeois constitutions may be divided into two groups: one group of constitutions openly denies, or actually nullifies, the equality of rights of citizens and democratic liberties. The other group of constitutions readily accepts and even advertises democratic principles, but at the same time it makes reservations and limitations which utterly mutilate democratic rights and liberties. They speak of equal suffrage for all citizens, but in the same breath limit it by residential, educational and even property qualifications. They speak of equal rights for citizens, but in the same breath they make the reservation that this does not apply to women or only partly applies to them. And so on and so forth.

The specific feature of the draft of the new Constitution of the U.S.S.R. is that it is free from such reservations and limitations. For it, active and passive citizens do not exist; for it, all citizens are active. It does not recognize any difference in rights as between men and women, "residents" and "non-residents," propertied and propertyless, educated and uneducated. For it, all citizens have equal rights. It is not property status, not national origin, not sex, not office that determines the position of every citizen in society, but personal ability and personal labor.

Lastly, there is still one other specific feature of the draft of the new Constitution. Bourgeois constitutions usually confine themselves to fixing the formal rights of citizens without bothering about the conditions for exercising these rights, about the possibility of exercising them, about the means by which they can be exercised. They speak of the equality of citizens, but forget that there cannot be real equality between master and workman, between landlord and peasant, if the former possess wealth and political weight in society while the latter are deprived of both, if the former are exploiters while the latter are exploited. Or again they speak of freedom of speech, assembly and the press, but forget that all these liberties may be merely a hollow sound for the working class if the latter cannot have access to suitable premises for meetings, good printshops, a sufficient quantity of printing paper, etc.

The specific feature of the draft of the new Constitution is that it does not confine itself to fixing the formal rights of citizens, but shifts the center of gravity to the guarantees of these rights, to the means by which these rights can be exercised. It does not simply proclaim the right to work, but ensures it by the legislative consolidation of the fact that crises do not exist in Soviet society, of the fact that unemployment has been abolished. It does not simply proclaim democratic liberties but legislatively ensures them by providing definite material resources. It is clear, therefore, that democracy in the draft of the new Constitution is not the "ordinary" and "universally recognized" democracy in general, but socialist democracy.

<hr />

MECHANICS OF A POLICE STATE *

Have the Soviets created a modern utopia, or is the Russian experiment another case of old wine in new bottles—dictatorship and totalitarianism under a different name? Independent observers, scholars, journalists, and foreign diplomats looking at this question not only deny the thesis that Russia has created the good society but indict the Soviet system as a travesty on freedom and democratic values. One of the most perceptive discussions of life in the U.S.S.R. is that written by the former United States Ambassador to the Soviet Union, Walter Bedell Smith. In the following selection Mr. Smith describes the political climate under the Communist regime as he experienced it during his three years in Moscow.

The Soviet state determines the behavior and activity of Soviet citizens in various ways. It educated the Soviet people in a spirit of Communist morality

* Condensed from *My Three Years in Moscow* by Walter Bedell Smith, pp. 111–30. Copyright, 1949, by Walter Bedell Smith, published by J. B. Lippincott Company.

of the system which introduces a series of legal norms regulating the life of the population, imposing interdictions, establishing encouragements, naming of punishment for the violation of these norms. The Soviet state stands guard over these legal norms with all its power. The conduct and activity of the Soviet people is also determined by the force of a public opinion which is created by the activity of numerous public organizations. In creating public opinion, the decisive role is played by the Communist party and the Soviet state, which, through various media, formulates public opinion and educates the workers in a spirit of Socialist awareness.

I am rather impressed by this introductory paragraph, because I think it is the suavest definition of national regimentation I have ever read, especially considering the source. I copied it verbatim from Issue No. 4 of Moscow *Bolshevik*, 1947, and it thus constitutes a Soviet description of the all-pervading police state—a system under which the state begins to determine and regulate the behavior and activities of its citizens almost from birth, continuing as long as they live. The Communist leadership disbelieves profoundly in the ability of the people to regulate their own lives or to govern themselves. I was startled by the evident sincerity with which individual party members subscribe to this theory, and to the police state methods by which the people are educated "in a spirit of political awareness." During the early days of our association, when personal relations were friendly and rather frank, Marshal Sokolovsky spent a week-end with me at my quarters in Frankfurt, Germany. During our conversation I spoke critically of the methods of political repression which the Communists already were employing in the occupied areas of Central Europe. Sokolovsky, who is an intelligent man and honest according to his principles, looked at me in surprise and said, "I don't see why you should criticize. We aren't doing anything there that we don't do at home."

The Communist Party of the Soviet Union still subscribes officially to the Marxian theory that as socialism develops, the state, which is an organ of class rule, will wither away. Since the contrary is obviously the case and the Soviet state is more robust than ever, Communist theoreticians explain the contradiction by pointing out to the Soviet people that they are living under the dangerous conditions of capitalist encirclement. Stalin was quoted in *Izvestia* in 1947 as saying that the state will continue to exist under communism unless capitalist encirclement is eliminated, unless the danger of armed attack from the outside is destroyed, and that the state will disappear and wither away if capitalist encirclement is eliminated and replaced by Communist encirclement. Thus the state is necessary just so long as the land of communism lives and develops in the conditions of capitalist encirclement. However, Stalin said last year that capitalist encirclement was no longer possible; yet the state continues to broaden its police authority. Party theoreticians haven't explained this yet. The words "police state" bring at once to mind the secret police organization itself. Actually the term means much more. In the Soviet Union, state control starts with the child, at a very early age. Soviet children are brought up as ideological Communists, and general education is a secondary consideration.

The Soviet child learns that the Soviet Union is the only nation which represents democracy and which stands for right, justice and peace. He is taught that the United States is an imperialistic, aggressive nation, where a small group of selfish, predatory millionaires dominate all capitalistic trusts, which in turn dominate the country, that workers are subjected to complete exploitation and literally kept in chains. When Anne O'Hare McCormick visited a Moscow school, one child asked her why the Americans kept their workers locked in dark cellars.

The child is told continually that the destruction of Soviet democracy is the primary objective of the capitalistic West, and that the attainment of this objective is frustrated only by the glorious Soviet Army and the strong and united determination of the great Soviet peoples. The educational system is designed to insure the perpetuation in power of the Communist Party and the exclusion of all political thought except that dictated by the party line.

The teaching of nationalism is intimately connected with political education. Its purpose is to arouse a boundless devotion to the Soviet Union in its struggle to establish the Soviet regime.

The Soviet child enters the Red Pioneers at about the same age that our boys and girls become Cub Scouts and Brownies. From the pioneers the children graduate into the Komsomol, or Communist youth organization, which admits young people from fourteen to twenty-six years of age. The Komsomol is the training school for future party members. The boy or girl receives a moral and political "shock group" training which at twenty-six will graduate the individual into the Communist Party if he or she has the intelligence, ability and response to discipline to qualify as a party member. Thus, from a very early age, Soviet youth is placed in an atmosphere which develops his "Socialist conscience" and the belief that he is above all a fighter for the defense of the Soviet regime, always menaced by capitalism.

Higher education is reserved for those who develop a "political consciousness" to a very high degree, or for the offspring of the new Soviet aristocracy. Indeed, the economic future of the Soviet young man or young woman depends to a large extent upon his political progress.

Aside from the evils inherent in its political aspects, there is nothing wrong with Soviet education in its primary stages that time and the constant attention given it by the government will not cure. In a country where work is obligatory for both parents, children become part-time wards of the state at an early age, and the Soviet state is a careful guardian of its most precious commodity. If the national average were taken as a basis of comparison, I believe that with certain clear exceptions the welfare of younger children in the Soviet Union would not be behind any other country in the world. The Soviet educational system is producing generations of serious-minded young people with a highly developed sense of responsibility, and illiteracy is being eradicated. In 1939 only 18.8 per cent of the total population of the Soviet Union was illiterate. Today's percentage would undoubtedly be appreciably less. The tragic thing about police state education is that all these young people are taught lies about the Western world, and there is no chance whatever for them to find out by observation and comparison that they are not being told the truth. The police state system molds the developing minds of its children for the loyal and enthusiastic support of a political regime that is basically evil.

When the young Soviet citizen leaves the direct supervision of his teachers, he comes, in one way or another, under the omnipotent eye of the secret police.

The Communists did not establish a secret police without apologies to the people, whose lives they intended to regulate. An early issue of the Soviet Encyclopedia states:

The apparatus of compulsion, the GPU, courts and prisons, is retained temporarily, only while the resistance of the bourgeois continues, but these instruments of struggle will wither away in proportion as the resistance declines. The state will disappear together with the division of society into classes.

And as long ago as 1939 no less a person than Stalin declared, "The function of compulsion inside the country has ceased, has withered away. The exploiters are no more, and there is no one to suppress any more."

But there is no slightest indication that the secret police are about to "wither away." On the contrary they have steadily increased in strength and power under Stalin's regime, and the organization has become a permanent and even a traditional feature of Soviet life, as it was in life under the Czars. The violent contradiction that involves between early Communist ideals and current Stalinist practice has had to be "resolved" dialectically. Therefore, the party line depicts the secret police of today as the guardian angels of the Soviet people against foreign machinations and enemy agents, foreign and domestic. The "organs of state security" are depicted as a beloved and benevolent feature of Socialist culture. But what colossal effrontery the writer must have had who described in Pravda recently the dread secret police organization in the following affectionate phrases:

For three decades the organs of Soviet intelligence have faithfully served our people. Soviet intelligence is surrounded by the well-deserved respect and confidence of the people of our country, and is called upon to stand guard over the historic achievements of October. The workers of the Soviet Union know very well that, reared and directed by the Bolshevik Party, the workers in the organs of state security, whom the Soviet people traditionally call Chekists, devotedly defend the vital interests of the people and vigilantly safeguard the security of the Socialist motherland. For this reason the Soviet people not only trust the iron talons of the Chekists but also help it actively every day in its noble work of protecting the creative activity of millions from the subversive activities of agents of the imperialist countries.

Such nonsense might convince some of the starry-eyed Communist sympathizers in this country who live far from the "iron talons" of the Cheka, but the Soviet people are well aware that the thousands of inmates of Lubianka and other prisons, and millions of laborers in prison camps, are Soviet nationals, many of whom have never seen a foreigner in their lives. So this must be explained, and the Moscow paper *Izvestia* undertakes to do it. "The attempts of world reaction have strengthened in recent times," says *Izvestia*. "American imperialism has turned to an aggressive, frankly expansionist course. The juridical trials which have taken place in Bulgaria, Rumania, Hungary and other countries, conclusively show how capitalist espionage makes use of the forces of internal reaction for its infamous, undermining purpose."

Thus the permanence of the secret police as a Soviet institution becomes undeniable, even to the easily deceived Soviet people, just at a time when the concept of capitalist espionage is becoming especially useful to the aggressive foreign policy of the rulers of the Soviet Union.

Many books have been written describing life in Soviet concentration camps and the summary forms of justice practiced in the Soviet Union, but they have not, I fear, entirely convinced the people of other countries of the lack of personal liberty in a police state. One of the most recent, and by our observation, the most accurate studies of the Soviet slave labor system, that by David Dallin, has been challenged because the statistics seem to exceed American credibility. Actually, from our point of view, whether there are one million or ten million political prisoners in the Soviet Union is relatively less important than is the simple fact that under the Soviet regime numbers of individuals are deprived of their liberty and sent to concentration camps solely for political and economic reasons.

Louis Fischer, in his book, *The Great Challenge*, repeats a story told him by his son, Captain George Fischer, who was one of our officers stationed at our shuttle bombing base at Poltava, in the Ukraine. Captain Fischer tried to explain to Soviet officers the purpose of the balloting conducted throughout our forces during the Presidential election of 1944. "I don't understand," said a Red Army lieutenant. "You mean that Roosevelt is a Democrat, and he has been President for several years, and there are still Republicans in the American Army?"

To an American who knows this, it is at first a surprise that the Soviet people show few outward signs of consciousness of omnipresent police surveillance or of the repressive activities of the agencies of internal security. I had lived in Moscow for some time before I began to appreciate the fact that the Soviet citizen is conditioned mentally to the chances of arrest and of "being sent away" just as we in this country are conditioned mentally to the chances of being struck by an automobile while crossing the street. His protective reactions to the one type of danger are as automatic and unostentatious as ours are to the other. For the true picture, one must look under the surface and this is hard to do. However, from a few among the stream of people who passed through the Consular Section of the Embassy, claiming American citizenship or seeking to enter the United States, I could at times get a glimpse of reality.

The most important function of the agencies of "security" of the police state, however, is the neutralization of political opposition, not only outside the party, but inside, and on the highest levels. The public and private life of every party member is under continuous scrutiny by the MVD, and the higher his position in the state, the more carefully he is watched. The average Soviet citizen, on the other hand, is conscious of the secret police only in a rather negative way, so long as he stays where he is registered, does his work, and refrains from comment or criticism of the Communist Party or the Soviet regime. But if he steps aside even the shortest distance from the routine path he is expected to follow, he is arrested at once, and his relatives and friends are likely to be arrested at the same time.

Arrests by the secret police are usually made at night and in an atmosphere of mystery that is terrifying, even to the foreigner with diplomatic immunity. A recurrent Moscow joke, told by Russians with a wry smile, describes the janitor of an apartment building walking through the halls at midnight knocking at the doors, and calling out loudly at the same time "Don't be afraid, comrades, it's only a fire."

A general "political crime" provision in Article 58 of the Soviet Criminal Code provides that for any acts disapproved by the Soviet authorities an accused can be tried *in camera,* and on the basis of entirely unpublished standards, by special MVD courts.

Two other provisions of Soviet law are particularly shocking to Westerners, but are essential to the operation of a police state system. The first of these, Article 58-1c of the Criminal Code, enacted July 20, 1934, reads as follows:

> In the event of escape or flight across the border of military service personnel, the adult members of his family, if they in any way facilitate the preparations for or committing of the act of treason, or even know about it but did not bring this to the attention of the authorities, are to be punished by deprivation of liberty for a term of five to ten years and the confiscation of all their property.
>
> The remainder of the traitor's family, who were residing with him or were dependent upon him at the time the crime was committed are subject to deprivation of voting rights and exile to remote regions of Siberia for five years.

The operations of Soviet law have a very different objective from the impartial administration of justice which is the ideal of the Anglo-Saxon jurisprudence. In his authoritative work on criminal procedure, Mr. Vishinsky says, "The primary duty of the Soviet judicial system lies in its protection of the class interests of the workers. Contrary to the bourgeois legal system which attempts to conceal its true nature of a class protection with only the pretense of independence of government policies, proletarian courts do not propose to disguise the fact that in their essence they are class protectors. The judicial system is the arm of the workers and peasants who dispose of the power of the state and use it to further their own interests against other classes." I agree with Mr. Vishinsky's definition of the Soviet law except for one thing. If he had substituted the words "Communist Party" for "workers and peasants" he would have been correct. They are not by any means synonymous.

The agencies of state security have complete supervision of every phase of national life. The Foreign Office cannot even give out an entry visa to a diplomatic attache without the approval of the men of the Lubianka, in the shadow of which the Foreign Office building stands. These men have a vested interest in insecurity, and the growth and influence of the police state machine have been directly proportional to the fears on which it feeds. The Soviet people have been for thirty years in what amounts, economically at least, to a state of siege. They have been called upon to work harder and get along with less in the way of material compensation for a longer period than any people will accept without protest, unless there is provided some powerful stimulus.

The state provides this stimulus in the form of a series of enemies. First, there were the bourgeoisie to be exterminated, then the Trotskyite wreckers, and then the actual and deadly threat of Germany. There has always been "capitalist encirclement," with the threat of sabotage, and lest this become shopworn, the new bogey of a warmongering United States now is brought out on parade daily. The statement that these threats existed has always necessitated strict and unquestioned obedience on the part of the population to the edicts of the state. Uncomplaining acceptance and hard work may bring the reward of a carrot in the form of a decoration or more material gain. Any other attitude is certain to bring the whip, and the whip is wielded by the secret police.

There is nothing that the people can do about it. They go to the polls and vote, but a Soviet election is simply a political puppet show, in which the masses dance to strings pulled by party bosses. Externally the purpose of elections is to conceal the reality of a police state behind the constitutional facade. Internally they constitute a gigantic organized demonstration in which the populace registers solidarity with the regime whether they like it or not. If any evidence of this is needed the Soviet election press provides ample quantity.

A good example of this is a pre-election editorial in *Culture and Life,* a copy of which I kept. This editorial contemptuously contrasts "bourgeois democracy" with that of the Soviet Union which is "based on genuine active participation of the people." This ideological hocus-pocus is followed by assertion that in the forthcoming election the Communist Party comes forth in "bloc" uniting "non-party people and Communists in one common collective of Soviet people." The paper then urges party agitators and the party press to redouble election propaganda work. It notes that 240,000 agitators are operating in Moscow, half a million in the Ukraine, etc. Tens of millions of political pamphlets have been published.

All this in a one-party election, where there is one ticket and one candidate for each office—an effort far beyond the wildest dreams of Tweed or Tammany in the old days. The press emphasizes that agitators must discuss subjects connected with the most important economic political tasks facing the country.

"They must ceaselessly wage the struggle for raising labor productivity, for labor discipline, educate workers in a spirit of selfless devotion to the cause of the party of Lenin and Stalin." The entire press, the radio and meetings must "urge all voters to vote unanimously for candidates of the bloc of Communist and non-party people." The editorial states that "forthcoming elections will demonstrate with new force the vitality and indestructibility of the Soviet multi-national state." The interesting fact is that there are no other candidates to vote for.

It is obvious to the most casual foreign observers that Soviet elections are not a contest as in a democracy but a carefully staged spectacle. The ruling party which controls the government, police, press and radio, uses its millions of members and the entire state machinery to get out one hundred per cent votes for its picked slated candidates. In these elections the public has no choice either on candidates or issues. Dissent from the party platform would of course be a matter for the secret police, but no Soviet citizen would dream of challenging publicly the party's choice of candidates or "issues." I say "no Soviet Citizen," but occasionally there is the rare exception. During the 1947 elections we visited several of the polling places and the Agitpunkt or party agitation centers. At one of the former, late in the evening, a little old Russian woman, dressed in a padded cotton coat, a gray wool skirt and the usual felt boots, and with her head wrapped in a shawl, walked in, advanced purposefully to the official in charge and demanded, "How do you vote 'NO'?"

There was a moment's silence, all eyebrows went up, and then the official, who undoubtedly had a sense of humor and realized that one little old woman did not provide a very serious threat to the regime, took a blank ballot and carefully instructed her. She took the ballot behind the curtained booth, which is provided for those who wish to change a ballot in secrecy and which few voters ever dare to enter, recorded her objection to conditions in general, and marched out with her head in the air. She had shown her independence and gotten away with it.

The foreigner who sees police state regimentation at close range might be able to regret it in a detached and impersonal way, return with relief and renewed confidence to his own democratic system, imperfect though it might be, and leave the whole thing for time and evolution, were it not for the sinister implications involved in a political religion that preaches hatred of all other political systems. It is this facet of communism that shocks Americans most. It is unwise and futile to disregard or to attempt to cheapen in any way a political ideology which, while it has in common with others the basic concept of overcoming the conflict of classes by transferring the means of production to national ownership, is unique in the profound belief that this end is attainable only by violent revolution, that subsequent to this revolution there must be a period of dictatorship based on open terror, and that the Socialist state can only be secure when capitalism is destroyed.

In 1947 the youth paper *Komsomol Pravda* featured an article on Leninism which contained this paragraph:

Love for the Socialist Motherland is undoubtedly linked with fostering hatred for all imperialists and reactionaries throughout the world. Hatred for enemies of the land of socialism is an inseparable feature of Socialist ideology and the ideology of Leninism. What is reactionary bourgeois ideology? One may briefly reply, "Look at the mighty armies of Hitlerite Germany." That is bourgeois ideology in action. Whom has this ideology trained, and whom is it now training? People devoid of conscience and honor, detachments of wild beasts, hordes of barbarians, hangmen.

Well! This is us, and people like us, whom *Komsomol Pravda* describes in these unflattering terms to its youthful readers, and they are beginning to believe it. Lenin was right in more ways than one when he said that the establishment of socialism would require the sacrifice of two generations, for these young people whose minds are being shaped into a pattern of hatred for all the things which we believe to be indispensable to real democracy are as lost to the world of human freedom as is the generation which was liquidated to secure the Bolshevik regime in its present position of power.

This propaganda is effective. I cannot accept the picture some writers have given of seething resentment against the Communist regime. The vast majority of people now living in the Soviet Union, in my opinion, have no idea of personal liberty or of the processes of democracy as we in America understand these things. Those Russians who did understand such things don't live there any more. They are in exile, in prison or dead.

In fact, the Soviet citizen today believes he has the fruits of democracy. He can vote, and the fact that he casts his ballot for one candidate selected by the only existing political party is without significance to him. He can be elected to and sit on the legislative body of his state, or of his national republic, or of the Soviet Union. The fact that in this capacity he acts only as a rubber stamp for the party and, as I myself have seen, would pass a national budget without question or discussion in the short space of fourteen minutes does not impress him as unusual. He has no standard of comparison.

He has in Stalin the "Little father" that the psychology of the Russian people seems always to have required—the demigod who represents all that is great and good in the national cosmos. Discontent exists, but I believe it is no more than the discontent which Lenin visualized when he said that "any regime that remains in power over a long period of time becomes unpopular."

Thus the Soviet regime is nailed in place by bayonets and held together by an omnipresent demonstration of force as well as by the psychological trickery of propaganda. The individual, his personal liberties and, to a considerable extent, his dignity as a human being, are submerged—all in the interest of the system as a whole, whose material achievements, particularly in vast stretches of backward territory, are ample evidence of impressive power.

————◆◆◆◆————

THE POLITICAL AND SOCIAL DOCTRINE OF FASCISM *

Unlike Communism in Russia, Fascism in Italy did not begin with a blueprint, a guidebook, or even a well-defined theory or philosophy. The movement came to Italy through the personage of Benito Mussolini. Capitalizing upon the economic distress and moral despair, Mussolini and his followers grew in strength with the failure of other groups to deal effectively with the chaos in postwar Italy. Finally in 1922, under the threat of force, the king appointed Mussolini prime minister. Once in power the Fascist Party systematically destroyed parliamentary government and democratic institutions. The ideology that developed was an evolving one. Mussolini did not know how many stories the structure was going to have when he started building. He acted and then sought the political rationale. Ultimately Fascist doctrine became a blending of a score of political and philosophical concepts and a travesty on all of them.

In addition to his political talents, Mussolini was also a writer of considerable ability and experience. In 1932 he contributed an article on Fascism to the *Enciclopedia Italiana*. The second part of this article, which is reprinted below, is generally considered a classic account of Fascist ideology. How do the claims made for Fascism compare with the observations of Herman Finer in the following article? Can any government which places itself above accountability operate efficiently for any long period of time? Is loyalty—true and lasting loyalty—secured by force and coercion? Can discipline, order, and obedience be superimposed upon a people even though these characteristics are not supported by the cultural traditions?

When, in the now distant March of 1919, I summoned a meeting at Milan through the columns of the *Popolo d'Italia* of the surviving members of the Interventionist Party who had themselves been in action, and who had followed me since the creation of the Fascist Revolutionary Party (which took place in January of 1915), I had no specific doctrinal attitude in my mind. I had a living experience of one doctrine only—that of Socialism, from 1903-4 to the winter of 1914—that is to say, about a decade: and from Socialism itself, even though I had taken part in the movement first as a member of the rank and file and then later as a leader, yet I had no experience of its doctrine in practice. My own doctrine, even in this period, had always been a doctrine of action. A unanimous universally ac-

* Benito Mussolini in Albert R. Chandler (ed.), *The Clash of Political Ideals*, New York, Revised Edition, 1949, Appleton-Century-Crofts, Inc., pp. 206–14.

cepted theory of Socialism did not exist after 1905, when the revisionist movement began in Germany under the leadership of Bernstein, while under pressure of the tendencies of the time, a Left Revolutionary movement also appeared, which though never getting further than talk in Italy, in Russian Socialistic circles laid the foundations of Bolshevism. Reformation, Revolution, Centralization—already the echoes of these terms are spent—while in the great stream of Fascism are to be found ideas which began with Sorel, Peguy, with Lagardelle in the "Mouvement Socialiste," and with the Italian trades-union movement which throughout the period 1904–14 was sounding a new note in Italian Socialist circles (already weakened by the betrayal of Giolitti) through Olivetti's *Pagine Libere*, Orano's *La Lupa*, and Enrico Leone's *Divenire Sociale*.

After the War, 1919, Socialism was already dead as a doctrine: it existed only as a hatred. There remained to it only one possibility of action, especially in Italy, reprisals against those who had desired the War and who must now be made to "expiate" its result. The *Popolo d'Italia* was then given the sub-title of "The newspaper of ex-service men and producers," and the word "producers" was already the expression of a mental attitude. Fascism was not the nursling of a doctrine worked out beforehand with detailed elaboration; it was born of the need for action and it was itself from the beginning practical rather than theoretical; it was not merely another political party but, even in the first two years, in opposition to all political parties as such, and itself a living movement. The name which I then gave to the organization fixed its character. And yet, if one were to re-read, in the now dusty columns of that date, the report of the meeting in which the *Fasci Italiani di combattimento* were constituted, one would there find no ordered expression of doctrine, but a series of aphorisms, anticipations, and aspirations which, when refined by time from the original ore, were destined after some years to develop into a series of doctrinal concepts, forming the Fascist political doctrine—different from all others either of the past or the present day.

"If the bourgeoisie," I said then, "think that they will find lightning-conductors in us, they are the more deceived; we must start work at once. . . . We want to accustom the working-class to real and effectual leadership, and also to convince them that it is no easy thing to direct an industry or a commercial enterprise successfully. . . . We shall combat every retrograde idea, technical or spiritual. . . . When the succession to the seat of government is open, we must not be unwilling to fight for it. We must make haste; when the present regime breaks down, we must be ready at once to take its place. It is we who have the right to the succession, because it was we who forced the country into the War, and led her to victory. The present method of political representation cannot suffice, we must have a representation direct from the individuals concerned. It may be objected against this program that it is a return to the conception of the corporation, but that is no matter. . . . Therefore, I desire that this assembly shall accept the claim of national trades-unionism from the economic point of view. . . ."

Now is it not a singular thing that even on this first day in the Piazza San Sepolcro that word "corporation" arose, which later, in the course of the Revolution, came to express one of the creations of social legislation at the very foundation of the regime?

Fascism is now a completely individual thing, not only as a regime but as a doctrine. And this means that today Fascism exercising its critical sense upon itself and upon others, has formed its own distinct and peculiar point of view, to which it can refer and upon which, therefore, it can act in the face of all problems, practical or intellectual, which confront the world.

And above all, Fascism, the more it considers and observes the future and the development of humanity quite apart from political considerations of the moment, believes neither in the possibility nor the utility of perpetual peace. It thus repudiates the doctrine of Pacifism—born of a renunciation of the struggle and an act of cowardice in the face of sacrifice. War alone brings up to its highest tension all human energy and puts the stamp of nobility upon the peoples who have the courage to meet it. All other trials are substitutes, which never really put men into the position where they have to make the great decision—the alternative of life or death. Thus a doctrine which is founded upon this harmful postulate of peace is hostile to Fascism. And thus hostile to the spirit of Fascism, though accepted for what use they can be in dealing with particular political situations, are all the international leagues and societies which, as history will show, can be scattered to the winds when once strong national feeling is aroused by any motive—sentimental, ideal or practical. This anti-pacifist spirit is carried by Fascism even into the life of the individual; the proud motto of the *Squadrista,* "Me ne frego" ("I don't give a damn"), written on the bandage of the wound, is an act of philosophy not only stoic, the summary of a doctrine not only political—it is the education to combat, the acceptation of the risks which combat implies, and a new way of life for Italy. Thus the Fascist accepts life and loves it, knowing nothing of and despising suicide; he rather conceives of life as duty and struggle and conquest, life which should be high and full, lived for oneself, but above all for others —those who are at hand and those who are far distant, contemporaries, and those who will come after.

Such a conception of life makes Fascism the complete opposite of that doctrine, the base of so-called scientific and Marxian Socialism, the materialist conception of history; according to which the history of human civilization can be explained simply through the conflict of interests among the various social groups and by the change and development in the means and instruments of production. That the changes in the economic field—new discoveries of raw materials, new methods of working them, and the inventions of science—have their importance no one can deny; but that these factors are sufficient to explain the history of humanity excluding all others is an absurd delusion. Fascism, now and always, believes in holiness and in heroism; that is to say, in actions influenced by no economic motive, direct or indirect. And if the economic conception of history be denied, according to which theory men are no more than puppets, carried to and fro by the waves of chance, while the real directing forces are quite out of their control, it follows that the existence of an unchangeable and unchanging class-war is also denied—the natural progeny of the economic conception of history. And above all Fascism denies that class-war can be the preponderant force in the transformation of society. These two fundamental concepts of Socialism being thus refuted, nothing is left of it but the sentimental aspiration—as old as humanity itself—towards a social system in which the sorrows and sufferings of the humblest shall be alleviated. But here again Fascism repudiates the conception of "economic" happiness, to be realized by Socialism and, as it were, at a given moment in economic evolution to assure to everyone the maximum of well-being. Fascism denies the materialist conception of happiness as a possibility, and abandons it to its inventors, the economists of the first half of the nineteenth century: that is to say, Fascism denies the validity of the equation, well-being—happiness, which would reduce men to the level of animals, caring for only one thing—to be fat and well fed—and would thus degrade humanity to a purely physical existence.

After Socialism, Fascism combats the whole complex system of democratic ideology, and repudiates it, whether in its theoretical premises or in its practical application. Fascism denies that the majority, by the simple fact that it is a majority, can direct human society; it denies that numbers alone can govern by means of periodical consultation, and it affirms the immutable, beneficial, and fruitful inequality of mankind, which can never be permanently leveled through the mere operation of a mechanical process such as universal suffrage. The democratic regime may be defined as from time to time giving the people the illusion of sovereignty, while the real effective sovereignty lies in the hands of other concealed and irresponsible forces. Democracy is a regime nominally without a king, but it is ruled by many kings—more absolute, tyrannical, and ruinous than one sole king, even though a tyrant. This explains why Fascism, having first in 1922 (for reasons of expediency) assumed an attitude tending towards republicanism, renounced this point of view before the march to Rome; being convinced that the question of political form is not today of prime importance, and after having studied the examples of monarchies and republics past and present reached the conclusion that monarchy or republicanism are not to be judged, as it were, by an absolute standard; but that they represent forms in which the evolution—political, historical, traditional, or psychological—of a particular country has expressed itself. Fascism supersedes the antithesis of monarchy or republicanism, while democracy still tarries beneath the domination of this idea, forever pointing out the insufficiency of the first and forever praising the second as the perfect regime. Today, it can be seen that there are republics innately reactionary and absolutist, and also monarchies which incorporate the most ardent social and political hopes of the future.

But the Fascist negation of Socialism, Democracy, and Liberalism must not be taken to mean that Fascism desires to lead the world back to the state of affairs before 1789, the date which seems to be indicated as the opening year of the succeeding semi-Liberal century: we do not desire to turn back; Fascism has not chosen De Maistre for its high priest. Absolute monarchy has been and can never return, any more than blind acceptance of ecclesiastical authority.

So, too, the privileges of the feudal system "have passed away," and the division of society into castes impenetrable from outside, and with no inter-communication among themselves: the Fascist conception of authority has nothing to do with such a policy. A party which entirely governs a nation is a fact entirely new to history; there are no possible references or parallels. Fascism uses in its construction whatever elements in the Liberal, Social, or Democratic doctrines still have a living value; it maintains what may be called the certainties which we owe to history, but it rejects all the rest—that is to say, the conception that there can be any doctrine of unquestioned efficacy for all times and all peoples. Given that the nineteenth century was the century of Socialism, of Liberalism, and of Democracy, it does not necessarily follow that the twentieth century must also be a century of Socialism, Liberalism, and Democracy: political doctrines pass, but humanity remains; and it may rather be expected that this will be a century of authority, a century of the Left, a century of Fascism. For if the nineteenth century was a century of individualism (Liberalism always signifying individualism) it may be expected that this will be the century of collectivism, and hence the century of the State. It is a perfectly logical deduction that a new doctrine can utilize all the still vital elements of previous doctrines.

The foundation of Fascism is the conception of the State, its character, its duty, and its aim. Fascism conceives of the State as an absolute, in comparison with which all individuals or groups are relative, only to be conceived of in their relation to the State. The conception of the Liberal State is not that of a directing force, guiding the play and development, both material and spiritual, of a collective body, but merely a force limited to the function of recording results: on the other hand, the Fascist State is itself conscious, and has itself a will and a personality—thus it may be called the "ethical" State.

From 1929 until today, evolution, both political and economic, has everywhere gone to prove the validity of these doctrinal premises. Of such gigantic importance is the State. It is the force which alone can provide a solution to the dramatic contradiction of capitalism, and that state of affairs which we call the crisis can only be dealt with by the State, as between other States. Where is the shade of Jules Simon, who in the dawn of Liberalism proclaimed that, "The State must labor to make itself unnecessary, and prepare the way for its own dismissal"? Or of McCulloch, who, in the second half of the last century, affirmed that the State must guard against the danger of governing too much? What would the Englishman, Bentham, say today to the continual and inevitably invoked intervention of the State in the sphere of economics, while according to his theories industry should ask no more of the State than to be left in peace? Or the German, Humboldt, according to whom the "lazy" State should be considered the best? It is true that the second wave of Liberal economists were less extreme than the first, and Adam Smith himself opened the door—if only very cautiously—which leads to State intervention in the economic field: but whoever says Liberalism implies individualism, and whoever says Fascism implies the State. Yet the Fascist State is unique, and an original creation. It is not reactionary, but revolutionary, in that it anticipates the solution of the universal political problems which elsewhere have to be settled in the political field by the rivalry of parties, the excessive power of the parliamentary regime and the irresponsibility of political assemblies; while it meets the problems of the economic field by a system of syndicalism which is continually increasing in importance, as much in the sphere of labor as of industry: and in the moral field enforces order, discipline, and obedience to that which is the determined moral code of the country. Fascism desires the State to be a strong and organic body, at the same time reposing upon broad and popular support. The Fascist State has drawn into itself even the economic activities of the nation, and, through the corporative social and educational institutions created by it, its influence reaches every aspect of the national life and includes, framed in their respective organizations, all the political, economic and spiritual forces of the nation. A State which reposes upon the support of millions of individuals who recognize its authority, are continually conscious of its power and are ready at once to serve it, is not the old tyranni-cal State of the medieval lord nor has it anything in common with the absolute governments either before or after 1789. The individual in the Fascist State is not annulled but rather multiplied, just in the same way that a soldier in a regiment is not diminished but rather increased by the number of his comrades. The Fascist State organizes the nation, but leaves a sufficient margin of liberty to the individual; the latter is deprived of all useless and possibly harmful freedom, but retains what is essential; the deciding power in this question cannot be the individual, but the State alone.

The Fascist State is not indifferent to the fact of religion in general, or to that particular and positive faith which is Italian Catholicism. The State professes no theology, but a morality, and in the Fascist State religion is considered as one of the deepest manifestations of the spirit of man, thus it is not only respected but defended and protected. The Fascist State has never tried to create its own God, as at one moment Robespierre and the wildest extremists of the Convention tried to do; nor does it vainly seek to obliterate religion from the hearts of men as does Bolshevism: Fascism respects the God of the ascetics, the saints and heroes, and equally, God as He is perceived and worshipped by simple people.

The Fascist State is an embodied will to power and government: the Roman tradition is here an ideal of force in action. According to Fascism, government is not so much a thing to be expressed in territorial or mili-tary terms as in terms of morality and the spirit. It must be thought of as an empire—that is to say, a nation which directly or indirectly rules other nations, without the need for conquering a single square yard of territory. For Fascism, the growth of empire, that is to say the expansion of the na-tion, is an essential manifestation of vitality, and its opposite a sign of decadence. Peoples which are rising, or rising again after a period of decadence, are always imperialist; any renunciation is a sign of decay and of death. Fascism is the doctrine best adapted to represent the tendencies and the aspirations of a people, like the people of Italy, who are rising again after many centuries of abasement and foreign servitude. But em-pire demands discipline, the coordination of all forces and a deeply felt sense of duty and sacrifice: this fact explains many aspects of the practical working of the regime, the character of many forces in the State, and the necessarily severe measures which must be taken against those who would oppose this spontaneous and inevitable movement of Italy in the twentieth century, and would oppose it by recalling the outworn ideology of the nineteenth century—repudiated wheresoever there has been the courage to undertake great experiments of social and political transformation: for never before has the nation stood more in need of authority, of direction, and of order. If every age has its own characteristic doctrine, there are a thousand signs which point to Fascism as the characteristic doctrine of our time. For if a doctrine must be a living thing, this is proved by the fact that Fascism has created a living faith; and that this faith is very powerful in the minds of men, is demonstrated by those who have suffered and died for it.

Fascism has henceforth in the world the universality of all those doctrines which, in realizing themselves, have represented a stage in the history of the human spirit.

THE SPIRITUAL GAINS AND LOSSES UNDER FASCISM *

In contrast to the commentary of Benito Mussolini on the accomplishments of Italian Fascism, the observations of Herman Finer present a far different evaluation. Unlike Mussolini, Finer has no axe to grind, no vested interest to defend. He writes simply as a political scientist with objectivity and perception, and the questions he raises are pertinent ones. What were the consequences of the taking away of liberty and the opportunity of self-questioning and public examination? Did the imposed order under Fascism compensate for the loss of freedom? Was the national unity achieved under Mussolini real or merely apparent? Is it not significant that Italy during this period produced nothing of worth in art or literature?

What has Fascism taken away from Italy's spiritual life, and what has it given? The answer depends on facts which cannot be measured exactly, like a temperature, and on the highly subjective judgment of their value to the individual. I believe that Italy has, on the balance, suffered a very serious loss.

Since it is dangerous to think in Italy, and there are abundant rewards for simply repeating what the leaders say, there is a loss of creative thought. The legal and the social sciences, which are supreme because they offer direction to humanity, have become merely slavish commentaries. The young men are anxious to justify the work of the regime in their theses and their lectures. The professors are anxious to expound to their students and to the public the absolute virtues of the official creed and works. The

* *Mussolini's Italy* by Professor Herman Finer, pp. 535-44, 546-50. Published by Victor Gollancz, Ltd., in 1935.

journalists use their literary power to popularise difficult conceptions, in repeating, ad nauseam, the same phrases. There is a philosophic inbreeding. There is no rationalist philosopher in Italy, no anti-Corporative economist, political scientist, or jurist. Not that there is no private philosophic discussion which does not seriously question the system. The freedom of small groups without organization and without public repercussion is permitted, because it would be impossible to root them out, and Mussolini is anxious to learn and by auto-criticism to keep the regime from stagnation. Yet considerable caution is required even among the chartered few. What is worse is that the rising generation, which should be marking out new paths in every field of the social sciences, is lost; and the older generation cannot, for its very life, do more than hint in private at the existence of things which are not to be found in the Fascist philosophy. What novel thought exists in Italy is of foreign origin, and here there is a surprising latitude: De Tocqueville's "Democracy in America," the "Communist Manifesto," "Trotsky's Life," and many books about America and Russia have recently been translated. The foreigners are the heretics; and the wish to read heretics evidently exists. The freedom to emulate them, and the products of such freedom, are lost.

The limitation of liberty has produced a corresponding loss in the quality of the governing class of the country. Many, of course, are excluded because they are hostile to the regime. Many who have had to leave the country have left behind no equals in intellect, nobility of conscience, or humane purpose. Within the Party itself there are no public elections of the governors; there is no open competition, or display of talents and public cross-examination. The method of selection is by hearsay, passed on in private letters and whispers. There is no public control, with all the fears of detection which that awakes in the potential slanderer, or even in the merely careless or mistaken. Those who are chosen may be good men; but there may be better. How do the leaders know that there are not? Those who make the ultimate choice do not need to be ruthlessly careful in their search for talent, for they themselves are not amenable to public criticism. Their power is not threatened.

Fascists say, in answer to these observations, that the Duce keeps on the watch for new men and for incompetents. The rejoinder to this is twofold. First, the Duce cannot be everywhere, to see and hear everything. One of the advantages of the democratic system is that democracy is everywhere, and can see and hear all that happens. Democracy has millions of eyes. Secondly, the assumption that Mussolini is miraculously vigilant settles the question of what will happen when he goes. The regime itself recognises what this means, and tries to overcome the difficulty. But from all sides one hears complaints of the incapacity of the system to produce a really competent governing class. Nor can time bring improvement, if we are to judge by the present products of Fascist education.

I will not pretend that a democratic system offers no scope for intrigue, or that considerations other than those of the capacity for office never decide who shall be the occupant. In democracies, however, the leaders of importance are the best that can be obtained in a system in which everyone strains to convince the public of his merits, publicly produces the evidence thereof, and is obliged to answer his opponents' evidence against him. It is true that the majority, at which Mussolini has so often sneered, makes the selection, but it does not lack sifted information, and there is a selected and responsible part of the majority which takes the lead.

Liberty in government is not important merely because the Government is compelled to explain and defend its policy, but equally because, as a by-product, it induces a very healthy process of self-questioning, and examination of the terms of its trust. In Italy, there is little to cause the Government to question its own assumptions, if we exclude Conscience, God, History, the Nation, the "objective will," and the possibly representative character of the men at the head. Outside such Fascist taskmasters there are neither spurs nor bridles.

It is true that Mussolini soon learned that his Revolution had not been a Revolution in the sense that the whole country was permeated, or quickly permeable, by an idea. He encountered opposition, from the leaders of industry in particular. Moreover the Party zealots and the bureaucracy have been obliged to act in economic matters considerably at the dictation of world influences. Yet it seems to me that Italy would have been better off if there had been free political opposition to call attention to impending errors. For example, the country would not have proceeded under more than full steam along the path of governmental expenditure for Public Works and other services, until a Budget deficit such as that reached in 1934 compelled a drastic reversal of general economic policy. So too with the valuation of the lira, which was made a matter of life and death by the Government at the end of 1927, to the immediate scoring of a vain triumph over France, but to the ultimate damage of Italian exports and the employers and employed who lived by them. Though the social services have been developed, in a free system much more might have been done, and much less spent on military forces to bolster up the quest for international "glory." If there had been free criticism in foreign affairs, the policy of aggrandising Germany in order to humble France would not have pursued as it was until early 1934, to the point where Germany was so truculent that she could break faith with Italy, cause her grave trouble on the Austrian Frontier, and insolently sneer at her objections (pitched now in a minor key) at unilateral denunciation of disarmament engagements.

The Fascists say they took away liberty from the Italian people because they were too ignorant to use it responsibly. They have erected a number of institutions, like the Corporations, intended, they allege, to educate the public in the affairs of the nation. What are the observed facts? Arguments are not pressed to their full limits, and the implications of the Government's decisions are as little appreciated as is the case against them. Even from the Fascist standpoint, propaganda is insufficiently thorough. There is only one Party, with two million members, a large proportion being merely passengers. How could there be sufficient advertisement to convince everybody, or even to reach everybody? It is not necessary to persuade all the people, although it is desirable to obtain a unanimous plebiscite. In a democratic system, as every candidate and election agent knows, it is necessary to do one's best to reach every voter, since any single vote may be the vote that secures the victory. Not so in Italy. It is enough to carry the more effective members of the Party with you, they must be kept in good humor; and if the rest of the population can be reached, well and good. Nothing, however, compels the regime to come down to them, and to demonstrate the value of its own proposals by comparison with others put before the public by a determined opponent.

It must further be remembered that public affairs in the modern State can only become known to the masses if there exist people with an interest in, and an ability to awake, questions in their minds. How can the masses, preoccupied with the care and toil of making a living, sometimes too poor of mind to think for themselves, seeking the fulfilment of their lives in family cares and non-political culture and recreation, ever achieve an insight into public affairs, which to-day embrace the whole world, unless there exist men and women with the stimulus to arouse a questioning attitude in them? For the mass of mankind the natural tendency is to take the things they encounter for granted, as much in the realm of political and social institutions as in the shape and actions of Nature. People with nascent ideas need great encouragement to dare to utter them. The comparatively small proportions of sensitive consciences and speculating minds must be let loose upon these to awaken doubts, and, as Lassalle once said, to shake their "damned wantlessness."

There is a graver count. The exclusion of publicity regarding the deciding reasons of many branches of public policy, and the deliberate distortion of facts and figures, deprive the social and economic scientists of the data indispensable to the progress of knowledge.

Therefore those in Italy who, perhaps quite sincerely, have all their lives cried out for the "elevation" of the people, have brought about a situation in which the rulers are elevated but the people palpably degraded. The leaders are not compelled to listen, and therefore there is no point in equipping one's self to achieve their conversion. The lower ranks are not encouraged to speak in perfect frankness, and it has been said by someone that the device which should be written up over the Federal offices of the Party should be, "Here nothing bad is said about anybody!"

The nation with the best prospects of civic education is the nation which can freely turn its public life into a nation-wide debating chamber. Such was Italy until 1922. It was rowdy, quarrelsome, slanderous, and sometimes violent. To cure its excesses the very system itself was swept away. In the new State the people do not learn the important art of composing their differences, which are inevitable, by free and reasonable argument and compromise. The Government steps in, and settles the matter out of hand. An example at the very root of Italian affairs is the problem of the class war. After so many years of coercion, Fascists admit, as though letting you into a profound secret, that the class war continues. They do not use the word "war" any longer, but replace it by "tension" or "differences." The only thing they have abolished is overt conflict. The class war mentality is still extant; distinct and hostile classes still confront each other. The war continues—but where? In the factories and agriculture, when bargains are made for wages and profits; in the Ministry of Corporations, when the interests come to plead their cases. Instead of letting both parties to the class war learn by experience how far their demands upon each other were just and practicable, even by violence to each other, the Fascist movement applied the violence, and this mainly to the workers, for whereas property is static, force resides in the masses. The lesson that had to be learnt has not been learnt. We concede, of course, the gain of ten years uninterrupted production. The Fascist may plead that propaganda in favour of national unity will in time accomplish the supersession of class. Will it?

In order to achieve its objects, Fascism has been obliged to dismiss the Past, or, when it remembers it, to slander history, which remains a silent but ever mocking observer. Happily, it is not entirely possible to destroy the cultural harvest of so many generations. The arts of printing and reading have made "totalitarian" and long-enduring Dictatorships impossible. If the Dictator is a well-read man they weaken even his resolution. The denunciation of democracy, for example, to the children simply arouses their curiosity. For the sake of efficiency Fascists are compelled to honour and admit intellect; and too many of them know that they have themselves not produced enough to justify the repudiation of the past. The libraries are still the organised opposition in the Fascist State. Yet the full effect of literature and history cannot be brought to bear upon the public mind.

Only the parts that support the Fascist view can seep through to form the mind of the adult population and the young. Half a brain is worse than none.

The control of the public mind is not absolute. To achieve that one would have needed at least to begin with an absolute Idea. Neither Mussolini nor his lieutenants possessed such an Idea, nor, in spite of ten thousand books including the Duce's has one yet been found. There is uncertainty and fumbling. Consequently, the light of the contemporary mind and the gleam of the ages still shine through the chinks, to Italy's great advantage. It is the heretic that blesses Italy, the non-Fascist who keeps the body politic healthy by his surreptitious pinches of salt. The Catholic Church is one such heretic, a powerful opponent of Mussolini's militarism. Here and there are economists, political scientists, and jurists, who, non-Fascist and anti-Fascist as they are, should be rewarded by the Government, because they save it from bad mistakes, and add to Italy's prestige wherever the learned congregate. For the rest, the regime is occupied in giving the Italian a character in place of brains, and in encouraging the flight from Reason.

The imminence of Force as the final argument in public affairs causes exclusion of the most sensitive consciences and scrupulous minds from full participation in them. These, who are the real elite of the world, and whose protection from the bullies should be the special concern of a civilization, must in self-defence retire from politics. What a loss to Italy! The jack-in-office who fills the subordinate roles in a Dictatorship does not need to satisfy himself, or others, of the objective rightness of his policy. Sheer anger with an opponent may be immediately transfigured into a political principle, and applied by main force. . . .

It is claimed that Italy is being moralised under the regime, ennobled, taken beyond the petty preoccupation with material welfare. I categorically affirm, from direct observation, and from the admissions of good Fascists, that Italy is being demoralised. The vacant-minded repetition of uniform phrases and songs and salutes, even when repeated by millions of people, cannot be called moralisation. To be moral is to have inwardly striven for the conviction of truth.

It is even strongly open to doubt whether the Fascists are able to secure what they allege to have most at heart: a sense of national unity. I suppose this would mean that all citizens should voluntarily and spontaneously think of their Nation as an entity, the preservation of whose claims on the rest of the world, and whose internal order and amenities, would merit ample sacrifices on their part. It is a sense of community, rather than of commanded uniformity. It is true that the Fascist regime teaches the idea of community, and of sacrifice on its behalf. True also, and beneficial, that reductions of railway fares and the work of the Dopolavoro enable Italians to get to know their country as never before. But what are the nation-building methods? As in other countries, they dwell on the nation's contributions to art, letters, and the sciences, the valour and devotion of its heroes. There is a strong emphasis on the past and potential hostility of the rest of the world, and the need for a belligerent attitude towards it. Let us admit that this educational process has some success.

Other factors in the dictatorship have tended to destroy such voluntary unity as before existed in the free association of men in their political parties and economic associations. The Dictatorship has rendered all individuals suspicious of each other. They may bring all sorts of trouble on themselves by a chance remark. The man you talk to in the park, the train, or the restaurant may cause you harm, and you must beware of him. The Italian in the Party is divided from the Italian outside it; the workman in the Fascist Unions is sundered from his fellows outside; the local political leaders are suspicious of each other. The Government is divorced from the people, though it renders services to it. The Corporations are held together very loosely, but each commands its own field of economic enterprise. Mussolini stands for national unity, but his system thrives on division. There is nothing to equal freedom as a builder of genuine fellowship.

If the Dictator pretends that he is the saviour of the country he must persuade his followers that there is something to be saved—the territory, the possibility of expansion, or the civilization. He must rouse in them a wish to maintain the values that he alleges are threatened. He must therefore make them proud of objects which they had previously taken for granted; and, I think it may be said, decent pride is not the word, but vanity, and even swollen-headedness, rising in the more susceptible to a veritable megalomania. Every simple difference becomes a superiority in favour of the Dictator's country. The Dictator is forced by his own position, and the continual need of stimulating the loyalties to him, to pursue a robust foreign policy. Hence Mussolini has taken the lead in European affairs wherever possible. Although many of his principles, such as the advocacy of the revision of the Treaty of Versailles and his plain outspoken comments on disarmament, are sound, his tactics have surely not been for the good of Italy or Europe. . . .

This is the nemesis of the nationalism which is artificially created to maintain a dictatorial system. It turned Mussolini against the Little Entente, when the Little Entente was Francophile; it turned him against the League of Nations, which suited Germany's book; it even makes him boil over with envy of England, which is too powerful to submit to his admonitions.

What is the end of such tactics, employed by a country whose resources are so modest? The honest broker will fall under international suspicion, or his speeches will be listened to with diplomatic courtesy but without practical effect. Does this serve Italy's interests in the long run, or her moral significance in the opinion of the world, or even the Dictator's personal position?

A nation can escape, and help other nations to escape, the danger of war by acting justly and modestly. If it chooses to pass into the sphere of active manipulation and wire-pulling it must be ready, if not to attack others, at least to defend itself from the anger of those who have been made catspaws. This inevitably implies armaments, military education, and expenditure.

I cannot believe that militarisation is a quality to be over encouraged in the warm-hearted, kindly, convivial, spontaneous Italian nature, which is so lovable. It is true that such people in the past have been liable to bullying by international brutes. The way to avoid the bullies, if this is all that is wanted, is to have an appropriate defence, and support the League of Nations. How strong can a country be when acting by itself? How strong can Italy be without impoverishing itself? Mussolini has said that a poor country cannot afford freedom, and he has abolished it; can a poor country afford a spirited foreign policy? . . .

The bourgeoisie are still in the land, a stumbling-block to the intentions of the régime. They are not prepared to sacrifice their goods, their positions, and the social and economic defences around their children, in order that others, of Mussolini's choosing, may replace them. Fascism, which has had twelve years of "high ideal tension" at its disposal, has so far done only three things to make their situation any different from that of their prototypes elsewhere. It has entrenched them in their positions of privilege, by protecting them from the pressure of the Socialist and Liberal movements. It has provided them with a large sackful of gifts and heroic catchwords, like authority, discipline, patriotism, private enterprise and sport, and made them feel glorious, where Socialism and Liberalism made them feel ashamed. Thirdly, it has in recent months begun to make them feel afraid that what was forbidden to the Socialist party may yet be undertaken by a dictatorial but mild Socialist—Mussolini.

What issue, if any, can there be from this state of affairs? Mussolini will have to lead the Revolution which the Socialists were leading. As Duce he will be obliged, if he is really intent on casting out the middle-class spirit, to lead the workers to the assault from which he had them bludgeoned thirteen years ago.

All the appeals to silent work, all the exhortations to stoic labour and a "lapidary style," are in practice, to an astonishing degree, contradicted.

I have made careful enquiries to discover whether the Italian before Fascism was so loud, bombastic, forced, sensational, and florid. I find that he was not. Since there can be no competition in the rivalry of ideas and criticism there is a rivalry in loud and superlative commentaries on the virtues of the régime. The superlative adjective and adverb have utterly expelled moderation and modesty. All of Mussolini's fulminations against the demagogues have recoiled upon his own head. As Mussolini says, the Dictatorship must go towards the people. Can it go towards the people unless it is prepared to stir them? Indeed, it flourishes largely by persuading people that without it even the most ordinary matters in the life of society could not be: it boasts that it is the primal and only cause, for example, of Civil Service examinations, of old-age pensions, of a work-free day in the week. A Dictatorship in the modern world makes an effective corner in demagoguery; and, like every monopolist, it sells inferior products at a high price.

Similarly of intrepidity. Mussolini has made current the two mottoes: "Live Dangerously!" and "Better a day's life as a lion, than the life of a sheep for a hundred years!" What shall Italians dare? To express their thoughts? They are asked for obedience and faith, and given medals and certificates for it; they are not asked for creativeness. In sport? Certainly, there is some improvement in Italy in the numbers participating, and, perhaps, in the spirit of sportsmanship. But this is hardly due to Fascist command, since a smiliar phenomenon has been world-wide since the War. There is a vocation to dangerous living, as there is to poetry or holiness. If dangerous living can be stimulated at all, this is done better in free societies, where allegiance is contingent, where people may change their minds and speak them, where no one is sheltered by the secrecy of the "reason of State." Whether they will or not, they are obliged to live dangerously. The first condition of human energy is challenge, not protection or repression. . . .

It is not surprising, therefore, that Fascist Italy has produced nothing new and valuable in any branch of art. It lives on its capital, and on the produce of other countries. The Fascist journals themselves ask, "Why has no Fascist art appeared?" But what, indeed, should its character be? The verbose journalese of the Fascist politician? Daring themes in the theatre? Only Pirandello produces and reproduces himself, and his genius is not Fascist. In general the stage-craft is worse than mediocre. Reinhardt and other foreign producers have led the way, even in the Italian theatre. Swiftness, energy and austere line in sculpture and architecture are foreign rather than Italian. The notable quality of Opera is not a Fascist virtue. The culture of Fascism has so far been the culture of a provincial middle-class. The newspapers are, with the exception of the Corriere della Sera, badly written, badly printed, badly set-out, and pretty provincial in character. The Cinema is very poor in every branch, from production to exhibition.

Perhaps there is more secular "charity" than before, but against this is the fact that the Party practically enforces it. There is, perhaps, more consciousness of being Italian, though not less of an attachment to the city and the region. There is more energy in government, but it is not spontaneous; the drive comes from an extraordinary man, and the public is not being trained to govern itself. Adam Smith said that there is a great deal of ruin in a country. Human nature is ingenious: when it is pursued it flees; when it is to be punished it hides; when its impulses are disparaged it gives them a mask and a pseudonym. That is what is occurring in Italy. . . .

Problem 6: How Can a Free Society Protect Itself from Conspiracy and Conformity?

In every society there is an inevitable conflict between liberty and authority. Too much liberty results in anarchy; too much authority terminates in absolutism. A government, like an individual, has the inherent right to defend itself. Freedom is not an absolute prerogative. Those who have a vested interest in the destruction of a government need not be given a complete and unrestricted opportunity to execute their designs. A real question, however, arises as to the measures that a government may properly take to defend itself. May not civil rights be jeopardized under the plea of national security? In times of hysteria and tension are we not likely to use more stringent methods than the situation warrants?

The threat of Communism is a serious one. Possessing missionary zeal and spurred on by resurgent Russian nationalism, the Communists have found good fishing in the troubled waters of the world. In appealing to rejected groups, they have something in every pocket—"a new day is coming" for the dispossessed and poverty stricken; the promise of equality for suppressed minority groups; a closed universe, in which one need not reason why but simply do or die, to the psychologically insecure. In addition the Communists have the advantage of selling gold bricks; they need not display their wares and the bargaining carries no warranty or money-back guarantee.

Until the depression years of the thirties there had never been an organized group of irreconcilables in this country. The United States, never having had many individuals who refused to accept the rules of the game, finds itself assuming a new role in attempting today to deal with the Communist conspiracy. The problem is further complicated by the difficulty involved in identifying true Communists and dealing with them within the framework of democratic procedures. With the Communists committed to a program of fraud and deceit, how can the real Communist be detected? Does the answer lie in loyalty oaths, congressional investigations, or the screening of magazines and textbooks? What happens to the individual with a roving mind, the person who thinks otherwise, when suspicion is based upon thought and speech? Who are the losers when traditional judicial procedures are bypassed for "guilt by association" methods? Someone has said that the great strength of the totalitarian state lies in the contingency that its opponents, out of fear, may seek to emulate it. Can we not eliminate Communist subversion without doing violence to democratic institutions? The program so far has produced a creeping climate of conformity, an increasing fear of unpopular ideas, and a tendency to proscribe minority views. These trends are difficult to understand in a country that should be the last to shrink from the competition of ideas; they are incompatible with democracy's struggle for the minds of men.

Who Is Loyal to America? *

Probably no other recent article on loyalty and freedom has been so widely publicized, quoted, and reprinted as this essay by Professor Commager. Written in 1946, it stands today as a brilliant testimonial of liberal-democratic faith. The author unconditionally rejects any definition formulated in group terms and makes a stirring plea for a concept of loyalty that not only respects but encourages individual disagreement and dissent. Loyalty, according to Professor Commager, can never be equated with conformity, status quo, superpatriotism, or

* Henry Steele Commager, Freedom, Loyalty, Dissent, Oxford University Press, Inc., 1954. Copyright 1947 by Henry Steele Commager. Reprinted from Harper's Magazine, September, 1947, pp. 193–99.

any particular economic system. It is instead a principle, an ideal, a tradition. Any attempt to reduce loyalty to a fixed formula is disloyal to everything the American tradition symbolizes.

In view of the comments made by Irving Kristol in the following article, are Commager's views unrealistic? Does Professor Commager fail to distinguish between the tradition of radicalism and protest, which up until now has always been honestly American, and the Communist conspiracy, which is dishonest, disloyal, and subversive? In protecting the right of nonconformity and disagreement, must we protect the Communist who would destroy the right of protest and dissent?

On May 6 a Russian-born girl, Mrs. Shura Lewis, gave a talk to the students of the Western High School of Washington, D.C. She talked about Russia—its school system, its public health program, the position of women, of the aged, of the workers, the farmers, and the professional classes—and compared, superficially and uncritically, some American and Russian social institutions. The most careful examination of the speech—happily reprinted for us in the *Congressional Record*—does not disclose a single disparagement of anything American unless it is a quasi-humorous reference to the cost of having a baby and of dental treatment in this country. Mrs. Lewis said nothing that had not been said a thousand times, in speeches, in newspapers, magazines, and books. She said nothing that any normal person could find objectionable.

Her speech, however, created a sensation. A few students walked out on it. Others improvised placards proclaiming their devotion to Americanism. Indignant mothers telephoned their protests. Newspapers took a strong stand against the outrage. Congress, rarely concerned for the political or economic welfare of the citizens of the capital city, reacted sharply when its intellectual welfare was at stake. Congressmen Rankin and Dirksen thundered and lightened; the District of Columbia Committee went into a huddle; there were demands for housecleaning in the whole school system, which was obviously shot through and through with Communism.

All this might be ignored, for we have learned not to expect either intelligence or understanding of Americanism from this element in our Congress. More ominous was the reaction of the educators entrusted with the high responsibility of guiding and guarding the intellectual welfare of our boys and girls. Did they stand up for intellectual freedom? Did they insist that high-school children had the right and the duty to learn about other countries? Did they protest that students were to be trusted to use intelligence and common sense? Did they affirm that the Americanism of their students was staunch enough to resist propaganda? Did they perform even the elementary task, expected of educators above all, of analyzing the much-criticised speech?

Not at all. The District Superintendent of Schools, Dr. Hobart Corning, hastened to agree with the animadversions of Representatives Rankin and Dirksen. The whole thing was, he confessed, "a very unfortunate occurrence," and had "shocked the whole school system." What Mrs. Lewis said, he added gratuitously, was "repugnant to all who are working with youth in the Washington schools," and "the entire affair contrary to the philosophy of education under which we operate." Mr. Danowsky, the hapless principal of the Western High School, was "the most shocked and regretful of all." The District of Columbia Committee would be happy to know that though he was innocent in the matter, he had been properly reprimanded!

It is the reaction of the educators that makes this episode more than a tempest in a teapot. We expect hysteria from Mr. Rankin and some newspapers; we are shocked when we see educators, timid before criticism and confused about first principles, betray their trust. And we wonder what can be that "Philosophy of education" which believes that young people can be trained to the duties of citizenship by wrapping their minds in cotton-wool.

Merely by talking about Russia Mrs. Lewis was thought to be attacking Americanism. It is indicative of the seriousness of the situation that during that same week the House found it necessary to take time out from the discussion of the labor bill, the tax bill, the International Trade Organization, and the world famine, to meet assaults upon Americanism from a new quarter. This time it was the artists who were undermining the American system, and members of the House spent some hours passing around reproductions of the paintings which the State Department had sent abroad as part of its program for advertising American culture. We need not pause over the exquisite humor which congressmen displayed in their comments on modern art: weary statesmen must have their fun. But we may profitably remark the major criticism which was directed against this unfortunate collection of paintings. What was wrong with these paintings, it shortly appeared, was that they were un-American. "No American drew those crazy pictures," said Mr. Rankin. Perhaps he was right. The copious files of the Committee on Un-American Activities were levied upon to prove that of the forty-five artists represented "no less than twenty were definitely New Deal in various shades of Communism." The damning facts are specified for each of the pernicious twenty; we can content ourselves with the first of them, Ben-Zion. What is the evidence here? "Ben-Zion was one of the signers of a letter sent to President Roosevelt by the United American Artists which urged help to the USSR and Britain after Hitler attacked Russia." He was, in short, a fellow-traveler of Churchill and Roosevelt.

The same day that Mr. Dirksen was denouncing the Washington school authorities for allowing students to hear about Russia ("In Russia equal right is granted to each nationality. There is no discrimination. Nobody says, you are a Negro, you are a Jew") Representative Williams of Mississippi rose to denounce the *Survey-Graphic* magazine and to add further to our understanding of Americanism. The *Survey-Graphic,* he said, "contained 129 pages of outrageously vile and nauseating anti-Southern, anti-Christian, un-American, and pro-Communist tripe, ostensibly directed toward the elimination of the custom of racial segregation in the South." It was written by "meddling un-American purveyors of hate and indecency."

All in all, a busy week for the House. Yet those who make a practice of reading their *Record* will agree that it was a typical week. For increasingly Congress is concerned with the eradication of disloyalty and the defense of Americanism, and scarcely a day passes that some congressman does not treat us to exhortations and admonitions, impassioned appeals and eloquent declamations, similar to those inspired by Mrs. Lewis, Mr. Ben-Zion, and the editors of the *Survey-Graphic.* And scarcely a day passes that the outlines of the new loyalty and the new Americanism are not etched more sharply in public policy.

And this is what is significant—the emergence of new patterns of Americanism and of loyalty, patterns radically different from those which have long been traditional. It is not only the Congress that is busy designing the new patterns. They are outlined in President Truman's recent disloyalty order; in similar orders formulated by the New York City Council and by state and local authorities throughout the country; in the programs of the D.A.R., the American Legion, and similar patriotic organizations; in the editorials of the Hearst and the McCormick-Patterson papers; and in an elaborate series of advertisements sponsored by large corporations and business organizations. In the making is a revival of the Red hysteria of the early 1920's, one of the shabbiest chapters in the history of American democracy; and more than a revival, for the new crusade is designed not merely to frustrate Communism but to formulate a positive definition of Americanism, and a positive concept of loyalty.

What is the new loyalty? It is, above all, conformity. It is the uncritical and unquestioning acceptance of America as it is—the political institutions, the social relationships, the economic practices. It rejects inquiry into race questions or socialized medicine, or public housing, or into the wisdom or validity of our foreign policy. It regards as particularly heinous any challenge to what is called "the system of private enterprise," identifying that system with Americanism. It abandons evolution, repudiates the once popular concept of progress, and regards America as a finished product, perfect and complete.

It is, it must be added, easily satisfied. For it wants not intellectual conviction nor spiritual conquest, but mere outward conformity. In matters of loyalty it takes the word for the deed, the gesture for the principle. It is content with the flag salute, and does not pause to consider the warning of our Supreme Court that "a person gets from a symbol the meaning he puts into it, and what is one man's comfort and inspiration is another's jest and scorn." It is satisfied with membership in respectable organizations and, as it assumes that every member of a liberal organization is a Communist, concludes that every member of a conservative one is a true American. It has not yet learned that not everyone who saith Lord, Lord, shall enter into the kingdom of Heaven. It is designed neither to discover real disloyalty nor to foster true loyalty.

What is wrong with this new concept of loyalty? What, fundamentally, is wrong with the pusillanimous retreat of the Washington educators, the barbarous antics of Washington legislators, the hysterical outbursts of the D.A.R., the gross and vulgar appeals of business corporations? It is not merely that these things are offensive. It is rather that they are wrong—morally, socially, and politically.

The concept of loyalty as conformity is a false one. It is narrow and restrictive, denies freedom of thought and of conscience, and is irremediably stained by private and selfish considerations. "Enlightened loyalty," wrote Josiah Royce, who made loyalty the very core of his philosophy, "means harm to no man's loyalty. It is at war only with disloyalty, and its warfare, unless necessity constrains, is only a spiritual warfare. It does not foster class hatreds; it knows of nothing reasonable about race prejudices; and it regards all races of men as one in their need of loyalty. It ignores mutual misunderstandings. It loves its own wherever upon earth its own, namely loyalty itself, is to be found." Justice, charity, wisdom, spirituality, he added, were all definable in terms of loyalty, and we may properly ask which of these qualities our contemporary champions of loyalty display.

Above all, loyalty must be to something larger than oneself, untainted by private purposes or selfish ends. But what are we to say of the attempts by the NAM and by individual corporations to identify loyalty with the system of private enterprise? Is it not as if officeholders should attempt to identify loyalty with their own party, their own political careers? Do not those corporations which pay for full-page advertisements associating Americanism with the competitive system expect, ultimately, to profit from that association? Do not those organizations that deplore, in the name of patriotism, the extension of government operation of hydro-electric power expect to profit from their campaign?

Certainly it is a gross perversion not only of the concept of loyalty but of the concept of Americanism to identify it with a particular economic system. This precise question, interestingly enough, came before the Supreme Court in the Schneiderman case not so long ago—and it was Wendell Willkie who was counsel for Schneiderman. Said the Court:

Throughout our history many sincere people whose attachment to the general Constitutional scheme cannot be doubted have, for various and even divergent reasons, urged differing degrees of governmental ownership and control of natural resources, basic means of production, and banks and the media of exchange, either with or without compensation. And something once regarded as a species of private property was abolished without compensating the owners when the institution of slavery was forbidden. Can it be said that the author of the Emancipation Proclamation and the supporters of the Thirteenth Amendment were not attached to the Constitution?

There is, it should be added, a further danger in the willful identification of Americanism with a particular body of economic practices. Many learned economists predict for the near future an economic crash similar to that of 1929. If Americanism is equated with competitive capitalism, what happens to it if competitive capitalism comes a cropper? If loyalty and private enterprise are inextricably associated, what is to preserve loyalty if private enterprise fails? Those who associate Americanism with a particular program of economic practices have a grave responsibility, for if their program should fail, they expose Americanism itself to disrepute.

The effort to equate loyalty with conformity is misguided because it assumes that there is a fixed content to loyalty and that this can be determined and defined. But loyalty is a principle, and eludes definition except in its own terms. It is devotion to the best interests of the commonwealth, and may require hostility to the particular policies which the government pursues, the particular practices which the economy undertakes, the particular institutions which society maintains. "If there is any fixed star in our Constitutional constellation," said the Supreme Court in the Barnette case, "it is that no official, high or petty, can prescribe what shall be orthodox in politics, nationalism, religion, or other matters of opinion, or force citizens to confess by work or act their faith therein. If there are any circumstances which permit an exception they do not now occur to us."

True loyalty may require, in fact, what appears to the naive to be disloyalty. It may require hostility to certain provisions of the Constitution itself, and historians have not concluded that those who subscribed to the "Higher Law" were lacking in patriotism. We should not forget that our tradition is one of protest and revolt, and it is stultifying to celebrate the rebels of the past—Jefferson and Paine, Emerson and Thoreau—while we silence the rebels of the present. "We are a rebellious nation," said

Theodore Parker, known in his day as the Great American Preacher, and went on:

Our whole history is treason; our blood was tainted before we were born; our creeds are infidelity to the mother church; our constitution, treason to our fatherland. What of that? Though all the governors in the world bid us commit treason against man, and set the example, let us never submit.

Those who would impose upon us a new concept of loyalty not only assume that this is possible, but have the presumption to believe that they are competent to write the definition. We are reminded of Whitman's defiance of the "never-ending audacity of elected persons." Who are those who would set the standards of loyalty? They are Rankins and Bilbos, officials of the D.A.R., and the Legion and the NAM, Hearsts and Mc-Cormicks. May we not say of Rankin's harangues on loyalty what Emerson said of Webster at the time of the Seventh of March Speech: "The word honor in the mouth of Mr. Webster is like the word love in the mouth of a whore."

What do men know of loyalty who make a mockery of the Declaration of Independence and the Bill of Rights, whose energies are dedicated to stirring up race and class hatreds, who would straitjacket the American spirit? What indeed do they know of America—the America of Sam Adams and Tom Paine, of Jackson's defiance of the Court and Lincoln's celebration of labor, of Thoreau's essay on Civil Disobedience and Emerson's championship of John Brown, of the America of the Fourierists and the Come-Outers, of cranks and fanatics, of socialists and anarchists? Who among American heroes could meet their tests, who would be cleared by their committees? Not Washington, who was a rebel. Not Jefferson, who wrote that all men are created equal and whose motto was "rebellion to tyrants is obedience to God." Not Garrison, who publicly burned the Constitution; or Wendell Philips, who spoke for the underprivileged everywhere and counted himself a philosophical anarchist; not Seward of the Higher Law or Sumner of racial equality. Not Lincoln, who admonished us to have malice toward none, charity for all; or Wilson, who warned that our flag was "a flag of liberty of opinion as well as of political liberty"; or Justice Holmes, who said that our Constitution is an experiment and that while that experiment is being made "we should be eternally vigilant against attempts to check the expression of opinions that we loathe and believe to be fraught with death."

There are further and more practical objections against the imposition of fixed concepts of loyalty or tests of disloyalty. The effort is itself a confession of fear, a declaration of insolvency. Those who are sure of themselves do not need reassurance, and those who have confidence in the strength and the virtue of America do not need to fear either criticism or competition. The effort is bound to miscarry. It will not apprehend those who are really disloyal, it will not even frighten them; it will affect only those who can be labeled "radical." It is sobering to recall that though the Japanese relocation program, carried through at such incalculable cost in misery and tragedy, was justified to us on the ground that the Japanese were potentially disloyal, the record does not disclose a single case of Japanese disloyalty or sabotage during the whole war. The warning sounded by the Supreme Court in the Barnette flag-salute case is a timely one:

Ultimate futility of such attempts to compel obedience is the lesson of every such effort from the Roman drive to stamp out Christianity as a disturber of pagan unity, the Inquisition as a means to religious and dynastic unity, the Siberian exiles as a means to Russian unity, down to the fast-failing efforts of our present totalitarian enemies. Those who begin coercive elimination of dissent soon find themselves exterminating dissenters. Compulsory unification of opinion achieves only the unanimity of the graveyard.

Nor are we left to idle conjecture in this matter; we have had experience enough. Let us limit ourselves to a single example, one that is wonderfully relevant. Back in 1943 the House Un-American Activities Committee, deeply disturbed by alleged disloyalty among government employees, wrote a definition of subversive activities and proceeded to apply it. The definition was admirable, and no one could challenge its logic or its symmetry:

Subversive activity derives from conduct intentionally destructive of or inimical to the Government of the United States—that which seeks to undermine its institutions, or to distort its functions, or to impede its projects, or to lessen its efforts, the ultimate end being to overturn it all.

Surely anyone guilty of activities so defined deserved not only dismissal but punishment. But how was the test applied? It was applied to two distinguished scholars, Robert Morss Lovett and Goodwin Watson, and to one able young historian William E. Dodd, Jr., son of our former Ambassador to Germany. Of almost three million persons employed by the government, these were the three whose subversive activities were deemed the most pernicious; the House cut them off the payroll. The sequel is familiar. The Senate concurred only to save a wartime appropriation; the President signed the bill under protest for the same reason. The Supreme Court declared the whole business a "bill of attainder" and therefore unconstitutional. Who was it, in the end, who engaged in "subversive activities"—Lovett, Dodd, and Watson, or the Congress which flagrantly violated Article One of the Constitution?

Finally, disloyalty tests are not only futile in application, they are pernicious in their consequences. They distract attention from activities that are really disloyal, and silence criticism inspired by true loyalty. That there are disloyal elements in America will not be denied, but there is no reason to suppose that any of the tests now formulated will ever be applied to them. It is relevant to remember that when Rankin was asked why his Committee did not investigate the Ku Klux Klan he replied that the Klan was not un-American, it was American!

Who are those who are really disloyal? Those who inflame racial hatreds, who sow religious and class dissentions. Those who subvert the Constitution by violating the freedom of the ballot box. Those who make a mockery of majority rule by the use of the filibuster. Those who impair democracy by denying equal educational facilities. Those who frustrate justice by lynch law or by making a farce of jury trials. Those who deny freedom of speech and of the press and of assembly. Those who press for special favors against the interest of the commonwealth. Those who regard public office as a source of private gain. Those who would exalt the military over the civil. Those who for selfish and private purposes stir up national antagonisms and expose the world to the ruin of war.

Will the House Committee on Un-American Activities interfere with the activities of these? Will Mr. Truman's disloyalty proclamation reach these? Will the current campaigns for Americanism convert these? If past experience is any guide, they will not. What they will do, if they are successful, is to silence criticism, stamp out dissent—or drive it underground. But if our democracy is to flourish it must have criticism, if our government is to function it must have dissent. Only totalitarian governments insist upon conformity and they—as we know—do so at their peril. Without criticism abuses will go unrebuked; without dissent our dynamic system will become static. The American people have a stake in the maintenance of the most thorough-going inquisition into American institutions. They have a stake in nonconformity, for they know that the American genius is nonconformist. They have a stake in experimentation of the most radical character, for they know that only those who prove all things can hold fast that which is good.

It is easier to say what loyalty is not than to say what it is. It is not conformity. It is not passive acquiescence in the status quo. It is not preference for everything American over everything foreign. It is not an ostrich-like ignorance of other countries and other institutions. It is not the indulgence in ceremony—a flag salute, an oath of allegiance, a fervid verbal declaration. It is not a particular creed, a particular version of history, a particular body of economic practices, a particular philosophy.

It is a tradition, an ideal, and a principle. It is a willingness to subordinate every private advantage for the larger good. It is an appreciation of the rich and diverse contributions that can come from the most varied sources. It is allegiance to the traditions that have guided our greatest statesmen and inspired our most eloquent poets—the traditions of freedom, equality, democracy, tolerance, the tradition of the higher law, of experimentation, cooperation, and pluralism. It is a realization that America was born of revolt, flourished on dissent, became great through experimentation.

Independence was an act of revolution; republicanism was something new under the sun; the federal system was a vast experimental laboratory. Physically Americans were pioneers; in the realm of social and economic institutions, too, their tradition has been one of pioneering. From the beginning, intellectual and spiritual diversity have been as characteristic of America as racial and linguistic. The most distinctively American philosophies have been transcendentalism—which is the philosophy of the Higher Law—and pragmatism—which is the philosophy of experimentation and pluralism. These two principles are the very core of Americanism: the principle of the Higher Law, or of obedience to the dictates of conscience rather than of statutes, and the principle of pragmatism, or the rejection of a single good and of the notion of a finished universe. From the beginning Americans have known that there were new worlds to conquer, new truths to be discovered. Every effort to confine Americanism to a single pattern, to constrain it to a single formula, is disloyalty to everything that is valid in Americanism.

———◄•••►———

CIVIL LIBERTIES TODAY: A STUDY IN CONFUSION *

The problem of maintaining our civil liberties during these turbulent times is not a simple one. In the preceding article Professor Commager makes an eloquent plea for liberalism and nonconformity in a democratic society. Many other voices have joined his in pointing out that both of these forces are jeopardized by the anti-Communist hysteria, which has reached epidemic proportions. In the following essay Irving Kristol, Managing Editor of *Commentary,* questions the validity of Mr. Commager's interpretations. Are liberals still unaware of the true nature of Communism, regarding it as the antithesis of

* Irving Kristol. Reprinted from *Commentary,* March, 1952, pp. 229–36. Copyright, 1952, by the American Jewish Committee.

Fascism? Do they believe that Communism is "a political trend continuous with liberalism and democratic socialism"? Do we defend our rights by protecting the Communists? Are liberals less critical of Communism, less ready to see Communism for what it really is, than conservatives and reactionaries?

. . . Perhaps it is a calamitous error to believe that because a vulgar demagogue lashes out at both Communism and liberalism as identical, it is necessary to protect Communism in order to defend liberalism. This way of putting the matter will surely shock liberals, who are convinced that it is only they who truly understand Communism and who thoughtfully oppose it. They are nonetheless mistaken, and it is a mistake on which McCarthyism waxes fat. For there is one thing that the American people know about Senator McCarthy: he, like them, is unequivocally anti-Communist. About the spokesmen for American liberalism, they feel they know no such thing. And with some justification.

With what justification, can be seen from an illustrative incident involving Professor Henry Steele Commager, a distinguished historian who never was a Communist and never will be. In the May 1947 issue of *Harper's,* Professor Commager wrote a spirited article that began as follows:

"On May 6 a Russian-born girl, Mrs. Shura Lewis, gave a talk to the students of the Western High School of Washington, D.C. She talked about Russia—its school system, its public health program, the position of women, of the aged, of the workers, the farmers, and the professional classes—and compared, superficially and uncritically, some American and Russian institutions. . . . Mrs. Lewis said nothing that had not been said a thousand times, in speeches, in newspapers, magazines and books. She said nothing that any normal person could find objectionable."

What greatly disturbed Professor Commager was that this inoffensive speech did give rise to a furor in Washington. Congressmen bellowed that our schools were being subverted, the principal of the school came forward with a humble apology, the superintendent of schools for the nation's capital swore it would never happen again, and the speech itself was reprinted (after some discussion of the wisdom of exposing the public to inflammation) in the *Congressional Record* as a horrible example. Professor Commager saw in this a reflection of an anti-Communist hysteria that threatened to engulf all civil liberties, and he pleaded earnestly that reason control the anti-Communist passion, lest we find ourselves saddled with an anti-Communist orthodoxy no less reprehensible than the Communist one. His article was hailed as a kind of liberal manifesto, and was reprinted—alongside John Stuart Mill and John Milton—in Howard

Mumford Jones' *Primer of Intellectual Freedom* (1949). Evil won a transient victory in the seats of power and Good won a permanent niche in the anthologies—a familiar tale.

Familiar, that is, until one goes to the *Congressional Record* and reads through this speech that no "normal person could find objectionable." Mrs. Lewis' English was broken, but her sentiments were whole:

They call it collective farm—the peasants farm and divide up products according to work put in by each individual during the years. As a result of planning, unemployment is completely wiped out. . . .

In Russia right now people absolutely do not worry about today or tomorrow. They never think "All of a sudden I lose a job." That fear doesn't exist among Russian people. . . .

No matter where you live you have to work. What the Russian people have, they are more secure about this. They work. They need not worry much about losing the job. They are free to travel from one place to another, and each person must work 25 years for after that he is able to get a pension. No matter where you work—in this plant or another, 25 years and then you get 50% of your salary and live the rest of your life. . . .

I never appreciated the life in Russia until I live here. Here you have to work hard in order to live, use all your courage not to die. . . .

I read all the papers here and occasionally I go to the Library of Congress and read all papers printed in Moscow. It is very interesting and when I read these papers always you can see here evidence of press where people talk all the time about having a war, to throw the atomic bomb on Russia, to destroy because they have a system which is very prideful. At the present time Russians are busy to restore all those houses, all those cities, all those towns. Russian people make streets, plants, produce new style of shoes, new fashion of dress, new production and never they talk about having a war.

The echoes this awakened in Congress may have been exaggerated, but they were not factitious or beside the point. Obviously, Professor Commager can argue that it will not harm American school children to encounter an occasional Communist apologist in the flesh; one may even go further and say it would do them good. However, in the first place, Mrs. Lewis was not introduced as a Communist apologist but as an informed reporter, and, in the second place, everything she said should have been objectionable to every normal person, and especially to a historian like Professor Commager—for the good and sufficient reason that it was a tissue of lies. For Professor Commager to defend the rights of Communists to free speech is one thing, for him to assert that there is nothing objectionable in mendacious pleading in support of Communism is quite another. The conclusion "any normal person" will draw from such behavior is that, for whatever reason, his critical faculties are less alert when he looks out of the left corner of his eye.

Indeed, the heart of the matter is exactly that he looks at Communism out of the *left* corner of his eye. Professor Commager seems to be seduced by the insidious myth according to which Communism is a political trend continuous with liberalism and democratic socialism, only more impatient and inclined to the fanatical, only more "radical" than its companions who are not quite so "left." It is a myth that Senator McCarthy, for his own ends, is happy to accept, since it allows him to tag a New Dealer as being by nature an embryonic Communist. Neither the Professor nor the Senator is concerned to see that the antithesis of "left" and "right" no longer suits the political realities; that measured by the ideals of the French or even Russian Revolution, Communism today is as counter-revolutionary as Louis XVI or Kolchak ever was; that if one wishes to defend the civil liberties of Communists (as the Senator does not), one must do so on the same grounds that one defends the civil liberties of Nazis and Fascists—no more, no less.

Professor Commager might retort that he knows all this full well, and that he is for civil liberties for everyone, Fascist, Communist, or what-have-you. But if a Nazi had, in 1938, addressed a high-school audience in this country, extolling the accomplishments of Hitler's regime, presenting a thoroughly fictitious account of life in Nazi Germany, never once mentioning the existence of concentration camps—would Professor Commager find in such a speech "nothing that any normal person could find objectionable"? It is doubtless an injustice to him even to conceive of the possibility. . . .

It is equally futile for liberals to try to match Senator McCarthy's irresponsible declamations with a crafty rhetoric of their own, especially when this rhetoric, while not designedly pro-Communist, is compelled by the logic of disingenuousness and special pleading to become so in effect. The need for disingenuousness arises out of a refusal to see Communism for what it is: a movement guided by conspiracy and aiming at totalitarianism, rather than merely another form of "dissent" or "nonconformity." Hence the liberal argument runs askew of reality and must clothe itself with neat obfuscation.

Once again Professor Commager obliges with a superior specimen:

The House Un-American Activities Committee has launched an attack on the Lawyers' Guild as a pro-Communist or "subversive" organization. The chief basis for this attack is, as far as we know, that the Guild has proffered its services to the defense of Communists under indictment for violation of the Smith Act. We need not inquire into the accuracy of this charge or into the degree of zeal displayed by the Lawyers' Guild. Let us ask rather what are the logical conclusions to be drawn by the position which the House Committee has adopted? They are two: that certain criminals are so despicable that they are not entitled to counsel, and that a lawyer who defends a criminal is himself sympathetic to crime.

That phrase in the second sentence, "as far as we know," is curious. It implies strongly that the only conceivable explanation of the Committee's attitude is the action of the Guild in providing lawyers to defend indicted Communists, and that there is no public information which gives plausibility to the Committee's belief that the Guild is a "front" organization, controlled and run by Communists. On the contrary, however, "as far as we know," and we know much further than Professor Commager suggests, the Lawyers' Guild is a Communist creation that, as A. A. Berle stated when he resigned from it in 1940, "is not prepared to take any stand which conflicts with the Communist party line." Moreover, the House Committee on Un-American Activities has collected and published sufficient evidence to demonstrate this beyond cavil—which leads one to think that if Professor Commager spent nearly as much time reading the records of Congressional hearings as he does denouncing them, we should all be better off.

The entire third sentence is even more curious: "We need not inquire into the accuracy of this charge or into the degree of zeal displayed by the Lawyers' Guild." If we take "zeal" to mean pro-Communism (in the context, that is all it can mean), then the degree of this zeal and the accuracy of the charge of pro-Communism are precisely what we *do* need to inquire into. How can we know whether to sanction or condemn the Committee's investigation of the Guild as a pro-Communist organization unless we make an effort to find out if the Guild is or is not, in fact, a pro-Communist organization? Even Professor Commanger surreptitiously ignores his own disclaimer, as the last two sentences of his paragraph show. Obviously, the two "logical conclusions" flow, not from the Committee's premise, but his own; namely, that the Lawyers' Guild is neither pro-Communist nor subversive. From the Committee's own premise, quite other logical conclusions may be inferred—one of them being that the Committee is engaged in showing up Communist fronts for what they are. Professor Commager's "logic" is a sleight-of-hand whereby premises that are prejudiced in favor of the Communist interpretation of affairs are made to pass for natural conclusions.

In the same vein, there is a liberal rhetoric of insinuation that works under cover of a high moral posture. Its net effect is to give a backhanded credence to the Communist assertion that it is impossible to oppose Communism vigorously without walking into the arms of Black Reaction. It is the kind of thing represented in the following observation of Alan Barth's:

In the New York trial of eleven Communist Party leaders in 1949, a number of FBI undercover operatives who had joined the party appeared as prosecution witnesses. How widely such agents have been dispersed in labor unions, in lawful voluntary associations, and in political groups is a matter of mere conjecture. But it is certainly a matter of legitimate concern to Americans who care about preservation of the traditional rights of privacy.

A noble sentiment, and the unwary reader assents—who is against the right to privacy, and who is not prepared to be concerned with its violation? Only the exceptionally attentive will note that the supposed threat to "the traditional rights of privacy" is "a matter of mere conjecture." Whose conjecture? We are not told. Is there any ground for such a conjecture? We are not told that either. Is Mr. Barth against the use of undercover agents in principle? He does not say so. Is he against the use of undercover agents in Communist organizations? He does not say this, either. He would seem to be against dispersing FBI agents in bona fide labor unions, lawful voluntary associations, and political groups, and reminds us of the consequences. But who is for it? The answer, which he does not bother to give, is: nobody—and that is why the FBI is doing no such thing and why the whole business is a "matter of conjecture." In the course of Mr. Barth's innuendoes, however, the onus has been neatly shifted from the Communist conspirators to the FBI agents who identified them.

The same technique of persuasion is at work in such a statement as this one by Professor Commager: "It will be useful to determine, a generation from now, whether those universities that have purged their faculties are actually stronger than they were before the purges occurred—stronger in those essentials that go to make a university." This has about it so trembling an air of bitter-sweet wisdom that it seems positively boorish to ask: just which universities would Professor Commager describe as "purged"? Surely Columbia is not one of them, for Professor Commager is not the kind of man who would retain his post on a "purged" faculty. Is it Yale? Princeton? Harvard? University of Chicago? The list could be extended indefinitely, and never provoke an affirmative response, for there is not a single university in the United States that can be said to have been, in any meaningful sense of the word, "purged." There has been no more than a handful of cases where Communist college teachers have been dismissed, and less than a handful of cases where non-Communists have been unjustly fired as "Reds." To call this a "purge"—even regardless of whether or not one thinks Communists have a right to teach in colleges— is to echo Communist propaganda.

Perhaps Professor Commager had in mind the University of California, where several dozen (out of a total of more than a thousand) teachers found the idea of a special loyalty oath—the content of which was irrelevant to their action—so offensive and intolerable that they exercised their constitutional right to refuse to swear it, and consequently had to seek other employment. Granting that the notion of a special oath for teachers is obnoxious, and even conceding that this minority was correct and courageous in its particular reaction to it—is it the part of sobriety to insist, as Professor Commager goes on to do, that the philosophy behind the actions of California's Board of Trustees does not differ "in any essentials" from the philosophy behind the totalitarian control of university teaching? One swallow does not make a spring, or one injustice an apocalypse.

Despite their fondness for cliches of Communist manufacture, all these liberal spokesmen are sincerely anti-Communist—otherwise, what they have to say would be of little interest to anyone. But their rejection of Communism has all the semblance of a preliminary gesture, a repudiation aiming to linger in the memory as a floating credential. It has little relation to all the ensuing scenes of the political drama, where bad conscience and stubborn pride join to guide the liberal through his role.

Did not the major segment of American liberalism, as a result of joining hands with the Communists in a Popular Front, go on record as denying the existence of Soviet concentration camps? Did it not give its blessing to the "liquidation" of millions of Soviet "kulaks"? Did it not apologize for the mass purges of 1936–38, and did it not solemnly approve the grotesque trials of the Old Bolsheviks? Did it not applaud the massacre of the non-Communist left by the GPU during the Spanish Civil War? All this carries no weight with Alan Barth who knows that, though a man repeat the Big Lie, so long as he is of a liberal intention he is saved. On the participation of non-Communists in Communist fronts during the 30's he writes: "In the main, their participation, while it lasted, was not only innocent but altogether praiseworthy."

Even Francis Biddle, who is generally cautious, remarks in his book *The Fear of Freedom*: "What makes an organization subversive? If a vast majority of its members are Communists but its conduct has always been exemplary, advocating desirable social reforms which Communists usually back, it can hardly fit the description."

One surmises that Mr. Biddle is not really so politically naive as this statement, on the face of it, would lead one to believe. He must know what it means to be "subversive," since it was he who, as Attorney General, sent eighteen members of a minuscule Trotskyist sect to jail in 1942 for being just that; he must know how Communists work, how front organizations act as an ancillary to the Communist party apparatus, since this is a matter of common knowledge and Mr. Biddle is uncommonly literate and intelligent. No, it was no elevated unsophistication that urged him on, but rather a sense of shame. Mr. Biddle, like Mr. Barth, refuses to admit what is now apparent: that a generation of earnest reformers who helped give this country a New Deal should find themselves in retrospect stained with the guilt of having lent aid and comfort to Stalinist tyranny. This is, to be sure, a truth of hindsight, an easy truth. But it is the truth nonetheless, and might as well be owned up to. If American liberalism is not willing to discriminate between its achievements and its sins, it only disarms itself before Senator McCarthy, who is eager to have it appear that its achievements are its sins.

There is a false pride, by which liberals persuade themselves that no matter what association a man has had with a Communist enterprise, he is absolutely guiltless of the crimes that Communism has committed so long as he was moved to this association by a generous idealism. There is a political mythology, by which liberals locate Communism over on the "left," in a zone exempt from the unsparing verdict directed against the totalitarian "right." There is also a fear, a fear that the American democracy in an excess of anti-Communism will gather its abundant energy into a wave of "conformism" that will drown all free thought. This pride, this mythology, this fear all unite for a liberal prejudgment of issues (*e.g.*, the cases of Alger Hiss, Owen Lattimore, William Remington, Harry Dexter White) which is not easy to explain on a purely rational view. It is what stimulates a flood of irrelevant and gaudy prose about loyalty in the abstract ("like love it must be given freely," etc.) while it shuns a careful discussion of Communist disloyalty in the concrete.

Of the three factors, the fear of "conformism" or "orthodoxy" is probably the most influential in its appeal, for it is founded in some degree on objective fact. Alexis de Tocqueville and John Stuart Mill, both friendly critics of the egalitarian trend, pointed out long ago that in every democratic society there is an inherent tendency toward a "despotism of public opinion"; where the majority makes the laws, it may also wish—especially in feverish and unsettled times—to make opinion, lauding the popular and extirpating the unpopular. In America, where the people are more powerful than elsewhere, and where there is, too, a significant tradition of vigilante-ism, the danger of despotism of public opinion is proportionately greater. When the State Department is forced to suspend an exhibition abroad of modern American art because some Congressmen denounce it as "communistic," the danger of such a despotism seems more than academic, and many otherwise sensible people are led to reprehend any attempt to unveil Communist activities or Communist beliefs as a malignant form of "punishment by publicity," which will soon be extended to all opinions that illiterate and narrow-minded Congressmen detest.

What these people do not see is that Communism, because it is a conspiratorial movement, has not the faintest interest in any genuine resistance to the despotism of public opinion. These martyrs whose testament is— "I refuse to answer on grounds that it might incriminate me"! These "intellectuals" of Hollywood and radio who are outraged at a Congressman's insistence that they say what they actually believe, and who wail that they are in danger of—being excluded from well-paying jobs! Is this the vibrant voice of "nonconformity" and "dissent"? Are these the American rebels of today? Oddly enough, the majority of American liberals seem to think so: they have been moved to indignation by the questions, but never moved to disgust by the answers. Presumably, this is what they think a dissenter looks like, and no sadder commentary is possible on the corruption they have inflicted on themselves. And not only on themselves —for this image of a dissenter happens to coincide with the image held by Joseph McCarthy and Pat McCarran, for whom the dissenter is *per se* a scheming subversive. No greater spur to the despotism of public opinion can be imagined than this identification of free thought with underground conspiracy.

There is only one way the despotism of public opinion can be resisted. That is for a person with unpopular views to express himself, loudly, brazenly, stubbornly, in disregard of the consequences. Such a person may have to suffer for his convictions, as others have suffered before him, and as others will suffer after. But the responsibility for the mind's freedom in a democracy lies with the intransigent thinker, with his courage to shout the truth in the face of the mob, with his faith that truth will win out, and with his maddening commitment to the truth, win or lose. Yet, during all the occasions of the past several years, not a single liberal voice was to say to these strange "victims"; "Speak up and damn the consequences! Let them take your job—as they certainly will anyway; tell the truth—you have nothing to lose and honor to gain!" Instead, there were erudite essays on the "right to a job" that would have corroborated William James in his mournful conviction that "the prevalent fear of poverty among our educated classes is the worst moral disease from which our civilization suffers."

Still, unworthy as these "victims" are, may they not, despite themselves, represent the right of the individual to hold whatever opinions he pleases without having to give a public accounting of them? Even if these Communists and Communist sympathizers are despicable, don't they have the right to believe privately anything they please? This is the way the question is frequently put, and it reveals a total misapprehension as to what Communism really is.

Communism is an Idea, beyond question. Indeed, it is an Idea, and it is of the essence of this Idea that it is also a conspiracy to subvert every social and political order it does not dominate. It is, furthermore, an Idea that has ceased to have any intellectual status but has become incarnate in the Soviet Union and the official Communist parties, to whose infallible directives unflinching devotion is owed. A person who is captive to this Idea can, at any time, in any place, be called upon to do whatever the Idea, *i.e.,* the Party, thinks necessary. Since this is so, it is of considerably more than private interest if a person is held by the Idea—he is, all appearances to the contrary, a person with different loyalties, and with different canons of scrupulousness, from ours. To grant him an "immunity by silence" is to concede the right to conspiracy, a concession no government ever has made or ever will make.

This sounds exaggerated, as it must, being so foreign to the nature of American political experience. Many of us have known Communists, and most of them conveyed no impression of being conspirators. But then, some of us have known Nazis too, and they conveyed no immediate association with gas chambers. It is quite impossible to judge a political movement by the personality of an individual member. Roosevelt certainly didn't see in Stalin any symptoms of blood lust. Hermann Goering in jail struck one as a clever clown. And there are still plenty of people who can't believe that Alger Hiss ever did any such thing.

No doubt there are some present members of the Communist party who would, in a showdown, break free of the Idea and rally to the democratic cause. Unfortunately, we have no way of knowing who they are. No doubt there are some present members and fellow-travelers of the Communist party who would sooner or later get disillusioned with Communism if they were permitted to hold down their present jobs as teachers, civil service workers, etc., whereas they are likely to harden in the face of persecution. Unfortunately, it is quite as impossible to tell the citizens of Oshkosh, some of whom have suffered personal loss as a result of the war in Korea, that there is no harm in having their children taught the three R's by a Communist, as it would have been to persuade the citizens of Flatbush in 1939 that there was no cause for excitement in their children being taught by a Nazi, or to convince a businessman that it is smart practice for him to pay a handsome salary to someone pledged to his "liquidation." No doubt some of these people became Communists after having suffered during the depression, or during a labor conflict, or as a result of race prejudice, and society must bear its share of the blame. Unfortunately, as Fitzjames Stephens remarked many decades ago: "It does not follow that because society caused a fault it is not to punish it. A man who breaks his arm when he is drunk may have to cut it off when he is sober."

The problem of fighting Communism while preserving civil liberties is no simple one, and there is no simple solution. A prerequisite for any solution, however, is, firstly, a proper understanding of Communism for what it is, and secondly, a sense of proportion. So long as liberals agree with Senator McCarthy that the fate of Communism involves the fate of liberalism, and that we must choose between complete civil liberties for everyone and a disregard for civil liberties entirely, we shall make no progress except to chaos. So long as one is either for or against "guilt by association," it is hopeless to try to distinguish between a sober and silly definition of that concept—sober when it is taken to mean, as for instance the Canwell Committee of the State of Washington took it to mean, that anyone who is a member of three or more organizations officially declared subversive is to be considered a Communist: silly when it is taken to mean, as many government loyalty boards take it to mean, that if you have a friend or a relation who is sympathetic to Communism, you are a "bad security risk." So long as Senator McCarthy and the liberals agree that the right of a Communist to teach or be a government employee is a matter of principle, we shall remain distant from the intelligent discrimination between one case and another, and one situation and another which alone can give us our true bearings. And so long as Senator McCarthy and the liberals are enmeshed in this confusion, the Senator will grow the stronger, for such confusion is the sap of his political life.

Inevitably, liberals will disagree among themselves about the appropriateness of specific actions with regard to Communism and Communists. Inevitably, too, there will always be a basic division and antagonism between liberalism (which is solicitous of freedom) and McCarthyism (which is not). But if a liberal wishes to defend the civil liberties of Communists or of Communist fellow-travelers, he must enter the court of American opinion with clean hands and a clear mind. He must show that he knows the existence of organized subversive movement such as Communism is a threat to the consensus on which civil society and its liberties are based. He must bluntly acknowledge Communists and fellow-travelers to be what they are, and then, if he so desires, defend the expediency in particular circumstances of allowing them the right to be what they are. He must speak as one of *us*, defending *their* liberties. To the extent he insists that they are on our side, that we can defend our liberties only by uncritically defending theirs, he will be taken as speaking as one of them.

Communists in a Free Society *

One of the most difficult problems facing Americans in the realm of civil liberties is how to handle domestic Communists without using undemocratic techniques. Is it possible to allow this group a measure of freedom and still keep a free society? If national security demands stern measures against Communism, how can we protect the rights of loyal but dissenting citizens? Professor Commager and Editor Kristol present varying approaches to this dilemma and to other issues associated with it. In the following essay Richard H. Rovere presents another possible solution to this complex problem.

. . . We have plenty to fear from Communist spying and, in the event of war or near-war, from Communist wrecking, but we have little or nothing to fear from Communist political agitation and propaganda. Even if there were five or six times as many Communists and fellow-travelers they would be powerless, in and of themselves, to do any serious damage to the fabric of American society. They were unable to do it when they were much stronger, and today, in spite of the lamentable fact that not all Americans are as wise in the ways of Communists as the editors of the *New Leader,* the country is pretty well alerted. Communists are now all but powerless in the trade unions; in the intellectual and educational world, they lead isolated, ineffectual lives; and the handful who may still hold government jobs must, in order to remain concealed, abandon all political activity. Here and there in American life there may remain a few small islands of Communist strength, but I fail to see how it can rationally be maintained that they meet any test of clear and present danger that would justify putting in jeopardy any element of civil liberty. To combat Communism in its political manifestations, no legal or governmental assistance of any sort is needed, no loyalty oaths, no star-chamber proceedings, no scoundrels like McCarthy, no lies, no euphemisms.

Espionage and sabotage are, of course, quite another matter. They are real dangers, and they are likely to grow with time. Sabotage is probably even more of a danger than espionage. In the event of war, the old, preposterous figure in the Hearst cartoons—the Communist fanatic planting a bomb in the heart of one of our large cities—would be no joke or fantasy. To avert a danger of this sort is well worth the calculated risk of a measure of freedom, and Mr. Barth is perfectly clear about this. He

* Richard H. Rovere, *Partisan Review,* May–June, 1952, pp. 343–46. Copyright, 1952, by *Partisan Review.*

feels, as I do, that the provision of the McCarran Act which calls for the internment of all Communists known to the F.B.I. immediately upon the outbreak of war is sound and necessary. It involves a violation of principle (though a less serious one than that involved in the internment of Japanese-Americans in the last war, for it would be based on the logic of politics rather than on the illogic of race), but the stakes would be high and the action would meet the test of clear and present danger.

In general, it happens that the most effective means of combating Communists in their role as conspirators are ones that do not involve civil liberties in any important way. The most effective means have been counter-espionage and due process of law. In every case but one, Communist spies have been apprehended by the F.B.I.   F.B.I. agents provided most of the evidence by which the Communist leaders were convicted under the Smith Act. Some of us may regard the Smith Act as bad law, but it has stood up in the courts so far, and certainly no one can say that the Communists convicted under it were denied their rights. The conviction of Alger Hiss was a triumph of due process, but his exposure was a triumph of the House Committee on Un-American Activities—its one significant triumph in fourteen years. Of the Hiss case, though, it can be said that if the Committee regularly conducted itself as it did then, no one could raise any reasonable objection to it. It subjected Whittaker Chambers to rigorous tests of credibility and gave Hiss a full, fair, prompt hearing and the opportunity to confront his accuser. It was solicitous in the extreme of Hiss's rights, allowing him to become almost the classic example of the man hoist by his own petard. But in every other case, the detection and punishment of Communist espionage agents has come about through the use of techniques whose legitimacy was recognized long before there was a Communist problem. Meanwhile, the loyalty and security programs have served as sieves through which Alger Hiss and Judith Coplon could easily pass. They have accomplished nothing but the harassment of government clerks, most of them in jobs that have no connection with national security, and have hugely magnified the timidity and irresoluteness that are occupational ailments of bureaucrats even when the atmosphere is not fouled by liars, bullies, and Holy Willies. The loyalty and security programs are not only ineffective and an affront to intelligence but have kept the F.B.I. so busy checking up on the political pasts of people whose political pasts don't matter—one thinks of a recent prolonged investigation of an elderly hedge-clipper at a National Historic Site hundreds of miles from Washington—that its director is frequently protesting that it can't get its really important work done.

"The problem of fighting Communism while preserving civil liberties is no simple one," Irving Kristol writes, "and there is no simple solution."

There is no simple solution to any problem that involves human beings, but it seems to me that many intellectuals today are devoting themselves to entangling this one to a fare-thee-well. I believe that an examination of the facts and an application to them of the principles shared by decent liberals and conservatives will yield not a simple solution but one not so hopelessly complicated that it is unworkable.

The key to it ought to be the Holmesian doctrine of clear and present danger, the validity of which has been frequently attacked but has never, to my knowledge, been destroyed. There are agencies of government in which the presence of Communists or Communist sympathizers is obviously intolerable; it is perfectly reasonable for these agencies—the State and Defense Departments, the White House, the Atomic Energy Commission, and perhaps a few others—to screen present and prospective employees, those at least whose jobs might enable them to jeopardize our security. Since no man has a right to a government job, or to any other kind of job for that matter, there should be no objection to the test of guilt by association in determining security risks, though the test should be soberly applied. Elsewhere in government, loyalty and security procedures ought to be abandoned on the ground that they are ridiculous. This is not to say that Communists should be handed jobs or should not be fired from jobs they hold in non-sensitive agencies. There is no reason why the government should hire anyone who has a vested interest in its failure. But the test of clear and present danger does not apply to most government agencies, and in consequence the rules of evidence should at least approximate judicial ones.

It is undoubtedly too much to hope that the Communist problem will in every case be solved with common sense and dignity. It is plain that among the rights of lard merchants are the right to make themselves absurd and the right to hire and fire radio performers as they please. It is plain that universities and school systems have the right, and it may be the duty, to keep Communist teachers out of their classrooms. In education, though, and in intellectual life in general, it would seem to me that it is the moral duty of those of us who serve our culture by being its critics to point out that the test of guilt by association is a bad test and that no present threat to our culture justifies it. It is very hard to conceive of a Communist writing a good book today or of a Communist teacher being a competent teacher, but where people are being dealt with in terms of their function in life, we should try to stick to the functional question. Communists, of course, make this difficult to do. For the good of our souls and of our society, we should attempt it anyway. When a Communist writer writes, we should deal with what he has written. We should deal with the individual Communist teacher as a teacher until he has demonstrated that he cannot be a teacher and must accordingly be treated only as a Communist. Once that has been shown, we need no longer defend his right to teach, but we must still defend his civil right to be a Communist and without apologizing for it to anyone. With the Communist as a political man, however, we have a really serious quarrel. We have been conducting it quite effectively for many years by debate, by exposure, and by political counterforce. We have needed no help from McCarthy, and we have gotten none, though we might, I suppose, acknowledge a good deal of unsolicited help from Stalin.

CHAPTER THREE

The Politics and Administration of American Government

Essentially, all government is a fusion of politics (policy making) and administration (execution of policy). It is this combination that converts wants, desires, and needs into official acts and regulated behavior. The process through which this conversion occurs involves policy determination and administrative fulfillment. Of the two, the political phase is of greater consequence. It is the procedure by which individuals and groups prevail upon others to share their views and act in concert with them. In a democracy the number of people who participate in the creation and dissemination of proposed government action is large. In a dictatorship the number is relatively small, but the political process is still present; even in the most authoritarian regime, the dictator is influenced to some degree by the thoughts and opinions of those about him.

The responsibility for transforming loyalties, ideas, and public opinion into specific acts, official policies, and governmental services lies in the province of administration. However, politics and administration are not completely separate and distinct; the line between them is often vague, fluctuating, and uncertain. Many acts impinge upon both areas. When, for example, does the President cease to act in a political capacity and function only as an administrator? At what point does Congress deviate from its policy-making function and enter the realm of administration?

The interplay between politics and administration is well illustrated in the operation of major institutions of American government. In this chapter political parties, Congress, the President, and the Supreme Court are discussed in terms of pressing problems. The questions raised are sharp and controversial. But underlying the specific questions are broader issues that run like bright threads through the entire government of the United States. Does the answer to spotlighting responsibility in Congress lie in tightening party discipline, by moving toward party government? Is the separation of powers concept still valid in the twentieth century, or does this principle paralyze the workings of an efficient administration? Does the independence from each other of the President and Congress constitute a handicap to responsible government? Is judicial review a pillar of democracy, or does it impede the development of political maturity? Can the reforms that are needed be found within the present framework, or does the solution lie in a major revision of the political system?

Problem 7: Political Parties-- Purposeful or Merely Partisan?

Writers on public affairs agree that political parties, at least in the United States, do not conform to Edmund Burke's description: "a body of men united for promoting the national interest upon some particular principle upon which they are agreed." Instead, there is more general approval for the observation that political parties are simply groups of people organized to win elections and to get control of the government.

Do political parties provide the voter with an opportunity to make real choices on significant issues, or are parties a snare and a delusion? Is the lack of uncompromising differences between the two major parties an indictment or a recommendation? Should political parties be more purposeful, stand on principles, reflect issues? Or is the great advantage of American parties related to their ability to keep the country from fighting over principles? In the first article, "American Political Parties," Herman Finer exposes the flabbiness of the American party system, the handicaps under which the parties labor, and the need for reform. Herbert Agar takes a different tack in "The Price of Union," contending that the alleged faults of the American party system are its virtues. The evasive, flexible, and coincidental nature of parties has served to strengthen the Federal Union by emphasizing compromise rather than conflict. Implementing these two general views are two case histories. In the first John Fischer analyzes the make-up of the Democratic Party, its sources of strength and weakness, and the dilemma of its future. In the second Walter Prescott Webb discusses the Republican Party from its origin down to the present and, like Fischer, attempts to analyze party composition, platforms, and future problems.

The two concluding articles treat the question, Should party lines be tightened? This is not an isolated inquiry, for overtones of the question of party responsibility extend into all phases of legislation and administration. Briefly stated, the issue is this: Would the injection of party government and stronger party discipline coordinate the functions of Congress and the Executive and create a more unified and efficient government? James MacGregor Burns states the affirmative answer clearly and concisely in "Toward Party Government." A case for the present status of the two-party system is resolutely presented by the editors of *Fortune* in "Political Parties and the Need for Moral Leadership."

American Political Parties *

Discussing American political parties in terms of values, power relationships, and constitutional restraints, Professor Finer takes a dim view of their present contributions to effective democratic government. Further, he notes the serious consequences that must result from the "flabbiness of party structure." Despite the range and authority of the article, one might question the severity of the author's judgment of American political parties. Does he not make an overly persuasive case for British parties and fail to make the necessary allowance for political and cultural differences between the United States and Great Britain?

Indifference to the Choice between Parties

It will have been observed that the distinguishing mark of political parties in Britain and Europe is that they are parties of principle: that is, they profess the purpose of governing or of opposing government in the name of a general design of political values. They may represent an interest—economic or of an historic power-position in society—and may prosecute it; of course, being men, they must and do. But over and above their special interest, they profess a broader special interest, they profess a broader social goal: that of conservatism, or liberalism, or communism, or Catholicism, or social democracy. Their interests are contained within a framework of value. They have made an order, or hierarchy, of items

---

* From *The Theory and Practice of Modern Government* by Herman Finer, Revised Edition, pp. 353–58. By permission of Methuen and Co., Ltd., London, and of Henry Holt and Company, Inc. Copyright, 1949.

in their program—what shall be done, to what degree the relationships between individual and society shall be fashioned by law and administration, and what things shall come first, middle, and last. A long cultural history has obscured the answer to whether material or more spiritual values came first or which were more masterful. But there is considerable firmness in the definition of the pattern of social values. The absence of firmly defined and broad social purpose, consistently pursued over many decades, is the diagnostic mark of political parties in the United States.

It is not possible within the compass of this volume to sketch the history of American political parties throughout their long career. Their chances and changes may be found in many other volumes. For long stretches they will be found saying the same thing, exactly, flatulent in phrase and combining the most inconsistent quasi-promises. So far is this the truth, especially for certain epochs, that cynical remarks have been made about the Republican and Democratic parties, the two which have held the field, gathering over 90 per cent of the votes cast, for about one hundred years. Bryce declared that they were like two bottles, each with different labels and both empty. Holcombe, American born and bred and a Harvard teacher for over forty years, says, some forty years after Bryce: Why, young men and women inquire of their elders and of one another with growing frequency, should a new voter become either a Democrat or a Republican? It is not easy—indeed, it is not possible—to give a convincing answer, if the reply is based upon no better evidence than is afforded by the planks of the party platforms and the declarations of the party candidates. Party platforms have tended to grow longer with the passing years, and less intelligible.

* * * * *

If the reader will compare two political biographies which came out within a year or two of each other, one English and the other American, they will appreciate the dismay with which American political parties may be regarded. In the biography of Neville Chamberlain they will find an intense concern and ambition for the highest office it is in the gift of the nation to bestow—but not a single page is without its deep anxiety about policy, the social purposes for which the premiership will be used. In the autobiography of James Farley they will see practically nothing but a concern for electoral victory, with hardly a trace of interest in a political program (except that the New Deal seems to jeopardize vote catching). In Mr. Farley's own cogitations about his ambitions for the Presidency, and in his estimates of his own qualifications, there is never a word about the presidency as a medium for the national good. The difference is not altogether a difference between men.

Causes and Consequences of Political Indifference

For good or ill, indifference to the choice between parties could not possibly be postulated of British or European parties. This is the striking and controlling truth about American political parties, and the causes and consequences deserve some brief consideration. Somewhere in his *Age of Reform,* Professor E. L. Woodward, speaking of English political parties in the eighteenth century, likens them to "two rival stagecoaches spattering each other with mud, going along the same road to the same destination." This is true of American political parties today, except that it is a little difficult to discern the destination, even as it was, perhaps, in the eighteenth century in England.

1. Let it be noticed that two parties dominate and organize American political life, not eight or ten. All the "occasional" parties, of a third- and fourth-party kind, have never, in any Presidential year, gained more than some 3 per cent of the vote. Nor have many of them lived for more than ten years. This at any rate, is an advantage to the nation, that its party organizations can gather the various sectional and occupational groupings into nation-wide confederations. Too many parties are confusing; the job of organizing the electorate must be done, the voters brought out, and provision made for a standing opposition of magnitude sufficient to threaten the government.

2. The "third" parties have in the main been sectional or occupational groupings; that is to say, they have emerged from a fairly definite area of the country, or from an economic interest. For example; Free Soil, Know-nothing, Greenback, Populist, Labor, Farm Labor, and—if we go beyond occupation—Prohibition and Communist. They have beset the other parties with some intensely passionate ideas and claims, and have persuaded (the word "forced" would not be too strong) one of them to carry into law its desires. Examples are antitrust legislation in the 1890's; the Greenbacks and silver-purchase legislation; the Nonpartisan League and government assistance of many kinds to farmers; and again, the Anti-Saloon League and Prohibition during World War I. The Political Action Committee of the CIO continues the old story, to waylay candidates of the two dominant parties and hold them to legislative ransom.

3. The two dominant parties have been round, firm, and fully packed on certain occasions which four are especially conspicuous: (1) Federalist and Anti-Federalist at the inception of the Republic; (2) the Jacksonian Democracy of 1828 and the opposition thereto; (3) Republicans and Demo-

crats on the issue of slavery and union; (4) Republicans and Democrats during the New Deal, 1933 to 1941. What were the characteristics of these periods? Each shows a compound of three elements: a moral and intellectual issue of the highest importance; an agonizing practical emergency; and on one side, at least, a "great" man, though the degrees of greatness vary. When these three elements coincide, American political parties assume the characteristics of British and European ones: they become for the time a purposive, partly ideological fellowship of like-minded persons throughout the country, inspiring an intense, sincere, and steady loyalty.

However, normally such conditions do not obtain, and American parties are at once without ideals or spine. They "straddle" in their policy, as the ironic saying goes. Many had hoped that the era of popular reform which the Great Depression of 1929 onwards necessitated and stimulated would have ushered in the rule of parties with a social purpose of an enduring kind, both loving their country, their whole country, but each with different but genuine gifts for it. The Democrats might have been the more "liberal" and concerned with mass welfare, the Republicans more stern and in favor of private enterprise and the limitation of governmental activity. But the mind and personality which had been able to attract to himself loyalties transcending those normally manipulated by the local bosses died. The grand national texture was involuntarily abandoned by Roosevelt's accidental successor, Harry Truman, who understood neither the nature of the weft and warp, nor the contribution that weaving from the center could make to the national welfare and liberty. Twenty-four million votes in 1948 could not supply moral stature at the point where Nature herself had stopped.

Why are American parties so full of electors that they are empty of sustained purpose? The answer is comparative and relative, a matter of degree.

1. Neither has as yet come to depend for its support on a distinctive gathering of interests: both appeal to all sections of a land of enormous territorial range, geographic diversity, economic interests, and racial and cultural groupings. Both are impelled to seek their support, since they long for office, not somewhere but everywhere. The exception to this is principally the hitherto "solid South" where, for reasons bygone of race, economic interest, and a fairly accidental party alignment in the 1850's and 1860's, the Democratic party has a monopoly. Something of an exception also is New England, where the Republican party, without anything like a monopoly, is particularly well-favored. First, then, the enormous geographical span and diversification of the nation.

2. The constitution has settled, or seems to have settled, a number of issues which continue to animate British and Continental parties: there

are limitations on the activity of state and national governments. Declarations may be made on these subjects in the platforms, but they are empty and not to be taken seriously. The party which gets the majority will never be sovereign in legislating on these matters, for the amending process and the Supreme Court enfeeble the party, its authority, and its sense of responsibility.

3. The vast size of the nation makes for localism. The United States is the largest area and population ever in all history to come under a single government in which the people rule. Extraordinary effort is required to overcome distances, density of population, and its variegated urban and rural patches. What do I mean by localism?—that people's interest, their everyday thoughts and pursuits, are largely focussed on and engaged by the life of their neighborhood. Since the constitution has considerably consecrated this by leaving to the states a very substantial range of authority, the natural localism is reinforced by elections, legislative authority and office and graft on the spot. This has two results:

One is to throw power into the hands of the local bosses—"machines" is no misnomer—especially those of the cities, from which their vote-gathering machine is operated—the Hagues, the Crumps, the Pendergasts, the Rorabacks, the Vares, the Kellys, the Curleys, and so through many generations. For they can deliver the vote at the state and national conventions, the primaries and general elections. The second result is to some degree to confuse and take the mind off the national, and, in our day, even the international issues. Washington is very far away, and therefore the nation as a unit also when the screen of local bossism, irresponsible for the national vision, not versed in its national and international problems, is set between the everyday mind of the voter and the central problems. (I learned first to appreciate this when I lived for a year in Knoxville, Tennessee.) In other words, the centralizing function of party, and therefore its purpose-determining, coherent-making, integrating function is riddled, torn, and obfuscated. If loyalties are nurtured and harvested by the local boss, and political office is impossible without him, why should a loyalty to the center be developed? It may be expensive.

4. The constitutional separation of powers and diverse terms of office break up the vision of unified purpose. Any vote cast at any election is not a vote which carries a total mandate. It is only a fraction of one, going to the House, the Senate, or the President. How it shall be cast is, therefore, not so momentous a consideration to a voter. So also, who shall be the trustee of its use at the center demands less searching of conscience and less purposive loyalty to the party as a creative association. This cause is accompanied by the disintegrating element of the variety of terms

for which the central legislative and executive body are elected, and the different election dates.   If they were all elected simultaneously at least, and for the same term (say, four years), a unity of judgment and decision, stimulated by an enforced unity of program, would result.

5. America has two assets as a polity which reduce party fever.   Its people are materially acquisitive in a specially high degree and, compared with the size of its population, the vast expanse and rich resources of the land offer an optimistic sense of continuing opportunity.   (The student must have lived in Europe to appreciate the tremendous power of these two factors.)   Hence, the electorate is of a middle-class, bourgeois type, even if its members are impoverished farmers or unskilled laborers.   They are not inspired by the heated winds of philosophic doctrine or transcendent ideology, which is more than wealth itself.   They are moderate and good-tempered, generally speaking and omitting a Huey Long, a Bilbo, or a Father Coughlin.   They do not take sides; and if the electorate does not take sides, there cannot be any sides.

American political parties cannot therefore have much gristle though they may be fat.   It is not possible to change this situation by constitutional fiat.   And if the people are broadly content, why should there be more than virtually one all-inclusive party: Serious consequences must flow from this flabbiness of party structure.   The parties being infirm of purpose, either party's legislative and executive policy and choice of men are rarely such as to meet the severe trials of modern statecraft.   Laws are not passed in time; or they are muddled with riders; or they are kept till the last moment of a session or confusion arises when a veto interposes itself between President and Congress and when party voting is unclear; or Congressional voting cuts extraordinarily across parties, thus making for electoral perplexity; or coordination fails between legislation and its execution, or even between the departments of the administration. A clear stream of controlling tendency is lacking.

What is worse, there is no central responsible thought for the future and the relationships of the various governmental decisions to each other. The best examples of the latter are the immediate lifting of many controls on V-J Day, and the impossibility of recovering the controls; the fumbling labor-management, wage-price relationship as the war ended; the different doctrines published by Truman and Wallace on the same subject of wages; the fumbling with OPA; the failure in deliveries of promised food contributions to Europe; the rise in prices and the effect on wage demands of central fumbling; and the consequent damage to all those countries to whom the foreign policy of the United States requires it to make loans—at one time, 50 per cent being the estimated loss in their value!   The position of labor in the nation—only a group, even if a very important group that deserves cherishing—is similarly the object of confused counsels, as the parties are morally flabby on this also. Labor is not a homogeneous body, but a number of occupations. Each and all have a responsibility to each other, without the understanding and fulfillment of which they cannot fail to do each other damage by making claims incompatible with the welfare of all and each. For the wages of each constitute part of the cost of production and the family budget of the others. And all of them have a responsibility to the nation as a body of consumers, a responsibility for using the investment of capital and invention in their industries to the maximum productivity and welfare of all. How can these responsibilities be explored and defined, and carried out, except through political parties? Unless political parties have a mind compact of standards of social justice, what kind of order can there possibly be in the tempestuous world of industry? The tergiversation of chief executive and Congress on labor legislation in 1948 and 1949 will long be remembered.

If no national disaster follows from all this, great damage does, losses of production and justice to social groups who vainly demand what is truly theirs. Often when government should give only a reason for saying "No" it yields against its own reason.

THE PARTIES AND THE UNION *

Viewing the situation somewhat differently from Professor Finer, Herbert Agar rejects the idea that political parties are unhealthy and inefficient. According to Agar, American parties are good; in fact, they are very good. Because of their undogmatic and compromising character, parties have preserved the Federal Union. They have harmonized the Federal system and tempered the clash between the Executive and Congress. They have kept classes and sections together. Every time one looks at the map of the United States he might say, in the words of Henry Steele Commager, "There, but for the Grace of God, the wisdom of the Fathers, and the work of political parties, goes South America."

Accepting the fact that parties have been a unifying influence, is this factor as vital today as it was a century ago? Has not the United States grown politically mature, and have not its cultural traditions developed sufficiently to withstand debate on controversial issues in the framework of a democratic election?

* Herbert Agar, *The Price of Union* (Houghton Mifflin, 1950), pp. 688–91.

During Grover Cleveland's first term in the White House, James Bryce published his remarkable book, *The American Commonwealth*. Surveying the party system from the English point of view, and with quiet surprise, he made the classic statement of the difference between the Republicans and the Democrats.

What are their principles [he wrote], their distinctive tenets, their tendencies? Which of them is for free trade, for civil-service reform, for a spirited foreign policy . . . for changes in the currency, for any other of the twenty issues which one hears discussed in the country as seriously involving its welfare? This is what a European is always asking of the intelligent Republicans and intelligent Democrats. He is always asking because he never gets an answer. The replies leave him in deeper perplexity. After some months the truth begins to dawn on him. Neither party has anything definite to say on these issues; neither party has any principles, any distinctive tenets. Both have traditions. Both claim to have tendencies. Both have certainly war cries, organizations, interests, enlisted in their support. But those interests are in the main the interests of getting or keeping the patronage of the government. Tenets and policies, points of political doctrine and points of political practice, have all but vanished. They have not been thrown away but have been stripped away by Time and the progress of events, fulfilling some policies, blotting out others. All has been lost, except office or the hope of it.

This is a true description of the parties as they were, and as they still are; but Bryce's explanation of how they came to be that way is misleading. He assumes that if the American parties were healthy they would resemble the parties of Great Britain. They would have "principles" and "tenets," and would thus be forced to take sides on all "the twenty issues that one hears discussed." And he assumes that "Time and the progress of events" have deprived the parties of their principles, leaving them with nothing but "office or the hope of it." But this is too short a view; Lord Bryce was confused by the brief history of the Republican Party, which possessed principles in 1856 and none in 1886. He thought this was a sign of failure and decay; but in fact it was a sign of health: 1856 had been the exception and the danger; 1886 was the reassuring norm.

The purpose—the important and healthy purpose—of an American party is to be exactly what Lord Bryce describes, and by implication deplores. The party is intended to be an organization for "getting or keeping the patronage of government." Instead of seeking "principles," or "distinctive tenets," which can only divide a federal union, the party is intended to seek bargains between the regions, the classes, and the other interest groups. It is intended to bring men and women of all beliefs, occupations, sections, racial backgrounds, into a combination for the pursuit of power. The combination is too various to possess firm convictions.

The members may have nothing in common except a desire for office. Unless driven by a forceful President they tend to do as little as possible. They tend to provide some small favor for each noisy group, and to call that a policy. They tend to ignore any issue that rouses deep passion. And by so doing they strengthen the Union.

The decisive American experience—the warning against politics based on principles—took place between 1850 and 1860. A subtle and healing compromise had been effected in 1850; yet year by year, whether through fate or through human folly, it slowly disintegrated. The best men watched in anguish but could not halt the ruin. In the name of principles and distinctive tenets the Whig Party was ground to bits. A new party was born which met Lord Bryce's requirements. The Republicans knew exactly where they stood on the major issue and would not give an inch. Finally, the same "principles" broke the Democratic Party, and the Union of 1789 perished.

The lesson which America learned was useful: in a large federal nation, when a problem is passionately felt, and is discussed in terms of morals, each party may divide within itself, against itself. And if the parties divide, the nation may divide; for the parties, with their enjoyable pursuit of power, are a unifying influence. Wise men, therefore, may seek to dodge such problems as long as possible. And the easiest way to dodge them is for both parties to take both sides. This is normal American practice, whether the issue turns section against section, like "cheap money"; or town against country, like Prohibition; or class against class like the use of injunctions in labor disputes. It is a sign of health when the Democrats choose a "sound-money" candidate for the presidency and a "cheap-money" platform, as they did in 1868; or when they choose a "wet" Eastern candidate for the presidency and a "dry" Western candidate for the vice-presidency, as they did in 1924. It is a sign of health when the Republicans choose a "sound-money" platform but cheerfully repudiate it throughout the "cheap-money" states, as they did in 1868.

A federal nation is safe so long as the parties are undogmatic and contain members with many contradictory views. But when the people begin to divide according to reason, with all the voters in one party who believe one way, the federal structure is strained. We saw this in 1896, during the last great fight for "free silver." To be sure, there remained some "gold Democrats" and some "silver Republicans" in 1896; yet the campaign produced the sharpest alignment on principle since the Civil War. And the fierce sectional passions racked the nation. Luckily, the silver issue soon settled itself, and removed itself from politics, so the parties could relapse into their saving illogicality.

The faults of such irrational parties are obvious. Brains and energy are lavished, not on the search for truth, but on the search for bargains, for concessions which will soothe well-organized minorities, for excuses to justify delay and denial. Unofficially, and in spite of any constitution, successful federal politics will tend to follow Calhoun's rule of concurrent majorities. Every interest which is strong enough to make trouble must usually be satisfied before anything can be done. This means great caution in attempting new policies, so that a whole ungainly continent may keep in step. Obstruction, evasion, well-nigh intolerable slowness—these are the costs of America's federal union. And the endless bartering of minor favors which we saw at its silliest in President Arthur's Congress is also part of the price. And so is the absence of a clear purpose whenever the President is weak or self-effacing, since the sum of sectional and class interests is not equal to the national interest, and the exchange of favors between blocs or pressure groups does not make a policy.

Yet no matter how high one puts the price of federal union, it is small compared to the price which other continents have paid for disunion, and for the little national states in which parties of principle can live (or more often die) for their clearly defined causes. And the price is small compared to what America paid for her own years of disunion. The United States, of course, may some day attain such uniformity (or have it thrust upon her) that she will abandon her federal structure; but until that happens she will be governed by concurrent majorities, by vetoes and filibusters, by parties which take both sides of every dangerous question, which are held together by the amusements and rewards of office-seeking, and which can only win an election by bringing many incompatible groups to accept a token triumph in the name of unity, instead of demanding their full "rights" at the cost of a fight.

The world today might do worse than study the curious methods by which such assuagements are effected.

------◆◆◆◆------

THE DEMOCRATIC PARTY: A CASE HISTORY *

John Fischer was a Stevenson aide during the 1952 presidential campaign. He was located at the Springfield headquarters of the Democratic candidate and witnessed from this ideal vantage point the inner workings of the party organization. Thus, as a participant-

* John Fischer, "What Do the Democrats Do Now?" *Harper's Magazine*, March, 1953, pp. 23–26, 28–30.

observer, Mr. Fischer can write with some authority on the present standing and future role of the Democratic Party. Nevertheless, his thesis that the Democratic Party is appealing to a diminishing base of public support is a controversial one. Are the shifting class loyalties and changing status of labor and the various ethnic groups strong enough to surmount the appeal of further social legislation? How do Fischer's conclusions compare with those of Professor Webb in the succeeding article?

When Adlai E. Stevenson gets back from his tour abroad late this spring, he will buckle down to the hardest job he has ever tackled—harder, even, than his campaign for the Presidency. He will start trying to rebuild the shattered remnants of the Democratic party, working under a set of hair-raising handicaps.

It is surprising that he should try at all. It would have been easy, and far more comfortable, for him to retire to his Libertyville farm, or to pick up the threads of his once-profitable law practice. It is even more surprising that a good many skeptical, hard-bitten Democratic politicians think he has a reasonable chance to succeed.

Long before the election, most people in the Democratic headquarters at Springfield had begun to suspect that their party was in a pretty gamy stage of decay. No one, so far as I know, foresaw the majestic weight of the Republican landslide, and two or three congenital optimists such as Wilson Wyatt and Clayton Fritchey bubbled with optimism to the very end—but very few Democrats in Springfield bet any money. I suspect that Governor Stevenson (notably a canny investor) never put up a dime. Certainly he showed no sign of being either astonished or over-whelmed by his defeat.

For almost every day of the campaign had uncovered additional symptoms that the party was suffering from two crippling ailments. Either of them might have killed off for good any organism less durable than the Democratic Party.

No political surgeon—not even the Old Wizard, FDR—could have cured them in the three and a half months between the convention and election day. Indeed, it probably will take at least four years of fasting, exercise, and meditation in the wilderness—plus massive doses of political vitamins and lots of luck—to get the patient in shape to fight another campaign on even terms. This article is an attempt at a diagnosis, with a very tentative guess at the chances for a cure.

One of the obvious troubles was intellectual anemia. For twenty years the party had been feeding on a batch of ideas whipped up in the first phase of the New Deal. This pantry was nearly emptied by 1940, and only the outbreak of World War II concealed for a while the Democrats' mental poverty.

Harry Truman's effort to warm up the leftovers under the guise of the Fair Deal didn't produce anything very appetizing—which was not surprising, since it is rare in this country for any political formula to work twice. (Van Buren's failure to coast on Jackson's program is a case in point; William Howard Taft's back-to-McKinley movement is another.) It is now clear that Truman's surprise victory in 1948 resulted, not from any wild popular enthusiasm for the menu he offered, but rather from the GOP failure that year to promise any nourishment at all.

Not that the Republicans did much better in 1952. The most painstaking analysis of their platform and campaign speeches discloses hardly a chemical trace of a new idea. But this time they didn't need any. Ike— plus a carefully vague promise to do something about Korea, plus the irritations and disappointments which had piled up during twenty years—were enough to lick the enfeebled Democrats.

It is only fair to note that Stevenson didn't offer much that was new either—aside from two significant but generally overlooked items which we shall note in a moment. He campaigned, in effect, on the proposition that the problems ahead of us are uncommonly tough ones; that he had no easy answer; but that he would take a fresh look at the entire agenda if he were elected. That was the only honest strategy, since any thoughtful long-range planning is impossible during the uproar of a campaign. But in the role of opposition leader, one of Stevenson's main tasks will be to equip his party with a new outlook and a new program.

The second malady which afflicted the Democrats was an almost total collapse of the party organization. Those of us who arrived in Springfield early in the campaign assumed that we would be working with a going party machine—ancient, of course, but presumably still serviceable. I had known something of the Roosevelt-Farley organization in prewar days, and took it for granted that at least a substantial remnant would still be in operation. After all, Mr. Truman prided himself on being an old-fashioned organization man, bulging with political know-how, who always Took Care of the Boys. The newspapers denounced the Big City Machines as if these monsters were still breathing fire and brimming with health. The columnists, including such shrewd old hands as Arthur Krock of *The New York Times*, talked knowingly about the 2,500,000 federal employees, who could be expected to deliver at least ten million Democratic votes come November.

All these assumptions turned out to be sadly naive. Some of those Washington bureaucrats may have been Democrats once, but as soon as they got civil service status and $4,600 a year they generally moved out to Montgomery County and registered as Republicans. The city machines proved to be a toothless and rheumatic team of dragons, far gone in senility and fatty degeneration. The old-time bosses—Crump, Arvey, De Sapio, Flynn, Kenny, Dever, and the rest—found they could no longer deliver the votes.

The only exception was Philadelphia, where a young, vigorous—and clean—Democratic organization, headed by Mayor Joe Clark and City Chairman James A. Finnegan, stacked up a 160,000 plurality for Stevenson: roughly twenty-three times as large as Truman's plurality in 1948.

The apparent reason for this decay was simply twenty years in power, during which the machines had grown flabby and encrusted with vermin. Perhaps the most noisome example was New York City; some of the goon types who hung around the corridors of the Democratic Headquarters in the Biltmore Hotel during the campaign would have frightened Boss Tweed. These Tammany dignitaries made awkward teammates in harness with the idealistic Junior League characters who largely made up the Volunteers for Stevenson. Moreover, their long record of corruption and incompetence had finally become too malodorous even for the complacent citizenry of New York; hundreds of thousands switched to the Republicans out of sheer revulsion.

A more fundamental reason for the breakup of the machines, however, lies in the revolutionary change in the structure of our urban society during the past two decades. Originally, the typical city boss had founded his power on the bewildered immigrants who streamed in from Europe during the past century. He gave them jobs, advice, protection, and a kind of rudimentary social status in a strange land. In grateful self-interest, they gave him votes.

This fountain of power began to run dry in the nineteen-twenties, as the immigration barriers went up. During the Depression it was replaced, temporarily, by the New Deal's bountiful pump; the hungry and friendless turned naturally to the local boss for handouts and WPA jobs. But by 1940 hardly anybody needed relief, and anyhow the Roosevelt version of the Welfare State had established itself on a permanent, non-patronage basis. Grandma no longer needed to see her precinct captain about that pension; instead she talked to a brisk civil servant with a Vassar degree in the neighborhood Social Security office.

Meanwhile, the broken-English laborers who had once formed the core of the Democratic city vote were dying off. When Giuseppe got off the boat, about 1919, he had been called a Dago and cuffed into the nearest slum. A few years later, he was proud and flattered when the Tammany district leader invited him to a clambake and spoke feelingly of "our sterling Italo-American citizens." But by the time Giuseppe's children had been through high school, and maybe college, they were neither Dagos nor Italo-Americans. They were Americans, period—and they resented the beef-headed ward heelers who were slow to realize that the hyphen had disappeared.

Moreover, this second generation has left both the slums and the laboring class. The new industry which has grown up since 1940 doesn't need many muscle workers; what it does need is a lot more engineers and chemists and accountants. So Giuseppe's children have moved simultaneously into the suburbs and into the middle class. Usually they register Republican, as the solid residents of Oakcrest and Westchester always have. The change in party is, quite simply, an outward badge of their progress up the ladder.

The sociologists have described this process as a broadening of the middle class to include virtually the whole of American society—accompanied by a massive flight away from the cities. The old-time Democratic boss merely knows that the cowed and poverty-haunted ethnic groups which once made up his army—the Poles, Irish, Italians, Germans, and East European Jews—have somehow deserted. The only such groups which stood firm last November were the two most recent batches of immigrants —the Puerto Ricans and the Negroes from the South—who have not yet had time to graduate into the middle class. The very success of the Democratic regime in raising living standards had undermined the structure of its power in the Northern and Eastern cities.

Much the same kind of thing happened in that other major stronghold of the old Roosevelt Coalition—the once solid South. The astonishingly swift spread of industry throughout the South during the past two decades has changed both its economy and its attitudes.

It is misleading to talk about "The South" as one piece, because any two of the states—say, Texas and South Carolina—differ just as much as Vermont and Ohio. But it is no wild oversimplification to say that as late as 1936 the South was still a semi-feudal society, scratching a thin living out of its cotton plantations and worshipping the political creed of John Calhoun. Its small governing class was of course profoundly conservative, but it called itself Democrat—out of habit, loyalty to the legend of Robert E. Lee, and a shrewd hunch that a one-party system was easier to control. It tolerated the New Deal (for a while) partly because it promised a way out of the South's ancient poverty, and partly because of a traditional Southern resentment for the Northern Republicans who had always treated the South like a conquered colony.

By 1952, however, all that was changed. Both cotton and the plantation aristocracy had shrunk to relatively minor importance. New crops, new farm machinery, a reshuffle of population, and—above all—new factories had transformed the South into a burgeoning industrial society, bustling with station wagons and junior executives.

It was this new business community, led by such young men as Governor Allen Shivers of Texas, which led the Southern defection from the Democrats. To them, a vote for the Business Man's Party was at once a gesture of independence, a symbol that the South was at last rejoining the Union, and a bid for an unhampered chance at the Big Money. They financed their revolt lavishly; in Texas, for example, the Shivers crowd spent more for confetti than the Stevenson people could raise there for their entire campaign.

The old-style Southern Conservatives, of the Byrd-Byrnes stamp, merely trailed along, with nervous misgivings, and some of them remained at least nominally true to the old faith. For they are not at all sure that they will like the New South. They suspect that it will destroy their cozy way of life—their tight one-party control, their Rule by Gentlemen—just as industrial revolutions have always destroyed the earlier feudal societies. And they realize, dimly, that even a Republican administration in Washington will not hold back the unwelcome stream of change.

So in Dixie, too, the New Deal has been destroyed by its own success. The spreading American middle class is swallowing up both the planter and his sharecroppers, much as it has absorbed Giuseppe's children in Detroit and Cleveland. Everywhere, the main building stones of the old Roosevelt Coalition have dissolved—and, barring a major depression, probably forever. . . .

If these guesses prove correct—if the centripetal forces of American politics shove both parties toward the center, in accordance with our historic tradition—then we can reasonably look forward to a period of relative harmony. No doubt the fanatic fringe of both parties—the McCarthys and Jenners of the right and professional Jeremiahs of the left—will continue to scream themselves hoarse. But the responsible men of each side appear closer to genuine national unity than at any time in our generation.

There will be plenty of room left, of course, for party differences. One fight seems likely to break out fairly soon over the question of giving away public assets. Ike already is committed to hand over the oil-rich tidelands to Louisiana, Texas, and California. That precedent may well encourage the Western sheep and cattle growers—one of the greediest of all special interests—to make another grab for the public forest and grazing lands they have long coveted. And some of the big utility men already are lusting openly for control of the great public power systems developed by the New Deal.

Agricultural policy may provide another battleground, particularly if farm prices keep falling. The long overdue revamping of our tax and immigration laws—if the Republicans dare tackle them—will offer still others. A serious economic slump before 1956 would, of course, give the Democrats the juiciest issue of all.

In the beginning, however, the big squabbles probably will arise in the field of foreign policy—and they will cut squarely across party lines. The new Administration has talked a lot about "trade, not aid" to support our European allies; but if Ike really tries to increase our imports, he is certain to run into heavy weather with the high-tariff Republicans. If he wins at all, it will be with the help of Democratic Congressional votes.

On many similar measures—economic and military—which will be needed to hold the Free World together, Eisenhower will find the GOP isolationists turning against him. As a consequence, he cannot depend solely on the ancient partnership of Republicans and conservative Democrats; he must bargain for the support of liberal Democrats as well.

Stevenson already has hinted at the strategy which might work best in these circumstances. It is the exact opposite of the strategy followed by most Republicans during their term in opposition. In place of nagging obstruction, he suggests that the Democrats adopt an attitude of sweet reasonableness. For any measure truly in the national interest, let Ike count on their cooperation. But in return, naturally, they would expect him to resist the more outrageous demands from the blind, the backward, and the fanatic elements within his own party.

Such tactics are nicely calculated to pry open the half-concealed fissures in the Republican leadership. These splits are bound to widen in any case. Already the Taft and Dewey factions are circling each other stifflegged, like a couple of bristling pups. The New England conscience of Senators Aiken, Saltonstall, Flanders, and Smith is revolted by the hate-mongering of the McCarthyites. Dirksen and the rest of the *Chicago Tribune* chorus distrust everybody east of the Alleghenies. The millionaires of Ike's gold-plated cabinet show little understanding of, or use for, the professional politicians on the Hill. And the veteran corporals of the Old Guard— Bricker, Taber, and Martin—nurse a profound suspicion of all their colleagues with an I.Q. above 85.

Even more distressing for the General will be the disillusion which is sure to infect his rank-and-file voters. It will be heart-breaking, in the months just ahead, to watch the anguish of those Ike-likers who counted on a simple and quick solution in Korea . . who expected all the world's troubles to evaporate as soon as that dreadful Acheson was ousted from the State Department . . . who were sure their hero could find a cheap method to hold the Kremlin at bay . . . who knew that high taxes were just an evil invention of New Deal socialists to destroy the Better Classes. . . .

Well, the Democrats can afford to listen to this moaning with Christian forbearance. They won't need to call Dulles a traitor, or accuse the General of plotting to destroy the American way of life. They might of course mention from time to time the campaign promises which inevitably get broken in the stern process of governing. They can also note the mistakes which Ike's Administration (like any other, short of Gabriel's) is certain to make. In this cheerful duty they may have the help, before long, of at least a few newspapers. Because it is the nature of newspapers to be agin the government, the one-party press isn't likely to remain that way forever.

Above all, the Democrats will need to keep on talking sense. The old reliable mixture of platitude and demagoguery won't turn the trick again for quite a while—not after the Stevenson campaign. But if the Democrats can combine fair criticism with a set of constructive alternatives— if they will continue to treat the voters as responsible and passably intelligent citizens—then they can be sure of picking up quite a lot of disappointed stragglers from the Eisenhower crusade.

Such a strategy would, of course, mean a sharp break away from the Democratic habit of the past two decades. It would mean more emphasis on the national interest, and less attention to the demands of special classes and pressure groups. It would force the party spokesmen to look at the electorate with fresh eyes. They could no longer view it merely as a loose confederation of farmers, war veterans, Catholics, union members, Southerners, second-generation immigrants, Negroes, and business men, but would have to regard it as a single community of Americans. This, I take it, was the gist of the Stevenson idea. He knew that the politics of the special groups is far from dead. Yet he had the courage to speak to the American People as mature and reasonably patriotic citizens, capable on occasion of rising above their selfish interests. He appealed, as few politicians ever have, to the solid moral sense which is the hidden foundation of our political life.

If Stevenson can persuade his fellow Democrats to join him in building on this foundation, the party can be confident about its future. In the process he may also restore politics to the honored place it has always held during the best days of our history—making it again, in E. B. White's words, "the noblest as well as the most dangerous of arts."

THE REPUBLICAN PARTY: A CASE HISTORY *

Professor Walter Prescott Webb wrote the following article as an analysis of the 1948 election. Although the point of the article, how the Republican Party lost its future, has been tarnished somewhat by the results in 1952, it has not been completely disproved. There is certainly much more evidence that the 1952 election was a personal triumph for General Eisenhower than that it was a victory for the Republican Party. On the other hand, the party did not behave like a defunct organization. Does the article fail to evaluate the changing economic, social, and political character of the times? Has the social state ceased to be a matter of political debate? Are not the Democrats, rather than the Republicans, now charged with the responsibility of coming up with a new principle, a fresh approach to the problems of government?

Senator Henry Cabot Lodge, Jr., published in the *Saturday Evening Post* of January 29, 1949, an article entitled "Does the Republican Party Have a Future?" Though he spoke with objectivity, the fact that he could ask the question indicates that he realizes the dilemma of the party of which he is a distinguished member. It is probably the first time in the history of the party that the question has been asked in such seriousness. Senator Lodge believes the party has a future, but he suggests that it can be realized only on condition that the Republicans clean house, discard old concepts, and adopt a program more in conformity with the will and the aspirations of the American people. In short he implies that the house is in disorder, that the party's present concepts are archaic, and that its program does not mesh with popular spirit and desires.

Many thoughtful persons have tried to explain the recent surprising defeat of the Republican party, but most of them have been content to do so by analysing the current situation in terms of such factors as the labor vote, the farm vote, or the Roosevelt vote. At least I have read no account that viewed the present state of the Republican party down the long gun-barrel of history. I believe the history throws a strong clear light on the problem and makes the eclipse of a once very powerful institution understandable.

It must be remembered that the Republican party set out as a great

* Walter Prescott Webb, "How the Republican Party Lost Its Future." Reprinted from *Southwest Review*, published at Southern Methodist University, Dallas, Texas, Autumn, 1949, pp. 329–39.

crusader bent on emancipating those Americans who were not yet free to enjoy the benefits of democratic life. The cause was one that made a tremendous appeal to the idealist and to the common man. The cause gathered that strength known as moral force. The party that espoused the cause became the champion of suffering humanity, of freedom, of real democracy extended to all men, even the most humble slave. There was something here of unselfishness, of humanitarianism, of philanthropy, and the appeal of it reached in some measure every man whose pecuniary interests did not outweigh his idealism. The party first appeared in 1852, and by 1860 it had enough strength to capture the national government.

As a result of its first success in the election of Lincoln, the southern states withdrew from the Union, giving the Republican party its second and its greatest opportunity, that of saving the Union. In saving the Union the party proved itself able to win the hardest war the nation has yet fought, and to add to the moral prestige it had exhibited in the election of Lincoln the prestige of physical force sufficient to hold the nation together in the gravest crisis. Here was the deed that stirred the patriotism and fervor of people everywhere, cementing their allegiance to the party with something approaching blind devotion. If you believed in freedom of men, you were a Republican, or should be; and if you believed in the Union and in loyalty to the flag, you could be nothing else. Thus it happened that the Republican party emerged from the four years of civil war triumphant in the shining armor of high moral purpose and armed with the keen sword of patriotic devotion. No political party ever set out on the path of peace—to last for more than three decades—under more favorable auspices. It had found in the shortest time the political holy grail.

But there was a structural weakness in the young party, a weakness which had considerable effect on policy for ten years after the war, and indirectly for a much longer period. The party was not geographically in the beginning a national party, and this despite the fact that it had kept the nation from dividing, had saved the Union. It originated as a sectional party, drew its total initial strength from the North, gained its first national election from northern votes, and had relatively little following elsewhere. Had its leaders inherited Lincoln's wisdom as they did his power, the party might in time have become truly national, but it never did. It has in essence always been sectional.

Because the South became so Democratic as to be known as the Solid South, it has been assumed in some quarters that the Democratic party was sectional. On the contrary it was a national party before the Civil War, through reconstruction, and remains so today. Its members were distributed over the whole nation, though for long they formed a minority in the more populous region. It was the sectional nature of the Republican party that led directly to the harsh reconstruction measures. The Republican leaders in Congress knew that they had no members in the South to speak of, and that if the southern states were permitted to return members to Congress, the Democrats would have a majority in the House of Representatives. The only safe thing they could do was to keep the southern Democrats out until the victorious Republicans could be assured of a majority in both houses of Congress. This political party maneuver, or gerrymander, was carried out under the guise of reconstruction with the result that no southern state really was represented in the national Congress for nearly a decade after the war closed.

In this decade the western states were not represented either. They were not represented because twelve of them had not yet been admitted to the Union. They existed as territories, and these territories were governed and administered by the national government, in this case the Republican party. When time came for the admission of new states, every step was taken to guarantee that they came into the Republican fold. By eliminating the South and conditioning the West, the Republicans built up their strength to a point where they could safely permit the southern states to send Democrats back to the Congress. But for a period of ten years the Republican party, operating from the northern states, had undisputed political control in theory and in fact over the entire nation— over the South because it was being reconstructed, over the West because it was largely unoccupied and still territorial in status.

The Republican party, having gained a breathing spell by disfranchising southern Democrats, set itself to the task of consolidating its strength and binding its membership to it before memory of its original high idealism and its patriotic achievement in saving the Union had faded into the background. It is perhaps a good political maxim that a party cannot live by its past alone. It must make good every day, at least every administration. This the party succeeded in doing.

Its position after Appomattox is probably unique in political history: Unique in that within five years from the time it came to power it had completed its program. It would be a mistake to assert that the Republican party of 1860 or 1864 had but one plank in its platform, but it is no mistake to say that it had only one that was important. The others were window dressing. By 1865 it had carried out the reform that gave it its birth and its original strength. As a reformer it had completed its mission and should have been ready to die, but the Republican party was not ready to die—as what party is? It was confronted with the necessity of finding another plank, evolving another program that would justify its existence and assure its growth. Fortunately its unlimited power and prestige at this juncture were matched by an unequaled opportunity, and that opportunity was seized with the unerring instinct which comes when the cards of success are falling right.

The whole nation lay at the feet of the Republican party for development and exploitation. The South was no longer a rival or even an obstructionist and the West was a fallow field with untouched and all but limitless resources. The nation was founded on agriculture, the farm and the plantation, but this old force was not the thing to build a program on. The South had tried that. The new force—with all its dynamic future before it—was the one for the new party to champion. The new force consisted of wheels, pulleys, belts, blades, gears, driven by water, steam, and electricity in the fabrication and distribution of goods and commodities. The North had made a considerable start in the development of technology before the Civil War, and in the war it had knocked out completely any competition that the South might have developed. It was in supreme command of the dynamic power generated by the Industrial Revolution.

The Republican party, in complete political control of the North, the South, and the West, was free to choose what it would go in for. It chose well. It embraced the new and most dynamic force, not the old agriculture which was mature and comparatively static, but rather that combination known as business meaning manufacturing, transportation, and distribution. Here was an alliance of a sectional economic power with a coterminous political power, a partnership for great achievement.

The program followed by the Republican party was designed, whether wittingly or not, to foster with loving care the economic power and smooth the way for its eager and powerful partner to seize the material resources of the nation and concentrate control in the North, and thus to make both economics and politics sectional. The policy of the Republican party was to make the North prosperous, and as long as the North prospered, the North would give its allegiance to the party and keep it in control. "The party of prosperity" was a good slogan to soothe a whole nation, but those inside know the real policy was Republican prosperity.

The assets of the party after the Civil War were staggering in their immensity, so enormous that they could not help but bring relative prosperity to all sections. The business interests had in hand the technology and skill to manufacture unlimited quantities of goods, enough for the entire nation. What business needed was protection from competition, domestic and foreign, and a system of transportation that would assure distribution. Government, in control of the Republican party, could protect against domestic competition by granting patents and against foreign competition by levying tariffs. Patents cannot be considered a party measure, but as luck would have it, they turned the chief benefits to the North where patentable articles were being devised and used. The Republican party made the protective tariff a broad plank in all its platforms, and throughout the Republican era the curve of the tariff was constantly upward, higher and higher. This tariff funneled the wealth of the nation into the Republican section and built up a surplus in the national treasury which was also dispensed for Republican and northern benefit.

Business needed railroads in order to transport the goods it manufactured to all parts of the nation, but the task of building them into the West was too great for business to undertake on its own hook. It did not need to. It called on government to finance the venture. The road to the Pacific—across the plains—was projected before the Civil War but was not built because the two sections could not agree on a route. The South wanted it; the North wanted it. Neither would yield, and so nothing was done. In 1862, with the South out of the Union, the Republican Congress authorized the building of the Union Pacific from the West into the northern region. From 1862 until building ceased, the whole railroad system was designed to feed into the northern section. And much of the building was done at government expense.

The government had in its possession after the Civil War two enormous tangible assets which the Republican party disposed of largely to its own benefit. The first asset and the larger one was the public lands comprising approximately one-half the continental area of the United States. Until 1862 the policy had been to sell the public lands to individuals, but in that year of fateful and far-reaching Republican legislation the Homestead Act was passed and the lands were given away. It was not difficult to convince any recipient of a homestead ranging from 160 to 640 acres that the Republican party was beneficent and worthy of support. Though small areas were given to individuals, much larger ones were given to corporations. The railroads received western lands equal to the area of France. This lavish distribution of the greatest relief fund in history to individuals and corporations took nothing away from the popularity of the Republican party, but it relieved the government of its landed estate and national resources and prepared the way for another and less popular form of relief.

The second asset in the hands of the government during this era was cash in the treasury, cash accumulated from the tariff proposed by the Republican party for the benefit of the infant industries of business. The question was not one of how this surplus cash could be returned to all the people, but rather how it could be placed safely in the hands of the chosen section and in the hands of good loyal Republicans. The solution was easy, the answer almost obvious. Give it to the Union soldiers of the Civil War in the form of pensions. Thus would it reward loyalty and strengthen business—and the Republican party. The pension rolls were set up during the war and increased constantly until 1923, nearly sixty years after the war ended. Here was a safety valve that would relieve the treasury of its surplus.

In any attempt to account for the deterioration of the Republican party the declining influence of these pensions cannot be ignored. Not only did the receipt of a pension check each month hold the member of the GAR to the Republican party, but it likewise held all his kith and kin, especially those on whom he might otherwise have been dependent, and friends whom he might influence. That this pension money, gathered from the pockets of the entire nation, flowed mainly into the pockets of one small section, the records in Washington will abundantly prove. Of each $100 paid in pensions about $85 went North and $15 was distributed to scattered Republicans in the South and West. Here was one of the most dependable blocs of votes that any party could hope to have.

It should not be difficult, then, to understand the loyalty of business to its political partner. Business had never known such opportunities, and nowhere in the world had it made more of the possibilities that lay before it. An increasing population in an expanding frontier lapped up all the commodities that could be produced and each year called for more. The resources were so great that there was something for all, enough to hide many inequalities. The Republican party rode this dynamic wave and won election after election. A part of its advantage was the fact that its position was positive; it was doing things and much was being done in its name. The opposition had to content itself with blocking, interfering, and protesting. What could you do with a party that had emancipated the slave, saved the union, given everybody a bounty in land or tariff, assured businessmen of prosperity and poor men of a full dinner pail?

The answer, as the opposition found out, was nothing—nothing but wait. The waiting was long. The South, sitting disconsolately outside the warmth of the charmed circle, sans tariff, sans pensions, was always in protest, but could be ignored. In the seventies and eighties the farmers of the West—though Republican by inheritance—raised their voices, against monopolies more than against the party that had fostered them. The Populists got nowhere. But the campaign of 1896—foreshadowing that of 1932—gave the Republicans a great scare and caused them to adopt, under the leadership of the able Mark Hanna, tactics as effective as they were reprehensible in order to win. This should have been a warning.

Despite the party's splendid record of achievement, keen observers might have detected by the turn of the century the deterioration that had set in, a deterioration in position. No party can live on its memories or expect to live on gratitude for past favors. By 1900 people were a little tired of hearing that Lincoln, the only great President the party has produced, had freed the slaves. By then the Union was so well saved that even the bloody shirt no longer evoked patriotic emotions. These things lay far in the past. The giving away of the public domain lay largely in the past too, and some were saying that the policy had been carried too far. The pensioners were dying rapidly, and the political loyalty of the GAR was becoming less important. The one vital force left to the Republican party was business.

Between the close of the Civil War and the eclipse of the Republican party in 1932, business made spectacular progress. As everyone knews, it got very big and more powerful than any other factor in American life. We emphasize this in books and politics by the use of capitals: Big Business. It has already been pointed out that business was the principal ally of the Republican party, the only one that survived the passage of years and retained its vitality. It crystallized around the corporations which the Republicans got the Supreme Court to define as individuals in order to override the will of the states and other protestants. The party did everything that could be done to clear the track and give cannon-ball right of way to the business special. The Republican boast, so effective in many campaigns, of being the party of business was sound and true.

This alliance between business and the dominant political party made an unbeatable combination as long as they could deliver prosperity and keep the factory wheels turning and the people employed. With the passage of time, subtle changes began to take place in the relationship between the two partners and also within the domain of each partner.

In the beginning both partners were young, each with its special vigor, but of the two the political partner was dominant. It was the Republican party that had the political power to grant the land to the railroads, to give a tariff bonus to manufacturers, and to grant pensions to the GAR. In the process of doing this it transferred the government's wealth—which theoretically belongs to all the people—into the hands of the party section, party members, and party supporters, that is, into the hands of business. The result was that business grew very powerful and became dominant. In the beginning the party had political power and economic assets; in the end it had only political power, the assets having been transferred. Therefore when it needed economic assets it became a supplicant before a power it had formerly controlled and helped to make.

Time brought changes in business and these changes compelled the Republican party to make two hard choices, neither of which was politically wise. Shortly after the Civil War the original numerous small businesses began to merge into fewer bigger businesses, forming trusts and approaching monopolies in one field after another. In the struggle that ensued the Republican party had to choose its destiny: would it champion the cause of small business or would it go where the power and money were, with Big Business? It is doubtful whether, given the background, the Republican party could have made any choice but the one it did. The choice in favor of Big Business was natural, logical, and under the circumstances inevitable. For as a matter of fact, the men who were operating Big Business were by that time the prime movers of the Republican party. They were on the board of directors of the corporation and of the party.

Another division in business compelled the Republican party to make a second choice. With the rise of the great industries, there was a sharp division between the owners or managers and the employees who did the work; there was capital on the one hand and labor on the other. The Republican party could not champion the cause of both. Its whole history of opposition in greater or less degree to the demands of organized labor indicates its decision in favor of capital.

The important thing to notice in both of these decisions is that the Republican party threw its support to the minority as against the majority. There were more small businesses than big businesses, and there were far more laborers than there were managements or managers. Slowly but surely the Republican party was narrowing the base of popular support upon which any party in a free democratic country must in the long run depend.

After it ran out of homesteads, the Republican party had no place at all for the farmer. It may have given him lip-service, but it never could accept the poignant plea of 1896 that the farmer too was a businessman. He was something else, a farmer. Even if it had granted him the status of a businessman, the party would have classed him as a small businessman, and his interest would still have been made secondary to those of Big Business. Throughout it compelled him to buy in a protected market and permitted him to sell in a free market with all the world as his competitor. For the farmer's mule or cow or cotton or tobacco there was neither tariff nor patent.

It is difficult to explain the long record of loyalty of middle western farmers to the Republican party, why they clung to it for three-quarters of a century to the detriment of their own welfare. The most reasonable explanation is that they inherited their Republicanism. The fact that their fathers received free homesteads and pensions brought them into the party and a loyal inertia held them there for a very long time—but not forever. They woke up at last to the fact that the party had done nothing for them lately.

Thus the Republican party successively turned its back on one great segment of society after another, on the farmer, on small business, on labor. The party quit the people long before the people quit it. Finding Big Business a jealous god, it gave it complete and undivided devotion, sacrificing its Lincolnian idealism and its early patriotic fervor for the downtrodden man, and thus cutting from under itself the foundation on which popular support could with any reason stand. It is not surprising that the Republican party eventually went down in defeat known to no other major party in history; the surprising fact, the one that needs explanation, is that its defeat was so long delayed. The explanation of the delay must be sought in the unbroken success of business.

The party was never really defeated in the sense that it lost prestige, until its main partner—and we might almost say its only one—collapsed. Since business near the end was the only ally of strength the party had, the condition for the continued dominance of the party hinged on the ability of business to provide prosperity. It was business that had to make and distribute the goods, maintain employment, and provide hope for the future. As long as business did this, the voters went along voting the Republicans into power with only an occasional interlude by protesters and reformers.

The union of business and the Republican party was never more felicitous than in the years following World War I. It is quite true that one President was not quite up to the standard expected, but the two that followed were well-nigh perfect. President Hoover, the engineer and humanitarian, was the ideal man for the party of business. And business was so good during the early part of his administration that the Republicans promised to make prosperity permanent and to put two cars in every garage. It would be hard to beat a party that does either.

Then it happened, overnight. The bottom fell out, not of the Republican party, but of business. From 1929 to 1933 the administration—representing the Republican party—moved around in a daze, completely stunned by the disaster that had come to its partner and main support. Though there was some vague talk about turning a corner, the Republicans were never able to make the turn. Their policy had been to let business take its course, and it was perhaps too much to expect a sudden reversal of a time-honored and well-established system.

In the next election the Republican party had nothing on which to base a campaign. Born on a platform of one plank, slavery, it died on a platform of one plank because that plank, business, had decomposed and fallen from under it. It began as a sectional party, carrying only northern states; it died as a sectional party carrying six states, all of them in the region of its original strength. Four years later it carried Maine and Vermont. Gone from it were the farmers of the Middle West, gone the votes of the laboring man, now jobless, around the silent factories of the industrial

North. Gone also the tradition of invincibility and the belief that the Republican party alone knew the magic formula of prosperity and success.

The collapse of business in 1929 and of the Republican party in 1932 gave the opposition the first opportunity it had had since long before the Civil War to seize the initiative and launch a constructive program. It is true that in a period of seventy-two years, from 1860 to 1932, the Democrats won four elections, serving sixteen years to fifty-six for the Republicans. But none of these victories gave the Democrats a broad initiative. They were due in Cleveland's case to protests against Republican rule, and in Wilson's case to disaffection in the Republican party and to war. The foundation under the Republicans in each case remained strong and sound, and as soon as the reformers had failed in their reforms, control slipped back into safe Republican hands. The party still stood for the constructive force, the development of business, and not for the complainers, obstructionists, and amorphous dissident elements which have always been a plague to the out party.

The entry of the Democratic party in 1932 was a triumphant entry such as it had not known before. Not only had the opposition been defeated, but its old sources of strength lay in complete ruins about it. The task was to build from the ground up on another principle. Twice before the Democrats had had the ball but had not known what to do with it. This time they had the ball and, as it turned out, they knew how to keep it and what to do with it.

What the Democrats did after 1932 was to launch a gold program much greater than but comparable to the one undertaken by Lincoln. And that program was based on an entirely new principle. The forces of government were directed, not to the restoration of business alone, but toward the rehabilitation of the suffering and destitute of the entire nation. It was in the words of Roosevelt himself a "crusade to restore America to its own people." That was a long-range program. In the short range it would give bread to the hungry, clothes to the naked, fuel to the freezing, jobs to the jobless, security to the aged, and insurance to the bankers; and, having no public domain to give away and no other government assets, it would pay for all this by taking money away from those who had it, mainly from the Republicans and Big Business, and giving it to those who needed it. It was the taking and not the giving that stirred the bitterness and acrimony, just as Lincoln's taking away property in slaves had stirred it three-quarters of a century earlier.

In this analysis we are not concerned with the merits of the program, its constitutionality, or its rightness or wrongness. We are concerned with its political effectiveness, with the broad appeal it had for the majority and its seemingly utter disregard for the powerful minority. This program gave the Democrats an initiative based on a new principle which for the time being the Republican party cannot possibly take from it and remain the Republican party. The Republican party for the first time in its history is now definitely on the outside. It can only complain, criticize, claim it can do the job better and more efficiently. It has as yet nothing constructive to offer, and under present conditions it seems doubtful whether it can find anything to offer that its members would accept or the American voters would take at face value. The Republican party worked out to the last grain its vein of success and for the present it is through. It carried to a logical conclusion the policy of taking from the many—either the government or the people—and giving to the few, taking from the three sections and giving to the favored one. Here was a principle that was good as long as it lasted, but it was not an eternal principle. Senator Lodge refers to archaic concepts of the party, but I would like to suggest to him that the great principle of the party is archaic and that therefore practically everything about it is now out of date. The old place may be tidied up a bit, but it will still be a Victorian palace with its gingerbread and gewgaws showing.

By way of being specific let us examine some of the cherished details of the establishment—relics of a dead past—that have no place save in a political antique shop. The first of these is the front porch. Now in its day that was quite an institution. It was a comfortable place for the presidential candidate who was sure of election to reside in dignity while the opposition beat its brains out trying to gain the attention of spellbound voters. It was a good place from which to make no mistakes, commit no errors. The front porch is one antique that the Republicans will have to give up until they get a house to go with it.

Another outworn formula has to do with the off-year elections. This formula held that if in the rare Democratic innings the Republicans gained control of Congress in the off-year election, that was a sure sign that the Democratic President was on his way out, come next election. In 1946 the Congress became Republican and it was taken for granted that the formula would work. The White House was as good as won.

So eager was the Eightieth Congress to please its favored constituents that it jumped the gun and began the work of destroying the principle which the Democrats had adopted and practiced for sixteen years. The result was that this Congress frightened the farmers, resolved labor's doubts, and lost the election of 1948. The formula did not work.

In the last election we did not hear much about the full dinner pail and sound money, the first a bauble for the workingman and the second a booby trap for small businessmen. For three years the workingman looked into the pail and found it always empty. And as for sound money, the Republican party ran out of money of any kind as did most of the voters. It appears that the dinner pail has been lost now and sound money, if not forgotten, is never mentioned.

It is customary for losers to quarrel among themselves in trying to apportion the blame for their defeat. According to news reports this jowering is going on now in the party high command. It seems that Mr. Dewey, who would have been so great if he had won, is taking the brunt of the attack. It may be pointed out that Mr. Dewey's whole campaign was in the very best Republican tradition. He conducted himself with the utmost propriety, said very little, and might even have remained on the front porch so far as results go. He was careful not to be specific or forthright but to depend on his supporters to make the commitments. He could not be expected to go over to the left of the Democrats, and his own party would not have followed him had he done so. His position was to the right of Mr. Truman's, and Mr. Truman's position was anchored firmly in the middle of the new principle of government. Actually Mr. Dewey had no principle. He was simply trying to get the voters to shoulder Mr. Truman out of his position, and the stubborn voters flatly refused to do it.

Nor can the Republicans find an alibi for their last defeat in the personality of the opposition. The two candidates were just about a hoss and a hoss in personality, though the man from New York is a little slicker than the man from Missouri. Certainly Mr. Truman's personality is not such as to give the opposition an inferiority complex. The people voted on the issues and not on the men.

President Truman's victory was so spectacular as to obscure important aspects of the last election. Had Mr. Truman been elected on personality, he might have found himself faced with a Republican Congress and with Republican governors in control of a majority of the states. The inarticulate but interested voters admired his courage and the desperate fight he made with practically nobody in his corner, but they did not vote for him through sympathy. They had simply had enough of the other party as it exhibited its program in the Eightieth Congress to know that they wanted no more of it. Wanting a modern government that will deal with modern problems and not an antiquity, they went to the polls and swept the little champ back to the White House, and with him they sent Democrats to Congress and into the governors' offices across the nation.

Of course we need two parties to debate the issues of the nation. It seems from our own political history that the debate swings around a principle. One party thinks the principle is right and the other is equally convinced that it is in great part wrong. The party that originates the principle and establishes it, does so in a national crisis. If the nation comes out of the crisis, the principle is accepted and the people go on supporting it for a long time, say until it runs into a crisis. This is what happened to the Republican party after the Civil War; it is what happened to the Democratic party in the Great Depression. During the time of trust and confidence in the principle, the party that originated it and put it into effect has a tremendous advantage, such an advantage that it may get away with almost anything. As long as the principle being acted upon works, it is almost impossible to dislodge the party that discovered it. This the Republicans need to bear in mind. They are going to have thin pickings until the present principle of developing a social state has failed. They are going to beat their brains out trying to get the attention of voters. They are going to quarrel, divide, complain, and criticize.

Their plight is like that of the man who had spent his life preparing for the future. It was his obsession. He awoke one morning on his birthday and began to appraise himself, his age which was considerable, his hair which had grown thin, his muscles a little flabby now, and his bones which seemed to have sand grains in the joints. After some contemplation, he struck his hand to his head and exclaimed, "Heavens! This is my future!" And so it may be for a considerable period with the Republican party.

TOWARD PARTY GOVERNMENT *

It is interesting but not at all curious that in his very perceptive book, *Congress on Trial,* Professor Burns should devote considerable attention to political parties. As he clearly demonstrates, parties are so closely interwoven with government that any discussion of a political system that neglects them is unrealistic. Our government is, to a large degree, a reflection of our parties, and our parties are what we make them. From this springboard Professor Burns launches a case for party government. Is the adoption of party government necessary or feasible in view of historical factors and constitutional limitations? Would not party government do violence to the separation of powers principle? May not the major defects of our parties be corrected without overhauling the present system?

The story goes that Daniel Webster's father Ebenezer, near death in a town given to anti-Federalist sentiments, begged to be carried back to New Hampshire, saying, "I was born a Federalist, I have lived a Federalist, and

---

* James MacGregor Burns, *Congress on Trial* (Harper, 1949), pp. 193–98. Copyright, 1949, by Harper and Brothers.

I won't die in a Democratic town." Later generations are inclined to scoff at such a show of party spirit. Many of us switch from party to party as blithely as we change fashions in clothes. We laud the statesmen who rise above party allegiances and we sneer at the faithful party hack. We pride ourselves on being "independents." The average American feels more loyal to the Elks or to the Legion than to his political party.

The argument . . . is that only by vitalizing our two-party system, by playing national party politics more zealously, and by centralizing control of our parties, will Americans be able to stabilize presidential leadership and foster teamwork in the federal government. The question, in short, is the prospect of party government in America—meaning by party government a condition where centralized and disciplined parties formulate national policy on key issues and use governmental machinery to carry out that policy. This term is used in contradistinction to presidential government, congressional government, and cabinet government, not one of which, it has been suggested above, can safely and effectively master the problems arising in an era of chronic crisis.

The Need for Extra-Constitutional Reform

Ideally, party government works as follows: As a result of winning a majority of the votes, one of two rival political parties wins power. Its platform is attuned to national needs. Its leaders are responsible to a majority of the people. The head of the party becomes President, and other high-ranking party officials assume key positions in Congress, in the Cabinet, and in state government. A group of national politicians tries to translate majority will into majority rule, and in doing so puts the general interest above special interest.

Since power is centered in the party leadership, there can be no shirking or concealing of responsibility. If affairs go badly, the voters know whom to blame. The opposition party, which has not shared power and which therefore has no responsibility for any unhappy turn of events, is waiting to take over the government if the next election gives it a majority of the votes.

Such a system has obvious advantages. It allows leadership. It gives responsibility. It harmonizes the various branches of government. It is simple in theory and in practice. Above all, it stresses national needs.

Party government has special meaning for Americans because of our urgent need of a way to stabilize the power of the Chief Executive without stunting him. If presidential power is now "dangerously personalized," the President must be made to share his authority with others. But he cannot share it with congressional leaders, cabinet members, or even the

Vice-President when these officials are blinded by particularist concerns of one kind or another, as they often are. He can, however, share that power with other party leaders who are as eager and able to take a national view of national problems as the President himself. He can do so without losing the flexibility of action that must remain in the White House. For the party leaders cannot check the President legally or constitutionally, but they can erect a "Stop" sign or at least a "Go Slow" sign that will have some chance of thwarting rash adventures.

And even more. By keeping in contact with his party, the President can more easily stay abreast of majority feeling during the years between elections. The party, with its tens of thousands of committees reaching into every corner of the land, has the potential machinery for grasping and analyzing shifts in public opinion across the nation. The party mobilizes and organizes political sentiment; the President influences majority opinion but he is also deeply influenced by it. In this sense the party is the institutionalization of majority action.

The best hope for the future of American politics and government lies in a fruitful union between presidential power and party government. The President needs the discipline involved in working with other national party politicians. He also needs their aid and expertise, especially as new problems emerge between elections. The party in turn requires presidential leadership to keep it alive to national needs, and it benefits from the capacity of the great President to draw the various elements of the party into some kind of harmony. In short, successful party government must have a sizable admixture of presidential government.

Although they have never seen it in action, American thinkers have often dreamed of party government. Thus Henry Jones Ford wrote many years ago of the "cardinal principle of American politics" that "party organization continues to be the sole efficient means of administrative union between the executive and legislative branches of government, and . . . whatever tends to maintain and perfect that union makes for orderly politics and constitutional progress; while whatever tends to impair that union, disturbs the constitutional poise of the government, obstructs its functions, and introduces an anarchic condition of affairs full of danger to all social interests."

More recently Finletter has written: "The national parties should be the force in this country which holds down the organized groups to their proper functions. They should be the link between the Executive and Congress which enables the government to work in the national interest and against the pressures of local interests, organized or not."

The central issue of American politics today is whether our parties can sustain party government in the above sense. Certainly they cannot do so in their present form. Party government assumes the existence of centralized, cohesive parties like the British ones. Ours are quite the reverse. . . . They cannot hold their lines in Congress on public policy. They cannot keep organized minorities in line. They give little help to their candidates at election time and they cannot discipline office-holders after election.

Our parties show many baffling traits. They form a web over the entire country, touching almost every town and hamlet; yet they are so weak at the top as to be virtually headless. They are many decades old and their names are on everyone's lips; yet as organizations they operate in a shadowland. It is safe to say that nine out of ten voters do not have a clear notion of the make-up of their local, state, and national party organizations; how party officials are appointed or elected; how the electoral machinery works. The major parties probably have more members than any other organization in the country; yet on important national policies they knuckle under to organized groups a third their size. Like the brontosaurus of old, the major party looms large on the landscape through sheer bulk, but it is often at the mercy of the more agile creatures around it.

Nevertheless, the American party system can be strengthened. It is raw material that can be worked with. Why?

In the first place, no impassable constitutional barrier stands in the way. It is true that our parties have had to adjust to the division of power between the nation and the states, and to the separation of power among President, Congress, and Judiciary. But our governmental forms have also had to conform to our party system. The American people through their parties have established a different order from that contemplated by the spirit or the letter of the Constitution. The parties have tremendous advantages in this sense. Since they are not constitutional organs, they can be changed without amendment. At the same time, they can influence what government is, as well as what government does.

Whether one is dealing with the one-party system of Soviet Russia, with the multi-party system of France or Italy, with the tightly knit two-party system of Great Britain, or with the decentralized two-party system of the United States, he finds that the nature of the parties is the key to the nature of the government. The parties are what we make them; the government, in part, is what we make the parties.

Another hopeful factor is the stamina and adaptability of our political forms. Our parties have had to make their own way from the beginning. The Constitution left no place for them. Most of the Framers feared the effects of "faction," and they set up machinery to dampen down those effects. Even Andy Jackson, some years before he became President, warned Monroe against "the monster called 'party spirit.'"

The people and the politicians, acting outside the Constitution, forged their own political arrangements out of their own needs and aspirations. Their job is not finished; we have reached a condition of equipoise where a jerry-built party structure has linked arms with a faulty system of government. To strengthen the party system involves an act of will on the part of politicians and voters today rivaling the earlier efforts of our forefathers.

An important consolidating force in the party is the President. His part in giving direction and meaning to the party in power, and indirectly to the opposition, can hardly be exaggerated. He serves as a polarizing element in national politics. As *de facto* leader of the party, he directs it through the national chairman. Planks of the national platform that otherwise would be obscure, he defines and projects before the public eye. He partially offsets the divisive effects of control of the party by scores of state and local organizations.

In trying to elect him the party gathers its far-flung forces every four years in a massive effort that does something to knit the party together, if only temporarily. President and party are essential to each other; because he must keep his party's support he is subject to a measure of party discipline; because the party needs his leadership it submits to a measure of national control.

Party government can be had. The question is whether the American people are willing to take the drastic steps necessary to create it.

POLITICAL PARTIES AND THE NEED FOR MORAL LEADERSHIP *

> In the nature of a rejoinder to the preceding "Toward Party Government," the following selection supports the present two-party system. The substance of the essay is that only through loosely knit and flexible parties can national unity be preserved and the rigidity of the separation of powers be overcome. The remedy for the defects of parties lies in increasing the moral leadership in the parties themselves. Is this proposal overly simple? Does not the proposition ignore the fact that good machinery is also necessary and that some methods of procedure are better than others?

The President is not responsible to the Congress, nor is his Cabinet. He is responsible directly to the people, but he is held accountable for his ac-

* "The Political Parties." Reprinted from the February, 1951, issue of *Fortune*, pp. 88–89, by special permission of the Editors. Copyright, 1951, Time, Inc.

tions only once every four years. He may, consequently, retain in power Cabinet officers who do not have the confidence of the people. In the meantime Congress may—and frequently does—become hostile to him as well as to members of his Cabinet.

This governmental system has its virtues, but it is characterized by a certain rigidity. If the American parties were divided into a party of the left and a party of the right, the result would be violent swings of policy as the powerful office of Chief Executive changed hands. Moreover, owing to the fact that Cabinet officers are appointed, no such thing as a coalition government is possible in the U.S. This was illustrated in 1940 when President Roosevelt appointed the Republican Henry L. Stimson as Secretary of War and the Republican Frank Knox as Secretary of the Navy. The move was theoretically shrewd, designed to enlist Republican support for the Roosevelt preparedness measures. But as soon as Messrs. Stimson and Knox moved into the Roosevelt Cabinet they lost their power within their own party—indeed in a fit of somewhat childish pique, the Republican leaders "read them out" of it. Were the conventional right-left split to give rise to several parties, under this rigid system orderly government would become almost impossible. Whichever party won, the presidency would win all the executive power, even though it represented only a small plurality of the voters.

Since flexibility is not provided by the American governmental structure it has to be provided by the parties themselves. Each party must have— and under healthy conditions always has had—a "right" wing and a "left" wing. The reason why the Democratic party appears to be the party of the "left" is that under Franklin Roosevelt the progressive or "liberal" wing of the party (the New Deal) won power within the party, and thereafter dictated the party's policies. It did not, however, eliminate the right wing of the party, which struggled against the New Deal throughout Roosevelt's administration, and which is still struggling—and even gaining ground. The situation within the Republican party is precisely the opposite. Here the conservative wing has been dominant. The progressive wing, however, has not been eliminated—indeed, with Wendell Willkie, it succeeded in capturing for a time the leadership of the party.

It is through this internal struggle that the American political party achieves its highest function, namely, that of national integration. The U.S., as has been so often pointed out in this issue, is a diverse land, with many different sectional interests competing against each other, many different popular groups, many racial strains. In terms of pure political theory all this should be integrated in the Congress where the people are officially represented. In practice it does not work out that way. For the most part the Congress solves these conflicts through logrolling, trad-

ing off one interest against the other, and sometimes yielding to overwhelming pressure. The political party, on the other hand, integrates in a positive way. To survive as a national party it must enlist the loyalty of at
least a minority of every group in every section. These organizational
minorities all have a common purpose: to win power at election time. To
this end sectional interests may have to be subordinated within the party.
It must nominate leaders and formulate policies that the people will follow.
And in doing so it integrates a vast number of conflicting interests in an
organic way.

Thus, the American political party has evolved into an almost ideal instrument for the type of government that Americans have chosen to adopt.
To compensate for the inherent rigidity of that government, it has enormous flexibility. When in power it must carry the burden of national
policy. When out of power its flexibility enables it to do a great deal of
experimenting. Thus it is possible for California to overindulge (under
a Republican governor) in state pensions and social security, without committing the whole party to an advocacy of the resulting deficits. The successful experiments are copied in other states and finally become official
doctrine.

The weakness of the American political party, on the other hand, is the
logical complement of its strength. The very fact that it is primarily an
organization of men and women bent on seizing power and patronage
leads to almost intolerable abuses. This is especially true, as Lord Bryce
noted, in the large cities, where the party machines, relieved of any responsibility toward national or even state policies, are free to go their own way
as pure power organizations. Such political "machines" exist to win votes
—and for almost literally nothing else. Corruption under those circumstances is inevitable. Then, in the national elections, the vote-getting power
of the machines is used to amass votes for a presidential candidate, who
is thus forced to tolerate among his own supporters a level of political morality that, were he to practice it himself, would result in his impeachment.

Even where actual "machines" are absent, the emphasis of the American
party system tends to fall much too heavily on vote getting at the expense
of matters of principle. One result is that local leadership deteriorates
in character, and with it the caliber of political debate. Orators resort
to a kind of emotional symbolism, hurling at the opposite party charges
that could not possibly be substantiated, even if anyone knew what they
really meant. The standard Republican attack on the Democrats as "socialists" is a case in point. On the other side, labor's attack on the Taft–Hartley
Act as a "slave labor law" is for the most part equally emotional.

The result of these abuses has been a decline in the prestige of both parties and what looks like a rise in the size of the "independent" vote. In the 1950 election, for example, the voters of New York City elected by overwhelming majorities a Republican Governor, a Democratic Senator, and a Mayor who was running on a hastily concocted Experience party ticket all by himself. Connecticut elected two Democratic Senators and a Republican Governor. Ohio elected a Republican Senator and a Democratic Governor. And so forth. Increasingly, people are complaining that the parties are corrupt, that they are not needed anyway, and that if they want to survive they must choose better leaders.

People who make this complaint are not always clear as to what they mean. It is plain foolishness to advocate, as many ill-informed Americans do, a rearrangement of the parties along doctrinaire lines . . . , both parties accept a set of principles and beliefs, . . . the Proposition and the System. The idea that one party could be for the Proposition and the other party against the Proposition would signal the end of American democracy as it has thus far developed. The task of the political parties, on the contrary, is to apply the Proposition, to concern themselves with its evolution, to reinterpret it courageously and with imagination. When either party deviates too far from this course, it is sure to fall.

What the critics of the parties really mean—or, at any rate, what they ought to mean—is something different. The parties have fallen into disrepute, not because they lack issues, but because they have failed to provide moral leadership. The constant temptation for candidates and officeholders is to listen to the counsels of compromise and political expediency—to mention nothing worse—that emanate constantly from the "organization crowd." The American people are so fed up with this that they will flock by the million to the support of candidates who dare to defy their own organization. The case of Mayor Impellitteri of New York City is a spectacular example; and in Pennsylvania, James Duff, who challenged and overthrew the Grundy machine, was swept into the Senate by an overwhelming majority. Yet outright defiance of the organization is not necessary. The people will follow a man who has moral convictions and who is not afraid to utter them. In 1950 Senator Taft was even able to capture some of the labor vote, which was supposedly solid against him, because he stood uncompromisingly for his principles.

Moral leadership in political affairs, in short, is the peculiar obligation of the American political party, transcending even parliamentary leadership. An American party must be prepared to nominate and back men who have beliefs, and who have also the courage and skill to convince others of their validity. For it is by such beliefs, sometimes reached through great struggle, sometimes uttered at great political risk, that the American Proposition has been successfully implemented, generation after generation. And deep in their hearts the American people know it is only in this way, and through the courage of such men, that the Proposition can endure.

Problem 8: Is the Office of the President Equal to the Job?

President Polk in a message to Congress wrote: "The President represents in the Executive department the whole people of the United States as each representative of the legislative department represents portions of them." Some eighty years later ex-President Coolidge commented that "the President comes more and more to stand as the champion of the rights of the whole country." Yet many Presidents have been unable to live up to this precept. During certain periods of American history effective presidential leadership has been frustrated by an all-powerful Congress.

Critics maintain that this condition is inherent in the system. They contend that the gap between the Executive and Congress is so wide that every vigorous program is bound to flounder on the rocks of congressional obstructionism. Moreover, the office has other deficiencies. The Executive is an isolated individual, lacking sufficient staff, and burdened by ceremonial duties and administrative detail. Under these conditions the President cannot do the job required of him. Proponents reply that these criticisms apply in large measure only to the occupant of the office, since, in Wilson's words: "The President is at liberty, both in law and conscience, to be as big a man as he can." They further note that the institution has functioned well, especially in times of emergency when the presidential system responds very quickly to new conditions. Furthermore, any other procedure would unwisely concentrate power and authority. Reorganization of the Executive's office is much more feasible as a solution to the shortcomings that do exist than are attempts at reconstruction along the lines of an untried system.

The discussion of the Presidency has two facets: the role of the President in his relations with Congress and the part that the Executive plays as an administrator. Alfred Steinberg's article, "A Day in the Life of the President," provides a background setting. Harold J. Laski then points the spotlight of criticism at the office. Pendleton Herring, in "The Strength of the Presidency," summarizes the benefits in the current allocation of power. As a suggested alternative, Henry Hazlitt argues for the parliamentary system, and Charles A. Beard gives the other side in "The Parliamentary System Is Not the Answer." Finally, Herman Miles Somers discusses the President as a political administrator and suggests workable reforms for this phase of the Executive's job.

A Day in the Life of the President *

Something of the magnitude of the President's task can be seen in this account of a typical presidential workday. Small wonder that the President's Committee on Administrative Management and the recent Hoover Commission unanimously agreed that the President needs assistance. Small wonder, too, that many observers regard the office as an impossible burden for one individual. Who can stand the pace? Or, more pointedly, who can rise above routine activity and provide the type of executive leadership that the times and the country demand?

Woodrow Wilson declared as long ago as 1907 that only "prudent athletes" should be considered for the presidency, and Franklin D. Roosevelt told a friend prior to World War II that "the detail of this job is killing me." Harry Truman, who has the preposterous burden of signing his name 600 times a day, on an average, just to keep current with the paper work required of him by law, is today an understandably grim, tired person most of the time.

The President usually sleeps six and one half hours at night, arising at 5:30 A.M.—a habit dating back to his days as a farmer. His bedroom on the second floor of Blair House, diagonally across Pennsylvania Avenue from the rebuilding White House, is simply furnished. Mr. Truman's bed is a four-poster, and the first thing be sees upon awakening is an assortment of pictures of preceding Presidents, including his hero, Andrew Jackson, who also had lots of troubles, a low boiling point and a gift for inelegant invective. . . .

The President's early-morning reading—a combination of headline skimming and quick but intensive absorption of selected items, including all mentions of himself—begins with the *Washington Post*. This was the

---

* Alfred Steinberg, "How Harry Truman Does His Job," *Saturday Evening Post,* March 3, 1951, pp. 18–19, 98–100.

newspaper, usually friendly to the Administration, which published the now-famous criticism of Margaret Truman's latest Washington concert. On that particular occasion, Mr. Truman didn't even wait until he reached his office to prepare his denunciatory letter. Without breakfast, mourning the death only thirteen hours earlier of Charlie Ross, and with both Clement Attlee and a military catastrophe on his hands, he wrote the note in a wrathful longhand on a White House memo pad in the Blair House study. He wrote as a father who adores his only child, and he also wrote as a man with the endless problems of the world on his shoulders who had, at last, found a concrete target.

If the *Washington Post* fails to set his circulation racing, the next paper he looks at certainly will. This is the *Washington Times-Herald,* Col. Robert R. McCormick's contribution to public enlightenment in darkest Washington, and strident little sister of the Colonel's better-known *Chicago Tribune.* Westbrook Pegler and George Sokolsky, enthusiastic nonadmirers of the President, are the *Times-Herald's* featured columnists, and if they fail to irritate Mr. Truman, the anonymous editorial writer is certain to fill the void. One recent morning, for example, the latter referred casually to the President as a "dishonest nincompoop," and urged him to resign the Presidency without further shilly-shallying.

The *Baltimore Sun, The New York Times* and the *New York Herald Tribune* round out the President's paper reading before he leaves Blair House at seven o'clock for his morning constitutional. Secret Service men pant at his side as Mr. Truman strides off two brisk miles at the old infantry pace of one hundred and twenty steps to the minute. He never follows the same route two days in a row—a concession to the nervous Secret Service—and early-rising Washingtonians are likely to bump into him almost anywhere. One morning the President interrupted his hike to walk down a stairway leading from Memorial Bridge and, on a lower landing, found the bridge tender with his breakfast spread before him on a newspaper. The President told him to finish eating and carried on a general discussion of life with him until he had done so. Then the bridge tender, Charles Barnhill, forty-five, showed Mr. Truman how to work the draw-bridge machinery.

The hike ends at the White House, where the President takes a ten-minute swim in the indoor pool in the west terrace. When he first became President, Mr. Truman swam late in the afternoon with members of his staff. Today he swims alone, no longer trying for twelve laps—one fourth of a mile—but still a curious sight with his unorthodox side stroke and head held high to keep the water off his glasses. After the swim, the President has a rubdown and weighs himself. . . .

Mrs. Truman and daughter Margaret, when she is in town, join the President for breakfast in Blair House at eight o'clock. When his family is out of town, he eats alone. Mr. Truman is a listless eater, unwilling to try new dishes. By 8:30 he is ready to cross Pennsylvania Avenue again to enter his office. With sight-seers and crowds of brief-case-carrying Government servants now on the avenue, he makes the trip in a heavily guarded limousine. . . .

Mr. Truman is so concerned with time and punctuality that he has six desk calendars, four clocks on his desk, three clocks on the wall, and a wrist watch. His telephone—National 1414, extension 32—sits precisely in the center of the desk when he is using it. When he is not telephoning, the instrument is out of reach on the far left corner of his vast mahogany working space. . . .

From 8:30 to nine o'clock, the President dictates personal correspondence to Miss Rose Conway, his private secretary. Many of his letters are only one or two sentences long. These include letters which go out without staff checking, leading at times to strange results, as in the case of the Marine Corps and John L. Lewis mash notes. Incidentally, Mr. Truman tried to get Miss Conway a raise in pay not long ago and was blocked by a Civil Service ruling that she was already getting the maximum for a Government secretary. The President finally solved this bureaucratic contretemps by making Miss Conway an administrative assistant in the President's office at a considerably higher salary. From nine to 9:30, Mr. Truman works on memoranda for the White House staff and Cabinet, and dictates his more official correspondence.

Gen. Omar N. Bradley, chairman of the Joint Chiefs of Staff, enters his office at 9:30 to brief him on the military situation, using a long pointer and a map set up on an easel about five feet from the President's desk. General Bradley is known for his soldierly seriousness, but one day when things were going well, he called Mr. Truman's attention to a dot of an island off the Korean coast which he explained had been captured that morning by twenty American soldiers.

"Now why did they ever bother to do that?" the President inquired.

"I really don't know unless the boys discovered there was a brewery on that island," Bradley said.

Shortly before ten o'clock, Mr. Truman's assistants congregate in the office next door to the President's which is occupied by Matthew J. Connelly, his appointments secretary. Virtually on the second that most of his seven clocks and his wrist watch point to ten A.M., Mr. Truman opens the door to Connelly's room and waves his staff into the presidential office. Mr. Truman never summons anyone by using a buzzer. If he wants to discuss something with an assistant at any time other than that set aside for the staff meetings, he will call him on the telephone or pop into his office in person.

Staff meetings are informal. In happier times, the President referred to his assembled helpers as "my class," and began the forty-five-minute session with a jocular "Are you ready, students?" The opening gambit today is more businesslike. Mr. Truman's aides seat themselves around his desk, while he opens a brown leather portfolio edged with tabs on which the names of the staff members are written. He flips through the folder first, handing out individual assignments, newspaper clippings or whatever else he may have put aside for reference to an assistant. Then he calls upon each staff member for a discussion of his problems of the day, beginning with the press secretary on his left. . . .

Staff meetings are delayed until eleven o'clock on Mondays, so the President can meet at ten with the Big Four, his congressional leaders. These include Vice President Alben W. Barkley, Speaker of the House Sam Rayburn, Senate Majority Leader Ernest W. McFarland and House Majority Leader John W. McCormack. At these meetings the President works from a staff-prepared memorandum noting which legislation is up at the moment, its urgency, probable amendments, who might raise objections, and the likely vote. Like the staff meetings, these sessions are informal. On a personal basis, they are also usually amiable, in spite of Mr. Truman's innumerable irritations and frustrations with Congress.

After the staff meetings, James S. Lay, Jr., executive secretary of the National Security Council, and Rear Admiral Sidney W. Souers, who formerly held Lay's job and now acts as consultant, brief the President on both national and international security problems. Then the President goes over his list of appointments with Connelly to see who is on tap for the day.

The President sets aside fifteen minutes for each appointment, and visitors have stayed overtime on not more than half a dozen occasions in the last five years. On most of these his guest was a reminiscing World War I veteran. Unlike President Roosevelt, who dominated most conversations, Mr. Truman is a listener. Visitors are asked to present a written memorandum on the subject to be discussed, and are required to do most of the talking, while Mr. Truman makes marginal notes on the memo which has just been handed to him. If action is required, he refers these annotated memos to the proper White House assistant or Government department. This system not only shortens appointments but lessens the drain on Mr. Truman from the endless contacts which have withered every President since Woodrow Wilson, with the possible exception of Calvin Coolidge.

Sometimes the system works so well—when the visitor, too, is a listener instead of a talker—that the appointment is embarrassingly brief. Mr. Truman bridges the gap by walking over to a large globe, which sits in front of a fireplace beneath a portrait of George Washington. On this globe, which General Eisenhower used in his World War II headquarters, the President points out the current trouble spots in the world, and thus extends the visit. Whatever may be left of the allotted fifteen minutes after the caller departs—Mr. Truman no longer walks to the door with every visitor because aides told him it was undignified—the President spends in working on the endless papers which require his personal signature, or in seeing intimates, such as Chief Justice Fred M. Vinson, who come and go unannounced.

Appointment hours generally are from eleven A.M. to one P.M., and from three P.M. to four. On an average, the President sees about 100 persons a week. Most appointments are made through Connelly, although personal friends may deal with the President directly, by mail or telephone, in arranging to see him. Certain appointments are fixtures, such as the 12:30 spot on Mondays and Thursdays with the Secretary of State, on Tuesday with the Secretary of Defense, and on Wednesday with the chairman of the National Security Resources Board. The President has a party-politics session on Wednesdays at 3:30. Press conferences are also usually held on Thursday, one week at 10:30 A.M. and the next week at four P.M. Cabinet meetings are held at four o'clock on Tuesday, and at ten A.M. on Friday, the latter again delaying the daily staff meeting until eleven.

Whole delegations often descend upon the President in his office. They may be Gold Star Mothers, or exchange teachers on their way to European schools, or visiting Elks. Generally, these occasions are three-ring circuses. If the weather is bad, scores of eager persons may crowd into his office like sardines to stare at him for a few minutes. Otherwise, the delegation files through the President's office while he stands in front of his desk, shaking hands with each visitor, and following the last person in line to the Rose Garden, outside his office, for a few general words of praise before sending them on their way.

When his morning appointments are out of the way, Mr. Truman returns to Blair House by automobile for lunch at one P.M. . . .

Before the Korean crisis, Mr. Truman had the Cabinet to lunch at Blair House every Monday. In those days, formal Cabinet meetings were held only once a week, on Friday. Now the Tuesday and Friday Cabinet sessions are all business, and the Monday lunch is eliminated. Cabinet meetings are attended by the nine Cabinet officers; by W. Stuart Symington, chairman of the National Security Resources Board; by W. Averell Harriman, his foreign-policy adviser; by Defense Mobilizer Charles E. Wilson; by Vice President Alben W. Barkley, Presidential Assistant John R. Steelman, and Connelly, the appointments secretary. Others are invited to attend from time to time; for example, General Bradley may be summoned to explain the military situation.

No minutes are kept of Cabinet meetings, and Connelly's presence is primarily for insurance in case Mr. Truman should have trouble remembering some detail later. In view of Mr. Truman's extraordinary memory, this is probably superfluous. The President remembers his high-school Latin perfectly, and can quote at length from Byron and Longfellow. One of his specialties is quoting Scripture to visiting clergymen. He has countless good-natured arguments with William D. Hassett, his venerable correspondence secretary, over details of history, Biblical quotations and poetry.

The Cabinet room is dominated by an immense table, an elongated octagon which looks vaguely like a huge coffin. The President sits in the center, on the window side of the room, facing the Vice President. Cabinet officers occupy the President's side and the ends of the table. Two cabinet members and the other high officials present are on the Vice President's side. The President has the only telephone in the room—extension 33—and occasionally receives calls during the Cabinet meetings.

Although the atmosphere is somewhat more formal, Mr. Truman follows much the same routine as that used for White House staff meetings. First he discusses the memoranda before him, then he calls on those present, in rotation. No votes are taken, and all decisions are left to the President. These meetings serve Mr. Truman primarily as a top-level listening post and as a forum for discussion of general Administration policy. They usually do not cover the individual problems of the participants. A Cabinet member will lag behind, at the close of the meeting, to discuss his department's business or may meet with the President by appointment later. Occasionally, Mr. Truman will set up a committee of several Cabinet members to investigate a specific problem. Sometimes he turns over domestic problems impinging upon the activities of more than one department to John Steelman for settlement.

Since the war crisis, most Cabinet meetings have held to a somber and serious tone. Occasionally, however, when things get too quiet or oppressive the President may lean back suddenly and say, "Barkley, tell us a story." The Vice President never fails him. Soon the entire room will be roaring with laughter, and the President always laughs the loudest. For a brief moment, the burdens of the world are set aside.

Such respites are all too few. By six o'clock, when the President is ready to return to Blair House for the evening, he may have spent the one or two hours following his last official appointment of the day at a score of different tasks. Some crisis is invariably at hand, which may require a hurried conference with the Secretary of State or the Secretary of Defense. Often there are speeches or public statements to be gone over with Charles S. Murphy, the presidential counsel who serves as his principal "ghost," and with others who may be called in to assist. And always there is the never-ending pile of papers to be signed—nominations to various Federal jobs, military commissions, pardons, statutes, documents in triplicate, documents *ad infinitum*.

When he leaves his oval office in the White House, for yet another limousine ride across the street, the President carries a brief case bulging with the papers which he wryly calls his "homework." The pile generally measures about six inches in depth. Once he is back in Blair House, the President likes a bourbon or two, and dinner at seven o'clock. Again he eats rather lightly and without much gusto. Except for occasions when he is giving a dinner in honor of a visiting dignitary—at Blair House if there are less than sixteen guests, or at the Carlton Hotel if there are more than sixteen—the President dines with his family or alone. By eight o'clock or shortly thereafter, he is back in the Blair House study, making notes on his working papers, drawing up memoranda, preparing for the grueling day which tomorrow certainly will be.

Shortly before his death, Charlie Ross told me of an occasion not long ago when the President summoned him and five others to Blair House after dinner to put the finishing touches on a public statement the President planned to make. As the six men filed into the study, the President looked up wearily from the pile of papers on his desk and straightened the position of the brief case in front of him.

"This room," Mr. Truman said sadly, "is just like the one over at the White House, except that this one is square."

In view of his burdens, it is understandable why the President's favorite story today is one which goes as follows:

A President was going over detailed matters of state with his staff. He happened to glance out the window just as the Vice President sauntered by.

"There goes the Vice President," he said, "with nothing on his mind but the health of the President."

THE AMERICAN EXECUTIVE *

Harold J. Laski, a brilliant political commentator, sets forth in considerable detail the structural weaknesses of the American political system. Essentially, Professor Laski believes, Americans are applying eighteenth-century institutions to the government of a twentieth-century democracy. Nowhere, according to Laski, is the absence of adequate governmental machinery more obvious than in the office of the President. Here the separation of powers between the President and the legislature creates antagonism, dissipates energy, and diverts responsibility. Although this article was written twenty-five years ago, Laski's discerning observations are still remarkably current.

Although many of Professor Laski's observations merit consideration, are not his conclusions too sweeping? Is not the office of the President the shadow of the man who occupies it? Does not the American Executive seem to rise to the exigencies of the situation in times of crisis and emergency?

. . . The Presidency is the most outstanding [institution of American government], for it has become the most powerful lever of authority there is in the modern world. Yet what is startling about its character is the haphazard way in which its occupant is chosen. An English Prime Minister serves a long apprenticeship before he reaches the pinnacle of a political career. Mr. Gladstone was thirty-five—Disraeli thirty years—in the House of Commons before he was so chosen; both had been for long years essential figures in public life whose qualities had long been tested in the House of Commons. Even Mr. MacDonald and Mr. Baldwin, who arrived at power through accident, had been members of Parliament for nearly twenty years. And each was able to retain office only on the exacting condition of being able to satisfy in debate a legislative assembly deliberately designed to maximize the consequence of his mistakes.

The American President is in no such position. No one knows who he is to be. He is only too often the product of a series of accidents in which what is most important is not his possession of quality or of ideas but public ignorance about him. He may well be quite unknown to the nation; he may even, like Mr. Roosevelt or President Coolidge, become President by the act of Heaven instead of by the choice of the American people. He has to assume the leadership of a party without, at least necessarily, being

* Harold J. Laski, *The Dangers of Obedience* (Harper, 1930). Copyright, 1930, by Harold J. Laski. Reprinted from *Harper's Magazine,* June, 1928, pp. 21–27.

trained to that delicate function. He has to influence a legislative assembly where each chamber is active and powerful; and, at the worst, he may have a majority in neither, or, at the best, be compelled to purchase acceptance of his policy by shifts and expedients which destroy its logic or weaken its application. He has never any assurance that his will must prevail. He lacks the exhilarating experience of defending his policy in the full light of day. He has not grown up in fellowship with the instruments he has to use; and the knowledge that a second term is almost certainly the maximum period of leadership does not make for that continuity of allegiance to him upon which the shaping of a great policy depends. He has even to gamble in a large degree upon the quality of his cabinet associates; and since they are rather his servants than his colleagues, he must inevitably bear the burden of their mistakes. Because, moreover, tradition has made the main embassies the reward of service in his election, he will be compelled to rely upon a diplomacy largely amateur in character; no American ambassador in Europe in 1914 had any previous experience of foreign affairs. He has to accept the personnel of Congress through which he must seek to work it; and, even then, he may find that the election in mid-term destroys the men whom he employs. Nor is this all. His period of office is so short that he has hardly become used to its exercise before he is driven to think of re-election; and if he is attracted by this notion, the price he must pay in complaisance and bargain will be well-nigh intolerable. And even if he is successful in forcing a policy upon Congress, he may well find that the exigencies of the spoils system, improved though it has been of recent years, fail to give him the instruments which might secure its successful application.

This, at least, is the logic of the system; and it is not an adequate defense of its deficiencies to urge that, despite them, men like Lincoln and Cleveland and Wilson have all been Presidents in the last seventy years. The fact is that anyone who studies in detail even the greatest of Presidential careers can hardly but be convinced that the necessary result of its environment is to minimize the best qualities of the occupant. He is fettered where he should be free; he is set apart where he should be in the midst. The absence of a clear organic relation between him and the legislature erodes his power while it destroys legislative responsibility. The rigidity of the system in which he is enclosed, the knowledge that his power is fugitive, the checks and balances which surround him on every hand, these serve only to illustrate the basic thesis that the separation of powers is the confusion of powers. No executive in the world disposes of greater authority; no executive, either, is so deliberately or perversely hampered in its fruitful exercise.

Nor is the position of an American cabinet member so much more attractive. It is only by presidential favor that he attains his office. Service to the party, outstanding ability, long experience in affairs, none of these things give him a prescriptive right to his position. He is a personal nomination of his master. He can make his policy effective only as he convinces the President on the one hand or placates Congress on the other. Resounding success may bring him no credit if President or Congress be jealous; and he has nothing to hope for from the prospect of resignation. Nothing, indeed, in the context of the cabinet has been more significant in recent years than the fact that Colonel House was able to do more than any member of the cabinet of his time without finding it necessary to assume office. For the work of a cabinet member is too little in the public view to count in any final way. Like a sudden tempest, they are come and gone. To occupy a place gives no lien on the gratitude of the party. The relationship to Congress is too tenuous and indirect to make it easy for them to impinge at all concretely on the public. A few men, like Mr. Hay and Mr. Root, have been significant in modern times; but, in general neither long experience nor outstanding qualities have been necessary for the tenure of cabinet office. The requirements of sectionalism, moreover, act as a deterrent to possible aspirants; the need to represent the West may check the ambition of youthful ability in New York or Cleveland long before cabinet office has become an object of conscious desire. The process of selection is far too haphazard; the prospect offers no such measure of reasonable certainty as parliamentary systems afford.

The power of the office, moreover, is only dubiously attractive as against some of the alternative political positions. A senator, for instance, need never resign in order to express dissent; and where he differs he can speak from one of the few political platforms in America to which attention is paid. But a cabinet member in retirement is, with rare exceptions, one of the unburied dead; and it is seldom that public opinion desires his emergence from the tomb.

Much, doubtless, would be altered if, as so many have desired, the cabinet member were to speak upon the floor of Congress. But, in that event, the whole character of the American system would necessarily change. For the articulation of the cabinet with the legislative assembly would compel the development in America of parliamentary government. To-day it is impossible to assess the qualities of a good American cabinet official. But if he were to sit in Congress, even to the limited extent that Chief Justice Taft has desired, the basis upon which he is selected would have to be completely changed. The ability to speak, the grasp of the subject, the knowledge of men, the instinct for administration, all these would become at once essential qualities. An outstanding secretary in Congress would immediately challenge the position of the President himself. Collective cabinet responsibility would automatically develop; and the resignation of a secretary whose authority in Congress was recognized would have important consequences upon the administration and its policy. The habit of debate in the House of Representatives would be restored, and, with its restoration, there would be both an increase in the significance of opposition, and a growth of public interest in the process of politics. A secretary charged with corruption, like Mr. Daugherty or Mr. Fall, would have to meet his accusers face to face—a fact which would, at a stroke, raise the level of political morality in America. Such a development as this, of course, is contrary to the whole tradition of the American system; and the possibility of its occurrence is obviously remote if only because, in a period of calm, peoples can rarely be persuaded to prepare themselves for times of storm. Yet it would be a service if an American statesman of authority were to remind his people how largely the present system was born of accident; had Madison and Jefferson taken a different view of Hamilton the lines of institutional evolution in America might have moved swiftly towards a neo-parliamentary form. . . .

But the American legislature must be judged less by its internal character than by its external relations. Here, of course, the Fathers proceeded upon assumptions which, in their own day, were judged exigent; and it is difficult to blame them for a construction which Montesquieu and Blackstone had canonized. Yet to-day it is supremely difficult for a foreigner to understand how Americans can remain satisfied with the institutional contact between executive and legislature. Here, once more, the system offends against every reasonable canon of political science. The separation of powers means that both legislature and executive must have fixed terms. Each lives a life in large part independent of the other, a life, indeed, that may well be conceived in antagonistic terms. Neither, as a result, has an interest in the other sufficient to secure a coherent and responsible policy. The legislature cannot get the executive which it wants; the executive is never sure of a legislature to its liking. The legislature never has its proper work to perform, which is to make a government to its liking; and the executive can never do its proper work of applying a policy which it fully approves. Each has a certain interest in the failure of the other. A President who always had his way with Congress would completely thwart its personality and purpose. A Congress which trampled on the President would—as the example of Andrew Johnson shows so well—make impossible a logical body of reasonable legislation. If either is to figure successfully in the public view, it must be at the expense of the other. And nothing that either can do will affect the life of the other. Each derives its power independently from the people, and each, whatever its character, must await the fixed period for a refreshment of power. The exigencies of party may, to some extent, mitigate the viciousness of the principle, but it can only obliterate in part the magnitude of the evil.

Nothing so well illustrates this radical defect as the realm of finance. In a parliamentary system, the minister has a plan and he stands or falls by it; if the legislature will not accept his proposals either it seeks a new government, or he demands a new legislature from the people. Whatever the choice, the result is at least logical and coherent. But in the American system nothing of the kind occurs. The minister makes his proposals; he seeks to placate the chairman of the appropriate committee. But the latter, however well intentioned, will not fully endorse the ministerial plan. He is himself, to begin with, a kind of quasi-minister, with a reputation to make. He has members on his committee who must be placated in turn. The member for Jacksonville thinks that something must be done for his constituents; and the member for Lincoln was promised a new Post Office. When the measure has been sufficiently mangled in the House, the process will be repeated in the Senate. A thousand competing interests, rarely related to the needs of efficient administration, must be conciliated. What emerges may even, as a total, look not unlike the original proposals of the executive; but it will be rare to find that the itemized details are the same. The truth is that for every subject, from finance downwards, the United States has at least three ministers; and neither the interest, nor the point of view, of any of them is identical. And since the cabinet lacks any collective responsibility, since the party caucus is far too big to give integration to policy, the result is a partial chaos in all that is done. The Presidential system, in brief, makes the executive and the legislature independent at exactly the point where dependence is required; and it secures their inevitable antagonism of interest where public policy requires a unity of interest. Nor can either, by the fact of independence, bring home responsibility effectively to the other. The power of punishment is outside in the nation; and the latter can speak, only not when the event requires, but when the constitution permits. But it may then be too late.

Other consequences of importance follow from this separation of Congress from the executive. No verdict can be sought from the people at a time when a verdict should be taken; and when the fixed epoch of judgment arrives events will have done much to obliterate the material upon which a verdict should be rendered. To an Englishman, for instance, it is literally incredible that no serious penalties should have been visited upon the Republican Party for the scandals of the Harding administration; but it was of the essence of the American system that when the American people, as here, was wanted, it could not be found. The result is an inevitable diminution of the popular interest in politics. The work of government requires a perspective of drama. The knowledge that grave error will precipitate a catastrophe keeps not only its members and the opposition alert, but also creates an active public opinion outside. For the latter feels that its influence may be creative. It may, by its approval or its antagonism, destroy the work in hand. It inquires into what is being done because it may affect what is being done. In America, that is only partially the case. Public opinion is special and interested rather than general and disinterested. It is a trade which wants a duty on the goods it manufactures, and the road to its wants is not through the channels of opinion but the avenue of the lobbyist. There is hardly a great subject of general import upon which an agitation in America can hope effectively to influence the government; for the maximum obtuseness on the part of the latter will not advance by one day the period of judgment at the polls.

Experience, in other words, seems to demand that the executive and the legislature should never be rivals for power. If that be the case, the mind of the public is confusion, and its confusion is destructive of its interest. Nor is that all. Their antagonism means that neither can perform its work effectively; each is continually tempted into regions outside its proper competence. A strong executive either reduces Congress to the level of a formless debating society, or is himself reduced by conflict to the position of an angry, if energetic man, declaiming, like Mr. Wilson in 1919, in a vacuum of futility. A weak executive becomes, almost necessarily, the creature of Congress; and there is never sufficient integration of purpose in the latter to make it a desirable master. The main business, indeed, of a legislature cannot be performed under American conditions. For that business is to find a suitable executive which the opposition can criticize, if occasion offers, to the point of defeat. A body of some four hundred and fifty men, like the House of Representatives, or even ninety-six, like the Senate, cannot hope to interfere successfully with the administrative process. The thing is too complex and delicate for anything more than general oversight. Yet it is to this that, under the given conditions, they are perpetually tempted; and the result is that they merely irritate and hamper where they should criticize to clarify. Nor can such a body legislate if it is able to substitute anyone's proposals for those submitted to it. Chaos is bound to result if the formal source of legislation is multiple in character. The executive ceases to be responsible because it does not create; and the legislature disavows responsibility because it does not apply. This has been the result of the American system, and increasingly the result in recent years. It is certainly difficult to reconcile its character with the possibility of adequate government.

A word is necessary upon what is the outstanding failure in the American federal scheme—the Vice Presidency. Tradition here has utterly undone the original purpose of the Constitution by reducing the Electoral College to a nullity. The result has been that every Vice President since the Civil War has been selected for reasons even worse, and more obscure, than those for which a President is chosen. No Vice Presidential candidate has ever been nominated with a view to his accession to the Presidency, though this has occurred on five occasions; and in each instance there has either, as with Andrew Johnson and (Theodore) Roosevelt, been a complete reversal of his predecessor's policy, or, as with Chester Arthur, an attitude of complete uncreativeness. The position, indeed, is utterly anomalous; and no experiment, like that of President Harding with Mr. Coolidge, which seeks to keep the Vice President in touch with policy has had any value. It is bad enough to have Presidents nominated systematically by interested wire-pullers; but it is surely worse to have Vice Presidents chosen by wire-pullers who are not even interested. Nothing in the working of the Constitution shows more lamentably the little respect of the system for the quality of men.

That is, indeed, throughout its capital defect. Granted the premise of the separation of powers, its formal aspects are logical enough. They are, indeed, politically dubious in the light of historic experience; but, more, they are politically vicious when they operate in the psychological penumbra of Jacksonian democracy. For the essential quality of the system is that it necessarily fails to elevate the temper of public life. The Presidency, of course, is an office as great as any in the gift of a democracy; but the terms of its conferment are, save by accident, fatal to its being occupied by the man who is fit to exercise its powers. To be a member of Congress, even to be a senator, will not often attract the highest talents in the Republic, for the simple reason that the separation of powers insulates the senator or representative from reasonable hope of any large and concrete achievement. The best members of the House of Commons go there because it is the highroad to the Cabinet, and a seat therein means that they put their hands upon a big machine of which the capacity for influence is enormous. The American legislator lacks almost entirely that prospect; and the American administrator is, on his side, similarly hampered by the knowledge that the machine he is to drive must run along a road largely indicated by others. There is not enough in such an outlook to attract from men of first quality their whole energy of mind throughout their lives. And it is, indeed, noteworthy that since the Civil War, at least, politics has rarely been the permanent vocation of the outstanding figures of American life. As with President Wilson, it has been the end of one career; or, as with Mr. Root and Mr. Hughes, it has been an interlude in another. There is, doubtless, the exceptional instance of Mr. Roosevelt;

but it is the general rule that the career of politician as a life-adventure is in America ample enough only to attract the men of routine mediocrity. . . .

———◆◆◆◆▶———

The Strength of the Presidency *

Franklin D. Roosevelt once described the office of the President as a "superb opportunity for reapplying, applying to new conditions, the simple rules of human conduct to which we always go back." Professor Herring accepts this concept and applies it to the relationship between the Executive and Congress. The President's power over Congress, Herring contends, is one of influence rather than authority. The power of the office depends upon the personality of the individual and the nature of the times. In periods of crisis the system adjusts very quickly; in intervals of tranquility the principle of divided power prevents undue concentration of power. Contrary to the charge that American political institutions are rigid and inflexible, governmental machinery is pliable and practical.

Does not the gap between the Executive and Congress paralyze leadership by preventing formulation of a vigorous program? Is Congress not encouraged under present conditions to invade the realm of the Executive and seek to conduct administration, a function that it is ill-fitted to perform?

Our government provides for an alternation of presidential and Congressional power. At times when authority and action are needed, the chief executive can be given scope; but at two-year intervals, when Congressional elections occur, the voters have the opportunity to judge his course. There is danger in this, to be sure, but we cannot preordain the success of popular government. We can, however, seek to improve the mechanics of legislative-executive relations so that if and when Congress impedes the president we may feel confident that this is in response to the will of the voters and not due to a lack of knowledge or to political trickery within Congress.

To generalize about a relationship so dynamic as that between Congress and the chief executive is dangerous. Congress is no fixed entity—it is a group of human beings reshuffled at regular intervals by popular elections

* Edward Pendleton Herring, *Presidential Leadership: The Political Relationships of Congress and the Chief Executive,* pp. 135–42. Copyright, 1940, by Pendleton Herring. New York: Rinehart and Company, Inc., 1940.

and shifted daily, even hourly, as different issues evoke varying reactions in the minds of individual members. The presidency is an office so colored by the personality of the incumbent and so affected by the current of the times that beyond the formal legal attributes of the position tremendous scope for self-expression remains. So in dealing with the president and Congress we face concomitant variables.

One of the most significant aspects of the relationships between the president and Congress is the ebb and flow of executive power. The increase in presidential authority comes as the result of popular demand for rapid and positive action. Powers are granted for temporary periods.

The need for fluidity in political relations can never safely be disregarded in the study of political institutions. There is no one best system. What is best suited for one set of conditions is ill adapted to others. To an extraordinary degree the relations between the chief executive and Congress are not spelled out in legal terms. Thus they become what the times and participants make them. Certain conditions clearly call for great power and initiative on the part of the president. Were his formal powers permanently increased to meet more easily the demands in times of crisis, would the nation rest content with such a concentration of authority in times of quietude? The answer may be made that the federal government has become committed to burdens of administration that call for positive leadership. There can be no doubt that the presidential office offers the only point for unified leadership. On the other hand, the whole concept of leadership in such terms is still tentative. Unless a rigid hierarchy is established and disciplined by adequate sanctions, leadership is not so much a matter of authority stretching downward as of loyalty extending upward. Even the general of an army, with all his means for control, is strongest when support is freely offered by each soldier, and the analogy is well applied to democratic government. Leadership is the obverse side of "followship" and fellowship. Hence the proposed strengthening of the presidential powers must be considered in relation to the circumstances which can make or break those powers.

In judging the adequacy of our institutions we are too inclined to look at the top and to ignore the substructure. Hopeful, some would make sweeping changes in the relations of Congress and the executive. Of greater intrinsic potentiality than such drastic and unpredictable changes are the minor changes that can be made further down, and that in their accumulated effect will preserve the structure and make it more effective at higher levels. This means multiplying the opportunities for each individual to contribute his own special skills and energies. These opportunities, however, cannot be written in terms of vague public spirit and the hollow hortatory ring of citizenship in the abstract, but of citizenship in terms of individual capacity and experience. In a society so constructed, the "checks and balances" at the top would have little use or meaning save as hypothetical safeguards against hypothetical abuses.

The fabric of democratic government can be pictured as composed of many strands. The strength of the fabric depends on the way in which these strands are interwoven. The integrity of these strands is best preserved not through isolation but through the skill with which they are related to the others: through the strength of the fabric as a whole the strength of each strand is maintained. As these threads are interwoven, different patterns emerge. In the intricacy and variety of these designs lies evidence of the imagination and vitality at work in our democratic society. Like the weavers of an Oriental carpet we sit close to our task, facing the seamy side of our designs and fingering the knots that make up the pattern.

But lack of perspective must not be allowed to detract from appreciation of the product. A broad view of the last few decades discloses a most impressive record of relatively peaceful political adjustment to great economic changes within the United States. Much of this adjustment has been piecemeal and unplanned, but advances have been made on a broad basis of consent. . . .

In constructing our Constitution the Founding Fathers built on the assumption that man is prone to abuse power. They drew their magic circles of separate areas of government and set up strong taboos against infringement. Under this institutional grant of power diverse economic systems have developed with monopolists, small shopkeepers, independent farmers, share croppers, trade-unionists and the unemployed jostling together and trying to argue their diverse ways into workable compromises. Tremendous racial variety, rapid industrial expansion, sporadic religious and intellectual ferment: in the face of this pluralism what assumptions of man and his objectives could be safely taken as the basis for an integrated political life?

By limiting the sphere of government, by incorporating within the Constitution itself fundamental safeguards to individual freedom and by centering in no single institution final authority, our political machinery has maintained an extraordinary amount of flexibility.

For everyday purposes the uncertain balance of power between the executive and the legislature has been of crucial significance. If the economic answers were clear and men were agreed in their objectives, we might with more confidence attempt to express through our governmental institutions unified power and direction. In the world as we find it there is much to

be said for a separation of powers which offers alternatives to a society uncertain of its direction but preferring to make its own mistakes rather than
relinquish this privilege to any single gang of rulers.

In our American striving for efficiency and our tendency to favor direct
action, we have at times been impatient with the conservatism of legal
institutions. Yet so great is the strength of tradition or inertia that usually
some way to achieve the desired goal has to be found short of tampering
with constitutional or other long-established legal forms. The cry of dictatorship raised against Franklin D. Roosevelt's "Court-packing" plan was
doubtless prompted by partisanship, and yet the widespread revulsion was
based on a habit of mind deeply ingrained. This profound and even
emotional conviction that the courts must not be interfered with is a factor
of the utmost importance in the continuity of constitutional government.
Legal conservatism says "Stop!—let political inventiveness look elsewhere
for ways and means." This puts a strain on ingenuity, but it removes
the pressure from deeply rooted institutions. Efficiency and action are important; but so is the continuity and stability of governmental institutions.

The extent to which a particular *modus operandi* should be institution-
alized is a matter for debate. Our Anglo-Saxon tradition tends to encourage an evolutionary approach. The governmental institutions that
have demonstrated the greatest lasting powers have not been those consciously established or syllogistically arranged.

In all the talk of separation of powers there is a great deal of artificiality.
In actual practice there must be a combination of the functions of legislating, executing, or adjudicating which in formal theory are supposed to
be kept distinct. In practice we have achieved this in sufficient degree to
weather an economic storm of awful magnitude and to face a world at war.

Why is it that the capacity of our system for action is so often underesti-
mated? One answer partially lies in the openness of our political squabbles. To the outsider, and even to ourselves, it is indeed a wonder that
out of so much loud talking and petty maneuvering decisions are made
and plans formulated. The matters that are quietly settled in parliamentary governments through discussion in cabinet meetings or in private
party conferences are paraded and debated in public here. Our political
leaders shout from one section of the country to another, from one end of
Pennsylvania Avenue to the other, and from the Senate to the House. If
we had well-articulated national party organizations, sternly disciplined,
if we had a national ministry formally and actually dealing with public
policy, if we had both legislative chambers held firmly in hand by this
ministry, we could proceed with greater decorum. Observers accustomed
to more orderly methods would then feel less dubious about the ability
of our institutions to meet the demands of the present day.

In actual practice our system can respond quickly to emergency conditions once the public is convinced of the need. Presidential leadership sustained by a united people has power for any crisis.

In a time of divided purposes Congress can so obstruct action that no president can have his will; but when the goal is clear the branches of government can move as one.

Our governmental structure does not condemn us to inaction and delay; we are able to transcend the institutional devices that provide for checks and balances and deliberation. In emergency we are free to improvise, but it does not follow from this that action and control are always to be given priority over deliberation and compromise.

Out of the infinite complexity of societal life, what phases are to be selected and built up into political institutions?

In our political institutions we have built on the assumption that concentrated power is dangerous in normal times. We have expressed our suspicion of strong leadership by hedging official position with various legal checks; but effective controls in time of emergency can be instituted with great rapidity. Once the general public realizes the need for united support behind the administration, the gap between Congress and the president is quickly closed. The concentration of authority is essential but its concentration in the wrong person is disastrous. This may be one consequence of a parliamentary system. It is a danger under our method of electing a president for a fixed term; but we have the great advantage of freshly surveying a wide field for selection. British leaders must serve a long apprenticeship to their parties. The fluidity of our system is a great safeguard.

The Parliamentary System *

Henry Hazlitt is only one of a number of distinguished writers who have suggested partial or complete adoption of the parliamentary system. In fact, so widely has this political institution been advocated that Don K. Price observes, "Perhaps only a psychoanalyst could explain America's peculiar nostalgia for the adolescent institution of the mother country."

Is the British success a ruling reason for adoption of the parliamen-

* Henry Hazlitt, *A New Constitution Now* (New York: Whittlesey House, 1942), pp. 19–22, 25–27.

tary system here? Do not transplanted institutions, like vegetables, often wither and die? Is the present American framework as rigid as the critics assert? Does the failure to provide for immediate elections mean that the presidential system is not responsible to public opinion?

The separation of the legislative and executive (and judicial) arms of the American Government . . . was not accidental but designed. It was based on a misunderstanding by the Founding Fathers of the real nature of the British Constitution—a misunderstanding not difficult to account for, because the modern British Constitution had not yet evolved. The real British executive at the time that our own Constitution was framed was not a prime minister chosen by the representatives of the people; he was still an hereditary monarch. George III chose and dismissed his own ministers. It was natural that our forefathers, when they came to frame our Constitution, should unconsciously regard the executive as an alien and outside force, and should come to think that liberty rested on the complete independence of the legislature from the executive. This natural inclination was strengthened by the influence of the theories of the French political philosopher Montesquieu, in his *Esprit de Lois* (1748), in which he originated the venerable principle of "the separation of powers," declaring: "There can be no liberty where the legislative and executive powers are united in the same person, or body of magistrates."

Bagehot was the first to make clear the impracticability of the doctrine of separation of powers. (Madison and other members of the American Constitutional Convention, it is true, sensed that impracticability, though only when the doctrine was carried to a more extreme form than in the Constitution they helped to frame.) "If the persons who have to do the work," Bagehot pointed out, "are not the same as those who have to make the laws, there will be a controversy between the two sets of persons. . . . The executive becomes unfit for its name since it cannot execute what it decides on; the legislature is demoralized by liberty, by taking decisions of which others (and not itself) will suffer the effects." The great defect of the American system is not merely that it can bring deadlock between Congress and the President (not to speak of deadlock between the two houses of Congress) but that it usually becomes impossible to fix the precise responsibility for that deadlock or to do anything about resolving it. "When a difference of opinion arises, the legislature is forced to fight the executive, and the executive is forced to fight the legislature; and so very likely they contend to the conclusion of their respective terms."

"Cabinet government," Bagehot went on to point out, "educates the nation; the presidential does not educate it, and may corrupt it." "It has been said that England invented the phrase, 'Her Majesty's Opposition';

that it was the first government which made a criticism of administration as much a part of the policy as administration itself." A debate in Parliament may immediately determine the decision on a great issue, and consequently everyone who participates in it, because his own political future may also be then and there involved, uses every faculty to present his case with as great effect as possible. There is no equal incentive behind the debates in Congress, and no equal incentive for public interest in them. . . .

There is no immediate constitutional method of changing the executive, as there is in England. Therefore patriotic men fear that criticism which brings responsibility home too closely to the President can only divide the country without effecting the change necessary. But this fear, only partly conscious, has a further effect: it leads men to wishful thinking; it leads them to tell themselves that the situation cannot be as bad as all that, and that the necessary changes can be effected by moderate arguments which do not urge a change in government but merely in the policies adopted by the existing government. Such a belief will continue to be held even though experience shows that the existing government will not modify its major policies, and may not even, however willing, know how to adopt and carry out the proper policies. The limitations imposed by a rigid constitution, in short, may pervert a nation's very thinking, leading it to a sort of national neurosis in which it refuses to face the truth about the situation that confronts it.

Continuing to press his criticism, Bagehot argued not only that the American system encourages deadlocks between the executive and the legislature, and fails properly to educate public opinion, that it tends, as compared with the cabinet system, to elect inferior men to office. One reason why Congressmen tend to be inferior to members of Parliament is that election to Congress offers far less chance of later promotion for an able man than does election to Parliament. A member of Parliament may nourish the hope, even during his first term, of being chosen for the Cabinet; such a prize seems always possible. No similar prize attaches to election to Congress.

"Unless a member of the legislature," wrote Bagehot, "be sure of something more than speech, unless he is incited by the hope of action, and chastened by the chance of responsibility, a first-rate man will not care to take the place, and will not do much if he does take it." Another kind of difficulty, he thought, affected our method of choosing presidents. The method of nomination by political conventions tended in most cases to become nomination by political wire pullers. The English Prime Minister is chosen by his colleagues in Parliament, who know his qualities intimately; usually he has spent some years as the leader of his party in Parliament when it was in the minority, or as a member of the Cabinet when his party was previously in power. His colleagues know what he will do, because they know what he has done. He is in nearly all cases, for the same reasons, a man whose record is known to the country. But presidential conventions often nominate "dark horses"—the selection of what Bagehot called "an unknown quantity." Even if the Americans scored an occasional success in such a lottery, he insisted, this was no argument for lotteries. Moreover, he pointed out, the very gifts that a particular statesman may have to rule in one set of circumstances may unfit him for rule in other circumstances. "By the structure of the world we often want, at the sudden occurrence of a grave tempest, to change the helmsman—to replace the pilot of the calm by the pilot of the storm." Summing up his indictment of the American system, Bagehot declared:

The American government calls itself a government of the supreme people; but at a quick crisis, the time when a sovereign power is most needed, you cannot find the supreme people. You have got a Congress elected for one fixed period, going out perhaps by fixed installments, which cannot be accelerated or retarded—you have a President chosen for a fixed period, and immovable during that period: all the arrangements are for stated times. There is no elastic element, everything is rigid, specified, dated. Come what may, you can quicken nothing and can retard nothing. You have bespoken your government in advance, and whether it suits you or not, whether it works well or works ill, whether it is what you want or not, by law you must keep it.

THE PARLIAMENTARY SYSTEM IS NOT ENOUGH *

Shortly before his death a few years ago, Professor Charles A. Beard wrote a lively commentary on American government entitled *The Republic*. Through the give-and-take discussion in a small circle of people, Beard explores numerous government problems. Among the issues that invoked spirited comment in the group was a query on the comparative merits of the presidential and the parliamentary systems. After explaining the theory of parliamentary government, Beard embarks upon a criticism of it as a solution to American problems of government. Much of his reasoning is directed toward the differences in cultural heritage between the United States and England. Also coming in for criticism is the concentration of power that occurs under the parliamentary system.

* From *The Republic* by Charles A. Beard, pp. 250–54. Copyright 1943 by Charles A. Beard. Reprinted by permission of the Viking Press, Inc., New York.

Is Beard completely objective or does he assume the role of a lawyer defending his client? Should all political institutions be retained, regardless of their effectiveness, solely on the basis of the social heritage? May not liberty be more strongly protected by responsibility and efficiency in government?

The theory of parliamentary government as I have formulated it rests upon certain fundamental assumptions. According to the theory, the legislature fresh from the people is sovereign, that is it can exercise practically all powers over the life, liberty, and property of the people. It is to be immediately and constantly responsive to the sentiments of the people as revealed in legislative elections. The will of the popular majority so disclosed is to be almost instantaneously expressed in the legislation and administration of the government. The responsibility of the executive to the legislature and to the country is clear and definite. The control the legislature has over the administration works for efficiency in administration. The power of the executive over legislation works for a concentration of talents on the business of legislating. In short, as the theory goes, parliamentary government is best adapted to eliminate deadlocks and confusion in government, to meet the needs of government in a complex industrial society, and to assure efficiency in administration.

MRS. SMYTH: So far you have spoken of the theory of parliamentary government. I can see that in fundamental points it is opposed to the features of our constitutional government as we have discussed them in our previous sessions. But what about practice in the long run?

BEARD: Ah, practice is another matter, even in Great Britain where the system is supposed to be in effect in its purest form. To go into practice would take months of our time. But I can declare with confidence that the introduction of parliamentary government in many other countries has not automatically worked according to the theory. The present state of France, Italy, Germany, and Yugoslavia, for instance, indicates that it may break down or may be incompetent to meet the needs of complex societies.

Parliamentary government is not like a good watch which runs regularly in all sorts of conditions. Its actual operation depends on the traditions of the country, on the experience of the people in self-government, on the number and character of the political parties or factions, and on obvious and subtle variations in civilization. Mark well, I do not say that parliamentary government was the cause of Hitler's rise to power in Germany or of France's collapse in 1940. That would be a ridiculous simplification. Nor do I say that our system of constitutional government would have worked as well or any better in Germany or France.

In the eighteenth century, radical political philosophers in Europe had a childlike faith in constitutions. Many believed that it was merely necessary to draw up the right kind of paper constitution in order to establish popular government and assure its success. More than a century's bitter experience has taught the portion of mankind capable of learning that this belief is utopian. No constitution works perfectly. To be workable, even in a limited sense, any form of government must be adapted to the traditions, political experience and habits, the prevailing economic interests, and the intellectual and moral values of the people for whom it is devised.

It is customary to speak of the common bonds of all humanity, of the natural rights all human beings enjoy, of the similarities among nations and peoples. Universal traits of mankind I have no desire to minimize or underestimate. But anybody who has studied the histories of the various nations and has traveled widely and observed closely cannot fail to be struck by fundamental divergences in the experiences, temper, economies, and social institutions of the various nations of the earth.

Civilization in the United States is by no means identical with civilization in Great Britain or any other country, despite similarities in specific features. Our history, our experience, have been in many ways unique. Our form of government has been adapted to our character and circumstances. Latin-American constitutions more or less modeled on our plan have not worked in the same way or encountered similar successes. To expect a common form of government for all nations of the earth is, in my view, a fantasy. To expect that the British parliamentary system, if adopted here, would work as it does in Great Britain, or indeed accomplish here the wonders attributed to it, is in my view also a fantasy.

DR. SMYTH: That is more gloom. You allow validity to many criticisms brought against our system. You picture the theory of parliamentary government as if it would introduce into government competency for dealing with the needs of a complex society, responsibility with reference to all official acts, and efficiency in administration. Then you straightaway declare that theory unworkable here and leave us stuck with our rigid Constitution which is responsible for our deadlocks, confusion, incompetency, and inefficiency. You admit that in a great national crisis it might break down for these very reasons. You offer no hope for adapting our form of government to the real needs of our industrial society. The chances are that in a real national calamity we may see established here a totalitarian government of one kind or another.

BEARD: You have said a great deal in a few words. Before I consider the whole bill of doubts, I want to correct one of your statements. When you say that our Constitution is rigid, you repeat an idea about the Constitution which was not written into the document by the framers. It is an idea created by partisan politicians for their own interests and later repeated by foreign critics like James Bryce and by citizens who pick up their views from conversations and stray bits of news and information.

In some few respects our Constitution is rigid. The number of Senators from each state is fixed at two. But in vital respects our Constitution is highly flexible. The elastic clause is not the only thing elastic in it. It was intended to be flexible, adapted, as John Marshall said, to the storms of the ages. It is as flexible as American intelligence and character may make it.

A great deal of the rigidity ascribed to it is not in the Constitution itself. It is in the huge body of congressional and executive practices built up under it—precedents and practices not imposed on the country by the Constitution but self-imposed by politicians, sometimes for the very purpose of escaping responsibility and preventing the introduction of efficiency. Our Constitution is encrusted with the accumulated impediments of one hundred and fifty years. If they were scraped off, and if we seized upon the freedom to which we are entitled under the letter and spirit of the Constitution, we could work wonders without altering a line of the document.

Here I should like to qualify another one of your statements. I do not believe that even in a great national crisis we shall necessarily subject ourselves to what you call a totalitarian government of some kind or other. My guess may be wrong, but that is my belief. We passed through the crisis of the American Revolution and the crisis of the Civil War without falling into a totalitarian system, though it was then freely predicted that we would.

This we have already discussed. We may have in a great national crisis a straight military dictatorship under the President or a joint committee of Congress. But I believe that it will prove to be temporary if it ever comes. The idea of our repeating all the mental imagery, ideas, rhetoric, sentiments, and hocus-pocus of totalitarianism in Germany, Russia, or Italy seems to me so highly fanciful as to be purely speculative, for America has not been and never can be Russia, Germany or Italy, through whatever variety of untried being we may pass in the indefinite future.

I agree with you that our fortunes will depend in some considerable measure upon what we do in the way of making our government competent to meet the needs of society, and at the same time efficient in administration. But competence and efficiency, though necessary for the perdurance of a government, are not the sole ends of guarantees of government. Besides, competence in what? In making laws against liberty of opinion, such as the Alien Registration Act of 1940? Efficiency of political police in suppressing liberty of opinion and action?

The end of government in the United States at least is not mere technical efficiency, nor mere competence in specific matters, nor speed of political action, nor instant responsiveness to the will of the majority, nor the unrestricted rule of simple majorities. For us the ends are not only a more perfect Union, the establishment of justice, provision for common defense and general welfare, but also—and don't forget it—the maintenance of the blessings of liberty and the long-run service of American society. Long-run efficiency, competence, action, and deference to temporary majorities or pluralities are devices we believe necessary to achieve the social ends of government.

The philosophy of parliamentary government presents many forms of contradiction to the American system. If we adopted that type of government, we should have to abolish the Senate or reduce it to the status of a mere advisory body, in order to prevent deadlocks between the two houses of Congress. This, I am convinced, is practically impossible, given the tenacity of underlying interests, and undesirable besides. We should also have to abrogate the power of the Supreme Court to declare void acts of Congress trenching upon personal liberty. This, too, I deem undesirable and dangerous.

Under our system, momentary efficiency, speed, or competence may be sacrificed, more or less, and rightly, in the interest of mature deliberation and civil liberty; but it is long-run efficiency and competence that count in the survival of our nation. Parliamentary government puts the great issues of life, liberty, economy, and the pursuit of happiness at stake in single popular elections and places them at the mercy of a majority of the people who take the trouble to vote after the heats and distempers of a campaign.

THE PRESIDENT AS ADMINISTRATOR *

In addition to the executive-legislative relationship, the second striking problem of the Presidency relates to the Chief Executive's function as an administrator. The Executive Branch of the government has grown enormously in recent years. Much of this growth was caused by emergency conditions and, as a result, lacked planning and integration. Efficient administration has also been handicapped by the creation of a large group of independent regulatory agencies and commissions. In 1937 the President's Committee on Administrative Manage-

* Herman Miles Somers, *The Annals* of the American Academy of Political and Social Science, September, 1952, pp. 104–5, 108–10, 112–14.

ment declared that these agencies constitute "a headless fourth branch of the government, responsible to no one." The build-up of agencies and officials continues to increase rather than diminish. Since the peak in World War II the scope of the job of the President has doubled.

Professor Herman Miles Somers discusses the role of the President as a political administrator, reviewing the findings of the Hoover Commission and suggesting other improvements. The question, however, remains: Is it possible to reorganize the office without a thorough-going reorganization of political parties and legislative procedure?

It may be that full performance of the duties which have accrued to the President is impossible. William Allen White, who knew the job in less frenetic days, thought "the devil invented the Presidency by combining all the futile despairs of Sisyphus with the agony of Tantalus and shaking in a jigger of the nervous irritation of a man with ants in his pants."

Even in days when the nation and its government were smaller and simpler, Presidents cried for help. Almost every President in this century has publicly complained that he could not fully cope with his administrative responsibilities. More than fifteen years ago, President Roosevelt transmitted to Congress the historic study of the Federal Government made by the Committee on Administrative Management, and added:

. . . they say, what has been common knowledge for twenty years, that the President cannot adequately handle his responsibilities, that he is overworked; that it is humanly impossible, under the system which we have, for him fully to carry out his Constitutional duty as Chief Executive, because he is overwhelmed with minor details and needless contacts arising directly from the bad organization and equipment of the Government. I can testify to this. With my predecessors who have said the same thing over and over, I plead guilty.

Twelve years later, the celebrated Hoover Commission reported as its first findings: (1) "The executive branch is not organized into a workable number of major departments and agencies which the President can effectively direct." (2) "The line of command and supervision from the President down through his department heads to every employee . . . has been weakened, or actually broken, in many places and in many ways." (3) "The President and the heads of departments lack the tools to frame programs and policies and to supervise their execution."

More recently *Fortune* reported that "according to old hands around the White House, the job of the Presidency has doubled in scope even since the peak effort of World War II."

Under the best of circumstances, the proper management of the executive branch alone, now numbering 2,500,000 civil servants, plus the military organization of which the President is also administrative chief, would be a backbreaking ordeal (quite aside from the President's other full-time jobs); but neither the Congress nor the American people seem interested in helping to create the best of circumstances.   On the contrary, a formidable array of obstacles, nettles, and mousetraps has been thrown in the President's path.   These are frequently called "safe-guards"; but just what or how they guard has never been made clear.   In fact, they are in part the painful expression by Congress of its own frustrations.   In part they represent the normal compromises, concessions, and contradictions of conflicting forces in a highly pluralistic society. . . .

The Hoover Commission's approach to problems of the Executive Office was generally similar to that of the Committee on Administrative Management.   It too recognized that the effectiveness of the Government of the United States rested on the ability of the Chief Executive to provide "firm direction to the departments and agencies" and orderly "organization for development and execution of policy."   It found the President still dangerously "handicapped" for the performance of his responsibilities.   In its first report the Commission submitted specific recommendations and valuable conceptual principles regarding the Office.   It said that the President must be boss of his own office and "should be given complete freedom to adjust the internal relationships."   It also said, "Statutory authority over the operating departments should not be vested in any staff or staff agency of the President's Office."

It appears that Congress does not intend to follow these recommendations.   In 1951, for example, it legislated that a Director for Mutual Security, who would serve as co-ordinator in this entire field, should be located in the Executive Office and that the same man who held this post should be the administrator of a large operating agency, the Mutual Security Agency.   Congress thereby flew in the face of the Hoover Commission precepts and violated other elementary principles of organization by making a single official both protagonist and umpire in interagency disputes.

The Hoover Commission enunciated the principles that multiheaded bodies, in the nature of full-time boards, could not serve effectively as Presidential staff, and that the heads of staff agencies in the President's Office "should be appointed by the President without confirmation by the Senate, except the Civil Service Commission."   It specifically pointed to the Council of Economic Advisers as an example of violation of both principles, and recommended that it be replaced by an Office of the Economic Adviser with a single head.   This was not done.   The authority of the National Security Resources Board was transferred from the Board to its chairman, but his appointment still requires Senate confirmation.

The Commission took cognizance of the lack of organization within the Executive Office, pointing out especially that there is no place in the Office where the President can look for a current summary of principal issues on staff work or assignment to departments and agencies. Its recommendation to meet this deficiency indicated that it is much easier to determine what is wrong than to reach agreement upon a solution. The compromise proposal was a new staff secretary whose prescribed functions suggest a high-class clerk for clearing and assembling papers for the President. Some of the Commission's members apparently hoped that such a position, once established, might grow into a more affirmative and influential role of "staff leader."

Meanwhile, the crucial issues of coherent organization and internal staff relationships in the Executive Office remain unresolved. This affects more than the adequacy of assistance. A Chief Executive can become a prisoner of the imbalances in his own organization. Ultimate decisions must rest upon the solitary figure of the President. He must therefore be sure that when issues reach him for decision they have had staff appraisal from all the different aspects of Presidential responsibility, and that all viewpoints on vital controversies reach him through persons representing such different views. This protects the President's judgments and his position.

The present deficiencies of the Executive Office should not, however, becloud the remarkable progress made during the last decade. The Executive Office is only thirteen years old. Large sectors are post-World War II developments. That it has not yet shaken down to a cohesive and orderly structure should not be discouraging. More informal coordination has been achieved internally than the formal structure suggests. In part, such institutions tend to achieve balance through an evolutionary process. For example, more and more of the legislative clearance function, basically located in the Bureau of the Budget, is passing into the hands of the White House staff without any formal ordering.

The general competence of the Executive Office is high. Acceptance of its Presidential functions are being achieved throughout the government. The present Chief Executive appears to make broader use of staff assistance than did his predecessor, and it may be as *Fortune* has optimistically noted, that this development "has provided the President of the United States for the first time with the machinery and manpower necessary to run an orderly government in these complex days."

Proper staffing of the Presidency will not alone provide a solution of the President's organization problems. Departmental organization is also vitally important. Three issues stand out:

1. The existence of commissions executing some of our most important statutes, claiming virtual independence of the Chief Executive, mocks at-

tempts at meaningful co-ordination of government policy and administration. The independent agencies are generally regulatory in nature. Regulation is essentially political; concerned with the formulation of public policies. Independence of the Executive and, in some cases, even of the legislature, makes these agencies essentially irresponsible. There is indeed "very great danger in any doctrine that pretends we can preserve democracy and still vest economic powers in a governmental agency that is not clearly subject to officials who in turn are responsible to the people."

2. There are entirely too many agencies for effective direction from the top. According to the Hoover Commission:

At the present time there are 65 departments, administrations, agencies, boards, and commissions engaged in executive work, all of which report directly to the President—if they report to anyone. This number does not include the "independent" regulatory agencies in their quasi-judicial or quasi-legislative functions. It is manifestly impossible for the President to give adequate supervision to so many agencies.

The Hoover Commission, like its predecessor Committee on Administrative Management, made useful recommendations for an orderly combining of agencies to reduce the total number. It is now clear that for the most part, Congress cannot heed such recommendations.

Recently, interesting proposals have been made for creation of a new echelon of command, between the departmental and Executive Office levels, through grouping of departments and agencies with particularly related activities. If modeled after the integrated structure of the Department of Defense in which are combined three administrative departments, as distinguished from its predecessor the National Military Establishment which had statutory authority only of a holding-company character and proved to have no basis of strength, such redesigning may have administrative merit. But, in any event, it is unlikely to appeal to congressional committees.

3. Authority within departments is diffused and uncertain, partly because of statutes through which Congress has too frequently spelled out the internal organization of departments and agencies and has given authority directly to subordinate officers. In part, the situation is due to the informal power relationships which align bureaus and agencies more closely with congressional committees than with their organizational superiors.

In greater or less degree, all three of these impediments to unified executive administration reflect the congressional-Presidential rivalry within our system. Even more, they reflect the lack of organization within Congress. As long as Congress remains a congeries of warring factions, its committees are encouraged to usurp powers properly belonging to the whole of Congress, and to divide up the executive branch into colonial empires directly subject to committee domination.

The danger is great on many scores. As one distinguished scholar recently warned,

It is extremely doubtful if government by congressional committees can be justified on either democratic or expediential grounds, because the standing committees of Congress are very nearly the least representative institutions in the government.

It is insufficiently recognized that the proper organization and functioning of the executive branch is greatly dependent upon the internal organization and management of the legislature. As long as Congress is disorganized, it will continue to promote the disorganization of the executive branch. As long as the executive branch is fragmented, it will be difficult if not impossible for the Congress to hold it accountable. Only by strengthening the control of the Chief Executive, with whom it can deal in direct and unitary fashion, can the Congress ever assure to itself administrative accountability of the bureaucracy. . . .

The combination of training in the school of electoral politics and experience as political executive appears generally to work out best [as qualifications for a successful President]. The successful administrator in business enterprise or in military combat generally finds that his skills are not directly transferable or convertible to political administration. The different kinds of administration not only represent different habit patterns, but seem to require different types of personality. The man accustomed to giving orders with the expectation that subordinates will automatically follow or bear the consequences will find the Presidency frustrating and baffling. The man who operates by making up his mind what is "right" and then driving ahead accordingly, irrespective of opposition, is likely to find the Presidency a strait jacket with taunting shackles.

The political administrator makes his leadership felt by media of persuasion, by winning wide public support, and by being a successful "lubricator of human relations." He cannot be doctrinaire or unyielding. He must be a man who can elevate compromise and draw out of it a creative principle. The necessity of harmonizing conflicting interests of functionally divergent groups in a pluralistic society is the most crucial task of top-level administration, just as it is of politics.

The President undertakes to coordinate not only the activities of an array of federal agencies but, through them, the conflicting tendencies and desires of our whole socioeconomic system. The basic conflicts cannot be "ordered" out of existence. Their reconciliation, issue by issue, is the keynote of democratic administration. And experience has taught us that "democracy is more efficient than efficiency."

Yet the great Presidents have also been strong and affirmative leaders. All were regarded as relatively "radical" in their own day. Each made the office as big as he could, and each left it more influential than he had found it.

However, it would be a mistake to attempt to fix the most desirable background for the Presidency into a mold, just as it is to fix the "right" procedures for him to follow. Human personality is flexible and unpredictable. Not every political background or business background or military background is the same as every other, nor does it have the same effect upon every man. For example, detractors of one of the possible candidates of 1952 (this is being written before either nominating convention), General Eisenhower, allege that he never was a real combat general, but rather a "chairman-of-the-board" commander or a political organizer in the military field. If true, this illustrates that intended derogation in one field may be commendation for another, as such talents are greater assets for the Presidency than those ordinarily associated with combat effectiveness.

Moreover, as President Franklin Roosevelt said of the Presidency, "It is pre-eminently a place of moral leadership." The consciousness of this fact and the searing responsibilities of the office have had a remarkable influence in molding the personality and the ability of men after they have assumed office. Presidents have often surprised themselves and their generations by their growth in office.

The Presidency is today the prime motive force in our Constitutional system. Our political and economic evolution and the nature of our party system have focused upon the President responsibility for the origin of major policies and programs and for the implementation and effectuation of policies approved by Congress. The American system, in which the Presidency is a representative institution—elected by universal suffrage—emphasizes the fact that co-ordination of politics and administration is necessary in a democratic nation.

In our complex society, responsible leadership must have the means of ensuring that policy will not be distorted in its administration, and must have control of the ever broadening areas of decision-making and policy determination which are implicit in the administrative process.

Presidential administrative difficulties are intertwined with the fundamental issues of political organization facing American society, including the complex problems of deficient party organization and party discipline. The basic factors are the same as those which encourage increasingly dangerous stalemates between President and Congress, which make the legislature and the bureaucracy unduly vulnerable to powerful private interests, and which give to extremists in Congress a disproportionate influence. The fate of the 'largest share of even so popularly dramatized reforms as those proposed by the Hoover Commission and endorsed by the leadership of both parties illustrates the unreality of treating administrative revisions as things distinct from the political environment.

Nevertheless, there are several administrative improvements which, on the basis of precedent or related experience, appear to have a chance for practical achievement if demanded by a new and popular President during his "honeymoon period." Among them are four points which ought to be regarded as a minimum program for early achievement.

1. The President should be given permanent authority to initiate plans for internal reorganization of the executive branch, such plans to take effect unless rejected by joint resolution of both houses of Congress within a specified time. Presidents have already been given similar authority for temporary periods. Congress has demonstrated that its power of veto under such an arrangement is amply adequate. Such permanent executive initiative would go far toward correlating authority and responsibility and would offer some operational basis for workable reordering of the executive branch structure. Considerable useful reorganization has already been achieved in this manner which could never have been accomplished otherwise; for example, placing the collectors of internal revenue under the merit system.

2. The highly successful operation of the National Security Council has provided a case study of how the Cabinet may be made a viable instrument for executive policy co-ordination and how the Executive Office may be molded into a coherent organization without the monolithic dangers of a single "chief-of-staff" arrangement.

The NSC has demonstrated that Cabinet-level committees, given a circumscribed area of jurisdiction and continuing responsibility, with members selected because of direct functional relationship to the committee's jurisdiction, can be effective instruments for Presidential counsel and co-ordination. One of the elements in its success has been the continuous efficient staff work of an able professional secretariat. The experience argues for similar Cabinet committees for other large areas of governmental responsibility which cut across departmental lines, each to be served by a full-time secretariat.

3. The various Cabinet committee secretariats should be interlocking and all attached to and assigned from the Executive Office, where they would be part of a central Presidential secretariat. The central secretariat would coordinate the work of the several committee secretariats, and, thereby, of the committees themselves. It should serve as a continuous

channel of communication to the President, to whom it would be responsible. The Executive Office would thereby acquire the integrating amalgam it has long needed.

4. The administrative structure is composed of people. If the President cannot reasonably control, within the law, the personnel system of government, it is difficult to conceive how adequate democratic control can be achieved. The merit system, now covering over 90 per cent of federal personnel, can become a boomerang, and is itself endangered, if it is independent of the political officers of government. The objective must be a reconciliation of the principle of merit with the principle of administrative control. Progress toward such an objective can begin by creating a director of personnel, directly accountable to the President. A continuing civil service commission or board should act only in an advisory capacity.

Such reforms are within the realm of possible realization by a new administration. Important in themselves, they can also serve as a vehicle for Presidential leadership in continuous administrative reform, with the target of bringing the total job under control. We must all realize that "the reality of responsible government is dependent upon the ability of the President to control the executive branch."

What I am placing before you is not a request for more power, but for the tools of management and the authority to distribute the work so that the President can effectively discharge those powers which the Constitution now places upon him.*

This is the type of plea the next President of the United States, whoever he is, is also likely to make. It would be well that he be heeded. It is tempting fate to continue to play the game of challenging greatness to surmount unnecessary and unreasonable barriers. The stakes of government are now too high!

———————◄••••►———————

Problem 9: Congress--
Confusion or Cultural Reflection?

The separation of powers principle has never operated in a properly adjusted, precisely balanced equilibrium. From time to time one of the three branches of government has exerted undue influence to tip the scales un-

* *Message,* The President of the United States to Congress, January 12, 1937.

evenly. For the greater part of our history Congress has occupied the power position in the American system. So apparent was the imbalance during the latter part of the nineteenth century that Woodrow Wilson wrote in 1885: "the actual form of our present government is simply a scheme of congressional supremacy." Three years later James Bryce noted that the President "has less influence on legislation . . . than the Speaker of the House of Representatives." Today, however, the roles of the Executive and Congress are somewhat reversed. The rise of the Presidency has been so great during the last two decades that the effect upon the constitutional system has been more loudly deplored than applauded. Some attribute the change to the ascendency of presidential government. Others, equally apprehensive, view the inefficiency and ineffectiveness of Congress as contributing to the trend. For these and other reasons many believe Congress to be at the crossroads.

This section deals with the problem of whether Congress is capable of doing the job of legislating for a large and powerful industrial democracy in the twentieth century. As a preface, "A Day in the Life of a Congressman" describes the work day of a Congressman. "Has Congress Broken Down?" shows the helplessness of an ill-equipped and unprepared legislative body's attempt to cope with technical problems. Robert Bendiner's "Just How Bad Is Congress?" reviews the case against Congress and concludes that the record does not justify the allegations. D. W. Brogan takes a different path in "How Congress Does It—And Parliament"; analyzing the Federal legislature in the framework of the parliamentary system, he criticizes lack of responsibility in the separation of powers. In "Custodian of Tender Consciences" T. V. Smith views the present institution rather favorably and utters a word of caution to those who would reform what is already satisfactory.

A DAY IN THE LIFE OF A CONGRESSMAN *

A Congressman is often confronted with a work load that makes his efforts to legislate creatively and intelligently very difficult. Appearing before the Joint Committee on the Organization of Congress in 1945, Senator Downey of California noted "even if I had four times the amount of time I have I could not possibly perform adequately and fully the duties rightfully imposed upon me as ambassador from my

* "Congressman: A Case History." Reprinted from the April, 1943, issue of *Fortune,* pp. 80, 177–78, by special permission of the Editors. Copyright, 1953, Time, Inc.

state." Other Congressmen could write similar testimonials. Several years ago *Fortune* sent a reporter to follow Representative (now Senator) Dirksen through a typical day. The reporter's account suggests that the prime requirement for all members of Congress should be a stringent physical examination.

Up at 6:15 A.M., he walked to the Carlton Hotel for a seven-fifteen breakfast date with the head of the industrial-relations department of an Illinois railroad. Mainly as a postwar project, the road hopes to get a lot of new industries established in the Peoria district and has made a thorough survey of its resources. Fortunately this visitor already knew a good many other interested government officials, so the Congressman did not have to take time to arrange a string of interviews for him.

Delayed by the long breakfast session, Dirksen arrived at his office in the Old House Office Building at eight-forty-five, three-quarters of an hour behind his usual time. His first visitor, after a less-experienced Congressman seeking advice, was a Chicago businessman. Chicago is outside Dirksen's district, but people often feel free to call on anyone in their state's congressional delegation. This one wanted to talk about home loan financing (Dirksen is trying to kill HOLC) and also about rent control on commercial properties in connection with a bill pending before the House Banking Committee. Dirksen pledged "sustained attention" to these matters.

On the heels of the banker came a distillers' representative, worried about the recent newspaper story that liquor consumption was to be cut 99 per cent for the duration. Dirksen promptly called Economic Czar Jimmy Byrnes, with whom he is on first-name terms. Byrnes laughed, said there was nothing to the report, and promised that a denial would be issued.

Meantime conversation, as always, was being continually interrupted by the ringing of the telephone. One after another, four other Congressmen called about items in pending bills under the jurisdiction of the Appropriations Committee, of which Dirksen is one of the most influential members. Between times throughout the day Dirksen made numerous telephone calls of his own, among them: (1) to *The New York Times* about an article it wanted him to write; (2) to the Civil Service Commission to get advance information for a constituent on her rating in a recent examination; (3) to a fellow member of the District of Columbia Committee about a pending bill that would permit Washington's charitable institutions to use oleomargarine instead of butter (Dirksen was against it); (4) to the Library of Congress for some data on public power that he could expect to receive in about two weeks.

Next visitor was a college trustee worried about what would happen to the college unless the Army or Navy selected it for one of their training programs. Could the Congressman help? The Congressman would try. After the trustee came a farm-organization representative concerned with price ceilings on farm commodities, who wanted to talk with Jimmy Byrnes, another official of the Economic Stabilization Board, and somebody in OPA [Office of Price Administration]. The Congressman arranged the appointments.

Normally, Dirksen spends the first hour in his office reading and answering his mail. But having lost the earlier hour, he turned now to this task and kept at it until 12:15 P.M. Then, in the outer office where secretary and stenographer work and visitors wait, he picked up two postwar planners and took them over to the Capitol for a quick lunch in the House restaurant.

The daily session of the House, which normally begins at noon, had been under way for an hour when Dirksen arrived on the floor. Debate on a merger of Western Union and Postal Telegraph was in progress. Dirksen's attendance was sporadic—the normal thing in Congress—for he was repeatedly called off the floor by visitors and telephone calls. In the course of a couple of hours messengers summoned him five times. Once was for a visitor, another college official with the same worries as the first. Two of the phone calls were from Illinois, one to announce that a college president would arrive next morning, another from a banker who wanted an appointment with Leo Crowley of the FDIC [Federal Deposit Insurance Corporation]. A third call was from an official of a steel company in his district, come to Washington to protest against his Lend-Lease quota of ingots and billets. A fourth took him to Union Station, where an entraining WPA [Works Progress Administration] official had a postwar project that he was impatient to discuss. In addition, the Congressman had to drop in at a meeting of the Appropriations Committee, return to his office for a little talk to a visiting college class in political science.

The telegraph debate was succeeded by a fiery one on renewing the Dies Committee for another two years. Dirksen, not much interested in hearing last year's arguments repeated, occasionally improved his time by retiring to the cloakroom to go over papers in his briefcase. After the Dies roll call, in which he voted yea, he went back to the Office Building and stopped by briefly at the office of another Congressman from Illinois who was giving a little farewell party honoring his secretary's departure for the Army.

Back in his own office, Dirksen cleared up details of dictating, letter signing, and telephoning, then packed his briefcase with his evening's reading. He reached the Mayflower at seven. As usual, several people were waiting to buttonhole him in the lobby. One was still another college trustee, two more were Navy officers on confidential business. He also stopped for a chat with the new chairman of the Republican National Committee, Harrison Spangler, about liaison between the Committee and the G.O.P. contingent in Congress.   Fed, he rolled up his sleeves, hooked on his spectacles, and settled down to read a file on the Independent Offices Appropriation Bill.   After a brisk walk and look at the evening papers, he turned out the lights at eleven-twenty—seventeen hours after he had turned them on. Except for dinner and his stop-off at the farewell party, he had been working all the time.

For busyness, this is a fair sample of Dirksen's days.   But it falls far short of covering the whole range of his activities and problems.   Like all Congressmen, he goes most mornings to a meeting of one of his committees beginning at ten.   (As do other major committees, Appropriations—probably the hardest working of the lot—also meets frequently in the afternoons.)   On an average of thirty times a month he goes along in person to introduce a constituent to some government official and help thrash out the problem.   In demand as a Republican speaker, he makes a good many appearances every year both in Illinois and around the country.   He also spends time investigating Washington's municipal affairs as a member of the District of Columbia Committee. . . .

HAS CONGRESS BROKEN DOWN? *

The relationship between the Executive and Congress has never been more important than it is today.   Pressing international and domestic problems demand leadership, efficiency, and concerted action.   Yet Congress continues to operate under impossible conditions —rules that date back to the eighteenth century and traditions that have long since outlived their usefulness.   As a result, it has lost ground to an expanding Executive.   The dilemma of Congress can be seen in the attempts of individual Congressmen, or even a congressional committee, to cope with a multi-billion-dollar budget.   Congress needs assistance if deadlocks, undue delays, and legislative inaction are to be avoided.   The editors of *Fortune* take a hard look at the Congress of the United States, diagnose some of its most serious ailments, and suggest a program for recovery.

Although the weight of evidence seems to indict congressional methods and rules of procedure, are we not judging this institution in

* Reprinted from the February, 1952, issue of *Fortune,* pp. 220–29, by special permission of the Editors.   Copyright, 1952, Time, Inc.

terms of emergency conditions? In such critical times as the depression of the thirties, World War II, and the present "cold war," is it not inevitable that Congress yield leadership to the President? Has not Congress undertaken critical reappraisal and achieved important reforms in the Legislative Reorganization Act of 1946?

The loud noises of the Eighty-second were like the rattling of overstrained parts; something was basically wrong with the legislative machinery. What was wrong was that it had become obsolete. Meanwhile, the federal government was generating more and more complex business, until that business was simply beyond Congress' power to control.

The situation was manifest in the House when a weary and bewildered subcommittee of seven members reported on the Administration's $56-billion defense bill.

"The sum of $56 billion is almost beyond comprehension," Mr. Wigglesworth, of Massachusetts, told the chamber. "I think it is probably easier for the average person to grasp the vastness of the universe than to picture this astronomical sum. . . . The justifications originally submitted to your committee, if piled on top of each other, would extend, I should judge, some twenty-four inches upward from the table. . . .

"The testimony submitted was in many cases highly unsatisfactory. Time and time again no breakdown was available; fundamental information was not forthcoming." He recalled then a discussion with an admiral over a certain request for $1,350,000. The admiral had made a particularly vague statement in trying to justify this item. Mr. Wigglesworth had said: "I would like to ask the admiral, if he were sitting on this side of the table, on the basis of that statement how he would determine whether you need $1,350,000 or $500,000 or $5,000,000?" The admiral answered blankly: "Sir, I would be at a loss."

Mr. Meader, of Michigan, summarized the situation. "Unless we have the facts we cannot act wisely and exercise effectively the power and authority which the Constitution vests in us." He called "as a witness" Mr. Truman himself. In 1943, when he was chairman of the committee investigating the defense program, Senator Truman reported hopelessly: "The Armed Forces know how to waste money better than any other organization I have ever had anything to do with. . . . Tremendous sums are simply being thrown away with a scoop shovel."

The House subcommittee in 1951 had only a dozen investigators on its staff. Mr. Meader cried:

The committee and the House are dealing with this huge and difficult task without adequate tools. Seven men almost with their bare hands are standing up to a huge organization with thousands of officials, both civilian and military,

devoting their full time to the presentation of self-serving statements and documents, and inundating the committee with a plethora of testimony and charts
and statistics which the committee is unable to digest, to say nothing of challenging. The Congress is at the mercy of the executive. . . . What if they had
asked for eighty billion instead of fifty-six billion? Would the committee have
been able to challenge and resist the request?

Hands in the Jam Pot

Nor were any of the other subcommittees and committees of Congress,
inundated with charts and statistics, able to do much more with twenty
other appropriation bills.

Adding to Congress' confusion in making new appropriations is Congress' lack of information on how last year's appropriations are being
spent. It has neither time nor facilities for careful examination of the
Administration's dispersal of tens of billions of dollars a year. The General Accounting Office's idea of a proper report is a lengthy document,
written in the abracadabra of auditors and designed to stand on its feet
for eternity, which Congressmen have neither time nor inclination to
digest. G.A.O. has not distinguished itself at hunting out people who
have their hands in the jam pot. Usually it just sticks to its chore of
recording, some time later, the consumption of jam. G.A.O. should have
spotted the misfeasance in RFC long before the Fulbright Committee did.

It should be recorded that G.A.O. has made some progress in reorganiz-
ing. It is shortening its reports in the hope that Congressmen will read
them. Once overmanned, it has cut personnel almost in half. It is persuading the executive agencies to use commercial accounting procedures
that will show immediately what an agency is doing with its money. It
is going into government corporations (e.g., Commodity Credit, Home
Owners Loan) with commercial auditing methods and in this field its audits
are up to date.

"The Moral Blindness"

Yet the Congressman's difficulty in finding out how the money he appropriated has been spent is only one measurement of his perplexity. Forget for the moment the question of what the various parts of government
are actually costing; can the Congressman find out what they are actually
doing? Here again, he is faced by maddening mysteries.

Congress sets up watchdog committees, but through all the vast area of
administrative activity Congress can only grope. Congressmen can and
do demand explanations, and sometimes Congressmen upset administration applecarts. Congress has a good nose for corruption, and is still highly

effective at keeping people, including its own members, fairly honest. The Eighty-second has so far conducted 130 separate investigations, most of them into the executive departments, and raked up widespread corruption. Not so prodigious as the great larcenies of Grant's day, or Harding's, nevertheless the graft in RFC, the Internal Revenue Bureau, etc., was in some ways more unsavory by reason of its very pettiness and multifariousness. "Civilizations have been destroyed," Senator Fulbright reminded the White House, "not as a result of external aggression but as a consequence of domestic corruption. . . . What seems to be new about these scandals is the moral blindness or callousness which allows those in responsible positions to accept the practices which the facts reveal."

Mr. Truman stood at bay. "If you want to have me impeached, you just go right ahead and I'll help you," he shouted over the telephone at New Hampshire's pious Senator Tobey. It was an extraordinary display of presidential rage in an extraordinary atmosphere. Not until too late in the game did Harry Truman turn his attention to his real enemies, the cronies and cronies of cronies who had betrayed him.

The Monster's Tracks

But unless there is some flagrant wrongdoing, by and large the great Administration machine, manned by some 2,500,000 people, clanks on without effective congressional surveillance or interference. The complexity of the mechanism, which begins with the pecking of a typewriter by the lowest-rated Civil Service employee in the Post Office Department and reaches a throbbing climax in that still uncomprehended powerhouse, the Atomic Energy Commission, thwarts all the skills of legislative control.

Now the monster itself even makes law. Robert Moss, Washington attorney and author of a textbook, *Cases and Materials on the Law of Government Contracts,* has been one of the numerous alarmed witnesses of a process that is growing more and more pervasive. Moss cites as example the way the executive agencies handled a number of small firms with claims against the government on World War II contracts. To be sure, Moss was involved as an attorney for the firms, but the whole incident is on the record.

A 1941 Act of Congress gave government agencies the right to reimburse manufacturers who had lost money on war contracts. Later, the Pentagon got out from under by announcing that its authority to make such settlements had run out with the end of the war. Congress renewed its authority, making it clear that claimants could still be reimbursed if their losses had been incurred through no fault of their own. The agencies tried to arrange an escape through an Executive Order that contained a legal knot-hole. Lawyers for the claimants, "in a sincere belief that the Executive Order was a direct emasculation of the statute," persuaded Congress to pass an amendment plugging the hole. The President vetoed the amendment. The veto message stated that if the statute were to cover seven specific points, he would sign it. Congress adopted another amendment covering the points. Again the President vetoed. Congressmen, apparently wearying of the game, this time let the veto ride. Out of some 350 claims, less than a dozen have so far been allowed. Thus the monster's tracks can be followed through legislative areas into judiciary areas as well. Executive agencies make rules that take on the actual force of statutes—and this practice is not confined to the seven regulatory commissions to which Congress specifically assigned certain semi-legislative and semi-judicial powers. Like a hierarchy concocted by W. S. Gilbert, the executive branch has become accuser, judge, and lord high executioner.

The executive banch, for its part, complains that Congress frequently usurps its functions, in some cases writing laws that leave too little play for administrative judgment (in the setting of OPS ceilings, allocation of ECA aid, etc.), or in other instances, through noisy public investigations or quiet pressure applied directly, seeking to control what are essentially administrative decisions. But the line between the legitimate investigative functions and unwarranted meddling is a hard one to draw, and a Congress too prompt to poke into the executive's performance is certainly preferable to one too slow.

"Now Who's Dead?"

A good part of the inability of Congress to deal with the inherent power of the executive lies in Congress' own inherent weakness. As the first session of the Eighty-second so painfully illustrated, Congress is tied down by its own rules. Members are shackled by committee chairmen who are chairmen by virtue of nothing but their seniority. The Senate wastes time in its interminable and unlimited debates. All members are burdened by what Edmund Burke called the legislator's "mean and petty business"—looking after the countless requests of constituents, running voters' errands, passing out patronage.

They are engulfed in the cumbersome legislative procedure, which has had no substantial improvement since the days of James Madison—as many as twenty-eight separate steps may be needed to pass an act.

Senators commute patiently back and forth from the Senate Office Building to the chamber on an underground subway, in electric charabancs. Representatives, with no subway, walk. Congressman Charles Elston, of Cincinnati, an active, muscular man, spends about eight brisk minutes on every trip he makes to the House floor from his office—No. 1717 in the New House Building and one of the farthest removed from the chamber. When Mr. Elston is trying to get some eminently necessary work done in his office while the House is meeting, quorum calls and roll calls may summon him as many as four times, requiring him to spend more than an hour in an afternoon just walking back and forth to have his nose counted. This does not include the time required to take an actual vote, when the clerk will read and reread the roll of 435 Representatives. It is estimated that the House of Representative used up the equivalent of one month last year just taking votes.

The business takes its toll. "What upset me coming to work," a Congress employee observed, "was to see the three flags on the Capitol at half-mast. I would think, 'Now who's dead?'" Eleven of the members, in fact, died during the year. The overwork and long hours were also felt by the staffs. "Two of my staff collapsed with coronaries," George Smith told the McClellan committee. "One of them died. I myself had a coronary and had to retire." So the survivors of the Eighty-second's first session adjourned wearily on October 20 and went home. A large number set out immediately to inspect parts of the world receiving large sums of money that they had voted. But most of them went back to their states and districts, like Antaeus, to regain their strength by touching earth.

They Don't Have Time to Listen

Congressman William B. Widnall, of New Jersey, packed his bags and took the train home to Hackensack. Mr. Widnall is something of a hero in his district. With the help of a group of amateur bushbeaters and doorbell ringers, mostly women, Mr. Widnall won the Republican nomination for the seat of J. Parnell Thomas, who had been sent to jail.

Leaving his wife and two schoolage children in New Jersey, Mr. Widnall had taken up bachelor quarters in Washington, renting a three-room apartment on Cathedral Avenue for $125 a month. It was an 80-cent cab ride or a 15-cent trolley ride from his office in the Old House Office Building; he usually took the trolley. Or he caught a free ride with his secretary and her husband, a Washington attorney.

He got to work every morning between eight-thirty and nine, and stayed at least until six, sometimes as late as eleven, and several times, during all-night sessions, until after three in the morning. He felt honored, considering his junior status, to be put on the important Banking and Currency Committee. Impressed by the great number of letters he was getting from veterans back home complaining that their new houses were shoddily constructed, improperly drained, and on the whole not worth anything

like the money the veterans had put up in VA loans, Mr. Widnall prepared a resolution calling for an investigation. Newcomer Widnall had
the unusual experience of getting a rule from the mighty Rules Committee
and actually seeing his resolution favorably voted on by the House. The
investigation will begin during the second session, he hopes. This triumph almost repaid him for seven-day work weeks, no vacation, his dreary
bachelor's existence, the lonesome restaurant suppers around the Hill, and
the financial loss he had incurred as a Congressman.

A Congressman's pay is $12,500, plus $2,500 tax-free expense money. Mr.
Widnall's outgo, originally based on an income of something like $15,000
from his law practice, included a $25,000 house in Saddle River, a growing
family, a 1946 Pontiac, the rent of a law office, and the salary of a secretary in Hackensack. These expenses went right on, while his law practice "went out the window," he says. "My best friends have forgotten that
I am in the law business."

In addition, he had the expense of the apartment in Washington, the
expense of eating out, of entertaining visitors, of contributing to hospital
balls and $100-a-plate political dinners, of phone calls to his district (about
$400 over his congressional allotment), and of weekend trips to see his
family and keep up his political connections. These trips cost him around
$1,500 a year. (Congressmen are allowed travel expense for one round
trip each session.) All together, the annual extra expense to Mr. Widnall
of living in Washington came to around $7,500. (After six years' service
he will be eligible for a pension, at age sixty-two, of $375 a year for each
year of service.)

Both in his office on the Hill and in his law office in Hackensack, Congressman Widnall saw and counseled an endless parade of angry and distracted constituents:

A deserted wife; service wives who had not received their allotments; a
man whose house was infested with worms; a diabetic who wanted his son
let out of the Army so the boy could run the store that was the family's
source of income; mothers asking, "Will you please tell me why my boy
is in Korea?"; people wanting work; people wanting help in getting relatives into the U.S. as immigrants ("A dishonest Congressman," said Mr.
Widnall, "can make himself thousands of dollars out of those people");
a delegation trying to get steel for a new school; citizens outraged by
swollen taxes, shouting: "You can't go on with this thing."

These were the voices of the voters, which Mr. Widnall heard every day
—begging and demanding, pleading and threatening. Mr. Congressman
was the government and could fix things up. With whom else did the
people's servant communicate? "One of the most discouraging things,"
said Mr. Widnall, "is to go to political meetings and see the same old party

job holders. You can't reach the people. They don't have time to listen to you, except when they want something for themselves."

At the beginning of the new year, Congressman Widnall packed his bags again and rejoined his colleagues on Capitol Hill, few of whom could boast of any regained strength—none of whom could argue very convincingly that the American system of representative government is, in fact, successfully meeting the test of modern times.

What's To Be Done?

Since 1789 there has been only one formal overhauling of the machinery of Congress. That was the La Follette–Monroney Reorganization Act of 1946. The act was passed after a long period of agitation by a committee of the American Political Science Association headed by Dr. George B. Galloway, senior specialist in the Legislative Reference Service of the Library of Congress, and after earnest crusading by the League of Women Voters, a National Planning Association Committee headed by Robert Heller, and a number of young Congressmen, including Mike Monroney, Estes Kefauver, and Everett Dirksen. Since then, Dr. Galloway, who is probably the foremost authority on the subject and claims to view the legislative scene with the detachment of "an anthropologist" viewing the customs of "primitive tribes," has gone right on writing books and pamphlets on the subject; Mr. Heller, a management engineer of Cleveland, has never quit issuing reports.

A multitude of standing committees were reduced by the Reorganization Act to fifteen in the Senate and nineteen in the House, with separate jurisdictions fairly well fixed. The act allowed some expansion in congressional staffs, called the "continuous watchfulness" on the part of committees over executive spending, strengthened the Legislative Reference Service as a source of needed information (Congressmen, said an observer, seldom read; they learn by listening), and raised congressional salaries (formerly $10,000).

It also provided that the House Ways and Means and Appropriations committees meet with the Senate's Finance and Appropriations committees at the beginning of each session and compile Congress' own budget. This legislative budget was to have fixed a ceiling on total spending, thus guiding Congressmen in their consideration of individual appropriations— and in the writing of a tax bill.

The act was only partially effective. Its chief failure was in the fiscal field. In 1947 the legislative budget died in a conference deadlock (Congress could not agree on what to do with an expected surplus!); in 1948 a legislative budget was actually delivered, but Congress thereupon appropriated $6 billion over its ceiling; in 1949 the House had passed eleven appropriation bills while the budget committee was still gestating a report; the legislative budget has not been heard of since.

In 1950 Congress decided to lump eleven supply bills into one omnibus bill, which worked out pretty well; the omnibus was passed a mere two months after the beginning of the fiscal year. The experiment was not repeated in 1951, largely because it limited congressional logrolling for favorite agencies and projects.

One fairly promising fiscal reform has been laid out in the McClellan bill, which would create a joint committee of five members from each house who would make a continuing, not just a spasmodic, study of finances. Federal agencies would have to show the committee a duplicate of every request made to the Budget Bureau. Congress could then, it was hoped, keep abreast of government business, and understand the figures on which it was basing decisions. This would not solve the problem of deficits, of course, which requires something more than an Act of Congress; i.e., skill, political nerve, and Hamiltonian wisdom.

A 2-Cent-a-Month Congress

Aside from the all-important fiscal problem, reformers addressed themselves to the other evident faults of the legislative machine and made many worthwhile suggestions. Mr. Heller, who became chairman of the National Committee for Strengthening Congress (bankers, businessmen, publishers, farm and labor leaders) recommended among other things: a relevancy rule for Senate debate; cloture by majority vote to shut off filibusters; committee chairmen to be elected by members or appointed by presiding officers on the basis of their competence rather than mere seniority; handling of picayune private bills by administrative and judicial authorities; larger congressional staffs, more facilities, electric voting equipment for the House; higher salaries ($25,000) for members. Several of these measures would provoke adamant resistance. Any majority leader who suggests a substitute for the seniority system, according to Senator Mike Monroney, "would be cutting his political throat." To a Congressman, says Monroney, seniority is "like money in the bank." A chairmanship for which he may have waited many years is a mark of prestige, an election asset. Majority cloture collides with the very stubborn ideas of some Americans. Advocates of such a measure must also be prepared to take the unquestioning position that the majority is always right. This weapon of a majority may sometimes be mere numbers.

Higher pay for Congressmen is long overdue. As to whether the nation can afford it, the present cost of keeping Congress—staff services, members' salaries, expenses, and all—is $36 million a year, approximately one-twentieth of 1 per cent of the federal budget; the cost to voters of maintaining their representation in Washington comes to 24 cents per American a year, or 2 cents a month. Congressmen could be expected to bow to a popular demand that they raise their own salaries. So far they have not detected any demand; last session, in fact, with almost excruciating political sensitivity, they cut their take-home pay about $1,000 by eliminating the tax exemption of their $2,500 expense money, beginning in 1953.

"If Men Were Angels . . ."

Montesquieu laid out the theory of checks and balances in good constitutional government—a theory that the Founding Fathers studied with great care.

It is ironic, in the light of history, that what James Madison feared most was the possibility of the legislative department "everywhere extending the sphere of its activity and drawing all power into its impetuous vortex." Madison did not foresee the revolution that began with Franklin Roosevelt. It is also ironic that while Mr. Truman was taking his thirteen defeats at the hands of the Eighty-second, real executive power was not disturbed. Mr. Truman himself may go down under the weight of scandal and blunders. But under him more and more power has been gathered into the executive vortex.

Something very drastic has to be done. The easiest thing would be to do nothing—that is, let an inefficient Congress surrender the country's fiscal policies to the Budget Bureau, surrender foreign policy to the President and his Secretaries of State and Defense, surrender law making to the agencies. Congress could continue to play its role as the country's great tattletale, busybody, and marathon talker. Then the revolution would be complete. Representative government would have ended in a babble of hoarse and meaningless voices.

The idea would be shocking to Americans. The idea is shocking to Congress. And yet this is the present course of American government, a course that only Congress still has the power to reverse. Congress must recognize that it is being overcome, in the final analysis, by its own inertia.

It is only Congress that can put to use the devices it was given to resist encroachment. The executive encroachment on its authority will continue to spread. It is the nature of political man to reach for power. As *The Federalist* pointed out: "It may be a reflection on human nature, that such devices should be necessary to control the abuses of government. But what is government itself but the greatest of all reflections on human nature? If men were angels, no government would be necessary. If angels were to govern men, neither external nor internal controls on government would be necessary. In framing a government which is to be administered by men over men, the great difficulty lies in this: you must first enable the government to control the governed; and in the next place oblige it to control itself." If Congress cannot control and manage itself, a long democratic struggle has been lost.

JUST HOW BAD IS CONGRESS? *

After surveying the recent record of Congress, Robert Bendiner concludes that representative government is far from deceased. On the contrary, the weaknesses that Congress exhibits are common to all parliamentary bodies in times of stress and conflict. Congress is simply reflecting the pressures that the country is facing both at home and on the international front.

Does the author attach too much importance to the cold war as explanation for the ills of Congress? What would be the consequences of a generation of international tension? Does the author ignore the impact of technology and scientific advance upon modern society? Can any government continue a policy of "muddling it through"?

When President Truman went through the country four years ago denouncing the "do-nothing, good-for-nothing 80th Congress," he was hardly setting a fresh pattern for a country in which Congress-baiting is a venerated pastime, going back to the dawn of the Republic and open to everyone from the Chief Executive down. Theodore Roosevelt habitually tried to by-pass the Senate as "a helpless body when efficient work for good is to be done." Wilson died embittered by that same "little group of willful men." As Jonathan Daniels has pointed out in his biography of Truman, the very phrase "do-nothing Congress" was borrowed by the President from his fellow Missourian Champ Clark, who applied it to the 54th Congress, of the Gay 90's. And a member of the Grant Cabinet used a figure peculiarly inappropriate for a spokesman of that corrupt administration. "You can't use tact with a Congressman," he explained to a questioner. "You must take a stick and hit him on the snout."

Yet before Truman, no president had ever waged an election campaign quite so concentrated on the derelictions of Congress. Justified as this

* Robert Bendiner. Reprinted from *Commentary*, February, 1952, pp. 135–41. Copyright, 1952, by the American Jewish Committee.

writer happens to think the President was, he undoubtedly furthered a trend which, viewed against the backdrop of the day's ideological warfare, has risky implications. At a moment when parliamentary institutions are under worldwide attack, when the whole democratic process is being systematically derided from Moscow, it is unfortunate, to say the least, that the Congress of the United States finds itself more and more on the defensive here at home, whatever the degree of its own responsibility.

Following the Republican "no-good 80th Congress," we had what some labor leaders called the "Eighty-worst Congress" because it failed to repeal the Taft-Hartley Act, and now we hear the 82nd described at a CIO Rubber Workers' Convention as "the worst in the history of the country." Even the journal of the temperate Americans for Democratic Action remarks that the first session of this Congress did "not match the mediocrity of the Republican-dominated Eightieth, but history will report the try as a near miss." To democrats elsewhere in the world it might well appear, discouragingly, that our legislative branch is deteriorating fast, even if they don't consult such irreverent works as *The Truman Merry-go-Round,* by Robert S. Allen and William V. Shannon, in which Representatives are discussed in all seriousness in a chapter headed "The Monkey House," while Senators, as a class, are referred to as "The Higher Primates."

Actually the criticisms of Congress, warranted and unwarranted alike, are almost never intended as attacks on that body as an institution. Usually, and naturally, they are partisan blasts, directed by Republicans at the Democratic majority or vice versa, or by Northern Democrats at the so-called Republican-Dixiecrat coalition. Sometimes they are charges hurled at a particular Congress as a whole by an economic group or special-interest bloc which has failed to get what it wants. Occasionally they are criticisms of specific practices fostered by one chamber or the other over the years— filibustering in the Senate, for example, or over-concentration of power in the Rules Committee of the House of Representatives, or abuse of the immunity privilege in both houses. Still, these complaints no matter what their merit, are rarely designed to weaken the system of checks and balances, much less bring the whole scheme of representative government into disrepute.

Yet carried too far, or misinterpreted, that can well be their effect, and for this Congressmen themselves are not without blame. There are always legislators who are ready to impute a destructive motive to their critics, equating attacks on themselves with hostility to the institution of Congress as such. Some even regard, or profess to regard, the growing practice of publicizing their voting records as somehow subversive. Others treat every attempt to curb the abuses committed by investigating committees as a blow at the foundations of government. Senator Robert A. Taft, typically, chose to interpret Truman's famous "non-political" trip in the spring of 1948 as an arraignment, not of the 80th Congress, but of the legislative system. "Our gallivanting President," he declared, "is blackguarding Congress at every whistle-stop in the West. . . . There is little use in keeping Congress in session while President Truman is delivering an attack on the principles of representative government itself."

For the most part we know how to discount this sort of by-play, though our friends abroad cannot be expected to. But even here at home it is becoming increasingly hard, in the fog of charge and countercharge, to maintain a fair perspective. Is it true that Congress as a branch of government has declined in comparison with the executive? If so, is its decline more than a passing phase in the historic tug of war between two frequently competitive branches of government? . . .

Beneath the emotionalism that marks the political exchanges of the day there lies, to begin with, a genuine and universal bewilderment in the face of the future. Congress merely reflects this. Far from not being representative enough, the national legislature is, in this sense at least, all too representative of a nation suffering from conflicting drives. The country ardently wants peace, yet it wants just as ardently to end the threat of Russian expansion and to check the spread of Communism. It still hankers after the old freedom from foreign "entanglements," yet it somewhat proudly accepts its inevitable role as the Number One Power of the non-Communist world. It wants to go on fulfilling the American dream of an ever rising standard of living, yet it wants also to be fully prepared for military operations of staggering cost. In a narrower sense it wants "free enterprise" and what Harding called "normalcy," yet no single special-interest group is ready to yield a fraction of what it has gained from government intervention since 1933. Moreover, as always, the minority party, by now desperate for the taste of victory, wants both to strengthen the nation in the face of Soviet challenge and yet harass its government at every turn for the sake of political advantage. That, too, is standard practice.

It is no wonder that on a score of issues Congress faces two ways at once. Neither is it to be wondered at that, with great changes sweeping over the world, with historic decisions to be made, members of Congress should put off those decisions as long as possible, should temporize and compromise, and channel most of their energies into the field of inquiry and investigation. On this score the first session of the 82nd Congress broke all records, with more than one hundred and thirty "special investigations"—that is, probes not connected with pending legislation.

Some of these investigations were irresponsibly conducted, and obviously conceived by individuals who had their own political fortunes exclusively in mind.   Others were calculated to use the abhorrence of Communism as a stick with which to beat the administration and block its program.   Still others were simply devices for marking time.   But there was far more to the trend than this.   Apart from the necessary airing of corruption in certain agencies, particularly the Reconstruction Finance Corporation and the Bureau of Internal Revenue, at least five of the investigations were basic in nature and of lasting importance.

No Congress can be brusquely dismissed that performed so remarkable a service as the hearings on the recall of General MacArthur.   Conducted in a fair and elevated manner by Senator Richard B. Russell of Georgia, these hearings before two top Senate committees were a unique achievement, even though they produced no notable findings and no concrete action whatever.   They served, first, to lower the national fever over the MacArthur affair, which was running so high that otherwise rational citizens completely forgot the proper relationship between military and civilian authority in a democracy.   More important in the long run, these hearings demonstrated to the country and to the world that we did, in fact, have a foreign policy which could be explained and defended, if not endorsed in all its particulars.   They gave men like Secretary Acheson and General Marshall an opportunity to defend themselves—and impressively —against the scurrilous assaults of the McCarthys and Jenners.   Not least, the investigation demonstrated to other nations, as few things American could, that, MacArthur notwithstanding, we were not hellbent for war; and that, Russian propaganda notwithstanding, we were still enough of a democracy to argue out basic conflicts of opinion in sober and responsible fashion.

Of the other significant investigations, the Kefauver inquiry into the operations of criminal rings was no doubt the most sensational, but others may prove more fruitful in the long run.   Exposure of the tactics used in the Maryland and Ohio election campaigns will very likely lead to revision of a thoroughly inadequate code.   Senator Douglas's inquiry into ethical standards in government, while less specific in nature, marked out an area of weakness which will have to be treated in all seriousness if we are to check corruption at the center of power.   Finally, Senator Benton's successful move to dig into the conduct of Senator McCarthy marked the turning point both in the career of that demagogue and in the decline of the Senate's reputation for courage and self-discipline.

Granted all that has been said of the inadequacies of recent Congresses, it is nevertheless true that in the most pressing area of legislation they have delivered to the President pretty much what he has asked for.   No one will doubt that this area is the field of foreign policy, and here the record of Congress is all the more remarkable in view of the passionate antagonism of so many of its members toward Secretary of State Acheson, his predecessor, and a good many of his colleagues. Here it is worth quoting Alistair Cooke . . . , in view of his over-all criticism: "Although the Congressional Record at times made it look as if the oratory of the Tafts, the Wherrys, and the Kems set the national temper, the fact is that troops were sent to Europe, grain was voted for India, prodigious military aid was granted to Europe and Asia, the Reciprocal Trade Act was extended again, as it has been every year since 1933. . . . For foreign aid, the original Presidential estimate of $8,600 million was reduced, after all the fuss and feathers about 'paying for European Socialism,' by only $1,300 millions." In other words, as Mr. Cooke freely admits, "Mr. Truman can get just about what any other President would get in this period of building up the Western defenses." A fair summary.

While no attempt will be offered here to defend the leadership of the Lucases, McFarlands, Tafts, and Wherrys, it is reasonable to admit that Congressional leadership inevitably diminishes as foreign policy grows in importance. The latter is largely, and necessarily, a function of the executive, and when it colors all other legislative activity, as is certainly the case today, Congress is bound to take a somewhat subordinate position and look to the White House for signals. This is a role that naturally irks legislators and offends their historic pride as a body. Which accounts for the tendency to go along with the President at a distance—grudgingly, with reservations, and with as much insistence on Congressional prerogative as can well be maintained. I think this is a fair description of the attitude of the past three Congresses. But in terms of world responsibility, who can say that they do not compare more than favorably with the one that wrecked Woodrow Wilson and reduced his dreams to rubble?

Man for man, the present Senate is no worse than dozens of its predecessors, and better than many. Alongside the McCarthy-for-LaFollette replacements, others must be considered which critics of Congress tend to overlook: a Kefauver in place of a long series of hacks sent to Washington by the Memphis machine of "Boss" Crump; Paul Douglas, who would have graced any Senate in our history, in place of Colonel McCormick's ineffable "Curly" Brooks; able Senators like Monroney of Oklahoma and Humphrey of Minnesota supplanting nonentities like Moore and Ball; a Sparkman and a Hill representing the state once served by Tom Heflin— not to mention young Russell B. Long, who now speaks soberly and ably on the spot where his father once jigged, clowned, and offered recipes for potlikker through a fifteen-hour filibuster.

Those who complain that the Senate no longer boasts men of the caliber of Clay, Calhoun, and Webster are referred to the similar plaint of Alexis de Tocqueville. When those giants still spoke in the land, the keen French observer commented sadly that "the race of American statesmen has evidently dwindled most remarkably in the course of the last fifty years." That would seem to argue that if we have been going downhill, there is at least nothing new about a decline that began in 1789. But the late Charles A. Beard did not see it that way at all. Surveying the work of the 76th Congress (1939–1941), he wrote:

As a more than casual student of the Congressional Record, I venture this opinion. It is possible to pick out of the Record for the past ten years addresses which, for breadth of knowledge, technical skill, analytical acumen, close reasoning, and dignified presentation, compare favorably with similar utterances made in the preceding century by the so-called great orators. . . . There is, to be sure, more trash—bad poetry, demagogic clap-trap, and clotted nonsense. . . . Yet after studying the operations of the first Congresses of the United States and the operations of the Seventy-sixth Congress, I am convinced that for disinterestedness, absence of corruption, and concern with the public good, the present body is of a higher order.

Improvement of personnel in individual instances, and the opposite, mean little as such; they tend generally to strike a balance. We are concerned here with Congress as an institution, and on this score it seems to me, in sum, far less accurate to say that Congress is going downhill, or even that its liberals are giving up the fight, than that it is going through a painful process of adjustment—to long-range changes within the country and to fearful uncertainties from without. The danger posed by Russia has already been mentioned, and the indecisiveness it causes is at least understandable. That Congresses basically hostile to the President and his diplomatic advisers should have gone along on the entire policy of "containment," from the Greek-Turkish program to the North Atlantic Treaty Organization, is a tribute to their awareness and responsibility, however grudging they have been in manner and in detail.

What is harder to appreciate, perhaps, is the difficulty of Congressmen in the face of the domestic changes brought on by the New Deal. Our national representatives have always had to do double duty, serving as errand boys for their constituents as well as legislators, but in the simpler days before 1933 government played only a small role in the daily lives of the voters, whose pressures on Representatives and Senators were mild and manageable. As Calvin Coolidge remarked in the 20's, the federal government could cease to operate and the average citizen wouldn't know the difference for three months. Today, with price controls, Social Security, an enormous defense program, huge federal power projects, comprehensive farm plans, loyalty probes, and all the other areas in which government operates extensively, millions of citizens have pressing business in Washington who never before gave more than a passing thought to government, and that only in election years.

Where a Senator once considered twenty letters a big day's mail, the average Congressman now gets a hundred a day, and during crucial debates he may get as many as seventy-five hundred. And they had better be answered. Where the First Congress passed 118 bills and resolutions, a Congress today grinds out more than a thousand, many of which are of enormous technical complexity. In his excellent book *Congress at the Crossroads,* George B. Galloway harks back to the life of a Congressman before World War I:

Congress was then in session only nine months out of twenty-four, and the members spent the remainder of their terms at home practicing law or attending to their private business. The mail they received then dealt largely with free seed, rural routes, Spanish War pensions, and occasionally a legislative matter. . . . "It was a pretty nice job that a member of Congress had in those days," Representative Ramspeck reminisced when he appeared thirty-four years later (1945) before a joint committee studying the burdens of legislation. "At that time the Government affected the people directly in only a minor way. . . . It was an entirely different job from the job we have to do today. It was primarily a legislative job, as the Constitution intended it to be."

As crisis followed crisis, the federal government expanded, and Congress, lacking the technical knowledge required, pressed for time, and harried by constituents, found itself forced "to place greater reliance upon the President and his well-staffed agencies for guidance and to delegate responsibility for policy-making, economic regulation, and social adjustment to a host of federal commissions, bureaus, and agencies."

To the extent that this occurred, and few observers will question that it was a significant extent, Congress has lost some ground as an institution. But it has not surrendered willingly or permanently, as the number of investigations eloquently testifies. Power has been delegated, but as the Roosevelt spell fades, Congress—jealous as always of its prerogatives—is attempting to limit and guide the exercise of that power. It has become as much the watchdog as the maker of policy. Where this takes the form of obstruction and infringement of the executive's rights, it is obviously harmful. Where it constitutes a reasonable assertion of what were Congressional prerogatives to begin with, it can be a healthy and democratic practice.

In the long run, the hope is that Congress itself will acquire, as it is now in the process of doing, the facilities for adequate knowledge, as well as devise parliamentary procedures geared to the swiftness of events. Beyond these, Congressmen sorely need freedom from the strain of having to spend half their time as lobbyists seeking favors and services for their constituents from the administrative agencies. While this period of adaptation continues, it is unlikely that Congress will take the lead. But, fortunately for its own integrity and the system of representative government, neither will it docilely follow the lead of the executive.

If generalizations are permissible at all, then, in a field as broad and fluid as this, the following ones would seem to be in order. Congress as a whole has been moving in a conservative direction since the death of Franklin D. Roosevelt, not to the point of having reversed the welfare program of the New Deal, or even trying to, but certainly to the extent of calling a halt to further experimentation. It is certainly arguable that this trend reflects a shift toward caution in the electorate. If Congress has been marking time, it is partly because the election results of 1946 and 1950 discouraged any further pressing for liberal measures, partly because President Truman's leadership has been less inspiring and less adroit than Roosevelt's, and partly because the unsettled state of the world has left Congressmen as uncertain of the future as the rest of us. Efforts to strengthen the structure of civil liberties by law have been paralyzed not only by the same Southern bloc that filibustered even in the days of the New Deal, but by the climate of opinion generated by Russian truculence, Communist behavior everywhere in the world, and the exploitation of those dangers by our own demagogues of the right. Finally, Congress as an institution is struggling, as we have suggested, to adjust itself to historic changes which have put upon its members so great a burden that a certain transfer of power to the executive branch has been inevitable.

Congress, in short, currently shows the weaknesses that always appear in parliamentary bodies in a period of uncertainty, fear, and swift change. We have had such times in the past, notably during the Civil War and its aftermath, and with similar—often worse—effect. In any case, there is little warrant for despair as to the capacity of Congress to assert itself as a working institution of democracy. In an immediate sense we have a right to expect, even to demand, that Congress bring itself, at the least, abreast of the times and to hope for a demonstration of the country's basic good sense at the polls—in Wisconsin, for example, that will assist the process. But in the long run we can look for relief in this area, as in so many others, only to a successful conclusion of the cold war, that prime source of the instability, fear, and confusion that feed the streams of political quackery and ineptitude.

HOW CONGRESS DOES IT—AND PARLIAMENT *

Professor Brogan offers wider insights into the role of Congress by comparing it with its counterpart, the British Parliament. In qualified and moderate terms he analyzes and evaluates corresponding functions of each institution. Neither institution is offered as a substitute for the other. Professor Brogan, however, does charge the American system with absence of identifiable responsibility. By its very nature, the system of divided power diffuses public attention. In compensation, the separation of powers deters the convergence of power in the hands of any one individual. Is this factor not important at a time when "faith in the magical powers of the state is the great modern disease"?

Few are the defenders of Congress, and they are fewer at the moment than even at other times. Senator Bilbo has not added to the dignity of the Senate and some members of the lower house have recalled that Congressman of whom the great Speaker Reed said that he never opened his mouth without subtracting from the sum of human knowledge.

Yet this contempt for Congress is not only bad for the processes of democracy, it is unjust and smug. The average American would do more good if he gave himself a good talking to, if he either rewarded Congressional virtue or punished Congressional vice with far more competence and zeal. For, as long as the average elector does no more than he does now in the way of intelligent and critical voting, the United States will get a better Congress than it deserves; it does so now, but it won't be as good a Congress as it needs.

I have never forgotten a party in which a group of intelligent and, in the ordinary sense of the term, well-informed and prosperous Americans were discussing (which is to say damning) Congress and the interruption that came from one of the party who was unknown to most of them but was in fact a (voluntarily) retired Congressman.

He pointed out that the critics had no real knowledge of Congress to back up their criticisms. He thought their classification of Congressmen showed no knowledge of the real character and usefulness of the more prominent members of the current Congress. And he pointed out that it was asking a lot of Congress to display all the highest virtues on behalf of such lazy citizens as were gathered there tonight.

"You come from X, don't you?" he asked one denouncer and deplorer.

* D. W. Brogan, *The New York Times Magazine*, July 7, 1946, pp. 8, 20, 21.

"Yes."

"Who is your Congressman?"

"I don't know; it's a new man."

"Who was your old Congressman?"

"I'm afraid I don't remember."

"Well, I'll tell you. I was, for four terms."

Now there might be plenty of parties in Britain where the knowledge of the facts of local political life was no more extensive than that shown at this party. But you don't need knowledge of the local facts of life, for an M.P. needn't be a local man whom you have got to watch and choose. He is in four cases out of five, a man chosen solely to vote as the national leaders tell him, and the vigilance that the American voter should, but does not, apply to the scrutiny of more than 500 members of both houses of Congress, need only be concentrated on the forty or fifty leaders at the top. And the local M.P. who defies local prejudices and loses his seat in a good cause, even if it is no more than the national party program, is not necessarily out forever; he can be found (if he rates the trouble) another seat.

Of course, local influence and local interests play and should play a great part in democratic politics in any country. There is a good deal of democratic sense in the retort of the old-time Irish M.P. who replied, "I don't care what *The* [London] *Times* is saying about me. I want to see what *The Skibbereen Eagle* is saying." But an American Congressman who, for the best of reasons, offends local pressure groups, or by not talking for Buncombe, wastes his time on mere national issues of the first order, may be out—and out forever. The history of Congress is full of martyrs to the general welfare, but any given Congress is full of men who have had more sense than to prefer the general welfare to the local interest.

Yet the experience of Canada shows that the American locality rule either in its constitutional or its stricter customary sense, is not necessary just because a country is big, a federation and deeply divided into sectional blocks. Canada is all of these and yet gets on very well without imposing on its Members of Parliament the necessity of being residents in the ridings they represent. But a century and a half of constitutional sanctity and rigorous tradition have made the locality rule sacred and in American eyes, "democratic," though a rigorist would point out that all it does is prohibit the electors electing men they might want, since if the intruder doesn't get elected, the rule is, in fact, observed in those districts that want to apply it.

The locality rule is one reason for the weakness of Congress. It keeps out of that body first-class Republicans from most parts of Manhattan; first-class Democrats in Vermont; and, in doubtful States, it makes a political career so hazardous that many men, otherwise well fitted for it and attracted by it, shy off. Congress is impoverished by a rule that 99 per cent of Americans think, in defiance of logic and relevant foreign experience, to be essential to democratic government. It is not the fault of Congress that this is so, but it is a fault all the same, the fault of "We the People of the United States."

Cabinet control on the English model does reduce the role of the mere private member to something much less interesting and important than that of the Congressman. He has to be content to be what a Conservative party spokesman is supposed to have called "The finest dumb votes in Christendom." It follows that, although Parliament is able to recruit from a more representative section of British talent than Congress can, the rank and file M.P. can be of a poorer intellectual type than the average Congressman without any visible consequences. In the past, he could also be a good deal idler and even be an absentee without his voters noticing it.

But the great growth of the social services has forced on every M.P. the need to act as an agent for his voters. A Liberal M.P. of the age before 1914 told me that with the passing of the first social security legislation in 1911, his mail multiplied fivefold. What the figures are now it is impossible to do more than guess, and the M.P. has no office building, no official secretarial staff and very inadequate facilities either for seeing or answering his voters. He is a kind of postoffice into which pour complaints that he passes on, a claims agent who is very much overworked. But he is not an independent legislator.

It is the Government which decides what measures must go through and whether a vote against them is a vote of "no-confidence" or not. And because of that, the Government cannot complain, as a President can, that it has had impossible legislation foisted on it or that it has been denied necessary powers. It has all the power—and all the responsibility.

So, too, with the slowness, the obstructiveness, the complexity of Congressional ways of business. They are, it is true, unnecessarily complicated, unnecessarily cumbrous. Much could be done inside the law and spirit of the Constitution to modernize them, but there are basic difficulties that would remain if the reforms were adopted and even if Mississippi sent only equivalents of John C. Calhoun or even Jefferson Davis to Congress instead of Bilbos, and Massachusetts only Daniel Websters or George Hoars instead of James M. Curleys.

If Congressional methods sometimes give to the outsider (and perhaps to the insider) the impression of a mechanical efficiency equivalent to that of the Toonerville trolley, the fault is not solely or mainly that of the members of Congress. It reflects the fact that the framers of the American Constitution (the half-foreign Hamilton excepted) did not want mere mechanical efficiency, did not want a smooth-running machine. They not only did not object to sand in the machine; they provided sand sprinklers. In this day and age, when faith in the magical powers of the state is the great modern disease, when it is reactionary, nay Fascist (in the new, meaningless sense of the word) even to wonder if the magic is not possibly black, not white, the Founding Fathers look like fools—or remarkably prescient fellows according to taste.

For they, most demonstrably, were not merely concerned to "get things done"; theirs was not the attitude of the brisk executive in the collar ads, his desk as clean as his shirt, commanding a series of bold, sweeping and rapid moves in the peanut business. No, the business methods suggested by the constitutional plan of the United States are more those of Postmaster Lincoln with the files in his hat. Indeed, that is to underestimate the business efficiency of Postmaster Lincoln for he had only one hat. The United States has three or four and finding the pea of responsibility is as difficult as is finding the pea under the thimble at the county fair.

Consider the life history of a statute, of the idea from the moment it is conceived in the mind of a Congressman, Senator, President, lobbyist, public-spirited citizen. One thing is certain about its fate: that if it ever comes to life in the great world at all, its parentage will be as uncertain as that of a character in a French farce or a new, powerful sociological novel about rural life in Georgia. There may be a few exceptions, a few measures like the Norris Amendment, that are children whose father is known. But there are not many. There may be a few occasions when the President's "must" legislation is really "must" and is really his. That, it seems to me, was true, by and large, of the Roosevelt "Hundred Days" in 1933.

But normally there is no doubt that even at the peak of Presidential "omnipotence" the President has to take adjustment from Congress that may make differences in degree that are close to differences in kind in his program. A British Prime Minister has, from time to time, to make concessions, too, though they are not necessarily concessions to Parliament. But, roughly speaking, the British Parliament has to take what the doctor orders.

So there is no passing the buck by the British executive which has never to put up with legislation it doesn't want and has very seldom to complain that it has not got the legislation and powers it does want. . . .

One explanation of the power of the British executive, which is not, I think, stressed enough, is the power of resignation. "Let George do it" is a possible Congressional attitude when it has passed, over the President's veto, an important measure that he has to administer or has cheerfully passed basically inconsistent pieces of legislation which the harrassed executive has to harmonize as best he can. . . .

But a British Parliament that does this is faced with the resignation of the Cabinet and has to provide a new Government. The party in power promptly votes itself out of office and the public and inescapable responsibility of the new policy falls on the new Government. An unfortunate President of the United States has no such chance of either threatening or getting out. For to whom is he to resign?

The nearest approach to identifiable responsibility in the American system is the general party responsibility. And that being so, a Republican House facing a Democratic President or vice versa has not merely a temptation to be obstructive, but a duty to be aggressive.

The motives that led the framers of the Constitution to give the House a two-year term are understandable. There was a prejudice, a reasonable one, against infrequent elections; some wanted annual elections and the comparatively long terms of the Senate and the President seemed to call for a counter-balance—if only to aid in getting the new Constitution adopted. The Founding Fathers thought of the Legislature as a coordinate and not over-busy branch, with a natural sphere of activity not bound closely to the President. They did not forsee the party system.

Were there no party system, a change in the majority of the House of Representatives would not be a "rebuke" to the President but to the former House; it would not be the first move in the next Presidential election, but a simple change of legislators. But the party system has changed all that, necessarily—and rightly—since otherwise the machine would not work at all. But although there is a great deal to be said for extending the term of the House to four years, it won't be done. And the possibility of two years of frustration will have to be faced as it is being faced now.

There is not much chance of any formal and fundamental changes. Some could only be made at the cost of a total change in the constitutional system and political habits of the American people, and such a change with such a risk of catastrophe will not and should not be made.

It should never be forgotten, as it often is by foreign and native critics, what an unprecedented success the Government of the United States is. No other country on this scale is so free and powerful. Possibly the United States would have grown to its present power, size and unity under another system, but we don't know that it would. Sic fortis Eturia crevit ("Thus Etruria grew strong").

But there are many modifications, not fundamental changes, that are worth making. One of the strong points of Congress could be, and sometimes is, its committee system. It makes Congress far more of a true legislative body than the House of Commons is. But the present committee system has too many defects: its excessive number of committees, its overlapping committees, its division of authority between the relevant committees in the two houses and the chairmanships going by mere seniority.

Since Congress must do its own business, it cannot afford to do it any longer on lines that suggest fraternity politics more than serious work. Whatever is done, the driving directing force will stay in the Presidency, though the office may know its periods of occultation.

Some parts of the parliamentary system might be grafted on (they would be grafted on a very different tree it should be remembered from the parent stock at Westminster). Cabinet officers might be allowed to address each house; there might be something like question time. But the American system will remain very American and there is more to be gained from a revival of party unity or a more rational division of party strength throughout the country than from mechanical adjustment.

Mr. Dooley once commented on the divorce wave in roughly these terms: "In the Archey Road, when a man and woman find they simply can't go on living together—they go on living together." So it is with Congress and the American people. But Congress must get her face lifted and recover some of the charm she must have had when every member of the lower house was a local hero and more Senators than Webster were godlike.

* * *

Custodian of the Tender Consciences *

As a practicing political scientist, T. V. Smith served in the Chicago city council and the Illinois legislature. In these capacities he had an opportunity to witness at close range the legislative way in action. He knows whereof he writes. Here politician-scholar Smith replies to the detractors of our national legislature with the novel suggestion that Congress already is doing a good job. The method by which Congress can be made better is neither technical nor mechanical. The problem of Congress, if one exists, is a moral one and as such is the responsibility of every individual in his capacity as a citizen. Is Professor Smith's analysis too pat and unsophisticated? Can skilled workmanship be achieved with inadequate tools? Or was Alexander Pope right when he wrote:

"For forms of government let fools contest
Whate'er is best administered is best"?

* T. V. Smith, *The Saturday Review of Literature,* December 14, 1946, pp. 12–13.

What needs reforming, if the criticism of Congress is to be stopped, is not reformable in a democratic society. Only a totalitarian society can enable one set of convictions to have its way. What "good" people want reformed is already good, is very good. It is this that they ask, and for the lack of which they blame Congress: to cease having differences of conviction over matters that seem to citizens most important, or if we must have such differences, to quit arguing about them in public, or if we must have major differences and must argue about them, then to settle the arguments "right," and not, as Congress does, make them worse by some hodge-podge compromise. That's what people want; that's what they, finding lacking, criticize Congress for. That's what Congress is not doing, because it does not know how. That's what Congress is not going to do, for nobody knows how, least of all the critics of Congress. That's what cannot be done without deserting democracy. If there is something that "should be done" which cannot be done collectively, then what should be done instead is for the critics of Congress to be brought to understand what democracy is, to understand how good a job Congress is already doing of it, and to quit applying private standards to public bodies if citizens are to remain both democratic and happy. It is a disservice to democracy to raise hope that by the reform of machinery citizens can get what they can get only by reforming themselves individually.

"For most of the things that properly can be called evils . . . ," says Justice Holmes, "the main remedy is for us to grow more civilized."

The crucial crossroads of Congress is, I repeat, moral, not technical. The business of this body is to turn inevitable conflicts of provincial interests and narrow consciences into compromises that create new standards of justice. So long as good men insist upon standards of justice antiquated by the very conflicts that call their reassertion forth, so long must Congress, as much by stalling as by legislating, be midwife to the ethically novel always straining at the birth. There is no other known way to keep conscience on the grow.

Someone has well said that there is no pain like the pain of a new idea; and we may add, as the proper sign to be hung at the main crossroads: "especially if the new idea be either a moral or a religious one." To budge the consciences of earnest men from rifts in the cake of custom created by honest conflict, leaving an anodyne to ease consciences too tender to bear up under their own self-built guilt,—this is the glory and the doom of Congress. The better it fulfils this, its moral vocation, the more noisily will it be criticized by those who admit themselves to be better than Congressmen, but the more gallantly will it be thanked in wise retrospect by the children of those self same critics. (There is much more profundity than cynicism in the wisecrack that the statesman is the dead politician.) In this game of disciplining honest men into accepting the utter minimum that is possible collectively, they also serve, often serve heroically, who only sit and stall.

Citizens, citizens, why do you ever kick against the collective goads of your own individual growth?

————◆••◆————

Problem 10: The Supreme Court--
Balance Wheel or Anchor Weight?

Throughout its history the Supreme Court has earned the confidence and respect of the American people. More than any other arm of the government, the Court has remained singularly free from graft, corruption, and maladministration. On the whole the caliber of its personnel has been able, and at times it has been distinguished. Yet the high prestige of the Supreme Court has not dispelled widespread criticism when its decisions seemed out of tune with the social and economic needs of the day. Such a condition occurred as the result of the Dred Scott case, the income tax decisions, and the opinions on child labor legislation. The most recent occasion of public dissatisfaction with the role of the Supreme Court occurred during the thirties when a series of major New Deal measures were held unconstitutional. This arrestment of social legislation prompted an outburst of critical comment. During the height of the dispute the Justices were called "the Nine Old Men" and their exercise of power was referred to as "the Divine Right of Judges." The center of the controversy was the nature and scope of judicial review.

It is paradoxical that in a country with a written constitution, and where judicial review has been developed most fully, the authorization for the practice should be so indefinite. Whether the Founding Fathers intended the courts to have this power is debatable. Actually, it is an academic rather than a realistic question. As Professor Corwin commented during the Senate hearings on Reorganization of the Federal Judiciary, "The people who say that the framers intended it are talking nonsense; and the people who say they did not intend it are talking nonsense. There is evidence on both sides. Why not deal with the question as it stands in the year of grace 1937?" In any event, judicial review is here to stay, and as a part of the American practice of government it remains the most striking characteristic of our political system.

The role of the Supreme Court is interlaced with the scope of judicial review. Charles Warren's article, "The Supreme Court Is the Corner-stone," espouses the traditional powers of the Court as the best guarantee of civil rights and liberties. A different interpretation of the effect of judicial review is presented by D. W. Brogan in "The Other Side of Judicial Review."   In the concluding article Robert H. Jackson criticizes any effort to evolve judicial review into judicial supremacy by showing the conse-quences of an all-powerful court.

THE SUPREME COURT IS THE CORNERSTONE OF THE AMERICAN SYSTEM *

There have been many eloquent treatises written in defense of the traditional role of the Supreme Court.   Close to the top among all of these is Charles Warren's two-volume history of the Supreme Court. The following selection from this work describes the Court as the bulwark of American government.   Warren regards judicial review as a democratic force, protecting the rights of minority groups from the tyranny of the majority.

Certain questions arise in the process of reading. Is it self-evident that constitutional rights are safer in the hands of the judiciary than in those of the legislature?   What explains the vitality of civil liberty in England where the concept of judicial review never developed? Finally, how does the advocacy of judicial review as a protection of minority rights square with the ideas advanced by D. W. Brogan in the succeeding article?

Whatever may be said of State Court Judges, those of the United States Supreme Court have been thoroughly and increasingly alive to the neces-sity of intellectual contact with new conditions and theories; and an earlier criticism of the Judiciary that cases are decided "upon the principles of the past . . . and the prejudices which the individualism of common law in-stitutional writers, the dogmas learned in a college course in economics, and habitual association with the business and professional class must in-evitably produce" is now by no means justified.

So thoroughly have the Judges, with very few exceptions, been imbued with this liberal spirit in later years, that the danger at present does not seem to lie in a reluctance of the Court to bow to the Legislative will, but

---

* From Charles Warren, *The Supreme Court in United States History*, Vol. II, pp. 750–56. By permission of Little, Brown and Company.

rather in a too facile readiness to confirm whatever the Legislature may have temporarily chosen to decree. There is some truth in Judge Dillon's words uttered as early as 1895: "If we are not struck with judicial blindness, we cannot fail to see that what is now to be feared and guarded against is the despotism of the many—of the majority." Restrictions of a temporary majority are as necessary now, as they were deemed to be when the founders of the Constitution deliberately and wisely included them in the frame of our Government. "The rights embodied in the Constitution . . . are as essential to the protection of the citizen against the tyranny of a hydra-headed tyrant of the future as they were against the monarchs of the past," said Attorney-General Wickersham at the meeting of the Bar on the death of Chief Justice Fuller. It is the chief and increasingly important function of the American Judiciary to disprove the prediction of that English historian, who wrote that "there is, in opposition to the will or passions of the majority, no lasting security, either for life or property, in America, in cases where the public mind is vehemently excited," and to confirm the happy phrase of James Russell Lowell that our written Constitutions are an obstacle "to the whim, but not to the will of the people." Legislative action is not always the height or essence of wisdom and justice. The needs or desires of the public are not always to be gratified, at the expense of individual rights and liberties; nor has the American people reached a stage where it is willing to surrender all such rights and liberties. There are still cases where "more is to be got for human happiness by private energy than by public legislation." It is of the greatest importance that the Judiciary should protect the rights of the minority, for otherwise they have no rights. In fact, the true test of a free government is the degree to which such protection is afforded. The majority must, of course, prevail in the long run, and eventually a Court must harmonize its juristic conceptions with the conception of liberty and right which public opinion sustains; but a majority is not always right temporarily. In view of the tendencies of legislation at the present time, the following views of a recent writer deserve earnest thought:

There has been some tendency in recent times to ignore the facts of majority tyranny, and to attribute the constitutional restraints adopted by the Fathers to certain monarchistic tendencies and an antipathy to the principles of democracy. But a careful study of the period would seem to indicate that the Fathers were animated mainly by a sane and practical fear of the evils of majority tyranny, with which they had considerable experience. The Revolutionary State Constitutions, with their provisions for legislative omnipotence, gave ample opportunities for the demonstration of the evils of unrestrained majorities. . . . The real importance of preventing majority tyranny does not become apparent, however, until we examine it in the light of its effect upon the existence of a true public opinion as a basis of popular government. We have seen that we cannot have true public opinion unless the minority feel themselves bound to acquiesce in the opinion of the majority. This attitude will never exist in regard to majority action which is tyrannical in nature, and which runs counter to the deeply embedded prejudices and convictions of the minority. In order to safeguard the very existence of popular government, therefore, it has been necessary to erect constitutional safeguards to protect the minority from such action by the majority as would lead the former to resistance or revolt.

Moreover, as Burke said, one hundred and thirty years ago: "The restraints on men, as well as their liberties, are to be reckoned among their rights."

That the Court, in its one hundred and thirty years' existence, has fully and worthily fulfilled the purposes for which it was designed by the framers of the Constitution, there can be no doubt; and De Tocqueville's words, written in 1835, are as true today as then:

The Supreme Court is placed at the head of all known tribunals, both by the nature of its rights and the class of justiciable parties which it controls. The peace, the prosperity and the very existence of the Union are placed in the hands of the Judges. Without their active cooperation, the Constitution would be a dead letter; the Executive appeals to them for protection against the encroachment of the Legislative power; the Legislature demands their protection against the designs of the Executive; they defend the Union against the disobedience of the States; the States, from the exaggerated claims of the Union; the public interests against the interests of private citizens; and the conservative spirit of order against the innovations of an excited democracy.

And as Judge Field wrote, on his resignation in 1897:

As I look back over the more than a third of a century that I have sat on this Bench, I am more and more impressed with the immeasurable importance of this Court. Now and then we hear it spoken of as an aristocratic feature of a republican government. But it is the most democratic of all. Senators represent their States, and Representatives their constituents; but this Court stands for the whole country, and as such it is truly "of the people, by the people and for the people." It has, indeed, no power to legislate. It cannot appropriate a dollar of money. It carries neither the purse nor the sword. But it possesses the power of declaring the law, and in that is found the safeguard which keeps the whole mighty fabric of government from rushing to destruction. This negative power, the power of resistance, is the only safety of a popular government.

That the Court is not infallible, that like all other human institutions it makes its mistakes may be acknowledged; yet in spite of the few instances in which it has run counter to the deliberate and better judgment of the community, the American people will unquestionably conclude that final judgment as to their constitutional rights is safer in the hands of the Judiciary than in those of the Legislature, and that if either body is to possess uncontrolled omnipotence, it should be reposed in the Court rather than in Congress, and in independent Judges rather than in Judges dependent on election by the people in passionate party campaigns and on partisan political issues.   In the words of Attorney-General Wickersham:

Mistakes have been made by the Judiciary.   Cases have been wrongly decided and the extension of legal principles to meet new conditions and judicial interpretation of the Constitution has often been slower than impatient reformers desirous of immediate results would wish.   Yet no candid critic can say that on the whole the history of the American Judiciary does not furnish as high, if not higher, example of adequate results than that of any other branch of the Government. . . .   They have no patronage with which to reward their followers, and no partisans to sustain them right or wrong; they have no interest except in common with their countrymen, and no ambition except to leave behind them an honored name.   Of all men in this world, they have the least temptation to do wrong and the greatest incentive to do right.   They are not infallible, and they make their mistakes, but they make fewer mistakes than other men; and so long as they can guard the Constitution of this Republic, it will protect the lives, the liberty and the property of the American people.

This book may well close with the eloquent appeal, written in 1856 at a time when American institutions seemed shaken:

Admit that the Federal Judiciary may in its time have been guilty of errors, that it has occasionally sought to wield more power than was safe, that it is as fallible as every other human institution.   Yet it has been, and is, a vast agency for good; it has averted many a storm which threatened our peace, and has lent its powerful aid in uniting us together in the bonds of law and justice.   Its very existence has proved a beacon of safety . . . and now let us ask ourselves, with all its imagined faults, what is there that can replace it: Strip it of its power, and what shall we get in exchange?   Discord and confusion, statutes without obedience, Courts without authority, an anarchy of principles and a chaos of decision, till all law at last shall be extinguished by an appeal to arms.

"If the Judiciary be struck from the system," said William Wirt in 1832, "what is there of any value that will remain?   The Government cannot subsist without it.   It would be as rational to talk of a solar system without a sun.   No, sir, the people of the United States know the value of this institution too well to suffer it to be put down or trammelled in its action by the dictates of others."

The Other Side of Judicial Review *

A persuasive argument in Charles Warren's "The Supreme Court is the Cornerstone of the American System" is that the courts and judicial review undergird American democracy. Professor Brogan turns the focus of American history upon the implications of this thesis. His conclusions cast doubt on the generally accepted assumptions that judicial review has insured minority rights, that it has protected property, and that it is a strong influence of democratization.

Is Professor Brogan right in suggesting that the Supreme Court and the principle of judicial review have tended to keep Americans in political tutelage? Would our political thinking have matured more quickly without judicial review? Let it be admitted that America has had its Klan, its America Firsters, its rabble rousers, its racists—nevertheless, is any country free from bigots? Has not the Supreme Court in upholding minority rights in the face of unsympathetic and sometimes hostile public opinion held the beachhead for the advance of democracy?

The final cause of judicial review is the preservation of the rights of minorities, of states, of individuals, against the ever-present danger of the tyranny of the majority. Has judicial review made more secure the rights guaranteed to the American citizen by the constitution? Has it saved the rights of the states against the Union? Only in a very limited degree can we answer "Yes." Certainly, the ordinary rights of the private citizen, in practice, are not more secure in the United States than in other countries, which have no such system of elaborate guarantees. Liberty of the Press, of petition, of public speech, are not particularly secure in some states at any time and in any state at a time of crisis. It may be answered that this is due to the temper of the people, that the tyrannies of the Ku Klux Klan were the work of individuals, the excesses of the Espionage Acts the works of a fever-heated Congress. Yet what are we to think of the educative effect of a century of judicial protection of individual liberty if the result was to make public opinion accept the preposterous tyranny with which, in the war to make the world safe for democracy, the people of America was plagued, three thousand miles from the battle front? Did England and France, and, for the matter, Germany, behave as badly in their treatment of unpopular minorities? Whatever else may be said for the American system, it has signally failed to tame the American people's

* D. W. Brogan, *Government of the People* (Harper, 1933), pp. 31–35.

passion for interference, with or without due process of law, with the rights of others. It has been argued, indeed, that it has lessened any initial tolerance and a plausible case can be made out for the thesis. Such rights as the courts do not protect are held on very poor security, whether they be of property or of liberty. The annihilation, without compensation, by the thirteenth amendment, of all slave property, not only in the revolted states, but in the loyal slave states, and by the eighteenth amendment, of the immense investment in breweries, distilleries, saloons, hardly suggest that unpopular forms of property can feel very secure in America, or, to put it at its lowest, that they would have been worse off in countries ruled by unlimited sovereign parliaments or by absolute monarchs. The record of the "Civil Liberties Union" is a long tale of attempts to make the letter of freedom do the work of the spirit. In this case, as in others, the letter killeth but the spirit giveth life.

The indignation aroused in radical breasts is not always justifiable, but it is understandable when we look at that sphere in which judicial control has been most effective. Liberty, political rights, the necessary guarantees of governmental efficiency may have little help from the courts, but how often has another cause been aided by the lawyers! The fourteenth amendment was passed, if not planned, to protect the freedmen after the Civil War and as such it was interpreted for ten years, till the court was induced to take up a strong attitude in defence of the corporations fearful of the political reactions that their assault on the old American economic system had provoked. How feeble was the amendment as a weapon to protect the Negro; how efficient in defence of the ideals of the rich! The contrast has led bitter critics to assail the courts with rather more heat than is justified. It might be argued indeed, that in nothing has the American constitution so met the wishes of its makers, as in its successful shielding of the rich from the consequences of the political power of the poor. That the contract clause, carefully imbedded in the instrument by its makers, should have had a more vigorous life than the "Bill of Rights," appended to placate the critics, is surely not surprising, but the fundamental weakness of constitutional guarantees of the American kind is their origin in a false, if noble, theory of government. It was in vain that the Massachusetts Declaration of Rights separated the judicial from the legislative and executive powers "to the end it may be a government of laws, and not of men," for all governments are governments of men; judicial review only ensures that the men must be lawyers.

This is not to say that the constitution, as interpreted by the courts, has not, at times, saved minorities, or individuals, even Negroes, from the anger of majorities expressed in statute or in more direct action. If we can assume (and it is not certain that we can) that the temper and standards of American legislation would have been as low without judicial review as with it, there is an obvious case for the Bill of Rights. It has been an obstacle to waves of tyranny when all other barriers failed. But it is possible that it would have worked as well had it been merely general counsel from the founding fathers, precepts without judicial sanction. Would it have been less effective if it had merely reminded Mr. Mitchell Palmer that the founder of his party had none of his dread of subversive propaganda or indifference to the rights of leaders of disreputable causes? Would a political reaction, such as stigmatized the Alien and Sedition Acts of 1798, have been less a tribute to the spirit of the constitution than belated protests of lawyers or decisions of the less panic-stricken federal judges? Would not more "Al" Smiths vetoing Lusk Acts in the height of the Red Panic of 1919–20, be more effective and lasting victories of the ideas of the Bill of Rights than an occasional Learned Hand on the federal bench?   But all this is guesswork; in the American situation the courts do at times defend private liberties and rights (other than property rights), and if we are to have judicial review at all, it is as well that there is the Bill of Rights as well as the "contract clause" and the fourteenth amendment.

Yet there is something to be said even against this side of judicial review, for the kind of rights that are protected are rights that can only be effectively protected by a spirit which judicial review does nothing to foster and possibly something to stifle. The Supreme Court will defend the rights of the Catholic minority in the Oregon schools case, but that does nothing to convict Oregon of sin and encourages, not only in Catholics, but in all other groups, that sectional feeling that is one of the banes of American politics. The slow growth of a real national feeling, of the give and take of a healthy commonwealth, of regard for a common consent, not for mere legal victories or majorities, is hindered by the attitude of mind that the recourse to legal, rather than political remedies, reveals. Yet in the present level of American political self-restraint, any suspicious minority may be pardoned for refusing to trust itself to the tender mercies of its fellows, and there is no likelihood that the reform of politics will be so rapid and evident that recourse to judicial review will seem unworthy of good citizens for a long time to come.

But there are two more exclusively political consequences of judicial review that wipe out much of the good the system may do: it encourages irresponsible legislation and it makes political objects too remote, and their attainment too uncertain, to make a healthy interest in politics easy to create or keep alive. The bad habit of relying on the judiciary to remedy the faults of the legislator is not the only cause of the low standard of much American legislation, but it contributes to it. This irresponsibility is possibly more dangerous than the occasional vagaries of unconstitutional legislation could be. Thanks to judicial review, the American legislator is kept permanently in a state of tutelage and he has, naturally, the ways of a child. It is possible that if he were trusted with a man's discretion he might put away childish things. If he did not, would the people not replace him, and if they cannot be trusted to show any passion for justice or liberty, can they be made to cherish either by any number of judicial vetoes? In all departments of American legislation, the encouragement to irresponsibility bred by judicial review is evident, the delusion that bad legislation does not matter, for if it is unconstitutional it will be nullified, if it is constitutional it cannot be really bad. Left to its own devices, the American people might learn that even if all things are lawful, all things are not expedient, but as it is they remain bound to the law. Even more enervating to sound politics is the uncertainty and remoteness that attaches to any political objective in the nation and the state. We cannot measure this by the number of federal or state acts invalidated, for we have no means of ascertaining the number of laws not passed, or not introduced, or not thought of, because of the possibility of judicial veto; nor can we assess the damage done to popular interest in politics by the widespread sense of futility that attaches to much legislative activity in America. The damage may be immeasurable and yet its existence certain. The politician and his electors are not the masters of their work or the judges of its limits and desirability. The futility that clings about all legislative chambers that have not a real final authority has sufficient cause for attaching to an American legislature, without the additional support of the consequences of judicial review. The politicians are playing an elaborate game whose rules they did not make and cannot alter, and which they are not even able to master thoroughly, since they are changed from time to time by the judicial masters of the constitution.

It is thus within the limits of the constitution, "as interpreted," that the politician must work and the forces making for artificiality, for slowness, for piecemeal adjustments rather than thorough schemes of reform or alteration, are powerfully reinforced by a habit of mind which goes very deep and whose ramifications are unseen by most Americans. It is the attitude of the American to the law-making process, the acceptance of the rule of lawyers conceived as being the rule of an objective wisdom above human criticism, that is least comprehensible by the European. Politically, the United States is a new "Country of the Blind"; along its narrow paths the politicians feel their way, never sure that they will not come suddenly to a dead end, for the guiding principles are feeble threads indeed. At any moment the whole path may have to be retraced and, for reasons that it is hoped are made plain elsewhere, it is hard enough to move American public opinion in any one direction at any time, almost impossible to start it off again on another slow advance, that may end as did the first. This gambling character of a great part of legislation, ranks with legislative irresponsibility as the chief sin against sound politics made easy or inevitable by judicial review. It is naturally hard to get the public to concentrate its attention on the legislative race when the winner may be disqualified for breach of undefined rules, for undefined they are and must be. The American political system is soaked in law, in lawyer's ideas and in the habits of mind bred by attention to the kind of thinking that legal training fosters. It is, of course, possible to think this a merit.

The spirit of the work of the Supreme Court permeates every legislative assembly and every important discussion of reforms by legislative action. We largely subject our political thinking to the conception of law, not as an arbitrary edict of power but as governed by the fundamental conceptions of justice.

To most Americans, this influence is a good thing; it is an example of their fear of the free action of the state and it has, in turn, encouraged that fear. To most Americans it seems obvious that "if either body is to possess uncontrolled omnipotence it should be reposed in the Court rather than in Congress." But the rest of the world sees no more reason to give the last word to a body of narrow specialists in general politics than it does to give them uncontrolled authority in their own speciality. We shall begin to adopt judicial review only after we have abandoned trial by jury.

———◆◆◆▶———

THE SUPREME COURT: JUDICIAL REVIEW OR JUDICIAL SUPREMACY? *

Taking a middle position between unconditional esteem and unqualified criticism, Robert H. Jackson discusses the Supreme Court as a crucible in which the shifting conflicts of economic, political, and social forces are balanced and blended. According to Jackson, the scales of adjudication are weighted in favor of conservative judgments because of the primacy of precedent, the recruitment of judges from the legal profession, and the age differential between the personnel in the Court and that in other branches of the government. Yet the author is quick to point out that no responsible critic has ever suggested abolishing the Court, and none has advanced a practical

* Reprinted from *The Struggle for Judicial Supremacy* by Robert H. Jackson, pp. vii–x, xii–xiv, 321–24, by permission of Alfred A. Knopf, Inc. Copyright, 1941, by Robert H. Jackson.

plan for reforming it. Jackson argues that the only workable reform must come from within the Court itself. Only through tolerance for the decisions of legislative bodies on controversial questions can judicial supremacy be avoided. Moreover, such forebearance keeps the avenues of compromise open. Judicial finality eliminates the opportunity for peaceful solution.

For a century every contest with the Supreme Court has ended in evading the basic inconsistency between popular government and judicial supremacy. None of the really influential critics of the Court have proposed destroying it or impairing its powers, and none have been able to suggest a hopeful formula for controlling it. None of the leaders of American democracy have yet been willing to risk democracy without some judicial restraint. So now, as always before, the struggle against judicial excess has ended by leaving it to the Justices themselves to correct the errors of the Court. It is certainly easier, and perhaps wiser, to let the Justices, when they have a will to do so, work out a corrected pattern of judicial restraint than to split our society as deeply as adoption of any formula for limiting judicial power would be likely to do.

But our history shows repeated disappointment of liberal Presidents in their efforts to effect a permanent or even long-enduring change of attitude or philosophy of the Court by additions to its personnel. Why is it that the Court influences appointees more consistently than appointees influence the Court? I point out certain sustained institutional and procedural pressures towards conservatism which only the most alert Justices will sense and only the most hardy will overcome. Because of these constant pressures I would underwrite no features even now.

Another generation may find itself fighting what is essentially the same conflict that we, under Roosevelt, and our fathers under Theodore Roosevelt and Wilson, and our grandfathers under Lincoln, and our great-grandfathers under Jackson, and our great-great-grandfathers under Jefferson, fought before them. The truce between judicial authority and popular will may, or may not, ripen into a permanent peace.

The proposal to reorganize the Supreme Court and the Court's self-reformation can only be understood as one chapter in the long and fascinating history of power politics in America. The seeds of a struggle for power were planted in the Constitution itself. That instrument set up a legislative and an executive branch, each in a large degree representative of popular will. It created on the other hand an appointive Court, whose Justices are chosen for life, and thus set up an overriding legal authority completely independent of popular will. These differently constituted institutions characteristically respond to the interests of different factions of society, as the founders foresaw they would. A struggle for power between these "equal" branches was inevitable. The Supreme Court has, from the very nature of its functions, been deep in power politics from the opening of the Court, and some of its leadership has been superb, notably so under Marshall and Hughes. It has moved with such mastery that by 1933 it had established a supremacy that could deny important powers to both state and nation on principles nowhere found in the Constitution itself, or could allocate powers as between state and nation, or between Congress and the executive departments, and could largely control the economic and social policy of the country. Exertion of such power was vigorously opposed, and the struggle for judicial supremacy aroused the most dramatic and persistent rivalry in our history.

As created, the Supreme Court seemed too anemic to endure a long contest for power. It has no function except to decide "cases" and "controversies," and its very jurisdiction to do that was left largely to the control of Congress. It has no force to execute its own commands, its judgments being handed over to the Executive for enforcement. Its Justices derive their offices from the favor of the other two branches by appointment and confirmation, and hold them subject to an undefined, unlimited, and unreviewable Congressional power of impeachment. They depend annually for the payment of their irreducible salaries and the housing and staffing of their Court upon appropriations by Congress. Certainly so dependent an institution would excite no fears.

Yet in spite of its apparently vulnerable position, this Court has repeatedly overruled and thwarted both the Congress and the Executive. It has been in angry collision with the most dynamic and popular Presidents in our history. Jefferson retaliated with impeachment; Jackson denied its authority; Lincoln disobeyed a writ of the Chief Justice; Theodore Roosevelt, after his Presidency, proposed recall of judicial decisions; Wilson tried to liberalize its membership; and Franklin D. Roosevelt proposed to "reorganize" it. It is surprising that it should not only survive but, with no might except the moral force of its judgments, should attain actual supremacy as a source of constitutional dogma.

Surprise turns to amazement when we reflect that time has proved that its judgment was wrong on the most outstanding issues upon which it has chosen to challenge the popular branches. Its judgment in the Dred Scott case was overruled by war. Its judgment that the currency that preserved the Union could not be made legal tender was overruled by Grant's selection of an additional Justice. Its judgment invalidating the income tax was overruled by the Sixteenth Amendment. Its judgments repressing labor and social legislation are now abandoned. Many of the judgments against New Deal legislation are rectified by confession of error. In no major conflict with the representative branches on any question of social or economic policy has time vindicated the Court. . . .

Nearly every significant decision of the Supreme Court has to do with power—power of government, power of officials—and hence it is always concerned with the social and economic interests involved in the allocation, denial, or recognition of power.

Two kinds of power seem always in competition in our democracy: there is political power, which is the power of the voters, and there is the economic power of property, which is the power of its owners. Conflicts between the two bring much grist to the judicial mill. The basic grievance of the New Deal was that the Court has seemed unduly to favor private economic power and always to find ways of circumventing the efforts of popular government to control or regulate it. . . .

The fight of 1937 was not a fight to destroy the Court or to impose legal limitations on its powers. The Roosevelt administration never refused obedience to any mandate of the Court. It made no attack on the tenure or integrity of any individual Justice. Its attack was on what it regarded as an abuse of power, not on the institution itself. It recognized the Supreme Court as a necessary institution in our federation and acknowledged its evolutionary accretions of customary authority to be quite as valid as its less specific written authority.

But liberal-minded lawyers also recognized that constitutional law is not a fixed body of immutable doctrine. We knew its rules had their beginnings and endings, their extensions and their recessions many times in the checkered history of the Court. We saw that those changes were identified with the predominant interests or currents of opinion of past epochs, though they were often made in the name of the Constitution itself. The peculiar character of judicial tenure had enabled a past that was dead and repudiated in the intellectual and political world to keep firm grip on the judicial world. What we demanded for our generation was the right consciously to influence the evolutionary progress of constitutional law, as other generations had done. And my generation has won its fight to make its own impression on the Court's constitutional doctrine. It has done it by marshalling the force of public opinion against the old Court through the court fight, by trying to influence the choice of forward-looking personnel, and, most of all, by persuasion of the Court itself. It must not be forgotten that many of the most important changes in legal theory were announced before there was any change in Justices. .

The Supreme Court can maintain itself and succeed in its tasks only if the counsels of self-restraint urged most earnestly by members of the Court itself are humbly and faithfully heeded. After the forces of conservatism and liberalism, of radicalism and reaction, of emotion and of self-interest are all caught up in the legislative process and averaged and come to rest in some compromise measure such as the Missouri Compromise, the N.R.A., the A.A.A., a minimum-wage law, or some other legislative policy, a decision striking it down closes an area of compromise in which conflicts have actually, if only temporarily, been composed. Each such decision takes away from our democratic federalism another of its defenses against domestic disorder and violence. The vice of judicial supremacy, as exerted for ninety years in the field of policy, has been its progressive closing of the avenues to peaceful and democratic conciliation of our social and economic conflicts.

In stressing this I do not join those who seek to deflate the whole judicial process. It is precisely because I value the role that the judiciary performs in the peaceful ordering of our society that I deprecate the ill-starred adventures of the judiciary that have recurringly jeopardized its essential usefulness. . . .

With us, what is wanted is not innovation, but a return to the spirit with which our early judges viewed the function of judicial review of legislation—the conviction that it is an awesome thing to strike down an act of the legislature approved by the Chief Executive, and that power so uncontrolled is not to be used save where the occasion is clear beyond fair debate.

If the judiciary attempts to enforce a judicial conservatism after legislative and political conservatism has decided to yield and compromise, it will jeopardize its power to serve the Republic in high and undisputed functions which only it can perform. By impairing its own prestige through risking it in the field of policy, it may impair its ability to defend our liberties.

CHAPTER FOUR

Personal Maladjustment and Crime

PERSONAL ADJUSTMENT to a rapidly changing and abundant culture in an era of declining primary social contacts and in an urbanized environment is more difficult to attain than under earlier conditions. There is a wealth of evidence to show that many of us are incapable of making that adjustment. Modern communications make us increasingly aware of the immensity of the problem. Murder and theft, alcoholism, mental aberrations, and homosexuality provide the material for many of our most widely read news stories and radio broadcasts. They are favorite themes for the modern novelist. That such problems are not foreign to the general population is further evidenced by the intense interest in and identification with all that is written and broadcast.

Inclusion of material concerning personal maladjustment in a book of social problems may seem, at first glance, to be inconsistent, but there are many justifications for it. Probably the most important is the growing realization that all individual problems tend to spring from the social setting. Even though there may be important hereditary connections, they become problematic only in terms of the individual's relationship with others—in social interaction. Individual behavior is seldom problematic unless the culture defines it as such. What is a problem in one culture may be accepted in another. An individual trait can become a problem only when social causation is at work.

A more easily recognized link between the individual and society is in terms of effect. Whatever may be the causes of personal maladjustments, there can be no question that their expression creates social problems. Society must deal with the neurotic and the psychotic, with the alcoholic and the sexual deviant, with the criminal and the delinquent. How it can deal most effectively with such deviants is not yet a closed subject. Numerous old methods have been subjected to close scrutiny and rejected. Certain substitutes for them have come forth, but many of these have not been fully tested because of public opposition or indifference.

Unsolved personal maladjustments and criminal activity are a great drain upon both our social and material resources. Millions of dollars are spent annually to erect and staff special institutions, such as mental hospitals and prisons. Our economy suffers from the loss of the productive efforts of those who are afflicted. And worst of all is the cost in terms of personal misery and personality distortion, which is not subject to dollar and cents measurement.

So we turn to the consideration of some of America's most serious *social and individual* problems. The accompanying readings are arranged under three major problems. The first concerns the matter of causation: What brings forth personal maladjustment? The second is concerned with the possible approaches to prevention and/or treatment of such maladjustments. Finally, special attention is centered upon the delinquent and the criminal in terms of causation, prevention, and rehabilitation.

Problem 11: What Are the Causes of Personal Maladjustment?

Having been "seized of a devil" was an early explanation of personal aberrations that were not acceptable to the social group. Although demonology is no longer considered to be an adequate explanation, vestiges of this point of view can still be found among certain portions of our population. Heredity has also been looked upon as the main source of such difficulties. However, as the social sciences have developed, we have come to understand that most, if not all, personal maladjustments are the product of social experiences in a specific cultural setting. This being true, it behooves us to know what experiences are most likely to produce personal disorganization and to contrast them with experiences that lead to personal balance. In the readings that follow several types of personal maladjustment are considered in terms of possible causative factors. Which explanation seems most convincing? Which require more careful analysis?

Mental Hygiene in the Atomic Age *

On every hand we see evidence of social maladjustment. So completely have we accepted the existence of personal and social disorganization that parrot-like we recite the statistics without thinking of their consequences—one out of every two hospital beds occupied by a mental patient, four million alcoholics, five million sleeping pills sold each day. Recently a speaker on "Town Meeting of the Air" stated that there are eight million persons receiving psychiatric treatment in America. The speaker then went on to declare, "The increasing dependence on the psychiatrist's couch is the mark of the decreasing dependence on the Christian church."

Individuals pondering these things have come up with various explanations. To some we are going crazy collectively. Others contend that social disorganization is no more common now than formerly, the only difference being that today we recognize cases that formerly went undetected. In the following article a thoughtful student of mental hygiene, Franz Alexander, analyzes our society and suggests some roads that we may travel in the future.

The central psychological difficulty of our industrial era consists essentially in the need for rapid adjustments to ever changing conditions. In times of slow social change—as for example the eight hundred years of feudal era in Europe—individual adjustments are supported by tradition as represented by attitudes in the family and in institutions like school and church. The life of everyone is rigidly determined by these traditions. A glance at the contours of history in the past one hundred and fifty years presents us with a sharp contrast to this picture. With the Industrial Revolution a fundamentally new era of civilization started, characterized by change and mobility. It is, however, erroneous to limit the extent of Industrial Revolution to the last decades of the 18th and the early part of the 19th centuries. Since those days we have never ceased to live in the era of industrial revolution, if we define the latter as sudden social changes resulting from rapid advancements of technology.

We have no methods to measure precisely the speed of social change, but it is certain that the rate of this already rapid change has been greatly accelerated in our present days. Our habits and views and our knowl-

* Franz Alexander in Lyman Bryson, Louis Finkelstein and Robert MacIver (eds.), *Conflicts of Power in Modern Culture* (Harper, 1947), pp. 276–79, 282–85. Copyright, 1947, by the Conference on Science, Philosophy and Religion in Their Relation to the Democratic Way of Life, Inc.

edge of yesterday are out of date today, and it seems that the demand for adjusting ourselves to an ever changing world exceeds our adaptability.

The birth of this nation coincided with the beginning of the Industrial Revolution. The American pioneer could turn to technology in his heroic task of conquering a vast, unexplored country. Just as the Spanish Civil War was a rehearsal for modern warfare, the conquest of the American continent was a grand rehearsal for modern technology—at first steam, then electricity, and eventually the combustion engine and electronic devices. The utilization of atomic energies will be the next step. The hero of this development was at first the settler in his steady movement toward the West, later the businessman, the mechanic, and the practical inventor, then the entrepreneur, and finally in our days of mass production, the organizer, the industrial executive. It is quite natural that the worship of industrial production and distribution of manufactured goods throughout the whole industrialized world became the ideological backbone of our times. A part of this cultural climate is the competitive spirit which has played such an important role in stimulating production and business in general. Accomplishment became the measure of public esteem, and accomplishment meant for the majority production and distribution of economic goods. And the production has gradually become an end in itself, overreaching its social usefulness.

Most people engrossed in their feverish race for achievement are truly terrified at the idea of leisure or inactivity. When the businessman successfully reaches his goal and can stop expanding his business, he does not dare to do so, lest his life become completely empty and senseless. Most of us behave as the tourist who makes a trip but concentrates only on driving his car. The places he includes in his itinerary are only illusory goals. When he arrives at one place, he scarcely notices it; he arrives in the evening, goes to his hotel, sleeps and eats, and starts out early the next morning in order to make the scheduled number of miles to the next stopping place. I can best illustrate the psychology behind this driving for its own sake with a clinical condition which can appropriately be called "retirement neurosis." I see an amazingly large number of these people. Such a patient is, as a rule, a successful businessman between the ages of fifty-five and seventy. For some reason he has to withdraw from active participation in business. His reaction is severe depression; life has ceased to have any meaning for him. From the time he started work as a boy his life has been concentrated on one single goal: financial success. Business has become a passion with him—an all-absorbing mad race. To a psychiatrist's remark that now, when he has to quit business, there might be something worthwhile left for him to do in life, the usual reply is that he has worked all his life, having had little time for other activities, and that if he can't work now, he'd prefer not to live.

One may raise the objection that these are exceptional cases, that for the majority life consists in a continuous effort to raise their standards of living. The embarrassment people feel if confronted with the question of what to do with their leisure time, however, is universal, a typical feature of our times. It is not so conspicuous in those who are struggling for their existence, but it becomes immediately manifest as soon as the necessity for struggle or the opportunity for the improvement of material standards disappears. We tell ourselves that we are striving for a state of affairs in which the material benefits of our technical advancements will be available to every member of society. Since we have not yet arrived at such a universal state of prosperity, we can evade the embarrassing question: What will then be the content of life for people who have prepared to use their prosperity for the enrichment of their lives? We look with complacency on our great material achievements and overlook the fact that, while we were achieving these things, we forgot the elementary art of living. We look condescendingly on the peasants of the feudal era because of their primitive material standards, and we overlook their superior capacity of creative expression in folk art, music, dance, handicraft, and folklore, the absence of which makes the life of our industrial masses so drab and colorless. I do not want to be misunderstood. I am not praising the bliss of feudal culture in contrast to industrial civilization. My point is that, while we were busy improving the material foundations of life, we became so engrossed in this endeavor, so fascinated by the possibilities which the machine offers, that we forgot the ultimate aim of all these improvements: a higher cultivation of our specifically human faculties. Eating, sleeping, and propagation are common to men and animals. Division of labor, the exchange of socially useful services, can even be observed in an insect society. But writing poems and novels, building cathedrals, producing plays and operas, discovering the laws of nature and inventing methods of healing, enjoying a landscape, educating and developing the powers of the mind, are specifically human faculties.

There is good evidence that these human faculties developed as a result of man's invention of the tool. The differentiation of the hand as a separate specific organ, relieved from its function of locomotion, together with a highly developed cortex in the brain, the site of the highest intellectual functions, made the discovery of the tool possible. From then on, the use of tools opened the road to an easier life and freed human energies for those higher functions which I have designated as "specifically human."

And now we are witnessing a curious turn in human development: the tool, originally developed to enable us to raise our heads and turn away, at least occasionally, from the struggle for existence, has become our master. For its sake, we are giving up the use of our higher faculties, our higher interests, and are devoting ourselves to improving the machine without ever enjoying its real benefits. We have been so preoccupied with the job of building a home through all these years that we have forgotten that we built it to live in. The industrial production of goods has become almost a form of idol worship with us. We are so absorbed in producing for the sake of production that we forget that the material goods were meant to make us free from the chores of material existence so that we might do something else. As a last result of this nonsensical development, we are faced with the ghastly prospect of using the tool to destroy each other together with all that we call civilization. Man invented a tool to make life easier for himself; he ends up using it to debase himself to a button-pushing automaton whose last act will be to push the button that will exterminate him.

. . . Social life consists in the mutual gratification of human needs by division of functions. It makes no difference what those needs are: whether food, or shoes, or lounging chairs, or poems. As soon as the needs of the body are satisfied, the satisfaction of our so-called higher needs must become our concern. Why should we consider the production of lounging chairs more basic than poems, when one can exist equally well without either of them? And yet the production of lounging chairs is considered productive, increasing the national wealth, while poetry, from the point of view of economics, is quite negligible and has nothing to do with increasing the national wealth except possibly through the paper on which it is printed. Yet if more people were interested in buying poetry than in buying lounging chairs, it would become a much more important national item in the national economy than the chairs.

The answer to this problem lies then in ideological changes—in a different scale of values appropriate to the phase of our social development. A country which has succeeded in such an unparalleled manner in laying down the material foundations of civilized life, is ripe for taking the next logical step in its development—the building of a high spiritual culture upon the material foundations. Productive energies can no longer concentrate exclusively on continuing to build the foundations because to a large extent they are already laid down. We shall have systematically to develop needs for less tangible goods which cannot be produced by machines. This can be done through education of the masses with a greater emphasis on the liberal arts and on the merits of esthetic appreciation and creative expression. Moreover, human energies can more and more turn toward such channels as teaching, healing, and all those human services which make for the enjoyment of life. Human energies liberated by advancing technology must be used either constructively or destructively. The choice is ours. If greater attention is not paid to cultural and moral values, it will lead to our destruction—either moral or physical. . . .

The aim of psychiatry is to help the individual who has failed to adjust himself to the conditions of his life. Mental hygiene attempts to accomplish the same on a large social scale. Like psychiatry it must begin with the diagnosis of trouble, finding those emotional difficulties of adjustment to which the majority of the people are exposed. In the above diagnosis my conclusion is that we are the victims of a cultural lag inasmuch as we still live emotionally in the past and have not caught up with the new conditions brought about by science and its technical achievements. Following the inertia of habit, instead of making use of labor-saving devices of industry for turning our creative capacities to other fields which lie outside the production of material goods, we are apt to follow traditional patterns and as a result more people will want to earn their living from industrial production than will be needed. This incongruity between ideology and economy will, with the further improvement of automatic tools, steadily increase in the future. The result will be that periodic unemployment will remain with us as a constant source of insecurity and a constant threat to self-esteem, arousing the feeling of having lost one's social usefulness. This insecurity and the frustration of having no opportunity to make use of one's productive capacities are the main source of emotional maladjustment in our times, taking the place of sexual repression which dominated the scene during the Victorian Era.

Another manifestation of this cultural lag is our addiction to competition, which makes a race track of our social scene. We live in a world of plenty, at least potentially we do, and yet emotionally we still follow the jungle pattern, "kill or be killed." We continue at home as well as abroad in the belief that it is necessary to prey upon each other. If we do not have to struggle and compete, life becomes empty for us and this feeling is a common cause of emotional maladjustment. We see then that no social group can escape the mentally unsettling consequences of the prevailing discrepancy between emotional orientation and social structure. The effect of this discrepancy upon the struggling masses is insecurity, loss of self-esteem, and frustration; its effect upon those who do not indulge any longer in the race for success is a feeling that life is empty and has lost its meaning. Indeed, machine civilization with all its magnificent material achievements has created a gap in our emotional household by liberating energies which we have not yet learned how to use in a constructive manner. To fill this gap with developing the higher creative faculties of man is the great future task of our era.

I have limited my remarks to defining the nature and source of the most common emotional problems of our times. Making such a diagnosis is one function of mental hygiene. The remedy lies obviously in an emotional reorientation restoring the disturbed relation between psychological attitudes and social structure. To accomplish this, lies not primarily in the field of psychiatry or mental hygiene. It is the function of the social institutions to which the shaping of the personality and social attitudes are traditionally entrusted—first of all the family, then the church and the school.

Don't Let Them Tell You We're All Going Crazy! *

Few topics have had greater publicity than the increasing incidence of mental illness and personal maladjustment. What is the true picture? Are Americans going crazy collectively rather than individually? Have the statistics been misinterpreted? Donald G. Cooley suggests a provocative explanation for the facts and figures that have had such wide circulation.

Are we all going quietly mad? Are you neurotic now? And if you are, does it mean that tomorrow you'll be psychotic, schizophrenic, or a victim of senile dementia? Or, to put it in plain language, will they be coming to get you one of these days in the little white wagon and put you where you can't hurt anybody, including yourself?

Maybe so. You hear plenty of gloomy reports on the mental state of the union. Surgeon General Thomas Parran tells us that mental disorders affect, to some degree, about 8,000,000 Americans and fill more than half the hospital beds of the country. Not only that, but nearly one-third of all men rejected under Selective Service were turned down for mental reasons. And almost half the disability discharges from the army—a whopping 44.6 per cent—were for neuropsychiatric reasons.

These are appalling figures. They shock. But do statistics imply what they seem to—that mental disorders are increasing by leaps and bounds? Frankly, some frightening interpretations are open to serious question.

For one thing, statistics represent mental cases that come to official notice. Not long ago, diagnosis of mental afflictions was a pretty haphazard

* Donald G. Cooley. Condensed from *Better Homes and Gardens,* July, 1947, pp. 33, 122, 124–26, 143. Copyright Meredith Publishing Company, 1947, Des Moines, Iowa.

affair. Only the most advanced cases wound up in hospitals. You may be old enough to remember cases like Gramp's. Gramp was well past 70, and his arteries, including those nourishing his brain, were getting brittle. He was untidy, forgetful, inclined to maunder, and needed the care and supervision a small child needs. But around the farm he was able to do a few chores, or, if he wasn't, he was still Gramp, who used to bring us hard candies in striped paper sacks, and there was a family tradition that we took care of our own.

Nowadays, Gramp would probably be bundled off to an institution. A three-room apartment doesn't have enough closets to hide a skeleton. The girls can't bring home their boy friends. They might set Gramp down as nuts and wonder if it ran in the family. Too, Gramp can't be cared for adequately in cramped family quarters nor allowed to wander at his peril on city streets. He's better off, gets better care, in an institution. In a small way, people like Gramp contribute to statistics on mental illness.

By far the largest part of what we loosely call mental illness is made up of the kind of statistics that surround you in the flesh. There's the over-suspicious associate who thinks you're out to get his job. The acquaintance who's an eager hater, the recluse who rarely comes out of the house, the neighbor who carries on a feud, the woman who seems normal until she gets off on some one subject where she doesn't make sense, the boy imprisoned in daydreams, the girl who rarely holds a job more than a week because "everybody hates her"—you can think of a hundred others like these without half trying. In general, they're the psychoneurotics who swell the mental statistics by hundreds of thousands.

We're all pretty glib in using words like psychoneurosis. The next movie you attend may have as its hero a psychiatrist, male or female, who fishes a complex out of the patient's past to set the stage for a satisfactory clinch. Books, novels, stage plays, even detective stories, deal with mental hospitals or have psychiatric twists. From these sources we pick up the jargon of the specialist, running the gamut from Id to Ego, but often with little understanding of specialized meanings.

. . . . . .

Take those army figures on hundreds of thousands of men discharged with the N.P. (neuropsychiatric) label. Blazoned in the press, they have intensified in the public mind the horrific stigma still unreasonably attached to mental disturbance. In all conscience, those figures compel intelligent attention to a serious problem. There is no reason to doubt that had women undergone the same mass examinations as men, they would have turned in equally depressing mental health cards. This isn't good, but a reasonable job of press agentry would have allayed the fears, in some quarters, that everybody's bound for Bedlam.

No one stresses the plain fact that only 1 out of 20 N.P. discharges had a psychosis—"insanity," if you want to put it crudely. The other 19 out of 20 were, in general, psychoneurotic, a long way short of being dangerous maniacs. But the damage was done. Stuck with a repugnant label, the boys didn't draw fine distinctions. As one serviceman remarked wryly, "It's psycho no matter how you slice it." Quite naturally, the public became skittish of the label, especially after the boys came home and tackled the big job of readjustment.

Of course, there were reasons for army procedure. In wartime a titanic job must be done in a hurry. There were only some two thousand trained psychiatrists in the service. In one large separation center, the psychiatric team had exactly two minutes to give each man a complete nervous and mental examination! Outranking the psychiatrists, in many cases, were medical officers with little psychiatric training. And in higher military echelons, the attitude was generally antagonistic. The N.P. was regarded as a gold-bricker, a weak sister, a malingerer who needed nothing but discipline.

Army statistics are a mare's nest of confusion. Case classifications are lumped together in bewildering fashion. Where the descriptions have specific meaning, much depends on the directive that happened to be in force at the moment, or upon varying exigencies such as the need to rustle troublemakers out of the front lines where they were disturbing morale. Fairly early in the game, it was recognized that the N.P. label was reacting badly upon the men and the folks back home. There was an abrupt change of face and terms such as "combat fatigue" or "battle fatigue" came into use. This was a sensible effort to focus attention on precipitating causes rather than character deficiencies. It didn't work too well, for the men were still routed thru psychiatric service and the whole thing was a little like those crushing words with which you dress down your wife: easy to issue, impossible to recall. Today, now that peace of a sort has come, the army is revising its psychiatric nomenclature along scientific lines.

What does the great army of psychoneurotics mean in human terms? Let's take a look at a hog. You don't think of a hog as being a natural candidate for a nervous breakdown. He has no way of knowing how unlucky he is to be a hog, and his pighood, as far as anyone knows, is unshadowed by an Oedipus complex or sense of sin.

Well at Cornell Behavior Farm, Dr. H. S. Liddell and his associates have been making neurotics out of hogs, not to mention dogs, goats, and sheep. They put a hog into a cage containing a box into which an apple falls when a bell rings. The animal lifts the box top and eats the apple. Later, an electric shock is added so he learns to forage only at the proper signal. Then the signals are crossed up. The hog can't tell if he'll get a shock, an apple, or a clout on the snout. His rational world collapses. He goes into a tantrum, squeals and rages, finally goes off and lies inert in a corner —a seclusive, schizophrenic pig. He acts exactly as if he had a nervous breakdown, and why not?

The analogy can be overstrained, but it is fair to point out that human beings have breaking points, even as the hog. When we are faced with situations we can't solve, or escape, when the rules we've learned don't seem to work, when our "enemy" is shapeless and we can't land a punch on him, the tensions pent up within us naturally explode in neurosis. This is much the sort of thing that happened to many N.P.'s, who had to face bombs and flak and jungles and see their comrades fall. A good many of these boys merely had transient personality reactions to situations of acute crisis. Not even the late General Patton, a soldier to the core if there ever was one, was immune to this sort of emotional explosion. The face-slapping incident in which he was involved was a consequence of long, unbearable stresses of frontline action that taxed even his steel-cable emotions.

To be sure, there is great variation in how much we can "take"—whether, as William James put it, we are tough-minded or tender-minded. When a man is emotionally immature, has weakened capacity to deal with reality, is without a bedrock philosophy to tie to, and has little sense of self-sufficiency, he's an easy collapser. But that's a long way from saying he's crazy, or even that he will exhibit overt signs of neurosis. In a placid job, surrounded by security and undemanding friends, he's likely to be an ordinary, if not too happy, citizen.

We're all interested, and rightly so, in learning how our minds get that way. The pity is that some aspects of psychiatry have been over-glamorized, while much of its finest and most quiet work is little known. Misconceptions are rampant. There are people who believe that psychiatrists are to blame for much mental illness because they diagnose it—a little like shooting your dentist because you have a toothache. In many ways the public relations of psychiatry are sorely in need of house cleaning, but you can't blame the psychiatrists for movie- or fiction-induced notions that psychoanalysis is the only tool they have to work with.

The psychoanalytic technique of dredging repressed ideas out of a patient's unconscious mind can be remarkably effective, but it means little to mass statistics of mental illness. Some cases may profit from a few psychoanalytic sessions, but on the whole, psychoanalysis is a matter of months or even years of treatment, far too costly for the run-of-the-mill patient. If every one of the country's 4,000 psychiatrists spent all his time on individual psychoanalysis, the effect on the reservoir of mental illness would be comparable to a $5 contribution in lowering the war debt.

Many psychiatrists feel that they have been dealing too largely with individuals, and that the next step is the prevention of mental illness by attacking on a broader base. They are agreed that the seeds of neurosis are sown in childhood. The neurotic is not necessarily born with defective mentality—indeed, he has a much keener mind than the slow, vegetative individual—but he is the product of his life experiences from childhood onward. He can't be detached from the society of which he is a part, and there are those who feel that our competitive, frustrating, high-pressure society needs a more intensive working-over than the patient.

A mentally healthy childhood should insure a mentally healthy adult. But parents and teachers who should provide a healthy atmosphere are more likely to be victims than good examples. Kids are brought up by the book, imbibe insecurities, are taught rigid dogmas and fixed ideas that are impossible to cling to in a changing world. In one Montreal mental hospital, there are patients whose parents taught them that the only decent way to take a bath is to wear long drawers that conceal the body from one's own gaze. No wonder they come down with an anxiety neurosis when they move to cities where such ideas are simply considered "screwball"!

Preventive psychiatry is making some encouraging starts. In several cities, Cornelian Corners have been established. These get their name from Cornelia, mother of the Gracchi, and the "corner" is the secluded one where, in a communal room, the mother used to turn her back while nursing her baby. Nursing is but one means of building security in the infant; it is deemed important to pick him up and cuddle him, for instance, not to let him squall if a cursory inspection shows that no pins are sticking him.

In industry, psychiatry is beginning to play a role in minimizing the sort of strikes and work difficulties that arise from insult to the worker's ego and disregard of him as a human being rather than from rates of pay. Some schools are taking advantage of child guidance clinics operated by public health services. There are local branches of mental hygiene associations, and municipal social service departments include psychiatrists as well as sociologists. Many courts, as well, have psychiatrists for helping delinquents and others in trouble. In most of these instances, the psychiatrist does not work alone, but as a member of a team that includes other specialists in social service. In mental hospitals, of course, the psychiatrist has made notable advances in the treatment of psychoses, by shock treatment and other methods. The popular idea that when the average psychotic patient is "sent to an asylum" he is there for life is far from true.

These are heartening steps forward. There will be more of them.

They're a long way removed from the popular notion of a beautiful patient on a couch, engaged in "transfer" to the psychiatrist—tho to dismiss psychoanalysis as nonsense is to confess, in a way, to a neurosis.

Nevertheless, psychiatry has important house-cleaning jobs ahead. The people who brag about consulting a psychiatrist are those who can afford psychoanalysis. The ideal will not be reached until people are as casual about seeking psychiatric help as they are in getting a diagnosis of sinus trouble. Psychiatrists still write mostly for themselves, in difficult jargon, and some of their words, filtered down—psychoneurosis is an example—frighten instead of helping, for words have an immense capacity to injure. Dr. Carl Binger is one eminent psychiatrist who has urged his colleagues to write in plain English if they're to enjoy reasonable public relations.

It is easy to forget that psychiatry is still very young as sciences go, and that it is still suffering growing pains as it emerges from early stages in which it was largely a classification of mental disturbances. There are plenty of intramural squabbles. The Freudians occupy one corner, exchanging clews with excommunicated disciples of Jung in another, and both crack down on followers of Adler. When the fists start flying, the innocent referee is as likely to be slugged as anybody. Some psychiatrists insist that it's silly to require medical study of neurology for their specialty; a few refuse to examine patients physically for fear they'll get the notion that something might be wrong with their bodies as well as their minds. This in spite of the fact that half the hospitalized psychoses have definite physical basis and, as the neurologists like to point out, the major advances of psychiatry such as shock treatments and brainwave patterns are based on the fact that the "mind" is a physically responding agent and that the brain can't have a thought of any kind that does not travel over a nerve pathway.

A widespread illusion is that by giving a name to some condition, we understand it. Psychiatrists can diagnose schizophrenia, manic depression psychosis, and a dozen other mental illnesses, but with a few exceptions they haven't any idea what causes them—at least, in the specific sense that a physician knows what causes typhoid fever. Fortunately, treatment can be effective even if causes are foggy. Yet treatment has a long way to go, too. Many psychiatrists are more successful in adjusting their patients to institutional life than to resuming their place in the world. And as Dr. C. C. Burlingame, himself a psychiatrist, has put it, "I doubt if merely talking with a patient, using so-called psychotherapy regarding hidden experiences which occurred to him at 2 or 3 years of age, is a practical solution to the problems of hundreds of thousands of psychiatric patients."

. . . . . .

There is still room for courage in human living. A man is knocked down, but he can rise again. Let's not trot out our little Ids and Egos for prideful pampering.

Let's refuse to be stampeded by "mental illness." Better yet, let's refuse to use that vague term, and give our cooperation to important community measures designed to put a foundation under mental health. Let's recognize that living is never a silver-platter job, that troubles are bound to arise. Let's admit that our only enduring defense is to develop means of meeting them realistically, without the buck-passing which is what a neurosis essentially boils down to.

That's a man-size and woman-size program, but, tackled in good faith, it will go a long way toward laying the bogey of overwhelming mental disaster.

CULTURE AND NEUROSIS *

The causes of neuroses are frequently apportioned according to the predilections of the expert involved. Since neurotic behavior represents a personal failure, much attention has been directed toward the easing of individual tensions. Thus the individual is frequently told to accept himself and his world; books advise him to relax, to develop a healthy personality, to avoid worry. In serious cases the neurotic may turn to professional psychological or psychiatric counselors for aid.

Implicit in much of this approach to neurosis is an unquestioning acceptance of existing social institutions. The possibility of modifying our social structure rather than individuals is often dismissed as theoretical, impractical, or far-fetched. In the following passage Dr. Horney suggests that much neurotic behavior is rooted in our present social organization, which breeds competitiveness, fear, lack of self-esteem, and emotional isolation.

There are certain typical difficulties inherent in our culture, which mirror themselves as conflicts in every individual's life and which, accumulated, may lead to the formation of neuroses. Since I am not a sociologist I shall merely point out briefly the main trends which have a bearing on the problem of neurosis and culture.

* Reprinted from *The Neurotic Personality of Our Time* by Karen Horney, pp. 284–90, by permission of W. W. Norton and Company, Inc. Copyright, 1937, by W. W. Norton and Company.

Modern culture is economically based on the principle of individual competition. The isolated individual has to fight with other individuals of the same group, has to surpass them and, frequently, thrust them aside. The advantage of the one is frequently the disadvantage of the other. The psychic result of this situation is a diffuse hostile tension between individuals. Everyone is the real or potential competitor of everyone else. This situation is clearly apparent among members of the same occupational group, regardless of strivings to be fair or of attempts to camouflage by polite considerateness. It must be emphasized, however, that competitiveness, and the potential hostility that accompanies it, pervades all human relationships. Competitiveness is one of the predominant factors in social relationships. It pervades the relationships between men and men, between women and women, and whether the point of competition be popularity, competence, attractiveness or any other social value it greatly impairs the possibilities of reliable friendship. It also . . . disturbs the relations between men and women, not only in the choice of the partner but in the entire struggle with him for superiority. It pervades the family situation, so that as a rule the child is inoculated with this germ from the very beginning. The rivalry between father and son, mother and daughter, one child and another, is not a general human phenomenon but is the response to culturally conditioned stimuli. It remains one of Freud's great achievements to have seen the role of rivalry in the family, as expressed in his concept of the Oedipus complex and in other hypotheses. It must be added, however, that this rivalry itself is not biologically conditioned but is a result of given cultural conditions and, furthermore, that the family situation is not the only one to stir up rivalry, but that the competitive stimuli are active from the cradle to the grave.

The potential hostile tension between individuals results in a constant generation of fear—fear of the potential hostility of others, reinforced by a fear of retaliation for hostilities of one's own. Another important source of fear in the normal individual is the prospect of failure. The fear of failure is a realistic one because, in general, the chances of failing are much greater than those of succeeding, and because failures in a competitive society entail a realistic frustration of needs. They mean not only economic insecurity, but also loss of prestige and all kinds of emotional frustrations.

Another reason why success is such a fascinating phantom is its effect on our self-esteem. It is not only by others that we are valued according to the degree of our success; willy-nilly our own self-evaluation follows the same pattern. According to existing ideologies success is due to our own intrinsic merits, or in religious terms, is a visible sign of the grace of God; in reality it is dependent on a number of factors independent of our control—fortuitous circumstances, unscrupulousness, and the like. Never-theless, under the pressure of the existing ideology, even the most normal person is constrained to feel that he amounts to something when successful, and is worthless if he is defeated. Needless to say, this presents a shaky basis for self-esteem.

All these factors together—competitiveness and its potential hostilities between fellow-beings, fears, diminished self-esteem—result psychologi-cally in the individual feeling that he is isolated. Even when he has many contacts with others, even when he is happily married, he is emotionally isolated. Emotional isolation is hard for anyone to endure; it becomes a calamity, however, if it coincides with apprehensions and uncertainties about one's self.

It is this situation which provokes, in the normal individual of our time, an intensified need for affection as a remedy. Obtaining affection makes him feel less isolated, less threatened by hostility and less uncertain of him-self. Because it corresponds to a vital need, love is overvalued in our culture. It becomes a phantom—like success—carrying with it the illusion that it is a solution for all problems. Love itself is not an illusion—al-though in our culture it is most often a screen for satisfying wishes that have nothing to do with it—but it is made an illusion by our expecting much more of it than it can possibly fulfill. And the ideological emphasis that we place on love serves to cover up the factors which create our exag-gerated need for it. Hence the individual—and I still mean the normal individual—is in the dilemma of needing a great deal of affection but find-ing difficulty in obtaining it.

The situation thus far represents a fertile ground for the development of neuroses. The same cultural factors that affect the normal person—leading him toward a shaky self-esteem, potential hostile tension, appre-hensiveness, competitiveness entailing fear and hostility, enhanced need for satisfactory personal relations—affect the neurotic to a higher degree and in him the same results are merely intensified—a crushed self-esteem, destructiveness, anxiety and destructive impulses, and excessive need for affection.

When we remember that in every neurosis there are contradictory tend-encies which the neurotic is unable to reconcile, the question arises as to whether there are not likewise certain definite contradictions in our cul-ture, which underlie the typical neurotic conflicts. It would be the task of the sociologist to study and describe these cultural contradictions. It must suffice for me to indicate briefly and schematically some of the main con-tradictory tendencies.

The first contradiction to be mentioned is that between competition and success on the one hand, and brotherly love and humility on the other.

On the one hand everything is done to spur us toward success, which means that we must be not only assertive but aggressive, able to push others out of the way. On the other hand we are deeply imbued with Christian ideals which declare that it is selfish to want anything for ourselves, that we should be humble, turn the other cheek, be yielding. For this contradiction there are only two solutions within the normal range: to take one of these strivings seriously and discard the other; or to take both seriously with the result that the individual is seriously inhibited in both directions.

The second contradiction is that between the stimulation of our needs and our factual frustrations in satisfying them. For economic reasons needs are constantly being stimulated in our culture by such means as advertisements, "conspicuous consumption," the ideal of "keeping up with the Joneses." For the great majority, however, the actual fulfillment of these needs is closely restricted. The psychic consequence for the individual is a constant discrepancy between his desires and their fulfillment.

Another contradiction exists between the alleged freedom of the individual and all his factual limitations. The individual is told by society that he is free, independent, can decide his life according to his own free will; "the great game of life" is open to him, and he can get what he wants if he is efficient and energetic. In actual fact, for the majority of people all these possibilities are limited. What has been said facetiously of impossibility of choosing one's parents can well be extended to life in general —choosing and succeeding in an occupation, choosing ways of recreation, choosing a mate. The result for the individual is a wavering between a feeling of boundless power in determining his own fate and a feeling of entire helplessness.

These contradictions embedded in our culture are precisely the conflicts which the neurotic struggles to reconcile: his tendencies toward aggressiveness and his tendencies toward yielding; his excessive demands and his fear of never getting anything; his striving toward self-aggrandizement and his feeling of personal helplessness. The difference from the normal is merely quantitative. While the normal person is able to cope with the difficulties without damage to his personality, in the neurotic all the conflicts are intensified to a degree that makes any satisfactory solution impossible.

It seems that the person who is likely to become neurotic is one who has experienced the culturally determined difficulties in an accentuated form, mostly through the medium of childhood experiences, and who has consequently been unable to solve them, or has solved them only at great cost to his personality. We might call him a stepchild of our culture.

Don't Call Me Broad-Minded *

One of the great discoveries of modern times is that of the intimate relationship between childhood experiences and adult behavior. Psychology has rendered us a real service in exploring the effect of insecurity, traumatic experiences, and unwholesome environment in the early, impressionable years. There is, however, the possibility that the psychological concept of childhood causation, like all great ideas, can be stretched to the breaking point. In this article Elizabeth Massey Hill points out with considerable force her reaction to the popular notion "It's too late to do much about our undesirable habits." Rather, the author serves notice that she is tired of hearing every imaginary weakness blamed on a bad case of childhood.

The most desirable trait now attainable, the ultimate accolade, seems to be that one be considered broad-minded. Beat your wife if you like; steal if you must; but never, never deviate from the path of broad-mindedness. It amounts to a fetish and I for one am sick of it. Friends for the Suppression of Broad-mindedness, unite!

I have been racking my brain unsuccessfully to discover any single thing —besides Communism and Communists, of course—which we are not supposed to tolerate today. Did your neighbor cheat his brother's widow and children out of their inheritance? Poor thing, he must have been the victim of some childhood insecurity which left him with a pathological craving for money. Has your cousin drunk himself and his family into poverty and broken the hearts of his parents? Well, everyone knows that alcoholism is a disease, probably caused by too much discipline in childhood, or is it too little? You can't blame him for that. Be broad-minded if your best friend runs off with your husband. Surely you must realize that monogamy is an unnatural state for the male animal and most likely your friend's mother didn't teach her when she was small that it is rude to grab. You didn't really expect your husband to feel any responsibility for the children he fathered did you? You must just indulgently get a divorce on polite grounds. If you are really big about it, give a party for the happy pair when they return from their flight. You will of course continue to be friends with them and teach Junior to call the lady "aunt."

For heaven's sake, how broad can you get? Every undesirable trait or act must be excused on the grounds of improper upbringing (or too proper,

* Elizabeth Massey Hill, *Woman's Home Companion*, November, 1950, p. 4.

which is apparently even worse) or a maladjustment of some kind, either mental or physical. Never suggest that just possibly a mature individual should be held responsible for his own acts, that he is given a brain with which to reason and control his appetites and desires, and that satisfying every urge and living entirely to please oneself is not always the ideal of life. Almost anything can be blamed on poor old Mom if you try hard enough; an inhibition is more to be feared than a thousand devils and duty is the last reason for any act. Individual freedom and human dignity are the cry when any question of restraint or discipline comes up. But how can anybody achieve either freedom or dignity without control, responsibility and consideration for other people?

Well, I for one am through being tolerant. It seems to me that a bit of insistence on the old-fashioned virtues might be a healthy change.

If my son should write home that he is flunking college or failing in whatever job he has because he has discovered that he has a mother fixation and must free himself of the desire to please me, I should be tempted to give him a swift kick where it would do the most good. Anyhow, I would arrange things so that he would have to spend more time earning his way and less dreaming up fixations to make himself more interesting. And I might point out in passing that it is not solely to bring a smile to my aging lips that he should try to make a success of his life.

I fully realize that alcoholism is a disease and a very unpleasant one. But is it too much to suggest that it need never develop? The first time a person drinks too much and wakes up the next morning with a throbbing head and the shameful knowledge that he has made a spectacle of himself or, worse still, doesn't know what he has done—right then is the time for him to say, "Never again" and mean it—to resolve to drink like a gentleman or not to drink at all.

And I think psychologists should make it quite clear that inhibition— that bugaboo of modern life—means not the conscious control of undesirable impulses and appetites, but rather the abnormal fear of them. And this fear is what causes the inhibited person to push them out of the conscious mind altogether, down into the subconscious to fester and infect the whole mind and body. Resisting a conscious desire is quite different and never did anyone any harm yet.

Even in smaller matters I am quitting the broad-minded group. I shall not force a lenient smile when some man who should know better tells an off-color story in my presence or uses words which wouldn't have been tolerated in a well-run saloon a generation ago. I shall do my bit to put discussions of marital relations back into the privacy they should never have left. (What I know about the husbands and wives of some of my friends would curl their hair!) When guests at my parties drink themselves into an objectionable state, I shall resolve never again to invite them. There is a line, and I am going to draw it.

All else aside, I fail to see that our vaunted modern tolerance and easy philosophy have made either society or individuals better or happier. Our parents and grandparents may not always have been as saintly as they pretended, but they did have definite standards which they insisted on and lived by in large part. Religion was large in their lives. And they were not afraid of inhibiting their children by teaching them to do their duty and strive after goodness, and by smacking their little bottoms when they didn't.

Yet the degree of stability and of human happiness generally was greater then, I think: and certainly our present appalling increase in crime and in neurotic and psychiatric cases is scarcely an argument for our modern way. We are trying to steer a course without a compass and it appears to me we are foundering.

It sifts down to the fact that broad-mindedness has come to mean moral apathy—either a complete lack of any standards of decency and principles of living or, at best, the lack of any convictions strong enough to fight for. Nothing worth building was ever founded on quicksand; no statue carved from putty; no enduring society or satisfactory life built on laziness, selfishness, irresponsibility and moral degradation.

So from now on, call me anything else you like, but don't call me broadminded. THOSE ARE FIGHTING WORDS!

Problem 12: Resolution of Maladjustment-- Personal or Social?

Granted that mental illness—psychosis, neurosis, psychotic behavior—is widespread in our urban, industrialized society, what can we do about it? Simply accepting the doctrine that personal maladjustment is socially produced leaves us far from a solution to the problem.

Essentially the solution is to bring the individual into accord with culture and society. Panaceas for accomplishing this objective are legion in our disordered world. In the main, however, they fall into one of three categories. One school of thought advocates the reordering of society. Is it possible to create a society whose culture will disorganize fewer people?

Another school suggests a more moderate program, that of reordering the primary social groups, such as the family.   Perhaps this is a way of working both ends at the same time, of changing both the individual and parts of the culture until they come into greater adjustment.   Finally, there are those who would direct their efforts almost entirely toward the individual, more or less accepting the dictates of the society and its culture, and attempting to mold the individual to conform or at least to accept his role in them.

The readings that follow explore these varying approaches in greater detail.

Society as the Patient *

Of the various approaches to the resolution of personal maladjustment, Dr. Frank chooses to emphasize the need for reordering culture and society. He seems to feel that with our present social and cultural conditions we should not be surprised at the amount of maladjustment that results. Is his diagnosis of our culture as "sick, disordered, and in need of treatment" a realistic one?   Does he hit upon the facets of our system that are the most damaging to personality? If his thesis is correct, is it possible to bring about the changes that he considers to be so imperative?

There is a growing realization among thoughtful persons that our culture is sick, mentally disordered, and in need of treatment. This belief finds expression in many different forms and from a variety of professions.

Anyone who reflects upon the present situation in which our Western European culture finds itself cannot fail to see that we have passed from the condition in which deviations from a social norm could be regarded as abnormal.   Today we have so many deviations and maladjustments that the term "normal" has lost almost all significance.   Indeed, we see efforts being made to erect many of the previously considered abnormalities into cultural patterns for general social adoption.

The disintegration of our traditional culture, with the decay of those ideas, conceptions and beliefs upon which our social and individual lives were organized, brings us face to face with the problem of treating society,

* Reprinted from Lawrence K. Frank, *Society as the Patient,* pp. 1, 2, 3, 4, 7, 8, 9, with the permission of the Rutgers University Press. Copyright, 1948, by the Trustees of Rutgers College in New Jersey.

since individual therapy or punishment no longer has any value beyond mere alleviation of our symptoms. No one can complain that we in America lack self-appointed physicians who are ready, nay eager, to doctor our own society; and abroad we can see various treatments in progress which we are being invited to emulate.

The conception of a sick society in need of treatment has many advantages for diagnosis of our individual and social difficulties and for constructive therapy, although we may find it necessary to prescribe a long period of preparation before the patient will be ready for the remedies indicated. Perhaps the most immediate gain from adopting this conception is the simplification it brings. Instead of thinking in terms of a multiplicity of so-called social problems, each demanding special attention and a different remedy, we can view all of them as different symptoms of the same disease. That would be a real gain even if we cannot entirely agree upon the exact nature of the disease. If, for example, we could regard crime, mental disorders, family disorganization, juvenile delinquency, prostitution and sex offenses, and much that now passes as the result of pathological processes (*e.g.*, gastric ulcer) as evidence, not of individual wickedness, incompetence, perversity, or pathology, but as human reactions to cultural disintegration, a forward step would be taken. At present we cherish a belief in a normal, intact society against which we see these criminals, these psychopaths, these warring husbands and wives, these recalcitrant adolescents, these shameless prostitutes and vicious sex offenders, as so many rebels who threaten society and so must be punished, disciplined, or otherwise individually treated. This assumption of individual depravity or perversity gives us a comfortable feeling that all is well socially, but that certain individuals are outrageously violating the laws and customs that all decent people uphold.

In every department and aspect of our social life we find the same pattern of thought about our society: that our social ills come from individual misconduct that must be corrected and punished so that these supposed underlying social forces and social laws can operate without hindrance, thereby solving our social problems. Nor is this point of view confined merely to the man in the street and the unscrupulous manipulator who has learned to utilize these social myths for his own purposes. Our social scientists, with few exceptions, are strong believers in these supposed social forces and laws and underlying natural processes that, if left unhindered, would operate smoothly. Much of our social research is a persistent search for these underlying social, political, and economic systems, the discovery of which will, it is expected, bring social progress, just as physical science revealed the underlying physical-chemical processes that gave us our modern industry and technology. Indeed, these conceptions of normality and inherent order in society have dominated both lay and professional thinking for many generations.

If, then, we abandon this social mythology, as a growing number of individuals are urging, for another view of the situation, what have we as an alternative? The term "society as the patient" is a good analogy for discussion, but we need something more than a clever phrase as a basis for reconsidering our social theory and revising our social objectives. The conception of culture and personality, emphasizing the patterned behavior of man toward his group and toward other individuals, offers some promise of help, for it indicates at once that our society is only one of numerous ways of patterning and organizing human life and that what individuals do, for good or evil, is in response to the cultural demands and opportunities offered them.

Instead of clinging to the traditional conception of individual autonomy and moral responsibility that were dependent upon a coherent culture for their effective operation, we must begin to think in terms of individuals caught in social confusion wherein individual conduct and ethics are no longer socially tolerable. The individual, instead of seeking his own personal salvation and security, must recognize his almost complete dependence upon the group life and see his only hope in and through cultural reorganization. The tradition of individual striving that was ushered in by the Renaissance has been the very process of this cultural disintegration, for the individual, in striving to be an individual, has broken down the inherited culture of common, shared beliefs and activities. Now that this necessary cultural disintegration has been accomplished, almost to the point of unbearable confusion, we must face the task of constructing a new culture, with new goals, new beliefs, new patterns and sanctions, but predicated upon the enduring human values that must be continually restated and given renewed expression.

We are, indeed, asked to give up these time-honored beliefs in human volition and responsibility, but only to replace them with a larger and humanly more valuable belief in cultural self-determination, social volition, and group responsibility. This idea that man can remake his culture is, in that form at least, relatively novel, although it has many antecedents in the utopias that have been proposed in the past. It repudiates the concept of purely individual responsibility and of personal salvation, regardless of the ruin of others, for the larger concept of social responsibility that directs attention to the creation of a culture to serve human needs and values—a culture with a "vital sensibility."

Just as the emergence of the doctrine of individual responsibility brought an enormous gain to the individual and to society, so the doctrine of cultural responsibility will bring another great step forward in human life.

It will give us both the courage and the faith to undertake the remaking of our culture, and it will provide the criteria for the new patterns and sanctions for the human needs of individuals who vary in capacities and skills but are basically alike in their physiological, psychological, and social requirements, and especially in their need of a common faith.

In the history of ideas and social development it is not improbable that this discovery of the plasticity of culture may rank as one of the greatest of man's achievements since, from the beginning of history, he has been at the mercy of supposed necessities—the divine right of kings, the power of the church, and all the other forms of sovereignty and their justification by social and religious theorists, with the continual sacrifice of the individual life to the most aggressive or unscrupulous.

Today we must face the task of reconstructing our culture and creating our own design for living, in which the age-old cruelties, frustrations, and deprivations may, we must hope, be mitigated, if not eliminated. For that task we have need of more understanding of personality and culture and, above all, of faith in the value of human life which the new culture must serve. Until the culture makes the conservation of human values the dominant theme, the individual cannot, or will not, find his fulfilment.

KEYSTONES OF HEALTHY LIVING *

The article that follows presents a less grandiose scheme than does Dr. Frank for bringing the individual and his society into greater adjustment. According to Dr. Schindler, most mental illness can be traced to an unwholesome family environment. Better families, he feels, will eradicate much of our personal maladjustment. If we accept this dictum, what are the earmarks of a happy home? May this approach not be an oversimplification of a complex problem? Admitting that cheerfulness, affection, and confidence are desirable objectives, how can we achieve them? Would the attitudes that Dr. Schindler suggests produce unreasoning Pollyannas? Would an emphasis on the present moment tend to de-emphasize foresight? Is the philosophy expounded here valid for both fair weather and foul?

Most family difficulties can be summed up in a nutshell. There is a common denominator that will cover 95 per cent of all family troubles.

* John A. Schindler. Reprinted from *The Progressive,* an independent monthly published at Madison, Wisconsin, November, 1952, pp. 15-17.

Keeping this common denominator in mind and steering clear of it simplifies successful homemaking. It is the same common denominator that is at the bottom of most of the functional disease we see. This common denominator in faulty families and in people with emotionally induced illness (EII) is that they lack the ability to enjoy life. Either they have never had it, or they have lost it.

A patient with EII under ordinary circumstances lacks cheerfulness and spontaneous pleasantness. His emotional color is anxious, fearful, worrisome, downhearted, or belligerent. Whether the situation is normal or an extraordinary event hits him, he is completely lost under an avalanche of unpleasant emotions. It has become his habit to have emotions of the overstimulating or stress variety. There are worse habits than drinking, and this one is the big destroyer of human value, human health, and human happiness.

This common denominator—this lack of the ability to enjoy the passing moment—can be turned into positive action by realizing and acting on the idea that the outstanding ingredients in family living should be cheerfulness and pleasantness, because cheerfulness and pleasantness, more than any of the other emotions, invite enjoyment. Cheerfulness and pleasantness should become the keystones in the arch through which our minds look out on the world. The other stones in the arch are hope, courage, resignation, and serenity.

One of the unfortunate trends in American living is our habit of putting so much emphasis on the means for enjoyment—fine houses, automobiles, radios, cameras, etc.—that in the process of getting the means we saddle ourselves with frustration and anxieties, forgetting that the most important element in living is the art of enjoyment. The trick is to develop the art of enjoyment first. Then get, if you must, the means later.

Actually the only necessary means are the simple facts and objects of existence. Practicing the art of enjoyment of simple grass when there isn't a horticultural show; the enjoyment of the green of the trees and the blue of the sky when there isn't an art gallery to go to; the sounds of nature, or your own whistle, when there isn't a symphony orchestra handy; enjoying people around you without needing a theatrical performance; enjoying yourself when you are alone.

Utilizing the common denominator in family living means simply getting enjoyment into family living, depending largely again upon a backdrop of cheerfulness and pleasantness.

A few of the indispensable ingredients that will bring these factors into being are these:

The Family Enterprise

The family is a cooperative effort in which father, mother, brother, and sister all have an active interest and responsibility. It is the primary duty of everyone in the family to see that the family succeeds.

Robert Frost defined Home as "the place, where, when you have to go there, they have to let you in." This may be paraphrased like this: "Home is the place where, when you need a lift, you'll always be able to find it." Such a place is necessarily a pleasant and cheerful place—a place of mutual endeavor, of things done together, games, stories, studies, Sunday afternoon projects, jaunts to the fair every year, a continual round of cooperative projects that everyone engages in and everyone helps everyone else to enjoy.

The Human Enterprise

A part of this same ingredient is to turn the vision of the Family Enterprise toward the wider community around the family so that the members of the family feel the added responsibility and the invitation to maturity of the Human Enterprise. Part of the process of maturity consists in turning our ego away from purely selfish considerations out toward the welfare of others. Not to have this sense of the human enterprise is to bury ourselves for life in a pit of very ugly emotions. Getting into the family the idea that the most important thing for anyone is the welfare and happiness of the other people around one, brings a maturity to the emotional color of that family that is highly satisfactory and filled with the highest kind of enjoyment. It brings into the members of the family a kindliness, a sympathy, and an understanding for other people without which you can't live happily; without such a spirit, there isn't much possibility of continued cheerfulness and pleasantness.

Turning Defeat Into Victory

As events transpire which could become disappointing or frustrating, the attitude should be, "We'll not let that get us down. We'll make the best of it, and the best is going to be pretty good!" It is easy to do this in the little things that we often let sour our entire day.

In the adversities of life this becomes harder, but it is, nevertheless, possible. Rastus was a man who had as much genuine trouble and adversity as any man alive. Yet through it all, Rastus would walk down the street whistling and, apparently, happy. This caused one of his neighbors to remark, "Rastus, you sure is a wonderful man. With all your trouble you is still happy. How does you do it?" Rastus replied, "Well, suh, when all this trouble started happening, I sat down and thought about it. When I got through thinking, I stood up and sez to myself, 'Rastus, you might just as well cooperate with the inevitable.' And that's just what I'ze been doin', suh—cooperatin' with the inevitable."

I saw this ability wondrously developed in a young mother with two children, to whom I had to break the news that her husband had suddenly dropped dead. The young woman's eyes filled with tears. For a few minutes she was silent. Then a magnificent act of her mind turned defeat into victory. A beautiful smile came to her lips and she said, "He was a wonderful man. It has been a great privilege to have lived with him. He has given me and the children such a wonderful spirit. And now I'm going to carry on. I'm going to keep carrying that spirit to the children. I'm going to give it to everyone I meet."

And she has. She is one of the truly fine, one of the truly great individuals now alive. Every place is immediately better and everyone is at once more cheerful for the simple reason that she is there. At a critical moment she turned defeat into victory. Such acts call for high thinking. What other kind is of any value?

Ingredient of Affection

No family can get along without this ingredient. A family without affection is a trap in whose jaws each is caught everytime he goes home, and everyone in that trap wants to get out just as soon as he can. General affection is easily generated in a family if there is affection between father and mother.

A doctor gets tired of seeing these silly nincompoops who lose all their affection after about a year of married life. It is so unnecessary. The only answer to marriage, any marriage, is that you rise above its problems. If these people had two cents' worth of good intentions, a nickel's worth of sympathy, and a dime's worth of understanding, their affection would grow through the years.

If there is bickering and strife in the top brass, the children are going to grow up to be Hatfields, McCoys, Stalins, and McCarthys. They can't help it. The only way to maintain a spirit of affection in the family is for the parents to have it. The example must come from the top.

Kindly Cheerfulness

It means so much in a family if the children are not crabbing and saying nasty things to each other. If the parents do not engage in this nefarious activity, the children can be taught not to. If the parents are continuously pleasant and cheerful to each other, then it can be a family rule that no one is to be nasty or mean to anyone else.

Reasonable, Yet Pleasant Discipline

Unhappy parents probably won't believe this, but in a happy family there isn't much call for discipline. Unhappy children are usually misbehaving children. If you provide for them a happy, pleasant atmosphere, two-thirds of your disciplinary problems disappear.

Discipline at times will be necessary, of course. It should be based on the reasonable ground that we act thus and so because it is good for us and do not act otherwise because it is bad for us and those around us. This basis should be explained pleasantly, not in a fit of splenic anger. The disciplining measure must be carried forward without wavering. Punishment for the same offense will seldom be necessary.

The Atmosphere of Confidence

This is a highly important ingredient, principally for the children—confidence not only in financial security, even if it isn't there, but confidence in their place in the family, the feeling that they have an important responsibility in contributing to the welfare and enjoyment of the family. No child, however awkward or backward, must be made to feel that he is thereby less useful or important to the family.

Mutual Enjoyment

This ingredient calls for more than cooperation in the Family Enterprise. It means mutual enjoyment, a pleasant quip or a jolly phrase when father passes one in the hall or when Mary comes into the kitchen with mother—the happy smile, a humorous sally, a glad word.

The Present Moment

By this I refer to the idea in the family, "What are we waiting for, this is the time—right now—to show affection. Now is the time to run the Family Enterprise, this is the moment, why wait any longer?" Thinking about the past is largely remorse, about the future mostly apprehension. It is permissible to plan for the future, but don't live in it. Live in the present and make this moment the one the whole family has been living for.

I have stressed the diseases produced by the wrong emotions. But we must not forget the beneficial effects produced by the right emotions. We must not forget that the pleasant emotions—cheerfulness, hope, courage, enthusiasm—are the best medicines we know anything about, again because of the physiological effects their manifestations produce.

A few weeks ago, one of our surgeons performed a very serious operation.

Four days later, the surgeon called me into consultation to say that the patient looked as though he were going to die. Indeed, imminent death was apparent on the hospital record sheet. But when I said to the patient, "Henry, how are you today?" he replied cheerfully and determinedly, "Fine. I'm getting up and out of here in a few days." I knew then he wasn't going to die, and he didn't.

Dr. Paul White, one of the country's greatest cardiologists, recently presented the same picture in a lecture at the University of Wisconsin. One of his illustrations was a young mother with severe rheumatic heart disease who had been in bed for three years, and who had, at the most, another year to live. One day, her no-good, no-account husband left home, leaving her and the two children. An emotional revolution occurred in the patient. She decided to go to work and support her children. When she was told her heart wouldn't stand it long, she said cheerfully, with determination and enthusiasm, "You watch me!" She supported the children for eighteen years on the beneficial effects her emotions had on her physiology.

Occasionally, then, it behooves us to take an objective look at our family and make an appraisal. Are we running the kind of an enterprise that is producing the wrong kind of emotions, functional disease, and personal maladjustments and unhappiness? The aim should be to run the kind of a family, the kind of a home, where, when your spirits are low, you are certain to find a lift.

Personal Peace of Mind *

In this final selection concerning the resolution of personal maladjustment Dr. Liebman maintains that efforts to bring about salvation for the individual personality must of necessity be directed toward the solitary individual himself. In general, Liebman stresses acceptance of and accommodation to existing conditions. Many ministers, psychologists, and psychiatrists champion this point of view. Is it possible for the individual to find such peace in a world filled with frustrations and barriers that stand in the way of personal achievement? Even if possible, is such peace desirable? Might it be a threat to progress by eliminating the reformer and others who attempt to alter existing conditions?

* Joshua Loth Liebman, *Peace of Mind* (Simon and Schuster, 1946). Copyright, 1946, by Joshua Loth Liebman. Reprinted by permission of Simon and Schuster, Publishers, from *Reader's Digest,* May, 1946, pp. 111–18.

Once, as a young man, I undertook to draw up a catalogue of the acknowledged "goods" of life. I set down my inventory of earthly desirables: *health, love, talent, power, riches,* and *fame.* Then I proudly showed it to a wise elder.

"An excellent list," said my old friend, "and set down in not unreasonable order. But it appears that you have omitted the one most important ingredient lacking which your list becomes an intolerable burden."

He crossed out my entire schedule. Then he wrote down three syllables: *peace of mind.*

"This is the gift that God reserves for His special proteges," he said. "Talent and health He gives to many. Wealth is commonplace, fame not rare. But peace of mind He bestows charily.

"This is no private opinion of mine," he explained. "I am merely paraphrasing from the Psalmists, Marcus Aurelius, Lao-tse. 'God, Lord of the universe,' say these wise ones, 'heap worldly gifts at the feet of foolish men. Give me the gift of the Untroubled Mind.'"

I found that difficult to accept; but now, after a quarter of a century of personal experience and professional observation, I have come to understand that peace of mind is the true goal of the considered life. I know now that the sum of all other possessions does not necessarily add up to peace of mind; on the other hand, I have seen this inner tranquility flourish without the personal supports of property or even the buttress of physical health. Peace of mind can transform a cottage into a spacious manor hall; the want of it can make a regal residence an imprisoning shell.

Analyze the prayers of mankind of all creeds, in every age—and their petitions come down to the common denominators of daily bread and inward peace. Such pleas for spiritual serenity must not be identified with ivory-tower escapism from the hurly-burly of life. Rather, they seek an inner equilibrium which enables us to overcome life's buffetings.

Peace of mind cannot be won by any brief or superficial effort. Association with noble works—literary, musical, artistic—helps to promote inward peace, but these alone cannot fully satisfy the dimensions of the soul. Certainly we shall not find peace in the furious pursuit of wealth which slips like quicksilver through our grasping fingers. And finally, not even in the sublime sharings of human love—that emotion which most powerfully conveys the illusion of perfect happiness—is peace of mind reliably to be found.

Where then shall we look for it? The key of the problem is to be found in Mathew Arnold's lines:

> "We would have inward peace
> But will not look within"

But will not look within! Here, in a single phrase, our willfulness is bared.

It is a striking irony that, while religious teaching emphasizes man's obligation to others, it says little about his obligation to himself. One of the great discoveries of modern psychology is that our attitudes toward ourselves are even more complicated than our attitudes toward others. The great commandment of religion, "Thou shalt love thy neighbor as thyself," might now be better interpreted to mean, "Thou shalt love thyself properly, and *then* thou wilt love thy neighbor."

A prominent social worker received a letter from a society woman who wanted to join in his crusade to help the poor of New York. She spoke at some length of her imperfections and ended by saying that perhaps her zeal for his cause would make up for her shortcomings. He wrote a brief reply: "Dear Madam, your truly magnificent shortcomings are too great. Nothing could prevent you from visiting them on the victims of your humility. I advise you to love yourself more before you squander any love on others."

Some will argue that this is a dangerous doctrine. "Human beings love themselves too much already," they will say. "The true goal of life is the rejection of self in the service of others." There are errors in this estimate of human nature. Is it true that we are spontaneously good to ourselves? The evidence points in quite the opposite direction. We often treat ourselves more rigidly, more vengefully, than we do others. Suicide and more subtle forms of self-degradation such as alcoholism, drug addiction, and promiscuity are extreme proofs of this. But all of the streets of the world are teeming with everyday men and women who mutilate themselves spiritually with self-criticism; who go through life committing partial suicide—destroying their own talents, energies, creative qualities.

Such actions constitute not only a crime against ourselves but against society. He who does not have proper regard for his own capacities can have no respect for others. By loving oneself I do not mean coddling oneself or engaging in self-glorification. I do, however, insist on the necessity of a proper self-regard as a prerequisite of the good and the moral life.

There are myriad ways in which we show contempt for ourselves rather than self-respect. Our feelings of inferiority, for instance: how often we attribute to our neighbors superior powers; we exaggerate their abilities, and sink into orgies of self-criticism. The fallacy here is that we see in others only the surface of assurance and poise. If we could look deeper and realize that all men and women bear within themselves the scars of many a lost battle, we would judge our own failures less harshly.

To one who goes through life hypnotized by thoughts of inferiority, I would say: "In actuality, you are quite strong and wise and successful.

You have done rather well in making a tolerable human existence out of the raw materials at your disposal. There are those who honor and love you for what you really are. Take off your dark-colored glasses, assume your place as an equal in the adult world, and realize that your strength is adequate to meet the problems of the world."

Another road to proper self-regard is the acceptance of our imperfections as well as our perfections. Most men have two pictures of themselves in separate rooms. In one room is hung the portrait of their virtues, done in bright, splashing colors. In the other room hangs the canvas of self-condemnation, painted equally as unrealistically in dark and morbid shades.

Instead of keeping these two pictures separate, we must look at them together and gradually blend them into one. We must begin to know and accept ourselves for what we are—a combination of strengths and weaknesses. It is enough if we learn to respect ourselves with all of our shortcomings and achievements; to know that true love of self neither exaggerates its powers nor minimizes its worth.

The great thing is that as long as we live we have the privilege of growing. We can learn new skills, engage in new kinds of work, devote ourselves to new causes, make new friends. Accepting, then, the truth that we are capable in some directions and limited in others, that genius is rare and that mediocrity is the portion of most of us, let us remember also that we can and must change ourselves. Until the day of our death we can grow, we can tap hidden resources in our make-up.

Every person who wishes to attain peace of mind must learn the art of renouncing many things in order to possess other things more fully. As young children our wishes were sovereign; we had only to wail and the adult world hastened to fulfill our every desire. We knew, at that stage of our development, very little about the postponement of satisfaction or the necessity of renunciation. But as we grow older we learn that every stage of human development calls upon us to weigh differing goods and to sacrifice some for the sake of others.

The philosopher Santayana pointed out that the great difficulty of life does not so much arise in the choice between good and evil as in the choice between good and good. In early life, however, we do not realize that one desire can be quite inconsistent with another. The young boy may vacillate between a dozen different plans for the future, but the mature man will have to renounce many careers in order to fulfill one. The same truth exists in the realm of emotions. It is fitting for the adolescent to transfer his love interest from one object of affection to another, but it is tragic when the grown man still plays the role of the adolescent. The man trying to wear youth's carefree clothing, the woman who costumes her emotions in doll's dresses—these are pathetic figures. They have not yet learned that human growth means the closing of many doors before one great door can be opened—the door of mature love and of adult achievement.

The first fundamental truth about our individual lives is the indispensability of love to every human being. By "love" I mean relatedness to some treasured person or group, the feeling of belonging to a larger whole, of being of value to others.

Our interdependence with others is the most encompassing fact of human reality: our personalities are made by contact with others. A boy may catch the contagion of courage from his father or the misery of fear from his mother. In a spiritual sense, we digest our heroes and heroines and make their way of life part of our own emotional substance. Thus every saint and every sinner affects those whom he will never see, because his words and his deeds stamp themselves upon the soft clay of human nature everywhere. There is, therefore, a duty that falls upon all of us— to become free, loving, warm, cooperative, affirmative personalities. If we understand this relatedness with others we shall get on noticeably better with our family, friends, business associates—and ourselves.

Next to bread, it is simple kindness that all mortals most hunger for. In times of catastrophe and disaster it finds a natural expression, good to contemplate in men's actions. But too often it is lacking in our daily lives. Many of us are dictatorial or bad-tempered toward others—employees, salespersons, domestic help. "I call no man charitable," said Thoreau, "who forgets that his barber, cook, and hostler are made of the same human clay as himself." When we fail to be kind to all men, we destroy our own peace of mind. The jeweled pivot on which our lives must turn is the realization that every person we meet during the day is a dignified, essential human soul.

In the exchange of simple affection lies the true secret of marriage— which at its best is mutual encouragement. When we are accepted, approved, *needed* by those who know all about us and like us anyway, we have the first inkling of the peace that transcends understanding.

To love one's neighbors is to achieve an inner tolerance for the uniqueness of others, to resist the temptation to private imperialism. Among our renunciations we must renounce undue possessiveness in relation to friends, children—yes, even our loves. The world is full of private imperialists—the father who forces his artistic son into his business, or the mother who rivets her daughter to her service by chains of pity, subtly refusing the daughter a life of her own.

When we insist that others conform to our ideas of what is proper, good, acceptable, we show that we ourselves are not certain of the rightness of our inner pattern. He who is sure of himself is deeply willing to let others be themselves. He who is unstable in his character must reassure himself by trying to compress others into his mold. We display true love when we cease to demand that our loved one become a revised edition of ourselves.

Every normal person experiences countless worries and fears. But it is possible to master these enemies of serenity.

It is true in a sense that man is blessed by his capacity to know fear. Fear is often the stimulus of growth, the goad of invention. Moreover, fear experienced in the presence of real danger is desirable. But are not most of our fears groundless? Scrutinize the large body of fears coming under the heading of "personal anxiety." Sometimes we are afraid about our health; we worry about our hearts, our lungs, our blood pressure, our insomnia. We begin to feel our pulse to find evidence of disease in every innocent or meaningless symptom. Or we become concerned about our personalities. We feel insecure, bemoan our failures, and imagine that others scorn or disapprove of us.

We must realize, of course, that our fears may disguise themselves. Some deep distrust may appear as an unreasoning fear of high places, of closed rooms. Again, our fears cunningly cloak themselves in the garments of physical pain. The new science of psychosomatic medicine has demonstrated that the whole gamut of illnesses, from the common cold to crippling arthritis, can often be traced to mental rather than physical troubles. It is much easier to be sick than to be courageous! The ill health enjoyed by some chronic invalids is no more than an elaborate disguise of deepseated fears.

Many such feelings of insecurity are hangovers from childhood when we really were inadequate and inferior, and knew that there was a vast difference between our weakness and the strength of the adult world. This difference disappears as we grow, but our childhood is a blackmailer that makes us pay over and over again for failures or mistakes that long ago have been outgrown.

Are we obsessed perhaps with a fear of death or the thought of punishment in an afterlife? Let us come to see that such fear is a projection from some early experience when we were punished by a parent, locked in a room, left alone. Are we continually haunted by the disapproval of others, frightened by social rejection? Let us look at these anxieties in the light of maturity, see that our neighbors are no less fallible than ourselves, and realize further that in the adult world we should not expect to be coddled as we were in childhood.

A source of hope lies also in the fact that our moods are temporary. This is a hard lesson to learn. When we are tired, every pinprick becomes the stab of a knife. But it is natural and normal to have depressed moods, and we should remember that we will come out into the light again. We human beings are very tough organisms, able to withstand many shocks, to shed many tears, to live through many tragedies without breaking. Let us learn not to take the depression of the day or month as the permanent state of our life.

It is natural to experience fear concerning our economic and social future. Countless people are frightened of unemployment or the collapse of their careers. These fears are very real. But firmly attached to them are highly neurotic residues. Americans particularly are engaged in a marathon race in which the runners are extremely anxious about those panting on their heels and envious of those ahead. This relentless race for economic success is the source of many breakdowns and premature cardiac deaths.

A yearning for achievement is an admirable attribute of human nature. Where, then, do we go wrong. We err in the excessive energy that we devote not to real accomplishment but to neurotic combat. A man may have a home, possessions, a charming family, and yet find all of these things ashy to his taste because he has been outstripped by some other runners in the race for material things. It is not that he does not possess enough for his own wants, but that others possess more. It is the *more* that haunts him and makes him minimize his real achievements.

The time has come to say: "I am no longer going to be interested in the power or wealth another man possesses so long as I can attain sufficient for the dignity and security of my family and myself. I am going to set goals for myself rather than borrowing them from others. I refuse any longer to destroy my peace of mind by striving only for money; I will also judge in the scale of goodness and culture."

We have learned that unexpressed emotions ultimately have their vengeance in the form of mental and physical illness. This truth illuminates for us the problems of achieving peace of mind in the face of bereavement and grief.

Dr. Erich Lindemann in clinical work at the Massachusetts General Hospital with hundreds of grief patients, has uncovered the basic fact that to repress feelings of grief may lead to morbid reactions later. Dr. Lindemann's patients included some who developed severe illness or depressions years after the loss of a loved one. Amazing curses of the mental and physical ills resulted when patients were persuaded to express the pain and sorrow that should normally have found outlet before.

How absurd is that notion which has gained currency in modern society that men and women should repress emotional outbursts. It is not those outbursts but the avoidance of them which scars the fabric of the soul.

The first law, then, which should be followed in the time of loss of a loved one is: give way to as much grief as you actually feel. Do not be ashamed of your emotions; released now, they will be the instrument of your later healing.

The discoveries of psychiatry—of how essential it is to express rather than repress grief, to talk about one's loss with friends and companions, to move step by step from inactivity to activity again—remind us that the ancient teachers of Judaism had an intuitive wisdom about human nature which our more sophisticated age has forgotten. The Bible records how open and unashamed was the expression of sorrow on the part of Abraham and Jacob and David. Our ancestors publicly wept, wore sackcloth, tore their garments, and fasted. It is unfortunate that in our time the expression of honest emotion has become taboo. Let us understand that the unrepressed experience of pain somehow has a curative function, and that any evasive detour around normal sorrow will bring us later to a tragic abyss.

Armed with such knowledge, if we are courageous and resolute we can live as our loved ones would wish us to live—not empty, morose, self-centered and self-pitying, but as brave and undismayed servants of the greater life.

It is not often that we are brave enough to come face to face with the thought of our own mortality. Yet man is not free in life unless he is also free from the fear of death.

As far as our own deaths are concerned, we should remember what science teaches about the process of dying. We needlessly frighten ourselves with anticipated horrors which never come to pass. As the famous physician, Sir William Osler, put it, "In my wide clinical experience most human beings die really without being in pain or fear. There is as much oblivion about the last hours as about the first."

Montaigne said a wonderfully wise thing about this: "When I have been in perfect health, I have been much more afraid of sickness than when I have really felt the sickness. . . Death is not to be feared. It is a friend."

No, death is not the enemy of life but its friend, for it is the knowledge that our years are limited that makes them so precious. Plato was right when he declared that infinite life on this earth would not be desirable, for a never-ending existence would be without heights or depths, without challenge or achievement. It is profoundly true that the joy of our striving and the zest of our aspirations would vanish if earthly immortality were our lot.

At the same time, we dare not ignore the hunger in the human heart for some kind of existence beyond this narrow span of life. There is an almost universal feeling that God could not shut the door completely upon our slowly developing talents—that there must be realms where we can use the powers achieved here. And one should not lightly dismiss the thoughts of the philosophers who insist that there is nothing inherently impossible about life in undreamed dimensions; that just as infra-red rays are invisible to our eyes, so a creative, growing universe might well have hidden continents beyond the perception of our senses.

Moreover, we should always remember that there are other forms of immortality besides personal survival. Man displays perhaps his most remarkable and his most unselfish genius when he turns from the thought of individual immortality and finds inspiration in the immortality of the human race. The more we concentrate upon the immortality of mankind, strangely enough, the richer becomes our own individual life. As we link ourselves to the heroes, and sages and martyrs, the poets and thinkers of every race, we come to share the wisest thoughts, the noblest ideals, the imperishable music of the centuries. Poor, indeed, is the man who lives only in his own time. Rich is the man who participates in the riches of the past and the promises of the future.

Both science and religion teach us, at last, that obstacles to serenity are not external. They lie within ourselves.

If we acquire the art of proper self-love; if, aided by religion, we free ourselves from shadow fears, and learn honestly to face grief and to transcend it; if we flee from immaturity and boldly shoulder adult responsibility; if we appraise and accept ourselves as we really are, how then can we fail to create a good life for ourselves? For then inward peace will be ours.

Problem 13: Crime in America— Custom or Conflict?

Trained criminologists are coming more and more to believe that a society has the amount of crime it deserves. In other words, under certain social and cultural conditions crime is to be expected. The loss of primary contacts and controls and the anonymity of modern life are sometimes cited as important sources of our "something for nothing" philosophy. White-collar crime—racketeering, gambling, exploitation of vice—are increasingly becoming looked upon as our more serious crimes, as much more damaging to society than the traditional crimes, such as murder, rape, and theft. Is the growth of the "something for nothing" philosophy an inevitable product of our variety of social and cultural organization? This subject is considered in the readings by Kefauver and Wilson.

Even if we accept this causal concept, it is still true that within that social and cultural organization some individuals become criminal and others remain, for the most part, law-abiding. Why? What are the experiences and associations that lead down these different paths? Several suggestions concerning the reasons for such differential behavior are put forward by Coulson, Panken, Winnet, and Martin.

Finally, given criminals, we must decide what to do with them. The philosophy of revenge and punishment has operated quite ineffectively for a long period in our history. Our prisons and reformatories are dedicated to these purposes. We sometimes rationalize our motives by saying we wish to prevent crime or that we are employing reformative devices in the prisons. However, even the best of our prisons and reformatories usually turn out to be training schools in crime, often accepting bewildered juveniles and adult first offenders only to graduate them as seasoned and effective criminals. If not, the inmates are often so broken and bitter that they turn to crime after release. What is wrong with our prisons? Or are prisons themselves wrong? Can their defects be corrected, or must we find new outlets for reformative purposes? Such questions are dealt with in the three concluding selections.

CRIME IN THE UNITED STATES *

Mention crime to the ordinary citizen and he is apt to picture a shadowy, solitary figure—a murderer, bank robber, embezzler, rapist, forger, or arsonist. Newspapers daily catalogue this kind of crime in great detail. Actually this type of law violation is the penny ante aspect of crime—fully visible, much discussed, keyed to personal violence.

A Senate crime investigating committee in 1950 lifted the lid from a totally different world of crime—a world where individualism was subordinated to mass organization; where terms like syndicate were commonplace. In this world the "take" ran into millions of dollars, and a close association had been built up between racketeers and

* From: *Crime in America* by Estes Kefauver. Copyright, 1951, by Estes Kefauver, reprinted by permission of the author and Doubleday and Company, Inc., from *The Saturday Evening Post*, April 7, 1951, pp. 19-21, 71-72, 76, 79.

ostensibly respectable business. The third figure in this sinister alliance was the venal politician. This unholy trio—politician, criminal, businessman—was actually levying a tariff upon society that made the old-fashioned "stick-up" man appear a rank amateur.

The work and finding of the Senate committee are given below in broad outline by its chairman, Senator Estes Kefauver of Tennessee.

My work as chairman of the United States Senate's Special Committee to Investigate Organized Crime in Interstate Commerce now is formally completed. Since May 26, 1950, when the committee held its first hearing in Miami, Florida, I have listened with mounting revulsion to the sordid story of the filth on America's doorstep. I have heard millions of words of shocking, at times incredible, testimony from approximately 450 witnesses. I have read additional hundreds of thousands of words in memoranda and exhibits backing up this oral testimony. I have seen and listened to persons who, in the eyes of most of their fellow members of society, are unquestionably the scum of the earth; and I have been heartened by the courageous appearances of upright citizens who are working tirelessly to cleanse our nation of this scum.

What I have learned scares me.

The facts uncovered by the Senate Investigating Committee plainly spell out that many acts of crime in the United States are not isolated, self-contained local activities. On the contrary, there is a nation-wide crime syndicate—loosely organized, but cohesive—in the United States. The activities of this syndicate are guided by an evil coalition—an alliance of conscienceless mobsters and of cynical, equally conscienceless, so-called "respectable" business and professional men.

There are some in our society—a strangely assorted company of criminals, self-serving politicians, plain blind fools and others who may be honestly misguided or misinformed—who pooh-pooh the existence of such a nation-wide crime syndicate. Some of these self-serving politicians—fortunately a small minority compared with the thousands of honest, devoted public servants—are full-fledged members of the crime syndicate. There is not much use in appealing to the criminals or to the dishonest politicians to drop their smoke screen. But I do urge those who may be merely misinformed to read the record of the Senate Crime Committee with an open mind. Then, I am confident, they will be willing to stand up and be counted among those in America who side with law and order and with the principles on which our democracy is founded, rather than on the side of the killers and the musclemen; the black-marketeers and "influence" peddlers; the thieves, big-time gamblers, pimps, sharpers and dope traffickers.

When I say that I am scared by what I have learned, I do not imply that I have lost faith in the ability of the American people to clean house, and to continue to clean it whenever the vermin attempt to creep back. This faith was bolstered, rather than weakened, by my experiences on the committee, because of the tremendous response and support of public opinion which we received. At times, when we were discouraged from wading through the record of the muck with which the committee dealt, I would restore my spirits by reading from the vast and inspiring file of letters we have received from housewives, mothers, storekeepers, bankers, clerks, ministers and professional men. It was a real cross section of America, and it gave us strength and encouragement for our task.

Nevertheless, as a realist, I still cannot shut out completely a feeling of fright as I contemplate how close America has come to the saturation point of criminal and political corruption which may pull us down entirely. I look about the world and see once-strong, once-proud nations of Europe and elsewhere where the infection of criminal and political corruption set in and progressed to the point where democracy and national strength were utterly lost. I ask myself—and it is a good question for every citizen to ask— Did the citizens and the legislative bodies of those ruined countries realize what was happening? Couldn't they sense that the mess of politico-criminal corruption would so weaken both the moral and economic fibers of their countries that their homelands inevitably must degenerate into ruined, impotent, third-class powers?

The big question—and I put it bluntly—is this: Has criminal and political corruption, which we now know is rampant in the United States, reached the point where this country, too, must follow the downward path after others? I say that we are dangerously close to that ruination point. However, though the hour is late, it is not yet too late. We can beat organized crime if all good citizens will open their eyes to the danger we are in. We can beat it if we recognize the unholy alliance of criminals and their "respectable" front men for what they are—hoodlums and despoilers rather than glamorous figures or heroes—and go after them with the same determination and ruthlessness that they employ in milking and perverting our society for their own gains.

The job, of course, is primarily a local, not a Federal, responsibility; and without the backing of citizens on the local level no laws, state or national, can be effective. However, buck-passing between Federal and state governments, of which there is entirely too much regarding the responsibility for crime eradication, is highly undesirable. If we are going to crack down effectively on organized crime, we must have all-out co-operation, all the way from Washington down to state capitals and county seats.

What, exactly, is this national crime syndicate which gave our committee such concern for the future well-being of America? Let me sketch the picture briefly in this opening article, in order that readers will understand why I personally think it so vital that all of us keep asking ourselves how corrupt America can get . . . and survive. Then, in ensuing articles, I shall develop in more detail various aspects of the crime syndicate. . . .

The national crime syndicate is an elusive and furtive but nonetheless tangible thing. Its organization and machinations are not always easy to pinpoint, for, obviously, it does not operate with the precise and open methods of, say, a large corporation, whose stockholders and whose operations are matters of record. However, through patient digging and by putting together little pieces of a huge and widely scattered puzzle, the picture can be made to emerge.

Actually, as Virgil W. Peterson, operating director of the Chicago Crime Commission, pointed out in his testimony before the committee, the crime syndicate had its genesis in the bloody gangs which took shape in the big cities of America—notably Chicago and New York—some thirty years ago. In those days, these gangs, built on the evil profits of prostitution, narcotics, bootlegging, blackmail, kidnaping and violence in general, fought one another. As the years went by, the mobsters, unfortunately, grew smarter; they realized that killings not only were bad business but bad public relations, that "in union there is strength." Gradually, they got together; they toned down on the violence, and, astounding as it seems, began reaching more or less peaceful agreements on divisions of territory and "spheres of influence."

Thus, crime became big business. Hoodlums—that is, the smart ones who lead the new-style gangs—began cleaning their fingernails, polishing up their language and aping the manners and sartorial trappings of captains of industry. While "muscle"—the willingness to bomb and kill without scruple—still remains an indispensable business accessory of the mobs, "brains" has supplanted "muscle" as the dominant factor in mob leadership. The new aristocrats of the criminal world are not the rough-talking, ape-like killers of the '20's. They have been replaced by the suave, soft-spoken, impeccably tailored Frank Costellos.

These new administrators of hoodlumdom are the kind of hypocrites who wail and figuratively bleed at every pore when you expose them for what they are—enemies of society. "We're businessmen!" they protest. "We live quietly, pay our income taxes and give the public only what it wants." Actually, however, because they are so smooth, because they have learned so well from certain lawyers, tax accountants and so-called "clean" businessmen who are affiliated with them, the new-style crimesters are more dangerous than the Al Capones and Dutch Schultzes of the earlier, rawer era.

Today, the two important points of the national-crime-syndicate axis are New York and Chicago and their satellite areas. As far as we have been able to determine, there is no absolute boss of the syndicate—that is, no single person who can give a flat order and have it carried out anywhere in the country. It doesn't operate quite like that; however, there are a handful of hoodlums whose influence, particularly since they work in close harmony, is all-powerful. At the top of that list is Frank Costello, the wily string-puller of what the underworld calls "The Combination" in New York City. Costello, who, according to Virgil Peterson's testimony, is "the most influential underworld leader in America," probably comes as close as anyone to being a man whose word is the law in the half-world where law as we know it does not exist. Costello doesn't have to issue orders or enforce his views with bombs or machine guns. When he talks, the underworld listens. The committee heard the story of how Costello quelled trouble at Roosevelt Raceway, a New York harness track, merely by "talking" to bookies around town; in return for his "conversation," he went on the race-track pay roll for $15,000 a year.

In Chicago, the mantle of leadership of Al Capone's old mob, which is now known as the "Capone Syndicate," is shared by a number of unsavory individuals, mostly ex-lieutenants of the late Scarface Al. Prominent among them are Jake ("Greasy Thumb") Guzik and Tony ("The Enforcer") Accardo, who appear on income-tax records as business partners. Guzik, a slippery character, is a manipulator rather than a muscleman and is credited with planning much of the intricate and profitable dirty work engaged in by the modern Capone Syndicate. I did not have the pleasure of interrogating him, for he was one of a number of witnesses who evaded our subpoenas and, at present writing, is still a fugitive. Accardo, on the other hand, is a prime example of the old-style hoodlum with the "new look"; he reminded me of a gorilla outfitted by a Bond Street tailor and fresh from a beauty parlor. Reputedly a onetime bodyguard for the late "Machine-Gun" Jack McGurn, Accardo, who was labeled a "public enemy" by the Chicago Crime Commission in 1931, has the reputation of being a killer; indeed, as Peterson testified, he was "one of the alleged plotters of the St. Valentine's Day massacre in 1929," though he never was convicted for it. More will be written about the infamous partnership of Guzik and Accardo as this story unfolds.

The hard core of the national crime syndicate is made up of this axis between the Costello-dominated "Combination" on the East Coast and the Capone Syndicate in Chicago. From these mobs, lines shoot out across state boundaries to every important crime center in the country. The links, of course, are by personal association, joint investments and mutual understanding between the mob leaders, rather than by constitution and by-laws.

The mob doesn't have to call conventions; its members meet automatically at Miami Beach or Hot Springs, depending on the season. . . .

There are two other factors that rank in importance with the New York–Chicago mob axis in keeping the national crime syndicate alive and powerful. One is the nationwide racing-news service known as Continental Press Service, about which I shall have more to say in a later article, and the other is the Mafia.

The Mafia is an organization so fantastic that most Americans find it difficult to believe it actually exists. In fact, one of the witnesses called before us sought to dismiss the Mafia as a sort of fairy tale or legend that children hear in Sicily, where the Mafia originated. The Mafia, however, is no fairy tale; it's real, all right, and it has left a trail of murder, kidnaping, narcotics smuggling, extortion, white-slavery traffic, labor racketeering and almost every other imaginable form of criminal violence across the country. . . .

As it functions today, the Mafia really is a secret international government-within-a-government. It has an international head in Italy—believed by the United States authorities to be Charles ("Lucky") Luciano, the notorious white-slaver and dope trafficker who was deported from this country. It has its grand council and its national and district heads in the countries in which it operates, including this nation. In the United States, Mafia members learned to infiltrate legitimate businesses—such as olive oil, cheese, candy, fruit and coffee importing agencies—as fronts for their nefarious deeds. . . .

KANSAS CITY—Tony Gizzo in the witness chair in executive session:

> Q.: Do you now belong to the Mafia?
> GIZZO: What is the Mafia? I don't even know what the Mafia is.

Elsewhere, however, Gizzo had slipped up:

> Q.: Do you know Balestrere? [Jim Balestrere, the reputed Mafia head in Kansas City.]
> GIZZO: Yes, sir. . . .
> Q.: He is rather widely known as a prominent man in the Mafia, isn't he?
> A.: That is what you hear.
> Q.: What do you hear?
> A.: The same thing that you just said there.

In the public hearings later, Gizzo was questioned again about his admission that rumor linked Balestrere with the Mafia. Gizzo, ordinarily a cool customer, got all flustered. He said he didn't remember giving these answers. At another point, he expostulated: "I wish to hell I know what the Mafia is!"

WASHINGTON—Salvatore Moretti, an extremely contemptuous New Jersey gambler and racketeer, testifying:

> Counsel Halley: Do you know what the Mafia is?
> Moretti: What?
> Q.: The Mafia?　M-a-f-i-a.
> A.: I am sorry.　I don't know what you are talking about. . . .
> Q.: You never heard that word before in your life?
> A.: No, sir, I did not.

At this Halley incredulously asked Moretti, "Do you read?" Moretti, practically sneering in his face, answered, "Nah—as I says before, I don't read very much on account of my eyes."

This then, is the sort of outlaw government-within-a-government that exists in the United States of America.

Early in our investigation, I began getting particularly irked by the obvious contempt which the coalition of criminals and political and business racketeers displayed for our society and our democratic institutions. I did my best during the course of our proceedings—and I hope the record will show I succeeded—to maintain a calm and judicial attitude in the face of these mocking disclosures. But many times my gorge rose. I felt sick when I heard testimony of how the murdered Charlie Binaggio threw the support of his Kansas City criminal gang behind the election of Gov. Forrest Smith in Missouri—even to the extent of offering Smith's rival $50,000 to quit the race—and of how, after Smith's election, Binaggio brazenly attempted to meddle in appointments of police officials.

The committee also was shocked to learn that the 1948 campaign of the successful gubernatorial candidate in Florida—Fuller Warren—was financed almost in its entirety by three men, who put up more than $400,-000. One of the three big contributors was Louis Wolfson, of Jacksonville, Washington and New York, who, at the age of thirty-eight, has had a phenomenally successful money-making career; he testified that he and his brothers paid tax on an income in excess of $7,000,000. Wolfson put up "in excess of $150,000"—he said he couldn't "recall exactly" how much. He sells supplies to the state, but said his only interest in making the contribution was to elect a man who would be an "outstanding salesman" for Florida.

It is little wonder that hoodlums and sharp businessmen think they can buy anybody. This might be a good place for me to relate an incident that I never before have revealed. One big business operator—I shall not mention his name, because as yet, so far as the law is concerned, there is nothing against him, except for some very shabby publicity—thought he could "buy" the chairman of the Senate Crime Investigating Committee, and attempted to do so. It came about in this way: One day I received a long-distance telephone call from an old acquaintance of mine, a former constituent from Tennessee, who had moved to another state. He wanted to come to Washington to see me right away on a matter of the utmost urgency. I gave him an appointment.

In the interim between the call and his arrival, I began to receive numerous telephone calls from constituents in Tennessee, telling me "what a fine fellow" my old acquaintance was. It was high pressure at its utmost.

Then the fellow arrived, and, to my amazement, he had in tow the aforementioned big business operator. This was a man whose name, in a collateral fashion, actually had been brought into our hearings. "Senator," the ex-Tennessee boy began, "I want you to get better acquainted with Mr. X—you and he have a lot in common!"

I sat there and listened. Mr. X was very persuasive. Item 1: He told me he wanted to make "a substantial contribution" to the Democratic National Committee—"in six figures," he said—but "only on the condition that they know I'm doing it on account of you." All he wanted was an O.K. from me to go to the committee and tell them he was my boy. I told him I didn't think the National Committee would care for that and that he was not to appear as "my boy" under any circumstances.

Item 2: He's been looking around my office and thought my staff was terribly overworked. Couldn't he send me two expert secretaries from his own office—"I'll pay them and nobody has to know anything about it"—to help me out? No, he couldn't.

Item 3: Well, he said, I must have a lot of "literature" to mail out. Why not let his big staff of office workers handle that for me? Again, no sale.

One would think that three strikes would spell "out," even to an unperceptive man. But Mr. X was persistent. If he couldn't give the contribution "in six figures" in my name; if he couldn't buy me two secretaries; if he couldn't even have his girls address envelopes for me, could he at least give "a big cocktail party for you and Mrs. Kefauver, or for any of your friends, and invite a lot of important people in Washington?"

Mr. X, I am sure, is going to continue to make a lot of money—at least, for a while. But for weeks after, I kept wondering—and I still wonder—just how cheap do these fellows think their public representatives and officials are? The shame of it, of course, is that the responsibility rests upon the heads of certain public servants who have let these Mr. X's come to believe that anyone and everyone can be bought, like a chattel, for a price ranging anywhere from "six figures" down to a cocktail party. . . .

CRIME AND AMERICAN SOCIETY *

The following article is essentially a critique of the Kefauver Committee. While admitting that its revelations had some value, Mr. Wilson insists that the committee stopped far short of a full analysis of crime.

Is it true that conclusions of the investigators were somewhat naive? Has the investigation resulted in any widespread, permanent eradication of crime? Do we really have a white-collar criminal class that feels itself above the law and its administrators? Are the basic causes of American crime those that Mr. Wilson suggests—disintegration of a traditional culture, social disorganization, the absence of common institutional or social ends? If this is true, can we do anything about the causes? Or is Mr. Wilson merely expressing what Robert Coulson would deride as "Rule 3" (see page 314)?

In January, 1950, Senator Estes Kefauver introduced a bill calling for a full-scale Senate investigation of crime in interstate commerce. After a hard struggle, first with those who sought to prevent such an investigation and then to see who would control it, Kefauver and his supporters, in May, 1950, succeeded in bringing into being the Special Committee to Investigate Organized Crime in Interstate Commerce.

For citizens desirous of having a permanent record of the committee's findings and recommendations the third interim report has been made available by two private publishers, and Senator Kefauver has prepared a useful summary of the coast-to-coast hearings in his "Crime in America." There is not, regrettably, in either his book or the committee report any significant analysis of the mass of facts, and there is little indication that either the Senators or their staff understood the implications of the material gathered.

While the hearings had vast entertainment value for newspaper readers and for the reported 20,000,000 to 30,000,000 television audience, it is doubtful that they contributed greatly to our understanding of the nature and sources of crime in American society or to our prospects for eliminating organized criminal activity. Only if the committee's findings are looked upon as a starting point, as a bringing up to date of one phase of the problem, will the $265,000 spent on the investigation during the first twelve months produce an adequate return.

* H. H. Wilson, "The Pressure to Buy and Corrupt." Reprinted from *The Nation*, July 21, 1951, pp. 45–48.

The statements of committee members reveal curiously naive assumptions about American society and the sources of deviant behavior. For example: that little was hitherto known of the extent of crime and political corruption; that the majority of citizens object to gambling, political favoritism, and the "fix"; that when aware of existing conditions people demand corrective reforms; that most anti-social behavior stems from the foreign-born and underprivileged; that personal pathologies are responsible for aberrant conduct; or that, as Senator Hunt observed, corruption exists "because the human heart is despicable and wicked in all things in its normal state." These assumptions are an inadequate framework for analysis of phenomena so widespread and also prevent the raising of various crucial questions. It would have been more productive, for example, to have tested the hypothesis that aberrant behavior is a symptom of conflict between culturally approved goals and narrowing opportunity for their achievement.

With no intention of belittling the sincere efforts of Senator Kefauver and his colleagues, it needs to be emphasized that the mere accumulation of additional evidence has little basic significance. Few adult citizens will be as astonished as Senator Tobey seems to have been by the committee's general conclusions: that "organized criminal gangs operating in interstate commerce are firmly intrenched in our large cities in the operation of many gambling enterprises"; that in some cities "law enforcement officials aided and protected gangsters and racketeers"; that "there is a sinister criminal organization known as the Mafia operating throughout the country"; that "the leading hoodlums in the country remain for the most part immune from prosecution and punishment"; that the "fix" may come about through tie-ups with political machines or apparently respectable business men, or through corruption of the public by charitable contributions and press relations; that "the backbone of the wire service which provides gambling information to bookmakers is the leased wires of the Western Union Telegraph Company"; that "legitimate business men have aided the interests of the underworld by awarding lucrative contracts to gangsters and mobsters in return for help in handling employees, defeating attempts at organization, and breaking strikes." Such facts have been repeatedly documented by scores of able newspapermen from Lincoln Steffens' day to this, as well as by such investigations as those of the Chicago Vice Commission, 1911, the Senate subcommittee on "so-called rackets," 1933, or the LaFollette committee, 1938.

Twenty years ago in a report written for the Wickersham Commission, Morris Ploscowe emphasized the need for fundamental social analysis:

It is in considering the social, economic, and political factors in crime causation that one is frequently confronted with the fact that the things which are considered as contributing to crime are merely the effects of larger and more fundamental causes. To explore these causes adequately demands a thorough-going examination of the criminal situation in the light of the social, political, and economic development of the country. This kind of examination has un-fortunately not been made, and one can merely speculate upon the effect upon crime of urban concentration, an industrial and acquisitive civilization, multi-plication of contacts through rapid communication and transportation, the ap-parent inefficacy of democratic government to cope with modern problems, a long tradition of lawlessness, a long history of violence, etc. Though it is ex-tremely difficult to make this kind of an examination, it is essential that it be done, so that a program of crime prevention can aim at fundamental causes and not at effects.

Despite the fact that Judge Ploscowe, now executive director of the American Bar Association's Commission on Organized Crime, worked with the Kefauver staff in preparing its final report, there is no evidence that the current Senate committee profited either by his advice or by the work of previous federal, state, and local crime studies. Similarly there is no evidence that use was made of such trenchant analyses as Edwin Suther-land's "White Color Crime," Thorsten Sellin's "Culture Conflict and Crime," Lawrence K. Frank's "Society as the Patient," or Robert K. Mer-ton's "Social Structure and Anomie."

Apparently emotional fervor and moral uplift got in the way of realistic appraisal of crime and delinquent conduct as an integral aspect of Ameri-can society. In the words of Senator Kefauver, "Serving on the Crime Committee was a tremendous emotional experience for all of us"; "emo-tional uplift came in the way that people from everywhere spoke of their approval of what we were trying to do"; and after the New York hearings, "my personal feelings were at a pitch of high moral indignation." It might have been more useful had the committee members remembered that people's indignation at anti-social or aberrant conduct, whether of private individuals or government officials, is rarely translated into positive action. Moral indignation may even serve as a convenient release for ten-sions and frustrations and, combined with our limited span of attention, provide a substitute for creative reform. As Frank has written, the "as-sumption of individual depravity or perversity gives us a comfortable feel-ing that all is well socially, but that certain individuals are outrageously violating the laws and customs that all decent people uphold."

In any case, in all the list of committee recommendations not one seems capable of rallying sustained public support or of providing opportunity for positive action. True, among its accomplishments the Crime Com-mittee does cite the "tremendous response in the nature of public awaken-ing and its constructive reaction to enlightenment . . . a far-reaching chain reaction" which is being expressed in grand-jury activity and "little Kefauver committees" in "many state legislatures." And it believes it "reasonable to forecast that venal politicians whose corruption has permitted the racketeers to become so firmly intrenched will in large measure be eliminated as aroused and awakened citizens go to the polls." A look at the record, however, arouses acute skepticism on this score. The history of almost any American city would show that "aroused and awakened citizens" seldom pursue reform for very long and almost never tackle the root sources of corruption. That Philadelphia has been corruptly governed for almost two generations is surely no secret to its inhabitants; James Michael Curley seems never to have been utterly repudiated by the citizens of Boston; even after the Kefauver investigation there is no obvious evidence of popular demand for the recall of Ambassador O'Dwyer; and if the people's representatives in Congress have demanded the resignation of the convicted Walter E. Brehm it has not come to notice. Nor has Congress displayed undue enthusiasm for prompt action on the legislative proposals of the Kefauver committee.

Evidence is also lacking for the committee's Jeffersonian tendency to believe that virtue resides in the small towns and rural areas. The hearings brought out that in the small towns of LaSalle and Streator, Illinois, gambler Thomas J. Cawley had been operating horse books, punchboards, baseball pools, roulette, and poker games for twenty-five years without apparent opposition from a majority of the citizens. And black-marketeer David Lubben had no difficulty in buying "a vast quantity of corn syrup in the Midwest by making under-the-table black-market payments to farmers."

"Political corruption," according to Lincoln Steffens, "is not a matter of men or classes or education or character of any sort; it is a matter of pressure. Wherever the pressure is brought to bear, society and government cave in. The problem, then, is one of dealing with the pressure, of discovering and dealing with the cause or the source of the pressure to buy and corrupt." We need to know what it is in society that forces individuals to pursue socially defined and approved goals by unlawful means. We have reached a stage in our national development where the exclusive pursuit of individual ends may well cause the disintegration of our society. It is not enough for the committee to say that success in the fight against crime and corruption "depends on the uplifting of standards of public and private morality, a rededication to basic spiritual values which will entail righteous indignation over" these conditions. Nor does Spruille Braden's suggestion—"I sometimes wonder if the Soviet is not, at least in some measure, inciting these vermin to defile our system of law and order"—advance our understanding. Let's face it: graft, crime, corruption, the "fix" are imbedded in the very fabric of our highly competitive society.

The closest Senator Kefauver comes to discussing this basic problem is when he writes: "In many big cities young people come to maturity with an attitude of contempt for law, because they see and hear almost daily of instances wherein criminals, through alliances with conniving politicians and crooked law-enforcement officers, are bigger than the law." He might usefully have gone on to discuss the impact on young people of the employment by the Phelps-Dodge Copper Products Company of gangster Anthony Anastasia (an incident which he does not treat in "Crime in America"), or of the Ford Motor Company's contract with Joe Adonis, or of the relations of the Detroit Stove Works and the Briggs Manufacturing Company with gangsters.

A certain naivete marks the report's treatment of business tie-ups with the underworld. We are told that "in fairness to Ford Motor Company it should be noted that it is taking vigorous steps to disassociate itself from these racketeer-held contracts." Apparently we are to assume that this represents revulsion from newly discovered contamination, although at least one of the contracts had existed for twenty years! At any rate we should be thankful that "Ford has publicly deplored this situation." In general it is puzzling that the Crime Committee should be so sanguine about the possibility of raising standards of public and private morality when the hearings reveal that business elites are not receptive to this rededication. "Practically every large distillery and brewery has granted franchises to racketeer dealers," but "they were almost all vague on the question of whether they would fire a distributor upon finding he had criminal association." Similarly, though Senator Kefauver was irritated by California's "Million-dollar lobbyist," Arthur H. Samish, he failed to develop the implications of the fact that Schenley Distillers of New York paid Samish $36,000 a year, or that the California State Brewers' Institute provided him with another $30,000 salary, "plus control of a $153,000-a-year slush fund."

The record of business during World War II suggests that even patriotism is inadequate to overcome other pressures operating in our society. The Senate National Defense Committee had no difficulty in compiling a list of major firms willing to take advantage of the national crisis, and Marshall Clinard has reported that at least 11 per cent of all retail firms violated OPA regulations in 1944. As a matter of fact, the million OPA violations in one year practically equaled the number of all other crimes known to the police in the same period. Though we do not place these white-collar criminals in the same category with violators of other laws, the financial loss from white-collar crime is probably greater than that from all other crimes combined. As Edwin Sutherland has demonstrated, its impact on our institutions and morale is infinitely greater. "The white-collar criminals resist efforts to enforce the criminal law against themselves by attacks, through the agencies of public opinion which they control, on the integrity of public officials and private parties who object to white-collar crime. These attacks result in further disintegration of the society."

Of the twenty-two recommendations of the Kefauver committee, one could be tremendously valuable—the creation of a Federal Crime Commission one of whose functions would be "the initiation and development of appropriate social study relating to crime, its punishment, and law enforcement." What is needed is a detailed analytical study of American society, its premises, values, institutions, and the forces operating to produce social disorganization and anomie. The findings of the Kefauver committee should be combined with those of the New York narcotics investigation, the Fulbright study of the Reconstruction Finance Corporation, the "five percenters" material, the studies of business men and the black market, relevant sections of the Truman committee findings, even the results of the Douglas committee on ethics and the Delaney committee on the use of chemicals in foodstuffs. Until the American public understands that these are all facets of the same problem—social disorganization, the disintegration of a traditional culture, the absence of common individual or social ends—investigations will do little more than compound the popular cynicism.

The narrow investigation of crime as the violation of law must be broadened to include the concept of delinquency—"those forms of behavior disorder which manifest themselves in injury to others or to society"—and the whole area of white-collar crime. That 350 unmarked trucks a month have been detected trying to enter the Holland and Lincoln tunnels carrying explosives or inflammable loads since the serious explosion in the Holland Tunnel in 1949 is more revealing of the general social malaise than is some individual's activity in betting on sporting events. The needed study of social morale would be aided by a comparative analysis of conditions in another society. A team of social scientists might therefore be sent to Great Britain, where some evidence suggests that deviant behavior is less common and that conflict between socially approved goals and means has been less acute. It would be a difficult assignment, for no culture can be realistically analyzed without a searching examination of its basic premises, institutions, and sacred idols—or without stepping on the toes of the righteous and the wielders of power. If this is too big or too delicate a task for the United States Congress, perhaps one of the foundations could be persuaded to do it.

LITTLE DONALD TOOK AN AXE *

In the following article, Robert E. Coulson criticizes some of the proposed changes in the handling of juvenile delinquents. He feels that our treatment has hindered the development of social responsibility and thereby fostered even greater delinquency.

Is he demanding a return to a strictly punitive philosophy, or does he himself bow to some of the dictates that he seems to oppose? Is he indicting a system that has not yet had a full and fair trial? Does he represent accurately the current sociological attitudes about delinquents, or does he seize upon only those portions that suit his purposes, thus misinterpreting the total of this philosophy? Is there a real difference between the sociological and psychological approaches to delinquency? These are among the questions that should be prompted by Mr. Coulson's account.

Almost every community now has a juvenile program and a group of advisers who assist the court in all cases where children are accused of misbehavior. For many years the police and courts have allowed the sociologist to have a controlling voice in the care and treatment of delinquent children. The motion pictures, radio programs, and writings on the subject have followed the line that these experts have chosen. Communities have spent millions of dollars doing the approved things, and propose to spend many more millions building playgrounds and recreation centers, forming off-the-street clubs and bicycle courts, and employing added personnel for their expanded programs.

Meanwhile the problem is growing worse. The number of offenses is increasing every year, the age horizon for the first offense is lowered, and the offenses themselves are changing. Never before have so many little children committed brutal assaults on their own parents and companions. For the first time in history we have in our court a twelve-year-old rapist, a nine-year-old robber, an eleven-year-old forger. Worse yet, the problem seems to increase in direct proportion to the amount of sociology applied to it. The fourteen-year-old sex murderer turns out to be the son of the court's adviser. Of fifteen kid murderers arrested in the past six months it appears that fourteen were in the middle of intensive sociological handling when their crimes were committed.

This does not necessarily mean that the present approach is all wrong; but it does suggest that there should be some measuring stick by which a

* Robert E. Coulson. *Harper's Magazine,* May, 1948, pp. 386-93.

good program can be recognized. Certainly it is possible that the sociologists are wrong, since figures indicate that delinquency is increasing. In such an emergency a fire-fighter should examine his equipment to make sure that his extinguishing fluid is not inflammable.

The test of a juvenile program should be its effect on juvenile crime. We should not be beguiled into accepting solutions which are merely kind or generous. It is easy for a speaker or writer to become an expert on the subject by simply urging more and more leniency, rewards instead of punishment, probations and releases indiscriminately in all cases, and an attitude of blaming environment for all difficulties. That's easy and safe for the expert; but it is unsound unless such an approach actually reduces the amount of misconduct. With all the magic solutions, the playgrounds and the forums, is there a community anywhere whose members are reasonably sure that no twelve-year-old is out cutting his buddy's throat; or do the sponsors of these projects sit around with their eyes shut and fingers crossed, hoping for a few weeks of applause before Donald disembowels grandmother in the back yard? Isn't it fair to measure their programs in terms of results rather than grand phrases?

Of course some communities have solved the problem temporarily—on paper. The City of Chicago did, a short time ago, by applying a new rule that held parents responsible for the children's misdeeds. In one month the delinquency problem was reduced by 579 cases and the number of adult crimes increased by the same number. The number of cars stolen was as great as usual, and the same number of storekeepers had bloody heads. This suggests another method by which the whole problem can be solved permanently. The police could simply fail to arrest any child for anything, and this would give the community a perfect score for the month.

However, it is more stimulating and challenging to attempt to reduce the total number of actual injuries; and this is not done by calling the conduct protest gestures or compensations rather than rapes and robberies.

The attitude toward juveniles which the sociologists have urged upon us is not merely a matter of leniency. Kindness to children is not some new device which they have invented. The oldest case books of English law contain references to children who were given the king's mercy or discharged through the indulgence of the court. Nor is the modern approach simply an opposition to reform schools and police and prosecutors, although this is the part that is most easily publicized. This also has existed since long before the days of Oliver Twist.

No, the approach which we have been led to accept as the only proper and scientific and true approach involves accepting certain rules and premises. Let us look at these one by one.

Rule 1. Children are a special kind of people, who need special rules and treatment different from that given to other people.

    Premise A. There is no such thing as a bad boy.

    Premise B. There are no delinquent children; there are only delinquent parents.

Rule 2. Delinquency is not the fault of the child, but is the fault of bad housing, lack of playgrounds, broken homes, drunken parents, movies, comic books, and similar specific factors in the child's environment.

Rule 3. Delinquency is the result of general vague factors in the child's environment, like the breakdown of the family structure, postwar excitement, and decline in the effectiveness of religious morality.

These are some of the propositions on which our juvenile programs are built. These are the "truths" which have been announced by sociologists, confirmed by best-selling novelists and professional lecturers, proved by the motion pictures and radio dramatizations, and finally, made a part of everyone's dinner table conversation. The kind intentions of this approach can hardly be denied, but our crime records cast some doubt on its efficiency. So let us look at the propositions again, and look at them more closely.

[First] Rule 1, "Children are a special kind of people." Donald is the delinquent boy. We do not call him just "a boy" or "a kid who sticks knives into people," for these labels lack human interest. He must have a name. Not a last name, for that would shame him and practically give him a criminal record. We use a first name and an initial, for spice. Sometimes we call him Harry J or Bobby L, but he is the same kid all the while. He gets into the wildest troubles, but when we see his wistful grin and learn that he comes from a poor family where the father drinks too much in a slum neighborhood where there are not enough playgrounds, we indict society and demand changes. I have found that it is simpler and more efficient if we call all these little fellows Donald.

Donald A stood at the rail of the court, slouching heavily so that his weight rested on his good right leg. His crippled left foot swung idly to and fro as he listened to the witnesses and lawyers. The police told about the burglaries he had committed, and described his habit of entering houses by way of the second-story window. Donald nodded his head in agreement. Yes, he had confessed to all that.

The probation officer of the court described Donald's loneliness and inability to find happiness in the company of others, and his wistful searches for companionship in the city's pool halls and saloons. Donald hung his head, nodding sadly to himself.

This was his first appearance in court, yet it appeared that he had committed seven burglaries. A psychologist waiting to assist the court in the next case remarked to his companion that this was a true example of compensatory activity. Donald committed burglaries to prove to himself that his lameness was not a handicap. He entered houses from the second-story windows to demonstrate that he was as strong and agile as any fellow. After he was sentenced to prison. . . .

Certainly he was sentenced. He was forty-two years of age. Now if he had been a juvenile we would have arranged for an operation on his leg. We would have built playgrounds for him, and invited him into clubs where he could find wholesome associates.

Even at that, being sentenced to prison at forty-two he was luckier than Donald L, who was only sixteen when he came into court. Donald L went to prison for fifty years. He had killed two people. The juvenile program doesn't work very well in the case of murderers and sex criminals. Of course the experts still insist that there is no such thing as a bad boy, but after he kills one or two people they sort of send him away quickly and hope that no one will interpret that as a lack of faith in the modern approach to juvenile delinquency. Perhaps the modern science is a luxury to be applied only when the community can afford to risk it.

There are many curious facets of the magic difference which separates juveniles from adults. The rules are different for every state and for almost every county within each state. Whether Donald is a juvenile does not depend on his education, size, experience, intelligence, or even his age; but rather upon the location of the city and county, the name of the judge, and the kind of offense or protest gesture he has committed. Donald may be a juvenile in Chicago for the automobile theft, and at the same time an adult in North Chicago as a sex offender. In a single court the distinctions are made by the judge and his expert advisers, and a sixteen-year-old may be a juvenile for the purpose of his thefts but an adult for sexual offenses. And any child anywhere can become an adult if he repeats his misconduct often enough; for then the experts look the other way while the judge sweeps the new grown-up into one of society's ashcans.

This same confusion exists where girls are involved. Here is Doris, whose parents complain that she refuses to go to school, charges expensive clothes to their accounts, keeps late hours, and finally last week left home to make her own way in the world. The general rule is that if such a girl is one day less than sixteen years of age she can be forced back into school, compelled to live at home or wherever the court wishes her to live, forbidden to marry, forbidden to work. She is imprisoned in childhood regardless of her physical, emotional, or mental development. If she is over sixteen she can win her own emancipation from her parents, and from then on she is treated like an adult, being eligible for the same jails as any other woman; and this too is regardless of her size or mental age.

Perhaps it is a belief of the experts that they can do nothing for the adults except punish them. The rigid classifications may be due to the belief that youngsters need and respond to facilities more than those over sixteen. If this is the basis, consider the case of Donald XX who has a long record of night-time wanderings and loafings. His home is not attractive, his parents are not well-to-do, and he has no spending money; so he loiters in front of disruptable establishments, begs from passersby, and naps in doorways. For such a Donald who is under the age of seventeen we blame the community, demand more playgrounds, and try to beguile the child from his boredom. For such a Donald who is a war veteran we blame society, demand medical care and occupational therapy, and try to obtain a pension. Donald XX, however, is fifty-four years of age, and began this course of behavior just after the death of his wife and the marriage of his youngest child; so we send this Donald to the state penal farm.

Why isn't it just as important and just as sound to have recreational facilities for fifty-year-old bums as for fifteen-year-old bums? Why blame environment for one and not for the other? What is the magic of being a juvenile which exempts from responsibility?

Inherent badness or hereditary weakness would be factors beyond the control of the expert, and no expert likes to have factors beyond his control. The sociologist has built his science around environmental badness, and he is reluctant to believe that there is any other kind.

So we come to Premise A: "There is no such thing as a bad boy." In the course of interviewing hundreds of criminals of every age, I have come to accept the statement that there is no such thing as a bad boy. I would carry the statement even further. There is no such thing as a bad anybody. About ninety per cent of the persons charged with crimes can present an account of their behavior which takes the badness from it, and the other ten per cent are mentally sick persons.

Doris the abortionist believes that her work saves her friends from shame and pain. Donald Dillinger believes that after one more unpleasant robbery he can buy a farm in some law-abiding community and become a taxpayer. Donald Capone doesn't agree with some of the laws of his state; he wouldn't think of violating the law he approves. Donald Burglar really believed that society owed him $34.00 because that was what he had lost in a dishonest gambling game the night before. Donald Adulterer and Donald Perjurer are always convinced of their righteousness.

One of the easiest and commonest methods of obtaining confessions from a person accused of crime is to search about for the rationalization which offers to the suspect a chance to appear to have done no wrong. If you tell Donald Burglar that you know how wretched was the lock and how fragile the back door and that you think people ought to be punished for leaving their property so poorly attended, pretty soon Donald claims a share of the reward for educating the storekeeper. If Donald hangs his head abjectly and says that there is no excuse for his behavior and if after questioning him it appears that he is sincerely unaware of any rationalization, then you send for the psychiatrist. Because you know that there is no such thing as real badness in any of us.

All of the social sciences combine to prove and emphasize the effect of environment; and whenever criminology crosses the path of sociology or psychology or economics crime is made to appear inevitable and hence unpunishable. The argument seems to be that if we were living in a perfect society there would be no crime, and since there are criminals we must not be living in a perfect society and you can't very well blame the poor criminal for that, can you?

But we live in a religious world, and our religions recognize the existence of badness and the separation of good people and sinful people. We have erected a punishment structure and built prisons and courtrooms. Perhaps it is not wise to cast all this away without considering the matter more carefully. Granted that there is no such thing as a bad boy and no such thing as a bad anybody; still, there are some people who must be detained, either for the protection of others or for revenge or for rehabilitation. If we use badness in this sense, there is a fair proportion of boys and girls who ought to be included.

When Donald H strikes his mother several hard blows with a pickaxe or drills holes in the church sexton or dismembers the neighbor's child, we put our respective theories to the test. If there is no such thing as a bad boy, and if that means that no child should be detained as adults are detained since he is a product of his environment and that wasn't his fault, was it?—then the subscribers to that statement should have some alternative or suggestion handy. If Donald's conduct was not badness, but merely a protest gesture, then what? Should we put a label on the child, saying "Lack of Playgrounds—please excuse bloodshed"? We have never tried that. Should we put his parents in jail and place the child in a foster home? We tried that, and Donald stabbed his nice new foster mother. Of course this also was simply a product of his past experiences; but how many such byproducts should be allowed, and what should be done then? How many murders should a child be allowed before he can be detained? How many robberies? How many burglaries?

Perhaps the sociologist is so intent on making man a creature of his environment that he is unable to draw the line anywhere. To him, bad housing is as much a defense for adult crime as for juvenile crime; and no sane person of any age is a criminal except as environmental factors drive him to commit "protest gestures." But this notion means a denial of the influence of heredity, and a denial of the freedom of the will. It runs counter to all moral codes except those which make allowance for broken homes and poverty. The sociologist is not quite ready to storm all these ramparts at once, so he is content that his theory shall be confined to children, trusting our mush-headed sentimentality to save him from criticism until his premise is established. Anyone who opposes this approach can be called a cruel reactionary and a torturer of children.

So let us look at the second premise of Rule 1: "There are no delinquent children; there are only delinquent parents."

Our police discovered a gang of petty thieves the other day, and it developed that three members were thirteen years old. A recent magazine article, a motion picture, a radio program had dealt with boy thieves of that age, and each had proved that the boy's trouble was the fault of his parents; so we tried to apply the modern program to our three boys. Here are the three.

Donald E is a child whose parents, after many years of quarreling and drinking were separated and divorced. The home was broken, and the boy lived with his mother. Obviously he had "lacked supervision," developed an "insecurity," and was "frustrated at being rejected." There were three brothers and sisters who had kept out of trouble, but the expert never considers successes when looking for the cause of failures. The cause was listed officially as "broken home," with no effort made to ascertain why the broken home had had its effect on only one of four children. The sociologist listed the case in its proper place among his statistics, and briskly snapped the book shut.

But we were left with the kid. There is no magic by which the child can be pushed five years back, his family forced to live happily together, and the child ordered to pass this way again. So far as divorce is concerned, the "parental delinquency" approach is a waste of time. Fathers and mothers will continue to be divorced. Should that be forbidden?

Look at Donald F. His parents are quarrelsome drunkards, too; but they have not been divorced. They continue to fight. They say they have sacrificed their happiness to keep the home together, for the sake of the children. Our experts nod knowingly and list the cause of Donald's trouble as "broken home"; and again they snap their books shut and walk away, leaving the little boy with us. Now if we blame Donald E's folks for breaking up the home, can we fairly blame F's parents for refusing to break up theirs? Certainly we should not have a legal system which offers to punish the parents whichever way they decide about a divorce. After a married couple have their first quarrel, they are now blamed if they see a lawyer and blamed if they don't. And the only purpose of the blame is for the sociologists' records. There is no remedy offered, and no prospect of one. The whole approach has the effect of advising the child of a convenient excuse for his misconduct in the future—and no further useful purpose.

The last of the thirteen-year-olds in this gang was Donald G, and his case was the hardest of all. Donald G is an orphan. Now if there are no delinquent children and only delinquent parents, who goes to jail when an orphan commits a crime? The superintendent of the orphanage? It is pretty hard to punish the real parents for dying, and there is no one else around. Yet if we put orphanage superintendents in jail whenever their charges go wrong, we would have them all in jail pretty quickly. If we did that, and then some other kid in the orphanage went wrong, perhaps the judge would have to send himself to jail, because it was he who deprived that kid of parental guidance.

Furthermore, in families where there are many children, if you jail the parents for contributing to the delinquency of one kid who then is to be blamed for the neglect of the others? And suppose that the very personality traits of the father which drove one boy into trouble were the traits necessary to keep the others out of trouble? If the parents of Donald N, a fourteen-year-old bandit, had lived in a better neighborhood it might have been better for him, but worse for his younger brother. If his father had spent less time in the saloons Donald might have been a better boy, but his sisters might have resented the old man's presence in the house. Should a parent be required to construct a new personality for each member of the family according to his individual needs, and tune in on them as he turns around the table? Is it punishable if he fails to do so?

These are the speculations around which the sociologist has built the modern approach. Our problem was what to do with Donald in the future, and that problem had to be resolved no matter where Donald belonged in the statistical analysis. So we arranged a foster home for him, and the fond foster parents protected him from the police and the reform school. They are fond of indicting "society" and themselves for every one of his misdeeds, and derive a masochistic satisfaction every time they make some restitution to some robbery victim in order to shield Donald and give him another chance.

But Donald's brothers have complained. The youngest won't mind his parents any more. He wants to be like Donald, and maybe go to college. The older brothers are no inspiration to him. They stayed out of trouble, but have factory jobs. The youngest brother wants to have all the chances that were given to Donald, and he knows that the best way to obtain them is to commit a few robberies. The older brothers are resentful because they feel that they have been penalized for having resisted the impulse to mischief and crime. It appears to them that society has selected the weakest and most vicious member of the family and heaped rewards upon him. Donald is going to have a car of his own next year. All the kids in the block want to be like Donald. If one of them becomes a delinquent who is to blame? Bad housing? Delinquent parents? Or maybe the modern sociological approach itself?

Eager as he is to prosecute the delinquent parents, the popular juvenile expert has other tricks in his briefcase which will serve to protect the child from the knowledge of evil. According to Rule 2 of his text, he recognizes a variety of sociological causes, and he can usually find one which is applicable. The one which remains after he has crossed out the others is the cause of the delinquency. If he finds that the boy's parents are happily married, both living, clean and homeloving, he looks to the other factors on his list.

First he checks over the specific causes, and of these the most stylish factor right now is bad housing. This is a popular argument because no one can refute it and it is a criticism of society itself. It is the style now for society to be self-accusatory; and we prefer to believe that slums and poverty are not only legitimate causal factors of delinquency but also the complete defense against any charge of crime. The sociologist is satisfied with an explanation such as this, because it enables him to catalogue the case properly. The prosecutor, the reform school manager, and the policeman must deal with the future lives of actual human beings, who cannot be buried in files, even if properly indexed. It appears that divorces between parents and deaths of parents are factors which are here to stay. In all probability poverty and inadequate housing are here to stay also. To list these as factors is not enough. We must find a solution in terms of communities as they actually exist and as they will exist in the foreseeable future; and that means communities which have poverty and divorces, where parents sometimes die and houses are often inadequate. If we cannot work with things as they are, then we must abandon slum areas to crime.

But slum areas produce ten good citizens for every bad one. Almost every delinquent who comes from a bad area has four or five brothers and sisters who stay out of trouble. The Horatio Alger success story occurs far more often than the sociologist is willing to admit. The child murderers do not often come from the slums. Chicago's last ten in a row came from good houses in respectable neighborhoods. Isn't there some other factor there which makes criminals out of one per cent of the kids in bad housing areas? And isn't it more profitable to look for that factor than to abandon the neighborhood until better houses are built? Why is it that the overwhelming majority of kids from the worst slum areas never become criminals?

The same thing is true of the second most popular "cause" of juvenile delinquency—lack of playgrounds. If we accept that as a valid cause, then we are helpless until the district is given more playgrounds. But there are two sides to the playground argument also. The classical pattern of conduct which the expert has in mind is that of a lonesome child, unable to entertain himself, who falls into the company of evil companions whom he meets in pool halls and alleys, or who commits lonely larcenies out of sheer boredom. Yet playgrounds are conducive to some kinds of crime. Donald Chicago, aged twelve, killed his nine-year-old companion in a forest preserve and hid the body for eight days in the thick undergrowth. It is arguable that such a pattern of conduct would have been impossible if the forest preserve had not been there. We have had many a frustrated and crippled and ugly child in our court who was driven to truancy and crime because he could not find acceptance at a playground. The play area itself solves nothing; for unless there is supervision it becomes the property of the strongest gang and forces the kid to join that gang or a rival group.

The need for playgrounds is supposed to be proved by the danger of bad companions. If there is no such thing as a bad boy, it is difficult to see how there can be such a thing as a bad companion, unless the experts are referring to the men who might influence lonesome Donald. But for every boy whose troubles the experts have blamed on lack of playgrounds there are a hundred who are just as far away from public recreation but who stay out of trouble. If a "cause" produces its "result" only once out of a hundred instances, is that a valid causal connection? Wouldn't it be more profitable to search into the mind of the hundredth boy to find out what made him differ from the other ninety-nine?

The same question can be asked of people who attack the movies, the radio programs, and the comic books. Donald GN in our city, attended the motion picture "Dillinger" and later that week committed a burglary. It would be easy to blame the burglary on the movie. But during that same week we had four other kid burglars who had not seen the movie, and I learned that over five hundred kids had seen the picture. Wasn't there some other factor which loaded the evil projectile, and for which the movie was only part of the pressure on the trigger? If Donald hadn't seen the movie he might have read some fairy stories and tried to push some friend into the furnace, or he might have read the Bible and learned of several ways to kill his brother. Shouldn't we look to the loading factors rather than the trigger cause? Once the mechanism is loaded and prepared for firing, any device—the falling of a leaf or the excitement of a home run—might set off the charge.

Possibly many children would stay out of trouble if they were insulated from all exciting material and provided with wholesome amusing entertainment and recreation, without cost and under public supervision.

Many middle-aged housewives would stay away from the gambling parlors and time-killers, and many elderly bums and drunkards would stay away from the saloons, and middle-aged men would stay away from other men's wives, and young punks would stay away from their questionable hang-outs—if they were provided supervised recreation programs and play areas. Most of our people have lost the ability to entertain themselves, and find their own company dull. But how far should the state go in providing these programs? Is it fair to the kids to carry them up to an arbitrary age limit and then abruptly push them out of the nest?

Certainly anyone who lacks faith in public playgrounds for children sounds like a cruel and miserly person. It should be easy to answer such a critic. There should be statistics and case histories by the bucketful to prove that children are driven into crime by a lack of playgrounds. It is not enough to have novels and motion pictures to prove the point. We thought we had a playground case a few months ago. Donald 12 and Donald 13, brothers, traveled a mile to a private swimming pool and there stole the wallets of their fellow guests. We found a swimming pool nearer home, and obtained a membership for them there. Now they don't have to carry the wallets so far.

The next line of causes submitted by the experts to account for juvenile delinquency are the vague generalizations, such as the breakdown of the family structure, postwar excitement, decline in the effectiveness of religious morality.

The truth or falsity of these vague generalizations can never be established. The factors are beyond our immediate control anyway. The real question is not whether these dinner table arguments are true, but whether we are helpless in the face of them. When the sociologist catalogues the case he is done with it, but the child still lives. A plan must be made for him. The past years cannot be erased from his memory.

Here is where the sociologist and the psychologist come into conflict. The sociologist has pretended to diagnose the case, and has announced that we would have no more juvenile crime if housing were adequate everywhere, if there were no divorces, no deaths of parents, no postwar or prewar periods, but plenty of playgrounds and strong family ties and religious morality. This is like saying that if we were all living in heaven we would be living in heaven; and quite possibly this is a true statement. But the sociologist interprets this to mean that so long as we don't have a heaven here on earth, then so long is all crime the product of the faulty environment. In the case of children, this seems to mean that crimes are unpunishable if there is a broken home or a lack of playgrounds or poverty in the background.

Psychologically this may be the worst sort of thing to say to a child. It is not kindness to teach the child that poverty is a defense against larceny, or that divorced parents make one immune from punishment for rape, or that burglaries are all right for cripples. Sooner or later the child must present himself to the outside world where such conduct is punished. Donald XR was in our court last week, charged with automobile theft for the fourth time. His father had abandoned the family many years ago and the youth passed his seventeenth birthday last month. Both of those facts are important, because in this modern program one cancels out the other. After the judge sentenced him to jail and while he waited with the deputy sheriff for the remand order to be written he looked at me mournfully and said, "Gee, I didn't know that stealing a car was that serious."

I am convinced that it is better to approach the whole problem of juvenile delinquency on the assumption that the children will grow up into a society which has jails and a legal code. The present system of tolerance and easy-going probation for juveniles is not working and offers no prospect that it ever will work. Automatic forgiveness is not a kindness; and rationalization of misbehavior often does the child more harm than good. For kids have a moral sense, sometimes stronger than their elders'. They can understand a punishment world, and they should be allowed to participate in it.

It is true that if childish offenses are overlooked they may not be repeated, and children may outgrow their habits of theft, truancy, or cruelty. But this is true in the adult world also. The murderer is in most cases a fellow who won't do it again. Many a thief will reform if let alone. Many a gangster and bandit wants to be forgiven and given a chance to start anew. But that is not the society we live in. We have a punishment society, and the child should be prepared for this. Give him probations again and again, give him psychiatric care, new environment and all—but always warn him that if he persists in his misconduct he will be punished. That is only fairness.

This is not a bestial argument in favor of corporal punishment for children. But we have gone too far in the other direction. Forgiveness is a weapon to deal with evil; and the weapon should not be blunted by its indiscriminate use everywhere so that all children come to expect it as a matter of right.

Finally, the moral question posed by the sociologist should be brought into the open and answered one way or another. Is poverty a defense to crime? Any crime? Even where the crippled father of four steals a loaf of bread for his family, is his poverty a defense? Has he done wrong, or hasn't he? Legally and traditionally, the difference between a defense and a plea for mercy is sharp. If we blur this distinction we are cheating our children—the one who commits the crime and the ninety-nine who do not. For even the delinquent boy is entitled to recognize the quality of mercy when it comes his way, and feel blessed.

------◆◆◆◆◆------

The Real Delinquent: The Parent *

In his article, "Little Donald Took an Axe," Robert Coulson makes a persuasive case for holding children responsible for their behavior. He argues that leaning over backwards to protect the juvenile offender from facing consequences may promote rather than prevent delinquency. Justice Jacob Panken takes a different position in indicting parents who fail to lead their children along the right path. Does the responsibility lie with the child, the parent, or society?

We have always had some delinquency on the part of children. We probably always shall have some until we root out the basic cause of this social disease. The best we have done so far is to attack the problem obliquely, seeking to cure and rehabilitate children who are already delinquent. Judges, social workers, psychiatrists and psychologists have developed techniques for their treatment, and these children should be treated by all techniques available.

But all delinquents cannot be cured by the methods at hand, nor do these methods eradicate the original cause and thus prevent development of new delinquencies. In the last five years juvenile delinquency has increased alarmingly, rising in some urban centers by more than 100 per cent. In New York City the number of court cases involving delinquent children jumped from 4,379 in 1940 to 6,975 in 1945, a rise of more than 50 per cent.

Obviously we have not been very successful in preventing juvenile delinquency. I think we can succeed in solving this community and nationwide problem with a long-range, permanent program of prevention. But, first, we must accept this fundamental premise: No child is born into the world to be bad or to be good. He is as bad or as good as we make it possible for him to be.

Under this premise the question, "What causes juvenile delinquency?" instead becomes, "Who, in the first instance, makes it possible for a child to be bad or good?" And there is only one answer—the parent.

* Jacob Panken, *The New York Times Magazine*, December 22, 1946, pp. 20, 48.

It may appear to be oversimplification to recommend improving the parent in order to bring up a younger generation that will not, except perhaps for a normal allowance for exceptions to the rule, become delinquent children. Yet a brief examination of the influences that shape the development of each of us, through childhood to responsible—or irresponsible—citizenship, supports this contention.

Most delinquent conduct and crime stem from neglect of children. Neglect is not merely failure to provide the physical needs, the clothing, shelter and medical care needed. Failure to provide proper supervision, leadership and guidance within the home is a more serious form of neglect; its consequences are often the most telling factor in the development of delinquency patterns in the child. The community may step in to cure sickness and supply physical needs; that is fairly easy. But anti-social characteristics learned in early childhood in the home are not easy to eliminate or even to modify. They are too deeply rooted.

For it is in his very early years that the child acquires the characteristics which fashion his personality and pattern his life. It might be said that he begins to learn how to live and how to act and react, and his personality begins to form at his mother's breast. The child's earliest teachers are his parents and his siblings.

His gods are his mother and father. If his gods are bad, he is going to be bad. If parents are inadequate to their responsibilities, their children will be the victims. If, therefore, parents are unfit because they were never taught how to guide their children, or if by their acts they inspire anti-social attitudes, prevention of juvenile delinquency by the community becomes—as it is now—merely an unrealized bit of wishful thinking.

Often delinquent conduct is a form of exhibitionism to compensate the child for a lack in his daily life—a feeling of rejection and insecurity. The human being is gregarious and the child wants to belong. We must bear in mind that children, no less than adults, are subject to conflicting emotions. There is always a conflict between the good that is awakened and the bad that beckons, the bad that gives a sense of belonging, of being sought after, or a sense of loyalty to the gang that provides interesting activity.

The resolution of this conflict decides where the child is to belong—with the good or the bad—and the direction, whichever path he takes, he learns from his home environment and the example and influence of his elders. He can be taught, and with not insurmountable difficulties, to respond to the finer things rather than to the evil in life.

Most delinquent children are asocial rather than anti-social; they have no moral sense because it was never taught them. They have no sense of responsibility, no consciousness of social cooperation, because these essentials were never taught them. But children can be taught not to become delinquents. There are exceptions, of course, where the individual is incapable of distinguishing right from wrong and is unable to appraise the quality of his acts because of mental defects or insanity.

Since it is the parent who makes it possible for children to grow up good or bad, training for parenthood is the road to prevention of juvenile delinquency. Parents, being the first teachers of children, must themselves be trained in their duties. We who work with children realize that anew as each delinquent child and his parents appear before us. Daily we see proof that the mere fact of parenthood does not automatically endow men and women with the knowledge and understanding mothers and fathers need.

I recall a boy who came before me charged with delinquency for having at the point of a knife robbed another child of his pennies and then beaten him. The relationship between his mother and father was revealed as contributing materially to the child's misconduct. The husband beat her repeatedly, the mother told the court. The husband denied this, explaining, "I only slap her."

"Do you think it proper for you to slap your wife?" he was asked. "You know that has a bad effect upon your children." His reply was shocking: "I think a woman should be slapped once in a while any time."

He had learned this precept, he said, as a child, from watching his father slap his mother "once in a while." And now his son is learning the "facts" of human relationship from his father, who learned them so badly from his father. A vicious circle!

So, too, is the case of a juvenile delinquent in which I punished the father—actually sent him to jail. I do not like to send anybody to jail, but this father had purchased from his son's friends the goods that they and his son had stolen. Children cannot be helped by punishment, nor can adults, but when an adult contributes to a child's delinquency it is a good thing to take him out of circulation for a while.

And yet I do not know that it was right. Can it be said that these untrained parents who contribute to the delinquency of their children by neglect or example are at fault? Were they not also neglected by their parents and by society so that they grew up to be maladjusted and in turn exposed their children to maladjustment?

Some think that the answer is schools for parents. San Francisco has established such a school. But in many cases it is too late to teach parental responsibility to those who are already parents. Many have first to unlearn bad techniques, others refuse to learn and many more cannot or will not attend such schools.

As I see it, the solution is to teach men and women how to be good parents before they become parents. The place to begin is with our children, teaching them now how to teach the children they will some day have. And the place to do that is in the schools.

Our high school pupils take courses in botany, science and higher mathematics. That is good. But only a small percentage of high school pupils carry on their studies in college, and a smaller number make use in later life of the knowledge they acquire in these subjects. I do not propose the elimination of these subjects from the curriculum. They are part of the process of education.

It is even more important, however, that our children receive training in the marriage relationship and parenthood, since nearly all of them will marry and have children. Yet nowhere in the high schools or junior high schools throughout the country are courses given to fit our young for the responsibilities of marriage and parenthood.

We train men and women to improve agricultural products, to become expert in animal husbandry and the care of trees. But we do nothing about preparing prospective fathers and mothers for the most important of all life's functions: the bringing-up of the next generation. If we would end juvenile delinquency, we must train parents-to-be in the art of helping their children grow up into good boys and girls rather than bad ones. To that end we should require all high school pupils to take courses in parent responsibility and child guidance.

They should be taught child psychology, hygiene, the care of the physical needs of the child; the effect upon children of the relationship of parents to each other; the ability to discover and encourage the child's talents and special interests; the child's proper place in the home as a personality and as a member of the social unit. It is in the latter field especially that the child develops a sense of security and respect for himself and for those around him.

What this amounts to is that, while teaching our children how to be good citizens, we teach them also how to be good parents. A comprehensive course covering the subjects mentioned above would awaken interest in the high school student body. The course should be required and graduation from high school should depend upon its satisfactory completion.

This may not be a cure-all, but it is certainly a long step in the right direction. In one generation we should be able to eliminate a high percentage of the original cause of juvenile delinquency—the delinquent parent—and thus solve the problem, in time, at its source.

While following such a program we must continue to work toward the cure and rehabilitation of the present generation's delinquent children. Elimination of poverty would help. Clearance of slum areas would contribute to rehabilitation and to permanent prevention. The use of public schools as cultural centers for parents and children, and as play, dance and sports centers under proper supervision would help to keep children off the streets. Another technique I have found to be valuable is suggested reading. This serves to improve the mind and to inspire the child with ambition by leading him to identify himself with the fine characters of history and literature.

But these, at best, are halfway measures. [The heart of the problem of juvenile delinquency is delinquent parents.] Left to chance and to themselves, good parents are more apt to have good children than bad; bad parents are more likely to have bad children than good. We can no longer leave it to chance. We must make it our business to see that all our children have good parents.

THE REAL DELINQUENTS: PARENTS OR SOCIETY? *

The two preceeding articles attribute the cause of juvenile delinquency to different factors. One of the discussions emphasizes the role of the individual; the other blames the parents. Judge Nochem Winnet replies to both viewpoints by placing the onus on society. To what extent is the problem one of multiple causation with parents, society, and the individual all sharing a measure of responsibility?

Six girls, aged fourteen to sixteen, were put on probation in the Juvenile Court for frequenting a neighborhood unlicensed juke-box dance joint. I became acquainted with the case when it reached the criminal court where the proprietor was on trial before me and a jury, charged with contributing to the delinquency of these minors. The police had raided the place on complaints from parents and neighbors. One of the girls, called as a prosecuting witness, was examined by the District Attorney and was asked what she was doing in a place of that sort. She answered: "I wanted to dance; I want to be with my friends. Where else can I go?"

Was it the fault of the parents who lived in a congested slum area that these girls went to this place for recreation?

On Christmas Eve a Philadelphia policeman was killed by two boys from outside the city. The policeman was in the act of taking them into custody to return them to their homes. According to newspaper reports

* Nochem S. Winnet, *The New York Times Magazine*, February 16, 1947, pp. 15, 56.

these homes are normal in every respect. The boys had received good home training, schooling and religious instruction. Was it the fault of these parents that these two adolescents started out seeking adventure on Christmas Eve?

A boy seventeen years old stood before me in Juvenile Court. He was charged with stealing an automobile, his first offense. He and an eighteen-year-old companion, both employed in a war plant, were coming from work and, having missed the bus, took the automobile. They were seen by a police car. A chase ensued. The automobile ended against a telegraph pole and the boys in a hospital. Months later they were in court. One boy's mother was a widow, herself employed. With tears in her eyes she explained that she thought she made a good home for her son and knew no reason why he should have committed the offense. Was it her fault that he stole the automobile?

What is it we mean by fault? Certainly, if we mean that parents are not wise enough to handle all the problems of their children, and particularly their adolescent children, then there can be no doubt that perhaps all of us as parents are at fault. "Being an effective parent involves knowledge concerning the problems of sex, hygiene, sanitation, growth, behavior, psychology, psychiatry, social relationships, education and so forth," says *Parent Education*. "If all this knowledge were required for professional training, years of intensive study would be necessary."

Is it any wonder that parents are often confused? The supervision of children and their guidance are a difficult assignment where there is no emotional involvement. And in the parent-child relationship there is always this complication. As a result our decisions as parents are not always the wisest. Sometimes we are too strict and overdiscipline our children; other times we are too lax and allow them too much freedom. This lack of wisdom may be called fault. But I do not call it fault. I have known too many parents who have given their best judgment and all their resources to their children and have failed. It is too cruel to characterize the delinquencies of their children as their fault.

If by fault we mean neglect, as recently stated by Justice Jacob Panken, then there are few such cases in comparison to the thousands that go through the courts. Where neglect is found, the solution is almost always rather simple. What the justice of the Domestic Relations Court finds confounding are the cases in which parents have done everything within their power to understand their children and to guide them, but where, nevertheless, the children have become delinquent.

And where does it get us to say that the parents are the real delinquents? It is very difficult to re-educate parents of adolescent children. The National Probation Association, after a four-month survey of special schools for parents set up in San Francisco and other cities, concluded that these court-ordered classes are not the answer to the delinquency problem. There were too many dangers to the family relationship in the stigma attached to court-ordered attendance. There was a break-down in the child's respect for the parent. And there was resentment by the parents at being ordered to listen to lectures.

Resentment does not help the fine relationship which must exist between parent and child, nor does it make for cooperation. In any event, if you could reeducate the parents, there would still be the many causes of delinquency and crime for which they as parents are not responsible. The real delinquent is society in tolerating conditions which are the basic causes of so much of our delinquency. Writers and judges who blame parents recognize this. They all say: "We must do this," "We must do that." And whom do they mean by "we" except society? Let us consider some concrete examples.

1. Justice Panken makes a good point in his indictment of the school system, which does not train our children for parenthood. But the blame for this lack lies not with the individual parent. The blame is society's; it failed to educate these parents. It is continuing its fault in neglecting to provide our future fathers and mothers with adequate education for marriage and parenthood.

2. There is general agreement that in the urban areas slums and substandard houses breed crime and delinquency. Parents do not live in them from choice. The rate of delinquency in such areas is sometimes ten times above the general average throughout a city. Society is at fault for these conditions. Only society can purge itself of this fault.

3. Children need recreational facilities, places where they can play, where there are normal and wholesome outlets for their energies. This is all the more important in our congested urban centers where the home is physically inadequate and the recreational facilities are nonexistent. There is little or nothing that the individual parent can do to supply this need of the child. But society, which has allowed cities to be built up in this manner, can do a great deal.

Philadelphia is recognizing this obligation. It is planning a broad extension of its recreational program. Some forty-six social and civic agencies, churches and schools are cooperating in this program. Gang projects are being developed to divert destructive activities of the street gang into constructive activities. Parents can do very little to destroy gang loyalty. But the community can do a lot to divert this loyalty to wholesome projects.

4. Every community has breeding places of crime and delinquency: the shady poolrooms, the taprooms which sell liquor to minors, the drugstore hangouts. Disrespect for law is bred by poor law enforcement. Only too

often a youth thinks he can get away with a violation of the law because he sees others doing so. Society can and must tighten its law enforcement. Police officials must be trained in the techniques of crime prevention.

During the war years there existed in Philadelphia a canteen in the very center of the city, operated by the USO and labor organizations, which was enjoyed by thousands of men in the services and their friends. Its gaiety and music attracted thousands of adolescent girls who came to the center of the city seeking adventure. The watchfulness of the men and women of the Crime Prevention Division of the Police Bureau in questioning, warning and sending home these young girls, did a great deal to prevent delinquency.

It is a good thing for our adolescent youths to realize that the "law" is on the job. Was it the fault of parents that these youngsters were found on the streets? Some came from the best homes, and the excuses they gave to their parents for being out was at least a tribute to their ingenuity if not to their good behavior.

5. Delinquency is also caused by the frustrations and insecurities which are the result of our economic system. Our educational system, certainly in the secondary school, does not discriminate. It teaches all our children that equality is the cardinal principle of our American life. Equal opportunity is open to all. A large segment of the population of any metropolitan city soon finds out that this is so only in theory. In practice they are condemned to live in the worst sections of the city and expected to do only the most menial jobs.

To some extent the war relaxed this practice. Peace has revived it. The frustration of the hopes and dreams of these youths leads to aggressive conduct, rebellion and hostility. It results in delinquency and crime. It does not lie in our mouths to blame the parents of these youths who themselves have experienced the same frustration. Society is at fault. Economic discrimination must end. It is just as much a crime to steal a person's birthright to equal opportunity as it is to steal an automobile.

6. Society can do much to destroy the basic fallacy in the thinking of almost every parent. It must bring home the lesson that having a problem of maladjustment at home is not a disgrace. The average parent runs to the physician for every physical ailment of his child. He will talk about it to friends and neighbors. But he buries within his breast a behavior problem and seeks advice and guidance only when it is too late.

Some behavior problems have more serious consequences than the ordinary physical ailment. Parents must be taught that every community has resources for guidance and advice. There are child guidance clinics, schools, churches, family societies, children's agencies, neurologists and physicians that can be consulted.

By no means do I minimize the importance of happy, well adjusted parents in bringing up their children. I know only too well the effect of broken homes, of conflicts between parents. Children need love and affection and an understanding father and mother. But we cannot have such parents by simply willing it. It does no good to repeat that it is their fault. Even good parents cannot imprison their children within the four walls of their homes. These children need the companionship and freedom which they now get in the streets for normal growth. Only society can meet the challenge of the hour in planning for understanding parents of the future and providing a safe and adequate community in which children can be reared.

CASE STUDY ON DELINQUENCY *

This is a story of crime and punishment, murder and the courts, a twelve-year-old boy and society. It is also a case study of juvenile delinquency. Here is a story filled with complicating factors. As you read it, you will be confronted with the question, Who was guilty: Howard? His father? His mother? His teachers? The police force? The recreational system? The social agencies? Society?

If the causes of Howard's crime are obscure, what of punishment? How should society have been protected? Should Howard have been executed? Imprisoned for life? For a shorter period? Released to foster parents? Some other device?

Lonnie Fellick was seven years old, and he'd been missing all day. At first the Chicago police figured he'd fallen asleep in a movie theater, the ushers would find him. At 1:10 A.M., however, he still hadn't turned up, so Lieutenant Thomas A. Sheridan of the North Avenue district station set in motion the machinery of search. A teletyped Missing Persons message to other district stations uncovered nothing. Sheridan assigned three squads to look for the boy. They looked all night but didn't find him.

About midmorning—the date was October 18, 1947—Lieutenant Dan Healy, acting captain in charge of the district, sent Detectives Paul Reser and Robert Fisher to Lonnie's home. His mother, a big Austrian immigrant who had borne nine children, said she was afraid Lonnie had run

---

* John Bartlow Martin, "End of a Boy's Life," *McCall's Magazine,* October, 1948, pp. 25–26, 38, 40, 54, 56–60, 62. Copyright, 1948, by McCall Corporation. Reprinted by permission of Harold Ober Associates and courtesy of *McCall's.*

away from home because they were about to be evicted and she was planning to put him in a foster home. She had last seen him Saturday morning, spinning tops and going off to play with Gerald Michalek, a neighbor boy of nine years; she since had learned that they had met a boy a few years older, Howard Lang, twelve. The police knew Howard Lang slightly—truancy, breaking windows, something about stealing pennies off a newsstand, none of it serious. The police went to his home but he wasn't there, he was at a show. His mother recalled that Howard, Lonnie and Mitch had left home about 10:30 A.M. the day before, headed for Von Humboldt Park. She promised to ask him about Lonnie when he came home.

Lieutenant Healy abandoned, after investigation, his first theory that Mrs. Fellick might have engineered the disappearance to win sympathy in her fight against being evicted from her flat. But he still thought it possible that the explanation lay in family troubles. Mrs. Fellick said her husband was in Los Angeles. Healy wired the Los Angeles police, who ascertained that Fellick knew nothing of the boy's disappearance. The pastor who was arranging to have Lonnie placed in a foster home could suggest nothing. The Fellicks' landlord had been hunting mushrooms at the time the boy disappeared. Healy sent detectives to search the many places where a runaway boy might hide—the dark hallways, the ruined basements and garages, the empty stores and vacant lots, the jalopies abandoned on the streets. No results.

By Monday Lieutenant Healy feared something serious had happened to Lonnie. He sent out squads to pick up men with records as sex offenders and purse snatchers. He sent detectives to search Von Humboldt Park, a vast area. They got a boat and dragged the lagoon. And, in an effort to trace Lonnie's movements Healy sent for Howard Lang and Gerald Michalek, Howard first since he was the older.

Lieutenant Healy was a chunky, cheerful, redfaced Irishman with short-cropped iron gray hair, the father of six children. Howard Lang was a polite clean-cut boy of twelve, slender, pale, nervous, with a quick smile. He said that Saturday morning he and Mitch and Lonnie had gone to Von Humboldt Park and three older boys had called Lonnie aside. "They were whispering," Howard recalled, "and they both were talking about me. . . . One of them gave me a dirty look . . . so I turned around and went." He didn't see Lonnie again. He'd never seen the three older boys before. He said one was about twelve or fifteen, black-haired, wearing a white shirt and overalls, the second boy was a little shorter though dressed similarly and also black-haired and the third boy "had blond hair. He was about my size; he had overalls on. . . . Shoes something like mine," and as he described this third lad, Howard stood up to demonstrate for the lieutenant, touching his own blond hair, his own T-shirt, his own blue jeans, his own brown shoes.

Gerald Michalek, swinging his feet and snapping his fingers, told Healy the same story. The detectives felt a vague disbelief. But the boys repeated the story flawlessly—once more Howard seemed to be describing himself as the third lad—and the police sent them home.

During the next two days the police interviewed crossing guards and other children, distributed pictures of Lonnie. Nobody had seen him. They picked up some older boys and about twenty-five men with prior arrest records, but neither Howard nor Mitch could identify any. Howard felt sure he could recognize the boys who had gone off with Lonnie, so the detectives took him around to about eight schools; they had the pupils of the fifth, sixth, seventh, and eighth grades march in and out of the classrooms while Howard watched, but he picked out no one. By now the neighborhood was in an uproar, and the newspapers were recalling recent sex crimes involving children.

The investigation had come to nothing when, at 11:30 A.M. on Wednesday, October 29, eleven days after Lonnie disappeared, his dead body was found.

It was found in Thatcher Woods, a forest preserve in a suburb about eight miles west of Lonnie's home, by a postman who later testified, "Well, it was my day off, and . . . I went out for a walk, which is my habit . . . on my day off . . . I noticed what seemed a heap of clothes, or something like a stuffed sawdust doll, at some distance. I hesitated a moment or two . . . I saw a pair of brown shoes, and as I got real close, it looked like there was legs in the shoes, and then I began to feel rather strange and horrified . . . I realized it was the body of a boy, and I immediately got out of there."

Soon a great crowd of officials had congregated in the wooded glade beside the Des Plaines River. Newspaper reporters took Mrs. Fellick to the scene: "I was under the impression that my baby was alive; I wanted to go to him. I thought perhaps he had stayed in the woods and was hungry and was cold . . . I thought perhaps he had gone out to . . . the end of the car line, because he has been out there, but when I seen they were going such a great distance, I said, 'How can a little boy get out there so far by himself . . . ?' We walked down the embankment, and somebody shouted, 'Who did this to this woman?'" So badly was the body battered and decomposed that identification was difficult. He had been stabbed with a Boy Scout knife and battered with a big chunk of concrete.

At the inquest Howard Lang said he himself had been in Thatcher Woods several times, building a fire and roasting potatoes, but always,

always alone. The coroner said that sounded unreasonable and Howard repeated, "I go all over by myself; I go all over by myself."

For days the officers had realized gradually that there was something wrong with Howard's story, that there was something wrong with Howard himself; and now back in the captain's little upstairs office at the dingy station they questioned him again. His manner had changed, he spoke coldly and carefully. Healy tripped him in a little lie, then switched the questioning to religion. Howard said he had gone to church last Sunday, though he rarely did so, because he'd heard that if something was bothering you church would help.

Healy said, "Tell me about it, there's something on our mind, it worries us, so we pray to God and it gives relief. Why not tell me about it, I could help you," and he thought the boy was about to confess, but instead Howard cried, "I want my Mommy."

Healy sent for her, sent too for the State's Attorney and juvenile authorities and men from the Homicide Squad, and he sent out for ice cream for Howard and Mitch. For four days Howard held out against the best efforts of the police, doctors, juvenile authorities, Assistant State's Attorneys, and experts with lie detectors and electroencephalographs. But the detectives were picking up his little friends, and one of these, Anna May Evans, seventeen, said that on the day after Lonnie disappeared Howard had told her he'd killed Lonnie. Now, to help the police, she talked to Howard and near daybreak on Sunday, two weeks after Lonnie disappeared, Howard confessed. He was transferred to the County jail and, as we shall see, brought to trial on an indictment charging first degree murder, a crime for which he could have been electrocuted.

What kind of a twelve-year-old was this who had murdered his playmate, a boy of seven? Let us study his life, his home, his neighborhood, his world. The world produced him. How? And now what is the world going to do with him?

Howard Lang was born December 22, 1934, at Chicago Lying-In Hospital. His mother went there in the seventh month of pregnancy after periodic hemorrhages; doctors diagnosed placentia previa and removed the baby, weighing only three and a half pounds, by Caesarian section. Howard's attorney said twelve years later, "By all the rules, he should have been a miscarriage—but here he is."

His mother, Alma Lang, was then thirty-nine years old. She had no other children. She came from a good German family. Her father was an embalmer who had saved his money and bought the two-room flat in which he lived. Both her parents were dead by the time Howard was born. His mother first had married when she was twenty-five. Howard's father was her fourth husband. She dislikes discussing her marriages saying, "I just had bad luck with men." She is a sharp-featured, blond, excitable woman, rapid of speech, nervous of gesture. Howard's father was a cook in a restaurant. They lived in a North Avenue rooming house; it overlooks Von Humboldt Park but the El trains clatter past the rear windows.

Howard has spent all his life here in the Von Humboldt Park area on the Northwest side of Chicago. Up broad North Avenue stretches a vista of steel trolley poles and neon signs and dingy red brick buildings, old buildings with peaked roofs topped by spires, the ground floors occupied by saloons and auto accessory stores and beauty shops, the narrow unmarked doors between the store fronts opening into black steep stairs that the inhabitants climb to their flats. In the jumbled traffic an old man wrapped in a comforter is driving a horse and wagon, and boys are skipping over the framework behind a billboard in a vacant lot, heading for the White Tower hamburger joint at North and Western, the main corner. Against the eastern sky rise the bell-shaped towers and spires of the churches of the foreign born, and not far beyond, near the dirty dock-lined Chicago River, lie the slums.

But the Von Humboldt Park area is no slum. If the sociologists find a juvenile delinquency rate of 4.9 here, they find one nearly three times as high near the River. The detective here says that major crime is relatively rare, that, indeed, "most of our business is 193–1's—the old man comes home drunk and beats up the old woman." True, it is not a pretty neighborhood—its aspect is bleak and flat and grimy—but it is nonetheless a neighborhood of the homes of working men. Probably the largest single element is Polish (does not Kosciusko, sword upraised, bestride a stone horse in the park?), but Jews and Germans are numerous, too, and there are a few Negroes, Italians, Filipinos, Chinese, and even American Indians.

The neighborhood is dotted with corner groceries, ice cream parlors and quiet taverns. The side streets are full of kids at play. Howard Lang played with a bunch of kids in Campbell Avenue, and near Lonnie Fellick's home neighbors painted a football field on the street; the parents here do not ignore their children. On Rockwell Street stands the huge old Von Humboldt School, red brick and dirty gray stone, signs "No Ball Playing Allowed" above the play yard fenced with iron. Here Howard Lang went to school.

Across the street is Smitty's Delicatessen, riotous at recess. Forty or fifty boys and girls jamming inside, the girls smelling strongly of perfume, the boys teasing them, a welter of children drinking sodas, snitching marbles, taking bites from each other's hot dogs, arguing over bubble gum, fingering the comic books strung on a wire, harassing the proprietor, who

is standing on a box policing them—"Hey Roy you smoking? Outside."
and "Hey, quit fighting" and "Thank you" to each child who hands him
a penny.

One day when Howard Lang was seventeen months old, his father went
to work and never came back. Mrs. Lang thinks he must be dead. Left
with an infant, she had to go to work—housework, cleaning work, a few
dollars a day. A meal with meat was a treat. They lived in three rooms
on Campbell Avenue. Mrs. Lang paid a woman thirty-five cents a day
to care for Howard. A neighbor recalls, "Weekends we took him out riding in our car. We did it to get him away from the city for a while. Gave
him food and clothes, too. ˙The relief only gave powdered milk." She
remembers Howard as a mischievous four-year-old, "like all boys." He let
the air out of auto tires, he swiped a bicycle and painted it with stove
blacking.

And how did his mother treat him? "She always swore at him," the
neighbor recalls. "She called him names out of the window. She'd tell
him she'd kill him . . . That word killing to him is nothing." But, she
added, Mrs. Lang "kept his little clothes clean, she never did let him go
dirty."

In 1940 when Howard was five, his mother married for the fifth time.
His new stepfather was a mild railroader in good circumstances. He recalls: "We had a nice car, a Buick trunk sedan, four doors, radio, heater,
we was out of debt, everything people could want." They moved into a
three-and-a-half-room apartment in a brick apartment building. It was
the nicest home Howard ever had.

For a time the new home was happy. Mrs. Lang had charge of Howard. When neighbors or other children complained of his conduct she
defended him fiercely. But she punished him severely even for getting
dirty. She had a temper and sometimes became enraged at him, and
though he loved her he also feared her.

Howard entered public kindergarten in September, 1940. He was
marked "Not Efficient" in the only two subjects on which he was graded
and was found to have an IQ of 86. This, though indicating "a somewhat
slower rate of mental growth than normal rate," put him in an IQ group
to which about 16 per cent of the population belongs. He was sick a good
deal and had his tonsils and adenoids removed (a neighbor stayed with him
during the operation because Mrs. Lang "couldn't go through with it").

On January 30, 1942, when he was in the first grade, his mother wrote
to his teacher to inquire whether Howard really had bought war-bond
stamps with two dimes she had given him, as he said he had. This was
the first of numerous maternal investigations. A few years later Howard's
attorney said they demonstrated "the stress she was applying to the boy"—

pressure, that is, which the defense claimed contributed ultimately to temporary insanity and produced the murder.

But though she seemed determined to police him, when it was the teachers who disciplined him she shielded him. Once she wrote to his teacher: ". . . Howard was saying that a certain teacher . . . had taken charge of him yesterday and pulled his ears, please show her this letter and tell her she is in that school, getting paid to teach the children not to abuse them . . . I'm his mother not HER and to keep her hands OFF of him." At least one of her numerous conferences at school involved physical violence. The principal found her unpredictable, inconsistent, difficult to deal with. She took part in Howard's childhood fights: "Dear Teacher, I wish you would please tell Charles or (Chucky) don't know his last name, to quit fighting with my youngster. He is bigger, and the way my son comes home is simply ridiculous."

In the spring of 1943 he failed grade 2A and was examined by the Bureau of Child Study of the Board of Education. The examiner thought Howard alert and cooperative but frail and thin and wrote: "The mother reports that the stepfather and Howard have never seemed to get along well together . . . He seemed very fond of his mother and expressed resentment of the way the stepfather treats his mother." (Remember, the psychologist did not have before her the stepfather's side of the story.) She wrote that Mrs. Lang "is greatly over-protective of Howard in many ways. She fusses a great deal over his meals, still bathes and dresses him, even though Howard insists that he can do it himself. In other ways she seems to expect maturity beyond his years. The school has felt that the mother has been anxious to have him placed in a foster home . . . [But she] stated that she would rather leave her husband and make a home for the child herself."

In summary the examiner said, "He is so greatly upset by conditions in his home that he has not been able to apply himself well to his school work. . . . Howard is under great strain and should be given as much security at school as possible . . . praise and encouragement."

But he kept on being "brought into the office." At home Mrs. Lang recalls, "He was driving me crazy, pestering me. He's a high-strung child, the show-off type." So, seeking outside help, she took him to the Institute for Juvenile Research, where she recalls, "two women watched him for a couple of hours with other kids and then said there was nothing much wrong with him except he didn't have a good home life and didn't like his stepfather. What good did that do?" She thinks the authorities should have taken over. But the Institute superintendent reported that nothing could be done till Mrs. Lang made up her own mind.

By this time she and her fifth husband were bickering almost constantly, usually over money, not infrequently over Howard, and about once a month they quarreled violently. Late one October night an hour-long fight ended when her husband got cut with a knife sharpener and the police arrived. Howard, who was nine, had been watching in silence from an indoor bed. Next day Mrs. Lang sued for divorce. A little later she took Howard and walked out.

From here on it was all downhill. For a time just living was a problem. They went to a ramshackle rooming house. Soon she was keeping company with a man who was mean when drunk; she and Howard hid from him fearfully all one night in a dark empty room, covered with their coats, the bedbugs so thick "it was just like a person took a handful of beans and threw 'em on the bed." They moved into a basement flat by an icehouse but it was infested with rats. Howard was hospitalized with "psychogenic diarrhea."

Finally the nightmare ended. A combination of events enabled them to move into a pleasant upstairs flat in a frame building at 2448 Le Moyne. The kitchen windows overlook a factory across the alley, but the bedroom is furnished with new blond wood twin beds, gay flowered wallpaper and venetian blinds. Here Howard moved in 1945 when he was ten, from here he went to big Von Humboldt School, and from here he was taken to face a murder charge.

Mrs. Lang worked, sometimes all day as a cleaning woman and all evening as a baby sitter, and Howard took care of himself. He was supposed to be in by 8:30 or 9 P.M. What did his mother do if he was late? "She hollered at me," he says—if she knew it. Sometimes for his supper he'd fix coffee and toast, even bacon and eggs. He could have eaten free lunch at school but he wouldn't, he was too proud, that was for poor kids.

His mother says, "That boy wasn't brought up, he was dragged up." She says, "I went out to work, he had to come home and let himself in with his own key, make his own meals, go to bed, and if I go out to work at night he has no mother, he tried to do the best he can, I'm working, I'm never here to help the child. Seven years I been laughed at and not helped. If the state would have helped me, let me stay home, they say he craves love and affection, this wouldn't have happened."

She is an intense bitter woman. The neighbors talked about her, and she hates them for it. "I work all night for two dollars, baby sitting. And be called a bum and say I go chasing in dance halls because I come home at two o'clock from being a sitter all night, that's the credit I get. I worked. I scrubbed, I did everything but steal for that boy. What I get? If you stay home and watch him, they say why don't you go out support the boy? If you go to work, why don't you stay home and watch him? What you supposed to do I don't know. That poor boy kicked around, dragged up, I don't know, poor child, never settled nowhere. I tell you if society had a helped me it wouldn't have a bad boy on its hands. That boy got such good quality in him."

The home, the school, the street—Howard's life ran on those three tracks. Mrs. Lang kept a roomer. Four times she had him arrested, and once she herself was placed under a peace bond. He is a shadowy character in Howard's life; by the time he entered it, Howard was lost to the streets. And yet one looks in vain for the usual "bad influence" of older boys. Howard's friends were mostly his own age. They played catch and tag and flew kites in Campbell Avenue. In summer Howard went fishing in Von Humboldt Park lagoon, swimming in Lake Michigan three miles east. He went to shows and read comic books. Sometimes he ate in other people's homes, especially, toward the end, the home of Anna May Evans. Her parents remember him as extremely polite, a boy who didn't jump all over the furniture, who helped with the dishes.

He could be kind. He was the first to leave the playing kids to help a blind neighbor across the street. He liked to brag. To Anna May he dramatized his home life—"My mother had my dad picked up by the cops"—and if he'd carried three or four cans of coal into a neighbor woman's flat, he'd tell Anna May he'd carried ten. He worried. He seemed to lack boyish spontaneity. He adopted adult attitudes: When another boy hit a girl, he went to her rescue, somewhat needlessly, and, later on, when his own attorney sought to question him about his relationship with Anna May, he replied coldly: "No gentleman talks about a lady."

He was slender but chesty. He had bold eyes. He had a nice quiet smile, a disarming way, but he could be cocky. When a neighbor woman rebuked him as he passed her swearing—"Just come from school, and such language"—he replied: "Who the hell goes to school?" He was baptized Howard Edward Louis Lang: confessing murder he volunteered, "My initials spell heck all together."

People remember him as very bright. He was "street-corner smart." Hauled in by the police and Juvenile Officer, he would sit beside the old rolltop desk and promise convincingly to "do better"—but a few hours later another neighbor would complain. The trouble was not very serious—breaking windows, throwing rocks, climbing on shed roofs—though once he was accused of pilfering money from bathers' clothing at the beach and once of stealing pennies from a news stand.

Once, too, he and another boy took a watch at school, sold it for fifty cents, spent fifteen cents and buried the rest in the schoolyard. The principal investigated, and Howard volunteered that though he didn't know the name of the thief he could point him out. While he was viewing child "suspects," his confederate confessed, but he skillfully maintained his own innocence until confronted with the burial place of the money. This happened only a few months before he killed Lonnie Fellick and buried him with leaves, then pretended to help the police, only to confess when trapped. One wonders whether he really understood the difference between a fifty-cent watch and a child's life.

Howard became known as a problem at Von Humboldt School almost as soon as he was transferred there in 1945. His 4B teacher that fall considered him "troublesome," a "nuisance," not "very much interested." When the teacher was out of the room he read comic books and threw spitballs. He was a good shot. The teacher asked that he be examined, and he was found to have an IQ of 75. He failed 4B. Mrs. Lang wrote, "He has worms and has been very sick and high strung, here lately. . . ." She still quarreled with the teachers. The psychologists said he needed to improve his initiative, industry, accuracy, reliability, and self-control.

In February of 1947 he was advanced to 5B, perhaps because he was so big. His new teacher was Miss Sophie Weiner, a kindly little woman. Testifying at his murder trial a year later, she recalled, "He was upset when he came into the room. He appeared to be undernourished . . . a nervous little boy . . . occasionally coughed . . ." She "told him about the evils of smoking." To allay his nervousness she placed him at the back of the room and told him he could move from one to another of the few vacant seats. She assigned him little tasks, such as pulling up the seats at the varnished desks and closing the windows; he didn't do them very well, and she had to get another boy to do them. His temper was easily aroused, she knew, and he lied.

He misbehaved, but only "naughty boy stuff." Once he brought a firecracker to school, and she took him "to the office," where it was confiscated. Once he wrote an essay: ". . . I do not like school and I do not like the office. I am in the office every day. What I do like about school is the vacation." He seemed most "upset" when he arrived at the classroom in the morning, improving as the day progressed. His stepfather said recently: "His mother would say 'Get outa here, I hope you get run over by a truck before you get across the street.' That's the way the boy went to school in the morning." Though in fifth grade, he was only doing third-grade work. Miss Weiner believed he could do better, and sometimes he did. She did all she could for him. "I had over forty children and I couldn't stop too long with any one child."

Nothing seemed to help much. His mother despaired of him. When he played hooky she turned him over to the police. In March she wrote a remarkable letter to Miss Weiner:

Sorry I had to keep my son Howard home from school, for two days. He had his attack of bronchitis so bad . . . You know, Mrs. Weiner, I sure don't like to keep him home unless it is absolutely necessary as I know he is a slow child in school to start with.

Now Mrs. Weiner, I want to face the facts with you. . . . He is getting to be entirely unmanageable, stays out till late at night until 10:30, 11 o'clock, goes to the show practically every day, where he gets the money is beyond me, as the note is on the table when I come home from work. I find cigarettes in his pockets and I ask him about the package, all I get is a lie, he is holding them for a certain boy friend.

He is hanging around with girls, has his face all lipstick when he comes tramping in at any hour. Now, if I have to be the man of the house, I can't lay awake, until that late hour to get up to wash him & get to bed at twelve or twelve-thirty.

He won't mind, slurrs me, talks back & humiliates me to the lowest in front of my friends. I think its ridiculous, to have to tolerate to such brutality from a youngster like that.

That child is just impossible and I can't keep it up much longer.

The principle said the next time I have trouble, I should go direct to the Juvenile Home. But, I really can't afford to lose any time off from work as I might just be working the day they would want me to come in for an interview. . . .

. . . could you get in touch with Mr. Duda [a Juvenile official] and have him come out to see me. . . .

. . . I'll work, & pay to have him put in a foster home, to see what somebody else can do with him.

That child don't let me sit down long enough to read my newspaper, he just seems to get a kick or thrill out of how much he can aggravate me. I am not a well woman, give that son of mine all the individual attention I can & what do I get in return, nothing.

. . . I am ready, to take & throw him out bodily, if I don't get some help some way. I have to beg him even to hang up his clothes, don't take enough pains even to wash himself, he is just absolutely good for nothing but shows & streets.

I've tried both ways to try & kill him with kindness or give him a whipping. I got nowhere. . . .

What should we do censor or pity him? Please read this to the principle. & do something. Excuse my pencil, as when I went to look for my penholder it was gone like everything else seems to disappear, in my home when he takes all his friends in, while I'm at work. . . ."

Once more the city's educational and legal machinery began to move. Upon request of the Von Humboldt principal, another Board of Education psychologist examined Howard. The previous findings and recommendations were confirmed. Mrs. Lang agreed to confer with Duda about putting Howard in a foster home. Duda sought information from the Von Humboldt principal. She wrote prophetically, "It was felt he was starved for affection and would do mischievous cruel things to get some notice," and she concluded that the school would be "gratified if Howard could be placed in a foster home. . . ." But nothing was done.

That summer he was on the streets most of the time—shows, beach, forest preserve, sleeping in parked cars.

In September, 1947, Howard entered 5A. Miss Weiner noted a change. "It was harder to get him down to work. It took more pressure." More conferences among her and the principal and the adjustment teacher, but efforts to interest him met little success. He kept getting in trouble, he was truant, his mother went fruitlessly to see the principal, and soon he was marked unsatisfactory in every subject except art and penmanship. Miss Weiner recalls, "At the very last he put his head down on his desk a few times. He was greatly troubled—as I knew, afterward."

The principal, contemplating official action that probably would have landed Howard in a disciplinary school, asked the police Juvenile Officer to take a hand. This man, deeply religious, rebuked Howard for his irreligion, threatened him with severe punishment and ordered him to report to him at the station every Saturday morning. Howard's first report was to be made on Saturday, October 18. But he did not report that day, instead he murdered Lonnie Fellick.

A couple of days earlier he broke some windows in the building where he lived, and the landlord sent his mother an eviction notice. She fainted, and while she was unconscious Howard stole ten dollars from her purse. Taking little Gerald Michalek with him, he bought a Boy Scout knife. "He left me hold [the ten dollars] for half an hour," Mitch recalls.

Saturday morning Howard, Mitch and Lonnie Fellick played a while in the neighborhood then caught a streetcar. They rode westward on North Avenue, past the Queen and the Crystal theaters where Howard had gone so often, past Von Humboldt Park where cops used to chase them off Kosciusko's stone horse, past the rooming house where Howard's mother had lived when he was born, past acres of wrecked autos rusting away beside the tracks, past bowling alleys and tattered billboards, past carbarns and factories and viaducts, the ugly brawny structures of Chicago. Presently the gray smoke pall lightened, the clash and shriek of traffic died, the streetcar went up a little hill and on its crest stopped. End of the line. End of the mesh of trolley wires, end of the factories and flats. The boys transferred to a bus, and it rolled on westward over North Avenue, now a broad boulevard, through the suburbs, Oak Park and River Forest. The buildings here were houses, widely spaced and new, where children played on spacious lawns; you could see all the way to the horizon. The sky was blue out here. There was no smoke. The sun shone. It was a Saturday in Indian summer.

Thatcher Woods is a narrow strip of forest preserve winding along the

Des Plaines River, and though it lies between two suburbs it seems remote from city places, a wildwood. The three city boys left the highway and walked down a dim trail through the woods beside the river. They came to a spidery steel railroad bridge and stopped to play on it.

Tiring of this presently they went on. From here the sequence of events is confused. They crossed a highway and descended into a glen in a bend of the river. They quarreled, Lonnie asked permission to use Howard's knife and Howard refused and Lonnie "called him a name." Mitch and Howard seem to have been picking on Lonnie, the smallest. "He always monkeys around too much," Mitch later said. They gathered paper and wood to make a fire. Howard told Lonnie he was going to kill him, but it was a make-believe killing. Howard recalled, "Well we kept walking down the path and I started smoking. . . . [Lonnie] asked for one, and I said no." Lonnie swore at him and Howard pushed him and Lonnie said, "If you don't quit pushing me around, I will tell your mother about the ten bucks you stole." Angered, Howard gave him a cigarette, saying, "This is your last cigarette." Lonnie "called me them three rotten names. . . . I had the knife in my hand, and I hit him with it."

He stabbed him first in the chest or side, "I was not sure, I was so excited." Lonnie doubled over and Howard stabbed him in the back. Lonnie fell on his face. Howard turned him over with his foot and cut his throat, ineffectually. In his fury he lost the knife. "He choked Lonnie and stepped on his mouth," Mitch recalled. Howard picked up a jagged 27 pound chunk of concrete. Lonnie was trying to get up, and Howard ordered Mitch to "hold his legs or else." Mitch did. Howard dropped the chunk of concrete on Lonnie's chest. ". . . it made a loud thump." Mitch said. ". . . he was—whatchamacall it—moving around, wriggling." Howard picked up the concrete and dropped it again on his chest, then several times on his face, leaving it there. Lonnie was barely breathing. Howard said, "Me and Mitch buried him with leaves." They hitched a ride on a truck that took them almost home. "We was tired," Howard recalled. "I told Mitch not to tell what happened. I told him to go over and call [Lonnie] just like he didn't know nothing happened."

Howard went home and changed his bloody clothing and went to a double-feature movie. "The one picture was a love picture, it was close to the end and there was some kind of a wedding like. It was not a wedding, it was a festival or something . . . they were throwing confetti around and stuff through the air like that there, and they are missing from home, and the girl and father, and the other son were looking all over for him. And there was a hotel guy and they were asking him questions, and they said they went to the airport, and he said they are up in a room . . . and

I went down and took a cigarette and had a smoke." He got to bed about 11:30.

Next morning Lonnie's brother telephoned; Howard told the story about having left Lonnie in the park with three older boys, and later called back to inquire if Lonnie had returned. He told Anna May Evans and two boys the truth ("can you keep a secret?"). They thought he was bragging, and he showed them his bloody clothes and offered to show them the body. Anna May threw away the clothes.

Right-thinkers were shocked by Howard's confession, and a great uproar ensued. Investigations of neighborhood and school were launched. A Parent-Teacher Association was hastily formed. Neighbors kept their kids in nights, and clubwomen complained that the children had no supervised place to play. Moralists inveighed against divorce, and experts on juvenile delinquency proposed ways to deal with Howard. One official commented bitterly, "Now everybody wants to put in his two cents' worth. Where were they before?" Everyone directly involved with Howard hastily sought to dodge responsibility. The school and the neighborhood blamed the home, and the home blamed the school and the neighborhood, and the police blamed the boy.

What was the motive for the crime? A detective said, "He was cunning, he wanted to get away with something to show he's smart." There is truth in this, but it seems to explain better Howard's efforts to escape detection than the murder itself. Howard killed in an ungovernable rage because Lonnie threatened to tell Howard's mother he stole ten dollars. Howard feared his mother. He loved his mother, felt an adult obligation to defend her, and Lonnie called him names abominable to any boy who loves his mother. As to why he so loved and feared her, and why the springs of rage inside him were coiled so taut, we can only recall the facts of his life as we have pieced them together.

Howard was lodged in the County Jail, a boy among men. The trial began before Criminal Court Judge Daniel A. Roberts, February 16, 1948. A large crowd was on hand, for a great many people wished to see Howard Lang, he was something odd, the youngest lad ever to go on trial for his life in Cook County. The courtroom was high-ceilinged, softly lit, paneled in marble and oak. A burly uniformed bailiff brought in the defendant, a boy with hair falling over his eyes, and he walked swiftly to the council table and sat there swinging his legs, a bailiff behind him, his lawyers in front of him, the Assistant State's Attorneys across the table.

And so proceedings were had, the life of a boy of the streets was straitjacketed into the hard ancient formulae: "Do you solemnly swear by the ever-living God . . . ," "Now if the court please we will ask that it be marked People's Exhibit One for identification and. . . ." Child followed child to the big witness chair, interspersed with an occasional bulky police-man. Mrs. Lang fainted. Howard caught cold passing through the prisoners' underground tunnel between the jail and the great gray Criminal Court building, and he coughed fitfully. After five days Assistant State's Attorney Alex J. Napoli rested his case.

Howard's attorneys had planned an elaborate defense of not guilty by reason of temporary insanity caused by the boy's environment. They hoped to prove that "murder, wild west, horror and gangster" movies and comic books filled with violence had tended to "aggravate the instability" of Howard's make-up. They planned to have sociologists, teachers, school psychologists, his mother and neighbors describe his life and environment. But the lucid forms of a murder trial, devised for adults, take on the unreal quality of a nightmare when applied to a child, as had become painfully apparent, and the question arose: What treatment would Howard receive if he pleaded guilty?

The Judge called in prison officials. Howard's chief counsel, Samuel J. Andalman, said he considered an outright acquittal undesirable—why free the boy without psychiatric treatment?—but on the other hand he opposed sending him to an adult prison. He asked leave to plead the boy guilty to manslaughter, which would have made probation possible, but the judge said the boy must plead guilty to murder or to nothing. The judge also showed the lawyers a note from the jurors, indicating they were anxious to end the case speedily. The conference broke up. At lunch in the little restaurant across the street Mrs. Lang said she didn't know what to do. Andalman was unwilling to accept alone the responsibility of continuing trial before an impatient jury that might send the boy to the electric chair. Andalman decided to plead guilty to the indictment. He has since said, "I was so heartsick I wouldn't make the motions, my associate made them."

At any rate the Judge received the guilty plea and called Mrs. Lang before him and asked if she understood what was going on. She did.

"Does Howard have a father who is available or present?"

"No, sir. . . ."

"There is no one other than you to speak for him?"

"That is right. . . ."

"And it is your thought that the better thing to be done in this matter is that he go to an institution of some type."

"Yes, sir."

"All right. . . . You may sit down, if you wish. Now then the boy. Your name is Howard Lang," and Howard stood up before him, very small in front of the high bench. The knot of the judge's necktie and a little of his white collar showed at his throat above the black robe. "You know what has happened here, don't you?"

"Yes, sir."

"The lawyers have spoken for you, and now they have indicated that they want to withdraw what is called a plea of not guilty and to enter a plea of guilty. Do you know what they mean by that?"

"Yes, sir."

"You say, 'Yes, sir'?"

"Yes, sir."

. . . . .

"Then the Court is required by law to advise you that you can be sent to an institution, and that you have to remain there for not less than fourteen years, and for more than that if the Court finds it necessary. . . ."

"Yes, sir."

"And your lawyers talked to you about that."

"Yes, sir."

"And they told you some people have to go to the electric chair?"

"Yes, sir."

. . . . .

"Now then, knowing that, do you still wish to say that you are guilty?"

"Yes, sir."

"You don't care at all, is that the way you feel?"

"No."

"Or are you sorry?"

"I am sorry for what I have done."

So the finding of guilty was entered, and the trial halted and the jury dismissed. Defense counsel made "the proper motions," and the clerk made rapid entries in the journal, and the three big men, judge and lawyers, conferred on a date for hearing evidence of mitigation and aggravation before the sentencing. Almost everyone seemed relieved.

But the hardest question of all remained: What was society to do with the boy? Nearly everyone agreed he must be put away somewhere—"If you send him back to his old neighborhood it's bad for him and for the other kids too, he committed murder." Put away, but where? "In a foster military school," his mother said. One teacher thought he needed "constructive training and constant supervision in an institution." The police agreed—they meant prison. But the Juvenile Officer said, "If somebody'd adopt him that're real people, which you won't get, there'd be a better chance he'd come out all right."

Howard was headed for the penitentiary. It was suggested he would receive an education there. His lawyer said, "He'll get an education, all right—a post-graduate course." Prison authorities described an elaborate system of screening new arrivals, but it meant little: Illinois has no reformatory. Incarceration, it appears, is for punishment alone, not rehabilitation, which is termed coddling. The educators who handled Howard Lang had known for several years that he presented a serious problem, yet they had done nothing effective. It seemed unlikely that the prison authorities would do better. Illinois' penal system was no better equipped to deal with him than Chicago's school system had been.

The world had produced him, and now he presented himself to the world, not as a child but as a Problem, and one beyond the pale. Turn him loose? Impossible. Imprison him—and would not the results be easily forseeable? Execute him? It hardly seemed fair. He waited patiently for the world to make up its mind. The hearings dragged out for weeks. The defense produced a long stream of teachers, psychologists, children, neighbors who had touched Howard Lang in his short passage through life; and as they moved through the courtroom in dull procession, Howard, squirming a little at the counsel table, made a sign to a little boy spectator meaning, in child sign language, "Horse manure." One teacher testified, "I set him over in a corner . . . and kept him in at recess," and another "The monitors brought him up," and sometimes it was hard to remember that the matter before the court was murder. The children, the old bunch from Campbell Avenue now waiting importantly to testify, giggled. A bailiff strode toward them menacingly, and Howard smirked.

At last it was over. On April 20, after long deliberation, the judge on his high bench read his findings, and there was no giggling now, there was only silence. The judge, blaming the mother mainly but censuring comic books and movies too, recounted the circumstances of this "abhorrent, gruesome, hideous murder which, if committed by an adult, would merit the extreme penalty of the law." But "we are confronted with a . . . mere slip of a boy. . . . To say that Lang is beyond redemption or is incapable of rehabilitation is to decry hope." The judge took note of his own "very grave duty." And he concluded: ". . . therefore the Court, after a review of all the evidence in the case, and all matters of mitigation, fixes the limit and duration of the sentence, under the Statutes of Illinois, of Howard Lang, for the murder of Lonnie Fellick, at twenty-two years in the penitentiary." A bailiff led the boy away.

Howard's little friends, the old bunch from Campbell Avenue, were not there at the end, though they had hoped to be. The most loyal of them was a little boy in glasses who had journeyed all the way out to the Criminal Court for every hearing. Once near dark, after a long day in court, he ran alone down the great stone steps. The streetcar came and he hopped onto the back platform and paid his fare, then stood there wedged among grownups, spindly legs braced, cap on the back of his head, his face expressionless but tear streaks running along the sides of his nose from his eyes.

Had Howard been a pretty nice kid? "He always was when I knew him." "What kind of a kid was he? A leader?"

"Well—no," And then. "He liked to swim. He played all kinds of sports."

"What happened to him? What went wrong?"

"I don't know."

"Do you live with your parents?"

"With my mother."

"Where's your father?"

"He—they're divorced. I'm sorry, I got to go here," and he jumped off alone at the Western Avenue viaduct and darted between two trucks and ran toward an onrushing streetcar, skipped around it perilously and leaped aboard, heading north, heading back to the Von Humboldt Park district, his home.

REVENGE COSTS TOO MUCH *

Professor Waite has written a sweeping indictment of our present prison system, declaring that our avowed objectives and methods are antithetical. In turn, he suggests a wholesale reorganization of the system and submits a tentative blueprint, under which punishment and revenge would be completely eliminated, leaving courts and social agencies to devote their full attention to rehabilitation.

Thoughtful readers will be forced to re-examine our treatment of criminals. Should society be cast in the role of an avenger—"an eye for an eye"? Are not potential criminals deterred by fear of punishment? Cannot revenge and reformation be profitably combined? Is Waite advocating a "soft" program such as that so roundly condemned by the author of "Little Donald Took an Axe"? Or is his program too tough in that many consistently minor offenders would be permanently imprisoned?

Ask a man on the street why the law punishes criminals and the answer will probably be, "To prevent crime, of course." Ask him how effectively it prevents crime and the answer will be profane. Certainly, as a preventive, punishment is in truth a farce.

Eddie Murphy recently made the headlines by his one hundredth conviction in a Detroit criminal court. But there are a hundred other petty

* John Barker Waite, *Harper's Magazine*, May, 1946, pp. 467–72.

criminals like him. Some have already beaten his record; some merely have not had time—Frank Evans, 54 years old, 76 convictions; J. W. Tyrrell, 50 convictions of crimes ranging from misdemeanor to felony, and imprisonments from Eastern jails to California's San Quentin; Kate Russell, 50 sentences in 30 years, nine years spent in jails. Eddie himself would undoubtedly soon have begun his second hundred had not the last conviction been for snatching a woman's purse—robbery—for which he was sentenced to a penitentiary term that will hold him from crime for several years. But most of Eddie's offenses, like those of any man who commits so many, were not serious. Not callous enough for a killer, not bold enough for a robber, he was just a confounded social nuisance. His record merely demonstrates that even trivial offenses may not be stopped by punishment.

Records of repeated punishment for more serious crimes obviously cannot run so high in a lifetime, though some criminals accomplish much. This is James Griffnor's:

1907, burglary, 2 years; 1908, burglary, 2 years; 1910, burglary, 5 years (all periods of confinement reduced by "good conduct" allowance, or parole); 1914, homicide, 10 years to life (escaped); 1915, rape, 12 years; 1923, burglary, "indeterminate" sentence; 1929, assault (penalty not recorded); 1933, burglary, 1 year to life.

. . . Penitentiary records are likewise illuminating. Thorsten Sellin, in his studies for the American Law Institute, discovered that more than half the inmates of our penitentiaries have been in penitentiaries one or more times before. The repetition is nation wide: 58 per cent in California and Indiana; 59 per cent in West Virginia and Pennsylvania, 64 per cent in Massachusetts, and 70 per cent in the District of Columbia. This is not the jail population, where the inmates run their repetitions into scores, but that of the penitentiaries wherein only serious offenders are confined. Moreover, it is the general average of young and old; of first offenders who have not yet had opportunity to repeat, as well as the few who may not. . . .

Small wonder that from many such data Mr. Sellin draws the pessimistic conclusion that punishment, instead of preventing crime, leaves men *seven times more likely to offend than those who have not been punished.* Thus from out of punishment—whether despite it or because of it—comes a stage-army of criminals, through the courts, into prison, back to freedom, through the courts, into prison, back to freedom; offending, punished, offending, punished again, again, and again until age itself ends the parade. It is pleasantest to express the evil lightly; in the rhymed philosophy of Ogden Nash:

> He who has never tasted jail
> Lives well within the legal pale,
> While he who's served a heavy sentence
> Renews the racket, not repentance.

The reason for punishment's failure is not difficult. Men do not expect to be caught and punished. That is only an aspect of the self-assurance that what happens to others will not happen to one's self, which enables men to go over the top into withering gunfire, to work in soft coal mines, to drive automobiles on the wrong side of curves—and to commit repeated crime, unafraid of its consequences.

Never in history have men been stayed from grasping at gain by the threat of pain or death. They sought Spanish gold in the face of the Inquisition and the exquisite pain of Comanche tortures. They climbed the Chilkoot Pass to the Yukon over the frozen bodies of their predecessors. In the days when punishment for theft was loss of an ear there were hundreds of men with both ears shorn. Pickpockets were active in the crowd at Tyburn watching the hanging of a pickpocket. No wonder, then, that crimes are committed somewhere in the country every minute and a half, many of them by men who have been in prison.

Effective prevention requires something other than punishment. Not something in addition to punishment; not correction by punishment; but an outright substitute for punishment. Punishment *and* prevention cannot exist together. Prevention needs methods which, while they may incidentally cause pain as a surgeon's knife in amputations causes pain, are specifically designed and intended for prevention instead of for punishment. It can operate satisfactorily only upon four basic principles, each of which is emphatically antithetic of punishment and inconsistent with it, namely:

That some offenders shall not be imprisoned at all;

That others shall never be allowed their freedom;

That in all offenders the causes of their criminality shall be sought for and if possible eliminated by any humane method;

That offenders who have been given their freedom shall be not merely watched lest they offend again, but shall be actively assisted to abstain from fresh offense.

Often, as a *preventive* measure, it may be both unnecessary and unwise to imprison a convict, as punishment would do. There is inevitably the danger that by imprisonment comparative innocence will be contaminated by wickedness, unsophistication be educated by experience, and what was mere casual or negligent wrongdoing be encouraged by evil association to an all pervading viciousness. In this respect, punishment has in fact yielded to prevention somewhat—but narrowly, grudgingly, and erratically. Connecticut and Florida allow convicts to be put on probation without imprisonment, not, oddly enough, when the interests of crime prevention so require, but whenever in the court's opinion the ends of justice do not require that he suffer a penalty. Generally, however, but with much state variance, probation is forbidden for most of the commoner crimes— burglary, rape, armed robbery, and the like. Wisconsin, in addition insists on punitive imprisonment without exception for desertion of a wife and child; Texas absolutely requires it for bigamy, incest, or abortion; Iowa demands it for certain liquor law offenses—and in Iowa the convict, whatever his offense, must be imprisoned unless he is free from venereal disease. Thus the penalty of imprisonment, regardless of its danger to the future in particular cases, is demanded or dispensed with by various state laws without rhyme, reason, consistency, or true regard for prevention.

On the other hand, punishment cannot logically keep an offender in prison for longer than his offense "deserves," no matter how dangerous he may be to the public. In this respect, punishment has yielded little if anything to prevention. Eddie Murphy is an illustration. After, shall we say, his twentieth demonstration of incapacity to live in conformity with group necessities, prevention would institutionalize him indefinitely—to the protection of society and, I suspect, to his own greater happiness. But punishment can do no more than imprison him briefly for the relatively light penalties his minor offenses deserve.

Dominick Piccone is an illustration of more serious evil consequences. When he had spent in a Michigan prison the four years of punishment which the court thought he deserved for attempted rape of a Negress, the psychologists recommended against his release. He was not frankly psychotic, they said, and hence was not committable to an institution for the insane, but he was "definitely assaultive and potentially homicidal." But Piccone had served his sentence and the authorities, against their will, were compelled to set him free. Within two weeks, he had murdered three good citizens. The only difference between Piccone and a thousand others, punished but not prevented, is that he killed three; they only assaulted, robbed, and raped.

Not even the so-called "fourth offender" statutes of many states are a manifestation of intent to prevent, through continued segregation, rather than merely to punish. They do, it is true, provide for life imprisonment after a fourth conviction of felony. But their purpose is primarily to scare the devil out of others by the harshness of their threatened penalty, rather than to keep provedly dangerous persons out of circulation—otherwise they would not be made to apply indiscriminately to every fourth offender, regardless of the circumstances or the high improbability in special cases of another offense. The very harshness of the statutes as punitive measures is the basis of criticism which is already driving them from the statute books. The only statutes I am aware of which seem really designed for prevention rather than punishment are those of nine states which, with greater or less limitation, contain the substance of the Michigan law that "any person who is suffering from a mental disorder and is not insane or feebleminded (in which case he could be confined in an insane asylum), which mental disorder . . . is coupled with criminal propensities to the commission of sex offenses" may be ordered confined after conviction of such an offense "until such person shall have fully and permanently recovered from such psychopathy." In these few states, the conventions of "deserved punishment" have given way to prevention insofar as the protection of womanhood is concerned—but to that extent only.

When a criminal is in custody, whether in prison or out, the common sense of prevention suggests that every effort be made to find the cause of his criminality and eliminate it. That can be done; not always, of course, but sometimes. The Rochester police were bothered years ago by a series of irrational burglaries. None of the stolen things appeared through fences nor in the pawnshops; the crimes did not look professional. Eventually a sixteen-year-old boy whom I shall call Joel Bagsby—that is not his real name—boasted too loudly and the police gathered him in. The loot from the burglaries was found in his closet, neatly packaged and labeled with time and place. Joel came before a juvenile court judge who was not obliged to inflict punishment and who was shrewd enough to see what was wrong. The boy was bald as an egg, and the constant butt of his fellows' ridicule. He defended himself by insistence that if he had less hair than they, he had more guts; which he sought to prove by burglarious daring. To have "punished" that boy would have made him a lifelong criminal. The judge ordered him given the realest wig obtainable and moved to the house of an aunt where nobody knew him. There is no record of further Bagsby crime.

In another case, a youngster who persisted in stealing money for candy, despite repeated chastisement, was, quite fortuitously, discovered to suffer from serious lack of sugar content in the blood stream. A sugar-inducing diet stopped his thievery. An adult's career of sex offenses was ended by discovery and surgical reduction of a chronic inflammation of his urethra. How many similar causes of repeated crime might be corrected by psychology, psychiatry, surgery, or other science, no one knows—because "punishment" is not concerned, and no attempt to find out has ever been made.

Punishment, indeed, is incapable of turning its victims back to freedom better able to live honestly than before. If it begets a strengthened will to refrain from crime, which I doubt, it does not develop a greater ability to do so.   On the contrary, it releases subjects as physically defective, as mentally backward, as psychologically obsessed, as subject to all the causes of crime as before it touched them.   They go forth, in fact, even less equipped to withstand the pressures of economic competition than before— the mechanic untutored in the development of his trade, the accountant's skill rusty from disuse, the laborer too soft for a full day's work.

The period following release is a critical time, when abstention from crime or repetition hangs in the balance.   Prevention demands every reasonable provision for helping the individual to abstain.   But "punishment" cannot help.   Nor does it.

Michigan and Iowa, most generous of the states, give the released convict a suit of clothes, $25 in money, and a railroad ticket, which Michigan fears to trust him with but hands to the conductor.   Indiana gives him ten dollars and a "durable" suit of clothes, which "shall not cost to exceed six dollars."   Florida presents him with "five dollars to provide the necessities of life until he can procure work"!   Then the state washes its hands of the ex-convict.

A Luke Lee, released from prison, is met with a brass band, a banquet, and presumably a job.   A Whitney is offered employment as manager of a friend's estate.   A Scarface Capone can retire to his own sea-island estate.   A Tenerowicz is sent to Congress.   But where does the run-of-the-mill offender find shelter and help?   With his five dollars or his twenty-five dollars, his shoddy clothes, his prison pallor; with no money for union dues in union-occupied trades, no money for the tools of his craft if he has one, no means of transportation to places where work may possibly be found; barred by his fingerprints from employment in many industries, unwanted in others, distrusted everywhere; he must turn perforce to the friends, the environment, the conditions which sent him to prison before and which will probably send him back.

The man on the street today justifies the use of punishment by the cliché that we want to prevent crime.   The philosophic contemporaries of Kant and Hegel justified it as a "religious duty"; as "a fulfillment of those metaphysical laws the meaning of which man, as a finite being cannot comprehend but to which he must conform" and as "a resolution of the discord with which an unrequited misdeed offends the sense of harmony and aesthetic consciousness."   Hammurabi and the writers of Deuteronomy more forthrightly decreed evil for evil without offering a justification. Childish indifference to subtlety says simply "Tit for Tat."

The frank truth is Sir James Stephens' assertion that "The criminal law stands to the passion of revenge in much the same relation as marriage does to the sexual appetite.') Nothing else will explain the now conventional legislation which punishes a successful crime twice as harshly as an unsuccessful attempt; the West Virginia Supreme Court's statement that a convicted murderer was to be hanged "in expiation" of his crime; or New Jersey judges' refusal to deal with a murderer who had struck his blow in New York, on the ground that "if New York does not choose to avenge the killing it is not for us to step in and do it for them." Nor will anything but the notion of punishment as the exaction of expiatory suffering, fit in with every newspaper's repeated reference to the convict who "has paid his debt to society." (Revenge must be accepted, I think, as the real basis of the law's punishments.)

That is why, when surgery or psychiatry is advocated for the correction of wrongdoing, when training of convicts in trade skills is seriously attempted, when material assistance in right living after release is urged, the demand for continuance of punishment fills legislative halls with opposition to making country clubs and hospitals out of penitentiaries, to turning prisons into schools whose admission fee is crime, to openly encouraging wrongdoing by rewarding the offender with advantages unavailable to the poor but honest. The advocacy of prevention is shouted down.

Will the man on the street, to whom legislatures look for approval, never forego the satisfaction of punishment and approve the measures of prevention? He has declined so far not, I think, because he is incapable of recognizing the value of prevention, but because the advocates of prevention have obscured the issue. They have overcautiously advocated new methods within the *framework of punishment*—probation as a mere exemption from punishment; long-continued segregation as an increased penalty; trade-training within the penitentiaries; penal-rehabilitation; penal-correction. All of which is penal-nonsense. The two ideas—prevention and punishment—cannot be combined. Their methods may at times look alike, as the breath-inducing slap on a new-born baby looks like the buttock slap of discipline; and as preventive segregation closely resembles today's mild penal incarcerations. But punishment and prevention are in truth by their natures and requisites inconsistent and uncombinable. To talk in the terminology of both is to advocate neither effectively.

Crime *can* be more effectively checked. But not by tinkering with the penal laws. Those laws must be boldly discarded. Crime must no longer be defined as an act which is punishable, but as something which demonstrates that the criminal is socially dangerous. "Shall be punished by imprisonment in the penitentiary" must be translated into "shall be treated in a manner designed to prevent further injurious activity." As thus stated, the one is specific, the other vague. It is the vagueness of brevity, however. There is no reason why prevention cannot be reduced to specific, practicable, operative detail.

In the punitive system certain legally specified activities make the offender subject to penalty. Following conviction the trial judge determines who shall go to prison, where, and for how long. Some judges rely upon pre-sentence investigation by a probation officer; some speculate on the criminal's looks and the evidence at the trial; one sometimes acted on the number of dried peas unpocketed by three fingers. One federal judge used probation in 62 per cent of his cases; another, on the same court, trying the same type of case, in four per cent. One judge's sentences of imprisonment averaged 851 days each; another's 40 days. After judicial commitment to prison a parole board takes over and determines how much less than the sentence a prisoner need stay. It cannot, however, hold him longer. Nobody at all is charged with responsibility for finding out why the convict offended and how he can be prevented from offending again. With rare exceptions, nobody attempts it. What help may be given a convict after release is likewise anyone's business—and no one's.

In a preventive system, I imagine, essentially the same specified activities —with some extension to cover persons who have clearly demonstrated a purpose toward evil . . . will make the offender legally subject to study and treatment. But the judge, trained only in law, instead of determining the treatment himself will commit every convicted person to the custody of a carefully chosen, highly trained, and well paid commission, sufficiently financed by the state for its purposes. It will be the commission's function, through its agencies, of course, to study each offender, not once, but continuously; to keep relative innocence apart from contaminating viciousness; to search out the cause of each convict's wrongdoing and the possibilities of correction; to set up facilities for the use of preventive medicine and psychiatry, for training toward economic self-sufficiency, and for whatever else may be requisite to effective prevention; and actively to assist convicts in law-abiding life after discharge.

The commission will release its wards as soon as release is safe—more wisely because more advisedly than parole boards do now. But so long as release affirmatively appears unsafe the commission will retain its control, by supervised freedom or actual confinement as necessity dictates. A power that could be abused. But I assume that its exercise will be safeguarded carefully; more carefully than today's power of the judge, who can, under some conditions, in his own sole and unrestricted discretion, choose whether a man shall spend the rest of his life in prison, or only fourteen years; who has power to keep a young boy confined as he himself thinks wise from a day to a decade.

Certainly the commission will be precluded from holding anyone more than a limited time except after a hearing in court and judicial approval. An Eddie Murphy will be given opportunity to convince the court, if he can, that despite a score of repetitions he is unlikely to repeat again; a Dominick Piccone may successfully dispute the opinions of psychiatrists. There will be no forgotten man in a sound preventive system. More costly initially, before its measures take effect, than the process of mass punishment, it need never be so potentially unfair to the individual.

This proposal for scrapping the traditional notions of the criminal law is revolutionary, I concede. But only so can society attain what it deserves from its Rizzos, Murphys, and Piccones, and displace the futility of seeking only what the Rizzos, Murphys, and Piccones deserve. Although for four thousand years we have sought satisfaction in punishing men like these— and have been dissatisfied—I think that we shall forego punishment when we truly appreciate the meaning of prevention and the cost of revenge.

AMERICA'S WORST PRISON *

Exposés of state penal institutions are a recurring phenomenon in American life. Since each exposé results in a measure of reformation, the title "America's Worst Prison" is unfair in that it describes past conditions. In reading the following article, therefore, you may be able to substitute for "Angola" the name of your own state prison. Although conditions there may not exactly duplicate those at the Louisiana institution, in most instances there are all-too-familiar similarities.

A description of such conditions should raise certain fundamental questions. Can we in all honesty call our present prisons reformatories? What do we actually expect of our prison system? The safety of society? Rehabilitation of the individual? Punishment? Revenge? If punishment is our objective, can we draw a line between approved corrective measures and ordinary brutality? Which is right —the "hard" or "soft" school of prison administrators?

All the prisoners were assigned to hard labor. Often the work was nothing more useful than cutting wild grass by hand. But it always began at "can see" and ended at "can't see," at times a twelve-hour stretch.

* Edward W. Stagg and John Lear, "A Riot Is an Unnecessary Evil," *Collier's,* November 22, 1952, pp. 13–16. Copyright John Lear.

A man was expected to keep up strength for this grinding toil on twenty-eight cents' worth of food a day.

His normal clothing ration was two suits of black-and-white-striped cloth a year. No underwear.

He was frequently permitted to leave the camp whenever the convenience of a politician outside demanded, undertake whatever job the politician had at hand and then return to his old work gang.

If he failed to follow orders, he often was flogged. Or fed a massive dose of salts or castor oil. Or thrown into a blank-walled dungeon on bread and water for weeks. Regulations forbidding such punishment were consistently ignored.

Did this happen on The Steppes of Soviet Russia? No. Right here in our own United States not long ago, in the prison called Angola.

Angola, the state penitentiary of Louisiana, is hidden in a big, looping bend of the Mississippi River just south of the line where the state of Mississippi ends. Shaped like an animal trap, with one side barricaded by a ten-mile arc of levees rimmed with quicksands, and the other cut off by the brush-tangled jaws of the Tunica Hills, it held within its gates in February, 1951, 2,640 humans—1,760 Negroes, 880 whites—and treated them as beasts.

"I have seen almost seven thousand men discharged from this institution," cried the first woman nurse who ever ventured into the place, "and I have never seen a man discharged . . . who was as qualified [for a place] in society as he was the day he was admitted. . . ."

By day, each prisoner lived in constant dread of his guards, some of whom were fellow convicts serving time for murder and other crimes of aggression. Despite their guns and authority, these guards ignored the existence of "harems" for all-male prostitution.

At night, he slept little better than a dog, lying in a tight-bedded pack with hundreds of his fellows snapping and snarling, under the steady glare of unshaded, never-dark light bulbs, keeping one eye open the night long against surprise sex assault by another male animal.

This ugly fester on the face of democracy stood untouched right up to last spring, a standing indictment of neglect and forgetfulness on the part of Louisiana citizens over more than half a century. Although the system is not yet destroyed, Angola's inmates have been freed from their former state of peonage. The dungeons have been dismantled. What remains of its terror has been thoroughly exposed, and is now in the course of what I believe will be total reformation. (I rely here on the conviction that my fellow citizens of Louisiana are too dedicated to humanity to consent to less.)

The story of how the exposure of Angola was brought about has meaning for you, wherever you live.   Angola is a telling example of man's habit of trying to get rid of problems by forgetting them. . . .

[The story is told from this point on in the first person because coauthor Stagg was a member of an investigating committee appointed by Governor Earl Long after Angola convicts repeatedly severed their own heel tendons with razor blades and so aroused the suspicion of Louisiana newspapers.]

We conducted "hearings" at Angola in March of 1951 in an almost dreamlike atmosphere of first come first served.   For two days we listened to men who were sent before us we know not whence, nor how, nor why. We were in a state of complete confusion until, just before going home, we turned wearily to listen to one more employee—a dark-eyed, gentle-voiced woman who had been waiting patiently to be heard.

She was Mrs. Mary Margaret Daughtry, Angola's first woman nurse. She had served the prison for seven years.   It was clear from what she said that she blamed Warden [Rudolph] Easterly for wrecking small humanitarianisms she had attempted among the prisoners when [Rollo C.] Lawrence [a distant relative of the late Kingfish Huey Long, appointed by Governor Earl Long as superintendent at Angola] had been the institution's only boss.

Her information consisted of a typewritten statement, which she presented without reading; two match-folder-size wax-paper decks of heroin she reported buying from a narcotics ring within the prison camp; the number of a five-dollar bill (H77490278A) she said she had paid for the dope through an intermediary; and a corner she had snipped from the bill before making the payment.

So quiet was her appearance that none of us realized she was making headlines until we got back to the Capitol pressroom in Baton Rouge that night and read her statement.

Days of the "Red Hats" Recalled

"No one has ever asked me if I have seen evidence of brutality," it declared.   "But I have seen plenty."   Referring explicitly to the heel slashings, she revealed that the first men to mutilate themselves included inmates then in solitary-confinement cells known as Red Hats in memory of the time when dangerous prisoners had to wear red hats to make their whereabouts constantly evident.   Some of the heel slashers had been sentenced to sixty days in Red Hats but had been kept there for as long as eight months.

"Angola is still in the Dark Ages," the nurse's statement went on.   "Degenerates of every type, . . . psychopaths and neurotics, are huddled in bedside companionship with the new arrivals, in huge dormitories that, as one inmate described to me, . . . 'stink like the hold of a slave ship.'

"There is . . . no trade school, no handicrafts or arts—not even a library. A man sentenced here who cannot read or write leaves here the same way. . . . No effort . . . is made to help him stay out of the penitentiary once he obtains his release . . . Their only choice is to steal or beg.

"Governor Long said the penitentiary has been a cancer on the state treasury—I say that the penitentiary is a cancer on the soul of every citizen in the state of Louisiana who knows of conditions at Angola and has made no effort to remedy them."

. . . . .

At the open meeting [called by the investigating committee at one point in the hearing to block an attempt at political intimidation through staged arrest of a committee member], a former prison captain (overseer) who was called admitted that he himself had flogged a prisoner until his arms were tired; and then given the whip to a younger relative, who had flogged until he was tired; and the younger man had returned the whip to the captain, who meanwhile had regained strength to finish the punishment. The victim of this outburst was a Negro. His offense, as stated by the captain: he "brushed against my daughter."

Political Hacks on Prison Payroll

A few of us slipped out of the hearing after that to pay a surprise visit to Angola. At the prison, we checked the records. They openly identified paid jobs as rewards for political hacks. They disclosed an accounting system so contrived that wholesale graft was possible without detection. There wasn't even an inventory. We couldn't determine what form of favoritism was used to choose the convict-guards, except that it clearly didn't reward good behavior. Punishment was medieval, one of the most pathetic victims being a sixty-one-year-old man who had been lashed with a leather strap fifteen or twenty times until he lost consciousness.

Prisoners who welcomed our prying didn't dare to betray it openly. But crude notes had a way of appearing in our hands as men brushed past us. The information set us stumbling blindly around the seven camps that are scattered over the prison farm's 18,000 acres, hunting this and that.

One of the peculiarities we came upon appeared to be a solid block of concrete. Three iron pipes stuck up from the top of it like periscopes.

On closer examination, we discovered three steel doors on one side of the block. Each was of solid metal, except for a small louvered rectangle near the bottom, similar to the draft vent beneath the grate of a furnace.

We banged on one door with our fists. A man's voice answered from within! We saw that the door was locked, and that there was no one around who could open it. We asked the man inside if he was all right, and he said he was. We saw that the second door was locked, and we assumed there was a man behind it, too. When we came to the third door, we found it unlocked and swung it open.

The walls and ceiling were painted black. There were no windows. The only sources of light or air were seven inch-wide, down-tilted slits in the bottom of the door and a two-inch hole in the ceiling. The hole led into a pipe on the roof that was bent in the opposite direction from the prevailing wind.

A bed stood along the wall. In an opposite corner was a concrete box for a toilet. The entire cubicle was the size of a small clothes closet. Into this stifling space as many as seven men were jammed at a time. At least one man had been removed in a state just short of roasting.

Back at the committee hearing in Baton Rouge that afternoon, Warden Easterly still insisted there was no justification for the heel slashings. He continued to insist there was nothing amiss at Angola even after this succession of events:

One of the heel slashers, William Richardson, twenty-two, summoned a lawyer to his hospital bed in New Orleans (he had been sent there from the prison to have his appendix removed; a simple operation Angola was powerless to cope with for lack of a surgeon). He sought a court injunction preventing his convict-guards and their "free people" bosses from carrying out threats to kill him. His application was denied on grounds that he had failed to establish a case. But—

A prisoner named Clifford Lacoste, thirty-seven, hanged himself in a Red Hats cell. And—

A West Feliciana Parish grand jury indicted Angola's machine-shop chief, J. D. Pearson, who had pleaded not guilty to a charge of soliciting $250 from a prisoner's family to "obtain a pardon" for the prisoner. The case is still pending at this writing.

Our committee didn't need those three events to be convinced that Angola really was, as Mrs. Daughtry had said, "a sewer of degradation."

Why a Capable Nurse Quit in Disgust

I personally shall always regret that we didn't get our backs up in time to prevent the resignation of Mrs. Daughtry. She quit her nurse's post in disgust early in April when it became apparent that Governor Long would transfer his kinsman, Superintendent Lawrence, who had been sympathetic to her efforts.

As we fitted together the terrible picture of Angola which Mrs. Daughtry had exposed, the thing that amazed us was not that there had been disturbances among the prisoners. What we couldn't understand was why the whole place hadn't either blown up or burned down.

Guns and ammunition were in the hands of trusties, some of whom were the very toughest inmates. Matches were strewn around the dilapidated old wooden shacks in which the men nested two and three tiers high— as many as 294 of them in a single room, locked behind steel doors to which a single guard had the keys. A half-dozen kitchen-size water faucets were the only means of fighting flame in barnlike shanties with wooden floors, crumbling plaster walls, and roofs whose corrugated iron shingles creaked loosely in the slightest breeze.

Motives for arson and murder were everywhere: favors peddled in return for cash . . . furloughs to work for pay outside the prison—for as much as six months to a year—granted in response to political pull . . . sexual perversion forced by assault . . . whisky making and dope peddling through connivance with the "free people" . . . open gambling, at crap tables patterned on those of fancy casinos . . . eight toilets for 300 men in the best dormitory, and often no toilet paper . . . government by buckshot, leather strap and rubber hose . . . many deaths by violence.

Our committee reported to Governor Long, recommending an end to corporal punishment, appointment of a trained prison man as warden, new and modern housing, and a positive program of rehabilitation of prisoners.

"You want us to teach those convicts . . . ping-pong, baseball, elocution, and gee-tar playin'?" he chortled. "Those fellow aren't up there for ringin' church bells."

· · · · ·

The people of Louisiana vigorously disagreed with Long's anachronistic thinking. They defeated his candidate for governor by electing Robert F. Kennon, who was first on the ballot to declare for penal reform. Recognizing publicly that "Angola was one of the big reasons why I was elected," Kennon stated his firm intent "to change Angola from one of the worst prisons in the country to one of the best."

· · · · ·

Already [Reed] Cozart [warden of the United States Prison Bureau's model penitentiary at Seagoville, Texas, whence Governor Kennon borrowed him to clean up Angola's horrors] and Sam A. Anderson, a Mississippi-born associate in the federal service whom he has brought in as the new warden, have prohibited private deals for use of prison labor outside the Angola farm. It is definitely understood by all that prisoners are no longer slaves. Stern orders have been posted against corporal punishment of any kind. A disciplinary board has been set up to take legitimate punishment out of the hands of convict-guards and brutal overseers. An assignment committee has been organized to classify the men according to their skills and give them work suited to their abilities. Blue denim cloth for suits has been ordered to replace the black and white stripes, which will go instead into mattress covers. A former Navy steward has been placed in charge of planning the farm's food production to meet the dietary needs of the prisoners, and of seeing to it that all prisoners get the same healthy food instead of whatever the individual overseers happen to throw together on any given day. Segregation of prisoners according to their behavior has been started. A man trained in vocational education has been hired to start a program. And the first corps of paid guards has passed its strenuous physical examination preparatory to taking the guns out of the hands of the convicts. We can take it for granted that Angola never will be allowed to revert to its former state of bestiality.

WHAT'S WRONG WITH OUR PRISONS? *

Riots, mass insubordination, and hunger strikes periodically have shattered the surface calm of American prisons. The increasing frequency with which these disturbances have made headlines and extra editions has caused both expert and layman alike to take another look at our penal institutions. In the following article two outstanding students of prisons, Donald Powell Wilson and Harry Elmer Barnes, survey the current status of state penitentiaries, point out glaring shortcomings, and suggest reasonable and practical remedies.

Inherent in the article are such questions as: What role should the prisons play? Are safe custody and the execution of court sentences the only responsibilities of our penitentiaries? Should the prisons merely "salt a man away" for a specified length of time, or should they build a rehabilitative program around the proven fact that 95 per cent of all convicts eventually return to society? What practical reforms can be undertaken to avoid the shameful disturbances that have occurred?

For the prisons of the U.S. 1952 is a year of shame. In no previous year have so many convicts been driven to setting off destructive, bloody riots.

* Donald Powell Wilson and Harry Elmer Barnes, *Life,* November 24, 1952. Copyright, Time, Inc.

So far there have been 20 major disturbances. In one short period of four months there were no fewer than 16. And several others were quelled before they could get out of hand and make national headlines.

Why the riots? Some prison officials blandly dismissed the violent series of uprisings that broke out last April as "spring fever." One official earnestly reported that the rioting convicts meant "to embarrass the administration." Another compared the murderous rebellions with the then current "panty-snatching" raids staged by the adolescents of many U.S. colleges. Another explained that one of the riots was "Communist-inspired."

Obviously we have to look much more deeply and scientifically if we are to find the causes and suggest remedies for this disgraceful record. . . .

Here, with suggestions for corrections, are the six major problems that visit our state prisons:

Brutality

One of the most colorful exponents of the treat-'em-rough policy is Roy Best, the arrogant, tough former warden of Colorado's Canon City Penitentiary. Warden Best was put on trial last summer, and although he was acquitted, this is some of the testimony of the prisoners and guards, as reported in the *Denver Post:* One summer day, a year before the trial, 50 guards and officials formed a ring around five Canon City prisoners in the penitentiary yard. The prisoners were stripped, forced to keep their hands high above their heads. Occasionally a guard knocked down one of the convicts, picked him up, knocked him down again and kicked him in the head and groin. The sun was so hot that the men's bare feet began to blister on the pavement. Sweat from their bodies formed tiny pools, but whenever one of the men tried to stand in a pool to cool his seared feet, he was forced back onto the dry, hot surface of the prison pavement. After about half an hour of this the five men were pushed into the prison gymnasium. One convict who had booed at this performance was added to the group. There the six men were chained over the "gray mare" and lashed. The various officials took turns wielding the whip, a six-inch-wide leather strap. At intervals a wire noose was slipped around a convict's neck and he was dragged across the floor. When a convict fainted, he was revived with a bucket of water so none of the punishment would be wasted on him. After each had received about 45 lashes, the men were unchained, stretched out on the floor while a guard whipped the bare soles of their feet with the strap.

At the trial Best denied everything but the lashings. But earlier he had boasted that he had been "spanking" convicts for 22 years. In a pretrial hearing Best's attorney maintained that a prisoner "is civilly dead. He has no civil rights." The way to handle a prison break, Mr. Best said, is simple: "Blow 'em to hell off the wall."

. . . . .

The first corrective measure to be taken against such brutality is obviously to get rid of those wardens and guards who are sadists. But they must first be exposed. Brutal conditions inside the state prisons are nearly always exposed by the inmates themselves, with the help of hardworking reporters.

. . . . .

Such conditions still exist behind the walls of many state prisons in the North as well as the South. They can only be smoked out by the state and only if the governor or legislature appoints an impartial group of investigators and guarantees them access to every dank cranny of every prison. This should be done at once. It is neither humane nor sensible to wait until the convicts riot before undertaking investigations.

Overcrowding

It is commonly accepted by penologists that the maximum number of inmates that can be efficiently handled in one institution, no matter how big, is about 1,200. But at the Jackson, Michigan, prison where one of the worst riots broke out this year, there were 4,800 prisoners inside the walls, with 600 of them sleeping in halls and corridors. In New Jersey, the scene of two other violent riots, there have been as many as three inmates crowded into cells built for one. In Ohio, where rebellion flared only three weeks ago, 150 convicts live in one dormitory room. There are about 148,000 prisoners in our state institutions; and when any group of murderers, psychopaths and sexual perverts are mixed together, there is bound to be trouble sooner or later. This is something wardens have every right to complain about. Governors and legislators usually answer that with rising costs and rising numbers of convictions, there is nothing they can do. But there are things that can be done about overcrowding without building new prisons. Any of the following measures would appreciably reduce the penitentiary load.

Better Probation and Parole Systems

The facilities a man needs for rehabilitation—guidance clinics, social settlements, night schools—are more accessible outside prisons than inside. Probation may make a man a good citizen, whereas prison can only make him a good convict—and at 10 times the cost of a good probation system.

The New York Court of General Sessions has had success in more than 90 per cent of its probation assignments. Los Angeles County has had about the same percentage of good results. Yet many judges still prefer prison sentences to probation.

Efficient parole systems after the convict's release have made as good a record as probation in many states. A good convict is fitted to live only in a tight totalitarian system, which is what the average prison is. If a prisoner is to become a law-abiding citizen of a democracy, he must be trained to re-enter society. Only a good parole system can provide such training. Yet there are not more than a dozen really good parole systems in the whole country. In nearly every major riot during 1951 and 1952 alleged abuses in the parole system were among the most common of convict grievances.

Instalment Plan for Fines

Although imprisonment for debt was supposedly outlawed more than a century ago, upwards of 40 per cent of the jail and penitentiary sentences today are levied for nonpayment of fines and nonsupport. In Maryland nearly 25 per cent of the prisoners are locked up for nonsupport alone. England and Ireland have long since solved this problem by instalment paying of fines. In the U.S., where you can finance almost anything on time, instalment paying of fines is a rare exception.

Classification and Segregation

Far too few prisons do any real diagnostic classification of prisoners. Convicts usually fall into one of three groups: those who are the easiest to rehabilitate and should really be on probation; those who ought to be in prison farms or camps or minimum-security institutions; and those so-called incorrigibles, the only ones who belong behind heavy bars. Better classification would at least help segregate the hardened criminals from those who are in prison because of one minor brush with the law.

Restatement of Laws

Criminal laws are a hodgepodge of inconsistencies. More than 500,000 new state laws have been passed since 1900. A man can be a criminal in one state and not in another; and ignorance of the local law is no excuse.

Idleness

One of the most destructive psychological forces at work on a man in prison is the futility he feels when he literally has nothing to do. When a warden claims that 75 per cent of the prisoners are working, he frequently means that four men are being "employed" on a one-man job. In the state penitentiary at Jackson, Michigan, 1,700 men were listed as "working" in the kitchen. Actually more than 50 per cent of today's prisoners in state institutions are idle, demoralized and ripe for riot.

The biggest single solution to idleness in state prisons would be the repeal of a lot of state legislation passed in the days when labor had some small reason to fear the competition of prisoners. Today no such reason exists.

There is more than enough work to keep all able-bodied state prisoners busy producing goods needed by prisons and other state institutions. But the present prison-labor laws are senseless. Prisons are limited by law to working on institutional goods and services. But state institutions are rarely, if ever, required to buy prison-made goods, even when available and of suitable quality. Until they are, prison idleness will continue and will defeat all efforts at convict rehabilitation. There would still remain plenty of markets for private business, for almost no state could produce by prison labor more than a fraction of the goods, services and food required by all its institutions.

．　．　．　．　．

Dangerously Low Budgets

One of the worst evils in the state prisons today cannot be blamed on the wardens. In the majority of states prison appropriations remain where they were in 1943, when prices were lower and prison populations were smaller than they are now. Consider the food problem alone. Despite inflation, the budgets for meals in the state prisons range from 37 cents a day per prisoner in the South to 60 cents per day per prisoner in Michigan. This 60 cents figure is only half what the Army spends on its ration. Figured on the average, the money appropriated by the states amounts to about 16 cents per meal for each convict.

A commissioner of corrections often works out a realistic, progressive plan for reforming the prison system of a state—and then finds he is wasting his time because a cost-cutting governor or legislature has allowed him barely enough money to keep the old regime functioning, much less introduce the new. In New Jersey, where two particularly serious outbreaks occurred this year, the Commissioner of Institutions and Agencies is Sanford Bates, one of the most enlightened American penologists. When Bates was director of the Federal Bureau of Prisons in 1930-37, Presidents Hoover and Roosevelt saw to it that he had adequate budgets, and he got results. But in New Jersey he has been crippled by the penurious budget and antiquated administrative system under which the big Trenton prison had to operate until last year.

Even where state legislatures can afford no larger budgets than they could in 1943, there are ways to save money without assuring more riots in the prisons.

One way is by better use of the classification system, to determine the small number of the prisoners who really need maximum-security institutions. The others can be more speedily put on probation or parole or put on work farms and in road camps. Maintenance for one man in a maximum-security penitentiary for a year comes to more than $1,500. A minimum-security institution can cut this cost in half. Probation and parole costs cut it down to 1/10th sometimes to 1/20th. Some states have already emphasized this method of cost-cutting, notably Rhode Island, New Hampshire, Ohio and Minnesota.

In Massachusetts the officials have learned how to use their appropriations constructively. There is, in Charlestown, Mass., a 147 year-old maximum-security fortress which was first condemned in 1878 but is still being used. Inmates carry food to their cells because there is no dining hall. Toilet facilities consist of a bucket in the cell corner. The walls actually drip and stink. Governor Dever, calling Charlestown "a disgrace —a bastille" got an appropriation of $8 million, which will be used for a new penitentiary. But the capacity of this maximum-security prison will be kept down to about 800. Prisoners who are good risks will be taken care of in a new system of prison camps. Instead of paring budgets for prisoners' food, medical care and rehabilitation, state legislatures could save money by following this example. Massachusetts has approached the long-term expense problem more realistically by deciding not to waste funds on maximum-security institutions. They cost as much as $15,000 per cell to build and the majority of convicts are only made worse by being confined in them.

Politics

Prison jobs in at least 26 of our states can still be handed out as political patronage. Even in the states where civil service operates at the working level, many of the top jobs can be appointive. One unfortunate result is that a prison administration can change with every new governor, with the inevitable result that penitentiary jobs are held by men with no training for them. Another drawback is that despite the great advances made in the science of penology in the last quarter of a century, wardens whose jobs depend upon political whim are afraid to advocate anything new; it is safer to follow the old pattern.

The solution to this problem is simple; put all the prison jobs under civil service and see that only qualified men hold them, without being subject to the whims of local or state politicians.

Poor Pay for Personnel

The sixth major problem of the state penitentiaries is just about the oldest. Salaries and general working conditions of prison employees have almost always been subnormal. Guards in some of the Southern prisons get as little as $100 a month. Even in the North the average is $200 a month. The employee turnover is so great, up to 300 per cent per year, that on-the-job training is virtually useless. The warden of one state institution, asked what the qualifications were for guards, replied candidly, "The ability to walk, see and hear."

The only solution to this problem is to convince the state legislatures that what they save on prisons they will spend on police, that the citizens will lose more from additional crimes than they will save in taxes. Maybe this lesson can be learned in most of the states as it has in California, New York and Wisconsin, where comparatively good salaries and working conditions have stabilized prison personnel and built up well qualified prison staffs.

These, then, are the six major problems of the state prisons today, the six main reasons why there have been penitentiary riots all across the nation this year—and the reasons why there will be more.

These conditions, which are reflected invariably in the grievances of rioting prisoners throughout the nation, show why we have prison riots at all. But they do not make it clear just why there has been such a unique wave of riots in the last year. Prison conditions are always bad enough, but increasing costs of prison food, clothing and other supplies and services have made the situation so much worse during the last six or seven years that rioting has become the inevitable convict answer to intolerable abuses.

Every state has it own problems; but every state should take a hard look at its prison establishment, whether the riot-warning has sounded or not. It must be a really penetrating investigation. Because of his frustrating situation, even the best state prison warden will try to conceal some of the shortcomings of his institution.

Reforms can be made. They have already been made in the federal prisons. Except for Alcatraz alone, the ill-famed "Isle of Dread" which holds the nation's most unsalvageable criminals, all of the federal prisons are being changed over from cages for beasts to places where men have a chance for rehabilitation.   And the bureau has a plan for a new and modernized institution to replace Alcatraz.   More than one-third of the federal prisoners are in active vocational training, learning some occupation by which they can at least hope to make an honest living when they get out.

The custodians of the old-style fortress prisons and fortress methods of handling prisoners are fond of claiming that the "do-gooders" sound fine but do not make practical sense.   It is true that the average convict is beyond the scoutmaster approach, but he is not an animal, and the application of humane principles sometimes works even with a tough con.

Take, for example, the work done at the federal minimum-security correctional institution at Seagoville, near Dallas, Texas, whose warden, Reed Cozart, is now helping the state of Louisiana clean up Angola.   In place of the old cell blocks, Seagoville has rows of cottages.   The steel "escape-proof" cells that convicts are always escaping from in the old-fashioned prisons do not exist at Seagoville; instead, each inmate has a private room, with a door that is never locked.   He has full freedom inside his cottage, restrained only by a minimum of rules necessary in any institution.   There are no walls at Seagoville, only a low fence around part of the area.   Escape would be fantastically easy.

Medical and psychiatric treatment is provided for every inmate.   A vocational training program prepares them for skilled jobs on the outside.   A 600-acre farm provides both training and healthy work.   There are no guards.   Most important is the atmosphere.   The inmates are assumed to have paid their debt to society by losing their freedom.   The staff's function is to see that prisoners are ready for the outside world when they are released.

The crux of this plan, of course, is the classification of inmates, to weed out the minority of men who appear unable to benefit by this rehabilitation.   Seagoville has had amazing results.   At its start it was naturally regarded as an experiment.   Its first inmates were conscientious objectors, the old, the infirm and the crippled.   But gradually more and more of the run of prison life was included.   Today 80 per cent of the men serving time at Seagoville were sent there from federal court, without having first proved "good behavior" elsewhere.   Seagoville's men are not "trusties." At least half of them would in most states be automatically regarded as poor security risks and clapped in a fortress hoosegow.   Some of them are unstable youthful offenders, the category of criminal most wardens regard as the worst of all security risks.

The real success of Seagoville is measured in some very encouraging statistics.   Of the 3,500 men who have served time at the institution, only

32 or 1 per cent have tried to walk away. All were caught. While more than 80 per cent of the "graduates" of most prisons return to crime after their release, Seagoville's record is less than 20 per cent.

This plan can work at the state level, too. The pioneer institution of the Seagoville type is Wallkill Prison in New York. Under the direction of Walter M. Wallack, Wallkill has become the model for progressive prisons both in this country and abroad.

Another excellent example of humane prison treatment is found in California, which, under Governor Warren's close leadership, has the best prison system of all 48 states. In California most lawbreakers are not given fixed prison sentences by the judges. Instead the state's Youth Authority or Adult Authority studies the cases and treats as many persons as possible outside the institutions. Those imprisoned are carefully classified, and the prisons are diversified. The prison at California's Soledad offers industrial training in 11 different trades. But to criminologists California's greatest distinction is the institution at Chino, directed by Kenyon J. Scudder. Here as at Wallkill and Seagoville, there are no walls, no bars, no locks, no guns. And here also there is rehabilitation, a minimum of walk-aways, a parole success of 75 per cent—and no riots.

Wallkill, Seagoville, Chino, a handful of other institutions like them, all seem to prove what a great many criminologists have been arguing for years: the old-style lockups, where a lawbreaker is simply salted away until his term is served, are the wrong approach. Most state prisons, as currently built and managed, are costing too much money and doing too little good. They are not deterring crime; instead they are hardening criminals. And so they cannot be said to protect law-abiding people. The simple truth has long since been appreciated by the officials and wardens who run the federal penitentiaries and the better state institutions. But many "hard-headed" penologists and "practical" wardens have not grasped the idea yet. Now they have riots on their hands, nearly two a month.

These officials will continue to have riots—until they realize that there are humane ways to handle prisoners, and that these methods have already been proved.

CHAPTER FIVE

The Family in a Changing Society

MOST OF US are prepared to adjust to change in many aspects of social behavior. If we are not pushed too hard or pressed too far, we make adjustments and declare them to be "progress"—label them "good." But at the same time we are often shocked and indignant at other shifts in our social life, particularly if they seem to challenge our traditional moral order —if they involve a radical departure from what has always been considered fine and inviolate.

Many of our most sacred moral sanctions are closely associated with the family and family life. We have felt, and probably quite accurately so, that changes in the family order presage more widespread change in the general social order. Recognizing the far-reaching consequences of changes in the family system, we are prone to move slowly and tentatively in our approval or disapproval of them.

Whatever our attitude toward it, the American family is undergoing a rapid transition. If the avalanche of public opinion expressed orally and in writing is any criterion, recognition of this change is proving to be a socially traumatic experience. And opinion is by no means consensus; the issue is shot through with intense controversy. Certain individuals and groups, shocked and upset by contemporary behavior patterns, insist that our only salvation, not only for the family but for the whole social order, is a return to traditional (but ill-defined) concepts of the family. At the other extreme are those who see the vestiges of tradition as the major barriers to an adjusted and coherent new order. In between, most of us grope blindly for some workable synthesis, some pattern of family life that does not call for the rejection of all that was once held dear but at the same time can embrace much of the new. The result is a widespread confusion. We are anxious to do the right thing, but as we have no clear chart to guide us, our worries, anxieties, and frustrations hamper effective action.

In the readings that follow we shall explore some of these areas of confusion and bewilderment. What is happening to the American family? Is it falling apart at the seams, or is it evolving into something finer and better? Do our child-care methods produce adjusted adults, or are we creating a generation of nonsocial individuals? Is "love" a sufficient basis for a good marriage? Is divorce the unmitigated evil it is often painted?

Problem 14: The Changing Family-- Adjustment or Decline?

The American family is changing in many ways. It is surrendering many of its functions to other institutions; it is becoming smaller; it is breaking up more frequently than in the past. Often drawing their arguments from the decline of Rome, some have predicted that such changes presage the downfall of our entire civilization, viewing the present situation as the final fling before oblivion. Others have maintained that the changes are simply signs of a transition period with eventual adjustment and stability, based upon a new and more realistic standard, in view. In the following readings we shall explore two matters pertaining to family life. What major changes are taking place in the American family? Are the changes totally detrimental, or do they contain the elements necessary for more adequate family living?

THE AMERICAN FAMILY IN TROUBLE *

The nature of the change that the American family is undergoing is not always clearly understood. In the following article *Life*, by comparing the American family at different stages in its evolutionary development, attempts to demonstrate change by the method of contrast. Following this illustration of changes, the article introduces the conflict over the meaning of these changes for the future—a subject that will be explored more fully in the readings that follow.

* *Life*, July 26, 1948. Copyright Time, Inc.

. . . The U.S. family, deep in the millrace of social and technological change, is itself deep in trouble.

The root of the trouble is found in another fact: in the last 100 years the pattern of American life has profoundly altered. A century ago the U.S. was largely agricultural, there were few great cities and industrialization was in its infancy. The average family lived on a farm or in a small town. The need for many hands to do the work produced large families of a type called by sociologists the trustee family. Life was not always easy, but economic interdependence and common interests formed a hard base for close family unity. But the trustee-type family could not withstand the march of industrialization. Its extra members went packing off to the booming cities to evolve a new family type, the so-called domestic family— small, no longer self-sufficient but still closely knit. Instead of making their own shoes and soap, individuals found they could buy these things with their high industrial wages and have time left over to develop a variety of social interests both within and outside of the family group.

Today the forces of social change have further broken down the family. It is now tiny—a husband, a wife and one or two children. Its members do little more than sleep and eat together. They buy everything—food, laundry, entertainment—and produce nothing but the money for these purchases. The outward pull of movies, automobiles, bridge clubs, and Elks constantly threatens what little family unity remains. The individual now looks outside his home for his interests. He is atomistic, an individualized fragment rather than part of a unified whole.

The Trustee-Type Family

. . . [The Russells of Belleview, Mo.] are the modern counterpart of the kind of family with which the U.S. began and which served as the strong backbone of American society until the industrial cities began to siphon its members away. The Ozark farm they live on has been in the family for 125 years, and in typical trustee fashion it has been passed on within the family from one member to another. Because they have had to work hard to make their farm pay, the Russells have always put a premium on children and on an efficient family economy. Two years ago Howard Russell persuaded his father to substitute more efficient tractors for horses. And to ease his womenfolk's work Russell has also bought an electric washing machine, a gas stove and a deep-freeze unit. But the freezer is stocked with home butchered meat (six hogs and a big beef each year) and the women put up a thousand quarts of food every summer. The family rises at 5 each morning and there is plenty of work for everyone to do. There are cows to milk, chickens, hogs and beef cattle to feed, corn to cultivate, machinery to repair, clothes to mend and bread to bake.

Despite their old-fashioned family existence, the Russells are beginning to show some of the signs of change which have produced the more modern family types shown on the following pages. Carson has a part-time job in a nearby ax-handle factory and is branching out on his own. A daughter has moved to St. Louis to work in a store. And Howard, who has been studying for the rural ministry, has not decided whether he will stay home to "plow corn" or move away to "preach Christ."

The Domestic-Type Family

The domestic-type family of Harry Frantz of Enid, Okla., is a closely knit one like the Russells, but has undergone considerable development from the rural family. It is cohesive, not from economic necessity but by choice, and has to be held together consciously. . . .

As the American family has changed, families like the Frantzes have hung on happily to what domestic ties they could. In place of food to grow and clothes to make and extra hands to raise for the harvest, they have developed mutual interests in fishing, church, shopping tours, and Sunday suppers. Their way of life is a good example of the middle ground which has had to be invented by many purposeful Americans who believe that the family is still worth worrying about.

The Atomistic-Type Family

. . . The Ward Parker family could probably be duplicated almost any evening in the majority of U.S. homes. The telephone has just rung. On the other end of the line there is undoubtedly a friend of some member of the family with an invitation to leave home for a few minutes or a few hours. During the day, when Mrs. Parker is alone, the telephone has still another use, for it leads to any number of outside services which she can summon to help her manage the family's needs. For the Parkers, like most U.S. families today, are what the social scientists have labeled atomistic. Which is to say that each member has his own separate interests and that the family's functions of household work, amusement and socialization have been taken over by outside agencies which are paid in cash from the family budget.

As a sales representative for Standard Brands, Ward Parker has moved his wife and two children five times to various company branches before settling down in Manhasset, near his New York home office. Each weekday morning he catches the 8:08 commuting train, not to return usually until 6:20 that night. And often he is called out of town on business trips to visit the company's offices. In the meantime his 14-year-old son, Cary, is usually off working out with whichever high school athletic team happens to be in season. Eleven-year-old Martha Anne juggles her time between music lessons, Girl Scout meetings, school play rehearsals, baby-sitting jobs and staying all night at the homes of her girl friends. Mrs. Parker has club and church activities and an occasional bridge game to keep her occupied in everyone else's absence. The Parkers are not as completely atomized as many American families, for the children still live at home and they go off together occasionally for a picnic, but the pattern of their living is vastly different from that of the Russells or the Frantzes. Like other couples who have given up the old family functions of home manufacture and even of much home recreation, Ward Parker and his wife have only one major function left: that of giving their children the affection and care they need until they leave home for college or a job that may be at the other end of the country.

The Romantic Dream

One of the most powerful forces at work today disrupting and disillusioning the atomistic family is the romantic dream fostered by movies, magazine serials, national advertising, and radio soap operas. More and more, as the result of such highly colored suggestion, young people have tended to rely impulsively on physical attraction and love at first sight. The idealistic belief in romantic love as the basis for marriage has become an almost universal American habit. There is nothing basically wrong with idealism in married love, but today it has been perverted until everyone is reminded constantly from all directions that wives must continue to be charming enough and husbands dandruff-free in order to be rechosen every day at breakfast. The sociologists point out that such hollow romance is by its very nature incompatible with the marriage it brings about. For marriage is nothing like this. It is a daily routine of facing small, realistic problems and of patient, selfless hard work.

A recent study by the Family Service Association of America, a clearing house for family research and welfare agencies, reported highest on its list of the usual causes of family troubles "the general immaturity of those people entering marriage." Some social scientists think now that America's youth, after a heavy postwar spurt of romanticism, is wisely beginning to substitute companionship for passion and temperamental congeniality for ecstatic castle-building. If this is so, perhaps there will be fewer tragic moments for the American family.

The Future of the Family

There are several divergent theories as to where the American family is going next now that it has reached its atomistic state and stands at a kind of sociological crossroads. As a matter of fact there is a great deal of disagreement among the experts even as to where it ought to go from here. Two of the leading men in the field of family sociology, Professor Carle C. Zimmerman of Harvard and Professor Joseph Kirk Folsom of Vassar, represent the major conflicting theories on the latter question. They both agree that the family is changing profoundly, but their books and speeches are diametrically opposed as to what values should be maintained as the changes take place.

In a book published last year, called *Family and Civilization,* Professor Zimmerman first gave the labels trustee, domestic, and atomistic to the main types of families which have been developed by Western civilization over centuries of social change. He then went on to sketch the development of each type as it had taken place twice before, among the Greeks and Romans. The moral of his history lesson is that the decline of each civilization to its collapse went hand in hand with the parallel disintegration of the Greek and Roman families from trustee to domestic to atomistic to chaos.

Zimmerman thinks he can see exactly the same signs of decay within the American family as plagued the ancients: the growing concept of marriage as a personal affair rather than one having real religious significance; the increased use of "causeless" divorce (for minor or meaningless grounds); the decreasing number of children per family (the average now is only about two); the "revolt of youth" against their parents and the growth of a youth class with idols and customs of its own; the rise of juvenile delinquency; the growing acceptance of sexual perversion. All of these signs Zimmerman lists as evidence of recurring atomism—of things which have happened before and which are happening again now. And atomism, he believes, is a chain-reaction breaking down of our society that will not stop with the family unit but will spread through the entire social structure until the modern world goes the dismal way of Greece and Rome.

Zimmerman has some immediate remedies for this danger. First of all he thinks the average family must begin having more children, preferably three or four, in order to reproduce itself. He would also like to see a revival of family spirit and activity among the learned and leadership classes, who were the first to weaken under the competition of outside forces like the school, the country club, and the sacrosanct adult bridge table. "We have on the one hand an institution which is breaking up because [people believe] it is not needed and, on the other hand, a great many juveniles who are breaking up because they do not have the proper family backgrounds." He does not expect the family to revert to the trustee form, for he regards that unit as having been most useful when the nation was young and struggling and so weak in the way of law and order that it depended upon the family to make and maintain its own laws. But he does think that the family should be pegged at least at the domestic level of unity, mutual interests and authority. As for the atomistic family, it is not so bad in itself, but it is a symptom of something which will wreck the society if it is not replaced by a strong family system, and that something is unbridled individualism. "There is little left now within the family," he warns, "or the moral code to hold [it] together. Mankind has consumed not only the crop but the seed for the next planting as well. The very continuation of our culture seems to be tied up with this nihilism in family behavior."

To all of this Professor Folsom of Vassar answers that the American family is not really disintegrating at all, but simply changing its form and its value to keep up with the permanent changes taking place in the society of which it is a part. "Something called 'the family' has survived all the revolutions of history. We need not worry about its continued existence," he writes in his book, *The Family and Democratic Society*. Folsom's reason for believing this is that the family fills too important a need for the people to allow it to collapse completely under the pressure of outside interests. With the increased mobility and complexity of our society, cooperation between individuals becomes more important and lifelong friendships with people outside the immediate family become difficult to maintain. The family will be preserved for the companionship it affords, if for nothing else.

"The problems of the modern family," he continues, "are similar in some respects to some which existed in Roman times. Does Roman history teach us any lessons by which we can profit? Some seem to think so, [saying that] we must not behave as the Romans did or we shall suffer their fate. But the conditions are different. The Romans lacked modern science. Our solution is not to preach against tendencies which cannot be checked but to do something additional which the Romans failed to do. Our job is to keep adjusting."

By this Folsom means that family atomization need not worry us into a frenzy of reform. Instead "when family members become more independent of one another economically and morally, their dependence upon one another for love may involve less frustration. It may be that further decline of the family as an economic unit may strengthen it as an emotional unit." The same holds true, he believes, for family authority. When family love was tied closely to authority and the parents ruled supreme, a threat to that authority brought anger and rebellion and love was smothered. When love is fully divorced from authority and coercion it may become more loyal and permanent. Even divorce comes in for a revaluation by Folsom. To make his point he tells the story of a cruel king who, as punishment to two lovers, ordered them tightly bound together for a period of several days. "It is said the lovers came to hate each other. We cannot verify the fact, but we know that it is quite in accord with known psychological processes. Thus does society, in the supposed interest of institutions called marriage and the family, sabotage that upon which modern marriage must rest: love."

The signs of change, therefore, which so worry Zimmerman, do not bother Folsom. In fact the very signs which worry Zimmerman the most —the splitting off of family members, the early growing up and moving away of the children, the growing strength of individualism—all these are to Folsom proof that the American society is actually progressing and reaching its goal of freedom. If the family as a unit is to be so sacrosanct as to stand in the way of allowing a growing child to develop his own contacts freely, to roam in search of fresh, private experiences and to strike out when he is ready to conquer his share of the world—then it has ceased to fulfill the functions for which it is intended in a democratic society.

That is why Folsom thinks that the atomistic atmosphere need not be harmful to children but will probably be healthier for them in the long run, despite the looseness of family ties and the present high incidence of divorce. He believes that the continued lessening of formal discipline (which leads to friction in the home) will result in an increase of parental affection and understanding, and hence to an increased feeling of responsibility. Says Folsom, "When parents respect the private world and personal values of their children, they may safely demand greater respect for their own needs. The mother will find she can afford to delegate some of her work and to be physically absent from the home for longer periods in order to enrich other aspects of her own personality if she has more sympathetic insight into the child's needs when she is present.

"The family is our most important primary group," he continues. "In large measure it determines personality development. If we believe in democracy we must promote freedom in the family and help parents build young personalities which will not sabotage democracy in the larger world through their frustrations and pent-up hostilities. This is the real significance of the family in modern society."

Folsom believes, finally, that if the American family is in deep trouble it is only because it has not realized the real meaning of the American democracy. When the people who show up in the divorce statistics learn how to live together and get along with themselves and their children the family will begin to find the changes taking place around it less disorganizing and confusing. "The modern family doesn't think of itself as 'atomistic.' People just don't live that way. Their strongest desires are to live together, and when they learn to do so the American family will be here to stay."

THE CRISIS OF THE CONTRACTUAL FAMILY *

Carle C. Zimmerman is not the only sociologist who decries the direction in which the American family is moving. From a somewhat different point of emphasis, Pitirim A. Sorokin has declared our family system to be sensate (based upon the idea that true reality and value are sensory) and contractual (free agreements of the parties for their mutual advantage, devoid of either love or hatred, but profitable to both husband and wife). His thesis is not that Western culture will come to an end, but that it will change and that the change will be exceedingly painful. In his own words, "the present disintegration of the sensate form is in no way identical with the end of Western society and culture. The tragedy and chaos, the horrors and sorrow of the transition period being over, they will evolve a new creative life, in a new integrated form, as magnificent in its own way as the five centuries of the sensate era." † But in the meantime we are near the transition period with its accompanying "horrors and sorrow."

. . . The decline of the contractual relationship in the *family* has assumed a different form from that obtaining in political and economic institutions. It manifests itself in a progressive disintegration of the contractual family, as a socially sanctioned union of husband and wife, of parents and children, and of the circle of the relatives. The disintegration shows itself in many forms, the tie binding husband and wife into one entity, normally for life, has weakened and is therefore sundered more and more frequently by divorces and separations. These have been rapidly increasing, especially in the last few decades. The bond uniting parents and children has likewise become weaker and weaker: first, because of an increasing percentage of marriages without children (in the United States 43 per cent of all married couples either are childless or have only one child); and,

---

* From the book *The Crisis of Our Age* by Pitirim A. Sorokin, pp. 187–92. Copyright, 1941, by E. P. Dutton & Co., Inc.
† *Ibid.*, p. 25.

second, because children now separate from their parents earlier than formerly: when they are grown, they remain much less frequently with their parents and especially their grandparents. Again, the cleavage between the mores, beliefs, mentality, and social forms of conduct of parents and children has progressively widened. The "conflict between fathers and sons" has become sharper and deeper than in the old-fashioned family. As a union of relatives beyond the circle of husband and wife and parents and children, the family is virtually non-existent nowadays, in contradistinction to the medieval family or even that of a century ago. As it has become more and more contractual, the family of the last few decades has grown ever more unstable, until it has reached the point of actual disintegration.

This disintegration manifests itself in many other ways, in the form of a shrinkage and atrophy of its size and functions. We all know that in the past few decades the number of children born to a family has been steadily decreasing, so that at the present time in most Western countries the births and survivals do not compensate for the deaths. As a result the population is now either stationary or on the decline. Contrary to all the assurances of the multitude of birth-control partisans, one should keep in mind that a period of depopulation has fairly uniformly been associated with a period of decline in the corresponding society and culture. The Greco-Roman cases for the epoch starting with the second century B. C. in Greece and a somewhat later epoch in Rome are typical. In addition, the number of childless marriages has been steadily mounting. This fact portends many social consequences, mainly negative ones. Childless marriages are more easily broken; the partners are more susceptible to suicide, and their outlook and attitudes are more egocentric than in marriages blessed with many children. Not only is the family becoming smaller and smaller in size, but it is growing by a striking reduction of almost all its functions.

In the past the family was the foremost educational agency for the young. Some hundred years ago it was well-nigh the sole educator for a vast proportion of the younger generation. At the present time its educational functions have shrunk enormously. Childless families obviously do not perform them at all; in families with children, the children are withdrawn from the educational influence of the home at a progressively younger and younger age, its place being taken by the nursery school, kindergarten, elementary school, high school, and college. Besides, even during the few years that a child remains in the home, the educational standards must comply to a large extent with the requirements of outside educational agencies. The actual shrinkage in the educational functions of the family is, accordingly, much greater than appears at first glance. In these respects the family has forfeited the greater part of its former prerogatives.

A similar thing has happened to the socio-moral education of children as *socii,* or members of society. In order to survive for any considerable period, the members of any society must possess a minimum of solidarity, altruism, and good will. An illiterate society can survive, but a thoroughly antisocial society cannot. Human beings are born mere biological organisms, devoid of solidary attitudes. Some agency must undertake the indispensable function of socializing them. Until recently the family was such an agency. It was the principal school of socialization for the new-born human animals, rendering them fit for social life. At present this vital mission is performed less and less by the family. Childless families, of course, do not fulfill it at all. Those with children perform it more and more inadequately: first, because the young are turned over at a very early age to such agencies as nursery schools and kindergartens; second, because an increasingly unstable family is a poor school for socialization. Instead of inculcating in its offspring a strong sense of moral and social integrity, it teaches them lessons of moral laxity and loose relationships, of antagonism and conflict between parents, of purely sensate egotism, and the like. Such a family cannot fail to produce, for the most part, unstable, loose, sensate persons. If outside agencies performed efficiently the former functions of the family, the defect might be remedied. Unfortunately, they have not successfully replaced the family in this mission. Even an illiterate mother, endowed with kindness and common sense, appears to have been a better moral educator of children than most of the highly trained educators of schools and correctional institutions. The result is a rapidly mounting juvenile delinquency, an increasing number of people without moral integrity, strength of character, a sense of social duty, or spontaneous altruism, who swell the ranks of criminals, of irresponsible persons, of paid minions of antisocial groups, from common murderers to the praetorian guards of the dictators.

Similarly, the family has sacrificed well-nigh all its other functions. It is less and less a *religious* agency, whereas in ancient times the head of the family was a priest (the *pater familias*). With the decline of religion, its place is taken either by nothing or by Sunday schools and similar institutions. Formerly the family supplied almost the only *means of subsistence* for its members. At the present time this function, too, is enormously reduced: hundreds of other agencies, including the state and philanthropic institutions, perform it. Other *economic* functions of the family have likewise either dwindled or disappeared: our meals we eat in cafeterias and restaurants; our bread comes from a bakers; our laundry is sent out; our clothes are bought in stores; and so on. So it is also with *recreational* functions. Formerly the family circle took care of these. Now we go to the movies, theaters, night clubs, and the like, instead of "wasting our time at home." Formerly the family was the principal agency for mitigating one's psycho-social isolation and loneliness. Now families are small, and their members are soon scattered. Even when they do live together, for the greater part of the day they work and live in separate places, and in the evening they again disperse in quest of recreation. The result is that the family home turns into a mere "over-night parking place"—not even for every night, and not always for the whole of any given night.

Accordingly, the contractual family in the process of its development has unexpectedly reached the point where it has lost most of its functions and prerogatives; even those that it retains are often atrophied and poorly performed. It has shrunk in size, it has become increasingly unstable and fragile. Less and less does it furnish even pleasure and comfort—the primary objectives of the sensate contractual family. When any institution finds itself in such a situation, it is in process of decay. This is precisely the position of the contractual sensate family today.

The Companionship Family [*]

Although he sees problems ahead for the American family, sociologist Ernest W. Burgess does not feel that it is doomed to extinction and disintegration if it continues to develop according to present tendencies. Perhaps the companionship family, with its emphasis on adjustment to changing conditions, is ideal for future stability in a society such as ours. Certainly Burgess would agree with Professor Folsom that many of the changes in the family have been beneficial rather than detrimental.

The Family and Society

With all the variations in American families, it is apparent that they are all in greater or less degree in a process of change toward an emerging type of family that is perhaps more aptly described as the "companionship" form. This term emphasizes the point that the essential bonds in the family are now found more and more in the inter-personal relationship of its members, as compared with those of law, custom, public opinion, and duty in the older institutional forms of the family.

The point is not that companionship, affection, and happiness are absent

[*] Ernest W. Burgess, "The Family in a Changing Society," *The American Journal of Sociology*, May, 1948 (The University of Chicago Press), pp. 418–21.

from the institutional family. They exist there in greater or less degree, but they are not its primary aims. The central objectives of the institutional family are children, status, and the fulfilment of its social and economic function in society.

The distinctive characteristics of the American family, as of the family in any society, are a resultant of (1) survivals from earlier forms of the family, developing under prior or different economic and social conditions; (2) the existing social and economic situation; and (3) the prevailing and evolving ideology of the society.

Survivals

The American family has had a rich and varied historical heritage, with strands going back to all European countries and to the religious ideologies of the Catholic, Jewish, and Protestant faiths. What is distinctive in the American family, however, has resulted from its role, first, in the early rural situation of the pioneer period, and, second, in the modern urban environment.

The growth of democracy in the family proceeded in interaction with the development of democracy in society. Pioneer conditions promoted the emancipation both of women and of youth from subordination to the family and to the community. Arrangements for marriage passed from the supervision of parents into the control of young people.

The rural family of the United States before World War I, however, had progressed toward, but had not achieved, democratic relations among its members. Control was centered in the father and husband as the head of the farm economy, with strict discipline and with familistic objectives still tending to be dominant over its members. Children were appraised in terms of their value for farm activities, and land tenure and farm operations were closely interrelated with family organization and objectives.

The Evolving Urban Environment

The modern city, growing up around the factory and serving as a trade center for a wide area, provided the necessary conditions for the development of the distinctive characteristics of the American family. It still further promoted the equality of family members and their democratic interrelationships, initiated and fostered to a certain degree by the rural pioneer environment. In the urban community the family lost the extrinsic functions which it had possessed from time immemorial and which continued, although in steadily diminishing degrees, in the rural family. The urban family ceased to be, to any appreciable extent, a unity of economic production. This change made possible a relaxation of authority and regimentation by the family head. Then, too, the actual or potential employment of wife and children outside the home signified their economic independence and created a new basis for family relations. In the city the members of the family tended to engage in recreational activities separately, in their appropriate sex and age groups. Each generation witnessed a decline of parental control over children.

This increased freedom and individualization of family members and their release from the strict supervision of the rural neighborhood was naturally reflected in the instability of the family. The divorce rate has averaged a 3 per cent increase each year since the Civil War.

Urbanization involves much more than the concentration and growth of population. It includes commercialization of activities, particularly recreational; specialization of vocations and interests; the development of new devices of communication: telephone, telegraph, motion picture, radio, the daily newspaper, and magazines of mass circulation. All these still further promote the urbanization and secularization of families residing not only in cities but even in remote rural settlements.

The Ideology of American Society

Democracy, freedom, and opportunity for self-expression are central concepts in the American ideology. The frontier situation favored their expression in the social, economic, and political life of the people. As they found articulation in the American creed, they reinforced existing tendencies toward democracy and companionship within the family.

Urban life in its economic aspects provided less opportunity than did the rural environment for the exemplification of the American ideology. For example, the development of big business and enormous industries decreased the opportunities for the husband and father to run his own business. But the city greatly increased the economic freedom and independence of the wife and children by providing employment outside the home. The social conditions of the modern city led to the emancipation of family members from the institutional controls of the rural family. The urban family tended to become an affectional and cultural group, united by the interpersonal relations of its members.

The Family in Process

The paradox between the unity and the diversity of the American family can be understood in large part by the conception of the family in process. This means, first of all, that it is in transition from earlier and existing divergent forms to an emergent generic type and, second, that it is in experimentation and is developing a variety of patterns corresponding to the subcultures in American society.

The Family in Transition

Much of what is termed the "instability" of the American family arises from the shift to the democratic companionship type from the old-time rural family of this country and the transplanted old-world forms of immigrant groups.

Many of the current problems within the family are to be explained by the resulting conflicting conceptions in expectations and roles of husbands and wives and of parents and children. The husband may expect his wife to be a devoted household slave like his mother, while she aspires to a career or to social or civic activities outside the home. Immigrant parents attempt to enforce old-world standards of behavior upon their children, who are determined to be American in appearance, behavior, and ideas.

The Family in Experimentation

The changes taking place in the family have constituted a vast experiment in democracy. Hundreds of thousands of husbands and wives, parents and children, have participated in it. Couples have refused to follow the pattern of the marriages of their parents and are engaged in working out new designs of family living more or less of their own devising. The behavior has been fully in accord with the ideals and practices of democracy and has exemplified the American ideology of individual initiative and opportunity for self-expression.

This experiment in family formation, while apparently proceeding by individual couples, has been essentially collectivistic rather than pluralistic behavior. Each couple has naturally cherished the illusion that it was acting on its own. To be sure, individual initiative and risk-taking were involved. Many individual ventures have ended in disaster. But actually it has been a collective experiment in the sense that the couples were acting under the stimulus of current criticisms of family life and were attempting to realize in their marriage the new conceptions of family living disseminated by the current literature, presented by the marriages of friends, or developed in discussion by groups of young people.

Adaptability Versus Stability

In the past, stability has been the great value exemplified by the family and expected of it by society. This was true because the family was the basic institution in a static society. American society, however, is not static but dynamic. The virtues of its institutions do not inhere in their rigid stability but in their adaptability to a rapid tempo of social change.

The findings of two recent studies underscore the significance of adaptability for the American family. Angell began his study of the family in the depression with the hypothesis that its degree of integration would determine its success or failure in adjustment to this crisis. He found, however, that he needed to introduce the concept of adaptability to explain why certain families, highly integrated and stable before the depression, failed, and why some moderately integrated families succeeded, in adjusting to the crisis. A restudy of these cases indicated that adaptability was more significant than integration in enabling families to adjust to the depression.

Another study arrived at a similar conclusion. In predicting success and failure in marriage, data were secured from couples during the engagement period. Certain couples with low prediction scores were later found to be well adjusted in their marriage. The explanation seemed to lie in the adaptability of one or both members of the couple, which enabled them to meet and solve successfully difficult problems as they developed in the marriage.

Adaptability as a personal characteristic has three components. One is psychogenic and represents the degree of flexibility in the emotional reaction of a person to a shift from an accustomed to a different situation. The second component is the tendency of the person as culturally or educationally determined to act in an appropriate way when entering a new situation. The third component of adaptability is the possession of knowledge and skills which make for successful adjustment to a new condition.

Successful marriage in modern society with its divergent personalities, diversity of cultural backgrounds, and changing conditions depends more and more upon the adaptability of husbands and wives and parents and children. The crucial matter, then, becomes the question of the adaptability of the family as a group, which may be something different from the adaptability of its members.

The growing adaptability of the companionship family makes for its stability in the long run. But it is a stability of a different kind from that of family organization in the past, which was in large part due to the external social pressures of public opinion, the mores, and law. The stability of the companionship family arises from the strength of the interpersonal relations of its members, as manifested in affection, rapport, common interests and objectives.

Flexibility of personality is not sufficient to insure adaptability of the family to a changing society. Its members should also be culturally and educationally oriented to the necessity for making adjustments. For example, the prospects of successful marriage would be greatly improved if husbands on entering wedded life were as predisposed in attitudes as are wives to be adjustable in the marital relation. Finally, adaptability in marriage and family living demands knowledge and skills on the part of family members. These are no longer transmitted adequately by tradition in the family. They can be acquired, of course, the hard way by experience. They can best be obtained through education and counseling based upon the findings of social science research.

Problem 15: Socialization of the Child-- What Are the Best Methods?

Although the family has surrendered many of its functions to other social institutions, it still retains the primary responsibility for socialization—for giving the young members of the society the cultural knowledge and the psychological traits that are essential if they are to become responsible, functioning members of that society. There are problems associated with learning the culture, but they are simple compared to the problem of developing acceptable, balanced psychological traits. We turn now to the study of this latter function. What do we know about the socialization process? How is it related to the formation of adult personality? Do some family group relationships bring about better results than others?

The literature of sociology and psychology in regard to the socialization process is abundant. It includes theories, research, and practical advice to parents. This literature, however, is neither clear nor consistent. Often one theory is opposed by another; research is inadequate, both in quantity and in quality; and guides for proper child care sometimes enunciate conflicting rules and principles. On only one aspect of the matter is there anything approaching consensus: few would disagree with the idea that the early years are extremely important in producing specific personality traits and general psychological organization in the individual. Beyond this point disagreements are numerous.

One of the first applications of science to the problem of socialization was that made by the behaviorist psychologists who emphasized, among other principles, the idea that personality is the result of habit formation. They insisted that the problem could be solved if we would discipline the individual through the development of early habit patterns. Based upon this principle and other associated theories, the "sterile" period of child care was initiated. Parents were told to see that the child was provided with the necessary physical care and then to leave him alone. Strict feeding schedules, early bowel and bladder control, proper ventilation and temperature, and refraining from unnecessary handling of the child were characteristic of the advice offered.   Since this point of view is no longer current, the readings that follow begin with an attack on this position and proceed to set forth some of the contemporary views about the proper socialization of the child.   The reader should thereby gain some insight into the nature of the problem and begin to formulate some concepts of his own for further analysis.

THE RIGHT TO A MOTHER *

One of the first voices to speak out strongly against the "sterile" approach in child care was that of Margaret Ribble.   In her book *The Rights of Infants* (of which the first chapter is reproduced below) she advocated the "mothering" approach and substantiated it with a theory of emotional needs.   The following comment, taken from the flyleaf of the jacket of her publication gives the key to her philosophy:

"Many a modern mother, impressed by certain twentieth-century theories of infant care, has given her baby expert physical attention, feeding and bathing him with clock-like regularity, while sternly denying any impulse to express her love for him.   Babies should not be fondled or fussed over—that was what the doctors said; and, against every instinct, mothers struggled to abide by their instructions.   But observation of nervous and unsocial children suggested, and experience in maternity hospitals has proved, that physical care is not enough. Babies need emotional care as well."

When science and "instinct" seem to clash, most of us are on both sides of the argument at once. . . . This is particularly true in the field of baby care, for here science is firmest, and Nature speaks with her most compelling voice.

The purpose of this book is to take up a vital aspect of infant care which is not covered in the manuals dealing with food and general hygiene—the feeding life of the baby, the human impulses which get their initial momentum in the primary relationship between the child and the mother. Modern science, when it considers the matter, assumes that this basic tie exists in order that the child may be fed and protected from harm during its helpless infancy.   This theory, if it stops here, makes the function of the mother that of a trustworthy nurse, who can be arbitrarily replaced.   It

---

* Margaret A. Ribble, *The Rights of Infants* (Columbia University Press, 1943), pp. 3–14.

leaves out of consideration the matter of a personal relationship on which the child's future emotional and social reactions are based.

This attitude is psychologically all wrong—so much so that the infant who is treated impersonally, however well nourished and clean he may be, is actually thwarted in his mental development and may suffer more cruelly than an adult locked up in solitary confinement. The experiences of infancy determine in no small way the evolution of individual personality. Certain studies of young children will illustrate the point.

Not many years ago one of the most baffling problems of child health was a disease known as marasmus. The name comes from the Greek word which means "wasting away." Sometimes it is called also infantile atrophy or debility. It affects particularly children in the first year of life, and less than three decades ago it was responsible for more than half the deaths in that age group.

To combat this tragic evil a special study of infant care was undertaken by both medical and social agencies, and the astonishing discovery was made that babies in the best homes and hospitals, given the most careful physical attention, often drifted into this condition of slow dying, while infants in the poorest homes, with a good mother, often overcame the handicaps of poverty and unhygienic surroundings and became bouncing babies. It was found that the element lacking in the sterilized lives of the babies of the former class, and generously supplied to those that flourished in spite of hit-or-miss environmental conditions, was mother love. In consequence of this new insight, science, without attempting to analyze the life-giving quality of mother love, came to terms with sense. Hospital authorities began looking around for a "Pharaoh's daughter" to care for the unloved children who fell into their hands. A new system of carefully selecting foster mothers was developed, and whenever an infant had no suitable person to care for him, he was sent to a foster home rather than to an institution unless the illness was acute. Young infants are now kept in hospitals for as short a time as possible. As a result marasmus is becoming a rare disease.

It is shocking that our ignorance endangered through neglect of the human element the lives of many infants we were trying to save, just at a time when science was making so much progress in other directions; yet the study of marasmus has added greatly to our understanding of infant nature. The disease showed in a dramatic way the meaning of hunger for mothering experiences and the effect on the child's mental as well as physical functions when this need is not satisfied. The typical life story of a baby who suffered from marasmus will help to make this clear.

Little Bob was born in the maternity hospital where the writer was making studies of infants at the time. He was a full-term child and weighed six pounds three ounces at birth. During the two weeks' stay in the hospital the baby was breast fed and there was no apparent difficulty with his body functions. The mother, a professional woman, had been reluctant about breast feeding because she wished to take up her work as soon as possible after the baby was born, but she yielded to the kindly encouragement of the hospital nurses, and the feeding was successful. Both mother and child were thriving when they left the hospital.

On returning home the mother found that her husband had suddenly deserted her—the climax of an unhappy and maladjusted marriage relationship. She discovered soon after that her milk did not agree with the baby. As is frequently the case the deep emotional reaction had affected her milk secretion. The infant refused the breast and began to vomit. Later he was taken to the hospital and the mother did not call to see him. At the end of a month she wrote that she had been seriously ill and asked the hospital to keep the child until further notice.

In spite of careful medical attention and skillful feeding, this baby remained for two months at practically the same weight. He was in a crowded ward and received very little personal attention. The busy nurses had no time to take him up and work with him as a mother would, by changing his position and making him comfortable at frequent intervals. The habit of finger sucking developed, and gradually the child became what is known as a ruminator, his food coming up and going down with equal ease. At the age of two months he weighed five pounds. The baby at this time was transferred to a small children's hospital, with the idea that this institution might be able to give him more individual care. It became apparent that the mother had abandoned the child altogether.

When seen by the writer, this baby actually looked like a seven months' foetus yet he had also a strange appearance of oldness. His arms and legs were wrinkled and wasted, his head large in proportion to the rest of the body, his chest round and flaring widely at the base over an enormous liver. His breathing was shallow, he was generally inactive, and his skin was cold and flabby. He took large quantities of milk but did not gain weight since most of it went through him with very little assimilation and with copious discharge of mucus from his intestines. The baby showed at this time the pallor which in our study we have found typical of infants who are not mothered, although careful examination of his blood did not indicate a serious degree of anemia. He was subject to severe sweating, particularly during sleep. A thorough study showed no indication of tuberculosis. The child's abdomen was large and protruding, but this proved to be due to lax intestinal muscles and consequent distention with gas and to a greatly enlarged and distended liver, which was actually in proportion to that of the foetus. There was no evidence of organic disease but growth and development were definitely at a standstill, and it appeared that the child was gradually slipping backward to lower and lower levels of body economy and function.

The routine treatment of this hospital for babies who are not gaining weight is to give him concentrated nursing care. They are held in the nurses' laps for feeding and allowed at least half an hour to take the bottle. From time to time their position in the crib is changed and when possible the nurse carries them about the ward for a few minutes before or after each feeding. This is the closest possible approach to mothering in a busy infants' ward. Medical treatment consists of frequent injections of salt solution under the skin to support the weakened circulation in the surface of the body.

With this treatment the child began to improve slowly. As his physical condition became better, it was possible for our research group to introduce the services of a volunteer "mother" who came to the hospital twice daily in order to give him some of the attention he so greatly needed. What she actually did was to hold him in her lap for a short period before his 10 A.M. and 6 P.M. feedings. She was told that he needed love more than he needed medicine, and she was instructed to stroke the child's head gently and speak or sing softly to him and walk him about. Her daily visits were gradually prolonged until she was spending an hour twice a day, giving the baby his artificial mothering. The result was good. The child remained in the hospital until he was five months of age, at which time he weighed nine pounds. All rumination and diarrhea had stopped, and he held up his head well and looked about, focusing his eyes and smiling in response to his familiar nurses; he could not yet grasp his own bottle or turn himself over, as is customary at this age. The finger sucking continued, as is usually the case with babies who have suffered early privation.

In accordance with the new hospital procedure, as soon as the child's life was no longer in danger, he was transferred to a good, supervised foster home in order that he might have still more individual attention. Under this regime his development proceeded well and gradually he mastered such functions as sitting, creeping, and standing. His speech was slow in developing, however, and he did not walk until after the second year. The general health of this child is now excellent at the end of his third year; also his "I.Q." is high on standard tests, but his emotional life is deeply damaged. With any change in his routine or with a prolonged absence of the foster mother, he goes into a state which is quite similar to a depression. He becomes inactive, eats very little, becomes constipated and extremely pale. When his foster mother goes away he usually reacts with a loss of body tone and alertness, rather than with a definite protest. His emotional relationship to the foster mother is receptive, like that of a young infant, but he makes little response to her mothering activities except to function better when she is there. He has little capacity to express affection, displays no initiative in seeking it, yet fails to thrive without it. This lack of response makes it difficult for the foster mother to show him the affection which he so deeply needs. Without the constant friendly explanation of the situation from the visiting nurse, she would probably have given up the care of the child.

This story, typical of the reaction of unmothered babies, throws light on the psychological importance of mothering. We have been too long inclined to see this only as a nursing problem involving routine physical care and not as an innate need for love, which is a necessary stimulus for psychological development. Most of the books on the care of infants deal almost exclusively with such matters as nutrition, fresh air and sunshine, immunization, and daily routine. Distracted young mothers who have given their earnest attention to watching the clock instead of the child sometimes treat the baby as if his mental and physical insides were run on the same principle as the clock's. . . .

All good science begins by defining its terms, so that it is essential to make clear first of all just what we mean by mothering. It is really a continuance of the closeness of the prenatal state, and the more clearly it imitates certain of the conditions before birth the more successful it is in the first weeks. The newborn baby still needs to be carried about at regular intervals until he can move and coordinate his own body. This helps to strengthen his sense of equilibrium and to give him a feeling of security. Also he must have frequent periods of actual contact with the mother because the warmth and the holding give him reassurance. Contact takes the place of the physical connection before birth when the child was like an organ of the mother's body. In addition mothering includes the whole gamut of small acts by means of which an emotionally healthy mother consistently shows her love for her child, thus instinctively stimulating his psychic development. Obviously, feeding, bathing, and all the details of physical care come in, but in addition to these duties which can easily become routine and perfunctory, we mean all of the small evidences of tender feeling—fondling, caressing, rocking, and singing or speaking to the baby. These activities have a deep significance.

Mothering also means understanding an infant's biological needs. The child has not one but three hungers; he has a hunger for oxygen, and a craving to feel as well as to eat. At the same time he needs help in strengthening through frequent use the organs and muscles through which those hungers are satisfied. His more specific psychological needs are to feel secure, to get pleasure from his body functions, and to feel that he is a going concern in the world of human beings. An important impetus to mental development is the appropriate stimulus of the senses, and this leads to getting a sense of self and of the world of physical objects, as well as to beginning to feel a sense of personal relationships.

A baby does not come into the world complete, like an adult on a small scale. Not by any means. The early painters took a long time to discover that a child does not look like a miniature man or woman, and some of their paintings of madonna and child are amusing to us for that reason. But we ourselves are even more obtuse when we think of a child's mental and nervous organization as being like that of an adult but on a small scale. Much of the brain substance, and particularly the gray matter, where we know higher mental activity takes place is quite incomplete at birth; the cells are unfinished and some of the blood vessels which feed and irrigate them are not yet developed. It is for this reason that the psychological task of the mother in helping the baby to adjust is so great. Very few mothers, and not too many scientists for that matter, seriously concern themselves with the fact of this immaturity of the human nervous system and the consequent helplessness of the infant. The baby is a potential person, but his mother must actually function for him for many months, and any separation from her at this time causes damage psychologically. The general tendency is to put emphasis exclusively on the nutritional aspects of development rather than on the integration of all body functions. Even among the most intelligent people of both scientific and lay groups the opinion is amazingly widespread that if an infant is properly fed and protected from cold and infection, he will develop as fully in body and mind as his native endowment of heredity warrants. The pediatrician thinks first in terms of calories, digestion, and regular gain in weight. Mothers and nurses are encouraged to focus their attention on formulas, cleanliness, and a host of other important but impersonal details, and our entire system of infant care has become a highly mechanical procedure.

The infant's mental functioning, the development of his emotional capacities and of his budding personality have been largely left in the hands of fate, with little or no contribution from doctors or parents. "Leave the child alone to grow and develop and do not spoil it," is supposed to be the advanced attitude of the nursery. The time-honored cradle and the comfortable rocking chair, as well as lullabies, are considered old-fashioned and even reprehensible from the modern scientific point of view. Let us, then, take a look in the direction of the baby's first psychological needs and the role of the mother in helping him to coordinate his primal body functions, as well as in bringing his feeling and perceptive life into action. . . .

When the umbilical cord is cut at birth, the child, as we have said, is far from being a complete and independent individual. The infant is peculiarly helpless, and it is not until after the faculties of speech and locomotion have developed that he can cope with any separation from the mother without danger. Mother and child after birth are psychologically still a unit, and close relationship is as important for early mental development as was the more primitive connection with the foetus for physiological development. As we have seen in the study of marasmus, interference with this natural relationship means that the infant starves for mothering, and as a result the vital activities, first of alimentation, then of breathing and circulation, get out of order, and we find the small body functioning much as it did before birth.

The infant appears, then, to have at birth a peculiarly human faculty for registering and associating sensory impressions from personal contact with the mother. Concomitant stimuli of touch, pressure, warmth, and of being moved about, together with the feelings which are aroused by suckling, come to form a nucleus of awareness to which sight, sound, taste, and smell are gradually added.

It is difficult to draw a clear line between the infant's physical and psychological needs, for the very act of making him more comfortable physically, if done by a kindly hand, may at the same time stimulate his sense of aliveness and his consciousness of personal contacts. Certainly we know now that the capacity for mature emotional relationships in adult life is a direct outgrowth of the parental care, more specifically the mothering, which an infant received. It is the first relationship of life which activates the feelings of the baby and primes his dormant nervous system into full functional activity, giving to each individual personality its original slant. Social impulses are part of the primary equipment; emotional hunger is an urge as definite and compelling as need for food. When we deny an infant fulfillment of these needs, we stifle his emotional and social life.

Sometimes we have to defend this point of view against vigorous and varied, and often quite violent, objections. The pediatrician is apt to be shocked by what appears to him a new menace in his hard-won fight against germs, and an inroad on the principles of nutrition and digestion that have been worked out so painstakingly. Trained nurses are disturbed because they have been rigidly taught that handling tends to spoil an infant, and that emotion, even when recognized and well controlled, is an influence that must not be allowed to enter the sacred halls of science. Parents on their part are bewildered because doctors seem to be at odds, and so are their own emotions. They are often given to understand that fondling or any show of affection will foster dependence, that evil thing that begins with feeding and behavior problems in childhood and flowers into the more serious forms of emotional dependencies in adult life.

It is obviously true that unwise attention prolongs dependency and thus spoils a baby. But mother love is a good deal like food; we do not stop giving it because the child may get too much or the wrong kind. It has to be expressed regularly so that the child expects it; a little at a time, and frequently is the emotional formula. When it is given in this way independence, rather than dependence, is fostered. For independence is the outgrowth of a feeling of security and completeness, whereas the deep dependency of the first months of life is a natural biological condition which characterizes babies, and not a trait which has been produced by too much care. Assurance comes with inner growth but only if this is accompanied by love which must not only be abundant but consistent. It cannot be given to the child simply because the mother happens to feel in the mood. Babies become demanding when they are given a great deal of attention and then deprived of it. The art of mothering is to discover and satisfy the particular need of the individual child.

Several highly intelligent mothers in discussing this fact made the statement, "My baby does not like mothering; he begins to cry and kick when I pick him up . . . he likes to be left alone." In such cases it was invariably found that a fundamental, though usually unconscious, dislike of children and a dislike for the feminine role, based on long-forgotten painful experiences in early life, featured in the attitude of the mother and was sensed by her child.

Not every woman can mother a child, even though biologically she may be capable of giving birth. The phase of mothering which comes immediately after birth reflects inevitably her own upbringing, to which other emotional relationships have contributed. The woman who is herself emotionally sound and whose deeper needs are satisfied in the marriage relationship gives her child this love without the help of a pediatrician or a psychiatrist, just as naturally as she secretes milk. Unfortunately, however, our highly impersonal civilization has insidiously damaged woman's instinctual nature and has deprived her of one of her most natural rights— that of teaching the small baby to love, by loving it consistently through the period of helpless infancy. It is for this reason that the modern woman may need help and guidance in her relationship with her baby. She needs reassurance that the handling and fondling which she gives are by no means casual expressions of sentiment but are biologically necessary for the healthy mental development of the baby.

Infant Training and the Personality of the Child *

Margaret Ribble's theory of emotional needs set the stage for the development of several ideas about the proper methods of socialization, which, it was claimed, would produce better adult personalities. One school of thought laid great emphasis upon the use of the proper specific *techniques*. Arising principally out of the observations of psychoanalysts and cultural anthropologists, this school maintained that the faults of the "sterile" philosophy could be overcome simply by reversing the techniques—by feeding on demand, by weaning late, by relaxed bowel and bladder training, and by generally less rigid treatment. The results of a recent research project to test this hypothesis are reported below.

In recent years a great deal has been written about the influence of child training on personality formation and development. In particular, these writings have stressed the crucial role of infant discipline in character formation and personality adjustment.

· · · · ·

The purpose of the present paper is to report the results of [a] study which bear directly on the relationship between the actual infant training of a group of children and their personality adjustments and traits, as indicated by scores on pencil-and-paper and projective personality tests, ratings by teachers, and behavioral information gained from interviews with their mothers.

The data for this study consist of detailed information on the infant-training experiences of 162 farm children of old American stock and the results of their ratings on various personality measures. In the design of the study an attempt was made to approximate experimental conditions by the prior control of several factors believed to be associated with personality adjustment. Thus diverse cultural influences were eliminated by selecting only children of old American cultural backgrounds in a predominately old American community. By selecting children from a single occupational group (farm children), occupational and socioeconomic influences were roughly controlled. Age was held constant by selecting only children in the age group five to six. Personal-social experiences were in some measure controlled by the selection of children who had not yet

* William H. Sewell, "Infant Training and the Personality of the Child," *American Journal of Sociology*, September, 1952 (The University of Chicago Press), pp. 150–59.

been subject to the socializing effects of school. Only the children of unbroken and never broken unions were selected; consequently disrupted family situations could not affect the findings.

. . . . .

The data on the infant-training practices which the children had undergone were obtained from a personal interview with the mother. The interview was conducted in the home of the child by a highly trained interviewer, using guided interviewing techniques. . . .

The data from these interviews were coded and punched on IBM cards. Examination of the schedules and preliminary analysis indicated that adequate data were available on the following specific infant-training practices: manner of nursing, nursing schedule, weaning, bowel training and bladder training, punishment for toilet accidents, and sleep security. Included in this list are most of the practices to which major attention has been given in the literature.

The personality data are of three types: (1) over-all ratings of personality adjustment based on scores on standardized and unstandardized personality tests of both the paper-and-pencil and the projective types; (2) scores or ratings on personality components derived from the personality adjustment tests; (3) personality behavioral manifestations, based on interviews with the mothers or on teachers' ratings of the child's behavior. These data were obtained from tests administered by a trained clinician, who tested the children early during their first year in school, from teachers' ratings of the child, and from information supplied by the mother in the course of the original interview. . . .

Because no great claim can be made for either the precision, the validity, or the reliability of any of the personality tests, indexes, or items and because the sample size is not great, no attempt is made in this study to use any of them as quantitative measures. Rather, each is used only as a crude indicator. Thus in the case of the tests and components, the child's score on each of the personality indexes was computed, an array of scores was cast for each measure, and two relative score groups of approximately equal size were established. The only assumption made was that those who made scores or ratings in the top half of the distribution were better adjusted as a group than those who made scores which placed them in the lower half of the distribution. Likewise, responses on the individual behavioral items were classified simply as "Favorable" or "Unfavorable." The categories derived from this process were then punched on the IBM cards containing the infant training data.

In the actual statistical analysis the association between each of the seven infant-training practices and each of the forty-six personality indicators was determined by applying the chi square test to the fourfold tables which were obtained by cross-sorting the training practice responses with the dichotomized personality variables. . . .*

The data from the foregoing analysis make possible the testing of a number of pertinent hypotheses about the influence of infant training on personality adjustment. . . . (O)ne general hypothesis concerning the relation of infant-training to personality adjustment and several specific hypotheses concerning the relation between particular training practices and personality adjustment were formulated. The general hypothesis, stated in the null form, is that *the personality adjustment and traits of children who have undergone varying infant-training experiences do not differ significantly from each other.* The specific null hypotheses covering each of the training practices are stated in the section on results, which follows.

• • • • •

On the basis of the results of the statistical tests, the first specific hypothesis that *the personality adjustments of the children who were breast fed do not differ significantly from those of the children who were bottle fed* cannot be rejected. . . .

Likewise, the second specific hypothesis that *the personality adjustments of the children who were fed on a self-demand nursing schedule do not differ significantly from those of the children who were fed on a regular schedule* cannot be rejected. . . .

The third specific hypothesis that *the personality adjustments and traits of the children who were weaned gradually do not differ significantly from those of the children who were weaned abruptly* cannot be rejected on the basis of statistical evidence. . . .

The fourth specific hypothesis that *the personality adjustments and traits of the children whose induction to bowel training was late do not differ significantly from those of the children whose induction was early* likewise must not be rejected. . . .

The fifth hypothesis that *the personality adjustments and traits of the children whose induction to bladder training was late do not differ significantly from those of the children whose induction was early* must not be rejected. . . .

The sixth hypothesis that *the personality adjustments and traits of the children who were not punished for toilet training accidents do not differ*

---

* This statistical method indicates the degree to which the relationships between the later personality characteristics and the training practices were of significance as compared to what would have been true of a chance relationship between these two factors.

significantly from those of the children who were punished must not be rejected. . . .

The seventh hypothesis that *the personality adjustments of the children who slept with their mothers during infancy do not differ significantly from those of the children who did not sleep with their mothers* must not be rejected. . . .

Because it was not possible on the basis of the analysis to reject any of the specific null hypotheses concerning the association between training experiences and personality adjustments and traits, the general null hypothesis that *the personality adjustments and traits of the children who have undergone varying infant-training experiences do not differ significantly* cannot be rejected.   However, before reaching this unequivocal conclusion, it was decided that some attempt should be made to determine the joint effects of several infancy experiences on personality adjustment. Consequently, a crude index was developed to indicate degree of infantile security. This index was based on the simple assumption that the combined effects of the various training experiences which are believed to be favorable would produce a more favorable infancy than would the combined effects of those training experiences which are assumed to be unfavorable. . . . This made possible the testing of an eighth null hypothesis that *the personality adjustments and traits of the children whose infantile security index scores are favorable do not differ significantly from those of the children whose scores are unfavorable.* This hypothesis, too, must not be rejected on the basis of the statistical analysis. . . .

As one phase of the larger study of social factors and personality adjustment of which the present paper is a part, a factor analysis has been made of thirty-eight child-training practices, in order to isolate meaningful constellations of practices. As a result of this analysis, six factors have been isolated, two of which contain items which are in the infant-training period; one on the toilet training complex and the other on the feeding training. This made possible the further testing of the original general hypothesis and a ninth and tenth hypothesis dealing with the specific factors. Thus, the ninth hypothesis is that *the personality adjustments and traits of the children whose toilet training factor scores are favorable do not differ significantly from those of the children whose scores are unfavorable.* This hypothesis cannot be rejected. . . . Likewise, the tenth hypothesis that *the personality adjustments and traits of the children whose feeding training factor scores are favorable do not differ significantly from those of the children whose scores are unfavorable* cannot be rejected. . . .

On the basis of the results of this study, the general null hypothesis that the personality adjustments and traits of children who have undergone varying training experiences do not differ significantly cannot be rejected.

. . . Such practices as breast-feeding, gradual weaning, demand schedule, and easy and late induction to bowel and bladder training, which have been so much emphasized in the psychoanalytic literature, were almost barren in terms of relation to personality adjustment as measured in this study. . . . The two factor indexes and the index constructed to measure the cumulative effects of the infant-training practices produce even more meager results.

It is also interesting to observe that none of the training experiences was significantly related to any of the major tests of personality adjustment. . . .

Certainly, the results of this study cast serious doubts on the validity of the psychoanalytic claims regarding the importance of the infant disciplines and on the efficacy of prescriptions based on them. However, it should not be concluded that these results unequivocally refute the claim that infancy is an important period in the development of the individual's personality, or even that the particular training practices studied have a bearing on personality formation and adjustments. To establish the first point would demand both controlled experiments and the study of other aspects of infancy. To establish the second point would demand the corroboration of the results of this study by many and better-designed studies of different culture and age groups.

It is entirely possible that the significant and crucial matter is not the practices themselves but the whole personal-social situation in which they find expression, including the attitudes and behavior of the mother. . . . Much work must be done to devise techniques which will give at least crude measures of these qualitative aspects of the personal-social situations if the importance of infancy on personality formation and adjustment is to be assessed adequately. However, assumptions about the importance of the personal-social situation should be put to scientific test before any more unfounded personality theories and practices are built upon them.

THEIR MOTHERS' SONS *

Whether or not specific techniques are responsible for differentials in personality development, the importance of the experiences of the early months and years may still be very great. Perhaps the most widespread point of view at present is that the differentials stem from the tenor of the child's emotional relationships with those about him.

* Edward A. Strecker, *Their Mothers' Sons* (J. B. Lippincott Co., 1951), pp. 23–37.

Edward A. Strecker, a psychiatrist who saw abundant evidence of in-adequate socialization among the psychoneurotics, alcoholics, homo-sexuals, and other maladjusted personalities in the armed forces, main-tains that the mother-child emotional relationship is the crucial factor in determining the degree of maturity the individual displays in his adult social relationships.

Maturity is not an inborn trait; it is not hereditary. It is the result of early background, environment, training and unselfish parental love.

Conversely, immaturity is caused by lack of a good intelligent foundation in this business of living. It is not difficult to find basic reasons for im-maturity. Often it is merely necessary to retrace the life of an immature person. Given the opportunity of having known when he was eight to twelve years old, any one of the men who failed in his opportunity to serve in the armed forces because of neuropsychiatric tendencies, and, particu-larly, of having known his mother, a competent psychiatrist could have forecast, with reasonable accuracy the boy's future immaturity. In the vast majority of case histories, a "mom" is at fault.

Every woman who bears children is confronted by a dilemma from which there is no escape. The dilemma is as old as the human race, yet its implications and its dangers are peculiarly a part of our closely knit modern civilization and its intricate social cultures. Upon the successful solution of the dilemma depends not only the welfare of a mother's chil-dren but, in a large part, the basic survival of the nation of which her children are to be the future citizens and statesmen. The solution is not easy and the stakes are high. No nation is in greater danger of failing to solve the mother-child dilemma than our own nation. No nation would have to pay as great a penalty as the United States for not solving it.

The future social behavior of a child has its beginnings and is patterned in the conflicting sensations and emotions that arise from the early relation-ship between the mother and child. For the child, the mother is not only the great Dispenser of pleasure and love and the great Protectress, but also the source of pain, the ruthless Thwarter and Frustrater. So the dilemma of the mother is likewise the dilemma of the child. It is a delicately balanced conflict of clinging and rejecting and, depending on which way the balance is tipped, the child either learns to meet successfully the larger give-and-take aspects of mature living or he doesn't. If the give-and-take capacity is not developed, the child will fail to adjust himself to his own life and to society. As a result, the child never grows up. He remains emo-tionally immature.

Weaning is as much a part of motherhood as is nursing. Taking away from a child is as important as giving to it. Rejecting and emancipating a child are as significant as clinging to it. Furthermore, these seemingly contradictory phases of motherhood belong to each other both in nature and in sequence.

A play would be incomplete and meaningless if it stopped at the end of the first act, or if the last act were given without the first. Likewise with the mother-child relationship. The phase of taking away from or the rejection of the child by the mother would not only be ineffective but also senseless cruelty unless it had been preceded by the clinging and protective phase. On the other hand, the child who has known nothing but protection and has only learned to take and not to give has been sadly defrauded by his mother—so badly cheated that it would have been better if he had never been born.

Within the limits of the sensory, emotional, and social motherhood-relationship, there is in miniature each child's future. The world we live in drives a hard bargain in the business of giving and taking. It never gives of the largeness of its satisfactions, unless it receives an equally valuable deposit in the general social account. The adult who as a child was never taught to share and give and concede or to think and act independently can almost never learn to do so later in life. There is a tragic finality about childhood. Unfortunately, the vast majority of men and women are made or broken before the first ten years of their lives have been completed.

What happens to the child whose mother not only has failed to sever the emotional apron strings but often has not even loosened them? His natural gregarious instincts lead him to seek social relations with his fellow man. But, because he has only learned to take, he sooner or later is rebuffed. He becomes a bystander in the game of life—a sad, disillusioned and envious spectator. He cannot be a lone wolf, living apart from his fellow man. Few men succeed in doing that and he least of all. Psychologically, it would mean his eventual emotional annihilation.

What constitutes a mom? How does she differ from a mother? Fundamentally, a mom is not a mother. Mom is a maternal parent who fails to prepare her offspring emotionally for living a productive adult life on an adult social plane. A mom does not untie the emotional apron string —the Silver Cord—which binds her children to her.

Moms are just about as old as parenthood. For years in my practice I have seen moms and the sad result of moms. My work in the Army and the Navy, because it gave me the chance to study over a short period thousands of psychoneurotics, served to add to my case histories of moms.

I look at mom without rancor or resentment and not without understanding. Mom is not of her own making. Various forces work together to produce her kind. The basic mosaic of her behavior in most cases was put together in her own childhood without her knowledge and without her consent. Furthermore, momism is the product of a social system veering toward a matriarchy in which each individual mom plays only a small part.

Outwardly, a mom is not distinctively marked. She may be fat or thin; tall or small; blond, brunette, or a redhead, or she may wear a halo of motherly silvered hair. She may be beautiful or uncomely, dress dashingly or dowdily. She may be a college graduate or she may not. She may be quite ignorant of Emily Post's dicta, or she may be gracious and charming.

However, she does have one thing in common—the emotional satisfaction, almost repletion, she derives from keeping her children paddling about in a kind of psychological amniotic fluid rather than letting them swim away with the bold and decisive strokes of maturity from the emotional maternal womb.

There is nothing stronger in this world than the child-mother cohesion. A mother song in a bar or from the stage of the cheapest burlesque will bring lumps in the throats and tears to the eyes of the roughest and toughest men. For all of us there is a natural pull back to mother.

. . . . .

A mom will take advantage of this natural mother urge to hold her child or children to her. The real mother fights the urge and lovingly does everything in her power to make her children stand on their own feet. She prepares them for an adult life. The mothers of men and women capable of facing life maturely are not apt to be the traditional mom type. More likely mom is sweet, doting, "self-sacrificing." But the obverse of this cast, the capable stern, self-contained domineering mom is not uncommon.

Silver cords come in varying lengths. Sometimes they are short, mere tether ropes, with both ends always in plain view. Not long ago I heard two moms boasting that their sixteen- and seventeen-year-old children had never slept a single night away from their homes. "When bedtime comes, kiddies want to be tucked in," they concluded with satisfaction.

More often, however, silver cords are much longer and much more difficult to trace. Seemingly they allow a wide range of freedom, but it is surprising how quickly they can be drawn taut and gathered in should the children roam too near strange pastures.

. . . . .

Theoretically, a mom is a woman whose maternal behavior is motivated by the seeking of emotional recompense for the buffets which life has dealt her own ego. In her relationship with her children, every deed and almost every breath are designed unconsciously but exclusively to absorb her children emotionally and to bind them to her securely. In order to achieve this purpose she must stamp a pattern of immature behavior in her children. Such a pattern is entirely inconsistent with even a minimum degree of adequacy and satisfaction and completely excludes the possibility of living life in an adult manner. With such a rigid criteria, probably there are not many bonafide moms, although I have known a few women who have almost succeeded in reaching the summit of momism.

Actually, in every mother, no matter how mature she may be, there are traces of moms. There should be. Likewise, in moms there are odds and ends and fragments of motherhood although sometimes they are ultra-microscopic. However, there is a deal of difference in the amounts of these ingredients in mothers and moms, and the driving forces which activate motherly and momish behaviors are as far apart as the poles.

The mature mother uses the emotional ingredients sparingly and wisely. Her major purpose is to produce a proper balance of give-and-take in her children, so that they may attain full-statured personal and social maturity and lead reasonably constructive and happy lives. The immature and insatiable mom, on the other hand, uses the ingredients lavishly and un-wisely, chiefly to bind her children with emotional coils. Being immature herself, she breeds immaturity in her children and, by and large, they are doomed to lives of personal and social insufficiency and unhappiness.

Do We Have a Science of Child Rearing? *

In the previous readings of this section we have noted some of the theories about the socialization of the child and some of the associated research. Let us now turn to a psychologist who views the situation with a broader perspective. Although he does arrive at some tentative conclusions, he also emphasizes the extreme importance of seeking more reliable information about this particular problem.

. . . Ultimately, the market for a science of child rearing is the parent, and especially the new parent. Discreet bits of excellent research, such as now exist, cannot be very serviceable to the parent. What he needs is a body of theory which covers just those circumstances to which he is ex-posed, namely, how to treat the child at this and that juncture in its growth

* John Dollard in Community Service Society, *The Family in a Democratic Society* (Columbia University Press, 1949), pp. 44–55.

so that some desired result in the child's character may be attained. A science of child rearing would provide a theory enabling the prediction of outcomes of different types of training at different ages. Does scheduled feeding, for instance, create such drives within the child as to set up bad emotional habits? Is the fact that the child can be led or forced to accept a feeding schedule germane to the discussion at all? When should cleanliness training be undertaken to get what results in child character? Under what circumstances may or must the parent physically punish the child's responses? How should parents react to the child's aggression, providing always that they can react as they are supposed to? How should taboos on the naive sex responses of the child be imposed? Does anxiety attached to the child's innocent masturbation generalize to the sex drive and thus operate as a factor in the later sexual life of the person? If anxiety is aroused, does it constitute a frustrating circumstance which, in turn, produces aggression? Is the cross-sex preference of the child a result of training or is it somehow instinctive? How can psychosexual attitudes which correspond with the bodily form of the child be engendered?

This seems like a raging mass of questions, and yet they are the very questions on which parents of our day are impaled. Advice on these important matters is now in the realm of hunch, fad, wisdom, guess, or clinical reconstruction. It should be possible to have a science of childhood which is nearer to fact. The theory should be consistent, as our present hunches are not consistent.

For example, many parents are advised today to give the child a kind of freedom which was not permitted in an earlier time, but they are not advised as to what necessary limits to put on this freedom. They must discover for themselves that small children cannot be allowed to play with matches, to manipulate the levers of the gas stove, to run with pointed instruments in the mouth, to move toward the traffic-laden streets, to use the carving knife as a plaything. These parents suffer at having to impose taboos on such actions because they are not told that such limitations are in the interest of the child and are necessary and inevitable. The parent, therefore, suffers from a bad conscience for doing what is his moral duty.

Perhaps it is a good thing to remove some of the taboos on childhood aggression, but I have seen parents struggling with the following dilemma. A child of four, blessed with the aforementioned freedom from parental restraint, had taken to bashing his one-year-old brother over the head with any handy metal object. The parents were embarrassed at the scenes created but tried to overlook the matter lest the four-year-old should suffer a paralyzing inhibition. At what risk for the future I do not know, these parents were not told that the removal of the taboo on aggression did not include allowing the older child to commit mayhem on his younger brother. They were asked rather, how much serious risk to the younger child they were willing to incur in order to follow their nonaggression pact. Naturally, I have discussed this incident in a one-sided and partisan manner. The parents were also told that they should study the situation and find out and alter, if possible, the factors that were producing such a degree of aggression in the other child. What I want to emphasize is that thanks to the lack of a science of child rearing the parents had received one bit of scientific lore which came inevitably into conflict with another necessity in the same situation. Where scientists must give such incomplete or contradictory advice we have, of course, no science.

That we have no science of child rearing is not due to the stupidity of child researchers of the past. The emergence of any science is in part a matter of luck. Until all the building blocks necessary for a theory have been assembled, it is difficult to give a consistent account of any natural process. It has been hard to have a science of child rearing without having an adequate theory of how human beings learn. Childhood is notoriously the time of intensive learning. How, then, could we build a science without learning theory?

The new variable of learning theory may indeed liberate child research in new directions and with a new force. As now assembled, learning theory stems from the great tradition in psychology—from Pavlov, Watson, Thorndike, Guthrie, Tolman, Hull, and the work and experiments of hundreds of others. At the Institute of Human Relations at Yale University this theory has received a strong impetus from Freudian theory. In the thought of early behaviorists there was a bias for identifying only the outside stimulus which became connected with a response. Freud's influence has been to identify and stress the importance of "inside" stimuli, of the drive stimuli which are so basic in the understanding of human behavior. This motivational emphasis, borrowed from Freud, has proved easy to naturalize in the field of behavior thinking.

Learning theory now implies that the fundamental variables of drive, response, cue, and reward are among the instruments with which the problem of child development must be attacked. I cannot elaborate them here, but these variables together with other principles and their necessary complications have given us a view of a psychology at once potent enough and flexible enough to deal with human behavior as we intuitively know it. The innate response hierarchy of the child is worked over by the conditions of social life, and in this working over the child's personality is produced.

I have already hinted at the questions which should guide the student of child learning. We need a better analysis of the tasks of childhood. We need to know the response units into which these tasks are broken up so that we can impose such tasks in an orderly manner and in a graded series. Until we have such knowledge we will never be free of the suspicion that we occasionally, and sometimes perhaps continuously over generations, attempt to impose insoluble tasks on our children. Possibly the conditions of cleanliness training, for instance, cannot be altered at the whim of adults or by any psychological fad. It may have its own laws both as to maturation and learning which are tinkered with only at the risk of producing confusions and trauma in the child.

We shall have to learn how language is acquired, since language units apparently function as thought units, and it may well be that the laws of mental life are, in part, those of language acquisition. Possibly in the same inquiry new perspectives on the nature of intelligence will emerge. We know little as yet about the effect of strong drive on the weak ego of very small children. It may be that hunger is an entirely different affair to the newborn child from what it is to the sophisticated adult. Hunger may have a savage and total impact and capacity to create alarm in the infant which have been long since lost to the adult character. Should anything like this be true, our view of the significance of deprivation, even simple-seeming deprivations, to the infant might be radically changed. I can only say that a few clinical experiences of my own have led me to refer to this very earliest period of life as a transitory period of psychosis, that is, a period of strong drive, great helplessness, and weak capacity to react to different real cues in the environment.

Our science-of-childhood-to-be should help us clearly to formulate the alternatives in child learning. We should, indeed, come to think, not of "child training," but rather of child learning. This science should also produce child specialists who can analyze behavior in just the detail here suggested, who have fewer general panaceas and many more detailed investigations of what the child has already learned and what is blocking further learning. The conditions-principles distinction should have great power in this field. Child rearing practice will turn out to be a choice of conditions which are selected to produce particular effects. The principles of learning would seem to be more or less immutable. Conditions are fortunately highly flexible and can be utilized to produce widely varying types of human beings.

A word about the techniques of research in child rearing: New scales will have to be invented. Anxiety, for instance, will have to be measured and its relation to other responses determined. Probably a whole host of new measuring instruments will have to be employed to build the science of child rearing. We should, therefore, have scientists at this work who know techniques of scale-making, of pioneering a scale, of testing it for reliability, of testing it for covariance with other scales. The researcher cannot expect that the instruments of other sciences will necessarily enable him to get ahead in this one. It might even be expedient if many of the instruments now in the hands of researchers could be knocked from their hands and they be prevented from measuring the nearest thing measurable in child behavior, letting them "soak" for a while in the problems of childhood, and requiring them to invent appropriate scales to measure the important variables. I do not decry the potential importance of any small bit of fact, but I do much doubt that a science is necessarily created by the accumulation of incidental measurements, however small the error thereof.

Another thing is crucial in regard to a science of child rearing. We may have to abandon the office, the clinic, the white coat, the convenient hours of our present research settings. If we are to study child learning we must study the child where he is learning, and children would seem to learn but precious little in the clinics. We must go to the home with the parents *in situ,* with their particular personalities, and watch their environing effects on the child. This house and these people set up the learning conditions for the child, and we cannot understand what the child learns and why he learns until we see him in relation to his actual home life.

The behavior of children is often mysterious because we do not understand the social conditions which are producing it. I believe child science, once achieved, will have the same magnificent simplicity that is shown by the physical sciences once they are achieved. In the absence of knowledge of the appropriate conditions of learning most human behavior is mysterious. We can sweat the mystery out of it by studying the conditions under which it is created.

In this connection I should like to use an analogy which arises in experimental work. Studying the behavior disorder of a child in a clinic is very much like the following fantastic situation. Suppose that after experimenters got through with their experimental rats all those rats were sent to a "rat reject center" and properly mixed up. If a sample of rats was daily withdrawn from this great pool and studied, it would be observed that some would dash down a lighted alley (though rats ordinarily seek the dark). Others would quake to a buzzer. Some would show great ingenuity in escaping from boxes with white walls. Others would jump to almost any sound stimulus. Obviously, little sense could be made out of the behavior of samples of such animals. However, if any of them were seen in the original experimental situation in which they were trained, the behavior would excite no comment. Naturally, the rat rushes down the lighted alley where it has been fed. It seeks to escape the stimuli of white walls where it has been shocked.

So also I presume it to be with children. If a child is dependent we should seek the circumstances under which such a mighty dependence was demanded of him. If he is aggressive we should learn why these behavior patterns helped the child to meet his life needs.   If the child lies we should search out the circumstances, probably inadvertently set up, which have rewarded lying.

Never was the prayer for a great philanthropist to sponsor a radical departure in child research more fervently uttered than now.   Research in the home is a time-taking task even if only behavior samples are taken. The work is probably sex specialized and must be carried on by women, since most men will not allow other men to browse around their households even under the noblest of pretexts.   Possibly the research operator should also have a conventional role in the household and possibly also should perform some helpful tasks.   In this connection I have thought of the registered nurse.   With some additional scientific training added to the curriculum of the modern university school of nursing, the nurse might have exactly the combination of qualities and talents needed.   Once the fundamental situation was established by the nurse, male researchers could presumably work with her from time to time and could certainly aid in the design of the research situation, the invention of the necessary scales, and the analysis of the data.

The urgency of developing a science of child rearing is emphasized by the many faddish innovations in our traditional child culture which have arisen from the partial sciences of the present day.   With each new idea, fad, or tendency in science new recommendations have been made to parents.   There has been a rapid turnover of such fads, but short-lived as they are, they have served to disrupt the traditional unity of our child rearing techniques.   It may well be that while our child rearing has gained something in flexibility it has lost much in unity and consistency since the days of our great-grandmothers, and it may also be that far from being ahead, we have a piecemeal, patchwork kind of child science which is actually less adaptive than the uninfluenced techniques of earlier times.

For example, Watson emphasized the importance of habit in human behavior.   As a result, parents were asked whether or not they stood for "habit" in the training of their children.   They answered, of course, that they did, and were given a good deal of advice on "regularity," "system," and organization which, for all we know, has been very bad for children. We now know, as scientists, that Watson's doctrine on habit omitted the crucial emotional elements of drive and reward and that inferences made from it in regard to the behavior of children were bound to be similarly biased.   There must be times when bad science is worse than no science at all.   Researchers must certainly be exceedingly careful not to give advice beyond the specific implications of their data.

Similarly, Adler's emphasis on the dangers of childish selfishness and the tendency to dominate has resulted in a ludicrous, counteractive atti-

tude. Parents have come to fear that early indulgence will create dependence and have inferred that the earlier the child is taught the bitter way
of the world the better it will be for the child. In some circles this amounts
almost to regarding the newborn child as a kind of enemy who must be
rapidly put in his place before he dominates the family entirely. We cannot say that Adler is wrong, but we can certainly offer an alternative point
of view (although it may be no better than his) to wit, that the child
should be granted the greatest indulgence when it exhibits the greatest
helplessness and that the straitjacket of reality should be only slowly
tightened around its body.

Similarly but conversely, the Freudian emphasis on the importance of
indulgence in early months and years may be incorrectly applied. Some
parents have extended the indulgence to later years when, not indulgence,
but proportionate enforcement of cultural demands is required. If the
child is to be made responsible and capable he must know at one and the
same time that he will get what he needs when need is desperate but that
under most circumstances he must work and bear and renounce in order
to live in the world as it is. When upon the base laid down by Freud, a
real science of childhood is built, it will be impossible for such confusing
interpretations to be made and for irresponsible interpretations of research
to get abroad. The great importance of science, as compared with a series
of isolated observations, is that it can give a proportionate and consistent
set of rules and study the alternatives in case this or that practice is followed. Since a science must deal with all the problems in a particular
culture at one time it is less likely to give inconsistent or whimsical advice.

Many now believe that our practices in the field of child rearing are to a
great extent related to the later happiness, freedom, and effectiveness of
individual personalities. This would render the creation of a child science
of highest importance even though there were no other issues at stake.
But there are other issues at stake.

It may be that in a time of crisis, such as the present, our child culture
may prove to be unexpectedly related to national survival itself. The reactions of childhood which become strong habits are believed to persist
into adult life and to be transferred to adult symbols and institutions.
Thus the child with a grudge against his parents may become the adult
with a grudge against his nation, his social group, his religion, or some
other aspect of adult social structure. If this were the case, the creation
of a science of child rearing would not be optional but would be felt by all
to be an urgent and even desperate need.

For example, in our time there has been a marked growth of antidemocratic ideology. This growth of antidemocratic sentiment is, in part, based
upon persisting injustices within the societies called "democratic." In the

United States we still suffer the abomination of a caste system. Many of the effects of a highly stratified class society are also with us, damaging the self-esteem and sense of worth of many citizens. These circumstances have promoted and seem to justify a degree of hostility toward our society which has, of course, taken the familiar form of suggestions for social change. If we may judge by the situation in the world today these suggestions have not been acted upon with sufficient rapidity, and many people sense a great disparity between the conditions which they are forced to bear and the possible social conditions which might now easily exist for them. In the United States we have means and techniques for producing social change, though some of our greatest changes seem to be coincidental with other great activities like the conduct of war. Nevertheless, the movement toward a square-deal society is clear today, though sometimes it seems to be unbearably slow. If our people are patient under this slowness it is possibly because "standing in line" is an American tradition along with dreaming of being at the ticket window.

However, by no means all the hostility toward our current society depends upon real, adult deprivations. Many hate our society for the "wrongs" done them in childhood, the stupidities of hunger and neglect all the more damnable because avoidable. A doctrine like that of Karl Marx acts to release these hatreds, to liberate the conscience to hate in the name of defending the weak, the helpless, and the exploited.

Many find our sexual mores hard to bear and develop a certain hostility toward society on the ground of frustration in this sphere. They have experienced the confusion and hardly tolerable privation produced by our sex training and have lived to be vaguely miserable adults, chronically resentful of they know not what. There is in them, nevertheless, a persisting hope for sexual liberation, a liberation which would seem possible within our present moral order, the goal of which might be conventionally expressed as the creation of husbands and wives who can make use of their sexual opportunities within marriage, to make the difficult married state bearable or even desirable.

I have often thought that the malcontents of our time do not so much want a better society as, really, no society at all, and therefore they wish to destroy our own. I think in this connection of the American physicist who at a public conference hoped that "others" would measure and publish the constants necessary to control the release of atomic energy. He thought it shameful that these were in American hands only and was apparently giving broad hints to fellow physicists in foreign lands who might be overhearing him. I for one felt that this man knew too much and that he expressed a petulant and dangerous impatience with "democratic" processes which seemed unreasonable and not intelligible on any rational ground.

The way before us is clear enough. The avoidable differences and discriminations must be avoided. The caste system must be abolished; anxieties about sheer physical survival must be ended. Status inequalities must be equalized, and where they do exist they must be placed on the basis of service, work, and talent. But these changes do not mean revolution and need not be achieved by revolutionary means. I believe that if democracy can intolerantly and ruthlessly demand the necessary time it can work itself over into a more satisfactory system. Anyone who pushes too hard in the line will have to be shown his place by the policeman. The line forms to the right and coils up and ever up the hill. That is the way, I take it, that we dream of working out our social salvation. If there are some ahead of us we will let them have their turn for the time being so long as the line does not form in the same order before every booth. That kind of line is gone forever.

Let me suppose for the moment that we know now what we are going to know in a hundred more years about a science of child rearing. What use would we make of our knowledge? Suppose that we could make our children more peaceable than present-day children, less dependent than present-day children, less inhibited than present-day children, less aggressive than present-day children, more reflective and planful than our children are now, would we dare do it, and if so, what parts of it?

It is hard to know. Certainly we do not wish to modify our child culture to the extent of national extinction. Possibly, for the world we now face, we should strive for yet more aggressive children. Perhaps they will be needed as adults if our society is to survive and have a chance to evolve. Possibly, in order even to try our own scheme, we must be ready to stamp out those who would move faster by violent means.

Perhaps, on the other hand, creating greater hostility might recoil on us. Hostile adults might take their own society as the target and thus be the death of us. Perhaps the correct move would be to make our children love their parents and our society more than they do now. For the supreme aggressions, should they be necessary, can occur only in the name of love.

This way of thought is dark indeed. Without knowledge of the kind of world the child will find when he becomes an adult we cannot choose the type of personality we will seek to develop. Even if we had a science of child rearing we could not use it in the absence of the ground plan of a specific adult society for which the child is being prepared. We might use our child science considerably to cut down individual misery in any particular society but we would always do this at the risk of changing characteristics which might be necessary for social survival.

Even though we were to let matters alone until social forces at the adult level had had a chance to shake down into a more stable order we would still be urgently impelled to create the science on the basis of which personality could be formed, for there is probably no form of overhead social system which can permanently maintain itself as a world-wide society if men are made intrinsically hostile and bellicose from their earliest experiences in life. Sooner or later the mischief-makers, the seekers after chaos, will creep into the control apparatus of the society and work their destruction there. If we are to build and maintain a peaceable society we must train men from earliest life in the habits of a peaceable society. This means creating the conditions from earliest life which will reward justice, sharing, bearing, waiting, foresight, and planning.

The vista has been opened to us of the creation of human personality and of a world order to match. The two supreme achievements awaiting the mind of man lie down the road. We know this road to be that of science. We do not expect that a peaceable society will necessarily be an idyllic one nor that a maximally healthy personality can exist without conflict and misery. Man in his social and personal life is bound to show the effects of his thousands of generations of struggle and passion. His intemperate nature will therefore leave its marks on his society and on his person. Common sense and mother wit have nevertheless advanced him a long way toward control of his environment and himself. In the more refined form of reasoning and foresight, with the aid of scientific control and caution, we believe that he can create a more bearable personal and social life. In the name of good men everywhere I propose that we get on with the task.

Problem 16: Choosing a Mate-- Impulse or Reason as a Basis for Marriage?

As the family has been subjected to research, we have become increasingly aware that the choice of a marriage partner is a key point at which satisfactory or unsatisfactory family relationships may begin. Americans, more than any other cultural group, have preferred to choose their mates on the basis of romantic love. Recently this process has been subjected to intense criticism and more "scientific" procedures have been suggested. Can we reduce family disorganization by a more rational selection of mates? Or, on the contrary, does the substitution of more rational procedures make marriage too much of a cold business proposition? Is there a middle ground?

The Romantic Illusion *

Romantic love, with its emphasis on emotional involvement, physical attractiveness, and the bliss of rapturous response, is prominent in American courtship practices. It has long been under attack by American social scientists as being an insecure basis for marriage. Because it does not provide any realistic conception of the real accommodative and adjustmental problems common to all marriages, it leads to the feeling that any problem in the marriage is a sign of the failure of the marriage rather than something to be worked out with a relative degree of mutual satisfaction. Some ramifications of this approach are presented in the following article.

Today, as never before, social workers, marriage counselors, family advisers, are using their skills to rehabilitate individual families in varying stages of conflict and disruption. They are more and more concerned with the prevention of this spreading phenomenon of family breakdown. Their efforts, like those of us in the colleges and universities, need to be grounded in a thorough and fundamental understanding of the pervasive and underlying influences which our superficial concept of "romance" has had upon the broad situation with which all of us are trying to cope.

Psychologically speaking, the trouble with our traditional "romantic concept" of marriage is that it puts a single-minded premium on complete emotional involvement. It reduces to a very subsidiary role the accommodation of life goals which the woman on her part and the man on his part have built into their separate personalities in the course of their experience from birth to maturity. In our society these life goals have become richer and more varied than ever before, for women as well as for men. When the illusory aspects of this emotional involvement evaporate, the long established personality goals of both husband and wife reassert

* Paul H. Landis, *Survey Midmonthly,* November, 1946, pp. 281–83.

themselves. If basic differences have been ignored, they become a threat to emotional compatability itself and may readily convert it to antagonism.

The war greatly intensified this problem of accommodation. It gave many women a new opportunity to realize their personal ambitions, and developed the masculine independence in men. As a result, members of both sexes find the requirements of marriage and family a greater threat than ever to the trend of their personality development.

For the modern woman who wishes to realize her own career and express her own creative force, the romantic theory of marriage offers no practical guide as to how she can reconcile these objectives with the role of wifehood and motherhood. The society in which she lives had long since discarded the point of view that her life should be built around the idea of being a help-mate to her husband, shielding him from the world, carrying the major burden of rearing the child and contributing to his social status in the community through her social activities and family management. It has encouraged her to be an individual in her own right: she is no longer resigned to accepting the common values which assured her that "the hand that rocks the cradle rules the world." Romance may be desirable and delightful but it gives her, of itself, no practical social pattern by which to compromise the conflict between her personal desires and her responsibilities as an equal partner in the family team.

Neither does his preoccupation with "romance" teach the husband much about the realities of his role in this modern partnership. Indeed, in general we find that he still expects from his wife many of the same emotional responses, worshipful attitudes, and submissive "clinging vine" reactions that were characteristic of the earlier traditional family. Paul Poponoe, director of the American Institute of Family Relations, has pointed out that the husbands of the more educated classes still look for wives who will bolster their egos. So they tend to marry women with less education than themselves, leaving the highly educated professional women to hope in vain for a mate of equal training. The educated husband, no less than others, still wants to be emotionally sheltered from the storm of a competitive business world, but the educated wife, frustrated in her own ambitions, is often incapable of giving these peculiarly feminine responses which men find in courtship and miss in marriage.

Louis M. Terman, in his book *Psychological Factors in Marital Happiness,* shows, for example, that the husband's most frequent source of serious complaint is lack of affection on the part of the wife. The husbands studied listed this item first among thirty-five grievances. In view of our emphasis on love as a basis for mate selection, this seems a surprising situation. Actually it was merely another evidence of the superficiality of our "romantic" theory of marriage. The competing life goals for women, which are now stressed by our culture, make inevitable some yielding on the part of the husband to her individualistic interests and ambitions.

Children may give some guarantee of family stability in the romantic marriage, but if one analyzes the underlying philosophy of the romantic marriage, one is bound to conclude that more often children hinder realization of the movie-made marital dreams of youth. The fact is that studies of marital happiness indicate that the happiest years are those which couples have to themselves before children are born.

To individualistic-minded parents the child may be a threat to the realization of their ambitions and goals rather than an aid to their attainment. Such was not the case in the rural family where the desire of the father to achieve economic success and ultimate economic security was supplemented by the wife and by the early work of the son or sons in the farm family enterprises. Children in this regime guaranteed economic security in old age. They also provided a kind of immortality by perpetuating the ancestral lines.

But today, the absorption of the child's time in school and the exclusion of adolescents from the work world, the disassociation of the child from the claims of kinship as he grows to maturity, his migration from the home neighborhood, threaten all these age long values of family patriarchs. Children in the average metropolitan community actually are of little help to the father in attaining his own goals. Rather, because of the economic drain on the family budget, they are apt to be a threat to their attainment.

Perhaps even more seriously, the child is a definite threat to the individualistic roles, goals, and ambitions of the wife. They are a factor in isolating her from her role as an independent woman and a mark of her inferiority to men. In a sense, childbearing itself becomes a humiliating concession to biological forces which automatically limit her chance of realizing the social and economic goals which she has been conditioned to desire.

The emotional security which she seeks in marriage is threatened by a new conflict. She can now choose whether or not she will have children. In all previous societies children were an inevitable counterpart of marriage. To fortify woman's role as childbearer a whole series of notions was built up about the concept of duty and obligation to children. Children fitted into this conception of life organization. If there were too many, one accepted them as the gift of an all-wise Providence. Today, it is not uncommon for women to bear children whom they actually do not love.

In the romantic family where tension reigns, the child is not protected by the marriage bond as such. There is considerable evidence that where severe conflict exists the marriage should end in divorce for the protection of the children. . . .

Writing from experience in a children's clinic, Dr. Plant tells judges that they often solve the most serious problem in the life of the child when they grant a divorce. He is not saying that the breakup of a family by divorce is good; he is merely stressing the significant fact that in many instances divorce has become the only possible solution in the interests of the child. His case is based on the fact that human beings in conflict are never fair. In the highly emotional, personalized relationship of the romantic marriage, the child becomes a pawn in the conflict. His sympathies are sought for the wrong of one parent against the other. The catastrophic effect on the personality of the child is obvious.

In considering the relations of men and women under the romantic family social system one cannot evade the sex issue. It has long been recognized as a critical point in family conflict and recent studies show it to be the most crucial point in marital adjustment.

The romantic marriage frankly recognizes the biological basis for marriage. Sex is treated candidly rather than prudishly. The traditional family system took it for granted as a means for siring the race; the romantic family system speaks much of sex as a means of recreation and of romantic fulfillment.

The double standard has long imposed virginity on the female sex only and penalized by social censure the pregnant unmarried girl, ignoring the responsibility of the offending male. At this point the relationships between men and women have suffered a severe strain for more than a generation. The first emphasis was on reforming men by removing prostitution and calling for a single standard of morality. World War II has hastened the acceptance of the philosophy that since man cannot be made pure, women should insist on a single standard by assuming the male prerogative of sex freedom. This new single standard, under which women approach the male's level of morality, is made possible by birth control, by the anonymity of urban living, and by extensive mobility which removes the personal relations of men and women from the surveillance of local groups. The extent of illicit sex relations inside and outside wedlock is anybody's guess, but all recognize that it has increased considerably, especially among those who are married.

While it is logical to hold that what is sauce for the gander is sauce for the goose, the application of such logic has failed to bring men and women closer together. For both in seeking sex pleasure within and outside marriage undermine the very foundations of the romantic theory of marriage. Where there is no confidence and no marital loyalty, there is in reality no marriage in the high spiritual sense—which the romantic marriage holds out as the basis for unity and stability.

Perhaps the wave of divorces that is following in the war's wake, the increasing concern about juvenile delinquency, the growing awareness of family conflict will bring us to the point where our society as a whole will take a more sane attitude toward marriage and family life. It is no doubt too much to expect the motion picture producers to discount their most marketable product, romantic love, but perhaps it is not unreasonable to expect them to present the stark realities of divorces which is so much an inherent part of this conception of marriage.

Perhaps even those in the market place will eventually realize that underlying forces are at work to bring us to a pattern of family life that is neither matriarchal nor patriarchal, but which will meet the demand for a flexible opportunity for the full development of individual personality within the family unit.

As an underpinning of all our particular efforts, teachers, social workers, clergymen, publicists, must join together to bring about a fundamental reorientation of our concept of the basis for satisfaction and happiness in marriage. Too casually, during this century, these concepts have been shaped by the movies, the popular magazines, romantic literature in its many facets. The philosophy of family life and family relationships on which they rest are unreal in the economic and social culture which produces the rich and varied personal interests, ambitions, and desires of individual men, women, and children. Yet these very romantic concepts create the greatest barrier to the development of that sanity of approach which is now imperative if we are to arrest the trend toward family breakdown. . . .

How To Pick a Mate *

It is something of a commentary that America, the land of romantic love and blissful marriage, has the highest divorce rate of any country in the world. Sociologists who have studied the subject feel that there is a close relationship between the two. The evidence is abundant that the romantic complex plus the conditions that foster it are incompatible with the marriage that results. In recent years a great deal

* Clifford R. Adams. Reprinted with permission from *The American Magazine*, December, 1944, as condensed in *The Reader's Digest*, January, 1945, pp. 19-22. Copyright Crowell-Collier Publishing Company.

has been written on the idea that factors other than the rate of one's heartbeat are important in picking a mate. Several authorities in impressive studies have concluded that it is possible to predict success or failure before marriage. In the following article Dr. Adams adds further substance to this thesis and, at the same time, raises some interesting questions. Can happiness or unhappiness in marriage be predicted? What are the positive and negative factors in the background of a successful marriage?

Today the chances that our young people will find happiness through marriage are slim, indeed. The rise of our divorce rate is frightening. One marriage in five or six landed on the rocks in 1940. And if long-range trends continue the rate will be one in two in 50 years.

There are deeper reasons than the war for the rising trends in divorce. Civilization, in becoming more complex, puts a greater strain on marriage.

Pennsylvania State College has tackled this problem at its roots by founding a marriage counseling service which students call "The Compatibility Clinic." It is available to students, faculty, and townsfolk alike. Some of our cases are married couples who are about ready to call it quits. We test them, talk to them, tell them the problems they are up against, and, unless they are hopelessly incompatible, try to find a solution. About 80 per cent of these cases are patched up successfully. In recent months couples all over America have been writing in for counsel.

Our main concern, however, is to work with young people *before* they marry and *before* the damage is done. We encourage both boys and girls to start thinking toward the day they will marry. And when they get down to specific cases we take the fellow and girl, probe their backgrounds, plot their personalities side by side on charts, and give them an over-all picture of their prospects for a happy marriage.

About one-fourth of such couples get our unqualified green light. A middle forty per cent are advised to proceed with caution because of certain important differences or shortcomings which we help to correct. The remainder are flatly warned to "go very slowly." We urge couples in the last two groups to hold off at least six months. During that time the obviously incompatible unions collapse from the weight of differences.

Many hundreds of couples we tested are married now, and we have the satisfaction of knowing that every prediction we made about them has proved to be substantially correct. Of the couples we encouraged not one is divorced or separated.

A great many of the young people who come to our clinic are either agitated or misty-eyed. They tell me that it was love at first sight. That always makes me wary; because "love at first sight" is either sheer sexual attraction or a matching of one's phantasy ideal. For example, a boy has in mind a Dream Girl with blonde hair, blue eyes, dimples, a turned-up nose, and a 24-inch waist. He falls in love with the first girl he meets who coincides with this description. It's a poor way to pick a life mate. When you marry you are taking unto yourself a lot more than a cute date.

At the clinic our greatest attention is devoted to finding whether the personalities of a couple harmonize. We test both of them for eleven different traits. The traits are scored between eleven sets of poles:

> Sociable—aloof; easily swayed—stubborn
> Irritable—settled; timid—bold
> Passionate—cold; idealistic—expedient
> Changeable—rigid; worrisome—carefree
> Conventional—unconventional
> Undependable—dependable
> Well-adjusted—badly adjusted

Congenial couples score fairly close on most of these and for the most part stay in the broad middle zone between these poles.

A person's scoring on these traits adds up to an accurate picture of his emotional maturity. Marriage experts agree that this is the most important factor in any marriage. People possessing it are free of complexes, neuroses, and phobias. In the same breath I will say that marriage happiness depends almost fifty per cent on sexual harmony of the married couple. Sexual harmony is obtainable only if the couple are sexually mature. And such maturity is present only with emotionally mature people.

Moralists have long contended that a vital requirement of any marriage is that neither partner have a record of physical intimacy before hand. Frankly, I don't know. Of the engaged couples contemplating early marriage I would estimate that seventy-five per cent have had such intimate relations with each other. Such relations do not seem to be an important factor in determining whether their eventual marriage will be happy or not.

Promiscuity, however, is another matter. I took at random twenty-five charts of girls who—according to our tests—were generally unstable emotionally. Later 21 of the 25 confided to me that they had been intimate with three or more boys during the preceding year. I would hesitate to recommend any one of them for marriage, not only because of their low moral standards but because of lack of emotional maturity.

There is a lot more, of course, to marriage happiness than matching up eleven personality traits. Here are some of the other things we take into consideration: First, the family background of the boy and girl. It is profoundly important to know whether the bride and groom had a happy childhood, whether they got along well with their parents, and whether their parents were well mated. *Happiness runs in families.* If you were reared in a happy home free of discord and conflict, you are more likely to be emotionally mature than if brought up amid bickering and tension.

Parents who were frank in talking to their children about the magic and mystery of sex contributed greatly to the emotional maturity and, therefore, to the eventual marital happiness of their children.

Another thing we are anxious to know is how the boy hopes to support his future wife. Occupations that involve regular office hours are the safest risks. These include doctors, bankers, teachers, ministers. The traveling salesmen is rightly considered one of the worst bets in marriage.

Third, we like to know whether their religions are the same. If the couple are of widely different religions they may be liable to constant friction unless they reach a tolerant understanding beforehand as to how their children will be reared.

Differences in age are not as important as many people imagine, so long as both man and woman are over twenty, under forty, and not more than ten years apart.

Three other things that we consider important to marriage success are: a courtship of at least a year, a sense of humor, which helps couples over many rough spots, and a desire on the part of both parties for children.

Now we come to some specific kinds of would-be spouses that should be treated with extreme caution. First are the neurotics. One type is the habitual heavy drinker. The girl who marries such a man on the assumption that she can reform him is due for a bitter awakening. Marriage rarely cures dipsomania or any other mania.

Any person who is a victim of a chronic desire is not normally a good risk.

Impotency and sterility have long been causes for heartaches among newlyweds. Now, however, such encouraging progress is being made by science that cures seem to be possible.

Finally, the jealous or suspicious person is a frequent marriage wrecker. In forty per cent of broken engagements or marriages, jealousy has been a big factor.

In making these warnings about poor mates I've left out one tremendously important qualification. No matter how bad the odds seem, happiness can be achieved by most of these couples if they face their dangers with open eyes and thresh out their mutual fears, problems, frustrations and strive to achieve a sensible solution. We call this by the high-sounding term of "mutual psychotherapy."

Are You Really in Love?

1. Do you have a great number of things that you like to do together?

2. Do you have a feeling of pride when you compare your friend with anyone else you know?

3. Do you suffer from a feeling of unrest when away from him or her?

4. Even when you quarrel, do you still enjoy being together?

5. Have you a strong desire to please him, or her, and are you quite glad to give way on your own preferences?

6. Do you actually want to marry this person?

7. Does he, or she, have the qualities you would like to have in your children?

8. Do your friends and associates admire this person and think it would be a good match for you?

9. Do your parents think you are in love? (They're very discerning about such things.)

10. Have you started planning, at least in your own mind, what kind of a wedding, children, and home you will have?

If you can truthfully answer *Yes* to at least seven of the above, then Dr. Adam's diagnosis would be that you *are* in love.

Predicting Success or Failure in Marriage *

A major landmark in marriage research was the publication in 1939 of *Predicting Success or Failure in Marriage*. Its authors, Professors Burgess and Cottrell, based their findings on extensive interviews with 526 married couples, thus securing a broad sampling base. Conclusions of their study, which are reproduced below, offer a yardstick by which individual students may measure their chances of marital success against established norms.

At the conclusion of a study the three following questions are almost always asked, and they are always well worth attention:

1. What, if any, contributions have been made to knowledge?
2. What is the significance of these contributions?
3. What further research is indicated?

The discussion of the third question upon further research will be reserved for the next and final chapter. An attempt will be made in this chapter to answer the first two questions by summarizing briefly the major findings of the study and by indicating their significance for an understanding of the way in which men and women adjust to each other in marriage.

* Ernest W. Burgess and Leonard S. Cottrell, Jr., *Predicting Success or Failure in Marriage* (Prentice-Hall, 1939), pp. 341–49. Copyright, 1939, by Prentice-Hall, Inc., New York. Reprinted by permission of the publisher.

Wives make the major adjustment in marriage. An outstanding, if not the most significant, finding of this study is that the background items of the husbands are much more important for adjustment in marriage than are the background items of the wives.

Why should the premarital characteristics of the husband be so much more closely correlated with marital adjustment than those of the wife? Perhaps in marriage the wife, on the average, makes much more of an adjustment to the husband than he makes to her.

On first thought the explanation that wives in the United States make the major adjustment in marriage is directly in contradiction to the American conception that marriage is a "fifty-fifty proposition" in which husband and wife make equal adaptations to one another. It might have been assumed that husbands in this country more than anywhere else in the world are disposed to cater to and comply with the wishes, attitudes, and even whims of their wives. European visitors to the United States are quick to point out the dominant position of the American wife in the home and the subservient or secondary role of her husband.

The findings of this study regarding the relatively greater weight of the characteristics of the husband in determining marital adjustment suggest that too much emphasis has been placed upon the superficial aspects of the American marital relationship. These aspects appear greater by contrast with the obvious and definite subordination of woman to man in Old-World marriages. Where the mores decree that the wife shall be submissive to the husband, as in Germany and to a lesser extent in England, all couples manifest a uniform pattern of behavior which corresponds to the approved forms.

In the United States, where the mores sanction equality in the marriage relation, the superficial forms of the husband's behavior may hide the actual situation. Since the mores do not demand the obvious display of the husband's dominance, wide individual differences in the marital relation are apparent. In many unions the wife is in fact, and not merely seemingly, superordinate. The domineering wife and the "henpecked" husband, to mention an extreme illustration, are much more evident in the United States than in Europe. The dictatorship of wives, however, is undoubtedly limited to a relatively small proportion of marriages. The majority of wives must still achieve their aims in subtle and indirect ways which evidence the dominant position of their husbands.

The statistical findings of this study deal with averages and obscure individual differences. Our problem is, then, to explain why so great an average discrepancy exists between the greater inferred adaptability of the wife than of the husband.

Two explanations are at hand which may operate independently or in conjunction. First, it may be assumed that the new mores emphasizing equality of the sexes in marriage have not as yet entirely displaced the old attitude that the husband should be dominant. Second, it may be asserted that the trait of dominance is, on the average, more marked in the male, and that of submission in the female. To the extent that this is true, the wife would be disposed to be subordinate and the husband superordinate.

To state that at present in American society dominance is in general a male, and submission a female, trait is not to imply that this difference is necessarily biological. It may, in fact, be social, not in the sense that it is commanded by the mores, but in that it persists in the attitudes arising out of our self-consciousness of sex differences and our conception of what is expected in the behavior of boys and girls, men and women.

Further research will be necessary to clarify the points raised by the discussion of these findings. If they actually measure present differences in the amount of adjustment made by man and woman in marriage, then it should be possible to determine the varying differences in adjustment between the husbands and wives in different sections of the United States. Comparative studies might be made to verify assumed differences between the East and the West, the North and the South, or between different districts within the city, as between equalitarian-family areas, semipatriarchal immigrant districts, and the matricentric suburban neighborhoods. It would be assumed, for example, that the Southern wife makes a greater adjustment in marriage than the Western wife, and that the immigrant wife living in the semipatriarchal-family neighborhood is more submissive to her husband than is the wife who is herself gainfully employed and residing in the apartment-house area with its equalitarian standards of family life.

The affectional relationships of childhood condition the love life of the adult. The response patterns of relationships established in childhood appear to be the dynamic factor determining the expression of affection in adult life. This finding is derived from the examination of 100 case studies in this investigation. It corresponds more or less closely to the conclusions reached by other workers in their clinical analysis of material obtained over a prolonged period by intensive psychiatric interviews. It is corroborated by the statistical evidence provided by this study.

Two general effects of the familial affectional environment upon the adjustment in marriage of young people have been independently established by Terman's study and by the present research:

1. Happy marriages of parents are correlated with happiness in the marriage of their children. This relationship is the outstanding association noticed in the study of the relation between background items of both husbands and wives and their adjustment in marriage.

2. Close attachment in childhood to father and mother and absence of conflict with them is positively correlated with the person's adjustment in marriage.

These two conclusions indicate the general correlation that obtains between a happy family relationship in childhood, with close attachment between parents and children, and a satisfactory adjustment as an adult in the marriage relationship itself.

Our case-study data enable us to proceed a step further and to make a specific formulation of a theory of childhood affectional attachment in relation to marital adjustment, as follows:

1. In childhood the person builds up a response relationship to the parent of the opposite sex which markedly influences his response to and selection of a love object in adult life.

2. If the childhood affectional relation to the parent of the opposite sex has been a satisfying one, the person will tend to fall in love with someone possessing temperamental and personality characteristics similar to those of the loved parent.

3. If the childhood affectional relation has been unsatisfactory, he is more likely to fall in love with a person of opposite temperamental and personality characteristics. An exception occurs where the relation in childhood has been one of frustration rather than of conflict, so that as a consequence of idealization the person seeks all the more in a loved one the personality type of the parent of the opposite sex. Where the attitude is ambivalent, then there may develop alternating attitudes of love and hatred toward the affectional object.

4. The childhood response fixation is generally, but not always, upon the parent of the opposite sex. It may under certain conditions be centered upon the parent of the same sex or upon a brother or sister.

5. The actual complex of attitudes in affectional relationships in adult life tends to reproduce all the significant response patterns of childhood. Thus the adult unconsciously strives to act in his love life not only his childhood role with regard to his sex-opposite parent but also his childhood roles with regard to his parent of the same sex, to his older brother or sister, and to his younger brother or sister. Where the relation has been ambivalent, as in the case of submissive and rebellious behavior, this pattern also tends to be expressed in the marital relation.

This theory of the nature of early childhood affectional relationships as determining the dynamics of adjustment in marriage is of such great significance, if correct, that systematic effort should be made to verify or disprove it by objective methods. Its validation would greatly simplify the understanding of a great field of behavior that otherwise seems to be hopelessly complex, complicated, and often contradictory.

Socialization of the person is significant for adjustment in marriage. A group of background items constituting what may be called the social factor in marital adjustment is found to be significantly related to success in marriage. Among these items are: higher level of education; objective evidence of religious activity, such as duration and frequency of attendance at Sunday school and church; the number and sex of friends; participation in social organizations; and residence in neighborhoods of single-family dwellings. These items taken together may be regarded as an index of sociability, or of socialization in respect to the degree of participation and achievement of the person in the activities of the community and its chief cultural institutions—the family, the school, and the church.

The impress of social institutions upon a person may be measured in terms of his conformity to social rules, his respect for conventions and his stability of character. The socialization of the person which results prepares him for adjustment in marriage.

The economic factor, in itself, is not significant for adjustment in marriage. A finding quite unexpected by the writers, and almost certain to be surprising to the public, is the virtual disappearance of the premarital economic items from the group of items significant in marital adjustment. It is true that several economic items such as moderate income, savings, occupations characterized by stability and social control, and regularity and continuity of employment are positively correlated with adjustment in marriage. But all these combined add very little to the effectiveness of the prediction that can be made without them. In fact, by the method of partial correlation whereby other factors are held constant, the discovery is made that the correlation of the economic factor with the prediction score is only .04 in comparison with .20 for the psychogenetic factor and the response factor, respectively; .18 for the socialization factor; and .14 for the cultural-impress factor.

The explanation for the very low weight to be assigned to the economic items in marital adjustment is that they add very little to the items included under psychogenetic, cultural-impress, social-type, and response factors. It may, indeed, be argued that the economic behavior of the person at least so far as it affects adjustment in marriage, is an expression of these noneconomic factors. Economic items such as moderate income, savings, occupations characterized by stability and social control, regularity and continuity of employment, may all be taken as indicating a stabilized and socialized personality which readily adjusts to the marriage situation. But this is a type of personality which is also strongly indicated by psychogenetic, cultural-impress, social-type, and response factors. The economic behavior of the person may therefore be thought of as the resultant of these noneconomic influences. In fact, the trait of personality which all our items are measuring may turn out to be *adjustability* or *socialization* that makes for adjustment in society, in industry, and in marriage. However, it must be remembered that the sample on which this study is based does not cover the entire range of economic groups in our culture.

With the majority of couples, sexual adjustment in marriage appears to be a resultant not so much of biological factors as of psychogenetic development and of cultural conditioning of attitudes toward sex. This finding is derived from case studies and, while rather clearly indicated, should not be taken as conclusively established. It is in harmony with the obvious generalization that the biological growth and maturation of the individual takes place in association and interaction with his emotional, intellectual, and social development. The understanding of any one of these aspects of human growth is necessarily to be arrived at in the context of the others.

Prediction before marriage of marital adjustment is feasible, and should and can be further developed through statistical and case-study techniques. This study has demonstrated the feasibility of predicting adjustment in marriage and has indicated the course of future research to improve the accuracy and significance of prediction.

With present methods it is entirely practicable to indicate the risk group into which any engaged person will fall, with a definite statement regarding the statistical probabilities of success or failure in marriage. This is, however, group prediction, as with life-expectancy tables which are used by life-insurance companies. But the prediction of marital adjustment has one advantage over that of a life-expectancy table: our study indicates that statistical prediction for all practical purposes can be applied to particular individuals at the two extremes where all, or at least 99 out of 100, persons assigned to the highest and to the lowest risk group will either succeed or fail in marriage, according to the predictions.

The most practical use of prediction will, however, undoubtedly be with individual cases. It is, therefore, the aim of research to increase the precision, reliability, and significance of prediction in individual cases.

Promising leads for investigators who want to achieve this objective lie in two opposite directions. One is the intensive study of relatively few cases to identify the chief dynamic factors operating in marriage relationships. An example of a dynamic factor which has already been isolated is that of the persistence in adult life of an affectional pattern which determines the object of the love response. Such a discovery may later be subjected to test by statistical procedure. Intensive studies of individual cases will, however, generally be necessary in order to identify the particular configuration of dynamic factors in the interpersonal relationships of a given couple.

A second direction of research will involve dealings with not hundreds and thousands but tens and hundreds of thousands of cases, so that signifi-

cant groupings of items may be identified by statistical methods.   Although
the obtaining of such large numbers of cases may not be feasible at the
present time, there is no reason why research in this field should not ultimately aspire to the amassing of the hundreds of thousands of cases that
are necessary to achieve the most significant results possible with statistical
procedures.

In conclusion, a recapitulation of the findings of this study shows the
following:

1. Contrary to prevailing opinion, American wives make the major adjustment in marriage.

2. Affectional relationships in childhood, typically of the son for the mother
and the daughter for the father, condition the love-object choice of the adult.

3. The socialization of the person, as indicated by his participation in social
life and social institutions, is significant for adjustment in marriage.

4. The economic factor in itself is not significant for adjustment in marriage,
since it is apparently fully accounted for by the other factors (impress of cultural background, psychogenetic characteristics, social type, and response patterns).

5. With the majority of couples, problems of sexual adjustment in marriage
appear to be a resultant not so much of biological factors as of psychological
characteristics and of cultural conditioning of attitudes toward sex.

6. Prediction before marriage of marital adjustment is feasible, and should
and can be further developed through statistical and case-study methods.

In short, the outstanding factors in marital adjustment seem to be those
of affection, temperamental compatibility, and social adaptability.   The
biological and economic factors are of less importance and appear to be
largely determined by these other factors.

These six major findings represent the outstanding contributions which
the present study makes to our knowledge of marital adjustment, particularly as adjustment may be predicted before marriage.   In this study, as in
many others, the most significant contribution is not to be found in any one
finding, nor even in the sum total of findings, but in the degree to which
the study opens up a new field to further research.   The next and final
chapter deals with this challenge.

Problem 17: Family Disorganization--Can Marital Stability Be Achieved?

Many American families are not ideal. Tensions, arguments, unhappiness, mental and physical cruelty, and other disorganizing elements are present in many homes. In the face of this reality, what is the way out? Must the unhappy partner bear with the situation "for the good of society"? Can such difficulties be worked out through the church, through family counseling agencies, or by other means? Is divorce a solution? If so, should divorce be made easier or more difficult? Or should divorce be allowed at all? These and related questions are discussed in the selections that follow.

MUST MARRIAGE BE FOR LIFE? *

Popular fancy has most often considered divorce to be the central problem of marriage and the family. More recently, experts on the subject have often thought of divorce as a solution to more deep-seated problems of the family. They sometimes feel that the prevailing popular opinions, which focus on the divorce itself, actually aggravate the problem because they support divorce laws calling for recrimination, accusation, and counteraccusation and because they leave the divorced (or those contemplating divorce) with intense guilt feelings because they have "failed."

This differential opinion highlights a difficult question in the study of any social problem: Are the facts (in this case, divorce statistics) the problem, or are the attitudes toward the facts actually the problem? Those who interpret the facts as the problem would attempt to bring forth programs that would change those facts (that is, result in fewer divorces). Those who feel that the actual problem is in the attitude toward the facts might well say, "Divorce is here to stay—let's adjust to it by forming new attitudes." The following article, subtitled "An Anthropologist Proposes a New Attitude toward Divorce," indicates which definition Margaret Mead makes of the problem and the way in which she would suggest that we "solve" it.

* Margaret Mead, '47, the Magazine of the Year, November, 1947, pp. 28–31.

When the question is asked, "Why do men and women get divorces?" the answer is usually expressed in terms of broken hearts, broken heads, or broken furniture. He drank or she drank; he gambled or she gambled; he outgrew her or she outgrew him; the difference in their backgrounds was too great; they were sexually incompatible; she had a job and was away from home too much; she was too much interested in her home and would never go out; she was too much interested in the children or he was too little interested in children; her mother interfered or his mother interfered; he met someone younger and smarter or she met someone richer and more successful—on and on through a series of one-sentence summaries of individual tragedies.

But do men and women really end their marriages because of heartbreak, betrayed hopes, or a reawakened wistful desire to begin life over again? Or do they get divorces because of the divorce rate?

There are the statistics; so many marriages will break up this month, next month, next year, and the partners will be of predictable ages, races, religious beliefs, and status in the community. Is there no choice except between thinking of one's own marriage as highly individual—quite independent of rates, trends, or other large abstractions—or as a punch hole in a tabulating card?

It is true that people follow a trend. But there is a difference between saying that Susan and Jim are willing to face a divorce because divorces have become a widely accepted solution, and saying that Susan and Jim are getting a divorce because so many other people have done so.

A divorce rate is merely an abstract way of recording the fact that in every community a great many marriages break up. Each such broken marriage does not necessarily cause more wife-beating or more adultery or more abuse of children. But each broken marriage does encourage in every human being who comes in contact with it as partner, relative, neighbor, or just newspaper reader, the attitude that marriage is a state which is terminable.

As more and more marriages break up, more and more young people enter marriage as something which is not necessarily permanent, as one moves into the home one has wanted all of one's life, but which one may, for any of a dozen reasons, have to leave after a while.

In a society with a divorce rate like ours (in 1946 there were 610,000 divorces to 2,300,000 marriages—a ratio of one to four) marriages have become a terminable state. Our religion, our poetry, most of our marriage and divorce laws, still assume that everyone who enters marriage does so with the expectation that the union will prove lifelong. Actually, although many starry-eyed young people and starrier-eyed middle-aged people enter marriage with the fervent hope it will last, almost no one, nowadays, even the most religious, enters it with the surety that it will last. So men and women get divorces because divorces are the expected end to a marriage which shows any one of a thousand sorts of maladjustment and misfortune, the very maladjustments and misfortunes which have accompanied marriage since it was invented as a means of assuring care for women and children.

Those who believe most fervently that it is better for a marriage to be legally dissolved than to be maintained in mutual hatred or fear, have felt very bitter toward the religious groups which oppose easy divorce laws. They ask: "Why can't the churches maintain their own religious codes over their own people? Why do they insist on laws which will interfere with the lives of people who don't subscribe to their religious attitudes on marriage?" But there is a reason for the attitude of the churches. They know quite well that the danger lies in the increasing recognition of terminability. They know that the belief in indissoluble marriage, once shattered for the community at large, is very hard to maintain in the hearts of the moderately or routinely devout. And so they have fought a vigorous battle. This battle has delayed our recognition of what has been happening, has slowed down the number of legal divorces in many states, and has postponed the development of new ethics to suit the new situation. But it hasn't kept the divorce rate down.

In the face of this rate, it is now possible to say clearly and definitely: Marriages in the United States are no longer the traditional Judeo-Christian-European contracts by which lifetime unions are established. They are terminable states to which both partners, no matter how loving, devoted, or convinced of the values of home and children can bring an expectation of only conditional fulfillment. If society as a whole could treat divorces not as a sordid mess but as just one more grievous event in a world of change, wouldn't we thereby increase the possibility for good relationships between those who come together in marriage?

Would the number of divorces increase if they were handled with dignified and admitted sorrow, rather than with anger, recrimination, and a sense of failure?

Those who are worried, for religious or moral or social reasons, about the steadily increasing disorganization of American family life, fear any step which may increase divorce. They cling to the hope that if we can keep divorce bitter and sordid, keep it labelled Failure, keep people unconscious that they are moving with a social stream, we can somehow keep down divorce.

It is a forlorn hope. How much better abandon it and recognize that divorce is no longer a rare socially repudiated tragedy, but the actual practice of our society. Such a recognition would hardly increase the number of divorces. But it might very well change the nature of divorces. Probably, too, it would have much effect on the kind of people who do the divorcing. Some of the Bills and Alices might find a divorce a less ready weapon to their hands if it were no longer defined as a weapon. Some of the marriages so torn with conflict that the children have no chance of good adjustment, could be broken up, and broken up gently, as one leaves a house one has loved. The move would be accepted as necessary and right.

Second marriages could be entered into minus the load of guilt and hostility which now hangs over them, thus making it doubly likely that those who have been divorced once will be divorced again. If we can change our attitude so that it is no longer necessary to blame people for acting as society has taught them they will be permitted to act, their friends and relatives will no longer need to take sides. Each former partner can retain the support and affection of his associates, and so stand a better chance of building on what was good in the past, instead of dwelling defensively on what was bad in it.

MAKING MARRIAGE STICK *

Although divorce is rapidly becoming an accepted practice in American society, some groups still look upon it as socially and morally wrong. The Roman Catholic Church, for example, recognizes marriage as a sacrament and regards it as a permanent union. Only under the most exceptional circumstances will the Church sanction divorce. The following article is condensed from a pamphlet that the Roman Catholic Church makes available to its members and uses for instruction programs in marriage.

Divorce No Solution

Divorce is not a satisfactory solution for the difficulties and trials that almost inevitably arise in marriage. If in later years you could talk with legions who rush to the divorce courts to find the "way out" of their discomforts, the overwhelming majority would tell you that it was the "way in" to deeper and more lasting sorrows. Such is the poignant testimony of a woman writing in *Harper's* with the disillusionment which comes from sad and bitter experience.

* Condensed and reprinted from *Making Marriage Stick*, by John A. O'Brien, Ave Maria Press, Notre Dame, Indiana, 1948, pp. 5–10, 14–15, 20, 25–29.

"If I had to do it over again," she says, "I would not divorce my husband. And I wonder how many divorcees wish that divorce had never been invented. Few will confess it because it is a human trait to disguise failure, to be reluctant to admit defeat even to oneself—and divorce is defeat. I am acknowledging that defeat, although even to my nearest friends I still carry through the stereotyped bluff, which indicates that I have borne unspeakable anguish with bravery."

She then tells how she divorced her husband because he drank. That was ten years ago, then she was thirty and her boy eight. The intervening years have been filled with loneliness, tears and aching regret. Everyone has shortcomings, she realizes now. Why hadn't she remained at his side, helping him to overcome his weakness instead of deserting him? It would have been better for her son, her husband and herself.

The son is permitted to spend one day a month with the father. When she calls at the country club to bring her boy home, she finds him on the tennis courts with the father. He is lighting his father's pipe, then his own cigarette. A camaraderie rooted deep in their kindred natures has blossomed forth. Suddenly she feels like a kidnapper. For she is severing one of the most fundamental kinships that exist.

Psychic Scars

When her son returns home from college, how desperately does she feel the need for someone to share her affection for him, her pride in the inches he has grown, her joy in his expanding maturity. The formal telephone call to let father know that he is safely home is to her a chill reminder of her self-imposed solitude. She had called it her "freedom" when she was seeking her divorce, but she knows it now for what it is—an exile, a nostalgia, an aching loneliness.

Hers are the haunting regrets, the frustrated hopes, which remain like scars upon the hearts and minds of all those who have known the rapture of conjugal love and the sharing of common dreams only to have them cruelly blasted by divorce. As she looks back at the hopes, dreams and aspirations once anchored in the beneficent institution of marriage, and then at the empty, futile days that stretch ahead, she wishes desperately that she had not made the fatal mistake which every divorced person makes —the mistake of seeking happiness where it can never be found. If she had again the chance of ten years ago, she knows now that she would continue in marriage even though a thorn were found here and there among its fragrant flowers.

"We could go on together," she concludes, "trying to understand each other, sometimes perhaps succeeding. Always we should wait for our boy's train together, and together do what we could to make the life for which we are mutually responsible a happy one. Together we should give him the comfort he now lacks of united parents—the tragic, desperate need of every child."

What pastor of souls has not listened to confessions of regret and disillusionment such as this?

The Best Preventive

"Father," said a young husband to me recently, "will you help Margie and me patch up our quarrel before it ends in divorce? I have a bad temper, and when angry say things I really don't mean. Margie has taken the baby home to mother. That was three days ago. I've been beside myself since. I haven't been able to eat or sleep. God! how desperately I want a chance to start over again."

His eyes were red from crying, and he made altogether a pathetic picture as he stood there fingering the rim of his hat.

When I called on Margie, her eyes were likewise red. Her boy of two was calling for "da da." She, too, was finding out that separation, instead of easing her pain, had intensified it. Yet humans are such strange mixtures of love and stubbornness and pride that she was determined not to return until Joe had begged her to do so. Like so many others, she was not going to make the first move.

How many marriages go upon the rocks of divorce through causes like this. Husband and wife, still desperately in love with each other, but each waiting for the other to make the first move toward reconciliation. Truly has it been observed that the hardest thing for most humans to say is:

"I was at fault. I'm sorry. Please forgive me."

But sometimes it is inescapably necessary. Always it is the mark of character and the badge of magnanimity. And usually it is the best preventive of divorce.

Every nation or society that wishes to survive must develop in its individual members a sense of social solidarity, and a willingness to sacrifice private interests for the public weal. In time of war the citizen is called upon to defend his country even at the risk of his life. The measure in which an individual is willing to subordinate his own selfish interests for the welfare of his family, his state, his nation, or humanity in general, is largely the measure of his usefulness and nobility of character.

When a marriage turns out badly, and the innocent victim feels tempted to have recourse to divorce and remarriage, Christ calls upon such a one to be willing to sacrifice his own selfish interests for the larger welfare of society as a whole. The divine Master would have him remember that if an exception were made in his case, there could be no drawing of the line, and that in consequence the unity and permanence of marriage would in a large measure be destroyed. An individual should recognize that in such circumstances he is called upon to play the role of a self-sacrificing hero and to place the public weal above his private interests. Such a one is no less worthy of the gratitude of his fellow-countrymen than is the soldier who defends his country from the attack of the enemy. Nor less worthy of the reward of Almighty God.

. . . But you may ask: Why is divorce such an evil? Why is it such a threat to the happiness of the people, to the welfare of society, and to the security of our nation?

First of all, it is the source of most of the juvenile delinquency and crime which has swept like a tidal wave across our nation. Eighty to ninety per cent of such delinquency stems from broken homes. When husband and wife are torn apart by the cruel hands of divorce, the children are thrown out upon a heartless world to shift for themselves. Deprived of the loving care of a father and a mother, they find the path to immorality and crime a short and slippery one. Filling our reformatories, our homes for incorrigible children, our jails, and our penitentiaries, teen-agers are leaving a wake of blood and tears across our land. Crime—and most of it committed by youth—is costing America more than two billion dollars a year. . . .

"But surely there are cases," people say, "where a person could be happier by getting a divorce and remarrying." Granted. There may be occasional instances where that would be true. The law has for its objective, however, the promotion of the welfare of society, the stability of the nation and the protection of the rights of the children. Hence an individual will be called upon now and then to sacrifice his private happiness for the common welfare.

Constructive Measures

The road ahead for America is the road to domestic peace and conjugal fidelity. It is the road flanked on both sides by happy homes, where peace and love abide. It is the road along which are found domestic shrines, where Christ's law of unity and permanence is the order of the day.

The greatest contribution we can make for the preservation of the safety of America, for the curbing of juvenile delinquency, for the strengthening of the family life and the deepening of its joys is the stemming of the mounting tide of divorces and the restoration of marriage to its indissoluble character. Such is the demand of patriotism, the dictate of reason and the mandate of Christ Himself. The Church calls upon all of you to fight in season and out of season for the permanence of the marriage bond and the sanctity of the Christian home. She calls upon all Christians to set the example for our non-Christian citizens and to plant in their minds and hearts the ideal of deathless love and loyalty given to us by Christ.

Let us work for the establishment of courts of conciliation where differences will be ironed out and couples headed for the divorce court will be reunited. Let us strive to set up a psychiatric department in connection with such courts of reconciliation to help mentally upset and distraught men and women and aid them in their struggle back to health, calmness and sanity. Here is one of the greatest services we can render to distressed people—a service that will redound to the social welfare and the moral and spiritual health of the American people.

Instruction—Before and After Marriage

Then there is prophylactic work to be done. An ounce of prevention is worth a pound of cure. We need to establish classes where young people going together would be given detailed instructions concerning marriage, its responsibilities and the manner of fulfilling them. A class or seminar in which are pooled the counsel of the pastor, physician, psychiatrist, and of parents who have made an outstanding success of marriage would give young couples a realistic understanding of the problems involved in raising a family and in the methods of solving them.

It would help to prevent many ill-considered unions where experienced counsellors would detect too many elements of uncongeniality, to which infatuation had blinded the young couple. Such courses as this are urgently needed in every city and town in America. In fact, before receiving a license to wed, a young couple might well be required to present a certificate showing they had completed such a course. It would screen out thousands of marriages which persons with one eye open could see were heavily weighted to end in the divorce court.

After the wedding there should be conferences given by the counsellors previously mentioned. In some cities they are known as Cana Conferences. In these conferences the married couples receive the guidance and help needed to solve any new problems which arise. The family life, like a tender plant, requires constant care and cultivation. The fragrance and bloom of the wedding day should be preserved through all the years. This can be done when young people receive from enlightened and sympathetic counsellors the guidance so often sorely needed to steer their marital barque safely between the Scylla of extravagance and the Charybdis of uncontrolled temper.

Archbishop Cushing Speaks

Archbishop Cushing proposes a twofold solution of the divorce problem: a new divorce law and new education for young people. "The civil law," he declared, "cries out for revision. Too often now it places false emphasis on personal and social duties. . . . If the law made the remarriage of divorced persons impossible, or at least more difficult, the motive for divorce among most of the flippant and superficial litigants who now are mobbing our divorce courts would be destroyed."

Urging new legislation to protect marriage against fraudulent exploitation of the existing grounds for divorce, Archbishop Cushing pointed out that there are too many accepted grounds for divorce, and that judges have the duty of interpreting divorce legislation strictly. "They must pay as much attention to the good of the community as is paid to the vaunted rights of those who cannot make successes of their marriages."

In developing the second remedy, the Archbishop asked that young people be better prepared for marriage, observing that it is rather late to prevent divorce after two people are already launched on an ill advised marriage. "Most unsuccessful marriages," he declared, "are doomed from the start, and I am convinced that the time to prevent divorce is before the marriage takes place instead of afterward. The most effective way to stop the growing prevalence of divorce would be to anticipate the conditions which make people seek divorce. That can be done only by an intelligent preparation for marriage on the part of those who intend to make marriage a vocation."

So pressing is the need for careful systematic pre-marital instruction that the enactment of legislation requiring it as a condition for obtaining a license is the urgent need of our day. Such instruction should be followed by Cana Conferences after the marriage so that every difficulty would be ironed out as soon as it arises and thus its disruptive power would be nipped in the bud.

DIVORCE WON'T HELP *

Those who approve of divorce look upon it as a "solution" to an unsatisfactory social situation. The assumption is that the marriage partners are better off for having separated than had they stayed together. In the article that follows, a psychiatrist challenges this assumption with his theory that many divorcees are neurotics and that their troubles lie, not in poor marriages, but in poor emotional adjustment, which is not improved by divorce.

A clever journalist once called marriage a two-dimensional study in frustration, an intimate relation without intimacy. Statistics seem to bear out this cynical opinion: the divorce rate has increased to the unprecedented point of one divorce to every three marriages. Statisticians claim that if the present rate of increase continues, the ratio in ten years will be 1:1—one divorce for every marriage.

What is the matter with marriage?

There is nothing the matter with marriage itself. Something is, however, very much the matter with the mental state of a high proportion of the people who enter into marriage. Too many of them are neurotic; and neurotics are not good material for marriage. Very conveniently, however, their underlying neuroticism is ignored and the institution of marriage itself is indicted.

Divorce is no longer regarded as an extreme remedy for an exceptional mistake, a situation encountered in normalcy, but rather as an everyday occurrence. I once asked a patient who was about to begin psychoanalytic treatment why he wanted to be divorced. "Why, practically everybody is either divorced or in the process of being divorced, or is thinking of divorce," he said. "Marriage seems to be an antiquated institution." When I told him that divorce, as a rule, was a neurotic solution adopted chiefly by neurotic persons, his response was one of mingled surprise and disbelief.

Not knowing where the blame actually lies, people blame both the institution of marriage and the marriage partner. If one listens to those who have made a failure of their marriage, one gains the impression that every divorced woman blames her husband and every divorced man blames his wife. The third and principal participant in every neurotic marriage, the neurosis which brought the couple together, in the first place, escapes detection.

* Edmund Bergler, *Divorce Won't Help* (Harper, 1948), pp. vii–x. Copyright, 1948, by Edmund Bergler.

The psychology of the divorcee has not yet been written. There is a superabundance of moral and statistical treatises; but the decisive argument against divorce—the futility of the whole procedure—is almost never stressed.

The futility of divorce can be established clinically: the second, third, and nth marriages are but repetitions of previous experiences. The partner is changed but that is the only difference. The institution of multiple marriage is a fiasco.

It cannot be emphasized enough that I am referring . . . exclusively to neurotics in a specific social setting: Scene, the United States of America; time, the present. In other cultures and at other times, the psychic components, always present, take different forms.

The overemphasis on the bad marriages, constructed unconsciously by neurotics and described here, should not detract from the fact that good marriages do exist in great numbers. They are not mentioned at length, because this volume focuses its attention on neurotic marriages.

. . . I have been frequently greeted with "So you are the fellow who objects to divorce on psychiatric grounds!" Being unable to answer such a question with a simple yes or no, I decided to use a simile. "Imagine," I said, "an engineer living in a superstitious environment. Popular opinion holds that the best way to prevent a threatening flood is to take laxatives. The engineer is asked what he thinks of this. The poor man must not necessarily be against castor oil if he states that castor oil is an ineffective means of preventing a flood. He will, perhaps, without personal malice toward castor oil, suggest the building of a dam as a less crude and more effective way to stop a flood."

In my opinion, chronic seekers of divorce are neurotics who should consult a psychiatrist before running to a lawyer.

. . . [The divorcee] is accused of almost everything—except her neurosis. But actually, she is an unhappy, struggling neurotic, misunderstood and maligned by herself and her environment. Even her frequent promiscuity is a neurotic symptom. No less significant is the fact that the "period between marriages," as one patient called her "post-Reno months," seems alluring to many a married woman. During that time she can do as she pleases—or so she believes. Precisely the opposite is actually the case: the "freedom" to do, without interference, whatever she pleases reduces itself in a divorcee to the slavery of having to do whatever her specific neurosis forces her to do. There is neither glamour nor freedom of will in divorce; no more, at any rate, than in a severe case of typhoid fever.

OUR LEGAL HORROR: DIVORCE *

Divorce itself is a problem, says Paul W. Alexander, judge of the Court of Common Pleas, Toledo, Ohio, in the following article—a view that runs somewhat counter to the suggestion of Margaret Mead in "Must Marriage Be for Life?" Judge Alexander proposes that we not only change our attitude about divorce but actually *do* something about it. Make divorce laws stiffer? No. Makes divorce laws "easier"? Not necessarily. Make divorce laws different? Yes!

"Mrs. Jones, will you describe in your own words what happened May 4, 1946?" the lawyer asked.

"My husband came home very late. He'd been drinking again. I knew he'd been running around and when I asked him where he'd been he got so abusive I made up my mind I just couldn't stand it any longer. Next day I left him," she answered.

"Thank you," and the lawyer motioned her to step down.

"Just a moment," said the judge, leaning forward. "You say he's been drinking the last three years?"

"Yes."

"Did he drink before you were married?"

"No."

"Did he drink or run around during the first six years of your marriage?"

"No."

"Then what got him started?"

"How should I know?" Mrs. Jones replied indignantly.

"Don't you have any idea what went wrong?" persisted the judge.

"All I know is he got to drinking and running around," Mrs. Jones told him. "And I couldn't take it any longer. He made a nervous wreck out of me."

"Yes," sighed the judge in a resigned voice. "The evidence shows he has been guilty on legal grounds, and under the law the court has to grant you a divorce."

Mrs. Jones is typical of millions of divorce seekers; aware only of another's guilt, of superficial symptoms, the outward manifestations; with little insight into the causative factors, the real roots of the trouble—and hence unable to do anything about it.

And the law is that way too!

* Paul W. Alexander, *Ladies Home Journal*, October, 1949, pp. 65, 122, 124–26. Reprinted by permission of *Ladies Home Journal*.

I am politely referred to as a "judge." Maybe that is one of those legal fictions. In reality I am just a faintly glorified public mortician. In the last dozen years I have presided over the final obsequies of more than 20,000 dead marriages.

For in reality, Jane and John kill off the marriage. The divorce trial is merely the autopsy, or post-mortem. The divorce decree is the burial certificate.

Now we public morticians are called upon to bury a lot of live corpses. We know there's still a spark of life in many a seemingly dead marriage. It's hard to discover, but it's there if only we had adequate time and resources to probe for it and bring it back to life.

Half a century ago, we started taking children out of the criminal courts and handling them in a brand-new kind of court, the juvenile court. In criminal court, the sole issues were guilt and punishment. In juvenile court these ideas were relegated so far into the background that in the more progessive courts now they have entirely disappeared.

They have been replaced by the new philosophy of diagnosis and therapy —healing, treatment. Instead of determining whether the child is guilty of an offense and then punishing him, the court tries to determine why the child behaves as he does and to correct his behavior.

The court over which I preside handles both juvenile delinquency and divorce. Years ago I became conscious that we were able to straighten out and help an impressive majority of the delinquent children, while at the same time a painful majority of the unhappy spouses got no help at all. Our work in juvenile court was constructive; in divorce court, destructive. The contrast was thought-provoking.

Much thought has been given this problem by the American Bar Association, the world's largest legal organization. It has a special committee on divorce and marriage laws and family courts. This committee has suggested patterning our divorce courts after our modern, progressive juvenile courts—handling our unhappy and delinquent spouses much as we handle our delinquent children. After all, their behavior is not unlike that of a delinquent child—and for much the same reasons! The committee asks:

Why not substitute in divorce courts the modern philosophy of diagnosis and therapy for that of guilt and punishment? Instead of determining whether a spouse is guilty, why not try to diagnose and treat, to discover the fundamental causes, then bring to bear all available community resources to remove or rectify them?

Today, the knowledge that one can always get a divorce without too much effort or expense or delay takes away much of the idea of the permanence of marriage. As a result, in many circles, marriage is no longer looked upon as a permanent affair. All John or Jane has to do is raise the necessary money to hire a lawyer, decide what "grounds" they are going to use, and then go into court. The grounds vary from state to state. In a few states, a wife can get a divorce simply by proving that her husband eats crackers in bed, and, although she has told him the habit annoyed her, he refused to quit. This comes under the heading of mental cruelty. In one state, divorce can be granted only if either spouse can prove his or her partner is unfaithful, and the proof must be in the form of pictures of the erring partner in a state of intimacy with a member of the opposite sex, or in statements from witnesses of such a situation. In every state, however, divorce grounds include infidelity; most add drunkenness, physical cruelty and desertion. These grounds stem from our traditional views on what constitutes "sin"—but are now merely pegs for the law to hang a divorce decree on.

To begin with, everybody believes divorces break up families. This is not so. The broken family is not the result of divorce. Divorce is the result of the broken family. In the last 12,000 cases coming before me the spouses had already been separated—the families broken—an average of over two years before getting their divorces.

Marriages fail because of the failure of the individuals who marry. Marital unhappiness must have a cause. That cause can be found with few exceptions, in the character defects of Jane or John or both. Here's a typical case I remember:

John was unfaithful. He was unfaithful because Jane wouldn't have "anything to do with him." She wouldn't have "anything to do with him" because John stayed out nights and got drunk. He stayed out and got drunk because Jane nagged. She nagged because John didn't make as much money as she wanted. John kept changing jobs and didn't provide well because he was discouraged. He was discouraged because Jane kept spending beyond his means. Jane was extravagant because she had been spoiled in her youth. John had never learned the virtues of hard work and perserverance; he preferred his own pleasures. Jane had never learned the virtues of encouragement, cooperation, and self-sacrifice. Both were fundamentally selfish. That's really why their marriage failed.

There is ample evidence that even sexual incompatibility is often merely the result of underlying selfishness, usually on the part of both spouses. In most cases it can be corrected, or greatly improved, by medical or psychological or psychiatric treatment—if the parties so desire. Moreover, there are still countless couples who have the strength of character—the selflessness—to put up with genuine sexual incompatibility.

However, the idea of guilt and punishment is so deep-rooted in all American thinking that perhaps we'd better go into a little detail to explain how this idea does more harm than good, how it is at the bottom of much that is wrong with divorce.

When Jane finally goes to court for a divorce, she thinks she is suing John. That's the way the papers read. That would be true if she were after alimony, for then she would ask the court to order John to pay money; she would get a judgment against John personally. But we're talking only about divorce, and in straight divorce Jane doesn't seek anything from John and she doesn't get a judgment or decree against him.

This is because a divorce suit is not a request for the state to do something to a person or to require a person to do something. It is not an action against a person. It is a suit against or upon a thing, a request that the state wipe out or remove or dissolve a thing. That thing is invisible, but the eyes of the law can see it. It is the legal marriage status.

Or we might say Jane asks the court to cut the purely legal tie still binding the parties, the thing the old judges with perhaps unconscious humor used to call the chain of matrimony.

The point is that Jane's divorce decree does not operate on John, but on a thing. The way it divorces Jane and John is by dissolving that legal status.

So what? Well, no self-respecting state would do anything to a person unless that person were guilty of something. Must we therefore find a thing guilty before we can dissolve it? Must that invisible, legal chain be a drunkard?

Now if, as the American Bar Association committee hopes, divorce is to be made helpful, constructive, preventive, what good can it do to find somebody guilty? In a way the shattered romance of Jane and John is like the shattered leg of a patient brought to the hospital. If the leg be hopelessly shattered, utterly beyond help, the surgeon will decide to amputate. That would be best for the patient and indirectly for society. But if the surgeon thinks the leg can be saved he will set the bones, cleanse the wounds, and give the healing power of Nature every possible chance to do its work. He doesn't have to know who was guilty of breaking the leg.

The idea of guilt isn't really necessary and it is really harmful. Since the law provides "no divorce without proving John guilty," many people have the idea that the converse should be true and that for every guilty John there ought to be a divorce. Appalling thought, but true!

People are learning fast how this antiquated idea actually serves to put a premium upon many forms of wickedness. The applicant who can testify to the most vilifying facts with the most vindictiveness comes through easiest and best; and if the true facts are trivial, the applicant exaggerates them until the stupid law is complied with; and in the many cases where there isn't even a trivial fact which can be magnified into something of sufficient legal weight, the applicant manufactures evidence out of whole cloth.

In the opinion of the ABA committee, these evils stem largely from our blind and useless adoption of and adherence to the doctrine of guilt and punishment; the idea that all we need do is prove somebody guilty in a sort of criminal trial. And the committee believes something should be done about it now. We suggest throwing out the window the whole false premise of guilt and punishment. (Don't be nervous! The committee has something better to offer.)

Is a divorce trial a contest, a court fight between a husband and wife, one seeking the other opposing the divorce? No. In an overwhelming majority of cases, the trial is a sham battle against the little man who isn't there. John really isn't there, literally, because he knows if he were to show up it might spoil everything. He wants the divorce as much as Jane—maybe more. So there is almost never a real contest on the question, "Shall there be a divorce?" Only one side is heard. (The court battles you read about are over dollars, not divorce—alimony, property, child support, and occasionally custody of children.)

Yet all the forms and procedures the law sets up are antagonistic lawsuits and they serve only to drive the parties farther apart. The law compels Jane to sue John. The case is titled: "Jane Doe vs. (against) John Doe." Jane must make public, written accusations against John. She must come into court and publicly swear to things against John. She must bring witnesses into court who likewise testify against him. And if, as happens once in a great while, she fails to paint John black enough the first time, she merely profits by her experience and comes back later with enough smear to blacken a regiment.

The ABA committee thinks it is unrealistic to wage sham battles; that it is silly to set the stage for a prize fight with referee, seconds and all the trappings, and then have only one fighter appear and engage in mere shadow boxing. It is positively harmful to have procedures that can only build up bitterness and intensify antagonism. The committee suggests doing away with false premise, these forms and procedures for contentious litigation, and substituting a realistic, sensible and positively helpful method.

A Nevada legislator recently introduced a bill to provide for divorce by slot machine: Divorce seekers reaching Nevada would register for a $5.00 fee. This fee would buy each a special key to a combination juke box, time clock and slot machine. They would be required to use their keys on the machines for 42 consecutive days. This would automatically record the fact they had spent the statutory six weeks in the state necessary for divorce. On the 42nd day the divorce seeker would insert in her machine

200 especially coined dollars, minted of Nevada silver.   Lights would flash. Wheels would spin.   The juke box section would give forth the first two lines of America.   As the music died away, a pretty divorce decree would pop out of a slot.   It would be complete with multicolored ribbons, the imprint of the great seal of Nevada, and the signature of the district judge.

Sound fantastic?   Well, it isn't.   We now have slot-machine divorce in almost every state.   Aside from the difference in time required, the only difference is that our divorce courts resemble human rather than mechanical slot machines.   First the divorce seeker inserts a petition into the legal machine.   Then she goes through an ordained ritual just as ignoble as the Nevada scheme.   Then out pops her decree.

Although divorce by mutual consent is common in almost every state, the idea is utterly abhorrent to the law.   The law goes to great lengths in an effort to avoid anything even faintly resembling divorce by mutual consent, but it is an ineffectual effort.   If both parties agree to a divorce, that is collusion and divorce is forbidden.   What is really forbidden is agreement.   Yet, as everybody knows, a vast majority of cases are agreed-to cases.   So, in a given case everybody must pretend not to know it.

Here are a few further samples of unsound thinking, firmly embedded in the law:

1. A divorce may be granted only in the state where the plaintiff has his legal domicile.   Now domicile is a state of mind.   You may be actually living in Ohio yet, because of your state of mind, choose to be "domiciled" in Florida. But it is the community where you actually live that is adversely affected by your marriage failure—not the distant state which you say is your home.   (Note: a social investigation of your marriage could be made only where you have been residing a reasonable length of time.)

2. If both parties are guilty, then by the doctrine of recrimination neither may be granted a divorce.   Yet when both are "guilty" there is often greater social need for divorce than when just one is proven "guilty."

3. If the "innocent" spouse forgives the "guilty" one, that is condonation, and there may be no divorce unless there is renewed "guilt." You and I were taught that to err is human, to forgive, divine.   But the law penalizes the spouse who forgives, and puts a premium upon vengefulness and vindictiveness. And thus the law punishes honest attempts at reconciliation.

In the thinking of the American Bar Association's special committee on divorce, all these examples of prevalent thinking, as embodied in the law, are fallacious.   They are vicious fictions, pernicious snares and delusions. We would utterly abolish them all—the doctrine of guilt and punishment, the forms and procedures of antagonistic litigation, the doctrines of domicile, collusion, recrimination, and condonation.

And what kind of divorces would we have instead?

To take care of family and personal problems, the progressive juvenile court is equipped with a staff of highly trained specialists. A family court for marital problems would have to be similarly staffed. It would probably require the social case worker, psychiatric case worker, marriage counselor, clinical psychologist, psychiatrist, and so on. In addition, like the juvenile court, it would regularly invoke the services of the legal profession, the church, school, private agency, public agency (police, recreation department and so on) and all available community and institutional resources.

In practice the new idea might work out something like this: When Jane decides the time has come, she retains a lawyer to "file for divorce." But instead of preparing a petition setting forth her bitter accusations against John, the lawyer takes Jane to the new Family Court, where she files an application for "help" or "remedial services" of the state. Instead of being a case titled: "Jane Doe vs. John Doe," it is titled: "In the interest of the John Doe Family." (This simple change is significant of the whole fresh approach.) The lawyer would remain definitely in the picture as both Jane's advocate and an officer of the court, playing a role beneficial to his client by assisting the court to get at the whole truth.

Immediately the trained personnel of the court would commence an investigation to determine not whether John or Jane had broken his or her marriage vows, not whether they—or either of them—are "guilty" but to get at the seat of the trouble, the underlying, fundamental factors causing the marital rift.

Following the diagnosis—and along with it—would come the therapy, the help, the healing. After a reasonable period of treatment—perhaps two months, possibly two years—final report of the investigation, with recommendations, would be submitted. The final report might read that the trouble had been located, the obstacles removed, and that all is now quiet on the Doe home front, whereupon the case would be dismissed.

On the other hand, the report might read that everything had been tried, every technique exhausted from simple case work to psychiatry, and the situation appears hopeless. Of course, the judge would not be bound by any recommendation and he would be free to pursue such further lines of inquiry as he saw fit. But in any event, his guiding star would be: "What is best for this family?"—and consequently, best for society—just as in juvenile court the guiding star is: "What is best for this child?"

If the judge be convinced that the case is utterly hopeless and that nothing can be gained by further efforts at marriage mending, something in the nature of "Banns of divorce" as suggested by Lord Merriman, President of the English Probate, Divorce, and Admiralty Division of the High

Court of Justice, would be issued. If nobody objected, a decree would be entered without the necessity of any verdict of guilt.

A public trial would be entirely eliminated by the plan just outlined. Once it has been clearly determined that Jane and John's marriage is unquestionably dead, that no spark of life remains which could by any amount of effort or skill be revived, there is no humane reason why the court should not be able to perform the necessary operation quietly and privately and mercifully, much as a surgeon operates upon a person. After all, what virtue is there in shaming, dishonoring, or humiliating the wretched and miserably unhappy persons who stand before the court?

We should also consider whether, if each state enacted a uniform divorce law, facing facts and aiming to protect family life, the "divorce mills" might not be put out of business.

The National Association of Women Lawyers has been valiantly in the forefront of the movement for uniform state laws on divorce. This is not just because our "sisters-in-law" dislike legal messes and feel sorry for unfortunate New Yorkers with Reno divorces who don't quite know whether they're single or still married. After all, these "migratory" divorces are only about three per cent of the grand total.

The women lawyers have a further aim—and their "brothers-in-law" join them. The drafting of a model state law on divorce and marriage would be a momentous undertaking. It would take some years of study and effort on the part of the best brains in law, religion, medicine, education, sociology, psychiatry, and other sciences. But it is certainly not unreasonable to expect a remarkably sensible, realistic, humane and constructive piece of legislation to emerge from so much talent and effort. Then if the legislature in only one state should adopt it, some good would have been accomplished, and when a number of states adopt it, a great stride will have been taken toward the protection of family life.

But do not think that when we get new divorce laws of the right kind the problem will be licked. The ABA committee cannot emphasize too strongly that laws alone solve no problems. It is the way a law is enforced, carried out, administered, that can make it a good law or a bad law.

The kind of law the ABA committee is thinking about would be worthless without the right kind of courts to administer it—the new-type Family Court. But the court would not be something made of stone or brick or mortar. It would be people—the trained specialists and their helpers. Everything would depend on the quality of the people. And the quality of the people would depend on their employer and superior officer, their judge. Thus everything would depend on the quality of the judge.

It is easier to stem a flood at the source than at the outlet. So the ABA committee has been thinking about marriage laws too.

England has a new provision in its divorce law affecting marriage. It forbids any person to seek divorce until after three years of marriage. This law was passed at least partly in the hope of putting the brakes on the hasty and ill-considered marriage. If Jane knows full well that when she marries John she will be stuck with him at least three years before she can get rid of him legally—no matter what a villain he may turn out to be— chances are she will use her head a little bit more, investigate a little more carefully, before plunging into matrimony. The ABA committee, knowing that close to one-fifth of American divorces occur while the parties have been married less than three years, believes this English plan is worthy of consideration.

Moreover, there must be some strengthening of our marriage laws. As the law now stands, if Jane and John can't get married when and where they want to, they never have to wait long or go very far or spend very much to get around the law where they live. Into the next county or across the state line they go and back they come married.

I call these elopements or runaways "migratory marriages." I mean a marriage in which the license is obtained or the ceremony performed in some place where neither Jane nor John lives. Few people realize how common this is or what a bad thing it is. In the last 12,000 divorce cases coming before me one out of three followed a migratory marriage!

Many times the evidence in court shows that the migratory marriage was not, in fact, a true marriage. Of the three things necessary to make a marriage, persons, sex, and duration—two were conspicuously absent. Sometimes almost any person of just a few hours' acquaintance would do. And the matter of duration or permanence was farthest from their thoughts. What the parties wanted above all else was to go to bed together without danger of interference.

So Jane and John slip off to their Gretna Green and call upon the state (through its marriage-license clerk and its justice of the peace) or the church (through some not-so-careful parson). And these agencies for sickly sentimental reasons—"all the world loves a lover"—or for money reasons, become parties to the evil transaction by giving their license and sanction and blessing, not to true marriage, but to legalized fornication. The ABA committee suggests that some attention be paid to a uniform law to curb the vicious migratory marriage.

The ABA committee recognizes the importance of education for marriage, but does not believe it is a cure-all. John and Jane once insisted upon consulting me under the mistaken notion I was a family counselor. Their marriage was fast going to pieces. This John was a Ph.D. and Jane had a master's degree. I got out books, pamphlets, articles. They had read them all. They knew the answers better than some of the authors. They had taken courses in college. Yet despite all their education their marriage ultimately crashed. Why? Because they didn't really want it to succeed.

So the ABA committee sees the need for something beyond mere education. For want of a better term it might be called inspiration. All the education in the books is useless unless Jane and John are inspired with an imperishable desire, an unquenchable urge to make a go of their marriage.

Of course the best education and inspiration for marriage stem from the church in the first instance, and from the home. The trouble is that the church just simply doesn't reach large segments of our population. In the past three years less than 10 per cent of the thousands seeking divorce before me have admitted that they attended any church—much less that they were communicants of any religious faith.

As to the home, the cold, hard fact is that too many parents are inadequate —just simply not equipped to do a good job of education and inspiration for marriage. If otherwise, where do all our divorce seekers come from?

When Jane and John appear at the window to apply for a license to enter upon the all-important career of marriage, all the state requires of them is that they have two dollars. In most states they also must pass a blood test to prove they do not have syphilis, but none to prove they are free from a hundred other diseases of soul or mind as well as body which could be far more damaging than syphilis.

The state is adversely affected by marriage failure. Every time a home is broken the state is hurt, as well as the children and the spouses. So why is it illogical for the state to step in and meet the deficiencies of the home and take care of those whom the church can't reach, by requiring preparation for the career of marriage—by compulsory education and inspiration for marriage? Many thoughtful persons have reached the conclusion that the state has not only the right but the duty to require a reasonable degree of education and inspiration for marriage on the part of each couple applying for a marriage license before issuing such license and conferring upon them the legal status of marriage.

The committee of the American Bar Association—an organization of over 40,000 of the country's leading lawyers—started by thinking about divorce from its beginning, getting right back to bedrock. Its principal aim is to protect family life by making our divorce laws helpful, not harmful; constructive, not destructive; preventive, not punitive. The unhappy folks who wind up in divorce court have for the most part been living in hell. What they need is not more hell, but help.

MEDICINE FOR SICK MARRIAGES *

Alarmed by the growing divorce rate and taking advantage of the volume of research about the family, interested citizens have created family counseling agencies, both public and private, in many American communities. Such agencies are so new that their philosophy and procedures are not yet standardized. But they have one common goal—to "save" marriages before the couples seek the divorce court. To indicate at least one philosophy and some of the methods of such an agency we now turn to a case study of a family in trouble. Our question might well be: If we had enough such agencies, could we hope to stem the tide of divorce?

Reorganization of a Family

Conflicts which, if continued, would undermine the unity of the family are generally solved by its members without obtaining outside advice. Certain critical situations, however, may arise with which the husband and wife or parents and children are unable to cope without assistance. The transition from a rural to an urban way of life has resulted in the rise of agencies like the marriage-counseling center and the child-guidance clinic to help the family solve its problems. The following case shows how a marriage-counseling center gave skilled and individualized consultation and treatment to a couple faced with a problem of marital adjustment:

First interview: Mr. Y and Mrs. Y came into the Marriage Counsel office and, at their request, were seen together. Mr. Y is six years older than his wife, and they have similar educational and religious backgrounds. Since Mr. Y's father died seven years ago, he has been the sole support of his mother, his brother, and his sister. Mrs. Y and her mother-in-law have had a most difficult time adjusting to each other.

Mr. Y's mother is a very dominating woman and speaks of her children as "babies." She controls them in every way possible and has kept them from mature development. Mr. Y had found it most difficult to contemplate marriage in view of his intense tie with his mother. During the five years before their marriage, when he was keeping company with Mrs. Y, he was never able to introduce his fiancee to his mother, or able to dis-

---

* Ernest W. Burgess and Harvey J. Locke, *The Family* (American Book Company, 1953), pp. 644–49. Except for an introductory paragraph and some concluding generalizations, the reading is composed of a case prepared especially for the authors by Mrs. Emily Hartshorn Mudd, director of the Marriage Counsel of Philadelphia.

cuss his problem with his fiancee. After a year and a half of marriage, he now recognizes that he will have to change his relationship with his mother if he is to establish a satisfactory relationship with his wife. As his wife puts it, "He really wants to make a break emotionally from his mother, but he hasn't got the guts."

Mr. Y explained, "We seem to be hitting a snag in relation to my mother. We get along beautifully in every other way. Mother has been most uncooperative and has made it very difficult for my wife." The counselor remarked that he seemed to be involved with two conflicting sets of responsibilities. He immediately answered that his first responsibility was to his wife. The counselor asked if he could withdraw his financial aid to his family. He said that this would place an undue hardship on his mother, as his sister and brother could not handle it.

Interviewed separately, Mrs. Y stated that, from the time she first knew her husband, he never really wanted to get married. It was always difficult for him to talk about taking her to meet his mother and to tell his mother about her. "His mother's thoughts are always his thoughts." Each time Mrs. Y came to see her mother-in-law she did all in her power to win her over with presents and to help her with the housework, but to no avail.

In talking with Mr. Y individually, the counselor pointed out the problem his wife was having in accepting his sense of responsibility for his family and asked if he, too, was not disturbed by the struggle. Mr. Y answered that he should never have gotten married, and that he always had a feeling of responsibility for his mother which is different from that of most men. The counselor asked if he would like to do anything about it. Mr. Y feels that this problem will interfere with all of their married life and that if it is possible to work it out, he would like to get help.

Both Mr. Y and Mrs. Y were rated by the Attitude Evaluation Scale. Mrs. Y's rating of —3 showed that she seemed to have in some degree many of the characteristics or attitudes which indicate difficulty in carrying on a constructive close relationship with other persons. Mr. Y's rating of +4 seemed to indicate more of the characteristics which make getting along with other people possible and constructive.

Second interview with Mrs. Y: Mrs. Y is exceedingly concerned about her whole married future and is becoming more and more pessimistic. She is beginning to feel that the problem is really with her and that she is about to have a nervous breakdown.

Third interview with Mrs. Y (two months later): Mrs. Y seems much happier. She couldn't say enough about the improvement both in herself and her husband. She knows that he is co-operating. Her brother-in-law is now working, which is unusual. Her husband has reduced his contribution to his family by $25 a month and is now about to take off another $25. "I am going to have to push him a bit on this, but I don't want to tackle it now, as it is our anniversary month. I have not been visiting his family; he goes about every ten days and tells me what he thinks I would like to know."

Mrs. Y isn't returning to her work, and this has created a real difference in their relationship. The first months of married life she was working and carrying a large share of financing the home. When she gave up her job her husband put great pressure on her to go back, which she did. But when they moved to Philadelphia she avoided facing the issue, and just didn't take a job. He is now beginning to see her in a different role. He likes the meals she cooks, is beginning to appreciate the home she is making for him, is taking much more interest in the house, and is constantly bringing home little knickknacks. They are now budgeting their money. They have been able to work this out comfortably, and are both thoroughly enjoying the sense of security it gives them.

In the last part of the interview Mrs. Y attempted to understand the difference now in their relationship. Previously she had always resented the fact that she had to furnish so much financial support for the home. However, she had never trusted her husband sufficiently to let him take over that responsibility. Last fall when their marriage came so close to going on the rocks, Mr. Y did a great deal to hold it together and change their relationship. Mrs. Y recognized his ability in working out the various situations and their complications.

Fourth interview with Mrs. Y: Mrs. Y described a painful and humiliating visit to Mr. Y, who was ill in the hospital. Both she and her mother-in-law had unintentionally arrived at the hospital at the same time. The mother-in-law shrieked and loudly accused her of many things. Mr. Y ignored this outburst, but Mrs. Y was "burnt up." As retribution, she wanted to force three specific demands on Mr. Y. The counselor pointed out the number of times Mrs. Y had compelled her husband to choose between his mother and her and that every time this issue was forced it resulted in greater mental conflict for her husband and, consequently, in greater discomfort for her. It was suggested that while there were certain issues she undoubtedly had to stand on, it was not wise to create an issue when she was feeling bitter.

Fifth interview with Mrs. Y: Mrs. Y expressed more dissatisfaction with Mr. Y's family and his attitude toward them, saying, "He can see things from only one angle." The counselor discussed with Mrs. Y the question of whether she was not trying too hard to make her husband's family into something she could like. Her desperate attempts to find her brother-in-law a job and her bitterness about his lack of gratitude were mentioned. The counselor brought out that, as hard as it was to accept the fact, Mr. Y's mother would never like her and that Mrs. Y would never like the mother-in-law. Also, Mr. Y would always be in the unhappy position of having to defend one against the other. Today, for the first time, Mrs. Y seemed to understand what the counselor was talking about and moved into an acceptance of the hard facts. Mrs. Y said that her husband had mentioned his desire to come to the Marriage Counsel.

Second interview with Mr. Y (several weeks after his wife's fifth interview): The counselor was amazed at the change in Mr. Y. He seems so much more certain of himself, so much more sure of his marriage, and faces the future with much confidence and courage. "I don't know that we will ever really iron out all our problems, but we are beginning to get started in working together and much of the bickering and upset has gone."

Mr. Y gave his version of the visit from his wife and his mother while he was in the hospital. He had looked forward to it, but "It was only intense pain for me. I was left feeling their hate for each other means more to them than their love for me." There followed a long discussion of the need to take into consideration the hate his mother and wife feel toward each other. The counselor suggested that perhaps he would have to face the fact that these two women never could accept each other. Perhaps his disillusionment would be less if he expected less from them. Mr. Y admitted that since the last interview he has come a long way in accepting this.

He feels that his wife has gotten much out of her interviews. It has meant much to her that she could pour out her feelings to a neutral person.

Sixth interview with Mrs. Y (immediately following above interview with Mr. Y and including him): Mrs. Y and her husband kissed each other fondly as they met in the interview room. The counselor restated the conclusion that as hard as we might want to help Mrs. Y to accept her mother-in-law and become fond of her, and her mother-in-law to become fond of Mrs. Y, it was almost a hopeless effort. Both Mr. Y and Mrs. Y agreed that in accepting this fact they were going a long way to remove the need to change it. The counselor repeated what each one had told her of their feelings about the hospital episode. Mrs. Y's resentment because of her husband's apparent preference for his mother was so keen that she had not been able even to consider his feelings. Mr. Y's resentment against the two women was so strong that he didn't really care how they were feeling. At no point had he been able to express his real feelings for his wife. Mr. Y and Mrs. Y then were able to discuss their feelings about the whole episode with warmth, understanding, and appreciation of each other's point of view.

Summary: This case illustrates the inevitable conflict which ensues when a man old enough and intellectually able to woo a wife and to establish a home is still tied emotionally to an overly possessive and jealous mother. He has never been allowed the opportunity to develop into an independent, mature individual; and, therefore, until he grows up he can never give to his mate the sharing, give-and-take, and mutually respecting love relationship which would bring to her the security she desires and needs. Without such security the wife feels continuously threatened and rejected. These feelings induce anxiety and fear, which in turn breed resentment, anger, and hate. She tries to force change by the very vehemence of her will, and when change does not ensue, her negative feelings are turned against herself and she becomes depressed and finally feels she must escape from an intolerable situation—her marriage.

The counselor recognized that both Mr. Y and Mrs. Y were lonely and anxious. She made them feel that she was interested and that she cared what happened to them. She allowed them, individually, an opportunity to express freely their resentment, anger, and aggression without fear of condemnation or manipulation.

Once relieved of much of these negative feelings, Mr. Y and Mrs. Y were able to develop new and constructive attitudes. By being able to discuss their problems together with the counselor, Mr. Y and Mrs. Y gained confidence in their own and in each other's true strength and ability. They now felt an assurance of their potentialities for making a success of their marriage, even though the conditions that had previously existed remained essentially the same.

The problem of the marital adjustment of the husband and the wife was complicated by deep personality and cultural problems with origins in their early childhood experiences in the family. The resolution of these and other conflicts generally involves the reshaping of attitudes and the redefinition of conceptions of roles of the husband and the wife.

Family reorganization is not a matter merely of the sum total of the readjustment of individual families. In America, as in other modern societies, modifications of attitudes, expectations, and roles are continuously taking place. Families and their members are interacting in situations that undermine traditional behavior and introduce modes of action adaptive to the new situation. The resulting general trend in family relationships is from the institutional to the companionship pattern.

Certain questions call for an answer in considering family reorganization: What is the relation of disorganization to reorganization? To what extent does the reshaping of the family take place without social intervention? Is governmental provision desirable and feasible to insure the economic security of the family, thereby decreasing its instability? Should conscious and concerted efforts be made to insure family welfare through education, religion, counseling, and research?

———————◄•••►———————

CHAPTER SIX

Racial and Cultural Minorities

"WE RESERVE the right to refuse service to anyone." Such a sign tacked above the counter in a restaurant may seem reasonable enough. But ask any Negro what it means and you will learn that it is a symbol of a highly emotional and controversial American problem. Or note the resort hotel advertisements in a New York paper—"churches nearby," "congenial atmosphere," "selected clientele," "club plan," "distinctive clientele," "screened clientele." These, too, sound innocent. But ask any well-traveled Jew— he can tell you what they mean.

And some of our "hints" aren't so subtle. There are such things as death-dealing bombs exploded in the home of a Negro schoolteacher in Florida, the broken and bleeding body of a bewildered Mexican boy on a Los Angeles street, the majority vote of a California community telling a Chinese-American war veteran that he is not wanted as a neighbor in the home he has purchased. Then there are fiery crosses and white-robed terrorists in Georgia.

Much as we would like to believe it is, the contemporary American scene is *not* all sweetness and light. American democracy is not complete, and one of its most obvious deficiencies is in the treatment of various racial, religious, and ethnic minority groups. The results of prejudice and bigotry are widespread and damaging. Human misery, wasted manpower, twisted personalities, and international disrepute are a part of the harvest of discrimination.

The sources of prejudice have been explored by many authorities. Evidence has been amassed to show that personal insecurity, the force of tradition, an exploitive capitalism, ignorance of facts, stereotyping, "social psychoses," and other factors, either singly or in combination, explain the presence of prejudice.

In the accounts that follow we shall center our attention on the contemporary scene and explore the nature and extent of American prejudices, particularly as they result in discriminatory practices. Just how far from America's democratic ideals are the behavior patterns of its citizens? Can the two be brought into agreement? What methods, if any, will hasten the process of change in attitudes and actions? What is to be the future of race and minority relations in the United States?

Problem 18: Democratic Equality- Myth or Goal?

Many well-meaning Americans feel that democratic theory was and is intended only for white, Protestant, Anglo-Saxon Americans. They reject with impatience or violence any suggestion that Negroes, Jews, Orientals, Indians, or later immigrant groups should have full and equal rights and privileges. But a democracy that grudgingly grants second-class citizenship to some fifty-five or sixty million of its one hundred and sixty million people is a democracy in a very limited sense. In this section we glance at the scientific truths concerning race and review the basic assumptions of American ideology, particularly as it pertains to minority groups. We also examine reality—the actual status of minorities. The central question is, Do present practices deny the democratic ideology that Americans profess?

MEN ARE MORE ALIKE *

Modern racial and minority tensions are rooted deep in custom, folklore, and superstition, rather than in scientific fact. Nevertheless, these beliefs at times have all the apparent validity of truth, and students concerned with problems in this area should review the facts. Below, in short compass, is summarized the little we actually know about physical and racial differences in man.

Men are all vertebrates and mammals. They are all multicellular animals with the same kinds of nervous, blood, respiratory, and reproductive

* Boyd C. Shafer, *The American Historical Review*, April, 1952, pp. 599–604.

systems. The same approximate percentages of chemical elements make up their bodies. So long as there are males and females reproduction between all varieties is possible, even probable. Their females all carry their young nine months and usually produce only one offspring at a time. Maturation for all offspring is comparatively slow. Unlike all other animals the desire of their adults for sexual activity is continuous: the adult male is normally capable of reproducing at any time and the adult female of about fifteen to forty-five years of age twelve times a year. Probably none of them, Lysenko notwithstanding, can inherit acquired characteristics. All of them, regardless of race or nationality, have the same few O, A, B, and AB blood types. Though learned studies use terms like brachycephalic and dolichocephalic their head shapes vary little, all being somewhat oblong. While their hair is round or oblong and straight or kinky, it is hair, and all usually have it in slightly varying intensities at the same points on their bodies. Their coloration runs from white to black but all gradations exist, while microscopic examinations shows but slight difference in pigmentation and even these differences seem rapidly to be fading.

Where differences occur, little is known of what they signify. On the basis of fact no one can say whether color, hair, head shape, or blood type have any relationship to the quality of a man, to his character, philosophy, and intelligence, or to how he will react in any circumstance. Observable differences like these may be easily classified and the classifications statistically presented in impressive, encyclopedic volumes. That is all. These particular differences occur. Nothing more can be added, no more meaning can be attached to them.

In intelligence, to be sure, the gap between moron and genius may be as wide as Galton's studies and Binet's tests have shown. But both occur in all national groupings, and the gap between them is not as wide as between man, moron or genius, and other forms of life. All men above the imbecilic seem to have greater facility, though they may not use it, for reflective intelligence than do the smartest chimpanzees. On the other hand all are a bit short of omniscient gods. Further, it is impossible to disentangle the environmental factors in the formation of intelligence. No one knows to what extent intelligence is a product of a good diet and to what extent it is a part of the inherited physiological structure of the individual. Nor does anyone know whether any particular kinds of intelligence are universally superior. In some primitive forest situations, in contemporary American college football, or in modern warfare, success most likely comes to the physically well-coordinated individual whom the imaginative poet might rightly consider dull and insensitive. As with intelligence so with emotions. All human creatures have the capacity for love, hate, and anger. While the depths and heights of their natures differ, capacity is common to all. The potential range and depth is greater in man than in any other animal, and which capacity is best in each situation has not been determined. . . .

What has been said above of the physiological diversities among men can be applied with greater force to the differences among the so-called races. We know that intelligence, emotional capacity, and bodily structure and size vary widely *within* each race. We also have solid grounds for believing that so far as we are able to measure these characteristics as well as other less obvious ones, they differ more widely within each race than they do from race to race. In all human characteristics there is overlapping among all races; the alleged differences are chiefly in statistical averages which hide the basic similarities.

That intelligent men should base any serious argument concerning men upon race is as absurd as to base diplomacy upon the consideration that one man likes his cottage cheese with garlic and another with onion. As everyone who reads can know, all races have ceaselessly intermixed and have become so "impure" that almost all the peculiarities of any importance ascribed to membership in these groupings are the fabrication of wish fancy. Ralph Linton, the anthropologist, neatly put it: "There is no human group whose ancestry is known for even five generations in the exact terms necessary for racial determinations."

In his zeal to make Christians out of heathens Paul preached that God "made of one blood all the nations of men for to dwell on all the face of the earth." His real converts at Athens may not have been many; his biology and sociology were good. Race usually cannot be distinguished because of visible, physical signs such as size, shape, or even color. Much less can it be determined by character and intelligence or any of the more esoteric classifications of dissimilarities. Conceivably, fundamental differences may be discovered. Our present scientific tools do not reveal them —even between "Slavic" Russians and "Anglo-Saxon" Americans. One may be able to tell something about a man by his shoes or by his color. The French children of the Third Republic, like the German children of the Third Reich, were told that their ancestors "were very tall, their eyes blue, and their hair was blond." The only known fact is that no one can know *who his* ancestors were nor can any group determine them with any exactitude except that they were men and before that—.

Few if any of the so-called racial characteristics tell anything of importance about a *man*. Men have been encyclopedically catalogued as to hair form and color, skin pigmentation, eye color and shape, stature, head form, size and structure of bones, and the way the head sits on the shoulders. What does this all mean? Simply that in these specific physical ways individual men vary and for this or that group there is a slightly different mean or average or deviation for each of the *particular* physical parts of the body. To ascribe greater weight to these differences than this would be as wrong as to assert that all men are exactly alike because all their bodily temperatures average around 98.6 degrees.

Systematic theories of racial differences are of recent origin, dating back for the most part only to the eighteenth century when it was becoming more important to be superior and powerful than to go to Heaven. The theories (they are only that by the grace of inaccurate terminology) have varied widely in time and often with the race or nationality of the investigator. Moreover, racial characters, if they exist, seem to have changed quite unbelievably through the years. Once ("Nordic") England was called "merry" but that was not the England of Attlee and Cripps. Once a Venetian ambassador spoke of the "low morals and excellent cooking" of the English but that was in the sixteenth not the nineteenth century. In praising folly, Erasmus spoke of the martial reputation of the ("Mediterranean") Spaniards, a characteristic few would accuse them of possessing in our times. Once what we call the northern Europeans ("Nordics?") were supposed to be "full of spirit" but unintelligent (Aristotle); the modern version is quite different. None of this proves that theories based upon race are completely untrue. It shows only that there is nothing scientific or God-given about them and that they are for the most part merely *a priori* guesses of men about other men. . . .

———◀••▶———

TO SECURE THESE RIGHTS *

Just what is the "race problem" in America? Most observers seem to agree that race relations are a problem because of the wide gap between American democratic ideology on the one hand and the undemocratic treatment of various minority groups on the other. This century-long lag in moral behavior is described in the opening portion of the report of the President's Committee on Civil Rights, which follows. The committee, appointed by President Truman to investigate the status of civil rights in America, was composed of distinguished scholars, private citizens, and public servants. Its comprehensive account indicates the nature and seriousness of the problem of civil rights, particularly as it applies to minority groups.

---

* *To Secure These Rights,* Report of the President's Committee on Civil Rights (Government Printing Office, 1947), pp. 1–10.

The American Heritage: The Promise of Freedom, Equality

In the time that it takes to read this report, 1,000 Americans will be born. These new Americans will come into families whose religious faiths are a roster of all those which men hold sacred. Their names will be strange and varied, echoes from every corner of the world. Their skins will range in color from black to white. A few will be born to riches, more to average comfort, and too many to poverty. All of them will be Americans.

These new Americans, drawn from all of the races of mankind, provide a challenge to our American democracy. We have a great heritage of freedom and equality for all men, sometimes called "the American way." Yet we cannot avoid the knowledge that the American ideal still awaits complete realization. . . .

If we are to judge with accuracy how far short we have fallen in living up to the ideals which comprise our American heritage of freedom and equality, we must first make it clear what that heritage is.

The Ideal of Freedom and Equality

The central theme in our American heritage is the importance of the individual person. From the earliest moment of our history we have believed that every human being has an essential dignity and integrity which must be respected and safeguarded. Moreover, we believe that the welfare of the individual is the final goal of group life. Our American heritage further teaches that to be secure in the rights he wishes for himself, each man must be willing to respect the rights of other men. This is the conscious recognition of a basic moral principle: that all men are created equal as well as free. Stemming from this principle is the obligation to build social institutions that will guarantee equality of opportunity to all men. Without this equality freedom becomes an illusion. Thus the only aristocracy that is consistent with the free way of life is an aristocracy of talent and achievement. The grounds on which our society accords respect, influence or reward to each of its citizens must be limited to the quality of his personal character and of his social contribution.

This concept of equality which is so vital a part of the American heritage knows no kinship with notions of human uniformity or regimentation. We abhor the totalitarian arrogance which makes one man say that he will respect another man as his equal only if he has "*my* race, *my* religion, *my* political views, *my* social position." In our land men are equal, but they are free to be different. From these very differences among our people has come the great human and national strength of America.

Thus, the aspirations and achievements of each member of our society are to be limited only by the skills and energies he brings to the opportunities equally offered to all Americans. We can tolerate no restrictions upon the individual which depend upon irrelevant factors such as his race, his color, his religion or the social position to which he is born.

Government and Freedom

The men who founded our Republic, as those who have built any constitutional democracy, faced the task of reconciling personal liberty and group authority, or of establishing an equilibrium between them. In a democratic state we recognize that the common interests of the people must be managed by laws and procedures established by majority rule. But a democratic majority, left unrestrained, may be as ruthless and tyrannical as were the earlier absolute monarchs. Seeing this clearly, and fearing it greatly, our forefathers built a constitutional system in which valued personal liberties, carefully enumerated in a Bill of Rights, were placed beyond the reach of popular majorities. Thus the people permanently denied the federal government power to interfere with certain personal rights and freedoms.

Freedom, however, as we now use the term, means even more than the traditional "freedoms" listed in our Bill of Rights—important as they are. Freedom has come to mean the right of a man to manage his own affairs as he sees fit up to the point where what he does interferes with the equal rights of others in the community to manage their affairs—or up to the point where he begins to injure the welfare of the whole group. It is clear that in modern democratic society a man's freedom in this broader sense is not and cannot be absolute—nor does it exist in a vacuum—but instead is hedged about by the competing rights of others and the demands of the social welfare. In this context it is government which must referee the clashes which arise among the freedoms of citizens, and protect each citizen in the enjoyment of the maximum freedom to which he is entitled.

There is no essential conflict between freedom and government. Bills of rights restrain government from abridging individual civil liberties, while government itself by sound legislative policies protects citizens against the aggressions of others seeking to push their freedoms too far. Thus in the words of the Declaration of Independence, "Man is endowed by his Creator with certain inalienable rights. Among these are life, liberty, and the pursuit of happiness. To secure these rights, *governments are instituted among men.*"

The Essential Rights

The rights essential to the citizen in a free society can be described in different words and in varying orders. The three great rights of the Declaration of Independence have just been mentioned. Another noble statement is made in the Bill of Rights of our Constitution. A more recent formulation is found in the Four Freedoms.

Four basic rights have seemed important to this Committee and have influenced its labors. We believe that each of these rights in essential to the well-being of the individual and to the progress of society.

1. The Right to Safety and Security of the Person

Freedom can exist only where the citizen is assured that his person is secure against bondage, lawless violence, and arbitrary arrest and punishment. Freedom from slavery in all its forms is clearly necessary if all men are to have equal opportunity to use their talents and to lead worthwhile lives. Moreover, to be free, men must be subject to discipline by society only for commission of offenses clearly defined by law and only after trial by due process of law. Where the administration of justice is discriminatory, no man can be sure of security. Where the threat of violence by private persons or mobs exists, a cruel inhibition of the sense of freedom of activity and security of the person inevitably results. Where a society permits private and arbitrary violence to be done to its members, its own integrity is inevitably corrupted. It cannot permit human beings to be imprisoned or killed in the absence of due process of law without degrading its entire fabric.

2. The Right to Citizenship and Its Privileges

Since it is a purpose of government in a democracy to regulate the activity of each man in the interest of all men, it follows that every mature and responsible person must be able to enjoy full citizenship and have an equal voice in his government. Because the right to participate in the political process is customarily limited to citizens there can be no denial of access to citizenship based upon race, color, creed, or national origin. Denial of citizenship for these reasons cheapens the personality of those who are confined to this inferior status and endangers the whole concept of a democratic society.

To deny qualified citizens the right to vote while others exercise it is to do violence to the principle of freedom and equality. Without the right to vote, the individual loses his voice in the group effort and is subjected to rule by a body from which he has been excluded. Likewise, the right of the individual to vote is important to the group itself. Democracy assumes that the majority is more likely as a general rule to make decisions which are wise and desirable from the point of view of the interests of the whole society than is any minority. Every time a qualified person is denied a voice in public affairs, one of the components of a potential majority is lost, and the formation of a sound public policy is endangered.

To the citizen in a democracy, freedom is a precious possession. Accordingly, all able-bodied citizens must enjoy the right to serve the nation and the cause of freedom in time of war. Any attempt to curb the right to fight in its defense can only lead the citizen to question the worth of the society in which he lives. A sense of frustration is created which is wholly alien to the normal emotions of a free man. In particular, any discrimination which, while imposing an obligation, prevents members of minority groups from rendering full military service in defense of their country is for them a peculiarly humiliating badge of inferiority. The nation also suffers a loss of manpower and is unable to marshal maximum strength at a moment when such strength is most needed.

3. The Right to Freedom of Conscience and Expression

In a free society there is faith in the ability of the people to make sound, rational judgments. But such judgments are possible only where the people have access to all relevant facts and to all prevailing interpretations of the facts. How can such judgments be formed on a sound basis if arguments, viewpoints, or opinions are arbitrarily suppressed? How can the concept of the market place of thought in which truth ultimately prevails retain its validity if the thought of certain individuals is denied the right of circulation? The Committee reaffirms our tradition that freedom of expression may be curbed by law only where the danger to the well-being of society is clear and present.

Our forefathers fought bloody wars and suffered torture and death for the right to worship God according to the varied dictates of conscience. Complete religious liberty has been accepted as an unquestioned personal freedom since our Bill of Rights was adopted. We have insisted only that religious freedom may not be pleaded as an excuse for criminal or clearly anti-social conduct.

4. The Right to Equality of Opportunity

It is not enough that full and equal membership in society entitles the individual to an equal voice in the control of his government; it must also give him the right to enjoy the benefits of society and to contribute to its progress. The opportunity of each individual to obtain useful employment, and to have access to services in the fields of education, housing, health, recreation and transportation whether available free or at a price, must be provided with complete disregard for race, color, creed, and national origin. Without this equality of opportunity the individual is deprived of the chance to develop his potentialities and to share the fruits of society. The group also suffers through the loss of the contributions which might have been made by persons excluded from the main channels of social and economic activity.

The Heritage and the Reality

Our American heritage of freedom and equality has given us prestige among the nations of the world and a strong feeling of national pride at home. There is much reason for that pride. But pride is no substitute for steady and honest performance, and the record shows that at varying times in American history the gulf between ideals and practice has been wide. We have had human slavery. We have had religious persecution. We have had mob rule. We still have their ideological remnants in the unwarrantable "pride and prejudice" of some of our people and practices.

From our work as a Committee, we have learned much that has shocked us, and much that has made us ashamed. But we have seen nothing to shake our conviction that the civil rights of the American people—all of them—can be strengthened quickly and effectively by the normal processes of democratic, constitutional government. That strengthening, we believe, will make our daily life more and more consonant with the spirit of the American heritage of freedom. But it will require as much courage, as much imagination, as much perseverance as anything which we have ever done together. The members of this Committee reaffirm their faith in the American heritage and in its promise. . . .

AN AMERICAN DILEMMA *

The word *dilemma* may be defined as a situation involving two alternative courses of action, either of which, if followed, brings dissatisfaction. Gunnar Myrdal, a Swedish social scientist brought to this country to study the role of the Negro in American life, gave the title *An American Dilemma* to his work, which is probably the most thorough and comprehensive account of the race problem in America.

* Gunnar Myrdal, *An American Dilemma* (Harper, 1944), Vol. I, pp. xli–31 (excerpts). Copyright, 1944, by Harper and Brothers.

The excerpts that follow are taken from the early portions of the book and indicate the philosophical framework in which Myrdal cast the problem.

The Negro Problem as a Moral Issue

There is a "Negro problem" in the United States and most Americans are aware of it, although it assumes varying forms and intensity in different regions of the country and among diverse groups of the American people. Americans have to react to it, politically as citizens and, where there are Negroes present in the community, privately as neighbors.

To the great majority of white Americans the Negro problem has distinctly negative connotations. It suggests something difficult to settle and equally difficult to leave alone. It is embarrassing. It makes for moral uneasiness. The very presence of the Negro in America, his fate in this country through slavery, Civil War and Reconstruction; his recent career and his present status; his accommodation; his protest and his aspiration; in fact his entire biological, historical and social existence as a participant American represent to the ordinary white man in the North as well as in the South an anomaly in the very structure of American society. To many, this takes on the proportion of a menace—biological, economic, social, cultural, and at times, political. This anxiety may be mingled with a feeling of individual and collective guilt. A few see the problem as a challenge to statesmanship. To all it is a trouble.

These and many other mutually inconsistent attitudes are blended into none too logical a scheme which, in turn, may be quite inconsistent with the wider personal, moral, religious, and civic sentiments and ideas of the Americans. Now and then, even the least sophisticated individual becomes aware of his own confusion and the contradiction in his attitudes. Occasionally he may recognize, even if only for a moment, the incongruence of his state of mind and find it so intolerable that the whole organization of his moral precepts is shaken. But most people, most of the time, suppress such threats to their moral integrity together with all of the confusion, the ambiguity, and inconsistency which lurks in the basement of man's soul. This, however, is rarely accomplished without mental strain. Out of the strain comes a sense of uneasiness and awkwardness which always seems attached to the Negro problem.

The strain is increased in democratic America by the freedom left open—even in the South, to a considerable extent—for the advocates of the Negro, his rights and welfare. All "pro-Negro" forces in American society, whether organized or not and irrespective of their wide differences in both strategy and tactics, sense that this is the situation. They all work on the national conscience. They all seek to fix everybody's attention on the suppressed moral conflict. No wonder they are often regarded as public nuisances, or worse—even when they succeed in getting grudging concessions to Negro rights and welfare.

. . . Moralism and rationalism are to many of us—among them the author of this book—the glory of the nation, its youthful strength, perhaps the salvation of mankind. The analysis of (the) "American Creed" and its implications have an important place in our inquiry. While on the one hand, to such a moralistic and rationalistic being as the ordinary American, the Negro problem and his own confused and contradictory attitudes toward it must be disturbing; on the other hand, the very mass of unsettled problems in his heterogeneous and changing culture, and the inherited liberalistic trust that things will ultimately take care of themselves and get settled in one way or another, enable the ordinary American to live on happily, with recognized contradictions around him and within him, in a kind of bright fatalism which is unmatched in the rest of the Western world. This fatalism . . . belongs to the national *ethos*.

The American Negro problem is a problem in the heart of the American. It is there that the interracial tension has its focus. It is there that the decisive struggle goes on. . . . Though our study includes economic, social, and political race relations, at bottom our problem is the moral dilemma of the American—the conflict between his moral valuation on various levels of consciousness and generality. The "American Dilemma," referred to in the title of this book, is the ever-raging conflict between, on the one hand, the valuations preserved on the general plane which we shall call the "American Creed," where the American thinks, talks, and acts under the influence of high national and Christian precepts, and, on the other hand, the valuations on specific planes of individual and group living, where personal and local interests; economic, social, and sexual jealousies; considerations of community prestige and conformity; group prejudice against particular persons or types of people; and all sorts of miscellaneous wants, impulses, and habits dominate his outlook.

Valuations and Beliefs

The Negro problem in America would be of a different nature, and, indeed, would be simpler to handle scientifically, if the moral conflict raged only between valuations held by different persons and groups of persons. The essence of the moral situation is, however, that the conflicting valuations are also held by the same person. The moral struggle goes on within people and not only between them. As people's valuations are conflicting, behavior normally becomes a moral compromise. There are no homogeneous "attitudes" behind human behavior but a mesh of struggling inclinations, interests, and ideals, some held conscious and some suppressed for long intervals but all active in bending behavior in their direction.

The unity of a culture consists in the fact that all valuations are mutually shared in some degree. . . . In America as everywhere else people agree, as an abstract proposition, that the more general valuations—those which refer to man as such and not to any particular group or temporary situation—are morally higher. These valuations are also given the sanction of religion and national legislation. They are incorporated into the American Creed. The other valuations—which refer to various smaller groups of mankind or to particular occasions—are commonly referred to as "irrational" or "prejudiced," sometimes even by people who express and stress them. They are defended in terms of tradition, expediency, or utility.

Trying to defend their behavior to others, and primarily to themselves, people will attempt to conceal the conflict between their different valuations of what is desirable and undesirable, right or wrong, by keeping away some valuations from awareness and by focusing attention on others. For the same opportune purpose, people will twist and mutilate their beliefs of how social reality actually is. In our study we encounter whole systems of firmly entrenched popular beliefs concerning the Negro and his relations to the larger society, which are bluntly false and which can only be understood when we remember the opportunistic *ad hoc* purposes they serve. These "popular theories," because of the rationalizing function they serve, are heavily loaded with emotions. But people also want to be rational. Scientific truth-seeking and education are slowly rectifying the beliefs and thereby also influencing the valuations. In a rationalistic civilization it is not only that the beliefs are shaped by the valuations, but also that the valuations depend upon the beliefs.

A White Man's Problem

Although the Negro problem is a moral issue both to Negroes and to whites in America, we shall in this book have to give primary attention to what goes on in the minds of white Americans. To explain this direction of our interest a general conclusion from our studies needs to be stated at this point. When the present writer started his inquiry, his preconception was that it had to be focused on the Negro people and their peculiarities. . . . But as he proceeded in his studies into the Negro problem it became increasingly evident that little, if anything, could be scientifically explained in terms of the peculiarities of the Negroes themselves.

As a matter of fact, in their basic human traits the Negroes are inherently not much different from other people. Neither are, incidentally, the white Americans. But Negroes and whites in the United States live in singular human relations with each other.   All the circumstances of life—the "environmental" conditions in the broadest meaning of that term—diverge more from the normal for the Negroes than for the whites, if only because of the statistical fact that the Negroes are the smaller group.   The average Negro must experience many times more of the "abnormal" interracial relations than the average white man in America.   The more important fact, however, is that practically all the economic, social, and political power is held by whites.   The Negroes do not by far have anything approaching a tenth of the things worth having in America.

It is thus the white majority group that naturally determines the Negro's "place."   All our attempts to reach scientific explanations of why the Negroes are what they are and why they live as they do have regularly led to determinants on the white side of the race line.   In the practical and political struggles of effecting changes, the views and attitudes of the white Americans are likewise strategic.   The Negro's entire life, and consequently, also his opinions on the Negro problem, are, in the main, to be considered as secondary reactions to more primary pressures from the side of the dominant white majority.

. . . The Negro, as a minority, and a poor and suppressed minority at that, in the final analysis, has had little other strategy open to him than to play on the conflicting values held in the white majority group.   In so doing, he has been able to identify his cause with broader issues in American politics and social life and with moral principles held dear by the white Americans.   This is the situation even today and will remain so in the foreseeable future.   In that sense, "This is a white man's country."

Not an Isolated Problem

Closely related to the thesis that the Negro problem is predominantly a white man's problem is another conclusion which slowly dawned upon the author, though it is undoubtedly not news to many of his American readers: The Negro problem is an integral part of, or a special phase of, the whole complex of problems in the larger American civilization.   It cannot be treated in isolation.   There is no single side of the Negro problem—whether it be the Negro's political status, the education he gets, his place in the labor market, his cultural and personality traits, or anything else—which is not predominantly determined by its total American setting. . . . The assumption underlying the approach to this book is . . . that the Negro problem exists and changes because of conditions and forces operating in the larger American society.   Establishing this integration is thought to make the analysis more realistic.   This will explain and, the author believes, justify the fact that in all parts of this inquiry attention is given to the characteristics of the American society at large in which the Negro becomes a problem.

The relationship between American society and the Negro problem is not one-sided. The entire structure of American society is itself greatly conditioned by the presence of the thirteen million Negro citizens. American politics, the labor market, education, religious life, civic ideals, art, and recreation are as they are partly because of the important conditioning factor working throughout the history of the nation. New impulses from the Negro people are constantly affecting the American way of life, bending in some degree all American institutions and bringing changes in every aspect of the American's complex world view. . . .

Unity of Ideals and Diversity of Culture

(In spite of the heterogeneity of the American people) there is evidently a strong unity in this nation and a basic homogeneity and stability in its valuations. Americans of all national origins, classes, regions, creeds, and colors, have something in common: a social ethos, a political creed. It is difficult to avoid the judgment that this "American Creed" is the cement in the structure of this great and disparate nation . . . America . . . has the most explicitly expressed system of general ideals in reference to human interrelations. This body of ideals is more widely understood and appreciated than similar ideals are anywhere else. The American Creed is not merely—as in some countries—the implicit background of the nation's political and judicial order as it functions. To be sure, the political creed of America is not very satisfactorily effectuated in actual social life. But as principles which ought to rule, the Creed has been made conscious to everyone in American society.

The ideals of the essential dignity of the individual human being, of the fundamental equality of all men, and of certain inalienable rights to freedom, justice, and a fair opportunity represent to the American people the essential meaning of the nation's early struggle for independence. . . . American nationalism is permeated by the American Creed, and therefore becomes international in its essence. . . . America got this dynamic creed much as a political convenience and a device of strategy during the long struggle with the English Crown, the London Parliament and the various British powerholders in the colonies. It served as the rallying center for the growing national unity that was needed. Later it was a necessary device for building up a national morale to enlist and sustain the people in the Revolutionary War. In this spirit the famous declarations were resolved, the glorious speeches made, the inciting pamphlets written and spread. . . . The Creed, once set forth and disseminated among the American people, became so strongly entrenched in their hearts and the circumstances have since then been so relatively favorable, that it has succeeded in keeping itself very much alive for more than a century and a half.

The Roots of the American Creed in the Philosophy of Enlightenment

The American Creed is a humanistic liberalism developing out of the epoch of Enlightenment when America received its national consciousness and its political structure. The Revolution did not stop short of anything less than the heroic desire for the "emancipation of human nature." The enticing flavor of the eighteenth century, so dear to every intellectual and rationalist, has not been lost on the long journey up to the present time. . . . For practical purposes the main norms of the American Creed as usually pronounced are centered in the belief in equality and in the rights to liberty. . . . In America as everywhere else—and sometimes, perhaps, on the average, a little more ruthlessly—liberty often provided opportunity for the stronger to rob the weaker. Against this, the equalitarianism in the Creed has been persistently revolting. The struggle is far from ended. The reason why American liberty was not more dangerous to equality was, of course, the open frontier and the free land. When opportunity became bounded in the last generation, the inherent conflict between equality and liberty flared up. Equality is slowly winning. . . .

The Roots in Christianity

If the European philosophy of Enlightenment was one of the ideological roots of the American Creed, another equally important one was Christianity, particularly as it took the form in the colonies of various lower class Protestant sects, split off from the Anglican Church. "Democracy was envisaged in religious terms long before it assumed a political terminology." . . . The basic teaching of Protestant Christianity is democratic. We are all poor sinners and have the same heavenly father. The concept of natural rights in the philosophy of Enlightenment corresponded rather closely with the idea of moral law in the Christian faith. . . . On the whole, church and religion in America are a force strengthening the American Creed. The fundamental tenets of Christianity press for expression even in the most bigoted setting.

The Roots in English Law

The third main ideological influence behind the American Creed is English law. . . . It established the principles of justice, equity, and equality before the law. . . . This concept of a government "of laws and not of men" contained certain fundamentals of both equality and liberty . . . these elemental demands are not nearly realized even in present-day America. But in the American Creed they have never been questioned.

Value Premises

The deeper reason for the technical simplicity of the value aspect of the Negro problem is this: From the point of view of the American Creed the status accorded the Negro in America represents nothing more and nothing less than a century-long lag of public morals. In principle the Negro problem was settled long ago; in practice the solution is not effectuated. The Negro in America has not yet been given the elemental civil and political rights of formal democracy, including fair opportunity to earn his living, upon which a general accord was already won when the American Creed was first taking form. And this anachronism constitutes the contemporary "problem" both to Negroes and to whites.

On the Minds of the Whites

The Negro problem is working on the white man's mind . . . even, and not least, when he wants to convince himself and others that it is settled for all time. . . . It is the writer's conclusion that even in those Northern states with few Negroes, the Negro problem is always present though relatively quiescent. Nearly everybody in America is prepared to discuss the issue, and almost nobody is entirely without opinions on it. . . . Few Americans are unaware of the Negro problem.

To the white Americans the possibilities of keeping the Negro problem out of their minds are, naturally, greater and, in addition, they have certainly good selfish reasons for keeping it below the level of consciousness. To be sure, it was a not unusual experience of the writer to be told confidently sometimes by the learned, but most often by the laity, that there is "no Negro problem" in America and that, if there ever was one, it is solved and settled for all time and to the full satisfaction of both parties. Everything is quiet on the racial front. We think the Negroes are all right in their place; and they on their part do not want things changed. In fact, they are the happiest lot on earth. Just look at them: how they laugh and enjoy themselves; how they sing and praise the Lord.

This attitude was met most frequently and expressed most emphatically in the Deep South. . . . All this is not true, of course. A contrary statement, that the white South is virtually obsessed by the Negro problem, that the South has allowed the Negro problem to rule its politics and its business, fetter its intelligence and human liberties, and hamper its progress in all directions, would be nearer the truth. . . . Apart from the few intellectuals of pronounced liberal leanings, however, statements to the effect that there really is no Negro problem have become part of the common stock of stereotyped opinions in the South, and they are not entirely absent from the North. But such statements cover a volcanic ground of doubt, disagreement, concern, and even anxiety—of moral tension and need for escape and defense. To furnish such a covering is, from a psychological point of view, their very "function." The prevalence of such opinions and the intensity with which they are expressed might serve as an index of the latent interracial tension felt in the white world.

Problem 19: What Are the Techniques of Discrimination?

How does discrimination operate? To this question we can secure one kind of answer by gathering statistics—so many lynchings, so much infant mortality, so many segregated schools, parks, buses, theaters.

Rather than this approach we have chosen highly personalized accounts of prejudice. What kind of justice did Roosevelt Wilson find? What is it like to be a Negro child in a white world? What does Josephine Baker remember? What experiences do Jews, Mexicans, and Japanese have in the American culture?

The record presented here poses an interesting question: Are the oft-proclaimed American ideals so much verbiage for Fourth of July orations? Do a majority of Americans find present practices to be a reasonable compromise with their avowed ideals?

THE ORDEAL OF ROOSEVELT WILSON *

Most Americans feel that they can get redress for wrongs through court action. This is a fundamental concept of the democratic ideology. Yet for the members of many minority groups the process is

* William B. Huie, "The South Kills Another Negro," *American Mercury*, November, 1941, pp. 535–45.

reversed; instead of a source of justice the court becomes a means of institutionalizing community prejudice. The Negro is condemned because he is a Negro—or, in another time and place, a Japanese simply because he is Japanese. Questions of guilt or innocence are disregarded, and blame is placed on the minority member regardless of the evidence and even (as in the following case) when his innocence is known to all—to judge, jury, witnesses, and courtroom listeners. Recent exposés of such practices, combined with the use of excellent legal talent provided by various organizations interested in civil rights for all, have perhaps reduced the number of such cases. However, real justice for minorities through the legal machinery of the United States is still far from complete.

You never heard of Roosevelt Wilson. I never saw him more than twice. But Roosevelt Wilson continues to disturb me. Whenever I try to feel that I am an honest and self-assured supporter of the American Dream, Roosevelt Wilson perches on my shoulder, laughs sardonically, and reminds me that I am just another lousy compromiser; that once when I had my chance to strike a blow in defense of the Great Dream, I turned aside with the Pontius Pilates and whimpered: "What the hell can I do?"

To understand Roosevelt Wilson you'll have to visualize the loneliest, most insignificant human being in the world. The cipher in a social system. He never knew who his mother was. He just appeared as a nameless black brat in a cotton patch. He breathed. He grew. He chopped cotton for bread. He stole. And somebody, somewhere, labeled him Roosevelt Wilson. Think of him as a black, burrheaded creature who felt no superior to a hound dog, and whose death would not have brought a waft of regret across any heart in America.

When I first heard of Roosevelt Wilson he was a dog being chased by other dogs. He was a scurrying black animal to be shot on sight and left naked to rot in a ditch and be picked by buzzards. He had raped a white woman in a potato patch at Bug Tussle, and bloodhounds and a posse were chasing him. It is the old familiar fabric to every Southern reporter, so I methodically ground out eight paragraphs on The Chase. And when the black quarry had been captured by a sheriff and "spirited away for safe-keeping," I ground out two editorial paragraphs congratulating the sheriff for preserving Alabama's proud record of not having had a lynching in three years.

When I arrived at the county courthouse to cover the trial, there was nothing unusual about the scene. The AP reporter and I sat in a dysentery parlor across the street, drank coffee, griped about the assignment, and hoped Justice would act swiftly so we could get back to Birmingham before night.

There were two or three thousand people massed in the streets leading up to the courthouse square. A scattering of sticks and shotguns. Two companies of National Guardsmen had mounted machine guns around the courthouse and an officer with a loud-speaker kept issuing warnings forbidding anyone to cross the street to the courthouse. Only those who had stood in line and obtained tickets for the two hundred seats in the courtroom were allowed to pass into the courthouse, and these—both men and women—were searched for weapons. The scene in the courtroom was usual for such trials. State police and Guardsmen, armed with side arms and nightsticks, were stationed around the walls and in the aisles.

The jury had been selected when I seated myself at the table which the sheriff had hastened to provide for the two out-of-town reporters. We had not been expected. It was a routine trial. We would not have been sent to cover it except for a dull news week. The jurors were farmers and townsmen, and I observed that they appeared more intelligent than the average Alabama jury. This was because the verdict was a foregone conclusion and thus counsel had not made the usual effort to strike the more intelligent men but had simply taken the first twelve in the venire.

I looked across at the plaintiff. She was a husky, loose-jointed farm woman, perhaps thirty, with big, red hands, big feet, and a matted mass of blonde hair which some amateur barber had chopped squarely and roughly off. She reminded me of a gangling battle-ax I had once seen in a brothel whom the madam used only as a shock trooper to take on the heavier and more bellicose clients who came in very late and very drunk. The two great press services dryly agreed that young Roosevelt had shown damn poor taste in his selection of a Queen Bee worthy of his life.

Next to the plaintiff sat her husband, a burly farmer whose cheap clothes were much too small for his bulging muscles and whose flushed face gave evidence of the great rage pent up inside him. Around the two sat an imposing array of counsel for the state. The Attorney General himself was on hand, his hackles up, and issuing brash statements by the bucketful. Every elected prosecutor in district and county was present, with assistants and volunteers, to see that swift justice was done. Such a case provides rare political opportunity and every attorney who plans to run for office rushes in to participate gratis in the prosecution and make a hellraising speech to the jury.

You had to look at counsel for the defense to appreciate the contrast. These two lawyers had been appointed by the court, their names drawn from a box containing a list of all practicing members of the bar. Fate had frowned on poor Roosevelt again. For he had drawn a couple of old men who had no stomach for trial procedure. They were in mortal fear the populace would get the idea that they had willingly taken Roosevelt's case and that they believed him innocent. Before the trial began, one of them rose and addressed the court.

"Your Honor," he stammered, "to avoid any misconceptions here, my colleague and I would like you to explain publicly that we have been drafted by the court to safeguard the constitutional rights of the defendant and that no sympathy for this defendant is implied by our actions."

This the judge did solemnly in the presence of the jury. But still the old fuddy-duddies weren't satisfied. They came over to us and requested we make clear in our stories that they were appearing only in compliance with constitutional requirement. The judge, a grayish politician of about sixty, tried nervously to rush the procedure. He wanted the trial over and the defendant safely back in state prison by nightfall.

There was a rumble in the courtroom. The big coppers and the Guardsmen hefted their nightsticks. You could feel the hackles rise and the hate charge the air. The defendant was trudging in with an escort of troopers. I gave him an unconcerned and half-amused glance and jotted down a note. Barefooted. Faded and patched pair of blue overalls and jumper. Hundred and thirty pounds. Five feet six. Burrheaded bastard. The troopers handcuffed him to a chair directly in front of us. With the trial about to start, his attorneys spoke contemptuously to him. It was the first time, apparently, that they had seen him.

"What's ya' name, boy?"

"Ruseyvelt Wilson."

"How old are ya?"

"Ah thinks ah's twenty-two."

Then they sat back and were ready. They assumed the defendant had no witnesses and that he should be pleaded not guilty so as to be certain of the death penalty.

The state called the plaintiff and recorded her story. Her husband had been working in another county. While she was digging potatoes in one of the more remote fields, the nigger had sneaked out of the thicket and accosted her with a shotgun. He had threatened to kill her if she didn't go into the thicket and submit to him. So, with a choice between death and such a sacrifice, she had complied with his demands. After he had run off, she had heard the yells of some women looking for her, and she had rushed to them and reported the crime.

The defense cross-examined softly and sympathetically, "Not that we doubt your story, ma'am," they explained, "but just for the record." The plaintiff agreed that the nigger had laid down his gun before the rape occurred, but the judge promptly explained to the jury that she had already been intimidated with the gun and was thus in mortal fear for her life, even though the gun had been cast aside. At this the irreverent AP cocked an eyebrow and shook his head. The plaintiff weighed a good thirty pounds more than the defendant and could obviously have smacked him silly when he laid the gun down.

Then followed a succession of witnesses who established that the defendant had run when approached by the posse, that he carried the gun, and that he had resisted arrest. Two women testified to the nervous state of the plaintiff after the crime.

At the noon recess I overheard a conversation between Roosevelt and his attorneys. They were telling him that there would be no need to take the stand, that it would be best just to submit the case when the state closed. But Roosevelt objected.

"Naw, suh, boss," he said. "De truf ain't being tole heah. Ah got to git up deah an' tell de truf. Ef dey kills me, ah got to git up deah an' tell de truf."

Believe me, it was no noble motive which inspired my intervention. I only wanted to blow up a dull story. I stepped up and said: "That's right, Roosevelt. If they're not telling the truth, you get up there and tell it. They've got to listen to you." The lawyers then admitted to him that "of course, the court couldn't deny him his constitutional right to testify in his own defense," but his testimony would do no good. When they had gone, I stepped back in and gave Roosevelt some more encouragement.

"Get in there and give it to them straight, Roosevelt," I said. Then, in that burrheaded nigger's face, I saw something I didn't want to see. I must have been the first white man ever to have spoken a civil word to him. He reacted like a dog when you pat him on the head. He let down his guard and I saw that he wasn't a nameless animal but a living, breathing, feeling—even aspiring—person. He showed me all the loneliness and fear of his wretched life. The loneliness of the cotton patch and a dog howling under the moon. The loneliness and fear of the swamp with bloodhounds baying. The loneliness and fear of a jail cell and a thunderbolt exploding in your body. I shrugged and turned away quickly.

Shortly after noon the state rested and defense counsel rose to inform the court solemnly that counsel had advised the defendant not to testify, but that he insisted on his constitutional right. The defense, therefore, was calling the defendant, Roosevelt Wilson, to the stand. If you had struck a match while that nigger was walking to the stand, the courtroom would have exploded. I have never felt such tension, such organized hate focused on one insignificant object. Troopers clutched their nightsticks and the judge unconsciously rapped for order, though the room was breathlessly silent.

"Now, Roosevelt, just go ahead and tell your story," defense counsel said.

"And make it short." There was no effort to guide his testimony or to help him in any way.

"Well, Jedge, it wuz lak dis," he began. "Ah got up dat mawnin' an' ah borr'd Sam Winson's gun to go rabbit huntin'. Ef Sam wuz heah he's tell ya ah did. Ah went ovah tow'd de nawth fawty an' ah seed dis lady a-diggin' taters. Ah'd seed her a time o' two befo' an' she'd tole me she wanted a ring ah had. Aw wawked up to her an' ah show'd her de ring an' we tawked a minute. Den ah axed her de question an' she lukked aroun' an' said she wuz willin' . . ."

The room exploded. In a split second the husband had yanked open his britches and from somewhere under or between his legs had come up with a forty-five. And he had come up shooting. The crowd rioted and the Guardsmen began laying them in the aisles with the nightsticks. Two big troopers jumped on the hate-crazed husband and wrested the gun from him. Two reporters who had been standing up, the better to hear Roosevelt's story, had done a dual jackknife under a table.

It was half an hour before order could be restored. The jury, the husband, and the defendant were removed from the courtroom, and AP and I began burning up the wires with flashes. I asked the judge if he wouldn't have to declare a mistrial. "I suppose I should," he said, "but, hell, we've got to get rid of this mess." He looked as if he were bothered by an offensive odor.

I went in to see Roosevelt, and his lawyers were upbraiding him. "We told you so. We told you not to get up there. Now you see we were right. When court goes back in session, we'll just close the case."

"Naw, suh, boss," Roosevelt objected. "Ah's jest got started good. De whole truf ain't been tole yit."

By now Roosevelt had me pulling for him. "Get back up there, Roosevelt," I told him. "Don't let 'em scare you. Tell it all."

When the trial was resumed, the defense apologized profusely and explained again that they had urged the defendant not to testify. Then they moved for a mistrial. The motion was denied, and Roosevelt went back to the stand, completely surrounded by troopers. In a deadly silence broken by heavy breathing, he finished the story of a mutual pine-needle affair, hastened near the end by "some women hollerin' fo' dis lady."

The cross-examination thunder began to roll. The prosecutors began jumping and yelling and shaking their fists.

"If you hadn't committed a crime," the Attorney General bellowed, "why did you run like a scared rabbit when these men found you over there in that field?"

The reply was cool. "Ah seed a buncha men come a-runnin' at me.

Dey wuz a-cussin' an' a-shootin'. So ah jest run. Dey kept a-chasin' me, so ah kept runnin'."

For an hour the state battery took turns working out on Roosevelt. They attempted to cross him in every way. But his story never changed. The woman had gone to the woods with him willingly in exchange for the ring he had given her.

During the impassioned oratory to the jury, I convinced myself that the woman—the plaintiff—had smuggled the gun into the courthouse. The husband could hardly have brought it in, for he was the most suspect of all the spectators and two deputies had searched him thoroughly. But the matron admitted her search of the woman had been perfunctory. The plaintiff had known the story the nigger might tell and she had brought the gun in to have her husband kill him before he could tell it.

The jury required four minutes to go out, organize, and bring back death. While it was out, I whispered to the judge: "Judge, I've lived around niggers all my life and if I ever heard one tell the truth, that little bastard was telling it this afternoon, wasn't he?" The judge crouched down low behind his desk, nodded his head, and grinned: "By God, he shore was, wasn't he?"

When the jury had been discharged, I spoke privately to several of the jurors. To each one I made the same statement I had made to the judge. In each case I got the same reply. "Shore he was telling the truth. But what the hell, he deserves the chair for messin' around with a white woman. Besides, if we'd turned him loose, that crowd outside woulda lynched us. We gotta live with these folks."

After the troopers had rushed Roosevelt through the crowds and away toward the penitentiary, the judge called the husband back to reprimand him for creating a disturbance, not to mention attempting to murder a man still presumed to be innocent. The husband told the judge:

"Judge, I felt like I had to kill that sonuvabitch. I intended to do it this mawnin' while he wuz a-settin' over there at the table. But ever' time I'd reach down to pull my gun, the Lawd would tell me not to do it, fo' them two newspapermen wuz a-settin' right smack behind him."

"Whew!" AP had turned white around the gills. "We got something to thank the Lord for, haven't we, boy?" he said.

As we rode back to Birmingham that night, I kept thinking of Roosevelt Wilson in his faded overalls and bare feet, riding alone toward Death Row with a hundred and twenty Guardsmen to see him safely in the chair. I thought of Pontius Pilate. I thought of Emile Zola and the few men who have had the courage to defy the mob. I sneered. What the hell! AP pulled in toward a roadhouse. "Let's have a drink," he said.

We had several drinks. We told the waitress some stories and pinched her on the thigh. To hell with Roosevelt Wilson. Smart guys don't go around butting their heads against stone walls. Smart guys make the most of the inevitable.

Next morning, in my clean-up story, I inserted two paragraphs about Roosevelt's testimony. In polite language I hinted at its substance. I watched the managing editor when he picked up the story at the copy desk. He looked over at me, made a wry face, and jerked his nose to tell me it stank. I saw his pencil go down in an impatient gesture, and I knew those two paragraphs would never see print. No one reading my story could have guessed on what claim Roosevelt based his plea of innocence. I suggested we use a picture of Roosevelt Wilson with the story. His face might impress somebody with his innocence. But my paper, like others in the South, had a policy against using pictures of Negroes. So we used the latest piece of Marlene Dietrich leg art instead.

I wish I could tell you that the case of Roosevelt Wilson perched on my shoulder like a raven, and that I never rested until I had freed him from his cell and thrown him back into the faces of the Pontius Pilates. I wish I could tell you that I made a brave speech to the editor of my paper; that I flung my job in his face; and that I fought for Roosevelt's freedom with pamphlets printed on a hand press. But none of these things happened. I told the editor the filthy facts and suggested a further story, but when he said, "Hell, Bill, you're crazy," I nodded and said, "Yeah, I guess you're right."

I told the Governor the same filthy facts. He shrugged and said: "Boy, you're crazy. What the hell can I do? You know what it would mean if I intervened in a case like this."

"Yeah, I guess you're right," I said. "But you know I've read of governors who couldn't sleep after they had let an innocent man go to his death."

He laughed. I laughed, too. The kind of laugh to keep from crying. Then—incredible as it seems—I forgot Roosevelt Wilson and it was quite by accident that I ever saw him again.

Thursday night is execution night at Alabama's big Kilby Prison. Most every week the state fries some black meat and occasionally a little white meat is thrown in for good measure. There was a young cop killer sent up from Birmingham. He was a white boy from somewhere out West. He had been in the Marines and had hit the highways. He had gone jittery during a holdup and plugged a cop. We had played the case with a lot of sob stuff, and I was sent down to Montgomery to cover his burning.

The warden was impatient. "Come on, you guys, let's get started," he said to the reporters. "We got eight black boys to burn after we finish off this yellow cop killer."

The cop killer was yellow, all right. There were six preachers with him when they brought him in the death house—all anxious to get their names spelled right—but he went hysterical and guards had to throw him in the chair.

I had filed my story and was ready to leave the prison when I remembered I had left my coat in the corridor near the death house. I went back for it and just happened to notice the black boy who was being led toward the green door.

It was Roosevelt Wilson.

In his white prison clothes the burrheaded little bastard looked smaller and less significant than he had looked in his overalls. Friendless and alone, he was going to his death. During his weeks of waiting he had not had a single visitor nor communication from the world outside. His eyeballs were rolling in fear, but he was walking without support. I tossed down my coat and called to the warden to wait a minute.

"You're Roosevelt Wilson, aren't you?" I said. "The boy from up in Webster County." He recognized me. I was still probably the only white man who had ever spoken civilly to him. "Yassuh, boss, ah is. And yo're de newspapah genmun who wuz at mah trial, ain'tcha?"

The warden was annoyed. "Come on, Huie," he snapped. "We're in a hurry. We got three more to go and it's gettin' late." But I insisted, and he reluctantly agreed to take another nigger on and get Roosevelt last. He locked us back in the cell and we had a few minutes to talk.

"Roosevelt, would you like to see a preacher before you go?" I asked him.

He said he would, so I called an attendant and sent him for a preacher. But the only preacher around now was a nigger preacher and he was in the death house. So I borrowed a greasy little Testament from an old white prisoner on the Row. I couldn't remember a suitable passage in the New Testament, so I opened the little Bible, pretended I was reading, and recited the first five verses of the Twenty-third Psalm. Roosevelt repeated after me.

I fumbled for something to say to that Negro boy. I wanted to say something that would give him faith and comfort and hope. Something he could understand. Finally, I said: "Roosevelt, before you go in there, I want to say this to you. You are not guilty of the crime for which this state is going to kill you. All of us who heard your story know that you are innocent. The judge knows you are innocent. The jurors know you are innocent."

"Den why is dey killin' me, boss? Fo' God, ah didn't fo'ce dat lady."

"I know you didn't. We all know you didn't. But we couldn't help it."

"Is dey killin' me jest fo' messin' aroun' wid dat lady?"

"Yes, that's one reason. And there's a bigger and more awful reason that I haven't time to explain. But what you want to do now is to buck up. Everybody has to die. It's not bad in there. You never feel it at all. So don't be afraid."

He thought for a minute. "Does ya reckon ah'll go to hebben, boss?"

"Well, Roosevelt," I answered, "I've heard it said that the folks here on earth who are done wrong like you, and the folks who have the worst luck —they are the folks who go to heaven, and they are the ones who get the biggest crowns and the most gold. So I think you deserve to go there and I believe you will."

"Thank ya, boss," he said. The warden was coming, and he turned and asked, "Will ya go in wif me, boss? It won't be so bad ef ya'll go wif me."

God, I hated to go back in there. It always makes me sick. But I nodded. My folks don't shake hands with Negroes, but I took Roosevelt by the hand and we walked down the corridor. An old whiteheaded Negro preacher joined us.

You would have been proud of Roosevelt in the death house. He was scared, but here were no hysterics. At the chair he turned around and said: "G'by boss. G'by parson." The attendants clapped on the hood and adjusted the electrodes and the old preacher broke into "I am the Resurrection and the Life. . . ." For a second the frail form quivered in the chair, and then the sovereign state of Alabama exploded twenty-three hundred volts of lightning.

They buried him in the prison plot for unclaimed bodies. My paper ran a story under my by-line. It was a stinking account of the execution of a yellow cop killer. "I have found God!" he was quoted as having said to the reporter before the switch was thrown. The last paragraph of the story was inconsequential. It would have been killed by the make-up man had it run over the column. It said: "Among the eight Negroes also executed last night was Roosevelt Wilson, twenty-two, convicted of rape in Webster County."

◆•••◆

BLACK BOUNDARIES IN BIG TEXAS *

Volumes have been written on the economic and political aspects of segregation, but the literature on the social and psychological effects

* Margaret L. Hartley, *Southwest Review,* published at Southern Methodist University, Dallas, Texas, Winter, 1952, pp. 69–71.

of discrimination is not nearly so impressive. Relatively little has been said about the day-to-day situations the Negro has to face and the cumulative effect of a lifetime of ridicule, disparagement, and patronization on his status as a human being. Yet it is in this area of personal relationships that the issues involving the dignity and worth of individual personality are most sharply defined. On this rock democracy will be built or will be destroyed.

In the following article Margaret L. Hartley points up the experiences that are the common lot of Negroes living in a large Southern city. The essay is unusually penetrating. It is particularly remarkable since the author, who is not a Negro, demonstrates acute insight into a virtually unthought-of segment of human relations.

. . . If a Negro child goes to town with his mother, he must never forget that only the back seats on the bus or streetcar are for him to sit on, no matter how many may be vacant farther up. Then when he gets to town and goes into a store where his mother is looking for some material for a dress, he must be very careful not to touch the pretty bolts of cloth. If he does, his mother may jerk him away with a roughness that is hard to understand. Across the aisle a white child may do the same thing and scarcely be spoken to. The difference is that if the white child "touches" too hard and pulls the cloth to the floor the saleswoman will give her a patient customer-smile and pick it up again, saying nothing—while if the Negro child had a similar mishap, chances would be good that his mother would be required to pay for all of the material thus "contaminated."

Shopping is long, and a child easily becomes thirsty. In a few stores his mother may find a drinking fountain marked "Colored," where she can take him to get a drink. He must learn on his first trip to town that all other fountains are forbidden to him—although his face may be scrubbed much cleaner than that of the white child he sees running freely to any fountain he pleases. If there is no fountain with the quarantining label, the dark-skinned child—and his mother—must go thirsty.

Or another and more urgent emergency may arise. Childlike, he may realize suddenly that he must go to the toilet without delay. In a very few stores there are "colored" restrooms to which he and his mother may make the familiar hurried journey of mothers and children everywhere. But if they are in any of the other stores he must simply wait in increasing discomfort until he can be taken somewhere—perhaps to a filthy public restroom "for colored" beneath a street—or else have a humiliating accident. He may take his embarrassment past the door of a clean restroom, big enough for everyone, but it is outside the invisible boundaries that hedge the dark child in and determine his actions at every turn.

Meanwhile, his mother too is experiencing in her adult fashion the binding of taboos. Texas cities vary in the difficulties their stores place in the way of Negro customers. In Fort Worth, for example, Negro women are allowed to try on dresses much more generally than is the case in Dallas. Those from Dallas who can afford to make the trip often go to Fort Worth to buy their clothes—even though this involves waiting in a tiny room at the back of the Dallas bus station, its windows piled high with empty bottles, its few feet of floor space crowded with people and food and all sorts of other things in an unsavory clogged-up mess.

But for most the problem of saving enough money for decent clothing is serious enough without the additional cost of bus fare to another city. So they must buy dresses they have not been allowed to try on, and then endure the amused condescension of their employers when what they have bought turns out to be ill-fitting or outrageously unbecoming. In the few stores in which trying on is permitted, a Negro customer may not, like the rest, go through the racks examining and choosing and then take the dresses of her choice to the dressing room. She must go straight to the dressing room and try on only what the saleswoman chooses to bring her— which may too easily be merchandise that she has had difficulty in selling to her white customers.

Humiliation is the chief effect of the taboo against trying on dresses. But with shoes, which may not be tried on in as many places as may dresses, discomfort and even real damage to health may be added to the feeling of being quarantined as if darkness of skin were a contagious disease. The fitting of shoes is a hard proposition at best, particularly for people who must be on their feet for long working hours. When they may not be fitted at all, an explanation becomes evident for some of the laughable makeshifts that seem quaint and scarcely civilized to white onlookers—the holes cut in the sides of shoes to ease the ache, or shoes bulging and cracking in odd places.

Meantime, while shoes and dresses and other things are being bought with difficulty and in constant awareness of barriers, there is the attitude of salespeople to be endured with patience, or at best met with humor subtle enough not to offend. It is not easy for a mature person to be called "gal" or "boy." For the elderly there may be the only slightly less disrespectful "Auntie" or "Uncle"—but the patronizing behind these originally harmless words strips dignity from both the language and the person to whom it is addressed. Or perhaps the form of address may be a completely random name, "Mary" or "George," as if the individual spoken to were not worthy of the distinction of a name of his own.

These are for transactions in which a white person would be addressed impersonally as "Ma'am" or "Sir." But when the business involved is somewhat more personal, where names are known and the white customer or client would be "Mrs. Smith" or "Mr. Brown," the indignity also becomes more personal. Now there is no "Mr." or "Mrs." or "Miss" for the Negro Texan, but only his or her first name. Some of the other taboos might be defended with some show of logic by the specious but attractive-sounding "separate but equal" principle. But here is one which can have no purpose but to degrade, and which can be taken in no other way by even the most charitably disposed of its victims. Because a man's name is his most intimate and prized possession, the seal of his identity, the wound dealt by its refusal is a particularly profound one.

It would be unfair to imply that all the white citizens of Texas (or any other state) concur in the cultivation of this thorny hedge of taboos surrounding the lives of their darker fellow-citizens. But those who would willingly help grub it out if they knew how are handicapped by still more taboos of a kind calculated to hinder the communication that is essential to understanding. When people may not sit together at church service, meetings, entertainments, or games—at any of the places where people commonly get to know each other—how are they to learn what is in each other's hearts so that good will may became effective?

While the penalties facing a white person who breaks the everyday taboos in order to gain this understanding are far from being as severe as those a Negro would encounter, the consequences in social disapproval are enough to give the ordinary citizen pause. One of the difficulties is, however, to a large extent imaginary. Many white people whose personal courage would be adequate to the effort to break a rule of tradition sit back and do nothing because they believe that what they would like to see done would be against the law. Thus they shrug the burden of their own uneasy consciences over onto the shoulders of the lawmakers, and feel that they themselves are powerless. Actually, this is true only in a limited area. The "Jim Crow" laws of Texas are no more than five in number. They require segregation in intrastate public transportation, schools, and state parks; forbid miscegenation; and require the separation of showers in coal mines.

Coal production in Texas being microscopic, the last of these is not apt to affect many people seriously. The other four statutes deal with "big" questions, those of which everyone is aware and which are subjects of nationwide discussion and debate. They do not touch the "little" things, so far from little in their aggregate effect, that go on unobtrusively but unremittingly, forming a pattern of life that is essentially negativistic and frustrating. Nor do they forbid, as is generally supposed, the unsegregated discussion groups, the common religious services, the friendly luncheon meetings, at which white and Negro individuals might learn how to change this pattern. Similarly, local ordinances do not go nearly as far in this direction as is popularly thought. The fact that city police have sometimes been used to enforce tradition rather than law has been to blame for misapprehensions on this point. The white citizen who takes the trouble to investigate will find that his uneasiness of conscience over prejudice and discrimination belongs where it originated, in his own heart. Laws may be hard to change, but taboos last only as long as the members of the group that established them continue to consent to them.

Josephine Baker Remembers St. Louis *

The following remarks, made in a curtain talk at Kiel Auditorium in St. Louis on February 3, 1952, provide an excellent counterpiece to "Black Boundaries in Big Texas." Many of the same ideas, for example, the feelings of a Negro living in a large Southern city, are discussed. However, in this case the presentation is sharpened by the fact that the author is herself a Negro. Josephine Baker has an international reputation not only as a singer but also as a spokesman for her people.

Strange, it seems just like yesterday that I ran away from home. It was not because I lived in poverty or because I was living in the slums. I have never been ashamed of my childhood surroundings. On the contrary, I have been very proud of my start, because it has made me understand my fellow brothers of misery.

I ran away from St. Louis, and then I ran away from the United States, because of that terror of discrimination, that horrible beast which paralyzes one's very soul and body. Those in this audience who have felt discrimination know what I am talking about, and those who understand human beings understand what I am talking about, too.

The hate directed against the colored people here in St. Louis has always given me a sad feeling. I remember the horror of the East St. Louis race riot when I was a little girl. I was very tiny, but the horror of the whole thing impressed me so that here today, at the age of 45, I can still see myself standing on the west bank of the Mississippi looking over into East St. Louis and watching the glow of the burning Negro homes lighting the sky.

We children stood huddled together in bewilderment, not being able to understand the horrible madness of mob violence. Here we were hiding

* Josephine Baker, *The St. Louis Post-Dispatch*, February 7, 1952.

behind the skirts of grownups, frightened to death with the screams of the Negro families running across the bridge with nothing but what they had on their backs as their worldly belongings.

To me for years St. Louis represented a city of fear, humiliation, misery and terror—a city where in the eyes of the white man a Negro should know his place and had better stay in it.

I wanted to get far away from those who believed in cruelty, so I went to France, a land of true freedom, democracy, equality and fraternity. There my soul was at ease, but after a time I started to wonder why it was that in St. Louis, which was at one time a French colony, the colored people have no equal rights, whereas in Paris we are loved and respected as human beings. In both cities, the majority of the population is white.

I was continuously unhappy. No one could understand why I should be, because at that time I was considered the greatest success in Europe. But that glow in the sky of burning houses, the screams, the terror, the tears of the unfortunate children who had lost their parents, kept coming before me on the stage, in the streets, in my sleep.

I remember when Lindbergh arrived in Paris, I was one of the first persons to know about his landing, because the French people, knowing I was born in St. Louis, thought I would be very proud to announce it to the public, and so gave me the news first. I was then starring in the Folies Bergeres. I was told to announce the great news to the public, which I did. The show stopped.

I forgot that Lindbergh was a white man and that he came from St. Louis and might not have liked Negroes. I only remembered that he was an American and that he had done something great for the progress of the world.

This happened at the height of the American tourist season in Paris. Half the people in the audience were Americans.

My heart almost burst with pride and joy. Americans and French alike were delirious with happiness. The celebration went on all night. My joy had no bounds. I kept thinking, "He is an American from St. Louis." Paris was going mad with joy.

Friends invited me to one of the most fashionable restaurants in Paris at that time. Everybody was drinking to the health of Lindbergh from St. Louis and America, when all of a sudden a clear and loud voice sounded. A white couple called the head waiter and told him not to serve me because in America this is not done. "At home," they said, "a nigger woman belongs in the kitchen."

This brought a great silence in the restaurant. I felt that if the floor could open and swallow me it would be a blessing. The manager, on hearing the disturbance, came over to find out what was going on. The white woman said, "I have never sat beside a nigger in my life—I never will."

The manager reminded them that they were in France, where human beings were equal, and if they wanted to leave he could give them their bill.

Americans, the eyes of the world are upon you. How can you expect the world to believe in you and respect your preaching of democracy when you yourself treat your colored brothers as you do?

Let us stop saying "White Americans" and "Colored Americans"; let us try once and for all saying, "Americans."

JAPANESE-AMERICAN RELOCATION *

A Jap's a Jap and it makes no difference whether he is an American citizen or not. . . . I don't want any of them. We got them out. They were a dangerous element. The West Coast is too vital and too vulnerable to take chances. . . . You can't change [a Jap] by giving him a piece of paper.

—GENERAL DeWITT †

It is a matter of record that no instance of espionage, sabotage, or other disloyal conduct was discovered on the part of any Japanese-American, either on the West Coast or in the Hawaiian Islands, during the war.

—ROBERT E. CUSHMAN ‡

Under peacetime conditions the United States government has rarely supported any outright "master race" theory. During World War II, however, the treatment of United States citizens of Japanese descent smacked strongly of a policy that equated race and behavior characteristics. How can the Japanese relocation policy be explained? Was the government "used" by the purveyors of racial intolerance? Did Americans as a people tacitly accept the fuzzy theories of the racists? Is it true that national safety demanded the scrapping of

* Eugene V. Rostow, "Our Worst Wartime Mistake," *Harper's Magazine*, September, 1945, pp. 193–201.

† Commanding General of the Western Defense Command, before a congressional committee (as quoted by Robert E. Cushman).

‡ "Civil Liberties in the Atomic Age," *The Annals* of the American Academy of Political and Social Science, January, 1947, p. 57.

constitutional guarantees for individuals? Or were the people hood-winked because they lacked information? Did California Japanese replace Tokyo Japanese as convenient symbols upon which to discharge Pearl Harbor frustrations? Were the basic motives greed, fear, hatred? Finally, did military necessity justify the action: who is right, General DeWitt or Robert Cushman?

During the bleak spring of 1942, the Japanese and the Japanese-Americans who lived on the West Coast of the United States were taken into custody and removed to camps in the interior. More than one hundred thousand men, women, and children were thus exiled and imprisoned. More than two-thirds of them were American citizens.

. . . They were arrested without warrants and were held without indictment or a statement of charges, although the courts were open and freely functioning. They were transported to camps far from their homes, and kept there under prison conditions, pending investigations of their "loyalty." Despite the good intentions of the chief relocation officers, the centers were little better than concentration camps.

If the evacuees were found "loyal," they were released only if they could find a job and a place to live, in a community where no hoodlums would come out at night to chalk up anti-Japanese slogans, break windows, or threaten riot. If found "disloyal" in their attitude toward the war, they were kept in the camps indefinitely—although sympathy with the enemy is no crime in the United States (for white people, at least) so long as it is not translated into deeds or the visible threat of deeds.

The original program of "relocation" was an injustice, in no way required or justified by the circumstances of war. But the Supreme Court, in three extraordinary decisions, has upheld its main features as constitutional. . . . It is having a sinister impact on the minority problem in every part of the country. It is giving aid to reactionary politicians who use social division and racial prejudice as their tools. The precedent is being used to encourage attacks on the civil rights of both citizens and aliens. As Mr. Justice Jackson has said, the principle of these decisions "lies about like a loaded weapon ready for the hand of any authority that can bring forward a plausible claim of an urgent need." All in all, the case of the Japanese-American is the worst blow our liberties have sustained in many years. Unless repudiated, it may support devastating and unforeseen social and political conflicts.

What was done in the name of military precaution on the West Coast was quite different from the security measures taken . . . on the East Coast, although (it was an) active theater of war in 1942.

On the East Coast enemy aliens were controlled without mass arrests or evacuations, despite their heavy concentration in and near shipping and manufacturing centers. Aliens had been registered, and the police had compiled information about fascist sympathizers, both aliens and citizens. "On the night of December 7, 1941," Attorney General Biddle reported, "the most dangerous of the persons in the group were taken into custody; in the following weeks a number of others were apprehended. Each arrest was made on the basis of information concerning the specific alien taken into custody. We have used no dragnet techniques and have conducted no indiscriminate, large-scale raids." General regulations were issued, somewhat restricting the freedom of all enemy aliens over fourteen years of age. They were forbidden to enter military areas; they had to get the District Attorney's permission before traveling; they were forbidden to own or use fire-arms, cameras, short-wave radio sets, codes, ciphers, or invisible ink. This control plan kept security officers informed, but otherwise allowed the aliens almost their normal share in the work and life of the community.

Enemy aliens under suspicion, and those who violated the regulations, were subject to summary arrest, and were then promptly examined by one of the special Alien Enemy Hearing Boards. Those boards could recommend that the individual alien be interned, paroled, or released unconditionally. The examinations were smoothly conducted, and they did nothing to lower prevailing standards of justice. Of the 1,100,000 enemy aliens in the country, 9,080 had been examined by the end of June, 1943, about 4,000 of them being then interned. By June 20, 1944, the number interned had been reduced to approximately 2,500.

In Hawaii a different procedure was followed, but one less drastic than the evacuation program pursued on the West Coast, although Hawaii was certainly a more active theater of war. Immediately after Pearl Harbor, martial law was installed in Hawaii, and the commanding general assumed the role of military governor. Yet, although about one-third the population of Hawaii is of Japanese descent, and although the tension was great after the Pearl Harbor raid, there was no mass roundup on the islands. Fewer than 800 Japanese aliens were sent to the mainland for internment, and fewer than 1,000 persons of Japanese ancestry, 912 of them being citizens, were sent to relocation centers on the mainland. Many of the latter group were families of interned aliens, and transferred voluntarily. Those arrested in Hawaii were taken into custody on the basis of individual suspicion, resting on previous examination or observed behavior. Even under a regime of martial law, men were arrested as individuals, and not because of the color of their skins. Safety was assured without mass arrests, or needless hardship.

On the West Coast the security program was something else again. Immediately after Pearl Harbor there were no special regulations for persons of Japanese extraction. Known enemy sympathizers among the Japanese, like white traitors and enemy agents, were arrested. *There was no sabotage by persons of Japanese ancestry.* [Italics ours.] There was no reason to suppose that the 112,000 persons of Japanese descent on the West Coast, less than 2 per cent of the population, constituted a greater menace than such persons in Hawaii, where they were 32 per cent of the population.

After a month's silence, *the organized minority whose business it has been to exploit racial tensions on the West Coast went to work.* [Italics ours.] They had strong support in the Hearst press and its equivalents. Politicians, fearful of an unknown public opinion, spoke out for white supremacy. West Coast Congressional delegations led by Senator Hiram Johnson, urged the administration to exclude all persons of Japanese blood from the coast states. Anti-Oriental spokesmen appeared before the special hearings of the Tolan Committee, and explained the situation as they conceived it to Lieutenant General J. L. DeWitt, commanding the Western Defense Command. Tension was intensified, and doubters, worried about the risks of another Pearl Harbor, remained silent, preferring too much caution to too little. An opinion crystallized in favor of evacuating the Japanese.

The history of law affords nothing more fantastic than the evidence which is supposed to justify this program. General DeWitt's final recommendation to the Secretary of War, dated February 14, 1942, but not made public until early in 1944, explains the basis of his decision.

"In the war in which we are now engaged," he said, "racial affinities are not severed by migration. The Japanese race is an enemy race and while many second and third generation Japanese born on United States soil, possessed of United States citizenship, have become 'Americanized,' the racial strains are undiluted." From the premise of a war of "races," the general had no difficulty reaching his conclusion. There is "no ground for assuming," he said, that Japanese-Americans will not turn against the United States. So much for the idea that men are presumed innocent until proved guilty, and that American citizens stand on an equal footing before the law without regard for race, color, or previous condition of servitude! "It therefore follows," the general added, "that along the vital Pacific Coast over 112,000 potential enemies, of Japanese extraction, are at large today. There are disturbing indications that these are organized and ready for concerted action at a favorable opportunity. The very fact that no sabotage has taken place to date is a disturbing and confirming indication that such action will be taken." [!!!!!]

There was somewhat more evidence than the absence of sabotage to prove its special danger. The Japanese lived closely together, often concentrated around harbors and other strategic areas. Japanese clubs and religious institutions played an important part in their segregated social life. Japanese language schools existed, to preserve for the American born something of the cultural heritage of Japan. The Japanese government, like that of many other countries, asserted a doctrine of nationality different from our own, which gave rise to possible claims of dual citizenship. Thus a long-standing conflict in international law, involving many countries other than Japan, was invoked to cast special doubt on the loyalty of American citizens of Japanese descent.

Much of the suspicion inferentially based on these statements disappears on closer examination. In many instances the concentration of Japanese homes around strategic areas had come about years before, and for entirely innocent reasons. Japanese cannery workers, for example, had had to live on the waterfront in order to be near the plants in which they worked. Japanese truck gardeners had rented land in the industrial outskirts of large cities to be close to their markets. They had rented land for gardening under high tension lines—regarded as a very suspicious circumstance—because the company could not use the land for other purposes; the initiative in starting this practice had come from the utility companies, not from the Japanese.

Despite discrimination against the Japanese, many had done well in America. They were substantial property owners. Their children participated normally and actively in the schools and universities of the West Coast. Their unions and social organizations had passed resolutions of loyalty in great number, before and after Pearl Harbor. It is difficult to find real evidence that either religious or social institutions among the Japanese had successfully fostered Japanese militarism or other dangerous sentiments. The Japanese language schools, which the Japanese-Americans themselves had long sought to put under state control, seem to represent little more than the familiar desire of many immigrant groups to keep alive the language and tradition of the "old country"; in the case of Japanese-Americans, knowledge of the Japanese language was of particular economic importance, since so much of their working life was spent with other Japanese on the West Coast.

Some elements among the Japanese were, of course, suspect. They were known to the authorities, who had for several years been checking on the Japanese-American population. Many had been individually arrested immediately after Pearl Harbor, and the others were under constant surveillance.

It is also true that a considerable percentage of the evacuees later gave negative answers to loyalty questions in the questionnaires they were asked to fill out while in camps. Many of these answers were expressly based upon the treatment the individuals had received; the same shock of evacuation and confinement undoubtedly was responsible for many more. Basically, however, the issue of abstract loyalty is irrelevant. Disloyalty even in the aggravated form of enthusiastic verbal support of the Axis cause, is not a crime in the United States. At most, it is a possible ground for interning enemy aliens. Citizens must do more than talk or think disloyal thoughts before being arrested and jailed.

Apart from the members of the group known to be under suspicion, there was no evidence beyond the vaguest fear to connect the Japanese on the West Coast with the unfavorable military events of 1941 and 1942. Both at Pearl Harbor and in sporadic attacks on the West Coast the enemy had shown that he had knowledge of our dispositions. There was some signaling to enemy ships at sea, both by radio and by lights, along the West Coast. There were several episodes of shelling the coast by submarine—although two of the three such cases mentioned by General DeWitt as tending to create suspicion of the Japanese-Americans took place *after* their removal from the coast. (These were the only such items in his report which were not identified by date.) And those subsequently arrested as Japanese agents in the Pearl Harbor areas were all white men.

The most striking comment on the quality of the evidence produced by General DeWitt to support his proposal was made by Solicitor General Fahy, whose job it was to defend the general's plan before the Supreme Court. He relied upon the general's report "only to the extent that it relates" statistics and other details concerning the actual evacuation and the events which took place after it. But the briefs that he himself presented were identical in the substance of their argument. The Japanese-Americans were an unknown, unknowable, foreign group, living together, and moving in mysterious ways, inscrutable to puzzled white men. Therefore, let them be imprisoned; let their property be taken into custody, sold off at bargain prices, dissipated, and lost; let their roots be torn up, let their children suffer the irreparable shock of life in a concentration camp; let their relation to society be distorted by the searing memory of humiliation, rejection, and punishment.

The evidence supports one conclusion only: the dominant element in the development of our relocation policy was race prejudice, not a military estimate of a military problem.

The Japanese exclusion program rests on five propositions of the utmost potential menace:

1. Protective custody, extending over three or four years, is a permitted form of imprisonment in the United States.

2. Political opinions, not criminal acts, may contain enough danger to justify such imprisonment.

3. Men, women, and children of a given racial group, both Americans and resident aliens, can be presumed to possess the kind of dangerous ideas which require their imprisonment.

4. In time of war or emergency the military—perhaps without even the concurrence of the legislature—can decide what political opinions require imprisonment, and which groups are infected with them.

5. The decision of the military can be carried out without indictment, trial, examination, jury, the confrontation of witnesses, counsel for the defense, the privilege against self-incrimination, or any of the other safeguards of the Bill of Rights.

The idea of punishment only for individual criminal behavior is basic to all systems of civilized law. A great principle was never lost so casually. Mr. Justice Black's comment was weak to the point of impotence: "Hardships are a part of war, and war is an aggregation of hardships." It was an answer in the spirit of the cliche: "Don't you know there's a war going on?" It ignores the rights of citizenship, and the safeguards of trial practice which have been the historical attributes of liberty.

We believe that the German people bear a common political responsibility for outrages secretly committed by the Gestapo and the SS. What are we to think of our own part in a program which violates every principle of our common life, yet has been approved by the President, Congress, and the Supreme Court?

BLOOD ON THE PAVEMENTS *

Damned at home because he does not respect the traditional controls, damned in public because he does not conform to a culture he has not been allowed to understand, the Mexican-American youth is confused and bewildered. He gropes blindly for a way out. One expression of this search for security and recognition was the zoot-suit and the group association it symbolized. But his Anglo-American neighbors, never having trusted him, interpreted his costume as a threat and turned upon him, used him as a scapegoat upon which to unload their own anxieties and frustrations, wreaked vicious physical violence upon him.

The following account of a Los Angeles riot centers upon a single expression of hostility and prejudice, but it touched off a chain of similar riots in other cities and led, eventually, to serious international complications.

* Condensed from *North from Mexico* by Carey McWilliams, pp. 244–53. Copyright, 1948, by Carey McWilliams, published by J. B. Lippincott Company.

On Thursday evening, June 3, 1943, the Alpine Club—made up of young-sters of Mexican descent—held a meeting in a police substation in Los Angeles. Usually these meetings were held in a nearby public school but, since the school was closed, the boys had accepted the invitation of a police captain to meet in the substation. The principal business of the meeting, conducted in the presence of the police captain, consisted in a discussion of how gang-strife could best be avoided in the neighborhood. After the meeting had adjourned, the boys were taken in squad cars to the street corner nearest the neighborhood in which most of them lived. The squad cars were scarcely out of sight, when the boys were assaulted, not by a rival "gang" or "club" but by hoodlum elements in the neighborhood. Of one thing the boys were sure; their assailants were not of Mexican descent.

Earlier the same evening a group of eleven sailors, on leave from their station in Los Angeles, were walking along the 1700 block on North Main Street in the center of one of the city's worst slum areas. The surrounding neighborhood is predominantly Mexican. . . . As they were walking along the street, so they later stated, the sailors were set upon by a gang of Mexican boys. One of the sailors was badly hurt; the others suffered minor cuts and bruises. According to their story, the sailors were outnumbered about three to one.

When the attack was reported to the nearest substation, the police adopted a curious attitude. Instead of attempting to find and arrest the assailants, fourteen policemen remained at the station after their regular duty was over for the night. Then, under the command of a detective lieutenant, the "Vengeance Squad" as they called themselves set out "to clean up" the gang that had attacked the sailors. But—miracle of miracles!—when they arrived at the scene of the attack they could find no one to arrest—not a single Mexican—on their favorite charge of "suspicion of assault." In itself this curious inability to find anyone to arrest—so strikingly at variance with what usually happened on raids of this sort—raises an inference that a larger strategy was involved. For the raid accomplished nothing except to get the names of the raiding officers in the newspapers and to whip up the anger of the community against the Mexican population, which may, per-haps, have been the reason for the raid. . . .

Thus began the so-called "Zoot-Suit Race Riots" which were to last, in one form or another, for a week in Los Angeles.

The Taxicab Brigade

Taking the police raid as an official cue,—a signal for action,—about two hundred sailors decided to take the law into their own hands on the follow-ing night. Coming down into the center of Los Angeles from the Naval

Armory in Chavez Ravine (near the "Chinatown" area), they hired a fleet of twenty taxicabs. Once assembled, the "task force" proceeded to cruise straight through the center of town en route to the east side of Los Angeles where the bulk of the Mexicans reside. Soon the sailors in the lead-car sighted a Mexican boy in a zoot-suit walking along the street. The "task force" immediately stopped and, in a few moments, the boy was lying on the pavement, badly beaten and bleeding. The sailors then piled back into the cabs and the caravan resumed its way until the next zoot-suiter was sighted, whereupon the same procedure was repeated. In these attacks, of course, the odds were pretty uneven: two hundred sailors to one Mexican boy. Four times this same treatment was meted out and four "gangsters," —two seventeen-year-old youngsters, one nineteen, and one twenty-three,— were left lying on the pavements for the ambulance to pick up.

It is indeed curious that in a city like Los Angeles, which boasts that it has more police cars equipped with two-way radio than any other city in the world (Los Angeles *Times,* September 2, 1947), the police were apparently unable to intercept a caravan of twenty taxicabs, loaded with two hundred uniformed, yelling bawdy sailors, as it cruised through the downtown and east-side sections of the city. At one point the police did happen to cross the trail of the caravan and the officers were apparently somewhat embarrassed over the meeting. For only nine of the sailors were taken into custody and the rest were permitted to continue on their merry way. No charges, however, were ever preferred against the nine.

Their evening's entertainment over, the sailors returned to the foot of Chavez Ravine. There they were met by the police and Shore Patrol. The Shore Patrol took seventeen of the sailors into custody and sent the rest up to the ravine to the Naval Armory. The petty officer who had led the expedition, and who was not among those arrested, gave the police a frank statement of things to come. "We're out to do what the police have failed to do," he said; "we're going to clean up this situation. . . . Tonight (by then it was the morning of June fifth) the sailors may have the marines along."

The next day the Los Angeles press pushed the war news from the front page as it proceeded to play up the pavement war in Los Angeles in screaming headlines. "Wild Night in L.A.—Sailor-Zooter Clash" was the headline in the *Daily News.* "Sailor Task Force Hits L.A. Zooters" bellowed the *Herald-Express.* A suburban newspaper gleefully reported that "zoot-suited roughnecks fled to cover before a task force of twenty taxicabs." None of these stories, however, reported the slightest resistance, up to this point, on the part of the Mexicans.

True to their promise, the sailors were joined that night, June fifth, by scores of soldiers and marines. Squads of servicemen, arms linked, paraded through downtown Los Angeles four abreast, stopping anyone wearing zoot-suits and ordering these individuals to put away their "drapes" by the following night or suffer the consequences. Aside from a few half-hearted admonitions, the police made no effort whatever to interfere with these heralds of disorder. However, twenty-seven Mexican boys, gathered on a street corner, were arrested and jailed that evening. While these boys were being booked "on suspicion" of various offenses, a mob of several hundred servicemen roamed the downtown section of a great city threatening members of the Mexican minority without hindrance or interference from the police, the Shore Patrol, or the Military Police.

On this same evening, a squad of sailors invaded a bar on the east side and carefully examined the clothes of the patrons. Two zoot-suit customers, drinking beer at a table, were peremptorily ordered to remove their clothes. One of them was beaten and his clothes were torn from his back when he refused to comply with the order. The other—they were both Mexicans—doffed his "drapes" which were promptly ripped to shreds. Similar occurrences in several parts of the city that evening were sufficiently alarming to have warranted some precautionary measures or to have justified an "out of bounds" order. All that the police officials did, however, was to call up some additional reserves and announce that any Mexicans involved in the rioting would be promptly arrested. That there had been no counterattacks by the Mexicans up to this point apparently did not enter into the police officers' appraisal of the situation. One thing must be said for the Los Angeles police: it is above all consistent. When it is wrong, it is consistently wrong; when it makes a mistake, it will be repeated.

By the night of June sixth the police had worked out a simple formula for action. Knowing that wherever the sailors went there would be trouble, the police simply followed the sailors at a conveniently spaced interval. Six carloads of sailors cruised down Brooklyn Avenue that evening. At Ramona Boulevard, they stopped and beat up eight teenage Mexicans. Failing to find any Mexican zoot-suiters in a bar on Indiana Street, they were so annoyed that they proceeded to wreck the establishment. In due course, the police made a leisurely appearance at the scene of the wreckage but could find no one to arrest. Carefully following the sailors, the police arrested eleven boys who had been beaten up on Carmelita Street; six more victims were arrested a few blocks further on, seven at Ford Boulevard, six at Gifford Street—and so on straight through the Mexican east-side settlements. Behind them came the police, stopping at the same street corners "to mop up" by arresting the injured victims of the mob. By morning, some forty-five Mexican boys, all severely beaten, were under arrest.

Operation "Dixie"

The stage was now set for the really serious rioting of June seventh and eighth. Having featured the preliminary rioting as an offensive launched by sailors, soldiers, and marines, the press now whipped public opinion into a frenzy by dire warnings that Mexican zoot-suiters planned mass retaliations. To insure a riot, the precise street corners were named at which retaliatory action was expected and the time of the anticipated action was carefully specified. In effect these stories announced a riot and invited public participation. "Zooters Planning to Attack More Servicemen," headlined the *Daily News;* "Would jab broken bottlenecks in the faces of their victims. . . . Beating sailors' brains out with hammers also on the program." Concerned for the safety of the Army, the Navy, and the Marine Corps, the *Herald-Express* warned that "Zooters . . . would mass 500 strong."

By way of explaining the action of the police throughout the subsequent rioting, it should be pointed out that, in June, 1943, the police were on a bad spot. A man by the name of Beebe, arrested on a drunk charge, had been kicked to death in the Central Jail by police officers. Through the excellent work of an alert police commissioner, the case had finally been broken and, at the time of the riots, a police officer by the name of Compton Dixon was on trial in the courts. While charges of police brutality had been bandied about for years, this was the first time that a seemingly airtight case had been prepared. Shortly after the riots, a Hollywood police captain told a motion picture director that the police had touched off the riots "in order to give Dixie (Dixon) a break." By staging a fake demonstration of the alleged necessity for harsh police methods, it was hoped that the jury would acquit Dixon. As a matter of fact, the jury did disagree and on July 2, 1943, the charges against Dixon were dismissed.

On Monday evening, June seventh, thousands of *Angelenos,* in response to twelve hours' advance notice in the press, turned out for a mass lynching. Marching through the streets of downtown Los Angeles, a mob of several thousand soldiers, sailors, and civilians, proceeded to beat up every zoot-suiter they could find. Pushing its way into the important motion picture theaters, the mob ordered the management to turn on the house lights and then ranged up and down the aisles dragging Mexicans out of their seats. Street cars were halted while Mexicans, and some Filipinos and Negroes, were jerked out of their seats, pushed into the streets, and beaten with sadistic frenzy. If the victims wore zoot-suits, they were stripped of their clothing and left naked or half-naked on the streets, bleeding and bruised. Proceeding down Main Street from First to Twelfth, the mob stopped on the edge of the Negro district. Learning that the Negroes planned a warm reception for them, the mobsters turned back and marched through the Mexican east side spreading panic and terror.

Here is one of numerous eye-witness accounts written by Al Waxman, editor of *The Eastside Journal:*

At Twelfth and Central I came upon a scene that will long live in my memory. Police were swinging clubs and servicemen were fighting with civilians. Wholesale arrests were being made by the officers.

Four boys came out of a pool hall. They were wearing zoot-suits that have become the symbol of a fighting flag. Police ordered them into arrest cars. One refused. He asked: "Why am I being arrested?" The police officer answered with three swift blows of the night-stick across the boy's head and he went down. As he sprawled, he was kicked in the face. Police had difficulty loading his body into the vehicle because he was one-legged and wore a wooden limb. Maybe the officer didn't know he was attacking a cripple.

At the next corner a Mexican mother cried out, "Don't take my boy, he did nothing. He's only fifteen years old. Don't take him." She was struck across the jaw with a night-stick and almost dropped the two and a half year old baby that was clinging in her arms. . . .

Rushing back to the east side to make sure that things were quiet here, I came upon a band of servicemen making a systematic tour of East First Street. They had just come out of a cocktail bar where four men were nursing bruises. Three autos loaded with Los Angeles policemen were on the scene but the soldiers were not molested. Farther down the street the men stopped a streetcar, forcing the motorman to open the door and proceeded to inspect the clothing of the male passengers. "We're looking for zoot-suits to burn," they shouted. Again the police did not interfere. . . . Half a block away . . . I pleaded with the men of the local police substation to put a stop to these activities. "It is a matter for the military police," they said.

Throughout the night the Mexican communities were in the wildest possible turmoil. Scores of Mexican mothers were trying to locate their youngsters and several hundred Mexicans milled around each of the police substations and the Central Jail trying to get word of missing members of their families. Boys came into the police stations saying: "Charge me with vagrancy or anything, but don't send me out there!" pointing to the streets where other boys, as young as twelve and thirteen years of age, were being beaten and stripped of their clothes. From affidavits which I helped prepare at the time, I should say that not more than half of the victims were actually wearing zoot-suits. A Negro defense worker, wearing a defense-plant identification badge on his workclothes, was taken from a street car and one of his eyes was gouged out with a knife. Huge half-page photographs, showing Mexican boys stripped of their clothes, cowering on the pavements, often bleeding profusely, surrounded by jeering mobs of men and women, appeared in all the Los Angeles newspapers. As Al Waxman most truthfully reported, blood had been "spilled on the streets of the city."

At midnight on June seventh, the military authorities decided that the local police were completely unable or unwilling to handle the situation, despite the fact that a thousand reserve officers had been called up. The entire downtown area of Los Angeles was then declared "out of bounds" for military personnel. This order immediately slowed down the pace of the rioting. The moment the Military Police and Shore Patrol went into action, the rioting quieted down. On June eighth the city officials brought their heads up out of the sand, took a look around, and began issuing statements. The district attorney, Fred N. Howser, announced that the "situation is getting entirely out of hand," while Mayor Fletcher Bowron thought that "sooner or later it will blow over." The chief of police, taking a count of the Mexicans in jail, cheerfully proclaimed that "the situation has now cleared up." All agreed however that it was quite "a situation."

Unfortunately "the situation" had not cleared up; nor did it blow over. It began to spread to the suburbs where the rioting continued for two more days. When it finally stopped, the Eagle Rock *Advertiser* mournfully editorialized: "It is too bad the servicemen were called off before they were able to complete the job. . . . Most of the citizens of the city have been delighted with what has been going on." County Supervisor Roger Jessup told the newsmen: "All that is needed to end lawlessness is more of the same action as is being exercised by the servicemen!" While the district attorney of Ventura, an outlying county, jumped on the bandwagon with a statement to the effect that "zoot suits are an open indication of subversive character." This was also the opinion of the Los Angeles City Council which adopted a resolution making the wearing of zoot-suits a misdemeanor! On June eleventh, hundreds of handbills were distributed to students and posted on bulletin boards in a high school attended by many Negroes and Mexicans which read: "Big Sale. Second-Hand Zoot Suits. Slightly Damaged. Apply at Nearest U.S. Naval Station. While they last we have your Size."

When the Devil Is Sick . . .

Egging on the mob to attack Mexicans in the most indiscriminate manner, the press developed a fine technique in reporting the riots. "44 Zooters Jailed in Attacks on Sailors" was the chief headline in the *Daily News* of June seventh; "Zoot Suit Chiefs Girding for War on Navy" was the headline in the same paper on the following day. The moralistic tone of this reporting is illustrated by a smug headline in the Los Angeles *Times* of June seventh: "Zoot Suiters Learn Lesson in Fight with Servicemen." The riots, according to the same paper, were having "a cleansing effect."

An editorial in the *Herald-Express* said that the riots "promise to rid the community of . . . those zoot-suited miscreants." While Mr. Manchester Boddy, in a signed editorial in the *Daily News* of June ninth excitedly announced that "the time for temporizing is past. . . . The time has come to serve notice that the City of Los Angeles will no longer be terrorized by a relatively small handful of morons parading as zoot suit hoodlums. To delay action *now* means to court disaster later on." As though there had been any "temporizing" in this sense for the prior two years!

But once the Navy had declared the downtown section of Los Angeles "out of bounds," once the Mexican ambassador in Washington had addressed a formal inquiry to Secretary of State Hull, and once official Washington began to advise the local minions of the press of the utterly disastrous international effects of the riots, in short when the local press realized the consequences of its own lawless action, a great thunderous cry for "unity," and "peace," and "order" went forth. One after the other, the editors began to disclaim all responsibility for the riots which, two days before, had been hailed for their "salutary" and "cleansing" effect.

Thus on June eleventh the Los Angeles *Times,* in a pious mood, wrote that,

at the outset, zoot-suiters were limited to no specific race; they were Anglo-Saxon, Latin and Negro. The fact that later on their numbers seemed to be predominately Latin was in itself no indictment of that race at all. No responsible person at any time condemned Latin-Americans as such.

Feeling a twinge of conscience, Mr. Boddy wrote that "only a ridiculously small percentage of the local Mexican population is involved in the so-called gang demonstrations. Every true Californian has an affection for his fellow citizens of Mexican ancestry that is as deep rooted as the Mexican culture that influences our way of living, our architecture, our music, our language, and even our food." This belated discovery of the Spanish-Mexican cultural heritage of California was, needless to say, rather ironic in view of the fact that the ink was not yet dry on Mr. Boddy's earlier editorial in which he had castigated the Mexican minority as "morons." To appreciate the ironic aspects of "the situation," the same newspapers that had been baiting Mexicans for nearly two years now began to extol them.

As might have been expected, this post-mortem mood of penitence and contrition survived just long enough for some of the international repercussions of the riots to quiet down. Within a year, the press and the police were back in the same old groove. On July 16, 1944, the Los Angeles *Times* gave front-page prominence to a curious story under the heading: "Youthful Gang Secrets Exposed." Indicating no source, identifying no spokesman, the story went on to say that "authorities of the Superior Court" had unearthed a dreadful "situation" among juvenile delinquents. Juveniles were using narcotics, marihuana, and smoking "reefers." Compelled to accept drug addiction, "unwilling neophytes" were dragooned into committing robberies and other crimes. Young girls were tatooed with various "secret cabalistic symbols" of gang membership. The high pompadours affected by the *cholitas,* it was said, were used to conceal knives and other "weapons." Two theories were advanced in the story by way of "explaining" the existence of these dangerous gangs: first, that "subversive groups" in Los Angeles had organized them; and, second, that "the gangs are the result of mollycoddling of racial groups." In view of the record, one is moved to inquire, what mollycoddling? by the police? by the juvenile authorities? by the courts? Backing up the news story, an editorial appeared in the *Times* on July eighteenth entitled: "It's Not a Nice Job But It Has To Be Done." Lashing out at "any maudlin and misguided sympathy for the 'poor juveniles,'" the editorial went on to say that "stern punishment is what is needed; stern and sure punishment. The police and the Sheriff's men should be given every encouragement to go after these young gangsters."

Problem 20: Future Prospects in Race Relations-- Democracy or Tradition?

If we, as Americans, admit to the prejudicial attitudes and the discriminatory practices recounted in the readings of the previous section, we are faced immediately with the problem of what we intend to do to bring practice into closer agreement with our ideals. There are, of course, those who feel that the United States has already moved too far in this direction and would like to backtrack to an earlier position. Our first reading in the present section represents this point of view.

A majority of American citizens, on the other hand, would agree that change in the direction of the fulfillment of the nation's democratic ideology is desirable. Here, however, the agreement ends. Many of those who agree that changes need to be made spend their energies defending one specific approach and objecting to others. Questions of How? and When? are the subject of much dispute. Shall we depend upon the slow and perhaps doubtful process of education? Shall we legislate? Are personal crusades effective? Should minority groups press their demands on the majority? The following articles embody, either explicitly or implicitly, most of the major recommendations about the means that have been advocated to extend the democratic philosophy.

SENATOR BILBO MEETS THE PRESS *

Although the myth of white, Protestant, Anglo-Saxon superiority has been unconsciously accepted by large numbers of people, the open espousal of white supremacy as a way of life is limited. Until his death a few years ago, Senator Bilbo of Mississippi was one of the most articulate advocates of white supremacy as a solution to problems arising out of social conflict. In a broadcast of "Meet the Press," the American press conference of the air, presented on a national network, Senator Bilbo virtually wrote an essay on this aspect of racism. The evidence that these were his views is irrefutable, since most of the exposition is by Bilbo himself.

The selection is inserted here because many of these concepts are still entertained and because the editors believe that only through an examination of undemocratic thought can the true value of democracy be appreciated.

Participants:
SENATOR THEODORE G. BILBO
BERT ANDREWS, New York *Herald Tribune*
CECIL B. DICKSON, Gannett Publications
ERNEST K. LINDLEY, *Newsweek*
LAWRENCE E. SPIVAK, Editor of *The American Mercury*
Presiding:
JACK PAGE, Mutual Broadcasting System

SPIVAK: Senator, are you or have you ever been a member of the Ku Klux Klan?
BILBO: I have—
SPIVAK: Do you think—
BILBO: —I am a member of the Ku Klux Klan No. 40, called Bilbo, Bilbo Klan No. 40, Poplarville, Mississippi. I attended one meeting and have

* *The American Mercury,* November, 1946, pp. 528–34.

not attended it since, because I was not in sympathy with some of the things in it.

SPIVAK: Are you in sympathy with what the Klan stands for now?

BILBO: I don't know what the present Klan stands for. I'm not advised. But if you pardon me, I heard Governor Talmadge tell some newspaper-men last Friday night, they could find out all about it by consulting Governor Arnall of Georgia. He is a member and received some kind of a plaque award as a member of the Klan.

ANDREWS: Do you think that Governor Arnall would get the Klan support now, Senator?

BILBO: How's that?

ANDREWS: Do you think Governor Arnall would get any Klan support now?

BILBO: No traitor of any organization or Klan, ever got any support.

ANDREWS: Do you think you would get any Klan support now, sir?

BILBO: I do.

ANDREWS: You have never left the Klan, in effect?

BILBO: No man can leave the Klan. He takes an oath to do that. He is —once a Ku Klux, always a Ku Klux.

SPIVAK: Senator, how can you take an oath to uphold the laws of your state and your country and be a member of an organization that secretly undermines those laws, as the Klan does?

BILBO: I am not informed that the Ku Klux Klan, as I know it, is seeking to undermine this government. It is only the Communist Party of the United States that is seeking to do that by force.

SPIVAK: Don't you think that any group that engages in lynching tends to undermine the laws of the government?

BILBO: I do not believe in lynch law, and as governor of the state I discouraged it—I was governor of my state for two terms, eight years—and I did everything in my power to do away with lynch law in my state. No good citizen of the South believes in lynch laws.

ANDREWS: Senator Bilbo, if you don't believe in lynch law, I wish you would explain in very simple terms to all of us what you meant by the statement that was several times attributed to you as having been made in campaign speeches down there: that the way to stop Negroes from voting was to stop them the night before.

BILBO: Evidently, Mr. Andrews, you have been reading the *Saturday Evening Post* and *Collier's* and *Time* and *Life, PM* and the *Voice,* and *Amsterdam News* and the New York *News*—

ANDREWS: No, Sir.

BILBO: —and others.

ANDREWS: No, sir, Senator, I have been reading the *Herald Tribune.* I have great faith in the *Herald Tribune's* honesty, and those quotes.

BILBO: The reporters may not be so reliable.

ANDREWS: I think that on this, sir, I would bet on the reporters' integrity against yours, because all of the reporters seem to agree on that particular quote. What did they all do: go out and manufacture it? Or what did you say that approximated that?

BILBO: I said the best time to keep a nigger away from a white Democratic primary in Mississippi was to see him the night before.

ANDREWS: Well, what did you mean by that? Doesn't that amount to lynch law to keep him away from the polls? To intimidate him?

BILBO: I did not, sir.

PAGE: Senator and others of the group, for the balance of the program we will have to ask you not to refer to any race, group or individual in any derogatory term.

BILBO: Very well.

SPIVAK: Senator—

BILBO: Wait a minute, I want to finish with Mr. Andrews. I meant by that, the time to keep a Negro from voting in a white Democratic primary in which, under the law, he had no right to vote, was to see him and advise with him the night before and tell him that he had no right, because I read the law, in practically every speech I made, passed in 1942, that disqualified every Negro in Mississippi from voting in our white Democratic primary. And I've got a copy of that law here.

ANDREWS: Wasn't that in effect to intimidate any Negroes who might have differed with your interpretation of the law and to keep them from the polls?

BILBO: Well, you can call it what you may. It's good diplomacy and good strategy to keep them from voting.

SPIVAK: Senator, do you believe in the Constitution of the United States? Did you as a Senator take an oath to uphold that?

BILBO: I have, repeatedly, sir, both as state senator, lieutenant governor, twice governor, and two times Senator.

SPIVAK: Do you remember Article XV, which says, "The right of a citizen to vote shall not be denied or abridged by the United States or by any state on account of race, color, or previous condition of servitude"? Did you take an oath to uphold the Fifteenth Amendment?

BILBO: Notwithstanding the fact that the Fourteenth and Fifteenth Amendments were adopted through fraud, I did take an oath to uphold it, and I am upholding it. I have not violated it.

SPIVAK: Do you believe, when you speak as you did in your primary, you are upholding the Fifteenth Amendment?

BILBO: I certainly was. There was nothing in violation of the provision of the Constitution in anything that I said; and I said further that it was the duty of every white Democrat in Mississippi to resort to every means within the law to keep the Negro from voting in our primary, because they were not qualified to vote.

LINDLEY: Senator Bilbo, once, I believe, perhaps more than once, you boasted on the floor of Congress that you ran for statewide office without ever having mentioned the Negroes or the race question. I don't know which of your several races you referred to. I suppose you got elected; you usually do. I wonder why you changed your tactics and have made the race question such a prominent thing in your campaign?

BILBO: Mr. Lindley, that's a very fine question, and it's timely and pertinent. That's true, I was elected state senator and lieutenant governor and twice governor and twice United States Senator, and never discussed the race question, had nothing to say, because, you must understand, in Mississippi the Negro has not voted in the white Democratic primary, in Mississippi, for fifty-six years; and it was just in this campaign that the CIO-PAC announced that they were setting aside a million dollas to organize the people of my state, in the South, in an effort to have the Negroes to participate in our white primary under the Texas law.

ANDREWS: Well, Senator—have you finished?

BILBO: And not only that. The activities of certain segments of our population, and certain organizations in our country, in their attempt to have the Negro to vote in our white Democratic primary, has been so persistent until the time had come for me to discuss an issue that was facing my people, if we proposed to hold and retain white control within our state, which we propose to do.

ANDREWS: Senator, leaving out the CIO and the PAC, hasn't the Supreme Court of the United States also upheld the right of the Negroes to vote in the white primaries?

BILBO: Yes. I think Hugo Black wrote an opinion in the Texas case that gave the Negroes the right. By the way, the Southern Conference for Human Welfare gave him a plaque, and one of the speakers on the occasion intimated that's why they were doing it, because of that opinion that he had delivered, giving the Negro a right to vote in the white Democratic primaries of the state of Texas.

ANDREWS: But then, in effect, sir, you don't recognize the Supreme Court's right to say what is constitutional and what is not constitutional?

BILBO: I'm not taking issue, and I said in all my speeches in this campaign that under the decisions of the Supreme Court, the Negro was qualified to vote in the primaries of Mississippi. But in 1942, the legislature in Mississippi passed a law, which they had a right to, that prohibited the Negro from voting at this time in our white Democratic primaries.

ANDREWS: Governor, you have had a white Democratic—

BILBO: Wait a minute. And this law provides that no party could vote in any primary, whether Democratic, Republican or Socialist, unless he had been in accord with that party in which he sought a chance to vote in for the last two preceding years, and there wasn't a Negro in Mississippi that could qualify under that law. Now, I was only trying to be law-abiding when I was trying to keep the Negro from voting in this primary.

ANDREWS: But when they are not allowed to vote in this primary or another primary a year from now, how could they ever qualify under that law?

BILBO: They'll never qualify to vote in the white Democratic primaries in Mississippi, because we are going to abolish the primary under the opinion of the Supreme Court and hold our own party elections so the Supreme Court can't monkey with our business.

SPIVAK: Senator, are you very proud of what white supremacy has done in your state? I have before me a quotation from a Pulitzer prize winner, Hodding Carter, publisher of the Greenville, Mississippi, *Times*—and I quote—he says: "My state is at or near the bottom of the list in literacy, venereal disease, low income per person, public health, unpunished crimes of violence, including lynching." Is that what white supremacy has done in the state of Mississippi?

BILBO: Mr. Spivak, I'm glad you brought up Mr. Carter's name, because it gives me an opportunity to tell you that he is the biggest liar in the South, and the A-number-1 quisling and betrayer and traitor to the South.

SPIVAK: Well, Governor—

BILBO: Now wait a minute; I'm not through. When he makes a statement, and when any newspaper makes a statement—and I regret very much that they don't stop to analyze the situation—when they talk about the low standards of the people of Mississippi, they predicate that by lumping the Negro race into our white population and consider them all together, which gives us a low rating. But, if you take the white people of Mississippi, the standard of the citizenship in literacy and in information and intelligence and patriotism is above the citizenship of Pennsylvania, New Jersey, New York or Massachusetts. Now I have campaigned in all those states, or part of them (I made three campaigns through Pennsylvania) and I think I know people when I speak to them.

DICKSON: Senator—

BILBO: Let me go a little further. We have in Mississippi the finest school system of any state in the Union. We have a half a dozen state-supported higher educational institutions—five, I believe it is—we have twelve junior colleges, and we have quite a bunch of agricultural high schools; and all our schools are graded schools, are consolidated, and the students are hauled to these schools, which gives us a very high percentage of literacy and general intelligent information.

SPIVAK: Governor, do you know the average of illiteracy—I just want to get this thing in—the average of illiteracy in the country is 14 per cent but Mississippi is 30 per cent?

DICKSON: Senator—

BILBO: Wait until I get through with Mr. Spivak. I just got through telling you that the Negro is counted in on the rating of Mississippi's literacy—

SPIVAK: These figures are on the whites.

BILBO: —Now, if you take the Negro out, if you take the white people alone, you will find they rate higher than Pennsylvania, New Jersey or Massachusetts.

SPIVAK: The figures I gave you were only on the whites.

DICKSON: Right here, Senator, in the median scores of the AEF intelligence test, Southern whites of Mississippi score 41.2. How do you reconcile your white supremacy theory with the fact that on an AEF intelligence test, Negroes living in the North showed a higher intelligence rating than did the whites of Mississippi?

BILBO: I recognize that by knowing all the time that it's not true. I've heard it, seen it, read it.

ANDREWS: In fact, anything that you don't agree with is either manufactured by some reporter or it is just plain not true; is that it?

BILBO: No, Sir! I'll back up my statements.

LINDLEY: Senator, what do you mean by "white" in connection with the "white" race? Do you include people of Italian descent as among the people of the white race?

BILBO: Most certainly. When I speak of the white race, I am not speaking about nationalities like Italians and Poles and Jews. We are all of the white race. When I speak of white and black, I am talking about the white races and the white race, which has lots of nationalities in it, and I think of them as white, as contrasted with the Africans in our citizenship.

LINDLEY: Didn't you, within recent months, address a letter to a person of Italian descent in which you saluted this person as "Dear Dago"?

BILBO: I did.

DICKSON: What was the idea, Senator?

BILBO: Mr. Dickson, I am sorry that you gentlemen haven't kept up on my former statements.

DICKSON: Inform us, please.

BILBO: I'll do it. While I was fighting the FEPC, which is a Communistic concoction—the purpose underlying it all is the integration of the Negro into the white race and forcing them to associate together in the offices and shops of the nation; that is the underlying purpose behind FEPC—I received a very insulting letter from a lady in New York, and she was very particular to tell me in her letter that she was neither a Negro or a Jew. Well—well, her letter was so insulting; she said she wasn't a Negro and she wasn't a Jew. I used an old Southern phrase that we always use when we speak of certain classes of Europeans: I just said "My dear Dago." And in that letter I said: "In this case if I am mistaken, please inform me." Now, I have never had a reply from her. She seemed to accept it without any correction, because I asked her in the salutation to give me a correction, which she did not.

LINDLEY: Senator on April 26th—

BILBO: Wait a minute. Now in that connection, I want to say that I have no prejudice whatever against the Italian people, because all the Italians in Mississippi support me, and all the high-class Jews support me.

LINDLEY: You have no prejudice against the Jews, either?

BILBO: No, sir, I have not, sir.

LINDLEY: On April 26th, according to the *Congressional Record,* you referred to some of the recent immigrants to this country as being the rabble of war-torn Europe. To whom did you refer?

BILBO: Well, I mean in comparison with the standards of our white people of America, with our education and culture and refinement and development. These people who were brought over here, some of them, were rabbles.

PAGE: Gentlemen, I am sorry, but our time is up.

◆◆◆◆

MRS. TILLY'S CRUSADE *

Too frequently race relations are discussed in terms of stereotypes, such as "Southern intolerance," "Southern indifference." What follows is an account of another South—one that is taking positive, constructive action in Negro-white relationships. To the recurring question "What can *I* do?" this story provides a concrete answer that is in accord with the best of American ideals and the tradition of individual initiative.

Outside the South, people hear about the floggings and the burning crosses, the intimidation at the polls, and the candidates who get elected by

* Helena Huntington Smith, *Collier's,* December 30, 1950, pp. 29, 66–67.

calling their opponents "nigger lovers." But they rarely hear about the sort of thing that happened last spring in Claxton, Georgia. Claxton is a rural county seat of 2,000 without any of the Southern liberal elements of big cities like Atlanta. But it had had its fill of Ku Klux Klan outrages: a pregnant woman flogged, an old preacher beaten up because he was accused—as it happens falsely—of teaching civil rights to his people. And so, early last year Claxton, by unanimous vote of its city council, slapped on an ordinance prohibiting the wearing of masks within its city limits. The Klan hasn't been back since.

Fewer than 40 of Georgia's 600 municipalities have passed such an anti-mask law. Yet there are those who detect, in Claxton's move to clean its own house, a bright new wave of the future.

For the good people of Claxton were not acting alone, but as part of a network with strands all over the South, a network of decent citizens opposed to violence and discrimination in their own communities. Many are church members, who believe in what they call "Christian race relations." Their headquarters is Atlanta, and their leader is a tiny and completely feminine woman who is as Southern as magnolia blossoms, yet, at the same time, a lionhearted champion of human rights.

The mere existence of Mrs. Milton E. Tilly makes Northerners rub their eyes. Born in Hampton, Georgia, raised on a plantation, sweet-voiced and with a fondness for roses in her hats, she is the perfect prototype of the Southern lady. But she has served on President Truman's civil rights commission—the only Southern woman on it—and has been paid the high compliment of receiving a Klan threat to blow up her house.

Mild-mannered Dorothy Tilly has been called "the most influential woman in the South." So great is her repute that some years ago, during the high-riding regime of the late Governor Eugene Talmadge, she obtained within a few brief weeks' time 28,000 signatures of Georgia women on a petition for a Negro training school, and then proceeded to stampede the appropriation for the school past a Talmadge veto.

Her answer to the invariable query by non-Southerners, "What's happening in Dixie?" is: "Nothing that wasn't happening in my girlhood," and she is in her sixties. "There have always been Southerners who put humanity above color."

If a Negro is held without charges in a county jail; if his lawyers are threatened with violence; if somebody has been killed or beaten and the law does nothing; if a DP family is kept in near peonage on a lonely farm, word somehow gets to Mrs. Tilly in Atlanta.

Sometimes it is brought by a relative of the victim, who turns up at the office of the Southern Regional Council, 63 Auburn Avenue, Atlanta, where she has her headquarters; often the messenger is waiting when Mrs.

Tilly, an early bird, arrives before eight in the morning. Or somebody drives across a county line or two—it is dangerous to use the phone near home on such an errand—and telephones her long-distance in the middle of the night. "Please come and help us," is the plea.

Mrs. Tilly has had these calls from all over the South. She always knows someone in the vicinity who will act, and usually she goes to the scene herself. Keeping in the background, careful never to appear as an outsider interfering in local affairs, she takes a group of local women with her. They're willing and glad to help; in their own words, they "don't know how to do" until someone shows them. Together with Mrs. Tilly, they call on the sheriff, the county judge and other influential local folk, pleading the cause of justice. Sometimes they succeed in getting the innocent out of jail and evildoers punished; sometimes they fail. Often they run into a political situation too tough to crack. But that doesn't stop them.

"We may not always get justice," Mrs. Tilly says, a shade defiantly, "but we can get public opinion so stirred up that the same thing can't ever happen in that community again."

During the first campaign of Herman Talmadge for governor, an Associated Press correspondent telephoned from the south Georgia turpentine country to tell her that a Negro schoolhouse had been burned. The story was pathetic. White people had moved away, so the plantation owner had turned over an empty school building to the Negroes. Out of their small earnings they had raised $100, and fixed up one of the two rooms as a community center. On the night of the gala opening a white man told them: "You will never hold another meeting in that schoolhouse." Next day it was a heap of ashes, and the odor of gasoline still lingered.

When Mrs. Tilly and two churchwomen from the neighborhood got there, even the local minister was unaware of the tragedy, and the sheriff explained: "I ain't never done nothin' because nobody asked me to." By the time the flying squad of three determined ladies got through, people were saying, "It's a shame!" and they raised money for a library "to build back race relations."

How does Mrs. Tilly do it? Simple, she says; merely set the facts before a few good people in the community, and they will stir up the consciences of the rest.

"There is not a spot in the South," she adds, "without its good, liberal-minded people who are terribly hurt when disaster and disgrace fall on the community through broken human relationships. They are eager to do something that will say to the Negroes and to the outside world: "We have had no part in this evil thing."

Her faith in goodness is awe-inspiring. But she backs it up with shrewd political know-how, and with a colossal card-index file, covering the whole

South, of what she calls "key people," principally ministers and leaders of churchwomen's societies. Most of us believe in virtue; but Mrs. Tilly has its address and telephone number.

For instance, when word reached Atlanta last year that a member of the South Carolina Assembly had invited Grand Dragon Sam Green of the Georgia Klan to speak to that legislative body, Alexander Miller, Southern regional director of the Anti-Defamation League, phoned Mrs. Tilly. Promptly she got out her South Carolina file, and within a week, 1,000 letters signed Dorothy Tilly poured out to "key people" in South Carolina church societies and civic groups. The Klanminded Assemblyman was so snowed under with protests that he made an indignant speech denouncing this foreign woman from Georgia for poking into South Carolina's affairs.

That was last year. This year South Carolina passed an anti-Klan law.

The bewildered Northerner, with certain Southern stereotypes embedded firmly in his mind, wonders why Mrs. Tilly isn't lynched, or at least ostracized. She goes down the line for even the most embittered aspects of the civil rights program, including FEPC, and she makes it plain that she thinks segregation nonsense.

Injustice Is the Nation's Business

The South's most cherished doctrine, "Just leave us alone to work out our own problems," leaves her cold. When something bad happens—like two little girls being imprisoned in a county jail to force their father to talk—she is on a plane and off to Washington, entreating her good friends the Attorney General or J. Edgar Hoover to put the resources of the FBI to work in Georgia. When people mutter about "Yankee interference," she retorts: "What happens to any person in this country is the business of the whole country."

Yet for all her bold trampling on tenderest Southern corns, she does it, somehow, as a member of the family. And instead of disowning her, the family showers her with honors.

In one month last spring, the Pi Sigma Alpha fraternity at Emory University, in Atlanta, made her an honorary member, and the North Georgia conference of her own Methodist Woman's Society gave her its highest award, "because you have stretched our minds and hearts to recognize our kinship with all men everywhere."

When a group of Southern women's organizations named her Woman of Achievement in Social Welfare two years ago, the Atlanta Women's Chamber of Commerce and the Atlanta Constitution backed it up handsomely with a chest of silver.

Not long ago I went with her to a meeting of the Georgia Interracial Committee in Macon. After it was over, an attractive young Negro couple drove us in their car to the bus terminal. My betrayal of surprise, after they left us, drew a gleam of amusement from Mrs. Tilly. Her whole family has long been the sort which always puts humanity first.

This definitely applies to Mr. Tilly, a tall, pleasant, easygoing gentleman who carries a pocketful of clippings about his wife's activities, and produces them, beaming, at the slightest excuse. He has backed her up in everything she has done.

When, in 1945, the White House called up to ask her to serve on the President's civil rights commission, Mr. Tilly stood beside his wife as she was gasping, "Who? Me?" into the telephone, urging her, "Say yes! You can do it!" They have one son and a nineteen-year-old grandson, also her stanch supporters. A devoted sister, who is a librarian for the blind, lives with them and takes over the house when Mrs. Tilly is on her frequent travels; she spoke in 30 of the 48 states last year.

Her father was a Methodist minister. "Throughout my youth," she recalls, "I saw and heard the troubles of the community, both Negro and white, pour over the doorstep of the parsonage." She learned there that, regardless of color, people were people first. Her mother and grandmother, women of independent mind, helped with the lesson.

After Dorothy graduated from Wesleyan College for Women, in Macon, her first work was among white children, under the sponsorship of the Methodist church. It was Mr. Tilly who set her on her present path.

"During the depression," she says, "he would drive me around Atlanta and show me things I couldn't bear to look at, like little Negro children eating out of garbage cans behind a downtown hotel. I said, 'I don't want to see it because it hurts me and I can't do anything about it.' He said, 'If it hurts you enough you will tell other people and they will do something.'"

She did and they are. But it took a long time.

For 20 years and more she has been traveling over the South as investigator for her various organizations, on the track of horror and injustice.

She was on the scene the second day after the quadruple lynching in Monroe, Georgia, in 1946. Driving from gas station to gas station and buying a gallon at a time, stopping for a soda here and a Coke there, she got the full story from stunned, horrified people—who a few days later had clammed up and would talk to nobody. A local woman told her how she had been on her way home from a church meeting a few nights before the thing happened, how she had passed some cars gathered on a lonely road, and how her heart had frozen, because she had heard rumors, and she felt that she was seeing a rehearsal of a lynching.

"What did you do?" Mrs. Tilly asked.

"Nothing," she replied. *"I didn't know what to do."*

Soon afterward Mrs. Tilly was in Columbia, Tennessee, in the wake of the race riot which wrecked the Negro community and cost the lives of two men killed in jail. A white minister told her sadly: "Our Negro maid called me that night and asked me to do something to stop the madness of the mob. *But I didn't know what to do.* So I went to bed."

With those words echoing in her ears, Dorothy Tilly prepared a leaflet which has since gone out through the Southern Regional Council, forearming members with a few simple rules in the event of a calamity: Call the sheriff and tell him you expect him to do his duty. Call and tell the state patrol the same. Call the local editor, the state-wide papers, the ministers, the civic leaders and the headquarters of the network—the Southern Regional Council in Atlanta.

The major part of her interracial work today is done as field representative of that organization. Beyond that, it is almost impossible to keep track of her connections. A colleague explains: "Mrs. Tilly goes and does what has to be done, and finds out later whom she did it for." She herself has a feminine vagueness about the jawbreaking names of the countless boards, committees, councils, conferences and associations to which she belongs.

But she has functioned, in a policymaking capacity, on the Georgia Interracial Committee, the Urban League of Atlanta, the Georgia Council of Church Women, the Georgia Conference of Social Work and a few dozen other organizations, and above all as a Methodist woman. From 1940 to 1948 she was secretary of Christian Social Relations of the Woman's Society of Christian Service of the Methodist Church, southeastern jurisdiction. They paid her travel expenses, but no salary. She has been some kind of officer of the Methodist organization ever since she became president of a juvenile missionary society at the age of twelve.

She is a national figure in all kinds of labor, social welfare, child welfare and rural welfare circles. In 1944 she went to Washington as a lobbyist to save the Farm Security Administration. Congress was going to let FSA die for lack of appropriations, so the Farmers Union, Catholic Rural Life Conference, Federal Council of Churches, AFL and CIO sent her off to the national capital to plead for its continuance. An ardent dry, Mrs. Tilly is probably the only successful lobbyist in recent history to entertain congressmen without a drop of liquor.

And then there was the affair of the 28,000 names. Georgia never had a training school for delinquent Negro girls until the middle thirties, when the Negro women themselves, through their state-wide Women's Club organization, raised the money for one. That is, they bought a plot of land,

and with WPA help built a building on it. Then they presented it to the state. But the legislature failed to pass an appropriation to open it.

"We were angry," Mrs. Tilly says quietly. "Next year we got the appropriation through and Eugene Talmadge vetoed the bill. Then we were angry sure enough."

She appealed to her old allies, the women's church organizations, and they came through. The signatures of twenty-eight thousand Georgia women, pleading for the Negro training school, were rounded up in time for the next opening of the legislature. The lawmakers fell over each other climbing on the band wagon.

"You should have seen the opening of that school," Mrs. Tilly smiles. "On the platform were Negro and white sponsors and speakers—no thought of segregation—and the pastor said: 'I dedicate that which has already been consecrated by the tears of the women of both races in Georgia.'"

Behind all this lies a historical fact: that the conscience of the South is its women, in church or out of it, as many a preacher will tell you, when it comes to courage to do the right thing, the women are far ahead of the men.

One of the first big steps toward interracial decency in the South was the formation, two decades ago, of the Association of Southern Women for the Prevention of Lynching.

Today—whether it is because men are made timid by their business and political connections—observers agree that in every county and little town, a handful of women and a preacher or two are first to point out right and wrong, boldly.

Courtroom Scene Shocked Her

In 1947, Mrs. Tilly sat in the courtroom in Greenville, South Carolina, during the trial of 31 taxi drivers for the lynch murder of a Negro named Willie Earle. It left a special kind of mark upon her to see the defendants and the jury making a brazen mockery of the trial, openly talking and cracking jokes back and forth. She thought: *People don't know about this. If they did they would stop it. If the good people were here, just their presence would stop it.*

So last year she and several other women launched an organization which they call the Fellowship of the Concerned, "because it was built on our concern over what had happened in Greenville and several places in Georgia." This idea was so simple it was genius—that if the good people would merely sit as observers in their courts, much evil would be avoided. This remarkable organization has no officers, no constitution and no dues, only a pledge which those "concerned" sign and send to the Southern Regional Council: "I will sit in the courts, and I will . . . learn how justice operates in my community. I will work with others in times of tension to see that the rights of all are protected."

Mrs. Tilly's aim is to recruit a membership covering every county seat in the South. "There's so much goodness everywhere," she says, "there's not a spot we can't reach."

The strange part of it is that she may be right. Within the first few months after the launching of the fellowship, women were signing up in all 12 Southern states. By now the whole northern half of Georgia is covered and most of the southern half. Twenty-five names came in from one cross-roads village of 500 during the first rush.

"We expect that in three years we can change the pattern of justice in the South," Mrs. Tilly serenely predicts.

Besides sitting in the courts, these women watch the polls to see that Negroes are allowed to vote; they work for a fair break for Negroes in housing and education. In Louisville a number of them got the idea of taking turns watching at the city hospital on Saturday nights—always a hot time, what with brawls and arrests for drunkenness—to gain an insight into community problems. The first problem they noticed was that no Negro doctor was admitted to practice at the hospital. The hospital board will have an uncomfortable time until this is remedied.

Enrolling the "Concerned"

Half of the counties in Kentucky are now organized into the unique net-work of the "concerned," 14 counties in South Carolina, seven in Tennessee, eight in North Carolina. Some time ago the enrollment passed the 3,000 mark, but when I asked Mrs. Tilly for the current membership she allowed she didn't know—she hadn't had time to count them lately!

Preposterous as it sounds, this all-woman network, a part of the Southern Regional Council program, is carried on singlehanded by Mrs. Tilly. The council, itself as poor as a church mouse, can pay little more than the cost of mimeographing and postage. What may be the most important single effort now being carried on in the field of race relations rests on one small, expendable woman who hasn't even a secretary.

She has had some rough experiences in the course of her work, "though I have never," she insists, "been in any real danger." While congress was discussing the FEPC a year or two ago, Atlanta papers carried an interview giving her views, "That night the phone never stopped ringing till we took the receiver off the hook. There were threats and snarls."

A bombing threat by the Klan came soon after publication of the report of the President's civil rights commission, which she signed. Mrs. Tilly was in Washington when Mr. Tilly received a phone call from a strange woman who was obviously in tears. "I want to warn Mrs. Tilly that the Klan is going to blow up her home," she quavered.

Meanwhile news of the threat had reached the mayor, who called up to offer police protection, and the Department of Justice, which posted FBI men around the place. Nothing came of it except a lost night's sleep for Mr. Tilly. "He didn't know whether the cars cruising the alley all night in back of our house were the police protecting us or the Klan coming to get us," his wife recalls.

She had another run-in with the Klan during Georgia's legislative hearings on a state-wide anti-mask bill, winter before last. The galleries were packed with Klan supporters, "rather pitiful-looking people," Mrs. Tilly describes them. Caught in the throng as they were leaving, she had heels ground into her instep, then was tripped up and thrown. She still has a lump on her wrist where it was stepped on.

Despite all evidence to the contrary, she holds fast to her Christian belief in the ultimate goodness of man—even the Klansman. Pitying the attacker along with the victim, she is convinced that the roots of hate lie in ignorance and poverty.

There are silent members of her network—people whose value to the movement lies in their keeping their eyes and ears open and their mouths shut. And Mrs. Tilly has had some curious experiences with the conscience-tortured wives of Klansmen. But of this she will say very little.

Behind the movement captained by Mrs. Tilly there stands a powerful element—the churches. And behind the churches is a ground swell—a stirring in the minds of the people.

In hundreds of big and little communities all over the South, Negro ministers are being invited to share white pulpits on "Brotherhood Sunday." Bible classes are worriedly discussing the pros and cons of segregation in the light of Christian teaching. When Dr. Ralph Bunche spoke in Atlanta last spring, Atlantans flocked to hear him, and there was a great deal of soul searching afterward. As one woman leader said, "They've come a long way."

A Challenge to Race Hatred

At the meeting of the North Georgia Conference of the Methodist Woman's Society last spring, the keynote address was made by one of Mrs. Tilly's ablest coworkers, Mrs. A. A. Hardy, of Thomaston. Her theme was: "Can the kingdom of God come in Georgia—when we have intimidation at the polls and a political campaign based on race hate?"

And speaking of waves of the future, an inconspicuous notice of a few lines appeared a short time ago in a Southern Baptist weekly, saying simply:

"If you want to know how to fight intolerance in your community, write for a booklet issued by the Anti-Defamation League." (The league is Jewish.) Five thousand post-card replies were received from hamlets and crossroads all over the South.

Gradually it is becoming fashionable to "do the right thing." More Southern communities are building good schools for Negroes and raising teachers' pay. After the Negro school burned down at Conyers, Georgia, this town of 2,300 floated a $50,000 bond issue for a modern consolidated school, and the vote was reported as "almost unanimous."

"You never saw such enthusiasm," said the woman who had led the drive. "They established a playground, too, and named it the Good Will Playground. They seemed to see that it was the only thing to do."

Later I had a talk with another woman member of Mrs. Tilly's astonishing network. She too came from a small town, one of those which are starting to "do the right thing," although it had had its incidents in the past—its floggings and cross-burnings.

After telling me enthusiastically about the various steps her fellow townsmen had taken to improve race relations, this woman said something that seemed to surprise her almost as much as it did me. She looked almost scared, as though she could not control or believe the words she heard issuing from her own lips.

"I tell you, change is coming in Georgia," she declared confidently. "Civil rights are coming. AND YOU CAN'T STOP IT!"

———◄••►———

THE LONELIEST MAN IN DIXIE *

Fighting discrimination against minority groups sometimes has unpleasant personal consequences, particularly if one lives in a community where prejudice is a part of the entrenched cultural pattern. According to the previous reading, Mrs. Tilly manages a personal crusade with considerable success and still retains her community status. But in the following case, the community reaction against Judge Waring took the form of social ostracism and denunciation. What are the differences in the two approaches? Suppose you were faced with a similar situation? Would you stand by your convictions even if you were rejected by your friends? Or would you bow to the dictates of the local prejudices? By what actions can individuals influence changes toward more democratic practices in regard to minority groups?

* Spencer R. McCulloch, *The St. Louis Post-Dispatch*, October 29, 1950.

Here in the heart of the Old South, where lineage counts more than dollars, United States District Judge Julius Waties Waring, son of a Confederate veteran and scion of an eighth generation of Charleston aristocracy, walks alone.

In this timeless city he lives in the limbo of social ostracism. Throughout the state, even at crossroads where social prestige counts for nothing, his name is anathema. He is the loneliest man in Dixie, a pariah in his own country.

So intense is anti-Waring feeling here—although the Judge is not without some southern sympathizers—that when lightning struck a house next to the Warings' summer cottage on an island near here, the owner put up a sign:

"Dear God, he lives next door."

For Judge Waring, at 70, is paying a harsh penalty for outraging southern custom through his celebrated 1947 opinion admitting Negroes to South Carolina's previously all-white Democratic primary.

His epochal decision, backed up by court action to protect Negroes who voted in what was once tantamount to a "white man's club," set a pattern for the South that no amount of subterfuge has succeeded in breaking. It was upheld by the Fourth Circuit Court of Appeals, at Richmond, Va., composed of southern jurists, and ultimately by the United States Supreme Court.

Judge Waring's original ruling was on statutes never before invoked. It brought about by an action by a group of Negroes with the support of the National Association for the Advancement of Colored People. He has not only backed it up but is unrelenting in what amounts to a public and private crusade for civil liberties. As a consequence, feeling against him is increasing rather than diminishing.

In unmistakable language, he issued his challenge. "It is time for South Carolina to rejoin the union. It is time to fall in step with the other states and to adopt the American way of conducting elections."

. . . . .

The South was further aroused when he ruled that Negroes must be admitted to the law school of the University of South Carolina unless facilities were afforded them at the State College for Negroes at Orangeburg.

When a law school was created at Orangeburg, staffed by as many instructors as students, Judge Waring drily remarked: "South Carolina apparently feels it can afford the luxury of a law school building for Negro students."

But, in Charleston, at least, his offense goes beyond his judicial actions. Two years before the first of his decisions that rocked Dixie, he alienated himself from his social class—as rigid, perhaps, as any in the world—when his wife, the former Miss Annie Gammell, daughter of an old Savannah family, obtained a Florida divorce after 32 years of marriage. Judge Waring, to the shock of a community where divorce is regarded askance, promptly married a twice-divorced northern woman, the former Mrs. Elizabeth Avery, of Detroit. She has added fuel to the flames by outspoken denunciations of segregation and criticisms of the southern way of life.

Since then, no white person has set foot socially in their Colonial house on Meeting Street in which the judge had lived for many years. As far as established social contacts go here, the Warings might as well live on another planet. Only summertime trips to California and New York, where the judge sometimes holds court, has enabled them to keep a sense of proportion.

. . . . .

Daily, when court is in session here, Judge Waring walks a short block to his chambers. Friends of yore, schoolmates of yesterday, look the other way. Attorneys and trades people may speak to him for diplomatic reasons, but even such conversations are strained and brief. Relatives, who once hailed him as an esteemed member of the family, now regard him in the light of a family cross.

To the outspoken disgust of Charlestonians, Negroes have been dinner guests at the Waring home. While traveling in the North the Warings have accepted awards and plaudits from Negro bodies and various humanitarian organizations. Each such award, together with the remarks of the recipients, is fully recorded in the southern press. The public reaction is often unprintable.

No longer do the sacrosanct portals of St. Cecelia's Society, symbol of top social recognition here, open for the Judge. One by one, he has resigned from his old clubs, surrendered the associations of a lifetime. Even St. Michael's Episcopal Church sees him seldom; nor is there a trace today, save in military bearing, of the former captain of the elite Charleston Light Dragoons.

. . . To the rank and file, from taxi driver to bartender, he's just "that guy who let the Nigger vote."

. . . Even attacks hurled at him, in public and private, ranging from a movement for impeachment to anonymous obscene telephone calls, have failed to turn him from a path regarded in the south as inexplicable for a man of his background.

"These actions attract attention," Judge Waring has observed, "for the eyes of the nation see what kind of people these so-called master race, white supremists are. I feel that the South has got to be cured. It needs treatment just as does an alcoholic or mental patient. American delegates in the United Nations are being asked by other nations 'where is democracy in South Carolina and Mississippi?' We cannot plant the garden of democracy in the world until we clean up our own back yard."

. . . . .

Replying to accusations that he advocates compulsory social equality between the races, Judge Waring explains that while he desires to abolish legal bars to association, he regards the choice of associates to be a matter of individual preference. . . .

So strong is the feeling here that 21,000 signatures were obtained last March to a petition seeking impeachment proceedings against Judge Waring although no legal basis has been found for such a move. The South Carolina House of Representatives voted $10,000 to defray costs of an impeachment attempt, stating that Judge Waring and "his northern-born wife have advocated a Negro revolution against white supremacy." The House also voted state funds to buy the couple a one-way ticket out of South Carolina.

Feeling against the Warings has been fanned by Mrs. Waring's public statements often delivered in belligerent fashion, sometimes with advance notice to the press. Mrs. Waring, comely and exuberant, has exhorted Negroes to a cold war "to attain the rights you already legally have" and has repeatedly denounced segregation. Before a Negro Y.W.C.A. audience here she described southern whites as "sick, confused and decadent people . . . full of pride and complacency, introverted, morally weak and low." . . .

The South Carolina Sheriffs' Association passed a resolution accusing the Judge and Mrs. Waring of making statements calculated to wreak vengeance upon the people of the South.

"These utterances, if followed to a logical conclusion," the sheriffs' resolution stated, "could but lead to mongrelization and bring about friction of a violent nature." . . .

. . . . .

Fiery crosses have not only been burned at Negro homes, but last March a small cross was burned on the lawn of Judge Waring's home here, while the jurist was in New York. Local authorities dismissed it as a "boyish prank," but Judge Waring saw it as "disheartening and disgusting; typical of the savagery of Southern white supremists."

Early this month the Warings were molested by unidentified intruders who threw bricks and a chunk of concrete through the window of their home and fired shots on the lawn.   Unable to reach the offices of the FBI, which were closed for the night, Judge Waring called the police.   The police department subsequently exhibited the thrown bricks and announced there was "nothing to the attack."

A full FBI investigation was subsequently authorized, however.   Deputy U. S. Marshals were assigned by Attorney General J. Howard McGrath to maintain a constant guard over Judge Waring, although he had not asked for it.

A SOUTHERN EDITOR ON SEGREGATION *

The great majority of Americans recognize the unjust and arbitrary character of the present status of race relations.   They agree on the necessity for change but differ radically on the velocity at which the desired change should come about.   Some believe in immediacy; others put their faith in gradualism with action.   In the following selection Mr. McKnight, Editor of *The Charlotte* (North Carolina) *News,* presents the viewpoint of the gradualists.

Three important Supreme Court decisions have chipped away at the structure of racial segregation without actually demolishing it.

All three test suits were brought by Negroes.   One plaintiff protested the separate seating facilities for whites and Negroes on railroad dining cars.   Another challenged the adequacy of a separate Texas law school for Negroes.   The third contended that he was discriminated against after being admitted to the University of Oklahoma graduate school.

The net effect of the court ruling in the railroad case is to abolish segregation on dining cars in interstate commerce, even if the "separate but equal" doctrine still stands.

In a second case, the court held unanimously that separate law school facilities were not equal to those provided for whites and ordered the State of Texas to admit Herman Marion Sweatt to the regular law school.

The Oklahoma ruling came even closer to upsetting the "separate but equal" doctrine.   To all intents and purposes, G. W. McLaurin has had equal educational opportunity.   He has sat in the same classroom, eaten in the same cafeteria, and studied in the same library with white students

* C. A. McKnight, "Handwriting on the Wall," *The Charlotte* (North Carolina) *News.* Reprinted from *The St. Louis Post-Dispatch.*

even if a certain physical segregation was preserved. Chief Justice Vinson, however, said for the majority that McLaurin "must receive the same treatment at the hands of the State as students of other races." Hence the "separate but equal" doctrine has virtually been reworded to include "the same treatment."

This topic is of paramount importance. North Carolina already faces four test suits. One demands the admittance of Negroes to the University of North Carolina law school. Three demand equal facilities in the public schools, or else the abolition of segregation.

And let us not be lulled into thinking that our public school facilities for Negroes are equal to whites. The Education Commission report in 1948 gave convincing, well-documented evidence that Negro school buildings and equipment are, in fact, woefully inferior to those for white students. No North Carolinian with any sense of justice can be happy over that.

What is pending in this state—if and when the proper test suits are fought through the Supreme Court—is a multi-million-dollar expenditure to bring Negro schools up to standard.

Up until 1949, such suits would have had to be filed on a county-by-county basis, since buildings and equipment were a local responsibility.

Now that the State Government has gone into the building of schools to the extent of $50,000,000, it is entirely possible that a single test suit could tie up the whole state appropriation and force it to be used for Negro schools.

We have said it before. We say it again today. Segregation, as an abstract moral principle, cannot be defended by any intellectually or spiritually honest person.

Yet we are dealing with more than an abstract moral principle. We are dealing with the realities of a system which dates back many generations.

That system can not be overturned by Congressional act or judicial interpretation without causing a degree of chaos that probably would be more detrimental to the national welfare and to that of the nation's citizens than a continuance of segregation practices would be. It can, however, be worked down bit by bit.

Hence, we are torn between gratification that the Supreme Court is gradually giving us a better standard for measuring real American democracy and apprehension that the Court or Congress might go too fast.

That having been said, we remind Tar Heels that the handwriting is on the wall, as far as our state educational system is concerned. The Supreme Court may leave the "separate but equal" doctrine on the books. But our state will have to get busy and make the facilities truly equal if it hopes to maintain its racial segregation.

Equality without Qualifications *

The relationship between Negroes and whites in the United States is undergoing constant change. This evolving relationship will probably be determined primarily by the dominant white majority. At the same time, it must not be overlooked that the attitudes and actions of the Negro can play an important role in giving this relationship purpose and direction, and a knowledge of Negro aspirations is therefore of prime importance. The following statement is a frank and cogent enunciation of Negro objectives by a distinguished American citizen. Dr. Bunche first presented these views before the convention of the National Association for the Advancement of Colored People at Atlanta, Georgia, July 1, 1951.

Let there be no doubt about the ends we seek.

I know, of course, that there are some Negroes who advocate, whether from cowardice or avarice, that it is harmful and bad tactics to run the risk of shocking some white Americans by stating our objectives bluntly and revealing all at once where we aim to go. I vigorously disagree with such views and have no respect for those who hold them. We shall never achieve our full rights unless we are willing to struggle and sacrifice for them. Indeed, unless we are willing to do so we are not deserving of them.

We Negroes need to learn one lesson better than we have: fate helps only those who help themselves. We are not helping ourselves as much as we should with our own resources of ability and wealth. We certainly do not give to the NAACP the full measure of our support, monetary and otherwise, which it deserves, which, in our interest, we should give. There are Negroes of substantial wealth all over America—quite a few of them right here in Atlanta—professional and business men, who could do much more to support this struggle than they have done. In my view, no Negro, however high he may think he has risen, no matter how much wealth he has amassed, is worth very much if he forgets his own people and holds himself aloof from the unrelenting struggle for full Negro emancipation.

The Negro should have no hesitation about stating in terms as clear as day what he demands, and should feel no self-consciousness in doing so. Why should any American feel timid about trying to make democracy work? If there are those who would be shocked at the demands of the American Negro, it is only because they do not believe in the democracy

* Ralph J. Bunche, *Phylon*, Atlanta University, Third Quarter, 1951, pp. 209–18.

which our Constitution prescribes. They are an even greater liability to the nation in these critical days than to the Negro.

I think that what the Negro demands is as simple as it is incontrovertible. He demands complete integration as an American citizen. That means simply that he insists upon his Constitutional heritage, without let or hindrance; equality, without qualification of race or color; an end to discrimination and segregation, for segregation itself, in any form, is discrimination. To speak of "segregated equality" among American citizens is to indulge in wanton sophistry.

Segregation by law, enforced segregation, in fact demeans the white southerner as well as the Negro. It is a form of state paternalism as outmoded in this day and age as feudalism. Its very existence in the South and its non-existence in the North, even in those communities where Negroes constitute a substantial element in population, implies that the Southern white citizen is considered to be less mature, less to be trusted, more in need of protection by the State, than the citizens of any other section of the country. An underlying assumption behind the segregation laws has to be that in the absence of such laws many Southern whites would voluntarily associate with Negroes.

There is a tyranny of law in the South, a tyranny over human relations which is all but unique in this twentieth century. The tyranny of the segregation laws of the South is designed to prohibit normal association between white and Negro Americans even in those instances where both may be willing if not eager to enjoy such association. This is a paternalistic tyranny of the law that is so arrogant as to defy description.

Equality is all the Negro citizen demands, and I am positive that the Negro will never give up this struggle until he achieves it. I am equally positive that he can and will achieve it, the hysterical antics of the racial bigots and demagogues notwithstanding. I am categorical about this because I have a deep faith in democracy. The force of democracy on the march is inexorable and democracy is on the march in the American society. It is the driving force of our society and if it should ever be lost it will be not only the Negro citizen who will suffer the loss of his freedom and individual liberty.

I am fully aware that there are some white folks down here who will argue, as on occasion they have argued with me, that what I have been saying is "dam Yankee" talk, uttered by a "black dam Yankee" at that, which is much worse, and that this does not represent at all the thinking of the "good Nigras" of the South. I would advise my good white friends that they are likely to discover sooner than later that they are gravely mistaken. They often claim to "know the Negro" but they should know that even most of those Negroes who seem to agree with them, or who at least do not oppose them, employ what might aptly be described as a "survival language." This is a form of double talk carefully selected according to the color of the listener. One thing may be said to the white man, solely for reasons of self-preservation. But it would be both revealing and painful to him if the white man could hear what is later said within the protective walls of the Negro home.

I have said earlier that the Negro problem is a national, not a sectional problem, and that it is a national responsibility. There have been in recent years not a few encouraging developments on the national level, as, for example, the progress being made toward full integration in the armed services. But in the field of national civil rights legislation the record is dismal.

Could there be any greater mockery of democracy than the performance of the national Senate with regard to civil rights legislation? Senators indulge themselves in breast-beating oratory about our democratic way of life; they embark upon rhetorical flights about the free world and free peoples; they threaten to use our growing military strength and our atomic weapons to protect the free world at large against any aggression; they declaim that our nation's God-given mission in the world is to protect and preserve freedom. But how transparent is this oratory, how blind, what a hollow ring it has, in the face of the fact that these same Senators cannot embrace the simple and mild civil rights program proposed by the President —a program designed to give only a minimum guarantee of civil rights for one out of every ten Americans, for one-tenth of the Senator's own constituents. There is an aggression on their own threshold which urgently demands their attention—a long continued and shameful aggression against the Constitutional rights of fifteen million hard-working, devoted and loyal American citizens, who work, pay taxes and shed their blood for their country exactly like all other American citizens, though their advantages from the society are arbitrarily restricted. Many of our Senators, and not a few of them from sections of the country other than the South, need to be vigorously reminded that freedom and justice must begin at home. All fair-minded Americans should mark well those Senators who are brave enough to have us risk a world war but who quail like chipmunks before our domestic racial prejudice. Does hypocrisy know no bounds? Can there be any greater devotion to flag and country than American Negroes fighting in Korea to protect rights and privileges for the Koreans which the Negroes who fight and die have never enjoyed at home?

We Negroes must suffer no illusions and expect no miracles. Grave social problems cannot be solved overnight, and the Negro problem will never be solved that way. But it can be solved, and the pace of progress toward its solution can be and must be greatly accelerated. It is not time that will solve the Negro problem; there is not time to wait, in any event.

That encouraging progress has been made and continues to be made is not to be denied. But time is much shorter than it has ever been before. It is shorter for the Negro, because he has become increasingly aware of the rights and privileges denied him, he also becomes increasingly aware that each day of his life he loses something that is irretrievable. It is shorter for the nation, precisely because the nation is confronted with its gravest international challenge and needs desperately its maximum strength, unity, moral position and prestige.

Indeed, it might well be said that rapid progress toward the full integration of the Negro in the society is of even greater urgency for the nation today than for the Negro. Who can deny that bad racial relations are a serious divisive factor and therefore weaken us when we most need unity? Who can deny that racial prejudice prevents one-tenth of the nation's manpower from being utilized to its maximum potential when we most need all of our manpower? Can it be doubted by anyone that our position of leadership of the free and democratic peoples of the world is subject to doubt, suspicion and even ridicule, because of our own inability to apply fully the democratic principles we so vigorously profess to one-tenth of our own citizenry? Can there be any question that our moral position and prestige in the world deeply suffer from these dangerous defects in the life of our society, defects which are known to all the world; and that this is so even among our friends? Can there be any question that undemocratic racial attitudes and practices are rich and fully exploited sources of effective propaganda for those who are opposed to us and all we stand for?

The costs to the nation of the Negro problem are incalculable. These costs are borne by every American, whatever his color or race.

In the struggle in which our nation is engaged it is the attitude of the peoples of the world which will be the decisive factor. We need many friends to win this struggle, and we seek friends. We would be short-sighted if we ignored the fact that the preponderance of the world's people are non-white, and that the vast millions of Asia, Africa, the Middle East, the Caribbean and Latin America are extremely sensitive to our undemocratic racial practices. In our design for democratic living by a free people we have something of compelling appeal for all people. But we must first demonstrate that this design can be applied to peoples of all colors.

We perhaps never will have and we need not expect a perfect society here. But it is imperative that we go much further than we have gone thus far in applied democracy for all Americans.

Full equality is the answer. There is no other. In a democracy there can be no substitute for equality. The Negro can never be content with less. I am sure you agree with me that we shall carry on this fight until we achieve full equality; until, Americans all, we are all free and equal.

◄•••►

FEPC THREATENS CIVIL RIGHTS *

Members of minority groups frequently encounter "closed" occupations. Or, if accepted for employment, they find the path to advancement barred. A long-standing complaint of the Negro is that he is "last hired, first fired."

All minority groups are embraced in one type of proposed Federal legislation—a Fair Employment Practices Commission. Such a commission would prevent discriminatory practices in the hiring and discharging of workers. No civil rights proposal has provoked greater heat in congressional debates. Implicit in nearly all discussion of this issue is the question, Can legislation solve or even mitigate racial-cultural patterns and tensions? Two divergent viewpoints on FEPC are presented in this and the succeeding article, the first by Senator Lister Hill of Alabama and the second by Representative Emanuel Celler of New York City.

Among the factors to be considered in connection with these two readings is the background of actual experience. The Federal government had a Fair Employment Practices Commission during World War II. In five years it satisfactorily settled 5,000 cases by peaceful negotiation. It held fifteen public hearings and docketed a total of 3,485 cases, settling 1,191 of them, during the last year of the war. "These settlements were not publicized and generally escaped attention. The contrary impression, that FEPC normally met with unyielding opposition, was created by the comparatively few difficult cases which received emphasis through public hearings and public expressions of defiance by some recalcitrant employers and unions." †

State Fair Employment Practices commissions have also met with general success. According to John H. Burma, "A survey of large employers in FEPC states, reported by *Business Week,* revealed that 'employers agree that FEPC laws haven't caused near the fuss that opponents predicted. Disgruntled jobseekers haven't swamped commissions with complaints. Personal friction hasn't been at all serious . . . even those who opposed FEPC aren't actively hostile now.' . . . In a survey made by this commission [New Jersey] seventy-nine em-

---

* Lister Hill, *Congressional Record,* Vol. 94, Pt. 10, p. A1866.
† *Final Report of the Fair Employment Practices Commission* (Government Printing Office, 1947), p. viii.

ployers indicated that there were no new difficulties or problems in business policy; that there was no interference with their 'basic right to select the most competent workers'; and that the law was being fairly and effectively administered. The commission further reported no complaints of FEPC-bred racial tension or of anyone refusing or vacating a job because of minority-group employment." *

The FEPC bill should be called a bill to destroy civil rights.

Under the guise of preventing discrimination in employment the bill actually contains the weapons for the complete destruction of many civil rights.

In the United States freedom of contract, freedom for a man to choose those who work for him or work with him, to exercise his own judgment in selecting those who occupy for him places of trust or responsibility, and a man's right to sell his services to whomever he will, are guaranteed us in the Bill of Rights of our Constitution.

Under FEPC these freedoms—the very foundation stones of our American political and economic system—would be denied.

Under the broad powers of the bill, failure to comply with the regulations laid down by the FEPC would be punishable by fine and even imprisonment. And that most precious of civil rights—the right of trial by jury—would be denied.

Under the inquiries and investigations directed by the bill, business would be vexed and harassed to the point where orderly plant management and efficient production would be impossible.

The small businessman, already overburdened, would encounter new regulations, investigation, hearings, and appeals far beyond his time, his energy, or his finances.

Labor organizations would be subject to interference and supervision of their internal affairs. The worker could not feel secure in his job. Employment and promotion based on merit would be superseded by government decrees, and the worker would be moved to look with distrust and suspicion on his fellow workers.

The bill actually takes away rights from the majority and gives special privilege to the minority.

Suppose a small plant employs fifty men. Ten of them can be identified with a minority group. If the employer has to lay off eight men, would he be likely to discharge any of the ten men who could claim discrimination —whether it existed or not—take the case to the commission and into the courts, causing the employer great expense and possible punishment?

* George E. Simpson and J. Milton Yinger, *Racial and Cultural Minorities* (Harper, 1953), pp. 412–13.

You and I know that the natural thing for the employer to do would be to avoid trouble and lay off eight of the average Americans who could not claim discrimination, even if they were better workmen than the employees who belonged to a minority group.

At a time when maximum production is so needed to fight inflation and keep our economy strong, the bill would create fear and suspicion, friction and division, in the business houses, plants, and factories of America.

It would weaken and imperil our national security at an hour of danger —a time when the peace of the world depends on America's strength.

The Atomic Energy Commission would be seriously handicapped in checking the loyalty of its employees. Companies manufacturing the most secret military equipment could not seek the information necessary to prevent disloyalty and sabotage.

The bill is an invitation to sabotage.

Presented with the antipoll tax bill and the antilynching bill, it is simply a political device for attracting votes.

It would obstruct the States in the substantial progress they are making in solving the question of discrimination.

The final result of this bill would be to substitute the edict of remote government for the personal judgment of the individual in matters of delicate human relationships and social customs—to bring thought control to the economic life of the United States.

The American people, with their love of freedom and their devotion to the rights of the individual, surely will not permit the FEPC bill to become law.

No Second-Class Citizens *

For an introductory statement to the following selection, see pages 529–30.

Mr. Speaker, you have heard the expression "second-class citizen." Have you given any serious thought to the implications of this designation? Do you realize that such a distinction could split our Nation in two? In view of the so-called revolt on the part of some southern Democrats, it is high time for each one of us to face the issue squarely. . . .

Americans are constantly orating about their great heritage of freedom and equality. It is a matter of extreme national pride. This is quite under-

* Emanuel Celler, *Congressional Record,* Vol. 94, Pt. 11, pp. A3434–35.

standable, as the record in this direction has been progressively good, but we must admit it has been spotty and any student of history will tell you that some of our performances have been disgraceful, to say the least. But we are entering a new era of human relationships—or rather, we hope we are—and we have this advantage. It is never too late to mend a mistake or curb an injustice. We know the problem. Racial hatreds and group intolerances must be eliminated. It is a challenging situation and one which we must meet head on or be defeated. Will intelligent Americans permit themselves to be victimized and degraded by malicious propaganda, whispering campaigns, directed against foreigners, against Jews, against Negroes, against Catholics? Will we permit the cherished American dream of freedom and equality for all our citizens to be perverted into a Fascist nightmare? . . .

My answer—and your answer—should be insistence upon the passage of legislation which will set up a Federal permanent fair employment practices committee. The right to a job, regardless of race or religion, is the right to life, liberty, and the pursuit of happiness. As some of us know, the opposition to FEPC is well organized but if the liberal elements in the community will take a lesson from our huge cooperative effort during the prosecution of the most complex war in history, we will avoid the strong undertow of anti-Semitism, anti-Negroism, anti-Catholicism, and other forms of racial and religious intolerances. We will not be overcome by the waves of bigotry. We will dig into this fight for a militant, dynamic, progressive democracy. Each attack on our objectives must be met with a counterattack, point and counterpoint, argument for argument. Freedom is everybody's business.

For instance, opponents to FEPC argue that such a law is futile, in that prejudice, they say, cannot be legislated out of existence. True, but this law will employ sanctions, a potent weapon, which will deter the biased employer or corporate entity from inflicting his or their prejudice upon the economic life of another, within the limits of Federal jurisdiction. We are told discrimination can best be eliminated by education, and I am all for it. I am the first to admit that considerable progress has been made in this field, aided and abetted by religious and educational leaders in many communities. But the problem is colossal, and this process is too pedestrian for the present crucial situation. It is a problem which requires an attack from a legislative approach as well.

The now defunct FEPC was established by President Roosevelt in an Executive order dated June 25, 1941. The effectiveness of the FEPC was due almost entirely to its success as a mediation body in persuading a union or employer to revise the particular policy or practice under complaint. Presently there are only six States which have laws directed against discrimination in private employment. The legislation enacted in New York, New Jersey, Massachusetts, and Connecticut have strong enforcement provisions. In those States an employer may no longer hire or fire an employee because he is a Jew, or an Italian, or a Negro, or a Catholic, or a Baptist. This does not mean that an employer must hire a Negro, or a Mexican, or a Presbyterian. He has the right of choice, depending upon the needs of his business and the quality of the service required, but he cannot reject an individual solely on the grounds of race or religion. In New York an employer or employment agency may not advertise, use application blanks, or question prospective applicants with the intention of discriminating in any way except on occupational qualifications.

A few cities—such as Chicago, Minneapolis, New York, Cincinnati, have enacted ordinances designed to prevent discrimination in employment practices, but such statutes vary and some are directed solely at municipal employment.

One does not have to do a great deal of addition and subtraction to appreciate that a more equitable solution would be a Federal statute. The opponents of such legislation advance the theory that a permanent FEPC would infringe on States rights. Let us examine this hoary argument for a moment, inasmuch as it is the bulwark of special interests and sectionalism.

States, under the Constitution, cannot regulate the areas of interstate commerce, Federal employment, and Federal contracts, which would be embraced by this bill. It should be stressed that purely local businesses would not be affected. A Federal FEPC would apply only to that portion of a State's industry which is in or which affects the stream of interstate commerce or under contract to the Federal Government.

We are also told that a permanent FEPC would interfere with private enterprise, that Government would step in and tell a man how to run his business. "Free enterprise," so-called, permits of considerable license, too much so in some instances, as witness our strangling monopolies but, nevertheless, such license is not unlimited. We have anti-trust laws which can be invoked and which should be invoked more frequently. Corporations and individual employers are subjected to the restrictions and requirements of the public welfare—under governmental supervision other free enterprise could easily descend into commercial cannibalism.

A permanent FEPC will establish impartial machinery for the satisfaction of grievances and for interpretation. This is a must. . . .

To the stubborn hate peddlers, to the despicable demagogs, let us give one firm answer: There shall be no second-class citizens in these United States.

SEGREGATION AND THE ARMED FORCES *

Arguments that changes in race relations will cause violence and great social upheaval are used by those who do not want change as weapons to win the timid to their side. The following article describes one of the most widespread changes in race relations in recent times— the integration of Negro and white troops in the Armed Forces. It clearly documents the fact that widespread change *can* occur without the violence and chaos which its opponents predict.

The Navy: From Exclusion to Integration

Since 1942 Navy policy concerning Negroes has changed from exclusion (except for mess attendant) to segregation and then to integration. The results of integration are reported as being uniformly satisfactory. No ship-board friction along racial lines has developed as some had feared; both Negro and white sailors seem well enough content with the arrangement; and no shattering complaints from civilian sources on this score have so far affected either the efficiency of or the appropriations for the Navy.

One observer, writing in 1947, tells of his visit aboard a battleship. In the crew were about a hundred Negroes, half of them in general service, as well as a Negro midshipman from Annapolis on a training cruise. "There was no sign of racial strain—in fact, the situation had been produced so quietly as a natural development of Navy policy that the public was un-aware of the changes and the men themselves were unconscious of the fact that they were making modern history."

The present policy of integration actually marks a return to the earlier Navy policy. The Navy had enlisted Negroes for general service from the earliest period of United States history until the end of World War I, and Negro sailors had served well throughout the naval establishment. It was only after World War I that the enlistment of Negroes was stopped and, when it was opened again in 1932, Negroes could only be recruited in the messman's branch.

This practice continued until 1942 when the Navy announced that Negroes would be enlisted for general service as well as for mess attendants. The Negroes thus accepted for general service were trained in segregated camps and schools, utilized in segregated units, and limited in assignment

* David G. Mandelbaum, *Soldier Groups and Negro Soldiers* (University of California Press, 1952), pp. 107–23.

to shore installations and harbor craft. But as the number of Negroes assigned to the Navy by Selective Service grew, employment could not be found for all of them in shore installations and on harbor craft. It was soon realized that many Negro recruits possessed technical skills which could not be put to use so long as Navy policy prevented the assignment of Negroes to seagoing vessels.

After considerable staff discussion and some tenative experiments, a decisive experiment was tried. In August, 1944, Negroes were assigned to twenty-five auxiliary ships of the fleet. Not more than 10 per cent of the enlisted personnel aboard any ship were Negroes, but these Negroes were integrated completely with white crews. From this experiment it was learned that Negroes could be placed in white crews without trouble. And in April, 1945, it was announced that Negro personnel would thenceforth be eligible for service in all auxiliary fleet vessels, though the 10 per cent quota for each ship would still be observed. By July, 1945, all segregated schools and camps were abolished. These modifications of segregation worked so well that the Navy abolished segregation entirely in February, 1946, and general service assignments have since been open to Negroes without restriction.

When the Fahy Committee made its thorough investigation in 1949–1950, it found that the new Navy directive had worked eminently well. The committee interviewed officers and enlisted men, both white and Negro; all those questioned said that there had been no racial friction rising out of integration. This evidence, the committee's report notes, serves to confirm the idea that respect created between individuals through competence on the job—the value which the workman sets upon workmanship—would translate itself over a period of time into personal respect and would facilitate the accommodation of the two races in their daily life, and thus act to break down artificial barriers.

The committee's report notes that in its about-face of policy the Navy had been chiefly influenced by considerations of military efficiency and the need to economize human resources. The findings on the results of the policy of integration in the Navy are summarized in the following words:

The Navy had defended the nonutilization of Negroes in general service by citing the lower level of Negro skills and by appealing to the necessity of maintaining ship efficiency and ship morale. It had discovered that, as individuals, Negroes could be trained and utilized in as wide a range of skills as whites, and that failure to use them as individuals resulted in a waste of manpower which neither the Navy nor the country could afford. Still driven by the imperative need for skilled men, the Navy had put Negro ratings aboard ship and found that no trouble resulted. In defense of its new policy the Navy now cites the skills of its Negro manpower and ship efficiency.

The Air Force: Toward the Abandonment of Segregation

Some military officials maintained that the happy experiences of the Navy with integration was not necessarily applicable to the Army and Air Force because in the Navy only small numbers of Negroes were involved whereas in the other services Negroes comprised 7 to 10 per cent of the total enlisted personnel. The recent record of the Air Force offers evidence that integration yields similarly satisfactory results even where larger numbers of Negroes are involved.

At the end of World War II the Air Force maintained the same policy on Negro manpower as the Army. Negro enlisted strength was restricted to 10 per cent, Negroes were utilized mainly in segregated units, and job opportunities for Negroes were greatly limited. Save for three all-Negro units—a fighter squadron, a fighter group, and a bombardment group— Negroes in the Air Force were used chiefly in service capacities and for heavy-duty work regardless of their individual skills and aptitudes. The great waste of this policy in the Army Air Corps was accurately predicted in a memorandum written early in 1941 by William H. Hastie, a Negro attorney and now a federal judge, who was then civilian aide to the secretary of war. Despite Hastie's well-considered—and as it turned out, prophetic—study, Air Corps planners made a series of inadequate compromises on the problem which intensified the waste.

In 1946 and 1947 a series of staff memoranda prepared in the Air Force pointed out that the established policy of segregation condemned men of superior skill to jobs where their abilities were wasted. It also forced the employment of men with lower skills in positions for which they were not equipped. Recommendations were made in these memoranda that Negroes in the Air Force be used only on the basis of their individual qualifications and that no job in the Air Force should carry a color bar.

However, these memoranda also recommended that segregation had to be maintained because of social custom and because of the possibility of difficulties between Negro and white airmen if they were placed in the same unit. In these latter recommendations the staff officers were dealing with social rather than purely military matters. As it turned out, they were as wrong in their judgments of the social situation as they were right in their appraisal of the military situation which maintained that there should be no race distinction made on the Air Force job.

In June, 1949, after a good deal of discussion within the Air Force staff and between the top Air Force officials and the secretary of defense, a new program for Negro manpower was instituted. It abolished enlistment quotas, job restrictions, and much of the segregation for Negroes, but did allow for the continued existence of some all-Negro units. But the three all-Negro combat units were disbanded and their personnel reassigned.

After the program had been in operation for six months, the staff of the Fahy Committee investigated seven major Air Force bases. It was found that complete integration had been reached as far as military duties were concerned and only one base still had a segregated unit.

In discussing the new program with commanding officers, the committee's staff brought forth significant evidence. These commanders, almost without exception, stated that they had put the new policy into effect with some misgivings. They had not questioned the fact that segregation constituted waste but they had doubted whether many Negroes would be able to qualify for technical positions in open competition with whites. In the words of the President's Committee: "They (had) questioned whether the gain in manpower utilization would be worth the trouble they expected from assigning Negroes to white units. Without exception commanding officers reported that their fears had not been borne out by events." Many more Negroes than the commanders had expected had demonstrated a capacity to compete on an equal basis, to absorb technical training successfully, and to perform ably in technical assignments. And the troubles they had feared had never materialized.

Furthermore, commanders testified that racial incidents had diminished, rather than increased, since the new policy had gone into effect. With all schools and jobs open on a basis of merit, officers were no longer plagued with complaints of discrimination. Some officers who candidly stated their personal preference for the old ways nevertheless volunteered that the new program benefited the service and caused less trouble.

At the time the Fahy Committee was making these studies in January, 1950, about three fourths of the Negroes in the Air Force performed their military duties side by side with white airmen. The presumably touchy matter of recreational facilities was left largely to the discretion of the individual commanding officer. The disposition of the commanding officers was to allow relationships to evolve according to the wishes of the men. And this led to a trend in the direction of shared facilities. There has since been an accelerating trend in the direction of complete integration in the Air Force both in regard to military duties and social and recreational facilities. This trend, far from bringing about any accentuation of interracial tension, has apparently diminished the incidence and the intensity of friction.

The Fahy Committee investigation led to a revision of Army procedure. In January, 1950, a new policy was published in Special Regulations 600-629-1. Under its terms the color bar was removed from all Army jobs and schools, all racial quotas were abolished including the former 10 per cent limit, and a Negro could now be assigned to any unit in the Army as his qualifications merit and as military considerations indicate. Segregated units were still maintained but would presumably decline in number and strength since a Negro no longer had to serve in a segregated unit only. The committee recognized that since all-Negro units were already attached or assigned to larger organizations which formed a part of the "immediate striking force," the problem of total abolition of segregation was more complicated in the Army than in the other services. On these grounds the committee did not press for complete integration and was satisfied that the new policy of January, 1950, was an effective step forward in the more efficient use of Negro manpower in the Army.

Results of the New Army Policy: Korean Combat

The first reports on the effects of the Army's new policy were entirely consistent with the evidence of earlier experience. Where segregation had been abolished, under carefully planned conditions, the Army has benefited by increased manpower efficiency and decreased racial conflict. Where segregation had been retained, complaints of discrimination continued to well up and interracial hostility sporadically broke out.

These reports are not complete or authoritative. They are mainly from journalistic sources and not based on long or extensive investigations. But they are congruent with the findings of such thorough studies as those conducted by the Research Branch.

Thus a Negro newspaperman, Collins C. George, made a tour of Army and Air Force installations in 1951. His articles, published in the *Pittsburgh Courier,* reflect an understandable tendency to see good in integration and bad in segregation, but the factual evidence he presents appears reliable. In the *Courier* of April 21, 1951, he describes his observations at Fort Jackson, South Carolina. Two divisions are in training there of which one, the Eighth (Golden Arrow) Division, is completely integrated. In this division a large proportion of the men, both white and Negro, are from the South. Whites and Negroes have the same barracks, the same mess; they work, study, and play side by side. Not only is there an absolute minimum of racial friction but, George notes with some surprise, some white soldiers whose speech indicates that they are from the deep South are becoming close buddies with Negro soldiers. "It seems that once the shock of the new experience wears off it is the southern white soldier who forms the warmest and closest personal friendships with the Negro G.I." One all-Negro unit is still maintained at Fort Jackson in the headquarters of the post complement. Of this unit George writes: "Just as in any segregated outfit, grievances fancied or real, become magnified and all is placed on a racial basis and just about all the stories of racial bias in the handling of men stemmed direct from the all-colored Section 2 of the Post headquarters unit."

. . . . .

At other Army installations in the South, as at Camp Gordon, Georgia, integration has been similarly successful on the job and in the schools, but has not been fully carried out in social and recreational matters because of civilian attitudes. However, in the *Pittsburgh Courier* of April 28, 1951, George reports two small but significant episodes which may portend future trends. A Negro second lieutenant was stationed as an instructor in one of the service schools in Camp Gordon. When the officers of his school complement sought to have a dance on the post, they found that no white girls from near-by Augusta would attend if the Negro lieutenant were present. The dance was held and he stayed away. But a good many of his white colleagues stayed away also rather than attend an affair from which a fellow officer was barred. Similarly, there was a Negro major among the students at another service school at Camp Gordon. When his fellow officers were refused permission to have a dance in the town if the major were present, the officers decided to hold their affair on the post where the Army, not the civilian, custom prevailed. Presumably this dance could be held without the presence of townspeople.

Trivial as these incidents are in themselves, they may indicate an important process. It can be stated in this way: When a Negro operates and is accepted as part of the primary group within a military unit, then an affront to him as a Negro is considered an affront to the group, and the other members will protect their colleague. Under such circumstances, neither the Negroes nor the whites of the unit are likely to encourage racial tension either within the unit or outside it.

All service clubs for enlisted men at Camp Gordon are open to Negroes. In only one of them, however, are Negro hostesses stationed, and to this center, naturally enough, most Negro enlisted men come. Even this minor kind of segregation in social facilities is considered undesirable by some commanding officers (as at Fort Dix, New Jersey), who obviate this situation by placing a Negro and a white hostess together in the same club.

A good deal of success of the integration program, according to George and other commentators, depends on the inclination and tact of the commanding officer. The smooth progress of the integration program at Fort Jackson, South Carolina, was attributed in no small part to the ability of the commanding general. Similarly at Fort Dix, New Jersey, where a program of integration has been in effect since January, 1951, the efforts of the commanding general are given full credit by George. At Fort Dix, indeed, the integration extends both to officers and enlisted men, on mili-

tary duty and off the job. Thus a Negro captain is in command of an integrated company, and mixed dances are held. The Negro newspaperman
writes that "almost no fault can now be found in the racial policies of the
post."

Whatever appraisal may be appropriate when better evidence is available,
these reports show that the Army's experience with a program of integration has been broadly the same as the Navy's. Few difficulties are encountered in having Negroes and whites work side by side in the performance
of military duties. Social and recreation integration is more complicated,
partly because of civilian influences, but no outraged outcry has arisen
from Southern white civilians in the neighborhood of Army posts where
integration has been effected.

In 1950–1951 both integration and segregation in combat as well as in
garrison were tested. Again the reports are fragmentary but again they
point to clear and consistent conclusions. In combat, integration is mili-
tarily more efficient than segregation. Expert testimony on this matter
comes from Colonel S. L. A. Marshall, who was placed on temporary active
duty in 1950 to study at first hand the effectiveness of U.S. Army tactics
in Korea. In an interview reported in the *New York Times* of December
17, 1950, Marshall said that a special study was made of companies in the
Second Division in which whites and Negroes were mixed, i.e., integrated.
"In my judgment those companies handled themselves as efficiently and
courageously as any companies in the war. In fact, the mixed Company B
of the 9th Infantry Regiment gave the bravest account of itself of any
company." When Company B's white commander was wounded in the
first hour of battle in the Kunu operation, where the Second Division
covered the Eighth Army's retreat before the big Chinese Communist
offensive, a Negro first lieutenant took over command for the rest of the
battle. He served with great distinction, Marshall notes.

One *New York Times* war correspondent with the Eighth Army in
Korea begins his report in the issue of February 9, 1951, as follows: "U.S.
Army Infantry outfits that are discarding Negro segregation practices
in Korea are discovering that removal of the color line among fighting
troops is paying good dividends both in morale and in battle." The evidence for this statement came from the reporter's observation that in some
units in Korea, white replacements are being assigned to Negro units
and Negro replacements to white units. This usually occurred because
local commanders had to take whatever replacements they could get without delay to bring their units back to fighting strength. And the commanders found that this practice had a beneficial rather than a detrimental
effect on the effectiveness of their units. As the replacements intermingled
more and more within the outfit, friendships were formed which were

in no wise hampered by the soldier's color. There had been instances of Negro officers having command of white troops and of Negro officers outranking white officers without any special friction in either case.

The correspondent cites an interview with a white lieutenant who said that when he was assigned to work with Negroes and whites together, he told his superiors that although he was a deeply indoctrinated Southerner he would try his best to go halfway and even more. Actually he found he had never had to go more than halfway. Usually he was not conscious of making any special effort at all. This interview indicates again that, once the color barrier is removed by order, a white soldier from the South generally finds few difficulties in working and fighting side by side with a Negro soldier—in accepting him as a fellow member of the primary group.

Similar conclusions were drawn by H. H. Martin, a correspondent whose article on the performance of Negro troops in Korea appeared in the *Saturday Evening Post* of June 16, 1951. At the time that article was written, some 25 per cent of the Negro infantry replacements in the Korean theater were assigned as individuals scattered throughout the Command and not to all-Negro units. At the same time, the all-Negro 24th Infantry Regiment and other segregated units were in the line. Thus, perhaps more by accident than design, there was at least an approach to controlled experiments on the combat performance of Negro soldiers in segregated and nonsegregated units.

The integration here was more thoroughgoing than in the World War II experiment in which Negro soldiers in line companies were still put in separate platoons. But the results, Martin writes, were generally the same: Officers commanding integrated units reported that Negro soldiers fought as well as the whites, and some proved to be outstanding combat leaders. "No disciplinary or morale problems have arisen by reason of the integration of Negro soldiers into white units, and there has been no friction between the troops that could be traced to differences in color."

As against these reports of the advantageous results of integration came evidence of the deleterious effects of segregation. The record of the 24th Infantry Regiment has been spotty. Every company in the regiment, Martin relates, has fought magnificently at one time or another, but, on the other hand, every unit but one broke and ran at one time or another. "Officers of line companies, though, never knew whether their men would fight or run."

In situations where the soldier needs special confidence in his fellows, in his primary group—as in night attacks—the men in all-Negro units were particularly vulnerable. As one battalion commander said, "The trouble was, not one of them had any confidence that the other man would stay and fight, and each one had a terror of being left up there alone."

The feeling of security which the soldier ordinarily gets from the others of the primary group was here negated by the doubt in those others implanted by the larger society and manifested to him by the facts of segregation. As insightful an explanation of this as any, is found in Martin's quotation of the words of a Negro captain of a combat company.

You put him in a white regiment, and he looks around him and sees white men and black men both, and he feel in his heart, 'now they are treating me like an American, not like a Negro.' But you put him in a Negro regiment, and he looks around him and sees nothing but Negroes, and he feels like somebody is using him as cannon fodder. He feels he is being treated not as an American soldier, but as a Negro soldier. And all the psychological inhibitions he has inherited through generations of living as a race apart—the lack of faith in himself, lack of confidence in his own race—take hold of him and he is hard to handle.

The combat record of the all-Negro regiment and its morale improved after better-educated and more highly skilled replacements came in, and during the term of command of an unusually able officer who effected notable improvements before he was invalided out with ulcers. However, the disrupting influences of segregation apparently continued in this regiment as in other all-Negro units.

INTEGRATION VS. SEGREGATION *

On May 17, 1954, the Supreme Court of the United States ruled that segregation of the races in the nation's schools was unconstitutional. The justices based their decision on the argument that segregated education was, in itself, a sign of inequality. At the date of this writing, methods of implementing the integration have not yet been set forth. Some states have declared, in defiance of the ruling, that they will find methods to keep segregated schools; other states have declared that they will comply with the ruling without attempting subterfuge. As he reads this decision, the student should make himself aware of developments that have occurred since the decision was made.

These cases come to us from the states of Kansas, South Carolina, Virginia, and Delaware. They are premised on different facts and different

* Text of the Supreme Court of the United States decision in the racial segregation cases as reprinted in the *Christian Science Monitor*, May 18, 1954.

local conditions, but a common legal question justifies their consideration together in this consolidated opinion.

In each of the cases, minors of the Negro race, through their legal representatives, seek the aid of the courts in obtaining admission to the public schools of their community on a non-segregated basis. In each instance, they had been denied admission to schools attended by white children under laws requiring or permitting segregation according to race. This segregation was alleged to deprive the plaintiffs of the equal protection of the laws under the Fourteenth Amendment. In each of the cases other than the Delaware case, a three-judge Federal district court denied relief to the plaintiffs on the so-called "separate but equal" doctrine announced by this court in Plessy v. Ferguson, 163 U.S. 537. Under that doctrine, equality of treatment is accorded when the races are provided substantially equal facilities, even though these facilities be separate. In the Delaware case, the Supreme Court of Delaware adhered to that doctrine, but ordered that the plaintiffs be admitted to the white schools because of their superiority to the Negro schools.

The plaintiffs contend that segregated public schools are not "equal" and cannot be made "equal," and that hence they are deprived of the equal protection of the laws. Because of the obvious importance of the question presented, the court took jurisdiction. Argument was heard in the 1952 term, and reargument was heard this term on certain questions propounded by the court.

Reargument was largely devoted to the circumstances surrounding the adoption of the Fourteenth Amendment in 1868. It covered exhaustively consideration of the amendment in Congress, ratification by the states, then existing practices in racial segregation, and the views of proponents and opponents of the amendment. This discussion and our own investigation convince us that, although these sources cast some light, it is not enough to resolve the problem with which we are faced. At best, they are inconclusive. The most avid proponents of the postwar amendments undoubtedly intended them to remove all legal distinctions among "all persons born or naturalized in the United States." Their opponents, just as certainly, were antagonistic to both the letter and the spirit of the amendments and wished them to have the most limited effect. What others in Congress and the state legislature had in mind cannot be determined with any degree of certainty.

An additional reason for the inclusive nature of the amendment's history, with respect to segregated schools, is the status of public education at that time. In the South, the movement toward free common schools, supported by general taxation, had not yet taken hold. Education of white children was largely in the hands of private groups. Education of

Negroes was almost nonexistent, and practically all of the race was illiterate. In fact, any education of Negroes was forbidden by law in some states. Today, in contrast, many Negroes have achieved outstanding success in the arts and sciences as well as in the business and professional world. It is true that public education has already advanced further in the North, but the effect of the amendment on northern states was generally ignored in the congressional debates. Even in the North, the conditions of public education did not approximate those existing today. The curriculum was usually rudimentary; ungraded schools were common in rural areas; the school term was but three months a year in many states; and compulsory school attendance was virtually unknown. As a consequence, it is not surprising that there should be so little in the history of the Fourteenth Amendment relating to its intended effect on public education.

In the first cases in this court construing the Fourteenth Amendment, decided shortly after its adoption, the court interpreted it as proscribing all state-imposed discriminations against the Negro race. The doctrine of "separate but equal" did not make its appearance in this court until 1896 in the case of Plessy v. Ferguson, supra, involving not education but transportation. American courts have since labored with the doctrine for over half a century. In this court, there have been six cases involving the "separate but equal" doctrine in the field of public education. In Cumming v. County Board of Education, 175 U.S. 528, and Gong Lum v. Rice, 275 U.S. 78, the validity of the doctrine itself was not challenged. In more recent cases, all on the graduate school level, inequality was found in that specific benefits enjoyed by white students were denied to Negro students of the same educational qualifications. Missouri ex rel. Gaines v. Canada, 305 U.S. 337; Sipuel v. Oklahoma, 332 U.S. 631; Sweatt v. Painter, 339 U.S. 629; McLaurin v. Oklahoma State Regents, 339 U.S. 637. In none of these cases was it necessary to reexamine the doctrine to grant relief to the Negro plaintiff. And in Sweatt v. Painter, supra, the court expressly reserved decision on the question whether Plessy v. Ferguson should be held inapplicable to public education.

In the instant cases, that question is directly presented. Here, unlike Sweatt v. Painter, there are findings below that the Negro and white schools involved have been equalized, or are being equalized, with respect to buildings, curricula, qualifications, and salaries of teachers, and other "tangible" factors. Our decision, therefore, cannot turn on merely a comparison of these tangible factors in the Negro and white schools involved in each of the cases. We must look instead to the effect of segregation itself on public education.

In approaching this problem, we cannot turn the clock back to 1868 when the amendment was adopted, or even to 1896 when Plessy v. Ferguson was written. We must consider public education in the light of its full development and its place in American life throughout the nation. Only in this way can it be determined if segregation in public schools deprives these plaintiffs of the equal protection of the laws.

Today, education is perhaps the most important function of state and local governments. Compulsory school attendance laws and the great expenditures for education both demonstrate our recognition of the importance of education to our democratic society. It is required in the performance of our most basic responsibilities, even service in the armed forces. It is the very foundation of good citizenship. Today, it is a principal instrument in awakening the child to cultural values, in preparing him for later professional training, and in helping him to adjust normally to his environment. In these days, it is doubtful that any child may reasonably be expected to succeed in life if he is denied the opportunity of an education. Such an opportunity, where the state has undertaken to provide it, is a right which must be made available to all on equal terms.

We come then to the question presented: Does segregation of children in public schools solely on the basis of race, even though the physical facilities and other "tangible" factors may be equal, deprive the children of the minority group of equal educational opportunities? We believe that it does.

In Sweatt v. Painter, supra, in finding that a segregated law school for Negroes could not provide them equal educational opportunities, this court relied in large part on "those qualities which are incapable of objective measurement but which make for greatness in a law school." In McLaurin v. Oklahoma State Regents, supra, the court, in requiring that a Negro admitted to a white graduate school be treated like all other students, again resorted to intangible considerations: ". . . his ability to study, engage in discussions and exchange views with other students, and, in general, to learn his profession." Such considerations apply with added force to children in grade and high schools. To separate them from others of similar age and qualifications solely because of their race generates a feeling of inferiority as to their status in the community that may affect their hearts and minds in a way unlikely ever to be undone. The effect of this separation on their educational opportunities was well stated by a finding in the Kansas case by a court which nevertheless felt compelled to rule against the Negro plaintiffs: "Segregation of white and colored children in public schools has a detrimental effect upon the colored children. The impact is greater when it has the sanction of the law; for the policy of separating the races is usually interpreted as denoting the inferiority of the Negro group. A sense of inferiority affects the motivation of a child to learn. Segregation with the sanction of law, therefore, has a tendency to retard the educational and mental development of Negro children and to deprive them of some of the benefits they would receive in a racially integrated school system."

Whatever may have been the extent of psychological knowledge at the time of Plessy v. Ferguson, this finding is amply supported by modern authority. Any language in Plessy v. Ferguson contrary to this finding is rejected.

We conclude that in the field of public education the doctrine of "separate but equal" has no place. Separate educational facilities are inherently unequal. Therefore, we hold that the plaintiffs and others similarly situated for whom the actions have been brought are, by reason of the segregation complained of, deprived of the equal protection of the laws guaranteed by the Fourteenth Amendment. This disposition makes unnecessary any discussion whether such segregation also violates the due process clause of the Fourteenth Amendment.

Because these are class actions, because of the wide applicability of this decision, and because of the great variety of local conditions, the formulation of decrees in these cases presents problems of considerable complexity. On reargument, the consideration of appropriate relief was necessarily subordinated to the primary question—the constitutionality of segregation in public education. We have now announced that such segregation is a denial of the equal protection of the laws. In order that we may have the full assistance of the parties in formulating decrees, the cases will be restored to the docket, and the parties are requested to present further argument on questions 4 and 5 previously propounded by the court for the reargument this term. The attorney general of the United States is again invited to participate. The attorney general of the state requiring or permitting segregation in public education will also be permitted to appear as amici curiae upon request to do so by Sept. 15, 1954, and submission of briefs by Oct. 1, 1954. It is so ordered.

TEN YEARS FROM TODAY *

Many white Americans comfortably assume that race relations will change only slowly; that they and their progeny will be exempt from violent change; that present patterns will disappear only under gradual social erosion. These "gradualists" have been accused of trying to

* Lillian Smith, *Vital Speeches,* August 15, 1951, pp. 669–72.

have their cake and eat it—to be liberal and yet defend the status quo. To such people Lillian Smith is anathema, while she in turn regards the "gradualists" as unrealistic dreamers. In the following article Mrs. Smith predicts an era of rapid change in race relationships—an era in which we will "gain a new, whole world for this split one that has warred with itself too long."

Ten years from today, racial segregation as a legal way of life will be gone from Dixie. Although signs will still be nailed to a few people's minds and hearts, the signs over doors, those words WHITE and COLORED that have cheapened democracy throughout the world will be down.

A prophet is not needed to forecast. Any one who looks closely at recent events here in the South and measures them against world events will know that the future holds no place in it for the philosophy and practice of segregation. Whether segregation takes the form of the iron curtain as it does in communist countries, or the familiar Jimcrow practices that we know in the South, or those severe restrictions that make up the pattern of life in South Africa, it is a belief, an act of the past which the future cannot use. . . .

Let us quickly remind ourselves of some of the barriers that are already down:

Hundreds of Negro students are now in southern white colleges and universities. The figure is often placed as high as a thousand. And there has been no tension on the campuses of these schools, despite the demagogues' warning that violence would come, were this to happen. Well, it has happened and there has been no violence. It is going to happen more and more until every state school and university in the South opens its doors to students regardless of their color. I believe, in less than five years, all our graduate and undergraduate schools will be open to Negroes and whites. Five years? Let's make it three—I doubt that even my state of Georgia can hold out three years. . . .

Where else are the walls coming down? In interstate travel, changes have come rather swiftly. Because of the old taboo about eating, we southerners know that the abolition of restrictions in dining cars is a profound cultural change. Today, it is a pleasant thing to report that southerners are now watching each other eat as they travel through Dixie and no one has felt violent about it, no one has fainted, no one has had acute indigestion. The sanity that our southern people possess has prevailed. . . .

We are changing down here, changing rapidly, and without violence. Let us name quickly other changes:

Negro policemen on nearly every southern city police force; Negro trained nurses fully integrated now into the national association of graduate nurses with their full rights as to equal salaries, etc., protected; Negroes on civic boards of many southern cities—the latest city to elect a Negro representative to a city board was Greensboro, North Carolina. The masks are off of the Klan in Georgia, in South Carolina, in other southern states also. Now without secrecy, the Klan will soon die out. Not only the new laws and the stripping off of those pillow-cases but the outspoken disapproval of the Klan by nearly all educated white persons in the South make their further activities almost an impossibility.

More than 750,000 Negroes voted in recent elections in the South. Indications are now that a million and a half will vote in 1952. There has been violence, now and then; a few Negroes have been killed or beaten up when attempting to vote. But always this violence comes where there are violent Negro-hating politicians stirring up the hate feelings of the people.

Many southern libraries have opened their research departments to Negro scholars. A few city libraries have opened their front doors to all citizens who want to read, regardless of race.

Unsegregated audiences are becoming more and more widespread. I have spoken to many unsegregated southern audiences within the past year and I am sure that other speakers have also.

In national sports, we have grown used to seeing Negroes and whites playing together. That is almost an old story now.

And yet, these changes may seem small—set against the tight rigid system of segregation in the South as you and I who were born here, know it. There is still so much to be done. Still so many barriers that seem as solid as concrete. But we must remember that each change is like a hole in a dam; the waters are pouring through; the hole is getting larger and larger; there is no way to plug it now, and soon the old dam will topple. There is no way—because the waters of change are in flood the world over.

Segregation in the South has been like a primitive taboo—different quantitatively and qualitatively, I think from segregation in the North. A taboo says: if you do this, you will die or those you love will die. Great disaster will befall you. A taboo says: you must never question, you must simply obey. A taboo's magic lies always in its ability to keep every one from daring to break it or talk about breaking it. If one person dares to question it aloud; if two question, three, four,—ah, then, the magic no longer "works." Those who support segregation have depended upon fear and silence to keep it strong in the South. Now the old silence is gone. Hundreds of men and women are saying their deep beliefs out loud. The old cliche, said so often in speeches and editorials, that "only a fool would question segregation" is not being heard much, this spring in Dixie. It is a statement not made even by the Dixiecrats. For we have grown such a big crop of "fools" lately who are questioning segregation not only in their letters to the press, and in speeches, but in casual conversations.

This breaking of the old conspiracy of silence in the South is big news, for when men talk, they change. Philosophers have often said that man is the only animal who talks to himself. He is certainly the only animal who talks *about* himself, about his past, his feelings, his dreams, his future. And he is the only animal who can change himself. Because he is a talking animal, he can talk about his dreams, and talking about his dreams makes him want those dreams to come true, and wanting those dreams to come true gives him the power to change himself, to draw upon hidden potentialities for growth within himself.

Dreaming, talking, acting: this is the way that free men bring change about, whether it is change within themselves, or within their culture or laws. . . .

We have two big jobs ahead of us, now that profound changes are taking place in our South, now that segregation is crumbling. The first job is to hasten the crumbling, for time is important. Walls are not only falling in the South they are falling everywhere, and American democracy can win the imagination of the world only by showing the world that within the strongest democracy on earth all of its citizens have been accepted and given their rights.

Our second job is a very important one also. And I stress it here because it is so easy to forget it. We must give back to our people, white and colored, in this time of severe change, something equal to or better than that which has been taken away from them. We must not let people feel cheated, if it can possibly be helped, when great change takes place. When old defenses are torn down within an individual's personality without building up new defenses, that personality is likely to collapse into mental illness. When such change takes place in a culture, there will be great trouble unless we build up new defenses as the old go down. . . .

Our new world will be a whole world; its people united under a democratic federation of nations; its unit will be the free individual, growing from childhood steadily toward a full maturity, accepting both freedom and responsibility, accepting all persons as human beings with the same right to grow and to be different as he has. A whole world requires that whole men live in it. To have whole men means that we must have integrated individuals. To have integrated individuals means that our children must be given the chance to grow not as split-up personalities in whom body, mind, and emotions are forever warring, but as children kept whole, with strong creative loving egoes that bind the body and personality together, and to their world.

Part of our fear today, part of the anxiety which so many feel, springs from the knowledge that this changing world requires that each of us change himself; that a world made whole means that each of us must be made whole, also. We want to be sure it is going to be worth it.

It seems worth it to me: to gain a new whole world for this split one that has warred with itself so long; to gain, in place of our split-up personalities, health and stability. We are making a good bargain in swapping our old segregated world, our segregated southern culture, our segregated personality, for love and wholeness and dignity in men's relationships with each other and with themselves.

Therefore it seems to me a fine time to be alive, in this age of falling walls—the greatest age that mankind has ever experienced. It is an age full of risks but the stakes are high and worth the risk.

Ten years from today, I hope that I shall still be alive and I hope you will, too, for it will be a fine thing to see this South of ours, if each of us does our share in bringing these changes about in a creative way. . . .

CHAPTER SEVEN

Rival Economic Ideologies

ECONOMIC THEORY and political theory are today intertwined in several doctrines that compete for man's favor. An earlier chapter of this book examines rival political doctrines. In this chapter we turn our attention to rival economic philosophies, bearing in mind, however, that political philosophy is commonly based on economic assumptions and economic theory is supported by political action. Nevertheless, the somewhat unrealistic cleavage of politics and economics followed here is a healthy antidote to those who insist that the two are bound together irrevocably—that every economic system must have its peculiar political counterpart.

Readings in this chapter center around two basic questions: What is the nature of capitalism? How do Socialism and Communism differ from capitalism in theory and practice?

We have not attempted to define capitalism as a finished, perfect doctrine; rather, it is considered as a process of "becoming" with its exact nature and future in dispute. Even a cursory glance at United States history makes evident that the American version of capitalism is, in the words of the editors of *Fortune,* "the permanent revolution." Certainly it is not a static force, once and for all embedded in an immutable philosophy; on the contrary, it is a growing, dynamic idea, reflecting the ever-changing economic and political realities of the 1950's. To make this statement is not to imply that all definition is impossible, however; exploration of the boundaries of capitalist philosophy is part of the central problem.

As for capitalism's rivals, we have selected two—Socialism and Communism. In considering these doctrines, too, we have assumed that an evolutionary situation exists—that theory is gradually shaped and changed by practice. Therefore, readings in these two sections emphasize both theory and evaluation of the systems in operation. The newness of British Socialism, American interest in it, and the attempt to draw "morals" applicable to the United States scene from British experience have been considered adequate justification for this emphasis. As for Communism, our selections contrast the Soviet and American systems and underline the difference between ideal and reality in the Russian economy.

Problem 21: Capitalism--
The Permanent Revolution?

What is American capitalism? Who holds the authorized patent, the mold by which all economic action must be measured and approved or rejected? Is so-called "classical" capitalism the only true faith? Or does the Fair Deal more closely approach the ideal?

To pose such questions is to suggest the wide diversity of answers that are proclaimed within the United States today. To those who revere the classical model, the United States deviated from the true course when it enacted the first protective tariff, provided the first business subsidy, or legalized the first public utility monopoly. Other spokesmen, however, would assign the time of America's departure from the rightful road to a much later date—specifically, 1933. Repudiating both these contentions, still other observers, represented by Nichols and Allen, suggest that American capitalism is a new creation, highly adaptable to world conditions, although even they would agree that capitalism—to be capitalism—must operate within certain prescribed limits. Hence the importance of definition.

THE AMERICAN FREE ENTERPRISE SYSTEM *

Any attempt to define the American economic system is apt to provoke argument today. Many of these disputes arise because we have no official dogma, no universally accepted "economic constitution" against which all puzzling questions can be measured. As a result Americans quarrel violently as to underlying economic theory, present economic relationships, and desirable future goals.

* *The American Economic System Compared with Collectivism and Dictatorship* (Chamber of Commerce of the United States, 1936), pp. 5, 7–13.

It was not always thus. The reading that follows expounds in brief compass the theory of "classical" economics—a theory presented by Adam Smith in his *Wealth of Nations* (1776) and refined by his successors. Historically, this theory has dominated American economic thought and is today widely advocated as the ideal that should govern relationships between producer, consumer, and government.

Under the American system of private initiative, land and natural wealth are owned mainly by private citizens, either individually or in groups. The establishment and conduct of industry, the employment of labor, the exchange of goods, and the organization and operation of various other types of business undertakings, are conducted by private enterprise under competitive conditions and under a system of free contract. The function of government is not to replace business but to create and maintain conditions in which business initiative may be successful in accordance with its own merits and may be free from predatory influences.

. . . . .

Maintenance of Competition

Of cardinal importance in the scheme of private enterprise is competition. Competition operates to bring about lower prices, better products, and better services, all for the enhancement of living standards and for the promotion of the public good. It is a constant incentive to invention, to the perfection of manufacturing and distributing processes, and to the elimination of economic waste.

Competition further acts to prevent monopolistic control—a control which under collectivism resides in the state, with only political means to assure that it will not be misused for political ends.

Consumer Preference

One important control in the system of private initiative is that exercised by the consumer. Every successful enterprise must produce a product or service so satisfactory to the free choice consumer that he will purchase it in such volume and at such a price as will compensate for the labor, materials, and management and capital service entering into it. Consumer preference constitutes one of the exacting tests of industrial and commercial efficiency, and gives to the system of private enterprise a flexible and automatic check upon its successful operation. Consumer demand, both in the free national market and in the world market, determines the character and objectives of the entire productive mechanism. Similarly, it determines not only the value of goods but also the value of factories, of distributing organizations, and of supplementary services; and, further, determines the rate of interest.

Elimination of Defects

Every system has its defects. There have been and still are weak spots in the American economic order, but they are weaknesses calling for the cure rather than for the killing of the patient. As mentioned above many of the imperfections in our economic order are automatically remedied through the operation of competitive enterprise, and through the force of consumer demand.

Defects in the system are also identified and cured through the application of industry's criticism of itself in its own self-interest, often through business men's organizations; the constant discussion in legislative halls of measures proposed for the elimination of actual or alleged defects; the administration of existing laws under democracy, for the elimination of weaknesses; and the constant contributions of scientific and economic thought to the improvement of our free economic order.

The Function of Government

Under the system of private initiative the function of government is to preserve opportunity for individual enterprise to develop, with protection against crime and predatory incursion. Where necessary, government sets up regulation to prevent actions inimical to the public interest. Governments have established many such checks and balances. Among limitations upon private enterprise might be mentioned, in this country, the anti-trust laws, laws governing shipment of commodities, child labor legislation, regulations in the interest of public health, legislation affecting the health of workers and relating to their working conditions.

Participation of Labor

Under collectivism the laborer is subordinate to the state; under the American order he is a free and independent participant in industrial and commercial life.

Under the American system the great bulk of the receipts of business, after the payment of taxes, tends to go directly or indirectly to wage and small-salary earners. The share paid to creditors, stockholders and large-salary earners is small in comparison.

An important forward advance in the system of private initiative—and one strikingly represented in the United States—is the increasing participation of labor in the financing of free enterprise, represented either by direct investments or by indirect investment through the millions of insurance policies and savings accounts the funds of which must largely be put to work in American economic undertakings. This partnership of capital and labor is further evidenced in the practice of holding joint conferences on questions of industrial management and distribution policy, and in the equitable adjustment of questions in the field of labor relations.

Profit and Capital

Profit—often made a target by the critics of the system of private initiative —is actually the life-blood of industry's expansion. The capital thus created seeks new usefulness, creates new enterprises, expands old enterprises, and in these processes creates ever-widening circles of employment for an expanding population.

Reasonable profit has, throughout history, been the most potent incentive to economic advancement. Whether privately-owned or state-owned, capital is essential to business conduct, improvement and expansion; but the use of state-owned capital, particularly under dictatorships, too frequently serves a political rather than an economic end.

International Trade

Under the private system international trade is created by the millions of individual contacts of citizens of one nation with citizens of another. These are important elements in creating world understanding of each other's aims and customs, and are thus a contributing factor to world peace. The concentration of economic power in the hands of autocratic dictators tends to the subordination of the ordinary citizen, to the temptation to use a nation's economic strength to bolster up the dictator's political aims, and thus to align nations under centralized control, one against the other, as great antagonistic units of economic wealth and economic interest backed by military force, with consequent impairment of friendly international relations and with the danger of war becoming proportionately greater.

Automatic Coordination

At times the system of private enterprise has been described as a *laissez faire* system. This creates the impression that there is chaos and lack of planning in it. As a matter of fact, the myriad adjustments and interrelations that have grown up throughout the years and that are daily in operation among the component parts of the free economic order represent a careful system of checks and balances, based on experience, to which even the collectivist-state planners themselves have to resort as a basis for their theories. Efforts to interfere arbitrarily with the normal operation of the system—an operation developed through trial and error—lead inevitably to major disturbances of economic well-being.

In the freedom of flexibility of the private initiative system is found an automatic mechanism for such effective distribution of labor and of capital funds, and stimulation of management and inventive genius, as normally to keep the economic order at high efficiency. . . .

Progress Under Private Initiative

Economic systems, based on the principle of private initiative, have been responsible for the great industrial and commercial advances made during the last century by the nations of Europe and America. Under conditions of free private operation, we have witnessed the great advances made in production, distribution, transportation, communication, banking, insurance, publicity, and the hundred and one other services that together have brought to the citizens of today a standard of living and of well-being never before attained in world civilization. And obviously such advances were possible only with a coincident wide diffusion of purchasing power.

In comparison with conditions a generation ago workers generally, even at the depths of the recent depression, have had better houses, better clothing, better food, better education, better protection against disease and risk, better pay for shorter hours, greater opportunities for leisure and enjoyment, and wide facilities for building up economic security against the future.

It has been private enterprise, with the use of accumulated private savings, that has given us in the United States such facilities as railroads, steamships, automobiles, telephones, radios, electric lighting, central heating, modern homes and apartments, modern office buildings and equipment, modern theaters and moving pictures, to mention only a few of the items which the operation of private business has taken from the realm of luxuries or undreamed-of conveniences and placed within the reach of the average citizen of present-day United States. The creative genius and the untiring initiative of individual Americans, often working against the dead weight of mass tradition, have been responsible for much of our invention and our progress.

No claim is made that improvements could have occurred *only* under the existing economic system, but, in considering the needs and opportunities of our country, it must be in the light of these established merits of our American system, proven by generations of substantial accomplishment, that we examine the theoretical standards and the work to date of the collectivist and the limitations upon the ordinary citizen under a dictatorship.

What Do You Mean, Free Enterprise? *

> Mr. Robertson attacks many of the concepts set forth in the preceding article, declaring that we have substituted for "free enterprise" a new reality—"safe enterprise." But, says the author, while we practice "safe enterprise," we preach "free enterprise," thereby producing a nation of schizophrenics in our economic thinking. Do you agree?

The United States today is in a condition comparable to that of a man suffering from schizophrenia. A few innocent fancies are safe enough in quiet times, but in a crisis, either the patient gives up his delusions, or society commits him to the firm hold of others. Our national phantasy, fateful in these edgy times, is our belief that we are living in a free-enterprise system. Since reality is quite the reverse, we are in no condition to make rational decisions. It is time to get wise to ourselves.

It is true that we have a free-enterprise system in the sense that if a man has enough money he can go into any work or any business he chooses. In most respects he can run his business to suit himself. He may make money or he may go under, depending upon the circumstances and his own ability. He can get out of one occupation or business and go into another whenever he can afford to.

But these are only the surface signs. Fundamentally, a free-enterprise system, as spelled out by Adam Smith, the great classical economist, is one in which there is a minimum of government or monopoly interference —in which the natural laws of supply and demand rule. In that kind of system an individual entrepreneur takes all the risks and, as a reward for beating those risks, is entitled to all the law of supply and demand will permit him to win.

America once had close to—although never completely—a free-enterprise system of that kind. Of course, from almost the beginning, this country had tariffs which interfered with the laws of supply and demand; subsidies to the railroads and to Western pioneers which fell considerably short of Adam Smith's ideal; prohibitions against some businesses regarded as

* Nathan Robertson, *Harper's Magazine*, November, 1948, pp. 70–75.

immoral, such as the slave trade; and government competition, such as the postal system in communications.

But except for a few interferences of this kind, the laws of supply and demand were in control, and we had something rather similar to a free-enterprise system. There was little government interference or monopoly. A man could go into any business he chose, pay any wages for which he could get men to work, charge any price he could get, and make as much money as the laws of supply and demand would permit. He could even throw away the nation's basic natural resources in the most profligate manner if he chose to do so in his grab for riches and power. He could make millions—or go bankrupt.

Today we have something quite different. The individual entrepreneur still faces the risk of competition within his own segment of the economy— if he happens to be in an area of business where competition still exists, such as farming or retailing. But in many segments of our industry, competition has been drastically restricted so that the laws of supply and demand no longer operate as they are supposed to. Many of our big manufacturing industries have price-fixing schemes of one kind or another. The steel, cement, and other heavy industries, until very recently, have had the basing-point system for controlling competition, and it is not yet clear to what extent the practice has been abandoned since it was outlawed by the Supreme Court. Price-fixing has extended clear down through the retail trades under the Miller-Tydings Act, which permits manufacturers to fix the price at which their products can be retailed to the public.* Patents have been used as the basis for widespread price-fixing.

Even beyond all this, American industry has become so big, with such huge industrial units, that only those with many millions of dollars to risk can enter into many fields of enterprise. This large scale, of course, limits competition. It takes huge aggregations of capital to enter most of the big industries like steel, automobile, machinery, or electrical equipment manufacturing—and even publishing. At least $10,000,000 is needed to launch a metropolitan newspaper today, and even then the chances of making a profit are slim—as Marshall Field can testify.

But a more important factor in changing our economic system is government. Today a business man, whether he is a manufacturer or retailer or farmer, no longer faces the biggest risk of all in a free-enterprise system— the risk of the uncontrolled ups-and-downs of the economy. No one believes that we have completely eliminated the business cycle, but we have today so vast a network of government supports that many economists believe we will never again have anything like the crash of 1929. Some of

---

* Aspects of this act have been declared unconstitutional since this article was written.—*Ed.*

these economists contend that this is the reason we escaped the postwar depression, which was expected to throw 8,000,000 men out of work after hostilities ceased.

So today, instead of having a nearly-free enterprise system in this country —as we used to have and as most people still seem to think we have—we are operating under something quite different. It is a drastically revised system—revised by monopoly and by government supports. Partly because we still have not recognized just how different our new system is, no one has yet named it—but it might be called the "safe-enterprise system."

This "safe-enterprise system" is almost as different from the one that Adam Smith talked about or the system we once had as the economy of Nazi Germany or of Soviet Russia. But it is just as American and goes along with democracy and liberty as naturally as the original. In fact, our democracy today is probably more complete than it ever was in the past. We still have free speech and free worship. We still can protest and vote "no" if we want, and more of us have the right to vote "no" than ever before. But we no longer have the freedom to pay workers five or ten dollars a week for a sixty-hour week, or to put millions of people into the breadlines.

The schizophrenic part about all of this is that we still talk and plan as though we had a system of the old kind. Proposals are rejected in Congress day after day because they will "interfere with the free-enterprise system." People tend to confuse the "free enterprise system" with basic Americanism and put it on the same pedestal as "liberty" or "democracy."

What makes this particularly strange is that we did not even begin to call our system a "free-enterprise system," or to use that phrase as almost synonymous with capitalism, until about ten or fifteen years ago. We had occasionally referred to it earlier as a system of "free competitive enterprise." But the more simple phrase with the competitive idea eliminated, was popularized by the business interests of this country about ten years ago, when they were fighting off some of the New Deal reforms. One of the bright young men then working for the National Association of Manufacturers is credited with promoting the new phrase.

The slogan had great value in fighting such innovations as the wage-hour law and the Wagner labor act. The business men were afraid that we were going to abolish the "free-enterprise system" which permitted them to pay their workers whatever they could get them to work for individually, and perhaps to regulate how much profit they could make. Actually we did abolish the first of these "rights"—but we never tampered with their profits, except to a limited extent during the war. So far, the changes in the "free enterprise system" have not hurt business. In fact, profitwise, business is going better today than ever before in history—with profits reaching more than $18,000,000,000 after taxes last year, or more than double what they were in the boom year of 1929.

Business pushed the phrase in speeches, advertisements, and propaganda. Politicians accepted it and won applause with it. Everything indicated that the American people wanted a free-enterprise system, except that by the time the phrase took hold we had moved on to another system without most people realizing it—although they had repeatedly approved the measures which brought the change about.

All the phrase did was to confuse America at a time when it could scarcely afford to be confused. It is important for the people of this country to get over their confusion—their schizophrenia—if they are to run the new system intelligently. Business men need to recognize the nature of the new system in order to adopt workable price policies, labor needs to recognize it to develop sound bargaining programs, and the public needs to recognize it to decide the issues of the day rationally. To decide some of the questions we now face without recognizing where we are or where we are going is like a ship captain trying to chart a course before he knows where he is or what port he wants to reach.

Most Americans seem to be in the same boat with the ship captain. Sensible and responsible men who are looking to the best interests of the country frequently take violently opposing stands on the same issues. People speak in the most glowing language about the free-enterprise system and then in almost the same breath show they really do not want it. Recently, for instance, one of the leading critics of the New Deal in Congress, a man who talks volubly about the glories of free enterprise, explained his constant support of the farm program by telling newspapermen that "certain parts of the New Deal have become a part of 'the American way of life.' "

The shape of our economy started to change in the last part of the 19th century with the growth of monopolies and the governmental steps to curb them. Actually the first big change came when we decided to place restrictions on some areas of free enterprise: the public utilities and the industries engaged in developing our natural resources. We decided that the railroads and the utilities, because of their subsidies and their monopoly positions, were secure and were not taking as big a risk as other businesses, and so should not be permitted to earn such rich rewards. We set up the Interstate Commerce Commission and the public utility commissions to regulate their profits and the services they provided the public. To protect our national resources, we gradually—and too late—enacted legislation limiting to some extent the aggressions of selfish entrepreneurs in the lumber and other natural resource industries. And as industry grew bigger and more powerful, we enacted the anti-trust laws, though we did not do much to enforce them.

In most areas of business we still maintained a system of comparatively free enterprise until the depression of 1929 shook America and the world to their economic and political foundations. Some governments and economic systems fell, and others came close to it. Desperately we began under Herbert Hoover to pour billions of dollars of government money into the railroads, the banks, and the insurance companies to shore up our economy. Franklin D. Roosevelt came into office and extended the same help to the average citizen.

We were so desperate that we didn't worry too much about abstract theories of government—although the Senate did debate for days over the question of whether we could feed hungry people as well as hungry cattle. There were warnings at the time that we were destroying our freedom, but we ignored them and probably would again under the same circumstances. We voted, or our representatives voted, a lot of changes in our system, piece by piece, in an effort to save various segments of the economy from ruin. These changes added up to a radical revision of the whole. But more important than any one of them, or all of them together, was the new principle of government Hoover and Roosevelt joined in writing into our system at that time—that the government stands back of our economy in time of trouble.

The men who initiated this fundamental change, and the other revisions of our system under the New Deal, believed in the free-enterprise system and were merely trying to save it by correcting isolated abuses or weaknesses. For instance, one of the most fundamental changes of all—the federal insurance of bank deposits—came not from the New Deal but from a conservative Republican, Senator Arthur H. Vandenberg of Michigan, who sponsored it and fought for it in Congress with only tacit approval from the Administration.

The farm program adopted in 1933 as one of the first acts of the Roosevelt Administration, and now accepted by both parties, was a drastic modification of free enterprise. It placed a government cushion, or guarantee, under our biggest industry—an industry which supports directly or indirectly about half the people of the country and vitally affects the rest. With the adoption of that law the "free-enterprise system" went at least half the way out of the window—without protest from anyone in authority except the Supreme Court. And even the Supreme Court changed its mind within a year or two.

In the face of such a law it is silly to talk of free enterprise in agriculture any longer. And yet that is just what the farm spokesmen do when they oppose ceilings on farm prices because they would "interfere with the free enterprise system." Like many of the rest of us the farmer wants floors, but no ceilings. The latest crop report points to the possibility of huge surpluses in some of the major crops, which may require the government to put up support money running past the billion dollar mark to hold prices up at a time when many of us would like them to go down. This is not free enterprise, under which prices can drop with a bang.

Our urban economy now has fully as many government cushions under it as the farm economy, although most business men do not feel them because they are more indirect. First there is the social security law, providing floors below which the incomes of our industrial workers cannot fall even during unemployment—and providing continuing income for the aged and infirm. Then, for those who work, the wage-and-hour law provides a floor under wages and a ceiling over the hours of work. What a change this is from the old free-enterprise days when men and women worked in sweatshops and cotton mills for seventy hours a week to earn perhaps seven dollars! These two measures alone protect millions of individuals. Together with the farm income guarantees, they provide a tremendous structure supporting national purchasing power—the foundation stone for our whole industrial prosperity.

Supplementing the social security law is the vast system of retirement plans set up by private industry during the recent war, when taxes were so high that it was almost as cheap to set up a lavish retirement system as to pay taxes on the income. These reserves—estimated to run into many hundreds of millions of dollars—are just as secure a bulwark to the individuals and the economy as the social security benefits.

There are besides a wide variety of government subsidies and cushions for specific industries. The air-transport industry, for instance, is subsidized through airmail contracts and when the TWA got into financial difficulties it rushed to Washington for a retroactive subsidy to pull it out of the hole. More recently the entire airtransport industry, with the exception of one or two companies, has been under financial strain. Instead of raising rates and competing under the rules of supply and demand the industry appealed to President Truman for help. Amid applause from the airlines, the President directed the RFC, the ever-ready crutch for industry, to study the situation, presumably as a preliminary to government loans. At the same time the Civil Aeronautics Board considered requests from the lines for bigger government subsidies—which would not be Adam Smith's solution to the problem.

The shipping industry has been subsidized by the government in one way or another for many years. Current subsidies to the merchant marine are running close to $100,000,000 a year on top of all the rich benefits provided these companies by the government in the past. Even the nation's press, which is founded on the word "free," is not free of subsidies. Newspapers and magazines enjoy the benefits of mail subsidies totaling many millions of dollars a year. Colonel Robert R. McCormick, of the Chicago *Tribune,* estimated not long ago that mail subsidies represented the entire profit of the prosperous *Time-Life-Fortune* enterprises.

Whether our banking system is subsidized is open to debate, but some economists contend that the banks got close to a billion dollars a year in subsidies during the war for handling the paper war debt. Government research subsidies are now reaching into almost every field of private enterprise and running into many hundreds of millions of dollars a year. They go not only to business concerns and educational institutions in the form of research grants, but even into the pockets of private physicians, the men who seem most determined to avoid government interference with their own profession (these payments come directly from the Public Health Service, which some physicians regard as an arch-enemy).

In some areas the definition of subsidies becomes difficult. Many industries benefit substantially from the government's weather reports, from the trade-promotion activities of the Commerce Department, from the improvements for the benefit of commerce in our rivers and harbors, from flood control expenditures, soil conservation, the establishment and maintenance of air navigation facilities, and a host of similar government operations including the production of cheap hydro-electric power. . . .

Government money has become such a major element in the American economy that one out of every six adults in this country now receives some of it in one form or another. Regular payments go to almost 16,000,000 individuals, including veterans and their dependents, members of the armed forces, government employees, federal pensioners, social security beneficiaries, and farmers.

Even more basic than any of these money payments, however, are the guarantees the federal government now offers to our credit structure. In addition to the federal insurance of bank deposits, which has eliminated the national fear of bank runs, the government offers ninety per cent guarantees on farms and urban mortgages. These guarantees, which cover a big segment of the private debt structure, have stabilized the mortgage market as it never was before—and to some extent, at least, have eliminated the wild ups-and-downs that have brought so much disaster in the past.

The federal government alone is now pumping into the economic system about $40,000,000,000 annually—most of which will have to continue unless we drastically modify the services our government provides, the military force, benefits to veterans, and foreign aid. This figure, which equals our total national income of only sixteen years ago, is for a period when we have been enjoying boom prosperity. State and local government expenditures swell the total beyond $50,000,000,000 a year.

Come a depression, the federal government's spending would go far beyond these figures, since it is legally obliged to cushion farm prices, pay unemployment benefits, and make good its guarantees. Furthermore, under the principle of government established by Hoover and Roosevelt in the past depression—that neither business nor people shall be permitted to go under *en masse*—the government would have an obligation to pour billions of dollars into financial and industrial enterprises and into relief of individual need. That it will do so is conceded.

What this all amounts to, in short, is not a free-enterprise system, but a comparatively safe-enterprise system under which our economic health is founded on government credit and government credit is used not only to battle depression but to avoid it. Even in good times the government will act to save an industry—as it did recently for the air-transport companies.

There is still risk in business, particularly in those areas where competition prevails. Many small businesses fail every day. Government does not guarantee a profit to every business man, or even to every farmer. An entrepreneur's rewards still depend considerably on his ability and his luck. But the risks in business today are far more limited than they were in the days when we really had the "free-enterprise system" we talk about so much. . . .

. . . . .

And the American people must admit that the safe-enterprise system under which they live requires certain adjustments. Does this system, for example, warrant such unlimited business profits as in the past, when business men risked all to win all? If business does not make the necessary adjustments in price and profit policies we must decide whether or not a large segment of industry has achieved the relative security of a public utility—a position where limited risks warrant legislation limiting profits. We will have to face up, also, to a permanent budget of $40,000,000,000 or more a year and pay the taxes that such a system of government services and supports require. In good years we will have to pay in taxes considerably more than that, so that the government will be sound enough to meet the extraordinary expenses it faces in bad times.

The old free-enterprise system exists only in our nostalgic imagination, and we have spent more than enough energy defending it. If we want to retain custody of our economic fate, the first step is to admit the facts.

WANTED: A NEW NAME FOR CAPITALISM *

Is "capitalism" a misnomer for the modern American economy? Does twentieth-century capitalism require a new term to differentiate it from the older system? More specifically, is the author correct in assuming that most criticism leveled against nineteenth-century capitalism is no longer valid—that a new word would mitigate criticism and gain supporters?

If the assumptions of the author are correct, why do we have a "reformed" capitalism in the United States? Why did other areas fail to reform? Would the author of "What Do You Mean, Free Enterprise?" attack Mr. Nichols' thesis? Would a Communist dispute his reasoning? Would a Socialist?

The redefinition of just one word could help change history.

Finding a new term to express a new idea could be a decisive factor in checking the world spread of Communism.

This is the report that comes back again and again from men and women who are engaged in the struggle of ideas between the free world and the Soviets. The word is "Capitalism."

It is the term used over and over by the Soviets as a smear word to describe our side; and, so far as that goes, Americans generally use it themselves when they try to describe their economic system. But in fact, and on both sides of the Iron Curtain, it is a misleading word because, when applied to America, it no longer fits the system it pretends to describe.

What is worse, to many people it carries negative overtones of old errors and old abuses. In no way does it imply the positive, dynamic, expanding system of today, constantly changing, but always moving toward one goal —to create more goods and greater well-being for more people.

Recently, a top official in our overseas Information Program put it this way: "In all propaganda broadcasts now, the two words which appear most frequently are 'Communism' and 'Capitalism.' I don't think we have half as much trouble with the word Communism as we do with Capitalism. It's relatively easy to expose the bad side of Communism and make it stick —so much so that when you say 'Communism' and 'Red Fascism' most people know you're talking about one and the same thing.

"But," he went on, "it's nowhere near as easy to make the good side of our society plain by using the word Capitalism. That's important. We

* William I. Nichols, *This Week Magazine,* March 4, 1951, pp. 7, 17, 19. Copyright, 1951, by the United Newspapers Magazine Corporation.

need a word to make people realize that the real source of hope, progress and prosperity rests with us."

The same thought has been expressed again and again by America's business leaders. "We only muddle our own thinking," they say, "when we use old words to describe new ideas."

To understand the problem, let's look back a bit. The word Capitalism came into being well over 100 years ago in the early days of the industrial revolution. At that time the basis of wealth shifted from land to money (that is, capital) invested in industrial and commercial ventures. Admittedly, during those years there were many abuses, errors and mistakes.

If you have read the novels of Charles Dickens—written 100 years ago —or the story of America's "Robber Barons" in the 1890's, you know what they were. There is no denying that Capitalism's primitive period contains many dark chapters of worker exploitation at home, and colonial expansion abroad.

We've Changed

All those memories are contained in the word Capitalism. The Communists are clever enough to seize on that fact. Hence their use of the word Capitalist as a dirty name, a smear word, for every aspect of our Western Civilization.

But what about us? Are we so stupid as to let them get away with it? In the face of their repressive, regressive slave system, we stand for a bold and imaginative society which has changed, developed and improved with the years. Are we imaginative enough to find a word for it?

Anyone who has eyes and looks around him knows how conditions today differ from those of 50 to 100 years ago. Here, for example, are 10 points based in large part on a listing recently prepared by Edward J. Meeman, Editor of the Memphis "Press-Scimitar":

1. Slavery, which antedates Capitalism, has been abolished in all Capitalist countries. In fact, and ironically, it is now practiced primarily in Communist countries, and on a wider scale than ever before in history.

2. In its early days Capitalism exploited the labor of women and children. This has nearly been abolished.

3. Capitalism once imposed overlong hours. These are now short, and growing shorter.

4. The standard of living under Capitalism has steadily risen. This is exactly contrary to Marx's prediction—and to the record of Communist countries.

5. Unemployment has been reduced and controlled and is now a diminishing problem.

6. The adulteration and misbranding of products have almost been eliminated.

7. Early Capitalist employers cared little about the health and safety of their workers. Today industrial safety has been carried to such a point that more accidents occur in our homes than in factories, offices and stores.

8. The slogan of Capitalism once was "The public be damned." Today all progressive companies know the importance of public opinion, and public relations have become an essential part of management.

9. Capitalism formerly produced crowded, unsanitary slums. Now employers know the value of better living conditions, and work for them.

10. Imperialist wars were once waged by Capitalists and colonial rule imposed on foreign peoples. Now country after country has given up its colonies.

That is a pretty impressive list of differences between "then" and "now." And the process is still going on. Up to the time of emergency controls (a result of Communist aggression, by the way) company after company was developing new plans for bonuses, pensions, incentive wages, "cost of living" wage raises, profit-sharing and other procedures.

In one form or another all these methods are designed to give more and more people an increasing share of production, whether in the form of higher wages, shorter hours, lower prices or better goods and services.

Most of us in America know all these facts. We know what our "New Capitalism" is producing for us and what it can produce anywhere if given a fair chance. But hundreds of millions of people throughout the world don't know this. We must find some way to make clear in their minds the distinction between (1) our system and Capitalism of the past, and, (2) between our system and Capitalism as it is practiced in some other parts of the world. Unfortunately, there are still areas where Capitalism operates in the old, primitive way, and a Capitalist is regarded as a member of a privileged upper group who dodges taxes, exploits his workers and overcharges his customers.

Europe's View

As was pointed out recently by French-American writer Lewis Galantiere, the average European "judges our capitalism in the light of what he knows about his own, and we have allowed him to remain in profound ignorance of the differences between the two."

A new name for our system would help make the distinctions clear. It would revive hope among the underprivileged. And at the same time it would be a spur toward more enlightened action by old-fashioned Capitalists wherever they may be.

Up to now Communism has claimed that it held out the only promise for a better future. But as soon as Communism takes over, the promises are forgotten. Then the Iron Curtain falls, the Security Police move in, the gates of the slave-labor camps swing open, and another helpless nation is trapped.

In a free world one can make no sweeping promises because people can come and go, and see for themselves. One can never claim that everything is, or will be, perfect for everybody, everywhere, at exactly the same time. But one *can* see with his own eyes that in most areas where true political and economic democracy is practiced, things are getting better; the direction is up. And it is the direction which counts.

Continuous Improvement

How shall we describe this system—imperfect, but always improving, and always capable of further improvement—where men move forward freely together, working together, building together, producing always more and more, and sharing together the rewards of their increased production? Capitalism is no longer the right word. In too many minds it stands for the primitive economic system of the 19th century when, all too often, employers were greedy and workers were oppressed. We need a new name to describe the new, expanding, and ever-self-renewing system. What shall it be? I have heard various suggestions. Here are a few of the best:

> The New Capitalism
> Democratic Capitalism
> Economic Democracy
> Industrial Democracy
> Distributism
> Mutualism
> Productivism

All have their points. All help catch and express the idea, or parts of it. But might there be something better? Some word which will catch hold and slip automatically into the language, giving that sense of birth, hope, promise and everlasting pushing forward which is the essence of every society of free men? . . .

THE ROAD AHEAD *

The Road Ahead represents a major landmark in the current dispute concerning national economic policy. Over 400,000 copies of the book were printed. A condensation appeared in *The Reader's Digest,* reprints of which reached every hamlet in the country. Opponents of recent economic trends hailed the book as a "shocking challenge which cannot be ignored by any citizen who wishes to preserve America's heritage of freedom." Certainly understanding of this point of view is essential if one is to comprehend fully the issues at stake in the great debate over the role of government in the American economy.

Most people in this country believe that the American Communist Party and its dupes are the chief internal enemy of our economic system and our form of government. This is a serious mistake. . . . If every Communist in America were rounded up and liquidated, the greatest menace to our form of social organization would be still among us.

This most dangerous enemy is the American counterpart of the British Fabian Socialist, who denies that he is a Socialist and operates behind a mask which he calls National Planning. These Socialist Planners are enticing us down the dark road that has led so many European nations to their doom. Unless they are recognized for what they are, and are stopped, they will destroy this country.

Of the countries in Europe which have moved into the Socialist camp, the two which concern us most are Russia and Great Britain. Each adopted Socialism by a different route; each organized its Socialist society upon a different model. But both are Socialist. . . .

We are following in the footsteps of Great Britain. We are much further along the road than we suspect. If we do not clearly recognize that fact and abandon that fatal road, we shall inevitably, perhaps in less than a decade, be in the condition the British now find themselves in.

In Great Britain we have a perfect case history of the infection and progress of the Socialist disease and, while this book is about America, we should briefly review the carefully concerted Socialist plan by which that once great country—the home of modern capitalism and modern free government—was led stealthily to her present state. . . .

Socialist propagandists from Britain are fond of claiming that they have

---

* John T. Flynn. From *The Road Ahead.* Copyright, 1949, by John T. Flynn, as condensed by *The Reader's Digest,* February, 1950, pp. 2, 4, 9–15, 18, 19. By permission of the Devin-Adair Company, Publishers, New York 10.

socialized only about 25 per cent of the economic system and that 75 per cent remains under capitalism. This is a distortion of the facts. Britain has "nationalized" about 25 per cent of her economic processes, but she has "socialized" almost the entire economic system.

The government has nationalized the following: the Bank of England (credit); cables and wireless (the overseas communications system); civil aviation; railways; bus transport and inland waterways; coal mines; electricity; the gas industry; medical services.

The rest of the economy has been socialized by a method under which the State makes the plans for all forms of business—farms, factories, shops. Government bureaus decide on production quotas for an industry as a whole and in many cases for the individual units. They fix the quotas, priorities and prices on raw materials; fix wages; determine who shall get credit at the banks and who shall not. In sum, the State generally makes the blueprints upon the basis of which all business operations are carried on and *polices* those operations to ensure faithful obedience to the State's plans.

If the British Socialist experiment were successful one would suppose that it would have produced more goods at lower prices, and workers would be better off than under the old capitalist regime; that the security of the nation would be advanced in every way.

But the promised benefits have not appeared. On the contrary, by every economic, physical and moral test, Socialism has been a tragic failure. It is already falling apart. The people cry out against impossible prices, against scarcities, oppressive taxation and bureaucratic oppressors. . . .

We have seen what Socialism means in Britain and the plan by which it was brought into effect and the consequences visited upon the British people. Do we have in America any movement comparable to the Fabian Socialist movement in Britain? And if so, what is it doing, how is it progressing and what are its chances of success here?

The answer is that we have precisely such a movement here; that it is making rapid strides; and that, unless it is soon arrested, nothing can prevent its extension here on the British model.

Do not confuse the present Socialist movement in America with what we have known for so long as the *Socialist Party*. This party has reached a low estate in numbers and in growth. I am referring to an entirely different movement led by entirely different men and under wholly different banners.

There are some persons who brand as Socialism almost any intervention by the State into the economic system. Many imagine that Socialism means confiscation by the State of the whole economic apparatus of the nation. These concepts are incorrect.

As we have seen in Britain, modern Socialism means the assumption by the State of the responsibility and authority for the control of the entire economic system. This does not mean that the State will take over every farm, mine, shop and factory. It will operate the great basic functions of credit, power, fuel, transportation and insurance. The rest of the economic system may be kept in private hands but must be operated according to plans made by the State and carried out under the supervision and compulsions of government bureaus.

This is the type of Socialism with which America is now threatened. And just as it fastened itself on Britain by a movement that avoided calling itself Socialist, so it is being promoted in America by persons and organizations that never use the word Socialism. They call their system the "Planned Economy." What that cunning label means is precisely the same thing that is now in operation in Britain.

The advocates of planning believe that the economic system must cease to be a free system and that the State, which under our system was forbidden to intervene in the management of industry, should be established as the master of industry with the power to make the plans for the whole economic system. . . .

At every stage of this subject the Communist issue arises to confuse us. The Communist Party in the United States is a political organization, but is not a party in the sense in which we understand that term. It is a secret, conspiratorial brotherhood, engaged in wrecking the American system as a prelude to making this country into a Socialist nation. (It is also the agent of a foreign power in carrying out the objectives of the Russian Government in this country, and to this extent it is organized treason.)

In a left-wing gathering it would be difficult to determine whether a given person is a Communist or a Socialist. They all believe that the capitalist system must go. They are agreed that Socialism in one form or another we must have, and on this plane all of them—Communists and Socialist Planners—must be grouped together as enemies of our traditional American system.

Communist Party members favor anything which will tend to wreck our private-enterprise system. For instance, they know that nothing will wreck it more quickly and more surely than extravagant spending and the accumulation of public debt. They are, therefore, for any program that will pile new tons of debt on the nation. Our less intelligent Socialist reformers, who know little about economics and despise its lessons, support public spending because the effects are immediately pleasant and because they have been persuaded by a new school of so-called economists that it is a sound policy. . . .

I have tried to make it clear that our American system is being destroyed by groups united in the design of luring this country into a socialist system on the British model. The Communist would like to ruin the American system by clubbing it over the head. The Socialist Planner does it by slow poison. Both types of assassin are at work here now, but the latter is by far the more dangerous. And their campaign is succeeding.

Just how far have the Planners advanced their program for socializing this country?

For one thing, our Government now has almost as large a control over our private banking system as England has over its banks. It has not yet the power to decide what types of loans may be made to private industry, but is geared now to assume that power with only a slight alteration in the setup. It would then possess the power of life and death over every industry.

The Government itself has moved into the business of banking, including money-lending, upon an astonishing scale, through a large number of major lending agencies whose loans and investments total $6,575,000,000, while the private banking system is at the Government's mercy because the Government is now the banks' biggest borrower and most powerful customer.

Next to credit, the most important key economic weapon is electric power. Our federal government's authority to engage in flood and navigation control has been seized on as a pretext for engaging in the manufacture of electrical power. The public has little conception of the extent to which our Government has penetrated that industry.

Up to now the Tennessee Valley Authority (TVA) has been the largest entry into that field. But President Truman has sent to Congress a demand for an extensive project on the Columbia River which would embrace river systems draining Washington, Oregon, Idaho, and western Montana. There are 16 other similar power projects. This is just the beginning of a program which is intended to cover America, take the power industry out of private hands and put it into the hands of the Government.

While Government power systems are to a great degree free of taxes and of interest charges on investment, amounting to countless millions a year, and are permitted bookkeeping practices which would land a private utility official in jail, the privately owned power companies are weighed down by every form of Government shackles. Private power systems must run at a profit or die. The federal power systems run at losses while loudly claiming fictitious profits.

The Socialist Planners believe they have the private power systems on the run. The total capacity of the private systems now is 45 million kilowatts. Present Government plans call for Government plants generating 41 million kilowatts. It is all being done in the name of reclamation and flood control. Little will be said about power, but the drive is to socialize the power industry.

Another project now heavily pressed by the Socialist Planners is socialized medicine. It is called "health insurance." The plan, which ostensibly came from Oscar R. Ewing, head of the Federal Security Agency, calls for an increase, with federal aid, of the number of hospitals, doctors and nurses and dentists, along with what he calls compulsory health insurance. This plan is similar to Britain's. Under it, all employers and their employes would be taxed at the payroll window for medical care.

The proponents of this scheme had the effrontery to call it "free" medical care. Of course it is not. It will be paid for by taxes from everyone's pocket. . . .

We must arrest the course of the social disease that is destroying us and set our hands to the hard task of lifting up and revivifying our shattered systems of free enterprise. If we do not, we shall go on stumbling down the path along which Europe has slipped.

It is not possible to lay down a program in detail for checking and reversing our direction. And it is not necessary. What is necessary is to see clearly the general principles which must govern our effort. These I shall now attempt to enumerate as briefly as possible.

We must put human freedom as the first of our demands. There can be no security in a nation without freedom. Let us work to make our country a more bountiful home for all to live in, but the first and indispensable test of every plan must be whether it will impair our freedom. A better life for all, yes—but not at the expense of our liberties.

We must stop apologizing for our capitalist society. It has made us strong, and has provided us the highest standard of living in world history.

Not one more step into Socialism. There is, of course, much to be done to repair all the damage already done to our system by the advocates of socialistic measures but the first militant maneuver must be to hold the line for the American way.

Get rid of compromising leaders. Let us put a mark upon every man in public life who is willing to surrender further.

We must recognize that we are in a social war, and that we must fight it as such. Our enemies have managed to capture many of the instrumentalities of the classroom, the platform, the pulpit, the movies and the radio upon an amazing scale, and to use them not for their traditional purposes but to carry on an attack upon the minds of the American people.

We must put an end to the orgy of spending that is rapidly bankrupting the nation. Among the most critical conditions that menace us are the fantastic commitments for spending countless billions and the crushing weight of our national debt upon our economic system. From July 1, 1945, to June 30, 1949—President Truman's years in power—he spent 184 billion dollars. This is 30 billion dollars more than was spent by this Government in all the 147 years of its existence from George Washington to the end of Franklin D. Roosevelt's first administration. We must not permit one more cent for any purpose beyond our present commitments.

We must stop "planning" for Socialism and begin planning to make our free system of private enterprise operate at its fullest capacity. Since 1933 the Government has waged relentless war upon the capitalist system—at first ignorantly, but recently with a definite design to cripple and destroy it. The man who runs a business has been pilloried as a criminal, and the Government has taken measures to prevent him from accumulating those savings which make expansion possible. It has held him up to public scorn and hatred. It has taxed away his savings, and it has so choked the streams through which savings flow into investment that our system is wilting away.

Our system is in an appalling mess now, what with the public debt, the confiscatory taxes which draw the blood from its very veins, Government intrusions and the threats of ultimate extinction that are taking ever more terrifying shape. The task calls for patriotism and courage; it must not be delayed another day.

We must set about rebuilding in its integrity our republican system of government. We cannot depend on any political party to save us. We must build a mass organization outside the parties so powerful that all parties will be compelled to yield to its demands. Our forefathers gave to the world the sublime example of statesmen who cast off the tyrant State and built up the sovereign people, unleashing the energies of free men. It was this historic experiment which set off the astonishing surge of human energy that created here such abundance and freedom as the world has never known.

The task before us is clear. For our principles of action we must go back to our Constitution, to our Declaration of Independence, to our history and to the example set by our national fathers. We must begin now to dismantle the tyrant State in America and to build up once again the energies of a free people.

THE UNSYSTEMATIC AMERICAN SYSTEM *

You will recall that in the ancient story of the seven blind men and the elephant, each examiner pronounced the beast to be something distinctly different. To John Flynn the road ahead leads to doom and destruction unless we take drastic action to reverse our present course. Frederick Lewis Allen suggests that this analysis is unconvincing and unrealistic. "It is time . . . we rid ourselves of the notion that the direction of change at home is toward socialism or communism, and that loyal Americans must stand pat." The reasoning that underlies this assertion is both optimistic and thought-provoking.

Have we actually evolved "beyond" Socialism and Communism without recognizing the course of our economic evolution? Have we entered into a new era of government-business relationships, with government providing the over-all direction and private business supplying the day-to-day decisions? Is it true that most Americans are in subconscious agreement as to the direction of economic change and that our quarrels are over relatively minor matters?

. . . At present we have a very large and powerful central government. It continues to expand as if in response to some irresistible law of growth— not only because of the obligations which war and cold war have imposed upon it, but because of our increasing interdependence as a more and more urbanized people with more and more complex institutions. The government regulates business in innumerable ways. It constantly interferes with the operations of the once almighty economic law of supply and demand, the law of the market place. It provides all sorts of subsidies and guarantees to groups who have convinced it, rightly or wrongly, that they need such help. And furthermore it acknowledges two great responsibilities, the recognition of which was forced upon us during the miserable years of the Great Depression. One of these is a responsibility for seeing that people in an economic jam are helped to their feet—if not by their relatives and friends, then by federal relief if necessary. And the other is a responsibility for seeing that the economic system as a whole does not break down.

The government therefore maintains certain control powers over the national economy as a whole; and in a time of emergency like that which has followed the onset of the Korean war, these powers are extended. But it does not try to run our individual businesses (with certain exceptions such

* Frederick Lewis Allen, *The Big Change* (Harper, 1952). Copyright, 1952, by Frederick Lewis Allen. Reprinted from *Harper's Magazine*, June, 1952, pp. 22–26.

as the atomic power industry, which for security purposes is an island of socialism in a sea of private management). For we recognize that our businesses are better run if they remain in private hands. The past dozen years or so have offered a triumphant demonstration of the validity of this belief. For they have seen privately managed American business not only do a brilliant job of huge-scale war production, but also foster a startling variety of advances in technology.

Nor, for that matter, does the federal government take over the power of our state and local governments, though it subsidizes them to do many things which they cannot adequately do unaided. So there is a wide distribution of government powers. Our road system, for instance, is part local, part state, and only in minor degree federal. Our university and college system is partly state-run, partly independent. And our school system is mostly locally run (by local public authority), partly church-run, partly independent.

Furthermore, we have an extraordinarily wide and proliferating assortment of voluntary institutions, associations, and societies which in their manifold ways contribute to the public good. Not only universities, schools, churches, hospitals, museums, libraries, and social agencies in great variety, but also societies for the protection or promotion of practically everything; if you want to feed European children, or protect our wild ducks, or promote zoning systems, or agitate for more freedom for corporations, or extend church work, or make boys into Boy Scouts, or save the redwoods, you will find a private organization dedicated to this purpose, and sometimes there will be several of them. There are also the foundations, offspring of idealism and the estate tax. And an endless range of trade associations, professional associations, alumni and alumnae associations, service clubs, and lodges. As a people we are great joiners, campaigners, and voluntary group helpers and savers and reformers and improvers and promoters. Get together half-a-dozen like-minded Americans and pretty soon you'll have an association, an executive secretary, a national program, and a fund-raising campaign. . . .

Over every proposal for a further change in the complicated design of the national economic machine there is hot argument. Will this measure undermine the incentive to work and save and invest and invent? Will it give tyrannical power to Washington? Does this group of people, or this industry, really need aid? Can the government afford it? Does it set a good or a bad precedent? People can get apoplectic over such issues—and no wonder, for the development of this new American system is highly experimental, and we don't know whether we can continue to make it work.

Take a look at a few of the uncertainties.

During the postwar years inflation, though never acute, has been almost uninterrupted, and in sum has been a serious menace to our economic health. We don't know whether we can maintain our fast pace without continuing inflation.

Even before the Korean war we had pretty nearly reached the limit of taxation—the limit beyond which the burden would become so intolerable that the incentive to produce would be weakened and tax evasion would become a monumental rather than a minor problem. We don't know whether we can reduce this load or increase our productivity fast enough to take care of it.

If the Soviets should change their policy so convincingly that we could ease up on military expenditures, we don't know whether we could step up domestic production fast enough to prevent a depression.

If total war should come, we don't know whether the federal debt would become so astronomical that the credit of the federal government would be shaken.

In any case, we don't know whether the government has taken on so many financial responsibilities, since it added to its own previous authority much of the authority once exercised by Wall Street, that there is not a danger of a new kind of panic and financial collapse at some time in the future—a panic resulting from the inability, not of private financiers, but of public financiers, to maintain the values they have undertaken to guarantee. We think we know a great deal more about economics than we did a generation ago, but we cannot be surer that we are living in a New Era than were the moguls of Wall Street who cherished that innocent faith in 1929.

And in addition, we don't know at exactly what point a policy of aid to disadvantaged men and women degenerates into a demoralizing policy of handouts to people who would rather accept federal bounties than extend themselves. Some are sure we have already crossed this line; others are sure we haven't.

So it is just as well that every time we tinker with this experimental system there should be energetic and protracted debate.

But the fury of our political campaigns, and the angry disputes over this or that congressional bill, detract our attention from a remarkable fact: that despite the purple language which is tossed about, very few Americans seriously propose any really wholesale change in our evolving American system. (And at that, our stormiest debates in recent years have not been over domestic policy but over foreign policy, or over the supposed influence of American Communists and their friends and alleged friends over foreign policy.) There is a large amount of antipathy to the Administration in power in Washington. There are numerous people who would like to curb federal power, repeal various laws now on the books, pare down the bureaucracy, minimize relief. There are others who want the government to take on new labors and new powers, like that of running a great medical insurance program. Yet the vast majority of Americans agree that the government should continue to accept an over-all responsibility for the satisfactory operation of the national economy; that it should continue to accept responsibility for relief when necessary; that it should supervise and regulate business to some extent—but that it should keep its intervention limited, and should let the great bulk of business remain under private management. The seething debate is over how much of this and how much of that we need, but the area of virtual agreement is very wide; and this includes allowing private business to remain in private hands.

For we believe we have demonstrated that business can be far more resourcefully and ingeniously run by private managers; and furthermore that these private managers can run most if not all of it with such consideration for the general public welfare that they can achieve for us all that government ownership would bring, plus the efficiency, flexibility, and adventurousness which government ownership would jeopardize—and without the danger of tyranny that government ownership might invite.

In short, there is subconscious agreement among the vast majority of Americans that the United States is not evolving toward socialism, but past socialism. I say subconscious agreement because in our conscious thought most of us still seem to be the victims of an old idea that has become a delusion. This is the idea that there is in the world a sort of inevitable trend of progress toward socialism; that people who want the government to do more than it is doing are therefore liberal (if they are polite about it) or radical (if they are aggressive about it); and that people who want the management of business to remain in private hands are therefore conservative (if polite) or reactionary (if aggressive).

Historically there has been ample warrant for this picture of the political spectrum. During the past century or so the principal political changes have been in the direction of getting the government to do more and more for what was thought to be the common weal; and the people who didn't want the government to act, who wanted to dig their heels in and stop it from acting, were rightly known as conservatives. By contrast the people who went whole hog for government intervention, to the point of wanting the government to take over virtually everything, by violent revolution if necessary, in short the Communists, were rightly known as extreme radicals. But now the United States has been demonstrating pretty convincingly that the system that works best of all, combining most of the genuine advantages of governmental responsibility and of private initiative, and avoiding the disadvantages of each, is one in which governmental intervention is limited and private industry and private associations have a great degree of freedom; and also that one of the mightiest advantages of this system is the way in which it diffuses very widely the decision-making power and the opportunities that go with it. In short, that the direction of progress is now different from what people had supposed it was.

Yet the delusion persists that the trend of the times is toward socialism, and perhaps even toward communism. Though our production, our wealth, our standard of living are the wonder of the world; though Britain under Socialist leadership had to come to us for financial aid; though, as Isabel Lundberg wrote in 1948, we are in a position to offer tangible goods and expert technological services to nations to whom the Russians, for all their loud talk of material benefits, could not offer so much as a shoelace; though our evolved and unsystematic system is potentially the most revolutionary force on earth, nevertheless so fixed in our minds is this delusion that when we face foreign problems we instinctively consider ourselves the natural allies of conservatism, and we tend to behave as if we wanted to stifle the natural hopes of mankind for a decenter way of life. Instinctively we set our faces against change. And preposterously many of us think of Soviet Russia—which has submerged the historic Communist aim of a better life for the masses of people in an aim of national aggrandizement through barbaric means—as if it and its allied zealots and dupes represented radicalism, represented a disposition of things toward which we ourselves might drift if we did not hold fast against change; as if Soviet Russia were something other than a despotic medievalism which has developed out of a revolutionary attempt to meet the problems of the nineteenth century—problems which we ourselves have long since surmounted.

It is time we rid ourselves of this notion about Russia. It is time we realize that when we battle against communism, we are battling against the past, not against the future. It is time, too, we rid ourselves of the notion that the direction of change at home is toward socialism or communism, and that therefore loyal Americans must stand pat. This notion is a stultifying force in our life. It causes well-meaning people to imagine that anyone with unorthodox ideas must be suspect of subversive intent. It tends to cramp men's imaginations into a timid conformity. It tends to constrict our generous impulses as a people. Combined with the fear of large-scale war, and especially of atomic war, it eats away at our bold confidence in ourselves and our destiny.

We would do better to put it out of our minds, and to realize that our sobering position of leadership in the world is founded upon the fact that we have not stood still. The story of the changes in the contours of American life that we have hammered out in the first half of this twentieth century is a triumphant story, however harsh may have been some of our experiences in the interim and however obscure may be the shape of the

future.   We would do well to think of our accomplishment thus far as but
the preface to what we may accomplish in the second half of the century
if we can continue to invent, improve, and change—and can keep a good
heart.   The courageous nation, like the courageous man, is not unhappy
at the thought of dangers beside the road ahead, but welcomes them as
challenges to be faced and overwhelmed along an adventurous course.

Problem 22: Socialism--
Progress or Decay?

It has been said that when two Socialists meet they immediately fall
to quarreling about the true nature of their doctrine.   Russians are apt to
declare that Communism is the only true version of Socialism; European
Socialists denounce the Soviet system as "Red Fascism"; conservative
Americans pin the Socialist label on the New Deal, thus infuriating the
members of minuscule Socialist Party, U.S.A., to whom the New Deal
was only an inept, half-way measure.   Some view Socialism as a half-way
station on the road to Communism; others profess to see no difference between Socialist and Communist systems.

Regardless of definitions, Socialism is one of the vital and important
economic doctrines of the twentieth century.   Because the Socialist Party
in this country is insignificant, Americans are apt to dismiss blithely the
Socialist philosophy as one held only by an erratic, crotchety minority.
Nothing is further from the truth.   It is a hard fact of modern history
that much of the world has rejected capitalism as Americans know it.
Most Western European nations are today governed by Socialists, or by
coalitions including Socialists.   Hence the importance of understanding
both the assumptions and results of Socialist rule.   Is Socialism (to mix
metaphors) "the Road to Serfdom" or "the Wave of the Future"?

The Moral Case for Socialism *

The virtues or shortcomings of socialism may be debated on many grounds. In presenting the following article to their readers the Editors of *Fortune* wrote:

"Is socialism all washed up as a political force? It has failed to solve Britain's central problem [as discussed in an article in the September, 1949, issue of *Fortune*]; it has lost ground on the Continent; everywhere intellectuals and the young are skeptical of its claims. Yet we have not heard the last of it, for politics is a branch of morals and there is a case for socialism that will survive its pragmatic failures.

"Those who hold that American-style capitalism is the better, safer, more hopeful system must meet this case. That is why we present the best statement of it that we could get. We urge our readers to work out their own answers to Mr. Williams. Part of the right answer, we believe, is the promise of future changes in American capitalism—changes for which it has always shown a capacity, but which are urgent if the socialist challenge is to be met. . . ."

The author of this article, Francis Williams, is a well-known British Socialist. He formerly edited the *Laborite Daily News* and during World War II served as Controller of News and Censorship. Recently he has been a British delegate to the United Nations Subcommittee on Freedom of Information and the Press.

I know of no better definition of the moral case for socialism than two sentences from the Declaration of Independence: "We hold these truths to be self-evident, that all men are created equal, that they are endowed by their Creator with certain inalienable Rights, that among these are Life, Liberty and the pursuit of Happiness. That to secure these rights Governments are instituted among Men deriving their just powers from the consent of the governed. . . ." I am a socialist because I believe that only within a socialist society can these rights be assured. Socialism, like all political systems, is a means. Its end is a democratic society recognizing the dignity of human personality and the uniqueness of the individual. Its specific contribution to the solution of these political problems, which are among the most intransigent facing mankind, arises from the belief

* Francis Williams. Reprinted from the October, 1949, issue of *Fortune*, pp. 120–22, 124, 126, by special permission of the Editors. Copyright, 1949, Time, Inc.

that man is not an economic but a moral being moved by ideals and aspirations more satisfying than those of the materialist conceptions that govern the other great political creeds of the modern world—capitalism and Communism. . . .

Capitalism, even when it outgrows its more ruthless manifestations and becomes benevolent and paternal, is rooted in the belief that the acquisitive instinct is the primary human instinct upon which a civilized community must depend. The socialist does not accept this profoundly skeptical and pessimistic view of human nature. He is no more prepared to accept the doctrine of economic man when it is presented to him in capitalist terms, than he is when it is presented to him in communist terms.

. . . The socialist rejects communism as a political method capable of achieving the good society because he cannot agree that economic interests, although important, are sufficiently absolute to justify the suppression of political and intellectual freedom and the concentration of all power in the hands of those who claim, rightly or wrongly, to represent the interests of the largest economic class. But he equally rejects capitalism as a means to the good society because he observes that by denying social control over economic power it reduces in practice the effectiveness of the very political liberties it claims to defend.

At the conclusion of the last meeting of the United States Chamber of Commerce, the United Press canvassed representative leaders of American business there present for their views on an unemployment total of over three million. "Unemployment is a natural and normal development of industrial readjustment," said one of these leaders. And a second one added, "Unemployment is a good thing in a dynamic free-enterprise economy."

Within the capitalist concept they were quite right: a system of private capitalism requires a reservoir of economically powerless and expendable human beings for its smooth functioning just as much as a communist system requires the existence of a politically powerless and expendable mass for its operations. The socialist, however, is concerned not with systems but with human beings. He says with all the force at his command that any system which can so dehumanize its leaders that they can regard as "a good thing" the infliction upon millions of their fellows of the mental and moral degradation and material suffering of unemployment—of being told by society that it has no use for them, that their strength and talents are valueless, that they are unfit to do what it is the right of all men to do, to support themselves and their families by their labor—that such a system is immoral; because it has altogether lost sight of the true values of human life. . . .

Capitalism, Road to Serfdom

The failure of communism to make men free needs no documentation by me in these pages. But let us briefly consider the record of modern capitalism. It has, it is true, immense material achievements to its credit. But since it developed out of the Industrial Revolution of the nineteenth century it has repeated a devastating pattern of boom and slump on a major scale no less than eighteen times. These recurring crises it has been able to solve only by the purges of bankruptcy and unemployment. It has required men and women to pay tribute to it by the most terrible of all submissions, the submission to blind economic forces generating their own crises and operating altogether outside the realms of logic or justice. The theoretical case for capitalism is that it rewards those who by their energy most deserve reward. But, in fact, depressions of capitalist economy are as undiscriminating as the plague. No man can build an individual barrier against their devastations however honestly he labors or however worthily he uses his talents. . . .

It may be that, as its defenders declare, American capitalism alone among the great capitalisms of the modern world can succeed in solving this dilemma. It may be that it can find a way to offer to all men and women not only that which all advanced capitalisms have been able to some degree to offer, a high standard of living in periods of prosperity, but also a bulwark against depression and a genuine hope of security against undeserved unemployment and poverty. It may be so. But I see little evidence of it so far. Nor is there in such pronouncements as those I have been quoting on the therapeutic of unemployment, anything to indicate even the beginnings of a real understanding of the nature of the human challenge capitalism has to meet.

But even if—which I repeat seems to me unlikely—American capitalism were able to solve the problem of security that has baffled all other capitalist societies; and even if, which is still more unlikely, it were able to pass on its solution to other capitalist societies with few of its advantages in vast national resources—the moral case for socialism would still remain.

For that case rests ultimately, as I stated earlier, on the belief that man is a moral being and not simply an economic being. The socialist case is thus a challenge to successful capitalism as well as to unsuccessful and is spiritual and in a wide sense religious in character. It is no accident that, as Prime Minister Attlee recently stated, "The first place in the influences that built up the British socialist movement must be given to religion." Nor is it an accident that many early leaders of British socialism were drawn from the churches and nonconformist chapels and that its present leaders include so many whose economic interests, taking into account the section of society into which they were born, gave them every reason to support the status quo. It was not personal economic interest but ethical compulsion that drove men like Attlee, Cripps, and others to try to build a more moral society.

Capitalism and Neurosis

. . . The socialist looking at modern capitalist societies sees them the prey of a profound neurosis. Their emphasis on a purely materialist standard of achievement, their insistence—inherent in the economic ideology that governs them—on competitive success as proof of character, so that men go through their lives hagridden by the fear that they may fail in almost the only test of manhood socially acceptable, that of the ability to earn a high income—all these confine human personality within a framework so rigid and so mutilating that the true values of civilization and the true warmths and generosities of human fellowship are lost. There is nothing so pitiable as the man who has no standards other than crudely material ones. Yet modern capitalism by its nature, by the credo at the heart of its philosophy, increasingly imposes these standards upon all men. Civilization is sick because the men and women who compose it are sick; forced into a mode of life unnatural to them and inimical to the profounder stirrings of the human spirit.

I do not think it is possible to look at American society, which is the product of modern capitalism at its most successful, without being made aware of the stresses and conflicts imposed upon men and women by the insistence upon materialist competitive success as the primary test of human value. The point of no return to which the salesman's philosophy brings those who give themselves wholly to the capitalist dream is not reassuring.

I am a visitor from a socialist country which is thought by many, because of the austerities that war and the change in international economic circumstances have imposed, to be a gray society and one hedged in with restrictions and controls. Yet I hope I shall be forgiven if I say that I am more conscious of strain and anxiety in American society than in British society. And of something perhaps more surprising—a sense of being imprisoned, confined within a pattern that has no mercy upon the nonconformist and dictates what it is socially acceptable to eat, to wear, to read, to say, to think, and above all to set as one's professional goal—to an extent that is not true of any European country I know. This dictation, this molding of the individual to a conventionally acceptable type, is not less significant nor less frightening because it is not the dictation of a man or of a group of men but of a philosophy. This philosophy sees people, as the believer in the capitalist thesis must, primarily as economic beings, as mass producers and mass consumers and as mass seekers after a social approval which is to be secured only by those who accept the standards of success that this philosophy lays down. I do not think this conformist pattern comes easily to American men and women—which is no doubt why neurosis seems to be assuming (if one can judge by newspaper reports, medical warnings, and what appears to be an almost universal preoccupation with digestion) the stature of a national disease.

Are Men Like Donkeys?

The moral case for socialism is simply that it is based on a philosophy of optimism about human nature, just as democracy is. That is, indeed, why it is the natural culmination of the democratic idea and why, if one is to be genuinely democratic, he ought also to be a socialist.

The democratic idea, which in its modern form is quite a new idea as political philosophies go, was quite a break with the past. This is true in the sense that it was an affirmation of faith in the ordinary man: in his ability to govern himself better than he could be governed by any hereditary or self-appointed ruler. And the democratic idea was also a revolutionary idea because it said that, however much men might differ in their individual talents and abilities, they were equals in their membership in a common society. It thus sought to transmit into the political sphere the Christian ethic of the uniqueness of the human personality and of the value of the individual—a value that is not to be judged solely by the standards of worldly success, but rather one by whose light all men are seen as equal in their common humanity. . . .

The socialist, imbued with the same faith in the ordinary human being as that possessed by the early democrat, seeks to widen the democratic domain. He does not accept the skeptical or the pessimistic view of human nature, which is the basis of the capitalist dependence upon economic self-interest and which holds that men, like donkeys, will not move unless they are alternately induced to do so by a carrot and driven to do so by a stick.

Nor does he accept the equally skeptical and pessimistic view, from which the capitalist theory of government flows, that men are unable to act wisely together in matters of major community concern or to elect representatives who will be honest and public-spirited in administering affairs, and that a government is the natural enemy of its citizens. Since he holds this view, it is natural that the advocate of capitalism as a political theory should believe that power cannot be tamed and must be dispersed. In his view a number of great corporations, wielding power uncontrolled by any authority other than the economic self-interest of their shareholders and managers, are less dangerous than one Department of State subject to the constant scrutiny of the legislature and the constant pressure of the public opinion of the electorate.

The socialist believes, however, that in matters of community concern the community is the best judge. Moreover, he holds that, as the quite short history of democratic government has shown, it is in fact able, within the framework of the democratic political method, to control its elected administrators and so ensure that the power delegated to them is used for the public good.

The business of supporting ourselves on this planet by using to the best advantages the natural resources with which it is endowed is not, to the socialist, an end in itself—as it is to those who hold to the capitalist theory as though it were a religion—but a means to an end. It is something to be solved in order that man may get on with the adventures of the soul and intellect, which are his real business. . . .

A MISSOURI MAILMAN IN CLEM ATTLEE'S BRITAIN *

The preceding article presents the philosophical case for Socialism, but final proof of an economic system must be based on its end results. What is Socialism actually like in practice? Is there a gap between theory and reality? If so, how widely are the two separated?

Such an analysis may take many forms—production tables, public opinion polls, statistical measurements of living standards, impressionistic accounts. The two selections that follow are diverse attempts to evaluate British Socialism. Mr. Kilby, a rural letter carrier from Vandalia, Missouri (pop. 2600), was commissioned by that town's Business and Professional Men's Club to investigate British Socialism in 1951. An avowed opponent of Socialism prior to his journey, Kilby spent fifty-five days in Britain—observing, comparing, taking notes, chatting with ordinary British citizens. His candid comments are those of an "ordinary" American citizen, rather than those of a trained analyst.

My first meal in Britain was that first day at the Cumberland with the two *Daily Graphic* men. We had some sort of fish—during the next two months I ate more fish than I had in all my life put together, meat being

* Abraham Lincoln Kilby, "Missouri Mailman Looks at Britain," *The Saturday Evening Post,* June 2, 1951, pp. 131, 132, 134.

scarce in Britain. I got real fond of smoked haddock. Another English dish that is right good is some sort of little minnows. I never did get just what they are called. What with the meat shortage and all, the British try to fill out their menus with French and other fancy-named dishes. So I was never sure exactly what I was getting.

There is also a lot of service going on in their dining rooms. At the Vandalia Hotel they have two or three waitresses to serve everybody. They just put the plates and things in front of you and take them away. But in England they seem to have two or three waiters for every eater. The waiters are dressed in hard-front shirts and long-tailed coats, and are always waving dishes and platters of heavy silver around your head. Some of these dishes and platters do not have too much food on them, and one thing they almost never have is an egg. I got four eggs the fifty-five days I was in Britain. The British say their damp climate is not good for raising poultry, and they have always imported most of their eggs from Denmark or Holland. Now the government doesn't want to let money for eggs get out of the country, so that during 1947 the average Englishman got only fifty-eight eggs. He got seventy-six in 1948 and 106 in 1949. The kind of meat I got most was sausage, and it wasn't usually very good. We had a small serving of bacon once a week at the hotel, and that was real good. When I mentioned this to the waiter, he reminded me that I would never get enough to tire of it. In England, each person is rationed to four ounces of bacon or ham per week, three ounces of cheese, two ounces of tea, four of butter, four of margarine and two of cooking fats, ten ounces of sugar, except during the spring and summer, when they get more, and twenty-two ounces of sweets a month. The most complaints are about the meat ration, which was nine and a half cents' worth a week for one person when I was there. You can buy a lamb chop or a large meat ball for that.

The way I understand it, the Ministry of Food buys all the meat that is imported into Britain, and turns it over to the public at controlled prices. This keeps the price of meat low, compared with our prices, but, of course, they get hardly enough to grease a skillet. Besides that, the government pays the butchers $42,000,000 a year because they can't handle enough meat to make a living.

The most the meat ration has been since the war was twenty-four cents' worth a week, in 1947. But that was whacked way down not long ago when the British Government fell out with its main meat supplier, Argentina, on a new contract. They had been paying $275 a long ton, but Peron at first wanted $350 on the new contract. After some horse trading, the British Government broke off the deal, calling Peron's price "quite excessive, quite unreasonable, quite unfair." Finally, on last April

23, the British Government signed a new agreement with Argentina to pay $352 to $410 per long ton of beef.

Most of the people I talked with over there thought this handling of the meat deal was the worst bungling the socialist government had done. I figured that if Attlee had come up for reelection at the time when the meat ration was nine and a half cents' worth he would have been beat.

The reason for handling food this way, as I suppose most folks know, is to keep living costs down, so wages can be kept low, so English-manufactured goods can be sold at a good profit on world markets. But the people who mentioned the matter to me said, in spite of this, they'd be happy to pay a few more cents a pound to get meat. I am no economist, but I know that the meat situation didn't make much sense to me.

I do not believe it is sensible or morally right for the government to deny its people the food they need for the sake of any economic plan. But I'll have to admit that the British economic planners have kept down a lot of the inflation we have at home. The hotel where I lived in London, for instance, was nice enough for anybody—a president or anybody else— and it cost $3.38 a day, compared with five dollars a day at the hotel I stayed in New York. And in London I got breakfast thrown in for the price of the room. Usually at breakfast I had smoked haddock, toast, tea and porridge. . . .

My nice hotel room had a good bed with plenty of covers. The only trouble was that I like to have frozen to death most of the time I was out of bed. I found all the houses and buildings over there pretty cold inside, and at first I blamed this on the coal shortage.

The coal industry was the first to be nationalized, in 1947, and this year England had to import coal for the first time in history. The government blamed the unusually cold winter, the fact that miners were leaving the mines, and indicated that the Labor Party has got industry booming so it's hard to keep it in coal. The government says that the amount of coal dug has increased from 175,000,000 tons in 1945 to 205,000,000 last year, under public ownership, and that miners' wages have been increased from about $17.25 a week in 1946 to $24.50 in 1949. The government also says the mines lost $65,000,000 in the last year they were under private ownership, but made a profit of $26,000,000 in 1949.

Well, the fact remains that coal is still rationed in Britain. While I was there, train services were cut for want of coal, and there were frequent power interruptions. Personally, I am against public ownership of industry, and I must say that the coal situation over there did not change my feelings. But even if they had coal to throw away, I doubt if the British would keep their buildings warm enough to suit me. I never saw people so fond of cold air inside the house. Over there most homes are heated by little coal fires. The hotel had central heating, but I'd come in shaking with cold and find that the maid, Mrs. Owen, had left my windows wide open, so plenty of nice, fresh, freezing air could blow in.

The heat was turned off in my room the first few days I was there. Since the radiator was hidden behind some draperies, I figured the only heat came from a little radiator in the bathroom. Mrs. Owen came in one day and found me sitting in the bathroom in my rocking chair, reading the paper. She asked if I thought the room was cold, and I said I knew it was cold. She then got a wrench and turned on the heat. After that, it was some better, but I never did get what you might call comfortable until the last two weeks that I spent in Britain. I guess I just got used to it.

I'd heard they were short on clothes in England, but this isn't so. Clothes are not rationed, but it's hard for them to buy many clothes, salaries being low and taxes high. But the people on the streets looked nice and neat, and I found out that they wouldn't be seen in some of the clothes we wear in this country.

Before I went over, I had bought a new hat of a dove-gray color with a wide brim and a band to match. I had some new loud ties, including a sunburst-silk and a hand-painted tie my son, Roger, had given me. As soon as I got to England, I noticed people stared at me and sometimes smiled. I asked about this of a waitress named Mrs. Cunningham, who worked in a restaurant near my hotel. She said the British looked down on people who dressed real loud, and that they could always tell Americans by the funny-looking hats we wear. She added that in England anybody who wears gaudy ties is considered a "spiv."

I found out "spiv" is a low character, like a black marketeer or a zoot-suiter. I certainly did not wish to look like one and, anyway, I had decided my gray hat and fancy ties made me too conspicuous. So I went down to Oxford Street and bought a black hat with one of those little, narrow, flimsy brims like they all wear over there. Then I bought two sober-looking ties.

After I put these on, I went to a bookstore to buy a dictionary. I was looking at a Webster's when the owner warned me that it was an American dictionary. I figured I really had them fooled about me being an American now, so I bought an English dictionary and left. No sooner had I got to the street than a drunk—one of the two drunks I saw the whole time I was in Britain—bumped into me.

He took one look and said, "Hello, pal. How are things in Detroit?" . . .

One of the most interesting places I visited in England was the city of Hornchurch. It is called that because a horned bull killed a priest there several centuries back. The people relate this with great pride and in an interesting way—the British are most interested in things that happened back in about the Year I. I visited two farms near Hornchurch and, like everything else over there, even farms have a lot of tradition. All the farming methods are very modern, except that they never grow corn, and I don't think anybody there ever heard of popcorn. It is something how the English farmers have solved the problem of erosion. The fields are rolling. Goodness knows, it rains enough, but the loam doesn't run off, as it does at home. They take care of every hatful of it. I was getting real encouraged about British agriculture until I learned that a farmer can't kill one of his own hogs without telling the government, or build on his own land without paying a "development tax." The farmers I talked with didn't think much of this. The disappointing thing about Britain is that when you get to enjoying yourself, you usually run into some depressing regulation.

I will say, though that socialism doesn't seem to have silenced free speech. It seemed to me that people there speak their minds more openly and intelligently about the government than our folks do. On my visit to Hornchurch, I went to see a socialist housing development—90 per cent of the new homes in Britain since the war have been built by the government—and the cooperative manager took me to see their druggist, or chemist, a young Scotsman. He didn't like socialism, and stood right there in front of his boss, a strong socialist, and gave it you-know-what. Also at Hornchurch I visited with the president of the Chamber of Trade, an undertaker named Mr. Rivett. He thought socialism ought to have ten more years for a fair trail. One thing he was sure of, though —that the British are way ahead of us in the art of embalming. He talked this more than he did socialism. . . .

I guess I talked with between three and four hundred people about socialism, and only three of them declined to say anything. One was a clerk, who said he didn't think he ought to chat on his employer's time. Another was a druggist, or chemist, as they call them, who was too busy. The other, a lady shopkeeper, who seemed suspicious of me.

When I first arrived, I asked one of my new friends how to begin without an introduction. He suggested something like, "I say, would you have time to chat a bit?" I tried that, but I guess it sounded so unnatural, coming from me, that it startled people. Then I switched to a more natural approach. I'd just say, "I'm Lincoln Kilby, from the States, and I'm over here making a study of your government under socialism. I'd like to discuss it with you, if you'd care to."

Most had definite opinions, but first wanted to know why I was over there on such a mission. I answered that so many times, I wished for a phonograph record. They always seemed surprised and pleased that a little town like Vandalia would be that interested.

Usually they'd start by saying, "Our health program has been a great thing for us." I found socialized medicine and the welfare program very popular, and I think it carries the rest of the socialistic program along, with the mass of the people. I just didn't find hardly anybody who was for the nationalization of industries. . . .

I left England on Wednesday, March fourteenth. On the return flight to New York I had a lot of time to form some conclusions about what I'd seen and been told. I understood now why England had gone socialist. Before, I had always thought of England in connection with manor houses and coats of arms and fox hunting. But I found that Britain is a very poor nation now, but still proud in spite of going socialistic. The average worker makes only about fifteen dollars a week, and a survey several years ago showed that nine out of ten die leaving less than $300.

Britain was also a sick nation, losing millions of pounds a year because workers were ill at home. I know they say there are a lot of abuses and wrongs in socialized medicine, but I still believe it has been a good thing for England.

In fairness, I'll have to say something I never thought I would, which is this: I believe that the English people are in better health, are better housed and have better working conditions than they would have had if the Labor Party had not come into power. From all I could learn, England had let herself drift into a pitiful economic and social condition that took something violent like socialism to flush out. Now that this has been done, I agree with those in England who think the reins ought to be handed back to free enterprise.

Certainly we in this country don't have the stagnant conditions that were plaguing Britain and that socialism has probably helped remedy. I can't see any reason why our Government ought to concern itself with socialism of any kind. The Labor Party has nationalized about 20 per cent of the nation's workers in the basic industries of coal, steel, transportation and communications. Their figures on the efficiency of these industries under public ownership look impressive on paper. But what doesn't show is the tendency that government ownership and paternalism have to kill the individual initiative and imagination that made England great.

I, who spent fifty-five days there, wouldn't have the gall to spout off like this alone. I am echoing the thoughts of some great Englishmen who know and love their country. Some of them were deeply impressed by what you might call the audacity of an unheard-of little town, like Vandalia, sitting in the flatlands of Missouri, in sending a clodhopper like me to

England to look around. Among those Englishmen who were impressed were the editors of the *Hornchurch and Upminster News*. They published an editorial about our project and part of it said:

What has Vandalia, Missouri, got over Hornchurch? Nothing, it would seem. Yet, would Hornchurch have been sufficiently farsighted to send an ambassador to Vandalia, if socialism had been in existence in America and not in Britain?
Bluntly, No.
What Vandalia has over us is merely a progressive spirit of enterprise, which, in a hundred and one different ways, is being stifled in Britain today.

------◆◆•◆------

THE FAILURE OF BRITISH SOCIALISM *

No economic experiment of the twentieth century has provoked more heated discussion in the United States than has British Socialism. To have their wartime ally reject capitalism in the moment of victory was an event for which most Americans were ill prepared. After their initial surprise some hailed the "experiment" as the wave of the future, and returned from visits to the new economic Mecca with glowing accounts. Other Americans found the British system to be a maze of red tape and contradictions—a solemn warning to their "Fair Dealing" countrymen. Thus Labour economics became an issue that reached far beyond the shores of Great Britain.

Williams' article makes the case for Socialism on the basis of its inevitability and moral superiority. These concepts are attacked by John Jewkes, a British economist, in an analysis penned shortly before the 1951 defeat of the British Labour Party. In a detailed study (here reproduced only in part) Jewkes declared the Labour record to be a failure in every respect—nationalization, social services, central planning, production, and balance of payments. In rebuttal, it is altogether possible that Socialists would now direct some of the following questions to Jewkes. Have Conservatives eliminated central planning since their victory? Have they improved British standards of living? If subsidized housing and health are wrong, why have the Tories kept them? Why have they retained nationalized industries?

* John Jewkes, "Socialism's Legacy to Churchill." Reprinted from the December, 1951, issue of *Fortune*, pp. 79–81, 183, 184, 186, 188, 190, 193, by special permission of the Editors. Copyright, 1951, Time, Inc.

The Standard of Living

The final test of the efficiency of any economic organization is provided by the standard of living it affords to the community. Of the British people it can broadly be said that they are now purchasing about the same quantity of goods and services as they did before the war but they have much less choice in what they can buy. The table below shows total personal expenditure per capita, at present prices, on goods and services:

1938	100.0
1947	98.7
1948	99.2
1949	100.6
1950	103.4

But the kind of living the British people maintain is much conditioned by the fact that the people are not allowed to spend their money as they would wish. The following foods are still rationed: meat, bacon, eggs, tea, sugar, butter, margarine, lard, sweets. It is virtually impossible for a private individual, unless he falls within one of a very limited number of priority classes, to buy a motorcar; the number of new motorcar registrations per month is less than half the prewar registrations. There is a great shortage of houses; the number of new houses now being built is only about two-thirds the prewar rate. It is impossible to measure statistically the loss of satisfaction that follows from this diversion of spending, by the state, from the things consumers would normally buy. The consequences are perhaps most marked in the consumption of meat and fats. Broadly speaking, it may be said that Great Britain has been forced onto the kind of diet traditional in the poorer countries. She is consuming per head much less meat and sugar, and more potatoes, cereals, and milk, than she did before the war.

The present standards of consumption are made possible only because the individual is saving much less. Personal saving is about 25 per cent lower than prewar. Also, there must be a great deal of unrecorded capital consumption going on, particularly among the middle classes, through failure to maintain property such as houses. On the other hand, the average person gets from the state more "free" services—"free" in the sense that he does not pay for them directly since they are provided out of general taxation or contributions to the social-insurance funds. The average annual value of the health services received by a family of man and wife and two children was, in 1950, about 36 pounds ($101). . . .

Stunted Production

It is commonly claimed by British socialists that production has increased rapidly since 1945 and that this fact in itself disposes of the arguments of their opponents. It cannot be true, they argue, that socialism stifles enterprise, reduces effort, and renders the whole system rigid if the records show that industrial output has been rising rapidly and steadily. This kind of propaganda has proved very effective. Visitors from abroad, as was the case with Henry Ford II recently, return to their own countries reporting that Britain has performed marvels in industrial production. The British Conservative party rarely challenges this reasoning and, even when it does, usually takes the negative and somewhat unconvincing line that the increased production has been achieved despite the socialist system, that a large part of the British economy still has some measure of economic freedom, and that the success achieved is a tribute to the effectiveness of private enterprise even when operating under the most serious disadvantages.

Has Great Britain a good record in production since 1945? In examining this question it is important to remember that output in one part of the economic system can always be increased if the cost need not be counted—in other words, if the effect upon production elsewhere need not be taken into account. In Great Britain, for instance, agricultural production is now about 20 per cent above the prewar level. This, however, has been made possible only by a policy of "featherbedding" the farmers—whose real income is now almost three times greater than before the war. The country has paid higher prices than those at which food might have been purchased abroad, and tax reliefs to farmers have meant higher taxes, and therefore reduced incentive, for other people. But it is production as a whole, and not production in any one section, that counts.

The figures most frequently quoted in support of the contention of increased British efficiency are those for the output of the manufacturing industry. But the same point holds here. Industrial production, within limits, can be measured. There are, however, many important parts of the system, such as transport, distribution, and commercial and financial services, in which the measurement of production is difficult if not impossible and on which additional burdens may be thrown in order to achieve increased industrial production. A case of special importance is that of employment in the civil service in Great Britain. The number of persons employed by the central government is now about one million more than before the war. A large number of these are undoubtedly employed in operating the planned economy. They constitute, therefore, a part of the cost of running the present kind of industrial system. But of course they are never counted in when measurements are made of productivity and output per head.

Since figures of total industrial production must necessarily be in the nature of estimates, different authorities and methods give different results. One possible comparison is that between British industrial production and that of other major industrial countries in recent years. It appears that the increase in industrial production in the United Kingdom as against prewar has, generally speaking, been higher only than in the countries very seriously dislocated by the war.

$$(1938 = 100)$$

U.S.	225
Canada	198
Sweden	165
Denmark	155
Norway	151
United Kingdom	150
Netherlands	139
France	121
Germany (W. Zone)	96
Japan	77

Statistics, however useful they may be, can give no real indication of the general atmosphere of uncertainty and frustration in which British industry is at present operating or of the long-term effects this may very well have upon the standard of living. It is not that profits cannot be made; owing to the high inflationary demand for commodities and services of all kinds, profits in British industry have not been unsatisfactory in the past few years. It is not that industry lacks men of ability. My own impression is that the younger British industrial executives are on the whole an extremely competent group who, under more favorable circumstances, might produce great results. It is not that industrial research is backward; some first-class work is going on in many industries. The real obstacles go deeper and spread wider than this.

Why Bother?

In Britain today there is a general feeling that pioneering does not pay, that everyone is working in a confined space, which it is almost impossible to enlarge, that foresight and forethought are likely to be rendered useless by sudden and unpredictable acts of the state. In short, there are no longer any premiums for the old-fashioned economic virtues of energy, tenacity, courage, and imagination. . . .

Dilemmas of Nationalization

I think it fair to put British feelings about the nationalization in this way: those who, at the outset, doubted the value of nationalization believe that their fears have proved real; those who welcomed nationalization five years ago are far from being satisfied with the results. . . .

What Test of Efficiency?

In a competitive system the test of efficiency is profitability. There are two very good reasons why this particular test cannot be applied to the Public Boards that control British nationalized industries. The first is that the industries are, in greater or less degree, monopolies. Profits, if any, could just as well be a measure of the degree of exploitation as of the effective working of the organization. But in fact the Public Boards have been virtually forbidden to make profits by the very laws under which they were set up.

For example, under the statute by which the National Coal Board was established, it is laid down that the coal-mining industry as a whole, taking good and bad years together, must cover its costs, including the charges on its original capital. In effect this means that the coal industry should not make profits over a period of years. If it did so it would almost certainly be charged with exploiting the public by fixing prices too high. Thus the line of least resistance clearly is to remain content with merging the profits of the good and bad mines and just keeping the head of the organization as a whole above water.

Another consequence of the absence of the normal profit motive is the weakening of managerial incentive. It seems to me fundamental for vigorous management that a surplus should be aimed at. Where there is a fixed and limited objective it is extremely tempting to go slow.

In the absence of the profit incentive, furthermore, the community now has no way of satisfying itself whether an industry is doing its job badly or well. If, for instance, the Coal Board is seeking to defend itself against the charge that it is losing money or raising its prices, it can argue that, after all, Great Britain is very short of coal and the present output cannot be maintained without using the inefficient mines. Or the board may say that on social grounds certain high-cost mines must be kept in existence, otherwise the displaced miners would have difficulty in finding employment elsewhere. Or the board may assert that its losses are due to high costs which it cannot control—a good deal of bickering is now going on between the boards of various nationalized industries, one accusing another of charging high prices. Or the board may say it has been forbidden by the government to raise prices because this would affect the cost-of-living index and lead to higher wages. Or the Coal Board may point out that it is selling coal abroad at a loss and that this is necessary to help reduce the adverse balance of trade.

When the boards were set up, it was commonly believed that, under the stimulus of public ownership and under the scrutiny of the public eye, the basic industries would become more efficient. Now apparently there is no way of deciding whether they are becoming more efficient or less. In that sense nationalization cannot be regarded as an experiment because one cannot have an experiment unless one can find some way of measuring its results. . . .

What Kind of Management?

Each one of the larger Public Boards in Great Britain has been severely criticized on the grounds that it was too centralized, that decisions were not being reached quickly enough, that the organization was becoming excessively rigid. Several boards, as a result of this criticism, have sought to adjust themselves and to decentralize their system of control. Those who still believe in nationalization argue that this open-minded quest for the right answer will undoubtedly bring about the right answer sooner or later. I myself would be doubtful about that.

The British Public Boards are very large indeed. The National Coal Board employs 800,000 workers, the Transport Commission almost as many. Now a large private company, of the type of General Motors in the United States, can decentralize almost indefinitely. Its different sections can be set to compete with each other even to the point where one drives another out of the market. One section need not buy from other parts of the organization if it can buy more cheaply outside. So the corporation can use the competitive process at all levels—and everything it involves in the way of constant testing and tuning up of efficiency. I do not believe the National Board can ever hope to do that in the same way. It runs counter to the whole rationale of nationalization, which is that size is good in itself and that competition and rivalry are something bad in themselves.

The Public Boards in Great Britain are clearly engaged in a seesaw. First the board establishes a highly centralized organization and is criticized because it is too rigid. Then it decentralizes and, of course, its different parts begin to operate in different ways and produce different results. The criticism then is that the board is not doing its job because of its not retaining that unifying grip upon the industry as a whole, which was the reason for setting it up. The seesaw may go on indefinitely but the right answer may be that the organization is too large ever to be effectively administered.

There is a further reason why the Public Board cannot adopt the devices for avoiding the dangers of excessive size that can be employed by a private business.

The boards are so large, their operations so vitally affect the running of the economy, their success or failure is so closely bound up with the political dogma, that the government will always be forced to interfere whenever it believes that anything is going wrong. That leads to a peculiar administrative problem: the demarcation between the administrative responsibilities of the Minister and the administrative responsibilities of the Public Board itself.

The statutes under which the boards were set up try to solve the problem by directing that the Minister is to be responsible for matters of major policy, matters that concern the national interest, and the board is to be free in day-to-day policy. In practice it proves difficult, if not impossible, to make this distinction between major and minor policy. Any question at any time, however trivial it seems to be, can in fact become a matter of national interest.

If a local train is consistently late, it might seem at first as if this were very clearly a matter of day-to-day policy. But if, as a result, workers in an export industry arrive at work late, public criticism may become so strong that the Minister will be forced to take up the matter as one of national interest or even of his own political reputation.

Easier Said Than Done

To conclude: nationalization in Great Britain has not, in my opinion, produced any new and superior ways of organizing production for the raising of standards of living. In the long history of the propaganda in favor of nationalization, emphasis has always been placed upon the gains from what is variously called "coordination," "integration," or "articulation." Those gains are easy to speak of but difficult to obtain. And it seems that the so-called wastes of competition are much easier to identify than to eliminate. I think one can go further than that and say that the British nationalization schemes have produced new industrial problems of their own to which we have not yet found the answers.

The Swollen Social Services

Perhaps the most spectacular change in postwar Britain has been the rapid growth of the social services. Although these were steadily expanding before the war, the main cost then was largely confined to unemployment relief, old-age pensions, and education. Now unemployment has virtually disappeared and education forms only about one-sixth, compared with a prewar figure of one-fourth, of the total social-service expenditure.

The social services can be described as the provision of goods or services by public authorities that would otherwise have to be (or perhaps, should be) provided by the individual. The bill is met from three sources: the central government, the local governments (partly financed by grants from the central government), and the National Insurance Funds (created by compulsory contributions from employees, employers, and the central government).

While prewar insurance schemes covered only a part of the population —workers earning less than a fixed sum—the National Insurance Act of 1948 embraced the whole population. It provided mothers with maternity benefits; the victims of industrial accidents and disease with compensation; the poor with a minimum income; the sick with sick pay; the bereaved with death grants; and everyone with free medical, hospital, and dental services, appliances, and medicines.

Workers are now paying, in compulsory insurance contributions, four and a half times what they paid in 1938—a point that is increasingly troubling them. Employers are paying in insurance contributions three and a half times more—which adds considerably to costs of production. In 1950 the sources of the National Insurance Funds were as follows: employees, 39 per cent; employers, 32 per cent; central government, 24 per cent; income from property, 5 per cent. It is important to bear in mind, however, that the immense National Health Service is financed almost wholly by the central government, i.e., by the taxpayers. In 1950 only one-tenth of the cost of the National Health Service was met by contributions from the National Insurance Funds.

The spectacular growth of the social services is shown below:

Gross Expenditure in Millions of Pounds

	1936	1946	1949
Food subsidies	—	331	465
National insurance and pensions	202	270	458
Health Service	41	76	414
Education	115	222	312
Family allowances	—	34	60
Assistance (poor relief)	52	85	59
Housing subsidies	21	35	65
Cost of social services per capita	9.7 *	21.7	36.7

* 1935–39 average.

Food: A Ministry Knows Best

Food subsidies were introduced during the war for the purpose of keeping down demands for wage increases—many wage rates were linked to the cost-of-living index—but the subsidies now appear to have become a permanent feature of the British economy, in fact an instrument of social policy. The Labor government, however, alarmed at the ever increasing burden, decided three years ago to stabilize these subsidies and pass on to the consumer any further price increases. In 1950 the subsidies were stabilized at about 410 million pounds and accounted for about one-quarter of the expenditure on the social services.

The anxiety of the government to place a ceiling on the total of food subsidies, combined with its equal anxiety to prevent any increase in the cost-of-living index number, has led to some very paradoxical and unpleasant consequences. There have been periods when the Ministry of Food has prevented food rations from rising, even though additional food was available, because as long as the cost-of-living index was not allowed to rise this would have increased food subsidies. The reduction of the meat ration in 1950 to unprecedented low levels is a striking case of the policy of "keeping down the cost of living by dispensing with the living."

Food subsidies and rationing go together; as long as the first continues, the second must. For by keeping the prices of food artificially low, thus giving a subsidy to everybody, rich and poor alike, the demand for food is increased. The Minister of Food admitted as long ago as September, 1949, that abolishing the food subsidies would go a long way toward abolishing the need for rationing. But the government is hardly likely to follow such a policy. It argues that, since this would bring about a rise in prices of food, it would bear heavily upon the poorer sections of the community and infringe the principle of "fair shares."

The absurdity of this contention is indicated by the fact that, in 1950, the British people spent 2,379,000,000 pounds on food but they also spent 1,518,000,000 pounds on drink and tobacco, the greater part of the cost of which was, of course, tax. To put the same point in another way: the food subsidies now amount to about 470 million pounds. The total taxes on beer and tobacco were 1 billion pounds. If the food subsidies were abolished, then the government could afford to reduce the taxes on beer and tobacco to about half their present level. People would be no worse off. They would pay a higher price for food, approximating its use; but they would buy their luxuries more cheaply. Only a government hopelessly trapped in the net of a "fair shares" policy and supremely confident that it knows better than the consumer what is good for him could deny the logic of this argument. The latter belief is probably a legacy from the bad old days of the nineteenth century when fathers could be found drinking away their wages in the pub while their families starved in garrets. Paradoxically enough, however, no one can be more acutely aware than the government of the serious problems that would emerge from a real drop in drinking and smoking; the revenue for the welfare state is dependent to a large degree on a high consumption of these luxuries.

Subsidized Housing

There is said to be a housing shortage in Great Britain and undoubtedly there is one in the sense that, with rents in general at their present levels, more people are anxious to obtain houses than there are houses available. The point often overlooked is that the housing shortage has been largely created by the policy of rent restriction, combined with the planning of the housing program. Rents have not been allowed to rise at anything like the rate of increase of general prices or of wages.

Index of Wages and Rents

	Wages	Rent of land and buildings
1938	100	100
1946	181	105
1950	251	119

A long string of undesirable consequences have followed from this:

1. Serious injustice has been done to property owners, whose incomes have not been allowed to follow the general movement of prices.

2. The demand for houses has been artificially increased because, in relation to other things, the cost of renting a house is low. There are very large numbers of houses in England on which the weekly rent is only about the cost of three packets of cigarettes. Those people who are fortunate enough to live in a house owned by someone else are, in effect, receiving a subsidy from the owner. There is no incentive to economize in housing space. No one stands to gain by moving from a house that is really too big for him. Wasteful use is being made of a facility that is in short supply.

3. No one can possibly build a house, at present costs, that would be profitable at the permitted rents. Accordingly, even where private enterprise is permitted to build houses, they cannot be built to rent.

The British housing subsidies must be seen against this background. About seven-eighths of the houses built in Britain are constructed under government auspices. The government restricts the number of houses built by private enterprise because, among other reasons, it is anxious that houses should be built to let at uneconomical rents. The houses built must, therefore, be subsidized.

In 1950 the housing subsidies amounted to 65 million pounds, of which 30 million pounds was provided by the central government and the rest found by local authorities. The system is inefficient, in that it almost certainly leads to fewer houses being built than might be built, and inequitable. The relatively few who manage to get a subsidized house are receiving a bounty, and the bounty is often paid to them by other people who are no richer but who, because they cannot rent a state-subsidized house, are forced to buy a house at the present very high purchase prices

Nationalized Health

It has been found extremely difficult to control the rising cost of the national health scheme. Each year the actual cost of the scheme proved higher than the estimated cost until finally, in 1950–51, a definite ceiling had to be imposed for the net cost of the scheme.

Net Cost of National Health Service to the Taxpayer
(millions of pounds)

	Estimate	Cost
1948–49	200	278
1949–50	260	359
1950–51	393	393
1951–52	400	—

The big and unexpected increases in cost have come in medical prescriptions, appliances such as spectacles and artificial teeth, and hospital services. Before the act, voluntary hospitals had been notoriously economical if not parsimonious, but with the passing of the act no special directive was issued on the need for economy. It should have been clear what would happen. Hospitals were in a bad state of repair owing to the war and the difficult years after the war. Renewals and repairs to buildings and equipment were ordered; staff were paid who formerly had worked for charity; numerous officials took over the many duties of the former secretary; and there was no inducement to prevent waste. Finally a limit of 274 million pounds was fixed in the estimate for hospitals in 1950, and hospitals were told not to expect any increase when drawing up their 1951–52 budgets. Special measures were taken by the Minister to limit expenditure—such as requests for detailed monthly statements, and the return of unspent balances under any heads to the Exchequer. This detailed and rigid budgeting has caused much troubled and probably resulted in overbudgeting and further waste.

A Nation of Hypochondriacs?

The new scheme threw a sudden and enormous burden on the various branches of the health services, and it is, of course, impossible to determine precisely how much of the increase was due to genuine ill-health concealed in the past because sufferers could not afford to pay for a doctor and how much was irresponsible abuse of the scheme simply because it was offered free. But there are ominous complaints that the British are becoming a nation of hypochondriacs and these complaints do not always come from those who are opposed to the scheme. The annual report of the Minister of Health tells what happened after the service was introduced in July, 1948: "The general experience was that doctors immediately began to have larger numbers in their surgeries although July and August are normally slack months. Some of these calls were unjustifiable, even frivolous, some patients seeking to obtain free supplies of simple medicaments such as are normally kept in any household."

Only three months later the Minister of Health was calling for restraint in the use of the health service, saying it would fail unless people used it "intelligently and sparingly . . . because things are free is no reason why people should abuse their opportunities." A year later the Minister was "shuddering to think of the ceaseless cascade of medicine which is pouring down British throats." In October, 1949, the Prime Minister reported that a charge for prescriptions was to be imposed (although, in fact, it never was imposed) in order "to reduce excessive and in some cases unnecessary resort to doctors and chemists of which there is evidence and which has for some time troubled the Minister of Health."

But the National Health Service has done little or nothing to increase the number of doctors and dentists available—the speed of introduction of the scheme made that impossible. Indeed, the increased time that must often be spent on committees, together with the increased work in filling in records, has no doubt considerably reduced the total time that the medical profession has available for treating the sick. The status of the general practitioner is being undermined, and unless things change he will become little more than a glorified medical clerk. As the *Lancet* points out, "Today half the practitioner's patients want some form of certificate—not medical service. That is not doctoring."

It is very easy to be biased, one way or the other, about the British National Health Service. The ideal that no one in the community should go without necessary and proper medical services because of lack of income is an appealing one. And there seems little doubt that many people, particularly women in the poorer classes, now receive desirable medical treatment that they would certainly not have received before. On the other hand the Health Service, in its present form, has proved immensely costly and has involved much waste. In the long run the heaviest cost may well be the serious deterioration in the standards and the efficiency of the medical profession itself.

To the economist the defects and difficulties really constitute a special case of a general problem: how can services be properly distributed and a proper economy exercised in their use unless a price is put upon them? All experience would suggest that when things are free they will be wasted. In the case of other goods and services that are sold below their market cost or are dispensed free, the usual answer of the Socialist is to ration in some rough-and-ready way. But medical services cannot be rationed; the essence of medical needs is that they vary from individual to individual. In the absence of rationing, there is only one other answer—the queue.

The doctor must inevitably see everybody—because any case may be a critical case. The queue, however, is so much lengthened by the presence of frivolous or pathological cases, encouraged by the fact that the service is free, that everybody gets less satisfactory treatment. The whole system is cluttered up with a type of inflationary pressure—too many patients chasing too few doctors and dentists.

Central Planning: Promise and Performance

When, in April, 1949, I spoke before the Economic Club in New York, I gave it as my opinion that central state planning was rapidly proving futile and was, indeed, losing any prestige it may have had in European countries. Events in Great Britain have more than confirmed that view; state planning has become almost a subject of ridicule. Of course, members of the Socialist Party must still pay lip service to the idea, although even here there has been a great deal of heart-searching.

But no one in this country really believes that a nation can be master of its own economic destiny, in the sense of being able to decide what its standard of living will be independently of its own exertions. No one believes that a nation can draw up, and carry into effect, a master economic plan without conscripting labor. Most people recognize that a master economic plan ties around the neck of the country which seeks to carry it into effect a millstone which endangers friendly relations with other countries. Experience has shown that attempts to keep rigid at one and the same time both the internal price level and the exchange rate are bound to fail. The myth that a government can run the economic affairs of a nation with the efficiency or rationality with which an individual controls his own financial affairs has been exploded.

The British economic planning authorities have never been able to predict the future course of events. Even when they have ostensibly been following a long-range plan they have never been able to depart from a "series of temporary expedients which led to a crisis as each expedient has been exhausted"—to use Sir Stafford Cripps's own words. But it is becoming obvious that the practices and habits of central planning render the crises more likely. The planners purport to operate without the assistance of, or even in defiance of, the normal forces of the free market. They are, therefore, working largely in the dark. They wake up late to find themselves in a crisis. They adhere to their plans so long that, when finally they are forced to act, they must act with a violence which would otherwise have been unnecessary. . . .

------◆◆◆◆------

Problem 23: Soviet Communism--
Utopia or Slave System?

Soviet Communism is today the great political, military, and economic rival of the United States. Merely to state this bald fact is to discard the optimistic view that Communism is nothing more than an unworkable economic theory. Somehow, in some fashion, the Soviet Union is able to operate an industrial state that, with its economic satellites, presents a grave challenge to the West.

What economic assumptions underlie the Communist system? Are such old Communist cliches as "From each according to his ability, to each according to his need" actually applied? Are goods shared in common? How is production mobilized? How is expansion capital acquired? How are management and the average worker rewarded? How do collective and state farms operate? What of Soviet forced labor camps? What does the system cost in human values? Wherein lie its weaknesses? How is capitalism portrayed in Russia?

The answers to these questions are far more valuable than the mass of hyperbole put forth to explain and defend Communism. Certainly the Soviet version of Communism is a far cry from British Socialism. Contrasted with the Soviet organization, basic outlines of American capitalism also stand out in bold relief, providing still greater clarification of our original question, What is the nature of capitalism?

THE COMMUNIST MANIFESTO *

Having entered its second century, the Communist Manifesto is now a somewhat ancient if not venerable document. Nevertheless, many of the Manifesto's phrases have a ring that is uncomfortably familiar in the contemporary world. Its opening paragraph declares that the specter of communism is haunting all Europe; its closing paragraph commits the party to the forcible overthrow of all existing social conditions. Although written relatively early in Marx's life, the Manifesto contains the basic components of his philosophy—the theory of the class struggle; the theory of value and surplus value; the alleged contradictions of competitive capitalism; depressions, monopoly, a rising proletariat.

Treated by leftist groups as a sort of Holy Writ, the Manifesto avows certain objectives that have an odd sound to the modern ear. Its advocacy of graduated income taxes, national banks, the abolition of child labor, free public education, and a plea for "suburbia" are indications of the bloodless changes that have been effected within the capitalistic system during the past hundred years.

A specter is haunting Europe—the specter of Communism. All the powers of old Europe have entered into a holy alliance to exorcise this specter: Pope and Tsar Metternich and Guizot, French Radicals and German police-spies.

Where is the party in opposition that has not been decried as communistic by its opponents in power? Where is the Opposition that has not hurled back the branding reproach of Communism, against the more advanced opposition parties, as well as against its reactionary adversaries?

Two things result from this fact:

1. Communism is already acknowledged by all European powers to be itself a power.

2. It is high time that Communists should openly, in the face of the whole world, publish their views, their aims, their tendencies, and meet this nursery tale of the specter of Communism with a manifesto of the party itself.

Bourgeois and Proletarians

The history of all hitherto existing society is the history of class struggles. Freeman and slave, patrician and plebeian, lord and serf, guild-master

* Karl Marx and Friedrich Engels, *The Manifesto of the Communist Party*, 1848.

and journeyman, in a word, oppressor and oppressed, stood in constant opposition to one another, carried on an uninterrupted, now hidden, now open fight, a fight that each time ended, either in a revolutionary reconstitution of society at large, or in the common ruin of the contending classes.

In the earlier epochs of history, we find almost everywhere a complicated arrangement of society into various orders, a manifold gradation of social rank. In ancient Rome we have patricians, knights, plebeians, slaves; in the Middle Ages, feudal lords, vassals, guild-masters, journeymen, apprentices, serfs; in almost all of these classes again, subordinate gradations.

The modern bourgeois society that has sprouted from the ruins of feudal society has not done away with class antagonisms. It has but established new classes, new conditions of oppression, new forms of struggle in place of the old ones.

Our epoch, the epoch of the bourgeoisie, possesses, however, this distinctive feature: it has simplified the class antagonisms. Society as a whole is more and more splitting up into two great hostile camps, into two great classes directly facing each other—bourgeoisie and proletarian.

. . . . .

The bourgeoisie, during its rule of scarce one hundred years, has created more massive and more colossal productive forces than have all preceding generations together. Subjection of nature's forces to man, machinery, application of chemistry to industry and agriculture, steam navigation, railways, electric telegraphs, clearing of whole continents for cultivation, canalization of rivers, whole populations conjured out of the ground—what earlier century had ever a presentiment that such productive forces slumbered in the lap of social labor?

We see then: the means of production and of exchange, on whose foundation the bourgeoisie built itself up, were generated in feudal society. At a certain stage in the development of these means of production and of exchange, the conditions under which feudal society produced and exchanged, the feudal organization of agriculture and manufacturing industry, in one word, the feudal relation of property became no longer compatible with the already developed productive forces; they became so many fetters. They had to be burst asunder; they were burst asunder.

Into their place stepped free competition, accompanied by a social and political constitution adapted to it, and by the economical and political sway of the bourgeois class.

A similar movement is going on before our own eyes. Modern bourgeois society with its relations of production, of exchange and of property, a society that has conjured up such gigantic means of production and of exchange, is like the sorcerer who is no longer able to control the powers of the nether world whom he has called up by his spells. For many a decade past the history of industry and commerce is but the history of the revolt of modern productive forces against modern conditions of production, against the property relations that are the conditions for the existence of the bourgeoisie and of its rule. It is enough to mention the commercial crises that by their periodical return put the existence of the entire bourgeois society on its trial, each time more threateningly. In these crises a great part not only of the existing products, but also of the previously created productive forces, are periodically destroyed. In these crises there breaks out an epidemic that, in all earlier epochs, would have seemed an absurdity—the epidemic of over-production. Society suddenly finds itself put back into a state of momentary barbarism; it appears as if a famine, a universal war of devastation, had cut off the supply of every means of subsistence; industry and commerce seem to be destroyed. And why? Because there is too much civilization, too much means of subsistence, too much industry, too much commerce. The productive forces at the disposal of society no longer tend to further the development of the conditions of bourgeois property; on the contrary, they have become too powerful for these conditions, by which they are fettered, and so soon as they overcome these fetters, they bring disorder into the whole of bourgeois society, endanger the existence of bourgeois property. The conditions of bourgeois society are too narrow to comprise the wealth created by them. And how does the bourgeoisie get over these crises? On the one hand by enforced destruction of a mass of productive forces; on the other, by the conquest of new markets, and by the more thorough exploitation of the old ones. That is to say, by paving the way for more extensive and more destructive crises, and by diminishing the means whereby crises are prevented.

The weapons with which the bourgeoisie felled feudalism to the ground are now turned against the bourgeoisie itself.

But not only has the bourgeoisie forged the weapons that bring death to itself; it has also called into existence the men who are to wield those weapons—the modern working class—the proletarians.

In proportion as the bourgeoisie, i.e., capital, is developed, in the same porportion is the proletariat, the modern working class, developed—a class of laborers, who live only so long as they find work, and who find work only so long as their labor increases capital. These laborers, who must sell themselves piecemeal, are a commodity, like every other article of commerce, and are consequently exposed to all the vicissitudes of competition, to all the fluctuations of the market.

Owing to the extensive use of machinery and to division of labor, the work of the proletarians has lost all individual character, and, consequently, all charm for the workman. He becomes an appendage of the machine, and it is only the most simple, most monotonous, and most easily acquired knack, that is required of him. Hence, the cost of production of a workman is restricted, almost entirely, to the means of subsistence that he requires for his maintenance, and for the propagation of his race. But the price of a commodity, and therefore, also of labor, is equal to its cost of production. In proportion, therefore, as the repulsiveness of the work increases, the wage decreases. Nay, more, in proportion as the use of machinery and division of labor increases, in the same proportion the burden of toil also increases, whether by prolongation of the working hours, by increase of the work exacted in a given time, or by increased speed of the machinery, etc.

Modern industry has converted the little workshop of the patriarchal master into the great factory of the industrial capitalist. Masses of laborers, crowded into the factory, are organized like soldiers. As privates of the industrial army they are placed under the command of a perfect hierarchy of officers and sergeants. Not only are they slaves of the bourgeois class, and of the bourgeois state; they are daily and hourly enslaved by the machine, by the overlooker, and, above all, by the individual bourgeois manufacturer himself. The more openly this despotism proclaims gain to be its end and aim, the more petty, the more hateful and the more embittering it is.

The less the skill and exertion of strength implied in manual labor, in other words, the more modern industry becomes developed, the more is the labor of men superseded by that of women. Differences of age and sex have no longer any distinctive social validity for the working class. All are the instruments of labor, more or less expensive to use, according to their age and sex.

No sooner is the exploitation of the laborer by the manufacturer so far at an end that he receives his wages in cash than he is set upon by the other portions of the bourgeoisie, the landlord, the shopkeeper, the pawnbroker, etc.

The lower strata of the middle class—the small tradespeople, shopkeepers, and retired tradesmen generally, the handicraftsmen and peasants—all these sink gradually into the proletariat, partly because their diminutive capital does not suffice for the scale on which modern industry is carried on, and is swamped in the competition with the large capitalists, partly because their specialized skill is rendered worthless by new methods of production. Thus the proletariat is recruited from all classes of the population.

.   .   .   .   .   .

Hitherto every form of society has been based, as we have already seen, on the antagonism of oppressing and oppressed classes. But in order to oppress a class, certain conditions must be assured to it under which it can, at least, continue its slavish existence. The serf, in the period of serfdom, raised himself to membership in the commune, just as the petty bourgeois, under the yoke of feudal absolutism, managed to develop into a bourgeois. The modern laborer, on the contrary, instead of rising with the progress of industry, sinks deeper and deeper below the conditions of existence of his own class. He becomes a pauper, and pauperism develops more rapidly than population and wealth. And here it becomes evident that the bourgeoisie is unfit any longer to be the ruling class in society and to impose its conditions of existence upon society as an overriding law. It is unfit to rule because it is incompetent to assure an existence to its slave within his slavery, because it cannot help letting him sink into such a state, that it has to feed him, instead of being fed by him. Society can no longer live under this bourgeoisie; in other words, its existence is no longer compatible with society.

The essential condition for the existence and for the sway of the bourgeois class is the formation and augmentation of capital; the condition for capital is wage labor. Wage labor rests exclusively on competition between the laborers. The advance of industry, whose involuntary promoter is the bourgeoisie, replaces the isolation of the laborers, due to competition, by their revolutionary combination, due to association. The development of modern industry, therefore, cuts from under its feet the very foundation on which the bourgeoisie produces and appropriates products. What the bourgeoisie therefore produces, above all, are its own gravediggers. Its fall and the victory of the proletariat are equally inevitable.

Proletarians and Communists

In what relation do the Communists stand to the proletarians as a whole?

The Communists do not form a separate party opposed to other working class parties.

They have no interests separate and apart from those of the proletariat as a whole.

They do not set up any sectarian principles of their own, by which to shape and mold the proletarian movement.

The Communists are distinguished from other working-class parties by this only: (1) In the national struggles of the proletarians of the different countries, they point out and bring to the front the common interests of the entire proletariat, independently of all nationality. (2) In the various stages of development which the struggle of the working class against the bourgeoisie has to pass through, they always and everywhere represent the interests of the movement as a whole.

The Communists, therefore, are on the one hand, practically, the most advanced and resolute section of the working-class parties of every country, that section which pushes forward all others; on the other hand, theoretically, they have over the great mass of the proletariat the advantage of clearly understanding the line of march, the conditions, and the ultimate general results of the proletarian movement.

The immediate aim of the Communists is the same as that of all the other proletarian parties: formation of the proletariat into a class, overthrow of the bourgeois supremacy, conquest of political power by the proletariat.

The theoretical conclusions of the Communists are in no way based on ideas or principles that have been invented, or discovered, by this or that would-be universal reformer.

They merely express, in general terms, actual relations springing from an existing class struggle, from a historical movement going on under our very eyes. The abolition of existing property relations is not at all a distinctive feature of Communism.

All property relations in the past have continually been subject to historical change consequent upon the change in historical conditions.

The French Revolution, for example, abolished feudal property in favor of bourgeois property.

The distinguishing feature of Communism is not the abolition of property generally but the abolition of bourgeois property. But modern bourgeois private property is the final and most complete expression of the system of producing and appropriating products that is based on class antagonisms, on the exploitation of the many by the few.

In this sense, the theory of the Communists may be summed up in the single sentence: Abolition of private property.

. . . . . .

We have seen above that the first step in the revolution by the working class is to raise the proletariat to the position of ruling class, to win the battle of democracy.

The proletariat will use its political supremacy to wrest, by degrees, all capital from the bourgeoisie, to centralize instruments of production in the hands of the state, *i. e.,* of the proletariat organized as the ruling class; and to increase the total of productive forces as rapidly as possible.

Of course in the beginning, this cannot be effected except by means of despotic inroads on the rights of property, and on the conditions of bourgeois production; by means of measures, therefore, which appear economically insufficient and untenable, but which, in the course of the movement, outstrip themselves, necessitate further inroads upon the old social order, and are unavoidable as a means of entirely revolutionizing the mode of production.

These measures will, of course, be different in different countries.

Nevertheless, in the most advanced countries, the following will be pretty generally applicable:

1. Abolition of property in land and application of all rents of land to public purposes.

2. A heavy progressive or graduated income tax.

3. Abolition of all right of inheritance.

4. Confiscation of the property of all emigrants and rebels.

5. Centralization of the means of communication and transport in the hands of the state.

6. Extension of factories and instruments of production owned by the state; the bringing into cultivation of waste lands, and the improvement of the soil generally in accordance with common plan.

7. Equal obligation of all to work. Establishment of industrial armies, especially for agriculture.

8. Combination of agriculture with manufacturing industries; gradual abolition of the distinction between town and country, by a more equable distribution of the population over the country.

9. Free education for all children in public schools. Abolition of children's factory labor in its present form. Combination of education with industrial production, etc.

When, in the course of development, class distinctions have disappeared, and all production has been concentrated in the hands of a vast association of the whole nation, the public power will lose its political character. Political power, properly so called, is merely the organized power of one class for oppressing another. If the proletariat during its contest with the bourgeoisie is compelled, by the force of circumstances, to organize itself as a class; if, by means of a revolution, it makes itself the ruling class, and, as such, sweep away by force the old conditions of production, then it will, along with these conditions, have swept away the conditions for the existence of class antagonisms and of classes generally, and will thereby have abolished its own supremacy as a class.

In place of the old bourgeois society, with its classes and class antagonisms, we shall have an association in which the free development of each is the condition for the free development of all.

Position of the Communist in Relation to Various Existing Opposition Parties

In short, the Communists everywhere support every revolutionary movement against the existing social and political order of things.

In all these movements they bring to the front, as the leading question in each, the property question, no matter what its degree of development at the time.

Finally, they labor everywhere for the union and agreement of the democratic parties of all countries.

The Communists disdain to conceal their views and aims. They openly declare that their ends can be attained only by the forcible overthrow of all existing social conditions. Let the ruling classes tremble at a Communist revolution. The proletarians have nothing to lose but their chains. They have a world to win.

Working men of all countries, unite!

Two Countries *

The contrast between economic organization in the Soviet Union and that in the United States has intrigued writers in both countries since 1917. Rightly, the Soviets recognize the United States as their great economic rival; American writers have reciprocated by praising their economy in contrast with that of the Soviets.

The selection that follows is a Russian analysis of economic differences between the two systems. It was originally prepared as a school text for children between the ages of 12 and 14. Hence the simplicity of its style and ideology. The American reader should bear in mind that this comparison was penned shortly after the inauguration of the First Five-Year Plan; the America with which Russia was contrasted was then in the throes of its Great Depression.

The Project of Our Country

The Five-Year Plan is a project: not of one factory, but of two thousand four hundred factories. And not only of factories, but also of cities, of electric stations, of bridges, of ships, of railroads, of mines, of state farms, of rural communes, of schools, of libraries. It is a project for the rebuild-

* Ilia Iakolevich Marshak, *New Russia's Primer,* tr. by George S. Counts and Nucia P. Lodge (Houghton Mifflin, 1931), pp. 5–17.

ing of our whole country, and was prepared, not by one man or by two men, but by thousands of trained persons. To the work of building came not tens, but millions of workers. All of us will help to build the Five-Year Plan.

The plan was first discussed in December, 1927, at the Fifteenth Congress of the Communist Party.

On the 1st of October, 1928, its fulfillment was begun.

And before the end of 1929 it became clear that the plan will be achieved, not in five years, but much more quickly.

Such a project has never been undertaken before. America has many large factories, many more than we have. There factories turn out four automobiles a minute; there some buildings are sixty stories high; there a huge steel bridge was built in one day; there a million tractors work in the fields. The Americans are proud of their machines, of their factories.

But how do these factories work? According to some general plan, do you suppose? No, they work without a general plan.

What Happens When They Work Without a Plan?

Mr. Fox acquires money—one million dollars. But money must not remain idle. Mr. Fox looks through newspapers, he consults friends, he employs agents. From morning till night the agents comb the city, look about, and make inquiries. What is to be done with the money of Mr. Fox?

At last a business is found. Hats! That is what one should make. Hats sell; men get rich.

There is nothing to hesitate about. Mr. Fox builds a hat factory.

The same idea occurs at the same time to Mr. Box, and Mr. Crox, and Mr. Nox. And they all begin to build hat factories simultaneously.

Within half a year there are several new hat factories in the country. Shops are filled to the ceiling with hat-boxes. Storerooms are bursting with them. Everywhere there are posters, signs, advertisements: HATS, HATS, HATS. A great many more hats are made than are needed— twice as many, three times as many. And the factories continue to work at full speed.

And here something happens that neither Mr. Fox, nor Mr. Box, nor Mr. Nox, nor Mr. Crox anticipated. The public stops buying hats. Mr. Nox lowers his price twenty cents; Mr. Crox, forty cents, Mr. Fox sells hats at a loss in order to get rid of them. But business grows worse and worse.

In all of the papers advertisements appear:

YOU MAY HAVE ONLY ONE HEAD, BUT THAT DOES NOT MEAN AT ALL THAT YOU SHOULD WEAR ONLY ONE HAT. EVERY AMERICAN SHOULD HAVE THREE HATS. BUY THE HATS OF MR. FOX!

Mr. Box offers to sell hats on a three-year installment plan.

Mr. Nox announces a sale:

ONLY ONE DAY! TAKE ADVANTAGE OF THIS OPPORTUNITY!

But this does not help. Mr. Fox lowers the wages of his workers one dollar a week. Mr. Crox lowers the wages two dollars a week. Again business grows worse and worse.

All at once—STOP! Mr. Fox closes his factory. Two thousand workers are discharged and permitted to go wherever they please. The following day the factory of Mr. Nox stops. In a week practically all hat factories are standing idle. Thousands of workers are without work. New machines grow rusty. Buildings are sold for wreckage.

A year or two pass. The hats bought from Nox, Fox, Box, and Crox, wear out. The public once more begins to buy hats. Hat stores become empty. From the top shelves dusty cartons are taken down. There are not enough hats. Prices go up on hats.

And now, not Mr. Fox, but a certain Mr. Doodle thinks of a profitable business—the building of a hat factory. The same idea also enters the heads of other wise and business-like people—Mr. Boodle, Mr. Foodle, and Mr. Noodle. And the old story begins over again.

The experience with hats is repeated with shoes, with sugar, with pig iron, with coal, with kerosene. Factories are blown up like soap bubbles and burst. One would think that people had lost their minds.

A Mad Country

On the 1st of September, 1920, a train left Washington: a locomotive and thirty cars. The cars were loaded to the top with watermelons. The melons were ripe and sound, and every one cost twenty-five cents—fifty kopecks in our money. The train went rapidly northward.

On the bank of the Potomac River, where the track passes along a cliff, the train stopped. Workers bustled about near one of the cars.

And all at once splash, splash! One melon fell into the water, a second, a third. A whole stream of melons rushed over the cliff into the river below. They jumped like croquet balls, collided, and broke into bits. Near the shore in the water a raft of melons was formed—a green floating island. And the melons continued to come. The first car was followed by a second, the second by a third. The work went on efficiently: a car in two minutes: thirty cars in an hour.

The locomotive blew the whistle, the people jumped aboard and the train disappeared. Slowly the watermelons floated with the current down the Potomac River.

I did not invent this story. If you do not believe it, get a book called "The Tragedy of Waste," written by Stuart Chase. He is an American and a member of the staff of the Labor Bureau in New York City. You will find the tale about the watermelons on page 193.

This book tells us many other interesting things:

In 1920 thousands of gallons of milk were poured into the rivers and creeks of southern Illinois.

In October, 1921, placards were placed along the highways in the Middle-Western States advising the farmers to burn corn instead of coal.

In June 24, 1924, the New York *World* announced: "Thousands of packages of cucumbers and other fresh vegetables were dumped on the offal dock today."

Every few years a large percentage of the Maine potato crop is left to rot in the ground.

And here is the very latest dispatch from the newspapers:

In the Western States again, as in 1921, grain is being burned in place of fuel.

On the cotton plantations they breed a weevil which destroys the cotton crop.

Automobile manufacturers spend millions of dollars for the purchase and destruction of used automobiles. Steamship companies wreck hundreds of the latest steamships.

What does this mean? Have the people lost their senses, or what is the matter? The burning of corn, the spilling of milk, the destruction of automobiles, the wrecking of steamships—why is this done? Who profits by it?

It is profitable to the Foxes and the Boxes. Mr. Fox burns a few train-loads of grain in order to raise the price of corn. Mr. Box gives orders to spill tens of thousands of bottles of milk into the river in order that milk may not be sold too cheaply. And in the meantime school physicians in New York report that one out of every four children in the city is under-nourished.

In a country boasting millions of machines, storerooms are bursting with goods; corn is burned in place of coal; milk is poured into the river. And at the very same time in this very same country, thousands of people go hungry.

Americans say with pride: "Every American worker has two hundred and thirty mechanical slaves." If we count the number of machines in the country and the number of workers they replace, then this statement is true.

Why, then, if this is so, are millions of American citizens in need of the most essential things?

What is the matter here?

The matter is that all these mechanical slaves, all these magnificent machines, belong, not to all Americans, but only to a very few. Just one "automobile king," Ford, owns sixty automobile factories in America and twenty-eight in other countries. He has his own railroads, his own steamships, his own mines, his own forests, his own mountains, his own rivers. If all of the workers in his factories with their families were brought together and put into one place, they would make a city with a population of three million persons. This is as if all Moscow and half of Leningrad in addition worked for one man.

Because one man owns the machines, millions must work for him.

The U.S.S.R. and the U.S.A.

Every American worker has two hundred and thirty mechanical helpers: every Soviet worker has only twenty.

But among us the mechanical helpers belong, not to Mr. Fox, and not to Mr. Box, but to the workers. And this at once changes the whole situation. Workers do not wish to break up automobiles; they do not wish to pour milk into the river; to burn corn in place of coal, to destroy sacks of cucumbers. Workers understand that automobiles, milk, corn, and cucumbers represent labor. They know that, if there is to be an automobile, some one must make it. Why then should labor and time be expended in vain?

> We have a plan.
> In America they work without a plan.
>
> We have a seeding campaign.
> In America they destroy crops.
>
> We increase production.
> In America they reduce production and increase unemployment.
>
> We make what is essential.
> In America hundreds of factories consume raw materials and
> energy in order to make what is altogether unnecessary.

Stuart Chase says: "We drown in a sea of things which we do not use, which we lose, which get out of style, which we give to friends and which they do not need, which disappear somewhere; fountain pens, cigar lighters, cheap rings, razors, endless trinkets, gew-gaws. We destroy mountains of good iron ore and an endless quantity of horse power in order in a few months to fill rubbish cans with them."

And how much money is spent for advertisement!

To read all of the advertisements which appear in one day in the American newspapers would require five hundred years. In picturesque places along the highways great colored placards are set up. At the edge of a beautiful forest you are urged to buy "Smith's Tooth Paste"; on the crest of a famous mountain you are greeted by a sign extolling the virtues of "Kickapoo Indian Sagwa." In the evening, cities are flooded with the light of innumerable electric signs and inscriptions. The roof of the Cleveland Company in a certain American city carries the advertisement: "This sign burns more electricity than a whole city."

Millions of tons of raw materials and fuel, millions of working days, are consumed in order to force people to buy what they do not need. Human labor is dissipated and expended for nothing.

And this happens because the mechanical slaves are the property of Mr. Fox and Mr. Box, and not of the workers. What these gentlemen make, if they only make money, is a matter of complete indifference to them.

For what purpose does Mr. Fox build a hat factory? Is it really in order to make hats? Not at all, but rather to make money. To him every factory is a money factory, a profits factory.

And for Mr. Fox and Mr. Box a worker is not a worker, not a man, but a machine for making profits. Of an ordinary machine made of iron and steel they take good care and do not overload it with work, because it costs too much money. But since a human machine in an American factory costs nothing, it is always overloaded with work. If it wears out or loses its strength—away with it. Others can be had.

Stuart Chase says that after his fortieth birthday a worker is no longer wanted in a factory. At this age the American worker is an old man.

In America the machine is not a helper to the worker, not a friend, but an enemy. Every new machine, every new invention, throws out upon the streets thousands of workers. In glass factories one person now makes three thousand bottles an hour. In former times such a task required seventy-seven men. This means that each machine for the making of bottles deprives seventy-six men of employment. And the American worker despises the machine which takes away his bread.

A certain American writer says: "Machines breed and multiply; there are more and more of them. We ourselves have nurtured them, but now they surround us like wild and dangerous beasts. And we are in their power."

But how is it with us? The more machines we have, the easier will be the work, the shorter will be the working day, the lighter and happier will be the lives of all.

We build factories in order that there may be no poverty, no filth, no sickness, no unemployment, no exhausting labor—in order that life may be rational and just. We build factories in order that we may have as many mechanical helpers as possible—machines in order that these mechanical helpers may belong to all and work for all equally. We build in our country a new, an unheard-of, a socialistic order.

Soviet Communism in Action *

At the suggestion of United States Representative (now Senator) Everett M. Dirksen of Illinois, the Legislative Reference Service of the Library of Congress in 1946 prepared a volume entitled *Communism in Action*. In the words of its editor, this book was designed "to explain to the lay reader, briefly and in simple terms how communism operates in the Soviet Union. . . . In order to help the reader to visualize the institutions, practices, and policies described, comparisons and analogies are frequently made with the United States."

The result is perhaps the most authoritative brief analysis of the Soviet economic system to appear thus far in English. Extracts that follow contrast the roles of managers, industrial laborers, and farmers in the two economies.

Contrasting Basic Principles of Soviet and American Economy

The workers (and peasants) of Russia have had a long memory of hostility and struggle against the Government of the country. In Czarist days it was the people against the Government. When they took over the Government and with it the expropriation and nationalization of the land and industrial property, the people were told there was nothing else to fight against. The people owned everything. The "dictatorship of the proletariat" was said to be a holding operation against the return of "bourgeois rule," of landlords and capitalists. In the first decade of the revolution the distinction and antagonism between the people and the Government broke down. It is true that a new governing class was being created—a class of

* *Communism in Action,* H. Doc. No. 754, 79th Cong. 2d sess. (Government Printing Office, 1946), pp. 23–24, 31–32, 44–45, 54–55, 74–75, 77–78.

politicians, commissars, planners, administrators, managers, Army officers, and intellectuals drawn from the Communist Party. These now make up the Government, and their Government runs industry and agriculture as well as the political activities of the State.

The Soviet Government which manages all industry is not, of course, a democracy in the American sense; but neither is it simply a personal dictatorship. It has developed many new forms in structure and organization in its three decades of history. It is operated in consultation with and with the cooperation of numerous representative bodies in their society. A Government decision is, however, final in realms in which Government does not operate in the United States. A course of action having been settled upon in accordance with the determined needs of the state (as viewed by the Communist Party hierarchy), it is carried out whether or not desired or repugnant to the persons or groups directly and indirectly affected. Forms and symbols of cooperation are set up and elaborate steps are taken to show the great benefit of the course of action to all and its superiority to the "capitalist methods." Thus all Government action in the economic sphere is always presented as the embodiment of the will of all the people—and this is true whether the decision, for example, is to spend vast sums for capital development rather than for consumers' goods, or to increase production quotas without increases in pay, to pay on a piecework rather than time basis, or to have greater inequality rather than relative equality of income for different categories of workers.

Government decisions may be debated thoroughly in the inner councils of the Communist Party; but once they are made, they are the official "Party Line," and the Party line brooks no "right deviationists" or "left deviationists." The new Party line may, indeed, be the opposite of the Party line of a year or two ago; but it is none the less true Marxism and Leninism. . . .

In contrast with centralized economic planning in Soviet Russia, the American system has left the initiative in industry to private planners, employers, and investors who are given an inducement to find new markets, reduce costs of production (but not at the expense of the highest wage levels of any country in the world), and meet the needs and predilections of their customers. When our system remains in balance, it is because the risks taken by thousands of independent enterprises or corporations either fill voids which exist or these enterprises contract or are eliminated when they do not find a profitable place for themselves in serving the consumer or as suppliers of other lines of business.

The phenomenon of the market is itself one of the most democratic forces ever devised. It determines whether there shall be more beer, more petroleum products, more retail outlets, and more housing rather than more industrial plants, more coal, more blacksmith shops, and more outmoded styles of apparel. It also determines the success of particular types of housing, particular styles of clothing, varied types of public eating accommodations, and public amusement. It depends upon the individual whether he spends more for milk or fruits and vegetables or liquor or household furnishings or books or the latest automatic fountain pen; whether he chooses to spend or save without regard to the standards or wishes of a Government department. Our choices are free, limited only by the amount of money we can make and the ingenuity of our collective intelligence to furnish anything the people may want to buy.

On the production side also there is no fixed way of doing things. Different producers obtain their own sources of materials and components, employ different processes, are at different degrees of mechanization, and are struggling for their existence and for ever wider markets. If they see an opportunity to reduce costs and widen their markets by substituting one material for another, substituting new machinery, rearranging the plant, using new fuels or byproducts, for the most part they need no one's permission beyond the management of the plant. If they lose, they lose only the company's money. If they win, others will soon be forced to make similar improvements, and the winning company will have to try again to keep ahead of the procession. This is called by Communists the "anarchism of capitalistic production."

General Contrasts Between Soviet and American Managers

The Soviet manager is a state official. His psychology must always remain that of an order taker. Goals are set for him. He agrees and he works hard to meet and surpass the tasks set for him. He wants to have a good reputation at headquarters and he tries to avoid mistakes. He is not working for big gains but for a good record or in fear that failure may result in serious punishment, such as social disgrace, exile to remote regions, or worse. At the same time, he has no sales or consumer problems and the market for his production is assured. There are no "unreasonable" unions demanding steep increases in pay, which will increase his labor costs at a time when higher prices are impossible. If the total wage bill is to be increased, the Soviet manager knows about it at the beginning of the year and provision is made for it in prices or production standards. He is given his "planned costs" and even his "planned profits," which together make up the fixed factory price, but if he is to get bonuses and promotions he has to reduce costs and increase profits above the planned figure.

The People's Commissar (Narkom) of a branch of industry is really the boss. He is the Soviet equivalent of the Fords, Graces, Girdlers, Wilsons, du Ponts, Sinclairs, and Averys, with the difference that they run whole industries rather than merely giant corporations and they are also part of the top machinery of Government and of the Communist Party as well. On this analogy the top executives on the level of the combine would be equivalent to the American director of an important subsidiary of a very large corporation, the director of a trust would be the counterpart of a chief executive officer of a representative American corporation, while the head of an enterprise would be represented by an American superintendent of a plant or a factory manager. The analogy is not a very good one because, except for the Commissar, all these Soviet executives are subordinate functionaries carrying out plans made largely by others from which they may generally not deviate. At the very top, however, even at the level of the Commissar, there is a greater concentration of power than under the American system.

While there has been some loosening of control from Moscow in intermediate and plant levels, the Soviet industrial operator is subject to the surveillance of both party representatives and the NKVD in the localities. The Soviet manager must always operate within the confines of the master and minor plans. There is real danger in experimenting because of the close oversight of the management hierarchy, the Party, and the NKVD. Lack of success according to plans could be interpreted as "wrecking." The Soviet manager can never have anything like the latitude and the freedom to experiment which his American counterpart has in laying out his ground, choosing his own course, arranging his production program, providing for materials, components, and supplies, and expanding his own customers.

The manager in the American economy may be self-elected, as when he risks his own capital, or appointed, as is more common in the large companies where other people's money has been acquired by the sale of bonds, stocks, and so forth. Such managers are tried and tested in the various divisions of management, like sales, production, purchasing, and so forth. Some are organizers, others are specialists, still others are executives—as such they can make a team work together more successfully than others. Managers are promoted to higher responsibilities within organizations and among organizations. Individually and severally they are subjected to the test which determines the constructive role they play in a capitalistic economy: that they can so organize and combine all the factors in production and execute the tasks undertaken that their total outlay is at least covered by their total sales. But that is not enough. If a manager wants to make real money he will find ways of reducing his costs below any of his competitors and he will have to keep ahead of them all the time. His self-interest is in every way tied up with the success of the enterprise he manages and thus he gives it all he has in ingenuity, energy, drive, and perserverance. The top men are judged by the expansion and profits of their enterprises, not by the meeting of formal requirements from a Government bureau or even by meeting or surpassing someone else's plans in accordance with more or less prescribed methods of operation.

Soviet Wage Scales

Despite the oft-repeated slogan that in a Communist society every value created by the worker redounds to his own personal advantage Stalinism has found it necessary to place before the worker the possibility of higher earnings for himself alone in order to induce him to undertake longer or more intensive training, greater risk, greater responsibility, to accept a harder or more disagreeable job, and to stick to his job with less idling, waste, and indifference.

There does not seem to be any national minimum wage in the Soviet Union. The lowest wage rate in different industries is determined by the industrial management, which has the problem of keeping within the pay-roll allowances fixed by the Plans.

Wages above the minimum are determined by a schedule of wage rates, expressed as multiples of the wage rate of the lowest-paid category. The range and number of categories above the minimum are determined by the Commissariats and approved by the Economsoviet, the body whose function is to coordinate the various Commissariats and act as a kind of economic general staff. The influence of trade-unions and plant committees on fixing wages and norms declined at the end of the 1920's. As collective contracts died away, trade-unions and plant committees gradually ceased to participate in fixing wages in the plant.

Wherever possible and more commonly than in the United States, wages are paid on a piecework basis or on some other form of measured production. The elements include "norms" of production or standard tasks, rates per unit of production, and bonuses for exceeding the norms. Even clerks in retail stores and in offices have norms. The differential rates or "categories," as they call them, are designed to induce workers with different degrees of skill and responsibility to do their very best and thus to assist in attaining the highest possible levels of production, while indirectly and as a result, they influence the availability of supply of workers in the different categories needed. In January 1938, according to a Soviet publication, 75 per cent of the total number or workers were paid on a piecework basis, with assigned standard tasks or norms. Of these 43 per cent were paid on straight piece rates plus bonuses while 32 per cent were paid at progressive piece rates—that is, higher rates for later increments or production beyond standard.

In setting wage scales all the familiar capitalist principles are given weight, since these measure the relative supply of different classes of labor or their relative productivity—the arduousness of the work, its riskiness or unpleasantness, its complexity or exactness; the degree of independence and responsibility borne by the worker; the education and experience required; the volume and quality produced. As in the United States, where competition and collective bargaining rather than the Government agencies fix wage rates, these principles work out in higher wages for heavy industry than for light industry, higher wages for men than for women, higher wages for all degrees of skill compared to unskilled labor, regardless of the family obligations of unskilled labor. The difference between the scales in the Soviet Union and the United States is one of degree and trend—the Soviet Union maintaining wider differentials and showing a definite tendency to increase differentials and inequalities, while in the United States, the widespread educational and training opportunities, the imposition of higher legal minimum wages, and the operating effect of wage adjustments based on the notion of a "living wage" are tending to narrow differentials and inequalities in wages among different classes of workers.

A further practice to encourage individual initiative on the part of workers in the Soviet Union, similar to that of a large percentage of private firms in the United States, is the practice of paying premiums for savings in fuel or materials, improvement in quality, in safety and sanitary techniques, and other technical improvements similar to those rewarded in American "suggestion systems."

Forced Labor

Undoubtedly the most troublesome of all the Soviet institutions to present and discuss without passion is the institution of forced labor. Although the Government publishes no statistics regarding the camps in which prisoners are concentrated—and thus confuses and throws out of line all its other employment statistics—there can be no reasonable doubt that in the Soviet Union several million workers are employed under police discipline and receive only miserable keep for their labor.

The Government makes every effort to conceal the existence of the camps. No foreigner or correspondent is ever permitted to see them. Correspondents accredited to the country do not dare to tangle with the censors and the NKVD regarding this matter. One Canadian newspaperwoman who succeeded by wile in gaining entrance to a concentration camp was quickly expelled from the Soviet Union. Our information comes from those who have escaped, from Russian writers now living abroad, from Americans who have worked, lived, or traveled in Soviet Russia, and from American correspondents who were able to write about the institution of forced labor after they left the Soviet Union.

The first correction labor camp was established in 1923. They grew rapidly in the 1930's, when it was apparently decided to keep most of the "liquidated" alive and working for the state rather than to kill them. The men and women—for there are very large numbers of women among them—work on railways, highways, and canals, cut timber, mine metals and minerals, fill swamplands, help on large construction projects, and open up new areas for settlement. Some are segregated in barracks and work in heavy industries.

The population of these camps was drawn from political offenders, nonconforming engineers and intellectuals, kulaks, recalcitrant peasants, former industrial and other officials, and deviating Communists of the right and of the left. They are exiles who are sent thousands of miles from the towns or villages of their birth. In later years the reserve of forced labor was increased by national groups believed to be hostile and populations residing along the many borders of the Soviet Union in Europe and Asia. There are apparently some differences in the treatment of the various groups which make up the forced labor of the Soviet Union from those living in the many concentration camps spread all over the land, to those exiled to work at reduced wages in the unsettled sections of the country, to those exiled as precautionary measures from frontier regions. Also, large numbers charged with or convicted of some unreliability by the authorities are permitted to work in established communities and factories at their old jobs at reduced pay.

We are concerned only to the extent that such camps exist in a country with the pretension of leading the world in improving the conditions of those who toil and labor. Nor does it matter in a sober comparison of industrial and social conditions whether those are called "correctional" or "educational" or "prison labor," "forced labor" or "slave labor." It is sufficient that for more than two decades reliance has been placed upon millions of involuntary workers who have produced enormous wealth practically at no cost to the state. Conditions, discipline, death rates, etc., in these camps will not be described. It is sufficient that millions who have been sentenced to them work for years or for life without wages and that they have no freedom to move out until their sentences are commuted or have run out. . . .

Government Control (of Farmers)

. . . the Government owns the land and the major instruments of production, the tractors and mechanized equipment being leased to the collectives by the Machine-Tractor Stations, which are part of the state administrative organization. The Government's influence, however, is not confined to ownership. Direct and important controls are exercised over nearly all phases of agricultural production. According to the Model Charter, the internal administration of the collectives is largely left to the General Assembly of the collective and the various officers and agencies selected by and responsible to it. Internal self-government is subject, however, to the conditions prescribed in the Charter itself and in subsequent decrees. The more significant limitation lies in the relatively restricted scope of a collective's "internal" concerns. Under the Soviet system of economic planning, the collective must adapt its operations to the state plan, and to the specific goals set for it in the plan.

Roughly speaking, the state prescribes annually the scope and nature of work for each collective, and sets certain "control figures" or goals. The collective then prepares a detailed production plan. The plan can make no changes in assignments or methods prescribed by the Government. Periodic reports must be made to the Government on the percentage of fulfillment of the plan. On the planning side, the collective's relations are primarily with the People's Commissariat (now Ministry) for Agriculture and its local and regional offices, and with the district and local Soviets (local government agencies).

In addition, a considerable measure of control, partly official and partly unofficial, is exercised by the Communist Party. On the average, collectives contain fewer Party members than are found in industrial organizations. Due to the importance of agriculture in the Soviet economy, however, the Party has taken an active interest in the collective and its operations, and it was, in fact, through the Party that the peasant holdings were collectivized.

Comparison of Government control of agriculture in the Soviet Union and in the United States indicates how inadequate the word "planning" is. We have seen in this country an increasing amount of planned agricultural production and prices since the great agricultural depression of the 1920's. We have had a great variety of price supporting measures and crop-control schemes, as well as the more traditional types of Government technical and financial assistance. With few exceptions, however, Government planning in this country has proceeded with the consent of the farmers. The Government has provided technical and scientific information and assistance and financial inducements, and has suggested methods and schemes by which production and demand might be brought into balance and agricultural income increased and stabilized. The decision whether or not to adopt the plans proposed, however, has remained largely with the farmers themselves. In the Soviet Union, on the other hand, the Government's "control figures" constitute the master plan to which the collective's operations must be geared.

CHAPTER EIGHT

Evolution of American Capitalism

MODERN AMERICAN CAPITALISM finds itself under fire from two divergent, conflicting sources. Rival ideologies attack the system as unorganized, chaotic, and exploitive; internally, capitalism is pushed to the right or left by citizen groups who differ widely in their philosophical approach to the problems of capitalism. Most internal disputes do not revolve around pure theory, however; on the contrary, theory commonly evolves from concrete situations, and an individual's attitude may vary from problem to problem. Of the multiple problems of American capitalism two major questions are considered in the following readings.

One underlying theme is the problem of bigness and how Americans propose to fit it into their political and economic life. Concerning bigness Americans have long had mixed reactions. Frequently, in a spirit of braggadocio, they have prided themselves on the size of their industry, their country, and their institutions. Obversely, Americans are confirmed supporters of little business, individual workers, small farmers, average consumers, and all manner of underdogs. At midpoint in the twentieth century it is obvious that big business, big agriculture, big labor, and even big government are established facts on the economic scene. Such a situation creates a deep conflict within American culture. Shall Americans dismiss their nostalgia for the "little fellow" as nineteenth-century romanticism, unrealistic in the modern world? Or shall they organize, promote, and legislate for the destruction of big unions, big industries, big farmers, and big bureaucracies?

The second underlying theme might be paraphrased as follows: Is big government an inevitable result of bigness elsewhere in the economy? This query is one of the fundamental questions of the twentieth century, which has witnessed the marriage of politics and economics on many fronts. Reared in a culture that long proclaimed the best government to be that which governed least, Americans have an uncomfortable feeling that politics is now "cluttered" with economic questions. Vital economic decisions are reached through the political process, rather than through the functioning of Adam Smith's *laissez faire*. This development means in practice, of course, that John Doe, average voter, is expected not only to have opinions on foreign policy, states' rights, and prohibition, but also on fair trade, the right to strike, parity prices, and health insurance. Apparently the major problems of business, labor, agriculture, and the consumer will ultimately be decided by the average citizen instead of through the operation of inexorable natural laws.

To summarize, this chapter deals with two basic problems: (1) bigness and its control, and (2) the relationship between government and various segments of America's capitalistic economy.

Problem 24: Big Business-- Menace or Promise?

For two generations Americans have watched with trepidation the expansion of big business in the United States. Against this trend they have created a dike of legislation—Sherman Anti-Trust Act, Clayton Act, Federal Trade Commission Act, Public Utility Holding Company Act, and Robinson-Patman Act.

Despite this mass of hostile legislation, business has continued to expand, merge, and consolidate. Thus, at mid-century the American attitude toward big business is mixed. Bigness has brought with it alleged economies of operation, and the further claim is made that big business provides the dynamic leadership that sparks the United States economy. In reverse, Americans are warned that monopolistic, soul-less corporations, the "Big Five," or "America's Sixty Families" will take over the country lock, stock, and barrel unless strenuous efforts are made to check bigness. Therefore, after sixty years of experimentation American citizens are again presented with a choice: Shall they make their peace with bigness as something inevitable and good? Or shall they continue the battle against it with redoubled vigor?

How Big Is Big Business? *

Like sin, monopoly is normally favored only by those who derive benefit from it. The following article levies a series of charges against big business and monopoly, dramatizing the problem by showing the effect of monopoly on the average man—Mr. Jones.

The average working man engaged in earning a living for himself and his family has little time to think about the mysterious problems of international finance, economic statistics or patent pools. His hours are crowded, and his first concerns are the achievement of better opportunities for himself, of education for his children and of making his dollars stretch farther and farther, as prices go bouncing beyond his reach. He has heard of monopoly and perhaps has formed some ideas about the ways in which monopoly should be treated. In fact, public opinion polls have indicated that eighty-five per cent of the American people do believe that monopolies are bad and that something should be done about them.

At the same time, Mr. Jones, our average man, seldom thinks about how monopolies affect him personally, or his employment, or the things he buys or what he pays for them. He has a feeling that monopolies, cartels and combines are far away from his own affairs. He realizes that monopolies are large, but in his thinking they are likely to be vast, nebulous and distant shapes in a remote part of the other fellow's economic life. It is probably for this reason more than any other that the real meaning of monopoly and a full understanding of such things as cartels and patent pools have not captured the attention of the ordinary citizen. Once this understanding becomes concrete in the thinking of the American people there is little question but that they will treat the subject as one of the two or three major economic issues of their lives.

For it is exactly that. The monopoly problem is one of the basic and central questions affecting the welfare and future of the ordinary citizen in the United States at the present time. In importance it ranks only below the improvement of industrial relations and preservation of civil liberties. It is tied up with both of them, yet monopoly can be understood by itself. Its effects are clear-cut. How important it is for the individual American to have this understanding can best be illustrated if we follow Mr. Jones in his daily life and see how often and in what various and sometimes unknown ways he meets monopoly and its effects.

* "A Day with Mr. Jones," *Economic Outlook*, August, 1946 (CIO Department of Education and Research), pp. 5-12.

From the time that he gets up in the morning until he goes to bed at night, Mr. Jones or some member of his family is face to face with monopoly in one of its many shapes. Before he eats his breakfast it is likely that Mr. Jones has brought in the morning milk. He knows that the price of milk has gone up and he thinks, rightly or wrongly, that rising costs of production and distribution are to be blamed. As a recent experience in New York City indicated, however, the price of butter, cheese, and other products may represent not any real increase in costs, nor even any reasonable increase in profits, but may be the result of a deliberate conspiracy to hold up the public and make them pay a dollar a pound for butter and extraordinary prices for cheese and milk. Such cases are nearly always tied into some form of monopoly control of the market.

But what about the bottle? It is quite unlikely that Mr. Jones has given the bottle any thought. The milkman brings the bottle and when it is empty he takes it away. If Mr. Jones buys his milk at a store he knows there is a deposit on the bottle but that is probably as far as his interest in the subject has gone. Nevertheless, if his curiosity should lead him to inquire into the origins of the milk bottle, Mr. Jones would discover that all the bottles delivered to him and thirty million other American families every morning were until very recently completely controlled products of one of the most tightly knit monopolies in existence.

After eating breakfast Jones probably relaxes a minute before going to work. He lights a cigarette and picks up a newspaper to look at the morning headlines. The match he strikes and the cigarette he smokes and the newspaper he reads are all either wholly or in part subject to monopolies which know his habits much better than he knows theirs. A match looks like a simple product, yet behind the history of a single match is one of the most complicated and involved stories of monopoly in modern times. The match may cost Mr. Jones nothing, or so he thinks, but it did cost somebody something. If he thinks about it long enough he will realize that, in one way or another, it is always the man who uses a product who pays for it. If he multiplies himself by several hundred million, he will begin to understand why a monopoly in matches can be Big Business. If he inquires far enough he will learn, in fact, that the entire match industry has been under the domination of an international monopoly, the match cartel. He may even recall the shadowy figure of Ivar Kreuger, the match king, whose suicide in the early '30s brought disaster to hundreds of thousands of people, toppled important banks and threatened to disrupt the internal affairs of half a dozen countries.

When it comes to his cigarette Mr. Jones is on firmer ground. He is well acquainted with the variations which occur in the price of a standard package of cigarettes from one month to another, and with the raucous but perhaps enjoyable advertising by which he is encouraged to use this or that particular brand. But if he ever stopped to think of the reason why all of his favorite brands of cigarettes cost him exactly the same, or why, for example, he should not be able to get his favorite brand for one-third of the price he does pay, he will again find that the answer is monopoly. "But how," he may ask, "is there a monopoly? They certainly make many more than one brand of cigarettes." Here complications set in. For what he will find if he carries his questions far enough is that he has been dealing with a form of monopoly by agreement maintained among the big companies of the American tobacco industry. The American people smoke billions of cigarettes and cigars in the course of a year and the tobacco industry is a billion dollar industry. Even though the average smoker might think that competition was unavoidable, the Supreme Court of the United States recently concluded, at the end of a long and difficult anti-trust case, that the tobacco industry was in fact controlled by monopoly power shared among the major producers who had, among other things, agreed in effect never to allow a good ten-cent package of cigarettes on the market. This country, in other words, will never get a good five-cent cigar or a ten-cent package of cigarettes as long as monopoly can prevent it.

As for his newspaper, a very brief inquiry would acquaint Mr. Jones with the fact that the paper upon which the news is printed and even the ink are or have been made in industries controlled by close-knit monopolies. In fact, even some of the press dispatches which come from distant places and are preceded by well-known initials of press associations, have in at least one instance been found to be a monopolized form of news.

Mr. Jones then goes to work. If he is in the electrical industry, the chemical industry, the machine tool industry, or a plant manufacturing steel or aluminum, or indeed any one of a host of other types of manufacturing, there is almost a one hundred per cent probability that the industry is dominated by a monopoly group. The concern of monopoly groups is with making higher and higher profits and only incidentally with maintaining jobs for Mr. Jones and his millions of fellow workers.

When he goes home at night, Mr. Jones may stay there and listen to the radio, or he may decide to go to the movies. If he does go to the movies he will enjoy one of the most pleasurable types of monopoly products, but a monopoly product nonetheless, for the motion picture industry has been found to be concentrated under the control of a few major producers who determine what pictures shall be made, when they shall be shown, and who may show them. In years past, major producers have exercised great control even over neighborhood theatres, and part of the admission price of a ticket has represented in effect a tax paid to monopoly.

If he stays at home, Mr. Jones will read his monopolized newspaper, with the aid of monopolized spectacles, smoking monopolized tobacco, in the light furnished by a conspicuous monopoly product, the electric light bulb. It may never occur to him that light bulbs are a special concern of one of the largest international monopolies and cartels in the world, for he thinks of light bulbs as efficient and economical. Within limits they are, but what Mr. Jones doesn't know is that because of monopoly he cannot get better light at lower cost, since monopoly procedure decided that he should normally use so many electric bulbs per month or per year at a certain price and, it may be added, at a certain level of revenue to utility companies.

If Mr. Jones turns on his radio he is aware of using a complicated mechanism which represents a major achievement of modern man. Yet his radio set represents a vast field in which industrial giants have fought, combined and fought again, both among themselves and with government. At the present moment the manufacture of radios is not monopolistic in any simple meaning of the term. Nevertheless, even the cheapest radio set is a product of many patent licenses, cross licenses and agreements floating in a pool of some fifteen to twenty thousand radio and communications patents. Again, the history of a modern radio set is the history of a struggle by and against monopoly power.

This struggle continues. Television, the wonder child of radio, is still [in 1946] a dream of the future to the householder. He will not get television until both the technical difficulties, which are relatively simple, and the complex contest among conflicting monopoly interests are overcome. The same condition holds true in nearly all of the much-vaunted postwar gadgets and improvements intended to make living more comfortable, housing more plentiful, and to place new marvels of convenience within the reach of all. Nearly every one of the fields in which these developments could occur is subject to control by monopoly groups. New and independent businesses cannot enter these fields. Until they can, the consumer will get new products only when, as, and if, monopoly decides that he should have them.

Mr. Jones may or may not know that he has had a busy day with monopoly. If he does know, it may give him a headache. In that case there is a simple remedy which monopoly past and present will place at his disposal. He can take an aspirin tablet—and then go to bed to dream of an economy of abundance.

THE GROWING CONCENTRATION OF ECONOMIC POWER *

The thesis set forth in the preceding article is here elaborated with specific statistics and examples. A thumbnail sketch of American big business is provided; the growing concentration of economic power is described; the necessity for additional curbs on bigness is argued. Not only are American consumers injured by big business, according to the viewpoint expressed here, but small business will inevitably be crushed by this modern Juggernaut. Mr. Harris is a Washington correspondent of the *St. Louis Post-Dispatch*. In 1946 he received a Pulitzer prize for distinguished reporting.

The concentration of aggressive political power in the hands of a few led the United States and its allies into World War II, fought over the face of the earth to preserve the freedom and rights of individuals. But a little-told paradox of transcending importance for the future is that this same mighty war, according to Congressional reports, served as an instrument for accelerating the trend in this nation toward concentration of economic power.

To the small businessman in every field of endeavor, economic freedom is fully as vital as political freedom. Yet as the country nears the end of the first half of the twentieth century, it is apparent, from official studies of the subject, that the anti-trust laws and popular devotion to the concept of really free enerprise have failed to stem the tide toward economic concentration.

Where does the road lead? Only an inspired crystal gazer can tell for sure, but economists do agree at least that the trend should be halted and reversed.

The economic picture since the turn of the century, with particular emphasis on the effects of two world wars, has been projected by authoritative groups in recent years, notably the Temporary National Economic Committee, the National Resources Committee, Commerce Department, Small War Plants Corporation, Twentieth Century Fund, Inc., and Congressional committees. A new report of the Smaller War Plants Corporation to the Senate Committee on Small Business sheds light especially on advantages given big business by the war.

---

* Edward A. Harris, *The St. Louis Post-Dispatch*, November 24, 1946.

Tendency Begins Shortly After Civil War

It is from these official and semi-official sources that the following facts and figures were compiled:

The tendency toward the combination of industrial units under centralized control began shortly after the Civil War and reached a peak in 1901 with the formation of the billion dollar United States Steel Corporation. By 1904 the trusts had control of 40 per cent of all manufacturing capital in the United States. But the stock market crash of 1903 and the business crisis of 1907 placed a temporary brake on the combination movement, then under attack by the Theodore Roosevelt administration.

Nevertheless, by 1909 it was estimated that the 200 largest non-financial (non-bank) corporations owned about one-third of the assets of all non-financial corporations. The large corporations had thus started to dominate the American economy long before the outbreak of World War I.

World War I stimulated the growth of big business. War contracts were issued predominately to the large corporations, and they accumulated huge profits for further expansion after the war. In 1909, the large manufacturing corporations (employing at least 1,000 persons) had on their payrolls 15.1 per cent of all the wage earners in the manufacturing industries; by 1919 this had risen to 26 per cent.

The wave of mergers and acquisitions that began at the close of World War I extended until 1921, when it was checked by the brief postwar depression. When better conditions returned in 1925 the merger movement was renewed, reaching white heat in 1928 and 1929, before the floor dropped out of the stock market.

Pre-War Concentration in Economy Considerable

While the precipitous depression of the thirties slowed mergers, the pre-World War II concentration in the economy as a whole was considerable, as shown by these figures compiled by the Temporary National Economic Committee, the Twentieth Century Fund and the National Resources Committee.

The 45 largest transportation corporations owned 92 per cent of all the transportation facilities of the nation;

The 40 largest public utility corporations owned more than 80 per cent of the public utility facilities.

The country's 20 largest banks held 27 per cent of the total loans and investments of all banks.

The 17 largest life insurance companies accounted for 81.5 per cent of all the assets of life insurance firms.

One-tenth of 1 per cent of all corporations owned 52 per cent of the total corporate assets;

Less than 4 per cent of all the manufacturing corporations earned 84 per cent of all the net profits of all manufacturing corporations.

One-tenth of one per cent of all the firms in the country in 1939 employed 500 or more workers (firms with less than 500 were considered small businesses) and accounted for 40 per cent of all the nonagricultural employment in the nation.

This prewar situation poses the question: Did the manner in which the nation's resources were mobilized for World War II place in the hands of Big Business the means of further increasing economic concentration in the years to come?

The recent report of the Small War Plants Corporation to the Senate showed that the war shoved small business into the background. Enormous gains were made by big business.

Small firms in war industries accounted for 52 per cent of total manufacturing employment in 1939; by 1944 this figure had declined to 38 per cent. In manufacturing as a whole, firms with 10,000 employees or more accounted for 13 per cent of total employment in 1939; after three years of war this had jumped to fully 31 per cent. Half a million small retail, service, and construction firms, moreover, disappeared entirely during the war.

Large Firms Get Bulk of Contracts During War

The increase in concentration that took place during the war, according to the Small War Plants Corporation, was due largely to the distribution of the great bulk of war contracts to a small number of very large firms. The key to the control of productive resources during the war was the distribution of nearly 200 billion dollars in prime supply contracts by the Government.

Statistics compiled by the War Production Board before its dissolution tell this story: From June, 1940, through September, 1944, prime contract awards totalling 175 billion dollars were made to 18,539 corporations. Two-thirds of this large amount went to the largest 100 firms. Nearly half of the value of the contracts awarded during this four-year period went to the top 30 corporations. The concentration of prime contracts remained fairly stable throughout the war.

In addition to this tremendous contract outlay, large corporations are in a position to consolidate their gains and to expand further as a result of the wartime facilities built largely with Federal funds.

The nation's manufacturing facilities in 1939 had cost about 40 billion dollars to build. To this was added during the war about 26 billion dollars of new plant and equipment, of which some two-thirds was provided directly from Federal funds and the balance from private funds.

Of the 26 billion, 14 billion was for new plant construction, 4.2 billion for expansion of prewar plants and 7.8 billion for conversion of prewar plants to war projects and for replacement of old equipment. The Small War Plants Corporation estimates that 20 billion dollars worth of wartime plants is usable for peacetime products.

Who controls this great productive plant? How much is held by big business and how much is held by smaller firms?

The 250 largest manufacturing corporations, says the Small War Plants Corporation, had 25.9 billion dollars of capital assets in 1939. They have added 3.7 billion dollars in privately owned new facilities, and have operated 8.9 billion dollars of the 11.5 billion dollars of Federally financed facilities which are estimated to be usable for peacetime production. . . . That big business is actually using its war-increased strength, especially in liquid funds, to improve its position and power over prewar levels is shown, the Small War Plants Corporation said, by the sharp rise in mergers and acquisitions that has taken place since the end of World War II. The current movement began in 1943 and swung into high speed in the fourth quarter of 1945, when the rate of mergers and acquisitions in manufacturing was higher than at any time in the preceding decade and a half.

Big Business Active in Acquiring Small Firms

In the late twenties, the merger movement embraced the linking together of large producers of the same items. In contrast, the present trend toward acquisition has been of the conglomerate type, in which large firms having established trade marks and distributing facilities have acquired smaller firms engaged in making auxiliary or unrelated products in order to round out their lines. . . .

Should the nation enjoy continuing prosperity in the years ahead, the giant corporations will dominate the economy more and more through the tremendous magnitude of their production capacity and accumulated working capital, in the opinion of the Small War Plants Corporation. On the other hand, if a depression sets in, big business will still be able to consolidate further its economic concentration because of its greater staying power in hard times, the Government agency declares. Thus the small business man faces a tighter squeeze in either contingency.

The Small War Plants Corporation conclusion is that it will take swift and drastic action to bring economic concentration back to its prewar level or reduce it substantially below the prewar level. It will require a more vigorous anti-trust program and a far more sweeping and effective program to aid small business than exists at present. Meanwhile, the record indicates, big business is getting bigger every day.

———◆◆◆◆———

Big Business for a Big Country *

In sharp contrast to Mr. Harris, David E. Lilienthal, the former head of the Tennessee Valley Authority and the Atomic Energy Commission, finds that Big Business is a positive good. Bigness is, in fact, "the key to our productive and distributive greatness, to our economic creativeness." Yet, like an elephant besieged by pygmies, Big Business finds itself hampered at every turn by antiquated, restrictive laws. Let us, Lilienthal suggests, abandon the negative, "thou shall not" attitude of our anti-trust laws and adopt a positive policy of encouraging all bigness that is not basically evil in intent.

The people of the United States of America now produce as much as all the rest of the world put together. This we do with a mere six per cent of the world's population and about the same per cent of its land area. And we are only at the beginning; we shall probably multiply this production over and over again in the next ten to twenty-five years.

At this moment this is the most important fact in the world. For it is America's mastery of productivity that stands between freedom and the tidal wave of Communist militarism threatening a new Era of Darkness.

This technique of production—and with it the equally important art of an ethical distribution of production—is a *creative* thing, a combination of poetry and sweat. It calls for imagination, vitality, faith, as well as the skills of science, management, human relations and modern governmental techniques. It is the most exciting spectacle in the history of the world—the unfolding of American productive and social genius.

Man has been working at wealth-creation since the beginning of time in order to fight off hunger, exposure, degradation. He has been trying to push back the enemy, poverty, trying for enough breathing space so the whole day and night would not be needed just to get enough food and

* David E. Lilienthal, *Big Business: A New Era* (Harper, 1952). Copyright, 1952, by David E. Lilienthal. Reprinted from *Collier's,* May 31, 1952, pp. 15–17, 74–75.

warmth and shelter to survive. He has been trying to get a margin so he could be a man, not merely an animal fighting to stay alive.

In America of the mid-fifties, twentieth century, we've done this wealth-creation job better by all odds than any generation ever did. Since 1939 we've doubled, trebled, quadrupled outputs, capacity, plants, and we go right on adding by a fifth, a fourth, a half every few years. More important still, we are learning, through an imaginative synthesis of private and public action, how to distribute the benefits of this vast flood of goods and services in a democratic and an ethical way. The result: fewer very poor and fewer very rich than in any comparably large community since the dawn of history.

We are well along toward the "formula," the *something* that men have been seeking these countless centuries.

What is this we've got? It is very important indeed that we try to understand what it is.

Why has this great and creative art come to fruition now, in U.S.A. 1952? What accounts for this almost-miracle? What can we do to stimulate and nourish this distinctive talent of ours? I've thought about this a great deal, as have ever so many other people.

Here is a summary of my views, boiled down and oversimplified:

First: The key to our productive and distributive greatness, to our economic creativeness, is Bigness—our special skill in creating and operating large-scale undertakings. Size is our greatest single functional asset.

Second: The hazards of Bigness are considerable. They are, chiefly, the dangers of concentration of economic power, and of overcentralization. These evils must be the object of our constant vigilance; from time to time correctives and safeguards against particular forms of these dangers will be urgently required in the public interest.

The dangers of Bigness, however, have, in my opinion, been reduced to manageable proportions. We can now enjoy the full benefits of Bigness— benefits we deny ourselves—because of recent almost revolutionary changes in the power of the public to protect itself against corporate excesses. Chief among these changes are: (a) a great increase in the strength and influence of organized labor; (b) the increased role of government, since 1933, in economic affairs; (c) the growing evidence of public responsibility on the part of business leadership; and (d) the development and increasing use of methods of decentralizing huge economic enterprises.

Third: We need badly to understand what an asset we have in this skill of large-scale management. We need to examine Bigness critically, but without old and outworn prejudices—need to be aware of its almost un-limited usefulness to us as a people. While always alive to its potential evils, I believe the time has come when it is in the interest of the whole country that we promote and encourage and nourish those principles and practices of Bigness that can bring us, in increasing measure, vast social and individual benefits.

Great as are the evident benefits of present-day Bigness, our public opinion, by and large, and our basic laws are both antagonistic to Bigness. Suspicions and fears bred in another period of our history carry over into the changed circumstances of this mid-century.

Our present public policy concerning Bigness is largely embodied in the Sherman and Clayton Antitrust laws. These were enacted many years ago as the creative Magna Charta of economic freedom for an America emerging from an agricultural economy in which small business was the norm. In 1952 our antitrust laws and their administration are still based on a nineteenth-century idea that Bigness in and of itself is dangerous to the public welfare.

But we live in a twentieth-century America. We are dependent upon big-scale undertakings. We are armed with new checks and balances to protect us. Our urgent need now is to recognize the great social asset we have in Bigness. Should we not, instead of attempting to inhibit and handicap and destroy Bigness, rather seek to find ways and means to retain and increase the benefits of Bigness, while safeguarding the public welfare against possible abuses? After twenty years of observation I am firmly of the opinion that the answer to this question should be a resounding "yes."

As they are applied to the principle of large-scale undertakings, both the basic business laws of the country and a substantial part of our public opinion are out of tune with the realities of the twentieth-century industrial and urban country we are today. This confusion and conflict between reality and doctrine prevent the full flowering of the advantages of Bigness so valuable to us, and so greatly needed for our national security.

It is to propose and to urge a fundamental re-examination and reappraisal of Bigness in the changed America of today that I write.

It is my conviction that America needs a new, fresh, realistic, *affirmative* Policy of Productivity, supported by public opinion and ultimately translated into law. That policy should rest upon and employ the dynamics of growth I have here designated as Bigness. America can, deliberately and consciously, fashion public safeguards and private incentives whereby, using that quality Walt Whitman called "amplitude," we can bring closer to reality the American Dream: individual freedom, social justice, material well-being, world moral leadership.

I am perfectly aware that in advocating better understanding and a more affirmative climate of opinion toward big-scale undertakings I move in a highly controversial field. It is an area where equally sensible and public-spirited men disagree, and where the memory of past corporate wrongs and abuses makes difficult a calm and objective analysis of today's circumstances. But these matters, controversial as they are, need to be discussed—and in the open air of reason. They need to be discussed widely, on their present merits, with a minimum of emotion, except the dominant emotion of furthering the strength and health of a country hard pressed with the increasing burdens of world leadership.

. . . I have tried to avoid reopening what I regard as a sterile quarrel between "little business" and "Big Business," as if we were faced with a choice of one or the other. That we need "little business" is too clear to require argument. What is more important is to realize that it is of the essence of growth through Bigness that it creates diversity—big and little —and nourishes diversity: diversity of size and of function, whereby what is small becomes bigger, whereby what is big in turn creates what is little, which in its turn stimulates and disciplines what is big.

Nor am I here concerned with economic prejudice, inflamed by dated oratorical flourishes and trumpetings that our fate is controlled by a "handful of rich and all-powerful men." This is a picture faded, unreal, a quaint daguerreotype of a world that is no more.

"As I belong to the class of people who have great faith in this country," wrote Henry Adams to his friend Charles Milnes Gaskell in 1877, "and who believe that in another century it will be saying, in its turn, the last word of civilization, I enjoy the expectation of the coming day. . . ."

I, too, "enjoy the expectation of the coming day." But whether such faith is sustained by the event depends upon the answer to this question: As a people will we be BIG enough? We have indeed climbed to new heights in human history, we Americans of the mid-twentieth century. Now what? Will we, too, lose our great chance because we do not ourselves understand and therefore cannot fully use the secret of our own strength?

An individual cannot do his best if he is confused about basic things. Neither can a nation. This nation *is* confused, for we say one thing about size in business, and we do another and almost opposite thing. We don't encourage and promote and strengthen, but on the contrary we continue to distrust and try to stunt and inhibit, and to penalize by law, the very economic talent that in considerable part makes us what we are—that talent which is one of our greatest sources of strength and freedom, our capacity for large-scale undertakings.

We distrust size in industry and business; our basic economic law, the Sherman Antitrust Act, symbolizes distrust, giving concrete expression to our temperamental aversion to Bigness and to our belief in competition. How sometimes confused and contradictory this idea is . . . [may be indicated by the fact] in U.S.A. 1952, Bigness in industry is itself one of the most effective ways—sometimes the only effective way—to maintain genuine competition.

Such contradictions and confusions as this are costly. We can scarcely expect other countries and peoples to "understand" us—which we try so desperately to have them do as part of the "cold war"—if we ourselves are mixed up about our own country on such basic issues as this. The only way out, for us, is to take a good hard look at the realities, to discuss and argue and think things through. These articles are an effort to bring about just such a discussion, and to focus that discussion not on technical details but on some fundamental propositions.

The belief that business Bigness is, in itself, something that must be curbed and restricted is a theme that has run throughout the governmental policy of this country for many years. The same theme, with only minor variations, has been repeated each four years in the political platforms and the speeches of Republicans and Democrats alike. Usually described as "concentration of economic power," the ever-mounting size of corporate undertakings has been, and continues to this day to be, the subject of un-remitting criticism, warning, attack and governmental action.

Almost 40 years ago—in 1914—at the time the Federal Trade Commission was established, a joint committee told Congress: "The concentration of wealth, money and property in the United States under the control and in the hands of a few individuals or great corporations has grown to such an enormous extent that unless checked it will ultimately threaten the perpetuity of our institutions."

In 1951, the Federal Trade Commission used almost the same words: "If nothing is done to check the growth in concentration, either the giant corporations will ultimately take over the country, or the government will be impelled to step in and impose some form of direct regulation." . . .

I suggest that in a changed America our present-day economic policy, the interpretation of our antitrust laws, and our emotional antipathy to Big-ness need careful re-examination and basic change. We have a right to insist that any proposal for a change in our economic and legal policy respecting business be based on the following propositions:

1. That the change suggested has as its evident purpose the promotion not of the welfare of business, big or small, or of labor or farmers or professional men, but the welfare of the country as a whole.

2. That the policy is designed to maintain and encourage competition in ideas and products as a fundamental tenet of American life.

3. That the policy proposed will help the American people secure the things they want. These things are in part material things. They are in part non-material.

In making my proposal for a change I have attempted to meet the fore-going tests. I was brought up, like most men and women of my genera-tion, to be suspicious and distrustful of things that are big. My father, and his friends who were small businessmen, spoke with deep apprehension of the trusts and cheered Teddy Roosevelt in his Bull Moose campaign; they thought the world was in a bad way when the first "five and ten" bought out an old individual family business and began the "chain-store" influx in our Indiana town.

At home and at school, my generation heard the same refrain of fear and antagonism and distrust of Bigness—though at the same time we bragged about things because they were big.

There were periodic curbs put on Big Business through the years. Woodrow Wilson created the Federal Trade Commission. Charles Evans Hughes, writing a great chapter of devoted public service, exposed the evils of big utilities and insurance companies. Louis D. Brandeis, with the power of his great spirit and mind, brought to light the "crime of Bigness," and it was anything but a pretty picture.

The depression of the thirties brought a resurgence of public condemna-tion and distrust of size: the Pecora investigation of Wall Street, the Temporary Economic Committee, the constructive and overdue reforms of the abuses of finance and large business during the first seven years of the administrations of Franklin Roosevelt.

In short, it has been part of the atmosphere of American life of my generation and the generation of my children to be emotionally and politically and economically critical of Bigness, and, more often than not, with good reason. Yet by the time I was forty, I found myself directing the biggest integrated power system in the world, the TVA, which was itself the creation of an old-time trust buster, George Norris, and of an outstanding opponent of Bigness, Franklin D. Roosevelt. For over thirteen years I helped develop, as a unit, a region larger geographically than Great Britain, that embraced parts of seven Southern states. And, in 1946, I was made head of the largest industrial monopoly of history, the Atomic Energy Commission of the United States.

The apparent contradictions of my own experience are but illustrative of those of almost everyone else. Despite our antagonism, despite the sore handicaps of law and public opinion, Bigness of units has nevertheless developed rapidly until today size is a chief and outstanding characteristic of the way we do business, the way we live. And we like the material fruits of size at the very same time that we continue to view it with dis-trust.

This is a country of Bigness. Even what is sometimes called "medium-sized" business is huge by almost any standard.

Why, then, are we so strongly suspicious and distrustful of Big Business, so defensive about it?

Part of the answer lies in this: that we so generally regard Bigness and Monopoly as synonymous. Or to put it another way, we favor competition: bigness and competition we regard as incompatible.

It is natural enough that we should think this way. During the first twenty years of this century, when many of us acquired our economic and political ideas, it was largely true that Bigness and Monopoly tended to be same.

We believe in competition in products, in services and—most important —in ideas. This is a central belief. If not carried to fanatic extremes it is one I firmly believe is just as sound and healthy today for America of 1952 as it was for America of 1890 when the Sherman Antitrust Act was passed.

We believe in competition and we are opposed to monopoly—this is clear. But we need to analyze this feeling rather closely.

We are certainly not for competition for competition's sake. We believe in competition not as a dogma but because we feel that it has been competition that has been in our interest and that it continues to be in our interest.

Our reasoning runs thus:

1. Anything that stifles or diminishes or impairs competition thereby stifles and diminishes and impairs our prospects of getting the things we want—things we want as customers, as businessmen, as citizens.

2. Bigness in business—so the argument runs—has sought to stifle competition and to cut down individual opportunity. By its very nature Bigness provides the opportunity to control and therefore to diminish competition.

But this line of thinking is essentially negative. What of the affirmative, positive side? How can we secure for ourselves those things we want and need? What is the functional, organizational characteristic of our system that can provide for us those things physical and intangible that we highly regard?

Generally speaking the answer is: Bigness. Without Bigness we simply *cannot* have a great many of these things we want and need. It is Bigness that is one of our chief assurances of even greater benefits in the future.

Here is an apparant contradiction between our deep fears of Bigness as monopolistic, and our need of it, that for a good many years has confused and troubled me. Can these two be reconciled? More narrowly, can Bigness and competition be reconciled? I submit the following for consideration.

1. Under the changed conditions of today, in many situations size has become an essential ingredient of competition.

2. The dangers of Bigness, in terms of concentrated power, are no longer

beyond handling, because of new tools of government social control and the increased power of labor and of large buyers in the market place.

If you were to take an opinion poll, asking a cross section of average Americans: "What do you think of the Sherman Act?" my guess is that at least 7 out of 10 would answer that they had never heard of it. And yet if any one law of the land can be said to sum up the economic views and philosophy of the ordinary man and woman—business people included—I suppose it is the Sherman Act. Under the Sherman Act, business combinations, trusts or contracts that fix prices, limit production, or otherwise put "restraints upon trade" are illegal. The act was directed against Big Business as it functioned when the law was passed in 1890, more than sixty years ago. The Sherman Act has been amended and strengthened, under Presidents Theodore Roosevelt, Woodrow Wilson, Franklin Roosevelt and Harry Truman; in most instances fear of Big Business and of its abuses of power was what was behind the drive to make the Sherman Act stronger, more inclusive; the penalties more severe.

The Sherman Antitrust Act has had a profound effect upon the course of American economic and social development. It was a great feat of statesmanship, an exhibition of remarkable insight into the needs of the United States for vigorous competition.

In the U.S.A. of Senator Sherman, in 1890, the country, just launched on its amazing career of industrialization, struck out almost by instinct against Bigness because it was tending to be synonymous with Monopoly. That Bigness must be "broken up" into smaller units was seen as the first big job of the antitrust enforcers; Big Oil, Big Steel, Big Railroads and so on.

But we are not living in Sherman's 1890, nor Teddy's 1906, nor Wilson's 1913, nor Roosevelt's 1933. This is 1952. The U.S.A. of 1952 bears little resemblance to the U.S.A. of those landmark years of the war on monopoly.

Of course, in 1952, many crimes against competition are still committed, and there exist all sorts of chicanery, deceit, economic coercion—the whole assortment of corporate and individual evasions or violations of the basic code of competition, what one might call the shoplifting, confidence-game and window-smashing episodes of the business world.

Here the policing functions of the Department of Justice's Antitrust Division have served in the past, and today continue to serve us well, as the FBI of the business world, to keep down the incidence of crime in the competitive system. This activity, and that of the Federal Trade Commission in the same area, is today of utmost importance to the maintenance of a healthy society.

But the policy of "don't do that" is not good enough for U.S.A. 1952.

Today the Sherman Act, though an essential of our business life, appears to me grossly inadequate and administered in a way that cripples America.

The need is not for repeal of the Sherman Act; its policing functions should be maintained and even strengthened in their administration. Those policing functions, however, should be only a part of a new, broader, and vigorously affirmative economic and legal policy that will release the potentialities of our asset of Bigness for the benefit of the whole country.

As applied to Bigness per se, the Sherman Act no longer lives up fully to the needs of U.S.A. 1952. It is a philosophy of a time when Bigness, in and of itself, was the symbol and even the synonym of Monopoly. For basic reasons going to the very dynamics of modern industry, this is no longer generally true—namely, that it is Bigness that helps keep competition a flourishing reality. . . .

It is not, however, with the provisions and interpretations of the Sherman Act that we laymen should be deeply concerned today, but with the underlying assumptions, "the picture in the mind," the philosophy for which that act stands as it is applied to large-scale undertakings. It is the economic and political philosophy behind it, affecting its present interpretation, that badly needs re-examination. It is by the new facts of 1952, in contrast to the essential facts about our country as it was a generation or two ago, that we need to judge whether Bigness should today be penalized or encouraged.

Is Bigness a good thing judged by economic standards—higher or lower costs to consumers, for example? Is it a good thing judged by its social consequences—does it hasten the wasting of our common natural resources of forests or mines, or does it serve to save and nourish them? Is Bigness a good thing for the average individual, not as a consumer of goods or a businessman or worker, but as a person—so that he is less fearful about his freedom, less subject to the arbitrary power of his boss or his government? Is Bigness a good thing for the nation's security, so it is better able to defend itself and defend its weaker friends against Communist aggression?

Weighed in the scales of such values as these, if (with appropriate safeguards) Bigness is a good thing, in 1952, then it is folly to cripple America and impede our progress by maintaining in full force the prejudices and penalties on size, and the economic and social opprobrium of 1890 and 1912 and 1933. If, on re-examination of the issue, it appears that Bigness is a great asset to us, then we need to have the courage and forthrightness to say so, to say why we so believe, and to adopt measures appropriate to that conviction.

This is particularly incumbent on liberals, we who have always insisted, wisely, that our policies must change with changing facts, that we must not cling to "horse-and-buggy" ideas in an automobile and jet-engine era.

What I am here discussing, and the changed policy I urge we examine, deals with some of the most fundamental things in our daily lives, with how we make our living, with the values we set for our individual lives, with the greatest productivity of our country not only in goods but in new ideas. I deal here with how we can best brace ourselves, industrially, against the great shock waves of organized tyranny that break against us in our no longer remote hemisphere.

The subject of Bigness, then, is not solely for the legal experts in anti-trust suits, and those well versed in economics. It concerns the direction of our lives and that of our children, the values we live by, the very shape of things to come.

Such fundamental re-examination is appropriate, indeed essential and vital, at a time like the present. In such a period of crisis and strain, of heart-searching and anxiety about basic things, we need to examine such an all-pervasive issue as this. If, by that inexplicable process of general public consensus by which Americans determine fundamental issues, we decide that Bigness is our ally, that its risk and dangers are now man-ageable and with wisdom can be surmounted, if we conclude to end this contradiction between our enjoyment of the fruits of Bigness and the sus-picions and penalties we visit on it, then in a decade we can accelerate our progress toward the goals of America in a way that takes one's breath away.

The wonders Bigness has been able to accomplish, despite having one hand tied behind its back, give some inkling of what benefits it could bring if we changed our policies and permitted and encouraged it to work with both hands.

Problem 25: Big Labor-- Can It Achieve Both Security and Industrial Peace?

Unionization of American labor has solved some problems, but has created new issues. Generally belonging to an earlier age are the ques-tions: Does labor have the right to organize? Are labor unions good or bad? Is labor a commodity, subject to the law of supply and demand? The least observant person now knows that unionized labor is a legalized fact of the American economy—despite the opposition to organization in new industrial regions—and that wages are determined at the plant or national level by collective bargaining, rather than through the operation of economic "law."

But still unanswered are such questions as: How can we humanize an industrial society, thus achieving the good as well as the abundant life? How can industrial peace be promoted without destroying employer-employee freedom? How can human personality and the dignity of the individual be preserved in an era of time clocks, production lines, and badge numbers? How can the consumer and management be protected against unions grown too powerful? What are the mutual rights and responsibilities of industry, labor, and government in American society? What are desirable long-range goals for labor? For management? For government? These issues, as yet only partially charted, are explored in this section.

HUMAN RELATIONS *

Oversimplified, the science of human relations is merely the Golden Rule writ large. Such nebulous doctrines have played but little part in traditional American labor policy, which has emphasized efficiency, financial incentives, and hard-handed supervision of the labor force. A shift away from this traditional policy is perhaps the most notable trend in labor-management relations during the past decade. Drawing heavily upon the findings of anthropology, sociology, and psychology, "enlightened" management has embarked upon experimental programs that are designed to create a happy, contented atmosphere within the industrial world. If widely adopted, such programs will revolutionize the American scene and pose new questions in the field of labor relations.

For instance, how should unions and their leaders react to management-sponsored programs of personnel counseling, loan services, and recreation? To the extent that such programs succeed, do they undermine union leadership? Do such programs actually pay? And who pays for them? Is this approach a frothy fringe benefit to be discarded at the first sign of widespread unemployment? Is social science

* *Time*, April 14, 1952, pp. 96–97. Courtesy *Time*, copyright Time, Inc., 1952.

being mobilized to exploit the workers? Or can this possibly be the American reply to the doctrine of class conflict? Finally, which incentive is the more effective—the carrot or the stick?

"If it were desired to reduce a man to nothing," wrote Fyodor Dostoevsky in *The House of the Dead,* ". . . it would be necessary only to give his work a character of uselessness." In the 20th century, such a character of uselessness was, in fact, imposed on much of the work done in American factories and offices. It was not a sudden occurrence; it was the result of a long historical process, sped by typical American haste and thoughtlessness.

The Industrial Revolution, which replaced the tools of the independent workmen with machines owned by lenders of capital, had transformed handicraftsmen who were their own bosses into hired hands subject to the orders of managers. Gradually, men felt themselves swallowed by a vast, impersonal machine, which rubbed away their self-respect and, in a way, their identities. In anger against this betrayal of the human spirit by the Industrial Revolution, millions of workers listened to the false promises of Marx's counterrevolution which, as Russia has proved, offered only greater loss of self-respect and, in the end, slavery.

Now a second Industrial Revolution, quieter but more profound, is sweeping through U.S. industry. Its name: Human Relations in Industry. Its purpose: to give the American worker a sense of usefulness and importance (and thus improve his work). Its goal (stated in one sentence); to make life more fun by making work more meaningful.

The Shovelers and the Spinners

. . . At a Pennsylvania textile plant where the labor turnover in one of the spinning departments was 41 times higher than elsewhere in the plant, efficiency experts in 1923 set up various wage incentives, yet production remained low and spinners kept quitting. When Elton Mayo was called in, he discovered the men were poor producers for a reason which had not occurred to anyone: they were unhappy. The machines had been set up so as to deprive the men of virtually all human contact with one another; lonely, they fell into melancholy and hypochondria. Mayo prescribed four daily rest periods when the workers could relax, brought in a nurse to whom they could complain. The change wrought by these two relatively minor steps was startling. Turnover immediately diminished; production for the first time reached the established quotas.

Four years later, something even more startling happened. At its Hawthorne Works near Chicago, Western Electric tried to determine the effects

of lighting on the worker and his output.   As a test, it moved a group of
girls into a special room with variable lighting, another group into a room
where lighting remained as before.   To its amazement, production shot
up in both rooms.   When the lighting was reduced in the first room, production continued to rise.   But it also kept rising in the second room.
Not until Mayo was called in to make tests of his own did the company discover what had happened.   The simple answer: both groups were producing more because they had been singled out for special attention.   The
excitement of the experiments made them feel they were no longer mere
cogs.

Mayo's Hawthorne experiments were widely hailed as a landmark in
social science.   Actually, they revealed nothing which could not have been
learned from any factory hand: every human being likes to feel that his
work is important, that the boss is interested in him, and appreciates what
he does.   In a sense, the importance attached to Mayo's findings is a measure of the indifference to people into which management has fallen in its
singleminded pursuit of Taylor's efficiency.   Because of this indifference,
the deep-rooted mutual interests of workers and management, as partners
in production, were lost in shallow attitudes of suspicion and hostility.
The folklore of each nourished a class warfare disturbingly like that which
Marx had predicated.

The Myths of Labor and Capital

In the accepted myths of hardheaded, hardfisted management, tender-
ness was weakness; workers could not be "coddled" lest they loaf; the
only drives to which they responded were greed (more money) or fear (of
dismissal).   To praise them was simply to invite increasing demands.
Workers, for their part, nursed long memories of hired spies who betrayed
their unions and of uniformed thugs (*e.g.,* "coal and iron police") who
smashed them.   In labor's mythology, management was a silk-hatted capitalist who automatically opposed anything good for the workingman; by
reflex, the worker opposed anything management favored.

For Mayo's new science to make headway in this charged atmosphere,
there had to be a great change in basic attitudes.   The change began with
the U. S. Supreme Court's 1937 decision upholding the Wagner Act; it
made management realize it had to learn to live with unions.   The change
was sped by World War II, which not only brought the patriotic necessity
for the U. S. industrial machine to achieve maximum output, but flooded
the labor force with millions of housewives and other new recruits relatively free of the old suspicions and hostilities.

Management began to learn that the once-feared unions themselves held potentials of higher production. In Pittsburgh, the United Steel Workers challenged one management to name its most productive department. Then the union boosted production there by 210% in a month. In the Toronto plant of Lever Brothers, union and management, working together, trimmed the payroll from 693 to 512, the wage bill by 17%, yet achieved greater output in a 40-hour week than in 48 before.

Moreover, housewives coming into war plants were amazed to discover that they could far exceed the normal output of old hands. At a big Cleveland war plant, one housewife found that she could easily produce 800 grenade pins daily, v. the plant quota of 500. When fellow workers warned her to slow down, she discovered another thing; old hands deliberately limited their output from fear that Taylor's time-and-motion study disciples would cut their pay rates by raising production quotas. More and more managers realized that maximum output could be realized only by finding ways to remove these old fears.

In dozens of plants, surveys of employees exploded the prize cliche of management's folklore—that workers wanted only more money. Actually, higher pay rated far down the list of workers' desires. For example, 100 shop workers who were polled by Psychologist S. N. F. Chant on twelve alternatives rated "high pay" as sixth. The Twentieth Century Fund found that wage disputes, the ostensible cause of 80% of all industrial conflicts, are only secondary causes: "Some of the industries most plagued by strikes . . . are among those where the highest wages are being paid." After ten years of polling workers, Elmo Roper concluded that their four chief desires are (1) security ("the right to work continuously at reasonably good wages"), (2) a chance to advance, (3) treatment as human beings, (4) dignity.

Yet the alarming fact, as agreed by all investigators, was that modern industry largely frustrates these desires. Detroit Edison, in a poll of its 11,000 employees found that 43% did not believe that the company was "really interested" in their ideas. After a study of the auto industry, Author Peter Drucker, management consultant, concluded that the average worker regards his status as frozen, with little hope of advancement, and hopes to keep his sons from doing the same work.

There was equal agreement on the causes of such widespread discontent and emotional frustration. Businesses had grown to such a size that the average worker lost all sense of personal contact with his employers. The constant increase in mechanization took away his sense of personal pride and self-identification with the final product; frequently he did not even know the use of the part he made. The robot nature of many tasks thwarted the craving for prestige; the hope of advancement was lost in the growing tendency to choose management material not from men up from the bench, but from young, college-trained technicians.

The New Managers

These discoveries came to a head at a time when U. S. management was best equipped to do something about them: management itself had undergone a revolution. Death and taxes had all but eclipsed the great owner-management dynasties epitomized by Carnegie, Ford and Rockefeller. In their place had come the professional managers, the engineer-trained technicians, *e.g.,* Du Pont's Crawford Greenewalt, General Electric's Philip Reed, General Motors' C. E. Wilson, Standard Oil's (N.J.) Frank Abrams. They took over industrial societies grown so huge that the average owner (*i.e.,* stockholder) seldom exercised more than theoretical control. Profits were still the test of efficiency, and a fair return to the stockholder a prime duty of management. But the tremendous diffusion of ownership enabled the professional manager to give first concern to the economic health of the whole corporate body, in which the welfare of workers was as vital as that of stockholders. Since increased welfare promised greater efficiency, the new managers welcomed experiments.

In Marion, Va., the Harwood Manufacturing Co., which had 600 employees, mostly women, making pajamas, discovered that whenever it changed the work, only one-third of the workers ever got back to their old output rate. Many others quit and most union grievances followed such changes. The company tried an experiment: one group was simply told of the change, another was told of the necessity for it and permitted to work out for itself the necessary revisions in quotas and rates. Result: its production quickly passed the old average of 60 hourly units per worker, and reached more than 80. The first group barely exceeded 50 units, and 17% of its members shortly quit. It also filed a complaint with the union that the new rate was "unjust," although investigations proved it generous. Yet when the survivors of this group were trained in the new way, they went up to a score of 73, within eight days.

At Detroit's Bundy Tubing Co., which had a history of ill will against the speed-up and fear of cuts in output rates, every attempt to boost production by special incentives had failed. The company offered the union a novel proposal: set a certain standard for labor costs, and let workers and management share all the savings when increased output drove costs below that figure. Not only did production beat all records, but the workers themselves began prodding slackers and berating absentees.

These lessons have borne fruit. In most big U.S. corporations, the new field of human relations is regarded as important, and equally as promising, as industrial research. Ford Motor Co. is spending millions to explore the untapped potentials of man. General Motors, the world's biggest industrial corporation, is drawing useful lessons from its World War II experience.

At one G. M. aircraft parts plant, the manager almost turned down the offer of a visit by a combat-scarred B-17 and crew; he feared it would disrupt production. Instead, output shot up, not because the workers were thrilled by the bomber, but because the maintenance crew told them for the first time what the parts they made were used for. Another G. M. plant, which had to train workers to make carbines, had each new employee shoot the actual carbine, take it apart to see the significance of the part he would make. Despite their lack of skill their output was high.

Other companies are tackling the problem of size and resulting loss of individual identity. Robert Wood Johnson, whose family's famed Johnson and Johnson had grown up as a huge plant at New Brunswick, N.J., decentralized much of it into small, new, ultra-modern factories, each making a single product line and small enough so that the president can usually call every worker by name. Not only has Johnson & Johnson been free of strikes, but the C.I.O. Textile Workers union is the first to praise its enlightened methods.

Many plants are encouraging their workers at self-government through broadening their corporate responsibilities. Parker Pen replaced the hated time-clock with an honor system, found that tardiness virtually vanished. The Commerce Trust Co. of Kansas City met the time loss from the morning "coffee rush" by providing free coffee.

A new concept of the rule of employers and employees in the corporation is being formed. Some examples: Pittsburgh's Wiegand Co. lends money, interest free, to employees who need it to buy homes, etc.; Allegheny Ludlum Steel holds "open houses" to let families see what their breadwinner does, and production goes up on visiting days; Weirton Steel now tags almost everything moving through the plant to let workers know what it will make.

The New Philosophy

Actually, far from being an occult science, human relations is nothing more than good will—and applied common sense. Much of it depends on simple things, such as making a plant more comfortable, and a friendlier place to work. Virtually every big company now sponsors plant bowling, baseball, dances, etc.; Westinghouse abets employee operettas, orchestras, picnics, even shows movies in its plants during lunch hours.

Yet that does not mean that every employer has seen the practical value of the new concept, or has accepted it. Some bitter-enders still regard any concession to the workers as a threat to their own authority. Others sometimes do more harm than good by doling out favors with an air of paternalism. Said one Kansas City industrialist: "We give our employees a Christmas party and that keeps 'em happy until we throw 'em a summer picnic." Still others have made the mistake of trying to create good human relations by mere words.

By and large the intent of this swiftly growing trend is not only genuine, but represents a movement toward an entirely new philosophy of management.

Nowhere has this new philosophy been better expressed than by General Foods' Chairman Clarence Francis at a postwar convention of the National Association of Manufacturers. Said Francis: "You can buy a man's time, you can buy a man's physical presence at a given place; you can even buy a measured number of skilled muscular motions per hour or day. But you cannot buy enthusiasm; you cannot buy initiative; you cannot buy loyalty; you cannot buy the devotion of hearts, minds and souls. You have to earn these things. . . . It is ironic that Americans—the most advanced people technically, mechanically and industrially—should have waited until a comparatively recent period to inquire into the most promising single source of productivity: Namely, the human will to work. It is hopeful, on the other hand, that the search is now under way."

In that search, at mid-century, lies the finest hope and promise of the Capitalist Revolution.

PRACTICAL AIMS AND PURPOSES OF AMERICAN LABOR *

What have labor unions achieved for their members on the American scene? What are their future objectives? These questions are answered below by one of labor's most powerful spokesmen, Walter Reuther, president of the Congress of Industrial Organizations.

We in the United Automobile Workers Union (Congress of Industrial Organizations) have worked hard in the vineyard of collective bargaining,

* Walter P. Reuther, *The Annals* of The American Academy of Political and Social Science, March, 1951, pp. 64–72.

and hundreds of thousands of workers and their families have won for themselves greater security and a richer, fuller life.

While our gains and achievements have been outstanding, we realize that collective bargaining is a never-ending struggle to make human progress. . . . There are still many problems unsolved and still many battles to be won before workers receive their full share of the fruits of American industry.

Changes Wrought by UAW-CIO

Perhaps the best way for me to discuss the practical aims and purposes of American labor is to recount some of the major achievements of the UAW-CIO, and some of its major goals and hopes for the future.

When our union was born fifteen years ago, working conditions in the automobile industry and the living standards of the workers in the industry were entirely different from the working conditions and living standards of the workers today. Workers had no job security. Old-age pensions financed by industry were, in most cases, not even a dream in those days. When a worker was too old to work but too young to die, he was dumped on the industrial scrap heap. Health plans, with hospital and medical coverage, and insurance programs were virtually unknown. There was no grievance procedure by which a worker could obtain redress for abuses suffered from supervision. There was no seniority system. Job security, layoffs, and recalls were determined by favoritism and what workers call "apple polishing." Paid vacations were unheard of. There was no overtime pay, no call-in pay, no paid holidays, and no night-shift premium.

The strength and solidarity of the UAW has brought about a great change. Our economic gains—higher wages, paid vacations, overtime, pensions, hospital-medical insurance program, and others—are important; but most important is the fact that we have won a measure of industrial democracy within our industries. We have won recognition of workers' rights. A worker is no longer a mere clock-card number; he is now a person—a human being, who can hold his head high and demand the respect and consideration to which he is entitled. We have in truth given substance to the old phrase, "the dignity of labor." . . .

UAW-CIO Basic Wage Policy

The UAW-CIO basic agreements, which now cover more than one million workers, translate into reality the economic and social principles which have been the foundation of the union's program during the last five years. They recognize that increased purchasing power—not just increased money wages—is the only basis for a higher standard of living. They recognize that workers have a right to a constantly improving standard of living and that they have a right to share in the benefits of greater production, made possible through technological progress, without additional human effort.

Our union was born out of the determination of the workers in our industry to build for themselves and their families a better life and a more secure future. The workers recognized that they could build a better world for themselves and their children only through the establishment of a powerful, militant, democratic, and progressive industrial union with the strength and vision to champion their cause.

Cost-of-Living Escalator Clause

Economically, the cost-of-living and annual wage improvement clauses in our contracts open up revolutionary new prospects for collective bargaining. . . .

Cost-of-living escalator clauses guarantee that economic gains won by our members will be worth their full face value at the grocery store. Inflation cannot rob them and their families of these gains. We have not forgotten that American wage earners during the period 1940 through 1950 won substantial money wage increases but little increase in purchasing power. Workers won in that period more than 50 cents per hour in their pay envelopes, but only 6 cents per hour increase in purchasing power at the grocery store.

Annual Wage Improvement Factor

The annual wage improvement factor in our agreements guarantees the workers a larger share in the benefits of the nation's technological progress. . . .

The recognition that technological progress rather than greater human effort through speed-up is the road toward higher living standards, and that wages can be increased without increasing prices, is of particular significance in the automobile industry and of historic importance in American industry in general.

While UAW-CIO contracts provide our membership with an increasing share of the nation's output, our workers still do not receive their full equity in our national economy. One of our next goals, when present contracts expire, will be to increase this equity by increasing the automatic annual improvement factor.

Taken together, the cost-of-living allowance and the annual wage improvement factor point the way toward creation of purchasing power for prosperity and full employment in the years ahead and bring nearer to balance the distorted wage-price-profit relationship that makes for economic instability and human insecurity. . . .

The development of our wage policy, on which we have made an important beginning, and the extension of our fundamental philosophy of progress with the community will be even more important in the future, because the impact of technological progress on production will be much greater in the future than in the past. The development of the science of electronics, the ultimate application of atomic power for peaceful purposes, and the development of other means of having machines do the work of men are opening whole new vistas of the possibility of greater human progress, provided we gear technical progress to the needs of all the people, rather than use it as a means whereby the wealthy few reap all the advantages and dictate the destinies and welfare of the many.

America, of all the nations in the world, has achieved the highest development of its economic resources and technical know-how. The world, however, will judge us, and we must judge ourselves, not by our technical progress, but by our ability to translate technical progress into human progress, human happiness, and human dignity. . . .

Under our five-year contracts, the million workers covered, since they are protected against the rise in the cost of living by the escalator clause, will have made during the five years a real economic gain of $2,700,000,000. If all of the 60 million gainfully employed people in America made comparable gains, they would gain $162 billion for the five-year period.

Old-Age Security

. . . The development of our complex industrial society has created many serious and challenging problems. One of the more serious and tragic problems resulted from the growing inability of millions of old workers and their wives to meet the cost of sustaining themselves in dignity and decency in the last years of their lives. Millions of old people who had worked hard all their lives, lived in constant fear of want and insecurity. Before the union won the job security of seniority protection, old workers were thrown on the industrial scrap heap after industry had robbed them of their youth and they could no longer keep up with the the speed of the lines.

Seniority protection stopped this inhuman practice, and older workers continued to work; but they also continued to grow old, and we had to meet the problem of giving workers security when they reached the age when they rightfully should be able to retire. This problem had to be met by having the corporation provide an adequate old-age pension to supplement the inadequate federal social security payments. . . .

Principles of a Sound Pension Plan

The Ford pension agreement was not only among the first pension plans won through collective bargaining in any mass production industry, but it was the first pension plan negotiated in which the three basic principles necessary to a sound pension plan were established.

1. It is a noncontributory plan (company to pay entire cost of pension).

2. Pension payments guaranteed by an actuarially sound pension trust fund into which the company is required to make payments to cover the cost of past as well as future service credits for all workers.

3. Joint board of administration to administer the plan, with equal representation from the union and the company. . . .

Take Price Tag Off Good Health

One of the tragic facts of life is that we in America have learned to split the atom, but we have not yet learned to care for people in times of illness and in cases of accident. The wealthiest nation in the world has permitted prohibitive economic barriers to deny millions of people needed hospital and medical care.

Many children grow up handicapped for life because their parents just could not afford to give them the benefits of modern medical care. Millions of workers and their families live in a state of fear and insecurity because the threat of illness or accidental injury hangs over their heads. Many a family has scraped and saved to get a few dollars laid aside to put the children through school or to buy a home, and one serious illness or accident has wiped out its life savings and destroyed its dreams.

The UAW-CIO understood the need for, and took up the fight to win, protection for workers and their families against the economic hazards of catastrophic sickness and accidents. . . .

At present, more than a million workers are covered by hospitalization and surgical programs in which the companies pay for one-half or more of the cost of such care for both the worker and his family. Our achievements in this field are substantial, and we have made a good beginning. We intend, however, to press forward both through collective bargaining and through legislation to remove the price tag completely from good health and to eliminate the economic hazards of sickness and accidents.

Sickness and Disability Insurance.

When sickness or accident strikes the breadwinner of a family, its members have not only the cost of hospital care to worry about, but the additional problem of loss of the weekly pay check. To meet this problem we have been working to provide more weekly sickness and disability benefits to the wage earner during periods of illness. The UAW-CIO has contracts covering nearly 1¼ million workers which provide for weekly sickness and disability benefits from $28 to $45 per week for a period of 13 to 52 weeks. The great majority of the covered workers get more than $32 for 26 weeks.

In this field we have laid a solid foundation upon which we can build larger benefits and greater protection to the worker and his family in the years ahead.

Life Insurance

As a part of our pension programs, we succeeded in getting the companies to meet the cost of a paid-up life insurance policy for workers on retirement. In recent collective bargaining agreements, we have both increased the amount of coverage and reduced the cost of such coverage to the worker by getting the companies to pay a larger share. Selling workers' insurance continues to be a very profitable business. Millions of dollars in profits and commission—all kinds of kickback arrangements where corporations get rebates from the insurance companies—are being paid for by our members in their part of the cost of their insurance. . . .

At the coming UAW-CIO convention, I propose to recommend to the delegates that they vote to authorize the International Executive Board to take appropriate steps to establish a UAW-CIO nonprofit insurance company to meet this problem.

Guaranteed Annual Wage

The most fundamental long-range economic problem faced by people in a free society is to find a way to maintain full employment and full protection, balanced by full and equitable distribution of the wealth created.

It is tragic that we have learned to solve the problem of unemployment in war, forging the weapons of destruction, but as yet we have not been able to provide jobs for everyone producing the things for a good life in peace. In 1939 we had approximately 9,000,000 unemployed, and in the early part of 1950 we had approximately 4,000,000 jobless. War and preparation for war solved the problem. Our basic problem flows from the fact that the tools of modern technology make it possible to create abundance, but the people have lacked the purchasing power to balance our productive power. The Great Depression following the crash of 1929 saw poverty and hunger in the midst of plenty.

We in America know how to split the atom. We must learn how to feed people when there is enough to eat. We must learn how to provide a job for every adult able and willing to work at wages geared to the wealth our economy creates. To find tools to do this job is part of the job of our union. It is a challenge to the vision and imagination of free men in every phase of our economic life. . . .

The guaranteed annual wage is next on our schedule in the UAW-CIO and certainly it constitutes one of the most important tools in finding the answer to full and continuous employment in a free society.

The guaranteed annual wage is more than a matter of economic justice to the wage earner; it is a matter of economic necessity to our nation, for freedom and unemployment cannot live together in democracy's house. Since a worker and his family must eat and be housed and clothed throughout twelve months of the year both logic and economic necessity demand that he should receive an annual wage. Corporation executives get paid by the year; why not a worker? . . .

This is a fundamental issue. The stakes are high, the obstacles great, and the fight will be hard; but I am confident that we have the will, the strength, the courage, and the basic understanding of the problem to win this further milestone in our forward march to a happier, more secure tomorrow.

Political Action and Legislation

Politics is the everyday housekeeping job of democracy. In a democratic society, politics is the people's business. Two basic problems confront labor in the field of political action:

1. We must do the practical day-to-day organizational work necessary to mobilize people and get them to register and then get them out to vote on election day. We must break down the indifference that millions of people have with respect to discharging their responsibility as democratic citizens. At a time when freedom and democracy are being threatened by the forces of Communist tyranny, millions of Americans still do not carry their part of democracy's responsibilities by getting out to vote on election day. In 1946, only 35,875,000 people voted out of a potential 91,634,000; in 1948, only 48,834,000 people out of 93,941,000; in 1950, only 42,324,000 people out of 96,753,000.

2. We must carry on a comprehensive educational campaign to develop an understanding among the people of the basic issues on which political decisions are being made and where the interest of the people lies. Millions of workers have not yet learned the relationship between the bread box and the ballot box. Millions of housewives have not yet learned that their failure to help fill the ballot boxes of America with good votes is in-

separably related to their problem of keeping their ice boxes filled with good food. . . .

The major items on our legislative agenda are: (1) effective price control and a fair tax program; (2) expanded social security; (3) national health program; (4) repeal of Taft-Hartley Law; (5) civil rights program; (6) adequate housing; (7) federal aid to education; (8) foreign policy program to strengthen America in the face of Communist aggression and to work with the free peoples of the world to win the peace.

NOT BY BREAD ALONE *

As this suggests, Professor Tannenbaum considers the modern labor union as far more than an economic bargaining agency. Status, and even the reconstitution of society, are perhaps more basic union functions than the routine, periodic arguments with employers over wages, hours, and working conditions. Viewed in this light, unions and the "new" management are both primarily engaged in the work of human relations. This assumption, in turn, poses several interesting queries. If man cannot live by bread alone, who is to supply his other needs? Can unions or management best supply status, a feeling of belonging, an ethical quality to economic relations that has hitherto been lacking? Or, do both groups aspire to roles they are ill-prepared to fill, over-emphasizing the worker-job relationship? Cannot such aspects of life as status be best supplied by the family, the community, the school, and the church?

The trade union is the conservative force of our time. It is conservative because, while endlessly bargaining, compromising, and battling for more pay, it is pushing to restore certain old values—self-respect, fellowship, and security—that men need in their work. These values were largely lost after the Industrial Revolution flung labor from field to factory, replaced the village with the city, and the master craftsman with the modern corporation.

Big industrialism can offer bread, or at best cake, but it has proved inadequate to meet the ethical and moral needs of men; the union, with all of its faults, may yet save the corporation, and the efficiency that goes with it. The unions are building their own natural "society," their own cohesive

* This article, based on Frank Tannenbaum's book, *A Philosophy of Labor* (Knopf, 1950), originally appeared in the April 11, 1950, issue of *The Reporter*.

labor force, which endows its members with a sense that they count, that they will be helped by their fellows in times of hardship. All real societies have possessed these values—values that give some ethical substance to man on his journey from the cradle to the grave. From this point of view, the challenge to management by the trade union is salutary and hopeful. It is the route—perhaps the only one—for saving our democratic society, and our contemporary industrial system as well. In some way, labor must achieve a genuine partnership with management and share more and more responsibility with it.

For the union is not an instrument against society; it is an additional way of organizing society, not merely as to its labor, but in all of its other forms. When a trade-union movement comes into being, the politics, the economy, the family, the morals, the status of men among men, the motivation and the ends, the very means of survival as we have formerly known them are modified.

The change that the trade union is making in the structure and spirit of our industrial community is world-wide in scope. Of course differences, and important ones, exist from country to country, but they are outweighed by similarities that are growing more visible every day.

What the change amounts to is a new pattern of industrial relations, which can be recognized as readily as the corporation, the trust, or the cartel. Its hallmark is the use of collective bargaining as the immediate instrumentality for easing the frictions, and adjusting the day-by-day differences, between labor and management. The end of this process is not industrial quietude; that is not to be had. But labor and management can achieve an acceptable way of dealing with the inevitable friction. The objective is a system of rules for resolving the differences that arise a thousand times a day in any concern. The object is to make strikes unnecessary by keeping the friction within a body of "common law" to which both sides subscribe.

Collective bargaining is now so far-reaching and widespread that basic questions constantly come up about it: Does it serve to protect the consumer against price gouging or lay him open to it? Does it help maintain full employment, sustain the pace of our technological improvements, and narrow the swing between inflation and deflation? Does it safeguard the individual against the loss of the freedoms which together make up democracy?

Anything for Security

All these concerns have become involved in the worker's search for "economic security" and his anxiety to hold on to it as the one certitude in a world where all else is confusion. His personal security is increasingly identified in his own mind with union security, the guarantee that his union can continue to exist in his plant—unmolested by outside attempts to break it up. It is the worker's sense of an identity between his own security and that of the union which accounts for the fact that seventy-seven per cent of the fifty thousand collective agreements in U.S. industry contain union-security provisions, such as the closed shop and the union hiring hall.

The quest for economic security is hardly confined to the union member. The harsh reality of our day is that when almost all men depend upon the money wage as their only resource, they are all subject to the threat of insecurity for which as individuals they have no remedy. It is this which explains the proposal of Senator Ives of New York for a universal hundred-dollar monthly pension for the aged. It explains the "Fair Deal" of President Truman, and the "socialism" of the British Labour Party, as well as the ever-increasing demands of the unions for old-age and retirement pensions.

All these derive logically from the disappearance of any source of real income for the majority of people. When most families lived on the land in whole or in part, they had (except for drought, earthquake, flood, insect blights, livestock epidemics, and other acts of God) a certain amount of economic security. They could raise their own food, build their own shelter, and weave their own clothing: This was real income.

The Tyranny of Cash

But the dweller in an urban industrial society has to have cash. Historically, this changeover from the real income of soil and handicraft to the money income of the mill and the mine coincided with the birth of a "contract" society and the death of a "status" society.

Under a society of "contract," a man is free to arrange, with anyone he can find, to sell his skill, his labor, or his goods for whatever price he can get. He can make a deal with an employer for his services, or with a merchant for his wares. If the two parties do not continue to agree, either can withdraw from the arrangement after a time, voiding their "contract."

The employee can look for another job, and the customer for another supplier. By contrast, in a society of "status," a person's economic condition is fixed, set within a hierarchy which is a stepladder on which he occupies always the same step. The serf and the guild member had security, but no freedom.

For both the serf and his successor, the freeholder, either the family (the full, extended family rather than the truncated family of today) or the local community acted as the natural "social-security" agency in times of emergency or misfortune. They took care of the orphan, the aged, the weak, and the sick, even as the guild took care of its members.

The free man of early and later capitalism had to face disaster on his own. His only source of income was the money wage, always precarious and unstable. The very onset of industrialism had destroyed the family, the village community, the parish, to which the serf and the freeholder had always turned in time of trouble.

To overcome this insecurity, the trade union from the first has sought to take control of the job away from the employer. Today it is the union which more often than not acts as the labor-supplying agency, and prescribes rules for hiring and firing. And as long as the union can limit the number of workers it will admit to membership, and at the same time insist upon membership as a condition of getting or keeping a job, it can effectively regulate the career of every union member in the factory, or even in the industry.

The courts have adjudged unions to be voluntary associations, but, actually, they possess compulsory power over both employer and employee. They are, in effect, private lawmaking bodies. Their rules influence the lives of millions of workers and thousands of industrial plants. A new and unsuspected issue has therefore come into being. It is the power of the union, as the disburser of job opportunities, to specify the place of the worker within his organization, and within the factory and industry where he makes his living.

Guilds—Old and New

Without intent or plan, proceeding always on the assumption that all men are free and equal before the law, the union is integrating the workers into what amounts to a series of separate social orders. It is re-creating a society based on status, and destroying the society based on contract. After a strange interlude of a hundred and fifty years, during which man existed without most of his age-old associations, the unions are developing a new system of "estates," which satisfies social and psychological, as well as economic, needs. In essential content and contours, they are like the old-time guilds.

If the historical record has any meaning, a sense of identity among men engaged in a common craft, trade, industry, or occupation is a "natural," or, better, an organic relationship to their function. There were guilds in India in 600 B.C.; in China at least a thousand years ago; they were prevalent in ancient Japan, widely scattered in the Islamic world, Greece, Rome, and the Europe of the Middle Ages and beyond. Wherever they have appeared, they had these features in common: They sought to control the labor supply. They specified the conditions (fees, dues, portions, apprenticeship) for entrance into a particular craft. They regulated wages, hours, quality, methods of work, and the tools used for it. Each was determined to protect its own job territory against the unfair competition of outsiders, of "foreigners," of non-guild members.

In medieval Europe every guild was a recognized and respected element in the community equation of manorial village and town. Every guild had its own saint, its own festivals, its own powers, its own laws, and its own mysteries, or skill secrets. (In England, the guild itself was often called the "mystery": "Artificers and men of mysteries shall each choose his own mystery before the next Candlemas, and having so chosen it he shall henceforth use no other," a fourteenth-century law says.)

The guild could enforce its decisions by means of boycott against a merchant who charged too high a price for imported materials; or a strike against a tax that discriminated against its members; or political pressure upon the community council; or ostracism of a member who did not live up to guild rules. (This last is still, of course, an effective tactic. James C. Petrillo, President of the American Federation of Musicians, recently said: "I don't know where he [the expelled musician] would get a job today. An expulsion is a very serious matter for a man who is making a living with his instrument.")

To belong to a guild was to belong to an order in an orderly life, to be part of a coherent pattern, to have place, face, and clearly-defined rights matched by clearly-defined responsibilities; and all of these were sustained by a sense of identity with the group, which protected one against competition, illness, and old age, and buried one honorably by intoning its own ritual along with the prayers of the priest.

The Isolated Man

The Industrial Revolution melted down the society of "status." Instead of fixity, it brought about mobility; instead of narrow, secure life-stations; wide, dangerous opportunities. Instead of clusters of human beings held together by tradition and function, there was a new isolated man, thrown upon his own resources. He was economically independent, but helpless in contracting or making a bargain for the sale of his labor-power to the employer. He was morally free, but adrift, without group supports and safeguards, on his own.

The source and symbol of this change from the group man of feudalism to the atomized individual of capitalism was the substitution of a money wage for the real wage. Under the manorial system, dues and services

were paid in produce and in labor, especially among the agricultural population.

Even as late as the mid-seventeenth century, the guildsman himself was
still partially attached to the land. He had his garden plot, and grazing
rights for his cattle. The baker and draper, the ironmonger and tanner,
were not a people apart. They did not depend for their income entirely
on the money wage. In hard times, they could always fall back upon the
subsistence security of the soil.

But when the Industrial Revolution drew men, women, and children
from farm and village into the mill, into the urban slum, it left them on
their own to find the good life previously provided by their organic connection with the land, the guild, the parish. More important, under the
new dispensation labor was paid for by a money wage.

For the masses of men, this new liberty to choose a master was not liberation but anarchy. The idea was that the right thing for every man was to
put his own financial gain first, that the race went to the swift and the
strong, to the upward-clawing and the ruthless. A few could use the new
freedom and the new equality to amass fortunes, build careers in politics.
But for the many, this new freedom and equality proved bitter and burden-
some.

The worker at the power loom was not an artisan. He was a name to
his foreman. He had lost not only the creative fulfillment of his handicraft,
but also his personality. He had no sense of participation in a larger purpose. He had no land to tide him over slack times; no guild to pay him
sickness allowance, to insure his regular employment. He had only his
ability to get and hold a job, to sell his labor and in exchange for it receive
shillings, francs, dollars. And as manufacturing units grew larger, the
gulf between employer and employee widened. The worker had less and
less contact with the boss, who determined the money wage, who hired
and fired, promoted and demoted, raised pay or cut it.

On the whole, the worker was powerless to modify the conditions of his
job. He had nothing except what he had in common with other workers:
the same employer, the same shop, the same foreman, the same factory
whistle. Gradually, a common setting made strangers companions. They
worked together along the same pit seam, and used the same tools to
subdue and shape materials. And as mechanization led to a complex
division of labor, they depended on each other more and more. A new
sense of identity was forged as workers congregated at building sites, in
mines, or in factories.

The process of atomization, the doctrine that each man stands or falls
alone, was reversed by the simple act of men working together. While
their lack of power as individuals was always apparent, their collective

strength was soon discovered. In time, they developed their own codes, their own lexicon, their own body of doctrine.

The original organizer of the trade-union movement is the shop, the mine, the plant, and the industry. It is not the theorist, the agitator, the orator, the professional missionary. They merely proclaim, each in his way, an already existing fact. The labor leader does not instill grievances; he merely articulates those already there.

The union represents the repudiation of the idea that labor is only a commodity, and that every man can be sufficient unto himself. It represents the striving to achieve a sense of unity with others, to belong, to participate, to share in a common cause, that men working together always find, because they need these feeling-attitudes, because they could not do without them.

It is these non-material motivations of unionism—its capacity to meet aspirations toward human dignity and self-respect, its creation of a real team—that accounts for its pivotal power in the modern world. That power is enabling unionism to foster a new system of human relationships which profoundly alters the substance and the standards of a free society, born and nurtured by a free-market economy.

Today, when membership in the union so often precedes the chance to work, when every union has its own rules of admission, dues, assessments, wage and promotion schedules, pensions and other benefits, then every union becomes in effect a differentiated order within the community. Like the guild before it, it endows its own members with rights and immunities shared only among themselves. Moreover, it is difficult and even impossible to leave the union since penalties for desertion are severe. The worker not only risks loss of a particular job, with its accretion and seniority and promotion rights, and retirement benefits; he also narrows the range of opportunity for finding a new job.

Unionism is thus developing a system of status in which the place and prerogatives of today's worker are becoming as firmly fixed in custom and precedent as were those of a cooper in medieval Lincoln or Lyons.

The theory that this status is voluntarily assumed makes little difference in practice. The penalties for not accepting this "voluntary" status can hardly be avoided. Actually, this institution of status already prevails throughout a vast number of industries, occupations, and professions. It includes barbers and steelworkers, musicians and airplane pilots, chorus girls and merchant seamen.

It should be noted that the growth of these "stratifications" is defended in the name of freedom, equality, and justice. But these have here only a functional rather than a political or civil context. They relate to rights and rules on the job.

In for Life

To be sure, the worker is free in that he can always resign; but where will he go if he does quit? Any other post he may acquire is likely to be less advantageous. Union seniority will impede his admission to a job of comparable earnings and expectancy. If he moves from one industry to another, he will stand to lose his accumulated priorities and privileges. If he moves from one plant to another, even in the same industry, the seniority and other rules still stand against him.

What is really involved is that the worker is changing a contract terminable at will, the contract of the free, mobile, independent individual, to a contract terminable only at death.

This is a result of the trade union's unceasing efforts to help the worker escape from a pecuniary, impersonal, and fluid relationship to his job. The trade union's every activity is a protest against such practices of a purely free-market economy. The whole trend of collective bargaining today is to expand the area in which men's lives are dominated by the "surety" of status and to shrink the area in which they are governed by the "liberty" of contract.

At the same time that the union seeks to buttress the economic security of the worker, it strengthens the idea that the work and the man belong to each other. It affirms—and management increasingly accepts—the concept that the connection between a worker and his job cannot be defined purely in monetary and temporary terms. It is reassuring that the human being at work must in some degree be allowed to feel that he has a share, a "concern"—in the old Quaker sense of the word—a concern with the future of the enterprise.

All this explains why, to the surprise of classical economists, the union insists on behaving as if it had a permanent stake in the business or industry. Even the quarrels over who gets what, the division of company income, testify to this fact.

The union quarrels over something that seems to belong to both owners and workers. If the workers are going to quarrel over the division of the yield, then they must in time, out of self-interest, become concerned with the production of the yield.

The claim that wages could be raised without raising prices, even when advanced purely for propaganda purposes, belongs in the same category. It recognizes the nexus between wages and prices, and between wages and operating costs, and so focuses the workers' attention upon output.

The recent growth of demands for an annual wage merely highlight this ever-increasing sense of interdependence between a union and a company. It is clear, indeed, that an annual wage can only be derived from a stable and profitable enterprise, and that it can be regularly sustained only if workers assume their responsibility for keeping the enterprise stable and profitable, and share with management some of the problems and the burdens of improving quality, increasing quantity, and cutting costs.

The same principle applies to the new demands for social security; for if, as the President's Fact-Finding Board suggested in the steel dispute of 1949, industry is to become the source, the primary source, of the worker's social security, if industry is to become responsible for the total well-being of its employees, then the latter have a very direct and continuing stake in the total well-being of the industry. For the proposal of the Board, which in its implications marks a new departure in the U.S. industrial relations pattern, is that a new program of social security, to be paid for by industry, with the blessing, if not the active support, of government, is now to be inaugurated. In broad outlines, this proposal has been adopted by the automobile, telephone, rubber, and other industries, even if in modified form. If it becomes more widespread it will hasten a vital change in our economic system, for it will in effect do much to freeze a worker in his job, and make his mobility all but meaningless.

Up till now, labor, in theory and in fact, has been mobile, for the contract on both sides could be disolved at will. The proposal set forth by the Presidential Steel Board amounts, in effect, to giving up the idea of mobility—a suggestion not intended by the Board—even though this will be the result of putting its precepts into action. For if industry is now to assume the obligation to provide the worker and his family with medical care, maternity and sickness insurance, retirement pensions, and many related benefits, his current wage will thus become only a part of his total income, and a decreasing part at that, as his years of service lengthen. If he wants to change his job, he will forfeit some very real and substantial material gains.

Basic to this whole doctrine is the unconscious substitution of the temporary contract for a life contract. To be sure, there is nothing novel or startling in this idea; its essence was explicit in John L. Lewis's first demand for a five-cent royalty per ton of coal. But the official acceptance of it is very new—and very far-reaching. It implies a good deal more than the immobilization of labor. It implies the identification of the worker's life-long interests with the fortunes of a company or an industry in which his lot happens to be cast. The future of the steel workers will be formally and irretrievably identified with the profits and losses of the owners of the coal mines; and the same will hold true of the textile, women's wear, rubber, automobile, and other workers.

Deep into Management

As the worker's concern for the prosperity and stability of his industry increases he will become more involved psychologically in the source of his livelihood. For unless his industry prospers, it will not be able to meet the demands on it, not only for the present but also in the future. This means a basic change in the mental-set of the worker, in his whole approach to "management," to the "company," to the "industry." This change, in turn, will vastly transform the role and functioning of the trade union. It will have to abandon the psychology and apparatus of combat and replace these by active and constructive co-operation with management.

All this would seem to imply a motivation, on the part of the unions, to get deeper into the issues of management. Actually the union is being pushed, usually without knowing why, into an increasing range of managerial activities by its original commitment to stabilize the security of its members. Its responsibilities increase with its growing powers. If the union agreed permanently to limit its field of activities, it would admit that it was an intruder, an outsider. But it is not; it is part of the industry; it is the other side of management.

The union is getting into management in an even more tangible way. Through its dues, it has become a repository of large and continuously growing funds. It has, in fact, like the insurance companies, become a semi-public savings--institution.

Some of these funds, logically enough, should be reinvested in the industry from which they are drawn. For the union cannot insist upon greater participation in, and concern for, the industry, except upon a proprietary basis. Some unions, like the United Automobile Workers, have bought into as many as sixty-eight companies with which they have collective agreements.

Thus a new source of industrial investment is being opened up at the very time when large private funds for new capital investment are dwindling. Hidden in the growth of trade unionism, then, is the re-establishment of the worker's interest in the industry from which he draws his living. If the worker has a pecuniary interest, he will also have to assume the moral responsibilities that go with it—responsibility for the property he owns, the work he does, the quality he produces.

The whole developing situation is often lost sight of in the persistent argument over wages, as if the union's role was chiefly occupied with pecuniary income. That is not the case. The economic ends are undeniable, but so are the purposes embraced by membership in a "society," and by the broad ethical objectives which define the conditions of the good life. The form the argument between management and labor takes is in some ways irrelevant to the inner bent of the union. Each separate dispute is over a specific issue. The underlying drive is increased participation in management, because whatever management does has a bearing not merely upon the future economic security of the members and the future role of the union, but also upon the undefinable but very real sense of membership in a going concern. The union may talk the language of the market, and be obsessed by economic objectives. That is part of the milieu as given, and it is a language both labor and management understand. But the underlying theme is the drive for moral status within the industry. A commitment to spend one's life in a job without moral status would be intolerable —equivalent to slavery.

<hr />

HOW TO PREVENT "NATIONAL EMERGENCY" STRIKES *

Americans are now generally agreed that the right to strike must be curtailed in some sections of our complex economy. The exact area embraced by "national emergency industries" is as yet ill-defined, however. To achieve industrial peace with justice, says the author, we must approach labor problems at two levels. First, there must be an improvement of the direct relations between labor and management and a further development of measuring rods to determine what is fair in this relationship. Second, government must take action to prevent strikes that truly threaten the national welfare. Mr. Raskin analyzes this dual program and offers devices and alternate solutions that might be employed to implement it.

Strikes and prospective strikes in steel, oil, railroads, aluminum, coal, communications and other basic industries have set the country off on a frantic new search for ways to keep labor-management conflict from undermining the national safety.

Congress, which has been busy looking the other way since it passed the Taft-Hartley Act as an answer to all labor problems five years ago, is trying hard to avoid anything fundamental in this election year. That probably is just as well because remedies adopted under the pressure of national emergencies seldom prove of lasting benefit. The urge is to "do something"—not necessarily something constructive. . . .

In one sense we are clearly making headway: unions and industry no

* A. H. Raskin, *The New York Times Magazine*, May 11, 1952, pp. 1, 55, 56, 58, 59.

longer fight with guns.   A major strike used to mean bloodshed and death;
now the picket lines are so placid that the strikers bring along portable
radios and listen to the ball games while they march.   But the fact that the
hand-to-hand fighting is gone does not mean that there is less bitterness between the parties—and it does not mean that strikes are less destructive in
their economic consequences.   On the contrary, our progress out of the
"armed warfare" stage of labor relations simply reflects the fact that unions
have become so big and so well entrenched in most basic industries that employers have recognized the futility of trying to keep plants operating in a
strike.

That does not mean everyone is fighting.   In the midst of the present
turmoil, there are great areas of calm—industries in which unions and employers have entered into harmonious wage agreements and are working
out their problems on a cooperative basis.   General Motors, once a bitter
battleground, is flourishing under a five-year peace pact that has protected
its workers against the impact of higher living costs and enabled them to
share in the fruits of increased industrial output.   In the textile and clothing
industries, hit by a slump in sales, unions are helping promote a revival by
refraining from new wage demands.

The advocates of class hatred on both sides are being pushed into the
ash can.   There is no 1952 labor counterpart of such revolutionary organizations as the old I.W.W., which called strikes with happy abandon and
was frankly dedicated to the overthrow of the bosses.   Communist influence is at low ebb and the few unions that remain under Communist
control hold their members by masking, rather than flaunting, their mili-
tancy.   On the employer side, even the most unreconstructed of the rugged
individualists have given up hope that they can ever run their plants without a union.

The underlying causes of strife are stubbornly embedded in our industrial
fabric.   They stem from mutual fear and distrust, from basic disagreements
on social, economic and political philosophy and from the absence of any
firm standards for determining what is fair in collective bargaining.

Too many unions are still oppressed by the belief that employers wish
to destroy them and too many employers by the fear that unions are out
to capture command of industry, provided they do not bankrupt it first.

The veneer of union-management amity cracks away at contract-writing
time.   Memories of old injustices inflame the minds of the negotiators; they
are back in the primordial ooze, ready to fight through again all the battles
that carried organized labor from the status of a criminal conspiracy a little
over a century ago to a membership of more than 15,000,000 today.

This fundamental hostility is aggravated by the absence of any mutually
acceptable yardsticks for deciding what is too little and what is too much

in a collective bargaining contract. Both sides bob and weave like fly-weight boxers when it comes to finding economic arguments for or against wage increases. When the business cycle is on the upgrade, labor leans heavily on "ability to pay." When the trend turns down, "inability to pay" becomes the principal shield on the employer side.

What can be done about improving things? The first thing to decide is whether our goal is to reduce strikes or to wipe them out. If we ever reach the "idyllic" state in which there are no strikes, we will probably discover we have acquired something much worse in the process. There is nothing impossible about eliminating strikes, but it is impossible to do it without a tyrannical concentration of power in the hands of government, industry or labor. Even if strikes were a hundred times more costly than they are, none of these would offer an acceptable way out.

There are other situations in which the preservation of industrial "peace" may be more unhealthy than open warfare. Powerful unions and employers, collaborating to restrict competition and inflate prices, are often in a position to buy peace at the expense of the public. From the standpoint of democratic values, such "cordial" relationships are as noisome as amity imposed through company domination of a supine union, union domination of a supine company or government domination of both.

What is needed in labor, as in international affairs, is not merely peace but peace with justice. And there must be enough justice to take care of the worker, the employer and the community as a whole.

The search for this Golden Rule in industrial relations must be carried forward at two levels. One is an improvement in the direct relations between labor and management and in the measuring rod they use to determine what is fair; the other is a program of government action to protect the nation against strikes so acute that they must be halted. In long-range terms, the first is the important one. The second is not a solution; it is simply a necessary safeguard in the absence of a solution.

There is no shortcut to good faith and mutual trust. It is the laborious product of living and working together and it can wither under a single cold blast of intemperance from either side. An angry remark or an indiscreet threat made in the excitement of a bargaining conference may poison the atmosphere in a plant for years.

A comprehensive analysis by the National Planning Association of the causes of industrial peace in factories with outstandingly good records highlights some of the elements that could promote sounder relations in all branches of industry. The companies involved gave full acceptance to collective bargaining, considered a strong union an asset and made no effort to interfere in the union's internal affairs.

The unions, for their part, proceeded on the basis that the welfare of their members depended on the prosperity of the business. Both sides took a "problem centered" approach to negotiations, spending more time on working out concrete problems than on arguing about "prerogatives" or abstract principles. Grievances were settled promptly and the unions functioned as two-way channels of communication between employers and employees.

There is nothing rare about such relationships. They exist in thousands of plants that have contracts providing machinery for arbitrating disputes that arise during the life of the agreement.

Substituting science for double talk in wage negotiations is a tougher problem. The General Motors formula, which has been adopted by many other companies, represents the closest approach to a scientific yardstick for wages that has yet been devised. It provides for automatic adjustments in pay scales when living costs go up or down. It also guarantees the G.M. workers a fixed increase in living standards each year over and above the changes in living costs. This increase of 4 cents an hour reflects the general improvement in the productivity of all American industry and is not tied to how much is produced by the individual G.M. workers. This gets away from the hated "speed-up" which made many workers fear they were working themselves out of a job when they worked under an incentive pay scale. . . .

What can Government do to safeguard the public without pulling the rug out from under the bargaining process? It can provide skilled mediators to assist in bringing about an agreement. More funds and more personnel for this important service is one area of helpfulness. But the effectiveness of mediators has been undercut by the assignment of disputes powers to the W.S.B. [Wage Stabilization Board] and by the increased tendency of the White House to take a direct hand in crucial disputes. In most big controversies mediation has become just a marking time period to be hurdled as swiftly as possible on the march to Washington. Even the most expert mediator can be no help under such conditions.

The important thing, from the standpoint of collective bargaining and the dignity of the mediation service, is to return to a situation in which Government intervention will not be automatic but will be confined to those situations that are genuinely essential to the national welfare. Government should not be used to help or hurt either side; it should not get in at all unless public necessity makes a strike unthinkable. The country has stood a lot of strikes in its time without cracking. In the year after V-J Day there were times when it appeared everybody was on strike, but our economy was resilient enough to stand it, even though we had been through a war that kept civilian goods off the market for four years. In a period of rearmament our ability to sustain crippling strikes is obviously less great, but there is reason to suspect that it is not nearly so limited as some of our recent gyrations might denote.

The reason for a "go slow" policy on Government intervention is that there is no way the Government can step in that will not torpedo collective bargaining. Four courses of possible action suggest themselves, and every one has bad features.

The first is an eighty-day no strike injunction of the type provided by the Taft-Hartley Act. This simply restrains the union; it does nothing to provide a possible basis for settlement. If it had been used in steel, the sole effect would have been to start the strike a month earlier. When it did start, the President would have had no further remedy to draw upon under the law.

The second is Federal seizure of plants, mills or mines. Even if this were based on specific legislative authority, it is a dubious expedient. If the President alters wages and working conditions during the seizure period, he reduces the pressure on the union to enter into a settlement and thus permit restoration of the property to its private owners. If the *status quo* is maintained and the old management continues to draw the profits and exercise the prerogatives of management, the whole operation becomes a fraud upon the workers who are barred from striking. It worked in wartime, but the restiveness on the railroads indicates it wears thin in a period of limited emergency that may last a lifetime.

The third is fact-finding recommendations of the type handed down by the W.S.B. in steel. The historic battle over the steel decision makes it plain that this is not the answer. For one thing, the refusal of the union to consider any modification in the board's report punctured the never-too-widely-held notion that the recommendations were advisory guideposts, rather than mandates. For another, the tripartite nature of the board, with the public, labor and industry equally represented, proved a handicap in the exercise of its judicial function. Many observers feel the decision would have had a much better chance of ultimate acceptance by both sides if the public members had not been obliged to get the support of either labor or industry for a majority report.

The fourth is fact-finding by a special panel appointed by the President and consisting exclusively of public members. To overcome the limitations that deprived the W.S.B. of much of its chance to make an acceptable settlement in steel, the special panel should have authority to make recommendations affecting both the price and wage aspects of the dispute. So long as we have controls, it is foolish to think we can settle wage disputes without a simultaneous determination on prices. That does not mean every wage rise must be accompanied by a price rise. It simply means that the merits of both positions have to be fully explored at the time the case is being decided.

The panel's report should not be compulsory, even though there is little reason to expect it will be much more subject to real bargaining than the W.S.B. steel report. The only time such a report ever gets into bargaining in any genuine sense is when both sides find it distasteful. Otherwise, the side that feels it came off best digs in and insists on getting everything the panel proposed. The things it doesn't want are usually the only ones the other side is prepared to concede.

The fact that the panel will have no partisanship in its makeup, that it will not be charged with responsibility for the day-to-day administration of controls and that it will be able to pass on both prices and wages should give its decisions a better chance of acceptance than those of the W.S.B., particularly under the conditions that now prevail.

The need may still arise for additional Government sanctions if the decision fails to bring a settlement and the national welfare forbids a strike. Students of labor relations would differ sharply on whether it was wise to take advance legislative action against that possibility. Some would feel it was smarter to wait until a crisis arrived before attempting to grapple with it.

If it was feared that such a crisis might come too swiftly for specific Congressional relief, the law should give the President the option of choosing between an injunction and seizure, depending on which course he felt was indicated by the situation that menaced the country. Such an alternative would make it impossible for either side to be deliberately obstructive in the belief that the President would be obliged to act to the detriment of the other.

It is not an ideal solution; there is no ideal solution that transfers the power of decision from the parties to Government. But it is not democratic to fail to do those things that are imperative for the public good. Labor and management cannot be permitted to carry their differences to the point of paralyzing the nation or leaving it defenseless before its enemies.

The less palatable and the less frequent we make Government intervention, the more chance there is for labor and industry to find their own road. If each would stop worrying about what it fears is in the mind of the other, we would already be a long way down that road.

Paths to Labor Peace *

The science of group relationships is admittedly still in swaddling clothes, its techniques, theories, and research patterns spread throughout half a dozen academic disciplines. Within the past decade, however, a more sophisticated approach to labor-management relationships has been evident in the United States. Stuart Chase has here synthesized current theories in this area of human relations. He also offers an optimistic view of the future, based on specific examples of industrial peace.

As mass transport and mass communication push the citizens of this unhappy planet ever closer together in the seventh year of the atomic age, I have been looking around for techniques of agreement. What methods and structures have social scientists and others discovered which might help us get along together better? We may or may not be our brothers' keepers, but we are increasingly in our brothers' laps.

The Quakers have a remarkable technique for reaching unanimous agreement in their business decisions, which has stood the test of three hundred years. The TVA has an equally remarkable method for getting on with the people of the Valley. The new studies in group dynamics give very promising leads. Semantics can be helpful in reducing certain kinds of conflict. Unesco's analysis of international conferences has good possibilities. And so on.

In the perpetual laboratory of labor-management relations, many unions, universities, business executives, are hard at work developing techniques. Some of the results have been spectacular, and I would like to tell you about one or two of them. First, however, let us look at various kinds of relationships which may exist between management and organized workers in the United States today.

Unions do not necessarily mean conflict, sometimes the reverse. There seems to be a regular progression from physical violence to active cooperation. Benjamin M. Selekman of the Harvard Business School, in a recent book, has described eight different stages.

In the long run relations will be determined by collective bargaining between union and management rather than by Taft-Hartley laws or similar legislation. The two parties at interest must work it out together. In four of the patterns of relationships conflict is implicit, ready to break out at any moment; in the other four agreement has been reached, but a dubi-

* Stuart Chase. Reprinted from *The Nation*, March 17, 1951, pp. 250-52.

ous agreement, in two categories. Beginning on the lowest rung, this is
how Selekman ranks the stages toward real understanding:

1. *Containment-aggression*—where management accepts the union under
protest but tries to limit its activities to bargaining over hours and wages.
The union is pressing to expand its power; tension is always high and
readily can become explosive.

2. *Class-struggle ideology*. In this pattern union leaders act along
Marxian lines. They may cooperate with management as a matter of
expediency or because Moscow tells them to for the moment—as in World
War II—but no real peace is possible. The union leaders, if not the rank
and file, are committed by their ideology to the elimination of the management class. This pattern is on the wane as C.I.O. and A.F. of L. purge
their red unions.

3. *Laissez-faire ideology*—which is the class struggle in reverse. Many
American managers, especially in the South, are convinced that unions
have no place in a free society. Though they will deal with unions if they
must, they are always on the alert for a chance to get rid of them once and
for all. Real cooperation is again impossible. This group was dealt a
mortal blow by the Wagner act and is gradually fading out.

4. *Power-bargaining*. By this Selekman means that the parties accept
each other as a necessary evil, but each tries to wrest from the other all
possible advantage. When winter comes and the need for coal is bitter,
then pull a strike! Base your strategy on the market and collect all the
traffic will bear. John L. Lewis, Caesar Petrillo, the dock workers of San
Francisco, teamsters in various cities, follow this pattern—tough leaders on
both sides, and the public be damned. Such a relationship is likely to
arouse the public's wrath and be followed by government intervention—
as when the army takes over the coal mines—and reduced power for both
men and management. The pattern can lead to the liquidation of collective bargaining.

Now we turn the corner from conflict to agreement. Here are four
types of relationships in which men and management really cooperate
without crossing their fingers. Observe, however, the mayhem practiced
on the public in numbers five and six!

5. *Deals*. Top union officials and top management make a deal about
wages, hours, and working conditions. The rank and file never know
the details, and of course neither do the stockholders; stockholders are
rarely supposed to know anything under our present business institutions.
Besides being utterly undemocratic, this is a pretty unreliable kind of cooperation, because if the rank and file *do* find out about the "deal" they
are likely to blow the roof off. Every now and then a labor big shot disappears into outer space.

6. *Collusion*—which differs from a deal in two ways. First, the rank and file are usually in on it; second, union and managers jointly seize control of the market and proceed to administer quotas, prices, quality, what not, in an air-tight monopoly. Collusion reaches its finest flowering in the building trades. Thurman Arnold in his "Bottlenecks of Business" can give you extensive documentation. It certainly reduces labor conflict, but at a cost to the consumer—sometimes a very high and fancy cost. The government is likely to move in here too, under the Sherman act.

7. *Accommodation.* Now we approach maturity. The term seems to have been invented by Selekman, and I find it very useful to indicate a process, not only in labor disputes, but in all sorts of human conflicts. It implies a degree of acceptance and an equilibrium. The idea is to live and let live; perhaps two parties cannot agree in all matters, but they can understand each other's point of view and accommodate their activities. Cyrus Ching described such a pattern to me, with a story from Mexico. Such is what Republicans and Democrats in the Senate will soon have to do if the Republic is to continue intact. Such is now the only hope in the cold war.

In labor relations accommodation means that while union and management are wary, while they still hold rigidly to the traditional methods of collective bargaining and attempt no "participation" plans at all, they have become used to one another. They "interact comfortably within a familiar pattern of behavior." In accommodation hope has been abandoned of liquidating the opponent; there he is and one must live with him.

8. *Cooperation,* or the Promised Land—to which accommodation is often the threshold. Gradually the old distrusts melt out, and each side comes to believe in the other's good faith. They feel so secure that they can go beyond the traditional agenda of collective bargaining. They can jointly consider matters of production, solvency, elimination of waste, introduction of new machines, and so on. "The union accepts managerial problems as being of concern to labor; management recognizes its stake in stable, effective unionism; together they dispose of problems as they arise." The Amalgamated Clothing Workers, for instance, would never attack Hart, Schaffner, and Marx as a "profit-swollen corporation" or a "greedy exploiter"—such adolescent name-calling has been outgrown. The union is pledged to keep the company solvent, while the company is pledged to union participation in certain well-defined managerial functions.

Stage eight will not arrive tomorrow for most American enterprise. Given the suddenness of union growth in this country—from fewer than three million members in 1934 to sixteen million today—and given the enduring rivalry between the C.I.O. and A.F. of L., accommodation seems to be the more realistic and promising objective. Selekman thinks we shall do well if we get stage seven over the greater part of industry by 1960.

What does stage eight look like? Both the Amalgamated and the International Ladies' Garment Workers' Union have been operating in it for years. Elsewhere Joseph Scanlon, a former steel-union official and now M.I.T. professor, has set up some forty "participating" plans in which union and management are jointly responsible for output.

There are plenty of examples available; suppose we pick a clothing manufacturer in Rochester, New York, where cooperation has been so effective that there has been no strike since the original contract was signed with Sidney Hillman in April, 1919. In the last eighteen years not a single grievance has gone to arbitration!

The Amalgamated was formed in 1914 when Hillman's group split off from the United Garment Workers, A.F. of L. He wanted to replace the craft union with an industrial union in which all crafts would be united, from messengers to skilled cutters. At first there were bloody strikes and many picket lines in New York, Philadelphia, Rochester, and elsewhere. Call it stage one, "containment-aggression."

A firm making top-quality men's suits in Rochester, the Hickey-Freeman Company, took a calculated risk and signed a contract with Hillman in 1919. It was a brief contract, providing for the settlement of grievances, a labor manager to be appointed by the firm, an open shop, and arbitration machinery. Dr. William Leiserson became the first impartial chairman under the arbitration clause, a post which was to win him national honor. Thirty-three cases came to him in the first year. Now grievances are settled so quickly at the point of origin in the shop that they seldom get to arbitration at all.

Gradually participation was introduced and increased until it became the fixed policy of Hickey-Freeman to consult the union before making any major decision affecting the workers. Such a policy clashes with the traditional prerogatives of the boss and is an acute issue in industry today. Employers are disposed to fight for what they consider their right to run the business. Unions are disposed to fight against what they consider unjust acts of management—rate-cutting, speed-ups, arbitrary firing. But at Hickey-Freeman "management prerogatives" carry no warlike connotation. Boundaries between managers and workers have been clearly defined and long since accepted. Stage eight is solidly established.

Let us look at an actual example of this kind of participation. Here is the "plant chairman," a union official, whose job it is to settle local grievances—the kind which the company personnel department or the company foreman tries to settle in most concerns. The chairman sits in a private office right in the factory.

A complaint comes in. "Julie" is making too many errors in stitching labels. He looks over the record and then summons the girl, the company foreman and the union shop steward. He shows them the figures. Nobody questions Julie's brilliant facility in wrecking labels. The plant chairman—a union official, remember—looks straight at her and says, "Julie, the company can't afford to pay you one cent a label to make mistakes, and then pay another girl six cents to correct them, can it?"

"No, sir."

"You know, Julie, you just weren't cut out to sit at a machine all day long. After you have been sitting for a while, your attention wanders, doesn't it?"

"Yes, I guess I'm not cut out for this job."

The company foreman then goes into action. "She used to be a good messenger when she first came here. How about shifting her to that job?"

"Would you like that?" says the plant chairman.

"Sure, I'd like it fine," says Julie.

And this grievance, an actual case, is settled by a union official to the complete satisfaction of the company foreman and of the girl herself. Julie is of course a union member.

When a new suit is designed, patterns are first taken to the operating department of the company for study. Then the union officers are called in for a joint conference. Piece rates, quality, the division of work, and other technical matters are thoroughly discussed. Patterns which raise objections go back to the designer for correction.

The new style, when ready, is a joint plan by both company and union, with all foreseeable grievances and conflicts removed. But that is not the end of the participation. A few suits are first manufactured in a kind of pilot plant. If the workers like the style—not the cut of the vest so much as the conditions of producing it—they tell the rest of the shop, aided by the plant chairman (union) and the labor manager (company). A better way to avoid later complaints and to encourage production would be difficult to imagine.

Perhaps the most striking example of participation came during the depression of the 1930's. Clothing firms were failing right and left. The Amalgamated became an industrial banker, loaning money out of the union treasury to keep the companies afloat! Hart, Schaffner, and Marx was said to have received a substantial loan in the nick of time.

In 1933 the Amalgamated at Rochester negotiated a wage cut—yes, cut wages 15 per cent. Later in that terrible year the union negotiated another cut of 15 per cent. In 1934 came a third cut of the same amount, later modified to 8 per cent. Thus the union had matured to the point of deliberately choosing the lesser evil—better a 45 per cent wage cut than unemployment. (The cost of living was falling too, of course.) Participation in the needle trades is a two-way street. Workers share in the high earnings of the good years and in the losses of the bad years. Both parties strive for a healthy industry.

Donald Straus, who has reported on Hickey-Freeman for the National Planning Association, sums up by saying that industrial peace rests on two foundations. First, the unreserved acceptance by management of the union and its functions, including participation in some managerial decisions. Second, the unreserved acceptance by the union of responsibility for the welfare and solvency of the industry. There are no "deals" and no collusive agreements.

The relationship between men and managers at Hickey-Freeman—and at most shops in the men's clothing industry—has been directed toward "solving mutual problems as they arise, not to winning arguments." As the relationship developed, increasing reliance was placed on collective bargaining at the local level, less on arbitration, far less on splitting legal hairs over the interpretation of the written contract.

The United Nations, by way of contrast, is still in the hair-splitting stage. But of course it is much younger than the union Sidney Hillman founded.

Hickey-Freeman is one of a dozen concerns now under intensive examination by the National Planning Association. Instead of studying labor wars the association is analyzing labor peace. In 1946 the papers printed more front-page news about strikes than ever before, but even in that turbulent year nine out of every ten labor contracts were renegotiated without a strike. In 1947 twenty-four out of twenty-five were so negotiated. The prevailing pattern is peace, even if the headlines make it look like war.

Peace is not news as defined by the newspapers; somebody has to bite somebody. Clinton Golden, who heads the N.P.A. research, said in launching the study: "The time has come when, instead of looking into the causes of conflict that we ought to try to discover how much peace there is, and what makes peace."

Let's End Labor Monopolies *

Mr. Hoover is in essential agreement with Mr. Kornhauser (see below, "Labor Disputes Should Be Settled by Law") in that he would pro-

* Glenn E. Hoover, "Our Major Economic Problems," *Vital Speeches*, July 1, 1950, pp. 569–70.

hibit strikes. However, Mr. Hoover would go further. Although he suggests no arrangement for compulsory arbitration of wage disputes, he would forbid unions to bargain by "strikes, threat of strikes, sabotage, or intimidation of other workers." Shorn of their economic power, unions would be permitted to retain their social and political functions—becoming, thus, solely human relations agencies. On the surface, at least, this proposal would relegate labor to the position it held in the capitalistic economy of a century ago.

One major problem, growing worse with the years, is what is loosely called the Labor Problem. It is most evident from the work stoppages which develop only in our unionized industries. It is proper therefore to say that the Labor Problem grows out of the existence—and acceptance—of labor unions. That great majority of workers who are not unionized present few, if any problems which can win our attention. We are always too distracted by the activities of the much smaller number of workers who are members of trade unions.

The simple truth is that labor unions are monopolies, and that the labor problem is essentially a monopoly problem. A labor union—like any other monopolist—has complete control over the price of its product, and may fix the price so high that the customary buyers will not pay it. If a normal buyer is a "little businessman"—a proprietor of a barbershop for example—the public is not much affected. However, if a firm such as General Motors, or U. S. Steel, or a railroad system, the telephone system, or the coal industry refuses to meet the union's terms, we are faced with national emergency.

Work stoppages in the mass production industries, the railroads or the coal mines are calamities of a kind that cannot be permitted to run their course. If the parties cannot reach agreement, then the terms of employment must be fixed by the government, as in the recent Steel Strike. Perhaps, as in the last Coal Strike, the threat of the government to "take over" the industry will force the parties to accept some temporary settlement, particularly if the increased labor costs can be passed on to the consumers in the form of higher prices. In our major labor disputes the government now plays the deciding role. In most of them, the collective bargaining device settles them only *pro forma,* if at all.

We must now adjust ourselves to the fact that in our major industries, "Collective Bargaining" has failed to live up to its billing. It was supposed to bring us a larger measure of industrial peace. It has, instead, since the war's end, brought us more serious work stoppages than in any comparable time in our nation's history. With increasing frequency, the federal government has had to determine, directly or indirectly, the terms of settle-

ment. So far as our major industries are concerned—if I may mix my
metaphors a little—the White Rabbit of collective bargaining is already
a dead duck.

No one, of course, really wanted the government to fix wages and other
terms of employment. The unions accept the inevitable—somewhat grudgingly—so long as the White House is occupied by a man who supports a
program and relies on their votes and campaign contributions. But what
our most powerful unions would do if we were ever again to have a
president somewhat more of the stamp of Grover Cleveland or Calvin
Coolidge is problematical, and not too pleasant to contemplate. We are,
therefore, giving that possibility the conventional American treatment,
that is, we refuse to even think about it.

Those who like to dig down to the root of any evil will find, I believe,
that our fundamental mistake was to permit either the organized employers or organized employees to use their monopoly power in determining the conditions of employment. The use of any form of power—
and particularly violence—should be reserved to the state, and neither
buyers nor sellers should ever be permitted to transform a free market into
a tug-of-war. It is a chief merit of free markets, that in their operations,
power plays no part. They provide a peaceful, automatic and impersonal
method for determining the terms of exchange between buyers and sellers
who have—so to speak—"parked their guns at the door." All our efforts
should be directed to restoring and perfecting such markets, both for
commodities and for the services of workers.

I am not proposing that labor unions be forbidden, for they have many
useful functions to perform. They serve as a channel for communicating
the grievances of the workers. Through them, too, a wise employer will
tell his workers of the problems confronting both them and the firm, such
as the outlook for expansion or curtailment, apprentice training, seniority
rights, etc.

The unions may also organize consumers' cooperatives, publish newspapers and make provision for incapacitated and aged members. Others
may follow the example set by some of the railway brotherhoods, and try
their hand at running banks or operating apartment houses. We should
be delighted everytime we hear of some union launching a business enterprise. We may not care to invest in many of them, but as a teacher I
appreciate the educational value of such undertakings.

And finally, as many unions are now showing us, there is the unlimited
field of politics to which they can devote their energies. The more farsighted labor leaders are aware that many of their aims can be achieved
only if they can gain control, or seriously influence, the whole apparatus of
government, particularly at national level. There are some who are

alarmed at the increasing political activity of labor unions. I do not share their fears. I believe, on the contrary, that such activity should be encouraged. Once it is provided that no worker shall be compelled to retain his membership in a union whose political activities he disapproves, I can see no objection to unions using their funds to support any candidate, political party, or legislative program they may choose.

What should be forbidden them is the use of their monopoly power, whether by strikes, threat of strikes, sabotage, or intimidation of other workers. They must not be permitted to extort a wage for their services above that which free markets provide. Except for public utilities, whose prices are regulated by public authority, we already prohibit the monopolistic price-fixing of commodities, and the same good rule should apply to wages, which are nothing but the price of labor services. . . .

Labor Disputes Should Be Settled by Law *

Mr. Kornhauser declares that strikes are an anachronism—a survival of private war in a society that has long since outlawed the dueling pistol. He would prohibit strikes and replace them with a form of compulsory arbitration. How do you believe that Mr. Kornhauser's program would be greeted by labor? Management? The public? If you find this program convincing, how would you answer a labor expert who recently wrote, "If we ever reach the 'idyllic' state in which there are no strikes, we will probably discover that we have acquired something much worse in the process." †

Despite the demonstrated futility of strikes, we permit our "domestic tranquility" to be incessantly and profoundly disturbed by these bitter industrial conflicts. It is time to bring to bear in the field of labor relations the time-tested methods by which we adjudicate most other differences between man and man.

Unfortunately, the obsolete "labor-is-a-commodity" heresy, which long delayed a rational solution of labor disputes, was succeeded by another no less tenacious and no less mischievous doctrine: "the right to strike." This doctrine, with all its implications, has become endowed with an air of sanctity. All labor legislation has been based on the premise that the right

* Samuel J. Kornhauser, *The Saturday Evening Post*. July 16, 1949, p. 12.
† A. H. Raskin, "How To Prevent 'National Emergency' Strikes," *The New York Times Magazine*, May 11, 1952.

to strike is untouchable, although the right to strike usually nullifies the right to work.

Most people agree that wage earners must have safeguards against exploitation by avaricious employers, but it does not follow that this object can be attained only by allowing them to redress their grievances by force at the expense of everybody else. A strike is a blockade of an establishment by a body of men having no legal right over the property, with the object of wearing down the owners till they capitulate. This is private war. When strikes paralyze transportation, communication or the distribution of food, they become nothing less than insurrections. And yet to outlaw strikes without insuring equitable treatment of wage earners would be to fly from one evil to another.

In other controversies, the parties go, as a matter of course, to the established judicial tribunal to have their rights adjudicated. They then abide by the result. That is because in their case we have duly constituted liberty under law. But we have no laws to enable the aggrieved wage earner to test in court his right to redress. Experience demonstrates that most aspects of labor relations are readily susceptible to regulation by law. Matters relating to the safety, health and convenience of men at work are now governed by statute. So, also, laws requiring compensation for personal injuries or illness sustained in the course of employment are practically universal in America. The right of workmen to organize and choose agents or agencies to represent them is basic under our Constitution.

My own feeling is that wage disputes likewise should come under the authority of legal rules. The first step toward establishing a real legal status for labor disputes would be to crystallize our best concepts in a code defining the rights and obligations of employers and employees. The principles embodied in such a code would not, at first, meet every possible contingency. Yet, definitions could be laid down with sufficient definiteness to enable courts to determine justly the basic controversies.

Suppose it were provided by law that an employer was required to pay the highest wages his business could afford, having due regard for returns to management and investors, reserves for suitable maintenance, replacements, expansion and other factors, including wages paid in his and other industries. Obviously, management must be left free to apply its knowledge to determine these requirements, subject to the qualification that the allowances made are reasonable in the light of honest business practice. It would be fatal to leave such matters to the whims of bureaucrats. On the other hand, the employer could not justly complain if the law prescribed judicial examination to determine whether he had acted in good faith.

A finding would then be made either that the employer had sufficient ground for refusing to grant higher wages, or that men were entitled to what they asked, or, more probably, that both were in error. The decision would be subject to review in higher courts. Meanwhile, there would be no strikes, lockouts or boycotts, no interruption of production or wages. Strikes would become as obsolete as dueling.

This would be no more an infringement on the legitimate privileges of employers than the requirement that they resort to the courts for settlement of conflicting claims under contracts, patents or antimonopoly laws. Labor leaders might declare that this would mean enslavement of the workers. Actually, a law to bar strikes is no more an infringement of legitimate freedom than a law against assault and battery. And a law requiring an employer to compensate his employees on a basis fairly consonant with the conditions of his business and general conditions in his locality is no more a trespass on his legitimate freedom than a safety-appliance law.

LAWS WON'T STOP STRIKES *

Mr. Kornhauser's enthusiasm for compulsory arbitration is not shared by Mr. Straus, who regards injunctions, compulsory arbitration, and government seizures as deceptively inadequate protection against serious strikes that undermine the constructive processes of collective bargaining. In their haste to "settle things" Americans tend to ignore the important role of the United States Mediation Service in helping disputants arrive at mutually satisfactory agreements. For true industrial peace this service should be granted additional prestige and be recognized for what it is—the last line of defense against disastrous work stoppages.

. . . We are accustomed in this country to having wages and working conditions set by collective bargaining, by give and take across a bargaining table on one side of which sit representatives of workers, on the other side representatives of management. If a deadlock in the discussions is reached, it is customary to have an impartial person, usually a government official, enter the conference room and try to mediate the differences. If his efforts fail, and if the company and the union are not willing to submit their differences to another impartial person, an arbitrator, for decision, then a strike results.

Many disputes today, however, hurt the public more than they hurt the

* Donald B. Straus, *Harper's Magazine*, July, 1952, pp. 21-27.

parties who are fighting each other. In such cases, when collective bargaining and mediation have failed, the government steps in and tries to avert a strike in order to keep production going. This has seemed especially necessary during the past decade, when continuous full-scale production in our key industries has been considered essential to our national defense. But it has proved bafflingly difficult.

During World War II, the ever-present danger from the foreign enemy, plus the dispute-settling machinery of the War Labor Board, maintained a fairly effective if uneasy peace on the domestic labor front. Since V-J Day, the government has tried out a series of increasingly restrictive devices to prevent strikes during a period when the danger from without, though real, has been less obvious. The list of devices is long, impressive, and varied. The results have been far from reassuring.

On several occasions, Taft-Hartley Law injunctions have run their eighty-day course and terminated with a strike. Presidentially-appointed boards have issued recommendations which have been rejected, sometimes by management, sometimes by unions; result—a strike. Even government seizure did not eliminate railroad strikes. Unions and managements in atomic energy pledged themselves not to strike or lock out without first resorting to a full course of mediatory procedures, with recommendations of an impartial panel as the last step. Compulsory arbitration of public-utility disputes has been tried in several states but strikes have not been eliminated. In several states, the laws themselves have been declared unconstitutional. Compulsory arbitration on a national scale has often been considered, but citizens of New Zealand, Australia, and Great Britain tell us that compulsory arbitration is no guarantee against strikes, because they have had many years of experience under this arrangement and have witnessed many work stoppages.

For a period of years, government use of these devices achieved, to be sure, a measure of success. But it now appears that this success may have been due in large part to novelty: the novelty of the devices used and the novelty of the situation which demanded such drastic government action. As the novelty of the drug wears off, so does its effectiveness. A strike in atomic energy today causes far less panic in the minds of the public than it did in the first few years following Hiroshima, even though the consequences are probably every bit as serious. And this spring a steel strike occurred after the President had tried numerous strike-stopping devices—including one which he thought he had but which the courts said he didn't have. . . .

Of all these many "final" solutions for labor troubles, not one can be counted upon to prevent strikes. That is the first flat fact with which we are confronted today.

But that isn't the half of it. For not only do these "final" solutions not work; the fact that both management and labor expect them to be applied gets in the way of any serious attempt to mediate their differences.

Always, when a srike appears to be in the wind, an attempt is made, first of all, to mediate the conflict. Mediation is the intervention of a "neutral" person in a dispute, a person skilled in resolving conflicts. A mediator has no power other than persuasion; the only hope he can offer to the public is his ability to resolve the conflict between the parties and thus get a voluntary agreement. In a dispute of possibly grave consequences to the nation, this process looks far too uncertain to provide adequate protection against a strike. Mediation has therefore often been a *pro-forma* procedure which is regarded by all concerned, including the hapless mediator, as a whistle-stop on the road to somewhere else—to some more final solution. The tougher the dispute appears to be, the more important its impact on the nation, the more casual will be the stop at this way station.

There is, however, a fundamental fallacy in considering mediation as a "whistle stop" on the road to strike prevention. In every dispute of national importance, there are two separate governmental responsibilities which must not be confused: first, the responsibility to get the dispute settled; and second, the responsibility to prevent a strike while the dispute-settling is going on. Mediation, fact-finding, even recommendations if wisely used, are among the mediator's tools for settling the dispute. Injunctions, seizure, appeals to patriotism are among the tools for strike-stopping. They are two different things. And what is more, *mediation is the final one*. For even if a strike is prevented we have now learned that an agreed settlement must be obtained before full production can be resumed. And of all possible government action it is the mediation process alone which leads toward an agreed settlement. The more coercive, more "final" sounding solutions of the strike-stopping variety may keep the men at work temporarily, but they are seldom of use in getting an agreement.

. . . We must have a better understanding of the role of the strike in our economy. The paradoxical truth of the matter is that under normal conditions there is no deterrent to strikes so effective as the strike itself. Governmentally created substitutes can as easily stimulate a strike threat as eliminate one. During World War II, William H. David, then Chairman of the War Labor Board, shocked the country by declaring that what the industrial relations of this country needed was a good strike. In midwar, this seemed to many an irresponsible statement for a highly-placed government official to make, but the deep wisdom of it was evident to all who were in the know. When government decisions replaced the strike, collective bargaining came to a standstill as managements and unions abandoned their responsibility to make decisions and laid their burdens on the doorstep of the War Labor Board. Strikes had all but disappeared, but so had collective bargaining. And today there is little disagreement over the proposition that collective bargaining must be preserved as an inherent part of our economy for the pricing of labor. Without it, our economy would evolve into something else, and the alternatives all appear to be a form of totalitarian state with individual freedoms drastically curtailed.

Under the collective-bargaining system the strike is the action of the free market on the price of labor. The strike is the seller's attempt to get higher prices, and the buyer's reluctance to pay them. If arbitration or government recommendations are substituted for collective bargaining, they become labor price-fixing by fiat—an aspect of a managed economy.

And so those on both sides of the table who prefer a free-enterprise system to a socialized one (and they number as many in ranks of labor as in management) abhor the inroads of government interference—even though the intensity of abhorrence may fluctuate, depending upon whether they think they can do better in the instant case without it than with it. Compulsory arbitration and its accompanying teeth—government seizure, injunctions, and anti-strike legislation—are all injurious to collective bargaining and, as a practical matter, are no positive guarantee against a strike. Of all possible alternatives for government intervention in a labor dispute, mediation alone can be a stimulant to the collective-bargaining process.

As our economy becomes more integrated, as more of us become dependent upon one another for even the most elementary necessities of living, the strike inevitably changes its character. When Mike Quill strikes New York's subways, or when Phil Murray shuts down Ben Fairless's steel mills, you and I will feel the pinch before either Phil, Ben, Mike, or the New York City Board of Transportation begins to suffer. When the nation must have steel for its defense, and wage and price increases will threaten it with inflation, a strike becomes still more damaging to all of us.

Under such circumstances the government may reasonably intervene to stop a strike in the public interest. But it must realize the grave consequences of such action. An injunction is close to a challenge of the constitutional guarantee against slavery. Government seizure invades basic property rights guaranteed by the Constitution. Compulsory arbitration dictates the terms of an agreement—a paradoxical concept if there ever was one. Furthermore, as we have seen, the government's supply of such drastic anti-strike measures is not limitless, and every time one of them is used, the supply diminishes. As we have also seen, when the threat of them hangs over the disputants, any attempt to bring them to a real agreement may be vitiated. And it is on agreement, and agreement only, that a continuation of steady and productive work will be premised. Even if the ultimate recourse to military force is used, the deciding vote still lies with the employer who manages the plants and with the workers who man them: do they choose to manage and to work under the conditions proposed, or do they prefer jail, fines, or—conceivably—death?

Production is creative and creation demands cooperative effort. You can kill or jail a man to prevent him from committing a crime, you can't jail or kill him in order to keep him at work. And the notion of terrorizing men into work is deeply repugnant anyhow to all our traditions of personal liberty. The consent of management and workers is as vital to our economic freedom as is the consent of the governed to our political freedom.

Therefore mediation—the effort to secure mutual consent—is not our first, but our last, line of defense against disastrous stoppages. It is not a whistle-stop on the road to somewhere else. It is the Grand Central Terminal of the dispute-settling process.

Problem 26: Big Agriculture-- Pillar or Parasite?

In one sense, American farmers and their families (23.3 million strong at last count) are a surviving remnant of Adam Smith's competitive economic system. By 1935 American industry was characterized by the multimillion dollar corporation, which, if it did not dominate its market, was apt to league itself with its fellows in trade associations. Labor, likewise, had combined in great unions that fixed wage rates on the basis of potential economic force (the strike), rather than by free market action. Farm prices, however, were established in a free, competitive market, with millions of producers making uncoordinated decisions as to prospective demand. These farmers differed from their industrial brethren, who seldom "overproduced" to the extent that they were compelled to sell below the cost of production.

During the past twenty years American agriculture has undergone a series of revolutions. First, farming has been revolutionized by an astounding technological transformation marked by greater capitalization, more machinery, and the widespread use of scientific knowledge. A parallel development has drastically reduced farm population and has concentrated land ownership into fewer hands. Thus in 1935 there were 6.8 million farms; in 1950 there were 5.4 million. Average acreage per farm in the same period mounted from 154 to 215 acres. Moreover, measured in terms of actual productivity, nearly half of the remaining farmers are unimportant. In 1950 some 40 per cent of them sold farm products valued at less than $1,000 in the course of an entire year.

Meanwhile, commercial farmers have leagued together in giant organizations that exercise great economic and political power. Membership in the National Grange totals 800,000; the American Farm Bureau represents 400,000 farmers; the National Farmers Union speaks for 100,000 farm families; and scattered throughout the United States are powerful regional organizations, such as the Missouri Farmers Association, which boasts a membership roll of 150,000. Through these organizations farmers have made themselves felt in congressional halls. At their demand a government-guaranteed floor has been placed under farm prices, and farm production has been regulated. So rapidly has the farm scene shifted that an American rural Rip Van Winkle of the 1920's, were he to awaken in the 1950's, would find his erstwhile friends talking an unintelligible gibberish that included such terms as power take-off, hybrid corn, parity payments, sliding supports, conservation practices, production quotas, the egg program, potato politics, and the Brannan Plan. Were he to inquire widely, he would discover that Americans are aligned in several rival camps over what is generally known as "the farm problem."

The Farmers Milk the Public Treasury *

In every debate over farm policy the word *parity* eventually emerges. To many farmers the term is a rallying cry—a government-backed promise that farm income will never again sag to depression levels. To many nonfarmers it seems evident that, by hook or by crook, the farmers have achieved a special, favored position in the American economy. What, specifically, is parity? Should a firm relationship be maintained between farm and nonfarm prices? If a floor is established, should there be a ceiling? What years are "normal" for establishing such a ratio?

The time has come for a showdown with the farm bloc. Judging from the sellout of the American consumer in the first session of the Eighty-first Congress, somebody will have to organize a pressure group for the four-fifths of our population which is still paying wartime peak prices for its

* Sam Shulsky, *The New American Mercury*, January, 1950. Reprinted from Robert E. Summers, *Subsidies for Farmers* (H. W. Wilson Co., 1951), pp. 66–69.

food. Every other basic industry has settled down to the give-and-take of a buyer's market, but the farm minority is still with congressional sanction, keeping its prices artificially inflated. . . .

As far back as the spring of 1948, the "inside dope" was that a "more realistic attitude is likely on farm supports." A lowering of supports to the old AAA levels of 52 to 75 per cent of parity was widely forecast. In fact, some even predicted that supports on a substantial list of items would disappear at the end of 1948. At that time, Congress extended the parity program another year. Even so, the cautious Dow Jones news service reported from Washington that the end was drawing near. "A move is quietly afoot among congressmen," it said on August 21, 1948, "to tackle the high cost of living next January by shortening the props under farm prices."

As recently as . . . October [1949], the Senate passed the Anderson bill which favored a sliding scale of price supports instead of the rigid 90 per cent support then in force. The New York *Times* warmly praised the "integrity" of the upper chamber for resisting President Truman's endorsement of the higher support level. But hardly had the rumble of its presses died down before the Washington wires were carrying the report that the provision had been defeated and that, despite the Democratic party's campaign oratory, the 90 per cent program had won. The farmer was once more encouraged to produce, not for the market, but for what he could get out of the government. . . .

The philosophy that the farmer is entitled to enjoy all the benefits of the private-enterprise system, but be subject to none of its vicissitudes, came into the national thinking in much humbler form in the early days of the New Deal. . . . With the gradual spread of a "riskless" philosophy, the farm bloc discovered "parity" in 1938 and arrived at a fixed price-support program in 1942. In less than a decade, the country's farm philosophy has undergone a complete reversal. What had started as a plan to save the farmer from bankruptcy became a scheme for raising him to the highest living standards in his history—and keeping him there. It was done through smart and timely political maneuvering. The clincher came in the 1942 Congress, when, with food of vital importance for ourselves and our allies, the farm bloc got what it wanted. No one was in a position to argue the point. Congress that year gave the American farmer a guarantee that the government would support the prices of major farm products until two years after the war. That deadline was reached more than two years ago. But the end is nowhere in sight.

It's all done with the magic word "parity." This measuring concept was evolved in the late 1930s, when farm prices were struggling up out of the morass of depression. In response to a demand for a comprehensive statistical index of agricultural prices the Agricultural Adjustment Act of 1938 defined parity as "that price for the commodity which will give to it a purchasing power [in the articles farmers buy] equivalent to the purchasing power of such commodity in the base period." Thus, if a farmer was able to buy a shirt with the proceeds of the sale of two bushels of corn during a period accepted as a fair standard, he should henceforth be guaranteed this purchasing power. For many commodities, this base covers the period August 1909 through July 1914, a period free from major economic and political disturbance and characterized by relative stability in all prices. This period, says the Federal Reserve Bank, "was generally a favorable one for agriculture."

In computing parity, the first step was to determine the average price received by the farmer during the base period. For instance, wheat averaged 88.4 cents a bushel at that time, corn 64.2 cents a bushel, and cotton 12.4 cents a pound. Parity levels for other commodities were based on later periods, owing to the lack of adequate price data before World War I, to extensive changes in consumer demand, or, as New York's Federal Reserve Bank blandly put it, "to the influence of pressure groups seeking a more favorable base period for their product."

As a second step, an index of prices paid by the farmer was arrived at by computing retail prices for 86 items used in family living (food, clothing, furniture, household supplies, etc.) and 96 items used in farm production (feed, fertilizer, machinery, etc.). In late 1949, the parity formula entitled the farmer to roughly two and one half times as much for his products as he got during the base period. If the free market for farm products falls 10 per cent below that level, it reaches the "support" level at which the government is pledged to step in and either buy or lend. If the government lends, the farmer has the choice of repaying the loan and reclaiming his produce (if the price subsequently goes up) or of keeping the money and letting the government keep his produce (if the price fails to rally). In either event, he has a call on the government to buy his produce at a price based on the wonderful days of 1909–14.

Nothing, of course, has been done about the fact that the farmer's labor time for growing and harvesting wheat, for example, has declined 60 per cent since the base period was set, or that potato production per acre has increased about fourfold. Nor has any erudite government economist exposed one absurdity in the system: since food itself is part of the parity index, the farmer is in the enviable position of raising his economic plane by his own bootstraps.

The results of such a program, sold to the American people in a time of great stress (at a time, in fact, when even labor—which is no shrinking violet—pledged it would not strike to better itself) are many, and varied, and all bad. Bad, that is, for the four-fifths of us who do not live on farms.

In the first place, there are the perils to our entire economy inherent in fitting such an inelastic policy to one of our basic needs. In the second place, there is the dishonesty involved in allowing a special group to profit at the expense of all. And finally, there is the simple objection that such arbitrary controls have solved nothing in the past and offer no proof that they will work any better in the future. . . .

The blatant stupidity which often accompanies bureaucratic attempts to regulate economic law is matched only by the arrogance with which such programs are propounded and than pushed forward to enactment. The farm program may once have been a scheme for saving the farmer from foreclosure and poverty. It is today, frankly, a scheme for keeping him prosperous in return for his support at the polls.

The Farmers' Side of the Farm Problem *

The farmer viewpoint on agricultural problems is for the most part buried in his professional or trade journals. Thus the farmer, like the businessman and union worker, often feels that he is misunderstood because of faulty communication. What is the case for farm subsidies? How much do they cost? Are they too expensive? Do nonfarmers also benefit from the government farm program? Could a more equitable system be devised?

Prompted by what appears to be a concerted attack on the farm program, I want to present the farmers' side of the argument. . . . Our farm price supports have not resulted in the exorbitant costs and surpluses you have heard about. For seventeen years the Commodity Credit Corporation has been acquiring surplus crops whenever gluts have threatened to cause market collapses which would bankrupt agriculture and throw the rest of our economy into a tail spin. The CCC has resold these surpluses on the open market if prices tended to climb out of balance because of scarcities; otherwise it has disposed of its stocks outside the normal channels of trade.

It was never intended, of course, that the government should make a profit on the price-support program in the usual sense. However, the CCC had to assume definite risks which might result in losses. It was reasonable, therefore, to permit the agency to use profits that might accrue

* Harold D. Cooley, *The Reader's Digest*, October, 1950, pp. 63–66.

on certain commodities to offset losses that might be suffered on others. During the seventeen years of CCC operations, price support has been extended on more than forty-three million bales of cotton—a normal four-year supply for our markets—nearly two billion bushels of corn and two and a half billion bushels of wheat.

This has not "coddled" farmers or made them rich; the per capita income of all persons living on farms was $763 last year *from all sources,* compared with $1555 for other people. But net farm income has risen since 1933 from slightly more than $2.5 billion to nearly $16 billion a year, which has benefited everyone. The increased farm income has meant extra cash for the city folk who sell radios, clothing and other wares. Moreover, the city man has benefited as a consumer of food. This year he has had to pay out only 18 per cent of his disposable income for the same diet which in 1935–39 took 23 per cent. Removal of price-support operations would not necessarily lower consumer costs; *beef, which is expensive, is the one major food item for which there is no price support.*

The program has been evolved and supported on a non-partisan basis by both Democrats and Republicans. It is approved by Congressmen representing city as well as rural constituencies. The farm program is not based on an economy of scarcity, nor was it inspired by a spirit of greed, nor has it been continued to satisfy the selfish desires of producers. It contemplates the production of an abundance of food and fiber, which is always in the interest of the consumer. Price supports mean to agriculture what minimum wages mean to labor—a reasonable security in producing needed commodities.

Carping critics of this program say that except for World War II's demands we would have smothered under the surpluses which up to that time had been accumulated through price-support activity. Why deal in "ifs"? Those surpluses turned out to be precious stock piles. We bartered our cotton for rubber. We sent corn and wheat to our allies. The reserves helped to keep the war going while we organized our agriculture to feed the world with record-breaking crops despite a shortage of manpower, machinery and fertilizer. Increased price supports provided the incentive.

Only in the last couple of years did world needs slacken enough so that we could begin to reconvert to a peacetime basis. Farmers then were required to cut their acreages to be eligible for price support, and that is the rule today. However, the Agriculture Department did not always reduce acreage sufficiently. As with potatoes, some farmers literally grew their crops in fertilizer so as to make their curtailed acreages produce an oversupply which could be unloaded on the government at a support price which represented guaranteed profit. The trend, though, has been toward normalcy. Cotton acreage has been reduced from nearly 28 million acres to 19 million in the last year. Thirteen million acres of wheat have been dropped in the same time. Eleven million acres of corn have been cancelled out since the war.

We now have $3.8 billion invested in price supports. This money is not lost, as some critics would have you believe. It is all secured by storable, staple commodities except for about $300 million worth of so-called perishables. Moreover, except for butter, these perishables have been processed and will keep. They include dried eggs, which the Secretary of Agriculture is supporting on his own initiative, dried milk and other commodities. To dispose of them now would involve losses.

And why dispose of these eggs and milk until we know that the world is to be at peace? We may have to help feed others once more. As for our staples, they should again be regarded as stock piles which we are fortunate to own. Already we are again bartering cotton abroad for materials of such direct military value that their identity must be kept secret. Our cotton surpluses are disappearing so rapidly on a boom market that our year-end inventories will be only a margin of safety against next year. Acreage curtailments already have removed tobacco from surplus. Our wheat stocks are so small that the Secretary of Agriculture recently rescinded a sharp cut in acreage. Too much emphasis has been placed upon the loses which we have sustained on perishables; too little mention has been made of the profits which we have realized on the price-support programs on the basic commodities.

Let's look at our profit and loss statements covering seventeen years of operations. We have given away $5 billion worth of commodities to feed areas occupied by our armed forces and to cover ECA commitments. We have sold other commodities abroad at a loss of $262 million, sometimes to compete with other sellers, sometimes because countries we wanted to aid could not pay full price. More than $890 million in food and other commodities has been distributed to our own people on relief, to welfare institutions and to schools for use in children's lunches. Another $103 million worth has been diverted to other than standard uses and to numerous programs of experimentation in the search of new utilizations. Eliminate such items and you find that we made a $248 million profit on cotton and a $5 million profit on tobacco. We lost $162 million on other commodities such as peanuts, wheat and corn. Thus we made a net profit of $91 million on basic commodities. On the other hand you find considerable losses in perishables—including the Irish potato program, which as handled was indefensible. It cost $400 million.

The evolution of the farm program was a work of pioneering. There was no blueprint available. If in this pioneering a miscalculation was made on one commodity—potatoes—this should not be seized upon as an excuse for discrediting the entire program. Nevertheless, even if you include the potato fiasco in the reckoning you find that all of our price supports over seventeen years represent a loss of but $547 million—only $32 million a year. In evaluating our overall program for the future, critics should be realistic enough to exclude the monstrous mistake of the potatoes, for Congress already has cut off all price support for them unless effective marketing controls are put on the books. If the potato deal is charged off to experience, the total loss on all other price supports has amounted to only $147 million. That averages about $8 million a year.

No one can fail to see the value of a farm program which, except for potatoes, has at a cost of only $8 million a year stabilized agriculture for the first time in history and added billions annually to national income for everybody's benefit. Critics should remember that farmers who do not abide by their acreage allotments are prohibited from receiving the program's protection. If producers of perishables such as eggs and dairy products do not bring production in line with reasonable consumer demands, such price supports should be abandoned.

This program has created reserve supplies of food and fiber against another emergency. In such an emergency we will be prepared for more than relief abroad. Our grain reserves can be used to maintain our meat supply. Other stocks can be filtered into the markets to offset prices if they tend to soar because of war demands or crop failures. They may well tend to retard the forces of inflation and stay the hand of government controls.

Price supports and quotas are not the permanent solution of the farm problem, but in the present situation they are necessary expedients. The ultimate answer will be found only in a wider distribution of both foodstuffs and fibers. Until we can expand markets at home and abroad, in a world at peace, we should retain and strive to perfect the program we now have in operation.

LET'S DEMAND OUR RIGHTS *

Even when reduced to writing, the following analysis preserves much of its intensity and oratorical flavor. It is, in fact, an eloquent statement of the farmer's case for government aid, delivered originally by President Heinkel before the annual meeting of the Missouri Farm-

* F. V. Heinkel, *The Missouri Farmer,* September, 1953, pp. 24–25.

ers' Association. That organization—150,000 strong—is the most powerful farm organization in Missouri and plays a potent role in state and national politics. Senators and the Secretary of Agriculture often appear on its platform, and association representatives frequently visit congressional halls. The allusion in the article to "so-called farm leaders" is to the Farm Bureau Federation and the National Grange—rival farm organizations that have favored a sliding scale of farm price supports.

Following World War I, when farm prices began to decline and a depression came upon agriculture, the farmers of America, through their leaders, appealed to both the Democratic and Republican conventions for help.

The farmers of America were turned away by reactionaries in both the political parties, and nothing was done to head off the farm collapse. It was allowed to develop into the awful general depression of the 1930's, and cost the Nation an estimated $500 billion in wealth that was not produced by our millions of unemployed.

I recall a statement made by a "moss-back" United States Senator at the time when the farmers were making an appeal for relief to one of the national political conventions. He said, "the farmers should stay at home and slop the hogs"!

This incident is mentioned because I fancy that I can feel some of that old "slop the hogs" attitude prevailing among many people to day. Either they sincerely believe that farmers are well off financially, or else they are interested in food being cheap so that labor can live on lower wages in order that their profits will be greater.

Whatever their reasons, they have been using scare words in an attempt to discredit any kind of governmental action in the farmers' behalf. They have been saying that farmers don't want "subsidies" and "regimentation" and that farmers should beware of "creeping socialism." They tell us that it is wrong for farmers to depend upon the government for anything, but that, instead, we should depend upon the "free market," where prices are supposedly to be arrived at as a result of supply and demand.

Farmers remember the free market that they had in the 1930's. Food was dirt cheap, but everybody went broke. Hogs became so cheap that market prognosticators were predicting the arrival of a time when there would be no market whatever for hogs!

As to subsidies and regimentation, look who's talking! The major oil companies are regimented and subsidized to the hilt. Not only have they been given a fast tax write-off of new facilities, totaling $750 million, plus a perpetual depletion tax allowance of 27 per cent of all crude oil produced, but their oil production (and hence their prices) are controlled by an inter-state compact commission.

That commission tells the companies just how much oil they can take out of the ground so that their prices will stay up and they won't suffer a debacle such as farmers are suffering right now. If you think that the oil companies don't just love this regimentation (and the subsidies) just try to get Congress to take it away from them, and you'll see how quickly their lobbyists can spring into action!

The railroads and telephone companies are all regimented and subsidized, and how they do love it! The railroads go before the Interstate Commerce Commission and argue for higher rates to cover their costs and give them a profit for their stockholders.

It should be mentioned that ICC has been exceedingly kind to them, having given them 12 freight increases since World War II. Last winter Senator Aiken remarked, "it's too bad farmers haven't an Interstate Commerce Commission to take care of them."

The telephone companies get their relief from the same public service commissions. There is hardly ever a time when one or more of the tele-phone companies isn't before a public service commission hollering for higher rates. A year or so ago the rate for a local phone call was a nickel in most towns. Now it costs you a dime. Moreover, these state commissions protect their respective trade territories. You can't start up a new telephone system where one already exists. So every time you make a phone call you partake of a little subsidy and regimentation.

Even the newspapers are subsidized through low postal rates. You often read an editorial telling how dreadful subsidies and regimentation are to farmers, but you never read an editorial advocating an increase in postal rates of newspapers.

Even the banks operate under a "legislated economy," which is supposed to be a bad thing for farmers. The Federal Reserve System is set up so that it has the authority legally to move interest rates up and down to suit the bankers.

The Sugar Act allows the sugar industry to be subsidized and regimented. Under it, the Secretary of Agriculture can and does, limit the amount of sugar that can come in from Cuba and elsewhere. We impose a tariff of so much per pound. We also put a tax on every pound of sugar refined in America. Then each year the government appropriates about the same amount of money that these taxes produce and hands it back to the pro-ducers and refiners of cane and beet sugar. So every time you put a spoon-ful of sugar in your coffee, you are swallowing just a little bit of regimenta-tion and subsidy.

Even labor is subsidized. Under the Wage and Hour Law enacted by

Congress, industry can't work a man more than 40 hours a week without paying him time and a half for each hour worked over 40. And under the Minimum Wage Law enacted by Congress, nearly all employers must pay at least 75 cents per hour.

I often wonder how astounded the labor union members would be if Walter Reuther, head of the CIO, or John L. Lewis, head of the Mine-workers, would get up in his respective national convention and tell the workers:

"We don't want the government to subsidize or regiment us. We believe that all labor laws should be repealed. Wages are too high. Labor is pricing itself out of the market. We must determine what parity shall be and then ask for sliding scale supports. We will allow wages to decline from 90 to 75 or 65 per cent of parity."

I can imagine what would happen when the meaning of these shocking words had penetrated the minds of the listening labor union members. Reuther and Lewis wouldn't only be fired, they would probably be tarred and feathered.

But that is exactly what some of the so-called farm leaders advocate! They openly and brazenly recommend such procedures. I keep wondering just how long the farmers of this country will continue to tolerate them as leaders.

The same line of argument is being put forth by the U. S. Department of Agriculture, which is purportedly looking after the best interests of the farmers.

What do you suppose organized labor would do if the U. S. Department of Labor advocated getting rid of all labor laws and allowing workers' wages to become fixed in a "free market"? Or if the Department contended that wages are too high, that labor is being priced out of the market, and that therefore wages ought to be allowed to decline to as much as 65 per cent of parity?

No industry has more protection in this country than the big private utilities. They are given monopolies by the government. Their trade territories are fixed, and no one else can enter. Their rates are fixed and protected by governmental agencies. They are steeped in subsidization and regimentation, and they like it so well that they maintain one of the biggest lobbies in Washington to protect it. They pay their head lobbyist $65,000 per year, plus expenses; and they maintain a lobby to protect their interests at nearly every state capital, if not every one.

But when it comes to the matter of farmers asking Uncle Sam to lend them money, at interest, with which to build REA cooperatives, transmission lines, power plants, or power dams (on the peoples' rivers) that is "creeping socialism"! Farmers should have none of it.

All of this talk about "subsidies," "regimentation," "free markets," and "creeping socialism" is simply something to anesthetize the farmers so that they will stand still while their pockets are being picked. Don't let these words fool you.

Farmers cannot live forever in an economy where every group except farmers is subsidized and given protection. If everything were free, if there were no protection whatever for the banks, the laborers, or any kind of industry, then I think the farmers would be willing to take their chance, too. But since that state of affairs is impossible, the farmers must have protection by government.

We must have price supports sufficiently high to give farmers equality with other segments of the American economy, and that is a floor of 90 per cent of parity. The average should be 100 per cent of parity.

Let's not allow scare words, false slogans, or bogeymen to keep us from seeing clearly the road ahead. We are entitled to protection by our government just as much as any other class of the American people. It's our government, isn't it? And I shall never worry about ills or dangers from "creeping socialism," "subsidies," or "regimentation" by our government so long as we have a Constitution and the right to vote on election day.

Let's not stay at home and "slop the hogs." Let's demand our rights!

Problem 27: Big Government-- The Welfare State, Nonsense or Necessity?

Implicit in nearly all United States political debates of the past twenty years is the question, "What role shall government play in economic affairs?" The conflict provoked by this question has already been examined in relation to the institutions of business, labor, and agriculture.

Another aspect of the question applies primarily to personal problems, such as unemployment, old age security, education, housing, and health. Thus far Americans have dealt with these problems piecemeal, and only in the past few years has the term *welfare state* been used to describe an over-all system under which government would play an active, positive role in resolving these issues.

Although welfare state has no universally accepted definition, it does imply government responsibility in the areas mentioned above. Legalists either advocate or oppose this concept, depending on their interpretation of a phrase in the United States Constitution: "The Congress shall have the power to lay and collect taxes, duties, imposts, and excises, to pay the debts and provide for the common defense and general welfare of the United States." Opponents of the welfare state have termed it "the Road to Serfdom," "Road to Hell," "creeping Socialism." Advocates have linked it with long-standing American traditions and the necessities of a technological age.

LIFE WITH THE GARLANDS *

In a democracy the average family is a social group of great moment. Because it holds the key to the ballot box, its ambitions, reactions, problems, and beliefs are reflected in both political and economic life. Final approval or rejection of the welfare-state philosophy is dependent upon the attitudes of millions of such families. Their decisions, in turn, will be based on their ability to solve their economic problems unaided.

Regarding the financial affairs of the average American family a great mass of statistical material has been compiled. We know its dollar income; its expenditures for insurance, books, food, clothing, and shelter; the size of its savings account; its church contributions; and its social security deductions. However, cloaked in statistical garb, this average family is something of a mythical skeleton, resembling in no way the flesh and blood family next door. To overcome this unreality the average family is here epitomized as the Garlands—a real-life family, complete with street address, telephone number, and a husband who likes to bowl. Are the Garlands shrewd consumers? How much education will their children probably receive? Will the Garlands become home owners? How effectively can they budget against unemployment, old age, sickness?

Tom Garland thinks it's time someone blew the whistle on prices. What Tom thinks is important. Not because there is anything exceptional about Tom, but because there is nothing exceptional about him. Tom comes as close to being Mr. Average Worker as it is possible to find among New York's army of wage earners. The State Labor Department picked Tom

* A. H. Raskin, *The New York Times Magazine*, April 6, 1952, pp. 12, 61, 63.

out as a man notable for his averageness—the holder of an average sort of job, in an average sort of company, with an average sort of pay envelope, and an average sort of family to feed and clothe. Nobody is exploiting Tom. He is not one of the ground-down wage slaves Moscow is always weeping over. The factory he works for prides itself on keeping its wages well ahead of its competitors, and it stays on cordial terms with the strong union to which Tom belongs.

Tom's pay as a stock selector at the Cutler-Hammer Electrical Company plant in the Bronx averages slightly less than $72 a week. That takes in his occasional overtime and the bonus the company distributes once a year. There was a time when Tom would have considered the $3,722 he earned last year a princely sum, but it doesn't seem to stretch very far these days. Tom is not used to lordly living. He has known a lot of poverty since he was born half a mile from the plant thirty-five years ago. His father, who had been a yard foreman for a coal company, lost his job during the depression and the family went on relief. Tom left school at 14 to take a job as a Western Union messenger.

He stayed at that for a year, making about $12 a week in delivery fees and tips, and then moved into a succession of off-and-on jobs as a grocery clerk, checkroom attendant, elevator operator and plumber's assistant. Nothing steady came along until he went to work for Cutler-Hammer in 1940 at 40 cents an hour. Uncle Sam pulled him out of that for four years of Army service, most of it in Panama and India. When he went back to making electrical switches in 1946, he found something besides his work to be interested in at the Bronx factory.

He fell in love with Helen Dippolito, a slim, brunette timekeeper, and they were married on St. Valentine's Day, 1948. Their first son, Thomas Joseph, is 3 years old; their second son, Gregory Robert, was born last October. Helen has to carry the baby up three flights of poorly lit stairs to the dingy six-room flat they share with her father and mother at 1244 Woodycrest Avenue in the Highbridge section of the Bronx. Helen's father used to be an iceman, but a spinal injury has kept him from working for the past fifteen years. Her mother makes umbrella straps and the Dippolitos pay the $43.55 monthly rent for the jointly occupied apartment. The Garlands pick up the bulk of the food bill by way of evening things.

They spend $8 a week for canned goods, coffee, cereals and other groceries. Butter is so high that Helen has switched to oleomargarine for her baking. The baking is an economy measure, too. Tom, a 200-pounder, has an insistent sweet tooth, and Helen has decided she can keep it satisfied herself for a good deal less money than the neighborhood baker charges. "Tom's favorite dessert is chocolate cream pie," Helen confides, "and a small one costs 85 cents at the bakery. I can make one twice as big for 50 or 60 cents."

Helen's hot oven doesn't shut the bakery shop out altogether. Tom still has to plank down $1 a week for bread and rolls. The butcher is a bigger problem. He puts a $6 dent in the family fortune. On weekends the Garlands splurge with round steak, roast fresh ham or chicken. Monday is left-over day. Tuesday they have pork chops, Wednesday chopped meat, and Thursday, spaghetti and meat balls. None of the family cares much for fish, so soup or eggs usually make up the main dish on Friday. Fruit and vegetables take another $6. The only reason it is not more, Tom explains, is that a brother-in-law runs the fruit store and gives them a break on prices. The milk-man leaves five quarts of milk every two days. That nicks the budget for $4 a week and $2.50 more goes into strained foods, evaporated milk and dextri-maltose for the baby.

Ever since their marriage four years ago the Garlands have been trying to get enough ahead of their food bills to buy an electric mixing machine to help Helen with her baking. They are still trying. Tom keeps a coin can at the factory and tosses some change into it every day or so toward the mixer. The total has got up close to $20 several times now, but some domestic emergency always comes along to empty the can before there is money enough for the machine.

The Garlands do have a washing machine, in which Helen does all the family laundry—including the baby's diapers and Tom's work clothes. Tom invested his $157 bonus check in the washing machine two years ago and the family would be lost without it. The other main prop of the Garland household is a $309 television set. Tom bought it on the installment plan in 1950. He made the last payment a few weeks ago.

Television is pretty much the beginning and end of the Garland entertainment program. They live half an hour by subway from Times Square, but they see less of the Great White Way than the average farmer from Pumpkin Corners. It has been so long since they went to a movie that Helen says she wouldn't know how to buy a ticket any more. Drama, musical comedy, opera and night clubs are part of a world they know only through TV.

Tom bowls every Wednesday night with some of the fellows from the shop. What with dinner and one thing or another, his evening away from the cathode tube costs him $3.60. That is as much as he spends each week on lunches—usually a meat sandwich, a slab of pie and a pot of tea, consumed in the stock room. When he has to work overtime, a dollar of his extra pay goes for supper at a diner near the plant. A co-worker drives him to and from home for the same $1 a week it would cost Tom to travel by subway.

Cigarettes are Tom's only vice. He smokes two packs a day. Forty-three cents burn away with the tobacco. There was a time when Tom drank a bit, but he has sworn off the stuff since his marriage. About the only time he touches whisky now is New Year's Eve, when he shakes hands with all the men, kisses all the women and passes out blissfully at a big family party at home.

Uncle Sam dips into Tom's pay envelope for $4.33 a week in income taxes and another $1.08 comes out for social security. The state takes 30 cents more for disability insurance, leaving him with a net of $66.29 to take home out of his $72 basic average. Tom doesn't take all of it home, however. As one who knows how tough it is to have no reserves to fall back on in a crisis, he believes in putting something aside on a systematic basis.

He has the company take out $5 a week for defense savings bonds. In addition, he puts $2 a week into a Christmas Club account at a neighborhood savings bank. That buys Yule gifts for all the family—gifts with a heavy accent on practicality. Tom got some underwear, a tie, and a handkerchief from Helen and the kids last year. Helen's portion was a skirt, a white satin blouse and a couple of pairs of stockings. Gregory was too young to care about anything except his bottle, but young Tom got a big bundle of toys.

Blue Cross hospital insurance for the family takes $6.12 a month of Tom's earnings. Another $2.50 a month goes for his dues as a member of the International Association of Machinists, A.F.L. Tom, who let his G. I. insurance lapse when he came out of the Army, has a $1,000 life insurance policy. So has Helen. They carry a $500 policy for young Tom and the same amount for Gregory. All told, the premiums come to $135.93 a year.

They have other fixed costs. Gas and electricity run to about $2.50 a week and the telephone costs half of that. It is harder to figure what they will have to pay the doctor and the dentist, to say nothing of the druggist. The other day Helen ran down to the drug store for a little salve and some odds and ends for Gregory. She returned with her purse $6.50 lighter.

The Garlands don't feel they have had more than their share of bad luck when it comes to illness, but they have had to go into hock several times to keep up with their medical charges. Their worst siege was when young Tom was born with a slight foot deformity. They took the boy to a specialist once or twice a week until he was a year and a half old. That cost about $30 a month. It cost $25 more to buy his first pair of shoes. Friends told them they could get equally good treatment at a clinic, but they are glad they handled the problem the way they did. Their son bounds around like a gazelle these days.

If anyone wonders why business is so anemic in the garment trades, the Garlands are part of the answer. Helen didn't buy any clothes last year because she was pregnant, and she hasn't bought any yet. She has a mouton coat her mother gave her as a wedding present. That keeps her warm in the cold weather. She is waiting to see how much it will cost to get young Tom's tonsils out before she decides whether she will do anything about a new spring wardrobe. In the house Helen usually wears slacks to save her dresses and bedroom slippers to save her shoes.

Tom is not much of a dresser, either. At the factory he wears a sports shirt and a pair of trousers. The only difference at home is that the shirt and pants are cleaner. He feels he will be really well dressed when he can go to the closet and choose between a blue suit and a brown suit.

The last suit he bought was not for himself but for his father-in-law. He bought it as a Christmas gift, along with two shirts for his brother Joe, and he is paying for it in installments of $5 a week. A snow suit for Tommy set the Garlands back $18 this winter. A department-store time payment account costs them another $1.50 a week for miscellaneous items of clothing and household supplies. One major expenditure they are putting off is a bed for Tommy. He still sleeps in a crib and his parents feel it is past time for a change.

Tom and Helen are not feeling sorry for themselves. They have been through enough to see their problems in perspective. They knew plenty of people with greater troubles. At Tom's own factory a few weeks ago, a hundred workers were laid off because the company could not get enough metal and other materials to keep everybody on the job.

Tom not only has his job, he has more money on the way, at least theoretically. The company and the union agreed on a wage increase of 8 cents an hour nearly a year ago, but the raise is tied up by Government red tape. The Wage Stabilization Board has to pass on the contract before the extra money can be paid to Cutler-Hammer employees. When the increase is approved, it will be retroactive to July 1 of last year. That means a lump sum of about $100 for Tom, and $3.50 a week more in each pay check from then on.

However, in the last few weeks, the same shortage of materials that forced the layoff of 100 Cutler-Hammer employees has cut Tom's working hours. The result is that his weekly pay, before taxes and other deductions, has been running a shade under $63, or $9 less than his year-round average. That makes it practically impossible to balance the family budget, and Tom has no way of knowing how long it will be before his checks fatten up again.

But, tough as life may get, the Garlands are glad they are Americans. "We're a lot better off than we would be anywhere else in the world," Tom says. "We may not get everything we want, but, at least we can choose what to do with our money. In other countries they don't even have a choice. No matter how bad things are, we're better off than they are."

Tom and Helen are happy about reports from Washington that the cost of living is coming down, but they would be happier if they saw the drop reflected in what they pay at the meat market and the grocery. Falling prices are still something they read about in the newspapers, and every optimistic report is counterbalanced by warnings of more inflation on the way.

Tom's idea is that the Government ought to put a stop sign somewhere along the road to higher living costs. "They should set a date six months from now," is the way Tom has it figured out, "and say on prices, that's it, and on wages, that's it. There's got to be a stopping point somewhere, or else we're all finished."

Helen has an even simpler idea. "I only wish the prices would come down," she says.

Who Are the American Poor? *

What is the American standard of living? Is there such a thing? Is the average American family portrayed accurately in advertising copy? Or is the drab picture painted by Communist propagandists closer to truth?

Any competent answer must be prefaced by a factual analysis of family income patterns. Mr. Heilbroner provides this analysis, which is made more vivid by his description of impoverished family groups. Going further, he suggests causes of low economic status in the United States and things that must be done to raise the American standard of living.

Unanswered, except by implication, in this article are two basic questions: Are individuals or society to blame for our poverty-stricken families? Are government-guaranteed minimum standards of living justified on the American scene?

In 1948—a year we are going to look back on fondly for quite a few to come—a hundred and forty-odd million Americans, digging and blasting, making and planting, clipping coupons, cornering markets, and begging on street corners, pulled down the staggering total personal income of $212,000,000,000.

If $212 billions is too large a number for you to imagine comfortably, you

* Robert L. Heilbroner, *Harper's Magazine,* June, 1950, pp. 27–33.

can settle for the fact that we receive the largest amount of purchasing power ever distributed in any nation in history and that our average standard of living was the highest ever achieved by any civilization of which we know.

All that is true and very reassuring.

But at the same time that our aggregate national income was making us the economic wonder of the age, these facts about our national state of well-being were also true and somewhat less reassuring:

One out of every two single-dwelling individuals lived on less than $1,000.

One family out of ten got along—to the extent that a family could get along—on $20 a week or less.

Out of forty million families in the nation, ten million shared in the greatest boom in history with an income of less than $40 a week—just over $13 per person.

These alarming statements should put you in a frame of mind to examine a curious table of statistics: the distribution of income among American families and individuals in 1948. And perhaps they will prompt you to look for something more in the columns of figures than just an impersonal collection of facts—for the distribution of income is *the* basic blueprint of the American economy.

It is an odd picture, both impressive and disturbing. Here is an industrial society which not so many years ago would have been thought Utopian: the better-off actually outnumber the poor. Here is the only society with a mass market for luxury goods; there are more Americans with incomes over $5,000 than the total populations of Canada and Australia put together. Here is also an unresolved hard core of poverty which in 1948 limited one-quarter of our citizens to a standard of living far short of that which we required for our national health, our social morale, or the mass market necessary to keep our farms and factories running at full production.

The Distribution of Income in the United States in 1948

Total Income Received During the Year	Total Number of Families	Total Single Individuals, Not Living with Families	Total Number of People (Family Members plus Individuals)
Under $1,000	4,020,000	4,090,000	16,220,000
$1,000–$2,000	5,580,000	1,830,000	20,160,000
$2,000–$3,000	7,950,000	1,240,000	28,470,000
$3,000–$5,000	12,970,000	810,000	
$5,000–$10,000	6,900,000	140,000	76,260,000
Over $10,000	1,110,000	30,000	

It is because our total national income is so large that the thinness of thirty million slices of the income cake at the bottom is disturbing and provoking.

What is disturbing is not that there is poverty in America—everyone with eyes to see knows that for himself. The provoking fact is that there is so much poverty, so much marginal living amidst so much plenty. One child in five lives in the heap of families in the bottom two layers of the nation's pile of incomes; something like five elderly persons out of ten scrimp along on a level well below the needs, not to say the rights, of the aged. Out of 140-odd million Americans on the march, thirty million have fallen out of step; in fact, fifteen million have dropped out of the parade altogether.

But there is no point in dramatizing further the fact that the statistical picture of America differs a good deal from the advertising man's conception of it. Nor are we ready for panaceas or polemics or politicking. These are unpleasant facts, to be sure, but before we lose our balance in outraged indignation, let us inquire why a country so rich and productive as our own can yet fail to provide a decent living for so large a fraction of its citizens.

One final word. You will want to know how much credence to place in the statistics themselves. They are the facts reported by a sub-committee of the Joint Committee on the Economic Report of the Congress of the United States, a sub-committee which is looking into the question of our low-income families. The data have been gathered by the Bureau of the Census and are public information. Other independent surveys tally very closely with the findings of the Census.

At the bottom of the nation's pile of incomes lie nearly ten million families and almost six million individuals whose earning in 1948 averaged under—well under $40 a week. But low incomes are all these people seem to have in common. For if you should take a family or an individual at random and look behind the bare statistics of their wealth, you would probably find that you were looking at Americans in one or more of six quite separate social or economic groups:

They might be rural poor. Just where the threshold of rural poverty lies is not an easy thing to say: $2,000 goes a lot further in rural Abilene, Kansas, than in urban Albany, New York, and most farm families provide some of their own food (not all, by a long shot) and usually they own their own homes and pay no rent. If we were to choose $2,000 as the threshold, we should have to judge *half* of America's six and a half million farm families to be badly off; that would obviously be a serious distortion of the facts.

But I think we can agree that an income of $1,000 is too little to keep a farming family of even the simplest tastes in decent food and clothing and medicine—not to mention feed and seed. There are over 1,700,000 farm families with incomes under that, a quarter of them with five or more mouths to feed. Counting only rural Americans with less than $1,000 income, there are well over six million farming poor—blacks, whites, share-croppers, Dust Bowlers, tenants.

They might be aged. Four and one half million families in the United States are headed by a person over sixty-five (who is not just "living with the family") and there are another two million single older folk who must live on what they make or get. *One out of every four elderly families and two out of every three single older men or women got along in 1948 on less than $20 a week.* The Social Security Administration tells us that in June, 1949, there were a quarter of a million Old-Age beneficiaries sub-sisting on less than $500! Here is one such case:

After working thirty-three years for the same company as a marble-worker, Mr. N. quit his job because of failing health and became entitled to monthly (Old Age) benefits of $10.93. The beneficiary, who is a widower, lives alone in an attic apartment for which he pays $10 a month rent. During the survey year he received $229 from public assistance and the payment of a $10 doctor bill by a lodge. He stated he needs more medical assistance, but hesitates to ask for more as he feels he is getting enough from public assistance. The bene-ficiary's only asset is a $200 bank account and a life-insurance policy with a face value of $250 on which he is still paying premiums.

They might be Negroes. Five million Negroes—mostly not on the farm —crowd into families in the brackets under $2,000; two of the five million have only one half of that. Not only is the Negro poor, but the fact that his chances for advancement are so closely circumscribed more or less con-demns him to a permanent continuance of his marginal economic status.

They might be broken families. No one knows exactly how many broken families are to be found in America—families headed by a widowed or deserted or divorced parents or even by an oldest child. We do know that out of 6.3 million urban families with incomes of less than $2,000, 1.5 million were headed by women, and that half a million of these families (with over one million children) depended in whole or in part on relief to stay alive. Even worse, half of these families on relief had total incomes of under $1,000.

They might be disabled. Disabled people—industrial casualties, social derelicts, the mentally and physically ill—number at any time about 4,500,000 people—and that excludes both the aged and the very young. Many of the disabled are living on charity, others are using up their savings; too many are destitute. About one third of the poor will mend its strength, rejoin the working force, and leave the lowest income brackets; another third will move up the economic scale *if* it receives the rehabilitative training that it needs. A final third—one and a half million people—will be wards of the community as long as they are alive.

Or they might belong to a sixth group. And the sixth group is different. For what we have been cataloguing hitherto are, so to speak, the economic and social problem children of our day. There is nothing new about rural poverty or impoverished old age, nor about Negro exploitation, nor about the social tragedies of broken families and disabled working people. What may be shocking for those who are not informed about these social problems is the number of our citizens who fall into one or another of these groups. Perhaps as many as ten to fifteen million Americans live on the edge of deprivation because they have literally dropped out of the industrial framework which keeps most of the rest of us comfortably above the water line.

But the sixth group is different because it is not the victim of social circumstances. It is simply a group that fails to earn a decent keep because the jobs it does are not sufficiently productive to warrant a decent wage.

In 1948 for every four workers who earned over one dollar an hour of work in a manufacturing industry, there was one worker who did not. Aside from the truly marginal jobs—the sweepers and the janitors and the cleaning women—here is just a sample of a few low-wage industries:

Percentage of Workers Making Less Than $1 per Hour

Men's seamless hosiery business	
Male workers	48
Female workers	84
Fertilizer plants	
All workers	69
Grain-milling industry	
All workers	54
Wood furniture industry	
All workers	60
Men's shoe industry	
Male workers	30
Female workers	64

And these are only small and scattered segments of our industrial machine. There are the tobacco plants where the *average* wage in 1950 was under $40. Among the poorest paid jobs in the country are broad sections of the textile industry, the hotel industry, the retail stores, the cleaning and dyeing industry, and still others. . . .

Poverty is nothing new to us Americans; we still have clear memories of breadlines and Hoovervilles and the stagnation of the thirties. But this poverty of which we have written is different. For in 1948—to all intents and purposes—there are no large-scale unemployed in America. At any-time during the year the number of people without jobs averaged just over two million, and this included the normal shifting about from job to job as well as the irreducible burden of the unemployables. It was rock-bottom unemployment for a dynamic economy.

So the fact that we suffered poverty amidst plenty was not an indictment of a system which did not work. On the contrary, from the point of view of the number of job opportunities offered, it never worked better. This was poverty which resulted from bumping up against the hard physical limits of an economy which many of us think as incredibly bountiful and inexhaustibly rich.

It isn't. Despite our billions of dollars of aggregate income, we are cramped and bound and sharply limited in the amount of real wealth we can scrape up and fashion from the resources at our command.

Nor is this an indictment of our distributive system. Fifty-five per cent of us lived on more than $3,000 a year—a figure which may seem modest enough, but which represents a new epoch in economic engineering. And although the few who were very rich received far more than the many who were very poor, the fact remains that many of the lower-income groups were subsidized by the transferred incomes of the wealthy. If it can truth-fully be said that not many moguls could justify their enormous (pre-tax) incomes before a court of social justice, it can also be maintained that many a typist, many a delivery-boy, many a salesgirl was grossly overpaid in that year of super-boom, in terms of the services which they actually rendered the community.

No, the distributive system was not too bad, and after taxes it was better yet. The fault must lie somewhere else.

The fault—if it is a fault, for no one is directly responsible—is not spec-tacular. It lies partly in the fact that our economy has not moved forward at an even pace throughout the ranks, that there have been laggard sectors which have failed to keep up with the general advance toward a better way of life. By now some of these sluggish backwaters of inactivity are almost detached from the rush of the main current. The old and the dis-abled, the victims of discrimination and rural isolation and decay, these and other groups will for many years need programs of special care if they are to share in our national prosperity. Few of us have squarely faced the scope and extent that these programs (if they are to be effective) must neces-sarily attain.

But there is another reason for our plight.

That reason is the low level of productivity at the bottom of the economic pyramid. By productivity I do not mean industriousness; low productivity does not just come from lazy backwoods farmers and unskilled workers who do nothing but lean on their shovels. Productivity means the ability to produce; and the ability to produce, in this industrialized world, means a chance to work with capital goods, with equipment and machines. After all, no one works harder than the Asiatic peasant who toils all day to stay alive. And yet no one is less productive. Add a little capital—in the shape of a bullock—to the primitive farmer, and watch his output shoot up ten- and twenty-fold. Add a couple of machines to our ditch-diggers and they will become crane operators, our share-croppers will become combine mechanics.

And underneath the whole, behind the ten million neediest cases, the misfits and the unproductive workers, lies the basic fact of scarcity. For what we are stricken with—at the lower levels of our economic structure—is the same disease that is eating all the world: a shortage of productive apparatus. We Americans—the most prodigious capital-builders the world has ever known—still lack the wealth—the real, hard, physical wealth, not the stocks and bonds—to make us all productive. And because the capital we have is unevenly spread from trade to trade, some sectors of the nation are badly undeveloped. Three-quarters of America has grown to an impressive stature; it can not only sustain itself in style but help the outside world as well. A laggard fourth remains. . . .

From the point of view of a world where living standards in the past half-century have actually *declined,* what is remarkable about America is not the fact that thirty million people do not have enough, but the fact that 120 million do.

. . . The disagreeable fact is that for this poverty of scarcity there are no miracle drugs. But that does not mean that nothing can be done—far from it. It means we need tonics more potent than relief and more specific than mere pumping, and that we must distinguish palliatives from cures.

Take, for example, the problem of our rural poor. We can help the blighted farmer by jacking up the prices of the crops he grows; we can buy endless quantities of potatoes in Aroostook County. This is welfare of a sort, particularly if you live in Maine. But for most of us it is nothing but a transfer of wealth from the nation at large to one small corner of it; if the potato-growers are better off it is because our income taxes have made them so.

But we can help the farmer in another way. When we bring in power to counties which have been without electric lights or pumps or generators, when we upgrade an entire region with a TVA, when we curb floods, terrace slopes, revitalize the soil—that is welfare of a different sort. That's the sort of welfare that does more than prop the farmer up; it puts him on his own two feet.

Or think about the question of our aged. We can face up to the problem of indigent old age by ladling out purchasing power with Old-Age Benefits and we can buy options on the future with old-age pension schemes. All that is well and good; at least it prevents the bottom from dropping out of the market as our population reaches sixty-five.

But can we do nothing better than give the old a helping taken from the plates of others? . . .

Is it not possible to have our aged *contribute* to our national wealth at the same time that we gladly contribute to their welfare? For example could we not—as Professor Slichter has suggested—pay to those employers who keep older workers on the job a portion of the Old-Age pensions which the government would save? Surely everyone might benefit from such a plan. And can we not find parttime work and special tasks to tap the earning power of those who want to supplement the pittance of government support? There must be some better way of using our old workers than making them night watchmen—and it is these better ways that we must plan (business and union leaders willing) if old age itself is to help us bear the cost of growing old. . . .

It is apparent that the disabled need retraining if they are to generate their own support: yet in 1948 we rehabilitated only 50,000 and left 1,500,000 on relief. And the Negro needs a foothold too: how can we build a market up when we hold a twelfth of the nation down? There is an economic cost to prejudice and measures like FEPC can build self-support along with self-respect.

The principle is clear. Static welfare by itself is not enough, handouts without a plan are little better than the dole—the last resort of a society which has given up the goal of progress for the three square meals and orderly existence of the Old People's Home. If we would harvest where we sow we must point our thinking toward making useful citizens out of those who have been cast aside.

But there is one group that we cannot help with welfare—the workers at the margin who do not earn enough. For while we can bolster up the chambermaids, the mill-hands, and the bellhops by legislating higher minimum wages, we cannot legislate ten millions at the margin into better jobs. . . .

To raise the margin, to make ten million better jobs, we have to grow. And growth is not an economic process that we can take for granted.

It was the fashion a few years ago to speak of America as an economy in which the hope for growth was gone. The bogy of maturity was at our heels: we talked of lost frontiers and stationary populations and gloomily debated whether air-conditioning and airplanes could supply the economic boost we had once got from the railroad and the automobile. The consensus was that we had reached the peak: the most we could look forward to was a dignified but cautious life—no violent exercise to be allowed and a regular diet of government pills to keep our energy at par.

Today that forecast seems a bit hasty. Our economy may be mature, but it is far from senile; perhaps it was the shock of the depression which made us myopic toward our past and caused us to forget the history of American production. For if any single feature characterizes our past one hundred years, it has been growth. Since 1850 we have given jobs to fifty million workers, cut their working time by nearly half, and upped the output of each man by 600 per cent.

And our technology has not lost its vigor: since the end of the war we have engineered at least two new *industries*—plastics and television—and the incalculable investment opportunities of an atomic age are dimly visible for the future. We have found that our frontiers are far from closed: American capital is wanted from the Ganges to the Rhine and we are seeking ways to overcome the risks of foreign lending. Even our population has taken a new spurt: since the outbreak of the war we have added the equivalent of Canada to our census.

But the fact that growth can give us what we need does not mean that we should lean back and wait for our salvation. *If* we keep on growing at our present pace—two per cent per year—we *can* double our real earnings in our lifetimes, and before the next decade is out the average family *can* enjoy an income of $5,000. The opportunities for growth are there: the man who operates a bulldozer worked with pick and shovel yesterday, and the man behind the hoe today *can* some day sit behind a tractor. The troubling challenge is whether we will *in fact* push against our boundaries.

And for that no complacent answer can be given.

For the real danger is that we will lose the fight against our poverty by default; not because our motors fail to deliver enough power, but because we fail to run them to capacity. Growth will only be a tantalizing vista unless we march resolutely down the road; if we do not find the sticks and carrots to keep us on the march, the problem of our poverty will be infinitely worse. We are the richest nation that the world has ever known, and yet we are not rich enough to give us all a decent living. If America at full production has thirty million poor, how will we fare at three-quarters speed ahead? To the honest poverty of not-enough-to-go-around let us not add the more dangerous and shameful poverty of failing to make vigorous and intelligent use of what we have.

Wards of the Government *

Essential to an understanding of the current debate over the welfare state is a definition of "slavery" and "freedom." What is "freedom" in the modern world? Does it mean liberty unrestrained by higher authority? Or does man achieve true freedom only when he accepts law and regulation? Does an absence of legislation confer freedom and choice on the powerful at the expense of the weak? May it not mean the freedom to starve for the aged, disabled, and unemployed? Does a society of urban, industrial workers require more legislation than a rural society of small, independent farmers. Does government intervention usually destroy the moral fiber of free citizens—making them wards of the government?

The constitutions of former American slave states generally specified that the masters must provide their slaves with adequate housing, food, medical care and old-age benefits. The Mississippi Constitution contained this additional sentence:

The legislature shall have no power to pass laws for the emancipation of slaves . . . [except] where the slave shall have rendered the State some distinguished service;

The highest honor that Mississippi could offer a man for distinguished service to his country was personal responsibility for his own welfare! His reward was freedom to find his own job and to have his own earnings, freedom to be responsible for his own housing, freedom to arrange for his own medical care, freedom to save for his own old age. In short, his reward was the individual opportunities—and the personal responsibilities—that have always distinguished a free man from a dependent.

What higher honor can any government offer?

The Rights of a Slave

Many present-day Americans are trying to avoid this personal responsibility that *is* freedom. They are voting for men who promise to install a system of compulsory, government-guaranteed "security"—a partial return to the old slave laws of Georgia that guaranteed to all slaves "the right to food and raiment, to kind attention when sick, to maintenance in old age. . . ." And the arguments used to defend this present-day trend

* Dean Russell, *Wards of the Government* (Foundation for Economic Education, 1950).

toward the bondage of a Welfare State are essentially the same arguments that were formerly used to defend the bondage of outright slavery.

For example, many of the slave-holders claimed that they knew what was "best for the slaves." After all, hadn't the masters "rescued" the slaves from a life of savagery? The advocates of government-guaranteed "security" also claim that they know what is best for the people. Many of them argue in this fashion: "After all, haven't the American people conclusively shown that they are incapable of handling the responsibility for their own welfare?"

Many of the slave-holders sincerely believed that the "dumb, ignorant slaves" would starve to death unless their welfare was guaranteed by the masters. And the advocates of compulsory "security" frequently say: "Are you in favor of letting people starve?"

Most Precious of All

But as proof of the fact that personal responsibility for one's own welfare brings increased material well-being, consider the emancipated slaves. Among them, there were old and crippled and sick people. They had no homes, no jobs, and little education. But—most precious of all—the former slaves were responsible for their own welfare. They were *free*. They had the privilege of finding their own security.

Now compare the remarkable progress of those former slaves to the lack of progress of the American Indians who were made wards of the government; who were given state guaranteed "security" instead of freedom with responsibility. In 1862, most American Negroes were slaves. Today they are about as self-supporting and responsible as other American citizens. Meanwhile the Indians as a group have become less self-supporting and more dependent on government aid. It has been claimed that many thousands of Indians will actually die of starvation unless the government feeds them. If this is true, why is it so? . . .

Instead of freedom, the Indian has government-guaranteed "security." Instead of individual responsibility, he has a government bureau to handle his personal affairs. There are special laws governing his right to own land and to spend tribal money. Under that system of bondage it should surprise no one to find that many thousands of Indians have remained uneducated, hungry, diseased, and mismanaged. . . .

A Return to Bondage

The advocates of this compulsory "security" honestly seem to believe that most Americans—including the Indians—are too ignorant, or lazy, or worthless to be trusted with their own destiny; that they will literally starve in the streets unless their welfare is guaranteed by a "benevolent" government. However good their intentions may be, these disciples of a Relief State are demanding that they be given the power to force mankind to follow their plans. In the name of liberty they advocate bondage!

This is true because the persons who receive support from the state are thereby led to expect—and then to demand—more support from the state. They become dependents. Thus they enter into a form of bondage. They lose their individual freedom of choice to whatever extent the state assumes responsibility for their personal welfare. In time, as is now the case in the Welfare State of Russia, the people become completely subservient to the state. In effect, they become slaves of the "benevolent" government that has promised to solve all of their personal problems for them!

Admittedly, this is not the intent of the planners. Apparently, most of the advocates of government paternalism really believe that they are able to know and to do what is "best" for all of the people. Most of them may honestly desire to help the people. But their efforts *always* result in some form of bondage. For example, the leaders of the Labor government in Britain probably never even dreamed of bringing compulsory labor to its supporters. Yet that is what they did. In England today the democratically elected leaders can—and do—force persons to work where the government decrees they are most needed. And if the person objects to his government's decision, force is used to make him conform.

The Road to Hell . . .

In Russia we find another example of the fact that good intentions are no guarantee of freedom. For instance, in the beginning Lenin and Stalin probably had no desire whatever to bring slavery to Russia. Their announced plan was to free the Russian people *from* the slavery of an all-powerful government. But look what happened!

We Americans of today are following this same path toward the bondage of a Welfare or Slave State. Just as the law once guaranteed "adequate" medical care for American slaves, so a law to guarantee adequate medical care for all Americans is being demanded today. And who will determine what is adequate medical care for a person? Not the person, but the governmental official who has the *authority*.

And jobs? Of course the government can guarantee every man a job —just as every slave was "guaranteed" a job; just as every Russian is "guaranteed" a job. But is is impossible, of course, for the government to guarantee everyone a job of his own choosing. Some persons may be guaranteed the scavenger jobs. They may not like it, but dependents have little choice.

The Only Hope

It is true that many citizens in this country are old and crippled and sick and homeless. Possibly some of them are jobless through no fault of their own. The same conditions existed during our Revolutionary War. But our ancestors knew that their only hope for permanent security lay in their own individual efforts. They knew that the main purpose of government should be to *protect* whatever security the people were able to attain individually or in voluntary cooperation. They knew that electing or appointing a man to public office cannot endow him with wisdom; it can endow him only with *power*. Thus they took no chances on this power of government being used to encroach upon their individual liberties and their personal responsibilities. In advance, they put positive restrictions on all office-holders. And as a final guarantee of freedom, they specified that any powers not expressly given to the federal officials were to remain with the individual citizens and their local governments.

The Use of Power

The American Constitution naturally did not list virtues—such as compassion, charity, and respect for one's fellow man—as functions of government. The statesmen who founded our government knew that *all* virtues are purely personal and voluntary. It is utter nonsense to imagine that a person can be *forced* to be good. Government can and should use force to punish a person who commits a crime. But this same force cannot be used to create kindness and compassion within the mind and heart of any person.

Thus the authors of our Constitution left compassion and charity—aid to the unfortunate—on a strictly voluntary basis. They designed a form of government based on individual freedom, personal responsibility, and equality before the law for all citizens. Wisely, they made no attempt whatever to separate freedom of choice from the resulting reward or punishment, success or failure. Since they recognized the absurdity of passing laws to protect a person from himself, they left all citizens free to make their own decisions concerning their own personal welfare. From all viewpoints, including that of material security for the so-called common man, those decisions concerning the proper functions of government proved to be the most effective that the world has ever known in this field.

Bread and Circus

If this state-guaranteed "security" idea were new, it might help explain why so many people insist on trying it. But it is not new. It was written into the Code of Hammurabi over 4,000 years ago.   In one form or another, it has been tried time and time again throughout history—always with the same result.   In the Roman Empire it was called "bread and circus."   More recently, Karl Marx called it socialism.   He believed that the state should take "from each according to his abilities" and give "to each according to his needs."

Marx said that it was the duty of government to provide all people with adequate housing, medical care, jobs and social security.   Word for word, the advocates of government "security" in this country are saying the same thing today.

And just as the Russians are enslaved to a Welfare State, so this country is being carried into bondage by accepting the same false principle.   Just as force is used in Russia to make the people conform to the security laws designed "for our own good."   And just as the Russian state punishes any objector, so the American state will now imprison us if we refuse to conform.

If you doubt that compulsory socialism has gone to that extreme in this country, just test it, for instance, by refusing to pay the social security tax that is taken from your salary.   The government will do the same thing to you that it did to the owner of a small battery shop in Pennsylvania who balked at the idea of compulsory social security.   First, the state confiscated his property.   Still he refused to obey.   Then the state preferred *criminal* charges against him.   And in January of 1943, the government gave him the choice of conforming or going to prison as a criminal—an enemy of the state because he refused to pay social security!   He paid.   And his six-months' prison sentence was suspended.

Next may come total government housing—"for our own good," of course.   Then the state will assign us so many square feet of "adequate" living space.   This is true because, under complete state ownership of housing, there is no other way that government can do it.   We may ask for more space, a different location, better service, or a choice of neighbors.   But we already know the government's answer.   Even today, a person has no real choice when he lives in government housing.

Next may come full employment with government-guaranteed jobs for everyone.   A person will say: "I don't want this job."   And as happened under England's program of government-guaranteed full employment, the American Welfare State will also answer: "We will put you in jail as a criminal unless you work at your assigned task."

Along about then, the advocates of government-guaranteed "security" may begin to understand the inevitable results of their ideas.   They may realize that it is *power* that makes a dictator, and not what he's called or how he's elected.   When that fact has become obvious to everyone, the advocates of compulsory "security" will then exclaim: "But we didn't mean this!" It will be too late to turn back at that point. Just as the night follows the day, so government aid *to* the individual is followed by government control *of* the individual, which necessarily means government force *against* the individual.

No Easy Way

Fortunately, it is not yet too late for America to turn away from the evil that is a Welfare State; a Slave State. But, unfortunately, there is no simple or easy way to do it. Both major political parties—along with the smaller ones—seem to be trying to outbid each other by promising more government housing, more social security, more "free" medical care, more government "welfare" projects, and more special privileges to various groups and interests.

Most of our movies, magazines, newspapers and radio programs generally endorse—directly or indirectly—the idea of some form of government-guaranteed "security." Even the few objections seem to be aimed mostly at the poor administration instead of a recognition that the theory is wrong in principle.

And, whether we like it or not, many of the instructors in our schools and colleges are teaching the desirability of the Relief State, the "planned economy" and government ownership in general.

Golden Rule Rejected

Finally, even some of our church leaders are teaching that the force of government should be used to make people charitable and good. Some of these Christian leaders seem to have forgotten that the principles of the Good Samaritan and each individual doing unto others as he would have others do unto him are voluntary principles. In many cases, these principles have now been discarded for this evil slogan: "It is the duty of government to care for the sick, to feed the hungry, to aid the unfortunate, and to build houses for those who need them." Probably one of the main reasons for the declining influence of the church is that the church is defaulting on many of its own responsibilities by turning them over to government. Many of our church leaders are rendering unto Caesar that which does not belong to Caesar.

But the politicians, periodicals, schools and churches generally reflect the opinions of the persons who support them. Thus the final decision rests on the attitude of each individual American. If enough of us accept the degrading idea of a Welfare State—a Relief State, a Slave State—the process will soon be completed. But if enough individual Americans desire a return to the personal responsibility that *is* freedom, we can have that, too.

The Choice Is Ours

Before choosing, however, consider this: When one chooses freedom— that is, personal responsibility—he should understand that his decision will not meet with popular approval. It is almost certain that he will be called vile names when he tries to explain that compulsory government "security" —jobs, medicine, housing, and all the rest—is bad in principle and in its total effect; it saps character and strength by encouraging greed and weakness; it destroys the individual's God-given responsibility for self-help, respect, compassion and charity; in some degree, it automatically turns all who accept it into wards of the government; it will eventually turn a proud and responsible people into cringing dependence upon the whims of an all-powerful state; it is the primrose path to serfdom.

No, the choice is not an easy one. But then, the choice of freedom never has been easy. Since this capacity for personal responsibility—freedom— is God's most precious gift to mankind, it requires the highest form of understanding and courage.

THE WELFARE STATE IS THE AMERICAN WAY *

Is not the welfare state a foreign importation, alien to historic American principles? Would its adoption spell the end of traditional American freedom? What was the attitude of such revered Americans as Jefferson, Madison, and Lincoln toward the general welfare? Senator Douglas suggests provocative answers to these questions—answers that in effect repudiate the position taken by Mr. Russell ("Wards of the Government"). Can the views of these two commentators be reconciled? If not, which writer has the better case? Is the welfare state the American Way or the Road to Hell?

During this last year many derisive criticisms have been made of federal and state action to improve the people and the term "welfare state" has been used as a derogatory term to describe these activities. It is implied

* Paul H. Douglas, "The Welfare State: Reflections on Its Paternity and Potentialities." Reprinted from *The Progressive,* an independent monthly published at Madison, Wisconsin, November, 1950, pp. 5–9.

that initiative and self-reliance are being badly injured by governmental action to help people and that unless this dangerous trend is reversed or at least halted, the character of our citizens will be almost totally undermined.

It is always hinted and, indeed, sometimes directly stated that such welfare activities have their ideological origins outside the United States; that their true father is either Karl Marx or Lenin, and that it is the duty of all red-blooded Americans to spurn these works of the evil one and, even more, to reject their present advocates.

These are horrendous if somewhat foggy charges. When one presses for particulars, the fog seems to thicken. For when the castigators of the welfare state are asked if they would have us close down our schools and colleges and put barricades across our roads they indignantly ask us not to be absurd.

When we inquire whether we should lock the doors of our hospitals and medical research centers, they say we are caricaturing them.

Then when we try to probe further and suggest that perhaps they do not believe in old age security or unemployment compensation, they say we are misrepresenting their position.

But when we ask if it would not be well to save government money by cutting outlays for rivers and harbors, and doing away with the postal subsidies to newspapers, magazines, direct mail advertisers, mail order houses, airlines, and railways, these opponents of the welfare state commonly become apoplectic in their indignation that we should even think of taking away such legitimate aid to free enterprise.

It is, indeed, hard to arrive at the precise position of this group for it is as misty as the Great Boy with which Ibsen's Peer Gynt contended. To the degree that there is substance to their position, it seems to be compounded of two parts:

First, that while we should keep the present welfare activities of our state and federal government, we should spend less money upon them, and hence relieve the tax-payers of much of the heavy burden which they are bearing.

Second, that the federal and state government should not take on any new welfare projects. In particular, it is urged that the federal government should not aid education in the states, should not help to make it easier for low and middle-income folks to get better housing, and under no conditions should it carry out the Ewing Plan for medical care or the Brannan Plan for farming.

Now let me hasten to say that I, too, am opposed to both the Ewing and the Brannan Plans, for reasons which I have not time fully to develop here. But I would like to point out, if I may, that so far as the federal budget is concerned, our total expenditures for pensions to the aged, to mothers and to the blind, for education, health, and housing comes to about 2½ billions of dollars a year, or about 6 per cent of the Federal budget.

This is in sharp contrast with the thirty and one-half billions which we are spending on arms for ourselves and our allies and for atomic energy, the four and one-half billions on foreign economic aid and occupation costs which we are spending to ward off Communism, or a total of thirty five billions to prepare us more effectively against a future war. If we add the costs of past wars in the form of five and one-quarter billions for interest on the war-incurred public debt and six billions for veterans, we come to a total of about forty-six billions which is being spent yearly for past and present wars. This is more than 76 per cent of the national budget. *It is the warfare world, therefore, and not the welfare state which causes our federal expenditures and taxes to be high.*

Suppose we consider now whether the functions of government should include the promotion of human welfare. I should like to advance the thesis that this not only should be one of the purposes of government, but that *throughout the history of our nation that has been one of the primary aims—perhaps, the most primary—of our national government.* So, far from the welfare state being of alien origin, it is a vital and integral part of the American tradition and ideal.

We can begin at no better place than with the soul-stirring Declaration of Independence composed by the young Jefferson. For the inalienable rights of men which Jefferson proclaimed and which stirred the pulses of the world were not life, liberty, and property, as John Locke had held, but rather Life, Liberty, and the Pursuit of Happiness. And "to secure these rights," Jefferson declared, "governments are instituted amongst men, deriving their just powers from the consent of the governed."

It is interesting that Jefferson did not say the "right to happiness." That is perhaps beyond the power of mortal man to attain by himself and certainly beyond the power of human government to guarantee. But what Jefferson was asserting is that men should have not only the right but the chance "to pursue" happiness—namely, to chase it. What is this but the right to seek human welfare? And let us note also that according to Jefferson, the only purpose of government, indeed *the* purpose for which government was instituted, was to secure these rights for *all* men—not only for the rich and well-born, but also for the poor and humble; not merely for the planters, but also for the small farmers and artisans—yes, and for the field-hands; not merely for white men, for Jefferson did not so restrict himself, but for black men as well; not merely for Protestants, but for Catholics, Jews, and free-thinkers in equal measure.

The Declaration of Independence was followed up two years later in

1778 by the adoption of the Articles of Confederation. It has been the fashion to disparage these Articles because of their manifest weakness in failing to create a sufficiently strong central government. This criticism is well-founded. The Articles were not adequate. But since newly born states, like persons, must creep before they can walk, so the adoption of the Constitution in 1787 would have been impossible had there not been the Articles of Confederation upon which to build.

And what did the all-too-neglected Articles of Confederation say were the purposes of the new confederacy—the United States of America—which was being born? Said Article III:

The said states hereby severally enter into a firm league of friendship with each other for their common defense, the security of their Liberties and their mutual and general welfare.

Thus, even though the "first, fine, careless rapture" of the Declaration of Independence had passed and the Continental Congress, in the terrible period of Valley Forge and after, was faced with the difficult task of getting the 13 separate states to work together, it kept a steady view of what it and the people were trying to do, namely to provide for their "common defense" (or to protect their lives), to "secure their liberties" and for their "mutual and general welfare."

Let us turn now to the Constitution itself. From the hands of one of the most unlikely of persons, peg-legged Gouverneur Morris, who out-Hamiltoned Hamilton in his devotion to the few, the rich, the well-born, and the well-educated, came the preamble summing up the decisions of nearly four months of heated and sharp debate.

We, the people of the United States, in order to form a more perfect union, establish justice, insure domestic tranquility, provide for the common defense, promote the general welfare and secure the blessings of liberty to ourselves and our Posterity, do ordain and establish this Constitution for the United States of America.

Thus the promotion of the general welfare was listed as one of the five fundamental purposes of that more perfect union which was being formed.

When critics of the welfare state are confronted with this fact, they commonly reply that the preamble is merely rhetoric and that it confers no specific powers. These, they say, must instead be sought within the body of the Constitution itself. In a strict legal sense, this is of course true. But the preamble is nevertheless of value, along with the debates and actions of the Constitutional Convention, in showing what was the actual legislative intent of the Founding Fathers. It certainly aids in giving significance to the specific powers granted to Congress by the Constitution in Article I, Section 8, which states in its first paragraph:

The Congress shall have power to lay and collect taxes, duties, imposts and excises, to pay the debts and provide for the common defense and general welfare of the United States.

. . . . .

I hope that this discussion should establish both the legitimate American paternity of the doctrine that it is proper for our government to concern itself with human welfare and that it is constitutional for it to spend money for furtherance of these ends. Far from springing from Marx and Lenin, it instead comes down to us from George Mason, Thomas Jefferson, and the younger Madison. It is eloquently re-stated by Lincoln, who at Gettysburg declared that ours was a government not only "of" and "by" the people but also "for" the people.

It has sprung from the well-springs of the American people themselves, the hardy frontiersmen and farmers, handicraftsmen, manual workers, and professional men—and never forgetting them, the women. For with all their proper emphasis upon individualism and self-reliance, the American people have always known that there are some burdens too heavy to be borne alone and some evils which can be removed only by collective action. To help bear these burdens and to help remove these evils, it is proper for the government, as one of the agencies for collective betterment to act.

So, far from being in the Marxist tradition, this is one of the very factors which has helped to give the lie to his predictions of an inevitable class struggle. Because the state has concerned itself with the troubles and difficulties of average people who have little property and low incomes, it has helped to win and retain their loyalty and devotion to the democratic principles, which, though under attack in most of the world, stand firm in America. They stand firm here because they are rooted in the hearts of the people who see in government, not an instrument of oppression, or an icy institution indifferent to their needs, but an agency which is carrying into effect at least some of the principles of human brotherhood.

There remains of course the practical question of what measures actually do serve human welfare and for how much welfare we can afford at any given time to pay. I do not want to minimize the importance of these questions but I would like to suggest that they are of a lower order of magnitude than the ideological issues, which, though vague, nevertheless disturb men's minds. The questions at stake are instead prudential issues. They are issues of fact and of judgment upon which men of probity may differ but about which disputes ought not to become too bitter. . . .

The areas where unmet needs are greatest are probably the rehabilitation of the physically handicapped, housing, and health.

It is only recently that we have begun to awaken to the very large number of severely handicapped people in this country. The number who are totally and more or less permanently disabled is probably close to half a million, while the number of severely handicapped is probably three times this number. By far the largest proportion of these unfortunates were not crippled in industry, but as a result of such diseases as infantile paralysis, cerebral palsy, arthritis, etc.

Adequate rehabilitation which will combine medical and surgical care, physiological stimulus, the provision of special apparatus, occupational training and placement will be a good investment. It will help reclaim for productive lives many who would otherwise be largely lost.

Housing is another pressing need for both low-income and middle-income families. A lowering of building costs is badly needed through improved methods such as fabrication and assembly on the job, prefabrication, the giving up of unreasonable restrictions by unions and of price agreements by the manufacturers and distributors of building materials. Even this, however, would not bring housing down within reach of the lowest income third of the population.

The slums of our cities where the urban portion of this group have to live are breeding places for juvenile delinquency, crime, and disease. They are at once a health hazard and an economic waste. Like cancer they need to be removed by a major surgical operation. The replacement of the slums by decent housing would reduce juvenile delinquency and crime, improve health, raise personal productivity, and immeasurably strengthen family life.

But the slums cannot be replaced with decent housing for the low-income groups by private capital. For one thing, slum land costs too much, and in the second place the incomes of the poor are still below the amount required for decent housing on low-cost land with adequate space per family. That is why the public housing law passed last year by the 81st Congress will be of help, since it will permit the localities to launch projects for 810,000 families in this group.

The middle income families can be helped not only by the lower construction costs which I have outlined, but also by lowering interest and maintenance costs. One of the best ways of effecting this reduction is through the formation of cooperatives, which, since they engage in wholesale operations, should be helped to obtain access to the capital market at wholesale interest rates and also be given the chance to maintain the properties in part by the personal services of the cooperators.

Finally, in the field of health, there are three admitted needs. First, more research is needed into the causes of such diseases as cancer, cerebral palsy, arthritis, rheumatic heart trouble, etc. This is a costly affair.

Secondly, we need much larger hospital facilities, particularly for the farming regions and the lower and middle income groups of our towns and cities. Finally, we need more physicians, especially to serve farm families and those with incomes under $3,500 or $4,000 a year in cities and towns.

It is a striking fact that we are graduating no more doctors today for our population of 150 million than we did a half century ago for a population which was only half as large. Certainly it would be worthwhile for us to finance the medical education of an additional 2,500 doctors a year for a period of 10 years on condition that at least nine-tenths of these spend a minimum of five years service in under-doctored areas and not more than a tenth in medical research as a return for the help thus given to them. Farm organizations can help in providing a market for the services of these doctors.

There remains the question of insurance against the cost of medical care. The Blue Cross and Blue Shield have been making real headway in dealing with this problem, partially stimulated, perhaps, by the threat of the so-called Ewing Plan for insurance against all medical and hospital costs. The Ewing Plan goes altogether too far in my judgment in providing for insurance against the cost of headaches, backaches, stomach-aches, the common cold and other minor ailments for which the major responsibility should fall upon the individual.

Since the Blue Cross and Blue Shield merely insure against the first portion of hospital and medical costs and since their coverage is at best imperfect, there is a real need for insurance against the catastrophic costs of sickness when costs run above 5 per cent of a family's income or, say, $150, whichever is smaller. This would use insurance for its real purpose, namely as a protection against heavy and unforeseeable losses.

I should like to suggest that here is a middle ground upon which the American Medical Association and Mr. Ewing might well meet, since it is the core of the real economic problem of sickness. It is not the small sicknesses which wreck families financially. They can generally care for these. It is instead the costs of catastrophic illness which cause the real trouble. We could deal with this problem at a third of the cost which the Ewing plan would entail and with a minimum of red tape if we could get the present contestants to get together on a constructive program such as I have suggested.

. . . I hope that this discussion of the historical background of the welfare concept and of some of the practical methods of administration whereby the good can be maximized and the possible abuses minimized, may take some of the heat out of the intellectual atmosphere and make it possible for us to deal in an open-minded manner with the concrete questions of what, if anything, should be done next.   There will still be differences of opinion, but they will not shatter men's souls nor rend the heavens.   That is proper, for they should not.

———◆◆◆———

BUSINESS HAS A MORAL CONTRACT *

Housing, health, education—can individual families best solve such problems?   Or are they so complex that they will yield only to governmental solutions?   Still a third point of view is here presented by a spokesman for business, who, while recognizing the problems, is opposed to government intervention in these areas.   Can you visualize how Mr. Hulcy's program might be implemented in providing housing, health, or education for low income families?

. . . When government operates on the theory of tax and spend, it multiplies the temptation to get our slice from the treasury while the getting is good.   We are inclined to use the cover-term of "federal aid," when we're on the receiving end; but when it's for the other fellow, we call it pork barrel stuff.

In the complex maze of big government, there is a constant temptation to cut corners with bribes.   The chance of being caught goes down as the size of government operation goes up.

Social erosion is a forerunner of socialistic government—and government has a perfect excuse to intrude into areas where private neglect has resulted in social erosion.   Here is an area where the sins of omission can be greater than the sin of commission.   The lethargic citizen throws open the gates to revolution.   The lethargic believer in free enterprise is hamstringing the ox of our economy as surely as if he hacked it with a tomahawk. . . .

I suggest that here is the chance of the century for business—as an institution—to fill a moral vacuum.   Business is the only economic segment of our society that fills a major role in the life of every American community. . . .

The stature of American business is high today.   It is too high for us to indulge in petty sniping.   Let us not condemn everything as socialistic because it costs money.   Let us remember that reformers have a useful function.   They are not all moony-minded or professional do-gooders.   Let us think of them as gadflies under the saddle of inertia.   If they fail to see any solution to inequities in our society except bigger government—why then,

* D. A. Hulcy, *Vital Speeches,* February 1, 1952, pp. 251–52.

gentlemen, isn't it up to this inventive and ingenious system of ours to invent workable solutions—the free enterprise way?

If there's a need for better health facilities, the need isn't going to go away because we don't like government control of health. If there's a need for better housing, the need won't disappear because we don't like government intrusion in the real estate business. If there's a need for better schools, the need won't cancel out because we deplore federal control of education.

In short, if there are cobwebs in the free enterprise household, we must find our own brooms to sweep them down, or government will do the sweeping.

The time to lick socialism in America is before it happens. It is an evil thing, for it trangresses the divine right of a man to be a man, independent in his judgment and with freedom of choice. It is a false god in its promise of justice to the individual—by the injustice of reducing him to a number in a card-index file. It is the green bay tree of our times. Let us, therefore, heed the message in the 37th Psalm and speak with wisdom as the righteous speak; depart from evil and do good—and with trust in the Lord—the workers of iniquity shall be cut down like the grass and wither as the green herb. . . .

MEDICAL PROGRESS VERSUS POLITICAL MEDICINE *

Compulsory health insurance has been bitterly debated on the American scene since it was first proposed to Congress by President Truman in 1945. To the American Medical Association the plan has been anathema, and they have expended as much as $1.5 million per year to prevent "socialized medicine." Some consumer and labor groups have spearheaded a countermovement to secure enactment of a national insurance plan. Dr. Henderson's speech, which gives the official position of the American Medical Association, was originally delivered at San Francisco, June 27, 1950. It has since been widely distributed in reprint form.

. . . American medicine has become the blazing focal point in a fundamental struggle which may determine whether America remains free, or whether we are to become a Socialist State, under the yoke of a Govern-

* Elmer L. Henderson, M.D., American Medical Association Presidential Inaugural Address, *The Journal of the American Medical Association*, July 1, 1950, pp. 783–85.

ment bureaucracy, dominated by selfish, cynical men who believe the American people are no longer competent to care for themselves.

. . . American medicine, which has led the world in medical advances, and which has helped to make this the healthiest, strongest Nation on the face of the globe, has been made the first major objective of those ambitious men in Washington who would make the American people walk in lock-step under a rigidly-controlled, Government-dominated economy.

The American medical system has been made a target for the barbs and criticisms of a comparatively small group of little men—little men whose lust for power is far out of proportion to their intellectual capacity, their spiritual understanding, their economic realism or their political honesty. These men of little faith in the American people propose to place all our people—doctors and patients alike—under a shabby, Government-dictated medical system which they call "Compulsory Health Insurance." And this, factually, is Socialized Medicine, regardless of how hard they try to disclaim it.

But it is not just "socialized medicine" which they seek; that is only their first goal. Their real objective is to gain control over all fields of human endeavor. Their real objective is to strip the American people of self-determination and self-Government and make this a Socialist State in the pathetic pattern of the socially and economically-bankrupt Nations of Europe, which we, the American people, are seeking to rescue from poverty and oppression.

This we must all recognize: There is only one essential difference between Socialism and Communism. Under State Socialism human liberty and human dignity die a little more slowly, but they die just as surely! Never will our people accept the Socialist program that grasping men in our Government have planned for them, if they once understand that fundamental fact. And tonight I call upon every doctor in the United States, no matter how heavy the burden of his practice may be, to dedicate himself, not only to the protection of the people's physical health, but also to the protection of our American way of life, which is the foundation of our economic health and our political freedom.

The moral and spiritual health of a people certainly is of equal importance with their physical well being.

It is not American medicine which has failed to measure up to its obligations. It is not American business nor American agriculture which has failed, nor the fine, loyal working people of America who have failed. It is the administrative arm of our Government in Washington which has failed us in this generation—a Government which is sick with intellectual dishonesty, with avarice, with moral laxity and with reckless excesses! That condition we simply must change, if we are to survive as a strong, free people, and all of us—everyone listening to me tonight, regardless of what his way of life may be—shares the responsibility.

·　·　·　·　·

The newspapers of America, with comparatively few exceptions have taken a strong stand, not only against socialized medicine, but against all forms of State Socialism in this country—and the doctors of America are proud to take their stand beside the fighting editors of America in the battle to save our freedom and the system of individual initiative which maintains it.

I am taking office as President of the American Medical Association at the half-way mark of the fabulous Twentieth Century—and I want to review briefly some of the advances we have made before turning to the goals which lie ahead.

The history of American medicine is a vibrant, continuing story of human progress. Because of that progress, millions of Americans are alive today who otherwise would have died at birth, during infancy, in childhood, in youth or in middle age. The story of never-ending medical progress in this country is not just a story of so-called "miracle drugs" and "miracle discoveries." The real miracle of American medical progress is the miracle of America itself—the motivating power of the American spirit, of free men, unshackled and unfettered, with freedom to think, to create, to cross new frontiers.

Part of the great miracle that is America is our freedom to share, to cooperate, to work together for the common good. That is the spirit which not only has provided the motive power for American medicine, but which has permeated the entire fabric of our American life—inspiring labor and business and industry—science and education, and all our fields of endeavor. It is only the course of wisdom and common sense, therefore, to examine the past, present and future of our medical system—to appraise what has been done, what is being done, and what can be done. For if Government—under the guise of misleading promises of health "security"—finally regiments physicians, dentists, nurses, druggists, scientists, hospitals, medical schools and patients under a totalitarian plan which Washington directs and the people pay for—the spirit of individual initiative not only will be killed in the realm of health. Gradually, it will die in all phases of American life, just as it is dying today in other Nations which first embarked on socialized medicine and then took the final, irrevocable steps down the path of State Socialism.

Let's look at the facts: In America, since the turn of this century, the death rate has been cut almost in half. In 1900, the average life expectancy at birth was only 49 years. Today, new born babies have a life expectancy of more than 68 years—a gift of 19 years of life! For American mothers and babies, the risks of childbirth have been greatly reduced. Both the maternal and infant mortality rates are the lowest in our history. The death rate for mothers in this country is the lowest reported by any Nation in the world! I wonder whether the politicians who want control over medicine can point to any comparable achievement.

At the turn of the century, pneumonia and influenza, taken together, and tuberculosis were far out ahead as the leading causes of death. Today they have been pushed down to sixth and seventh places, respectively, with death rates less than one-fifth and one-sixth of what they were in 1900. If our would-be overseers in Washington had made similar progress in the art of Government, we might look upon their pretensions in the field of health with less fear of the consequences! Dread diseases like typhoid fever, diphtheria, and smallpox—which 50 years ago took a heavy toll in sickness and death—virtually have been eliminated as National health problems. And all of the infectious diseases have been brought under effective methods of prevention, control and treatment.

The fight against disease and premature death is of significance and dramatic interest to every man, woman and child in our country. It is being waged today with weapons which were largely unknown or undeveloped in 1900—new and revolutionary methods of examination, diagnosis and treatment; new drugs, new anesthetics, new surgical techniques, new vaccines and serums, new facts about nutrition, new kinds of equipment and facilities, new methods of sanitation, public hygiene and medical education.

A vital part of the great advance has been the continual expansion and improvement of our hospital system, and the constant raising of standards in our medical schools. Yet only recently, the advocates of a Government-controlled medical system had the amazing effrontery to castigate American medicine because, they asserted, there were more schools of medicine in 1900 than there are today!

The truth is that in 1900, the American landscape was dotted with scores of unaccredited, second-and-third rate medical schools, many of which were actually diploma mills for the production of quack doctors! Is that the condition to which these political medicine men would have us return? Today, as a result of the American Medical Association's fight for higher standards, that dangerously deplorable situation has been eradicated—and we now have 79 Class A medical schools with approximately 25,000 students. And the number of doctors in America is increasing at a more rapid rate than the general population!

The misleading propaganda which has emanated from Washington on this issue is an affront to the American people's intelligence. Typical of this flagrant misrepresentation is the attempt to create a crisis over an alleged "doctor-shortage" in this country. The simple truth is that the ratio of doctors to population is higher in the United States than in any Nation on earth except Israel, where the unfortunate refugee doctors of all Europe are gathered. It is equally true, as we are confident most of the people are aware, that the individual physician today can provide far more medical service than even a decade ago, because of technological improvements.

Now let's look at a half century of progress in the hospital field. In 1900, there were less than 1,000 approved hospitals, with approximately 400,000 beds. Today there are more than 6,300 registered hospitals, with almost 1,500,000 beds, serving more than 16,000,000 patients a year. And the number of hospitals also is increasing steadily.

Finally, in the field of medical economics, the past twenty years have given our Nation the new instrument of Voluntary Health Insurance to provide people with prepaid medical care and thereby take the economic shock out of illness. Today, hundreds of excellent Voluntary Health Insurance plans are available. There are non-profit plans sponsored by doctors and hospitals. There are commercial plans offered by insurance companies. There are fraternal group plans, labor-sponsored plans and industry-sponsored plans.

This has been one of the great advances in medicine in our times, because it is increasing the availability of medical care to people in all income groups. Compulsory Health Insurance is not the answer to this problem. The Voluntary way is the American way to cope with the problem—and the people, by their support of the Voluntary systems, are demonstrating that fact. In 1946, there were 40 million Americans enrolled in the Voluntary Health Insurance plans. In 1949, the number had increased to 61 million—and now it is approximately 70 million. Within the next three years, in the opinion of leading medical economists, 90 million persons will be enrolled in the Voluntary prepaid medical plans—and when that number has been reached, the problem will have been largely resolved.

This, then, is a brief, over-all picture of just one chapter of American accomplishment—the stimulating hopeful march of medical progress in the past half-century.

Mindful of that astounding progress, we can look forward to even more amazing medical progress in the next half-century, if the American spirit of freedom, initiative and adventure is kept alive. The doctors believe that solutions to current problems of medical care and service can be reached without recourse to legislation, without compulsory payroll taxes and without political pressure!

In the half-century ahead, I think we can expect that doctors and their scientific allies will achieve victory over cancer. I think we will conquer infantile paralysis, arthritis, rheumatic fever, premature heart disease and high blood pressure. It is reasonable to expect that pneumonia, influenza, tuberculosis, the common cold and other infectious conditions will be reduced to an absolute minimum by new methods of prevention, control, and treatment. And certainly the years ahead will bring a wealth of new knowledge concerning the human mind as well as the human body.

We are on the threshold of great progress which will do much to alleviate human suffering and to prolong human life. But if we are to achieve this maximum progress in the future, we must keep alive the American spirit and the American methods which have made possible the progress of the past and present! This is the spirit, and these are the very methods, which Government domination of medical practice would destroy! In behalf of American medicine, I want to express my deep appreciation of the wonderful support the medical profession has received from civic groups all over America in its fight for liberty.

Today nearly 10,000 National, State and local organizations, with many millions of members, have taken positive action against socialized medicine —and there is a rapidly broadening front against all forms of State Socialism as a result of the fight that American medicine has been making. We are proud to have such outstanding organizations as the American Farm Bureau Federation, the American Legion, the National Grange, the Veterans of Foreign Wars, the General Federation of Women's Clubs, the American Bar Association, the American Council of Christian Churches, and thousands of other groups, standing beside us in this battle for good medicine and sound Americanism!

With the help of God and the American people, the medical profession will continue to minister to the sick, to relieve human suffering—and to uphold the ideals which have made America the hope of freedom-loving people everywhere.

LETTER TO A FAMILY DOCTOR *

In direct rebuttal to the foregoing article, Mr. De Voto savagely attacks the position of the American Medical Association. Is it true that the AMA publicity program has consisted of distortion and demagoguery? Are most doctors politically naive? What has sparked

* Bernard De Voto, *Harper's Magazine*, January, 1951, pp. 56–60.

medical research—private contributions or government grants? If you find the positions of Dr. Henderson and Mr. De Voto extreme, is there a middle ground? Assuming that a health problem exists in the United States, is there no compromise solution between full government intervention and a hands-off policy? Is our only choice an either-or proposition?

Dear Doctor Jay:

My check for $14.45 accompanies this letter. I have taken two deductions from the $15 for which you billed me. The first one, thirty cents, is the 2 per cent for current payment customary in commercial transactions; business ethics, I gather, now govern our relationship. I will explain the remaining twenty-five cents in a moment.

I fully understand why you have been forced to raise your fee for house calls from $10 to $15, though I am not able to adjust my own professional fees so readily to the rise in living costs. I am still being paid for "The Easy Chair" just what I was getting in June, 1946, when I wrote a piece attacking the anti-vivisectionists for which you and about a thousand other medical men wrote me letters of approval. (Many of them phrased so similarly as to suggest that someone had sent out word to give me a hand.) Still, though my income is not large enough to enable me to pay for my children's education this year without dipping into savings, I realize that it is large enough to put me, statistically, in the topmost 5 per cent of Americans. I am therefore glad to send you the $15, less deductions, as payment for your treatment of my son's cold plus my share of your treatment of others who cannot afford your full fee or perhaps any of it. I will help American medicine take care of them—as long as I can.

I do not know how long that will be. This month the hospital to whose staff you belong asked me to contribute to its endowment drive. The last time it did so I sent what was for me a thumping big check, much larger than I could really afford. I would be glad to contribute now, all the more glad because of the magnificent care I received during the three weeks I spent there last April. But this year I cannot afford to give the hospital a dime. One reason, besides taxes and the inflation, is that the cost of those three weeks, the fee of the surgeon who operated on me, and the loss of income while I was convalescing used up all my margin. The chairman of the drive tells me that it is going to fall far short of its goal; many people on whom it could once depend for contributions can no longer afford them. He, you, and I all know how grave a danger this is to the hospital, to your profession, and to the public. Who is going to pay the hospital's deficits and who is going to support its medical research now that we of the middle class no longer can? I understand your trade association, the AMA, to say that though it cannot answer that question it will not permit the government to pay for them.

I thank you for the publicity matter which you inclosed with your statement. I am especially glad to have the copy of Dr. Elmer L. Henderson's inaugural address, "Medical Progress versus Political Medicine." I understand that in sending me this material you were helping in the crusade which Messrs. Whitaker and Baxter outlined for you in "A Simplified Blueprint of the Campaign against Compulsory Health Insurance." You must, they tell you there, "do double duty until this issue is resolved." You must, they say, "help in treating the ills of the body politic." But I must tell you that as part of the body politic I do not think you are qualified either to diagnose or to treat such illnesses, and I know that advertising agencies will make any diagnosis asked for on a fee-for-service basis.

Your proprietary advertising reached me opportunely. I was following the ads which you were running in the Boston newspapers. I found them dishonest, and they further annoyed me by the copywriter's assumption that I am a fool. But they harmonized well with the ads on the opposite page, which were trying to sell me water from a radium spring that is guaranteed to cure everything from impotence to cancer. They set out to rouse the same fears to the same ends. Your radio commercials interested me, too. Little dramatic sketches presented you as the old family doctor, with the nobility and self-sacrifice which copywriters now have you wearing like a streetwalker's smile, and assured me that you were guarding my health (without fee, the implication was) and simultaneously protecting me from political enslavement. I observed that as soon as you signed off, another little drama came on. There was a woman who was very, very tired. She was so exhausted and suffered so much from backache that she could not greet her husband with the loving eagerness which alone could save their marriage. It turned out that she needed the dollar economy-size of a cathartic which acts painlessly, and I rejoiced that the advertising agencies were saving freedom, monogamy, and peristalsis in the same half-hour.

You and a tobacco company will relieve throat irritation; you and Seneca Snake Oil will get rid of gallstones. Your advertising has already cost you a very great deal of the prestige which the advertising agency told you would put your campaign over. And it has radically changed the relationship between you and me. Your ad speaks of the trust between physician and patient, so noble it says here, so sacred, so certain to be destroyed by what the propaganda calls socialism. But I do not like any kind of solicitation that trades on prestige or on such fears and hopes as illness necessarily involves, and I will not tolerate political solicitation in a relationship of trust. Solicitors who call at my house must use the back door.

My second deduction, the twenty-five cents, signifies that I will not help pay for the $25 assessment you sent to the AMA to run these ads and print these pamphlets. I will not help you finance distortion and demagoguery. In an envelope that has your name and degree on it you tell me by way of Dr. Henderson that "all infectious diseases have been brought under effective methods of prevention, control, and treatment." I am to have no more colds, then, and my friend's daughter need not have died of poliomyelitis last summer. Cure guaranteed, Dr. Henderson's ad says in effect, and it was only through inadvertence that he did not mention the great increase in chronic diseases, especially among the elderly, and that he did not point out how our increased longevity makes more medical service necessary, not less. There is much further disingenuousness in his anthem of self-praise but let us pass over it. I am willing to grant him that on the whole "the history of American medicine is a vibrant, continuing story of human progress." But when you follow him into a political agitation that is at once arrogant, insolent, and dishonest, someone has got to call you.

"It is," the two of you say, "the administrative arm of our Government in Washington which has failed us in this generation—a Government which is sick with intellectual dishonesty, with avarice, with moral laxity, and with reckless excesses." You say that to me when you send me his speech, Doctor. You sound like Mr. Vishinsky, and that eloquent rabble-rouser was surely pleased by your allusion to "the totalitarian plan which Washington directs and the people pay for." You and Dr. Henderson are to be highlighted in your nobility against the government's viciousness, and I am to rejoice that, all other moral heroisms having been defeated, yours will keep us free. And the conspiracy, though so powerful, is so small. You tell me that the people who do not stand on the AMA's party line are "a comparatively small group of little men—little men whose lust for power is far out of proportion to their intellectual capacity, their spiritual understanding, their economic realism, or their political honesty." Expert hysterical rabble-rousing Doctor, and you add, "Their real objective is to gain control over all fields of human endeavor. Their real objective is to strip the American people of self-determination and self-government and make them a Socialist State in the pathetic pattern of the socially and economically bankrupt Nations of Europe which we, the American people, are seeking to rescue from poverty and oppression." You go on to say that the issue is "whether we are to become a Socialist State, under the yoke of a Government bureaucracy, dominated by selfish, cynical men who believe the American people are no longer competent to care for themselves." You and Dr. Henderson and his publicity adviser, from your advertising agency I suppose, appear to believe that the American people are no longer competent to think for themselves. But you make me wonder how competent you are.

Much might be said about this delirious rant, which would have landed Dr. Henderson before the Un-American Activities Committee if it had been circulated by a group of excited college boys who had just heard of Marx. One thing is this: you and Dr. Henderson are saying what is not so. Another is this: Dr. Henderson acquires no immunity by wrapping the flag around the vested interest of AMA's bureaucracy and trustees. Your acquiescence in his claptrap withdraws you from my respect but I take it to be a consequence of the fact that you have not done much thinking about the subject he is misrepresenting. Medicine is your field, not economics, sociology, or government. You come innocent and virginal to social thinking. It is a fair bet that, like thousands of other physicians whose rage Dr. Henderson is whipping up, you have not even read the bills for compulsory payroll deductions for medical insurance which, after all, are what he is talking about. You probably do not know what the bills say, and you had to work so hard on biochemistry at college that you did not learn to detect the propaganda in such phrases as "socialized medicine," "statism," "socialism," and "totalitarianism." With what valorous stupidity you charge head down at those red rags—and all they are concealing is certain bills which would require some people to take out medical insurance. Bills that are an admittedly clumsy attempt to remedy an intolerable situation which your trade association refuses to face realistically and which, it makes clear, must be solved without its help.

You are a busy man, I know. You have not got time to find out for yourself, though every day you see some of the conditions that the bills are trying to alleviate. So you check your intelligence with the AMA, whose refusal to do anything grows more reactionary as conditions grow more alarming. And with your intelligence and your $25 in its pocket, the AMA systematically distorts the facts and misrepresents the conditions to you. You docilely swallow the cure-guaranteed elixir which your propagandists prescribe. And, docile to them but truculent to me, you send me Dr. Henderson's nonsense and forfeit your status.

A friend of mine, a Vermonter, has a useful locution. He does not say, "Joe is a damned fool." Knowing the mixed nature of the human being and the fallibility of human judgment, he says instead, "Joe puts me in mind of a damned fool." What you put me in mind of, Doctor, is a sap.

You had better stop acting like a sap. Our constitutionally elected government, which has to do something about an increasingly alarming social situation that the AMA refuses to deal with at all except on its own long-obsolete terms—do you really think it is what Dr. Henderson says it is? You had better think again, fast and hard. And this pamphlet called "Old Doc Truman's Pink Pills." Have you read it Doctor? Take the passage that begins on page 27. It equates the Democrats, the party which a majority of our citizens have maintained in power, with Communists, and in doing so it makes some of the most scabrous and feculent statements I have ever seen in print. Its distributors have learned a little caution, but not much, from the public outrage that followed the notorious "Dear Christian Colleague" letter which one of your propaganda organizations sent out. As it describes the plot of various committees and learned foundations to deliver medicine and the United States over to Stalin, it insistently repeats Jewish names. It never quite says right out that the Democrat-Communist plot is a Jewish plot, but it is so written as to make many a reader believe that it is. Thus it arrives at a standard technique of totalitarianism: anti-Semitism. Do you accept responsibility for this? You will be held responsible. I got the pamphlet from the office of your State medical society and the girl there said that it was for distribution to patients. You paid the $25 assessment. The noble old family friend has corrupted the relationship of trust with anti-Semitism.

I know that you, personally, do not approve of this, but there it is. Thousands of your colleagues do not, either, and still there it is. Take a tumble to yourself.

And take a tumble to your leaders. Dr. Henderson says that in three more years ninety million people will be enrolled in voluntary health-insurance plans and that "when that number has been reached, the problem will be largely resolved." Even if his wild guess should prove accurate, and even if all those voluntary plans should prove adequate, *will* the problem be "largely resolved"? Dr. Henderson will be satisfied if the remaining 40 per cent of the population are without insurance—will you be satisfied? And are you sure that the AMA will support the voluntary plans which it is now praising? For years it opposed voluntary health insurance as violently as it now opposes payroll deductions. Twenty-six state medical societies, I make it, have sponsored legislation which limits such plans to those that are controlled wholly by physicians. That is, plans in which neither the public nor the subscriber has effective power. Many medical societies have threatened disciplinary action—up to measures which would make practice impossible—against any of their members who participate in any other kind of plan. Some have been convicted of conspiracy in restraint of trade—which is a crime, Doctor—and others are under indictment for such interference with *voluntary* prepayment plans. The AMA has fought hard against comprehensive prepayment plans. It has tried to kill those that have succeeded. On the showing so far, is it honest about voluntary insurance or is it throwing dust in my eyes and yours?

Like a lot of physicians, a lot of us laymen are fed to the teeth with the AMA's methods. With its persistently negative approach to everything.

With its unvarying misrepresentation of the efforts other countries are making to solve the problem.   With its "crusade" and its "battle" and its vilification of the government, the public, and its own members who speak out. With its uniformly misleading attack on "government medicine."   Everyone in the military services is under a system of "government medicine"; so is everyone in a veterans' hospital or receiving out-patient treatment from one.   The Public Health Service is "government medicine."   Several thousand of your colleagues who have had the best training available are practicing "government medicine."   Are they venal, inferior, and suppressed?

One of your ads listed "damage to research" among the ills certain to follow "government domination of the people's medical affairs under compulsory health insurance."   What about that?   The hospital which asked me for a contribution is carrying out fundamentally important researches that are being paid for by the government.   They are entirely in the hospital's hands.   Have they been damaged?   As a member of a committee of the National Research Council, you regularly go to Washington to appraise projects in medical research for which the government is to pay. Your committee is composed exclusively of medical men who are not in the government service.   You decide whether a project is valuable and how much ought to be spent on it; the project then passes to representatives of the government just long enough for them to allocate the money for it; it then passes entirely out of their hands and the government has no more to do with it till private medicine has finished the job. . . . Why do you submit to a patent misrepresentation?   Why do you try to deceive me?

The advertising, propaganda, and vilification which the AMA conducts is steadily, and now seriously, undermining your professional standing and prestige.   The public very much needs both.   The traditional system of medical practice has burst its seams; it is now inadequate and outworn. We are going to have something different.   No matter what your propagandists say, it is certain to be not a single system but multiple and mixed. And there is no chance whatever that the AMA will get what it demands —no chance that the mixed system will be developed and administered solely by doctors.   This is a public matter, a community and national matter.   It requires innumerable skills which medical men simply have not got, and it must be under the unremitting scrutiny of representatives of the public with power to act.   Medical knowledge is only one of many kinds of knowledge that are required for social action.

But you and your colleagues can shape the future of American medicine if you will accept the responsibility.   If you study the problem and act to solve it, not to prevent its being solved.   If you turn back the AMA's headlong opposition to every change not approved by the extremely small group of men who enforce its reactionary policy on its whole membership.   (Is there no lust for power on the top level of the AMA? And how much of this policy is designed to secure to a very few men the largest possible incomes while the average income of medical men is smaller than it would be if people could afford to pay their doctors' bills?) If you stop acting like a sap, then you can count on shaping the solution. But time passes, the problem grows more desperate all the time, and a solution will be worked out somehow—with, without, or in spite of you. It had better be with your help.

Desperate social problems have to be solved, Doctor; they are solved as needs must, if it comes to that. Even if we accept Dr. Henderson's figures, 40 per cent of the population will have no insurance protection against medical expense. Of his 60 per cent, only a part will have adequate insurance. Ward service in the hospital that is trying to raise funds now costs $10 a day, the cheapest room $18 a day. Last week in the out-patient department I saw a patient getting a prescription filled at a drug window. It called for six capsules of aureomycin a day for ten days. The hospital was selling him the capsules at cost, forty cents a piece, $24. If his job paid him $40 a week, he could not afford them. In that case the hospital had to pay $24 for them—and it can no longer get its deficits paid by contribution. Yet aureomycin is cheap compared to certain other remedies which medical research—in part supported by government appropriation—has developed. How could he afford ACTH, or the hospital afford it for him?

There are other considerations too. You know that, in spite of what your advertising says, the only places where American medicine can fully live up to its possibilities are the teaching hospitals. You know that elsewhere it is not doing so well as it wants to and must. You know that there are areas inadequately provided with doctors, hospitals, and the proper equipment for tests, treatment, and research. You know that some doctors are not well enough trained—with the cost of training climbing before your eyes—and that some hospitals are not good enough—with the cost of making them better steadily mounting.

You know too that thousands of physicians disapprove of the AMA policy, are alarmed by it, and want to substitute for it one which will enable the profession to grapple successfully with all these problems. And you know that the hard facts of a rapidly changing world are forcing thousands of other physicians into activities—contract practice is one of them—which the AMA condemns. You know that many thousands of your colleagues agree with Dr. James Howard Means, who is not a Communist, who I think is not a Democrat either, but who *is* Chief of Medicine at a great hospital and Professor of Clinical Medicine at a great medical school. "A learned profession has sunk, or been dragged, in its political sphere, to a distressingly low level," Dr. Means wrote, and he went on, "What organized medicine needs . . . is a new and more enlightened leadership."

That puts it up to you, Doctor.   For the campaign of what the AMA calls "public education" run by an advertising agency, you had better substitute one of self-education.   You had better adopt the scientific attitude and find out what the facts are and what, besides propaganda, can be done about them.   You might begin by reminding Dr. Henderson of his oath: "I shall strive constantly to maintain the ethics of the medical profession and to promote the public health and welfare."   The public does not consider misrepresentation ethical.   The AMA is not promoting public health and welfare by intimidating its members, trying to frighten laymen, lapsing into anti-Semitism, and accusing a government which has also sworn to promote the public welfare, of conspiring with Communists to stamp out freedom in the United States.

You can hold your leadership to proper ends, Doctor, or you can repudiate it.   You have that option.   But if you are to retain the public respect that has been yours or if you are to do your part in guiding the future of medicine in the United States, you have no other choice.

The Old Fear of New Ideas *

What follows is an attempt to draw a parallel between public education and national health insurance, with the implication that cultural lag is the basic problem in the debate over "socialized medicine." Is the comparison valid?   Or is there little relationship between education and medicine?   Can you offer support or rebuttal to implications of the article?

Americans a century ago were fiercely divided on the question of tax-supported education for all children.   No punches were pulled.   The opponents had 10 main arguments and in flowing oratory they presented them.

History seems to be running the film over again today, this time on national health insurance.   The strange thing is that the arguments are exactly the same as those of a hundred years ago.   The quotations in the column to the left, with one exception, are from the Philadelphia National Gazette, 1830.

* Shirley Basch, "The Pains of a New Idea," reprinted from the *Survey Graphic*, February, 1948, pp. 78–79.

Universal Education	National Health Insurance

1. Only those who can pay have a right to it.

The "peasant" must labor during those hours of the day which his wealthy neighbor can give to the abstract culture of his mind; otherwise the earth would not yield enough for the subsistence of all. Languor, decay, poverty, discontent would soon be visible among all classes.

The assumption that people have a "right" to health is as false as the notion that everyone is entitled to freedom from want. Nothing could be more viciously destructive of initiative, effort and progress. Health is a privilege, not a right. (Edward J. Stieglitz, M.D., in "A Future for Preventive Medicine." 1945.)

2. The idea is foreign to our country.

Some of the writers about universal public instruction and discipline seem to forget the constitution of modern society and declaim as if our communities could receive institutions . . . like those of Sparta. . . . No government, no statesman, no philanthropist can furnish what is incompatible . . . civil society.

We need look no further for evidence that this legislation embodies proposals which find no roots in the soil of free America. . . . The system here proposed is alien to the deepest instincts of the American people. (National Physicians' Committee in "Compulsion the Key to Collectivism," 1946.)

3. It should be left to private enterprise.

Education generally, to be effective, must be left to the enterprise and competition of individuals. . . . The whole business of teaching school should be thrown open to private enterprise and free competition, just like . . . running a shoe factory. (Zachery Montgomery in "The School Question," 1866.)

The broad purpose is nothing less than the shifting of responsibility from its threefold traditional base—the individual, the medical profession, and the local community—to the Federal Government and the States. (The Nation's Business, 1940.)

4. Government must not concern itself with it .

It is an old and sound remark that government cannot provide for the necessities of the people, that it is they who maintain the government, and not the latter the people.

That the protection of the health of the citizen is a natural function of government is debatable. The best government is that which governs least, and all history persuades us that freedom is smothered by increasing government paternalism. (L. S. Goin, M.D., California Medical Society.)

Universal Education	National Health Insurance

5. *Political bureaucracy will be rampant.*

In this country nothing could prevent (Public education) from becoming a political job, if a government concern.

Shall patients and doctors retain their freedom of judgment, or shall this freedom be surrendered to a federal bureaucracy? (H. H. Shoulders, M.D., 1946 presidential address to American Medical Association.)

6. *Requiring people to pay for its support is dangerous.*

Authority—that is, the State—is to force the more eligibly situated citizens to contribute a part . . . of their means for the accommodation of the rest, and this is equivalent to the idea of an actual, compulsory partition of their substance.

Compulsion is the key to Collectivism. . . . The Wagner-Murray-Dingell proposals . . . would introduce a compulsory tax to pay for a compulsory service . . . directly affecting the most vital and most sacred function of each individual citizen. (National Physicians' Committee, 1946.)

7. *It is "Agrarianism"—or "Socialism."*

The scheme of Universal Equal Education at the expense of the State is virtually Agrarianism. It would be a compulsory application of the means of the richer for the direct use of the poorer classes.

Frauds like compulsory health insurance . . . anticipate . . . State medical service for everybody. That is Socialism, as unadulterated as if it came from the sanctified pen of Karl Marx. (The Nation's Business, 1940.)

8. *It will destroy initiative and ambition.*

One of the chief excitements to industry among the working classes is the hope of earning the means of educating their children respectably and liberally; that incentive would be removed, and the scheme of State and equal education be thus a premium for comparative idleness, to be taken out of the pockets of the laborious and conscientious.

Ambition is destroyed . . . when all the provisions of socialized medicine are put into effect. . . . The proposed bill . . . makes it possible for the Government to take . . . earnings . . . of conscientious moral workmen . . . and give them to the lazy, shiftless, immoral individuals for sickness which they may have largely brought on themselves by riotous, immoral living. (Edward H. Ochsner, M.D., Chicago Medical Society, 1946.)

Universal Education	National Health Insurance

9. It will lower standards.

Universal Equal Education is impossible . . . unless the standard of education be greatly lowered and narrowed.	Compulsory health insurance . . . would inevitably result in a serious— even criminal—deterioration in . . . medical care. (National Physicians' Committee, 1946.)

10. It is best to insure it only for the needy.

State and National Governments may endow public schools for the indigent . . . But to create or sustain seminaries for the tuition of all classes . . . is beyond their province and power.	It is our recommendation that the Federal Government consider some plan for aid to the states in taking care of those persons who cannot pay for it. (Peter D. Ward, M.D., American Hospital Association, 1946.)

And after all the smoke of the century-old battle cleared away, we had the start of a public school system unsurpassed in the world. The dire predictions of its calamitous effect are now a shadowy memory.

------◆◆◆◆------

PUBLIC HOUSING—WRONG-WAY PROGRAM *

The housing debate, reduced to simple terms, centers around such questions as: How can we best eliminate slums and provide decent housing accommodations for Americans? With whom does responsibility for good housing rest? The individual family? The housing industry? The national government?

To the extent that the Federal government assumes responsibility for the shelter of its impoverished citizens, housing becomes part of the welfare-state philosophy. Such a program is rejected on both practical and philosophical grounds by Mr. Stewart, an official of the National Association of Real Estate Boards.

There is a national unity as far as housing goals are concerned. Private industry, government and social organizations, as well as Mr. and Mrs. America, want more housing, and more home ownership. Those are the only housing goals there are. The question is how to reach them, and government ownership and operation of family shelter in many

* Charles T. Stewart. Condensed from USA, June, 1952, pp. 91–98.

ways is an obstacle rather than a help to their direct and full attainment.

The private housing industry, on the other hand, has been doing a monumental job in moving toward the nation's housing goals. Its widespread utilization of the insured home mortgage program, along with its development of new materials, techniques, and equipment items, has cut the cost of family shelter while improving its quality. A considerably smaller proportion of the average family's budget is required for good housing today than was the case 10 or 20 years ago. . . .

Figures of the United States Bureau of the Census show (1) that we now have more family dwellings per thousand of population than we have ever had since records began; (2) that there has been a dramatic improvement in the quality of our housing supply since the first housing census of 1940; (3) that we have been increasing our housing supply at a rate greater than the rate of population increase; and, (4) that we have made unprecedented gains in home ownership since 1940.

This substantial progress toward our housing goals affects many millions of American families of low and moderate income. While we cannot congratulate ourselves on having removed all the unsatisfactory housing conditions in America, we are far and away the best-housed nation on earth.

In a number of ways public housing is a negative force which keeps us from attaining the quality and quantity of housing that is within reach of our people. Its most pervasive effect is to build a public conviction that good housing is not worth paying for.

While only a small fraction of American families can benefit from public housing, it gives the average citizen ground for thinking that society owes him housing at a lush discount; that he is not expected to pay his full fare in housing even though he is able to; that housing should be, somehow, just "available," like tax-supported public utilities such as the sewer system. While there are some people who clearly need some form of assistance, private or public, in obtaining housing, the vast majority can afford to house themselves adequately, and frequently in better homes than they now occupy.

In cities all over the United States there can be found some housing that most of us deplore, but it is a fact that, in far too many such cases, people living in that deplorable housing do not deplore it—or do not deplore it enough to forego nonessential things in order to obtain the best housing they could otherwise afford.

In 1936, a study by the United States Department of Agriculture showed that American families with average annual incomes ranging from $1,250 to $2,000 were spending more on automobiles than for their homes. In 1941, the United States Department of Labor studied the expenditures of families whose total incomes were under $500 per year, and found that 25.4 per cent of them owned automobiles. . . .

Clearly these people were more interested in automobiles than in the best housing within their reach. They deliberately chose lower housing standards. Other figures compiled by the Federal Government show that in 1949 Americans as a group were spending more for alcoholic beverages than for rent.

Human tastes, likes, and dislikes strongly influence the distribution of a family's budget and many families put trivial and relatively unimportant things ahead of housing in their own scale of values. Good homes are of civic importance to the community and nation, as well as to good family life. Consequently, something should be done about it.

Providing publicly owned housing at a tax-fed loss is the wrong thing to do, since it aggravates the basic trouble. To the family that really needs to be shown why it should rearrange its scale of values, public housing—in effect—says: "Don't frustrate your desire for a car or a TV set just for the sake of good housing. We have a plan that lets you use your income for these things and also gets you the latest in housing at such a discount that you will have practically effortless access to it as a social right."

· · · · ·

Today in the United States, our public housing program, with some 700,000 units built, owned, subsidized, and operated by government, is in fact a socialized housing program. There is just no unsocialistic way of socializing the ownership of even 700,000 family dwellings. The inability of public housing to draw a significant line between beneficiaries and non-beneficiaries among the citizens will be a steady force pushing it along the pattern of European public housing in seeking greater and greater expansion until it is producing virtually all the nation's housing.

· · · · ·

When it is suggested that the best way to meet the needs of families who should have housing help is to provide direct assistance through appropriate private or public local agencies instead of building government-owned projects, it is said that the system doesn't work. The fact is that it not only works, but as the situation in Washington showed, it is being used in the nation's capital itself. It is also the system used, and used successfully, in the well-housed nation of Switzerland.

Aiding the needy family to get private housing is a more effective system than building and operating government neighborhoods for the needy. In the first place, the private and public funds available will go further and help a greater number of families. Aid can be geared to the duration of a particular family's need more readily than in the case of public housing. In our land of opportunity, family distress is usually temporary and, under the direct aid plan, when a family's circumstances improve, it can stay where it is on a self-supporting basis.

Finally, this method of meeting genuine need does not contain the dangers to public attitudes toward housing, or the political dangers of concentrated government ownership of property, that are inherent in public housing.

Families being aided in this manner should not be compelled to put up with substandard housing. They cannot if all dwellings are required to meet standards set by city governments. Every city and town in the country has ample authority to prevent the use of substandard housing or to require it to be brought up to standard by its owners.

. . . . . .

Freedom and civilization depend upon the widespread ownership of property. It is the highest, most urgent, economic goal we can seek.

One thoughtful observer of a growing animalism that has accompanied the attempt to make social planning the be-all and end-all of human existence, has referred to property ownership as the "last metaphysical right" of mankind. (Richard M. Weaver, in "Ideas Have Consequences.")

While we still have a great deal of room in the United States for more family-sized business, family-sized farms, and even family-sized industry, we must look to more home ownership as the principle means of attaining the maximum diffusion of property ownership.

Numerous factors have boosted home ownership in the United States until it now extends to 55 per cent of the families. The latest survey of consumer finances by the Federal Reserve Board shows that 60 per cent of all purchasers of homes in 1950 had average annual incomes, before taxes, of $3,999. Families or other spending units with incomes of $2,999 or less accounted for 29 per cent of home purchases in 1950. These figures furnish ample evidence that, with the modern financing plans available today, home ownership is well within the reach of even the moderate income families.

Even though the increase in home ownership represents a robust 54 per cent in a decade, and even though it may be far beyond the dreams of other nations, we should be restless to extend it much, much further.

Public housing has a definite wrong-way influence on home ownership. Hundreds of thousands of families in the same income group as typical public housing tenants are soundly working toward home ownership under the FHA and VA insured and guaranteed mortgage programs. The instinct for home ownership is a fundamental one, but naturally those who get a direct housing discount at the hands of the taxpayers are inclined to take the line of least resistance and to hold on to it.

Little, if anything, worth having is achieved through the line of least resistance. We will not extend home ownership most effectively to a greater proportion of the nation's families if a substitute—even a poor substitute—for it is made available through the line of least resistance.

Public housing builds that line, even for families not living in it, by the promise and expectation it extends to all families in the income group of those it does house. The more public housing extends, the wider is this promise extended. Its final triumph, achieved under Socialism in England, was to make the production of homes for private ownership or owner-occupancy almost illegal.

Instead of spreading the ownership of property to millions of free-acting, responsible individuals, public housing concentrates more and more property ownership under the centralized control of the state. That, we should learn from history, is a dangerous and antisocial tendency.

———◆◆◆◆◆———

DEMOCRACY CAN'T LIVE IN THESE HOUSES *

In the continuing debate over the welfare state, public housing has been a major bone of contention. Are government slum-clearance programs "creeping socialism"? Or are they, as Senator Douglas contends, an aid in the preservation of democracy? Which is the more dangerous—slums or Federal housing projects? Which course will best preserve a strong, free America?

Whatever the federal government has done or proposes to do about housing, it is a dangerous fact that millions of Americans are shabbily sheltered and living in filthy, malignant slum areas that are growing both in size and in their threat to the physical and political health of our country. Any slum-clearance legislation passed by Congress would have to be followed up by action in states and cities, and by continuous Congressional action.

We Americans like to think of the typical home as a vine-clad cottage, with roses growing on trellises, and trees and grass in the yards; and with all this we associate the pleasing and lively sounds of healthy children at

* Paul H. Douglas, *Collier's*, July 9, 1949, pp. 22, 23.

play. It is one of the glories of America that so many of our homes are of that kind—or, at least, equally attractive.

But it is one of our moral, political and economic responsibilities to do something to lift more homes at least to the minimum level for satisfactory living. The 15,000,000 or more Americans who live in the blighted areas are not inferior to the rest of us. They are only less fortunate. Imagine how you would feel if you and your family were housed as they are. Trouble does not come from men who live agreeable lives. It breeds among men who are frustrated, ashamed and envious.

Some people seem to think that slums are what they are because of the character and capacity of the people who live in them. That is not true. Environment to a considerable degree determines the way men act. The extremely strong or the extremely lucky can break free from the handicaps which surround them. Unfortunately not many have exceptional luck or strength.

Clifford R. Shaw made a careful study of bad localities in Chicago, and in his book, *Delinquency Areas,* he presents some facts that will bring you up short.

For example, he found slum areas in which years ago most of the residents were Irish. The juvenile delinquency rate was from 12 to 14 times that of normal neighborhoods. The Irish in these blighted areas began rising in the world, and moved out. Italians moved in. Juvenile delinquency among Italian youth was almost exactly what it had been when the Irish were there. The Italians moved out and Jews moved in. The delinquency story was repeated. The Jews moved out, and Negroes moved in. Again, the delinquency rate in these blighted sections was some 12 to 14 times that of cleaner neighborhoods.

If I can interpret facts, this means that the living conditions, and not race or religion or color, largely determine delinquency rates.

When the Farm Security Administration began its relief activities in the days of the depression, only rural families who were completely down and out could qualify for its program. If a farmer had means or could get credit, Farm Security could not take him on. Failure was the qualification for getting in under Farm Security. In the South, and elsewhere, this meant that only those who generally were thought of as "shiftless" or "worthless" were assisted. And what do you think happened?

Faith in Human Nature Justified

When the government helped them, about 90 per cent of these people moved swiftly to better living than they ever had known, and paid back the loans the government had made to them. Of those who did not make good, some were sick, and a few—perhaps 5 per cent—were shiftless and worthless.

Farm Security first found reasonably fertile land and reasonably habitable houses for those in need of help. Then it set them up with loans for equipment and work clothes, and even a few dollars for window curtains.

That window curtain item evoked some loud yells of protest, but it was wise. Curtains, bright colors, mean something to women. These people, who had not imagined they ever could have such a luxury as curtains, aspired to new heights of living when they saw them in their own homes. Hundreds of thousands of "shiftless" and "worthless" rural slum dwellers, who never had known the possibility or even the meaning of thrift, became thrifty producers and canners of food. Never before had they had a reason for storage shelves.

These people could not have done this by themselves, and private landlords could not have done it for them. They had to have help, and the national government was the only source from which effective help could come at that time.

The people who dwell in the urban slums today can't get out by themselves, either. They require help. Where is it to come from?

The fact that upward of 4,000,000 dwelling units exist in blighted areas —and many of them are very old—is pretty good evidence that private capital cannot solve the housing problem.

Private enterprise is always alert for profitable investment. It must make a profit in order to survive. If slums could have been cleared and decent dwellings put up for the slum families, at a profit to private investors, it would have been done. But private enterprise should not be expected to commit suicide by plunging into enterprises that cannot possibly pay out. Men who finance great private works do so, usually, partly with the money of other persons. They have no right deliberately to lose it, even for the worthiest of social causes.

I would favor solving the housing problem by private effort, if it could be done that way. But since it cannot, I think the national government must do it. When the soil resources of this nation were threatened by erosion, the national government properly set to work to save them. It must act similarly when human resources are threatened. States and municipalities generally have not the means to do what must be done.

Anyway, the problem, the responsibility and the danger are national.

A Tide That Does Not Turn

. . . You have seen some wonderful illustrations of private enterprise at work in our great cities—for example, the erection of Stuyvesant Town in New York. But, to assure a reasonable profit, the buildings had to be so high as to create other problems of congestion. And the number of persons benefited is a tiny portion of the total who need better shelter.

Perhaps you think of slums as evils confined to some of the big cities of the industrial North and Middle West. . . . The situation is not mainly Northern or Southern, or Eastern or Western, and neither is the problem. It is national.

The Danger of Complacency

Some of you may imagine that because you live in nice small towns where the refreshing air of heaven circulates freely, the cleansing rays of the sun penetrate every room and yard, and rats do not congregate nightly around garbage cans and outside privies, you are immune to the threat of the blighted areas. I beg you, if you imagine yourself safe, to stop and think. If, because of depression in some future decade, we should have dangerous unrest, the consequences would not be confined to the areas where the unrest is most likely to develop first. If some dreadful disease should begin in one area, it might spread anywhere.

Responsibility to do something to clear the blighted living areas is not limited to morality or to national pride. National internal security demands that something effective be done. National health demands it. Protection of your own health and protection of you and your family from crime require it.

A number of years ago several cases of elephantiasis were discovered in widely scattered parts of the United States. Health authorities, alarmed at this alien disease in our midst, began careful studies to learn the source of the trouble, and every case was traced to the city dump in Charleston, South Carolina.

Senator Burnet R. Maybank, now chairman of the Senate Committee on Banking and Currency, was mayor of Charleston when those cases of elephantiasis were traced to his city. That situation, plus a personal experience, started him on the lines of thought and of action that have brought him today to be one of the foremost figures in the United States in the fight to provide for all Americans the kinds of houses which minimum standards of decency and safety require.

One day the public health officer of Charleston reported to young Mayor Maybank that the mayor's laundress was ill with meningitis. The laundress had just returned to the Maybank home the weekly baskets piled with freshly washed and ironed linen and clothes. When the mayor told Mrs. Maybank the disturbing news, she placed those baskets of clothes and sheets and towels and what not in the yard and burned them. Inci-

dentally, like the noble woman she was, she went to the laundress' home
and helped to nurse her.

Mayor Maybank came to Washington and called on the President. He
told the story of the Charleston dump. He told of his personal experience. He explained that the city was broke. It could not act alone, nor
could its businessmen remove the dreadful peril of the dump. He is a
mighty man when aroused, as all of us who serve with him on his committee are aware, and when he went back to Charleston he had a relief
appropriation for clearing away the city's dump. It was a stinking, un-
sightly and horrible spot frequented by buzzards and rats and disease
germs—but it was no worse than other city dumps.

He transformed it into one of the first public housing developments for
Negroes; and the neat buildings stand today as evidence of what can be
done, and what must be done on a vast scale for the public safety. . . .

Slums Cost Taxpayers Plenty

. . . But the slums must be licked, the rise of new slums must be
prevented, by eternal vigilance on the part of citizens, manifested in local
and national action. The apparent cost of the entire job will rise into
the billions, but the benefits will be inestimable. A government investment in slum clearance, which I support, is not a dollar investment in the
narrow sense. It is an investment in American ways of living, and in
ever-rising American aspirations. It is an investment in social and political stability. It is an investment in the fundamental resource of this
free country—the people.

A primary function of our representative and free government is "to
promote the general welfare." When our nation was young, that did not
demand as much government activity as is required now. In those simple, frontier days men were much on their own. But it is foolish for us
to talk now about "going back" to simpler days and simpler ways. The
basic principles of representative government do not change, but the
application of those principles is constantly changing. Otherwise, our
free government would have perished long ago because of a failure to
promote the public welfare as it must be promoted in each generation—in
the bright light of existing conditions, not in the nostalgia afterglow of
conditions as they once were.

I think our government has been dangerously slow in recognizing that
decent housing is a basic necessity for the public welfare. The public
must urge that more be done for those who are caught in the slums.
There is no sense in waiting longer, because it now is plain that only
governmental aid can solve this national problem.

Such aid is not a threat to our free enterprise system. On the contrary, it provides families with decent homes upon which a better system of free enterprise can be built. The choice before us is slum clearance and rehousing by cities and the nation, or mounting millions of Americans living in slums. Which is the real threat? Think it over, in all of its implications.

CHAPTER NINE

The United States in World Affairs

THE CONTEMPORARY AGE is so obviously one of international tension, violence, and warfare that documentation seems unnecessary. Within the memory of middle-aged men two of the most destructive wars in history have been fought; perhaps 50 million men, women, and children—soldiers and civilians—have been killed by their fellow men; seven great empires —the Turkish, Austrian, French, Dutch, German, Japanese, and British —have either been destroyed or are apparently crumbling. It is, indeed, a time when terms such as "chaos," "crisis," and "destiny" have the ring of reality.

From this holocaust the United States has not escaped. Among the major revolutions of the twentieth century is that combination of destruction and growth that has thrust up the United States as the most powerful of all nations. So sudden and so drastic is this change that America appears on the world stage, caught full in the floodlights, without adequate training or rehearsal for the role it is required to play. American history has, until recently, been one of semi-isolation from the main stream of world events. This fact is particularly noteworthy since the other major performer on the world stage is the Soviet Union, another ingenue but recently removed from isolation. Each star in this drama insists on top billing and demands that the remainder of the cast follow its lead.

Stripped of all verbiage, certain elementary facts emerge. Only two first-rate powers remain in the world—the United States and the Soviet Union. Russian and American foreign policies clash at every turn, while each country seeks the allegiance of smaller nations. Each leader represents a complete political and economic ideology; each possesses tremendous military strength; each claims that its way should be the World Way. Above these two national giants is the dream of world unity, expressed in the United Nations.

The future of a world such as that described here is certainly in doubt. At least five possibilities suggest themselves: (1) a Soviet world, organized after defeat of the United States in war; (2) a United States world, organized after defeat of the Soviet Union; (3) a "Third Force" world, in which smaller nations caught between the rival camps organize and secure the balance of power; (4) an uneasy truce, stretching into the unforeseeable future, filled with rumors, excursions, and alarms; (5) the gradual consolidation and strengthening of the United Nations or some substitute Parliament of Man.

From this confused international picture three fundamental questions have been selected as worthy of special emphasis: First, what are the objectives and principles upon which Soviet foreign policy is founded? Second, how can the United States as a sovereign nation best insure its peace, prosperity, influence, and chances of survival? Third, what are the possibilities of peace and justice through international cooperation? These questions are not mutually exclusive. Soviet and United States foreign policies obviously affect each other; both the United States and Russia participate in activities of the United Nations. Nevertheless, the three queries posed above represent basic issues in international relations.

Problem 28: What Are the Objectives of Soviet Foreign Policy?

Regarding Soviet foreign policy there is much loose talk and confused thinking. The bare historical record suggests why this is true. Immediately after the Russian Revolution (1917) the Soviet Union was an outcast, pariah nation that anticipated and advocated the immediate overthrow of all capitalistic governments. Later the Soviets concentrated on internal affairs, until the advent of Adolph Hitler made them turn to collective security. Nevertheless, from 1939 to 1941 the Soviet Union was linked by treaty with Nazi Germany, while Denmark, Norway, Poland, Belgium, Yugoslavia, Greece, and France were falling before the German war machine. From 1941 to 1945, however, it fought side by side with the United States and Great Britain against Germany. Today, having reduced eastern Europe to satellite status and having made a junior partner of Red China, Russia remains a question mark. In one hand it clutches the dove of peace; in the other, an atom bomb. Which is symbolic of the true Russia? Or are both devices part of Soviet tactics?

Other questions will occur to the student. Who makes ultimate decisions in the Soviet system? How closely is Russia committed to the Marx-Lenin projections of future history? Can the Soviet Union and the United States coexist in the same world? Or must it be—"We or they"?

RUSSIA STANDS FOR PEACE *

Most Americans know somewhat vaguely that their role in international affairs is subjected to a constant barrage of criticism from the Soviet camp. Secure in the belief that their country is a constructive, humanitarian force in world affairs, Americans are apt airily to dismiss all such criticism as "just propaganda." This complacent attitude underrates the appeal to other peoples of the Russian version of the world—a scene in which the dove of peace is Russian and the United States becomes the leading warmonger.

An old adage of the prize ring runs thus—"Never underestimate your opponent." Granted that Mr. Vyshinsky's analysis has little appeal in Boston, what about Bombay? If not in San Francisco, what of Shanghai? Note that many of Vyshinsky's isolated facts are in themselves true, only the interpretation being Communist. How can the United States most effectively reply to such Russian publicity?

. . . At present the United Nations Organization is confronted with a number of important tasks which call for very thorough attention on the part of the Assembly and on the part of all peaceloving states. . . . The soviet delegation now, as at the previous sessions, sees its task as the directing of the Assembly's efforts toward the elimination of the obstacles which hamper the strengthening of peace and international cooperation and toward the removal of the menace of another world war. At present this is the most important and primary task which calls for an immediate decision on the part of the United Nations. We are convinced that there

---

* Extracts from a speech delivered by the Russian Foreign Minister, A. Y. Vyshinsky, at the Paris meeting of the United Nations General Assembly, November 8, 1951. Translated from the Russian and distributed by the Embassy of the Union of Soviet Socialist Republics.

is no other task whose successful accomplishment is so eagerly awaited and demanded by millions and millions of people, by all the peace-loving peoples.

This task becomes all the more important, for the international situation has become even more complicated, both economically and politically, in the course of the period that has elapsed since the Fifth Session of the Assembly.

During this time the economic situation in the capitalist countries has deteriorated still further as a direct result of the aggressive policy of the Atlantic bloc, headed by the United States, and also of a number of other countries which are compelled to pursue such a policy under constant pressure on the part of the United States of America. The United States economy at present has assumed an unhealthy military-inflationary nature, being characterized by a steady growth of armaments production with a simultaneous curtailment of the civilian industries. The armaments drive entails the growth of military budgets as well as the growth of direct and indirect taxes, even further worsening the material conditions of the population of those countries. . . .

As regards the economic situation of the West European countries and, specifically, in Great Britain and France, this can be judged, for instance, by the conclusions of the United Nations Economic Commission for Europe, about which one can read in the September issues of *New Statesman and Nation* that in the United Kingdom "the economy is showing every sign of suffering from severe strain. Cost inflation is rampant, and towards the end of the year may well be enhanced by demand inflation flowing from the heaviest rearmament program in Europe."

. . . Even more definite in this regard was the program speech of the new British Prime Minister, made in the House of Commons only two days ago, in which, according to official organs of the press, Mr. Churchill said:

. . . The latest estimates show that in 1952, on present trends and policies and without making any allowance for further speculative losses, the United Kingdom would have a deficit on its general balance of overseas payments of between 500,000,000 and 600,000,000 pounds, and the loss to the central gold and dollar reserves in the transactions of the sterling areas as a whole with the rest of the world might be appreciably more. These figures mean, in short, that we are buying much more than we can afford to pay for from current earnings, and this can only in time lead to national bankruptcy.

. . . The political situation, too, has become more complicated in the past year. The Anglo-American aggressive Atlantic bloc brought about a further deterioration of international relations among countries which are put to serious trials under the pressure of the unbridled war hysteria, the armaments drive, and the attempts to intimidate other nations with atom and hydrogen bombs, with which the American reactionary leaders are constantly threatening.

The United States and Great Britain, which head this bloc, have been waging an aggressive war in Korea for almost a year and a half.

Mr. Acheson made an attempt to relieve the United States Government, which has unleashed this aggressive war, of the responsibility for the war in Korea by repeating the already exposed slander about aggression from North Korea. There is no need to dwell on this now. As regards the negotiations in Kaesong of which Mr. Acheson also spoke, can there be any doubt indeed that it is precisely the Messrs. American generals—the Mac-Arthurs and the Ridgeways—and their Washington protectors, who are stubbornly thwarting all attempts of the other side to achieve success in these negotiations? Is it not the American Command that hampers the progress of the negotiations by all sorts of delays, bombings of the neutral zone and similar methods of so-called "negotiations" in the course of which, for example, the absurd demand that the Kaesong area, which is in the hands of the North Korean troops, be handed over to the American troops was recently put forth on the pretext of an adjustment of the line of contact of troops.

. . . In order to deceive public opinion and to camouflage their actual aggressive aims, the President, the Cabinet Members, Senators and other political and public leaders in the United States are raising a hue and cry about the threat to United States security emanating from the USSR. With this end in view they are trying to make use also of the recent test of the atom bomb in the USSR, tests of different sizes of which, as J. V. Stalin said in his reply to a *Pravda* correspondent concerning the atomic weapon, shall be carried out in the future as well, in conformity with the plan for the defense of our country against attack by the Anglo-American aggressive bloc.

In his reply to the *Pravda* correspondent, J. V. Stalin exposed the utter groundlessness of this alarm pointing out that there is no basis for this alarm.

United States leaders . . . "cannot but know that the Soviet Union is not only opposed to the employment of atomic weapons, but is in favor of having them banned and their production discontinued" and that "if the United States is not thinking of attacking the Soviet Union, then the alarm of the United States leaders must be regarded as baseless and false, since the Soviet Union has no intention of ever attacking the United States or any other country."

In its hostile policy toward the Soviet Union and the People's Democracies, the Atlantic bloc, under the pressure mainly, in these cases again, of the United States, is trying to make use also of the United Nations by imposing on the General Assembly and other United Nations bodies decisions canceling the rulings adopted at the previous sessions of the Assembly. With a view to eliminating the threat of another war and assuring the peace and security of nations, at the Fifth Session of the Assembly the delegation of the Soviet Union pointed out that the Assembly was thus violating the basic principles of the United Nations and insisted on the adoption of the proposals submitted by the Soviet Union and the People's Democracies, aimed at strengthening peace, at prohibition—I stress—not at the reduction of which Truman and Acheson speak, but at prohibiting, completely and unconditionally, the atomic weapon and establishing strict international control over the utilization of atomic energy for peaceful purposes, and at prohibiting war propaganda. The Soviet delegation at the same time insisted that the Assembly pass decisions on the immediate cessation of the war in Korea, thrust on the Korean people by the American-British interventionists, on the cessation of aggressive actions toward the People's Republic of China and on a number of other important questions.

. . . It is sufficient to recall the above-mentioned facts to have no doubt that the elementary principles and standards of the international law are being trampled upon in the United Nations, that the American policy in the United Nations is inflicting tremendous damage on the moral prestige of the United Nations.

Instead of solving important tasks, promoting the establishment of conditions necessary for peaceful and friendly relations among nations, raising the living standards, ensuring full employment, etc., the Economic and Social Council has been fully engrossed in elaborating measures designed to facilitate Anglo-American aggression in Korea. . . . Thus, from year to year, the United Nations, step by step, departs more and more from the principles of the Charter, from the aims and tasks set before the United Nations. It has strayed far from the path of strengthening peace and promoting the development of friendly relations among countries. It is guided now by other interests. It is being impelled toward other aims by aggressive forces in the United States, Great Britain, France and in the Latin American countries, which are now deciding matters of war and peace in the United Nations. These aims and interests are the craving for a new war, the craving to fatten on another war, to make huge profits on war. Herein is the source of inspiration of the gentlemen monopolists who regard "war as an item of income which gives colossal profits" as the head of the Soviet Government, J. V. Stalin, has said.

. . . The aggressive nature of the United States foreign policy is clear to the entire world, despite the efforts of the American Government to conceal this from the world public, presenting the new war it is preparing as a defensive war and presenting the peaceful policy of the USSR and other peace-loving countries as an aggressive one, although it is known to all that the Soviet Union, as I have already said, citing the authoritative statements of Generalissimo J. V. Stalin, does not contemplate ever attacking the United States or any other country.

The United States is increasing its army, navy and air force from year to year, is building hundreds of new naval and air bases on foreign territories, is establishing a whole system of military alliances to bring countries of the former "axis"—Japan and Italy as well as Western Germany—into these alliances.

The entire economy of the United States, as well as of Great Britain, France and of a number of other countries, is geared to war. The lion's share of expenditures in state budgets goes for war preparations. Military expenditures in the budget of the United States in the fiscal year 1951–1952 comprise, according to official American data, 81.8 billion dollars, i.e., 76 times more than in 1939.

According to the admission made by Mr. Truman in a message to Congress last April, during the preceding 10 months the United States more than doubled the numerical strength of its armed forces and was planning to increase them further the next fiscal year—up to 3,500,000 men, not counting 2,000,000 men in the various military reserve formations and in the national guard units. Thus, the numerical strength of the armed forces of the United States, Great Britain and France is now already several times greater than their armed forces were before the Second World War in 1939, and more than twice as large as the numerical strength of the armed forces of the Soviet Union. Nevertheless the armed forces of these countries are being increased more and more.

The United States continues to expand its war industry, which is absorbing ever more billions of dollars, covering this up with references to the interests of the "defense" and of the "national security" of the United States.

. . . The entire foreign policy of the United States is based on preparation for another world war with the object of gaining world domination for American monopolies and making gigantic profits on war. It is for this reason that the foreign policy of the United States is directed not at developing and strengthening friendly relations with the other countries and international cooperation, but at subordinating the other countries through economic enslavement or military coercion.

. . . As in the period preceding the Second World War, American gold has already for several years, since the end of this war, been flowing again in a broad stream into the German war industry in order to place it at the service of the American monopolists, who are craving for more and more profits, even at the price of inflicting great calamities and sacrifices on all mankind.

What the aim of the United States policy toward Japan is and what it leads to can be seen without any explanation from the farce of signing the so-called peace treaty with Japan, staged under the direction of the United States in San Francisco. This treaty fully contradicts the principles upon which a real peace treaty should be based, a treaty that could ensure peace in the Far East and provide a guarantee against the recurrence of Japanese aggression. Not only the Government of the United States, but also the Governments of Great Britain, France, Canada, Australia and certain other states that signed the San Francisco treaty violated the commitments they had assumed in 1947 as members of the Far Eastern Commission in the decision on the basic policy for Japan. This decision declared that the above states undertake to carry out reforms in Japan in order to eliminate the militaristic influence, effect complete disarmament and deprive Japan of the opportunity to wage aggressive wars in the future.

Instead, the initiators and inspirers of the so-called peace treaty with Japan have taken the path of reviving all kinds of militaristic organization, of establishing and expanding military, naval and air bases in Japan; they have taken the path of restoring the Japanese army, navy and air force, the path of securing Japan as an American arsenal and springboard in the Far East.

. . . The basis of the present foreign policy of the United States is the fear of a possible peaceful development of international relations and of the strengthening of international cooperation.

It is frankly admitted in United States "business" circles that fear of the "danger of peace" prevails there, that, as repeatedly stated in the American press, the price of stocks goes up on the American Exchange when a continuation of the war in Korea looks probable and, on the contrary, falls when a prospect for the establishment of peace arises.

Having launched the aggressive war in Korea, which brings them enormous profits, the American billionaires and millionaires are holding on tightly to this source of income and have no desire to let go of this "golden opportunity" of multiplying their billions and millions. They meet every hint at the possibility of an armistice in Korea with alarm, doing everything to wreck the negotiations in Kaesong even though the American people, like all the peace-loving people, thirst for and demand the cessation of the war and the establishment of peace in the Far East.

It was openly stated in the July issue of the bulletin published by the American First National Bank of New York, controlled by the Morgan group, that any reduction in expenditures on armaments will complicate the monopolists' position.

At one of his numerous press conferences, United States President Truman declared that the armistice in Korea might cause a delay in the implementation of the American arms program and that this would be the most disastrous thing that could happen in the United States.

At a conference of bankers in Los Angeles, Edward Rubin, President of the large investment company, Selected American Shares Incorporated, openly said that if peace were attained, it would be difficult to imagine what would replace the defense program as the prop of the United States economy.

. . . Do not these facts sufficiently prove that the real direction of United States foreign policy is aggressive, that its purpose is not the maintenance of peace, but the instigation of another world war regardless of the fresh disasters and rivers of blood it will cost mankind?

The foreign policy of the Soviet Union is a policy of peace. [*Prolonged applause*] The Soviet Union indefatigably strives to eliminate the threat of war, strives for peace, for strengthening friendly relations among the countries, for close international cooperation based on mutual respect for the independence of nations and the sovereign equality of states. . . .

Pursuing its peaceful policy the Soviet Union employs all its resources not to increase its armed forces or to carry out an armaments drive, not to expand war industry and not to organize military bases on foreign territories, but to develop civilian industry to the utmost and to further advance the entire national economy.

Successes achieved in the rehabilitation and development of the postwar economy have enabled the Soviet Union to start the implementation of a great task—the task of the extensive complex utilization of the Volga, Don, Dnieper and Amu Darya rivers for the power, agricultural, transportation, and other needs of the national economy. The great projects which the Soviet Union has already set about carrying out—the Kuibyshev, Stalingrad and other hydropower stations, the Main Turkmenian, South Ukrainian and other canals—are widely known. The new power plants will produce 22 billion kilowatt hours of cheap electric power annually which, as the Vice-Chairman of the Council of Ministers of the USSR L. P. Beria pointed out in his report is equal to the entire annual production of electric power in Italy; the new irrigation systems will make it possible to irrigate and water more than 28 million hectares of land, which is equal to the area of several European states. The object of these great projects is to advance further the peaceful economy of our country, to raise the standard of living of the Soviet people still more. The Soviet Union is investing thousands of millions of rubles in the aforementioned great projects.

In the Soviet Union the entire nation is engaged in constructive labor, directing all its energies toward a further development of the national economy and attaining ever new achievements in the further progress of culture, engineering, science and art.

In its foreign political relations with other countries the Soviet Union stands for friendly cooperation, opposes all kinds of discrimination, all kinds of artificial barriers which hamper free association of the Soviet people with other peoples, and stands for the friendship of nations. . . .

. . . Mr. Acheson permitted himself to repeat the disgusting slander about the violation of human rights in an extensive area of the world, as he put it, mentioning Hungary and Czechoslovakia. I shall not dwell on this matter specially, for slanders of this type, spread by the Acheson camp, have already been completely disproved many times. You, Mr. Acheson, talk about violation of human rights in other countries. I too should like to tell you what I read today in a French evening newspaper about an outrageous crime committed a few days ago in Florida when two Negroes—Samuel Shephard and Walter Irvin—charged by an American court with raping a white woman and acquitted by the United States Supreme Court because of an inordinate number of violations of the law during their trial—were shot before the eyes of all by the Sheriff of Eustis, Florida, after they were acquitted by the American Court, and a third Negro was shot by a policeman in the presence of the Sheriff.

At the same time racists burned down several houses in the Negro quarter of Eustis where this tragedy took place. This incensed the American people so much that, according to the press reports, the President of the United Automobile Workers of America, Walter Reuther, was compelled to say at the CIO Congress in New York: "But we know that in state after state in America that it has been the practice where Negroes come before the bar of justice there are two standards of justice, one for Negroes and one for white citizens." This is not an isolated fact. It is an illustration, and a very common one, of the American human rights, of the American way of life which we so firmly reject.

We spoke above of the immediate necessity of taking all measures to eliminate the threat of another war and to ensure the peace and security of nations.

It is necessary immediately to terminate the war forced upon the Korean people and other regions of the Pacific Ocean.

It is necessary to take immediate measures against the preparation of a new world war being made in certain countries and especially in the United States, Great Britain and also in France and other states belonging to the aggressive Atlantic bloc, membership in which is incompatible with membership in the United Nations.

It is necessary immediately to prohibit the manufacture of the atomic weapon and to establish strict international control ensuring the fulfillment of this decision, so that atomic energy and the atomic bombs already produced be utilized exclusively for civilian purposes.

It is necessary to terminate the armaments drive, to discontinue the establishment of military bases on foreign territories and to withdraw foreign troops therefrom.

It is necessary that all the states immediately take measures to reduce the armed forces and expend funds now used for military purposes on the needs of the people, to improve their living standard and ensure their well-being.

It is necessary that the United States, Great Britain, France, China and the USSR combine their efforts and conclude a Pact of Peace, urging all peace-loving nations to join it. Such measures should undermine the aggressive plans of the ruling circles of the United States, Great Britain and certain other states, and eliminate the threat of a new world war. [*Applause*]

On instructions of the Soviet Government, the delegation of the USSR submits proposals which it is deeply convinced are an important means for achieving the goal which millions upon millions of people dream of, live and work for in all corners of the earth.

The Soviet delegation is certain that the struggle for peace will terminate in the complete victory of peace.

"Peace," as the head of the Soviet Government J. V. Stalin said, "will be preserved and consolidated if the peoples take the cause of preserving peace into their own hands and uphold it to the end." [*Applause*]

The General Assembly should harken to the voice of the peoples and fulfill its duty in this great and noble cause.

Stalin on Revolution *

Although an understanding of Russian policy is vital to their own security and survival, most Americans are inclined to dismiss the matter with a fatalistic shrug of the shoulders and the cliche that Russian actions are "a mystery wrapped in an enigma." The following article attempts to sort fact from fiction, "strategy" from "tactics," and reduce Soviet philosophy to a predictable system. As such it merits the careful consideration of every United States citizen—particularly since its anonymous authorship suggests that the author was a Russian expert in the American State Department when the article was penned (1948).

* Historicus.   Condensed from *Foreign Affairs*, January, 1949, pp. 176, 178–99, 202–14.

It is, of course, possible that the death of Stalin has radically altered the course of Soviet diplomacy. In any event this article serves as a yardstick by which the new regime may be measured.

The stress laid by Stalin on the importance of theory is so foreign to American habits of mind that we are prone to underestimate the influence which theory plays in determining his action. Any such tendency would lead us into especially grave error when we come to estimating the importance of his theoretical conception of the nature of revolution; for on this he has been amazingly consistent. . . .

The present study summarizes the body of ideas on revolution which has presumably played a part in Stalin's thought and action, as revealed in his published writings and statements. Except for two reports of interviews with Stalin published in the United States but apparently not in the Soviet Union, it makes use of Russian sources only. . . .

The Science of Revolution

In outlining Stalin's revolutionary theory, we shall first consider his views on those determinants of revolution which he calls "objective," *i.e.,* those historical forces which, though modified by the action of conscious human will, determine the basic pattern of history regardless of human will.

Stalin calls the philosophical framework of his theory "dialectical and historical materialism." It is, in effect, revolution writ large into the cosmos; its basic postulates are so many reasons why "the bourgeoisie" are on the way down and "the proletariat" on the way up, why "capitalism" must inevitably give way to "Socialism" everywhere, and why this must occur by violent revolution. It is sufficient for our present purposes to state briefly those postulates which are most important for Stalin's theory of revolution.

Change

Nature is constantly changing; "there is always something arising and evolving, something declining and living out its time." This means that "the dying off of what is old and the growth of something new is the law of evolution," hence that there are no "'stable' social orders" or "'eternal principles' of private property." It means further that "only that which is rising and developing is invincible," *i.e.* that a rising class, though yet relatively weak, is a better bet politically than one which has had its rise and, though still relatively powerful, is beginning to decline. Hence, according to Stalin, the Marxists were right in basing their policy on the proletariat even in Russia in the 1880's, because it was evolving as a class, while the peasantry, though in the enormous majority, was declining as a class.

Contradiction and Struggle

". . . the process of evolution from the lower to the higher takes place not as a harmonious unfolding of phenomena but . . . as a 'struggle' of opposite tendencies which operate on the basis of these contradictions . . . in order to overcome these contradictions." This means that "the class struggle of the proletariat is a perfectly natural and inevitable phenomenon, that we must not cover up the contradictions of the capitalist system but uncover and draw them out, not extinguish the class struggle but carry it to its conclusion." Here . . . is Stalin's philosophical ground for his position that a basic policy (as distinguished from temporary tactics) of compromise and reform is a mistake.

The Primary Contradiction of Capitalism

The prime mover of social progress is change in the productive forces, especially tools: as new types of tools develop they enter into "contradiction" or "nonconformity" with the increasingly outmoded productive relations, until the latter are demolished and new ones created. . . . With this "sudden, qualitative" change comes a change in the whole social system. Such is the inmost dynamic of revolution. Capitalism, for example, develops large-scale industrial plants as productive forces; but "by gathering millions of workers together in enormous factories and plants, capitalism gives a social character to the process of production and thereby undermines its own basis," namely, the productive relations that center around private ownership of industry. Thus the primary contradiction that develops inside capitalism as it evolves is that between actual private ownership and the new productive forces which require social ownership for their full expansion. This maladjustment expresses itself in the periodic crises of overproduction familiar to capitalism, and finally in revolution which resolves the contradiction by socializing the means of production.

The Class Struggle

It is ultimately from the growing contradiction between social productive forces and private property productive relations that the class struggle receives the dynamism, the increasing tension, which impels it toward revolution. . . . That earlier Marxist doctrine of "increasing misery" of the proletariat was modified by Lenin and others in view of the observable fact that workers were not getting poorer. Stalin does not discuss this topic; but possibly he, too, as a disciple of Lenin, does not hold the earlier view. What certainly does increase, according to Stalin, is tension between the two classes—the bourgeoisie put more and more "pressure" on the proletariat, which the proletariat meets with growing resistance and resentment. The "pressure" or "oppression" by the bourgeoisie takes various forms. One is the effort to reduce wages or hold them down, which becomes ever more powerful as capitalism enters its monopoly stage. Another is the actual misery caused by falling wages and unemployment in times of economic crisis—the recurrent crises being due to the fact that the capitalists do not allow wages to rise in proportion to production, thus curtailing purchasing power and resulting in "overproduction." Another form of pressure by the bourgeoisie is Fascism, which deprives workers of important means of resistance—labor unions, parliaments, the freedom to form labor or Communist parties.

As will be explained later, the tension between bourgeoisie and proletariat does not increase uniformly but is a wave-like ebb and flow. While tension mounts, the social system nears the flashpoint of revolution. . . .

The Imperialist Stage of Capitalism

Stalin, following Lenin, holds that capitalism in its last stage, when it becomes ripe for revolution, turns monopolist and imperialist. The scene is dominated by giant trusts and combinations of international finance which rival each other for control of world markets, raw materials and opportunities for investment of surplus capital. This means that there is no longer an assortment of capitalist systems, one for each country, but one world capitalist system. Revolution accordingly occurs in particular countries as a result of the total interplay of forces within the world system and not, as earlier Marxists expected, simply as the result of local conditions. "Formerly it was usual to speak of the presence or absence of objective conditions for proletarian revolution . . . in one or another well developed country. . . . Now we must speak of the presence of objective conditions of revolution in the entire system . . . *because* the system as a whole is already ripe for revolution.". . .

The direct effect of the rise of monopoly capitalism on the contradiction between bourgeoisie and proletariat has been mentioned. In addition, two further contradictions are now generated within the capitalist system.

One of these is the international counterpart of the class struggle: the great monopolies seek to exploit the foreign as well as the domestic field, which leads to a few powerful capitalist countries dividing up the world as colonial possessions and spheres of influence. Thus arises a contradiction within the capitalist world economy between the exploiting imperialists and the exploited colonies. As tension rises, a revolutionary crisis developed in the exploited countries, taking the form primarily of movements for national liberation from imperialism.

The other contradiction develops between rival capitalist countries. Since some evolve more rapidly than others, they come to demand a larger share of colonies and spheres of influence than the one allotted on the basis of their former power. Since no country will voluntarily hand over part of its present share, tension mounts until imperialist war—for example, the First and Second World Wars—inevitably breaks out as the sole means of redividing the world and restoring equilibrium. In Stalin's thinking, the importance of war as a midwife of revolution can scarcely be exaggerated.

The Contradiction Between Capitalist and Socialist Systems

According to Stalin, the contradictions above described created . . . yet another contradiction, that between the capitalist and Socialist systems. For henceforth the system of world capitalism has lost its monopoly of the world and its claim to be the latest work in progress. Beside it grows a Socialist system which "by the very fact of its existence demonstrates the rottenness of capitalism and shakes loose its foundations." This predicament, together with the loss both of economic equilibrium and of authority in colonial areas occasioned by the war of 1914, constitutes what Stalin calls the "general crisis of capitalism," a condition of permanently impaired health. The capitalist system will never recover its pre-1914 stability and self-assurance.

Increasing tension grows from both sides of this contradiction between the social systems. It is an axiom with Stalin that capitalists are filled with envy and hatred, and that whenever they can and dare they will seek to intervene in the Socialist country and restore capitalism. This danger he dramatizes as "capitalist encirclement," declaring that Socialism cannot be considered finally achieved as long as this danger of intervention and restoration persists. From the other side of the contradiction, every triumph of the Soviet Socialist system is considered by Stalin to have a profoundly revolutionizing effect on capitalist countries. . . .

The primary and secondary contradictions of capitalist society, which we have just described, interact upon one another to produce revolution. There are three chief types of interaction.

Productive Forces vs. Productive Relations: Economic Crises

. . . This doctrine is an integral part of the bedrock of Marxist "scientific" certainty about the future course of history on which Stalin evidently bases his entire life work. It is his cardinal reason for holding that, no matter what happens, in the long run all the contradictions of capitalism will get

worse and worse until revolution cures the source of trouble by substituting
Socialism . . . As capitalism evolves, productive forces (*i.e.* productive
capacity) are dynamically expanded but wages are kept as low as possible
in order to make more profits.   The result is a "relative curtailment of
purchasing power"; goods accumulate for which there is no market and a
crisis of overproduction is precipitated; finished goods and even productive
forces are destroyed, factories are closed and millions suffer unemployment
and hunger not because goods are scarce but because they are plentiful.
Stalin stresses the destruction of productive forces as conspicuous evidence
of the way in which their development is hampered by capitalist productive
relations.   His account in 1930 concludes: "If capitalism could adapt
production not to getting maximum profit but to the systematic improvement of the material conditions of the masses of the people . . . then there
would not be any crises.   But then also capitalism would not be capitalism."

The "Objective" Conditions for Revolution: War

We have seen that, for Stalin, capitalism in its imperialist stage has become a single world system in which the total interplay of forces determines
the ripeness of conditions for revolution in particular countries, revolutions
actually occurring where the world front of capitalism is weakest in relation
to the forces of revolution. . . .

The primary contradiction, both chronically and in its acute manifestation as economic crisis, impels the bourgeoisie to increase pressure against
the proletariat, against colonial peoples, against each other (in rivalry for
spheres of influence) and against the Soviet Union.   The culmination of
these trends is war of one kind or another: the colonies fight for liberation,
the capitalist nations who demand greater spheres of influence fight to get
them or capitalist countries attack the Soviet Union as the major threat to
their whole system and also as another big area to be exploited.   Preparation for war on the part of the bourgeoisie further arouses the proletariat
and the other masses who desire peace and resent having to die for their
masters, and who also resent the added economic and political pressures—
including Fascism, in some cases—which are imposed in order to prepare
for war.   When the war is to be directed against the Socialist Fatherland,
this fact of course greatly adds to the resentment of the proletariat, whose
deeper sympathies are on the side of the Soviet Union. Bourgeois preparation for war likewise leads to increased pressure on colonies, with a corre-
spondingly greater tendency of colonies to rebel.

Actual war, however, is the crux of the matter.   Stalin writes of the relation of the First World War to the contradictions of capitalism that "the
imperialist war . . . gathered all these contradictions into one bundle and

threw them onto the scales, thereby accelerating and facilitating the revolutionary battles of the proletariat." . . .

. . . For the past quarter century, according to the overwhelming testimony of his writings, Stalin has expected the next crop of revolutions to come during, or in the immediate aftermath of, the Second World War. To the Seventeenth Party Congress in 1934 he stated that a new imperialist war "will surely turn loose revolution and place in jeopardy the very existence of capitalism in a number of countries, as happened in the course of the first imperialist war." . . . Though Stalin hopes for proletariat revolutions in certain colonial areas, he values all local movements for national liberation, whether proletarian or not: in any case, each step they take toward emancipation is "a steam-hammer blow against imperialism" and thus has "objective" revolutionary significance, *i.e.,* weakens the bourgeoisie of imperialist countries by depriving them of markets and raw materials. Hence a colonial war would become an added factor promoting a revolutionary crisis in the metropolitan country.

The Law of Ebb and Flow

According to Stalin, the October Revolution of 1917 ushered in "a new era in the history of humanity—the era of proletarian revolutions," in fact, "the epoch of world revolution." This means, in terms of his theory, that the contradictions in the world system of capitalism have evolved to the point where revolutions are generally in order. Actual revolution, however, occurred first in only one country, and Stalin expects further revolutions usually to occur in one country at a time, as state after state breaks away from the capitalist system and joins the Socialist one.

But the course of the revolutionary movement is not expected to be uniform. Stalin notes that it has always moved in a wavelike rhythm of ebb and flow, rise and fall. . . . Under the stress of the First World War a major crest came with the two revolutions of 1917 . . . and the wave spread out to Europe in the years immediately following. In 1925 Stalin announces that another decline has set in, corresponding to a "partial and temporary stabilization of capitalism," but he now generalizes the alternation of ebb and flow in a prediction of the future: "The epoch of world revolution . . . is a whole strategic period, embracing a whole series of years and, I dare say, even a number of decades. In the course of this period there can and must be ebbings and flowings."

Up to March, 1948, Stalin has published nothing to indicate that the revolutionary wave—so long expected in connection with World War II—has passed its crest, though his doctrine of ebb and flow suggests that he must expect another ebb within a few years unless capitalism collapses completely in the meantime. Thus the entire period from 1929 to March 1948 moves before Stalin's eyes on a rising tide of revolutionary opportunities.

The Art of Revolution

Having outlined Stalin's conception of the "objective" determinants of revolution, our inquiry now turns to the "subjective" side: the role of conscious organization.

Communist Leadership

Notwithstanding the remorseless and unavoidable evolution of the contradictions of capitalism, making Socialist revolution sooner or later inevitable, Stalin holds that actual revolution can occur only through conscious human efforts. In this he is a disciple of Lenin, and his history of the Party records with sympathy Lenin's battles against "reformist" Marxists, compromisers, opportunists, gradualists—any and all who held that the "objective" factors would automatically bring about the change to Socialism, or that anything short of the most resolute and uncompromising revolutionary policy should be adopted. . . .

Stalin expresses the contrast between Bolshevism and western Socialism most vividly in his 1934 interview with H. G. Wells. . . . Wells approaches Stalin from the point of view of a western Socialist; he states that conceptions of violent class war are obsolete; leading businessmen are not ruled wholly (or even primarily in many cases) by the profit motive and there is therefore no radical conflict of interest between capital and labor; modern technology makes Socialism inevitable through gradual extension of government controls; hence the need is for intelligent direction, not violent revolution; eastern and western Socialists should develop a common language and work together rather than emphasize their historic antagonisms. Stalin replies with denial on all points and puts the crux of the matter as he sees it thus: ". . . the replacement of one social system by another social system is a complicated and protracted revolutionary process. It is not a merely spontaneous process. . . . No—revolution . . . has always been struggle, an excruciating and cruel struggle, struggle for life and death."

Communists, he continues, do not idealize force and violence: they would gladly dispense with them if the bourgeoisie would consent to turn things over peaceably to the proletariat. But abundant historical experience teaches (as he said to Wells) that "classes which have had their day do not leave the stage of history voluntarily." . . .

The "combat Staff" of the new political army is the Communist Party. Effective Communist Party action is Stalin's "subjective" condition for revolution which, when timed with the "objective" conditions previously described, actually brings revolutions to pass. . . . Moments occur when the situation is revolutionary, the power of the bourgeoisie is shaken to its very foundations, and yet the victory of the revolution does not come, because there is no revolutionary party of the proletariat sufficiently strong and authoritative to lead the masses and take power in its own hands."

World Strategy: The Soviet Union as Base

. . . "*The goal is to consolidate the dictatorship of the proletariat in one country, using it as a base for the overthrow of imperialism in all countries.* Revolution spreads beyond the limits of one country; the epoch of world revolution has begun."

The fundamental, not merely incidental, intention to use the Soviet Union as the base for world revolution has been on the record in Stalin's most important doctrinal work, repeatedly republished for mass circulation from 1924 to the present time. . . . The supreme aim of world revolution is the logical outcome of Stalin's entire theoretical position as outlined in the present study—notably the thesis that capitalism is a single *world-system* fatally torn by contradictions which can be cured only by a consciously directed Socialist revolution. Granted these assumptions, the determination to use the foothold won in the Soviet Union as a base for world revolution is elementary common sense. . . .

. . . The problem of the "final" victory of Socialism in one country within the wider context of world revolution . . . marks the outer limit of Stalin's program for Communist expansion. Further . . . the Soviet Union will first be prepared as a base, and only then, "*After* organizing its own Socialist production," will be used more aggressively to aid revolution abroad. This tallies with the predominant absorption of the Soviets with internal affairs during the earlier five-year plans. Further, the phrase does not define the stage at which production is to be considered adequately organized. Hence the prospect of three or more additional five-year plans, as announced in 1938 and again in 1946, may indicate that the base is still not ready for contemplated operations.

Finally, the passage definitely states that armed force will be used against capitalist governments if necessary. There thus is nothing except expediency to limit the aid which Stalin contemplates giving to revolutions abroad. However, the phrase "if necessary" indicates that armed force is not to be used by preference; ahead of it come propaganda and Communist Party control, by which is meant that the Soviet Union should attract to itself "the oppressed classes of other countries, raising revolts in these countries against the capitalists."

The ultimate resort to armed force is a logical development of the Leninist thesis that only consciously-led revolution can drive the capitalists from the stage of history, as explained in the preceding section. The assumption that the world has been fundamentally divided into two camps since the October Revolution runs through Stalin's writings from his early days and is grounded in his Marxist philosophy. Stalin pictures the long-range evolution of the two camps as follows:

Most probably, in the course of development of the world revolution, side by side with the centers of imperialism in individual capitalist countries and the system of these countries throughout the world, centers of Socialism will be created in individual Soviet countries and a system of these centers throughout the world, and the struggle between these two systems will fill up the history of the development of the world revolution.

The systems are expected to be organized around two centers:

Thus in the course of further development of international revolution two centers will form on a world scale: a Socialist center, binding to itself the countries that gravitate to Socialism, and a capitalist center, binding to itself the countries that gravitate to capitalism. The struggle between these two centers for the possession of the world economy will decide the fate of capitalism and Communism in the whole world.

The plan to make the Soviet Union the base for world revolution implies that it will be one of the two centers. Evidence will be presented later that the United States is expected to be the other. The ultimate inevitability of war to the finish between the two camps is made clear in one of Stalin's favorite quotations from Lenin: "We live . . . not only in a state but in a system of states, and the existence of the Soviet Republic side by side with the imperialist states for a long time is unthinkable. In the end either one or the other will conquer. And until that end comes, a series of the most terrible collisions between the Soviet Republic and the bourgeois states is inevitable." Stalin appended to this forecast of inexorable wars a succinct, "Clear, one would think." Thus Stalin expects not merely one but several world wars before the end of capitalism.

Flexibility of Strategy and Tactics

We are now in a position to . . . link Stalin's strategy and tactics with his conception of the "objective" conditions making for revolution. . . .

In general, despite his comparatively rigid doctrinal framework, Stalin's conception of Communist strategy and tactics is highly flexible. It rests on a continual assessment of the status of forces in both the capitalist and the Socialist systems. . . .

For the period of world revolution, Stalin's grand strategy is to use the Soviet Union as a base linking the proletariat of the west with the movements for national liberation from imperialism in the east into "a single world front against the world front of imperialism." In this way he harnesses two of the major contradictions of capitalism to his chariot—contradictions between the proletariat and bourgeoisie, and contradictions between capitalist and colonial countries. The front thus formed is to be used to exploit the third contradiction of capitalism—that between capitalist countries, whose rivalry for spheres of influence must lead periodically to war, the event most propitious for revolution.

One of the chief conditions to which tactics must be adjusted, according to Stalin, is the ebb and flow of the forces favoring revolution. Aggressive tactics should be timed with a rising tide; tactics of defense, the assemblage of forces, and even retreat go with an ebbing tide. . . .

Stalin's insistence on flexibility of tactics is ground for a very important maxim in the interpretation of his public statements; one must avoid, if possible, mistaking a change in tactics for a change in fundamental doctrine and strategic objectives. The example of a change in tactics often thus mistaken is Stalin's remarks about peaceful coexistence of and cooperation between the Socialist and capitalist systems. The whole body of mutually reinforcing propositions in Stalin's philosophy adds up to a veritable religion of conflict and contradiction. This is described as not only inevitable but desirable, until revolution is achieved. Here we find further strong evidence that Stalin's statements on cooperation represent nothing deeper than a tactic.

Stalin first announced a period of "peaceful coexistence" for proletarian and bourgeois worlds in 1925, saying that the revolutionary movement was ebbing and capitalism achieving a temporary stabilization. But the context of his statement makes plain that he expected peaceful coexistence to be as temporary as the stabilization. . . .

The peace policy has another tactical function in Stalin's strategy of revolution. He notes how successfully the Communists capitalized on the general popular craving for peace during the October Revolution; accordingly he manoeuvres the Soviet Union and the Communist Parties into position as apostles of peace, unmasking the imperialist "warmongers" in order to profit by popular sentiments for peace in the future. . . .

Revolution in the United States

In a speech in the Comintern in May, 1929, Stalin rebukes representatives of the American Communist Party for exaggerating the "specific traits" of American capitalism. The basis for the activities of all Communist Parties, he states, is the "common traits" of capitalism, which are fundamentally the same for all countries—the specific traits of capitalism in a particular country merely supplement the general traits. This implies that Stalin makes no major exceptions on behalf of the United States in regard to the application of his theory of capitalism and his objective of world revolution. . . .

As we have noted, Stalin's portrait of the capitalists paints them as utterly unprincipled and ruthless men, dominated by the lust for profits, to which they are willing to sacrifice all else. . . . To Wells in 1934, he says that American or other capitalists will never permit abolition of unemployment because they need a "reserve army of unemployed" to ensure cheap labor; capitalists are "riveted to profit" and "see nothing except their own interest." The government is merely their tool: if Roosevelt seriously threatens private property and the profit system, they will put in another president.

How does Stalin regard Americans in general? His admiration for American technological prowess and business efficiency are well known. To Ludwig in 1931 he also mentions the democratic simplicity of American manners; but he denies "worship of everything American." . . . On no occasion does Stalin appeal to lasting ties of sentiment or culture as a basis for cooperation with the United States. Even to Howard in 1936 he specifies that neither of the rival systems will evolve into the other. "The Soviet system will not grow into American democracy, and vice versa." The utterly unsentimental basis of Stalin's approach to cooperation despite ideological differences is made particularly clear by his statement to Stassen in 1947 that the Soviet Union would have cooperated with Germany as much as with any other capitalist country if Germany had desired. Stalin bids for cooperation on the basis of interest, such as maintaining peace and securing profitable trade.

Stalin has long evinced a belief that proletarian forces are backward in the United States. To the American Labor Delegation in 1927 he comments that American labor leaders are "reactionary" and "reformist," and points to the small fraction of workers who are unionized. He also observes that both political parties are bourgeois, and asks: "Don't you Comrades consider that the absence of your own mass workers' party, if only one like the English (Labor Party), weakens the strength of the working class in its political struggle with capitalism?" In 1947 he remarks to Stassen that he sees little difference between Democrats and Republicans. Likewise in speaking to American Communist Party representatives in 1929 he attacks them for "rightist Factionalism," saying: "It cannot be denied that American life offers an environment which favors the Communist Party's falling into error and exaggerating the strength and stability of American capitalism." He has said nothing since to indicate a change of opinion. Thus such evidence as his writings afford points to an expectation that the United States will be one of the last countries to go Communist.

This conclusion is reinforced by Stalin's views on the American economy. He notes that the United States—"the chief country of capitalism, its stronghold"—is hardest hit by the economic crisis of 1929, and that the crisis of 1937 originates here. But he also observes that the country leads world recovery in 1925 and 1933, and in 1939 he implies that it will pull out of the later crisis. Thus the United States is the center of the capitalist world system, its "stronghold," and, though affected by the general decadence of capitalism, shows some remnants of health in its powers of recovery. As early as 1925 Stalin observes that the center of capitalist financial power is moving across the Atlantic, and he describes how the United States, with England as partner, is becoming the hub of the capitalist system . . . "two chief, but opposed, centers of attraction are being formed," he writes, "and, in conformity with this, two directions of pull toward these centers throughout the world: Anglo-America . . . and the Soviet Union. . . ." In the years immediately following, Stalin sees the United States and England becoming rivals rather than partners, but at no time up to the present has he implied that the United States has ceased to be the center of world capitalism. . . .

Thus Stalin's conception of the United States as the "stronghold of capitalism dovetails with his picture of the future course of world revolution. The United States is expected to be the center of the rival world system which finally must clash with the Soviet system until capitalism goes down and Socialism conquers the world. This means that Stalin expects revolution in the United States only near the end of the "epoch of world revolution." As he declares . . . in 1929, "when a revolutionary crisis has developed in America, that will be the beginning of the end of all world capitalism."

The Next Phase

Thus it is probable that Stalin hardly expected revolution to occur in the United States during World War II or its aftermath. But the evidence presented in the present article makes it likely that his perspective on this period was (and is) as follows:

1. The time for the next harvest of revolution is at hand. The world war, predicted since 1927, has come to pass, and the upheaval it has created will bring to a climax the contradictions of capitalism in a way that will make revolution possible in "a number of countries in Europe and Asia." Precisely such revolution is required to guarantee once and for all that the

forces of capitalism will not obliterate Socialism (even in the U.S.S.R. itself) and compel the whole process to begin again from scratch. Therefore the minimum revolutionary objective for World War II and its aftermath is to bring enough countries into the Soviet camp to effect such a guarantee.

2. The "law of ebb and flow" implies that unless the whole of capitalism collapses under the present revolutionary wave, the surviving remnant will temporarily stabilize itself a few years after the end of the war and an ebb in the tide of revolution will set in: the revolutionary objective of World War II must therefore be consolidated before the tide begins to ebb. This imparts a certain urgency to revolutionary tactics in the immediate postwar period.

3. Though the Soviet Union has not yet equalled the United States in industrial production per capita, its industrial and military strength has increased greatly since 1928, and with the defeat of Germany and Japan its relative strength among the Powers of Europe and Asia will be enormous. Therefore the Soviet Union will be in position to serve as base for much more active fostering of revolutionary movements in other countries, though not ready to establish Communism throughout the world. This indicates a much more aggressive tactic toward other countries, but not so aggressive as deliberately to bring on war for world hegemony in the immediate future.

The success of this tactic would depend in part, according to Stalin's theory of revolution, on the extent to which the critical areas were isolated from foreign influences hostile to revolution. This gives a major clue to Stalin's war and postwar policies toward Britain and the United States. Many of them can be regarded as a delaying action: by retarding realization on the part of these countries of what is really going on, then minimizing efforts to intervene . . . in the countries singled out for revolution until Communist control is established. Stalin's profession of nonaggressive war aims served to lull suspicion. So did the dissolution of the Comintern and his comments thereon. So did his statements on the possibility of coexistence and cooperation and the necessity for unanimity among the big Powers after the war. These and similar moves imposed a serious reluctance on the part of the Allies to do or say anything that could be construed as a breach in the spirit of wartime collaboration. When at last Allied public opinion began to denounce Soviet or Communist actions, the same statements served as a basis for propaganda counter attack. Stalin launched this attack with his comments on Churchill's speech at Fulton, declaring it a "dangerous act," sowing discord among the Allies, harming the cause of peace and security, in short, warmongering. Thereafter those who like Churchill object to Soviet policies in Eastern Europe and elsewhere are denounced as "warmongers," and an attempt is made to mobilize against them the popular craving for peace.

Even the United Nations has to some extent been exploited by Stalin's tactics. The possibility of using the veto to cripple Allied action in revolutionary areas is obvious. But if, as some think, Stalin might prefer a deal based on spheres of influence . . . such an arrangement could be depended on to further, not to limit, revolutionary operations. Within his sphere Stalin would have a free hand, and Communist action would also continue across the demarcation line into the other sphere.

When Stalin looks to the more distant future, the United States, which has emerged from the last war more truly than ever the "stronghold of capitalism," probably continues to figure in his thinking as it has done in his basic writings since the mid-1920's—as the center around which the capitalist system will form for the final war to the death between the two systems. Meanwhile, Stalin projects further industrial expansion in the Soviet Union on a scale which suggests, other factors aside, that the climactic struggle will not be risked before 15 or 20 years have elapsed. Stalin's theory of "ebb and flow" would lead him to expect a new stabilization of capitalism within a few years, followed some years later by another wave of crisis and revolution generated by capitalism's inexorable contradictions. He apparently is timing completion of the Soviet base of operations for the crest of this next wave. Tactics of the moment may swing this way or that, but the Marxist doctrine to which he is committed is uncompromisingly revolutionary. In that doctrine, world Communism is the supreme aim, Soviet power the major instrument by which it will be achieved.

Problem 29: How Can the United States Best Insure Its Liberty and Survival?

The preceding chapters of this book are concerned only with United States internal problems—individual maladjustment, family reorganization, crime, race and minority relations, the role of big business, the welfare state, political bosses, and pressure groups. Such study is unrealistic, however, unless we heavily underscore the fact that the United States is not an isolated laboratory—that Americans live in a belligerent, warlike world peopled by sovereign national states. Nearly 85 per cent of the Federal government's expenditures are for wars—past, present, and future. Defense activities claim energy, materials, and money that might otherwise be devoted to domestic improvements. Hence, foreign policy has important internal repercussions in addition to its external effects.

Cynical Americans are apt to dismiss United States foreign affairs with a pat declaration that this country has no foreign policy, that its diplomats conduct international relations by ear, rather than in the light of a carefully formulated philosophy. Like most aphorisms, this is true only in a limited sense. Certainly most Americans recognize such long-range programs as the Monroe Doctrine, "freedom of the seas," and the Open Door.

Since 1939, however, there has been a general reshuffling of the world power structure, as a result of which the United States has been forced to redefine its relations with the world. In a sense America has continued its normal routine of foreign affairs while the structure erected by earlier generations was remodeled. During World War II the future was much too uncertain for reordering foreign affairs, although the United States did make a tentative commitment to abandon isolation. Much of the "new" American foreign policy, therefore, was drafted under the Truman Administration, when a whole host of policies was initiated—the Marshall Plan, Point Four, the Truman Doctrine, the North Atlantic Treaty Organization, the Organization of American States, and the Mutual Security program.

Although its authors no longer govern, this new internationalism has an official status that makes it the focal point of the debates that follow. Is American foreign policy—Truman and post-Truman—an epitome of wisdom, a compound of despair and disaster, or something between these extremes? Is this the American century, and, if so, what should the United States do about it? Should it substitute Gibraltarism for a global approach to world affairs? Is Point Four visionary, or is it a realistic cure for low living standards throughout the world? Should the United States defend the *status quo* in Asia and Africa, or should it promote world revolution? These are the foreign policy issues that Americans debate at mid-century.

PRINCIPAL INGREDIENTS OF AMERICAN FOREIGN POLICY *

American foreign policy is actually a synthesis of many programs welded together to form an over-all pattern. The following analysis of that policy, presented before an Americans for Democratic Action

* Adrian Fisher, *Department of State Bulletin*, February 18, 1952, pp. 244–48.

dinner at Chicago in early 1952 by a legal adviser of the State Department, is a friendly one. It is interesting to compare present policy with this definition of the Truman program. What parts of the Truman master plan survive? Which parts are essentially the same except for name? What policies, if any, have been abandoned?

. . . During World War II and after it, the United States adopted a policy which held that peace was best secured through collective security. Fundamentally, that policy accepted the thesis that world peace could not be broken down into compartments, that a threat to peace in one region was a threat to the peace of all regions. In practical terms the immediate application of that policy called for the United States to shoulder the burden of world leadership which had been thrust upon it and to join with other nations who valued liberty in immunizing the free world against Soviet encroachment. This was indicated in the simple interest of saving our own necks. And now at a crucial stage in putting this policy across when perhaps for the first time we can see the outlines of success on the horizon, some groups in this country are actually suggesting retreat. This tactic denies all the lessons of the past and breeds doubt and terror throughout the free world.

We have heard further outcries recently against our efforts to fight aggression in Korea. We might have washed our hands of Korea, but what would have been the result? Instead of being halted in its tracks, Communist aggression might by now have made a clean sweep of southeast Asia. Indochina, Malaya, Burma could not have withstood the tide. These countries are not yet free of threat, but if we had not taken our stand in Korea, they might have been engulfed long months ago. . . .

Our action in Korea was unavoidable, if the Truman Doctrine with reference to Greece and Turkey meant anything. When we undertook in southeast Europe to halt Communist penetration, the great majority of Americans understood and approved the step. When we undertook to halt Communist penetration in Korea, most Americans understood and approved. In the one instance, we saved Greece and Turkey from the jaws of the Russian bear. In the other instance, we upset his program, notified him that he could trespass only at his peril, instilled threatened peoples with a fresh courage, and gave ourselves an opportunity to gird our loins. . . .

The Faith of Our Fathers

The men who wrote our Constitution and set the feet of this Republic on the road to greatness had a lively sense of the example the United States was setting. From his retirement, James Madison wrote to a friend:

The free system of government we have established is so congenial with reason, with common sense, and with a universal feeling, that it must produce approbation. . . . Our country, if it does justice to itself, will be the workshop of liberty to the civilized world, and do more than any other for the uncivilized.

That phrase, "workshop of liberty," is projected in twentieth-century terms by our present foreign policy. We have through trial and error, through adversity mixed with hard work and good fortune managed to reach a plateau of freedom from which we can view the posture of world affairs through the wisdom gained by our own experience. Our fortunate situation and what we have learned along the hard road that brought us to it imposes upon us an obligation to the rest of mankind. That obligation requires us to do what we can to help them to a similar position. This is not as unselfish as it appears on the surface. We have learned that we cannot live unto ourselves alone. We realize that insofar as we are concerned our freedom cannot be preserved if the freedom of other nations is snuffed out.

This is the essence of the American idea and is the wellspring of the enormous vitality which has enabled the United States to surmount every emergency which it has encountered and continue to grow and prosper. . . . Our domestic critics are fond of reproaching America for moralizing in the field of foreign policy. I contend that our national interest is best looked after when we are guided by the fusion of moral values and practical consideration. Those who discuss power politics as though it were something removed and separate from the things we live by spiritually seem to me to be at odds with all that has made America what it is today.

Application of the Policy of Containment

In terms of our present objectives, the moral values as well as the material are essential to success. We are engaging at this moment in a determined struggle to contain communism and to prevent its poison spreading into new areas. This effort at containment involves military, economic, and political reconstruction in areas endangered by the Soviet drive. In toto it is the negative phase of U. S. policy. It includes the situations of strength which we are building in Western Europe, at key points in the Mediterranean, in the Middle East, and in the Far East. It is based on three major premises. These premises are of equal importance and are completely interdependent. The Soviet Union bases its foreign policy to a very large degree on the harsh fact of military power. Therefore, if a nation or a group of nations is to stand up to Moscow or deal with Stalin with any semblance of parity, that nation or group of nations must be able to call upon sufficient military strength to command the respect of the Kremlin.

As long as the appeal of communism is strongest in areas where there is hardship and want, that appeal must be combated by an improved standard of living so that a man's work produces the necessities of life and perhaps a few luxuries as well.

Finally, as long as communism depends on robbing a person of his faith in the future of the free world and on creating social chaos and confusion, that tactic must be countered by building the individual's confidence, in his ability to manage his own affairs and by instilling in him the will to resist Soviet encroachment.

The foregoing summary will serve our purpose here, although it involves some oversimplification and—insofar as it labels the last two premises as merely negative—is inaccurate. Obviously, economic and social rehabilitation have important positive facets.

In applying this policy of containment, the Government of the United States embarked on a series of moves which are unequaled for boldness and imagination in this country's history. Although it is practically forgotten in the present emergency, the interim-aid program, a forerunner of the Marshall Plan, was instrumental in checking a Communist threat in both Italy and France. Shortly thereafter, Greece and Turkey were gravely menaced by Soviet pressure. Greece had to contend with a communist-instigated revolt within its own borders and at the same time refused to be cowed by the sabre rattling of the Soviet puppets across its borders. Because of threatened Soviet moves against its northern provinces, Turkey was maintaining a military force on a scale far beyond the power of the nation's economy to sustain.

The Truman Doctrine: Military and Economic Aid

The United States responded with the Truman Doctrine of combined military and economic aid. The success of this action is now a matter of history. The Greek revolt was crushed and the present Government is far stronger than the earlier regime. Turkey is a stable and determined friend in a highly strategic area.

I do not think I need to do more than remind you of the Marshall Plan and its great effectiveness in aiding the reconstruction of Western Europe. There were other steps taken to give needed economic assistance to friendly free nations in southeast Asia and in the Pacific area which were effective in checking internal Communist threats and in strengthening and stabilizing the governments concerned.

When then Secretary of State Marshall launched the program, now known by his name, at Harvard University in June, 1947, he identified its purpose as "the revival of a working economy in the world so as to permit the emergence of political and social conditions in which the free institutions can exist." To a considerable degree this purpose has been achieved.

Despite a reluctance on the part of the free nations to again engage in raising a military force, realism required that all hands take into account the potential menace of the Red army and the Kremlin's habit of using its military force as a blackjack in dealing with other nations. Plain common sense dictated that defenses be erected. If the underlying principle of collective security—a joint defense based on self-help and mutual aid—was to be applied, a political framework had first to be put together. This framework was developed through the regional defense agreements exemplified by the Organization of American States, the North Atlantic Pact, the proposed Federated Command for the Middle East, and the Pacific security arrangements.

To give the initial impetus to these defense agreements, the United States launched the U. S. Mutual Defense Assistance Program and followed up with the combined economic and military aid which is now going forward under the Mutual Security Program.

.   .   .   .   .

With these provisions for the setting up of a defensive shield which would deter Communist aggression and make impossible the bargain-basement conquest so dear to their hearts what might be called the holding aspect of American policy is rounded off. But in terms of what Monroe described as a "workshop of liberty" it is only a part of the necessary program.

There must be essential positive factors which meet the challenge of communism and demonstrate the immeasurably greater values of freedom and democracy. A part of this program is economic in nature, but the type of assistance that we were able to offer through the Marshall Plan does not suffice. The Marshall Plan and kindred programs were intended mainly for economically advanced countries and peoples victimized by war; countries with economies which had once been staunch, people who had known prosperity, enjoyed political and social stability, pursued the arts of successful living.

Point Four: Assistance to the Underdeveloped Areas

But what about that vast multitude who belong to an entirely different category, the underprivileged billions who for one reason or another have never been emancipated from poverty, disease, and ignorance, the men and women of the world who fit Edwin Markham's line from the "Man with the Hoe": "Humanity betrayed, plundered, profaned, and disinherited." I direct your attention to the concluding stanza of that poem:

> O masters, lords and rulers in all lands,
> How will the future reckon with this man?
> How answer his brute question in that hour
> When whirlwinds of rebellion shake all shores?

The whirlwinds of revolt are shaking the shores and hinterlands of Asia and Africa. Nationalism is giving a special edge to the long frustration of the past. How are we to deal with this ferment? We cannot afford to be indifferent to it. We can be sure the Communists are not indifferent. The people of underdeveloped areas are meat and wine for the Commies— not because the poor devils yearn for Stalin but because the promises for Stalinism offer at least the appearance of an escape from the wrongs and sorrows of their existence. . . .

In proposing the Point Four Program President Truman called for democracy to attack those ancient tyrants, "hunger, misery, and despair." That call has not yet been fully heeded. But even a year and a half of limited effort has already revealed a feasible way of extricating helpless human beings from the fell clutch of circumstances. Already our specialists and experts working at the grass-roots level have shown that they can clear the way to a new earth for forgotten men and women. And this is possible without any great outlay of money, without imposing our will on anyone, merely through combining technical knowledge with a certain missionary zeal to help people help themselves. . . .

The Campaign of Truth

In practical terms the debate over these issues goes deeper than the question of this country's course in world affairs. Like it or not, we are locked in a struggle for the minds of men. The outcome of this struggle will determine whether or not men shall remain masters of their individual destinies or shall become the pawns of totalitarianism.

At this moment the heavy artillery that the United States can bring to bear is that which fires ideas. In a manner of speaking, the American guns are transmitters, moving pictures, and the printed matter which carry the news and the ideas that are components of the Campaign of Truth. In popular terms we are speaking of the propaganda that is beamed through the Iron Curtain, but we are dealing in the facts of American life and telling the story of the ways of men in societies where men are free. We are thus striking at the soft spot in the monolith of communism. The Iron Curtain was dropped to prevent the penetration of these ideas because they constitute the one area where rigid Soviet controls cannot be applied.

The Soviet Union has built jamming mechanisms by the hundreds in a vain attempt to silence the Voice of America, but despite this all-out-effort, we know that we are getting through to the satellites and to the Russian people. We know also that pictures and printed material, detailing the differences between a life in the West and life in the Kremlin, have reached areas in the Soviet sphere. Testimony to the impact that this material is having on the subject peoples is provided by the strenuous Soviet methods to keep it out. Every month, this drive to reach into the heart of Soviet territory with the facts and the ideas that unmask communism, and its betrayal of human dignity, is increased. A few weeks ago "Operation Vagabond" was launched. I say launched because the *Vagabond* is a ship, or more accurately, a floating transmitter which will cruise the seas off Soviet shores and provide a mobile barrage for the news-starved subjects of the Politburo.

We believe the injunction, "Know the truth and the truth shall set ye free." And we are doing all in our power to help the people of the Soviet Union know it.

A third element in the free world counteroffensive is the United Nations organization. Here we have a force for peace which has gained steadily in strength and effectiveness since its inception. In its beginnings it provided the conference table over which international disputes could be settled without resort to force. It was also a highly effective form for the airing of differences between nations so that world opinion could gain an unprejudiced evaluation of the rights and wrongs of a particular issue. In June of 1950 the United Nations matured. Confronted with a flagrant breach of peace, the representatives of 54 nations joined forces to condemn the aggression and then urged the membership to meet force with force. The membership responded, and as a result, for the first time in the history of the modern world, troops of nearly a score of nations are fighting to beat back an aggression and preserve peace.

It is conceded that all participants in this action have not contributed the maximum according to their capacity. That is something which the United States is doing everything in its power to remedy. But it is not as important as the implications of the action itself. In its true meaning the Korean move signifies that the principle of collective security has been translated into an actuality. That in itself is an accomplishment of huge proportions.

The point we have now reached recalls a situation which prevailed more than 30 years ago when another debate involving the similar issue of American leadership and support for an international organization was raging. On this occasion Woodrow Wilson said:

The world outside of America is asking itself the question "Is America going to stand by us now, or is it at this moment of final crisis going to draw apart and desert us?" I can answer this question here and now. It is not going to draw apart and it is not going to desert the nations of the world. America responds to nothing so quickly or unanimously as a great moral challenge. It is much more ready to carry through what now lies before it than it was even to carry through what was before it when we took up arms in behalf of the freedom of the world.

But Wilson's affirmation of faith came too soon. The bitter-enders in the Senate played upon popular lethargy, and our country rejected the role of leadership. It took a depression and another World War to drive home to the American people a full realization of the part they had to play. But, by then, what would have been relatively simple had grown formidably complicated. A new factor had been injected into the international equation. Soviet imperialism had emerged to bedevil the situation. Now nothing could be tried or done without having to contend with the ruthless, unpredictable hostility of Moscow.

I believe that Wilson's declaration of faith is now being redeemed. I feel that in the marrow of their bones the American people know that what we are testing is the validity and strength, and the endurance of the principles of American democracy against the dogma of communism.

I feel, also, that in the marrow of their bones the American people are determined that the way of life which they represent will be the one which will endure.

A Reappraisal of American Foreign Policy *

Does the United States have a bipartisan foreign policy? Is such a policy desirable? Or must foreign policy of necessity be either Republican or Democratic? A preceding article by Adrian Fisher explained and defended the Truman record in foreign affairs. What major changes, if any, did a Republican administration bring? The following analysis was delivered by Secretary of State Dulles before the Council on Foreign Relations at New York, January 12, 1954. Are the changes noted here of a basic nature? Or do they merely represent a shift in emphasis? Can partisanship be eliminated from foreign policy? Should voters be given a choice of foreign policies

* Text of speech by John Foster Dulles, Secretary of State, before the Council on Foreign Relations, New York, N.Y., January 12, 1954.

at the polls? Does a divergence of American public opinion indicate
weakness? What are the basic tenets of Republican policy in foreign
affairs?

It is now nearly a year since the Eisenhower Administration took office.
During that year I have often spoken of various parts of our foreign policies.
Tonight I should like to present an over-all view of those policies which
relate to our security.

The Good in Past Policies

First of all, let us recognize that many of the preceding foreign policies
were good. Aid to Greece and Turkey had checked the Communist drive
to the Mediterranean. The European Recovery Program had helped the
peoples of Western Europe to pull out of the post-war morass. The
Western powers were steadfast in Berlin and overcame the blockade with
their airlift. As a loyal member of the United Nations, we had reacted
with force to repel the Communist attack in Korea. When that effort exposed our military weakness, we rebuilt rapidly our military establishment. We also sought a quick buildup of armed strength in Western
Europe.

These were the acts of a nation which saw the danger of Soviet Communism; which realized that its own safety was tied up with that of others;
which was capable of responding boldly and promptly to emergencies.
These are precious values to be acclaimed. Also, we can pay tribute to
Congressional bipartisanship which puts the nation above politics.

The Insufficiency of Past Policies

But we need to recall that what we did was in the main emergency action,
imposed on us by our enemies.

Let me illustrate.

1. We did not send our army into Korea because we judged, in advance,
that it was sound military strategy to commit our Army to fight land battles
in Asia. Our decision had been to pull out of Korea. It was Soviet-in-
spired action that pulled us back.

2. We did not decide in advance that it was wise to grant billions
annually as foreign economic aid. We adopted that policy in response to
the Communist efforts to sabotage the free economies of Western Europe.

3. We did not build up our military establishment at a rate which involved huge budget deficits, a depreciating currency and a feverish economy,
because this seemed, in advance, a good policy. Indeed, we decided otherwise until the Soviet military threat was clearly revealed.

We live in a world where emergencies are always possible and our survival may depend upon our capacity to meet emergencies. Let us pray that we shall always have that capacity. But, having said that, it is necessary also to say that emergency measures—however good for the emergency —do not necessarily make good permanent policies. Emergency measures are costly, they are superficial and they imply that the enemy has the initiative. They cannot be depended on to serve our long-time interests.

The Need for Long-Range Policies

This "long time" factor is of critical importance.

The Soviet Communists are planning for what they call "an entire historical era," and we should do the same. They seek, through many types of maneuvers, gradually to divide and weaken the free nations by overextending them in efforts which, as Lenin put it, are "beyond their strength, so that they come to practical bankruptcy." Then, said Lenin, "our victory is assured." Then, said Stalin, will be "the moment for the decisive blow."

In the face of this strategy, measures cannot be judged adequate merely because they ward off an immediate danger. It is essential to do this, but it is also essential to do so without exhausting ourselves.

When the Eisenhower Administration applied this test, we felt that some transformations were needed.

It is not sound military strategy permanently to commit U. S. land forces to Asia to a degree that leaves us no strategic reserves.

It is not sound economics, or good foreign policy, to support permanently other countries; for in the long run, that creates as much ill will as good will.

Also, it is not sound to become permanently committed to military expenditures so vast that they lead to "practical bankruptcy."

Change was imperative to assure the stamina needed for permanent security. But it was equally imperative that change should be accompanied by understanding of our true purposes. Sudden and spectacular change had to be avoided. Otherwise, there might have been a panic among our friends, and miscalculated aggression by our enemies.

We can, I believe, make a good report in these respects.

Collective Security

We need allies and collective security. Our purpose is to make these relations more effective, less costly. This can be done by placing more reliance on deterrent power, and less dependence on local defensive power.

This is accepted practice so far as local communities are concerned. We keep locks on our doors; but we do not have an armed guard in every home.

We rely principally on a community security system so well equipped to punish any who break in and steal that, in fact, would-be aggressors are generally deterred. That is the modern way of getting maximum protection at a bearable cost.

What the Eisenhower Administration seeks is a similar international security system. We want, for ourselves and the other free nations, a maximum deterrent at a bearable cost.

Local defense will always be important. But there is no local defense which alone will contain the mighty land power of the Communist world. Local defenses must be reinforced by the further deterrent of massive retaliatory power. A potential aggressor must know that he cannot always prescribe battle conditions that suit him. Otherwise, for example, a potential aggressor, who is glutted with manpower, might be tempted to attack in confidence that resistance would be confined to manpower. He might be tempted to attack in places where his superiority was decisive.

The way to deter aggression is for the free community to be willing and able to respond vigorously at places and with means of its own choosing.

So long as our basic policy concepts were unclear, our military leaders could not be selective in building our military power. If an enemy could pick his time and place and method of warfare—and if our policy was to remain the traditional one of meeting aggression by direct and local opposition—then we needed to be ready to fight in the arctic and in the tropics; in Asia, the Near East and in Europe; by sea, by land and by air; with old weapons and with new weapons.

The total cost of our security efforts, at home and abroad, was over $50,000,000,000 per annum, and involved, for 1953, a projected budgetary deficit of $9,000,000,000; and $11,000,000,000 for 1954. This was on top of taxes comparable to wartime taxes; and the dollar was depreciating in effective value. Our allies were similarly weighed down. This could not be continued for long without grave budgetary, economic and social consequences.

But before military planning could be changed, the President and his advisers, as represented by the National Security Council, had to make some basic policy decisions. This has been done. The basic decision was to depend primarily upon a great capacity to retaliate, instantly, by means and at places of our choosing. Now the Department of Defense and the Joint Chiefs of Staff can shape our military establishment to fit what is *our* policy, instead of having to try to be ready to meet the enemy's many choices. That permits of a selection of military means instead of a multiplication of means. As a result, it is now possible to get, and share, more basic security at less cost.

The Far East

Let us now see how this concept has been applied to foreign policy, taking first the Far East.

In Korea this Administration effected a major transformation. The fighting has been stopped on honorable terms. That was possible because the aggressor, already thrown back to and behind his place of beginning, was faced with the possibility that the fighting might, to his own great peril, soon spread beyond the limits and methods which he had selected.

The cruel toll of American youth, and the non-productive expenditure of many billions has been stopped. Also our armed forces are no longer largely committed to the Asian mainland. We can begin to create a strategic reserve which greatly improves our defensive posture.

This change gives added authority to the warning of the members of the United Nations which fought in Korea that if the Communists renewed the aggression, the United Nations response would not necessarily be confined to Korea.

I have said, in relation to Indochina, that if there were open Red Chinese Army aggression there, that would have "grave consequences which might not be confined to Indochina."

I expressed last month the intention of the United States to maintain its position in Okinawa. This is needed to ensure adequate striking power to implement the collective security concept which I describe.

All of this is summed up in President Eisenhower's important statement of December 26. He announced the progressive reduction of the United States ground forces in Korea. He pointed out that United States military forces in the Far East will now feature "highly mobile naval, air and amphibious units"; and he said in this way, despite some withdrawal of land forces, the United States will have a capacity to oppose aggression "with even greater effect than heretofore."

The bringing home of some of our land forces also provides a most eloquent rebuttal to the Communist charge of "imperialism."

NATO

If we turn to Europe, we see readjustments in the NATO collective security effort. Senator Vandenberg called the North Atlantic Treaty pledges "the most practical deterrent and discouragement to war which the wit of man has yet devised." But he said also that "if the concept and objective are to build sufficient forces in being to hold the Russian line . . . it presents ruinous corollaries both at home and abroad."

In the first years of the North Atlantic Treaty Organization, after the aggression in Korea, its members made an emergency buildup of military strength. I do not question the judgment of that time. The strength thus built has served well the cause of peace. But the pace originally set could not be maintained indefinitely.

At the April meeting of the NATO Council, the United States put forward a new concept, now known as that of the "long haul." That meant a steady development of defensive strength at a rate which will preserve and not exhaust the economic strength of our allies and ourselves. This would be reinforced by the striking power of a strategic air force based on internationally agreed positions.

We found, at the Council of last December, that there was general acceptance of the "long haul" concept, and recognition that it better served the probable needs than an effort to create full defensive land strength at a ruinous price.

EDC

One of the emergency aspects of NATO is that it was begun before there was a solid foundation.

For example, Western Europe cannot be successfully defended without a defense of West Germany. West Germany cannot be defended without help from the Germans. German participation is excluded by the armistice arrangements still in force.

The West German Republic needs to be freed from the armistice; and new political arrangements should be made to assure that rearmed Germans will serve the common cause and never serve German militarism.

The French produced a plan to take care of this matter. It was to create a European Defense Community, composed of France, Italy, Belgium, the Netherlands, Luxembourg, and West Germany. They would have a European Army, including Germans, but there would be no national armies in West Europe.

A treaty to create this Defense Community was signed in May, 1952. But when the Eisenhower Administration took office last January, no Government had sought parliamentary ratification, and the project was nigh unto death.

President Eisenhower is deeply convinced that there can be no long-term assurance of security and vitality for Europe, and therefore for the Western world including the United States, unless there is a unity which will include France and Germany and end the disunity which has led to recurrent wars, and in our generation to two World Wars. As NATO's Chief Commander, and now as President, he continues to make clear the importance which the United States attached to the consummation of the

European Defense Community and, we would hope thereafter, a Political Community.

Until the goals of EDC are achieved, NATO, and indeed future peace, are in jeopardy. Distrust between France and Germany is inflammable and already Communist agents are looking to it as a means for international arson.

There are of course immense difficulties in the way of the final consummation of Franco-German unity. But we have confidence that peace will soon have the indispensable foundation of the EDC.

Economic Aid

New collective security concepts reduce non-productive military expenses of our allies to a point where it is desirable and practicable also to reduce economic aid. There was need of a more self-respecting relationship, and that, indeed, is what our allies wanted. Trade, broader markets and a flow of investments are far more healthy than inter-governmental grants-in-aid.

There are still some strategic spots where the local governments cannot maintain adequate armed forces without some financial support from us. In these cases, we take the judgment of our military advisers as to how to proceed in the common interest. For example, we have contributed largely, ungrudgingly, and I hope constructively, to end aggression and advance freedom in Indochina.

The Technical Assistance Program is being continued, and we stand ready to meet non-recurrent needs due to crop failures or like disasters.

But, broadly speaking, foreign budgetary aid is being limited to situations where it clearly contributes to military strength.

In the ways I outlined we gather strength for the long-term defense of freedom.

We do not, of course, claim to have found some magic formula that ensures against all forms of Communist successes. It is normal that at some times and at some places there may be setbacks to the cause of freedom. What we do expect to ensure is that any setbacks will have only temporary and local significance because they will leave unimpaired those free world assets which in the long run will prevail.

If we can deter such aggression as would mean general war, and that is our confident resolve, then we can let time and fundamentals work for us. We do not need self-imposed policies which sap our strength.

The Hope

The fundamental hope, on our side, is the richness—spiritual, intellectual and material—that freedom can produce and the irresistible attraction it then sets up. That is why we do not plan ourselves to shackle freedom to preserve freedom. We intend that our conduct and example shall continue, as in the past, to show all men how good can be the fruits of freedom.

If we rely on freedom, then it follows that we must abstain from diplomatic moves which would seem to endorse captivity. That would, in effect, be a conspiracy against freedom. I can assure you that we shall never seek illusory security for ourselves by such a "deal."

We do negotiate about specific matters but only to advance the cause of human welfare.

President Eisenhower electrified the world with his proposal to lift a great weight of fear by turning atomic energy from a means of death into a source of life. Yesterday, I started procedural talks with the Soviet Government on that topic.

We have persisted, with our Allies, in seeking the unification of Germany and the liberation of Austria. Now the Soviet rulers have agreed to discuss these questions. We expect to meet them soon in Berlin. I hope they will come with a sincerity which will equal our own.

We have sought a conference to unify Korea and relieve it of foreign troops. So far, our persistence is unrewarded; but we have not given up.

These efforts at negotiation are normal initiatives that breathe the spirit of freedom. They involve no plan for a partnership division of world power with those who suppress freedom.

If we persist in the courses I outline we shall confront dictatorship with a task that is, in the long run, beyond its strength. For unless it changes, it must suppress the human desires that freedom satisfies—as we shall be demonstrating.

If the dictators persist in their present course then it is they who will be limited to superficial successes, while their foundation crumbles under the tread of their iron boots.

Human beings, for the most part, want simple things. They want to worship God in accordance with the dictates of their conscience. But that is not easily granted by those who promote an atheistic creed.

They want to think in accordance with the dictates of their reason. But that is not easily granted by those who represent an authoritarian system.

They want to exchange views with others and to persuade and to be persuaded by what appeals to their reason and their conscience. But that is not easily granted by those who believe in a society of conformity.

They want to live in their homes without fear. But that is not easily granted by those who believe in a police state system.

They want to be able to work productively and creatively and to enjoy the fruits of their labor. But that is not easily granted by those who look upon human beings as a means to create a powerhouse to dominate the world.

We can be sure that there is going on, even within Russia, a silent test of strength between the powerful rulers and the multitudes of human beings. Each individual no doubt seems by himself to be helpless in this struggle. But their aspirations in the aggregate make up a mighty force.

There are signs that the rulers are bending to some of the human desires of their people. There are promises of more food, more household goods, more economic freedom.

That does not prove that the Soviet rulers have themselves been converted. It is rather that they may be dimly perceiving a basic fact, that is that there are limits to the power of any rulers indefinitely to suppress the human spirit.

In that God-given fact lies our greatest hope. It is a hope that can sustain us. For even if the path ahead be long and hard, it need not be a war-like path; and we can know that at the end may be found the blessedness of peace.

Revolution Is Our Business *

Clearly the contemporary scene is one of revolution—technological, political, social, and economic. Most Americans recognize that the world is seething with unrest, that rapid or violent change is the order of the day. Regarding America's role in this tumultuous process there is less agreement. Should the foreign policy of the United States be a brake, designed to prevent change and preserve old institutions? Or should America actively encourage and give direction to aspirations of the world's people? Should America serve as a counterrevolution-ary force or abet revolution? Mr. Douglas, who advocates the latter course, is an Associate Justice of the United States Supreme Court who has traveled extensively in Asia. Perhaps the key to his philosophy is found in the question, "Why aren't we in America standing in the villages of the Middle East and Asia and saying that we are for economic justice and social justice and we are going to help you, the peasants, achieve your revolution?"

* William O. Douglas. A condensation of "The Battle for the Minds of Men," an address delivered before the biennial convention of the Amalgamated Clothing Workers of America, CIO, May 14, 1952.

There is much talk these days of war. And the prospects of war seem to grow and grow and grow as the world lines up in a struggle between Communism and Freedom. I, of course, am not in a position to know, but I have a feeling that the fears of America are often misplaced. I have a feeling that we have misinterpreted and misjudged some of the forces in the world.

Soviet Russia, with its hungry appetite for imperialistic expansion, is a military threat, and America must be prepared, of course. But I don't think there is going to be war at this time. And why?

I think the stakes involved, the immediate stakes are the stakes of Asia and the Middle East. I think that Soviet Russia will not move in a military way until Soviet Russia has on her side the balance of the people of the world. I think that the great issues of the day are, who are going to get the hearts and the minds of the peoples of the world?

The great struggles for the world today are at the political level.

The battle for Asia is at the political level, and in that sense, I think we in America have misinterpreted the signs of the times.

Reliance on Guns, Dollars

So much depends on our own attitudes. We have to date gone to the world largely with the great wealth of America, billions upon billions of dollars and with the great military strength of America. We have placed our reliance primarily upon guns and upon dollars.

It is my deep conviction that Asia, the peoples of Asia, cannot be won by guns or by dollars. The peoples of Asia must be won, if they are to be won, with ideas. What ideas?

I suppose that each of us projects into his personal relationships and into his community relationships the same conflicts that he has within himself.

That is inevitable because, after all, we are human beings. If you do not believe in free speech, if you are afraid of new ideas, of course, you will be panicky and alarmed of people like Nehru of India, who believes in experimentation.

If you are afraid to stand up at home and fight for your civil rights, you will be afraid to stand up abroad in Asia and in the Middle East and speak for the peoples who are oppressed.

Effects of Suspicion

If you are suspicious that everyone who has a new idea may be a secret Communist agent representing the Kremlin, of course you will be suspicious of the peoples and the peasants of the Middle East who are speaking and working and striving for a higher standard of living for themselves.

And, if you practice in your union racial discrimination, if you do not believe that a man is entitled to the same opportunities, whatever his religion, whatever his race, whatever his creed, when you turn to the colored people of Asia, you will be confused and in trouble, because you who are not able to recognize equality at home will not be able to recognize equality abroad.

The worst provincialism of which America can be guilty is the provincialism of prejudice, racial prejudice, prejudice against new and challenging ideas.

The Power of Ideas

The most powerful things in the world are ideas, more powerful than all of the atomic bombs, all of the big guns, all of the airplanes.

The most powerful things in the world are ideas. They are the most dangerous things in the world, too.

What is this hold that Communism has on people? Mostly ideas, and rather shabby ones at that—ideas borrowed from the West and perverted to the Communist goal.

What is the great powerful thing of which we are proud in America? What is it that we represent, of which we are so proud? It is the standards of the Christian faith, the standards of decency and brotherhood that have come down to us in the channels of literature and religion. Those are the things which make America great and strong.

It is our Declaration of Independence, it is our Constitution, it is our Bill of Rights. Those are the things that set us apart, not our television sets, not our bathroom facilities, not our motor cars, not our buildings and paved streets. And when the atomic dust settles, if it ever does, we will still have our ideas of brotherhood and freedom and justice and we will go on from there and not turn back.

Dangers in Ideas

Ideas are the most powerful things in the world and the most dangerous things in the world. We, being afraid of ideas at home, get afraid of ideas abroad.

There are revolutions that are sweeping the world and we in America have been in a position of trying to stop them. With all the wealth of America, with all of the military strength of America, those revolutions cannot be stopped. Those revolutions are revolutions against a form of political and economic organization in the countries of Asia and the Middle East that are oppressive. They are revolutions against feudalism.

What was it that begat Communism in Russia? Feudalism. It is feudalism that is feeding the fires of Communism in the Middle East and Asia.

When I say feudalism, I mean a system of economic organization whereby a few men own the wealth of the country, where a few men run the politics of a country and where there is a government of the landlords and by the landlords and for the landlords. We do not have that in America. We have in America a broad base for participation in all affairs by everyone. We in America are not perfect. We have much to do, but our standards are right and our ideas are good, and we are striving to live up to them.

Middle East Situation

But out there in the Middle East and Asia, people like us who have come from the bottom of society, as all of us have, would not have any opportunity.

We would have no schools for our children; we would have no doctors or dentists to take care of ourselves or our families; we would have no hospitals; our income would be enough to barely live on.

We would be tied in to a farm tenancy system whereby the owner of the land would get a net return of about 90 per cent or 95 per cent on the crop and we would get 5 per cent or 10 per cent—a bare subsistence. He would own our land, our houses, our oxen, our plows, our water. He would own our souls.

That kind of a system is not going to survive. It is on its way out.

People are on the move. I did not fully appreciate that until I got to the Middle East and spent three summers there and saw what was happening in the villages. People are on the march. They are going to be free from that feudalistic system.

Who are their champions today? The underground Communist Party. Why aren't we their champions? Why aren't we in America standing in the villages of the Middle East and Asia and saying we are for economic justice and social justice and we are going to help you, the peasants, achieve your revolution. Not by throwing bombs, of course. Not by smuggling in guns. Not by leading armed insurrections. But through revolutions in the political sense.

We Support Reaction

What do we do instead? We have been supporting corrupt reactionary regimes, pouring monies behind governments that are vicious governments, reactionary governments, wasting the wealth of America, trying to underwrite the status quo, trying to stabilize the situation, as our officials sometimes say.

The situation cannot be stabilized with all the wealth of the world, with all the guns of the world. Things are on the move. Revolutions are in the making. The stakes are civilization.

Russia is not going to move in a military way, in my opinion, until the balance of power politically swings to Russia in Asia.

So I say, let us concentrate our thinking upon Asia and the Middle East and decide, as a result of our own soul-searching, what we do really stand for. If we stand abroad for the things that this great Union stands for at home, then the political victory in Asia is going to be easy. Then we are going to have more to offer the people of Asia not in terms of dollars, not in terms of guns, but in terms of ideas—than all the Communists in the world can deliver.

Undercurrent at Home

This is a great country and the people are generous and warm-hearted and idealistic. There is today, I think, a great groping for something that is constructive and positive. There is a growing feeling in this country of futility, of frustration. What we are doing is not succeeding while Russia seems to be having political successes after political successes.

Russia has been winning by default. With very few exceptions, there is no such thing in the Middle East as political parties as we know them. The only political alternative that the people have had, who have been trying to escape from their misery and their poverty, has been the Communist Party. There are exceptions, but the exceptions are not many. We, in our generosity, go to these countries with a vast Point Four program from a technical point of view. With all of our medical skills and public health services, we can move into these areas of the Middle East and Asia and we can improve conditions substantially.

In many parts of the Middle East and Asia, eight out of 10 babies die before they reach the age of 1, and it would not take very many American technicians to move through that part of the world and to stop that, by cleaning up water supplies, by teaching vaccination, and so on.

But if that is all that is done, if all you do is keep the babies from dying before they reach the age of 1, you have done nothing but increase the number of people among whom you will have to ration the poverty.

You can move in to your agricultural areas of Asia and the Middle East with our wonderful Point Four program and increase the production of the land. But if the net return through the tenant is still only 5 per cent, all you are doing is making a few landlords richer.

Feudalism Rampant

I am not exaggerating. I do not think we have any idea of the extent to which the feudal system has fastened itself upon that part of the world. It is about the way Europe was before 1000 A.D.

I met men out there who own farming land greater in acreage than the entire State of Switzerland. One man owned 1,600 villages lock, stock and barrel. Go into those villages with your Point Four program and increase the production of the land and if the owner takes 95 per cent, what have you gained in the struggle against Communism?

There are many raw materials in Asia and the Middle East. There are tremendous industrial possibilities there. Those industrial possibilities fill men like Nehru with alarm and deep concern. Why? Unskilled labor in that part of the world gets around 25 cents a day. Skilled labor in that part of the world gets about $1 a day.

The standards are not the same as they are here. Conditions are vastly different. Of course, Asia needs industrialization. Of course, the Middle East does too. But it will take years and years to get it, in the American sense, unless there is going to be tremendous exploitation.

Patience Essential

Those who know the Middle East and Asia are filled with great concern to hear people talk glibly in Washington, in New York and in other places where plans are being formulated about industrializing that part of the world.

It cannot be done quickly. It cannot be done in the typical American way of doing things. It must be slow. One of the things that must be imported along with capital are the kind of skills that you people have in the organization of unions for the protection of the rights of labor.

What the Middle East and Asia need is union know-how. There is no such thing as the tradition of trade unionism that a person acquires at birth. It is a matter of experience.

As you know, the people out there have had no such experience. They need help. There are some union men out there. They need more union men working among them. I hope that some day this great union will have many out there, showing the working people of Asia and the Middle East the democratic way of organizing and promoting their interests.

When one sees how far back in the train of things the peoples of Asia are, industrially speaking, one begins to appreciate the wisdom of Gandhi when he was arguing for the development of home industries and village industries, rather than these tremendous social cancers that would fasten themselves on Asia and India for the benefit of a few men.

Our Help Needed

Yes, we must go to the Middle East and we must go to Asia. We must help them. We must go with technical programs. If we are going, we must also go with more than that. We must also go with social and political ideas. If we do not go with social and political ideas, our technical program will be of little value in saving that part of the world from Soviet imperialism.

The things that make America great are the ideas of freedom and justice and opportunity. Those are the things that inspire people the world around. Those are things that people in the Middle East and Asia want.

Abraham Lincoln said that the Declaration of Independence was an instrument forged not only for the benefit of Americans on this continent, but one destined to lift the weight off the shoulders of men the world around. That is what people in the backward areas think.

Let us be true to our great traditions. Let us go to the world with ideas of freedom and justice. Let us make the revolutions. Let us make sure that when our technical people go into the villages of the Middle East and Asia that the people of the villages will know on which side America stands.

Impartiality Impossible

You cannot go into those villages and be there a week without taking sides. You are either for the landlord or you are for the peasants. Before we go, let us make up our mind whom we are for; and if we cannot make up our mind, we should not go.

Program for U.S.

And if we can hitch the few dollars that we have and the much knowledge that we have to a few simple ideas of economic democracy and political democracy and social justice, and be heard in that part of the world as the advocates of economic and social and political democracy, this red tide of Communism will turn. Then we of the West will make a political victory; we of the West will have Asia and the Middle East on our side. We of the West will save those people from the curse of Soviet imperialism.

Those are things that we must go to the world with.

We have been hesitant, we have been afraid. We have poured billions of dollars into Europe, and we did necessarily, I think; but we have never hitched much of our European dollars to ideas.

Why do you think the number of Communists have been increasing in France and in Italy? Why do you think they have been growing? Because we have not hitched our dollars to ideas. Unless we hitch our few dollars to ideas, unless we are forthright in our dealings in the Middle East and in Asia, we are going to go down in history as identified with the worst reactionary imperialistic forces, apart from Soviet Russia, that the world has known. That is not fair to America nor to her people, because America is not made up of people who want to do that kind of thing.

My pleas to you is this: carry into the field of international relations your ideas of social and economic and political democracy. Make those ideas vocal in our foreign affairs as you have made them vocal at home. If you do, this spectre of Soviet imperialism will shrink and recede and disappear, because there is strength in the ideas that we have here in America, strength that no Communist people have ever known.

We believe not in terror, but in tolerance; we believe in justice for everyone, regardless of his political faith, his racial origins, or his religious creeds. Those are the strongest ideas that have ever been let loose in the world.

Hang on to them, promote them, and you and the other people like you can save the world from Communism.

That is the only way it can be done.

GIBRALTARISM—AN AMERICAN FOREIGN POLICY *

Some of the bitterest debates on the American scene have centered around foreign policy. "Internationalist," "American Firster," and "Isolationist" have provoked both loyalty and scorn. When, in the winter of 1950–1951, United Nations forces in Korea were faced with disaster, former president Hoover took to the air to proclaim a policy that was immediately dubbed "Gibraltarism." In the supercharged political atmosphere, his speech was labelled "Statesmanship," "Neo-Isolation," and "Realism." Regardless of the wisdom of his stand, it is certain that Hoover spoke for millions of Americans.

I have received hundreds of requests that I appraise the present situation and give my conclusions as to our national policies. I speak with a deep

* Herbert Hoover, "Our National Policies in This Crisis," *Vital Speeches*, January, 1951, pp. 165–67.

sense of responsibility. And I speak tonight under the anxieties of every American for the nations' sons who are fighting and dying on a mission of peace and the honor of our country.

No appraisal of the world situation can be final in an unstable world. However, to find our national path we must constantly re-examine where we have arrived and at times revise our direction. I do not propose to traverse the disastrous road by which we reached this point.

The Global Military Situation

We may first survey the global military situation. There is today only one center of aggression on the earth. That is the Communist-controlled Asian-European land mass of 800,000,000 people. They have probably over 300 trained and equipped combat divisions with over 30,000 tanks, 10,000 tactical planes and further large reserves they can put in action in 90 days. But they are not a great sea power. Their long-range air power is limited. These congeries of over 30 different races will some day go to pieces. But in the meantime they are cannon fodder.

Facing this menace on the Eastern front there are about 100,000,000 non-Communist island peoples in Japan, Formosa, the Philippines, and Korea. Aside from Korea, which I discuss later, they have probably 12 effective combat divisions with practically no tanks, air force or navy.

Facing this land mass on the South are the Indies and the Middle East of about 600,000,000 non-Communist peoples. There are about 150,000,000 non-Communist peoples in North Africa and Latin America. Except Turkey and Formosa, these 850,000,000 people have little military force which they would or could spare. But they could contribute vital economic and moral strength.

Facing this menace on the Continental European front there are about 160,000,000 non-Communist people who, excluding Spain, have less than 20 combat divisions now available, few tanks and little air or naval force. But their will to defend themselves is feeble and their disunities are manifest.

Of importance in military weight at this moment there is the British Commonwealth of 150,000,000 people, with probably 30 combat divisions under arms, a superior navy, considerable air force and a few tanks.

And there are 150,000,000 people in the United States preparing 3,500,000 men into a gigantic air force and navy, with about 30 equipped combat divisions.

Some Military Conclusions

If we weigh these military forces as they stand today we must arrive at certain basic conclusions.

(a) We must face the fact that to commit the sparse ground forces of the non-Communist nations into a land war against this Communist land mass would be a war without victory, a war without a successful political terminal. Any attempt to make war on the Communist mass by land invasion, through the quicksands of China, India or Western Europe is sheer folly. That would be the graveyard of millions of American boys and would end in the exhaustion of this Gibraltar of Western Civilization.

Even were Western Europe armed far beyond any contemplated program, we could never reach Moscow. The Germans failed with a magnificent army of 240 combat divisions and with powerful air and tank forces.

(b) Equally, we Americans alone with sea and air power can so control the Atlantic and Pacific Oceans that there can be no possible invasion of the Western Hemisphere by Communist armies. They can no more reach Washington in force than we can reach Moscow.

(c) In this military connection we must realize the fact that the Atomic Bomb is a far less dominant weapon than it was once thought to be.

(d) It is obvious that the United Nations has been defeated in Korea by the aggression of Communist China. There are no adequate forces in the world to repel them.

Even if we sacrifice more American boys to hold a bridgehead, we know we shall not succeed at the present time in the mission given to us by the 50 members of the United Nations.

Our Economic Strength

We may explore the American situation still further. The 150,000,000 American people are already economically strained by government expenditures. It must not be forgotten that we are carrying huge burdens from previous wars including obligations to veterans and $260 billions of bond and currency issues from those wars. In the fiscal year 1952, federal and local expenditures are likely to exceed $90 billions. That is more than our total savings. We must finance huge deficits by further government issues. Inflation is already moving but we might with stern measures avoid the economic disintegration of such a load for a few years. If we continue long on this road the one center of resistance in the world will collapse in economic disaster.

The Diplomatic Front

We may appraise the diplomatic front. Our great hope was in the United Nations. We have witnessed the sabotage of its primary purpose of preserving peace. It has been, down to last week, a forum for continuous smear on our honor, our ideals and our purposes.

It did stiffen up against raw aggression last July in Korea. But in its call for that military action, America had to furnish over 90 per cent of the foreign forces and suffer over 90 per cent of their dead and injured. That effort now comes at least to a measurable military defeat by the aggression of Communist hordes.

Whether or not the United Nations is to have a moral defeat and suffer the collapse of its whole moral stature now depends on whether it has the courage to

(a) Declare Communist China an aggressor.

(b) Refuse admission of this agressor to its membership.

(c) Demand that each member of the United Nations cease to furnish or transport supplies of any kind to Communist China that can aid in their military operations. Such a course honestly carried out by the non-Communist nations is not economic sanctions nor does it require military actions. But it would constitute a great pressure for rectitude.

(d) For once, pass a resolution condemning the infamous lies about the United States.

Any course short of this is appeasement.

What Should Our Policies Be?

And now I come to where we should go from here.

Two months ago I suggested a tentative alternate policy for the United States. It received a favorable reception from the large majority of our press.

Since then the crisis in the world has become even more acute. It is clear that the United Nations are defeated in Korea. It is also clear that other non-Communist nations did not or could not substantially respond to the U.N. call for arms to Korea. It is clear the U.N. cannot mobilize substantial military forces. It is clear Continental Europe has not in the three years of our aid developed that unity of purpose, and that will power necessary for its own defense. It is clear that our British friends are flirting with appeasment of Communist China. It is clear that the U.N. is in a fog of debate and indecision on whether to appease or not to appease.

In expansion of my proposals of two months ago, I now propose certain principles and action.

First. The foundation of our national policies must be to preserve for the world this Western Hemisphere Gibraltar of Western Civilization.

Second. We can, without any measure of doubt, with our own air and naval forces, hold the Atlantic and Pacific Oceans with one frontier on Britain (if she wishes to cooperate); the other, on Japan, Formosa and the Philippines. We can hold open the sea lanes for our supplies. I devoutly hope that a maximum of cooperation can be established between the British Commonwealth and ourselves.

Third. To do this we should arm our air and naval forces to the teeth. We have little need for large armies unless we are going to Europe or China. We should give Japan her independence and aid her in arms to defend herself. We should stiffen the defenses of our Pacific frontier in Formosa and the Philippines. We can protect this island chain by our sea and air power.

Fourth. We could, after initial outlays for more air and navy equipment, greatly reduce our expenditures, balance our budget and free ourselves from the dangers of inflation and economic degeneration.

Fifth. If we toil and sacrifice as the President has asked, we can continue aid to the hungry of the world. Out of our productivity, we can give aid to other nations when they have already displayed spirit and strength in defense against Communism. We have the stern duty to work and sacrifice to do it.

Sixth. We should have none of appeasement. Morally there is no appeasement of Communism. Appeasement contains more danger than Dunkirks. We want no more Teherans and Yaltas. We can retrieve a battle, but we cannot retrieve an appeasement. We are grateful that President Truman has denounced such a course.

Seventh. We are not blind to the need to preserve Western Civilization on the Continent of Europe or to our cultural and religious ties to it. But the prime obligation of defense of Western Continental Europe rests upon the nations of Europe. The test is whether they have the spiritual force, the will and acceptance of unity among them to achieve this by their own volition. America cannot create their spiritual forces; we cannot buy them with money.

You can search all the history of mankind and there is no parallel to the effort and sacrifice we have made to elevate their spirit and to achieve their unity. To this date it has failed. Their minds are confused with fears and disunities. They exclude Spain, although she has the will and means to fight. They haggle with Germany, although she is their frontier. They vacillate in the belief that they are in little danger and they hope to avoid again being a theatre of war. And Karl Marx has added to their confusions. They still suffer from battle shock. Their highly organized Communist parties are a menace we must not ignore.

In both World War I and World War II they (including West Germany) placed more than 250 trained and equipped combat divisions in the field within sixty days with strong air and naval forces. They have more manpower and more productive capacity today than in either one of those wars. To warrant our further aid they should show they have spiritual strength and unity to avail themselves of their own resources. But it must be far more than pacts, conferences, paper promises and declarations. Today it must express itself in organized and equipped combat divisions of such huge numbers as would erect a sure dam against the red flood. And that before we land another man or another dollar on their shores. Otherwise we shall be inviting another Korea. That would be a calamity to Europe as well as to us.

Our policy in this quarter of the world should be confined to a period of watchful waiting.

National Unity

There is a proper urge in all Americans for unity in troubled times. But unless unity is based on right principles and right action it is a vain and dangerous thing.

Honest difference of views and honest debate are not disunity. They are the vital process of policy making among free men.

A right, a specific, an open foreign policy must be formulated which gives confidence in our own security before we can get behind it.

Conclusions

American eyes should now be opened to those hordes in Asia.

These policies I have suggested would be no isolationism. Indeed they are the opposite. They would avoid rash involvement of our military forces in hopeless campaigns. They do not relieve us of working to our utmost. They would preserve a stronghold of Christian civilization in the world against any preadventure.

With the policies I have outlined, even without Europe, Americans have no reason for hysteria or loss of confidence in our security or our future. And in American security rests the future security of all mankind.

It would be an uneasy peace but we could carry it on with these policies indefinitely even if the Communists should attack our lines on the seas.

We can hope that in time the millions of other non-Communist peoples of the world will rise to their dangers.

We can hope that sometime the evils of Communism and the disintegration of their racial controls will bring their own disintegration. It is a remote consolation, but twice before in world history Asiatic hordes have swept over a large part of the world and their racial dissensions dissolved their empire.

Our people have braved difficult and distressing situations in these three centuries we have been on this continent. We have faced our troubles without fear and we have not failed.

We shall not fail in this, even if we have to stand alone. But we need to realize the whole truth and gird ourselves for troubled times. The truth is ugly. We face it with prayer and courage.

THE UNITED STATES MUST PROVIDE ECONOMIC LEADERSHIP [*]

Assuming that Justice Douglas is right, how can the United States provide economic and intellectual leadership for backward areas? Certainly American resources and factories are not equal to the job, nor can the nation's financial structure stand the strain of such an undertaking. Faced with this dilemma, President Truman first proposed a "bold new program" in his inaugural address of 1949. Outlining United States foreign policy under four major points (hence "Point Four"), he proposed a new program "for making the benefits of our scientific advance and industrial progress available for the growth and development of underdeveloped areas. . . . Our aim should be to help the free peoples of the world, through their own efforts, to produce more food, more clothing, more materials for housing, and more mechanical power to lighten their burdens."

Despite a political turnover within the United States, the problems that originally prompted Point Four remain. What major barriers stand between the great mass of mankind and economic plenty? What obligation does the United States have to promote higher living standards throughout the world? Can the American people afford such a program? Conversely, can they afford to maintain a "hands off" policy in the face of world-wide poverty? Will not military aid promote the same ends and yet give more concrete rewards to the United States? If technical assistance is given to backward areas, may they not emerge as competitors for world markets? The following spirited defense of Point Four by Dean Acheson, then Secretary of State, will suggest still other questions.

Today, Democracy is on trial for its life. The free way of life is under attack in every part of the world, including those areas of the world which we call "underdeveloped."

These areas include parts of Latin America, Africa, the Middle East, and the Far East, where two-thirds of the world's people live, many of them in the shadow of hunger, poverty, and disease.

Increasing numbers of these people no longer accept poverty as an in-

[*] Dean Acheson, *Department of State Bulletin,* April 10, 1950, pp. 552–55.

evitable fact of life. They are becoming aware of the gap between their living standards and those in the more highly developed countries. They are looking for a way out of their misery. They are interested in practical solutions to their problems in terms of food, shelter, and a decent livelihood. When the Communists offer quick and easy remedies for all their ills, they make a strong appeal to these people.

There are the facts we must face. What do they mean to our national security, to the peace and well-being and freedom of the American people—in short, to the fundamental aims of our foreign policy?

We are spending billions for military defense—as we must. We are spending other billions for economic reconstruction in Europe and vital points in the Far East—as we must. We are organizing joint defense through the North Atlantic Treaty and the Military Assistance Program. We are organizing joint action to remove trade barriers through tariff and Reciprocal Trade Agreements and through the International Trade Organization. We are attempting to remove the causes of international friction and misunderstanding by playing an active role in the United Nations.

All the things we do are, in the last analysis, measures of national security—the broadest kind of security for our free and democratic way of life.

[The] Act for International Development [authorizing the Point Four Program] has the same broad purpose. In a very real sense, it is a security measure. And as a security measure it is an essential arm of our foreign policy. For our military and economic security is vitally dependent on the economic security of other people.

But our foreign policy is not based on security alone. We have never been satisfied merely to resist a threat—of Communism or any other ism. Our policy is broader than this. It is essentially constructive. It is based on the assumption that, in the world today, our own welfare is closely related to that of other peoples. We can participate in this kind of program because it serves both the interest of other peoples and our own interest as well.

Economic development will bring us certain practical material benefits. It will open up new sources of materials and goods we need and new markets for the products of our farms and factories. Our friends in Europe, who depend far more than we do on foreign goods and markets, will benefit in similar ways. The volume of world trade will inevitably expand.

And finally, the peoples of the underdeveloped areas will begin to see new opportunities for a better life, and they will associate those opportunities in their minds with the helping hand of the American people. Even more important, they will associate economic progress with an approach to the problems of daily life that preserves and enlarges the initiative, dignity, and freedom of the individual.

The bill now before [the Congress] establishes economic development of underdeveloped areas for the first time as a national policy. Its purpose is to encourage the exchange of technical skills and promote the flow of private investment capital where these skills and capital can help to raise standards of living, create new wealth, increase productivity, and expand purchasing power.

There are other conditions. American aid will be furnished only where it contributes to the development of a balanced economy. It may go only where it is actually needed and where the country receiving it cannot provide skills and capital for itself.

Most of the capital needed for economic development must come from the underdeveloped areas themselves. However, foreign capital will be needed from three main sources: from private investors, from the International Bank for Reconstruction and Development, and from the Export-Import Bank. The latter two should supplement, not compete, with private capital. They should finance projects, such as transportation and irrigation, which are foundations for economic development and which are not ordinarily attractive to private investment. We put primary emphasis, however, on the need for stimulating an expansion of private investment not only to provide capital but also to provide the technical and managerial skills that come with capital.

If investment is to do its job, the people of these underdeveloped areas must have confidence that foreign investors will not squander their natural resources, will pay taxes, will obey the local laws, and will provide decent wages and working conditions.

At the same time investors must have confidence that their property will not be confiscated without fair compensation, that they can take their legitimate profits and their capital out of the country, and that they can have reasonable freedom to manage their business, subject to local laws that apply to everybody equally.

This, in a nutshell, is the essence of the investment problem, and, as you see, it is a problem of confidence. I don't think there is any quick or easy solution to this problem. We are, however, taking steps which seem likely to help solve it. We are negotiating for treaties with other countries which will protect our investors from some of the risks I have mentioned. But protection from some of the risks cannot be provided by treaty no matter how sincere the intentions of the participating governments. Therefore, a bill has been introduced and favorably reported by the Senate Banking and Currency Committee which would permit the Export-Import Bank to sell certain kinds of guaranties—in other words, insurance—to investors, specifically against expropriation, confiscation, and seizure and against inability to convert local currencies. We are trying to work out proposals to amend our tax laws to give some measure of tax relief as an added incentive to investors. We are also trying to make treaties to avoid the hardship of double taxation.

But when you put all these things together, I think you will find that there is no foolproof way of guaranteeing investors against the variety of non-business risks that they face in many parts of the world today.

Fortunately, we can go ahead with a program of technical cooperation while we are trying to develop what the economists call a "favorable climate" for investment. In fact, it seems clear that one of the best possible ways to help create that climate is to get on just as energetically as possible with technical cooperation.

As you know, the United States Government has been in the business of technical cooperation for ten years. Most of the work has been concentrated in Latin America. A little has been done in the Far East. [The Act for International Development] authorizes the President to do three important and necessary things.

First, it authorizes him to expand the work and to spread it to other underdeveloped areas where the right conditions prevail.

Second, it authorizes him to coordinate all the work of our Government in this field.

Third, the President may contribute funds and personnel to the United Nations and to other international organizations for such technical cooperation programs as he is convinced they can carry on as well as we can—or better.

Now I think there are obvious advantages in giving vigorous support to the work of the United Nations in this field. Anything that gives the organization greater authority and experience is good for the United Nations and good for us. There are other compelling reasons. The United Nations and particularly the related agencies like the World Health and Food and Agriculture Organizations are set up to do certain things we cannot do.

They can, for example, mobilize the resources of many countries, some of which have skills that we don't have. We certainly do not claim to have a monopoly of skills. Nor do we flatter ourselves that we are superior in all fields. The Norwegians, for example, are expert in the science of fishery—and our technical people are glad to admit that they have much to learn from foreign technicians.

Moreover, some of the members of the United Nations are closer to the problems of the underdeveloped peoples than we are. Just because some of them are less advanced, technically, than we, they have a better understanding of the basic needs of these people.

We need have no fear in contributing to the United Nations technical-cooperation programs, since we ourselves are well represented in the United Nations agencies and will cooperate with other contributing nations in keeping watch over the programs. It should be remembered that our contributions to the work of the United Nations and its agencies are purely voluntary and that their continuation and size will depend on the effectiveness of the programs to which they are applied.

I think there is a pretty widely held idea that we are going to build large mills, mines, and factories for these underdeveloped peoples. This is not true. In most cases what we need to do and what we are going to do is to try to help these people satisfy their growing desire to learn to do things for themselves which will lighten their burden of poverty. A remarkable thing about this kind of help is that you can get big results by making a comparatively small outlay of dollars for the services of skilled people.

Let me give you some examples, based on what we have been doing.

In the San Andres Valley in El Salvador there is an agricultural experiment station in which some American technical experts work side by side with local technicians. A farmer, troubled by poor crops, came to this station for advice. One of these specialists studied conditions on the farm and recommended the use of sodium nitrate fertilizer. Following his advice, the farmer reported that his corn yield had been tripled. Now this is a simple story, and the kind of advice offered would not seem very advanced to an American farmer. But the point is that for the farmer in El Salvador it brought all the best of modern knowledge. Repeated many hundreds of times, this kind of help can change the lives of many people.

Another example: The Institute of Inter-American Affairs has been collaborating with the Brazilian Government, which is vitally interested in economic development, in the Amazon Valley of Brazil. When we went into that area, which is two-thirds the size of the United States, only two cities had safe water supplies. Typhoid fever and dysentery were all over the valley, and children were dying off in a shocking manner. A few experienced sanitation engineers went in there and showed the people how to plan and build safe water systems. The results in Aimores, a little town of 5,000 inhabitants, are typical of what has been accomplished. These people used to have from 20 to 30 cases of typhoid a year—not to mention the other diseases from polluted water. They built a small, economical, public water system, under expert guidance, and the next year not a single case of typhoid developed.

The Brazilian Government also invited three American Government geologists to help their own experts locate new deposits of strategic materials. This comparatively trivial investment in technical ability has resulted in uncovering two of the largest deposits of manganese in the Western Hemisphere, of untold value.

One of the greatest needs in the underdeveloped areas is to train people in the simple basic practices of public administration. We can, for example, help people from those areas in such things as techniques of census taking and keeping vital statistics. You don't need investment capital to do these things. You need some skilled people, people who literally talk the language of the country they are working with.

To get the technical-cooperation program rolling, we are going to have to comb the United States for people with all kinds of skills. They don't all need to be top authorities in their fields. This work should appeal to young people with some competence and experience. I suspect we will find hundreds of good people in State and municipal governments, on farms, in schools and universities, factories, and private research organizations. The problem is to seek out these people, give them a little extra training, and persuade them to go abroad in the service of their country.

Now I want to talk briefly about the cost of the Point Four enterprise. We are requesting a total authorization of 45 million dollars for the first fiscal year, ending June 30, 1951. Of this, 10 million dollars has been included in the President's budget for technical assistance activities under the Institute of Inter-American Affairs and the Information and Educational Exchange Act of 1948. Thirty-five million dollars is requested for new activities.

This figure is a result of very careful planning on the part of agencies of the United States Government which have been participating in this kind of activity in the past. It takes into consideration the excellent experience which the Institute of Inter-American Affairs and other agencies have had in Latin America. It is based on a careful study of the most urgent problems of the areas involved after consultation with representatives of those countries and an appraisal of the number and type of experts which could be recruited and effectively organized in the various fields of activity.

In all honesty I wish we could effectively spend more. I say this because I know of no better investment for the American people at this time. Any action reducing this amount would, in my opinion, have two most unfortunate results. It would undoubtedly be interpreted by the peoples of the free countries of Asia, the Middle East, and other underdeveloped areas as indicating a lack of interest in a program upon which they have been putting a very great hope. It would also seriously handicap the undertaking of specific activities which can effectively be organized during the coming year.

By its very nature, this is not and never will be a big-money enterprise. It is cooperative, which means that a considerable part of the expense should be borne by the countries with which we work. It involves salaries and expenses of people—not vast purchases of machinery and raw materials. Its objective is to show other people how to meet their own needs, not to attempt to meet those needs ourselves. For this reason the cost of technical cooperation will always be modest, compared with the cost of other types of foreign-aid programs.

Now I want to make one last observation. We talk about this program as a long-term business—which it must be. But the fact is, we are not going to have to wait long to get results. Some results can be seen in a year, as in the little town of Aimores. Others may take 5 or 10 years or even longer to produce tangible benefits.

Well, 10 years is a minute in the life of a nation—and less than a second in the life of a civilization. The fight for freedom and democracy has been going on for more than 2,000 years. It will not be won in a decade. The question that concerns us is whether it will be going our way 10 years from now. And part of the answer, I am convinced, lies in the energy, the skill, and the faith we put into this Point Four Program.

Here, indeed, is a chance to prove that our civilization, which has grown to vigor and maturity with the help of science, can bend science to its will— not to destroy but to serve humanity.

———————◆◆◆◆———————

Point Four Propaganda and Reality *

> Searching criticism of Point Four is advanced by William Vogt, author of *Road to Survival*. Disregarding political implications of the program, he declares that it is unworkable in backward areas on four counts: (1) population is outdistancing food supply; (2) these are areas of high illiteracy; (3) these regions lack capital; (4) they have a feudalistic political and economic organization.

At no period in the history of the human race has the power of the lie been so great as it is today. This is a simple effect of exponential increase in human communication facilities. The untruth need not be malicious, nor even understood by its originator. It is enough that it can be transmitted to human beings who have not the wisdom to evaluate it; and wisdom has not begun to keep up with the techniques of communication.

The influential groups in world society, whether they be the American hucksters or the international Cominform, depend on this power of the lie to peddle their particular product. If the listeners can't read, their sales

---

* William Vogt, *American Perspective*, Spring, 1950, pp. 122–29.

resistance will be lower. You can't fool all of the people all of the time, but you can fool an appalling number of them long enough to create extremely dangerous situations.

The fault is in no sense intrinsically that of the people. When they have enough facts their collective judgment is sound. Hitler knew this well, and concealed or perverted the facts. The same thing is true of Stalin. And the same thing, unhappily, is true of the State Department of the United States. We have adopted the policy of trying to outlie the Communists, apparently with the hope that our falsehoods will be more acceptable than those of the Communists.

In a sense, the fault is not that of the State Department. They were pushed out on the end of a rotten limb by the President when he promised a "bold new program" to provide "triumphant action . . . against hunger, misery, and despair" and "growing abundance." Obviously the Department couldn't repudiate the President, and some of them have been trying to figure out how to climb off that limb ever since. Others, suffering from delusions, have sincerely espoused the President's proposals and are busily trying to create substance out of void, order out of chaos. Their alchemy, they believe, will not only achieve the objectives stated by the President. The benefits that will accrue to the people of the world will be so great that they will no longer be beguiled by the promises of Stalin.

The first wave of enthusiasm, that set the Treasury Secretaries of all the "backward" countries drooling, was dashed when the Truman administration announced that it would ask for $35 million to initiate Point IV in the entire world. But the bullish trend was somewhat reestablished with the more recent suggestion that the American people put $50 billion on the black, as a bet against the red.

What are these various people—from the President down—talking about? Can triumphant action against despair be achieved, in fact, by the shotgun wedding of Economics and Technology? What, aside from words and other symbols do economics and technology have to work with? What processes are involved, and how are they to be set in motion and directed to the desired ends? More space than is available would be needed to give approximately complete answers, but we can throw some of the more important ones into relief.

Triumphant action against hunger and misery, which we may assume to be antecedent to triumph over despair, at least in the minds of President Truman and other leaders both in our government and in international organizations, depends upon the access of every human being to an adequate supply of certain substances. These include, in the first instance, between 1000 and 2000 pounds of food a year, and food in sufficient variety to provide more than calorie-bearing carbohydrates; there will be required the proteins that provide energy, protective foods such as green fruits and vegetables, minerals, and vitamins. Some of our technologists have seemed to imply that the food problem could be solved with hybrid corn, but while it is true that rats get along fairly well on such a diet, it is not likely to satisfy the human animal.

Will the people of the world be fed—through a Point IV program, or any other that is likely to be developed? Since food is basic to any plan of human betterment, this is a fair question. And it should be answered as it is asked—not in terms of the subjunctive mood and conditional tense. What the agronomists and economists might do, in an ideal situation, or even under American conditions, has nothing to do with the actual processes that are going on—and will continue to go on—in the soils of the world, and in the churning stomachs of children and women and men.

My own answer to the question is based on more than six years of actual field work in so-called backward countries, plus more years of study of scientific reports on other areas. And, much as I regret it, my answer has to be in the negative. Many people who know the backward areas agree.

"Can you tell me," I asked a very knowledgeable agronomist on the staff of FAO, "of a single one of the so-called backward countries of the world, where the increase in food production is even beginning to keep pace with the increase in population?"

His answer was a reluctant, "No." Such increase as there has been in food production has, of course, taken place mostly in the technologically advanced areas that do not need it. The backward peoples of the world, by and large, simply do not have enough of land, skill, tools and fertilizers, and—above all—socio-economic flexibility, to increase their production as fast as is necessary. Where, in backward areas, there is no large outlet for cash crops, farmers cannot secure the means of filling these needs. Years of costly, high power extension work and agricultural education in the literate United States have made good farmers out of only a small fraction of our farm population; some who know the situation place the estimate as low as ten per cent. It is utterly unrealistic to talk about meeting the demand for an adequate diet within a decade or two; and since people live and suffer in a real world, not in the promised world of technicians and bureaucrats, making promises that cannot possibly be kept seems to me downright cruel and vicious.

The United Press recently reported on a United Nations survey stating that the production of a number of basic commodities, including wheat, potatoes and barley, in 1947, was below the 1928 level. Meanwhile, of course, the world population had grown enormously—probably by more than 300 million of those churning stomachs. And while we are failing —and failing miserably—in our efforts to meet the world demand for food, we are not trying to reduce the demand. We are actually expanding it. There is grim humor in the fact that on this policy the Cominform and the Catholic Church agree—even in Italy.

Nor is food the only problem. In the long run, it may not even be the most important. In this world of accelerated communication, where people give words a hard-currency value, it is difficult to see how democracy can survive unless men and women everywhere are able to evaluate those words. And few of us in this country doubt, I think that the fall of democracy would be tantamount to the beginning of a new Dark Ages.

If people are not to be made mere captives of the words of the Cominform, or the Hitlers of tomorrow, they must be able to distinguish fact from fiction, sound inference from delusion. This requires an irreducible minimum of education.

Yet education costs money. Teachers must be paid. Schools must be built. Books must be available. And these books must be based on scholarship and research. There must be good teachers and good books, or only negative literacy will be developed.

In the rice bowl economy, there is not enough surplus wealth to provide these indispensables. There is not enough in Mississippi and Louisiana, some Fair Dealers tell us; the deficit must be made up by New York and California. How, then, is there likely to be enough in Haiti, where the income is seven cents a day, in India where it is five cents—in China and Borneo and Africa where, if it is any more, the increase is not significant?

When in the relatively simple matter of food production we are not keeping up with demand, how can we hope to provide the water (where and when it is needed), the timber for hundreds of uses from railroad ties to the paper for the printing of books and newspapers? How are we to find the surplus wealth to build the roads that permit the integration of economics, the shipment of raw materials? Where we start with populations that are 50–90 per cent illiterate, how are we to educate not only the masses of the people, but their leaders? Where are the teachers, the scientists, the technicians, the doctors, the newspapermen, coming from? These, too, are the product of wealth above and beyond the mere subsistence level.

Approximately every second and a half the world population increases by one of these empty stomachs. By far the biggest proportion of this increase takes place in the so-called backward countries. Most of them have geographic limitations that combine into far more resistant environments than ours. In nearly all of them, farmers, lumbermen, cattle-, sheep- and goatmen are reducing the productivity of the environment that exists. Nor are they likely to stop—even if we offer our assistance. For few of these countries are in the hands of the people. They are, by and large, controlled by colonial powers—or by oligarchies of powerful business groups and big landowners, operating through the instrumentality of armies and police forces. Unless Point IV aid by-passes these groups—which means by-passing governments—the people of the world are not likely to profit by our efforts. In much of Latin America, for example, any successful effort to end the misery and despair of the people, would have to be preceded by social revolution. It is not without reason that many Latin American leaders fear democracy more than they do Communism.

Unless we establish such controls over the use of American capital, and other developmental forces, Point IV activities are likely to benefit chiefly those who are already comfortably situated in the backward areas. And unless we control the exploiters of natural resources—both Americans and nationals of the countries involved—the net result is likely to be something approaching permanent destruction.

The chances of "triumphant action against misery and despair" are minute. The possibility of success within a period shorter than a number of decades is virtually non-existent. Yet we are largely relying on promises of such progress as our answer to Communism.

Communism is not going to solve the problems of the peoples of the world—and they will eventually find it out. Neither will democracy solve these problems, in the terms stated by the United States government and its President. Unless production is rapidly increased on a long range basis, of which there seems to be no likelihood at the present time, and the demand is effectively reduced, increasing poverty and not prosperity will be the lot of the people. As Walter Lowdermilk has expressed it, we are engaged in a race between food and population. And the population is drawing steadily ahead.

We are also involved in a race between truth and lies—two lies. Our lie, with Freedom up, may for a time outrun the Communist lie. But there is no possibility that we can provide abundance for burgeoning populations in 24, or 40 or 50 years. Perhaps the Communist lie will become the favorite as, in the next decade or so the futility of our efforts becomes patent. Whatever happens, in the home stretch, Truth is sure to be ahead. And in a world whose exploding populations insist on making impossible demands on a resistant environment, Truth is virtually certain to be a bony steed with a bony rider, scythe in hand.

Few words in history have been more foolish than President Truman's Point IV remarks. It is, perhaps, not too late to correct the harm they have done. We shall lose face in doing it; but this, it seems to me, would be far preferable to leading hundreds of millions of people through the Valley of Despair to ultimate destruction. Faith among the people of the world in the integrity of the United States has been deteriorating since the latter days of President Roosevelt's administration. The Point IV hoax will not improve the situation. Nor, parenthetically, will the logorrhea that seems to be a chronic American disease.

I do not mean to suggest that we should withdraw from the world, in a Wherry-like retreat to the womb. We have so much to give the world that we really don't need to present it as though it were the Hollywood version of a soap opera. It is of critical importance, both to other countries and to our own, that we do not make impossible promises. We have been going "to make the world safe for democracy," establish "freedom from want and fear," abolish "hunger, misery and despair" so often, during the past 35 years, it is a wonder that even the non-Communist countries have not begun to give us the Bronx cheer.

Secretary Acheson, wiser than most of his critics, has stated that our foreign policy must be adjusted to particular circumstances and particular times. Development, operation and expectation under the Point IV program, must be similarly adaptable. But there are, it seems to me, certain requirements and yardsticks that should be set up in agreement with the governments controlling the respective "backward" areas; furthermore, these requirements and yardsticks should be given the widest possible publicity, especially within the areas concerned. They should include:

1. *An estimate of demand.* This should be based, primarily, upon expected population trends, and should be revised annually. It should also include estimates of the amounts and kinds of foodstuffs required to meet the demand; educational facilities; housing; water-supplies; hospitalization, etc. In other words, the best possible approximation of what will be needed to provide a stated standard of living, within given periods, for expected numbers of people.

2. *An inventory of resources, showing trends.* This will show what the cooperating agencies have to work with (including human resources) and will keep before the people of the world the potentials and limits of resources for any area—either within the area, or by exchange; will show whether or not resources are being utilized on a sustained-yield or destructive basis; and will indicate whether or not production can be expected to keep up with demand. News reports that Spain was seeking hundreds of millions of bushels of wheat failed to remind their readers that, a fortnight or so previously, publication of the Spanish budget had shown only one per cent of the total devoted to agriculture. Obviously, before aid is given to any area, it should be required to take reasonable steps to help itself. Spain, it seems to me, in the face of this irresponsibility deserves no outside help.

3. *Full and free dissemination of these estimates, or inventories,* both in publications and over the radio—so that the people of the areas involved may know what to expect, and why they cannot expect more.

Spot-checks must frequently be made of the estimates by independent, technical groups. Obviously, since the State Department, Institute of Inter-American Affairs or Office of Foreign Agricultural Relations must come to heel when the Administration whistles, they cannot be depended upon for honest evaluation. The United Nations, the FAO and Organization of American States, are at even more of a disadvantage; they have a plethora of masters, some of them statesmen, but many who are unfortunately pipsqueak politicians who cannot permit the organizations they control to say anything that might offend national prestige or sensibilities. Evaluations might be made under a non-political National Science Foundation, if one can be established; or, failing this, by scientific committees drawn from outside government and responsible directly to Congress.

Such bilaterality will shock those who put their faith in international bodies; unfortunately, when facts may be suppressed or perverted because of political expediency, it is impossible to maintain faith in the capacity of international bodies to deal with facts. And, whether they are palatable or not, those facts stay with us.

In every case—accepting Secretary Acheson's formulation—we must make sure, before we undertake it, that the people and governments of the various areas will want strongly enough what we consider development to do their part. Incredible though it may seem to large numbers of Americans, not all the people in the world want the education that we have made a shibboleth; not all of them want our material standard of living enough to accept the hard work and self-discipline on which it must be based; nor will many governments be willing to jettison such waste and extravagance as corruption and useless military organizations in the interest of citizen welfare. These are limiting factors powerful enough to wreck any "development" program.

The nub of the matter is facts. They go on—such facts as 55,000 more people in the world every day, in the face of wasting soils, water and forests —and words either do not change them or else change them only with glacial slowness. No matter how fast we talk, the facts remain. If we do enough talking, the people of the world will finally see through our verbalizing, and realize that empty bellies are not filled with words, nor even dollars.

One need not travel very far beyond our borders to realize that some of them already realize it. When that understanding sweeps the world, it will be too late for us to do anything about it.

Problem 30: Can International Cooperation Provide Peace and Justice?

Broadly speaking, we may divide all movements toward international unity into two types: expansion based on force, or union through agreement. Throughout history, regions and continents have been consolidated into empires, with a homeland extending its dominion through conquest of other areas. Through an evolutionary process some empires have even reduced the distinction between conqueror and conquered. Thus, in the case of Rome, a common citizenship was eventually created, while Great Britain transformed several of her major colonies into the British Commonwealth of Nations. Such a version of "One World" is of current significance, for on the modern scene it would probably mean world domination by either the Soviet Union or the United States.

The second type of international unity was confined to the realm of theory until the twentieth century. An international organization, with member states sacrificing part of their peacetime sovereignty to the group, is something very new in the world. Earlier leagues were actually military alliances, designed to either preserve or overthrow the *status quo.*

The failure of the first genuine international organization, the League of Nations, is an oft-told tale that needs no repeating here. The League's successor, the United Nations, has already suffered many of the strains and stresses to which the League succumbed. What hope can one entertain for UN success? Should the UN, rather than military alliances, be the chief bulwark of American foreign policy? Or has the UN proved to be nothing but a soapbox for Russian oratory? Should the great power veto be eliminated? Rather than the UN, do we need an all-powerful world government? Are Americans willing to forego in some measure the national independence and sovereignty that spell international anarchy? How can chauvinism and nationalism be curbed in the interests of peace? Shall we train American or world citizens in our schools? Is "Americanism" threatened by the ideal of "One World"?

A PLEA FOR WORLD GOVERNMENT *

> In their restless mid-century search for security, the American people are bombarded with many programs of action—"isolation," "Gibraltarism," "American Century," "Russian Century," "security through the UN," "Western alliance." Still another alternative is proposed by the United World Federalists, who declare that they are the true realists—that only a wholesale reorganization of society can bring peace in our time.
>
> Do supporters of the various types of world federalism ignore some elementary, harsh truths? Would federalism mitigate or increase world tensions? Have not international relationships always been based on power politics and military force? Is not the United States primarily interested in preserving our "way of life" and only secondarily in maintaining peace?

The creation by peaceful consent in our time of some form of world government is a tremendously difficult undertaking and success is obviously uncertain. Because of that fact a good many people feel that those who are practically working today for world government must be utopian idealists.

Yet in spite of the monumental difficulties and in the face of active opposition by official policy makers, the popular movements that are working for world government continue to grow, and at the same time an increasing number of able and respected men are devoting their energies and time to it.

Before all this activity can be dismissed as irrelevant, as escapism from the problems of the real world, it seems to me that the objective observer should take a moment to consider the facts and the logic which force the United World Federalists to the position they take today. A process of elimination and a thorough analysis of the other available courses of action and their consequences have led the federalists to believe that the only way to preserve peace and the values of civilized life is through the creation of a structure of enforceable world law above the nations.

Let me briefly review, therefore, the reasons that we have for rejecting as inadequate the usual courses of action that are advocated for our country and the world.

Futility of Armament Policy

First, there is the present policy of the American Government. I will define that policy as an attempt to maintain a preponderance of power so great that no nation will dare to attack us. Thereby it is hoped that

* Cord Meyer, Jr., *The Annals* of the American Academy of Political and Social Science, July, 1949, pp. 1–13.

peace will be maintained. In following that policy we are pursuing a program of domestic rearmament at the cost of fifteen billion dollars a year.

We are also engaged in a program of economic and military aid in order to ensure strong and loyal allies when the war starts, and we are using an economic boycott in an attempt to weaken the economies of our probable opponents.

Finally, we are forming military alliances, such as the Atlantic Pact, in order to gain strategic bases.

Now, given the nation-state system in which we live, granted the fact that every nation today is free to prepare for war, in view of the fact there is no assurance in the world that aggression can be effectively dealt with, we in this country have no choice, it seems to me, but to maintain our military defenses. I think most federalists would agree with that.

However, to admit that arms, bases, and allies are necessary today is not to prove that they can ensure either peace or American security in the future. They cannot. They are only temporary, dangerous, stopgap expedients to buy time; and the question is, What are we going to do with the time that we are buying by building up a military force sufficient for a temporary period to stop aggression?

The reasons why we can decide conclusively that military rearmament and bases are not enough are well known to most of us. First, of course, there is the revolution that has taken place in the nature of war itself—a revolution characterized by the new weapons, atomic and biological, and the long range aircraft. We can have no lasting monopoly on these weapons. The informed military observers and the scientists are in agreement that there can be no effective defense against an air attack launched with atomic and biological weapons against the cities of a modern nation.

Therefore, our present preparations for war are not designed to defend our people and our cities. What we are trying to do is build up so great a striking force, so well dispersed, that even after we have lost our major cities and most of their people, we can counterattack from the ruins and wreak equal or greater devastation on the opposition. And the hope is expressed that fear of our ability to counterattack will prevent any nation from destroying our cities in the first place.

Costs of Armament Policy

The full cost of this program is becoming evident. We have to keep ahead of all other nations in the production of ever more destructive weapons. We are faced with the necessity of maintaining a large standing army. We must in the immediate future undertake a program of industrial dispersal and decentralization if we seek to keep any part of our war industry functioning after the war has started. And all this costs astronomical sums, fifteen billion dollars this year and an increasing amount in the years to come, which means a steady decline in our living standards.

At the same time, the building of an armed camp to enable this country to carry on a war after it has lost its two hundred major cities is necessarily going to demand a steady loss of democratic practice and of civil liberties, and is now doing so, as I think most of us are aware.

Every country where effective preparation for modern war is undertaken must in the process become a barracks society, with its people regimented and disciplined, its living standards steadily depressed, and its liberties lost.

The obvious reaction of other nations in the world to this program is to follow the same course, they also believing that they can be safe only if they are stronger than we are, they also feel that the only security is preponderant power. They regiment their people, spend increasing sums on armaments, disperse their industries, and the result is not security for any one of the separate nations, but increasing insecurity for all, mutual fear, hysteria, incidents, and eventual war.

If that war is allowed to occur, we can say with assurance that it will be the most destructive war in history. The large-scale use of atomic weapons will involve the destruction of most of our urban and industrial society. The survivors will have little left but ruins to live with, and the whole course of human events and history will be set back many, many years.

In the light of these facts we must conclude that military preparedness in this country is necessary today but that it is not enough.

Support of United Nations

There is another course of action that is often proposed. It is urged that we support to the limit the United Nations as it is presently constituted; that we try through every possible economic and social means to improve the living standards in the world and to spread a general sense of world community and good will, and that no attempt be made to change the structure of the U.N. for a long time—until, in fact, a general sense of world community is built up throughout the earth.

The hope expressed by the people who follow this line of thought is that gradually differences will be compromised, and living standards will be improved to the point where at some future, indeterminate date, say some hundred years from now, we can move to the establishment of some form of government for the world.

In speaking to that position, let me say that the World Federalists have supported the United Nations as a first step. . . .

Weakness of United Nations

But we have never felt that the best way to support the U.N. is to give it blind and uncritical worship. We feel that in the field of security the U.N. is fatally weak. We feel that the events of the last three years and the size of the present competitive national armament budgets are a measure of its weakness and its failure to protect its members and provide genuine international security. We also feel that only by understanding what its weaknesses are and by taking energetic and immediate action to remedy them can we in fact save the U.N. and end the arms race that threatens it. Our analysis of the weakness of the U.N. is somewhat as follows.

The General Assembly was designed as the town meeting of the world, but its recommendations are not binding on any member nation. As a result, they have been consistently ignored whenever it has been to the national interest of a country to ignore them.

The Security Council is the agency with the obligation to enforce the peace. However, it cannot act except against a small state that is without the support of any of the larger ones. As a result, the Security Council is incapable of dealing with the real problems that lead to major war, because a small country that is without the support of any of the Big Five is not a nation that is likely to provoke the third world war.

The International Court of Justice lacks compulsory jurisdiction in the sense that a nation need not appear before it unless it wishes to, and it lacks jurisdiction over the individual. In other words, the U.N. is founded on the concept of collective guilt, on the idea that sanctions are to be directed against an entire people—the men, women, and children of a whole nation. The U.N. is not founded on the principle that we tried to establish at Nuremberg, the principle of individual responsibility under the law.

Finally, there is no U.N. police force. Under the U.N. every nation is free to arm, and therefore every nation has to arm in self-defense against the armament of others.

As a result of these weaknesses it is evident that no nation can depend upon the U.N. as it is today for protection. All nations must depend on their own competitive national armaments, on rival military alliances, on strategic bases.

Transform the United Nations

The fact that neither American military power nor the U.N.'s present structure can in the long run preserve peace or end the arms race has led us, the federalists, to advocate immediate steps to strengthen the U.N. and to transform it, giving it the power of a federal government stronger than its members and capable of protecting them as against each other.

In the last three years there has been a great deal of debate and discussion as to what changes are necessary in the U.N., what kind of a government it should become, and what powers should be given to it. Very briefly I wish to discuss from my own personal point of view those problems, because there are real and meaningful differences of opinions on these issues among men who share a common belief in the necessity of some type of world federal government.

Proposed Powers of the United Nations

If the U.N. is to be able to protect its members, it must be given the constitutional authority to make and enforce law that is binding on national governments and on their individual citizens as their first duty. But once one has said that, one must add that this lawmaking power must be very clearly defined and strictly limited.

I think much of the opposition to the cause of world government comes from the fact that people do not understand what is actually being advocated. We do not advocate the creation of a world superstate with vast power to change the domestic institutions of the various nations and stamp out the differences between peoples and impose a common form of economic and social structure on the world. That is neither desirable nor necessary nor possible.

What we do advocate is that the U.N. should be given certain clearly defined and limited lawmaking powers sufficient to preserve the peace between the member states, and no more than that. The powers specifically necessary in the security field seem to be the following:

1. Power to prohibit the use of force by national governments in the settlement of their disputes, and to require the peaceful arbitration or judicial settlement of those disputes.

2. Power to control effectively the means of making war.

3. Power to limit and regulate national armed forces so that no nation is permitted to maintain more military power than it needs for preservation of order among its own citizens.

4. Power to control atomic energy in its potentially dangerous aspects, and to control certain other types of scientific development that can be easily diverted secretly to mass destruction.

5. Power to levy taxes to provide a dependable source of revenue, independent of the action taken by national governments.

Proposed Changes in United Nations Structure

If even these minimum powers are to be given to the U.N., some change in its structure is required.

The present system of representation in the General Assembly is indefensible. One nation, one vote: Luxembourg one vote; Great Britain one vote; Nicaragua one vote; the United States one vote. We cannot expect any real authority ever to be given to an assembly based on that system of representation.

On the other hand, representation cannot be based on population alone. There are too many differences in the level of development between countries to permit that at this time, although it is an end toward which we must work.

It seems to me that a possible compromise can be found in a weighted system of representation in which population, literacy, and levels of economic development are taken together to determine the actual voting strength to which each country would be entitled.

Now, the Security Council. Obviously, the Security Council under its present structure is not an effective executive agency. It should be replaced by a cabinet responsible for the execution of the laws, operating without veto.

World courts are required with compulsory jurisdiction over the individual. We must recognize once and for all the futility of attempting to prevent war by trying to enforce sanctions against entire countries. We must base the enforcement procedure of any workable international organization on the principle of individual responsibility, which can be determined only in a court, according to known and established laws.

Finally, law is meaningless unless it can be promptly and decisively enforced. Therefore a world police force is required larger than the forces maintained by any separate state, and world inspection forces are needed with free access into every country to make sure that the prohibited armament is not being secretly manufactured.

That, very briefly, is the kind of security structure that seems to be the skeleton of any workable organization having a chance of keeping the peace. . . .

Steps toward Goal

Here are the objectives toward which we in the United World Federalists are working, and these are the practical steps that we think are necessary to reach these objectives.

First, we see the obvious need for an informed and aroused American public opinion, an insistent popular demand, focused on our legislators. And that demand is growing today. In Connecticut in an official ballot we got an eleven-to-one majority on a question as to whether our country should take the lead in the transformation of the U.N. into a world federal government. Similar majorities occur when the question is put elsewhere, as in Massachusetts, where the majority was nine to one. We think that is an impressive indication of the fact that the people are ahead of their leaders on this issue, that they are ready now to pay the price in terms of some limitation of national sovereignty in order to get a chance to live in peace.

This aroused opinion must then be focused through effective political action, so that we can be assured of a majority in the House and the Senate. We have now, I would say, about sixty men in the House and about eight Senators who are informed and active on our side. Our supporters expect in the near future to introduce a bill in the House which will, if passed, put the Congress on record on this issue. We hope and expect to get fifty to sixty men behind that bill when it is introduced, and we think we have a chance of passage.

In the state legislatures we are sponsoring a number of different types of legislation. Particularly interesting is the fact that recently the legislatures of Maine and California passed legislation calling upon the Congress to initiate a National Constitutional Convention under Article 5 of our Constitution for the purpose of making such amendments as are necessary to enable the United States to ratify and enter a world federal structure.

Once we have an assured majority in the House and the Senate, we can expect and demand action by the administration and the President, and we feel that that action should be a declaration that it is the goal of American foreign policy to move steadily toward the transformation and strengthening of the U.N. into an actual federation. Once that declaration is made, the next step is a careful and patient negotiation with all the other members of the U.N. to see if we can get initial broad agreement. If we can get that agreement, then and only then should a General Conference be called under Article 109 of the Charter of the United Nations.

A review conference under Article 109 would act as a constitutional convention, and the results would have to be referred to each country for ratification; and in this country that would necessarily involve some amendment of our Constitution. It is a hard road and a long one, and we know it. But we really see no other way out of the dilemmas that we now face. . . .

The Case of Russia

The problem of Russia remains. First, we know that Russia is a dictatorship, not a democracy, that is has no civil liberties as we know them. But we also feel that democracy is not going to be established in Russia by conquest through atomic war nor by threatening such a war. The effect of that kind of action is to strengthen the position of the present leaders in relation to their own people, since it gives the leaders the best propaganda card they have in trying to convince their people that our intentions are aggressive and that they must band together for defense against us.

Second, it seems to me quite clear that it would be much better and safer all around to have Russia in a world federation rather than outside. Outside it, she would remain free to compete for armament and prepare for war and she would be capable of secret and sudden attack. Inside it, she, together with other nations, would be subject to a common law; she would be subject to substantial national disarmament controlled by the world police force, the courts, and the inspectors.

Once all those assumptions have been made, I have to admit that the present leadership in the Kremlin is opposed to the idea of world government. As a matter of fact, the Moscow radio has spent some time attacking us, and it attacked me personally not so long ago as the fig leaf of American imperialism; I think that was the nice phrase used.

But it seems to me that we cannot assume that this opposition will last forever, and there is a chance of acceptance by the Kremlin. That chance depends on how the proposal is made.

We must recognize that the transformation of the U.N. into a working security structure capable of making and enforcing law cannot be made without some kind of general statement of the outstanding specific issues, and that, in fact, the two things are interdependent. There is no chance of settling specific issues such as Germany and Korea as separate problems; they are part of the over-all power struggle.

The chance of a settlement rests on an agreement to a working security structure that can guarantee that settlement. A mere treaty that can be torn up ten days after it is made is inadequate because there is too much distrust for nations to go into that kind of a treaty again. There must be assurance of effective enforcement if any settlement is to be made, and it is in that context that the proposal should be made.

The possibility of acceptance by Russian leaders is due simply to the fact that in an atomic and biological war they stand to lose as much as or more than we do. They stand to be totally destroyed—their people, their cities, and the industries they have built up. There is a possibility that they may be realistic enough to change some parts of their present doctrine to conform to the facts, the reality being that war is no longer a means of advancing the national interests of any country, but has become a method of collective suicide for entire nations. There is a chance that both we and they may recognize that fact in time.

If Russia Stays Out

If at first, after patient negotiation, the Russians do not come in, I think we should then have no choice but to hold the U.N. together for all it is worth as a forum for discussion, but proceeding with it to form a federation of all those nations willing to join, providing that a majority are ready to go ahead. We should have to maintain the military strength of that partial federation; we should have to improve its economic health; we should have to demonstrate that it was not an instrument for American domination and control; and, most important of all, we should have to hold out a standing offer of membership to those who remained outside, and reach the people of those countries with the knowledge that here was a fair and honorable opportunity to end the arms race that was continually open to them. We could then hope, over a period of time, through a wise course in the pursuit of that policy, to gain either a change of policy or leadership on the part of those nations that at first might remain outside.

The Chance of Success

This sequence of action provides the best practical chance of success. It is that for which we, the United World Federalists, are working, and we are encouraged by the growing popular support we are receiving and by the political support we are winning in Washington.

Our most effective opposition is not our active opposition, such as the extreme right and the extreme left. Our most effective opposition is the despair and the resignation to inevitable war of able and intelligent men who could do much if they were on our side.

We must act and think and live in the profound conviction that men are neither so stupid nor so brutal as to be condemned to self-destruction. There were good words written recently by Robert Oppenheimer; they express hope and warning: "It is in our hands to see that the hope of the future is not lost because we were too sure that we knew the answers, too sure that there was no hope."

Objections to World Government *

In the wake of the first atomic bomb blast, many Americans declared that the only choice in foreign policy was between one world and none. State legislatures committed themselves to world government, the United World Federalists flourished, Congressmen pledged their allegiance to the new ideal. This initial enthusiasm was later to diminish somewhat.

The more telling arguments used against world government are here summarized by Elmer Davis, noted radio commentator and news analyst. World unity, he suggests, can be achieved neither with nor without the Russians. Therefore, we have no choice for the immediate future but to maintain a vigorous, intelligent foreign policy, backed by powerful armaments.

. . . If the United Nations had seriously tried to solve the one great and dangerous problem of international relations, the antagonism between the Russian empire and the free world, the result would probably have been a world war. If the United Nations were replaced, before the antagonism has been resolved, by a world organization with paramount authority and the power to enforce it, the result would be either global civil war or global tyranny.

Yet many high-minded and intelligent people insist that we must have something stronger than the United Nations. Their proposals run all the way from strengthening the present organization to the establishment of a full-fledged world government, with such authority in its field over the individual citizens of its component nations as the United States Government has, in its field, over the individual citizens of its component states. Such a government, if the Russians and their satellites had a share in it, would be as open to subversion, and to the same kind of subversion, as was the government of the late Czechoslovak Republic. And no world government that could conceivably be safe for democracy could be established now, unless at the price of war. It may be that we shall eventually have to fight a war, though I am far from convinced of that; but there is no sense in asking for it.

Of course the advocates of world government do not see it that way. I have many friends among them—men and women of patriotism and good will, who see world government as the only hope of preventing war; a war that would be made more horrible by the reciprocal use of the pluto-

* Elmer Davis, *The New Republic*, February 27, 1950, pp. 10-11, 13.

nium bomb, with the still more appalling possibility of the hydrogen bomb in the background. (And don't forget biological warfare, which might prove worse than either.) Four and a half years ago, the first revulsion of the atomic scientists from their own achievement produced a well-intentioned but hysterical and illogical book entitled *One World or None.* Time has taught most people that the problem is not so simple; a document I have just been reading observes that "the prevention of atomic-age warfare is unquestionably a paramount problem." The language is well chosen; this is indeed a paramount problem. *The* paramount problem, however, is the preservation of the freedom of the mind, already in eclipse over large parts of the earth's surface. Unless that is our primary objective, whatever the preservation may cost, then George Orwell's *1984* is a preview of the history of the future. . . .

At this point I had better pause to thin out my audience. If you do not believe that the aggressive expansionism of Russia, an empire using a world religion as an instrument for softening up its intended victims, is the major problem in the world today; if you think that Stalin, when he talks to visiting Americans about the peaceful coexistence of the two systems, is saying what he means and not indulging in a tactical expedient; if you do not believe Stalin when, teaching *ex cathedra* on faith and morals, he says the exact opposite to his disciples—why, then you need read no farther. If the history of the past five years has not convinced you, I can't. To the remnant that remains, I may offer some comment on a few of these problems [of world government].

. . . Of these world government organizations the best known is that of the United World Federalists. Nineteen Senators and 100 Representatives have supported its resolution declaring that it should be a fundamental objective of American foreign policy to seek the development of the United Nations into a world federation, open to all nations. How many of these gentlemen would actually vote for a constitutional amendment taking the United States into such a federation is another matter; a good many Congressmen, to oblige a pressure group, will come out for almost anything so long as they don't have to do anything about it. The UWF plan is sweeping enough—a world legislature in which representation would be determined according to the principles of justice (whatever they may turn out to be); a world judiciary to interpret the federal constitution and laws, with compulsory jurisdiction over individuals; and a world executive, controlling all weapons of mass destruction, with an armed force sufficient to lick any national forces.

There is logic in this, if nothing else; a government which does not possess sufficient power to execute its policies is not a government. But who would operate this world executive possessing all the atomic bombs?

The proponents of this program are afraid that the Russians might not be willing to come into such a world government; as they were unwilling to accept the Baruch Plan for control of atomic energy, which would have been a long step toward it. In that case, say the World Federalists, let the rest of the world set up the government and remain armed until the Russians realize that they might as well climb aboard the bandwagon. But what I am afraid of is not that the Russians would not join, but that they would.

They might not, in view of the persistent stupidity of their foreign policy since the end of the war—a policy which obligingly provided a new provocation every time Congress was beginning to wonder if we weren't spending more money than was necessary on trying to stop them. But surely there must be somebody in the Kremlin bright enough to realize that a government with such powers, in which Russia, on the basis both of population and of industrial development, would be heavily represented in the executive as well as the legislative branch, would offer an opportunity to repeat on a global scale the performance so successfully put over in Prague in February, 1948. . . .

A world government would have to be a coalition government, in which the Russians and their acolytes (now including the rulers of China) would have a large share. There is no reason to suppose they would behave differently in a world government from the way Communists have behaved in every national coalition government, or for that matter in every labor-union coalition government. Every such government has eventually been faced with a choice between throwing them out and letting them take over. To throw them out of a world government would be difficult and dangerous; it would mean a world civil war, with the odds heavily against the democracies. It seems simpler, and safer, to keep them out in the first place.

But, say the world-government advocates, consider the frightful alternative—atomic war. It would be frightful, but I am not persuaded that it is the necessary alternative; either/or thinking is seldom applicable to the complexities of politics. By a vigorous and intelligent political policy, reinforced by the maintenance of powerful armaments, we may be able to convince the Russians that they cannot get what they want without war, and that they could not possibly win a war; so eventually they might decide to settle down with what they have.

This policy is open to objections too. It offers no hope for the liberation of the peoples now enslaved by the Kremlin—unless the Russian empire should fall apart from its own internal contradictions, which is possible but not at all probable. Also, this policy would take a long time and would cost a great deal of money. But it would cost far less than a war. As for the time, no one can say how long it might take; decades, I should think, rather than centuries; but a long time on the individual life-scale, and a time in which we could never afford to relax our vigilance, and would probably be unable to relax our tension. We shall all have to get used to living in the kind of world we don't like much—living in it, and working hard to keep it from becoming the kind of world we should not like at all. But that is not without precedent. When the Ice Age was coming on, it did no good to pretend that the glaciers weren't there, or that this weather was very unusual; you had to get used to living with the conditions that actually existed.

Such a life (we are getting a taste of it already, and it is likely to become less comfortable and more expensive) would with all its drawbacks be better than an atomic war. Unfortunately, we cannot be sure it would prevent war, though it looks to me like the best prospect for so doing. And if war came? Well, there is only one thing worse than atomic war and that is the loss of freedom—the total loss of freedom, of the body and of the mind, that you get in a totalitarian police state.

We know all about the evils of nationalism; and there are many. But when a nation has lost its freedom, it may hope some day to recover it; at worst, some of its more fortunate citizens can get out to regions that are still free. If the whole world loses its freedom, whence comes salvation? Some day, no doubt, we shall have world government; but it will have to be a different kind of world—either far better than the world we live in, or far worse.

————◄••••►————

THE UNITED NATIONS: PATHWAY TO A PEACEFUL WORLD *

An official of the United Nations Secretariat, Dr. Bunche has been an active participant in work of that organization for several years. The speech reproduced below was given at Oslo, Norway, December 11, 1950, at which time its author was awarded the Nobel Peace Prize. As an examination of the text will show, Dr. Bunche is convinced that only through the United Nations can a peaceful world be achieved. By stressing accomplishments of the UN he builds a case for that organization as the avenue through which world peace efforts should be channeled. Is this attitude one of idealism or realism? Is Dr. Bunche an uncritical defender of the UN? Or does he fully recognize the barriers to world peace?

* Ralph J. Bunche. Condensed and reprinted with permission of the author.

If today we speak of peace, we also speak of the United Nations, for in this era, peace and the United Nations have become inseparable. If the United Nations cannot ensure peace, there will be none. If war should come, it will be only because the United Nations has failed. But the United Nations need not fail. Surely, every man of reason must work and pray to the end that it will not fail.

In these critical days, it is a high privilege and a most rewarding experience to be associated with the United Nations—the greatest peace effort in human history. Those who work in and with the organization, perhaps inevitably, tend to develop a professional optimism with regard to the prospects for the United Nations, and therefore, to the prospects for peace. But there is also a sense of deep frustration, which flows from the knowledge that mankind could readily live in peace and freedom and good neighbourliness if there were but a minimum of will to do so. There is the ever-present, simple but stark truth that though the peoples long primarily for peace, they may be prodded by their leaders and governments into needless war, which may at worst destroy them, at best lead them once again to barbarism.

The United Nations strives to be realistic. It understands well the frailties of man. It is realized that if there is to be peace in the world, it must be attained through men and with man, in his nature and mores, just about as he now is. Intensive effort is exerted to reach the hearts and minds of men with the vital pleas for peace and human understanding, to the end that human attitudes and relations may be steadily improved. But this is a process of international education, or better, education for international living, and it is at best gradual. Men change their attitudes and habits slowly, but grudgingly divorce their minds from fears, suspicions and prejudices.

The United Nations itself is but a cross-section of the world's peoples. It reflects, therefore, the typical fears, suspicions and prejudices which bedevil human relations throughout the world. In the delegations from the sixty member states, and in the international Secretariat in which most of them are represented, may be found individual qualities of goodness and badness, honesty and subterfuge, courage and timorousness, internationalism and chauvinism. It could not be otherwise. Still, the activities of all are within the framework of a great international organization dedicated to the imperative causes of peace, freedom and justice in the world.

The United Nations, inescapably, is an organization at once of great weakness and great strength.

Its powers of action are sharply limited by the exigencies of national sovereignties. With nationalism *per se* there may be no quarrel. But narrow, exclusively self-centered nationalism persists as the outstanding dynamic of world politics and is the prime obstacle to enduring peace. The international well-being on the one hand, and national egocentrism on the other, are inevitably at cross-purposes. The procedures and processes of the United Nations as a circumscribed international parliament, are unavoidably complex and tedious.

The United Nations was established in the hope, if not on the assumption, that the five great powers would work harmoniously toward an increasingly better world order. The existing impasse between West and East and the resultant "cold war" were not foreseen by those who formulated the United Nations Charter in the spring of 1945 in the misleading, but understandably jubilant, atmosphere of war's triumphant end. Nevertheless, the United Nations has exhibited a fortunate flexibility which has enabled it to adjust to the regrettable circumstances of the discord among the great powers and to continue to function effectively.

Reflecting the hopes and aspirations of all peoples for peace, security, freedom and justice, the foundations of the United Nations are firmly anchored and its moral sanctions are strong. It is served by a fully competent international Secretariat which is devoted to the high principles and purposes of the Organization. At the head of this Secretariat is the Secretary-General of the United Nations, Trygve Lie, a great son of Norway, and a man whose name will be writ large in the annals of world statesmanship and peace-making. No living man has worked more persistently or courageously to save the world from the scourge of war than Trygve Lie.

In its short but turbulent five years, the United Nations, until the past few weeks, at least, has demonstrated a comforting ability to cope with every dangerous crisis that has erupted into violence or threatened to do so. It has never been easily done nor as well as might be hoped for, but the fact remains that it has been done. In these post-war years, the United Nations, in the interest of peace, has been called upon to eliminate the threat of local wars, to stop local wars already underway, and now in Korea, itself to undertake an international police action which amounts to full-scale war. Its record has been impressive. Its interventions have been directly responsible for checking and containing dangerous armed conflicts in Indonesia, Kashmir, and Palestine, and to only a lesser extent in Greece.

That the United Nations has been able to serve the cause of peace in this way has been due in large measure to the determination of its members to reject the use of armed force as an instrument of national policy, and to the new techniques of international intervention which it has employed. In each instance of a threat to the peace, the United Nations projects itself directly into the area of conflict by sending United Nations representatives to the area for the purpose of mediation and conciliation.

It was as the head of a United Nations mission of this kind that Count

Folke Bernadotte went to Palestine in the spring of 1948. On his arrival in the Near East, he found the Arabs and Jews locked in a bitter, bloody and highly emotional war in Palestine. He was armed only with the strong demand of the United Nations that in the interest of world peace the Palestine problem must be settled by peaceful means.

In one of the most brilliant individual feats of diplomatic history, Count Bernadotte, within two weeks of his arrival on the scene of conflict, had negotiated a four weeks' truce and the guns had ceased firing. In order to supervise that truce, he requested of the Secretary-General and promptly received, an international team of civilian and military personnel, numbering some seven hundred men and women. The members of this compact and devoted United Nations "peace army" in Palestine, many of whom were from the Scandinavian countries, and all of whom were unarmed, under the early leadership of Count Bernadotte wrote a heroic chapter in the cause of peace. The peace-loving world must ever be grateful to them. We who had the privilege to serve under the leadership of Count Bernadotte revere his name. He was a great internationalist, a warm-hearted humanitarian, a warrior of unflinching courage in the cause of peace, and a truly noble man. We who carried on after him were inspired by his self-sacrifice, and were determined to pay him the one tribute which he would have appreciated above all others—the successful completion of the task which he had begun, the restoration of peace to Palestine.

In Korea, for the first, and it may be fervently hoped, the last time, the United Nations processes of peaceful intervention to settle disputes failed. They failed only because the North Korean regime stubbornly refused to afford them the chance to work, and resorted to aggressive force as the means of attaining its ends. Confronted with this, the gravest challenge to its mandate to preserve the peace of the world, the United Nations had no reasonable alternative but to check aggressive national force with decisive international force. This it has attempted to do and it was enabled to do so only by the firm resolve of the overwhelming majority of its members that the peace must be preserved, and that aggression shall be struck down wherever undertaken, or by whom.

By virtue of recent set-backs to United Nations forces in Korea, as a result of the injection of vast numbers of Chinese troops into the conflict, it becomes clear that this resolve of its members has not been backed by sufficient armed strength to ensure that the right shall prevail. In the future, it must be the forces of peace that are overwhelming.

But whatever the outcome of the present military struggle in Korea in which the United Nations and Chinese troops are now locked, Korea provides the lesson which can save peace and freedom in the world if nations and peoples will but learn that lesson, and learn it quickly. To make peace in the world secure, the United Nations must have readily at its disposal, as a result of firm commitments undertaken by all of its members, military strength of sufficient dimensions to make it certain that it can meet aggressive military force with international military force, speedily and conclusively.

If that kind of strength is made available to the United Nations—and under action taken by the General Assembly this fall it can be made available—in my view that strength will never again be challenged in war, and therefore need never be employed.

But military strength will not be enough. The moral position of the United Nations must ever be strong and unassailable; it must stand steadfastly, always, for the right.

The international problems with which the United Nations is concerned are the problems of the inter-relations of the peoples of the world. They are human problems. The United Nations is entitled to believe, and it does believe, that there are no insoluble problems of human relations, and that there is none which cannot be solved by peaceful means. The United Nations—in Indonesia, Palestine and Kashmir—has demonstrated convincingly that parties to the most severe conflict may be induced to abandon war as the method of settlement in favour of mediation and conciliation, at a merciful saving of untold lives and acute suffering.

Unfortunately, there may yet be some in the world who have not learned that today war can settle nothing, that aggressive force can never be enough, nor will it be tolerated. If this should be so, the pitiless wrath of the organized world must fall upon those who would endanger the peace for selfish ends. For in this advanced day, there is no excuse, no justification for nations resorting to force except to repel armed attack.

The world and its peoples being as they are, there is no easy or quick or infallible approach to a secure peace. It is only by patient, persistent, undismayed effort, by trial and error, that peace can be true. Nor can it be won cheaply, as the taxpayer is learning. In the existing world tension, there will be rebuffs and set-backs, dangerous crises and episodes of violence. But the United Nations, with unshakeable resolution, in the future as in the past, will continue to man the dykes of peace. In this common purpose, all states, irrespective of size, are vital.

The small nations, which constitute the overwhelming majority in its membership, are a great source of strength for the United Nations. Their desire for peace is deep-seated and constant. The fear, suspicion and conflict which characterize the relations among the great powers, and the resultant uncertainty, keep them and their peoples in a state of anxious tension and suspense. For the relations among the great powers will largely determine their future. A third world war would quickly engulf the smaller states, and many of them would again provide the battlefields. On many of them, now as before, the impact of war would be even more severe than upon the great powers. They, in particular, therefore, support and often initiate measures designed to ensure that the United Nations shall be increasingly effective as a practical instrumentality for peace. In this regard, the Scandinavian countries contribute signally to the constructive effort of the United Nations.

One legacy of the recent past greatly handicaps the work of the United Nations. It can never realize its maximum potential for peace until the Second World War is fully liquidated. The impasse between West and East has prevented the great powers from concluding the peace treaties which would finally terminate that last war. It can be little doubted that the United Nations, if called upon, could afford valuable aid toward this end. At present, the United Nations must work for future peace in the unhappy atmosphere of an unconcluded great war, while precluded from rendering any assistance toward the liquidation of that war. These, obviously, are matters of direct and vital concern to all peace-loving nations, whatever their size.

At the moment, in view of the disturbing events in Korea and Indo-China, the attention of a fearful world is focused on Asia, seeking an answer to the fateful question "peace or war?" But the intrinsic importance of Europe in the world peace equation cannot be ignored. The peace of Europe, and therefore of the world, can never be secure so long as the problem of Germany remains unsolved.

In this regard, those who at the end of the last war were inclined to dismiss Europe as a vital factor in reckoning the future security and prosperity of the world, have had to revise their calculations. For Europe, grievously wounded though it was, has displayed a remarkable resiliency, and has quickly regained its place in the orbit of world affairs.

But Europe, and the western world generally, must become fully aware that the massive and restive millions of Asia and Africa are henceforth a new and highly significant factor in all peace calculations. These hitherto suppressed masses are rapidly awakening and are demanding, and are entitled to enjoy a full share in the future fruits of peace, freedom and security.

Very many of these millions are experiencing a new-found freedom. Many other millions are still in subject states, as colonials. The aspirations and demands of those who have achieved freedom and those who seek it are the same: security, treatment as equals, and their rightful place in the brotherhood of nations.

It is truer today than when Alfred Nobel realized it a half-century ago, that peace cannot be achieved in a vacuum. Peace must be paced by human progress. Peace is no mere matter of men fighting or not fighting. Peace, to have meaning for many who have known only suffering in both peace and war, must be translated into bread or rice, shelter, health and education, as well as freedom and human dignity—a steadily better life. If peace is to be secure, long-suffering and long-starved forgotten peoples of the world, the under-privileged and the under-nourished, must begin to realize without delay the promise of a new day and a new life.

In the world of today, Europe, like the rest of the west, is confronted with the urgent necessity of a new orientation—a global orientation. The pre-war outlook is as obsolete as the pre-war world. There must be an awakening to the incontestable fact that the far away, little known and little understood peoples of Asia and Africa, who constitute the majority of the world's population, are no longer passive and no longer to be ignored. The fury of the world ideological struggle swirls about them. Their vast numbers will prove a dominant factor in the future world pattern of life. They provide virgin soil for the growth of democracy, but the west must first learn how to approach them understandingly and how to win their trust and friendship. There is a long and unsavory history of western imperialism, suppression and exploitation to be overcome, despite the un-denied benefits which the west also brought to them. There must be an acceleration in the liquidation of colonialism. A friendly hand must be extended to the peoples who are labouring under the heavy burden of newly won independence, as well as to those who aspire to it. And in that hand must be tangible aid in generous quantity—funds, goods, foodstuffs, equipment, technical assistance.

There are great issues demanding resolution in the world: the clash of the rather loosely defined concepts and systems of capitalism and communism; the radically contrasted conceptions of democracy, posing extreme views of individualism against extreme views of statism; the widespread denials of human rights; the understandable impatience of many among some two hundred million colonial peoples for the early realization of their aspirations toward emancipation; and others.

But these are issues which in no sense may be considered as defying solution. The issue of capitalism versus communism is one of ideology which in the world of today cannot, in fact, be clearly defined. It cannot be clearly defined because there are not two worlds, one "capitalist" and one "communist." There is but one world—a world of sharp clashes to be sure—with these two doctrines at the opposite ideological poles. In between these extremes are found many gradations of the two systems and ideologies.

There is room in the world for both capitalism and communism and all gradations of them, provided only that neither system is set upon pursuing an aggressively imperialistic course.

The United Nations is opposed to imperialism of any kind, ideological or otherwise. The United Nations stands for the freedom and equality of all peoples, irrespective of race, religion, or ideology. It is for the peoples of every society to make their own choices with regard to ideologies, economic systems and the relationship which is to prevail between the state and the individual. The United Nations is engaged in an historic effort to underwrite the rights of man. It is also attempting to give reassurance to the colonial peoples that their aspirations for freedom can be realized, if only gradually, by processes.

There can be peace and a better life for all men. Given adequate authority and support, the United Nations can ensure this. The decision really rests with the peoples of the world. The United Nations belongs to the people, but it is not yet as close to them, as much a part of their conscious interest, as it must come to be. The United Nations must always be on the people's side. Where their fundamental rights and interests are involved, it must never act from mere expediency. At times, perhaps, it has done so, but never to its own advantage, nor to that of the sacred causes of peace and freedom. If the peoples of the world are strong in their resolve, and if they speak through the United Nations, they need never be confronted with the tragic alternatives of war or dishonourable appeasement, death or enslavement.

Amidst the frenzy and irrationality of a topsy-turvy world, some simple truths would appear to be self-evident.

As Alfred Nobel finally discerned, people are never deterred from the folly of war by the stark terror of it. But it is nonetheless true that if in atomic war there would be survivors there could be no victors. What then, could war achieve which could not be better gained by peaceful means? There are, to be sure, vital differences and wide areas of conflict among the nations, but there is utterly none which could not be settled peacefully—by negotiation and mediation—given a genuine will for peace and even a modicum of mutual good faith.

But there would appear to be little hope that efforts to break the great power impasse could be very fruitful in the current atmosphere of fear, suspicion and mutual recrimination. Fear, suspicion and recrimination in the relations among nations tend to be dangerously self-compounding. They induce that national hysteria which, in its rejection of poise and rationality, can itself be the fatal prelude to war. A favorable climate for peaceful negotiation must be created and can only be created by painstaking, unremitting effort. Conflicting parties must be led to realize that the road to peace can never be traversed by threatening to fight at every bend, by merely being armed to the teeth, or by flushing every bush to find an enemy. An essential first step in a civilized approach to peace in these times would call for a moratorium on recrimination and reproach.

There are some in the world who are prematurely resigned to the inevitability of war. Among them are the advocates of the so-called "preventive war," who, in their resignation to war, wish merely to select their own time for initiating it. To suggest that war can prevent war is a base play on words and a despicable form of war-mongering. The objective of any who sincerely believe in peace clearly must be to exhaust every honorable recourse in the effort to save the peace. The world has had ample evidence that war begets only conditions which beget further war.

In the final analysis, the acid test of a genuine will to peace is the willingness of disputing parties to expose their differences to the peaceful processes of the United Nations and to the bar of international public opinion which the United Nations reflects. It is only in this way that truth, reason, and justice may come to prevail over the shrill and blatant voice of propaganda; that a wholesome international morality can be cultivated.

It is worthy of emphasis that the United Nations exists not merely to preserve the peace but also to make change—even radical change—possible without violent upheaval. The United Nations has no vested interest in the status quo. It seeks a more secure world, a better world, a world of progress for all peoples. In the dynamic world society which is the objective of the United Nations, all peoples must have quality and equal rights. The rights of those who at any given time may be in the minority —whether for reasons of race, religion or ideology—are as important as those of the majority, and the minorities must enjoy the same respect and protection. The United Nations does not seek a world cut after a single pattern, nor does it consider this desirable. The United Nations seeks only unity, not uniformity, out of the world's diversity.

There will be no security in our world, no release from agonizing tension, no genuine progress, no enduring peace, until, in Shelley's fine words, "reason's voice, loud as the voice of nature, shall have waked the nations."

RE-EXAMINING THE U.N. *

Long before the end of World War II a large segment of the American people became convinced that some type of world organization was necessary to solve the ever-recurring problem of aggression. Two

* Walter Lippmann, *The New York Herald Tribune,* January 15, 1951. Copyright, 1951, New York Herald Tribune, Inc. All rights reserved.

major wars within a single generation engraved in the minds of men the futility of attempting to achieve peace through isolation. As a consequence the United Nations at birth was hailed, if not as a panacea for the ills of the world, as an agency that would preserve peace through collective security. However, events since 1945 have served as a checkrein on uncontrolled enthusiasm for the UN.

In the following essay Walter Lippmann, a widely syndicated political columnist, points up the pitfalls that face any world organization that is dependent on the action of member states. Can the United Nations survive if it is expected to maintain collective security? Is disillusionment inevitable when a world organization attempts to enforce peace through collective action? Does the real contribution of the United Nations lie in the fields of diplomacy, negotiation, and collective discussion where it can serve as a world forum?

The Korean War is naturally enough bringing with it a reexamination of the United Nations. The crucial question, which no one of us ought to answer quickly or excitedly, is whether the failure to repel aggression in Korea by collective action is a demonstration that the United Nations should be written off, allowed to dissolve or even dissolved deliberately.

This question—whether peace can be enforced by the united actions of all nations against an aggressor nation—is not a new one. I myself, for example, heard it argued pro and con in the presence of President Wilson some two years before we entered the first world war, and I can remember how reluctantly and with what misgivings President Wilson accepted the idea, which in point of fact was first given wide currency in this country by ex-President Theodore Roosevelt.

. . . It has long seemed to me . . . that no universal society like the United Nations can survive if it is expected to execute the principle of collective security. The general and official view ever since President Wilson's time has been, I am fully aware, that unless the United Nations is able to suppress aggression by collective action, it has no reason for existence. But the truth, as I see it, was demonstrated by the League of Nations and is now, I believe, confirmed in Korea. It is that a universal society cannot enforce peace by collective action and will be destroyed if it tries to.

The reason why collective security is an unworkable principle was expounded by Alexander Hamilton in the fifteenth of the Federalist Papers: "Every breach of the laws must involve a state of war; and military execution must become the only instrument of . . . obedience." The old League in respect to Manchuria and Ethiopia, the United Nations in respect to Korea and China, have shown up collective security—they have shown that you cannot rally all the nations to a collective war to enforce peace and that you cannot get peace if you rally only some of them.

The trouble with collective security is, if I may reprint something I wrote back in 1946, that "when the issue is less than the survival of the *great* nations, the method of collective security will not be used because it is just as terrifying to the policeman as it is to the lawbreakers. It punishes the law-enforcing states, at least until they have paid the awful price of victory, as much as the law-breaking states. Therefore it cannot be used as a method of ordinary and continuing enforcement, for example as a means of insuring the inspection of laboratories and plants working with fissionable materials. There would be little surgery if the surgeon had to amputate his own arm when he was called upon to amputate his patient's leg. There would be little enforcement of law in our cities if in order to arrest burglars, murderers and violators of the traffic ordinances police had to start a fight in which the courthouse, the jail, and their own homes were likely to be demolished. Men will not burn down the barn in order to roast a pig: the method of collective security is, I repeat, too crude, too expensive, and too unreliable for general and regular use. It proposes to achieve peace through law by calling upon great masses of innocent people to stand ready to exterminate great masses of innocent people. No world order can be founded upon such a principle: it cannot command the support of civilized men, least of all of democratic men who respect the individual and consider it the very essence of justice to distinguish between the guilty and the innocent, the responsible and the irresponsible."

Survival of the United Nations depends, it seems to me, on a general recognition of the fact that, while it is not a policeman and cannot be made into a policeman, not even if the Russians were expelled, it is still, and none the less, an invaluable, indeed an indispensable diplomatic meeting place. Were it dissolved, we should be asking where and how we can achieve general contact and diplomatic intercourse not merely without Soviet adversaries but with the great number of states in Asia, the Middle East, Europe, and Africa who are our allies or are friendly neutrals.

Let us then be very careful not to sacrifice all that, which is most important though it is largely invisible, on the altar of the principle of collective security—which in practice is not collective and does not bring security.

Index